PREHISTORIC CANNIBALISM

AT MANCOS 5MTUMR–2346

PREHISTORIC CANNIBALISM AT MANCOS 5MTUMR-2346

Tim D. White

• PRINCETON UNIVERSITY PRESS •

Published by Princeton University Press, 41 William Street,
Princeton, New Jersey 08540
In the United Kingdom: Princeton University Press, Oxford

Library of Congress Cataloging-in-Publication Data
White, T. D. (Tim D.).
Prehistoric cannibalism at Mancos 5MTUMR–2346 / Tim D. White.
p. cm.
Includes bibliographical references and index.
ISBN 0–691–09467–5
1. Mancos Site (Colo.) 2. Pueblo Indians—Anthropometry.
3. Cannibalism—Colorado—History. 4. Pueblo Indians—Antiquities.
I. Title.
E99.P9W49 1992
978.8'27—dc20 91–23953 CIP

This book has been composed in Times Roman Expanded

Princeton University Press books are printed on acid-free paper, and meet the guidelines for permanence and durability of the Committee on Production Guidelines for Book Longevity of the Council on Library Resources

Printed in the United States of America

10 9 8 7 6 5 4 3 2 1

Contents

Figures

Tables

Ute Mountain Tribal Park

Research and Education Center

Towaoc, Colorado 81334
(303) 565-3751, Ext. 282

July 31, 1991

Professor Tim D. White
Department of Anthropology
University of California
Berkeley, California 94720

Dear Tim,

Your extensive discussion of Mancos Canyon 5MTUMR-2346 gives all of us a keen interest in the Future Excavations on the Ute Tribal Lands, especially with the recent (1990) Excavation of 5MT-1207 and the discovery of similar skeletal material. We will begin the excavation of fifty-three additional sites in 1992-94, and notify you immediately if additional material is found. You have made a significant contribution to Southwest Archaeology.

Thank you,

Doug Bowman

Doug Bowman
Director, Ute Mountain
Tribal Park Research
and Education Center

Preface

Cannibalism is a globally claimed but sparsely documented human behavior. Its spatial and temporal dimensions, situational contexts, and archaeological signatures are poorly understood. This book presents the inference, based on contextual and osteological evidence, that an episode of cannibalism took place nearly nine hundred years ago in the Mancos Canyon of southwestern Colorado.

The cultural systems that we now call "Anasazi" flourished in the American Southwest for hundreds of years. Complex religion developed there, as well as works of art and architecture that captivate us even today. Archaeology and physical anthropology are means of revealing the cultural and biological dimensions of these people and their environments. These disciplines have yielded the knowledge that Anasazi mortuary practice usually took the form of primary burial, with the body of the deceased often accompanied by items of material culture. In contrast, there are relatively few cases in which cannibalism has been inferred from Anasazi remains. Just as no person characterizes all American pioneers of the last century as cannibals on the basis of cannibalism among the Donner party (Grayson, 1990), no person should characterize all Anasazi as cannibals.

Some will undoubtedly question the inference of cannibalism at Mancos 5MTUMR–2346. Some may prefer to take comfort or refuge in the fact that archaeological evidence is often circumstantial, and archaeological proof is consistently elusive.

Present-day perceptions of cannibalism are heavily value-laden. These perceptions carry with them the strong potential for biasing both the researcher's and the audience's conclusions about the behavior. We must recognize these biases, but proceed to study the phenomenon with the same theoretical and methodological rigor that we would employ in studying any other aspect of human behavior. The late George Gaylord Simpson put it well in another context: "I have nothing for those whose only approach is emotional and who will always believe what is pleasant in preference to what is true, but if anyone cares for the facts, I intend to know them."[1]

Here, then, are the facts about Mancos 5MTUMR–2346, and the inferences to which they have led.

[1] George Gaylord Simpson, in *Simple Curiosity: Letters from G.G. Simpson to His Family, 1921–1970*, ed. Leo Laporte (Berkeley: University of California Press, 1987), p. 67.

Acknowledgments

My work on the skeletal remains from Mancos Canyon site 5MTUMR–2346 was made possible by the generosity of many individuals and institutions. The Harry Frank Guggenheim Foundation provided financial support, administered by the Institute of Human Origins, for the research described here. Additional support came from the UC Berkeley Committee on Research.

Paul Nickens provided constant encouragement and was a source of invaluable information regarding the excavation and earlier analysis of the material. Allen Bohnert provided assistance in obtaining loans. Jack Smith kindly provided necessary records and photographs for the Mancos assemblage, uncovered previously undocumented assemblages with similar attributes, and patiently answered innumerable questions about the Southwest, giving me the benefit of his experience and knowledge in the archaeology of this region. He and Rosie made my Mesa Verde visits most memorable.

When my estimated dates of completion proved inaccurate, Allen Bohnert showed the understanding and patience that let the work go on. Thanks also go to Art Cuthair and the Ute Mountain Tribe for providing permission to study the material, and to Doug Bowman for the visit to Mancos Canyon in the Ute Mountain Tribal Park. Superintendent Robert Heyder greatly facilitated my visits to Mesa Verde National Park. I thank David Breternitz and Margo Surovik of the Dolores Archaeological Project, Jerry Fetterman of Woods Canyon Archaeological Consultants, and Larry Hammack of CASA for assistance in understanding other related occurrences. Dana Hartman helped me to view collections in the Museum of Northern Arizona. The Lowie Museum in Berkeley provided comparative material. Roger Green provided assistance in obtaining and interpreting evidence from Largo-Gallina and from the Pacific. Thanks are extended to Carmen Ma. Pijoan A. and other colleagues of the Departamento de Antropología Física of the Instituto Nacional de Antropologia e Historia in Mexico. They provided access to Mesoamerican skeletal remains and Carmen helped greatly in directing me to the appropriate literature. Thanks also go to Andy Darling of the University of Michigan, and to Fred Lange and Nancy Malville of the University of Colorado, Boulder, who made it possible for me to study the recently excavated Yellow Jacket 5MT–3 assemblage. The Yellow Jacket project is under the overall direction of Joe Ben Wheat. Thanks also go to Nancy A. Harris of the Mesa Verde Research Center for her assistance in the Badger House zooarchaeological analysis, and to Elizabeth Bauer for her assistance in study of material housed under her curatorial care.

Bruce and Cindy Bradley of the Crow Canyon Archaeological Center provided me with permission to study the Wallace Ruin skeletal material, and provided the deer metapodials used in bone-boiling experiments. I am grateful to Leander Gridley of Ute Mountain Pottery, who loaned me the corrugated cooking vessel used in these experiments.

I have had the good fortune to study fossil and subfossil material in Africa, Europe, Asia, and North America. To all the curators who have made my visits so valuable I extend my sincere thanks. I have learned a great deal from friends and colleagues in physical anthropology and archaeology while working on the Mancos collection. In particular I would like to thank Peter Andrews, Bill Arens, Shane Baker, Frank Bayham, John Beaton, Amilcare Bietti, Lewis Binford, Rob Blumenschine, Jane Buikstra, Desmond Clark, Jill Cook, Hilary Deacon, Milan Dokládal, Dave Doyel, Jerry Fetterman, John Graham, Tom Hester, Clark Howell, Winston Hurst, Frank Ivanhoe, Jan Jelinek, Don Johanson, Rhys Jones, Dick Jordan, Bill Kimbel, Pat Kirch, Tony Klesert, Clark Larsen, Bob Leonard, Kent Lightfoot, Mike Love, Owen Lovejoy, R. Lee Lyman, Curtis Marean, Alex Marshack, Katherine Milton, Jim O'Connell, John Olson, Michael Pietrusewsky, Cedric Poggenpoel, Yoel Rak, Jeff Reid, John Roe, Carmel Schrire, Sileshi Semaw, Pat Shipman, Andy Sillen, Fred Smith, Dirk Spennemann, Nancy Stone, Doug Sutton, Christine Szuter, Erv Taylor, Erik Trinkaus, Christy Turner, Herbert Ullrich, Elizabeth Voigt, Bob Walter, and Steve Ward for discussions. Drs. Mehdi Tavassoli and George F. Cahill provided valuable information on human bone marrow. Many of these colleagues provided invaluable references and assistance to my navigation of the archaeological and ethnographic literature. The recording procedures employed were developed in collaboration with Nick Toth and Kathy Schick, whose insights and help are greatly appreciated. I am particularly grateful to Nick for his work on the scanning electron microscope. The SEM work on pot polish was made possible through the assistance of Donald L. Pardoe and Jorge A. Santiago-Blay of the Robert D. Ogg Electron Microscope Laboratory of the University of California. Thanks to the Institute of Human Origins and to Apple Computer for the computing backup necessary for the completion of the project.

The research described in this book is founded in large part on the skill and time of several colleagues. Roberta Jewett's critical reading and commentary on the initial, partial manuscript helped the work immeasurably. R. Lee Lyman, Diane Gifford-Gonzalez, Bruce Bradley, and Bill Arens critically read the incomplete manuscript in 1989, thereby greatly helping to improve the final product. The hours of data entry required by the analysis were made bearable by the invaluable assistance of Betty Schmucker on Mancos and Reina Milligan on Yellow Jacket. David Symonik printed the many photographs used to illustrate the text. Terrence Speed of the Department of Statistics, UC Berkeley, provided timely assistance with quantitative aspects of the analysis. Thanks go to Bill Kimbel for copiloting the Chevy from Berkeley to Mesa Verde and back. Efforts of Berkeley students made possible the major time investment in sorting, numbering, conjoining, checking, and rechecking. Thanks go to Natalie Anikouchine, Raymond Cheung, James Foster, Charlane Gross, Todd Rae, Melody Tannam, Reina Wong, and Tracey Zaher. James Mills helped with the Cottonwood sample. In particular, Susan

Chin made major contributions in all the Mancos laboratory effort and provided crucial library assistance. Avis Worthington typed the bibliography. Dorothy Koenig, Anthropology Librarian, and the staff of the UCB Interlibrary Loan Department provided extensive bibliographic assistance. I also wish to thank Lewis R. Binford, Kent V. Flannery, R. Lee Lyman, Paul R. Nickens, James F. O'Connell, Jack E. Smith, and other anonymous reviewers who read the manuscript for Princeton University Press. Bill Woodcock's advice, encouragement, and hard work in bringing this project to publication is gratefully acknowledged. To the many other colleagues I have had the pleasure to work with in faunal analysis, Paleolithic and Southwest archaeology, paleontology, geology, physical anthropology, and anatomy, I extend my thanks. I take full responsibility for the ideas and conclusions expressed here.

PREHISTORIC
CANNIBALISM
AT MANCOS 5MTUMR–2346

CHAPTER

1

The Trail to Mancos

Why would a physical anthropologist who has worked primarily on Pliocene hominid fossils from Africa be drawn to the archaeology of the American Southwest? There is a vast gulf between the hominids of Ethiopia's Afar depression and the Anasazi inhabitants of southwestern Colorado in the dimensions of time, space, anatomy, and behavior. Yet a fossil from the Afar posed questions that led me down a trail to Mancos Canyon.

ETHIOPIA

In several respects, this study is rooted in the year 1973. That year French geologist Maurice Taieb was joined in Ethiopia by American graduate student Donald Johanson. They discovered remains of the first hominid from Hadar, Ethiopia—a knee joint. Taieb had surveyed much of the area to the north and south of Hadar—thousands of square kilometers—but had chosen Hadar as a place to begin the research because of its diverse Pliocene fossils. The choice was a good one and by the late 1970s the abundant harvest of fossils from Hadar provided fresh insights into human evolution (Johanson *et al.*, 1982, and references therein). The area along the Awash River to the immediate south of Hadar is called the Middle Awash. It was not until work was well underway at Hadar that the Middle Awash yielded its first hominid fossil, a nearly complete cranium associated with Acheulean artifacts at a site called Bodo. The work there was led by Jon Kalb, a former associate of Johanson and Taieb at Hadar.

The Bodo cranium was described as a late *Homo erectus*, or "archaic" *Homo sapiens*, by its discoverers (Conroy *et al.*, 1978). In 1981 I was asked by Desmond Clark to accompany him on a survey of the Middle Awash at Bodo and other sites. Before departing from the capitol, Addis Ababa, Clark asked to have a look at the Bodo cranium housed at the National Museum of Ethiopia. It was an unforgettable introduction. The massive specimen was completely fossilized, its surface almost perfectly preserved. As it was lifted out of its carrying case and rested upon the table in one of the old museum laboratories, I noticed a set of fine, deep incisions that crossed the left zygomaticomaxillary suture below the orbit. These were obviously not preparator's marks and did not resemble carnivore damage. Further cleaning and analysis revealed the striae to be cutmarks made before the cranium had been fossilized. More marks were found beneath the matrix, inside the orbit, and on the vault (White, 1985, 1986).

The 1981 field season in the Middle

Awash was very productive. An additional hominid was found at Bodo, Pliocene hominid fossils were recovered, excavations were undertaken, and the first samples to yield radiometric dates were analyzed (Clark *et al.*, 1984). When the Bodo scratches were confirmed as cutmarks after our return to Berkeley, the question of what they meant continued to haunt us.

ANCIENT CANNIBALS?

I first turned to the literature on fossil hominids to see whether similar marks had been reported elsewhere. The search revealed an abundance of claims about early hominid violence. The tales of cannibalistic feasts at Choukoutien and other sites that are part of every beginning student's introduction to anthropology were repeated more emphatically the farther one got from the original source. Lewis Binford's *Bones: Ancient Men and Modern Myths* (1981) had been published by this time, and it was clear that a study of perimortem and postmortem trauma to original hominid fossils from *Australopithecus* to Neanderthal was called for. As background to that research, conducted by myself and Nick Toth in 1986, I began a survey of the ethnographic literature dealing with postmortem modification of human skeletal remains. I got about as far as Bill Arens' *The Man Eating Myth* (1979) before realizing that the contemporary record was essentially mute regarding the osteological manifestations of cannibalism. Knowing of Christy Turner's conclusions on cannibalism drawn from recent osteological material in the American Southwest, I turned to that part of the archaeological record.

MANCOS CANYON

The year 1973 had been an auspicious one in southwestern Colorado as well as in the Afar. During salvage excavation of an Anasazi pueblo (site 5MTUMR–2346; c. A.D. 1100) broken and scattered bones representing approximately thirty humans had been recovered by a team from the University of Colorado Mesa Verde Research Center under the general supervision of David Breternitz. The sample of over two thousand bone fragments was first reported on by Nickens (1975).

I was introduced to the Mancos Canyon 5MTUMR–2346 human bone collection in 1984. In comparing this sample with several others from the Southwest I concluded that it represented a unique research opportunity. The Mancos materials were excellently preserved and the sample was large enough for particular bones of the skeleton to be represented multiple times in different age groups. The bones had been recovered *in situ* during a modern archaeological excavation. The assemblage was essentially unmixed with other fauna and the entire pueblo had been excavated. The integrity of the assemblage promised to reveal insights into its formation.

I borrowed the Mancos Canyon 5MTUMR–2346 collection in the summer of 1985 and worked on it through 1990. Initial consultation of the Mancos sample was made to provide a background for work on Neanderthal fossils. It was apparent on my introduction to the Mancos assemblage that it would yield significant additional data in several areas of prehistoric studies, building on the excellent work of Paul Nickens. In the years that followed, the significance of the Anasazi bones seemed to grow with each round of analysis.

OVERVIEW

This study of the Mancos 5MTUMR–2346 skeletal remains began as a way to probe the issue of Paleolithic cannibalism. The results of the study also may help to advance our understanding of the Anasazi. Of more general archaeological significance is the issue of how cannibalism is recognized in a prehistoric context.

The detailed analysis of the large Mancos sample represented a chance for physical anthropology to interface productively with prehistoric archaeology. The methods introduced in this book and the findings of the analysis have applications across the spatial breadth and temporal sweep of archaeological studies. The results of the analysis should be of interest to an audience beyond the geographic area of the American Southwest. Osteologists studying both modern and fossil hominid remains and archaeologists working on sites spanning the Paleolithic to the ethnographic present may find that these results have analytical and comparative relevance to their work.

The questions the Mancos analysis raised and the insights it provided about recording and quantification in faunal analysis are common to all archaeologists. For example, problems of identifying burning on osteological material are of general archaeological concern. The recognition of new categories of bone damage, such as the pot polish and peeling described in Chapter 6, also has general significance. The unmixed nature of the Mancos sample provided a chance to study the effects of different levels of identification in archaeological faunal analysis. For this study the collection was maximally conjoined during the analysis and the results of this full conjoining are compared to the information available from the unconjoined sample. Comparable analytical detail is rarely available for single-taxon faunal assemblages of this size.

The Mancos study, as noted above, was initiated and driven by the need for critical analysis of the fossil evidence. The Mancos assemblage can form a part of the comparative foundation on which studies of hominid fossils can be built. Because of this, results of analysis on fossil hominids will be presented elsewhere.

Chapter 2 provides a background to questions involved with historic and prehistoric cannibalism. The record of cannibalism in the prehistoric Southwest is reviewed in Chapter 3, where the archaeological context of the Mancos assemblage is also outlined. In Chapter 4 the analytical background to the assemblage is detailed, as well as the methods and results of conjoining (refitting the bone fragments). Chapter 5 introduces the skeletal biology of the Mancos people. In Chapter 6 the methodological background to the study of the Mancos osteological material is outlined and the attributes used in this analysis are defined, with an assessment of each attribute as it relates to work in zooarchaeology. Chapters 7 through 11 present the Mancos assemblage in an element-by-element manner, segregating the skeletal elements within the head, trunk, arm, leg, and hand/foot. Further quantitative aspects of the Mancos collection are outlined in Chapter 12, which compares results with those generated by more traditional zooarchaeological analyses. The concluding chapter summarizes the Mancos results and suggests some further applications in physical anthropology and archaeology. Appendix 1 provides a catalog of sites in the American Southwest from which evidence interpreted as consistent with prehistoric cannibalism has been recovered. Appendix 2 is a full catalog and data set for the Mancos 5MTUMR–2346 human bone assemblage. Appendix 3 provides a field and laboratory guide to the recovery and analysis of this kind of bone assemblage.

Discoveries in the Afar posed questions that formed a pathway leading to the Mancos Canyon sample. The significance of cutmarks on the Bodo cranium continues to be elusive, whereas the analytical methodology with which to assess future discoveries has grown. To Desmond Clark, who asked me to join him in Ethiopia, whose passion for prehistory knows no boundaries in time or space, and who was there when the trail began, I dedicate this book.

CHAPTER

2

Cannibalism Past and Present

Cannibalism, ancestral or contemporary, fascinates. One human's consumption of another is an activity, whether in fact or fantasy, which undoubtedly held the attention of the public and the scholarly community long before Herodotus provided us with the first written, but secondhand accounts. Human cannibalism is a behavior that continues to hold considerable interest for the anthropologist. Indeed, the study of cannibalism might appear to be one of the only remnants of anthropological turf on which the research of ethnologists, archaeologists, and physical anthropologists might still be supported simultaneously (see Figure 2.1). Hayden succinctly (1981:344) reminds us, however, of the diminishing role of ethnography: ". . . hunter/gatherer societies are passing rapidly into the province of the archeologist and the prehistorian." That passage is now complete for human groups including, perhaps, hunter-gatherers who might have practiced cannibalism. As Wobst (1978:307) has noted:

> Archaeologists are the only anthropologists whose data contain information about behavioral variance in all its dimensions. . . . Long after the ethnographic era of hunter-gatherer research will have passed into history, archaeologists will be busy removing the ethnographically imposed form and structure from their data and retrodicting both the ethnographic and archaeological record.

This is a book about 2,106 bone fragments from an Anasazi archaeological site in the Mancos Canyon of southwestern Colorado. It is a book about recognizing cannibalism in an archaeological context. Cannibalism is defined in this chapter and its potential signatures in the archaeological record are considered. To provide a global perspective on the Mancos assemblage, the claims and evidence for cannibalism in the hominid fossil record are briefly touched upon, some historical accounts of cannibalism are reviewed, and the archaeological record for this activity outside the American Southwest is briefly sampled.

DEFINING CANNIBALISM AND RECOGNIZING IT IN AN ARCHAEOLOGICAL CONTEXT

Coping with Bias

The accuracy of any reconstruction of prehistoric activities depends entirely upon the extent to which unambiguous interpretations can be based on material remains from archaeological contexts. Before proceeding to discuss standards of evidence

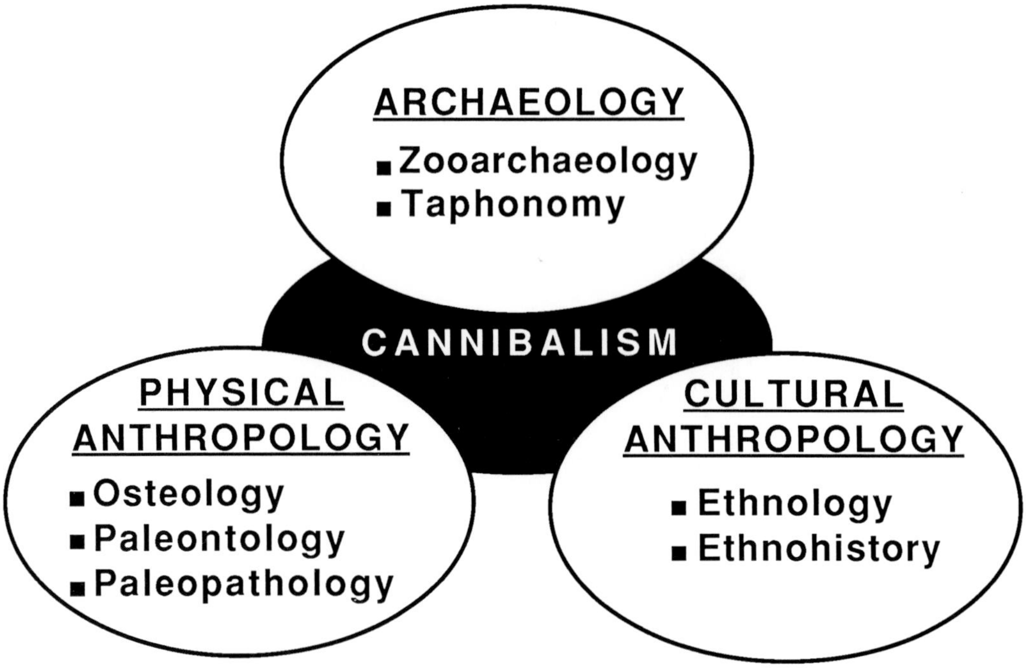

Fig. 2.1 The study of human cannibalism draws on data, method, and theory from all three subdisciplines of anthropology.

to be used in the study of past human cannibalism, it is important to address the potential for modern human emotion and preconception to interfere with a rigorous analysis of the data. In a recent article considering a variety of responses to Arens' (1979) contention that cannibalism was never so widespread as portrayed, Kolata (1986:1500) notes that calling other people cannibals is "perhaps the ultimate derogatory comment." Given Arens' demonstration of how widespread such comment has been, it is no surprise that at least one anthropologist has stated: "The question of whether people are or ever were cannibals is very much tied into our views of who we are and what we are" (Trinkaus, in Kolata, 1986:1497). This describes a counterproductive posture. The question of whether people are or were cannibals may be "tied into" our modern values, but our effectiveness as scientists is grounded on our ability to recognize such bias and avoid it in our research. We must study the material evidence for cannibalism as we would study that left by any other human activity.

Defining Cannibalism

The first step in meeting the challenge of recognizing cannibalism in the archaeological record comes in defining the object of study, cannibalism. As Myers (1984:149) notes:

> There is an absence of a clear definition of cannibalism, a practice encompassing an extremely broad and sometimes ambiguous range of behaviors. Cannibalism can include

drinking waterdiluted ashes of a cremated relative, licking blood off a sword in warfare (Sagan 1974:56), masticating and subsequently vomiting a snippet of flesh (Brown and Tuzin 1983), celebrating Christian communion, or gnawing on entire barbecued limbs as De Bry depicts Caribs doing (1590–95). Accompanying these behaviors is a display of affect ranging from revulsion to reverence and enthusiasm.

In this book, human cannibalism is defined as the conspecific consumption of human tissue. Such intraspecific consumption is widespread in mammals and this definition is taken for granted by zoologists. In a recent literature survey, Polis *et al.* (1984) found 146 references documenting intraspecific predation in 75 species of mammals distributed among 7 orders. In the 15 primate species for which cannibalism has been observed, it is attributed to conspecific density factors, nutritional stress, or reproductive strategy. For humans, the definition of cannibalism used here encompasses all motives and functions of the consumption.

Criteria of Recognition

Binford (1978, 1981, 1984) has recently made major theoretical and empirical contributions to the ability of Paleolithic archaeologists to recognize patterns of damage and element representation in the skeletal remains of fauna recovered from archaeological sites. This work is built upon a long history of research that includes the important studies of Martin (1907), Pei (1938), Dart (1957a), Brain (1981a), and many others. These workers have inspired dozens of modern scholars in the active pursuit of methods to identify the variety of nonhuman agents that can modify archaeological bone assemblages. The result of this combined research is that it is increasingly possible to examine the context of bone assemblages, their composition, and the modification of their elements (cutmarks and hammerstone percussion, for example, versus trampling and/or carnivore and rodent gnawing) in order to illuminate past human activities. Attributes allowing the discrimination between perimortem bone modification (alteration of fresh bone either just before, at, or immediately after the time of death; Turner, 1983) and postdepositional alterations, and among various agencies of bone modification are better defined today as a result of research in the last two decades.

A recent paper entitled "Cannibalism in the Neolithic" by Villa *et al.* (1986a:431) proposes four lines of evidence important in the verification of cannibalism in an archaeological context:

> **(i)** Similar butchering techniques in human and animal remains. Thus frequency, location, and type of verified cut marks and chop marks on human and animal bones must be similar, but we should allow for anatomical differences between humans and animals;
>
> **(ii)** Similar patterns of long bone breakage that might facilitate marrow extraction;
>
> **(iii)** Identical patterns of postprocessing discard of human and animal remains;
>
> **(iv)** Evidence of cooking; if present, such evidence should indicate comparable treatment of human and animal remains.

The comparison of human remains with other faunal residues from the same archaeological context is hardly a novel approach to demonstrating cannibalism in the human past. Fully 112 years before Villa *et al.* proposed these four lines of evidence, Jeffries Wyman concluded that human remains from aboriginal Floridan middens indicated prehistoric cannibalism. Wyman (1874:33) listed four reasons underlying his conclusions:

> 1. The bones . . . were not deposited there at an ordinary burial of a dead body.
>
> 2. The bones were broken as in the case of those of edible animals, as the deer, alligator, etc.
>
> 3. The breaking up of the bones had a certain amount of method.
>
> 4. There is no evidence that the bones were broken up while lying exposed on the ground by wild animals.

In this remarkable early analysis, brought to my attention by John Rowe, Wyman goes on to note that careful examination of the assemblage showed evidence of neither patterned spongy bone destruction nor carnivore toothmarks.

Another example of the early use of the basic principle of faunal comparison for identifying cannibalism archaeologically comes with Somers' (1892) treatment of the archaeological site of Aztalan, Wisconsin. Describing what we now call middens, Somers (1892:20–21) states:

> In these heaps one generally learns more of the manner and means of subsistence of the prehistoric people than from all other sources of conjecture combined, for in them are thrown the bones and refuse of their meat supply, and the broken cooking and other utensils. . . . The human bones in this heap were subject to the same treatment of those of the beast, and lay often in actual contact with them, and in every one of the strata. The bones containing marrow were all either broken into short pieces or split open. The mark of the stone knife and axe is to be seen on most of them, where they were hit to break or split them, or in severing the joints. The ribs were cut into short bits, seldom over three inches in length; and always the knife-marks are seen on the inside, except where they are severed from the vertebral connection. This treatment is the same in both those of the beasts and men.

In yet another early, but completely independent analysis of an Algonkian site at Cayuga, New York, Skinner (1919:52) used the same criteria of recognition when he observed:

> Traces of animals used as food were very abundant, and throughout the midden were encountered bones of deer, elk, bear, birds, tortoises, and fish, and mingled with them no small quantity of human bones, split, cracked, and charred in the same way as those of the beasts. . . .

It is beyond the scope of the present work to review the theoretical literature on what, if anything, constitutes "proof" in archaeological research. Suffice it to say that when archaeologists find *faunal* remains whose context, element representation, and damage patterns are in accordance with exploitation for nutritional benefit, these remains are interpreted to represent evidence of human consumption. When *human* remains are found in similar contexts, with similar patterns of exploitation, they are best interpreted as evidence of conspecific consumption, or cannibalism as defined here. An alternate interpretation would suggest that we cannot say anything about diet from the archaeological record—an alternative espoused by few archaeologists (Lyman, 1982).

Key elements in the archaeological recognition of cannibalism as defined here are the patterns of surface modification (cutmarks, percussion damage, fracture, burning) and *representation* of human skeletal remains. Bones are embedded under varying amounts of soft tissue, much of it with nutritive value. When the tissue is removed and/or prepared, the embedded bones often retain characteristic signatures of this processing in the form of scrapemarks, cutmarks, and burning. Furthermore, bones envelop tissues, including fatty marrow, with considerable nutritional value. The removal of these tissues from the bones by percussion leads to diagnostic patterns of bone damage. For archaeological bone, when damage patterns caused by human efforts to prepare and remove tissues reflect a functional exploitation of the body and its elements that is consistent with the extraction of nutrition, the argument for cannibalism is made.

Judgments on what patterns are consistent with nutritionally motivated processing can be based on the associated archaeological record (particularly the nonhuman faunal record) or with ethnohistorical accounts. This definition, using a pattern-recognition, comparative approach that emphasizes multiple types of osteological damage, is very restrictive, artificially elevating the threshold for recognizing cannibalism. Under this approach, discoveries of cutmarked, articulated (Allen *et al.*, 1985) or partially articulated (Zimmerman *et al.*, 1980) skeletal remains are not considered evidence of cannibalism when the contextual and traumatic patterns are inconsistent with a nutritionally motivated exploitation of bone tissue. Given the recognition criteria outlined here, there are severe restrictions on the interpretation of archaeological evidence for cannibalism.

Difficulties in Applying the Definitions

Use of the procedures outlined above will usually lead to a serious underestimation of the amount of cannibalism in the past. It is easy to imagine (and slightly more difficult to document ethnographically) the ritual consumption of small parts of dead humans as part of funerary activities. Such activities are almost always archaeologically invisible. It is obvious that there will be many other occurrences for which the interpretation of damaged skeletal remains is not as straightforward as desired by a skeptical community. It is also evident that an assessment of multiple lines of evidence on a case-by-case basis will provide the most objective and accurate answers to questions about cannibalism in the past, even if this assessment underestimates its extent. Furthermore, because of the stringent recognition criteria for cannibalism followed here, cases in which the bones suffer the most damage during nutritional exploitation (predicted to be cases in which the processing was motivated by starvation) are more likely to be interpreted as evidence of cannibalism. A lowering of the cannibalism recognition threshold, however, only invites more problems.

There are two additional areas of concern in applying the principles derived here to the interpretation of the archaeological record. First, specific cultural rules may affect the exploitation of faunal material in unusual ways that could prove confusing to an interpretation of bones in an archaeological context. As an illustrative example, John Tanner's 1830 narrative is appropriate. He notes that among some North American Indians, a war feast was staged, whereupon all the meat from a deer, bear, or moose carcass was consumed. Cultural rules, however, prescribed that "no bone of the animal eaten shall be broken." After the flesh was removed, Tanner relates that the bones were bundled together and hung in a tree. Archaeologically, such treatment parallels mortuary rather than dietary practices. In the unlikely event that the unbroken, but defleshed and disarticulated bones of these nonhuman mammals were actually recovered by an archaeologist, it would prove difficult to argue for consumption. This concern is mitigated by the observation that large mammal bone found in most archaeological contexts has usually been processed to remove tissues of nutritive value, resulting in nearly universal fragmentation of, for example, crania or limb bones of large mammals.

The second area of concern in the archaeological analysis of human skeletal material involves ethnographically and archaeologically documented mortuary practices. Modern humans dispose of the dead in an almost unbelievable variety of ways (Czaplicka, 1914; Kroeber, 1927; Métraux, 1946; Gorecki, 1979; Bartel, 1982; O'Shea, 1984). Bodies may be buried, burned, placed on scaffolding, set adrift, put in tree trunks, or fed to dogs. Bones may be disinterred, washed, painted, or buried in bundles. All of these practices have potential archaeological signatures. In Tibet, future archaeologists will have difficulty recognizing any mortuary practice at all. Here, some corpses are dismembered and fed to vultures and other carnivores; the bones are then collected, ground to powder, mixed with barley and flour, and again fed to vultures (Tucci, 1967; Tomasevic, 1981). As recognized by Black (1967:204) while describing a prehistoric American Indian village, some mortuary practices can lead to high frequencies of isolated human bones in archaeological contexts without requiring an interpretation of cannibalism:

> In the absence of human bones cracked for marrow extraction we would be inclined to think of our random finds as representing trophies or skirmishes. But such consideration even would be secondary to the possibility of burial disruption as a normal result of people living their daily lives upon a cemetery containing shallow graves.

CLASSIFICATIONS OF CANNIBALISM

It may seem premature to discuss classifying different kinds of cannibalism, given the nature of the controversy about its prevalence discussed below. It is, however, a useful step, if still theoretical, in considering the kinds of signatures that cannibalism might leave in the archaeological record. Arens (1979) notes that classifications of cannibalism have usually proceeded along two cross-cutting lines based on group affiliation and motive (or function). Some taxonomies divide the activity according to the group affiliation of the people being consumed. Thus, endocannibalism refers to consumption of individuals within the group, exocannibalism indicates consumption of outsiders, and autocannibalism covers everything from nail biting to torture-induced self-consumption. Concern with motive and/or function has led to another set of terms in the anthropological literature. All authors agree on the dimensions of survival, obligatory, or emergency-ration cannibalism—cases in which actual or perceived starvation leads to consumption. Historically documented cases include pioneers trapped in high mountains and shipwreck or airplane crash survivors (Gzowski, 1980; Lopez, 1973; Read, 1974). The agreement of most taxonomically inclined writers on cannibalism ends at this basic level of classification.

A fundamental division recognized implicitly by most, and explicitly by others such as Stothers *et al.* (1982), is best seen in the work of Sagan (1974), who recognizes the contrast between aggressive and affectionate cannibalism (consuming your enemies versus consuming your friends or relatives). Flinn *et al.* (1976) prefer a four-way breakdown, with ritual, revenge, gustatory, and survival cannibalism. Nickens (1975) follows Hogg (1966) in recognizing obligatory, dietary, and ceremonial cannibalism. Arens (1979), Shipman (1987), and Villa *et al.* (1986a) call the latter "ritual" or "magical" cannibalism, a practice often identified with the consumption of human flesh (and even bone material) in affectionate funerary situations. Helmuth (1973) adds "funerary" and "juridicial," whereas Myers (1984) adds "institutional" and "symbolic" to the taxonomic mix.

For many people, "cannibalism" is equated with activities in which there is regular and culturally encouraged consumption of human flesh. This "dietary," "customary," "gourmet," or "gustatory" cannibalism is the phenomenon of which Arens is so skeptical.

Most of the terms associated with cannibalism are actually very misleading. The words "ritual," "ceremonial," or "magical" are inappropriate in describing the funerary cannibalism noted above. As Sahlins (1983:88) points out, sorting the "real" from the "ritual" is problematical: "The problem, of course, is that cannibalism is always 'symbolic,' even when it is 'real.' " Indeed, strong "religious," "symbolic," "ritual," or "ceremonial" dimensions are emphatically present even in all historically documented cases of survival cannibalism. In fact, it is very difficult to contemplate cannibalism, whatever the motivation, without involving these aspects in one way or another. In a similar vein, the label "dietary cannibalism" is particularly misleading because whatever the cause, the tissue ingested is part of the diet!

For these reasons, this book will refer to starvation-induced cannibalism as "survival" cannibalism. Cannibalism of deceased, usually within-group members in which affectionate motivation is present will be called "funerary" cannibalism. Nonfunerary cannibalism practiced under nonstarvation conditions will be called "gastronomic" cannibalism. The challenges posed in differentiating among these categories based on archaeological evidence are considerable.

CANNIBALISM AND THE HUMAN FOSSIL RECORD

Almost as soon as human fossils were recovered from Paleolithic contexts in Europe, speculations were generated about cannibalism in the distant past. In a classic examination of the rules of paleontological evidence, Mark Twain skeptically responded to such claims in 1871 as follows:

> Here is a pile of bones of primeval man and beast all mixed together, with no more damning evidence that the man ate the bears than that the bears ate the man—yet paleontology holds a coroner's inquest in the fifth geologic period on an "unpleasantness" which transpired in the quaternary, and calmly lays it on the MAN, and then adds to it what purports to be evidence of CANNIBALISM. I ask the candid reader, Does not this look like taking advantage of a gentleman who has been dead two million years, and whose surviving friends and relatives—. But the subject is too painful. . . . Here are the savage ways and atrocious appetites attributed to the dead and helpless Primeval Man—have we any assurance that the same hand will not fling mud at the Primeval Man's mother, next? (Twain, 1871 in Neider, 1961:135–136)

Twain's attitude was late in taking hold, and by the time Binford published his *Bones* book 110 years later, archaeologists and physical anthropologists had discovered and described, in one scholarly publication or another, *Australopithecus africanus*, *Homo erectus*, and *Homo neanderthalensis* as cannibalistic ancestors. Montagu (1937) echoed Twain in calling on prehistorians to stop attributing cannibalism to fossils who could not defend themselves. Brothwell (1961:304) advocated a critical view of more recent archaeological reports of cannibalism. He was so influenced by the strong tide of paleontological thought, however, as to concede that "There are, of course, strong indications of this practice in the early African hominids." Later hominids did not escape this interpretation. Indeed, popular and textbook accounts almost universally depict the situation at Choukoutien as demonstrating cannibalism. Some authors go as far as examining cognitive aspects of *Homo erectus*: "This implies not only that he was prepared to eat his fellows when the hunting was poor, but that he ate them without much more compunction than he ate deer, otter, or wild sheep" (Tannahill, 1975:3). Indonesian remains of *Homo erectus* were once interpreted as indicating cannibalism, although more recent authors have adopted skepticism in this regard (Jacob, 1972). Introductory anthropology students are normally presented with the *fact* of cannibalism at Choukoutien and then presented with explanatory *hypotheses* that often include speculations about the origin of ritual and religion! Suffice it to say that a critical review of the evidence behind the "fact" is clearly in order.

A review of the historical context of arguments over cannibalism in fossil hominids will not be attempted here. Rather, the reader is referred to Binford (1981) for an insightful but perhaps unnecessarily peremptory look at some claims for cannibalism among fossil hominids. A spate of recent publications of variable quality on perimortem and postmortem trauma to fossil hominid remains has followed Binford's lead (Russell and LeMort, 1986; LeMort, 1988; Marshack, 1988; Shipman, 1987; Trinkaus, 1985; Ullrich, 1986; White, 1986).

Problems involved with the reconstruction of hominid behavior at the African Plio-Pleistocene boundary are the same, in many ways, as those encountered in the investigation of archaeological manifestations of cannibalism. The analogy is worth pursuing. As Binford (1985) points out, there developed during the late 1970s a consensus view of hominid ancestors as hunters who lived in social groups and shared their food at home bases. From the static evidence of scatters of broken stones and bones at sites like Olduvai and Koobi Fora, this dynamic portrait of life in the past had been created. Arguing that expectations of the investigators had colored interpretations of the evidence, Binford (1981) challenged this model of Paleolithic existence. He noted that the model, like many other myths founded on a mixture of archaeological fact and modern opinion, was really little more than an accommodation of the Oldowan evidence to preconceived notions about early hominids based mostly on ethnographic accounts. Binford asked how unambiguous meaning could be assigned to the archaeological evidence of the objects and their contexts.

Binford (1981:26) presents a strong case for building a dialog between the modern world and the archaeological record. He argues that to give meaning to the static record of the past,

> First, we must attempt to isolate the different agents or forces that might be expected to contribute to or "cause" a given pattern. Second, we would have to conduct studies of these agents or processes in the contemporary world so as to develop criteria of recognition. In short, we need to specify criteria for recognizing traces, "signature patterns" apt to be preserved in the archaeological record, of the agents likely to have contributed to deposits in which hominid remains might also occur. . . . The problem is one of pattern recognition

> linked with the demonstration that the pattern is redundant and unambiguous, a diagnostic signature that discriminates one agent or set of agents from another.

Using the analogy of a bear (an actor who performed past activities) and its footprint (evidence of its past activities after the bear has departed), Binford (1981:29) concludes that "The reason that middle range research must be basically actualistic is that only in the present can we observe the bear and the footprint together, the coincidence of the dynamic and static derivatives."

What are the archaeological signatures of cannibalism? Can we "anchor our interpretations" (Binford, 1987b) of cannibalism in middle-range studies, actualistic research "where controlled information about causes and effects could be evaluated experientally rather than inferentially" (Binford, 1981:32)? To employ Binford's uniformitarian "middle-range research" in the archaeological investigation of cannibalism, we would like to observe instances in which the cannibal and his leftovers can be observed together. This turns out to be a tall order.

CANNIBALISM AND THE HISTORICAL RECORD

Two years before Binford launched his attack on what he considered to be myths about early hominid behavior Arens sparked controversy and consternation within the anthropological community with another assault on myth, *The Man Eating Myth: Anthropology and Anthropophagy* (1979). A decade earlier Shankman, in his critique of Levi-Strauss' theories regarding cannibalism, conveniently presaged the response to Arens and epitomized the status quo that Arens set out to challenge: "Long before academics were devouring each other, people around the world were using their stomachs as cemeteries" (Shankman, 1969:54). The extent to which the latter statement was true was critically examined by Arens. It was by no means, however, the first time cannibalism as a general human activity had been questioned. Montagu (1937:57) had set the tone with his statement: "In fact, cannibalism is a pure traveler's myth."

Arens (1979) stopped far short of the latter position. It is worth examining what his book does and does not say about cannibalism. According to Arens (1979:9):

> . . . this essay has a dual purpose. First, to assess critically the instances of and documentation for cannibalism, and second, by examining this material and the theoretical explanations offered, to arrive at some broader understanding of the nature and function of anthropology over the past century. In other words, the question of whether or not people eat each other is taken as interesting, but moot. But if the idea that they do is commonly accepted without adequate documentation, then the reason for this state of affairs is an even more intriguing problem.

Arens' 1979 book is really about anthropology. He reviews the record of cannibalism, attempting to choose the most popular and best documented cases and to examine these critically. Excluding survival conditions, Arens did not uncover adequate documentation of cannibalism as a custom in any form for any society:

> Rumors, suspicions, fears and accusations abound, but no satisfactory first-hand accounts. Learned essays by professionals are unending but the sustaining ethnography is lacking (p. 21). . . . The most certain thing to be said is that all cultures, subcultures, religions, sects, secret societies and every other possible human association have been labeled

> anthropophagic by someone. In this light, the contemporary, though neglected, anthropological problem emerges more clearly. The idea of ''others'' as cannibals, rather than the act, is the universal phenomenon. (Arens, 1979:139)

Arens (1979:9–10) goes on to question how cannibalism grew as conventional wisdom in anthropology, concluding that the situation is ''astonishing'':

> Anthropology has not maintained the usual standards of documentation and intellectual rigor expected when other topics are being considered. Instead, it has chosen uncritically to lend its support to the collective representations and thinly disguised prejudices of western culture about others.

These conclusions evoked responses across the anthropological community. Many of them were negative, focusing on Arens' denial of evidence (Crapanzano, 1979; Wagner, 1979; Sahlins, 1979). These responses were predictable and understandable given Arens' proclivity for overstatement. For example, Turner (1983) calls Arens' work a tree-falling-in-the-woods-noiselessly argument. Springer's review concludes: ''The difficulty with the book is that Arens is almost certainly wrong'' (1980:148). A variety of anthropologists have come forward with ethnohistorical evidence of one sort or another for the existence of cannibalism among the Maori (Bowden, 1984; Sahlins, 1979), in South America (Forsyth, 1985; Rivière, 1980; Durham, in preparation), in Fiji (Sahlins, 1979, 1983), and in North America (Abler, 1980). Some reviewers, however, have come closer to grappling with the significance of the gulf between the myth and the evidence that Arens has identified and emphasized. For example, Brady (1982:601) states:

> It should be remembered that Arens's book is less an attempt to set the record straight on cannibalism (where it does or does not occur and why) than it is an indictment of anthropology for swallowing such tales whole and parading them around in the literature as facts when most of the evidence turns out on close inspection to be unsubstantiated impressions, rumors, innuendo, ethnocentrism, plagiarism, and so forth.

Needham's (1980) thoughtful review of Arens (1979) makes the substantive criticism that the book lacks a precise definition of cannibalism (a point also made by Myers, 1984). Needham (1980:76) accurately describes the Arens position as a ''modest proposal that cannibalism, though perhaps sporadically carried out, is far less common than Europeans, and especially anthropologists, have been more than willing to suppose.'' Furthermore, Needham correctly points out Arens' lack of precision about exactly what would count as evidence for cannibalism. The practice, if it existed, was usually history by the time modern anthropologists came along, yet most of the written histories are unacceptable to Arens.

The anthropologist's interest in cannibalism continues unabated (Harris, 1977; Sahlins, 1978). A recent book entitled *The Ethnography of Cannibalism* (Brown and Tuzin, 1983:1) is prefaced with the thought that

> Until about one hundred years ago, knowledge of actual cannibal practices rested on a heap of traveler's tales, missionary testimonies, conquerors' apologetics, diplomatic and administrative reports and the like . . . there are many other societies closer in time to their cannibal traditions—societies in which living informants still remember how, why, and under what circumstances humans were eaten, or for which the relevant documentation is relatively rich and reliable.

When it comes to our ability to study cannibals, Brown and Tuzin seem as optimistic as Arens is skeptical. Contrast their view with that of Arens (1979:183):

> . . . the general tone of modern anthropological commentary on cannibalism emerges as little more than nineteenth-century reinterpretations in contemporary scientific jargon.

In another review of 156 societies by Sanday (1986), 109 were found to yield information bearing on cannibalism. Of these, cannibalism was indicated for 34 percent. The strength of these data is suspect, given the frequency with which people talk about cannibals and cannibalism and the ease and frequency with which they accuse others of this activity (for example, 62 percent of California Indian groups had cannibal tales; Groff, 1960).

The impact of Arens' book probably will take a long time to register in the popular literature. A brief perusal of professional and popular anthropology brings evidence of a continuing fascination with cannibalism. Accounts range from tabloid announcements ("Cannibals Shrink Space Alien's Head," Anon. 1986) through secondhand recitations (Anglo, 1979), to more semipopular treatises (Harris, 1977; Davies, 1981; Eckholm, 1986) and uncritical scientific papers (Neuman, 1987).

Charles Darwin, in *The Descent of Man* (1871:327), said that ". . . without doubting there can be no progress. . . ." Modern doubts about historical and prehistoric cannibalism force a reconsideration of the standards for applicable archaeological evidence. Binford (1981) contends that the classic cannibals of the Paleolithic are myths created by modern prehistorians. Arens (1979:120) contends that the cannibalism so commonly found in our ethnographies has been built with a set of linking preconceptions:

> In this fashion, an equation was made between nineteenth-century primitives and prehistoric man. Both creatures were assumed to be almost devoid of culture as conceived by the European mind of the last century; and in this savage state, the worst could be expected. This line of reasoning inevitably led to the second reason for the *a priori* assumption of cannibalism on the part of early man.

Arens uses Loeb's *The Blood Sacrifice Complex* (1927) to illustrate the misplaced evolutionary underpinnings of the linkage of the modern "savage" with the ancient hominid by pointing out that the evidence employed in this classic study was *prehistoric* evidence of cannibalism in Europe and *ethnographic* evidence in the rest of the world.

Any contemporary undergraduate student familiar with anthropology through textbooks probably would agree with Merbs and Steadman (1982) that Arens' failure to find documented, customary cannibalism was "amazing." My review of the literature was mercifully shortened when it was realized that Arens and his reviewers had already beaten that path to little avail. There is little hope of conducting actualistic, ethnoarchaeological research to ascertain cannibalism's osteological/archaeological signature. Experimental studies may have difficulty clearing human subjects committees.

CANNIBALISM AND THE ARCHAEOLOGICAL RECORD

As Arens has suggested, many, if not most, historical sources on cannibalism are inadequate or inaccurate. Because ethnographic research no longer seems possible, the study of cannibalism must, of necessity, be accomplished by a historical science. A man in a position to know, Matos Moctezuma, the excavator of a site at which Spanish accounts suggest that human sacrifice took place (the Aztec Templo Mayor in Mexico City), puts it this way (Matos Moctezuma, 1987:185):

> Archaeology and the study of documentary sources are two of these mutually reinforcing fields. Documentary sources provide us with historical information that is either exaggerated or faithful to observations, depending on the bias of the chronicler and how he has chosen to present his material. Such ethnohistorical information serves as a basis for the hypotheses that are corroborated or invalidated by excavation and archaeological evidence. Archaeology then either validates the written information or demonstrates its unreliability.

Archaeology seems, therefore, to be the only remaining tool for investigating the existence and extent of cannibalism. Arens assessed the track record of archaeologists on cannibalism as follows (1979:133):

> Although some may be improvident in their interpretation of the prehistoric evidence, by and large they are much more cautious in drawing conclusions than their colleagues who study historic and contemporary non-western societies. . . . Stricter scholarly standards may have something to do with this condition, but equally significant is the existence of observable concrete artifacts. . . . Indeed the archeologists and paleontologists arrive at some of their more indefensible deductions by their unsuspecting reliance on the contributions of social anthropologists whose research methods are not as rigorous.

The study of human mortuary practices has been an area of archaeological concern for as long as there have been archaeologists. Arens (1979) recognizes the value of physical evidence for the accurate reconstruction of past human behaviors and considers a few examples from the prehistoric record, but, by his own admission, does not pursue the archaeological evidence to any great length. Archaeological response to Arens has been very limited. Rathje set Arens' thesis against the archaeological evidence on cannibalism in two popular papers (1981, 1985), concluding that there was fertile ground for investigation. It was not Arens' intent to create work for archaeologists, but it is likely that archaeology will be the final arbiter of his ideas.

The stances taken by Arens and Binford are arguably extreme, but the accumulated bias of several centuries of "study" of cannibalism is not easily corrected. Clearly a balance remains to be achieved. These authors have effectively set the cannibal ledger to zero. In so doing, they have challenged their respective academic communities to raise the standards of their evidence and scholarship.

ASSESSING A SAMPLE OF CLAIMS FOR CANNIBALISM IN THE ARCHAEOLOGICAL RECORD

It is beyond the scope of this book to undertake a complete review of the archaeological literature on every claim for, or mention of, cannibalism made in the last two centuries of archaeological research. It is valuable, however, to consider a sample of claims that have been made, in different parts of the world, for cannibalism in the post-Pleistocene archaeological record. Mention also will be made of areas in which ethnohistorical documents predict that evidence for cannibalism might be abundant. This is a useful exercise for a variety of reasons. First, it places the evidence from the American Southwest presented in this book into a more global perspective. Second, it illustrates the nature of the problems in identifying cannibalism in archaeological contexts. Finally, because the cases cited here are among the best documented instances of cannibalism in the record, this section should help illustrate why the Mancos 5MTUMR–2346 assemblage is such an important one.

Before presenting the results of the survey, however, it should be noted that for some areas in which cannibalism is "documented" or alluded to in the ethnographic or ethnohistorical records, evidence of burned and broken human bone in archaeological context is far more likely to be interpreted as cannibalism than in cases in which analogous material evidence is found in regions with little or no such "documentary" evidence of cannibalism. In other words, expectations can often steer interpretations.

The willingness to accept cannibalism as responsible for damaged human bones in areas or time ranges in which cannibalism is "expected" contrasts with a skepticism about so interpreting similar remains in areas where cannibalism is not so "expected." This reliance on ethnographic records in the interpretation of prehistoric data can lead to dramatically disparate interpretations of the same data. Thus, the spatial distribution of archaeological evidence *interpreted* to signal cannibalism is expected to coincide with the distribution of ethnohistorical/ethnological accounts of cannibalism. This phenomenon has been termed the "tyranny" of ethnographic analogy (Wobst, 1978; Upham, 1987), carrying with it the assumption of stasis. The American Southwest is one region (among many) with relatively little record of circum-contact cannibalism, on the opposite end of the ethnohistorical backdrop from New Guinea, where we start the survey.

New Guinea and the Pacific

As discussed above, the potential for ethnoarchaeological research on cannibalism is small. This may come as a surprise because ethnographic accounts of this activity in New Guinea are so widespread and because 20th-century reports suggest the persistence of the activity into the 1960s. Koch (1970), for example, describes the activities associated with processing the deceased among the Jalé in some detail, including a description of the midsagittal incision lines made across the head. Zegwaard (1959) provides similar detail for the Asmat. In addition to such accounts, there is a common assumption that the slow viral disease Kuru is linked to cannibalism. The Nobel Prize-winning Gajdusek has been attacked by Arens (1979) on this issue, the latter holding that such linkage has been a "compulsion," and yet evidence that *ingestion* of human tissue spreads the virus has not been forthcoming. Merbs and Steadman (1982) suggest that handling corpses during mortuary practices rather than cannibalism is responsible for the spread of the disease. Gajdusek has proven reluctant to provide documentation of cannibalism despite the insistence of Arens and others, maintaining that "The whole of Australia knows these people are cannibals. It is 100% documented" (Gajdusek in Kolata, 1986:1499). As Schryer (1986) notes, however, the whole of Europe once "knew" that witches existed. Durham's (1991) account summarizes the ethnohistorical and biological backgrounds to cannibalism in this part of the world.

It is very well documented that many aboriginal people in New Guinea displayed human skeletal remains in and around their houses and sometimes wore them on their bodies. Toth and I examined a series of crania collected in the late 1800s from around the Dawson Straits, D'Entrecasteaux Islands, off the southeast tip of Papua New Guinea (Pietrusewsky, 1985; White and Toth, 1991). The damage patterning implied that these crania had been defleshed, and the bases were then carefully struck to create a hole that would simplify mounting on a pole. Many crania were decorated with painted lines and showed polish clearly resulting from extensive handling. The trauma to these remains was consistent with postmortem use of the skull as an ornament. The consistent processing (foramen magnum enlargement) of the cranial bases has no necessary implication for cannibalism—yet this skeletal series inspired Sergi and others to conclude that Neanderthal specimens without cranial bases resulted from cannibalistic feasts (White and Toth, 1991).

Elsewhere in the Pacific there is a detailed ethnohistorical record of cannibalism. This is one area of the world that Arens covers in only a cursory manner. Bowden (1984), for example, has drawn attention to an "abundance" of "reliable" historical and ethnographic evidence for cannibalism among the Maori of New Zealand. Archaeological evidence of this is more limited. In reviewing the prehistory of New Zealand, Davidson (1979a) notes that secondary burial practices were present. The Whangamata Wharf site on the Coromandel Peninsula has very weak evidence in the form of "burnt and scattered" human bones found among dog bones and interpreted as "probably evidence of cannibalism" (Allo, 1972:76). Davidson (1984) briefly reviews possible occurrences of cannibalism in New Zealand, noting the difficulty in determining whether isolated human remains represent cannibalism or result from postburial disturbance. She grounds her review ethnohistorically, citing "indisputable" evidence of cannibalism. For archaeological occurrences, she accepts as evidence of cannibalism incomplete burials and charred bones in firepits, noting that ". . . the few occurrences are hardly sufficient to suggest a significant contribution to the diet, even during late prehistoric times" (Davidson, 1984:137). The Pouerua project in central Northland, New Zealand, was undertaken to define the origin and operation of the northern Maori chiefdom as it was in 1840. Sutton's (1990) work on the rim of Pouerua has revealed small pits filled with burnt and fragmentary human bone, male and female, representing a mixture of individual developmental ages. This late-precontact/early-historic evidence is interpreted by Sutton as indicative of cannibalism.

Davidson (1979b) also reports an oven containing human bone at the base of the Lotofaga midden on Samoa (A.D. 1215). Sinoto (1979) maintains that a Phase III (A.D. 1300–1600) midden on the Marquesas is dominated by shellfish and human bone that suggests cannibalism. Kirch's (1973) work at Marquesan site MUH1, sand dunes with much domestic cultural content, indicates that broken, scattered, and sometimes charred human bone occurred in quantity in the upper layers. Kirch (1973:38) suggests that this evidence indicates ". . . the growth of intertribal warfare and cannibalism, ethnohistorically well-documented aspects of Marquesas culture." Poulsen (1968) describes a similar situation of scattered, broken bone in the middens of Tongatapu, saying that cannibalism was "possibly" present. In the New Hebrides, Garanger (1972) notes that the fragmentary human remains at Mangaasi indicate cannibalism. In New Caledonia, Gifford and Shutler (1956) report that similar evidence for cannibalism was found, but that it was not as extensive as that on Fiji.

Cannibalism is not reported for Hawaii although cautionary tales abound. Many human bones bear cutmarks, and evidence for widespread manufacture of human bone tools is present (Snow, 1974). The situation on Easter Island is similar, but Heyerdahl and Ferdon (1961) cautiously approach the discovery of human bones and marine shells in the middens, noting the need for detailed study. They note that "Human teeth and small fragments of human bones were encountered at all levels. Some human bones were used in the manufacture of fishhooks, but whether or not cannibalism was practiced at the site cannot be determined" (Heyerdahl and Ferdon, 1961:263). McCoy (1979:142) reviews the archaeological evidence for Easter Island cannibalism, concluding that "Food shortages are reflected in the emergence of cannibalism, to which there are numerous references in traditions on warfare."

Fiji is the area in which cannibalism is most widely accepted as having been practiced at contact. As noted above, Sahlins (1979, 1983) has used the ethnohistorical record for Fiji to attack Arens' contentions. Spennemann (1987) also labels Arens' claims as "naive and ethnocentric." Citing ethnohistorical sources, he claims that evidence for Fijian cannibalism over the last 2,500 years is "ample" and "firm." Spennemann analyzes thirteen bones from four human individuals found in a tree-fork trophy, noting cut- and chopmarks on the bones. He comments on the faintness of the cutmarks, attributing this to earth-oven cooking and use of bamboo knives. Spennemann notes the surprising lack of ethnohistorical reference to procurement of marrow from the bones of cannibalized humans. He goes on to "match" the elbow, hip, and knee joint cutmarks with ethnohistorical accounts and proceeds with experimental butchery with bamboo to "confirm" the existence of cannibal butchery. Spennemann (1987:44) concludes that, although now scanty, archaeological data on Fijian cannibalism will "undoubtedly be gathered in time."

Gifford (1951) reports evidence of burned, fragmented human bone from the Vunda site on Fiji as follows: "Except for fish, man was the most popular of the vertebrate animals used for food" (Gifford, 1951:208). True burials found in the middens were excluded from consideration by Gifford. I have examined the vertebrate fauna from the Uluvinavatu and Vunda sites housed in the Lowie Museum of Anthropology. The human remains have evidence of perimortem cutmarks and fracture, but the samples are very small. Considerably more work could be done with these materials, but more excavation is obviously needed to increase sample size in an effort to unravel the history of these mixed human and faunal assemblages.

Best's work at Lakeba (1984) contributes additional information to the subject of cannibalism on Fiji. In describing the mammalian faunal remains from four sites, Best notes very limited evidence of disturbed burials contributing to the bulk of the human remains that he considers to represent "food remains" because of ". . . the small size of most of the fragments, charring on many of them, cut marks on some, and the under representation of hands, feet and heads" (Best [1984:535] cites ethnohistorical accounts suggesting that hands, feet, and heads were disposed of or fed to the pigs after large massacres). Plotting "calorific values" of the eleven "main meat resources" from the large rock shelter site 197, Best notes the importance of the human component. Houghton's assessments are cited in Appendix O, where Best describes the skeletal material as follows (1984:A84): "The material is extremely fragmented, without a single intact long bone. The majority of fragments are from long bones, many are charred. . . ."

Across the Pacific archaeologists have worked in contexts where ethnohistorical accounts predict cannibalism. Fragmentary human bone has often been found in midden contexts and interpreted to represent cannibalism. The latter activity has never really been questioned by archaeologists. Therefore, the primary analysis of the human remains has been at an understandably superficial level, and summary accounts (Cram, 1975) accept the conclusions of the primary workers. A major work on Fijiian archaeological bone assemblages by Bob Rechtman (n.d.) promises to dramatically change this situation.

Australia

Early Australian narratives and ethnographies are replete with tales of cannibalism (Lumholtz, 1890; Elkin, 1937). Archaeologically, there are accounts of charred, fragmented human bone remains from middens, mingled with fauna (for example, Schrire, 1982). Given the amount of secondary burial practiced ethnographically in Australia, the paucity of discussion of the phenomenon is perhaps not surprising. In fact, Australia is the continent on which archaeological and ethnohistorical data provide the most serious challenge to disentangling cannibalism from other mortuary practices. Bowler *et al.* (1970:57) report that even for Mungo, some of the earliest human remains from Australia, there is evidence for cremation and a ". . . total and thorough smashing of the burnt skeleton, particularly the face and vault." The longest long-bone fragment from this postcremation processing was 11 cm. Ash and smashed bones were gathered and deposited in a conical hole. Hiatt (1969) summarizes the distribution of ethnographically and ethnohistorically documented cremation practices in Australia. Mortuary practices here were diverse, and in cremations, bones not completely consumed by fire were often bashed to make further burning or burial easier. The hollow log burial documented by McKenzie (1980) is another example. Here, after the bones from the primary exhumation have been excavated, scraped free of adhering tissue remains, and painted with red ochre, group members use a hammer and anvil technique to fracture all the bones into pieces smaller than approximately 8 cm, finally placing them in a painted, hollowed tree trunk that is erected as a monument. In spite of the ethnohistorical "expectations" for cannibalism, Australian archaeologists have been very reluctant to interpret skeletal remains that they discover as evidence of cannibalism, perhaps because of the parallel detailed ethnographic knowledge about mortuary practices.

Africa

Despite many ethnohistorical accounts (for example, Hibbert, 1983), the archaeological evidence of cannibalism in Africa is minimal. For example, at Hyrax Hill, an Iron Age site in Kenya, a series of burials described as "apparently hasty" was interpreted to show dismemberment and decapitation. This evidence was interpreted as follows by Leakey (1945:373): "Nor is it impossible either that these remains are the result of cannibalism."

Klapwijk's (1989) description of "pot burials" in the Transvaal includes reference to possible human sacrifice, and the remains are clearly the result of mortuary practices. There is no reference to cannibalism, nor any reason to suspect it in this case. Given the background discussed above, perhaps the only surprise about these finds is that the presence of fragmentary human remains interred in large pots did not lead the investigator to claim that cannibalism was indicated!

Europe

Contrary to the biases of many investigators, ethnohistorical accounts of European cannibalism are surprisingly easy to come by. In fact, medicinal cannibalism was practiced extensively in Europe during the 16th, 17th, and 18th centuries. Tissues involved included flesh, blood, and even bone marrow (Gordon-Grube, 1988). There is no archaeological documentation of these practices.

Archaeological evidence for cannibalism in Europe is rare, but very important. In many instances human skeletal material has been found scattered across site surfaces, sometimes with carnivore gnawing. For example, Larsson *et al.* (1981) describe nearly 40 percent of 59 faunal-bearing Mesolithic Scandinavian sites with such remains. These authors prudently take the position that it is unsafe to ascribe such remains to cannibalism. Wall *et al.* (1986) describe an occurrence of bones in a Late Minoan IB (1450 B.C.) site in which over 35 percent of the disarticulated human bones from four children have cutmarks. The context of discovery and damage patterns are well documented and illustrated. The authors conclude that the children were likely killed, that the killings may have been sacrificial, that the butchery is similar to that done on the associated fauna, and that the context suggests cooking of the human remains in a ritual.

In 1957 Jan Jelinek reviewed the Czechoslovakian evidence for Bronze Age and "Hallstatt" cannibalism. In this excellent review he compiled evidence for a funerary rite ". . . remarkable for its irreverent burial of human remains often accompanied by anthropophagy" (Jelinek, 1957:130). This evidence takes the form of faunal and human material from archaeological excavations. The human bones were cut, fractured, and disposed of in the same manner as the faunal remains. Jelinek comments that the evidence is widespread geographically and temporally, and he provides illustrations to support his views.

Villa and colleagues (Villa *et al.*, 1986a, 1986b, 1987, 1988) provide one of the world's best documented archaeological occurrences consistent with cannibalism. This is the Neolithic (3000–4000 B.C.) site of Fontbrégoua Cave in southeastern France. These "post-Arens" authors emphasize the Fontbrégoua evidence by dismissing or ignoring (in the case of the American Southwest) previous archaeological interpretations of cannibalism. Although the basic data are incompletely reported, recovery, documentation, and analysis of the Fontbrégoua bone materials are sound. Direct comparison with processed faunal remains was possible at the site. The depositional context and damage patterns on the human and animal remains were essentially the same. Villa *et al.* (1986a:436) conclude:

> Our inference that animal and human meat was eaten is based on the evidence of ordinary butchering practices and unceremonial patterns of discard in a domestic setting. Similarities in the treatment of animal and human remains are striking. The evidence of breakage to extract marrow and the mode of discard contrast strongly with known secondary burial practices. . . . Taphonomic studies of human bones at additional Stone Age French sites should help to establish whether our findings represent isolated events or institutionalized practices.

Thus, at Fontbrégoua the evidence for cannibalism was excellent, but this occurrence is unique in its preservation of contextual evidence so critical to the interpretation. Even here, however, the nature of historical evidence remains at odds with the conclusion of the primary investigators that ". . . cannibalism is *proven beyond doubt* . . ." (Villa *et al.*, 1988:57; italics mine).

The Caribbean

Cannibalism derives its name from aboriginal inhabitants of the Caribbean. Arens (1979) considered this region in some detail. His book drew a response from Myers (1984) who, like Arens, considers cannibalism as an epithet that helped to justify slaughter and enslavement of the indigenous Island Carib populations. After reviewing the ethnohistorical and archaeological record, Myers concludes that there is little evidence of cannibalism in the Caribbean, but concedes that late Carib sites have not been excavated.

South America

Response to Arens' (1979) contentions about the lack of institutionalized cannibalism in South America has been far less sympathetic. Both Forsyth (1985) and Rivière (1980) have concluded that the ethnohistoric record for cannibalism was dismissed too lightly by Arens. Forsyth (1985:31) calls Arens' effort "poor ethnohistoric scholarship" and concludes that it "cannot be taken seriously." He is willing, however, to take 16th-century sources far more seriously than Arens is, and the result is a deadlock. Archaeological evidence has not yet figured in the debate, probably because not enough of it is available. Work in progress by William Durham of Stanford University promises to add more light to the issue of cannibalism in South America (Durham, 1991).

Mesoamerica

Nowhere has the debate about the extent and functions of cannibalism been as extensive as it has been for Mesoamerica. Contact and postcontact accounts of the Aztec are voluminous. There is no doubt that there was extensive human sacrifice in the region, and archaeological evidence for this is widespread (Fowler, 1984; Berrelleza, 1986; Agrinier, 1978). Harner (1977:119) has relied heavily on the chronicles of the Spanish in his contention that Aztec cannibalism has been ". . . largely ignored or consciously or unconsciously covered up." His functionally oriented analysis of the Aztec maintains that their system was driven by the subsistence requirements of a large human population in the Valley of Mexico. Ortiz de Montellano (1978) has attacked this idea by attempting to show that protein requirements were not as Harner imagines. Sahlins (1979) has also attacked the idea by reviewing the religious aspects of Aztec cannibalism. Gould and Lewontin (1978) suggest that the cannibalism was a "secondary epiphenomenon" rather than a cause of the system. Arens (1979) doubts that much Aztec cannibalism existed *at all* and contends that the scale imagined by Harner is a myth promulgated by the European colonists.

It is obvious that archaeological evidence could have a major impact in resolving these very different views of the past. Harner (1977) does refer to limbless skeletal torsos and piles of skulls found at the Aztec site of Tlatelolco (now part of Mexico City and, at contact, a site strongly tied to the Aztec capitol) in the context of his arguments about widespread cannibalism. Pijoan and Pastrana (1985) and Pijoan *et al.* (1989) have now analyzed osteological evidence from 1962 excavations that revealed 170 tzompantli crania (trophy skulls placed on wooden racks) at Tlatelolco. They conclude that the patterning is consistent with accounts of human sacrifice. Pijoan has shown me some of these materials housed in the National Anthropological Museum in Mexico City. The patterning is impressive, with clear cutmarks. There is an obvious patterning of the percussion on these crania. The crania were carefully struck multiple times on the sides of the vaults, the smaller impact holes coalescing into large openings in the temporoparietal regions. Many of these crania were found in linear juxtaposition consistent with the ethnohistorical accounts of vast skull racks that dominated some major plazas described in the Spanish chronicles. The skulls were probably ligamentous when displayed as may be inferred from the fact that the mandibles are still attached. As in the New Guinea collections described above, percussion of the vault was accomplished in a careful, controlled manner that left the cranium intact for display. This is hardly evidence of cannibalism. The postcranial portions of the skeletons are not present. Recent work (Pijoan *et al.*, in press) on postcranial specimens from another area of the Tlatelolco site promises to reveal additional information on prehistoric activities there.

Harner (1977) cites the Spanish chronicles in his contention that limbs were cut from captive sacrificial victims and distributed among the Aztec captors. If protein and fats were at the shortages suggested by Harner, the archaeological signature should be straightforward: broken and scattered human remains in food refuse deposits. Such evidence has not been reported. In Mexico City, it is very unlikely that such evidence will become available because much of the ancient city is now covered by its modern descendant. In other Aztec sites, however, a test of the various contending ideas about cannibalism is possible but so far unperformed.

Coe and Diehl (1980:386), based on a modest sample of incompletely analyzed, fragmentary human bone from excavations, suggest that *Homo sapiens* was a major dietary element in the Chicharras and San Lorenzo diet, concluding that "The Olmec appear to have been thoroughgoing cannibals, on the basis of this evidence." For the Toltec, Diehl (1983:98) interprets burned human bones found in excavations at Tula as evidence of cannibalism, but goes on to suggest that the situation regarding the frequency of cannibalism can ". . . only be clarified by additional research." Sanders (1972:131–132) reports on the excavation of an Early Classic, small, compact "corporate community" site (TC–8) of 200 x 400 m. Here in the Teotihuacán Valley, Sanders reports a

> . . . rarity of bone other than human and dog in the midden. . . . Human bone was common, and scattered through the kitchen refuse. Isolated mandibles were particularly common and several pieces of worked skull fragments were found. In several cases more direct evidence of cannibalism was revealed, i.e., human bone in cooking pots. Warfare with its attendant ritual practices seem to parallel very closely those reported by the Spaniards of the Aztec.

It is evident that archaeologists in Mesoamerica have encountered isolated, fragmentary, sometimes burned human bone in refuse deposits, and have attributed their discoveries to the activities of cannibals. Rather than interpreting such discoveries as evidence of cremation, as might be done in other parts of the world, the Mesoamerican archaeologist may sometimes be drawn by ethnohistory to interpret the evidence as cannibalism. Systematic, critical investigation of these bony remains seems not to have been given high priority by archaeologists working in the region, but physical anthropologists Pijoan and Pastrana and colleagues at the Instituto Nacional de Antropologia e Historia have made excellent progress on several assemblages.

Although advances in the interpretation of Mayan art and iconography have revealed the practice of ritual sacrifice, the first to address this argument, based on burial data and skeletal remains, is Welsh (1988). He marshals considerable evidence for sacrifice, but his analysis was of archaeologically recognized burials and did not consider cannibalism.

The best evidence of cannibalism (as I have defined it) from Mesoamerica comes from the site of Tlatelcomila, Teltelpan. This Upper Preclassic (500–700 B.C.) occurrence has the remains of a minimum of 18 human individuals described by Pijoan and Pastrana (1987, 1989). The assemblage includes four infants, two subadults, and ten adults. It shows a pattern of burning, fragmentation, percussion, and cutmarks that is consistent with the nutritional exploitation of the skeletal parts. Contextual details of the occurrence are not, however, as well documented as is the case of Fontbrégoua, France. A recent review of human skeletal remains from northeastern Mesoamerica has revealed additional specimens with suggestive cutmarks and fracture patterns (Pijoan and Mansilla, 1990).

America North of Mexico

Apart from Europe, North America has experienced more archaeological research per area and time horizon than most of the other areas discussed above. In North America there is a large ethnohistorical literature and a well studied archaeological record that, in many regions, extends from contact down into the late Pleistocene. Human skeletal remains were the focus of a diversity of mortuary practices, including primary burial, secondary burial, and cremation. Tools made of human bone have been recovered from many areas. Cutmarks on human skeletal material have been reported from Clarksville and Potomac Creek in Virginia (St. Hoyme and Bass, 1962; Ubelaker, 1989) through Indian Knoll in Kentucky (Snow, 1948), Juntunen in Michigan (McPherron, 1967; Russell, 1987), and at a variety of Woodland period sites (see Brown, 1979; Graves, 1984; Molto *et al.*, 1986 for references). In these and other instances, much of the cutmark activity seems related to disarticulation associated with mortuary practices. In other instances, skeletal trauma is present as a result of warfare (Owsley *et al.*, 1977). Postmortem bone preparation involving cranial parts is present at many sites. For example, Redmond (1982) discusses the evidence for Late Woodland practices that included perforation of crania by percussion and drilling, punching, rearticulation and clay masking of bones, and the manufacture of ornaments made from human bone. As with scalping (Axtell and Sturtevant, 1980), none of this constitutes evidence of cannibalism as I have defined it. It is important to note, however, that European explorers who contacted similar practices for the first time during the seventeenth and eighteenth centuries may have had some of their preconceptions about cannibalism strengthened when faced with an abundance of unburied human osteological material. Again, archaeology is the most appropriate medium for investigating many ethnohistorical accounts of cannibalism at contact and for establishing the degree of cannibalism prior to contact. This brief survey of some relevant North American literature begins in the far north and moves to the Pacific Northwest, the Plains, the Midwest, and the East.

Several archaeological investigations centered on Kodiak Island and Cook Inlet, Alaska, have resulted in the discovery of human remains (deLaguna, 1934;

Hrdlicka, 1944; Heizer, 1956; Lobdell, 1975; Jordan, 1988). Partial skeletons, articulated segments of skeletons, and many isolated skeletal elements have been found at Kachemak sites. The isolated elements are often broken, cut, and burned in a fashion similar to that seen for nonhuman remains from the same middens. Hrdlicka (1944) saw this as undoubted evidence for cannibalism although studies aimed at testing this interpretation in a more rigorous fashion are currently underway (Jordan, personal communication).

Some of the earliest North American remains interpreted as cannibalized are from the Marmes site in the Pacific Northwest. Krantz (1979:174) describes this heavily fragmented material as bearing cutmarks and being burned. He concludes: "Frankly, the whole picture presented is that of a cannibalistic feast during which over half of the food was removed from the immediate area and some of the leftovers thrown back into the fire." Further documentation is not available.

The early history of the Texas Gulf coast is dominated by accounts of aboriginal man-eaters. Knowles (1940:202) describes the inhabitants as "undoubtedly voracious cannibals." A book by Kilman (1959) entitled *The Cannibal Coast* is a popularistic historical account of the region. It provides much assertion and little archaeological documentation. Pearce reported human remains excavated at a site near Robstown, Texas, on the Agua Dulce Bayou. In what is, to my knowledge, the only published account of the occurrence, Pearce (1932:672) describes the remains as follows:

> . . . about twenty-five butchered human bodies buried in a wide shallow pit possibly the refuse of a characteristic Karankawa cannibal feast. Many bones show marks of axes and all long bones had been broken into at least two or three pieces. This find tends to confirm the historical reputation of the Indians of this region for cannibalism.

A 1987 check of this skeletal material at the University of Texas failed to reveal any evidence of bone modification (Tom Hester, personal communication). In addition, Pearce illustrates broken human bones from a site on the San Gabriel River, central Texas, in his book *Tales That Dead Men Tell* (1935:10). Judging from the lack of details on damage recorded by Pearce, contentions about cannibalism appear to have been inspired more by tales told by pioneers than by the archaeological evidence itself—another case of ethnohistorical expectations biasing archaeological interpretation.

Zimmerman *et al.* (1980) and Zimmerman and Alex (1981) describe another discovery of a mass deposit of human bone in the American West, this one at Crow Creek. This site (c. A.D. 1300) was a 50-lodge village overlooking the Missouri River in South Dakota. Part of the site was excavated in the 1970s, leading to the recovery of a minimum of 486 individuals from a fortification ditch around the village. The semiarticulated skeletons were found in a bone bed of up to 1.5-m thickness. There was extensive evidence for perimortem trauma. There had been decapitation and some dismemberment, with carnivore damage superimposed. Large numbers of crania showed cutmarks interpreted as evidence of scalping. Cannibalism has never been suggested for this assemblage. Contextual information and the nature of osteological trauma are consistent with a prehistoric Arikara massacre associated with intergroup conflict. This important assemblage has now been reburied and is unavailable for further study. Other examples of ossuaries (O'Shea and Bridges, 1989) from the Plains show the disarticulated remains of multiple individuals with cutmarks—cases of secondary burial with no indication of cannibalism as defined here.

Moving to a consideration of the eastern half of North America, we find ethnohistorical accounts stressing cannibalism among the aboriginals. For example, Knowles (1940) describes torture of captives among eastern Indian tribes, and contends that among Iroquois-speaking tribes, cannibalism "invariably" accompanied this activity. Archaeological research has been sufficient in central and eastern North America that such practices, if prehistorically or ethnohistorically present, should be archaeologically visible.

Robbins (1974) provides two "interpretational hypotheses" to account for the nearly 2,000 fragments and fewer than 50 complete bones from a minimum of 41 human individuals in Salts Cave, Kentucky. This material showed cutmarks and burning, and was recovered from excavations in a context containing animal bones with the same preservational characteristics. The interpretation favored by Robbins is cannibalism, but an alternate is one of defleshing and cremation. The latter alternative is favored in a recent review of Early Woodland archaeology by Seeman (1986). Unfortunately, the published analysis of the Salts Cave material is so poorly illustrated and quantified that it is impossible to make a proper evaluation of this important evidence.

Phelps and Burgess (1964) report another possible case of cannibalism, this time from Early Woodland eastern Georgia. This much smaller sample is also highly fragmentary except for the mandibles (suggested to be "trophies"). There are cutmarks, and there is some burning. The lack of illustration or quantification, again, makes analysis difficult.

Any sampler of the archaeological evidence of cannibalism should consider the Northeast and the Great Lakes region. It is in these areas that the ethnohistorical accounts of North American cannibalism are most detailed. In the *Handbook of North American Indians*, Heidenreich (1978:386) completely accepts accounts of cannibalism in the *Jesuit Relations*, contending for the Huron that "Archaeological proof of this activity is sometimes found in middens in the form of bits of human bone (Wright, 1966)." His informant, Wright (1966), relies mostly on other sources for evidence and is not particularly convincing.

Stothers *et al.* (1982) and Abler (1980) both take strong issue with Arens' dismissal of the ethnohistorical sources, particularly the *Jesuit Relations*. Abler (1980:311) insists that the archaeological evidence for cannibalism among the Huron is supportive, but holds that ". . . proof of the case must rest with historical documentation." To the contrary, it is the written records that have been contested and the archaeological record that may be expected to provide a means of resolution.

Saul (1968) describes scattered human bone from Sheep Rock Shelter in Pennsylvania, but that cautious author did not feel personally competent to verify the "worked" and/or "cooked" characteristics of the bone in question. Brose *et al.* (1976), and Stothers *et al.* (1982) say unambiguous evidence for cannibalism in the area exists, but neither account provides the primary evidence.

Arens' (1979) treatment of the archaeological record for Iroquois cannibalism has been criticized by Abler (1980), who cites a variety of works in which cannibalism has been claimed. As mentioned above, Skinner (1919) interpreted the human skeletal remains from Cayuga, New York, as evidence for cannibalism because of their context and condition. Skinner (1919:52) concludes:

> There can be no doubt of the cannibalistic tendencies of the inhabitants of this site, since human bones were abundant throughout the refuse. . . . The long-bones had been cracked for the purpose of extracting the marrow.

The New York site held out by Arens as poor evidence of cannibalism in the Northeast is the Bloody Hill site (A.D. 1480) in which fragmented bones were found in a "roasting pit." The illustrations suggest dry, rather than fresh, bone fracture for at least some of these materials (see Chapter 6). As Abler notes, however, if the Bloody Hill fragments were an isolated find, Arens' dismissals would be more warranted. The evidence for late prehistoric cannibalism in Ontario and Wisconsin, however, cannot be so lightly dismissed.

In separate publications on the Roebuck and Lawson prehistoric village sites in Ontario, Canada, Wintemberg (1936, 1939) describes an abundance of broken and scattered bone remains in nearly all refuse deposits excavated. He notes cutmarks, burning, and breakage patterns analogous to the fauna found in the same deposits. He also notes worked human bone and some canid gnawing on the bones. Wintemberg interprets the remains as representing cannibalism. Knowles (1937) pursues the analysis of the Roebuck human remains, noting that this Iroquoian assemblage includes two bone sets, one from burials and the other from broken and scattered remains from 25 large refuse deposits. The latter set included bone tools made from human remains. Eighty-four individuals from burials were the focus of this physical anthropological analysis, but Knowles estimates a minimum number of 35 individuals in the refuse deposits and suggests that all but four of these were adult males.

The site of Aztalan in Wisconsin was introduced above in the discussion about recognizing cannibalism archaeologically. Somers collected nearly 2,000 bones from refuse deposits at this large Middle Mississippian (A.D. 1100–1150) site in the 1880s. Forty percent of these were human and interpreted as evidence of cannibalism by Somers (1892:23):

> That the flesh of those bodies was eaten there can be no doubt, for no savage would go to the trouble to mutilate the dead bodies of friend or foe, to the extent of separating all the joints with a knife, chopping the bones three or four inches long, and splitting all those and only those containing marrow, and then finally mixing them with the bones of the animals he undoubtedly used as food, and throwing them into one common heap.

Barrett (1933) suggests that the cited human bone percentage might be somewhat exaggerated because human bone may have been preferentially collected by Somers. Barrett's own excavations were conducted at Aztalan nearly fifty years later to test the conclusions about cannibalism. Barrett (1933:358–359) stresses that he went into the excavations with an open mind. He relates: "Very shortly after commencing the work in the first season, our first unmistakable evidence of the practise of eating human flesh was encountered." Barrett's excavations had again uncovered human and animal bone material at Aztalan treated in

> . . . precisely the same manner, broken and split for the marrow, and finally cast into the refuse heap, together with ashes, shells, fish bones and scales, and all the ordinary kitchen refuse of the village. No more consideration was given to these human bones than to those

> of any animal used as food. There can be no doubt whatever, therefore, that these remains represent the meals of the early inhabitants of Aztalan.

This time the fragmented human bone was found in refuse pits with other fauna. Barrett argues against an interpretation of "ceremonial" cannibalism at the site, noting that the human bone fragments were "almost unbelievably numerous" and citing the rarity of intact bones. Bennett (1952:120) goes a bit beyond Barrett's evidence when he notes that "One of the stimulating aspects of life in ancient Aztalan was the practice of cannibalism. . . ." The evidence marshaled by Somers and Barrett has stimulated little further work on cannibalism at the site. Parmalee (1960) simply accepts the practice of cannibalism as fact, but prefers to question the extent of the practice in view of the amount of human bone and numbers of human individuals being "not comparable in amount" to deer bone from the site. In a 1986 review of the work at Aztalan, Freeman questions Barrett's conclusions, noting the lack of quantification in the 1930s accounts and suggesting that a detailed comparison of the faunal and human bones from this site is necessary to determine the extent of cannibalism.

Thus, in eastern North America there is evidence that human and faunal osteological material received similar treatment at several sites. Several of these sites are located in a region known for ethnohistorical accounts of cannibalism. In none of the cases, however, are the published accounts definitive enough to match the standards of evidence advocated above.

Colorado's Mancos Canyon 5MTUMR–2346 site and its osteological content represent a prehistoric occurrence indicating cannibalism. The regional context necessary for interpreting this evidence is presented in the next chapter, where claims for cannibalism in the American Southwest will be considered in detail.

SUMMARY

The sample of published archaeological evidence for cannibalism presented here is emphatically incomplete. Nevertheless, some important conclusions can be drawn from the survey. Archaeology has played a small role in the testing of ethnohistorical accounts of cannibalism. As Arens (1979) maintained, archaeologists have often been willing to accept the ethnohistorical accounts at face value. Given the methods of modern zooarchaeology and physical anthropology, the archaeological record stands ready for use in the investigation of historical and prehistoric cannibalism.

CHAPTER

3

Cannibalism in the Prehistoric Southwest: Mancos 5MTUMR–2346 and Its Context

Evidence of cannibalism in the archaeological record is far more restricted than ethnohistorical accounts of the practice would predict. Ironically, some of the most secure evidence for cannibalism comes from *pre*historic contexts. Compounding the irony is the fact that the best evidence is from Europe and the American Southwest—geographic areas in which the ethnohistorical record on cannibalism is limited (see Volhard, 1939 for a global overview).

The European Neolithic site of Fontbrégoua provides excellent, but unique, data bearing on prehistoric cannibalism. Besides the thorough analysis of the recovered skeletal material, the strength of the case for cannibalism at this French site stems from two basic dimensions of the site's archaeology. The first dimension is what Binford (1981) calls "historical *integrity*." Deposits resulting from the combined action of various depositional and attritional agencies besides human behavior have low integrity. Sites such as Fontbrégoua that show minimal geological disturbance and little carnivore activity are said to have a high degree of integrity. In this high-integrity site, *both the artifacts and their contexts are products largely or exclusively derived from past human actions*.

A second critical dimension complementing the integrity of the Fontbrégoua archaeological occurrence and making this site so informative is the "*fine-grained*" nature of the archaeological assemblages recovered there. Binford (1981) describes a fine-grained assemblage as *one in which the archaeological record results from a limited number of events or episodes*.

Fontbrégoua is the only archaeological site surveyed in Chapter 2 that has both integrity and a fine-grained archaeological assemblage. It contrasts in these important dimensions with the middens of Alaska, eastern North America (except for some Aztalan refuse pits), and the Pacific where archaeological evidence has been interpreted to represent cannibalism.

The authors of the Fontbrégoua analysis (Villa *et al.*, 1986a) failed to mention evidence of cannibalism from the American Southwest. Nevertheless, an important series of discoveries in a number of sites centered geographically on the "Four Corners" area, in which the western states of Utah, Colorado, New Mexico, and Arizona meet, has yielded evidence interpreted as indicating cannibalism. In this chapter the late prehistoric archaeology of the Four Corners area is introduced to provide a regional perspective on the Mancos Canyon site 5MTUMR–2346 human bone assemblage.

Most of the sites in the American Southwest excavated over the last century contain at least some components with integrity and fine-grained assemblages. The Southwest evidence, for these reasons, is some of the most important archaeological data bearing on prehistoric cannibalism. Even the skeptical Arens (1979) admits the strength of this evidence, choosing to interpret and characterize it as relating to survival cannibalism.

THE ANASAZI

The Anasazi are one of four major cultural traditions of the American Southwest (Cordell, 1984). Centered on the geographic point at which the states of Utah, Colorado, New Mexico, and Arizona meet, the Anasazi inhabited much of the Colorado Plateau—a geographic area bounded by the Rocky Mountains to the north and east, the Great Basin to the west, and the Sonoran desert to the south. The Anasazi are considered to be some of the ancestors of modern Pueblo Indians. The most impressive archaeological manifestations of Anasazi culture in the Four Corners region are the spectacular cliff-dwellings constructed before abandonment of the region during the late prehistoric period. Several signatures allow the archaeological identification of Anasazi in the Four Corners area (but not Kayenta; Ambler, 1989). These include the "kiva," a circular subterranean or semi-subterranean structure; the "unit pueblo," a modular building unit made up of a room block, plaza, kiva, and trash dump; and the characteristic Anasazi black-and-white pottery and gray and corrugated utility pottery. The name "Anasazi" is translated from the Navajo term for "the old ones," "the ones who went before" (Martin and Plog, 1973:107), or as "enemy ancestors" (Plog, 1979:108). The historical use of the word is summarized by Collins (1983).

The Colorado Plateau province is characterized by high elevations ranging from 1,500 to 3,000 m, mostly drained by the Colorado River and its tributaries—deeply entrenched rivers with high gradients. The geography is dominated by mesas, plateaus, and steep-walled canyons incised into sedimentary rocks. As Plog (1979) points out, this region is considered marginal for agriculture because of topographic, hydrological, and climatic characteristics.

Professional research has been conducted on the archaeology of the Anasazi for over a century. More research has been done here than on any other area of comparable size in North America (Plog, 1979). The Mesa Verde region has been studied particularly intensively. The wealth of data on the Anasazi occupation of the Four Corners region is derived from the exceptional preservation of normally perishable remains and from the excellent opportunity for chronological control through dendrochronology, radiocarbon chronometry, and ceramic analysis. As Berry (1982) points out, the Anasazi archaeological sequence is held to be one of the most securely documented examples of prehistoric cultural evolution in the New World.

The interpretive framework for the archaeology of the Four Corners region was established with the formation of the Pecos Conference chronology in 1927 (Kidder, 1927). This chronology was a heuristic device used to classify regional prehistory into eight stages of "cultural evolution" based on settlement or village patterns and technology. This classification had a major impact on subsequent archaeological work in the Southwest. It was originally devised as an evolutionary typology rather than as a chronology. Only later were dates affixed to the stages, and usage of the stage names today carries no necessary implications for a specific stage of settlement pattern or technology.

Plog (1979), Martin and Plog (1973), Cordell (1984), Euler (1988), and Vivian (1990) provide general reviews of all or parts of the Anasazi archaeological record. Before turning to a site-by-site assessment of the human osteological material that has been interpreted as evidence of cannibalism, however, it is useful to review briefly the regional evidence for those periods that have yielded this material evidence. This review is mainly extracted from Plog and Cordell and is focused on the Anasazi of the Mesa Verde area, in the northeast part of the area traditionally considered to be "Anasazi."

Anasazi subsistence primarily involved hunting and gathering of native foodstuffs until agricultural food production based on maize became the dominant element of subsistence, well before A.D. 1000. The Pueblo I period, lasting from c. A.D. 750 to 900 in the Mesa Verde area (Cordell, 1984:103), marked the introduction of above-ground masonry rooms from the preceding Basketmaker phases in which pithouses were predominant. An increasing reliance on agriculture is evidenced in Pueblo I times (Plog, 1979:115). Corn, beans, squash, dogs, and possibly turkeys were the primary domesticates.

Pueblo II lasted from c. A.D. 900 to 1100, whereas the succeeding Pueblo III lasted from c. A.D. 1100 to 1300 (Plog, 1979:115; Cordell, 1984:103–104). Settlements grew larger in many areas, and subsistence was increasingly derived from agriculture. Pueblo IV spanned the period from A.D. 1300 until the time of Spanish contact (Plog, 1979:115). During this stage there was abandonment of much of the Colorado Plateau.

In the Mesa Verde area, and on the Colorado Plateau in general, the 5-stage, Basketmaker III, Pueblo I to IV classification system has enjoyed wide acceptance for decades and most sites have been accommodated in this succession. The succession across the Anasazi area has traditionally been seen as a series of smoothly intergraded stages of cultural development superimposed across local phases. The textbook scenario is one of gradual population increase and a subsequent crash at the end of the 13th-Century "Great Drought"—an event that brought about the demise of the classic Anasazi centers (Willey, 1966). The degree and directness of Mesoamerican influence on the development and decline of the Anasazi is an ongoing research question (DiPeso, 1974; Kelley and Kelley, 1975; Plog, 1979; Weigand *et al.*, 1977; Riley and Hedrick, 1978; Mathien and McGuire, 1986).

Berry (1982) has questioned the existence of the gradual Basketmaker I to Pueblo IV continuum of cultural evolution, calling the textbook version of Anasazi prehistory into question. He contends that the textbook view outlined above is empirically false and conceptually misleading. He contends that the Basketmaker through late Pueblo evolutionary sequence comprises a series of temporally discrete stages separated by abrupt transition events that were induced by Plateau-wide droughts that caused considerable population dislocation. The parallel to the debate within evolutionary biology about punctuated equilibrium versus Darwinian gradualism is not lost on Berry.

Anasazi cultural evolution will be considered again after the evidence for cannibalism in the prehistoric Southwest has been presented. Before turning to that evidence, however, it is important to note that thousands of Anasazi burials have been excavated over the last century. Mortuary practices are widely documented, if incompletely understood, for the Anasazi. Grave goods frequently accompanied primary, flexed or unflexed burials that often were placed in refuse areas next to pueblos or in the room fill in the dwelling structures themselves (Stodder, 1987). Ceremonial burial of dogs is also found in Anasazi sites (Emslie, 1978). For a review of ethnohistorical accounts of mortuary practices in the Southwest, see Ellis (1968).

The Dolores Archaeological Project in the Mesa Verde area provides an exemplary sketch of mortuary practices among the Anasazi. Here, skeletal remains representing 115 individuals were recovered from 92 archaeological sites as part of the project's activities. The burials were single, double, and multiple, most dating from A.D. 650 to 975. Eighty percent of the burials were primary and only 14 percent secondary. Burials were found in simple graves dug into the postoccupational fill of habitation and storage structures and less frequently in refuse middens (Stodder, 1986). Turner and Turner (1990) report that the Museum of Northern Arizona's skeletal series from about 250 Anasazi/Sinagua sites includes 98.4 percent formal burials on a by-site basis. Only 1.6 percent of these sites yielded skeletal remains suggesting possible violence and/or cannibalism. The recovery of human remains in Southwest archaeology is commonplace; compared to the very large number of well-documented primary and secondary interments, the occurrences described below are very unusual. They are, however, frequent enough and patterned enough to command archaeological attention.

CANNIBALISM IN THE SOUTHWEST: SURVEYING THE EVIDENCE

Skeletal evidence for interpersonal violence in the prehistoric Southwest was discovered early in archaeological investigations of this area. Before the turn of the century, for example, Wetherill (1894) described traumatized skeletons placed "haphazardly" in a structure at Snider's Well, a deep, circular room southwest of Yucca House National Monument (formerly Aztec Springs), Montezuma County, Colorado. Dozens of other examples of skeletons or skeletal portions found in contexts not associated with formal, mortuary interment have been found in Anasazi sites. Morris (1939) describes such occurrences from Mesa Verde, West Pueblo at Aztec Ruin, Acowitz, Animas Valley, La Plata Site 33, and Old Fort. Occurrences are also known from Charnel House Tower (Martin, 1929), Cottonwood Creek Cave 7 (Turner, 1983), the Coombs Site (Lister and Lister, 1961), Bancos Village (Eddy, 1974), Smokey Bear Ruin (Wiseman, 1976), Canyon de Chelly (McDonald, 1976), Pueblo Bonito (Pepper, 1920, Akins, 1986), and several Largo-Gallina sites (Mackey and Green, 1979). Many of these occurrences are described as articulated or partially articulated skeletons, sometimes with evidence of violent perimortem trauma, including embedded projectile points. Others are described as cremations. It is beyond the scope of the present work to assess such occurrences and their significance, but some of them may represent phenomena that are reported from the sites detailed below. Mackey and Green (1979) and Eddy (1974) as well as J. Haas (1990) deal with aspects of warfare and other forms of violence in Southwest prehistory.

The assemblages detailed below also show evidence of perimortem trauma, but disarticulation is usually much more complete, and a pattern of fracture of the skeletal elements while they were fresh is documented. Burning and cutmarks are also part of the evidence. Furthermore, for many of these assemblages, the patterns of trauma and element representation as well as the contextual circumstances in which they are found provide evidence that they are not secondary or disturbed burials. Almost all of these assemblages have been described as indicative of prehistoric cannibalism.

In the Turner and Morris (1970) publication on one of these, the Polacca Wash human skeletal assemblage, the terms "grave," "multiple burial site," and "mass burial" were all used to describe the occurrence. Turner and other authors have consistently continued to refer to similar occurrences as "mass burials." There is no evidence, however, that several of the assemblages, including the Polacca Wash and Mancos assemblages, were intentionally buried, as the term "mass burial" implies. "Mass burial" implies an ossuary situation resulting from intentional mortuary practices. Again, for several assemblages, there is no evidence that this was the case. The description of these and other similar bone sets as "human bone assemblages" is a terminological shift that may help to avoid difficulties of prejudging the circumstances surrounding the occurrences in question.

Turner (1983) presents the most comprehensive review of the evidence for cannibalism in the Southwest, having personally examined six of the ten assemblages that he considers as evidence of cannibalism. Fink's (1989) tabulation, although presented as a listing of eighteen localities with "possible cannibalism," includes assemblages that neither Turner nor I consider to be appropriately included. Turner (1983) did not examine the Mancos 5MTUMR–2346 assemblage, although he noted its presence.

In Appendix 1 a survey of assemblages of broken and scattered human bones that have been interpreted as evidence for cannibalism in the prehistoric American Southwest is presented. The reader is urged to consult Appendix 1 to gain a full appreciation of the diversity of ages, architectures, quantities, and individual ages of the skeletal remains, and history of interpretations assigned to these cases of possible cannibalism in the prehistoric Southwest. My survey of this evidence is, in large part, based on the foundation laid by Turner. I have not personally studied all of the bone assemblages detailed in Appendix 1, only those of Mancos, Cottonwood Canyon, Yellow Jacket, and Bluff. I have only cursorily examined the Marshview Hamlet, Leroux Wash, and Polacca Wash assemblages, observed the 5MT–10207 assemblage as it was being excavated, and noticed the Coyote Village occurrence. The information presented in Appendix 1 is, therefore, taken mainly from primary publications.

The survey should not be seen as a comprehensive accounting of all possible occurrences of this kind. As discussed in the final chapter of this book, several additional assemblages that share characteristics with those described below have already been identified. It is likely that others have gone unrecognized and/or unpublished. The survey of the nineteen better documented assemblages, however, provides a geographically and chronologically representative sample of occurrences in the Southwest and introduces the reader to the variation present in the assemblages already described.

Appendix 1 is organized in order of discovery, to give the reader a sense of how the evidence for cannibalism has accumulated and been interpreted. For each occurrence the following information is compiled: the site name and identification number; its location, excavator, date(s) of excavation, and completeness of excavation; the primary archaeological and skeletal report(s); the site type; the local and regional chronological determinations and their basis; the chronometric age(s); the context(s) of the human remains; the number of human skeletal pieces and individuals; the age and sex of these individuals; the damage patterns observed on the remains; the excavator's interpretation of the occurrence; and other published reports and interpretations. A summary discussion for each of the occurrences is included.

A guide to the geographic placement of sites with osteological evidence for cannibalism detailed in Appendix 1 is provided in Figure 3.1. This map is accompanied by a diagram (Figure 3.2) that places each occurrence chronologically.

CANNIBALISM IN THE SOUTHWEST: A SYNOPSIS

The catalog presented in Appendix 1 provides essential data on a series of nineteen occurrences centered on the Four Corners area, but spread across large parts of the states of Colorado, New Mexico, Arizona, and Utah. As noted above, the catalog is not comprehensive but includes the major assemblages that have been interpreted as producing evidence of cannibalism among the Anasazi.

The concluding chapter of this book examines the phenomenon of cannibalism among the Anasazi in a comprehensive regional sense. As a prelude to the detailed examination of the Mancos 5MTUMR–2346 remains that follows, however, it is appropriate to review briefly the history of the discovery and interpretation of the assemblages outlined above and to consider some important questions raised by previous analyses of this material.

Although the first documented archaeological investigation of broken and scattered human remains in Anasazi contexts dates to work by Pepper, Hough, Shapiro, and Morris at the turn of the century, systematic study of the phenomenon did not begin until the 1960s, with the discovery and analysis of the Polacca Wash sample. The most comprehensive work has been done by Turner, who suggested in 1961 that skeletal remains from the Coomb's site might be the result of cannibalism (Lister and Lister, 1961; Appendix 2). Not until the Turner and Morris (1970) publication on the Polacca Wash assemblage, however, did he began to outline a methodology for the study of such fragmentary human material. Combining

Opposite page:

Fig. 3.1 A map of the 19 sites yielding assemblages of broken, scattered, human-modified skeletal remains interpreted as evidence of human cannibalism. Each site is indicated by a number, and the number order corresponds to the order in which the sites were discovered. This numbering scheme is also used in Figure 3.2 (temporal placement), and it represents the order in which the sites are described in Appendix 1.

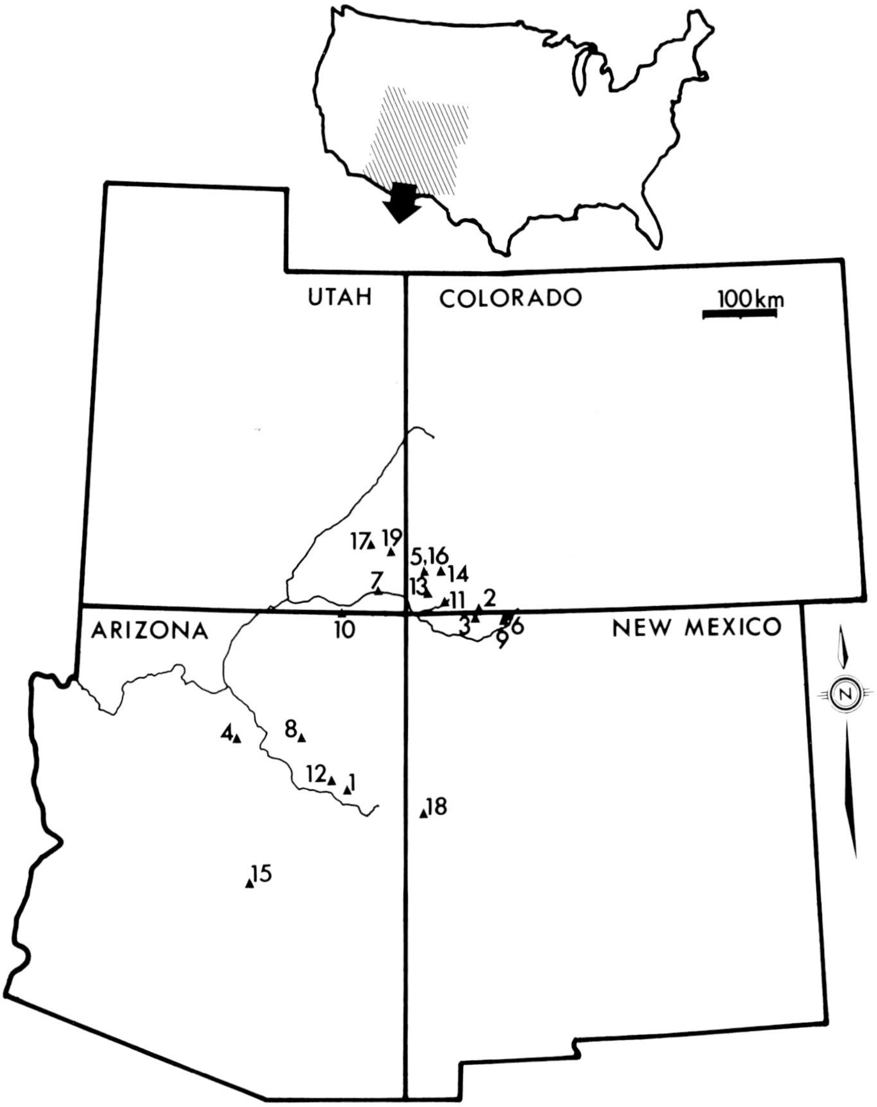

	SITE	Date Found	Immat. MNI	Adult MNI	Total MNI	Females	Males	Total Pieces
1	Canyon Butte Ruin 3	1901	-	3	-	-	-	-
2	La Plata 23	1927	1	1	2	-	1	-
3	La Plata 41	1930	2	4	6	-	-	-
4	Big Hawk Valley NA-682	1948	-	-	-	-	-	-
5	Yellow Jacket Porter Pueblo 5MT-1	1959	3	1	4	-	-	-
6	Sambrito Village LA-4195	1960-61	6	6	14	-	-	474
7	Bluff	1961	3	1	4	1	-	202
8	Polacca Wash NA-8502	1964	12	18	30	3	1	-
9	Burnt Mesa LA-4528	1969	4	7	11	2	4	3,389
10	Monument Valley	1970	4	3	7	1	2	644
11	**Mancos 5MTUMR-2346**	1974	14	15	29	-	-	2,106
12	Leroux Wash NA-12854	1974	-	-	>16	-	-	3,443
13	Grinnell	1974	3	4	7	1	-	380
14	Marshview Hamlet 5MT-2235	1978-80	3	3	6	1	1	528
15	Ash Creek AZ:U:3:49	1982-83	1	4	5	-	-	212
16	Yellow Jacket 5MT-3	1985-87	4	6	10	1	2	1,556
17	Cottonwood Canyon	1987	2	2	4	1	1	693
18	Fence Lake Area	1988	1	4	5	2	2	1,088
19	Verdure Canyon	1989	-	1	1	-	1	19
		TOTALS:	63	83	145	13	15	14,734

	SITE	Architecture/Associations
1	Canyon Butte Ruin 3	Cemetery in trash mound of 20-room pueblo
2	La Plata 23	Rockshelter, in firepit and corrugated jar
3	La Plata 41	In pit beneath 2 rooms of > 13-room, 2-kiva pueblo
4	Big Hawk Valley NA-682	Below stone slab on storage pit of 5-room pueblo
5	Yellow Jacket Porter Pueblo 5MT-1	In storage pit below house floor
6	Sambrito Village LA-4195	In fill of 2 pithouses of 38-house pithouse village
7	Bluff	Undetermined, unassociated with buildings
8	Polacca Wash NA-8502	No associated features
9	Burnt Mesa LA-4528	On 1 pithouse floor in 3-pithouse pueblo
10	Monument Valley	In isolated slab-lined pit
11	**Mancos 5MTUMR-2346**	On floors, in fill of rooms and kiva of small unit pueblo
12	Leroux Wash NA-12854	In large pit near small pueblo
13	Grinnell	On floor, cist, and jar fill of 2-kiva "ceremonial center"
14	Marshview Hamlet 5MT-2235	In and around a large pithouse
15	Ash Creek AZ:U:3:49	On floor of 1 room in 6-room unit pueblo
16	Yellow Jacket 5MT-3	On kiva floor
17	Cottonwood Canyon 42SA-12209	In shallow pit in room of small pueblo
18	Fence Lake Area	Undetermined
19	Verdure Canyon 42SA-3724	In a small cave/crevice

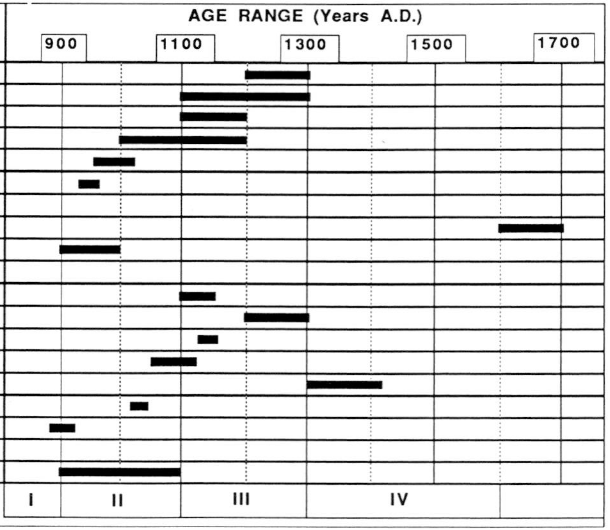

Fig. 3.2 Temporal placement of the sites whose spatial position is shown in Figure 3.1. Appendix 1 provides a full catalog of these occurrences.

physical anthropological analysis of the assemblage's age and sex composition with a forensic consideration of patterns of bone trauma and element representation in an archaeological context, Turner and Morris (1970) concluded that an interpretation of cannibalism was reasonable. Flinn, Turner, and Brew employed the same basic methods in their 1976 analysis of the Burnt Mesa occurrence.

Additional bone assemblages similar to that from Polacca Wash were found during the 1970s at a variety of other sites, including Mancos Canyon. By 1983, Turner was able to summarize the evidence from ten Southwest bone assemblages that he interpreted as producing evidence of cannibalism. These assemblages, according to Turner (1983), exhibit fourteen characteristics:

1. A single short-term depositional episode
2. Good to excellent bone preservation
3. Specimen counts between 400 and 3,500
4. Nearly complete disarticulation of elements
5. Relative lack of vertebrae
6. Massive perimortem breakage of most elements
7. Breakage by percussion hammering
8. Almost universal breakage of the head, face, and long bones
9. 2 to 35 percent burning after butchering and breaking
10. Butchering and skinning cutmarks on 1 to 5 percent of all specimens
11. Gnawing on fewer than 5 percent of all specimens
12. A damage sequence of cutting-breaking-burning-gnawing
13. An extremely low incidence of bone tools among the assemblages
14. A ratio of alteration to the bone lots as follows: perimortem breakage = 95; burning = 20; cutmarks = 3; and possible gnawing = 2

The degree to which these "characteristics" actually diagnose the phenomenon under study is investigated in the concluding chapter. Turner (1983) pointed to a number of important but unexplained aspects of this widespread pattern of bone modification, including aspects of bone fragmentation and element representation. Skeletal element loss was left unexplained, particularly the loss of pelves and vertebrae. This phenomenon was noted by Turner and Morris in the first study (1970; Polacca Wash) and attributed to export by assailants or scavengers. Disproportions have led others to posit butchery activity away from the site of deposition (Flinn *et al.*, 1976) and to deduce differential import of elements to and from the site (Nickens, 1975). Nass and Bellantoni (1982) suggest that dismemberment of pectoral and pelvic girdles was difficult and that these elements may have been discarded intact to be later dispersed by scavenging animals. Regarding the relative scarcity of vertebrae, Turner (1983:232) comments: "An unexplainable aspect of mass burials is the marked deficiency of vertebral elements. I am at a loss to explain this characteristic, but it is undoubtedly important."

Other aspects that remain unresolved are the heavy damage to cranial vaults and facial regions, particularly perimortem tooth evulsion, by means of percussion. The phrase "intentional and violent mutilation" was introduced by the Turner and Morris (1970) paper on Polacca Wash and has been used in this regard to imply that destruction of skeletal remains had a non-nutritional component. These authors note that distal and proximal limb-bone ends, condyles, processes, and articular surfaces were consistently broken away. They attribute this damage to disarticulation with inadequate tools or an inaccurate knowledge of human anatomy. Nass and

Bellantoni (1982) wonder why it was necessary to break the skeletal remains from Monument Valley into such small pieces, citing "mutilation" as a possible rationale. In his 1983 paper, Turner states that he is still searching for an explanation for such complete destruction of the skeletal remains from Polacca Wash. The analysis of the Mancos 5MTUMR–2346 assemblage has resulted in possible resolution of some of these questions. This will become apparent during the discussions of Chapters 7 to 11, and these findings are summarized in Chapter 13.

Contextually, the ten assemblages considered by Turner (1983) and the other occurrences presented in Figures 3.1 and 3.2 and cataloged in Appendix 1 cover a wide range, from isolated rockshelters and crypts to trash mounds and kiva floors associated with unit pueblos. The occurrences range from Pueblo I (c. A.D. 900) to late Pueblo IV (c. A.D. 1650), and are centered in the Four Corners area. The assemblages share a virtual absence of associated nonhuman fauna. Skeletal elements in them display perimortem damage attributes that include burning, cutmarks, and percussion-induced fracture. Minimum numbers of individuals range from 1 to 30, and the individuals comprise roughly equal mixtures of subadult and adult, male and female individuals.

Turner interprets these assemblages as evidence of cannibalism, but does not speculate upon the reasons behind this prehistoric activity in his 1983 summary. In a 1986 contribution, Turner includes the activities under "prehistoric social paleopathology." A fuller consideration of the context and causes linked to the entire series of assemblages in the Southwest will be presented in the concluding chapter. Although work on the Mancos Canyon 5MTUMR–2346 assemblage may have resolved several questions posed by previous investigators, full understanding of the activities that resulted in the assemblages described above is clearly not at hand. Before turning to a consideration of the theory and method behind the analysis of the Mancos 5MTUMR–2346 human bone assemblage, it is necessary to describe the archaeological context of these remains.

MANCOS CANYON SITE 5MTUMR–2346

Historical Context

The archaeological occurrences reviewed above and presented in Appendix 1, despite their wide chronological and geographic distribution, share basic patterns of bone modification and element representation. These patterns have been interpreted as evidence of cannibalism in the American Southwest by Turner (1983) and others. Several occurrences were discovered early in this century when archaeological recovery and documentation methods were still being developed. Others were discovered by accident or during vandalism. In several cases, unknown portions of the original human osteological assemblages were removed by erosion or vandals. Some assemblages were only partially excavated. Still other samples have suffered considerable postdepositional modification by root damage. Only a few of the assemblages comprise an adequate number of individuals to warrant a detailed search for patterns of element composition and perimortem trauma.

The large bone assemblage from Mancos Canyon site 5MTUMR–2346 is derived from approximately thirty individuals (hereafter the text will often refer to this site and its human bone assemblage as "Mancos"). It was recovered during controlled excavations, and there is excellent bone preservation. There is little evidence for pre- or postdepositional disturbance of the assemblage. Recovery was fairly complete. For all of these reasons, the Mancos Canyon bone assemblage is an appropriate vehicle with which to examine the phenomenon of cannibalism in the archaeological record in general and in the American Southwest in particular.

The Mancos human bone assemblage described in this book was recovered in 1973. Over a decade later, in 1985, I first became acquainted with the assemblage. Here, details of the setting, excavation, and earlier interpretations of the evidence are reported and the more recent analysis of the assemblage is introduced. This background is essential to the interpretations that follow. It relies heavily on accounts by the principal investigators of the site, Larry Nordby (1974) and Paul Nickens (1974, 1975), and on original "Burial Forms" completed by the field excavators in 1973 and made available by David Breternitz and the Mesa Verde National Park.

Archaeological salvage work in Mancos Canyon, funded by the Bureau of Indian Affairs, was conducted during the summers of 1972 and 1973. Road construction involving access to a proposed Mancos Canyon Indian Park endangered several sites, including a site found during a survey in 1969 and designated 5MTUMR–1272. The site designation was later changed to 5MTUMR–2346, one of five sites tested during the summer of 1973. Archaeological work was done under the auspices of the Mesa Verde Research Center, Department of Anthropology, the University of Colorado at Boulder.

Setting

The site is located in Mancos Canyon on the Ute Mountain Indian Reservation in Montezuma County, southwestern Colorado, approximately 10 km south of the southern boundary of the Mesa Verde National Park (Figure 3.3). The unexcavated site appeared as a low mound on the first terrace above the right (north) bank floodplain of the Mancos River (Figures 3.4–3.5). The river channel is approximately 75 m southwest of the excavated area. The mesas of the Mesa Verde form cliffs and talus slopes approximately 50 m north of the site. The site itself is at the foot of the talus slope, and its placement would have situated the inhabitants on high ground as well as affording them ready access to a water supply. Site cover today is primarily sage, grass, and cactus, with juniper and pinyon pine scattered over the slope.

Excavations

Excavation was conducted in the summer of 1973 by a crew under the direction of field foreman Larry Nordby, who worked under the supervision of D. Breternitz and J. Lancaster. The unexcavated site formed a low mound. It was revealed by excavation to be complex, with one multiroom habitation superimposed over another earlier one. Surface masonry structures for both occupations included several rooms, an associated kiva structure, and a refuse deposit. The refuse deposit was tested with exploratory trenches that revealed typical burials. The main architectural units were completely excavated, but discovery of retaining walls and possible additional buried structures was made at the end of the 1973 fieldwork, and Nordby (1974) noted the need for further work at the site. He also noted the presence of a small pueblo located about 10 m north of 5MTUMR–2346, a pueblo whose trash mound edges underlay rooms of the early 5MTUMR–2346 pueblo.

Excavations followed standard procedure in Southwest archaeology at the time, involving excavation by trowel and broom. As Plog (1979:110) noted for

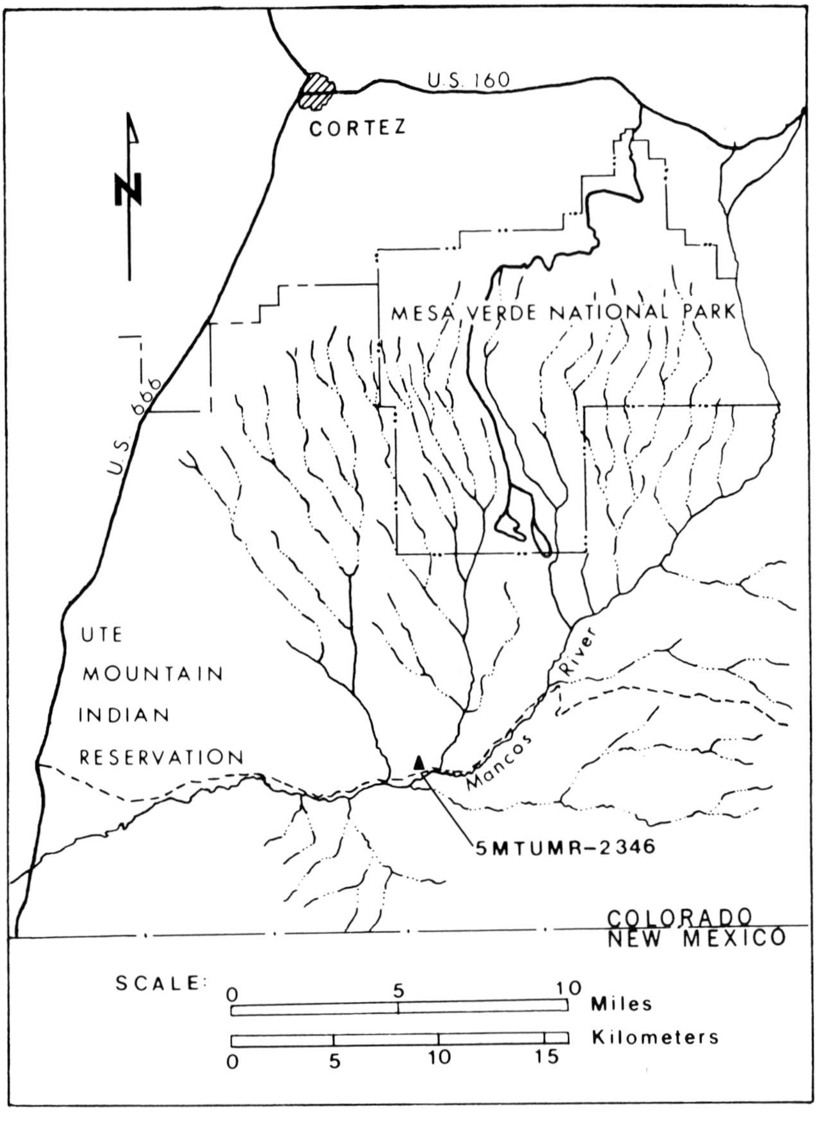

Fig. 3.3 Geographic placement of the Mancos 5MTUMR–2346 site in the Mancos Canyon, southwestern Colorado. From Nickens (1975), with permission.

Southwest archaeology, "The use of screens, of a square grid system, and of natural levels has not been characteristic." At Mancos 5MTUMR–2346, rooms were excavated in levels separated by floors lettered from the top down, so that "Level A" refers to the fill above "Floor A," and "Floor A Floor Contact" refers to material within 10 cm of the actual floor. Attention was paid to the superimposed floors and walls of the excavated structures, and, as a result, some details

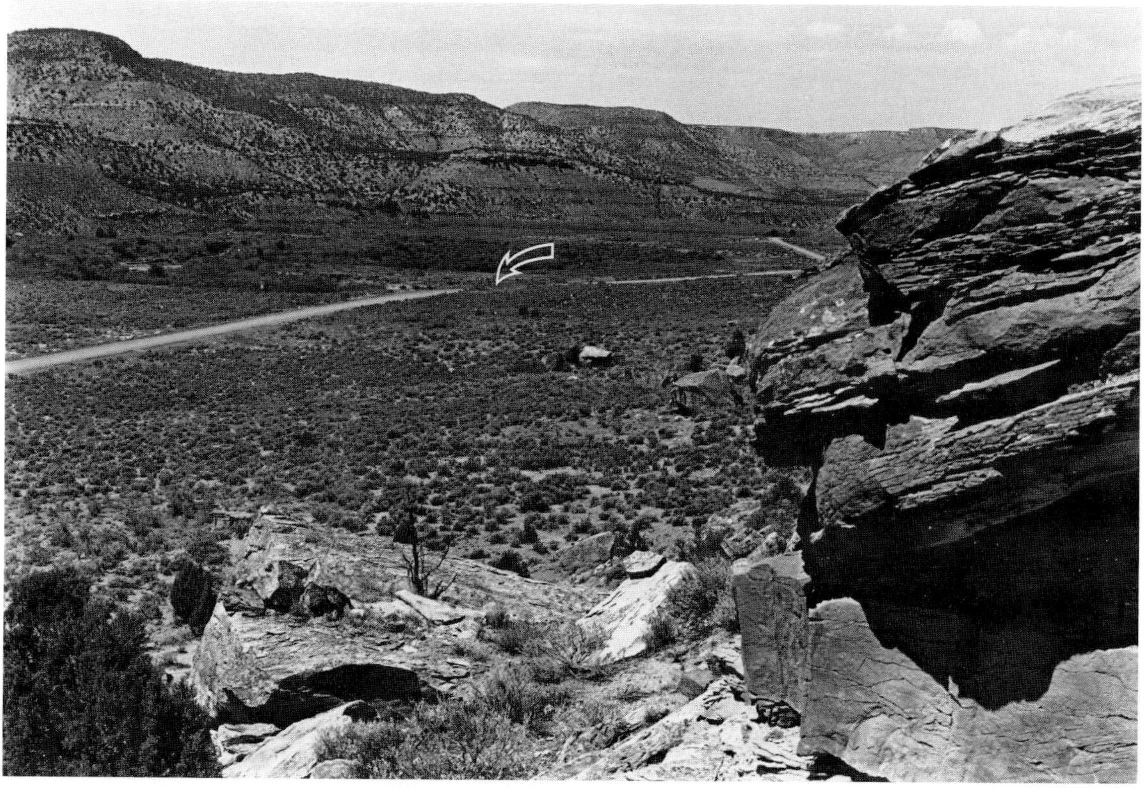

Fig. 3.4 View down the Mancos Canyon, looking toward the southwest. Vegetation associated with the Mancos River is visible south of the road, away from the viewer. The 5MTUMR–2346 site is cut into by the road at the position indicated by the arrow. Anasazi occupation in this region was very dense, and the 5MTUMR–2346 pueblo would have been but one element of a large farming community in this area during prehistoric times.

about the sequence of occupation are available.

Rooms were numbered in order of discovery. Burials were numbered successively, with B (''burial''), FS (''field specimen''), or FA (''floor artifact'') numbers (see the section on human skeletal remains below). It is evident from the field notes that the human skeletal remains that were encountered in room fill and on room floors were initially considered by the excavators to be secondary or disturbed burials. This is not surprising, given that primary burials were present at 5MTUMR–2346 and are ubiquitous in Anasazi sites.

Site Layout and Building Sequence

Nordby (1974:52) describes the site as comprising one multiroom pueblo superimposed over another, slightly earlier one. The later pueblo was, according to this excavator, ''. . . erected subsequent

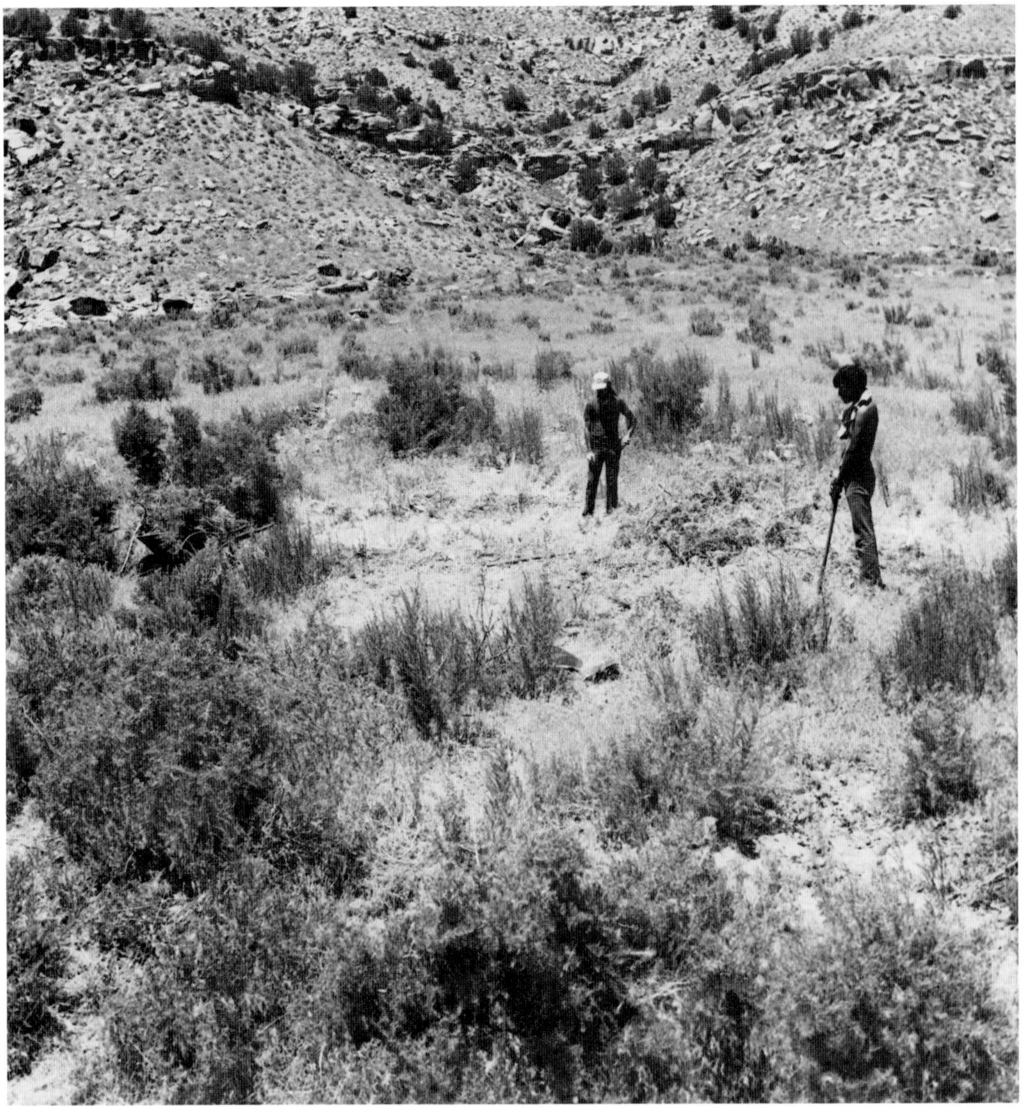

Fig. 3.5 Clearing brush at the 5MTUMR–2346 site before excavation in 1973.

to either natural breakdown or purposeful razing by the new population. . . .'' Both pueblos consisted of a small room block and associated structures.

The earlier habitation (Figure 3.6) consisted of twelve roughly rectangular rooms defined by stone walls whose construction sequence is described by Nordby (1974). The rooms were arranged in an L-shape, with a circular, semisubterranean structure incorporated into the long arm of the L (an atypical, intramural ''kiva,''

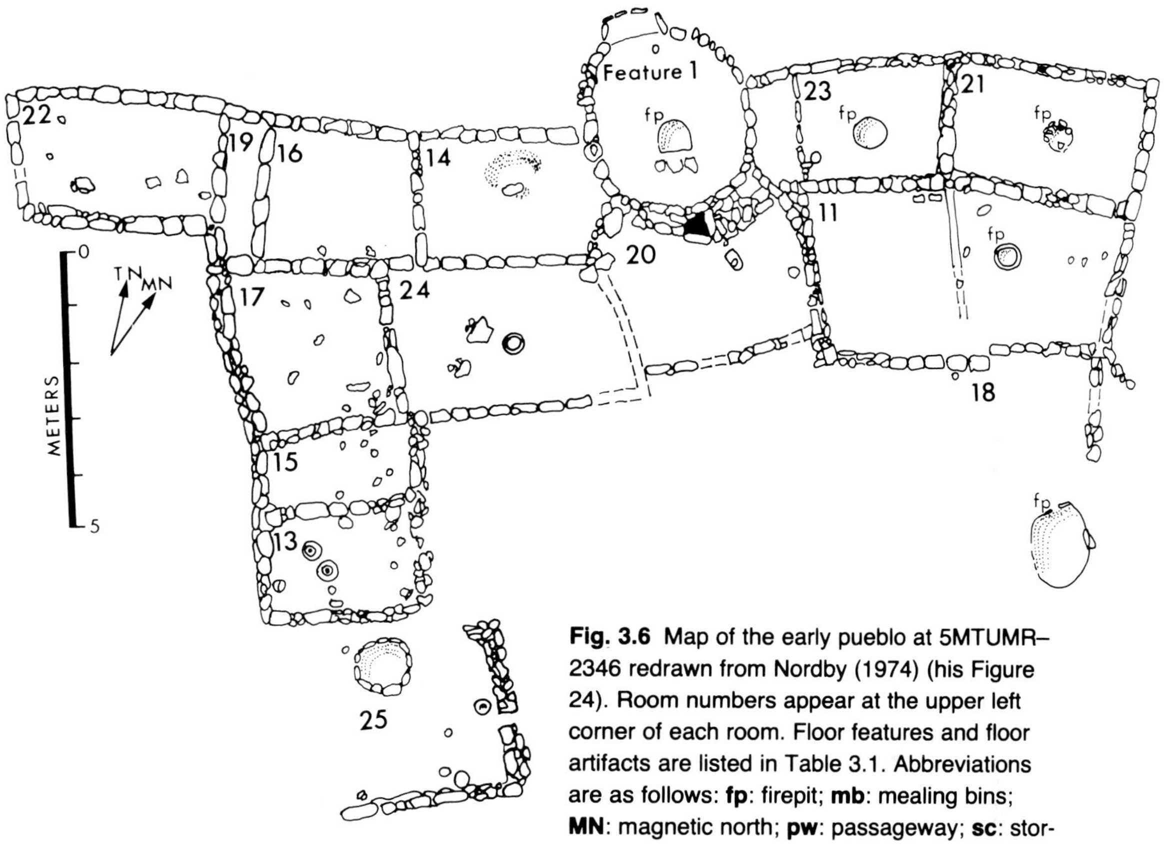

Fig. 3.6 Map of the early pueblo at 5MTUMR–2346 redrawn from Nordby (1974) (his Figure 24). Room numbers appear at the upper left corner of each room. Floor features and floor artifacts are listed in Table 3.1. Abbreviations are as follows: **fp**: firepit; **mb**: mealing bins; **MN**: magnetic north; **pw**: passageway; **sc**: storage cist; **TN**: true north; **tnl**: tunnel.

called "Feature 1" by Nordby, 1974). Only the lower portions of the first pueblo's walls were found in the excavation, the upper parts having been eroded or used by later inhabitants for construction. Rooms assignable to the earlier habitation included Rooms 11, 13, 14, 15, 16, 17, 19, 20, 21, 22, 23, and 24. Possibly also included were "Rooms" 18 and 25. Five types of masonry were defined by Nordby for the early pueblo. A floor artifact list is presented in Table 3.1, compiled from Nordby (1974:61). Only 2 of 2,106 specimens in the human bone assemblage under consideration come from provenances that are clearly attributable to the second occupation; the bulk of the assemblage was, therefore, contained in rooms of the first habitation.

Nordby describes the interval between the first and second phases of occupation as follows (1974:112): "After enough time had elapsed to permit natural erosional elements to deteriorate the masonry of the early component, at the same time permitting the broken down rooms to be filled with colluvium, alluvium, and refuse, a second occupation took place. That some of the previous walls still stood is indicated by the re-use of a number of them by later occupants when they constructed the new pueblo." He does not

Table 3.1

Room 11	Room 13			Room 14	Room 15	Room 16	Room 17		Room 18
Floor Artifacts	*Floor "A" Artifacts*	*Floor "B" Artifacts*	*Floor "C" Artifacts*	*Floor Artifacts*	*Floor Artifacts*	*Floor Artifacts*	*Floor A Artifacts*	*Floor A cont'd*	*Floor Artifacts*
1. McElmo B/W bowl 2. Chapin Gray jar 3. Mancos B/W bowl 4. Axe 5. Palette 6. Mano 7. Core-hammerstone 8. Mano 9. Unutilized river cobble 10. Mano	+3 unutilized flakes +1 bone tool +9 potsherds	1, 2. Mesa V. corrugated jars 3. Chapin Gray jar 4. McElmo B/W bowl	5. Mancos corrugated jar 6, 8. Unutilized cobbles 7. Mano 9. McElmo B/W bowl 10. Corner cist cover 11-15. Manos 16. Tchamahia 17-19. Manos	+1 unutilized flake *+Most of 858 pieces of broken human bone*	1. Lap anvil 2-6. Manos	1. Human "cranium": this is 21 total pieces, and includes postcrania 2. Lap anvil 3. Polishing stone	1. Axe blank 2. Mano 3. Unutilized flake 4. Mano frag. 5. Door closure slab 6-8. Unspecified 9, 13. McElmo B/W seed jar 10, 11. Mancos corrugated jar 12. Unutilized turkey bone 13. Bone awl 14. Polishing stone 15. Axe	+11 unutilized flakes +1 core +1 utilized flake +2 manos +1 frag. Tchamahia +1 polished stone +1 seed +1 broken awl +284 potsherds	None

	Room 11		Room 13			Room 14		Room 15		Room 16		Room 17		Room 18	
	Floor Contact	*Fill*	*Level A Fill*	*Level B Fill and Floor*	*Levels C,D, and E Fill*	*Floor Contact*	*Fill*	*Floor*	*Floor Contact + Fill*	*Floor Contact*	*Upper Fill*	*Fill A*	*Floor B + Fill B*	*Floor Contact*	*Firepit*
Broken human bone	*None*	*None*	*58 specimens without level data reported*			*See above*	*Some*	*None*	*620 specimens in fill*	*94 specimens in FC and fill*		*7 specimens without level data reported*		*None*	*None*
Unutilized flakes	6	12	23	2	20	6	39	-	42	4	9	43	2	6	2
Rejuvenation flakes	-	2	1	-	1	1	1	-	4	1	1	1	-	-	1
Flake/choppers	-	-	1	-	-	-	-	-	1	-	-	-	-	-	-
Utilized flakes	-	1	-	-	1	-	1	-	-	-	-	2	-	-	-
Scrapers/flake scrapers	-	-	-	-	-	-	1	-	-	-	-	-	-	-	-
Projectile points	-	-	-	-	-	-	-	-	-	-	-	-	-	-	-
Cores	-	1	-	-	-	-	2	-	2	-	1	2	-	-	1
Worked pebbles	-	-	1	-	-	-	-	-	-	-	-	-	-	-	-
Hafted stone hammer	-	-	-	-	-	-	-	-	-	-	1	-	-	-	-
Axes	-	-	-	-	-	-	-	-	-	-	-	-	-	-	-
Axe fragments	-	-	-	-	-	-	-	-	1	-	-	-	-	-	-
Chop/core-Hammerstone	-	-	1	-	-	-	1	-	-	-	-	-	-	-	-
Hammerstones	-	-	3	-	2	-	1	-	-	-	2	3	-	-	-
Metates	-	-	-	-	-	-	1	-	1	-	-	4	-	-	-
Metate fragments	-	-	-	-	-	-	-	-	-	-	-	-	-	-	-
Manos	-	5	3	-	3	-	5	-	2	1	4	5	-	-	-
Mano/paint grinders	-	1	-	-	-	-	-	-	-	-	-	-	-	-	-
Polishing stones	-	1	-	-	1	-	-	-	1	-	-	1	-	-	1
Ground/shaped slabs	-	-	1	-	-	-	-	-	-	1	-	-	-	1	-
Shell beads	-	-	-	1	-	-	-	-	-	-	-	-	-	-	-
Lap anvils	-	-	-	-	-	-	-	1	1	-	-	-	-	-	-
Ground shale	1	-	-	-	-	-	-	-	-	-	-	-	-	-	-
Bone tools	-	2	-	-	1	-	1	-	-	-	2	-	1	-	-
Corncobs	1	-	-	-	-	-	-	-	-	-	1	-	-	-	-
Seeds	1	-	-	-	-	-	-	-	-	-	+	-	-	-	-
Jar lids	-	-	-	-	-	-	-	-	-	-	1	-	-	-	-
Potsherds	144	496	183	36	160	18	141	-	301	64	104	287	130	43	20

Table 3.1 *(continued)*

Room 19	Room 20		Room 21		Room 22		Room 23		Room 24		Feature 1				
Floor Artifacts	*Floor B Artifacts*	*Floor A Artifacts*	*Floor Artifacts*		*Floor A Artifacts*		*Floor Artifacts*		*Floor Artifacts*						
None	1. Slab metate 2. Mano 3. Pitted pounding stone 4. McElmo B/W Bowl	+28 potsherds	None		1, 2. Pottery concentration 3. Maul 4. Eggshell 5. Lap anvil 6. Mano 7. Cornmeal 8. Polishing stone 9. Bone awl +65 potsherds		1. Trough metate fragment 2, 3. McElmo B/W pottery concentration		1, 2. Mancos corrugated jars 3. Bone reamer 4. McElmo B/W bowl +22 potsherds						
Floor and Fill	*Level A*	*Level B + Floor*	*Fill*	*Floor Contact*	*A Fill/Floor Contact*	*B Fill*	*Floor Contact*	*Fill*	*Fill A*	*Fill B*	*Floor Contact*	*Lower Fill*	*Overburden*	*Ventilator 2*	
44 specimens	*None*	*None*	*None*	*None*	*None*	*None*	*None*	*176 specimens*	*41 specimens without level*		*None*	*None*	*1 specimen*	*None*	*Broken human bone*
-	1	-	-	-	3	3	1	10	37	3	8	14	8	2	Unutilized flakes
1	-	-	-	-	-	-	-	-	5	-	1	3	-	-	Rejuvenation flakes
-	-	-	-	-	-	-	-	-	-	-	-	-	-	-	Flake/choppers
1	-	-	-	-	-	-	-	-	-	1	-	-	-	-	Utilized flakes
1	-	1	-	-	-	-	-	-	3	-	-	1	-	-	Scrapers/flake scrapers
1	-	-	-	-	-	-	-	-	-	-	-	-	-	-	Projectile points
-	-	-	-	-	1	-	-	-	2	-	-	-	1	-	Cores
-	1	-	-	-	-	-	-	-	-	-	-	-	-	-	Worked pebbles
-	-	-	-	-	-	-	-	-	-	-	-	-	-	-	Hafted stone hammer
-	-	-	-	-	-	-	-	-	2	-	-	-	-	-	Axes
-	-	-	-	-	-	-	-	-	-	-	-	1	-	-	Axe fragments
-	-	-	-	-	-	-	-	-	-	-	-	-	-	-	Chop/core-Hammerstone
1	-	-	-	-	-	-	-	1	-	-	1	3	2	1	Hammerstones
-	-	-	-	-	1	-	1	-	1	-	-	-	-	-	Metates
-	-	-	-	-	-	-	-	1	-	-	-	-	-	-	Metate fragments
-	1	-	-	-	-	-	-	1	1	-	5	-	-	1	Manos
-	-	-	-	-	-	-	-	-	-	-	-	-	-	-	Mano/paint grinders
-	-	-	-	-	-	-	-	-	1	-	-	1	-	-	Polishing stones
-	2	-	-	-	-	-	-	-	4	-	-	-	-	-	Ground/shaped slabs
-	-	-	-	-	-	-	-	-	1	-	-	-	-	-	Shell beads
-	-	-	-	-	-	-	-	-	-	-	-	-	-	-	Lap anvils
-	-	-	-	-	-	-	-	-	-	-	-	-	-	-	Ground shale
-	-	-	-	-	-	-	-	-	5	1	-	1	-	-	Bone tools
-	-	+	-	-	-	-	+	-	-	-	-	-	-	-	Corncobs
some	-	-	-	-	-	-	-	-	+	-	-	-	-	-	Seeds
-	-	-	-	-	-	-	-	-	1 or 2	-	-	1	-	-	Jar lids
108	141	54	59	23	107	90	9	205	147	6	58	196	99	7	Potsherds

Table 3.1 The combined floor artifact (FA) and overall artifact list by room for the earlier Mancos 5MTUMR–2346 occupation. Numbered items correspond to Figure 3.6. Rooms of the later pueblo and Room 25 (whose age was indeterminate) are not included for reasons specified in the text. Data are from Nordby (1974).

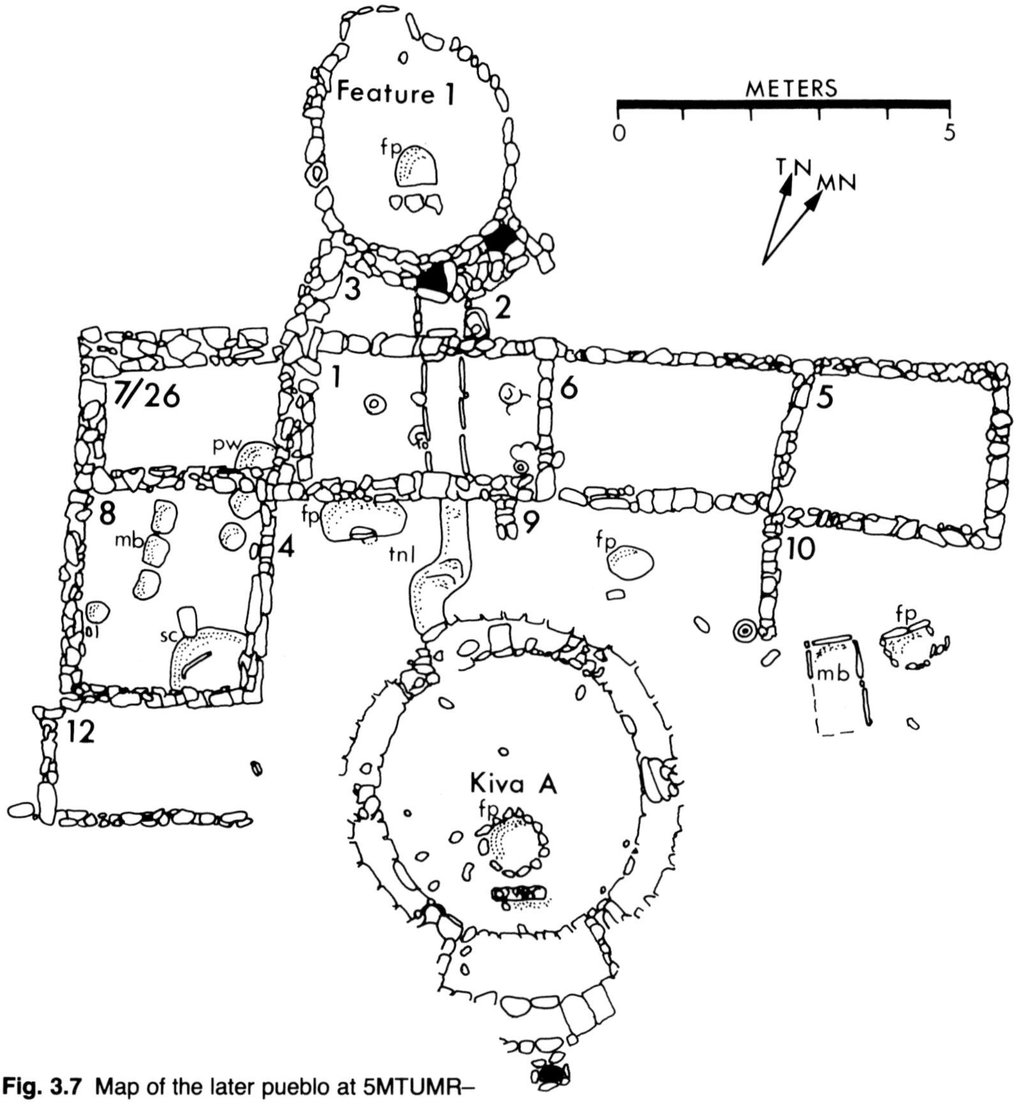

Fig. 3.7 Map of the later pueblo at 5MTUMR–2346, redrawn from Nordby (1974) (his Figure 32). Conventions used in Figure 3.6 are also employed here.

make clear by whom the interoccupational "refuse" was generated.

It is evident that when people later returned to the site to construct the adjacent, contiguous, partly superimposed pueblo structure (Figure 3.7) after the first habitation was abandoned, some abandoned walls stood high enough to form foundations for the new walls. Structures carried over from the first pueblo into the second include the original "kiva" (Feature 1) as well as walls of Rooms 7, 15, and 13. The later habitation added a larger, isolated, more typical kiva but continued to use the smaller original, remodeled "Feature 1" structure as well. The second pueblo was smaller than the first, and five or six of its ten rooms were nestled into the space between the arms of the original "L." The new, standard kiva was constructed to the immediate south, and the ventilator system of the "Feature 1" structure was modified and linked to this new kiva.

Estimated Number of Inhabitants

The number of people who lived at an archaeological site can be estimated through the assessment of a variety of attributes, including dwelling or floor space, site area, number of dwellings per site, number of rooms per dwelling or site, number of persons per room, volume of site deposits, and number of hearths (Hassan, 1978 and references therein; Schlanger, 1987). For multichamber buildings such as the early and late pueblos at 5MTUMR–2346, it is necessary to have a good estimate of the number of rooms used for "habitation" rather than storage or other purposes, to determine how many rooms were simultaneously occupied, and to determine the family size. Hill (1970), Clarke (1974), Longacre (1976), Plog (1975), and Sebastian (1986) have all attempted to determine the number of inhabitants at various prehistoric dwelling sites in the Southwest.

If Sebastian's estimate of 5 to 6 persons per apartment or dwelling unit is accepted, and if it is estimated that the larger, earlier pueblo had 4 family habitations based on 4 rooms with firepits (11, 21, 22, 23), a pueblo population estimate of 20 to 24 persons is obtained. Three or 4 rooms of the later pueblo have firepits, indicating 15 to 24 people. If the total number of rooms is used to estimate population size, using Hill's (1970) average of 2.8 persons per room (and not including the kivas and rooms that are not fully enclosed), the early pueblo is estimated to have 12 rooms and 33 people, the later pueblo 5 rooms and 14 people. Alternatively, if we calculate the total number of households by assuming one storage area for each, the early pueblo was occupied by 3 households, whereas the later pueblo's rooms interpreted to function for storage suggest 2 households. Either of the latter estimates could be an underestimate of one to 2 households because of rooms with unknown functions. Nevertheless, minimal population size estimates for the early and later pueblos, based on 6.1 people per household (Hill, 1970), are 18 and 12 people, respectively.

The assumptions upon which these estimates rest are very open to question, but it is very probable that more than two and fewer than six families lived in each pueblo at Mancos site 5MTUMR–2346.

Artifacts

Nordby (1974) provides an extensive analysis of the artifact assemblages recovered from both components of the site. Nickens (1974) provides a preliminary analysis of the human remains. Ceramics, both intact and fragmentary, were abundant in both pueblos. The chipped stone assemblage includes cores manufactured primarily from river cobbles of siltstone and chert, and abundant flakes of these materials, as well as a minor component of jasper, quartzite, quartz, ironstone, and shale flakes. Ground and pecked stone artifacts include manos, metates, and hammerstones, the former mostly in sandstone and silicified sandstone and the latter mostly in siltstone. Additional tools include abraders, paint palettes, mauls, and hafted stone hammers. Awls and needles of bone were recovered. A few specimens of wood were found, including what appear to be digging stick portions. *Olivella* beads, bone tubes, and pottery pendants were also found.

Nonhuman Faunal Remains

Nordby (1974) reports that a "variety of unworked bone detritus" was found on the site. He gives some details on bone artifacts, but provides no faunal analysis. The field catalog shows an abundance of lagomorph and turkey remains, and relatively few artiodactyl bones. Emslie's (1977) report is the best guide to the artiodactyl bone component of the site's zooarchaeological assemblage. The combined phases of the occupation yield the following results, based on Emslie's account. Elk are represented by one proximal humeral epiphysis and one proximal ulna. Bighorn sheep are represented by one complete phalanx, an intact scapula, a distal radius, a calcaneum, and a proximal metatarsal fragment. Pronghorn are represented by a single scapula. Mule deer remains are more abundant, with two mandible fragments and one edentulous mandible, a maxilla fragment with two molars, half an atlas, a fragment of scapular blade, a proximal radius, nine metapodial fragments, and a complete phalanx. Ten additional fragments attributed to "unidentifiable artiodactyl" are described by Emslie (1977).

The nonhuman faunal assemblage is limited in size because the site's refuse deposits were only sampled by small tests. The nonhuman osteological collections have been returned to the Ute Mountain Tribe and are presently housed in Towaoc, Colorado. A search of that collection in June 1990 failed to locate any nonhuman remains besides bone artifacts. Analysis of the Mancos human bone collection by Nickens identified a total of only eight certain nonhuman specimens (see Chapter 6 for a discussion of identification in the assemblage). Nordby (1974) noted the presence of some unmodified animal bone in most of the excavation units that yielded the fragmented human bone, but provided no further details. Additional nonhuman remains were recovered from the site and are listed in artifact catalogs. It is likely that much of this bone was human. Nickens (personal communication), who excavated most of the primary bone groups at the site, does not recall the presence of any identifiable nonhuman osteological elements besides the obvious bone tools. Furthermore, in cases such as Feature 1 and Room 17, it is evident that many bone fragments thought to be nonhuman during excavation were later recognized as human and included in the assemblage under consideration here. Even if more nonhuman remains existed among the site collections than are presently available, it is evident that they would have been insufficient for a productive comparative analysis with the Mancos human remains. For these reasons, other assemblages of nonhuman faunal remains from Anasazi contexts were used in the comparative work described in Chapter 12.

Human Skeletal Remains

As with typical Southwestern archaeological practice, most of the Mancos Canyon human bone occurrences were given field identifications as "burials." Several typical primary interments (articulated, most elements intact) were recovered from the site (Figure 3.8). These include Burials 1, 2, 4, and 12. Burial 1 was found on the floor of Room 1 of the later pueblo, a complete skeleton, semiflexed on the left side with associated grave goods, including McElmo black-on-white ceramic bowls (5) and plain (1) and effigy (1)

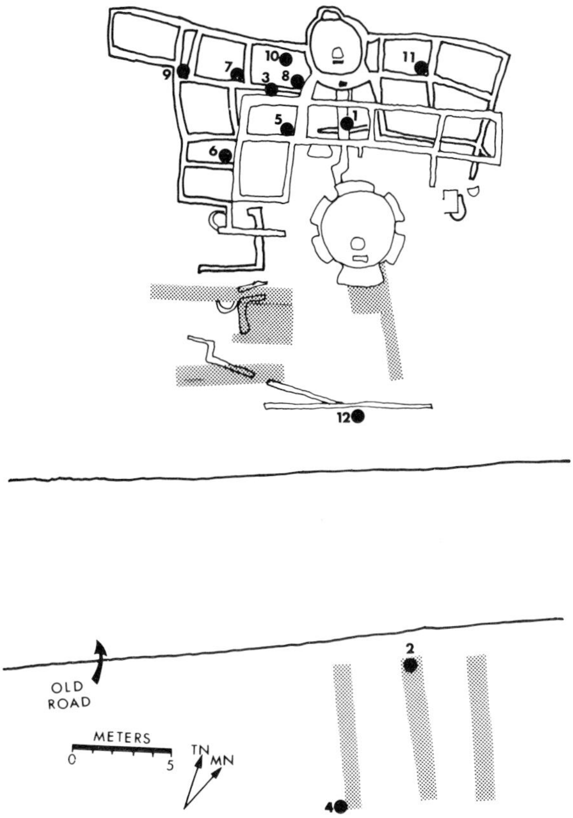

Fig. 3.8 This map of 5MTUMR–2346, redrawn from Nordby (1974) (his Figure 17), indicates the position of the various numbered "burials" recovered from the site. Some of the "burials" were formal, primary interments (numbers 1, 2, 4, 12), whereas others were concentrations of fragmented human bone. The shaded areas indicate test trenches.

Fig. 3.9 Burial 1, a primary interment, *in situ*. Note the accompanying grave goods at the feet of this individual, and the intact nature of her long bones. The elements of this skeleton are illustrated in Figure 3.19.

mugs as well as a St. Johns Polychrome bowl (Figure 3.9). Burial 2 was found in the trial trench. It was a primary extended burial without grave goods, whose head was oriented west and whose arms were crossed beneath the body. This individual was judged by Nickens (1974) to be an adult male (Figure 3.10). Burial 4 (Figure 3.11), also found without grave goods in the heart of the refuse deposit, was found on the bottom of an oven, Feature 2 of test trench 1. It was a young female individual (Nickens, 1974), buried in a tightly flexed position on her right side, with the head oriented to the north and facing west. Burial 12, another adult male (Nickens, 1974), was found on the northern margins of the midden, but was so poorly preserved as to make identification of burial position impossible. There were undoubtedly many more typical primary burials at the site, the available ones having been exposed only by limited testing of the refuse deposit. As Nordby (1974) points out, these primary interments all occur in common loci for Anasazi burials in the area. Their position and mortuary accom-

Fig. 3.10 Burial 2, a primary interment, *in situ*.

paniments also follow local convention, in stark contrast with the other human remains from the site.

Besides the more typical burials described above, scattered "bone beds" were found in several locations on the site. There is a clear dichotomy between these remains and the intentional, primary burials. Unlike the primary burials, there was no association or articulation of skeletal elements, and multiple individuals were mixed together in the scattered bone beds. It is inferred that fragmentation of these remains was not a result of sediment pressure because fragments of individual skeletal elements were found widely separated. Further support for this inference comes from the fact that the thin long bone shafts (particularly the fibula) were recovered intact, whereas bones that are much larger, more robust, and more resistant to fragmentation (tibia and femur)

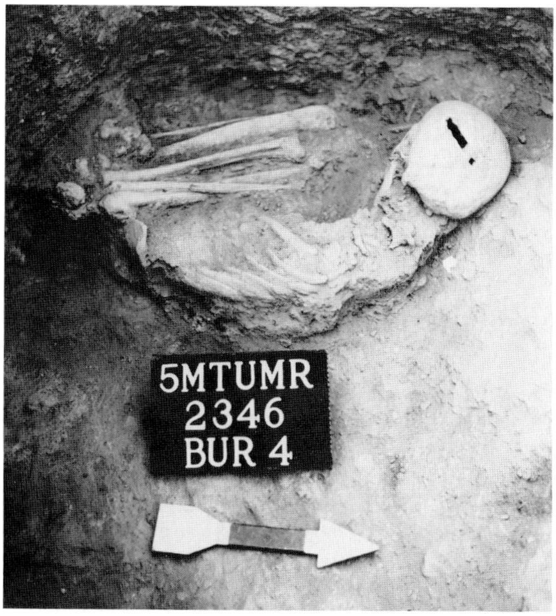

Fig. 3.11 Burial 4, a tightly flexed primary interment, *in situ*. The rectangular defect in the rear of the cranium was the result of excavation trauma.

were highly fragmented. Furthermore, elements in the bone beds manifest burning and trauma. There is no evidence of purposive burial, and no evidence of *in situ* burning. For these reasons, it is clear that the term "burial" should not be applied to the broken and scattered remains. The primary provenance for the fragmented bone lots comprising the Mancos assemblage, however, is in the form of "burial" numbers assigned to more or less discrete patches of broken bone. Field excavation forms were made out according to these "burial" identifications.

Nickens (1974, 1975) describes the Mancos 5MTUMR–2346 assemblage in nine separate "bone units" that correspond to the original field specimen, floor artifact, or "burial" numbers. Although inappropriate, the "burial" numbers constitute the most precise provenance available for the fragmented human bone from the site. As described in Chapter 4, each specimen in the assemblage was individually numbered, but all specimens may easily be related back to "burial" numbers in Appendix 2. It is valuable to summarize the "by-burial" information presented by the excavation forms and by Nickens (1974). Table 3.2 provides data on original "burial" number, FS and FA numbers, room numbers, specimen counts, and contextual notes.

Nordby (1974:237) describes the picture of how the broken and scattered human remains fit into the history of site occupation as ". . . unfortunately none too clear." He describes bone beds and other, more diffuse deposits with human bone. As noted above, most deposits of fragmented human bone were located in rooms of the earlier pueblo (Figure 3.12). Exceptions are the few specimens represented by FS19, Floor Artifact 3 of Room 8, and Burial 5 of Room 7. Dense bone beds are reported by Nordby (1974) to have been "banked up" against walls of various rooms, indicating that the walls stood above the level the bones were deposited on. According to Nordby (1974:239), the bone concentrations were of two kinds—vertically spread in some cases, and vertically discrete in others (specifically "Burials" 6 and 11, in Rooms 15 and 23, respectively). Both kinds of concentrations were spatially patterned:

> Like the concentrated bone beds, these bone deposits are usually found in the portion of the room facing the exterior of the later pueblo. For example, deposits in rooms to the west of the later pueblo tend to be more dense in the eastern parts of these rooms, as though thrown out by the inhabitants of the later pueblo.

Table 3.2

ROOM NUMBER	"BURIAL" NUMBER	OTHER NUMBERS	TOTAL SPECIMENS	FLOOR[a]	CONTEXT: FILL	COMMENTS
Feature 1	—	**FS18**	**1**	**no**	**yes**	Reported from upper fill, only one cranial fragment.
2 + 3	—	**FS19**	**40**	**no**	**yes**	Room 2 is not a room, but a space.
7/26	**5**	**FS30, 37**	**128**	**sub**	**yes**	Bone from fill of passageway to Room 8, cut below floor level.
8	—	**FA3**	**2**	**yes**	**no**	Both bone pieces polished, from floor on SW room corner.
13	—	**FS50**	**58**	**?**	**yes**	Unreported.
14	**8**	**FS49, 117**	**855**	**most**	**some**	Fallen roof adobe mixed with bones concentrated 2 to 4 cm above floor.
14	**10**	**FS138**	**Incl. in 8**	**sub**	**?no**	Bone in floor depression, covered with hard, adobe-like material.
14	—	**FS82**	**3**	**?**	**?**	Unreported.
15	**6**	**FS52**	**620**	**no**	**yes**	Numerous potsherds and lithics mixed in, ash and charcoal throughout.
16	**7**	**FS90**	**94**	**yes**	**yes**	Organics (wood) reported, some bones vertical, 25-cm thickness.
16	—	**FA1**	**21**	**yes**	**no**	Nordby identifies as "human cranium," but other elements present.
17	—	**FS65**	**7**	**?**	**?**	Unreported, probably from upper floor and overlying fill.
19	**9**	**FS123**	**44**	**yes**	**no**	Found beneath a large rectangular stone slab, 15-cm thickness.
23	**11**	**FS156**	**176**	**no**	**yes**	Hard material above, softer below, 8-cm thickness, level with wall top.
24	**3**	**FS23**	**41**	**?**	**yes**	Outside of Room 7, otherwise unreported.
Indet.	**0**	—	**16**	—	—	—

[a] Includes "Floor Contact."

Table 3.2 A compilation of information on the context of the various subassemblages of the Mancos 5MTUMR–2346 human bone assemblage. Data were taken from Nordby (1974) and Nickens (1974).

Nordby (1974) points out that remains in Rooms 15 and 23 (yielding bones of "Burials" 6 and 11, respectively) were found in levels substantially above the floor. He concludes that some time had passed between the abandonment of Rooms 15 and 23 and the deposition of "Burials" 6 and 11. As noted below and discussed further in Chapter 5, this observation corresponds to a fact noted by the present analysis—that bones from these particular subassemblages have different preservational characteristics from the remainder of the broken and scattered human bone from the site.

Several bone deposits were not as concentrated as the "bone beds." In these cases, the bone fragments were found throughout the fill above the floors, extending from the floor itself through the

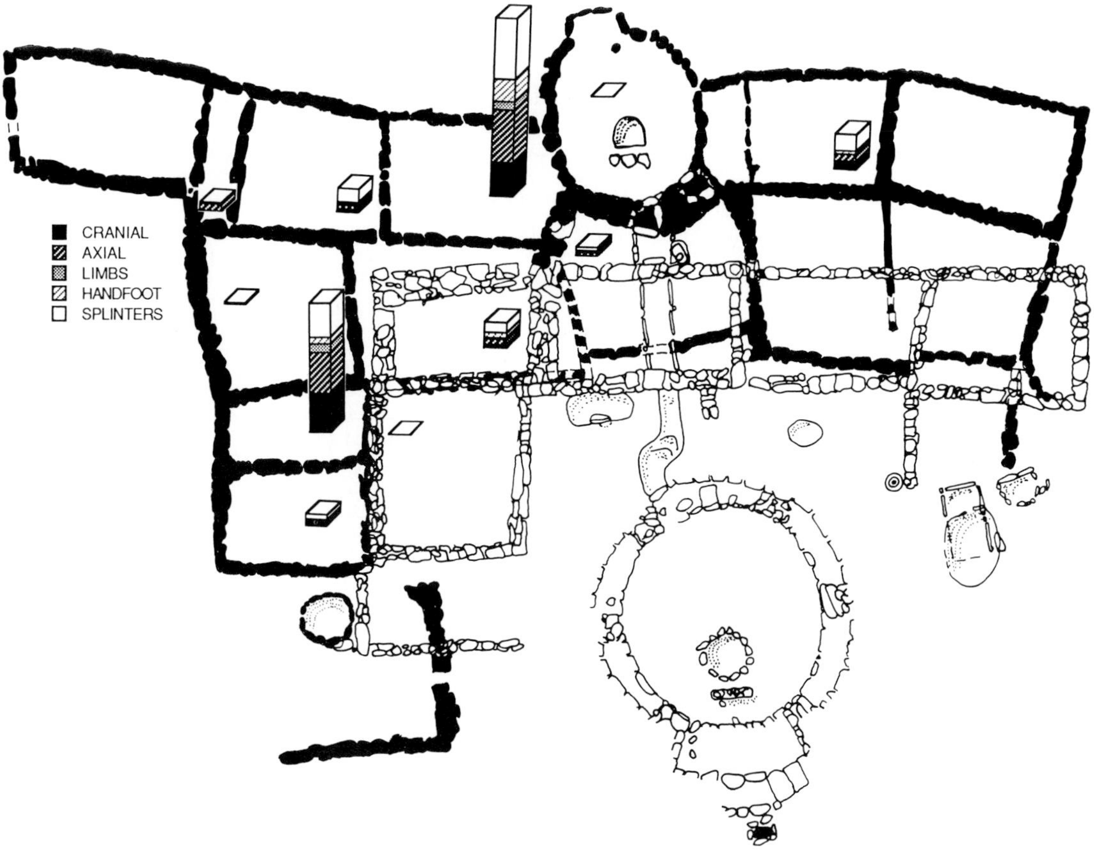

Fig. 3.12 Map of the combined older and younger pueblos at 5MTUMR–2346. The older pueblo is indicated in black. Provenience for the broken, scattered human skeletal remains is indicated by the base of the vertical columns. Specimen counts are indicated by height of each column, segmented by element groupings used in the database. Original "Burials" 8 and 10 were pooled in compiling these data. Note that virtually all of the broken, scattered human skeletal remains recovered from the site come from rooms of the older settlement.

"floor contact," and into the fill. Bones in the "unconcentrated" bone beds were mixed with substantial amounts of organic debris (wood), earth, potsherds, flakes, ground stone, and pecked stone artifacts. For example, "Burial" 7 (Figure 3.13) came from Room 16, a room inferred by Nordby (1974) to have been a sleeping area because the only two floor artifacts found there were a lap anvil and a polishing stone. The subassemblage from this room comprised 94 fragments of human bone found in the two arbitrary stratigraphic levels of "fill" and "floor contact." Commingled with the human bone were 168 potsherds, 13 utilized flakes, 2 rejuvenation flakes, a core, a jar lid, 2 hammerstones, a hafted stone hammer, 5 manos, a shaped stone slab, 2 bone tools, a corncob, and some seeds. The

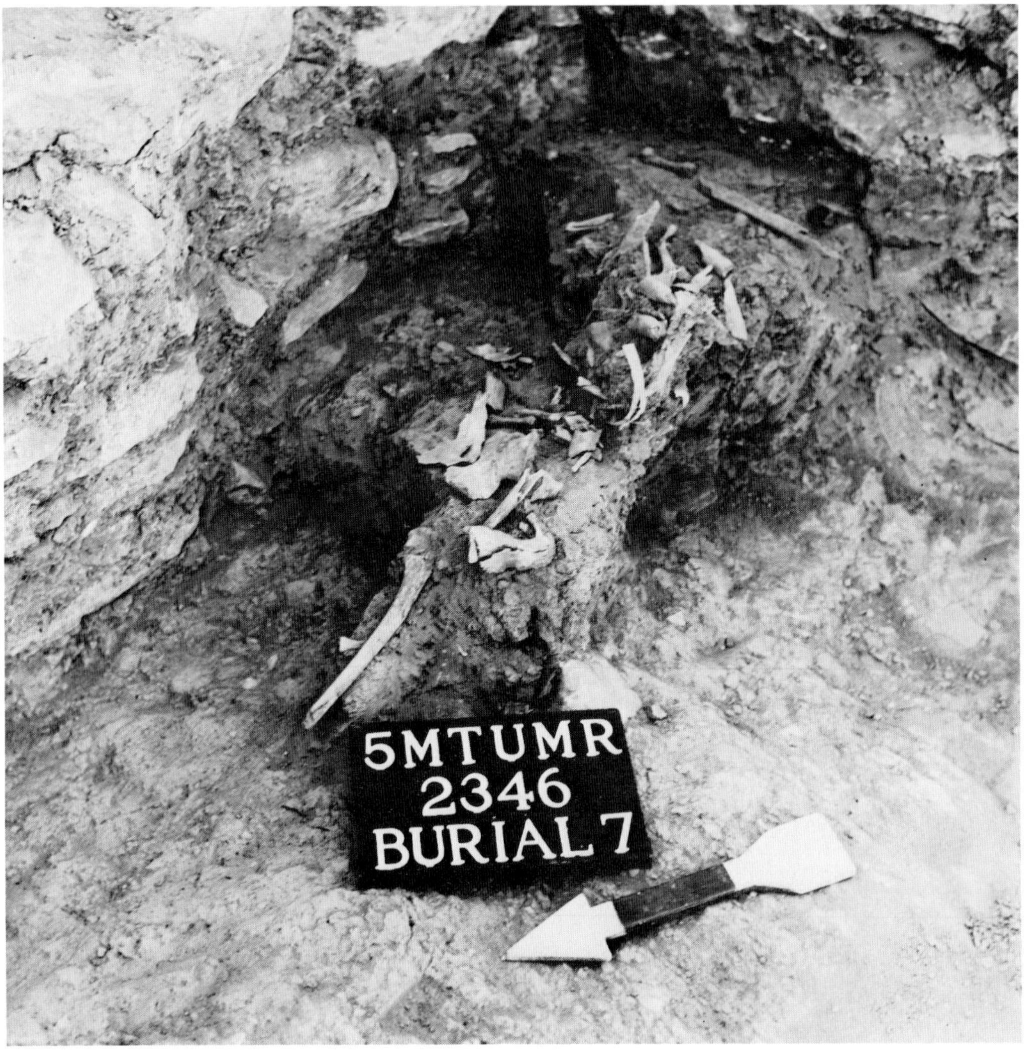

Fig. 3.13 "Burial" 7 *in situ* in Room 16.

fragmented human bone was found throughout the floor contact and upper fill. Similar artifact complements were found with the other bone concentrations. Figures 3.13 through 3.18 illustrate the contextual background of several bone sets contained in the Mancos assemblage. Figure 3.19 illustrates the bony elements of the formal Burial 1 from the pueblo. The contrast between the bones of this individual and the human bone fragments from the Mancos assemblage is great, as described and illustrated in previous figures and in chapters to follow.

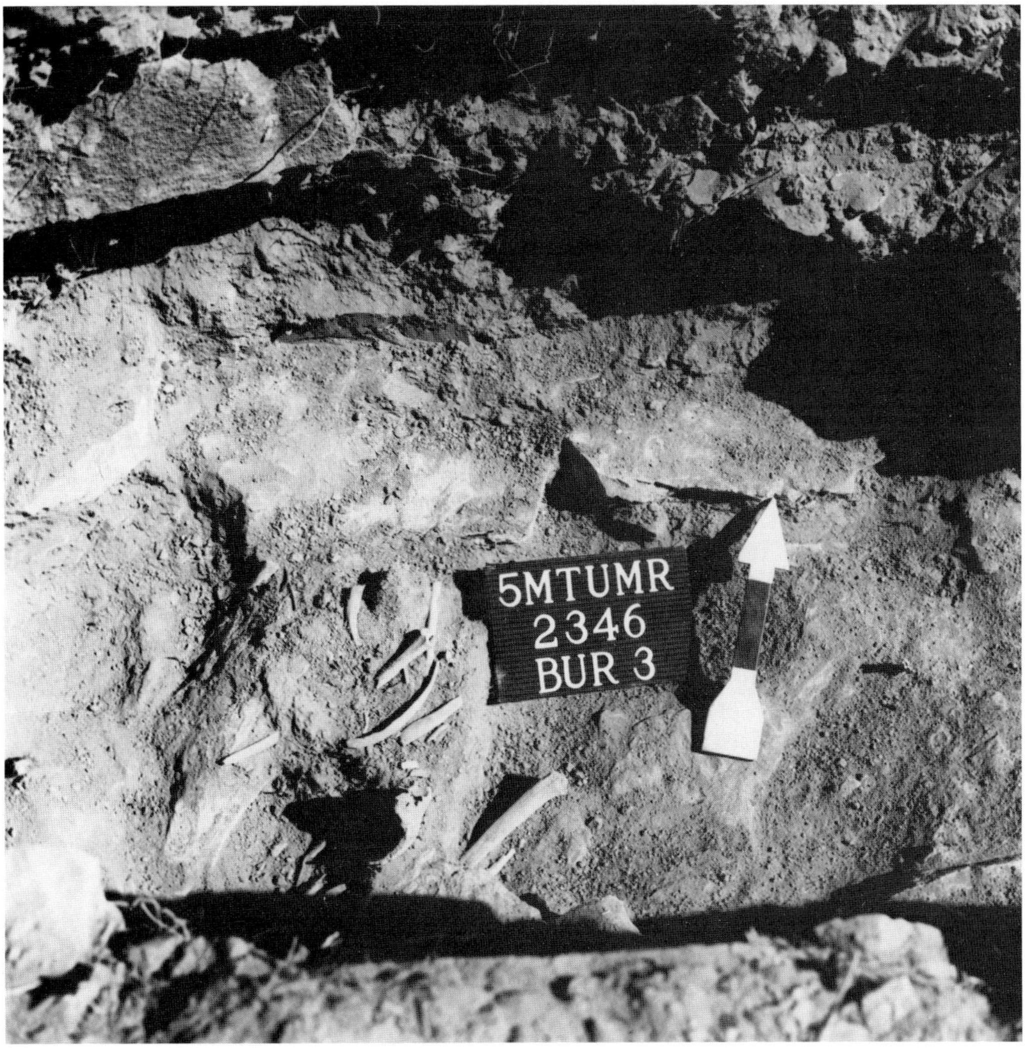

Fig. 3.14 "Burial" 3 *in situ* in Room 24.

Chronology

Since few tree-ring specimens were obtained from the site, chronological placement by comparative architectural considerations and artifact analysis has been attempted by Nordby (1974). Based on kiva form and the predominance of McElmo black-on-white ceramics, Nordby suggests that the construction date of the early site component was slightly after A.D. 1100 and that the later component was constructed about A.D. 1150 (very late Pueblo II or early Pueblo III).

5MTUMR
2346
BURIAL 11

5MTUMR
2346
BURIAL 10

Opposite page top:

Fig. 3.15 "Burial" 11 *in situ*. This was a bone "bed" above the floor level of Room 23. Note the corrugated pottery sherds intimately associated with the skeletal remains.

Opposite page bottom:

Fig. 3.16 "Burial" 10 as it was encountered *in situ* in Room 14.

Fig. 3.17 "Burial" 8 *in situ* in Room 14.

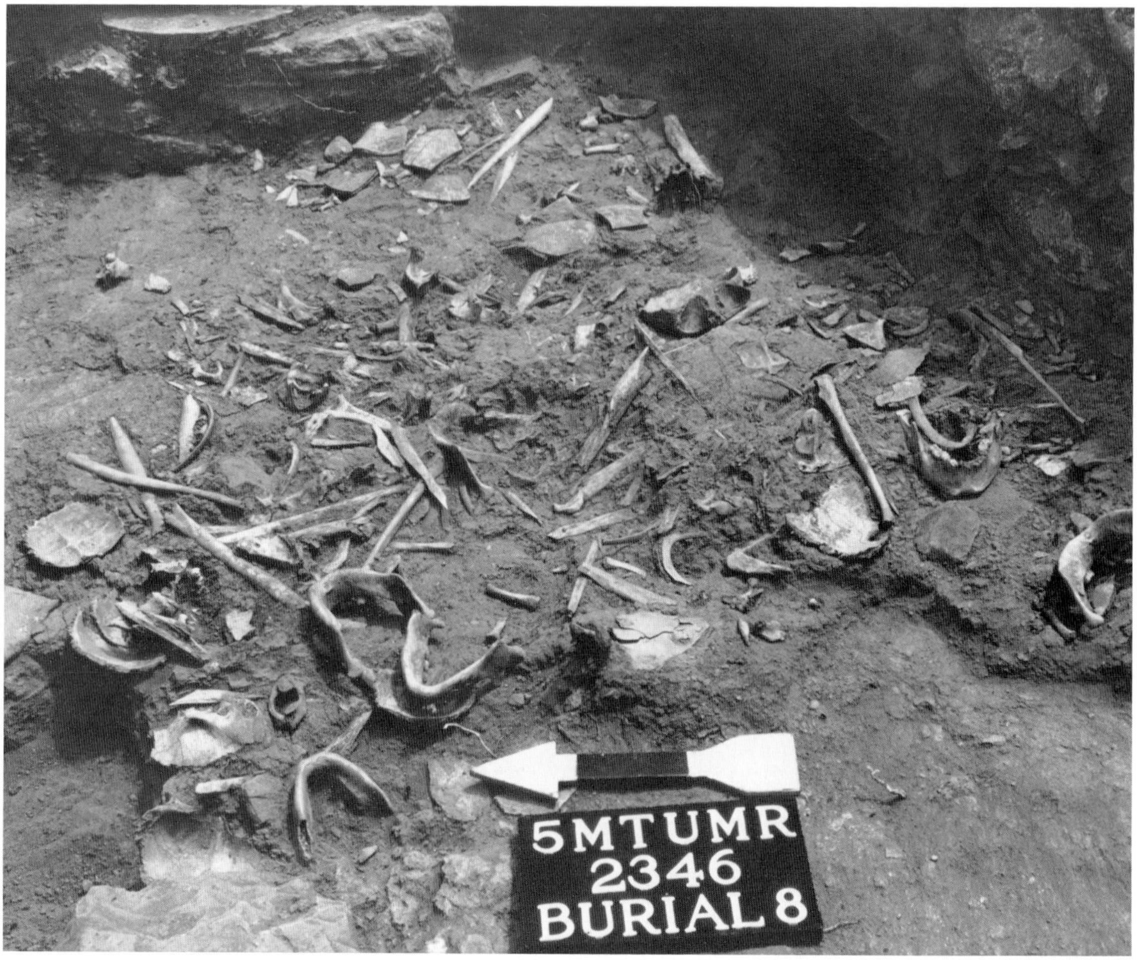

Fig. 3.18 Closeup of "Burial" 8 remains. Note the fragmentary and scattered nature of the non-mandibular cranial remains and tibial and femoral shafts compared to the mandibles and the ulnae and fibulae. Fragmentation of this assemblage clearly did not take place *in situ*.

PUBLISHED INTERPRETATIONS OF MANCOS 5MTUMR–2346

Nordby (1974:240) comments on four hypotheses to account for the evidence from Mancos Canyon 5MTUMR–2346. It is useful to quote extensively from his conclusions because he was responsible for the recovery of the material and had full command of the archaeological context of the human bone material.

> Unfortunately, it is difficult to settle upon a single explanation for these various occurrences. Various hypotheses that became evident during examination of the facts did not reconcile all of the conditions involved.

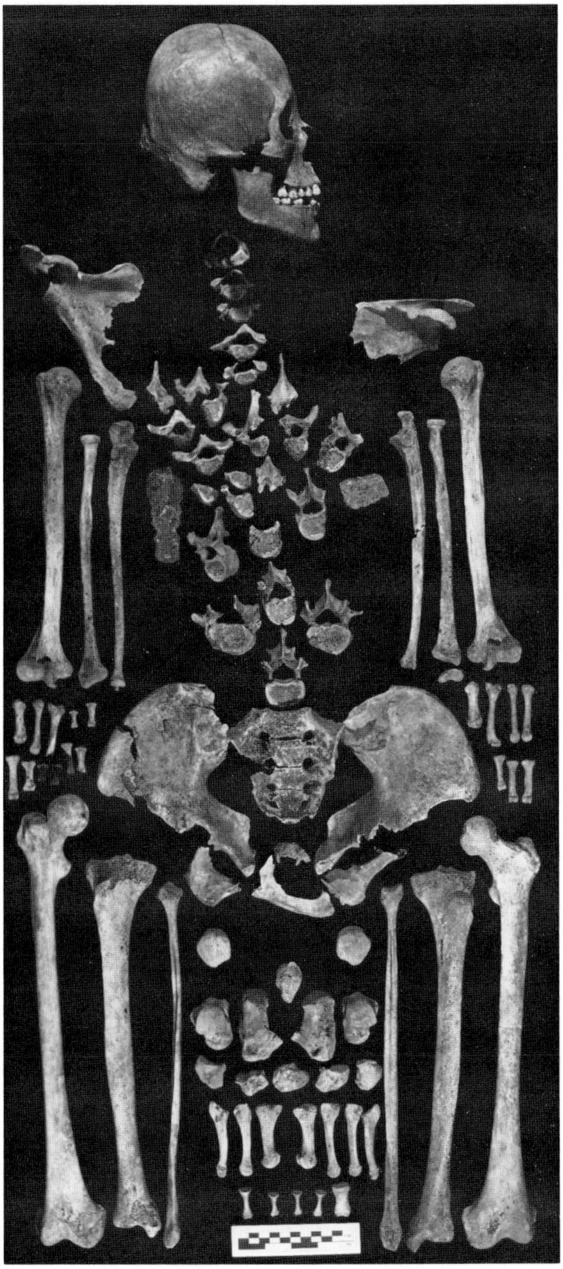

Fig. 3.19 The skeleton of the formal Burial 1 individual from site 5MTUMR–2346. Fragmentation among these skeletal elements was far less than among the nonburial remains described in this book as the "assemblage."

Nordby considers two hypotheses involving secondary burial. These suggest the possibility that excavation into older rooms by later occupants resulted in the discovery of primary burials, which were disinterred or cleaned out of abandoned rooms and tossed into older rooms that were not reoccupied. He rejects such ideas based on the nature and degree of fragmentation of the specimens.

Nordby (1974:240–241) goes on to consider two other hypotheses:

> Site 5MTUMR 2346 was attacked by people who killed the inhabitants, dismembered the corpses, and cannibalized the flesh of the long bones, and the brains of the skull, carrying the torsos, particularly the pelves, back to their own pueblo for ritual or consumption. Unfortunately, this explanation does not explain the specific location of the bones at the unused portion of the pueblo. Presumably, the attacking group would not have been overly conscious of the cleanliness of the courtyard surrounding the kiva. . . . More than thirty individuals are represented by the bone remains, a number which was too large to have lived in the eight-room later pueblo. . . .

Another hypothesis forwarded by Nordby (1974:240–241) is as follows:

> The people from 5MTUMR 2346 attacked a somewhat larger pueblo, killed an extensive number of young adults and children, decapitated the bodies, removed some of the appendages, and returned to 5MTUMR 2346, either for an unknown cannibalistic ritual or because of famine. . . . This explanation fits well with what is known of cases of cannibalism throughout other parts of the world, especially the tendency to collect the heads of enemies, either for consumption of the brains or as trophy heads. . . . Summarily, this hypothesis fits well with all of the conditions so far noted. Unfortunately, none of the skulls show definite breakage of the calotte through use of a

club or other heavy implement. Victims may have been killed by projectiles of some sort, which would thus have left the evidential projectile points at some other as yet undiscovered site. The skull bones do, however, show questionable alteration. There are minor and infrequent places on several skulls which might have been subjected to blows on the cranium. A more frequent occurrence is slight scratching upon the brain case. It is unlikely that the butchers were attempting to cut their way through the thick brain cases of the victims, especially in light of the increased thickness resulting from osteoporosis. It is possible that some trophy scalp removal or skinning practice could account for such scratching. . . .

Nordby (1974:242–243) goes on to suggest brain extraction by levering or hammering through the cranial base, concluding:

> Although alternative methods of death for the victims, such as death from famine or disease, might be imagined, it appears that this hypothesis most closely approximates the explanation needed to produce the condition and location of the bone remains. These bones were deposited when the abandoned rooms of the early pueblo were roofless, with walls still standing, by occupants of the later pueblo.

Nickens (1974) performed the analysis of the skeletal remains themselves and provided some background on biases in element representation that lie behind Nordby's (1974) interpretation. By the time of the 1973 discovery of fragmented human bone at Mancos, there were several reported cases of cannibalism in the American Southwest that Nickens could use for comparison. Nickens (1974) interpreted the Mancos Canyon assemblage as follows. Thirty-three individuals had been found in bone units, most units representing more than one person's bones. He noted the discrepancies, with a low abundance of certain skeletal elements relative to others. For example, intact mandibles were abundant, whereas pelves were poorly represented even though there was excellent bone preservation at the site. Nickens attempted to match bone fragments from "burials" from different rooms, but the experiment provided no associations. He noted the absence of carnivore damage to the bones and the overall similarity of the assemblage to that described by Turner and Morris (1970) for Polacca Wash. About preservation, Nickens (1974:51–52) states:

> In general appearance, the bones included in these remains are quite different from those in other burials at the site. They are well preserved and heavy, indicating a high mineral content. All are "bleached" to a very light color, a characteristic also noted in other cannibalism reports and which is probably due to being interred with no organic material adhering to the bones. Evidence of direct contact with fire is present, particularly in Burials 6 and 8, a few bones being thoroughly calcined. For the most part, the bones show evidence of being scorched in small areas which suggests that the bones may still have been partly covered with flesh at the time of their incineration. For example, several mandibles were found to be burnt only on the outside of the bone and on one side only. The complete or nearly whole mandibles may have some significance. . . . Damage to some of the mandibles and the fact that they are dumped in with the rest of the bone fragments argue against this practice and probably indicate that during dissection of the bodies, the jaw was removed and thrown aside in one piece.

Nickens (1975:290–291) perceptively points out for the Mancos assemblage that

> It is realized that there is no concrete evidence of actual cannibalism accompanying these re-

> mains, for the dismemberment of bodies and breakage of bones do not signify concomitant consumption of flesh. In this series, however, the degree of fragmentation, the apparent careful and patterned fracturing of the long bone shafts resulting in the exposure of the marrow cavity, and the evidence for contact with fire, are viewed as indications of something beyond merely mutilation of individuals in a postmortem condition. Cannibalistic motives are proposed to explain the condition of the human remains from 5MTUMR 2346.

Nickens (1974:52–53) discusses this interpretation of cannibalism as follows:

> In summary, the evidence points to the practice of cannibalism, albeit the type cannot be ascertained. No magico-religious connections are seen in the material. There seems to be a good distribution of age groups ranging from children to one individual over the age of 35 among the thirty-three individuals, but a predominance of young adults exists. There is no evidence that indicates violent death or that all these individuals died at the same point in time.

Nickens (1974:56) concludes his preliminary report with the following plea for further research:

> There is good evidence that some form of cannibalism was practiced at 5MTUMR 2346. While the occurrence of such a practice is not unique to the Anasazi culture area, there exists a need to reexamine the available data concerning cannibalism in the Southwest and to make an attempt to determine what purpose it served within prehistoric Pueblo society.

Nickens (1975:292) judiciously discusses the possible motivation for the behaviors he inferred as follows:

> While the presence of cannibalism in the Southwest is established in the archaeological record, its significance remains to be determined. Half of the total occurrences . . . report evidence of violent death in association with cannibalized remains, however, no definite magico-religious significance is apparent at any of the sites. This information coupled with the vagaries of food supply during Pueblo times probably indicates that obligatory or emergency ration cannibalism was practiced during hard times although this hypothesis cannot be considered conclusive at this time.

The results of a complete conjoining exercise on the Mancos assemblage are described in Chapter 4. These data, when combined with the excavator's observations outlined above, allow further investigation of the sequence of events leading to the deposition of the fragmented and scattered bone from the Mancos site.

POSTRECOVERY HISTORY OF THE MANCOS ASSEMBLAGE

As related above, the Mancos assemblage was recovered in the summer of 1973. Paul Nickens took responsibility for the analysis of the collection, aiming to determine its biological and behavioral backgrounds. His unpublished paper reporting on the remains was finished in 1974, and the main points of his analysis were published in *The Kiva* in 1975. The artifactual material from the Mancos Canyon sites excavated by Breternitz and associates was returned to the Ute Mountain tribe in Towaoc, Colorado. The human remains were stored temporarily at Mesa Verde National Park.

SUMMARY

As described in the introduction to this book, my purpose in studying the skeletal remains from the Southwest was to learn about the signature of cannibalism in the archaeological record in order to compare it to patterns of Paleolithic bone damage. It soon became evident, however, that additional analysis of the patterns evident in the osteological remains from the American Southwest might make significant contributions to regional archaeology and to the more general methodology of osteological analysis in archaeology. This was evident the first time I visually compared the Mancos and Leroux Wash assemblages in 1984, noting strong parallels in burning, cutmarks, crushing, and element representation. The pursuit of this patterning is the subject of the following chapters.

The research described here represents an attempt to extend the pioneering work of Paul Nickens and Christy Turner by intensively focusing on the human bone assemblage from 5MTUMR–2346. This work was designed as another step in the ongoing effort to unravel some of the mysteries surrounding this and other similar assemblages from the Southwest, and to illuminate prehistoric cannibalism in general.

CHAPTER

4

Analytical Background and Conjoining

In 1984 I visited Mesa Verde to view the Mancos 5MTUMR–2346 collection. Upon noting striking similarities between undocumented damage patterns on the Mancos collection and the collections from Polacca and Leroux washes stored at the Museum of Northern Arizona, permission to borrow the Mancos 5MTUMR–2346 material from the Ute Mountain Tribe and Mesa Verde National Park was sought. The assistance of Robert Heyder, Jack Smith, and Allen Bohnert at Mesa Verde; David Breternitz, Paul Nickens, and Larry Nordby of the original excavation team; and Art Cuthair of the Ute Mountain Tribe was important in arranging the loan and facilitating the 1985–1990 Berkeley analysis. Jack Smith provided me with copies of all relevant excavation records and photographs from the Mesa Verde archives. While working with the Mancos assemblage, I had the good fortune to be able to assess similar collections from Cottonwood Wash and Bluff, Utah, and Yellow Jacket, Colorado.

ANALYTICAL BACKGROUND

The procedures outlined in this chapter are not necessarily the most efficient nor the most desirable ones for assessing similar skeletal collections. The analysis described below evolved between 1985 and 1989 to deal with a fair share of false starts and emerging questions. The results of this study have made it possible to outline a recommended, streamlined procedure for excavating and analyzing similar skeletal collections (an outline is provided in Appendix 3). This procedure was tested with the Yellow Jacket 5MT–3 human bone assemblage (see Appendix 1) and found to be satisfactory. Work on the Yellow Jacket assemblage was done in the summer of 1989, as this book was being written.

When the analysis was begun in 1985, the bone from 5MTUMR–2346 was stored in paper bags that bore the original "burial" and feature numbers (see Table 3.2 and Chapter 3 for a discussion of what the term "burial" means for most Mancos specimens—it is a spatial term only). Bones of the formal burials from the site are not included in the "assemblage" described below and were used only in the comparative physical anthropological analysis of Chapter 5.

All the Mancos human bones had been washed, but none was individually labeled. Nickens had glued many cranial remains in the assemblage together (50 joins), but only one postcranial join and no cross-''burial'' joins had been noted. As a first step in the analysis, the glued joins were dissolved, returning the collection to its previous unjoined, *in situ* status. Many isolated teeth had become dislodged in the transport bags, and these were returned to their sockets and glued into place at this stage of the analysis. Several recent (as opposed to ancient) breaks were easy to diagnose by color and topography of the broken surfaces, and these breaks were joined with glue before further analysis. It should be emphasized that no gluing across a break that was not certainly of recent (as opposed to ancient) fracture (see Chapter 6) was done.

Dozens of small bone fragments with recent breaks had chipped off the larger specimens, particularly the burned cranial vaults, during their residence in the paper bags. Residues (including bone powder as well as freshly fractured pieces smaller than 1 cm^2) that could not be rejoined to the pieces from which they had chipped away were not included in the analysis. The small-fragment component of the Mancos assemblage was already biased by recovery technique so the inclusion of dozens of small tabular pieces of external and internal vault would have yielded no significant change in results.

An important early step in the analysis was to insure that no mixing of specimens from different provenances occurred during the extensive manipulations required by full analysis, including conjoining. Each specimen was therefore labeled with its provenance as determined by the bag in which it was contained. Bones of a left arm, right and left clavicles, ribs, hand bones, and vertebrae found in Room 1 with Burial 1 (FS7) were not included in the analysis due to uncertain provenance. Nickens describes the less complete set as FS17, but it was bagged as FS7.

In this analysis, the term ''specimen'' refers to a singular, isolated, nonconjoined whole or partial bone or tooth. Mixing of specimens among bags before the Berkeley analysis was possible, but unlikely, as the collection had not been intensively studied since the Nickens analysis.

After provenance labeling, each ''burial'' subassemblage was assessed separately. The analysis followed the basic outline established by T. E. White (1956)—segregating the specimens by element, side, maturity, and taxon. Each specimen was identified and sorted by designations in the element code described in Chapter 6. The term ''element'' refers to the intact bone as it occurs in the adult skeleton. Elements of the skull are considered separately. The term ''piece'' refers to specimens that do not join with others and to pieces composed of sets of specimens that do join.

After sorting by element, each piece was checked for evidence of recent (as opposed to ancient, see Chapter 6) fracture. Where fracture surface characteristics showed unequivocally that there was a recent break, this surface was checked against all appropriate specimens to see where the opposite surface was. When such recently fractured, matching surfaces were found, they were glued together. This procedure insured that the collection to be analyzed was as close as possible to the original, fractured assemblage that had been deposited in the site.

Systematic maximal checking for possible joins was performed for each element category. The conjoining (refitting) methodology is described below. For cases in which fits between individual specimens were found, temporary joins were forged with masking tape. Minimum numbers estimations were then made for individuals and elements within both the ''burial'' subassemblages and the assemblage as a whole. At this maximally conjoined stage, the remains were as close to their prebreakage condition as was possible. Individual aging was performed at this maximally conjoined stage. Observations on the maximally conjoined collection were made to assess and record patterns of perimortem trauma in a narrative fashion for each element and for the skull as a unit (the results of this work are presented in Chapters 7–11).

After the assessment of biological features and perimortem alteration patterns of the maximally conjoined collection, all joins were separated. Each separate specimen was given an individual specimen number. Consequently, each piece in the collection now bears two numbers, a provenance (''burial'') number from the original excavators and an individual specimen number assigned at Berkeley.

After deconjoining, a full set of observations from a zooarchaeological viewpoint was made for each specimen. The large amount of data generated from analysis of the nonconjoined assemblage was entered in 5 separate database files (Appendix 2): ''CRANIAL,'' ''AXIAL,'' ''LIMBS,'' ''HANDFOOT,'' and ''SPLINTERS.'' The division of the collection into these five databases was made only for analytical convenience, and the files and their organization are described in detail in Chapter 6.

Each attribute recorded in the database files is defined and discussed in Chapter 6, with an accounting of relevant published work and a consideration of some results generated by this study. A chapter is devoted to the discussion, definition, and illustration of the attributes because of the general lack of standardization in faunal analysis, and because many of these attributes were recognized for the first time in the Mancos study.

BACKGROUND TO THE CONJOINING STUDY

Most archaeological bone assemblages represent a mixture of taxa, some deposited as the result of human activity and some as the result of the actions of other biological or geological agents. Rare are those sites that contain few vertebrate taxa, accumulated over a short period, with minimal postdiscard disturbance. Those that exist provide the analyst with unique opportunities to investigate past activities through the restoration of bones from the recovered fragments. As Hofman (1986:170) has noted for artifact refitting, ''Piecing things together is not an analytical end point, but it should put us in a position to develop and evaluate increasingly sophisticated models of past behavior and culture change.''

Such restoration involves steps designed to reassemble (Schiffer, 1987) the bones in order to learn about the *sequence of processing* and *the nature of discard* that characterized past butchery activities. By refitting (the terms ''reassembling,'' ''refitting,'' and ''conjoining'' are used here synonymously) fragments to reconstruct bony elements, it is possible to gain insight into how the individual elements were processed. As Lyman (1978) notes, this working ''backwards'' to get at the *butchering process* is a very effective methodology so long as data presentation is not incomplete or inaccurate (Johnson, 1978).

Complementing the insights that conjoining affords into the butchery process, conjoining can be employed across horizontal space in an effort to infer activity areas and gauge the degree of postdiscard disturbance, whether with stone tools or faunal remains (as in Schild, 1976; Stahl and Zeidler, 1988; Hofman, 1986; Villa, 1990). The reassembly of skeletal elements can thereby provide insights into the *spatial patterning* of past activities. In addition, the joining of specimens in different strata may yield understanding of postdepositional disturbance or reuse of resources. Thus, the degree to which reassembly is possible is often a good indication of the degree to which an assemblage has suffered *postdiscard disturbance*. As Villa *et al.* (1988) point out, mapping bone fragments that participate in joins allows the investigator to exclude the possibility of bone breakage resulting from sediment pressure.

Except for Nickens' (1974) attempts to derive behavioral information from the spatial assessment of conjoining among the Mancos 5MTUMR–2346 remains, the Southwest human bone assemblages summarized in Chapter 3 and interpreted as evidence of cannibalism by Turner and others have been subjected to a minimum of refitting analysis—all of it directed at obtaining more complete crania and long bones for standard physical anthropological analyses. Because conjoining studies offered to yield information about the processes of bone modification and discard in these assemblages, the Mancos assemblage was subjected to a thorough refitting exercise.

PREVIOUS CONJOINING STUDIES

An early example of the conjoining approach to vertebrate fauna is found in Frison's (1971) work at Eden-Farson, a protohistoric Shoshonean procurement site that yielded the remains of more than 200 antelope in Wyoming. Here, bones from lodges at the site were "reconstructed" to show that bone processing took place on an intralodge basis. Leroi-Gourhan and Brezillon (1972) focus on similar spatial problems in their conjoining work on the fauna from the European Paleolithic site of Pincevent, but go on to look at the reassembled bones in an effort to understand fracture patterns. Enloe and David (1989) pursue additional work at Pincevent.

Bunn *et al.* (1980) extend similar techniques to an analysis of much earlier material from Koobi Fora, Kenya. These authors note that their search for bone-refitting sets was very time-consuming, but like the other authors cited above, their refitting methods are left unspecified. In 1984 Kroll and Isaac described their refitting studies as a "most exciting new line of spatial evidence" (p. 21). They cited a personal communication from the investigator responsible for the bone-refitting work, Henry Bunn, to the effect that up to 4 percent of the identifiable bones recovered from the FxJj–50 site at Koobi Fora and the FLK "*Zinj*" site at Olduvai had been found to join. Bunn's Ph.D. dissertation (1982) details his methodology. He subdivided the assemblage by "particular skeletal category" and sought matches of broken surfaces, interproximal tooth facets, and articular anatomy within each category. He included nonphysical matches of dental wear, tooth eruption, and morphology in his "conjoining" analysis, making his results somewhat incompatible with other work that relies strictly on refitting edges from bone elements that have actually been broken. Bunn's description does not identify what his "particular skeletal categories" are, nor does it specify how systematically specimens in the assemblages were checked for all possible joins.

Beebe's (1983) conjoining work on the Canadian Bluefish Cave bone assemblage was directed at identifying the agent of fracture, but the methodology of conjoining was not specified.

Villa's work (Villa, 1982; Villa *et al.*, 1985, 1986a, 1986b, 1987) on both Paleolithic and Neolithic bone and stone assemblages has demonstrated the utility of conjoining studies in understanding spatial patterning within archaeological sites. The methodology of conjoining, however, is again left unspecified.

Todd's (1987) work on the Horner II bone bed from Wyoming is the most precise methodological statement available for reassembly methods in faunal analysis. Todd points out that refitting in lithics is essentially a mechanical process once raw material has been controlled for. In faunal studies, bilateral symmetry in morphology, articular surface topography, and age-related characteristics such as tooth eruption and wear, or epiphyseal fusion, allow for further reassembly of an assemblage. Todd makes the very useful distinction between "anatomical refitting studies" using the latter criteria and "mechanical" (conjoining) refitting studies in which skeletal and dental elements are restored from reassembly of fragments along lines of fracture. Conjoining, or mechanical refitting, is used by Todd in his analysis of the Horner assemblage. Although his *anatomical* refitting procedure is elaborated upon, his *mechanical* (conjoining) methodology is not described in detail. Todd's terminology is used here when describing the analysis of the Mancos assemblage—the term "conjoining" refers only to the refitting of fragments along lines of perimortem (ancient, see Chapter 6) breakage.

Perhaps the conjoining studies cited above do not precisely specify the conjoining methodology employed because each exercise actually explored the possibility that every single fragment under consideration was fully and systematically checked against every other piece in the collection that afforded a conceivable join. On the other hand, because such an approach is extremely time-consuming, perhaps such maximal, systematic conjoining has not been attempted in many analyses. Whatever the case, the failure to specify the degree to which a conjoining exercise was systematic renders many data generated by such exercises difficult to use comparatively. For example, one investigator might check an assemblage fully for every single possible join, whereas another investigator "eyeballs" it, finds a few joins, and reports a much lower total. In an effort to avoid such problems, the Mancos assemblage was put through a maximal, systematic conjoining exercise according to the procedure described below. The objective of this exercise was to learn as much as possible about the processing and discard activities that played roles in creating and shaping the Mancos assemblage.

THE MANCOS CANYON 5MTUMR–2346 CONJOINING EXERCISE

The total 2,106-piece Mancos assemblage was sorted by element as described above. All specimens were separated by element and by side for nonmidline elements. At this stage, each broken edge of each specimen was physically checked against all other broken edges on all other specimens in the same element and side category, as well as against indeterminate side and IP1–IP4 categories where appropriate. The IP (indeterminate postcrania) categories were created for pieces whose element identity could not be established precisely. IP1 specimens are fragments of smaller diameter long-bone shaft attributable to the radius, ulna, or fibula. IP2 specimens are fragments of larger shafts that could belong to the humerus, tibia, or femur; and IP3 specimens are shaft fragments that belong either to the tibia or the femur. IP4 specimens cannot be taken beyond postcranial identification. An example of this conjoining methodology is provided in Figure 4.1.

When a few specimens are involved in a conjoining exercise, the procedure outlined above is fast and easy. For a collection like Mancos, the procedure involved a large time investment. The estimated time spent fully conjoining the Mancos Canyon 5MTUMR–2346 assemblage totaled 245 person-hours. This expenditure was made by experienced human osteologists (Susan Chin, Susan Anton, and the author) *after* detailed, physical anthropological identifications had been made for all the specimens, each had been sorted by

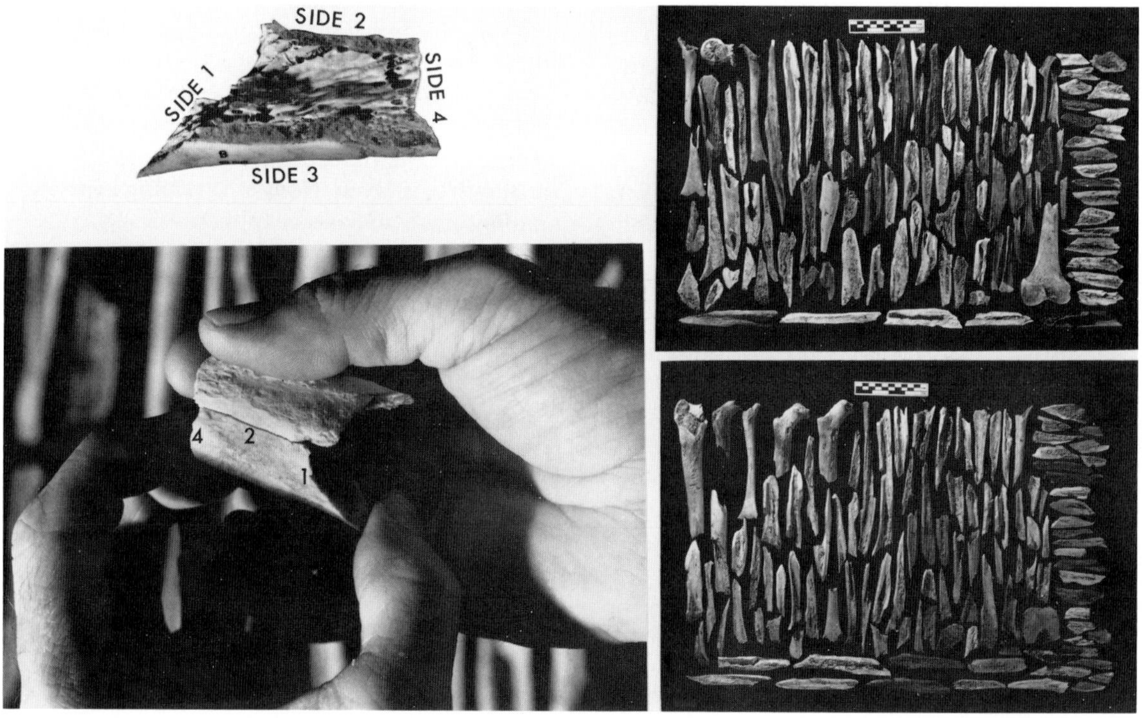

Fig. 4.1 This figure illustrates the conjoining methodology as applied to a specimen identified as a femur fragment, side indeterminate. *All* broken edges of this femur specimen were checked to see if they joined *any* of the broken edges of *any* specimens identified as belonging to a right or left femur (boxes on right). This did not exhaust all the potential joins, however, requiring that the specimen also be checked against all other femur, side-indeterminate specimens. Furthermore, because indeterminate postcranial element categories IP2, IP3, and IP4 (Figures 12.4–12.6) also contained potential femur fragments, the specimen was also checked for joins with each fragment from these categories. In this systematic, maximal checking methodology, all possible joins were found. Where joins were positively established, the joining bones were temporarily taped (not glued) together and assigned arbitrarily designated "conjoining set" numbers.

side and element, and obvious "anatomical" joins had been made in an unsystematic fashion. In theory, if the 2,106 specimens averaged four broken edges each, and if each specimen was checked against every other specimen in the assemblage (16 surface checks per pair) with no matches found, the total number of surfaces checked against one another would equal 35,465,040. This staggering sum represents an underestimate in the sense that it does not account for the fact that checking two broken edges for possible joins requires that the fractured surfaces be checked along their entire lengths for joins. This is because the fragments often share only a few millimeters of joining surface along the fractured edges being checked (Figure 4.1).

In practice, the intimidating total of over 35 million is lowered dramatically by the extent to which specimens are identifiable to element. This is because specimens properly identified as left femur fragments will, for example, never join with specimens in the humerus element subsample, the tibia subsample, the right femur subsample, or any other element subsample except the left femur sample (and IP1, IP3, and IP4). Furthermore, within each element category reside segments of bone identifiable as, for example, proximal or distal ends. It is possible to exclude many possible joins by recognizing this, despite the fact that many of these specimens cannot be sided. This is even true of fragments not identified to element. An example would be the case in which the investigator is able to determine that *if* the IP2 specimen is from a tibia, it can *only* have come from the region of the anterior tibial crest.

The *accuracy* with which specimens are assigned to element is a critical foundation for conjoining studies. The *underidentification* of elements will greatly increase the number of edges requiring checking, whereas element *misidentification* will eliminate the possibility that joins will be found. For these reasons, elements should be carefully and maximally identified, without guesswork, before refitting begins.

Another practical consideration that dramatically limits the number of necessary checks among individual specimens is the fact that specimens differ in ontogenetic age, cortical thickness, and external and internal morphology (including surface texture and porosity). These features may easily be used to immediately rule out the possibility of any join between many specimens. On the other hand, it is not permissible to use nonfracture attributes of perimortem and postmortem surface alteration in conjoining exercises. Bone color, rootmarking, burning, and other preservational attributes are apt to be extremely misleading if used during conjoining, as illustrated by Figure 4.2. This is because once broken, the different bone pieces can suffer very different prerecovery histories.

One additional beneficial feature of assemblages with many refitting pieces is the fact that each join established reduces the number of necessary cross-checks because no other pieces can join that particular edge. The analyst must be careful, however, to systematically control exactly which specimens within conjoining sets have been checked against other joined and isolated specimens.

The best procedure for this kind of work is to initially perform "anatomical" refitting within each sided element category before systematically checking the remaining pieces. The use of anatomy represents a shortcut for the skilled analyst, and when the sample to be refit is small (few individuals represented) and the assemblage has a high integrity, ana-

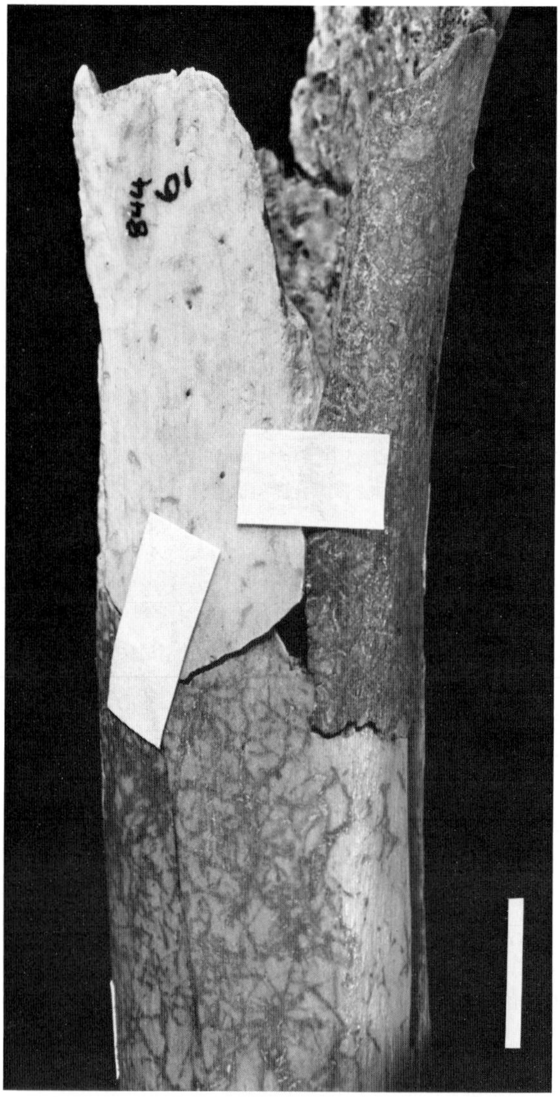

Fig. 4.2 This conjoined femoral Set 67 shows the different preservational characteristics of fragments derived from the same bone. This differential indicates variation in postfracture history and cautions against the use of color and preservation in seeking joins during refitting exercises. Bar = 1 cm.

tomically based joining is a very fast method of finding many joins, reducing the tedious work of edge checking.

Once all the "easy," anatomically guided joins have been found, then all possible joins within each *sided* piece in an element category should be checked for. After this, all *unsided* pieces within each element category must be checked against all the remaining pieces in both of the right and left side categories. Conjoining within an element category, "internal" conjoining, is finished only with the completion of this work. All element categories, including IP1–IP4, should be internally joined prior to checking for between-category joins. By definition, after internal conjoining, the only possible remaining joins will be between pieces attributed to element and pieces attributed to the IP1, IP2, IP3, and IP4 "element" categories. Because all elements have the potential to join with specimens in the IP4 (totally indeterminate postcranial) category, these IP4 pieces must be checked against all specimens and sets in all other element categories. Group IP3, on the other hand, contains pieces that can only join with specimens in the tibia, femur, or other IP categories.

CONJOINING RESULTS: A QUANTITATIVE ASSESSMENT

Even when the methodology is standardized, the number of joins found in a refitting exercise will depend upon many factors, including the degree to which postdiscard fracture has modified the assemblage. Such fractures can result from different agencies, including trampling, carnivore activity, *in situ* crushing, and excavation/transport breakage. The latter did occur on the Mancos assemblage, but all such fractures were recognized and repaired prior to the refitting work. For the Mancos assemblage, there is no evidence of postdepositional, *in situ* fragmentation due to the weight of overlying sediment. Such crushing would have been evident during excavation. As noted in Chapter 6, there is no evidence of carnivore modification, and the contextual circumstances described in Chapter 3 make trampling seem an unlikely factor in fragmentation of the human remains. Therefore, it is likely that the conjoining work described above was done across ancient fractures that were induced by human activity (see Chapters 6–11 for further evidence of human modification).

All specimens that were found to join at least one other specimen in the Mancos assemblage are identified with the conjoining set number in column 14 of the database files of Appendix 2. The term "conjoining set" as used in this study is the equivalent to, but preferred over, Schild's (1976) "articulation net" used in stone tool conjoining. The latter term has osteological implications that might create confusion when applied to bones. Since dislodged teeth may have become separated from the jaw after recovery, no tooth root/socket fits were counted as conjoining sets. Also, antimeres were not sought nor were they counted as conjoining sets. Figures 4.3 to 4.6 show the effects of conjoining upon some pieces from the Mancos 5MTUMR–2346 assemblage.

Table 4.1 gives refitting data extracted from the Mancos databases, showing a total of 551 specimens participating in joins that resulted in 186 total conjoining sets. Thus, 26.2 percent of the 2,106-piece Mancos assemblage was found to conjoin mechanically across perimortem (ancient, see Chapter 6) fracture surfaces. Nickens (1974, 1975) reported 1,899 pieces in the assemblage, but his count was made after he refitted many vault specimens. The counts reported in Table 4.1 were made after all of Nickens' conjoins were disassociated and independently reconjoined with tape.

Fig. 4.3 Fully conjoined Sets 67 (femur, n = 11 specimens) and 96 (tibia, n = 10 specimens).

Nearly 62 percent (116 of 186) of the conjoining sets consisted of pairs of linked specimens (sets of 2 pieces united by single joins), whereas the largest set consisted of 11 specimens belonging to a single femur (conjoining Set 67). Cranial

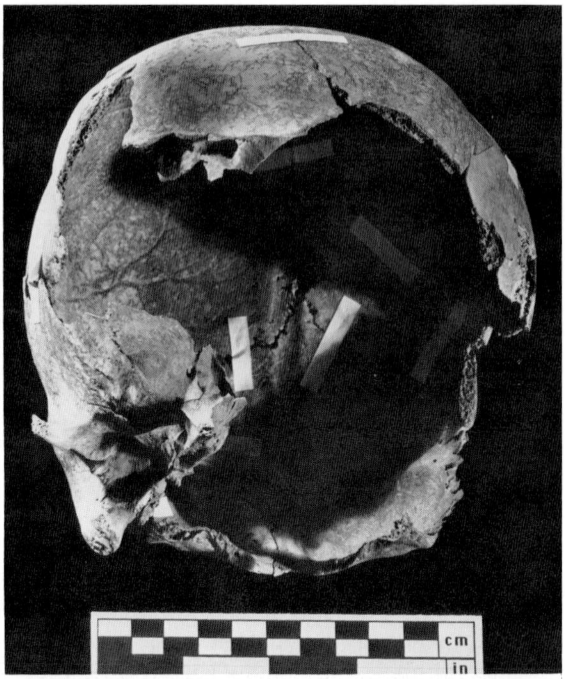

Fig. 4.4 Deconjoined Sets 67 (femur, n = 11 specimens) and 96 (tibia, n = 10 specimens).

Top right:

Fig. 4.5 Fully conjoined Set 152 (cranium, n = 10 specimens).

Bottom right:

Fig. 4.6 Deconjoined Set 152 (cranium, n = 10 specimens).

Table 4.1

	NUMBER OF SETS OF (*n*) PIECES										TOTAL SPECIMENS
ELEMENT	*2*	*3*	*4*	*5*	*6*	*7*	*8*	*9*	*10*	*11*	*CONJOINED*
FOOT	1										**2**
INDET. POSTCR. 4	1										**2**
CLAVICLE	1	1									**5**
INDET. POSTCR. 3	4										**8**
INDET. POSTCR. 2	3	1									**9**
ULNA	5	1									**13**
MANDIBLE	5	1									**13**
RADIUS	6	2									**18**
FIBULA	8	2									**22**
RIB	15										**30**
HUMERUS	7	4	1	1	2						**47**
TIBIA	16	3	3	4	2		1		1		**103**
FEMUR	25	8	6	3		1	1			1	**139**
CRANIUM	19	6	4	3	1	3	2		1		**140**
TOTALS	**116**	**29**	**14**	**11**	**5**	**4**	**4**		**2**	**1**	**551**

Table 4.1 Joins by element within the Mancos 5MTUMR–2346 human bone assemblage. A total of 551 specimens, or 26.2 percent of the human bone assemblage, conjoins in a total of 186 conjoining sets. Conjoining sets average 2.96 pieces per set, but some sets are considerably larger.

and femoral elements contributed the most conjoining specimens to the assemblage—140 and 139 of the total 551 pieces, respectively. Note that only the cranium, femur, tibia, and humerus contributed to conjoining sets that comprised more than 3 specimens each, and that these 4 elements were responsible for nearly 80 percent of the total number of conjoining specimens. The disproportionately large contribution of the femur and tibia to the conjoining exercise is evidenced by the following: the 18 specimens representing these elements and "identifiable" in a standard faunal analysis (see Chapter 6) comprise less than one percent of the entire assemblage, yet the 242 joining specimens representing the femur and tibia comprise 43.9 percent of the total conjoining specimens in the Mancos assemblage.

It is very difficult to compare the Mancos conjoining results with data from other analyses because other investigators fail to report their methods. As noted above, the number of joins in Plio-Pleistocene assemblages is often substantially less than reported here. Bunn *et al.* (1980), for example, report a 3.9 percent value for a 2,100-piece collection from the Lower Pleistocene site of FxJj–50 at Koobi Fora.

The best study of a bone assemblage of human remains attributed to cannibalism is the French Neolithic site of Fontbrégoua reported by Villa *et al.* (Villa *et al.*, 1985, 1986a, 1986b, 1987; the data and much of the text of the 1986 papers are identical, but the French translation is better illustrated). These investigators dealt with three clusters consisting exclusively of human remains: H1, H2, and H3. These clusters were tied together via conjoining, but the reporting of data makes quantitative assessment difficult.

The least disturbed feature, H3, contained remains representing at least 6 individuals. The specimens are reported as "134 fragments of postcranial bones that lack most of the articular ends" (Villa *et al.*, 1986a:432) and 134 *"identifiable"* fragments of postcranial bones after refitting (Villa *et al.*, 1986a: Table 2). The latter value, listed as a NISP value (number of identified specimens), is a count apparently made by Villa *et al. after refitting*. Conjoining results, in this case, create a potential trap for the unwary. The NISP value tabulates as pieces some sets comprising more than one specimen. It is unclear, however, whether the number of preconjoined identified specimens was identical with the reported value after joins were made. Without this information, comparisons with NISP values on unconjoined collections is fraught with risk. Grayson (1984) and Klein and Cruz-Uribe (1984) provide detailed discussions of NISP values in faunal analysis. Chapter 12 includes a fuller discussion of the problems in quantitative work with the reported Fontbrégoua data.

Villa *et al.* (1986a) report 20 conjoining sets for H3, comprising 59 pieces. Complete data on the numbers of specimens making up each set are not provided. The investigators do, however, record 33.9 percent conjointness for the H3 feature, the number of conjoined fragments divided by the total number of bone fragments. This total excludes unidentified splinters, and it is unclear whether the splinters were excluded from the conjoining exercise itself. Similarly derived conjoining values for other features with both human and animal remains at Fontbrégoua lie between 30 and 70 percent.

Because *all specimens* (including unidentified ones) were used in the refitting exercise that led to the 26.2 percent Mancos conjoining value, for comparative purposes it becomes important to estimate the *total* number of pieces in Fontbrégoua Feature H3. Footnote (18) of the Villa *et al.* (1986a:436) report states: "For example, feature H3 contained 154 indeterminate bone fragments > 2 cm and 133 g of small bone chips. . . ." Apparently, some unspecified number of these indeterminate fragments were conjoined in units counted as part of the 134-piece value described as "NISP." It is unclear whether these specimens were included in the 154-piece indeterminate category, or became part of the "NISP" value. Without this information, it is impossible to determine how the 33.9 percent conjoining number was arrived at for the Fontbrégoua H3 sample.

As the previous example illustrates, it is extremely difficult to make comparisons between the extent of Mancos conjointness and the extent of conjointness in other human and faunal assemblages due to the lack of published data. Over a quarter of the Mancos specimens, however, were found to join one another. This is a high value compared to other reported archaeological assemblages. On the other hand, the conjoining value for the Cottonwood Wash site in Utah (White, 1988) is placed at 19.5 percent, and maximal conjoining was not done for that collection. The Yellow Jacket assemblage from site 5MT–3 was maximally conjoined for the cranial skeleton (including teeth, but not ICR [cranial element indeterminate] and for the limbs (except IP4). A total of 317 joining specimens of 1,556 total Yellow Jacket 5MT–3 specimens (20.4%) compares with the relevant Mancos value of 24.6 percent for the same elements (the Mancos value is actually slightly inflated by the ICR and IP4 pieces that it contains). Although this kind of systematic conjoining has not been performed on other assemblages from the Southwest described in Chapter 3, these limited data suggest that conjointness is high in these samples.

CONJOINING RESULTS: ENHANCING SPECIMEN IDENTIFICATION

It is evident from the discussion above that the conjoining exercise for the Fontbrégoua H3 assemblage enhanced identification of some specimens, but quantitative information on this aspect is impossible to derive from the data reported. As Bunn (1981:40) notes for his analysis of Plio-Pleistocene bone assemblages, conjoining can dramatically alter a specimen's identity: ". . . a minimally identifiable miscellaneous limb shaft specimen could be instantly and unambiguously propelled to the higher status. . . ."

Because enhancement of the identity of specimens assists the faunal analyst, it is important to establish the degree of identification enhancement that results from refitting. In other words, if enhancement of identity is a goal, what are the costs (mostly in time) versus the benefits of better identification made possible by such work? Data on this are not available outside the current study. The conjoining study provides information on conjointness and identifiability for the Mancos assemblage. Of the total 551 specimens that participated in joins, 123 might have been considered "identifiable" by a faunal analyst (see Chapter 6 for a full discussion of the difference between what a faunal analyst and a physical anthropologist consider "identifiable"). The remaining 428 join-participating specimens in the assemblage probably would have been designated "unidentifiable" by a faunal analyst because they lacked "diagnostic" features. Of these, conjoining had no effect on the identity of 300. Conjoining enhanced *only* the physical anthropological identification of 117 specimens. It enhanced *only* the faunal analytical identification of 70 specimens. It enhanced *both* faunal and physical anthropological identification of 64 specimens. To summarize, based on this single assemblage, conjoining exercises in faunal analysis might be expected to increase the element identification of specimens in a collection like Mancos by 6.4 percent. The overwhelming majority (95.5%) of these identification enhancements would come in the attribution of long-bone splinters to individual long-bone element. A comparable figure for the Yellow Jacket 5MT–3 assemblage is approximately 4.4 percent. These limited benefits will be considered against the costs of the refitting exercise below.

CONJOINING RESULTS: SPATIAL, TEMPORAL, AND BEHAVIORAL IMPLICATIONS

The conjoining exercise on the Mancos assemblage generated spatial data important in any consideration of the temporal and behavioral background of the assemblage. As noted above, Nickens attempted to find cross-"Burial" and cross-room joins, but found no examples (see Chapter 3 for a discussion of the peculiar meaning of "Burial" for the Mancos assemblage). The systematic, maximal conjoining exercise described here identified 186 sets among the 551 specimens that participated in joins, an average of 2.96 specimens per set (the Yellow Jacket 5MT–3 figure, inflated by the lack of internal IP4, ICR, and rib refitting, is 4.88 specimens per set). Of the Mancos conjoining sets, 155 (83.3%) were *within spatial provenance unit* joins. Only 31 sets were cross-unit joins. Of these, one cross-''Burial'' join was between synonymous ''field specimen'' and ''Burial'' numbers. Cross-''Burial'' joins between ''Burials'' 8 and 10 from Room 14 were present, according to Nickens (1974), but his pooling of specimens from the ''Burial'' 10 and ''Burial'' 8 spatial loci in Room 14 precluded further analysis. All the cross-''Burial'' joins in my analysis were, therefore, also cross-room joins. Thus, only 16.7 percent of all conjoining sets involved specimens from different rooms.

Table 4.2 provides data on the intra-''Burial'' and cross-''Burial'' conjoining sets. As expected from sample size alone, it is evident that the ''Burials'' with the largest numbers of pieces (''Burials'' 6, 8, and 11, from Rooms 15, 14, and 23, respectively—see Chapter 3) also contained the largest number of conjoining sets. The conjoining data also show a clear and unmistakable tendency for pieces in the same spatial clusters to join, a tendency also present within the features at Fontbrégoua. In the context of the Mancos assemblage, these data may help to elucidate aspects of the bone fracture episode(s). As noted above, postdiscard, *in situ* fragmentation due to crushing by sediment probably does not account for this pattern of elevated intra-''Burial'' conjoining because all conjoins were made across ancient fractures judged to have formed when the bone was fresh.

Figure 4.7 tabulates all conjoining sets that include five or more joining specimens. It is evident that the spatial composition of these sets is highly patterned—most of the sets, particularly those with large numbers of specimens participating, are made up of specimens from the same ''Burial'' provenance. There are relatively few joins between specimens from different rooms. It is evident that the cranial and long-bone fragments that go into the reassembled bones did not haphazardly end up in different rooms of the pueblo. Furthermore, work

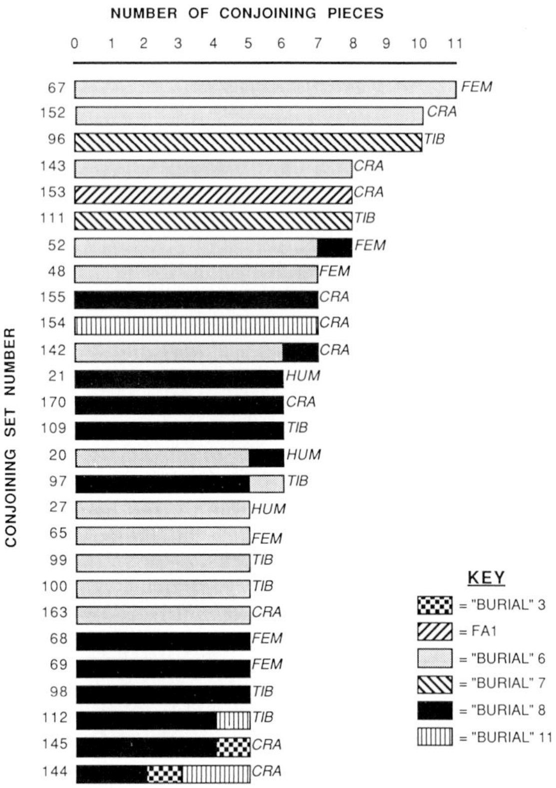

Fig. 4.7 Chart showing the conjoining sets by provenance. Note the integrity of the spatial provenience for the individual conjoining sets. Few conjoining sets contain elements from different spatial provenience, suggesting that fragments of single elements tended to stay together after fracture and through discard. See the text for a discussion of the behavioral significance of these data.

Table 4.2

WITHIN "BURIAL" *"Burial"*	*Rooms*	*NUMBER OF SETS OF (n) PIECES* 2	3	4	5	6	7	8	9	10	11	*TOTAL NUMBER OF SETS*
3	24	2										**2**
6	15	18	7	2	5		1	1		1	1	**35**
7	16	6	1	1				1		1		**10**
8	14	46	10	5	3	3	1					**69**
9	19	3										**3**
FS11	23	8	3	2			1					**14**
FS19	2 + 3	1										**1**
FS30	?26	11		1								**12**
FS50	13	2	1									**3**
FS52	15	3										**3**
FA1	16	1		1				1				**3**
TOTALS		**100**	**22**	**12**	**8**	**3**	**3**	**3**		**2**	**1**	**155**
BETWEEN "BURIAL" *"Burial"*	*Rooms*											
3 + 6	24 + 15	1	1	1								**3**
3 + 8	24 + 14	1		1	1							**3**
5 + FS65	26? + 17	1										**1**
6 + 8	15 + 14	3	3			2	1	1				**10**
6 + FS50	15 + 13	2										**2**
7 + 8	16 + 14	1										**1**
8 + 11	14 + 23				1							**1**
8 + FS19	14 + (2 + 3)	2										**2**
8 + FS30	14 + ?26	3	2									**5**
11 + FS50	23 + 13	2										**2**
FS82 + FA1	14 + 16	1										**1**
3 + 8 + 11	24 + 14 + 23				1							**1**
TOTALS		**17**	**6**	**2**	**2**	**2**	**1**	**1**				**31**

Table 4.2 Conjoining within and between "burials" in the Mancos 5MTUMR–2346 human bone assemblage. Only 31 of the 186 conjoining sets (16.7%) and 97 of the 551 specimens (17.4%) cross between rooms.

on associating mandibles and maxillae in the collection (Chapter 7) strengthens this conclusion. Of the five matched maxillary and mandibular specimens, four were within "Burial" 8 and one was within "Burial" 6. No certain maxilla-to-mandible matches were found between rooms.

Figure 4.7, however, shows sufficient cross-room specimen joining to suggest that the bone clusters in the various rooms ("Burials") were not completely discrete. The strong indication from these

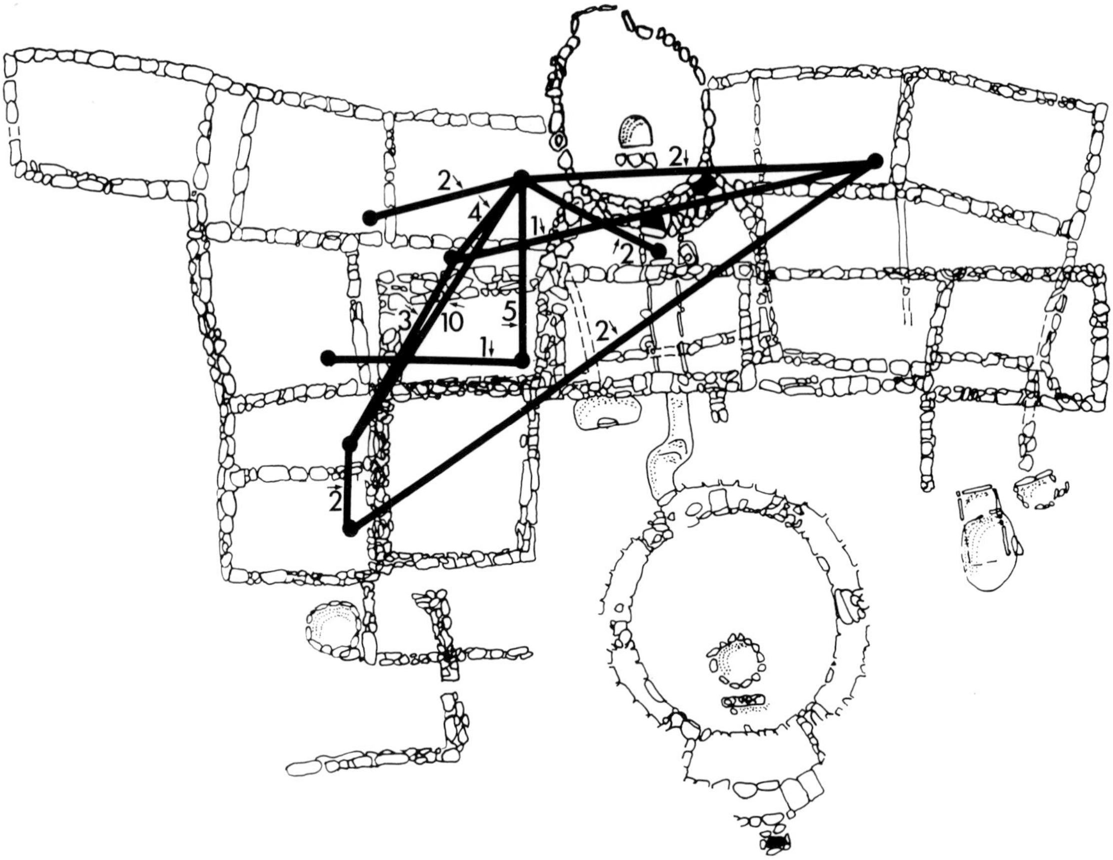

Fig. 4.8 Map of the superimposed older and newer 5MTUMR–2346 pueblos showing refitting links between human bone fragments from various proveniences. The number associated with each line shows the number of links between fragments from the proveniences indicated by the terminus of each line. Note that the greatest number of links (10, between "Burials" 8 and 6) are between the units with the greatest number of specimens (as indicated in Figure 3.12).

data is that the fragments from individual broken crania and limb bones remained in proximity after perimortem fracture. Figure 4.8 maps the cross-room joins and shows the dominance of "old pueblo" cross-room joins (23 sets; 79 specimens), as expected from the fact that most of the specimens were deposited in rooms of the earlier occupation. Only one join crosses between rooms of the first and second pueblos. This pair involves material from the fill of "Room" 2, an architectural niche that Nordby (1974) characterizes as not a valid room at all, but a small "surplus area." All other joins between "new" and "old" pueblo rooms involve specimens found within Room 7/26, a reoccupied unit within which the discrimination between early and late occupation strata could not be firmly established (Nordby, 1974:130).

These findings offer the opportunity to help clarify the sequence of events at the site. As noted in Chapter 3, the timing of bone assemblage discard relative to the earlier and later pueblos was unclear to the original investigators. For the second pueblo, Nordby (1974) notes the discrepancy between the large number of human individuals represented by the Mancos bone assemblage and the small size of the habitation. Nevertheless, he concludes that the depositional episode was during the smaller, second occupation. Nordby (1974:241) postulates that the inhabitants of the second pueblo deposited the Mancos assemblage as follows: "Judiciously preserving the courtyard around Kiva A, the bone debris was then thrown into the still defined rooms of the earlier pueblo, perhaps from the roofs of the later pueblo."

Data on bone trauma suggest that the fracture of bones in the Mancos assemblage was a perimortem, human-induced phenomenon. The data on refitting presented above indicate that fragments of most conjoining sets, up to 11 fragments at a time, came to rest in spatial proximity to one another, the relative spatial integrity of the conjoining sets suggesting that bone fragments were not haphazardly, randomly tossed into abandoned rooms of the pueblo after fracture. Bones from Rooms 15 and 23 ("Burials" 6 and 11) were not found on the floor, but were instead concentrated in bone beds within the fill. These two rooms had obviously been abandoned when deposition took place. In the other rooms where bones were found, the bone fragments were in both the fill and at the floor level in all cases, and were usually mixed with roof fall debris, charcoal, and artifacts as described in Chapter 3. Room 14, from which much of the remaining assemblage was recovered, contained bones found primarily on and immediately above the floor. These bones, in contrast to those deposited in the abandoned Rooms 15 and 23, show different preservational characteristics, lacking the brown staining and weathering seen on the bones from the abandoned rooms. Another contrast between the subassemblage from Room 14 ("Burial" 8) and the abandoned Room 15 ("Burial" 6) comes in the segregation of immature individuals between these rooms. As is shown in Chapter 5, there is an inverse relationship between the ages of children from the two units, with children of 6 years and younger being highly over-represented in Room 15 on the basis of MNI and total specimen counts.

Any interpretation of the deposition of the Mancos 5MTUMR–2346 human bone assemblage must take these facts and others into account. For example, there is no case in which bone material underlies an early pueblo occupation floor. The only case in which specimens in the assemblage are definitely associated with the second occupation comes with Room 8, where Floor Artifact 3 comprises two large pieces of human cranium (a frontal and a broken vault portion). These are the only pieces in the entire assemblage that show a uniform polishing effect along their entire broken edges. This room (Room 8) of the second pueblo was interpreted by Nordby (1974) as having been used for storage during early habitation of the second pueblo. Other cases in which specimens from the human bone assemblage are found in rooms of the newer pueblo are the one specimen in the overburden of Feature 1; 40 specimens in debris fill from a surplus space and a room ("Room" 2 and Room 3) superimposed on Room 20 of the old pueblo; and 128 specimens reported from Room 7, a room whose lower contents could not be stratigraphically discriminated from those of the older Room 26 upon which it was superimposed.

Table 3.1 of Chapter 3 details the artifact content of rooms in the earlier pueblo. The room with the best preserved bone, Room 14, yielded over 40 percent of the Mancos human bone assemblage. Abandoned Rooms 15 and 23 yielded another 40 percent of the total assemblage. The floor of Room 14 stands in contrast to many other rooms that contained larger assemblages of floor artifacts—only 8 flakes and 18 potsherds were direct floor associations with the "Burial" 8 and 10 bone samples from Room 14, but the stone and ceramic assemblage in the fill above the bones was typical of the pueblo as a whole. A comparison between rooms with and without broken and scattered human bone reveals no apparent difference in artifact contents. Artifact associations with the bone assemblages are similar and appear to be unpatterned.

The patterning of the conjoining results, in contrast, suggests that postdiscard disturbance of the various subassemblages of human bone at 5MTUMR–2346 was limited. Establishing the time of deposition is very difficult given these facts. Deposition was not necessarily one event, although cross-room specimen joins suggest that it was. If it were a single episode of deposition, it must have come near the end of occupation of the earlier pueblo or after abandonment, due to the lack of superimposed early pueblo floors. Deposition of the assemblage could therefore have come at abandonment, or during the occupational hiatus between the earlier and later pueblo, a hiatus whose duration is estimated as less than fifty years. Such timing would be just as consistent with the available evidence as Nordby's (1974) interpretation of deposition during the second habitation of the site. In fact, the presence of the largest bone bed on the floor of an unabandoned room of the earlier pueblo and the data from refitting cast some doubts on Nordby's scenario.

The dominance of within-room joins can be explained in several (not mutually exclusive) ways. Fracture of specimens may have taken place at a location removed from the locus of deposition, followed by the broken bone being transported in units (pots, baskets?) to disposal sites in the various rooms. Fracture and subsequent deposition within the rooms (the unabandoned rooms) is a second possibility. Fracture on the rooftops adjacent to abandoned rooms (in the case of "Burials" 6 and 11), with subsequent discard of the bone off the roof edge or through roof openings into the rooms below (in the case of "Burial" 8) is a third possibility.

These various ideas would best be tested by analysis of the component of very small pieces of the assemblage. The small bone flakes might provide clues as to whether the bone was fractured in place or transported into the rooms from elsewhere (for Room 14, with no directly associated hammerstones, choppers, manos, metates, or anvils, the latter appears to be a reasonable interpretation). Analysis of the lithic tools for residues of crushed bone would be another means of further assessing the spatial configuration of the bone assemblage. Patterns of within-room conjoining (if there were any) might establish whether the remains were secondarily deposited in the rooms as the result of a cleanup operation, or were dumped there to begin with. Unfortunately, none of these paths of investigation remains open for the Mancos assemblage. The deposition of this assemblage within the context of a multihabitation, remodeled dwelling site makes interpretation difficult. It seems probable that the exact sequence of events that led to deposition of the human bone assemblage at 5MTUMR–2346 will remain obscure for this site.

CONJOINING BONE ASSEMBLAGES: COSTS AND BENEFITS

The time costs of a maximal, systematic conjoining of the Mancos assemblage, as described above, were great. They could have been considerably higher for investigators less proficient in identifying fragments of the human skeleton.

The conjoining exercise adds support to the argument that the assemblage resulted primarily from the actions of a single agency (human behavior), probably over a relatively short period, and that it was little disturbed once deposited. Compared to the few other archaeological occurrences where this sort of work has been done, the Mancos assemblage showed a high degree of conjointness.

Identification of specimens was enhanced only marginally by the conjoining exercise. This enhancement, in itself, is not deemed worth the cost of the analysis, particularly as it applies to more typical, mixed faunal collections.

As expected, an important class of information coming from the conjoining exercise was spatial. Here, the demonstration that fracture of the bones was not followed by spatially random discard has important implications for the overall behavioral context of the assemblage. The ideas about bone fragment discard generated by the conjoining exercise are, unfortunately, not further testable for this assemblage. The Mancos analysis points the way, however, for the recovery and assessment of similar occurrences in the future. This will be discussed further in the final chapter.

As Lyman (1987a) has pointed out, a major role that conjoining can play in faunal analysis is in elucidating the butchery process. The demonstration that humans were responsible for the damage patterns observed on the Mancos bones (see Chapters 6 and 7–11) may be coupled with the conjoining data to allow a very detailed understanding of the processes by which the assemblage was generated. As a first step in working toward that understanding, Chapter 5 presents a consideration of the underpinnings of health and demography among the people represented by the Mancos 5MTUMR–2346 assemblage.

CHAPTER

5

The Mancos 5MTUMR–2346 Sample: A Biological Background

Over 25 percent of the 2,106 specimens constituting the Mancos 5MTUMR–2346 assemblage participated in joins. Although this value is high for an archaeological assemblage, the results of the conjoining exercise fell far short of providing a series of intact skeletons for analysis. Rather, the conjoining made the specimens under analysis somewhat less fragmentary. The nature of the bone fragmentation and other damage attributes and patterns are dealt with in detail in the chapters that follow. Here the Mancos assemblage is assessed from a more traditional physical anthropological perspective, assessing the number of individuals and the skeletal biology of these individuals.

THE MINIMUM NUMBER OF INDIVIDUALS: BACKGROUND

The minimum number of individuals (MNI) in the Mancos assemblage is a critical variable in any further assessment of these remains. A variety of techniques allows the archaeologist and physical anthropologist to quantify bone assemblages, and a large literature has developed to describe and assess these techniques. In the analysis of the Mancos assemblage, one of the primary goals was to determine the number of individuals represented by the osteological sample recovered. This is a trivial question for most physical anthropological analyses of Southwest human osteological remains recovered from primary burials. For assemblages like the one from Mancos, however, the extreme fragmentation and spatial mixing of the osteological material make minimum numbers assessment a difficult endeavor. The application of techniques most often used in zooarchaeology is called for under these circumstances.

As discussed in Chapter 6, the science of identifying damage attributes is underdeveloped in zooarchaeology relative to the area of quantitative analysis, particularly as the latter concerns relative abundance in vertebrate assemblages. Faunal analysts have often used MNI values to estimate the relative abundance of different species in an assemblage. Since its introduction to archaeology from paleontology in the 1950s, many workers have noted the relative value of the minimum numbers approach compared, for example, to using the number of identified specimens (NISP) per taxon to quantify assemblage characteristics. Indeed, MNI has become the most common statistic employed in zooarchaeology, whereas a substantial critical literature has developed around the whole topic of minimum numbers analysis. Many works consider MNI values, both in general (Ducos, 1968; Casteel, 1976–77, 1977; Holtzman, 1979; Watson, 1979; Turner, 1981; Damuth, 1982; Hesse, 1982; Poplin, 1983; Grayson, 1984; Klein and Cruz-Uribe, 1984; Lyman, 1985; During, 1986; Badgley, 1986a; Rackham, 1983), and with respect to the calculation of relative species abundance (Grayson, 1973, 1979, 1981; Gilbert *et al.*, 1981; Bobrowsky, 1982; Plug and Plug, 1990). Considerable attention has also been given to methods of MNI estimation, including computer-based techniques (Krantz, 1968; Lie, 1980; Poplin, 1981; Fieller and Turner, 1982; Wild and Nichol, 1983a, 1983b; Turner, 1983, 1984; Horton, 1984; Cruz-Uribe and Klein, 1986).

For the basically single-taxon Mancos assemblage, considerations of relative species abundance are minimized, whereas concerns with the total number of individuals are paramount. It is here that minimum numbers analysis is a very appropriate tool of estimation.

Before introducing the Mancos MNI analysis, it is important to emphasize what MNI is, and what it is not. Concise definitions are offered by Hesse (1982) and Grayson (1984). For Hesse (1982:61), a species MNI value ". . . represents the smallest number of animals necessary to produce the sample of bones observed." For Grayson, the definition of the MNI is best taken from Shotwell (1955:272) as ". . . that number of individuals which are necessary to account for all of the skeletal elements (specimens) found in the site."

It is important to note that the MNI does not represent the original number of carcasses available to the inhabitants of the site or provenance unit (although it may approach this value under some archaeological circumstances). Rather, the MNI is the minimum number of individuals required to account for all the specimens in the assemblage. In the words of Allen and Guy (1984:41),

> The central problem with the MNI is that it says nothing about the distance between itself and reality—it is merely the number of animals needed to account for the faunal components in the sample and gives no indication of how many animals might have contributed to that sample.

For any given assemblage, there is one (and only one) valid MNI value. Various investigators, however, will estimate this value using different methods as described below. Failure to consider data on age, sex, antimeres, occlusion, and articulation will always tend to produce MNI estimates that are too low when compared to the actual MNI value.

As pointed out by Casteel (1977), despite the long history of use and the wide acceptance of the MNI in archaeological faunal analysis, there is a considerable amount of variation in the manner in which this value is calculated. Medlock (1975:224) shares this view, describing the basis of the variation as follows:

> One major source of variability is the degree of detail used in comparing elements. The simplest method is to determine the most common elements (e.g., left humerus) and let the count of that element represent the minimum number. A slightly more complex method is to compare all specimens of the same element as to age and sex and reduce the count by one whenever a possible match is discovered. A still more complex method involves comparing all elements as to sex, age, and other rele-

vant criteria. Thus, a right humerus that could not be matched with any of the left humeri would represent a new individual.

Horton (1984) reviews a variety of MNI estimation methods, concluding that there is no single "best" method of estimating the MNI, but that the method chosen should depend on the desired result and particular contextual features of the assemblage. Klein's (1977) method of MNI calculation is clearly stated and probably represents the procedure in widest use in faunal analysis. Klein divides the assemblage into identifiable specimens and then sorts these specimens into taxa. Within each taxon, he divides the elements into left and right sides and into age groups where feasible. After these divisions he calculates the MNI for each taxon. Other investigators follow Parmalee (1977) in considering whether left and right side elements might be paired (Higham, 1968). Some have inappropriately carried the search for pairing into the realm of the computer (Nichol and Creak, 1979), despite the fact that arranging the specimens in age and size series and matching them by hand is faster, easier, and more accurate.

Medlock (1975) outlines a "maximum distinction" MNI approach that uses age, sex, and other attributes to match or preclude matches between right and left sides, articular, and occlusal surfaces. This matching departs from White's (1953) suggestion that matching right and left sides represented a vast time expenditure with only a small return. Flannery (1967) was one of the first to make this time investment and altered his MNI values accordingly in his elegant work on prehistoric Mesoamerican faunas. Bunn's (1982:33–34) description of work with the Olduvai Bed I assemblages shows his appreciation of the utility of matching age and side in the accurate estimation of MNI:

> As approximations or best estimates, MNI values should be determined in as thorough, consistent, and careful a manner as possible. . . . The MNI values presented in Chapters 3–5 are maximum MNI estimates. That is not the same as saying maximum possible number of individuals, in which case one would simply be counting bone fragments. Maximum MNI estimates rely on the cumulative indications which the different identifying characteristics provide, when they are used in combination. To accomplish that, simultaneous examination of all bones within a particular taxonomic and skeletal category is important. With all of the relevant bones out on the table at one time each bone can be compared with the rest. Examination of each bone in isolation from the rest, and reliance on written data manipulations for MNI values will lead to superficial under-estimates. With all relevant bones laid out on the table at one time, it is possible to make comparisons of the size of particular morphological features, relative tooth wear patterns, and the more subtle features, many of which would be overlooked in manipulations of recorded data rather than of actual bones.

THE MINIMUM NUMBER OF INDIVIDUALS IN THE MANCOS 5MTUMR–2346 ASSEMBLAGE

Given the archaeological context of the Mancos assemblage and the demonstration that the rooms of the Mancos pueblo were linked by refitting pieces from the same skeletal element (see Chapter 4), the main objective of work on individual identification was to determine the correct, maximal MNI value for the entire Mancos assemblage.

The minimum number of human individuals can be calculated for the Mancos

Table 5.1

ROOM NUMBER	*"BURIAL" NUMBER*	*OTHER NUMBERS*	*NICKENS (1974) MNI: IMMAT.*	*ADULT*	*THIS STUDY: IMMAT.*	*ADULT*	*TOTAL SPECIMENS*
Feature 1	—	FS18	0	1	0	1	1
2 + 3	—	FS19	0	2	1	2	40
7/26	5	FS30, 37	1	1	2	2	128
8	—	FA3	0	1	0	2	2
13	—	FS50	1	1	1	2	58
14	8	FS49, 117	3	8	6	9	855
14	10	FS138	incl. in B8		—	—	0
14	—	FS82	not included		1	0	3
15	6	FS52	3	4	6	5	620
16	7	FS90	0	2	1	2	94
16, fill	—	FA1	0	1	1	1	21
17, fill	—	FS65	1	0	2	1	7
19	9	FS123	1	0	2	2	44
23	11	FS156	3	0	3	3	176
26 (outside 7)	3	FS23	1	1	1	1	41
No Provenance	0	—	—	—	—	—	16

Table 5.1 Minimum numbers of human individuals by spatial provenance within the Mancos 5MTUMR–2346 site.

assemblage both within each "burial" and within the site as a whole. Table 5.1 gives original Nickens (1974) minimum number of individuals (MNI) estimates by "Burial" for the Mancos assemblage. His 1974 and 1975 MNI value of 33 for the total assemblage was generated by summing all individuals in each of his "Burial" subsamples (the total in Table 5.1 is higher because he left FS18 and FS65 as well as FA1 and FA3 out of the 1974 counts). Because the individual "Burial" MNI values were derived for each "Burial" based on different skeletal elements, however, these values are valid only within each "Burial" assemblage. They therefore cannot be used additively for the entire site. For example, Nickens (1974) reports that 2 of his minimum of 33 individuals come from the 78 postcranial fragments that constitute "Burial" 7. Either one of these 2 "individuals," however, could possibly have belonged to one of the 11 individuals, for example, reported from "Burial" 8. This would, of course, lead to the smaller MNI value of 11, rather than 13. Given the refitting data of Chapter 4, which indicate that different "Burials" contain parts of the same element from single individuals, it is evident that a valid total MNI can only be determined for the entire assemblage. The MNI was therefore determined by considering all the bones simultaneously.

The MNIs were determined in a maximal manner for both the Mancos assemblage as a whole and for its subsets (i.e., "Burials"). In these analyses the assemblage and subassemblages were in their maximally conjoined state, including both single and joined specimens. I employed full matching of age and occlusion as well as antimeric size and morphology in all MNI work.

For the subassemblage analysis, where conjoining sets comprised specimens from different provenances, the individual was allocated to the "Burial" with greatest number of specimens included in the set. These subassemblage (within-"Burial") MNIs are provided in Table 5.1. They are very close to those obtained by Nickens (1975). For reasons outlined above, an additive MNI totaled from the MNIs of different subassemblages (different "Burials") is inflated.

The maximally conjoined Mancos assemblage was divided into element categories. Once divided in this manner, it was obvious that the most commonly represented elements were gnathic. As in most other vertebrate assemblages, the minimum number of individuals was maximized for the total Mancos assemblage in dental, mandibular, and maxillary element categories.

The first step in determining the Mancos MNI was the seriation of all available mandibles according to dental eruption and tooth wear. Isolated lower teeth were assigned to the seriated mandibular specimens according to antimeric associations and interproximal contact facets. The remaining isolated lower teeth were accommodated in the mandibular series, except in cases where eruption or wear status precluded any plausible association with the mandibles, and only in such cases were additional mandibulodental individuals created. A total minimum number of 25 mandibulodental individuals was recognized in this manner. These procedures were repeated for the maxillae and isolated maxillary teeth. The maxillodental seriation produced a MNI value of 23 (Figure 5.1).

Because lower teeth are implanted in dense, thick mandibular bodies instead of thinner maxillary bone, mandibulodental MNI values are usually higher than maxillodental MNI values in assemblages

Fig. 5.1 Seriation of the mandibular and maxillary specimens from the Mancos assemblage. Tooth eruption and wear were used to seriate both upper and lower dental sets. Minimum numbers (MNI) determinations for both the maxillary and mandibular sets were then made, yielding 25 "mandibular" individuals and 23 "maxillary" individuals. These two sets were then checked against each other, and 4 maxillary individuals that could not belong to any of the 25 mandibular individuals were identified, increasing the total MNI to 29 for the assemblage. Figure 5.2 identifies the specimens involved in this exercise.

suffering postmortem attrition. The close match between maxillodental and mandibulodental MNI counts for the Mancos assemblage suggests that despite the extreme fragmentation of the assemblage, this postmortem attrition did not lead to differential representation between maxillary and mandibular parts as is so common in altered paleontological and archaeological assemblages.

Following the calculation of maxillodental and mandibulodental MNIs, all plausible maxillary and mandibular associations were entertained to see whether the maxillary and mandibular series, when considered together, could increase the MNI. This procedure resulted in five fairly certain occlusal associations between mandibular and maxillary teeth. This left 14 maxillodental specimens with permissible associations with the mandibulodental series, and four maxillodental nonmatches (maxillodental specimens that definitely do not belong to any of the 25 mandibulodental individuals). Thus, a total MNI value for the total Mancos assemblage is set at 29. Figure 5.2 shows the results of the Mancos MNI analysis and provides the background to the demographic considerations discussed below. The Mancos postcranial element categories contained no specimens that could not belong to individuals in the dentognathic series on which the MNI was based. One set of fetal/newborn parietal bone fragments (specimen 1703) was not included in this MNI analysis.

DEMOGRAPHY

Assessment of the demographic structure of the human sample represented by the human bone assemblage from Mancos 5MTUMR–2346 is constrained by the small size of the sample and by the extremely fragmentary nature of the remains themselves. Demographic analysis is difficult enough for cemetery populations where individuals are represented by intact skeletons. In a collection such as the one from Mancos, individual elements originally from a single skeleton retain no articulations or other associations. One of the elements most important for aging and sexing, the os coxae, is under-represented, and portions of it are virtually nonexistent due to the fragmentation.

Mancos MNI values are based on dentognathic evidence. Fortunately, the ages for each individual based on these specimens could be established by applying standards of tooth eruption and wear. Ages for individuals represented by the mandibular and maxillary seriation are based on the dental eruption standards of Ubelaker (1989) and the dental wear standards of Lovejoy (1985).

The age order and estimated ages for all maxillodental and mandibulodental individuals are shown in Figure 5.2. Note that the age precision drops significantly for the adult material where aging was done only on the basis of occlusal attrition. The wider confidence intervals in adult ages are due to interindividual variation in tooth wear. Because the goal of this analysis was to deduce the age profile of the sample, not the precise age at death of any individual, these wider intervals are acceptable. The comparative seriation holds the relative ages of the included individuals accurate.

Assessment of the maximally conjoined, aged mandibulodental and maxillodental minimum individuals by room (Table 5.1, Figure 5.2) reveals some correlation between spatial patterning and individual skeletal age. The subassemblage from abandoned Room 14 (''Burial'' 6) contains 10 of the Mancos assemblage's 29 minimum individuals. The subassem-

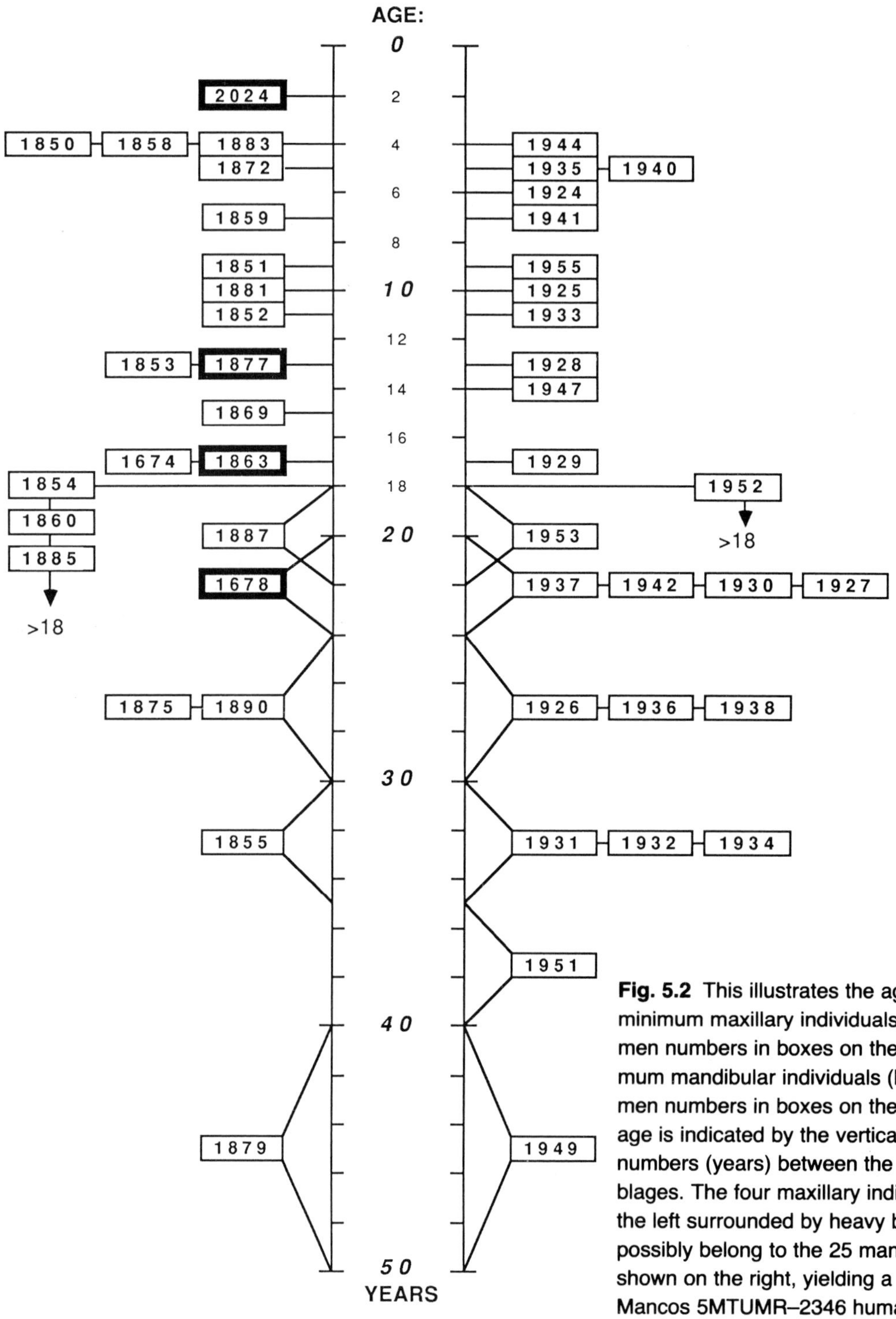

Fig. 5.2 This illustrates the age placement of minimum maxillary individuals (based on specimen numbers in boxes on the left) and minimum mandibular individuals (based on specimen numbers in boxes on the right). Individual age is indicated by the vertically arranged scale numbers (years) between the two subassemblages. The four maxillary individuals shown on the left surrounded by heavy borders cannot possibly belong to the 25 mandibular individuals shown on the right, yielding a total MNI for the Mancos 5MTUMR–2346 human bone assemblage of 29 people (25 mandibular; 4 maxillary).

blage from the floor and floor contact of Room 15 (''Burial'' 8 and FS82) includes 13 of the 29. Together these rooms yield approximately 70 percent of the Mancos total specimen count. A full 75 percent of the total Mancos assemblage MNI and *all* 5 individuals age 6 years and younger come from these two rooms. Rather than an even mixture of immature individuals in each room, however, 4 of 5 children age 6 or younger derive from the subassemblage from abandoned Room 14. The Room 15 subassemblage, on the other hand, yields 5 of 8 total assemblage individuals between 6 and 18 years, whereas Room 14 yields none. Room 15 yields 7 of the 15 remaining adults in the total assemblage, and Room 14 yields 6.

The pattern of segregation by age between Rooms 14 and 15 (as exposed by the dentognathic MNI analysis) was further assessed by examining specimen counts by age. In this analysis, all immature individuals whose age was estimated with a numerical value in the 5 database files were counted by room. Figure 5.3 shows the results in graphic form. These results provide overwhelming support for the proposition that very young individuals were deposited preferentially in the abandoned Room 14. Figure 5.3 combines specimen counts from all 5 database files, because the counts in each of the five showed the same pattern. With increasing age, immature individuals stood a much higher chance of having their remains deposited in Room 14 than in Room 15. Some selection for 4- and 6-year-old children being deposited in the bone bed in Room 14 was taking place. This finding provides further support to the conjoining data (see Chapter 4) in demonstrating that

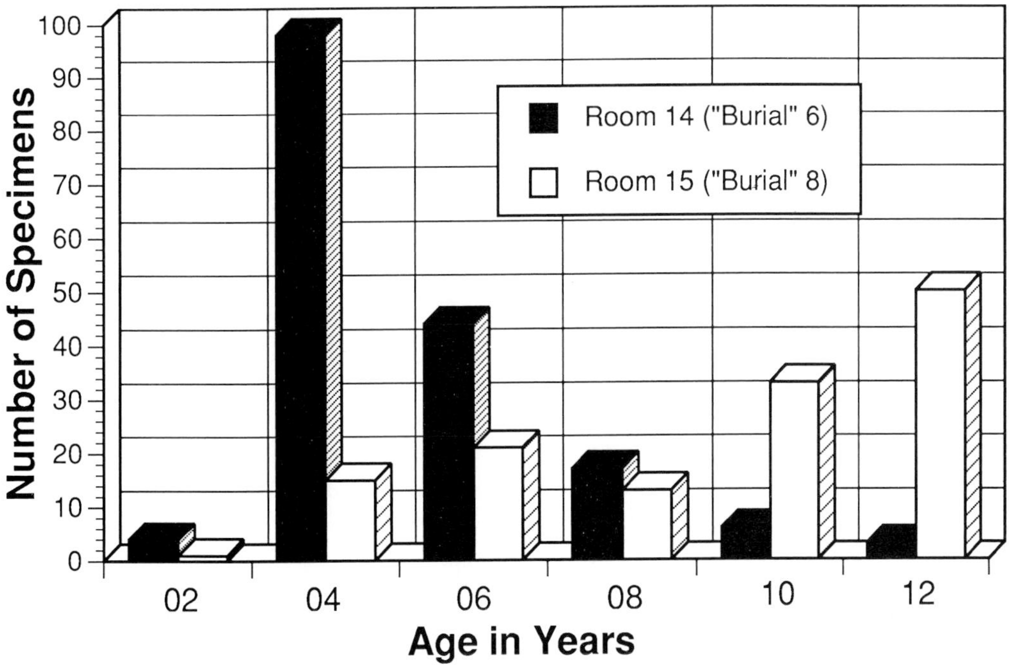

Fig. 5.3 Age segregation by room. Note the relatively large number of specimens from younger individuals from Room 14.

deposition of bones within the rooms of the older Mancos pueblo was nonrandom.

In his assessment of the age profile in the Mancos Canyon population, Nickens (1974) combined the fragmented 5MTUMR–2346 assemblage with the material from the formal burials in this and other Mancos Canyon sites. Although he did not assess the fragmented assemblage from 5MTUMR–2346 as a unit, he noted that there was a "high mortality of young adults" in this collection.

Figure 5.4 compares the survivorship profile determined for the 29 aged individuals of the Mancos assemblage with age profiles for two prehistoric Native American cemeteries. The first of these is a well established and accurate profile for the large Libben collection from Ohio (Lovejoy *et al.*, 1977; Mensforth and Lovejoy, 1985). Although these population-based data are not derived from a Southwest U.S. aboriginal sample, the standards of their recovery, age assessment, and recording surpass all other skeletal collections of adequate size. To gain the Southwest perspective, however, the second profile is from Arroyo Hondo, a 14th-century pueblo in the northern Rio Grande (adjusted from Palkovich, 1984; the figures from Hooton's 1930 study of the Pecos Pueblo population are less reliable; Ruff, 1981). The two cemetery populations show the expected attritional survivorship curve seen in most archaeological cemeteries and ossuaries (Pfeiffer, 1986; Paine, 1989 shows additional data); the steepest segments are in the young ages. The Mancos sample, although limited to a relatively small number of individuals, shows a more catastrophic (in the sense of Klein and Cruz-Uribe, 1984; Klein, 1987) survivorship profile, with a relatively large number of individuals dying in the prime of life, and very few old individuals. This profile is not typical of a cemetery population.

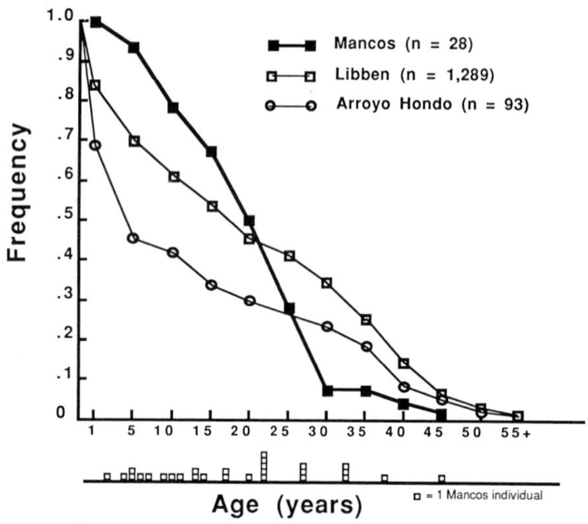

Fig. 5.4 Survivorship curve and age histogram for the Mancos 5MTUMR–2346 human skeletal assemblage (based on dentognathic minimum individuals) compared with curves from Arroyo Hondo and Libben, two cemetery assemblages chosen for the broad perspective they provide (see text). Note the large number of Mancos individuals who perished when they were young adults.

Determining the sex of the Mancos individuals proved considerably more difficult than determining the age. This is because the most accurate sex indicator of the skeleton is the pubis, and intact specimens retaining this portion of the skeleton were not recovered. Nickens (1974) noted the presence of both male and female individuals in the assemblage, an observation confirmed by this analysis. The fragments of os coxae available for analysis included specimens 145, 156, and 162, which showed wide sciatic notches. Specimens 146, 154, and 158 showed narrow sciatic notches. Only this trait was available for sexing on the pelvis, and the small sample should be taken to indicate only that both males and females are represented in the sample.

It is a given in human osteology that cranial and dental remains exhibit considerably less sexual dimorphism than the pelvis. Physical anthropologists have employed characters of mandibular size, shape, and robusticity, however, to determine sex from isolated mandibles (see Buikstra and Miekle's 1985 review of sexing osteological remains). In the Mancos assemblage, I seriated the adult mandibles according to these criteria. The smaller, more gracile end of the range was held by specimen 1952 (Room 15). The largest, most robust mandible was 1938 + 50 (Room 15). I am confident that these range endpoints represent male and female individuals. Two probable males, both from Room 8 (1934 and 1926), and two probable females (1931, Room 13; 1927, Room 7/26) were identified in this analysis. Further attribution of the remaining mandibles to sex is considered unreplicable. The remaining available cranial remains showed both sexes present, based on size and robusticity of the mastoid processes, the supraorbital tori, and the like, but sample sizes are so limited as to make further conclusions unwarranted. Radius specimens also indicate probable male and female individuals on the basis of size and robusticity (Berrizbeitia, 1989).

On a percentage basis, the human canine is the most dimorphic tooth in the dentition (Garn *et al.*, 1967), with male lower canine crown breadth averaging from about 103 to about 111 percent the size of the female tooth dimension (Frayer and Wolpoff, 1985). Studies of prehistoric (Perzigian, 1976) and modern (Garn *et al.*, 1967; Hanihara, 1976) American Indians indicate that average male lower canine breadths are about 6 percent larger than female lower canine breadths. For example, among Pima Indians, Hanihara reports that the average lower canine breadth in a sample of 60 males was 7.77 mm (one standard deviation = 0.3975) whereas the female mean in a sample of 60 was 7.16 mm (one standard deviation = 0.2963). Ten Mancos individuals provided permanent lower canine breadths ranging from a low of 7.0 mm to a high of 8.4 mm. As in the other skeletal parts discussed above, it is evident that both sexes are represented in the assemblage. There is no evidence that either sex is more abundant in the sample.

An analysis of the sexed os coxae and mandibular remains described above showed 2 specimens from males and none from females in Room 14, and 3 from males and 4 from females in Room 15. Other provenanced samples were too small for such considerations. Although they might indicate some room segregation between the deposition of male and female parts, the small number of specimens from Rooms 14 and 15 hardly provide conclusive evidence. Furthermore, these small samples include individuals whose sex is not certain, only "probable" as described above. Finally, many unsexed individuals are also derived from each room's subassemblages.

A variety of architectural and demographic considerations based on ethnographic analogy and room, firepit, and storage room counts for the Mancos 5MTUMR–2346 pueblo led to estimates of the total population (Chapter 3). A total of 4 to 5 households with between 20 and 33 people were estimated for the earlier pueblo on the site. The age and sex profiles described above may be compared with these estimates. There are 14 people represented by the bone assemblage who died as adults between the ages of 17 and 35. With an even sex ratio, these individuals could have represented 7 mother/father pairs. Factoring the 12 immature individuals into such a structure results in fewer than 2 children per family. It is within the limits of possibility to conclude that the broken and scattered human bone assemblage constitutes an accurate representation of the population that actually inhabited the early 5MTUMR–2346 pueblo. Both the total number of 29 individuals and the adult:immature ratio of 14:12 are, however, at the high ends of their respective ranges as predicted by ethnographic analogy. These data may be hinting, however inconclusively, that more than just the original inhabitants are represented here.

ARTIFICIAL DEFORMATION AND PATHOLOGY

In contrast to most aboriginal skeletal populations from the American Southwest, the Mancos assemblage, because of the intensive fragmentation seen in the series, reveals little in the way of diagnosable pathology on an element-by-element basis. Paul Nicken's 1974 report on the Mancos Canyon skeletal material included treatment of pathology and anomaly in the Mancos assemblage under review here (many of the other reports on similar occurrences do not consider these dimensions; see Appendix 1), as well as the formal burials from the site. His most consistent finding was that of cranial deformation in the Mancos series. Of the six individuals included in the assemblage of broken and scattered human remains, Nickens found only one cranially undeformed individual, three individuals with symmetrical lambdoidal flattening, two with asymmetrical lambdoidal flattening, and one with unspecified flattening. As Nickens pointed out, this kind of deformation is found at high frequencies in all Mancos Canyon skeletal material, with the flattening inclined at an angle of 45 to 60° to the Frankfurt Horizontal. Figure 5.5 shows one of the restored Mancos vaults with cranial deformation. Nickens (1974) noted only minor evidence of antemortem skeletal trauma on the assemblage bones, including two fractured ribs and cranial lesions on one vault. I agree with his assessment. Nickens (1974) also noted caries in the dental series from the Mancos assemblage. This is associated with abscessing in two mandibles. Robinson (1974) reports 18.8 percent specimens with abscessing at the time of death among the general Mancos Canyon skeletal population.

As recognized by Nickens, there are also cases of dental enamel hypoplasia in the Mancos assemblage, best exemplified in specimen on the 1853, where there are

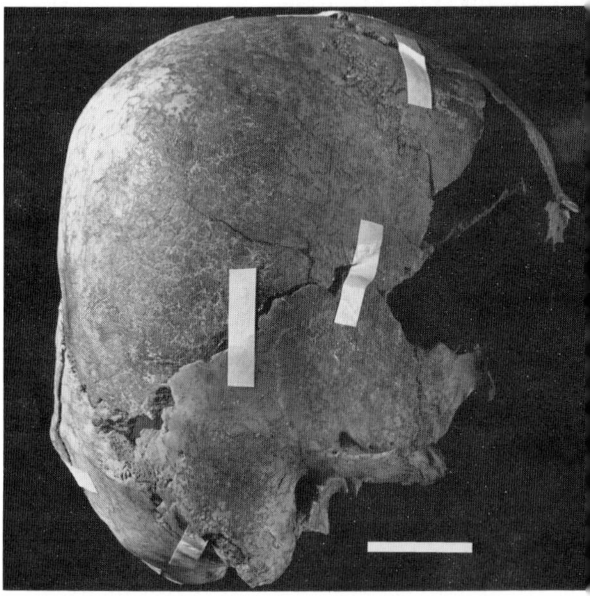

Fig. 5.5 Cranial deformation on the cranium of conjoining Set 152. This deformation is typical of Anasazi skeletal remains. Bar = 3 cm.

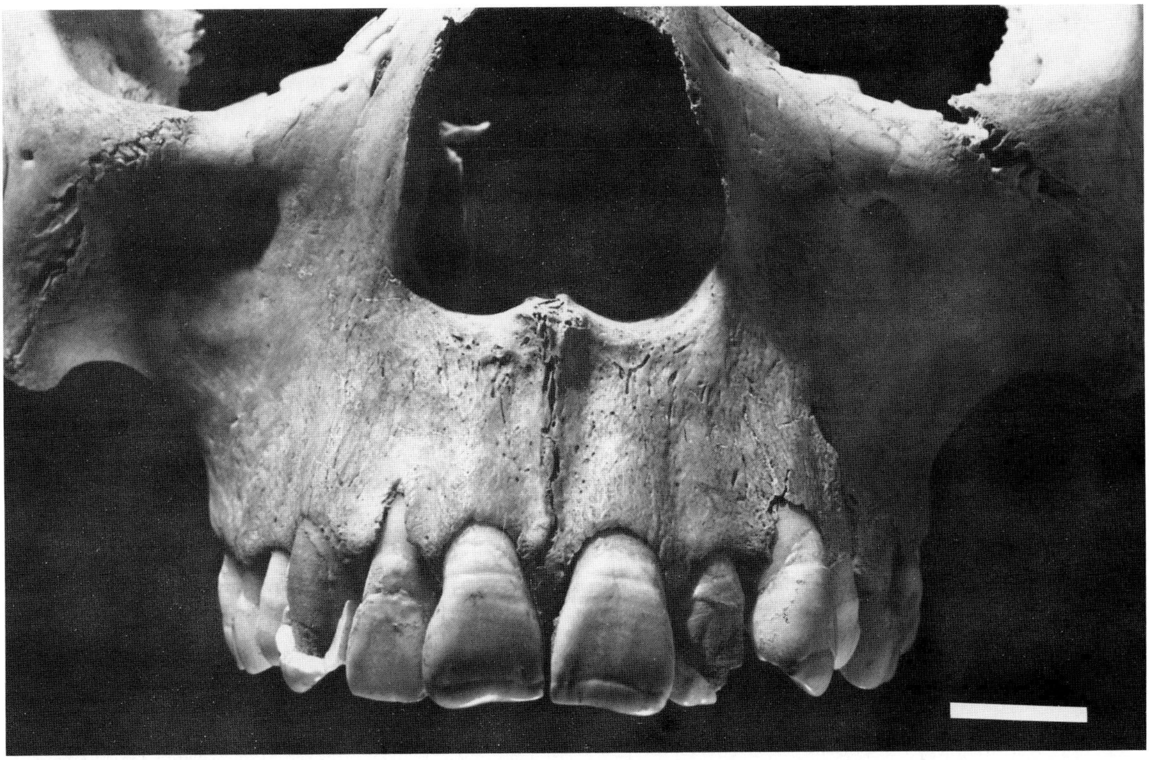

Fig. 5.6 Hypoplasia on maxillary specimen 1852. The linear rings around the incisors and canines demonstrate metabolic system upsets that resulted in disturbances of enamel formation when this 11-year-old individual (see Figure 5.2) was 2-3 years old (lower line on incisors, single line on canine) and 3-4 years old (upper lines). Bar = 1 cm.

deep transverse lines at formation positions between two and four years (Figure 5.6). Dental hypoplasia is associated with a variety of diseases and nutritional deficiencies (Goodman *et al.*, 1984; Rose *et al.*, 1985; Stodder, 1987).

Another osteological marker of stress to the individual is porotic hyperostosis, a term describing the pathological condition in which cranial lesions affect the anterior portion of the supraorbital plate and the pericranial surfaces of the frontal, parietal, and occipital. The lesions are the consequence of bone marrow proliferation (Mensforth *et al.*, 1978). They are thought to relate to iron deficiency anemia associated with metabolic insults to the individual associated with dietary inadequacy, nutritional stress, and infectious diseases—in other words, they are multifactorial in origin (Palkovich, 1984; Martin *et al.*, 1985; Walker, 1985; Stodder, 1987).

Porotic hyperostosis is manifested in the Mancos collection in several ways. In specimens such as adult 1670, the thickening of the vault to nearly 1.0 cm indicates a widening of the spongy diploe. The immature occipital specimen 1800 is a classic surface porosity manifestation of hyperostosis. Such ectocranial hyperostosis is very rare in the Mancos sample, but fragmentation of the remains makes meaningful quantification impossible.

When hyperostotic lesions occupy the external, anterior portion of the supraorbital plate of the frontal, they are often referred to as cribra orbitalia or cribrotic hyperostosis. Mensforth *et al.* (1978) and Martin *et al.* (1985) illustrate these lesions, recommending that a distinction be made between active (unremodeled) and healed (remodeled) states, the former indicating that disease processes were occurring at the time of death.

Cribra orbitalia is common on human osteological remains from Southwest archaeological contexts. For example, Palkovich's (1984) analysis of Pueblo Bonito showed 4 of the 20 juvenile individuals (age 10 or below) with the lesions. Akins (1986) reports that over half the zero-to-ten-year-olds from the Chacoan context had these lesions. Robinson (1974) reports 3 of 11 Mancos Canyon individuals younger than 11 years show such lesions. In the Mancos series assessed here, there is evidence of active cribra orbitalia on 2 of 9 adult right side frontals, and evidence of the resorbed lesions on 3 of these 9. All the immature frontal pieces (3 left and 2 right sides) show evidence of the lesions, and only one of these is resorbed. None of the lesions is severe. Figure 5.7 illustrates two of these cases.

Fig. 5.7 Cribra orbitalia on Mancos frontals 1673 and 1648. These lesions are thought to be related to iron deficiency anemia associated with metabolic insults to the individual associated with dietary inadequacy, nutritional stress, and infectious diseases (Palkovich, 1984; Martin *et al.*, 1985). Bar = 1 cm.

A final type of nonspecific skeletal lesion observed on Mancos assemblage individuals is periosteal reaction, a "scab" of coarsely woven bone sometimes found over normal cortex (Mensforth *et al.*, 1978). Like porotic hyperostosis, this lesion can be common in skeletal collections. Mensforth *et al.* (1978) illustrate severe cases of this on the endocranial surface of an immature specimen, but the Mancos collection shows only comparatively minor periosteal reaction, centered mostly on the frontals, temporals, and occipitals, and manifested as very thin layers of reactive bone concentrated in the depths of the sagittal and transverse sulci associated with venous drainage of the brain. Where samples are adequate for quantification, as in the case of the temporals, such periosteal reaction is seen in 7 of 18 sigmoid sulci, both adult and immature. Palkovich reports 8 of 49 Arroyo Hondo juveniles with presumably similar endocranial lesions, and Mensforth *et al.* (1978) report a 64 percent incidence of endocranial periosteal reactions in the 86 subadult crania they examined.

AFFINITY

The first reference to the biological affinity of people represented by the nineteen

Southwest human bone assemblages named in Chapter 3 and Appendix 1 was that of Morris (1939). He noted that an artificially deformed cranium from the La Plata 23 rockshelter probably was not related to the inhabitants of nearby dwellings. Turner and Morris, in their 1970 work on the Polacca Wash assemblage, provide what is still the most complete assessment of biological affinity among the assemblages under study. They sought to demonstrate that the Polacca remains were more closely related to Hopi rather than to the Gran Quivera Eastern pueblo people by using four nonmetric traits, three-rooted lower first molars, mylohyoid arches, temporal dehiscence, and mandibular torus. Their specific question was whether the skeletal series represented a Hopi legend, as related in Chapter 3. Nass and Bellantoni (1982), mostly on the basis of asymmetrical lambdoidal flattening, link the Monument Valley remains to "Anasazi" of Kayenta, Navajo Mountain, or San Juan River. Turner's 1983 synthesis of information on Southwestern assemblages thought to represent evidence of cannibalism does not consider the question of affinity, and none of the other publications on this subject specifically address the question of biological affinity. Most of the reports on the individual assemblages attempt to provide sex and age estimations for the skeletal remains, but stature estimates are not usually provided due to the fragmentary nature of the major limb bones.

Nickens pooled the Mancos Canyon skeletal remains from several sites, including 5MTUMR–2346, in his 1974 analysis. He estimated stature for the formal Burial 1 female at 159 ± 3.5 cm, and for the formal Burial 4 female at 158.6 ± 3.5 cm. These estimates are within 2 cm of Robinson's (1974) female means for 6 Mancos Canyon females. Comparison of major limb-bone lengths in these two Mancos individuals (humerus, femur, tibia) with those reported by Bennett (1975) for the Mesa Verde sample shows no significant differences in estimated stature, all the Mancos metrics falling within one standard deviation of the Mesa Verde mean when the latter is reported.

Nickens noted the fairly ubiquitous artificial lambdoidal flattening in the Mancos Canyon composite series. Mandibular third molar agenesis and one pair of serially fused ribs were also noted. Neither caries nor agenesis differ in kind or degree from what is reported from other skeletal populations from the Southwest (Nelson, 1938).

A variety of cranial (Molto, 1983), dental (Scott, 1973; Turner, 1979, 1986b; Scott and Dahlberg, 1982) and postcranial (Finnegan, 1978) nonmetric traits are available for comparisons among skeletal populations. Saunders (1989) reviews the use of such traits in assessing population affinity, noting the theoretical hurdle contained in the silent assumption that interpopulation variability detected by dental and osteological variables may be translated into genetic distance and other methodological difficulties involved in such work. Table 5.2 tabulates the results of a nonmetric analyses of the Mancos formal burial population and the broken, scattered remains of the "assemblage" from 5MTUMR–2346.

The most important consideration to give the data presented in Table 5.2 is the very small sample sizes for the formal burial and "assemblage" human remains from Mancos site 5MTUMR–2346. Comparison between the formal burials and the nonburial assemblage from this site fails to show any biologically significant differences. Comparison of the Mancos data with those available for the general Mancos Canyon skeletal population (Robin-

Table 5.2

POSTCRANIAL TRAIT	Burial	Assemblage	CRANIAL TRAIT	Burial	Assemblage
Allen's fossa	0/2	0/0	Mandibular torus	2/3	3/15
Poirier's facet	0/1	0/0	Mylohyoid bridge	0/3	0/14
Plaque	0/1	0/0	Mental foramen multiple	0/3	4/14
Hypotrochanteric fossa	2/2	1/1	Palatine torus	1/1	6/12
Troch. fossa exostosis	0/2	0/1	Access. less. pal. foram.	1/1	6/7
Third trochanter	1/2	2/2	Infraorbital suture	1/2	6/6
Med. tibial squat. facet	0/2	0/0	Infraorbital foram. mult.	0/2	1/8
Lat. tibial squat. facet	1/2	2/2	Multiple zygomfac. foram.	2/2	8/8
Supracondylod process	0/3	0/1	Os japonicum	0/2	0/6
Septal aperture	2/4	3/8	Nasal foramen	2/2	4/5
Acetabular crease	2/2	1/2	Upper nasal overlap	1/2	5/9
Preauricular sulcus	3/3	1/1	Supraorbital foramen	2/2	7/11
Accessory sacral facets	0/1	0/1	Supraorbital notch	2/2	8/11
Acromial articular facet	0/2	0/0	Frontotemporal articulation	0/2	0/5
Suprascapular foramen	0/3	0/3	Epipteric bone	0/2	1/5
Circumflex sulcus	0/1	0/3	Metopic suture	0/2	0/11
Vastus notch	1/2	0/3	Parietal notch bone	0/2	0/2
Vastus fossa	1/2	0/3	Auditory exostosis	0/2	0/7
Emarginate patella	0/1	0/3	Asterionic ossicle	1/2	2/4
Os trigonum	0/2	0/2	Mendosal suture	0/2	1/3
Medial talar facet	0/2	0/3	Occipitomastoid ossicle	0/2	0/3
Lateral talar extension	0/2	0/3	Inca bone	1/2	1/2
Inf. talar artic. surface	2×3	2×3	Wormian bones	1/2	4/4
Ant. calcaneal facet double	1/3	1/2	Lambda ossicle	0/2	2/3
Ant. calcaneal facet absent	0/3	0/2	Parietal foramen	1/2	3/3
Peroneal tubercle	0/3	1/2	Posterior condylar canal	2/2	7/7
Atlas facet form	1×1	1×5	Condylar facet double	0/1	0/5
Posterior bridge	0/1	0/3	Precondylar tubercle	0/1	0/4
Lateral bridge	0/1	0/3	Double ant. condy. canal	0/0	3/6
Transv. foram. bipartite	1/3	0/2	Tympanic dehiscence	1/2	9/15

Table 5.2 Nonmetric traits. *Left columns*: Nonmetric traits of the postcranial skeleton in the Mancos 5MTUMR–2346 formal burials and the assemblage of broken human bones. The number in the numerator of each fraction represents the number of individuals displaying the trait, the number in the denominator is the total number of individuals available for observation. The traits scored are those of Finnegan (1978), scored for the right side unless only the left side was present. *Central columns*: Nonmetric traits of the cranial skeleton in the Mancos 5MTUMR–2346 formal burials and the assemblage of broken human bones. The traits are scored as above and are a combination of traits from Palkovich (1980), Stodder (1987), and Molto (1983). *Right columns*: Nonmetric traits of the dentition in the Mancos 5MTUMR–2346 formal burials and the assemblage of broken human bones. The traits are scored as above and are those used by Scott (1973) and Turner (1979).

Table 5.2 *(continued)*

MAXILLARY DENTAL TRAIT	*Burial*	*Assemblage*
I1 shovel	1/1	5/5
I1 winging	0/0	1/1
I1 double shovel	1/1	4/5
C tubercle	1/3	3/9
P3 1 root	1	14
2 root	1	1
M1 hypocone	2/2	15/23
M1 Carabelli's	0/0	6/8
M1 4 cusps	1/1	14/15
M1 enamel extension	2/2	6/12
M2 3 roots	2/2	7/9
M2 3 cusps	0	2
4 cusps	1	11
5 cusps	0	1
M2 cusp pattern +	0/1	2/14
M3 3 cusps	0	5
4 cusps	1	5
M3 cusp pattern +	1/1	6/10
M3 agenesis	1/2	3/15
MANDIBULAR DENTAL TRAIT		
P4 1 lingual cusp	0	6
2 lingual cusps	1	3
M1 deflecting wrinkle	0/0	1/4
M1 C6	0	1
C7	0	0
M1 +5 cusp pattern	1	2
Y5 cusp pattern	0	9
×5 cusp pattern	0	2
M2 C5	1	8
C6	0	0
M2 +4 cusp pattern	2	0
×4 cusp pattern	0	1
×5 cusp pattern	0	5
M3 C5	1	7
C6	0	3
M3 ×4 cusp pattern	0	1
×5 cusp pattern	1	3
×6 cusp pattern	1	3

son, 1974), the Dolores Project sample (Stodder, 1987), and the remains from Mesa Verde National Park (Bennett, 1975; Miles, 1975) also fails to reveal evidence for distinctiveness of the Mancos assemblage remains. There is no evidence to suggest that these are the remains of outsiders to the region, and limited evidence in the form of cranial deformation to suggest that the 29 Mancos assemblage individuals are local Anasazi.

SUMMARY

The Mancos Canyon 5MTUMR–2346 assemblage is typical for an Anasazi population in its osteological and dental pathologies. There is clear evidence that the population had been stressed nutritionally. The sample includes a minimum of 29 men, women, and children whose remains were mixed within and between rooms with respect to age and sex. The age profile of this sample, with many young adults relative to old adults, is unexpected for a cemetery population.

CHAPTER

6

Method and Theory: Physical Anthropology Meets Zooarchaeology

Investigation of the Mancos assemblage called for a combination of faunal analysis (the study of nonhuman animal remains from archaeological sites, or "zooarchaeology"; Olsen and Olsen, 1981) and human osteology (traditionally the work of the physical anthropologist). In this chapter I provide the methodological background for the Mancos analysis, defining the attributes used and introducing the occurrence of these attributes within the assemblage. These attributes are used in Chapters 7 to 11 for a functional assessment of damage patterns to the Mancos assemblage, and in Chapter 12 for a comparison of the Mancos assemblage to other assemblages.

As Yellen (1977) notes, work on faunal remains in archaeology is usually undertaken for three basic reasons: nonhuman remains from archaeological contexts may be used to elucidate dating and past environments, to determine the use of animal products in material culture, and to understand human activity, including diet. It is in the area of investigating past human behavior that the Mancos skeletal sample is most informative.

INTEGRATING ZOOARCHAEOLOGY AND PHYSICAL ANTHROPOLOGY

Because the Mancos skeletal sample is composed almost exclusively of human remains, a detailed physical anthropological assessment is possible. At the same time, the perimortem trauma and the skewed element representations exhibited by the collection make a zooarchaeological assessment essential. These attributes allow the two subdisciplines to be integrated in a way that will illuminate some of the things that happened nearly 900 years ago in the Mancos Canyon.

The Mancos Canyon assemblage is similar to many of the occurrences of broken and scattered human bone introduced in Chapter 3. The 2,106-specimen sample of human dental and skeletal remains recovered from the Mancos Canyon site does not constitute the largest series attributed to cannibalism in the Southwest. The Mancos find derives its value as a reference collection from its context.

The Mancos assemblage, like other Southwest assemblages described in Chapter 3, differs in several important ways from samples of vertebrate skeletal remains derived from most archaeological settings. The assemblage analyzed (excluding the artifacts made of nonhuman bone) included only 8 identifiably nonhuman fragments. Single-taxon osteological assemblages in archaeology usually derive from mass kill sites such as bison jumps. Recovery of such samples is extremely rare for dwelling or habitation sites in which most vertebrate faunal remains are found in middens and represent multiple taxa. The faunal analyst (zooarchaeologist) is usually responsible for sorting the various taxa present and interpreting the assemblage as a whole. For the Mancos and similar assemblages from the Southwest, the taxon involved, *Homo sapiens*, has been the object of detailed study for centuries by anatomists, forensic scientists, and physical anthropologists. The resulting specialized knowledge makes it easier to identify and interpret human remains from these occurrences in a very precise manner.

Other unusual analytical aspects of the Mancos assemblage include its "fine-grained" nature and high historical "integrity" (see Chapter 3). The bases for this statement are the extensive conjoining within the assemblage (Chapter 4), and the evidence for human-induced perimortem trauma (presented in subsequent chapters).

There are additional advantages to working with human skeletal collections like the one from Mancos. For many skeletal collections from both archaeological and paleontological contexts, it is often very difficult to strip away the taphonomic overprint of postmortem events that bias and blur the assemblages under consideration (Lawrence, 1968). This often constrains interpretations because it is difficult to determine accurately the relative impact of nonhuman agents on element representation and perimortem damage. The concern for "taphonomic" factors is today widespread in zooarchaeological studies at all time levels (Noe-Nygaard, 1987).

Brain (1981b, 1985) describes the "crystallization" of a "discipline" of "taphonomy" as beginning in the 1940s with Efremov's work. According to Brain, "taphonomy" achieved the status of a "science" in 1976 at a conference that he helped to organize. As Koch (1986) describes, many early investigators like Duckworth (1904), Breuil (1938), Pei (1938), and Leroi-Gourhan (1952) were deeply concerned with the "overprint" of geological and nonhuman alterations to archaeological bone assemblages. For these workers and many others in paleontology and archaeology, "taphonomy" was just part of what they did to better know the past—it needed no special name or status. Nevertheless, "taphonomy" is now a widely employed term to describe an area of research that has evolved its own jargon—what Lyman (1987b) aptly identifies as a "pedantic terminology," which I shall attempt to avoid in the present account.

Bones may be modified after death by human agents and by other biological agents or physical processes, either before (primary modification) or after (secondary modification) burial. In the Mancos sample, virtually all the damage to the skeletal elements is attributable to human agency. There is no evidence that carnivores modified this assemblage (see below). Weathering on most bone surfaces is very limited in degree. Preservation of surface detail on the bones and the presence of delicate bone elements suggests that postdepositional destruction was minimal. Conjoining data and observations made during excavation indicate that the bones were not fragmented by overlying sediment. The apparent absence of the effects of nonhuman biological and geological agents of bone alteration (besides readily interpretable excavation trauma and rootmarking) provides an unusual opportunity to study *perimortem* damage (alteration of fresh bone either just before, at, or after the time of death; Turner, 1983). Knowledge of human soft and hard tissue anatomy aids in the interpretation. Furthermore, the virtual absence of nonhuman skeletal elements in the assemblage makes it possible to assess more fully the patterns of damage and element representation for a single taxon. In this manner, physical anthropological identifications and other data are integrated with the zooarchaeological results. The fact that the taxon involved in *generating* the assemblage was the same as the taxon *comprising* the assemblage thus becomes an advantage and an opportunity.

LIMITATIONS OF THE MANCOS ASSEMBLAGE

Despite the specific advantages of working with an assemblage comprising a single, intensively studied taxon from a well-established archaeological context, there are some limitations to a full assessment of the Mancos sample.

The effect of bias introduced at the recovery level in both paleontology (Clark and Kietzke, 1967) and zooarchaeology (Watson, 1972) is well known. Yet surprisingly many primary reports in both disciplines leave recovery method unspecified or incompletely described.

As Medlock (1975) points out, *any* excavation technique will bias an archaeological sample. Many studies address the effects of different recovery methods on zooarchaeological assemblages (Clason and Prummel, 1977; Payne, 1972a, 1975; Barker, 1975; Avery, 1984). As Payne (1972a:49) puts it, there is need for concern here because "The value of any analysis depends on the quality of the sample on which it is based." For example, what is the significance of Potts' (1982) statement that 54 percent of the FLK "*Zinjanthropus*" assemblage consists of bone fragments less than 1 cm in length when the recovery method itself is so critical in establishing this percentage? Of what significance are "identifiable" versus "nonidentifiable" specimen ratios for Chencherere II (Crader, 1984) without basic information on the screen size used in recovery? Because the Mancos sample was recovered without water screening, analysis of the small end of the fragment size range is not appropriate.

The debate over archaeological recovery methods is tied to the issue of what merits collection (and, ultimately, to the question of what is "identifiable"). Yet there has been little noticeable progress a decade after Legge (1978:129) wrote: "Archaeology has, in fact, been very slow to adopt even the simplest standards of recovery, a point that will puzzle any worker familiar with the methodology of any science. This failing remains the most obvious deficiency in archaeological methods. . . ." Schmid (1972:2) only partially exaggerates in concluding that "Only complete animal skeletons and exceptional marked bones and skulls can arouse the conscience of the archaeologist to the point that he will collect them." On a more pragmatic level, Olsen (1961:538) contends that too much recovery can result in an "overwhelming problem" for the archaeologist. He even ranks the relative zooarchaeological merit of various skeletal elements, suggesting that limb-bone shaft fragments, for example, should be discarded on the site (1971).

Olsen's viewpoint is driven more by his

focus on taxonomic identification than by a consideration of prehistoric behavior. Casteel (1972) says that the view of an archaeologist going to the field to recover "everything" is misleading at best and an impossibility in practice. Payne (1975:16) outlines the archaeologist's dilemma this way: "For the future, we have first to recognize that total recovery, though the ideal aim, is impracticable. Even if we were able to excavate in such a way as to recover every bat incisor and pollen grain this would normally be a misuse of limited resources." Such statements are reactions to the sentiment expressed by Chaplin (1971:24): "Every scrap of bone found must be kept for examination. There is no room for argument on this point. Unless this is done no one will be able to produce valid information." Brain (1981a:10) echoes this sentiment: ". . . it is remarkable how much information can be obtained from the study of bone accumulations—often from those parts of the assemblage that, in the past, have been ignored or discarded by paleontologists. It is desirable that *all* bone fragments from an excavation be retained, as the seemingly uninteresting fragments often provide clues vital to the interpretation."

The debate over which faunal remains to collect from an archaeological context seems destined to continue indefinitely (Gamble, 1978). It is fair to generalize that more and more material has been collected from archaeological excavation as methods have been refined in the discipline, particularly in the last two decades. For a Paleolithic example of the more traditional practice of zooarchaeological discard, we can turn to Breuil (1939:30). At least he made explicit the bias in bone collections from Choukoutien when he noted that "The collecting of those fragments which are valueless to palaeontology has not been carried out systematically. . . ." Most paleolithic archaeologists of Breuil's day and even some more current practitioners continue to leave uncollected and unreported the smaller or less identifiable fragments. Examples include some of the most important Paleolithic collections (such as Combe Grenal, Chase, 1986; and Klasies River, White, 1987). In the early 1960s, faunal analyst Charles Reed joked about archaeologists and faunal remains (1963:205): "Who—except possibly archeologists—would dig for artifacts when there are bones to be salvaged?" Today, as Gamble (1978:346) points out, "The recovery of bones is now one of the primary aims of archaeological excavation and is no longer regarded as one of the side effects of digging." As one veteran faunal analyst recently characterized the situation, most archaeologists now take a pragmatic approach to the recovery of osteological remains, saving all that time and circumstances allow (Parmalee, 1985). Multidisciplinary approaches are increasingly common, with faunal analysts participating in the actual recovery of remains (instead of just analysis), and with sampling strategies that ensure that no class of remains is lost in recovery (Payne, 1975; Huelsbeck and Wesson, 1982).

The architecturally and stratigraphically constrained situation at Mancos 5MTUMR–2346 allowed for recovery of all large fragments of the human bone assemblage (> c. 4.5 × c. 3.0 cm; some identifiable human bones and fragments of this size were observed in the backdirt at 5MTUMR–2346 in June 1990), and all recovered fragments were saved for analysis. The recovery methods employed at the Mancos Canyon 5MTUMR–2346 site were standard in Southwest archaeology (see Chapter 3). Trowels and whisk brooms were used to expose skeletal specimens for drawing and photography, and the remains were then lifted by spatial unit. This unit lifting rather than piece plotting eliminated some spatial information from the results of conjoining exercises described in Chapter 4. True bone flakes and other fragments with dimensions of less than 1 cm were probably lost during recovery.

Although its recovery was less than ideal, with a bias toward sizes greater than 3.0 cm, the failure to recover the very small component of the assemblage cuts both ways—for analytical time considerations, this "defect" actually represents a hidden benefit when one considers time expenditure in the conjoining analysis of the sample (see Chapter 4).

A final disadvantage to working with the Mancos sample involves the uncertainty surrounding the limited faunal remains "associated" with the assemblage. The trash mound, normal resting place of Anasazi faunal remains, was hardly touched by excavation. Nonhuman remains mentioned in the initial field report were not accessible for analysis, nor were they well described by Nordby (1974). Nordby's section on nonhuman bone and antler (1974) describes the bone tools from the site (awls, reamers, weaving tools, spatulas, etc.), but the only account of unmodified nonhuman bone comes in his individual room descriptions, under "Observations during Excavation." Reference here is made to "unmodified animal bone," in small quantities when specified, that often accompanied the human remains. The only taxon identified is turkey. Indeed, for unmodified fragments of bone described as nonhuman, it is reasonable to suspect that specimens attributed to nonhuman macromammalian taxa actually belonged in the human assemblage, but were misidentified in the field. As noted previously, Paul Nickens excavated most of the bone concentrations in the 5MTUMR–2346 site. He did not note any unmodified bone that was diagnostically nonhuman (personal communication). Subsequent work with the available sample identified only 8 diagnostically nonhuman fragments—3 fragments from medium- to large-sized mammals, and 5 fragments of turkey. It is reasonable to conclude that these pieces represent a background scatter mixed by chance with the human sample. Henceforth, the term "assemblage" will refer only to the 2,106 Mancos specimens attributed to the taxon *Homo sapiens*.

ANALYTICAL PROCEDURES: SOME INITIAL CONSIDERATIONS

As Yesner (1978) points out, it is possible to envision three steps by which any assemblage of skeletal remains can be transformed by analysis into data relevant to human behavior—identification, quantification, and interpretation. The fact that both cultural and natural agents can alter bone assemblages is widely appreciated, but few have considered the degree to which the *analysis* of an assemblage itself can bias our perspective on the past (Whitlam, 1982).

Unfortunately, even when reporting formats for faunal data are similar, different standards of recovery and different analytical methodologies usually make it difficult or impossible to make valid comparisons between archaeological bone assemblages (Legge, 1978). Many authors have lamented the lack of methodological standardization in zooarchaeology (Clason, 1972; Payne, 1972b; Lawrence, 1973; Clutton-Brock, 1975; Munthe and McLeod, 1975; McArdle, 1975–77; Redding *et al.*, 1978; Grigson, 1978; Driver, 1982; Emslie, 1984; Reitz *et al.*, 1987). As Maltby (1985) has appreciated, differentials in analyst skill and experience, working conditions, available time, and even recording methods can lead to incompatibility among the results of different zooarchaeologists. Furthermore, Marshall (1989) contends that the study of bone modification (alteration in size, structure, or texture of bone by an external agent) is still in its infancy. Perhaps "adolescence" would be a more appropriate term, but the point is well taken because a basic set of modification attributes used in zooarchaeological work has yet to be established.

This state of affairs has been explained in various ways. Clason (1972), for example, attributed the lack of standardization to rapid progress in the field. The lack of analytical standards is more reliably traced, however, to the wide range of problems and questions addressed by archaeologists using vertebrate faunal remains. Dealing with the material from a Mesopotamian city site is a very different theoretical, methodological, and logistical exercise from assessing a sample recovered from a sealed Mousterian unit or an open-air assemblage from a Pleistocene land surface. In short, faunal analysts tailor their methods to the samples with which they deal and to the research questions at hand.

Some zooarchaeological studies are "paleontological" in focus, almost exclusively concerned with the taxonomic identity of the remains—the species composition of the faunal assemblage—with little regard to the damage patterns on the bones (Baynes *et al.*, 1975). Others use similar data and address the taxa involved from a more ecological point of view in an effort to resolve questions about past environments and procurement strategies (Freeman, 1973; Straus, 1977). Still other analysts are extremely concerned with the quantification and assessment of element representation within a few taxa, placing less emphasis on the details of surface modifications to bone (Speth, 1983).

The addition of computing power to the archaeologist's arsenal has brought the faunal analyst a tool of great flexibility and importance when dealing with large collections of vertebrate remains. Yet in some faunal analyses, inappropriate quantification is pursued obsessively without due regard being given to the observational data that are being compiled, manipulated, and compared. Often the very research questions that the analyses should be designed to answer seem lost in the push to quantify. In his appeal for more rigorous observational and control studies, Yellen (1977:328) notes:

> . . . in faunal studies which attempt cultural reconstruction of this type, it will be necessary to shift the basic unit of analysis from entire bones, or even the heads of bones themselves, to smaller units and to devise smaller categories, or attribute systems which will permit one to ask the question of how—by what steps—was the bone broken. . . . I am struck by the fact that interpretation based on the counting of anatomical parts provides the least trustworthy information. . . .

The human osteological remains from the Mancos site bear evidence of human modification. Lyman (1987a) defines butchery as the human reduction of animal carcasses into consumable parts, as a *process* rather than an act (contra Noe-Nyggard, 1989). The consumable products of vertebrate carcasses include hide, hair, meat, blood, brains, marrow, grease, juice, sinew, bone, teeth, and viscera and their contents (Lyman, 1987a). As Lyman points out, butchery involves carcass-processing activities directed toward the extraction of these products. Butchery activities include skinning, evisceration, disarticulation (dismemberment), defleshing (filleting), bone extraction, marrow and brain extraction, and bone grease extraction. The activities result in patterns observable in the faunal assemblage, making the osteological study, for Lyman, a special kind of taphonomic study through which the process of butchery is reconstructed. The goal of the analysis of the Mancos assemblage was the reconstruction and understanding of prehistoric human activity. The analysis was driven, in all the stages described below, by a desire to learn as much as possible about the events that structured the assemblage.

ANALYTICAL BACKGROUND AND DEFINITIONS

Any analyst facing an assemblage of bones from an archaeological site is faced with the related questions of what attributes to record and how to record them. As discussed above, there are no standard answers. While there are no recognized standards for analyzing an assemblage like the one from Mancos, I endorse the calls of Casteel and Grayson (1977) for explicit definition of analytical methods. Unfortunately, Bayham's (1987) suggestion that there is a uniform agreement that explicit description is a part of all faunal analyses remains too optimistic in 1992.

As with most other zooarchaeological studies, the methods described below emerged from a combination of the author's own background and skills and the specific characteristics of the assemblages studied. This has undoubtedly led to some incompatibility between these results and those of other analysts, and an attempt to identify these is made below. In the spirit of uniformity, what follows is an attempt to outline and illustrate in detail the methods employed in studying the Mancos assemblage.

The lack of a standardized recording system for zooarchaeological attributes is a hindrance. A variety of techniques exists for the actual recording of zooarchaeological data, but none of these has been very widely accepted. In the middle and late 1970s, a flurry of publications describing computer data entry techniques emerged (Clutton-Brock, 1975; McArdle, 1975–77; Bonnichsen and Sanger, 1977; Redding *et al.*, 1977, 1978; Gifford and Crader, 1977; Meadow, 1978; Armitage, 1978; Uerpmann, 1978). What were state-of-the-art computing techniques a decade ago are no more than a string of historically interesting references today. Computing has become accessible and affordable to the archaeologist (Dibble and McPherron, 1988). A new generation of computer hardware and software threatens to unleash another complement of "how-to" programs for the zooarchaeologist. With sophistication gained from experience with the systems of yesteryear, the newer recording systems promise to give the zooarchaeologist far more power in dealing with quantitative data (Klein and Cruz-Uribe, 1984; Aaris-Sorensen, 1982; Campana and Crabtree, 1987; Gifford and Wright, 1986). I have no desire to formalize a format for recording data on osteological assemblages. Instead, I prefer to take advantage of the flexibility made possible by today's computing machines in tailoring the recording procedure to individual research problems. On the other hand, it is essential that there be some uniformity in what is being recorded so that data can be compared between investigators and assemblages. For these reasons, I will describe in some detail the attributes used in the analysis of the Mancos human bone assemblage reported in Chapters 7 to 11 and in the unconjoined assemblage reported as Appendix 2 of this book.

Summaries of relevant quantitative data

on the Mancos assemblage are presented in the chapters to follow, particularly Chapter 12. Besides tabulating data to describe a vertebrate assemblage, a variety of graphic methods, some of them excellent, are available (Inskeep and Hendey, 1966; Kehoe, 1967; Brain, 1981a; Fisher, 1984; Scott, 1986) and will be used below. The presentation of original observational and metric data in Appendix 2 allows analysts to explore and use the data in any way they please. To make these data most useful, however, it is necessary to provide explicit information on how they were gathered.

PARTS AND ATTRIBUTES: A REVIEW

Recent work on prehistoric bone assemblages shows a clear trend toward the recording of more and more attributes. Once, the faunal analyst's work was finished when the identifiable pieces were assigned to taxa and a faunal list generated. Taxonomic presence/absence data continue to be important for purposes of environmental reconstruction. The overall concern for quantification has increased in archaeology in general and in faunal studies in particular. Questions of how and what to count in terms of specimens and elements are reviewed in Grayson (1984) and dealt with in some detail below.

Paralleling and complementing the increasing concern for quantification of the various *parts* of archaeological and paleontological bone assemblages (Klein and Cruz-Uribe, 1984), has been a focus on the identification and quantification of *damage* to these parts. Following on the pioneering work in this area by Buckland (1822), Lartet (1860), Martin (1907), Bouyssonie *et al.* (1913), Pei (1938), Dart (1957a), and others, studies attempting to distinguish natural modifications on bone surfaces from modifications made by humans have burgeoned in recent years. These studies stem from several areas of inquiry (see Gifford, 1981 for a more detailed review). Some analyses investigate the activities of early hominids (Binford, 1981, 1984; Brain, 1981a; Bunn, 1982), and others the presence of people in the New World (Bonnichsen, 1983; Shipman *et al.*, 1984). As a result of the critical approach best exemplified by Binford's work, reports describing "butchery sites" without reference to bone surface modification (Shipman *et al.*, 1983) are now rare.

Most of the more recent, comprehensive studies cited here show some concern with all aspects of perimortem and postmortem bone damage in the form of weathering, burning, cutmarks, percussion marks, mammalian gnawing marks, rootmarks, trampling marks, and fracture patterns. Intensive study of such bone surface damage has been carried out on a variety of bone assemblages spanning the late Pliocene (Bunn, 1983; Potts, 1982), Pleistocene (Binford, 1984, 1990; Binford and Stone, 1986; Koch, 1986), Holocene (Zimmerman *et al.*, 1980; Marshall, 1986a; Voigt, 1983; G. Turner, 1986; Lyman, 1987a), and recent (Andrews and Cook, 1985; Blumenschine, 1988; Gifford-Gonzalez, 1989a).

The available terminology involving bone modification is often imprecise and misleading, the nomenclature unworkable. Few would disagree with Chase (1986) that the three agencies involved with bone modification can be classified as chemical, mechanical, and biological (little *cannot* be classified this way). Some agents lead to the disintegration of the bone surface (weathering, burning), whereas others leave evidence of their contact with the bone surface in the form of marks (human-induced marks, toothmarks made by various taxa, marks made by contact with the substrate, marks left by root etching). Beyond this, however, there is little uniformity in the approach to the identification, description, or quantification of surface modifications to bones. One analyst's cutmark is another's scrapemark, someone else's chopmark or tooth scratch. This means that any really meaningful comparison of the results of different observers depends on rigorous definitions of how attributes were scored. This is where standardization and control of the inevitable subjectivity involved in dividing a continuum are essential, but currently unavailable.

The choice of attributes for observation and recording is a function of the research questions being asked for any vertebrate assemblage under consideration. Brain, in a 1974 paper on procedures, suggests that all bone be collected and each piece be maximally identified and thoroughly analyzed. His is a general statement, but it can be seen as an early template for the kind of analysis that the Mancos collection was subjected to. For the Mancos collection, concern centered on the kinds and patterns of perimortem and postmortem damage to the bones. The attributes chosen for observation reflect this concern.

Data generated from analysis of the Mancos assemblage in its nonconjoined state were recorded in five databases for analytical convenience. Each specimen is listed in one of these databases—collectively they make up a catalog of the entire assemblage. As used in the analysis that follows, the term "specimen" refers to a nonconjoined whole or partial bone or tooth. The term "element" refers to an intact bone as it occurs in the adult skeleton.

The CRANIAL database file includes all cranial bones and teeth. The AXIAL database contains all vertebrae, pelvic portions, sternal portions, scapulae, ribs, carpals, tarsals, and patellae (note that not all specimens listed in this database are "axial" parts). The HANDFOOT database contains all tubular bones of the hand and foot. The LIMBS database contains all specimens of clavicle, humerus, radius, ulna, femur, tibia, and fibula that an archaeological faunal analyst might set aside for genus- or species-level taxonomic identity study (see below). The SPLINTERS database includes portions of the same bones that might be classified by an archaeological faunal analyst as "unidentifiable" (note that only some specimens listed in this database are actually splinters; see the discussion of identifiability below for the rationale for the divisions adopted here). The database program known as Reflex™ for the Macintosh computer was chosen to cope with these data. Attributes for each specimen were entered, one specimen at a time. Appendix 2 of this book gives a full report of all 5 database files.

The five databases presented in Appendix 2 consist of alphanumeric data organized in the form of observations entered in a horizontal line (a "record") for each specimen. Each vertical column, therefore, records the values for each observation (a "field"). The observations recorded in this study are numbered from 1 through 98. For ease of reference, these numbers are provided in the discussions below. The observations are most effectively considered in 8 *attribute groups*:

1. identification
2. preservation
3. fracture
4. toolmarks
5. percussion striae
6. mammalian chewing
7. burning
8. specimen dimensions

Within each attribute group, different *observation numbers* often differentiate the locations of the observations on elements. Many of the observations are not routinely recorded in zooarchaeological analyses, and several of them have not, to my knowledge, been described before now.

The extensive assistance of Nick Toth and Kathy Schick in developing the recording routine and database system for quantifying the faunal analytical results is gratefully acknowledged. What follows represents many difficult decisions reached jointly about where and how to best draw the lines between recording valuable data and engaging in osteological overkill.

Table 6.1 is a representation of the data entry form used to construct the databases in Appendix 2. A total of 98 observations are potentially recordable in this system. The system was designed for use on a variety of assemblage types, including Plio/Pleistocene, recent archaeological, and actualistic. Not all the observations are applicable to any given element, taxon, or assemblage, and Mancos was no exception. A streamlined data acquisition procedure is presented later in this book (Appendix 3) for standard analyses of assemblages similar to Mancos.

ANALYTICAL CONDITIONS

Each piece was examined at low magnification under harsh incandescent illumination. Observations were made in a darkened room with no fluorescent lighting. The fluorescent lighting ubiquitous in laboratories is highly detrimental to proper analysis, a point correctly noted by Bunn (1982). This is because fluorescent lights give diffuse illumination that subdues topographic detail critical to the interpretation of alteration to the bone surface.

Some recent workers contend that various forms of surface modification, particularly cutmarks, are best diagnosed with the use of a scanning electron microscope (SEM), and SEM images have accompanied many recent analyses of modern and archaeological bone (Brothwell, 1969; Shipman, 1981a; White, 1986; Cook, 1986; Blumenschine and Selvaggio, 1988; Olsen, 1988). Although little cited by modern Africanist practitioners, as early as 1972 Wyckoff advocated the use of the SEM on fossils, noting that the value of this instrument lies in its ability to display photographically low magnification microscopic detail on modified bone surfaces. Topography is easy to see in SEM images and the depth of field is excellent. The technique, however, is expensive, time-consuming, and usually unnecessary except in cases in which confirmation of visual identification is necessary (Olivier, 1989). Furthermore, it has been shown that microscopic details of human-induced cutmarks are mimicked by a variety of natural processes, rendering reliance on SEM images alone a dubious practice. Finally, blind tests conducted by Nick Toth and the author show that even novice archaeologists and osteologists with minimal training can readily and highly accurately discriminate between cutmarks made with stone tools and carnivore gnawing marks. For these reasons, only small samples of Mancos specimens related to specific problems were chosen for SEM analysis.

Where discernible patterns of perimortem damage were present (cutmarks, burning, percussion, etc.), quantification of these proceeded in the maximally conjoined state. The number of individual specimens or conjoined sets *exhibiting* the attribute relative to the total specimens *capable of exhibiting* the relevant attribute were noted. In other words, the real incidence of the damage was assessed. This observation is sometimes neglected in quantitatively oriented reports that observe, for example, that "X-percent of all

Table 6.1

1. SITE NAME ___
2. BURIAL NUMBER ___
3. SPECIMEN NUMBER ___
4. SIDE (R, L, B = if midline, or I = indeterminate) ___
5. FRAGMENTATION (W or F) ___
6. ELEMENT (T.W. code) ___
7. AGE (00 - 99, AD, IM, and ?? = indeterminate) ___
8. TAXON (I = indeterminate, H = H. sap.) ___

Enter 9-14 only for specimens not identifiable by faunal analyst

9. SIDE (R, L, B = if midline, or I = indeterminate) ___
10. FRAGMENTATION (W or F) ___
11. ELEMENT (T.W. system) ___
12. AGE (00 - 99, AD, IM, and ?? = indeterminate) ___
13. TAXON (I = indeterminate, H. = H. sap.) ___
14. CONJOINING SET NUMBER ___
15. INTACT OUTER CORTEX (0–100%) ___
16. ROLLING OR POLISH (+, -, or P = pot polish) ___
17. WEATHERING (0-5, see code) ___
18. PREPARATION DAMAGE (+ or -) ___
19. RANDOM STRIAE (+ or -) ___

Enter 20-22 for identifiable appendicular specimens

20. ELEMENT PORTION (see code, "I" if 6 is indet.) ___
21. SHAFT CIRCUMFERENCE (1, 2, or 3, see code) ___
22. SHAFT LENGTH (1, 2, or 3, see code) ___
23. MODERN FRACTURE (+ or -) ___
24. ANCIENT FRACTURE (+ or -) ___
25. FRACTURE TIME INDETERMINATE (+ or -) ___

Enter 26-28 for cranial vault only

26. EXTERNAL VAULT RELEASE (+ or -) ___
27. INTERNAL VAULT RELEASE (+ or -) ___
28. SUTURAL RELEASE (+ or -) ___

Enter 29-36 for fractured shafts only

29. PROXIMAL FRACTURE MODERN (+ or -) ___
30. PROXIMAL FRACTURE ANCIENT (+ or -) ___
31. PROXIMAL FRACTURE INDET. (+ or -) ___
32. PROXIMAL FRACTURE INDET. (see code) ___
33. DISTAL FRACTURE MODERN (+ or -) ___
34. DISTAL FRACTURE ANCIENT (+ or -) ___
35. DISTAL FRACTURE TIME INDET. (+ or -) ___
36. DISTAL FRACTURE PATTERN (see code) ___
37. OUTER CONCHOIDAL SCARS (No.) ___
38. INNER CONCHOIDAL SCARS (No.) ___
39. TRUE BONE FLAKE (+ or -) ___
40. INCIPIENT FRACTURE CRACKS (No.) ___
41. CRUSHING (+ or -) ___
42. PERCUSSION PITS (No.) ___
43. ADHERING FLAKES (No.) ___
44. PEELING (+ or -) ___

45-98: Enter (-) where not applicable, and (0) if not present

45. PROXIMAL SHAFT CUTS (No.) ___
46. DISTAL SHAFT CUTS (No.) ___
47. CUTS ON BONE ENDS (No.) ___
48. MIDSHAFT CUTS (No.) ___
49. CUTS ON NONLIMB ELEMENTS (No.) ___
50. PROXIMAL SHAFT CHOPMARKS (No.) ___
51. DISTAL SHAFT CHOPMARKS (No.) ___
52. CHOPMARKS ON BONE ENDS (No.) ___
53. MIDSHAFT CHOPMARKS (No.) ___
54. CHOPMARKS ON NONLIMB ELEMENTS (No.) ___
55. PROXIMAL SHAFT SCRAPEMARKS (+ or -) ___
56. DISTAL SHAFT SCRAPEMARKS (+ or -) ___
57. SCRAPEMARKS ON BONE ENDS (+ or -) ___
58. MIDSHAFT SCRAPEMARKS (+ or -) ___
59. SCRAPEMARKS ON NONLIMB ELEMENTS (+ or -) ___

60-64: Percussion striae can be anvil– or hammer–related

60. PROXIMAL SHAFT PERCUSSION STRIAE (+ or -) ___
61. DISTAL SHAFT PERCUSSION STRIAE (+ or -) ___
62. PERCUSSION STRIAE ON BONE ENDS (+ or -) ___
63. MIDSHAFT PERCUSSION STRIAE (+ or -) ___
64. STRIAE ON NONLIMB ELEMENTS (+ or -) ___

Enter 65-80 for mammalian chewing damage

65. PROXIMAL SHAFT TOOTH SCRATCHES (No.) ___
66. DISTAL SHAFT TOOTH SCRATCHES (No.) ___
67. TOOTH SCRATCHES ON BONE ENDS (No.) ___
68. MIDSHAFT TOOTH PUNCTURES (No.) ___
69. SCRATCHES ON NONLIMB ELEMENTS (No.) ___
70. PROXIMAL SHAFT TOOTH PUNCTURES (No.) ___
71. DISTAL SHAFT TOOTH PUNCTURES (No.) ___
72. TOOTH PUNCTURES ON BONE ENDS (No.) ___
73. MIDSHAFT TOOTH PUNCTURES (No.) ___
74. PUNCTURES ON NONLIMB ELEMENTS (No.) ___
75. PROXIMAL SHAFT TOOTH PITS (No.) ___
76. DISTAL SHAFT TOOTH PITS (No.) ___
77. TOOTH PITS ON BONE ENDS (No.) ___
78. MIDSHAFT TOOTH PITS (No.) ___
79. TOOTH PITS ON NONLIMB ELEMENTS (No.) ___
80. RODENT GNAWING (+ or -) ___

Enter 81-85 for evidence of thermal alteration (burning)

81. PROXIMAL SHAFT DISCOLORATION (+ or -) ___
82. PROXIMAL SHAFT EXFOLIATION (+ or -) ___
83. PROXIMAL SHAFT CRACKING/CRAZING (+ or -) ___
84. DISTAL SHAFT DISCOLORATION (+ or -) ___
85. DISTAL SHAFT EXFOLIATION (+ or -) ___
86. DISTAL SHAFT CRACKING/CRAZING (+ or -) ___
87. DISCOLORATION ON BONE END (+ or -) ___
88. EXFOLIATION ON BONE END (+ or -) ___
89. CRACKING/CRAZING ON BONE END (+ or -) ___
90. DISCOLORATION AT MIDSHAFT (+ or -) ___
91. EXFOLIATION AT MIDSHAFT (+ or -) ___
92. CRACKING/CRAZING AT MIDSHAFT (+ or -) ___
93. DISCOLORATION: NONLIMB ELEMENTS (+ or -) ___
94. EXFOLIATION: NONLIMB ELEMENTS (+ or -) ___
95. CRACKING: NONLIMB ELEMENTS (+ or -) ___
96. SHAFT SPLINTER LENGTH (in mm) ___
97. SHAFT SPLINTER BREADTH (in mm) ___
98. SPLINTER CORTEX THICKNESS (max., in mm) ___

Table 6.1 The data entry form used to record attributes of each specimen in the Mancos 5MTUMR–2346 analysis. Data recorded appear as Appendix 2 of this book. A simplified recording form to save analysis time is presented as an illustration in Appendix 3.

femora show proximal cutmarks.'' Such observations are of dubious meaning unless accompanied by data on how many femora were *preserved* (and thus capable of displaying such trauma in the relevant area; Von den Driesch and Boessneck, 1975; Vigne and Marinval-Vigne, 1983). Lyman (1987a) appreciates this point when he calls for increased attention to the unmodified bones in archaeological faunal assemblages.

IDENTIFICATION

Background

Identification of osteological specimens is done at many levels. As Medlock (1975:228) outlines; ''The primary meaning of 'identification' to many faunal analysts is to locate the animal within the Linnean taxonomy. However, the complete identification of a specimen also includes the element (such as 'mandible'), the anatomical position (such as 'left'), the portion of the element (such as 'alveolar'), the sex of the animal, and the age of the animal.'' Lyman (1979a:23) accurately characterizes the fundamental problem of identifiability in faunal analysis as follows: ''The near universal neglect to define explicitly what authors mean by 'identifiable' has led to a near impossible situation when attempting to compare published analyses and interpretations.'' Driver (1982:203) echoes this view: ''. . . one is frequently impressed by the fact that bone fragments are divided into 'identifiable' and 'unidentifiable' without any criteria of identification being presented.'' These authors are concerned with identification because the number of identified specimens (NISP; see Klein and Cruz-Uribe, 1984; Grayson, 1984) is so universally reported in zooarchaeology, and yet identifiability continues to be an almost entirely subjective judgment. Considerable doubt about the significance of ratios of NISP to *un*identified specimens results from this subjectivity. Further complicating the situation is the fact that there is no simple dichotomy between identifiable and unidentifiable (Hesse, 1982; Klein and Cruz-Uribe, 1984). Lyman (1979a), for example, describes seven levels of identifiability, ranging from completely unidentifiable through levels of identification that include: size only; size and element; size, element, and side; and all of the latter plus family, genus, and species.

Most discussion about the utility of NISP values in faunal analysis has focused on the degree to which these values can be used to evaluate proportions of taxa in the assemblages under consideration (to calculate relative element and taxonomic abundance in assemblages). It is obvious that differences in competence and conditions of faunal analyses render suspect the NISP values themselves. This is an area in which fruitful research could be undertaken as carefully controlled analyses of the same assemblages by different analysts. Such research would be critical in elucidating the degree to which comparisons of NISP versus total piece count ratios could be used to compare the degree of fragmentation in different assemblages.

As noted above, identification of specimens in the Mancos Canyon 5MTUMR-2346 assemblage was approached both from the perspective of a physical anthropologist and from the perspective of a zooarchaeologist. These approaches have forced close attention to the problem of identifiability in reporting the element and taxonomic status of the specimens comprising this assemblage. The following discussion of identification, forced by these complementary approaches, should not be interpreted as an effort to belittle the work of any school of analysts, but rather as an attempt to illuminate the issue of interanalyst variation and its potential effects on comparative osteological work. For a fuller discussion of the general problem of bias in archaeological classification, see Beck and Jones (1989).

Problems of identification were exacerbated in the Mancos analysis by the unusual situation of a single-taxon assemblage being assessed by a specialist on the osteology of that taxon. The pioneer T. E. White presaged the implications of this situation (1956:402):

> Many archaeologists, because they have not given the problem much thought, do not know which elements are identifiable and which are not, and in order to play it safe they bring everything in. Others, because they lack the moral courage to make a decision, bring in everything and justify their action by boasting of the capabilities of the physical anthropologist. They forget that physical anthropologists deal with minute differences of only a single species while paleontologists and zoologists deal with only slightly greater differences in several hundred species.

I am a physical anthropologist who specializes in human osteology, but I attempted to allow other investigators in both physical anthropology and archaeology to use the data from the Mancos study comparatively.

The degree to which any specimen can be identified by element and taxon depends upon three factors: competence, conditions, and context. It is extremely difficult, if not impossible, to control for interinvestigator variation in these factors. The results of any analysis may consequently be biased, with specimens being overidentified (attributed to the wrong element, side, or taxon) or underidentified (identified as indeterminate for element, side, or taxon when more precise allocation is possible).

Analyst competence, or skill, is the first key to the identification of fragmentary osteological remains. This skill rests upon twin pillars—experience and the innate aptitude for morphologically based work. What is unidentifiable for one analyst is readily attributed to element, side, and taxon by a more experienced analyst with a higher aptitude for morphological differentiation who works under ideal conditions (including comparative specimens and time to use them). For the latter analyst, Binford and Bertram's (1977:125) contention seems plausible: ". . . there *is no unidentifiable bone*. All bones, even the smallest fragments, may be identified with sufficient training in osteology." We might agree, "Identifiable as *bones*—of course!," but experience, ability, and conditions are rarely so good as to allow so much as element identification of all fragments, leading to Lyman's (1982:368) characterization of Binford and Bertram's position as demonstrating "remarkable naiveté."

Most accounts of procedure in faunal analysis begin with the sorting of "identifiable" from "unidentifiable" specimens (Ziegler, 1973; Brain, 1981a), and it is here that problems stem from variation in analyst competence. What is unidentifiable for one analyst is identifiable to the element for another, identifiable to the family to a third, and identifiable to the species for a fourth. Each of these analysts will report different data for the same specimen.

The nature of the faunal analyst's *experience* is important in establishing the ability to identify specimens. Small fragments from an archaeological context will seem hardly "identifiable" to a novice whose only experience is in recognizing intact elements in a laboratory collection. The same specimens may, however, be readily attributed to species by an experienced professional who has spent years identifying fragments. Klein (1980) notes that the accuracy of identification generally increases with the experience of the analyst, and that this can lead to significant bias in the results of any analysis.

Cornwall (1956) draws attention to the second dimension of competence when he recognizes what all teachers of osteology know. He describes a "feeling" or "intuitive perception" for bones that no great paleontologist is without, and that some students never get. The analyst with high *aptitude* for morphological study will find fragments of skeleton easily identifiable, whereas an equally experienced analyst with low aptitude will be baffled. Recombination and environment can both produce differentials in competence, differentials with the potential to produce very different data about the identity of the same osteological specimen.

Conditions of analysis are the second major factor that determines the degree to which fragmentary osteological specimens can be identified. The amount of time available for the analysis, and the bench space and lighting available to the analyst can both seriously affect the accuracy and degree to which fragmentary material is identified. The nature of available comparative collections is yet another element of analytical conditions that influences identifiability.

The precision of identification in faunal analysis depends on two main factors discussed above, conditions and competence. Klein and Cruz-Uribe (1984:19–20) make a valuable observation on a third factor relevant to the identification of osteological specimens (particularly from assemblages such as the Mancos one)—context:

> Often, however, the most important factor is what the analyst expects or assumes. Thus, few analysts would hesitate to assign isolated bovine teeth in a prehistoric North American sample to bison, even though the teeth may be morphologically indistinguishable from the teeth of the European aurochs or the African buffalo. Similarly, otherwise "unidentifiable" ribs, vertebrae, sesamoids, and small long-bone shaft fragments may readily be assigned to species in a fossil sample in which cranial parts suggest there is only one species of the appropriate size and morphology. In short, form is only one criterion used to determine whether a bone is identifiable. . . . Clearly, to avoid potentially misleading comparisons between samples, faunal analysts should make their criteria for identifiability as explicit as possible. It is especially important to note what identifications were based on assumptions about the population from which the fossil sample was drawn.

For the Mancos collection, all identification was done by the author in excellent laboratory conditions. Identification was simplified by the fact that the assemblage comprised, almost exclusively, one taxon. In such a situation, identification of specimens is a different sort of undertaking than the usual faunal analysis, a point appreciated by other archaeologists. For example, in dealing with a large sample of artiodactyl bones from one horizon at Gatecliff Shelter, Thomas and Mayer (1983:353) noted the special nature of single-taxon assemblages in categorical levels of identification: "Because we explicitly assume that all artiodactyl remains in this horizon are bighorn, the term *unidentified* takes on a different meaning. 'Unidentified' in this sense means that an individual bone is 'unidentifiable' relative to skeletal element, rather than being 'unidentifiable' to genus."

Only 8 of the 2,114 specimens in the

Mancos assemblage considered here showed diagnostic features excluding them from *Homo sapiens*. These nonhuman specimens are not counted in the analysis that follows. All the remaining 2,106 specimens are designated as human. The recording format used gives maximum identification using physical anthropological, postconjoining knowledge. Simultaneously, it identifies all specimens that an "average" (based on my limited experience) archaeological faunal analyst probably would place in the traditional "unidentifiable" category. Thus, both the maximal *physical anthropological* identity and the *faunal analytical* identity are recorded for each specimen.

Observations 1–3: Provenance (Table 6.1)

Observation 1 is a *site* indicator, "**M**," describing Mancos. Observation 2 is the "burial" number (spatial *provenance* indicator; see Chapter 3). Observation 3 provides the arbitrarily assigned *specimen number* that uniquely identifies each specimen.

Observations 4–13: Identity (Table 6.1)

It was evident from the beginning of the Mancos analysis that the author, based on his specialty in human osteology and experience with fragmentary skeletal remains, could identify element, side, age, and taxon for many specimens that some faunal analysts working with an archaeological assemblage might designate as "unidentifiable." To record both the author's guess at a *faunal analytical* identification, as well as the more precise *physical anthropological* identification, Observations 4–8 and 9–13 duplicate each other. Observations 4–8 record only specimens that a faunal analyst working on a mixed archaeological faunal collection would typically designate as identifiable (would set aside for search of a comparative collection with the objective of identifying taxon to at least the level of genus). These are generally cranial specimens retaining substantial segments of major skull bones, and postcranial specimens with most or all of at least one articular surface. The judgment is obviously a highly subjective one, and among practicing faunal analysts there is an extremely wide range in what is termed "identifiable." I have tested my ability to make the discrimination between specimens that are, or are not, "identifiable" in standard, traditional faunal analysis. This I have done by checking my identifications against those made by several archaeologists. Reasonable agreement about what usually is designated "unidentifiable" by zooarchaeologists was found on all such tests.

Because I judged no specimen in the SPLINTERS database to be "identifiable" by an "average" faunal analyst, Observations 4–8 do not appear in SPLINTERS. Because all specimens in the LIMBS database would be judged identifiable by a faunal analyst, Observations 9–13 do not appear in LIMBS. In the CRANIAL, AXIAL, and HANDFOOT databases, specimens that a faunal analyst would judge to be unidentifiable are entered only under Observations 9–13, where they are identified to the fullest possible extent. Some identifications here are the result of information gathered during the conjoining exercise (see Chapter 4); the element identifications in 9–13 are therefore maximal.

Observations 4, 9: Side (Table 6.1)

Observations 4 and 9 refer to the *side* of the body that a specimen comes from as follows: **L** for left, **R** for right, **B** for both (in which midline is present), or **I** for indeterminate.

Observations 5, 10: Fragmentation (Table 6.1)

Observations 5 and 10 provide a very rough measure of *fragmentation*. Here, specimens for which more than half the original element is preserved are recorded as **W** for whole, and those with less than half the original element as **F** for fragmentary. "Half," of course, is a subjective judgment roughly based on the volume of an intact, undamaged element.

To describe the patterning seen in rib and vertebral fragmentation, a one-letter code using the letters **A** through **F** was used. For vertebrae, **A** designates only the complete (> 50 percent) arch; **B** designates only the intact (> 50 percent) body; **C** indicates that both the arch and body are present (> 50 percent of each preserved); **D** designates fragments in which both body and arch portions are present but less than half of either is preserved; **E** designates a fragment of the arch/spine complex; and **F** designates a fragment of the body.

For ribs, a similar code is used, in which **A** designates the head, neck, tubercle, *and* greater than 50 percent of the shaft; **B** designates "**A**" without the head; **C** designates greater than 50 percent of the shaft only; **D** designates less than 50 percent of the shaft only; **E** designates "**A**" with less than 50 percent of the shaft; and **F** designates "**E**" without the head.

All of these designations were made in an effort to describe conveniently patterns of fragmentation across the assemblage and within any element category.

Observations 6, 11: Element (Table 6.1)

Observations 6 and 11 identify the *element* that the specimen represents. The code used here approximates that used by Gifford and Crader (1977), but it has been modified so that each element is identified in a three-letter format most readily recognizable by human osteologists (Table 6.2). Four additional indeterminate postcranial element categories (IP1–IP4) were created to reflect the varying degrees of identifiability of some limb-bone fragments. It was always possible to distinguish between cranial and postcranial remains in the analysis. Cranial fragments that could not be assigned to an element were given the designation **ICR** (indeterminate cranial). The **IP1** specimens are fragments of smaller diameter long-bone shafts attributable to the radius, ulna, or fibula. The **IP2** specimens are fragments of larger shafts that could belong to the humerus, tibia, or femur; and the **IP3** specimens are shaft fragments that belong either to the tibia or to the femur. The **IP4** specimens cannot be taken beyond postcranial identification. Finally, the **IND** (for completely indeterminate) category includes those fragments that cannot be attributed to cranial or postcranial elements. There were none of these in the Mancos assemblage. These numbered "indeterminate" element identification categories were used only when physical anthropological and conjoining analyses failed to attribute the specimen to a more specific element. The specimens placed in the ICR and IP4 categories in any assemblage will tend to include many small

Table 6.2 The element code used in the Mancos 5MTUMR–2346 analysis. This shorthand notation system is a very efficient means of coding for element attribution of isolated specimens.

ELEMENT CODE

SIDE: L, R, B (Both where midline present), or **I** (indeterminate).

FRAGMENTATION: W (> 1/2 bone), or **F** (< 1/2 bone). See rib and vertebra codes for **"A** to **F"** breakdown.

ELEMENT: By the code given below–where the specimen consists of multiple elements, it is indicated by a slash (/) between the 3-letter codes. Extrasutural bones and < 1.0 cm attached elements not entered.

AGE: 00, 02, 04, 06, 08, 10, 12, AD (Adult), **IM** (Immature).

SUMMARY EXAMPLES:

R F TIB AD is a fragment of right tibia from an adult individual (> 12 years old).

B W OCC / R F PAR O6 is an occipital (with midline) attached to a fragment of right parietal of a six-year-old child.

CRANIAL

FRO	FRONTAL
PAR	PARIETAL
OCC	OCCIPITAL
TEM	TEMPORAL
MAX	MAXILLA
ZYG	ZYGOMATIC
SPH	SPHENOID
NAS	NASAL
ETH	ETHMOID
VOM	VOMER
PAL	PALATINE
HYO	HYOID
INC	INFERIOR NASAL CONCHA
MAN	MANDIBLE
CRA	CRANIAL PORTIONS, MULTIPLE ELEMENTS
ICR	INDETERMINATE CRANIAL
DUT	DECIDUOUS UPPER TOOTH
DLT	DECIDUOUS LOWER TOOTH
PUT	PERMANENT UPPER TOOTH
PLT	PERMANENT LOWER TOOTH
ITO	INDETERMINATE TOOTH
(+)	OTHER BONES ATTACHED

POSTCRANIA

ATL	ATLAS
AXI	AXIS
CER	CERVICAL VERTEBRAE 3+
THO	THORACIC VERTEBRAE
LUM	LUMBAR VERTEBRAE
VER	VERTEBRA
A	> 1/2 arch only
B	> 1/2 body only
C	> 1/2, arch and body
D	< 1/2, arch and body
E	fragment of arch/spine complex (< 1/2)
F	fragment of body (< 1/2)
SAC	SACRUM
COC	COCCYX
OCX	OS COXAE
STE	STERNUM
R#1	FIRST RIB
A RIB	head, neck, tubercle, > 1/2 shaft
B RIB	RIB A without head
C RIB	> 1/2 shaft only
D RIB	< 1/2 shaft only
E RIB	RIB A with < 1/2 shaft
F RIB	RIB E without head
SCA	SCAPULA
CLA	CLAVICLE
HUM	HUMERUS
ULN	ULNA
RAD	RADIUS
FEM	FEMUR
PAT	PATELLA
TIB	TIBIA
FIB	FIBULA
CAR	CARPAL
MC0 to 5	METACARPAL 1 TO 5
PHP	PROXIMAL HAND PHALANX
IHP	INTERMEDIATE HAND PHALANX
THP	TERMINAL HAND PHALANX
CAL	CALCANEUS
TAL	TALUS
TAR	OTHER TARSALS
MT0 to 5	METATARSAL 1 TO 5
PFP	PROXIMAL FOOT PHALANX
IFP	INTERMEDIATE FOOT PHALANX
TFP	TERMINAL FOOT PHALANX
IP1	RADIUS, or ULNA, or FIBULA
IP2	HUMERUS, or TIBIA, or FEMUR
IP3	FEMUR or TIBIA
IP4	INDETERMINATE POSTCRANIAL
IND	COMPLETELY INDETERMINATE

fragments that became detached from larger specimens, particularly burned, exfoliating cranial vault pieces. These should usually not be included in the analysis because their existence is related to recovery or postrecovery influences rather than prehistoric bone modification. One rib crushed in a transport bag, for example, can artificially inflate the IP4 count by 10 or 20 specimens. On the other hand, small unidentified specimen counts are also extremely sensitive to the degree to which the small isolated fragments deposited in a site were recovered, and when such recovery is good, the ICR and IP4 counts will skyrocket. In the final analysis, caution in the use of data derived from these "element" categories is urged for any assemblage.

Observations 7, 12: Age (Table 6.1)

Observations 7 and 12 record the *age* of the specimen as determined by comparison with a representative series of intact skeletons from the Lowie Museum prehistoric California skeletal collections. These specimens were chosen to match the dental eruption standards of Ubelaker (1989). All Mancos specimens were compared to this series and segregated into one of 9 age categories: **00**, **02**, **04**, **06**, **08**, **10**, **12**, **IM** (immature, $\leq$ 12), and **AD** (adult, $>$ 12). In practice, for fragmentary specimens, it was often difficult to sort between subadults of different age categories, and between adults and 12-year-olds (it is, for example, inevitable that some fragments from 12-year-old individuals are recorded as adult). The subadult age determinations for nongnathic specimens in the assemblage, therefore, should be seen as rough approximations of age rather than precise estimates. Analytically, this has little significance for the fragmentary postcrania for two reasons. Functionally, the processing of bones of a 12-year-old individual would have been more similar to that employed on an adult individual than that employed on a 6-year-old. Furthermore, none of the postcranial specimens involved is used in any quantitative analysis in which an age discrimination within a 4-year interval is significant. Greater precision of age estimation in fragmentary subadult postcrania would have required an expenditure of analytical time that was judged to be wasteful.

Observations 8, 13: Taxon (Table 6.1)

Observations 8 and 13 indicate the *taxonomic attribution* for each specimen. For the Mancos assemblage, human status (**H**) was determined for all zooarchaeologically identifiable specimens. For many other specimens, conjoining or the physical anthropological analysis demonstrated human status. For specimens in the IP1 through IP4 categories, and for small rib and vertebral specimens, a human status was *assumed* on the basis that less than one–half of one percent of the overall assemblage was identifiably nonhuman. Thus, as discussed above, context played a role in identification at the taxonomic level. Given the virtual absence of identifiable nonhuman remains in the assemblage, it was judged highly unlikely the indeterminate postcranial samples include nonhuman specimens. In a mixed assemblage, this assumption would be less warranted. Observations 8 and 13 are given the **H** designation for all five databases.

Observation 14: Conjoining (Table 6.1)

Observation 14 provides unique numbers to identify all *sets of conjoining bone fragments*. These sets and their construction are more fully described in Chapter 4.

PRESERVATION

Background

Bone preservation in archaeological contexts varies along a continuum, ranging from greasy bone with adhering flesh to bone that crumbles when touched. This preservation depends, in great measure, on the degree to which the organic components of bone remain. It has long been noted that human bone thought to represent the remains of cannibalized individuals is often excellently preserved. Wintemberg (1936) and Knowles (1937) both note this phenomenon. The latter author attributed the better preservation in bones from refuse heaps to some property of the surrounding ashy deposit. He goes on to suggest that boiling might expel some fats from the bone, arresting or retarding the process of disintegration. Morris (1939) was the first to describe the excellent bone preservation in fragmentary human remains from the Southwest summarized in Chapter 3. He noted the "dead white appearance" of bone from the La Plata human bone assemblages, calling it "cooked." Turner and Morris (1970) stated that the Polacca infant bones were as well preserved as the adults. Other investigators such as Nickens (1974, 1975) and Malville (1989) have noted that the fragmentary bone from similar assemblages is usually better preserved than bone from formally buried individuals at the same site. Nickens attributes the difference to burial with or without flesh adhering to the bones. Hohmann *et al.* (1985) followed other authors assessing human bone assemblages from the Southwest when they noted that the fragmented and disarticulated bones were better preserved than those from inhumation contexts at the same site. Whether boiling or interment without fleshy cover is responsible for the characteristics of these assemblages, excellent preservation of the bone material itself is ubiquitous. Subjective analysis and comparison of the Mancos nonburial bone specimens indicate that they are no exception to the rule of excellent preservation in broken, scattered assemblages of human bones. Quantification of bone material preservation was not attempted.

Bone *surface* preservation, as opposed to bone material preservation, is an important variable influencing zooarchaeological analyses. The recording and assessment of surface modification are rapidly developing specialties in archaeological faunal analysis. For example, the quantification of butchery marks lies at the heart of the debate over the subsistence activities of the earliest hominids (Potts and Shipman, 1981; Koch, 1986; Bunn and Kroll, 1988; Binford, 1988), and weathering patterns have been used to estimate perimortem exposure of assemblages (Potts, 1986; but see Lyman and Fox, 1989).

Whereas a good deal of attention has been given to discriminating among cutmarks, rootmarks, preparation damage, and other agents of surface modification, one issue that has been widely overlooked involves the impact of differing bone surface preservation on cutmark frequencies in any assemblage (but see Grayson, 1988). Both perimortem and postdepositional factors can modify the bone surface, erasing signs of human modification. Exfoliation due to weathering, abrasion due to hydraulic transport, subaerial sandblasting, and root acid etching all have the capacity to eliminate both carnivore gnawing and/or human-induced cutmarks. Given the increasing importance of assessing human-induced trauma on bone surfaces and the poor reporting of surface preservation itself, I attempted to take some tentative steps toward quantifying five preservational observations in the Mancos analysis (see, in particular, the description of Observation 15, below). Olsen (1989) has also taken first steps in this direction in her work on the archaeological faunal assemblages from Solutré.

Andrews and Cook (1985) and Grayson (1988) note the value of using rootmarks in faunal analysis. For good illustrations of rootmarks on bones, see Binford (1981), Baud (1982), and Johnson (1983). The presence of rootmarks on fracture surfaces or on the internal surface of limb-bone shafts can be essential clues about the relative timing of bone fracture. They can aid in discriminating recent excavation and preparation damage from ancient, perimortem damage. Rootmarks were not recorded separately in the Mancos analysis, but they were ubiquitous among specimens in the collection, crossing many fracture surfaces and found equally on original external and internal surfaces of the bones. The intensity of the rootmarking at Mancos, however, is relatively low and serves to obscure little of the human-induced surface modification (see Figure 6.1 for a 5MTUMR–2346 example). The contrast among the Mancos assemblage, the heavily root etched collection from Cottonwood Canyon, Utah, (White, 1988), and the more lightly-etched collection from Yellow Jacket (this study) emphasizes the need for faunal analysts to take steps toward specifying the degree of bone surface preservation as an

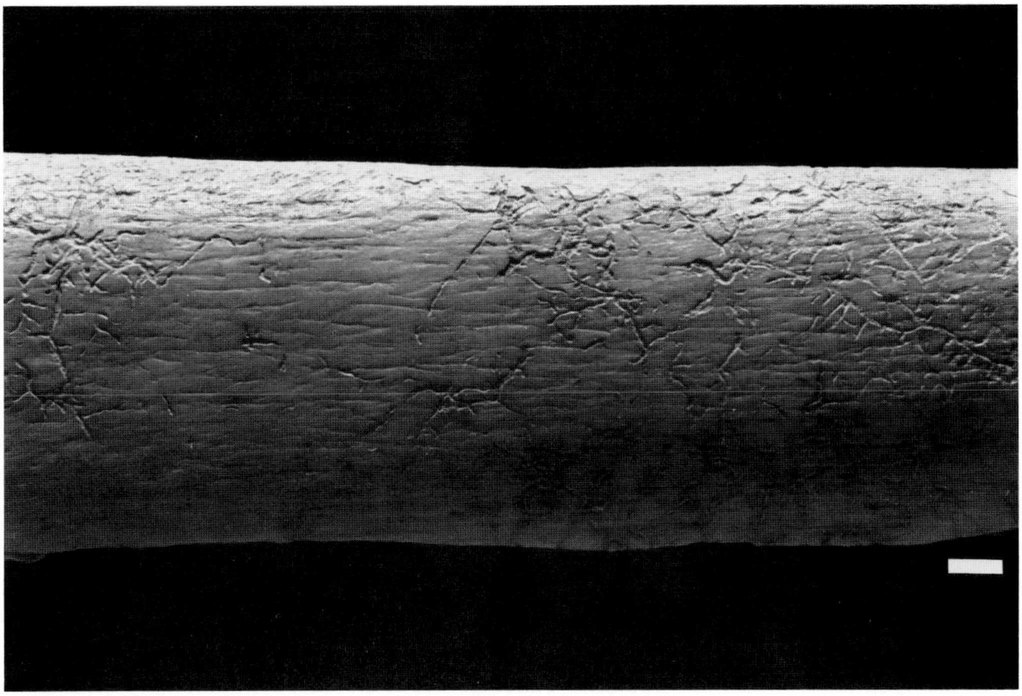

Fig. 6.1 Rootmarking on a tibial splinter (1057). Bar = 3 mm.

essential companion to any quantitative presentation of human-induced surface modification.

Observation 15: Percentage Intact Surface (Table 6.1)

Observation 15 records the *percentage of intact surface*, a rough percentage estimate of how much of the specimen's original outer cortical bone surface remains to retain evidence of cutmarks, if such marks had been present. Thus, a value of **100** indicates that the entire outer surface of the specimen is perfectly preserved, whereas a value of **50** indicates that half the specimen's outer surface is etched, abraded, weathered, exfoliated, or otherwise missing. Where the entire inner table of cranial bone is exfoliated, this is not entered into the recorded percentage, but where half the ectocranial table of bone that might have borne cutmarks is exfoliated, for example, the value of 50 percent is entered. It is recognized that this is a very crude method of estimating damage to an assemblage's cortical surface, but it is seen as a step in the right direction.

In comparing data on bone surface modification, the percentage intact surface observation is critical. For example, assemblages comprising weathered, rolled, or root-etched specimens will give lower values of cutmarks and other surface modification because of postdiscard surface degradation rather than as a reflection of different human behavior. The Mancos assemblage shows high values for this observation, reflecting the fact that the outer bone surface is, in general, excellently preserved.

A total of 86.3 percent of the nontooth specimens in the Mancos assemblage scored 100 percent intact on this measure, and the nontooth assemblage of 2,027 specimens averaged 94.9 percent intact. The only comparative human data available were generated for the Yellow Jacket 5MT–3 assemblage, in which the comparable percentages were 93.7 and 98.7 percent, respectively. The Badger House zooarchaeological assemblage (see Chapter 12) gave analogous values of 85.9 and 90.8 percent, respectively. Ultimately, if other analysts record this variable, interassemblage comparisons among the incidence of various bone modifications will become increasingly valid. Meanwhile, the cited values imply that few prediscard bone modifications have been erased from the Mancos assemblage.

Observation 16: Polish (Table 6.1)

Observation 16 began as a presence/absence (+, −) indicator of *rolling* or *polish* that was judged, by its distribution across the bone, to derive from natural causes (usually fluviatile or aeolian sediment transport, or the passage of animal or human traffic, particularly in caves; Buckland, 1822; Leroi-Gourhan, 1952). Only two specimens in the entire Mancos collection were recorded as exhibiting such damage, and the unusual context of these is described in Chapter 3. These two cranial specimens are noted with a + in the CRANIAL database file and one is illustrated in Figure 6.2.

During the course of the study, many other specimens (particularly limb-bone shaft splinters and ribs) in the Mancos assemblage were noted to display polish/-abrasion on their projecting parts. Some long-bone splinters showed beveled abrasion and polishing at their tips. This modification was initially interpreted to be the result of these specimens having been used as tools. After the Mancos analysis, similar artificially polished specimens were found in the Yellow Jacket 5MT–3 assemblage. This polish/abrasion was fo-

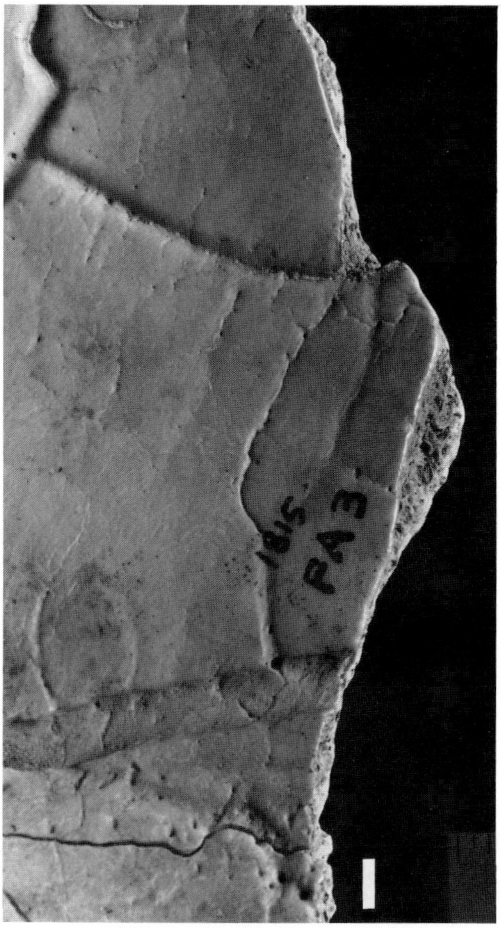

Fig. 6.2 Polishing on the broken edge of a left temporal (1815). Consult Chapter 3 for a discussion of the unique provenance of this specimen, and one associated with it that showed the same kind of modification. These two specimens were the only ones in the assemblage that showed this kind of whole-specimen polishing. Bar = 3 mm.

cused on tips of the specimens in question, and its absence on other parts of the same specimens represented a patterning of modification that suggested hominid involvement. Similarly modified bone splinters are sometimes considered "expediency tools" (see Lyman, 1984a for a critical review) or, in some cases, crude protoawls, or variants of digging tools such as those described by Brain *et al.* (1988).

In 1990, in an effort to obtain comparative data for the Mancos analysis, I studied the artiodactyl remains from an Anasazi midden at Badger House, Mesa Verde (see Chapter 12). This study revealed similar modification of the projecting parts of some large artiodactyl bones in the assemblage. Given the ubiquity of the modification on these different assemblages, and the minimal extent of damage to any particular specimen, an alternate interpretation to the "bone utensil" inference was born. It was hypothesized that this bone polish (rounding and beveling with associated microscopic striae) was the result of the bone fragments being boiled in pottery cooking vessels. To further explore the patterning of damage observed on the archaeological remains, a replication experiment was conducted.

Several mule deer metapodials were broken into splinters and articular ends by hard hammer, over-anvil percussion. Eighteen fragments were isolated as controls. The remaining 69 specimens, ranging in length from 12 to 133 mm, were placed in a replica of a corrugated Anasazi cooking vessel measuring c. 28-cm maximum diameter by c. 30-cm maximum height. The bone fragment assemblage was submerged in water within the vessel, the water filling it to the three-quarter mark. The pot and its contents were stabilized on a Coleman® stove and heated on full burner for three hours. A wooden stick was used to stir the contents for approximately 15 minutes of the total cooking period. The water eventually (barely) reached a slow boil (with consequent implications for firewood consumption among Anasazi—the thermal inertia of this vessel and its contents was surprisingly high!—see Kohler and Matthews, 1988).

The deer metapodials were from ligamentous specimens that contained virtually no marrow, but some fat was nevertheless rendered by the cooking experiment. This fat rose to the surface of the water and coagulated around the waterline of the pot, forming a ring of grease measuring up to 1 cm in thickness. After heating, the water was cooled and the contents of the pot were decanted. One experimental bone splinter was used to scrape the ring of fat from the inside surface of the pot. The other bone splinters were assessed for damage.

The results of the experiment closely replicated the pattern of bone modification observed on the archaeological specimens. Beveling and rounding on the projecting ends of the bone splinters were observed with the naked eye, checked with a 10-power hand lens, and scored. All of the 29 specimens showing beveling also displayed rounding. An additional 12 of the 69 fragments showed some polish/abrasion in the form of rounding. The degree of modification was clearly related to the length and weight of the specimen—of the 17 specimens measuring less than 30 mm in length, only one showed obvious pot-related modification. All this damage was recognized on broken bone surfaces. None was visible on the articular ends of bones, but proximity of an articular end and a broken shaft surface often led to a ''control'' of the bevel angle to the polish/abrasion facet. The specimen used to scrape fat from the pot displayed strong unifacial abrasion/polishing with a uniformity of microscopic striae orientation perpendicular to the axis of the edge. This pattern of modification matched that observed on one Mancos bone splinter (1489) and on several Badger House rib specimens.

These results are not surprising given a consideration of the mechanics of boiling within ceramic vessels. The inner surfaces of such vessels present an abrasive surface with which the bone ends come into contact (Figure 6.3). For longer bone splinters contacting the pot's inner surface, the angle between the long axis of the splinter and the side of the pot is acute. The shorter the piece, the more oblique this angle. The contact between the broken edge of the bone and the pot side tends to abrade ''facets'' on the bone ends, and these facets may be seen with the naked eye (Figure 6.4). They are shiny relative to the remainder of the broken bone edge; they are placed at the most projecting points of the bone; and they are most easily recognized as modifications to sharp broken edges, seen by orienting the bone relative to the incident light source and looking for reflected light from the polished surface(s). Microscopic examination of the polished/abraded surfaces shows, as predicted from the mechanics of contact, that there are striae on the polished surfaces formed by individual grains of temper in the inner vessel wall (Figures 6.5–6.8).

This form of modification, to my knowledge, has not been described as the result of cooking in ceramic vessels. The bone modification resulting from the replication experiment fits very well with that observed among the archaeological specimens. The degree of modification and the incidence of this damage in the experimental cervid bone assemblage are greater than observed in the archaeological material from Badger House or the Mancos assemblage. This may stem from a combination of excessive stirring in the experiment, edge chipping and loss in the archaeological remains, or a comparison between 100 percent boiled experimental specimens versus a lower percentage of prehistorically boiled specimens. Addi-

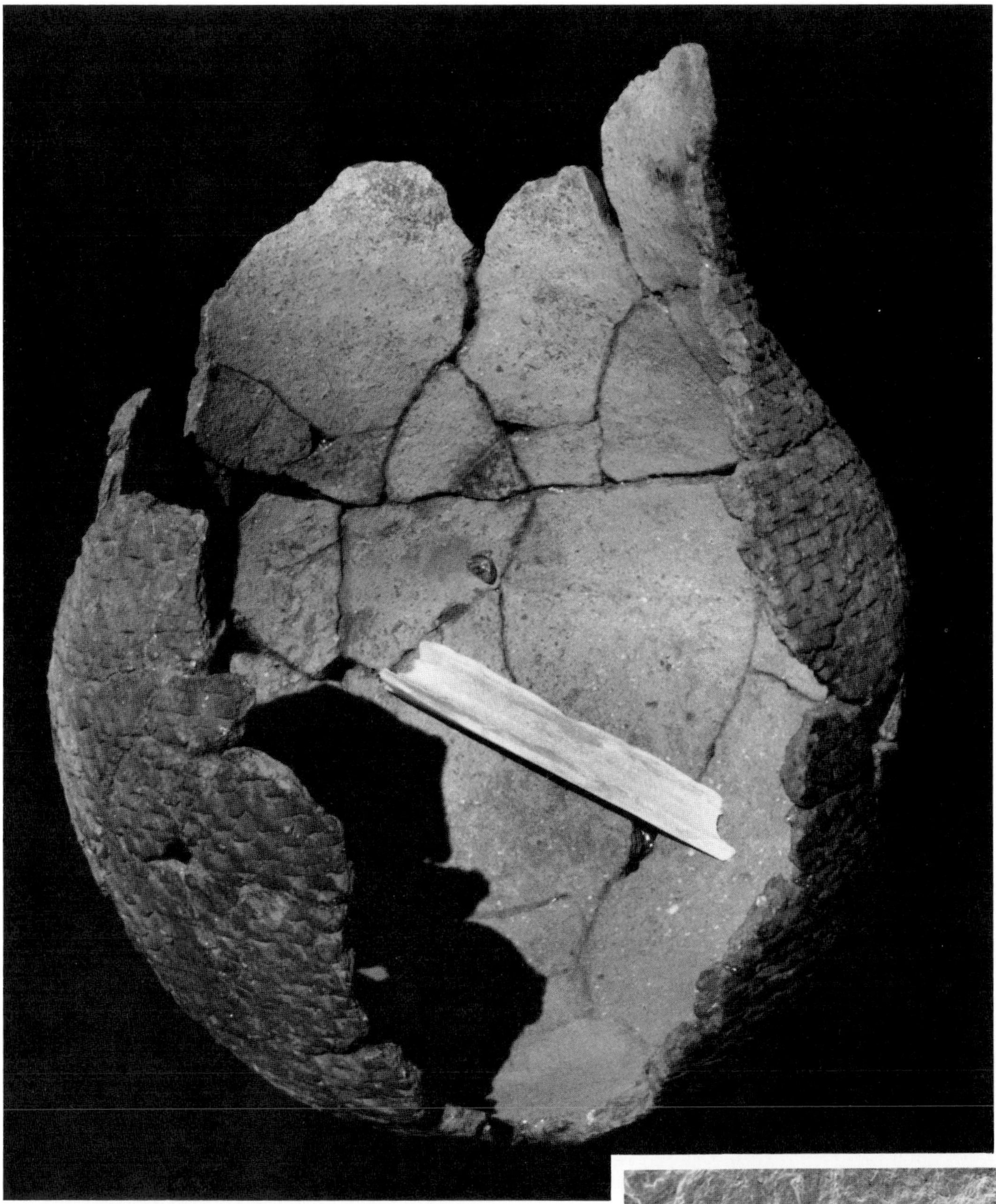

Fig. 6.3 A fragmentary corrugated vessel (archaeological specimen, Mesa Verde National Park collection) allows the viewer to observe the contact points between the deer metapodial splinter and the vessel wall. The inner wall of the vessel, with its embedded grains of temper (inset Scanning Electron Micrograph SEM image), creates an abrasive surface that interfaces with the bone during cooking to produce polish and beveling—a phenomenon termed "pot polish." See the text for a discussion of experimental work on pot polish.

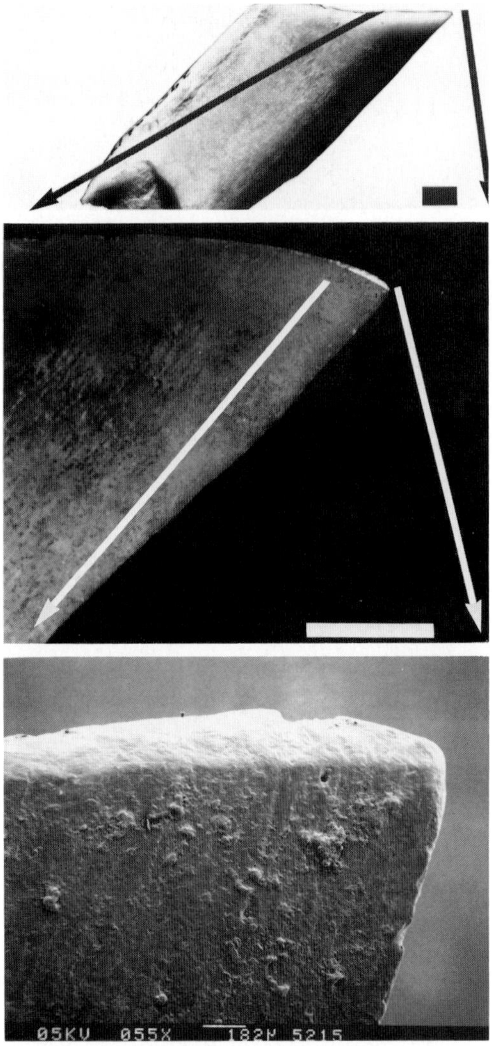

Fig. 6.4 Successive blowups of specimen 29513aa, an artiodactyl (probably cervid) limb-bone shaft splinter from the Badger House zooarchaeological assemblage. The beveled, polished area is evident as a shiny curved facet in gross view (center). Bars = 5 mm.

tional experimentation is necessary to resolve these problems. Meanwhile, the presence of this form of bone modification may be an effective means of recognizing boiling of osteological material in the archaeological record. The kind of polish/abrasion described above is termed "pot polish" and its presence entered as a "**P**" under Observation 16. Scoring of this damage attribute as present was highly conservative because there is a chance for superficially similar damage to occur as a result of recovery and transport. It is likely, because of this conservative approach, that pot polish damage has been underestimated for the Mancos assemblage. What is most significant is the presence of the damage rather than the relative amount. This damage, after all, will exist along a continuum depending upon the length of cooking time, the amount of grit in the vessel bed load, the roughness of the vessel's inner surface, and the amount of stirring. Beveling was not scored as pot polish if there were adjacent percussion striae (see below) that suggested that the bone was abraded during fracture rather than by cooking.

Observation 17: Weathering (Table 6.1)

Observation 17 indicates *weathering* damage to a specimen. The values recorded here are numbers corresponding to the six "stages" of weathering postulated by Behrensmeyer (1978; **0** = unweathered). With Mancos, these values carry absolutely no connotation about the time over which the bones were exposed, and they are recorded only for the sake of completeness. This is because it is uncertain how applicable Behrensmeyer's observations are to bone assemblages under differing environmental conditions. Second, microhabitat differences within a few meters can dramatically influence the rate of bone weathering (Haynes, 1981, 1988; Gifford, 1981). Dust cover, litter cover, humidity, temperature, and incident sunlight all seem likely to affect the

Fig. 6.5 The cervid metapodial splinter (A) on the left was a control specimen not subjected to boiling during the experiment. The large arrow indicates placement of the SEM image (B). The SEM image of this specimen's pointed end (B) shows a sharp, ragged edge with no polish. The pointed end of another cervid metapodial splinter circulated in the experimental ceramic vessel shows bevel, polishing, and striae indicative of contact with the inner vessel wall. Bar = 5 mm.

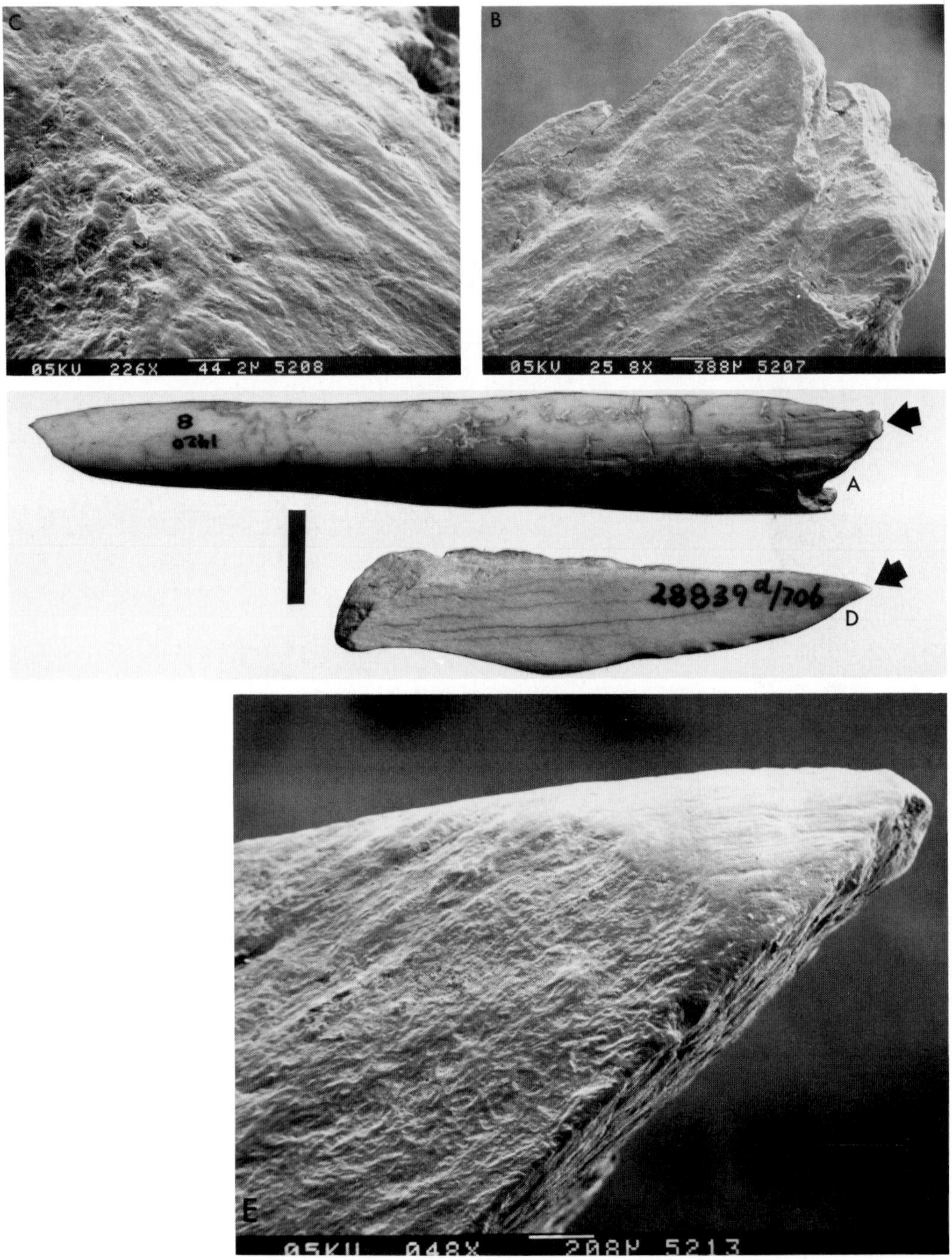

Fig. 6.6 The upper bone splinter (A) is specimen 1420 from the Mancos human bone assemblage. SEM images of its end (B and C are successive blowups) show bevel, polish, and striae that match those seen in the experiment. The lower bone splinter (D) is specimen 28839d from the artiodactyl assemblage of Badger House. The bevel, polish, and striae displayed by this specimen (SEM image E) are also inferred to indicate circulation within a ceramic vessel. Bar = 1 cm.

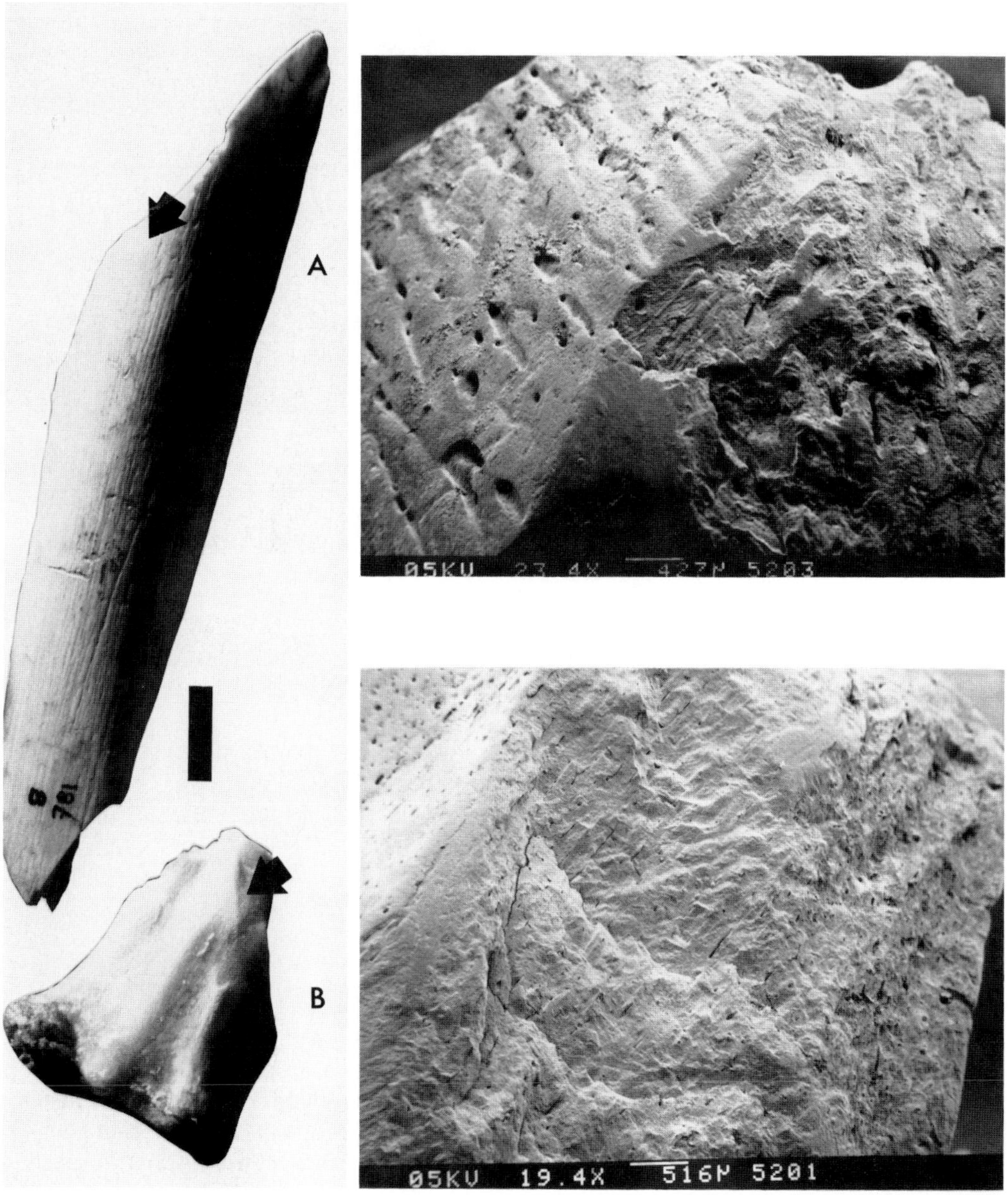

Fig. 6.7 The upper bone splinter (A) is specimen 781, a femoral shaft fragment from the Mancos human bone assemblage. The lower bone fragment (B) is from a deer metapodial used in the experiment. The large arrows indicate the placement of the SEM images accompanying each specimen. These images show beveling of the broken edges as well as planar facets abraded onto high points of the rough, broken cortical surface of these limb-bone shaft fragments. Bar = 1 cm.

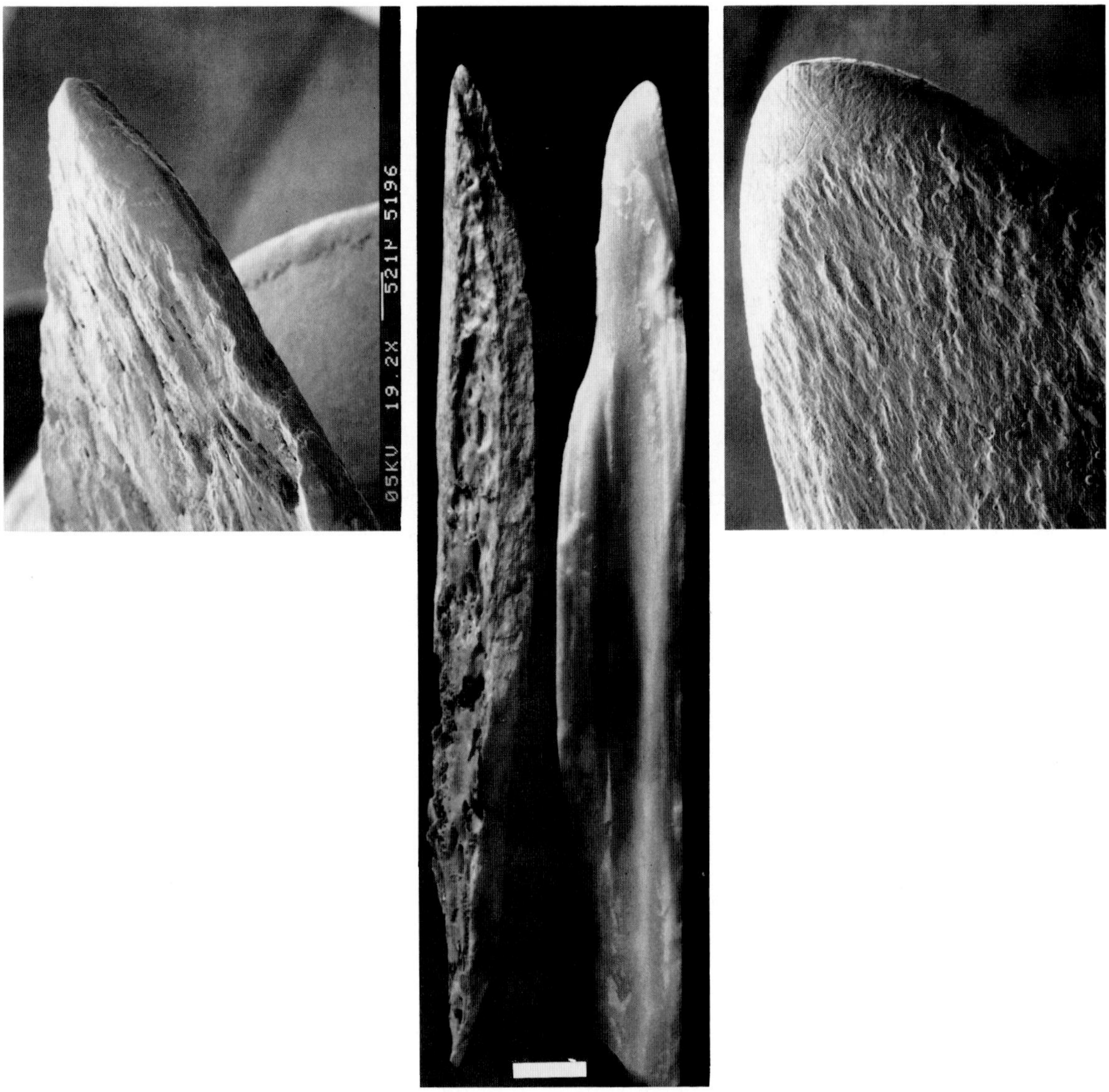

Fig. 6.8 The femur splinter and accompanying SEM image on the left are from the Mancos human bone assemblage. The metapodial splinter and accompanying SEM image on the right are from the cervid bones used in the experimental study. Note that the polish and beveling on both specimens are focused on the tip of each specimen. Bar = 1 cm.

rate of bone weathering. Lyman and Fox (1989:313) reach similar conclusions in their review of the evidence, which bear repeating here: "We conclude that bone weathering data do not in any simple and direct fashion reflect Time, particularly the duration of bone assemblage formation." Finally, as discussed below, the Mancos study demonstrates that burning may mimic bone weathering in some details, potentially increasing estimates of surface exposure. The overall weathering stage average for the Mancos collection is extremely low—the assemblage is effectively unweathered. Potts (1986, 1988) provides data on weathering in the Olduvai bone assemblages, focusing only on specimens with major long-bone pieces possessing at least a partial diaphysis and an articular end, whereas Gifford-Gonzalez (1989a) uses the same scale, also on long bones.

I have assessed weathering for all specimens in the Mancos non-tooth assemblage. A total of 1,988 specimens were scored as stage 0, 22 specimens were placed in stage 1, 11 specimens in stage 2, and 4 specimens in stage 3. It is possible that the stage 1–3 values are inflated by misreading burning damage as weathering (see below).

A small number of human bone fragments from the surface of the 5MTUMR–2346 backdirt heaps was collected during a site visit in 1990. The considerable weathering damage shown by the surfaces of these bones indicated what 17 years of exposure can do. It resulted in stage 3–4 weathering (Figure 6.9), a degree of weathering damage not seen among the 2,106 excavated specimens from the site. This fortuitous "experiment" in weathering lends support to Turner and Morris' (1970) observations of fairly high weathering rate in this region. Indeed, given the circumstances of discovery of the Polacca Wash remains, it is possible that some weathering that afflicted that assemblage came about because of recent surface exposure prior to discovery.

All indications are that the Mancos assemblage was not exposed to weathering of more than a few years before deposition. Depositional burial for most of the assemblage could have immediately followed processing. For further discussion of the identification of weathering, see the section below on burning.

Observation 18: Preparation and Excavation Damage (Table 6.1)

Observation 18 records the presence or absence of preparation and/or excavation damage to the Mancos specimens caused by recovery and/or cleaning. This observation records surface modifications that are distinguishable based on their color, surface characteristics, and microscopic topography (Bromage, 1984). Most of the preparation damage on the collection seems to have come from digging implements coming into contact with the bones. It is easy to sort this kind of damage from perimortem bone modification. There was very little of this preparation or excavation damage on the Mancos assemblage, with only 65 specimens (3%) scored positively for this attribute. The higher values for metal tool damage to specimens reported by Potts (1982; 8%) for the FLK "Zinj" assemblage may relate to the latter bones being excavated from more consolidated sediment than the Mancos assemblage.

Observation 19: Random Striae (Table 6.1)

Observation 19 records the presence or absence of *random striae* on the Mancos bone surfaces. These are marks that may mimic cutmarks (Fiorillo, 1989; Olivier, 1989). Compared to human-produced cutmarks, however, random striae occur in highest frequency on the most elevated portions of an element. They are more superficial than cutmarks (usually less deeply incised). Quantification of mark depth was not attempted during the study, but the much deeper actual cutmarks (see below) made by stone tools have previ-

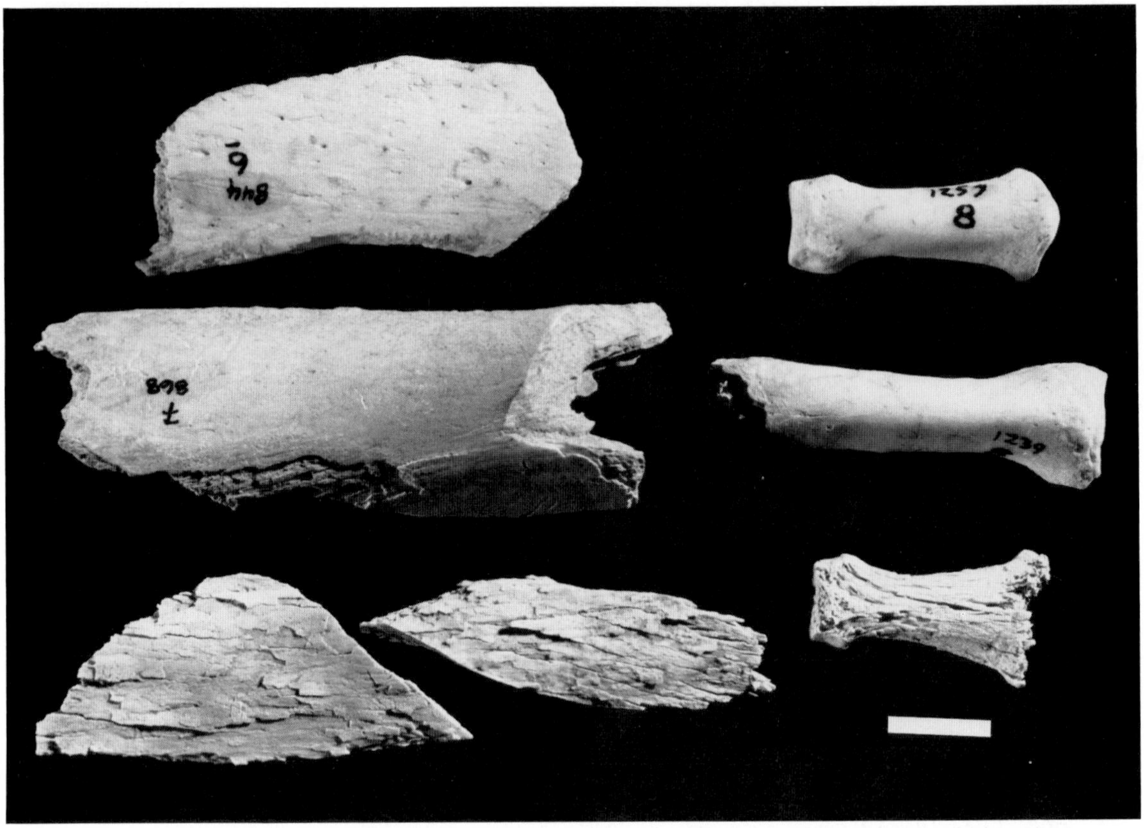

Fig. 6.9 The limb-bone shaft splinter and phalanx in the top row are unaltered (884, 1259). The splinter and phalanx in the central row show bone deterioration and exfoliation interpreted to represent exposure to high heat (burning, 868, 1239). The splinters and phalanx in the lower row show cracking and exfoliation typical of weathering damage. The latter three specimens were recovered from the surface of the backdirt at site 5MTUMR–2346 in July 1990 (unnumbered, not included in the 2,106 bones of the "assemblage"). None of the 2,106 specimens recovered during the excavation at Mancos showed this degree of weathering. Bar = 1 cm.

ously been noted to vary in depth according to the amount of force applied, and have been measured at a maximum depth of .21 mm (Walker and Long 1977). Besides being shallower than most cutmarks, random striae are random in placement and orientation with respect to soft tissue, and are often (but not always, see Haynes, 1988) associated with other parallel striae and most intensive on the most projecting areas of the bone. Random striae may be impossible to discriminate from hammerstone and anvil-related striae fields (percussion striae, see below). Some random striae are also microscopically difficult to distinguish from some human-induced cutmarks, but they do not show the patterning that usually characterizes true cutmarks (see the discussion below for a full account of cutmark recognition). An assessment of the context is, of course, critical in assessing these and other similar modifications to bones (Olivier, 1989).

Random striae are most often seen in bone assemblages from caves in which the specimens were subjected to animal movement and rockfall (Chmielewsky, 1958; Dixon, 1984; Olivier, 1989), but they also may be found on open-air assemblages; they have been observed paleontologically (Fiorillo, 1984, 1987a, 1987b, 1987c; Behrensmeyer *et al.*, 1989), documented actualistically (Haynes and Stanford, 1984; Andrews and Cook, 1985; Haynes, 1988; Avery, personal communication), and replicated experimentally (Myers *et al.*, 1980; Behrensmeyer *et al.*, 1986; Fiorillo, 1989). These marks are characteristic of bone surfaces in assemblages that have been in contact with a stony or sandy substrate. Random striae were not found on the Mancos assemblage. In conjunction with the near absence of rolling on the bones, the lack of demonstrable random striae on the collection suggests that postmortem trampling was minimal.

FRACTURE

Background

As discussed by Binford (1981), bone fracture patterns have been used uncritically by many workers positing the early presence of man in the New World and the behaviors of early man in the Old. The need for methods to discriminate between human and nonhuman bone fracture was stated by Nelson (1928:317): "But who is prepared to tell us of the finer distinctions—if any—between fresh bone crushed by a carnivore and fresh bone crushed by a man between two stones?" Many workers were willing to posit fracture criteria that allegedly allowed the diagnosis. Early experimentation by Martin (1910) was not followed up. Pei's 1938 caution that bone naturally breaks into regular forms deterred neither his contemporaries nor subsequent workers who accommodated the bone fragmentation to the human or protohuman agent thought responsible for the assemblage in question. It is remarkable that to this day, few controlled actualistic studies have been conducted. Appreciation of the extensive overlap between the results of carnivore- and hominid-induced bone fracture has come with the realization that multiple agents are often responsible for the formation and modification of archaeological bone assemblages. Koch (1986) and Lyman (1987a) provide summaries of research in this area; Potts (1988) contributes to and tabulates the discussions; and Binford (1978, 1981) and Haynes (1983) begin to research the problem actualistically.

Gifford (1981:405) succinctly summarizes the problems involved in fracture attribute recording as follows: "Nearly all the literature on bone fracture patterns has employed very general descriptive categories, often simply classifying gross fracture patterns according to the segment represented (e.g., proximal, distal, or shaft) or by general and often poorly defined descriptions of the shape of the break (e.g., spiral or transverse)." Gifford criticizes the Sadek-Kooros (1972, 1975) and Bonnichsen (1979) descriptive terminologies of bone damage, pointing out the fact that inadequate actualistic controls were employed by these workers. Indeed, a variety of templates for the recording of bone breakage attributes has been forwarded (Biddick and Tomenchuck, 1975; Tomenchuck and Tomenchuck, 1976; Ghaleb, 1983; Johnson, 1983; Aird, 1985). Many of these are detailed to the point of overkill, extremely cumbersome, and ill-suited for application across a range of taxa or to more than a few specimens. More to the point, however, because it is not yet clear what features discriminate among geological, carnivore-induced, and human-induced bone fracture, any standardization of attribute recording is premature. As Hill (1980:135) puts it: "Most existing classifications of bone damage are unsatisfactory in some way. The main determinant of the way a bone is damaged seems to be the anatomy of the bone itself. . . ."

Some of the observations recorded in the Mancos analysis, such as "spiral fracture," are widely reported in the archaeological literature. Others, such as "peeling," are never mentioned. Several of the fracture observations recorded here were chosen only because their presence/absence or frequencies have been interpreted by other workers as indicative of human modification of bone assemblages.

Observation 20: Fractured Tubular Element Portion (Table 6.1)

Data entered in Observations 20–22 describe which part of an element each specimen represents in its unconjoined state. These data are recorded for limbs, tubular hand and foot bones, and postcranial specimens classed as indeterminate by faunal analysis (LIMBS, HANDFOOT, SPLINTERS). Observation 20 records the *element portion* for tubular bones judged as identifiable (LIMBS, HANDFOOT) according to the following six-division, two–letter code: **PO** = proximal only, the specimen including some part of the articular surface or epiphyseal plate; **PS** = proximal plus shaft, the specimen retaining proximal end plus at least half the length of the original shaft; **DO** = distal only, defined as for proximal; **DS** = distal plus shaft, defined as for proximal plus shaft; **SO** = shaft only (the specimen lacks epiphysis or articular surface); and **CO** = complete (the specimen has greater than half of all three segments, proximal, distal, and shaft). The Observation 20 code is slightly different for "faunally" unidentified specimens (SPLINTERS), with **S** designating a true splinter without complete enclosure of the marrow cavity; **T** designating a bone tube (cylinder) with complete enclosure of the marrow cavity; and **0** designating a non-shaft fragment. Note that all specimens indicated by **S** would be considered by Brain (1981a) to be bone "flakes" (see below). This classification system was developed to compare the Mancos assemblage with others in an effort to assess quantitatively the pattern of limb-bone shaft entry.

Observation 21: Shaft Circumference (Table 6.1)

Observations 21 and 22 are recorded only for tubular bone specimens that are identifiable to a faunal analyst (LIMBS, HANDFOOT). Observation 21 provides an estimate of *shaft circumference*. The numbers refer to the maximum enclosure of marrow cavity at any point along the preserved shaft as follows: **1** = $<$ 50 percent of the shaft circumference preserved; **2** = $>$ 50 percent but $<$ 100 percent of the shaft circumference preserved; and **3** = marrow cavity completely ringed by preserved bone somewhere along the shaft. These data were recorded in an attempt to gauge the degree to which shafts versus ends of bones were targets of percussion-related entry. Carnivores with potential perimortem access to the assemblage (dogs, coyotes) were predicted to first attack the limb-bone ends and leave abundant bone cylinders.

Observation 22: Fractured Shaft Length (Table 6.1)

Observation 22 provides an estimate for preserved *length of shaft* as follows: **1** = < 50 percent of the complete bone length; **2** = > 50 percent of the complete bone length (but missing a significant part of the length); and **3** = complete length of the shaft preserved. The rationale for this attribute is like that for Observation 20.

Observations 23–25: Fracture Antiquity (Table 6.1)

Observations 23 to 25 are presence/absence indicators of *fracture antiquity*. Fractures on any specimen may be "ancient" (perimortem), "recent" (postdepositional), or impossible to diagnose (indeterminate). One specimen may show all three fracture types. Diagnosing time of fracture is usually a simple procedure in cases such as Mancos in which there has been minimal *in situ* fracture of specimens. The color of the broken surface relative to the external and internal bone surfaces is the best guide to fracture time determination (Lyman and O'Brien, 1987). Bone surfaces broken recently (during or after recovery) are recognizable because their color, texture, and patina are different from the original unbroken bone surfaces and because they lack any matrix. In the Mancos assemblage, fracture surfaces of indeterminate relative antiquity were rare. It should be noted that a positive indication for ancient fracture cannot distinguish whether the fracture occurred just before the time of death, at the time of death, or after the time of death of the individual. The failure of many studies to exclude recently broken specimens from quantitative summaries is a major source of bias in faunal analyses in which quantification of piece size has been undertaken (see Lyman and O'Brien, 1987).

Although not presently quantifiable or otherwise systematically recordable, it is appropriate to note that the fracture of the Mancos assemblage was overwhelmingly "perimortem" in the sense of Turner (1983), the bone obviously having been broken while fresh. This evaluation, a subjective one, is usually based on a "configurational" approach (see the section below on cutmarks for a parallel discussion and a definition of this term in a related context) in which the investigator evaluates the fracture surfaces on the archaeological specimen (whose fracture time is unknown) in light of actualistic knowledge about breakage of fresh versus ancient bone. As Lyman and Fox (1989) point out, however, bone can remain "fresh" for several years after death (or for even longer, depending on the environment of deposition).

Observations 26–28: Cranial Fracture (Table 6.1)

Observations 26 to 28 are specific to *cranial bone fracture*. Human cranial vault bone, relative to that of other mammals, is thick, covering a large brain volume. Forensic studies of blunt trauma to the frontal, parietal, occipital, and temporal bones have shown that fracture of the cranium can propagate either across a vault bone or along a suture. Fracture across a vault bone may result in the inner (endocranial) table of compact vault bone releasing from the spongy bone superficial to it (the diploe). This phenomenon occurs most often as a result of impact to the ectocranial surface, and is the functional equivalent to "peeling" associated with

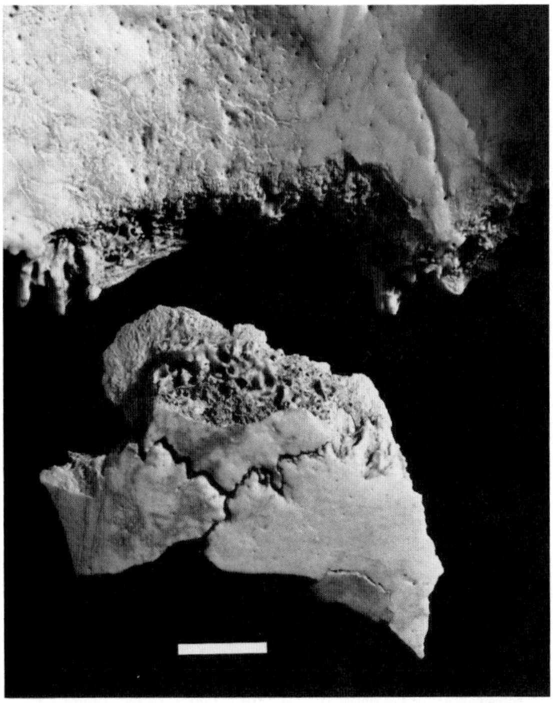

Fig. 6.10 Internal vault release on two frontal bones (1700 and 1670). Note that another view of the larger specimen is given in Figure 7.3, where the blow causing the fracture at the bregmatic edge is evidenced by the ectocranial surface being driven inward, as seen along the edge of the smaller fragment illustrated here. Bar = 1 cm.

postcranial fracture (see below). It is recorded in Observation 27 as the presence or absence of *internal vault release*. Internal vault release is a fracture pattern commonly recorded in forensic cases of cranial trauma (Spitz, 1980). The converse fracture type, in which ectocranial compact bone releases from its superficial interface with the spongy bone, is recorded in Observation 26 as the presence or absence of *external vault release*. The fracture type recorded as present or absent in Observation 28 is *sutural release*, in which fragmentation of the vault has been at least partially accomplished by fracture along the sutures. Sutural and internal vault release are the dominant fracture types seen in the Mancos cranial bones and these are illustrated in Figure 6.10.

Observations 29–36: Limb Shaft Fracture (Table 6.1)

Data for Observations 29 to 36, fractures of limb shafts, were gathered only for faunally identifiable specimens (LIMBS database). Observations 29 to 31 and 33 to 35 record whether the fracture in question is of modern, ancient, indeterminate, or composite nature as described above. For proximal (Observation 32) and distal (Observation 36) shaft fractures, the *fracture pattern* itself is recorded according to a two-letter code as follows: **ST** = step or olumnar; **SW** = sawtooth; **VS** = V-shaped; **DV** = double V; **TS** = typical spiral; **IS** = irregular spiral; **TP** = typical, smooth perpendicular; **IP** = irregular perpendicular; and **IR** = irregular, atypical. Only the **DV**, **TS**, **IS**, **TP**, and **IR** shapes were found in the Mancos collection, and these are illustrated in Figure 6.11. These shape types were chosen for convenience and ease of analysis and are based largely on the scheme used by Shipman *et al.* (1982). They carry with them, however, no implications regarding the agent of fracture. As noted earlier, fracture morphology has been used and abused for decades as an indicator of human bone modification. The most widely used term is the "spiral fracture," defined as a descriptive rather than explanatory term by Haynes (1988). His definition is adequate, except for the unnecessary inclusion of criteria on adjacent mammalian chewing damage. The spiral fracture type has convincingly been shown to result from both natural (carnivore, weathering) and human influence on bones (Leroi-

Fig. 6.11 Shaft breakage types. From left to right: double V (DV; 1159 fibula), typical spiral (TS; 703 radius), irregular spiral (IS; 704 radius), typical perpendicular (TP; 641 humerus), irregular (IR 588; humerus). Bar = 1 cm.

Gourhan, 1952; Hendey and Singer, 1965; Hill, 1976; Myers *et al.*, 1980; Haynes, 1980, 1983).

Observations 37–39: Fracture Products of Percussion (Table 6.1)

Observations 37 to 39 record the fracture products of percussion to bones. These data are recorded for tubular bones (LIMBS, HANDFOOT, SPLINTERS) because axial elements do not share these fracture characteristics. For cranial elements, it was only possible to identify this type of damage when the original flake adhered (see Observation 43 below) because fracture through the diploe of cranial elements differs in quality from fracture through shaft cortex. Observation 37 records the number of *outer conchoidal scars*—conchoidal flake scars on the external cortical surface of the bone shaft. Observation 38 records the number of *inner conchoidal scars*. Measurements of the sizes of these percussion scars were recorded elsewhere and are reported in Chapter 12. Examples of these scars are shown in Figure 6.12.

Hammerstone percussion damage has been investigated archaeologically, eth-

Fig. 6.12 Inner conchoidal percussion scars on right femoral specimens (from left to right: 752, 753, 789, 805, 847, 885). Note the wide range in dimensions of these scars. Bar = 1 cm.

nographically, and experimentally. In an assemblage for which the loading objective is the fracture of the bone shaft for marrow extraction, inner conchoidal scars are predicted to dominate quantitatively. Binford (1981) describes these as "percussion impact notches," Archer *et al.* (1980) as "fracture cones," Fisher (1984) as "impact cones," Bonnichsen (1979) and Villa *et al.* (1986a) as "impact scars"; Haynes and Stanford (1984) differentiate "impact notches" and "flake scars." On a more general level, Lyman (1987a) makes the distinction between "lineal" (linear) scratches ("striae") and marks created by impact ("scars").

Blumenschine (1988) follows several other authors (for instance, Bunn and Kroll, 1988; Bunn, 1989) in referring to these fracture features as "impact notches" and "carnivore notches." Blumenschine contends that these differ qualitatively. Brain (1981a) suggests that hyaena and hammerstone notches are difficult to sort; Binford (1981) and Haynes (1982a) illustrate such scars from carnivore-ravaged assemblages; and Maguire *et al.* (1980) illustrate the same internal conchoidal fracture pattern induced by hyaenas, pointing out that only 3 of 451 recorded cases came without other signs of carnivore damage on adjacent bone surfaces. Bunn (1981) contends that carnivore breakage of shafts is similar to hominid percussion, but that the scars and flakes are much smaller. He provides no data. Bunn (1982) notes that hammerstone and carnivore "impact" phenomena can overlap in quality and metrics. Thomas and Mayer (1983), on the other hand, illustrate impact scars that they interpret as the result of "channeling" by carnivores rather than marrow breakage by humans, citing Binford (1981) in support of their view that human-produced scars generally occur in isolation rather than in a series. They go on to attribute scars in their sample to carnivores based on the "alignment" of scars. This is a questionable practice, and the illustrated specimens attributed to carnivore damage (their Figure 186) are more probably the result of percussion directed by humans (for a discussion, see Lyman, 1987a).

My scoring of a conchoidal scar is based on the conchoidal nature of the entire scar, not simply the crescentic shape of the impact scar's edge when viewed from the direction of the blow. This distinction is not often made clear when various analysts count impact scars. I have avoided the terms "impact" and "percussion" in the classification of these marks simply because of the possible overlap between static (carnivore) and dynamic (hammerstone) loading in producing them. As discussed below, there are many inner conchoidal scars in the Mancos assemblage related to percussion of the long-bone shafts. Furthermore, it should be noted that the Mancos assemblage has several specimens for which hammerstone strike is indicated and the resulting internal conchoidal scar is extremely diffuse (extending for many centimeters along a broken edge). It is likely that there is a wide continuum in the shape of these scars, from the well-defined to the very diffuse, depending upon the bone struck and the characteristics of the blow and the percussor.

Observation 39, for counting the number of *true bone flakes*, does not appear in the Mancos databases because no true flakes were recovered in the Mancos assemblage (except as they adhered to larger specimens). Potts (1988) illustrates such flakes.

It should be noted that C.K. Brain consistently (for example, 1974, 1975a, 1981a) uses the term "bone flakes" to refer to specimens that are limb-bone shaft fragments lacking articular ends and preserving less than half the circumference of the long-bone shaft. Similar specimens with more than half the circumference Brain terms "shaft pieces." Few analysts have embraced this terminology (Voigt, 1983), and most workers prefer the term "splinters" to refer to both kinds of fragments. I follow this preference, defining bone flakes as those bone fragments exhibiting evidence of statically (for example, by tooth cusp) or dynamically (for example, by hammerstone strike) induced fracture that results in solid cortical bone flakes with the typical striking platform and bulb of percussion that characterize true lithic flakes for the archaeologist (see Blumenschine, 1988; Bunn, 1989).

Observation 40: Incipient Fracture Cracks (Table 6.1)

Data on attributes 40 through 44 were entered for all specimens even though these four attributes are rarely or never considered in faunal analysis. Observation 40

Fig. 6.13 Incipient fracture cracks on right femoral splinters (758, 798). Bar = 1 cm.

records the number of *incipient fracture cracks* that partly or completely cross a specimen. These cracks are not minor, hairline cracks except at their terminus on the bone. Fracture lines demarcating adhering flakes (see below) are not counted here. Incipient cracks are cracks judged to have been present when the bone was buried, and data for this attribute were considered worth gathering and examining for exploratory purposes. Incipient fracture cracks are illustrated in Figure 6.13.

Observation 41: Crushing (Table 6.1)

Observation 41 records the presence or absence of a very important phenomenon described here as *crushing*. This refers to the inward crushing or displacement of bone cortex into the spongy bone space within. It commonly occurs in the metaphyseal articular areas of the long bones, but it is seen in cranial and axial bones as well. It is simply the inward crushing of the outer bone cortex. It is probably the same thing that Binford (1981:164) terms "a splintered and depressed margin." This attribute is not recorded when the crushed area is small and surrounded by uncrushed bone surface as is true of carnivore-induced perforations or percussion pits (see below). Zimmerman *et al.* (1980) differentiate, but do not diagnose, "splintering" and "crushing" as damage that sorts between the fragmentation of fresh and dry bone, but these terms have not enjoyed any wider use in the literature and they are not used here in this sense. Turner (1983) refers to "percussion denting" and "crushing," but does not define these terms. His use suggests that our definitions of crushing match, whereas his term "percussion denting" probably corresponds to my term "hammerstone pit" (below). Crushing damage is a common and important damage type on the Mancos assemblage, and examples of it are shown in Figure 6.14.

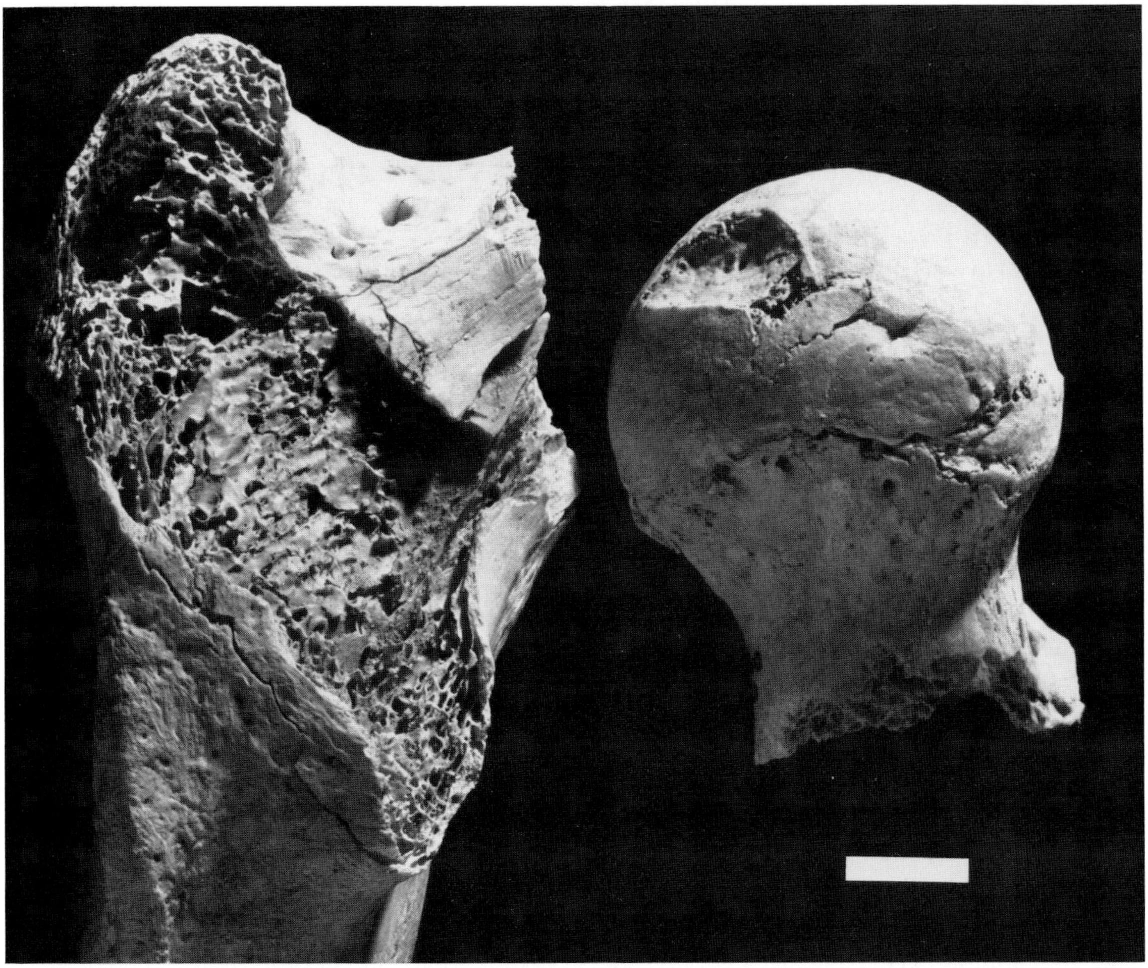

Fig. 6.14 Crushing on proximal femora (760, 870). Bar = 1 cm.

Observation 42: Percussion Pits (Table 6.1)

Observation 42 records the number of *percussion pits* on the bone surface. These pits vary in size and are usually recordable as discrete entities in which the hammerstone (this term used in a functional, not morphological sense) has struck solid cortical bone and scarred this bone without causing inward crushing of the bone cortex. Blumenschine and Selvaggio (1988) describe "percussion pits" as areas that are roughly circular in plan and capable of mimicking carnivore tooth pits. Their assessment of percussion damage is discussed below. Some percussion pits may be impossible to sort from pits created by carnivore tooth cusps, but the former will usually be more irregular in internal topography and outline (corresponding to the tip of the hammerstone that is only sometimes circular), and are usually accompanied by abrasion rather than by tooth striae (see below). Each hammerstone tip will leave a different ''signature'' on the bone, a fact that one of the conjoined human femora from the Yellow Jacket 5MT–3 assemblage shows very well—the hammerstone used on this femur shaft had a double tip, and the distinctive impressions left by its impact are seen in at least 5 separate places, proximal and distal, anterior and posterior, on this restored (by refitting) bone's shaft.

When percussion results in its desired effect (fracture of the bone), half the percussion pit is carried on one specimen, and half on another. Rather than recording these pits twice, I adopted the rule of recording percussion pits situated on a broken edge only in those cases in which I estimated that more than half the pit seemed to be present along the edge. In some cases, estimating how much of the total pit extended onto the missing adjacent shaft fragment was extremely difficult. This problem may result in an inaccurate estimate of the actual number of percussor blows.

A sharp-edged ''hammerstone'' (for example, a chopper used as a percussor to fracture a limb-bone shaft) will often leave a chopmark on the bone. Distinguishing between percussion pits and chopmarks associated with soft tissue removal is therefore rendered extremely difficult, and must be constrained by functional considerations alone, because the resulting mark morphologies will often be indistinguishable. The distinction between the two is sometimes aided by the fact that it is possible to see several successive ''failed'' percussion pits adjacent to the pit associated with the bone fracture. The problem of distinguishing percussion pits from chopmarks is most likely to have artificially lowered the percussion pit frequencies in the Mancos data.

Percussion pits are present, but not particularly common on the Mancos assemblage. They are illustrated in Figures 6.15 and 6.16.

Observation 43: Adhering Flakes (Table 6.1)

Observation 43 records the number of *adhering flakes*, the number of true bone flakes (see above) that adhere to the fracture surface of a specimen. These flakes are set off by curving incipient fracture lines, often hairline, which subparallel the fracture edge. They are often adjacent to points of percussion. Villa *et al.* (1986a:436) describe ''wide impact scars'' in about 20 percent of the limb bones in one of their samples: ''. . . half of these are characterized by broad, thin spalls still attached to the bone, with platforms bounded by arcuate fissure lines behind the point of impact.'' These adhering flakes are present at highest frequencies on the cranial vault bones and shaft fragments of the Mancos assemblage. They are illustrated in Figure 6.17.

Observation 44: Peeling (Table 6.1)

Observation 44 records a phenomenon described here as *peeling*. The most effective way to visualize this is to imagine bending a popsicle stick or a small fresh twig from a tree branch between two hands. Stripped of its bark, the twig can be bent until it snaps. When the wood is fresh, however, the two pieces will tend to remain attached by a fibrous connection until ''peeled'' apart. The peeling apart of the two pieces leaves a distinctive pattern (a roughened surface with parallel grooves left as the two halves are pulled apart). This pattern observed on wood is very similar to the same phenomenon on fractured and peeled fresh bone. This

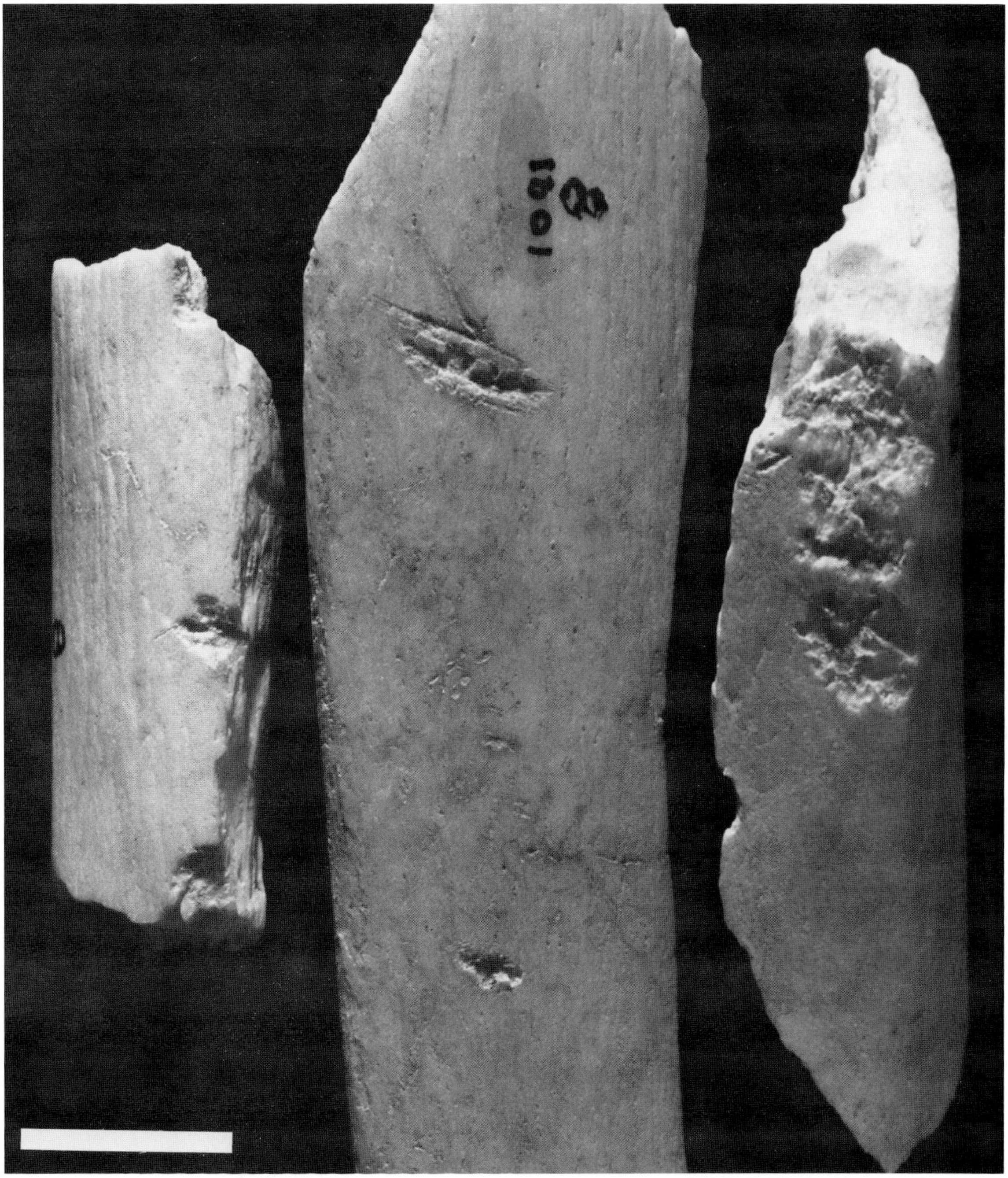

Fig. 6.15 Percussion pits on the eternal surface of long-bone shafts (IP3 1552, 1531; femur splinter 1091, center). Note the linearity in some of these impact marks. See the text for a discussion of diagnosing percussion marks and chopmarks. Bar = 1 cm.

Fig. 6.16 Scanning Electron Micrograph of a percussion mark on femur specimen 870.

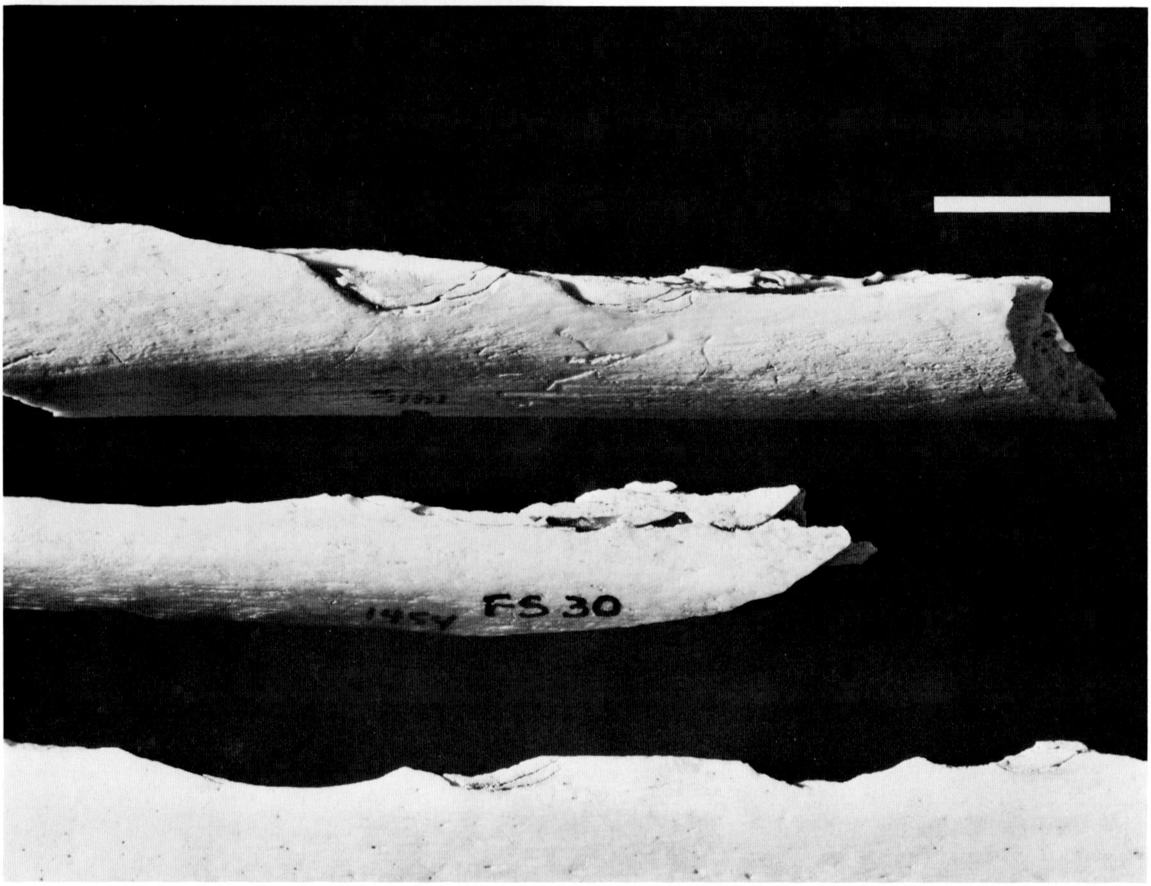

Fig. 6.17 Adhering flakes on long-bone shaft fragments (IP2 1416, top; humeral splinter 648, middle bottom; IP2 1454). Bar = 1 cm.

fracture-related pattern in fibrous material, including bone, is described as "peeling" and recorded as present or absent for each Mancos specimen. Evidence can be on the external or internal bone surface. Peeling is common on the Mancos assemblage and can be used to judge the direction of force applied to some bones during their fracture. Examples of peeling on this assemblage are illustrated in Figure 6.18.

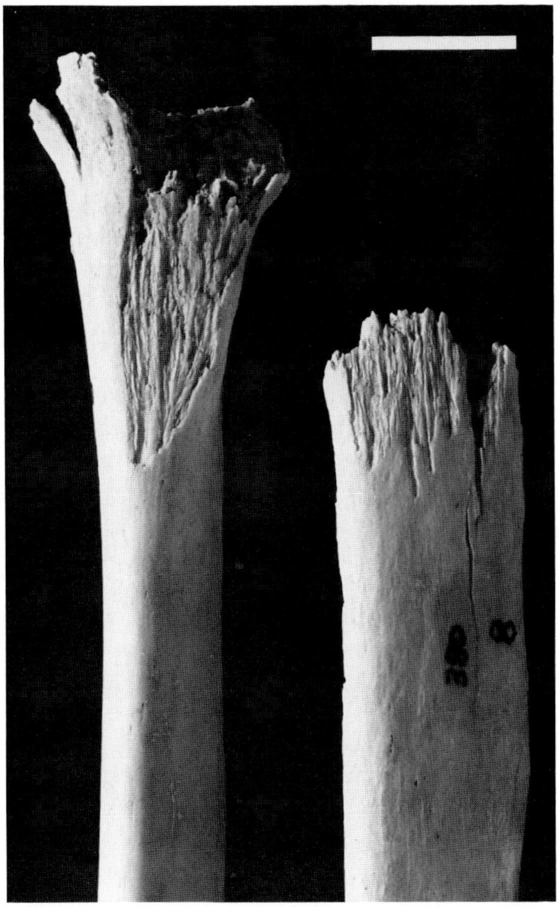

Fig. 6.18 Peeling on a rib and proximal ulna (380; 671). Bar = 1 cm.

TOOL-INDUCED MODIFICATIONS: CUTMARKS, CHOPMARKS, AND SCRAPEMARKS

Background

Since well before the turn of the century, prehistorians have used cutmarks on bone surfaces to infer human activities in the past (for example, Lartet, 1860). As Lyman's excellent recent review of research in this area notes (1987a:260); "Reference to butchering marks became commonplace in the late 1960s, and today these marks form a major portion of the data used in butchery analysis. . . ." Early work by Guilday *et al.* (1962), Guilday (1963), and Parmalee (1965) set standards for cutmark data collection in faunal analysis, with close attention paid to the goal of elucidating the butchery process based on the marks. As Lyman notes, the criteria used by these workers to identify butchery marks were difficult to operationalize analytically, and the rise of critical studies of early man in both the New and Old Worlds in the 1970s brought an intense focus on the unit of analysis, the mark itself.

Much of a voluminous zooarchaeological literature has been concerned with cutmarks (slicing marks) to the exclusion of other marks made by sharp-edged objects such as bone, shell, and bamboo (Toth, 1989). Much of the literature revolves around the identification of cutmarks on fossilized ungulate bones from early archaeological occurrences in eastern Africa. At the center of the debate has been the argument about how to distinguish human-created cutmarks from a host of other marks made by biological and physical agents such as carnivore and rodent tooth scratches, root etching, abrasion, trampling marks, preparation scratches, vascular grooves, and so on (Potts and Shipman, 1981; Shipman and Rose, 1984). Some workers contend that macroscopic examination of these linear features is sufficient to diagnose cutmarks (Bunn, 1981; Binford and Stone, 1986). Others hold that many different alterations to bone surfaces are macroscopically similar to cutmarks, requiring a microscopic approach (Shipman, 1981a, 1988). Different researchers draw different conclusions regarding cutmark frequency (Guthrie, 1982; Shipman, 1983, 1986).

Difficulty in the identification of the various kinds of trauma on bones has led some investigators to employ the scanning electron microscope, or SEM (Shipman, 1981a; Potts and Shipman, 1981; Shipman and Rose, 1983; Cook, 1986; Potts, 1987) to enhance viewing of damaged bone surfaces. With the concern for discriminating between human-induced cutmarks and other "natural" damage, attributes visible in the SEM were put forward as unambiguous markers of human-induced cutmarks. For some, the focus on cutmarks was narrowed appreciably by considering only the features visible within the boundaries of the SEM image. The SEM was heralded as able to distinguish directionality of cutmarks (Bromage and Boyde, 1984) and to sort cutmarks made on fresh versus dried bone tissue (Russell *et al.*, 1985; Shipman, 1987). Many criteria put forward as diagnostic of human-induced cutmarks have been shown to be otherwise by further work (Eickhoff and Herrmann, 1985; Andrews and Cook, 1985; Behrensmeyer *et al.*, 1986; Haynes, 1988; Shipman, 1988). What began as a hunt for the diagnostics to resolve ambiguity has led to even more ambiguity. As Lyman perceived in 1982 and later charitably stated (1987a:281); ". . . exclusive focus on the morphology of marks (whether macroscopic or microscopic) on bones can be fraught with difficulties." Olivier (1989) provides further insight on the issue, and Lyman (1987a) provides a long summary of signature criteria for marks on bones in his Table 5.6. White summarizes some of the problems in his work on the Bodo cranium (1985:18–19):

> The features observed in slicing marks (striations within striations, variable "V"-shapes, shoulder effects) are all explained by the nature of the stone tool edge. Each microscopic "peak" or irregularity along the stone tool edge has the potential to make its own impression as the tool edge contacts and is drawn across the bone. The "diagnostic" nature of cutmarks, both scraping and slicing, is thus simply the reflection of the mechanical interaction of bone and stone. It is important to note however, that the nature of this relationship carries with it certain consequences. For instance, it is possible for non-hominid agencies to create marks which mimic those produced by hominids using stone tools. Thus, occasional stray marks are predicted to occur on bones which have come into contact with stones during trampling by other organisms or by hydraulic movement. Such "accidental" marks may be morphologically similar to hominid-induced cutmarks, particularly when only short segments of the marks are considered under the microscope. . . . It is already evident on simple theoretical grounds that there will be no absolutely diagnostic set of criteria that will always allow a clear choice between causal agents for single striae.

Given this background, how, in analytical terms, are cutmarks to be recognized (diagnosed)? Shipman (1986:29), the main advocate of the SEM approach, suggests that the use of this instrument is ". . . not generally warranted if (1) the assemblage was created or modified by *Homo sapiens*, a species of known habits and (2) the observed patterning of presumed cut marks conforms to ethnographic reports for that region." This reasoning is completely unacceptable in an archaeological context for which knowledge about past behavior is not presumed before the analysis. More pragmatically, Shipman has employed an SEM sampling approach to confirm her diagnosis of cutmarks in archaeological assemblages (Villa *et al.*, 1986a).

Morlan (1984) suggests that chewing and cutting marks may be distinguished by a combination of attributes that includes the anatomical element marked, the position of the mark on the element, the gross and microscopic morphology of the mark, and a comparison between the contour of the mark and that of the bone surface. These are the basic recognition criteria that archaeologists have used for decades. Haynes and Stanford (1984:226) characterize cutmarks as follows:

> Cut marks should be found on parts of bones where a sharp edge would have been necessary to separate meat from bone, bone from bone, or hide from carcass. Cut marks should be clean incisions with V-shaped cross sections. True cut marks should be discontinuous or unconformable on bone surfaces where the topography is uneven, because inflexible tool edges skip over minor depressions when applied to bone surfaces. It must be kept in mind that cut marks are the result of plausible, practical human motor actions such as sawing, scraping, or slicing. Most butchering cut marks are sets of a few short, parallel, linear incisions.

Olsen and Shipman (1988:549) urge investigators to examine the sedimentary context of the assemblage under consideration, and to examine a range of features for each possible cutmark. These include "frequency of modified bone in the assemblage; number of marks per bone and their locations on the bone; their orientation; their morphology and depth; and their association with polish."

Binford (1985) has championed what he terms a "configurational approach" to cutmark recognition, an approach based on experience. He is skeptical of Shipman's claims for lack of ambiguity and he disagrees with Bunn's differentiation between cutmarks and the chewing marks left by young carnivores. Binford and Stone (1986:472) provide their reaction to the recent work described above as follows:

> Recently there has been a "high-tech" craze among many researchers of East African materials who have sought to develop identification procedures enabling them to recognize cut marks solely in terms of the formal properties of a single, discrete mark. . . . The operational procedure for generating data is an expensive, high-tech process. . . . The attempt to discriminate was in my opinion made at the wrong observational level. Discrimination must rest in a general understanding of the patterned placement of marks, their form relative to one another, and their associations with other types of marks, such as pitting, scooping out, breakage, and, most important, anatomical placement and shape of the bone surface. For several years I have been engaged in building up this type of knowledge (see Binford 1981 and more to come), and I am very confident of my ability to recognize *patterned* bone modification by rodents of many types, carnivores, and tool-using humans, as well as that produced by trampling. I have referred earlier to this as a configurational approach to data production as opposed to approaches that seek to identify a single mark by its internal morphology alone. . . . What provides a configurational approach with increasing reliability is the demonstration through *comparative studies* that the patterns are redundant and recurrent and covary with other indicators of the agents one infers from the patterns.

Experience of the investigator, as discussed above in matters of element and taxonomic identification, is notably difficult to control for. Martin (1907), Binford (1981), Ubelaker (1989), and a host of other investigators provide illustrations of cutmarks, and the same is done here. The author is confident in his ability to identify cutmarks accurately, and this confidence is based on comparative studies, experimentation, and blind tests. In fact, such a diagnosis is not difficult given familiarity with bone modifications of known origin (Toth and White, in preparation).

My approach to cutmark (synonymous with slicing marks; a "sawing" motion of a blade causes multiple slicing marks) identification in the Mancos assemblage was conservative. Any mark that was ambiguous as to origin was not identified as a cutmark. I used a configurational approach supplemented by SEM analysis designed to illustrate the microscopic detail of the cutmarks found on the assemblage. All the observations in this part of the Mancos analysis are described functionally based on the inferred force directed at the bone via a stone tool. Criteria for diagnosing cutmarks are given below. Shipman (1988) and Villa *et al.* (1986) claim to be able to diagnose delayed from immediate processing by microscopic analysis of cutmarks, but no criteria have been published to support this distinction, and I have not attempted to make such a diagnosis.

Observations 45 to 49 involve *cutmarks*, Observations 50–54 involve *chopmarks*, and Observations 55 to 59 involve *scrapemarks*. This division is widely used in faunal analysis. Discussion of chopmarks and slicing marks appears in the observation descriptions below.

Observations 45–49: Cutmarks (Table 6.1)

Observations 45 to 48 were made only for faunally identifiable tubular bones (HANDFOOT and LIMBS). They record the *number of cutmarks* by anatomical region. Elements of cutmarks such as barbs and shoulder effects (Shipman and Rose, 1983) assisted in diagnosing cutmarks, but were not recorded separately. Anatomical regions were defined as follows: proximal = the proximal quarter of the bone's length (shaft and end); distal = the distal quarter of the bone's length (shaft and end); and shaft = the central half of the bone. Observation 49 records the number of cutmarks on all other bone specimens (specimens in SPLINTERS, AXIAL, CRANIAL).

Identifying cutmarks is relatively easy, whereas counting them is exceedingly difficult. In a cluster of roughly parallel marks, deciding exactly which marks to count individually as cutmarks becomes arbitrary. For this reason, the values entered in Observations 45 to 49 must be considered approximate. I attempted to estimate the number of cutting strokes involved in the production of each cutmark cluster, and rough estimates are indicated by the numbers entered. Examples of cutmarks identified on specimens in the Mancos assemblage are illustrated in Figures 6.19 and 6.20.

Observations 50–54: Chopmarks (Table 6.1)

Observations 50 to 54 record the *number of chopmarks*. Shipman (1981a:366) defines these marks as follows: "*Chopping marks* are produced in a manner functionally similar to that responsible for punctures: a stone artifact is used to strike a bone surface with a blow directed roughly perpendicular to the bone surface. . . . Chopping marks are broad and V-shaped in cross section. . . ." Cook (1986:151) defines chopping marks as follows: "Chopping marks are created by the impact of the edge of a stone artefact used

Fig. 6.19 Cutmarks on shaft fragments (femur splinter 928; clavicle 551; IP3 1510). Bar = 1 cm.

with a striking action. They may be simply characterised as broad wedge shaped depressed fractures. . . ." Voigt (1983) uses the term similarly, separating it from "chisel" marks or "cleancuts." Most faunal analysts follow these definitions of chopmarks (Noe-Nyggard, 1989), and there is little disagreement over their iden-

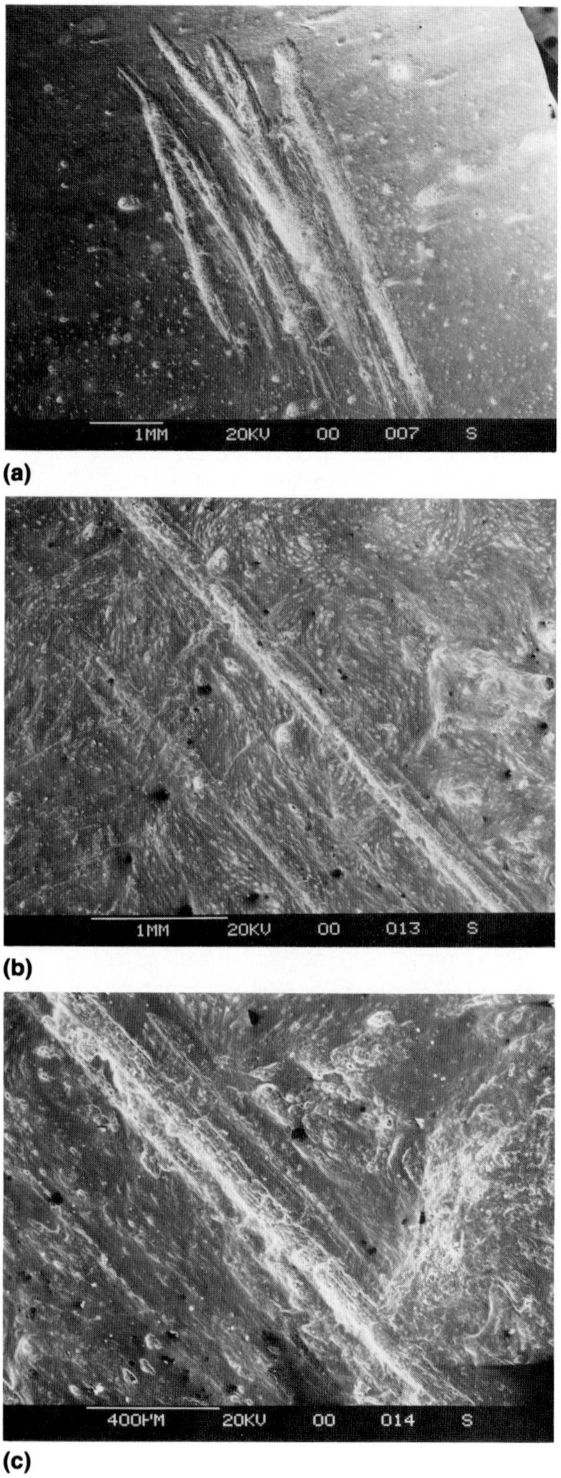

Fig. 6.20 Scanning Electron Micrograph of transverse cutmarks on distal humerus specimen 588 (a) (see Figure 9.5 for a photograph). Scanning Electron Micrographs of cutmarks on frontal specimen 1670 (b and c).

tification. Binford (1984) and Flinn *et al.* (1976) differ only in terminology, describing and illustrating such marks as "*hackmarks*."

As discussed above, however, there remains a problem that few have satisfactorily considered. This concerns the ambiguity between some percussion pits and hackmarks. All agree that both marks are made by percussion. If we define a "hammerstone" functionally as a percussor, when percussion by a *V-edged hammerstone* fails to crack the bone, it is obvious that a V-shaped pit will result. Should this be termed a percussion pit or a chopmark? Ambiguity persists because such marks are functional impact points directed at bone fracture, whereas morphologically, they are chopmarks. In practice, it may be possible to reduce the ambiguity in a functional sense by defining chopmarks to be the result of soft tissue manipulation and percussion pits to be the result of blows aimed at bone fracture. Nonetheless, for reasons outlined here, I am very skeptical of my ability to diagnose chopmarks and percussion scars made by a sharp percussor. The data recorded for Mancos should be used with these cautions in mind. Examples of Mancos chopmarks are shown in Figure 6.21.

Observations 55–59: Scraping Marks (Table 6.1)

Observations 55 to 59 record the presence or absence of scraping marks on bone surfaces associated with the functional removal of tissue, particularly periosteum, from the surface of a bone. Shipman

Fig. 6.21 Chopmarks on a tibia fragment (1037). Bar = 1 cm.

(1981a:369) defines the production of scraping marks as follows:

> They are produced by drawing an artifact across a bone surface in a direction roughly perpendicular to the long axis of the edge. The result is a dense series of usually superficial, parallel striations across a broad area of bone. . . . In contrast to slicing marks, then, scraping marks are not confined to a main groove.

Cook (1986) and Noe-Nyggard (1989) offer similar descriptions, and Binford (1981) describes and illustrates these marks, attributing them to periosteum removal. Cook points out the potential for human-induced scrapemarks to be mimicked by scrapes produced by trampling. Such confusion might result from a microscopic focus on a small sample, but as Cook notes, scrapemarks generally differ from random or percussion striae in being longer and more patterned. In the Mancos assemblage, very little typical scraping by an implement held perpendicular to a bone was noted. Rather, examples of scraping caused by oblique contact with a rough surface were noted. These are similar to percussion striae described below, but, based on the location and directionality of the marks, the proposed objective of the contact was not judged to be fracture of the bone in these cases; these marks were therefore described as scraping marks. Nothing like the periosteal removal by scraping described by Binford was observed on the Mancos assemblage. An example of scraping damage is illustrated in Figure 6.22. On a presence/absence basis, the Mancos assemblage shows far more cutmarks than chopmarks or scraping marks.

Observations 45–49: Percussion Striae (Table 6.1)

It was noted above that when the surface of a bone is struck by or dragged along an

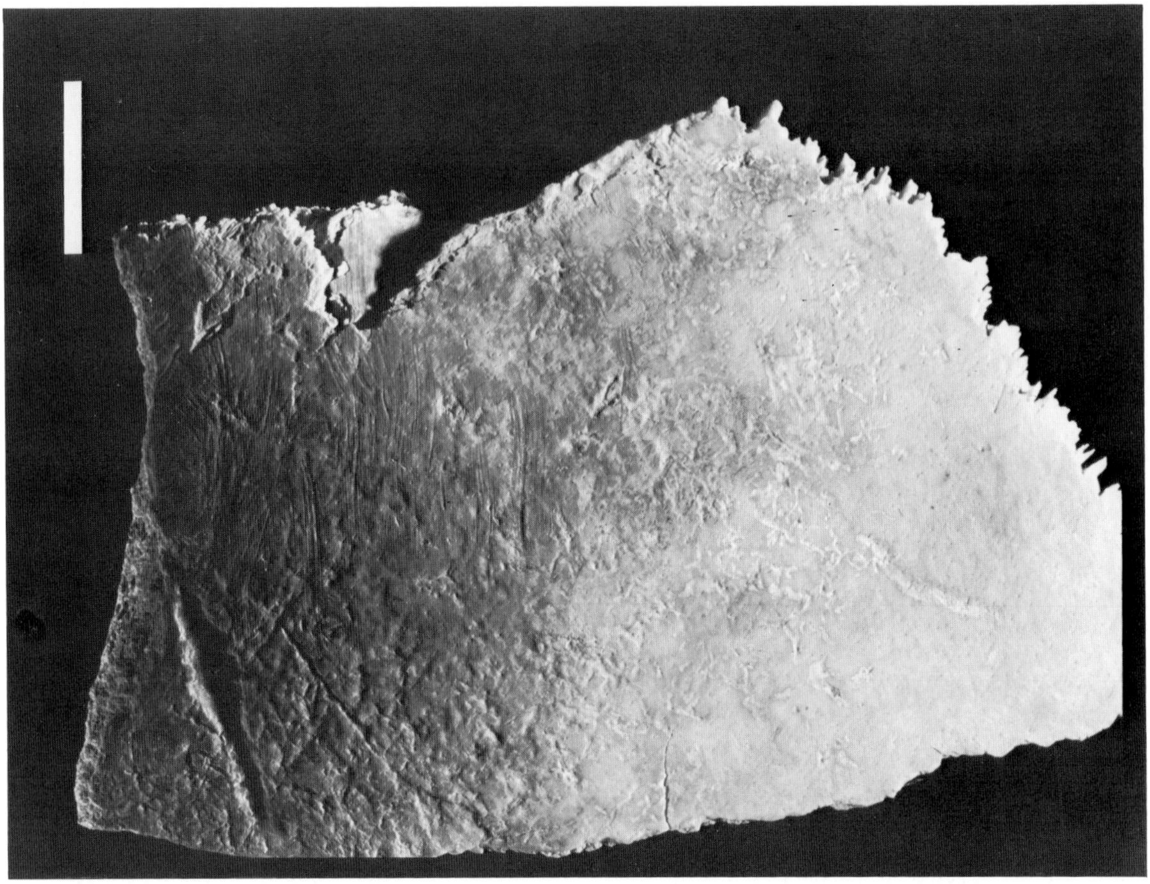

Fig. 6.22 Scraping on an immature frontal (1752). Bar = 1 cm.

irregular stone surface, pits and one or more grooves of varying dimensions may result. *Dragging* contact may have nothing to do with human intervention, and such surface modification I have termed "random striae" (see Observation 19 above). Alternatively, the dragging contact between a bone and a stone edge may be directed by a human hand, resulting in striae on the bone surface that I refer to as "cutmarks" and "scrapemarks." Because the contacting materials in both instances are the same, the resulting marks may sometimes be microscopically identical. Similarly, the *impact* of a stone on a bone surface, whether directed by gravity (rarely) or by a human hand, may cause percussion pits (hammerstone or anvil) or chopmarks. During stone-on-bone contact percussion pits, fracture impact scars, and a class of damage described here as *percussion striae* are often produced. These aid in the diagnosis of human-implemented bone fracture.

A considerable amount of attention has been paid to the conchoidal fracture and surface notching caused by percussion fracture of bones. The dynamic hammerstone loading of bones resting on an anvil may result in a primary conchoidal scar, particularly in the shaft portions of long bones. A similar, but less distinct fracture on the anvil side of the bone (''contre-coup'' marks; Leroi-Gourhan and Brezillon, 1972) also may result. In those rare instances in which the bone does not slip on either the anvil or hammerstone surface during impact, the resulting percussion pits are unaccompanied by striations caused by the stone surface scratching the bone. Such striae ''fields,'' however, occur on impact-fractured assemblages and were described and illustrated by Turner (1983:236) as ''anvil scratches,'' ''. . . tightly compacted fine multiple incisions occur only in association with an impact fracture.'' Microscopically these striae fields are indistinguishable from marks described as resulting from dragging contact with stone surfaces during trampling and gravitational movement (Cook, 1986). Investigators have focused on the lone, isolated mark in trampling studies to show its microscopic similarity to human cutmarks (Behrensmeyer *et al.*, 1986; Haynes, 1988), but such marks clearly represent one end of a continuum on whose other end lie striae fields that are indistinguishable from human-induced percussion striae.

Blumenschine and Selvaggio (1988) have recently rediscovered percussion striae and describe them as a ''new diagnostic'' of human behavior. Their terminology lumps the striae and the percussion pits into a single inappropriate category, ''percussion marks.'' My analysis keeps these separate, with the recognition that they are part of the same phenomenon and may overlap on the bone. The most valuable parts of Blumenschine and Selvaggio's work are the experimental control over these marks and the recognition that the *association* of percussion striae and pits with internal conchoidal flake scars is a very good diagnostic tool for separating carnivore from hominid fracture of bone. Further work in this area that measures the direction of the striae relative to the long axis of long bones may ultimately afford a technique through which to distinguish, by frequency, between random striae (see above, and Fiorillo, 1989) and percussion striae. Meanwhile, the former are predicted to concentrate on the more prominent areas of a bone and be less frequently associated with fracture of the bone, whereas the latter are predicted to focus on the areas where percussion leads to exposure of marrow.

As Blumenschine and Selvaggio (1988: 764) indicate, percussion striae may microscopically mimic cutmarks or random striae caused by trampling, particularly when adjacent pits and conchoidal scars are not considered. They assert that ''Percussion microstriations differ from stone tool-cut marks in being shallower, narrower, and usually shorter and occurring in dense unidirectional patches.'' Nevertheless, microscopic assessment of anvil- or hammerstone-induced percussion striae shows considerable overlap of characteristics with actual cutmark damage. The reportedly high frequency of ''cutmarks'' (chopping and slicing marks) on ''non-meaty,'' midshaft areas of Plio-Pleistocene and more recent archaeological bones (Potts and Shipman, 1981; Potts, 1982; Marshall, 1986b) may reflect this overlap. Rather than explaining such marks as reflecting skin and ligament procurement for tying bundles together (Shipman in Lewin, 1981; Shipman, 1984; but see Binford, 1985) or skin peeling and/or detachment (Behrensmeyer, 1987), it seems possible that at least some of these ''cutmarks'' are damage patterns (percussion striae) incidental to percussion fracture of the bones.

Observations on percussion striae are entered as numbers 60 to 64 in Appendix

2 according to the same distributional format described for Observations 45 to 59 above. The Mancos assemblage exhibits an abundance of percussion striae associated with crushing and conchoidal fracture scars. These are illustrated in Figures 6.23 through 6.26.

MAMMALIAN CHEWING

Background

Evidence of mammalian chewing on bones has been well documented since Buckland's pioneering work in 1822. Pei's (1938) caution that errors of interpretation can result from carnivore damage being attributed to human agents has been neglected by a few workers (for example, Singer, 1956; Straus, 1957), but the last two decades of experimental and archaeological studies in this area have significantly advanced knowledge, showing a wide range of damage types resulting from mammalian chewing. The effects of carnivores on element representation and element portion representation in the faunal record of archaeological sites have been widely noted and debated (Lyon, 1970; Casteel, 1971; Binford, 1981). Attributes allowing the faunal analyst to recognize carnivore, rodent, and even ungulate chewing damage on bone assemblages have been identified, described, and illustrated both actualistically (Bonnichsen, 1973; Richardson, 1980; Haynes, 1980, 1981, 1982a, 1983; Binford, 1978, 1981; Cook, 1986) and archaeologically (Pei, 1938; Bunn, 1981; Scott and Klein, 1981; Wilson, 1983). Mammalian chewing has even been documented on human bones in forensic (Haglund *et al.*, 1988) and archaeological (Constandse-Westermann and Meiklejohn, 1979; Gregg *et al.*,

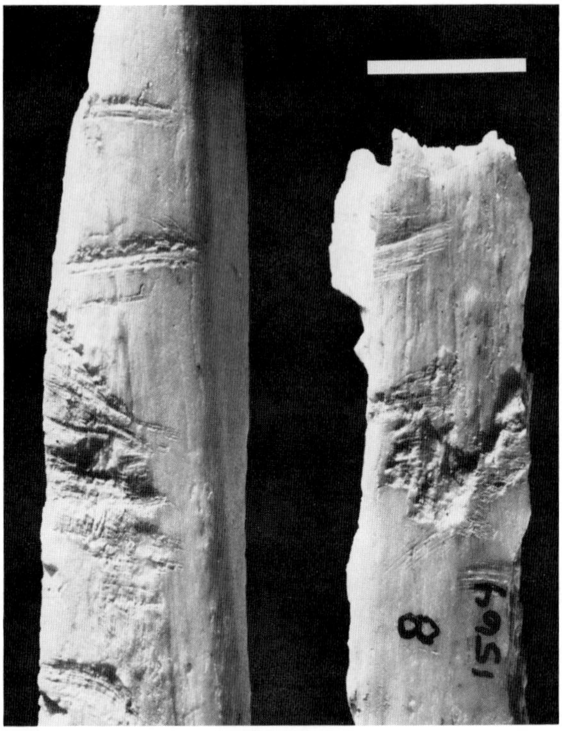

Fig. 6.23 Hammerstone pit associated with percussion striae on long-bone shaft fragments (IP3 1564 and 1515). Bar = 1 cm.

Fig. 6.24 Percussion striae on left femur splinters (875 and 892). Bar = 1 cm.

Fig. 6.25 Percussion striae and cutmarks on a femur splinter. Very oblique light is needed to observe the percussion striae because they are more superficial than cutmarks (femur 900). Bar = 1 cm.

1981; Turner, 1983; Binford, 1984; Milner and Smith, 1989) contexts.

Some investigators use the term "gnawing" to describe any damage caused by teeth of rodents, carnivores, ungulates, and even humans (Gifford, 1981; Binford, 1981; Turner, 1983; Bunn and Kroll, 1986). Other workers are explicit in applying the term "gnawing" only to the damage caused by rodent incisor chewing (Johnson, 1983; Shipman, 1981a). Because of the ambiguity surrounding the term "gnawing," this term is used here only when accompanied by the word "rodent" in order to avoid confusion. In the Mancos analysis, individual mammalian chewing attributes such as scooping, channeling, chipping back, scoring, furrowing, or abrasion (Binford, 1981) were not recorded independently. Instead, three main, discrete types of carnivore damage were chosen, employing a configurational approach when any ambiguity about the agent of modification was involved. The carnivore damage patterns recorded in the Mancos analysis were tooth scratches, tooth punctures, and tooth pits. These are described below and are agreed upon as specific damage types by all investigators (for example, Binford, 1981; Shipman, 1981a; Cook, 1986; Lyman, 1987a; and see Marshall, 1989 for a summary of recent descriptions of carnivore damage). I will not describe these damage types below because they are so well covered in these other works. I have not included Todd's (1987) "erose" category. Rodent gnawing,

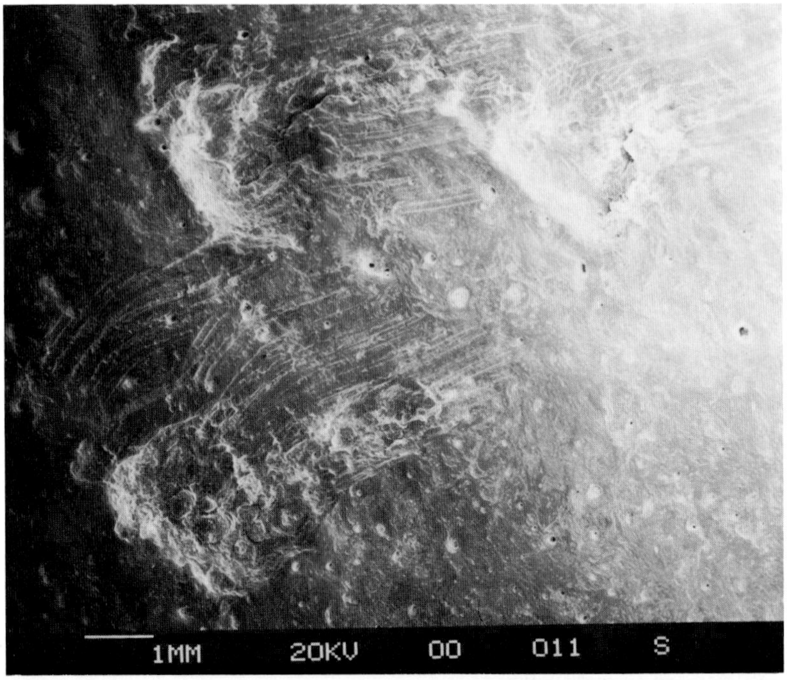

(a)

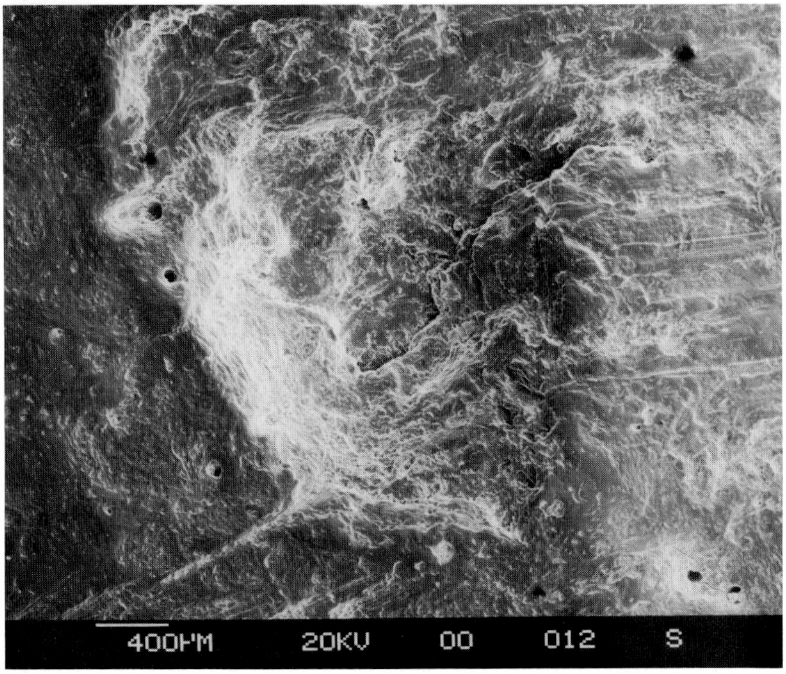

(b)

Fig. 6.26 Scanning Electron Micrographs of hammerstone pits and associated percussion striae on frontal specimen 1661 (a and b) (see Figure 8.4 for a photograph of this percussion-related modification).

which is also a distinctive, readily diagnosed pattern, was recorded as a separate observation.

Before describing the observations made on mammalian chewing, however, it is important to consider what is known about the signature of a particular mammal's chewing, human chewing, on bone. This is an extremely underdeveloped, but important area of potential actualistic research. An early, amusing, and still current reference to the problem of differentiating human and carnivore chewmarks on archaeological bone assemblages is Mark Twain's 1871 comment: "If the student should ask me how the paleontologist tells the difference between hyaena and human teeth-marks on a *bone*, and particularly a bone that has been rotting in a cave since the everlasting hills were builded, I should answer that I don't know" (in Neider, 1961:136).

Brain (1981a), to separate the damage done to bones by Hottentot dogs from that created by the Hottentots themselves, gave one subadult male goat to these people. They returned the bones to him after traditional processing and consumption of the animal. Brain's concern was more with element deletion than surface damage, but Maguire *et al.* (1980) describe these goat remains, referring to the considerable amount of damage to the bones done by bunodont human teeth. Gifford-Gonzalez (1989a) describes, for goat bones, damage that she attributes to humans. She notes the difficulty of finding incontrovertible evidence of human modification as opposed to carnivore gnawing. Binford (1981) describes his results as paralleling those of Maguire *et al.*, noting the absence of punctures and scoring on human-chewed bones. Binford notes that data from carefully controlled studies are required (1981:148) ". . . before tooth modifications on bones can be assigned to nonhuman agents in a totally reliable manner." In 1984, however, Binford described and illustrated damage on archaeological bone specimens from Klasies River as hominid toothmarks!

It is evident from simple mechanical considerations that substantial overlap between human and carnivore chewing damage on bones will be shown by future research in this area. Patterned incisal striations resulting from periosteum removal by hominids may be the most appropriate kind of damage to examine from the point of view of diagnostics. Meanwhile, tooth striae, punctures, and tooth pits should not be attributed to taxon in archaeological bone assemblages until further actualistic work is completed. Chapter 12 deals with the issue of possible human chewing damage to specimens in the Mancos assemblage.

Observations 65–80: Nonhuman Chewing Damage (Table 6.1)

Observations 65 to 79 were recorded for various elements and element parts in the same manner that other modifications described above were recorded. Observations 65 to 69 record the number of tooth scratches. Observations 70 to 74 record the number of tooth punctures. Observations 75 to 79 record the number of pits made by teeth. The latter damage might be mistaken for hammerstone pits, but the configuration of other damage types attributable exclusively to mammalian chewing on the specimen usually renders diagnosis straightforward. Finally, Observation 80 records the presence or absence of rodent gnawing on a specimen. In the Mancos assemblage, no nonhuman mammalian chewing attributes were recorded because the only nonhuman mammalian chewing was recent rodent gnawing of a few fragments. The assemblage of human bones is notable for the absence of any carnivore damage.

BURNING

Background

In contrast to the extensive research that has identified diagnostic criteria of mammalian chewing damage to bones, issues of thermal alteration of faunal remains are unsettled, and this area of study is a relatively immature one. This is true despite early (Black, 1931) and more recent (James, 1989) claims about the antiquity of fire in prehistory, and Brothwell's (1961) early plea for more research on burned bone. The recognition of burning damage to bones is important in revealing food-processing strategies. Additionally, assessment of this damage on a spatial basis, with special attention to *in situ* burning associated with hearths or other features, can assist in taphonomic and conjoining studies using vertebrate remains. Buikstra and Swegle (1989) provide an introductory orientation to the modification of bone by heat.

Marshall (1989) offers a sound point of departure for any discussion of thermally induced bone modification in the archaeological record, differentiating between *cooking* (preparation for eating by a heating process, such as boiling, roasting, or baking), *heating* (making warm or hot), and *burning* (injuring or damaging by exposure to fire/heat). In an archaeological bone assemblage, cooking and heating must be inferred from evidence of burning. Archaeologists are not reluctant to identify burning on bones, and the characteristics that they use are probably first assimilated in their introduction to cremated human remains (Ubelaker, 1989; technically, ''cremation'' implies complete incineration of the organic phase of bone and quantitative sintering, so some refer to the bones routinely recovered by archaeologists as ''incompletely burned'' or ''smoked'' rather than ''cremated'' [Hummel *et al.*, 1988]). This aspect of training is unfortunate because, as a funerary practice, the purpose of crematorial burning is usually to eliminate the corpse, rather than to warm its flesh, as is true with roasting (note that roasting is but one form of cooking, a point not often explicitly recognized). Cremation requires larger fuel supplies than most cooking does. Roasting on an open flame or on coals, with less thermal input than most cremations, is not as likely to powder or calcine large segments of bone, and is more likely to result in differential burning on and between anatomical parts of bones. As Szuter (1989:306–312) puts it, ''Roasting meat long enough for the bone to burn would result in an inedible meal.''

Even the most critical and rigorous faunal analysts may implicitly assume, on the basis of familiarity with bone from cremations, that burning is recognized easily and identification criteria are straightforward (Lyman, 1982). Still others provide extensive reviews of perimortem bone damage that do not include fire (Gifford, 1981). Many faunal analyses quantify ''burning'' without making explicit the criteria used in its recognition (Gifford *et al.*, 1980; Turner, 1983; Crader, 1984; Gifford-Gonzalez, 1985; Callow *et al.*, 1986; Marshall, 1986). Those who specify the attributes used to recognize burning usually employ color, sometimes discriminating between ''smoked'' and ''calcined'' on the basis of whether the bone is blackened or whitened (Theler and Harris, 1988). Voigt (1983:11) attempts to *specify* how she identified burning at Mapungubwe and *identify* uncertainty in some identifications: ''When bone was dark brown, black or calcined white, it was assumed that the specimens had been subjected to burning. Some of the less severely burnt material was not always easy to identify since the only modification was a slight darkening of the bone.''

Given such a background, it is not surprising that the diagnostic nature of some criteria used to identify burning, particularly in paleontological assemblages, has been questioned (Binford and Ho, 1985; Binford and Stone, 1986). Most analysts classify evidence of bone burning in archaeological assemblages based on gross, macroscopic characteristics. These usually include color, although this is known to vary widely in forensic contexts (see below) and to be susceptible to nonthermal, diagenetic processes in archaeological contexts. The terms ''carbonized'' and ''calcined'' (Hakiel *et al.*, 1983) are widely used, but usually undefined. Buikstra and Goldstein's (1973) analysis of a crematory follows Baby's (1954) three-way burning classification, identifying ''calcined,'' ''smoked,'' and ''unburned'' bones. Brain (1981a) follows this basic division, illustrating a specimen with ''unburned,'' ''carbonized,'' and ''calcined'' sections, whereas Todd (1987a) adds a fourth category, ''localized carbonization.''

More recent assessments of burning in archaeological contexts have begun to focus on microscopic attributes in an effort to get beyond the inherent subjectivity involved with identifications at the gross level. Work by Bonucci and Graziani (1975), Shipman *et al.* (1984), Brain and Sillen (1988), and Susini *et al.* (1988) represents initial steps in the identification of diagnostic indicators of bone burning, but there is a clear need for further work, including the assessment of diagenetic processes that might mimic the features that these workers identify.

The patterns of burning reported by archaeologists are often implicitly linked to cooking activities in prehistory, despite the fact that the criteria used to diagnose burning have been developed through actualistic studies of burning of *defleshed* bones (Shipman, 1981a; Spennemann and Colley, 1980) or of cremations. Bones may be burnt as fuel (Payne, 1983), in rubbish disposal (Davis and Wilson, 1978), or accidentally. None of these activities has any necessary tie to culinary practices. Balme's (1980) question over how bones could have become charred after the animal was cooked whole is readily answered by Brooks and Yellen (1987), who describe the ethnoarchaeological discard of bones into hearths after consumption of the soft tissues. Bone burning may, but does not necessarily, correspond to the roasting of flesh or to the heating of bones prior to marrow extraction (Binford, 1981; Yellen, 1977; Johnson, 1983). It is evident that conclusions such as those of Crader (1984), that the high proportion of burned bone at a site indicates systematic roasting, are unwarranted.

Some of the best understanding of thermal alteration to bones comes from actualistic sources. Experiments in extreme incineration of human cadavers by Dokládal (1970, 1971) have shown the effect of 600–1000°C burning on human bone. Forensic work has elucidated the macroscopic modification of bone (Stewart, 1979; Krogman and Işçan, 1986, Spitz, 1980; Hegler, 1984) and teeth (Furuhata and Yamamoto, 1967) due to burning. Additionally, the study of cremation and allied actualistic studies provide an important background for the study of bone burning (Franchet, 1933; Wells, 1960; Merbs, 1967; Gejvall, 1969; Thurman and Willmore, 1981; Buikstra and Swegle, 1989).

Baby, in a 1954 attempt to decipher Hopewell cremation practices, examined cremated bones and noted a close correspondence between soft tissue coverage and burning on bones. A similar finding was made by Zimmerman *et al.* (1980), who found that the burned parts of the Crow Creek massacre bones were from those areas not covered with much soft tissue. The identification of patterned burning corresponding to flesh coverage is also made by Nass and Bellantoni (1982) for burned human remains from the Southwest. Binford (1963), in an early actualistic study of burning, noted that the degree of burning on experimental subjects (he did not include colleagues at this early stage of his career) was a function of the length of time on the fire, the intensity of the heat, the thickness of the protecting muscle tissue, and the position of the bone in relation to the point of oxidation of the consuming flame. Other work has shown that the amount of residual carbon from the organic components of bone causes the color changes in heat-exposed bones. Low temperatures turn the bone brownish, followed by dark brown to black. With rising temperatures, the carbon is burnt to CO_2, leading to a bluish and then chalky white appearance at temperatures above 600° to 700°C. Above 700° to 800°, the structure of the bone is changed. Because the burning of carbon depends on the amount of added oxygen, it is not reasonable to judge burning temperature from residual carbon coloration of the burned bone (Hummel *et al.*, 1988).

Early in the Mancos analysis it became evident that there was a very strong patterning of burning damage on the bones. This patterning corresponded closely to the flesh cover of the bones in the human body—the more superficial a bone, the more burning. Thus, anterior tibial crests and mandibular gonial angles showed a high frequency of burning damage, whereas posterior tibial surfaces and mandibular coronoid processes (covered by musculature) were unaffected (see Chapters 7–11). Much of the evidence for burning took the form of discoloration, exfoliation, and cracking/crazing that usually leads to an identification of bone as burned. Rather than fitting the model of calcining and charring that is usually used to identify burning in the archaeological record, however, much of the patterned damage on the Mancos bones superficially resembled weathering in gross appearance (Behrensmeyer, 1978; Brain, 1980). In some cases there was associated blackening (char), but in most cases, discoloration, exfoliation, and general deterioration of the bone were the most apparent signatures of burning. Indeed, had the relationship between element soft tissue coverage and burning not been recognized by assessment of unambiguously burned specimens (based on carbonized or calcined bone adjacent to the affected surface), many of the other specimens might have been identified as weathered. Gifford-Gonzalez (1989) has also noted instances of burning damage mimicking weathering. The temperatures required to produce the patterned damage to the Mancos assemblage were probably not very high (Andrew Sillen, personal communication). It is unlikely that crystallographic work will differentiate the damage from diagenetic changes. Scanning electron micrographs were taken across a transect from burned to unburned bone on a parietal fragment (1657) in an effort to match the effects documented by Shipman *et al.* (1984). The results, at magnifications of up to 3,500×, were not comparable to those reported by these authors. The areas that I interpreted to have been burned showed degradation of surface morphology, a smoother, more amorphous texture, but not the extreme modification illustrated by Shipman *et al.* (1984).

It is not surprising that archaeological manifestations of bone burning should, on a gross level, overlap with weathering characteristics. Hare (1980) notes that the degree of preservation of bone is a function of time and environment and that many chemical changes observed in laboratory treatments of bone at 75° to 150°C within minutes and hours are only observable after years at lower ambient temperatures (15°–20°C). Von Endt and Ortner (1984) also speak of simulating bone diagenesis with high temperatures in the laboratory. Bell (1990) has studied the microscopic effects of diagenesis on cortical bone, finding them to be nonrandomly distributed.

The finding that bone burning may superficially mimic bone weathering has important archaeological implications. Analyses that exclude "weathered" bone specimens before burning evidence is quantified (Marshall, 1986a; 1986b) may inadvertently record erroneous results. Because of the Mancos work, I suggest that burning may be dramatically under-reported in faunal analysis and probably in human osteological studies. Furthermore, what burning *is* recorded in zooarchaeological studies is probably often the result of small bone fragments becoming calcined as they are incidentally incorporated into hearths. Yet, this places the faunal analyst in a serious dilemma in the case of mixed assemblages (especially assemblages of fossilized bones) without the preservational and analytical backgrounds of Mancos. It is both premature and impractical to assess each "weathered" specimen microscopically for evidence of burning. In the Mancos study, an attempt was made to employ short-wave ultraviolet light to segregate burned and unburned specimens (McKern, 1958). The results were negative. There is an urgent need to develop techniques based on the change in the organic phase of bone due to heat and combustion that will allow unambiguous recognition of thermal alteration in both recent and fossil bone.

Until such methods exist, the most practical solution to the problem of burning damage mimicking weathering is to pay close attention to the relationship between the soft tissue cover that once invested the bone and evidence of thermal bone alteration observed on the osteological specimen(s). This approach has been employed by a few zooarchaeologists (Gifford *et al.*, 1980). Although bone surface modification by burning may be confused, in the gross aspect, with "weathering," the latter agent will leave a random pattern of surface modification across an assemblage, whereas the burning will leave a signature highly correlated with expectations derived from soft tissue anatomy. Roasting as a culinary behavior may be indicated by the presence of such correlations. For assemblages such as Mancos, in which bones with a highly weathered appearance are found commingled with perfectly preserved bones in a single stratum, damage by burning may be responsible: in such cases, particular attention should be paid to the soft tissue relationships of each bone.

It might be argued that much of what is recognized here as burning damage is, indeed, weathering. This possibility is deemed to be extremely unlikely for several reasons. First, although the surface damage may be similar on a gross level, the character of the damage differs in several ways, even though these observational differences are difficult to quantify. In weathering, split lines develop and ramify through time, and long-bone surfaces disintegrate through a process of exfoliation of thin spalls of bone (see Figure 6.9). This modification is usually distributed fairly uniformly across one or all of the bone specimen's surfaces. In contrast, burning damage results in very steep gradients (rapid transitions) between the damaged and undamaged bone surfaces. In general, for bare bones, weathering damage is independent of soft tissue cover. It is possible that adhering, dessicated soft tissue could differentially protect various bone surfaces from weathering, but there is no evidence of this, and it is not expected except under extremely unusual preservational conditions (in which weathering itself is predicted to be absent or extremely slow). For the Mancos assemblage, the distribution of damaged areas attributed to burning was assessed relative to the upper or lower surface of the bone as it rested *in situ* as ascertained through photographs made during exposure of the assemblage. There is no relationship between the damaged surface and its orientation. If weathering of the bones had taken place prior to burial, it might be predicted that the altered surfaces would have been predominantly the upper surfaces. This was not so. Furthermore, if weathering were responsible for the observed damage, the inner surfaces of bones (inner cortex of broken long bones, endocranial surface of vault bones) would have been equally prone to alteration as the outer surfaces. This was not the case with the damage attributed to burning.

Finally, I know of no tested method to ascertain whether bone has been boiled in prehistory (but see Observation 16 above). Coy's (1975) anecdotes about "the longer the cooking the softer the bone" are self-admittedly speculative. Akins (1982) describes the phenomenon of "cooking brown" and attributes this to boiling, but it is clear from her discussion that soil staining can mimic this modification. Furthermore, the attribution of this bone darkening to boiling is presumptive. Should diagnostic criteria of boiling become available, it would be very interesting to employ them to a wide range of faunal remains from archaeological contexts.

Observations 81–95: Burning (Table 6.1)

When bone is burned, the macroscopic alterations include discoloration (charring and calcining), cracking, and exfoliation. The presence or absence of each of these changes was recorded independently in the Mancos analysis. Another feature associated with burning is the affinity of matrix for the burned bone surface, an affinity that renders complete cleaning in these areas very difficult, as a thin clay residue often adheres in such cases (see Mancos specimen 1505, Figure 6.27). Figures 6.28 and 6.29 illustrate the deterioration of the bone surface interpreted to represent thermal trauma. Another observation made during the analysis involved the opacity that burning brought to the bone (see Mancos specimens 1485, 1822, 1846; Figure 6.30). As noted above, these attributes are continuously variable and may not be tied exclusively to thermal alteration. Identification of these changes was recorded only for those cases in which the damage was judged to be unambiguously attributable to burning (Figure 6.31); therefore it is very likely to be an underestimate of the amount of burning on the assemblage. Location of the changes on each element was made according to the same procedure outlined for recording toolmarks and mammalian chewing described above.

SPECIMEN DIMENSIONS

Observations 96 to 98 record the dimensions of true bone splinters. These are defined as fragments of shaft that do not retain significant areas of metaphysis, epiphysis, or articular surface. Measure-

Fig. 6.27 Adherence of a thin residue of clay on a burned long-bone shaft fragment (IP3 1505). Bar = 1 cm.

Fig. 6.28 Burning damage mimicking weathering (1003). Bar = 1 cm.

Fig. 6.29 Burning damage to two tibial crests (top tibia splinter 0994 and bottom tibia splinter 1052). Note the abrupt transition between deeply exfoliated, chalky bone at the subcutaneous anterior tibial crest, and the perfectly preserved bone immediately adjacent to it. Bone weathering does not typically produce such gradients. Bar = 1 cm.

ments are all maxima, recorded in millimeters. No other measurements of specimen size were taken for the assemblage because it was evident that such data would not be particularly meaningful. The length, breadth, and thickness measurements were taken to explore the possibility that these might differ significantly from those derived from nonhuman archaeological assemblages.

A PRELIMINARY SUMMARY OF TRAUMA TO THE MANCOS 5MTUMR–2346 BONES

This review of attributes recorded for the Mancos assemblage has previewed the extensive perimortem fragmentation of the skeletal elements. There is much evidence of human-induced toolmarks resulting from defleshing, disarticulation, and per-

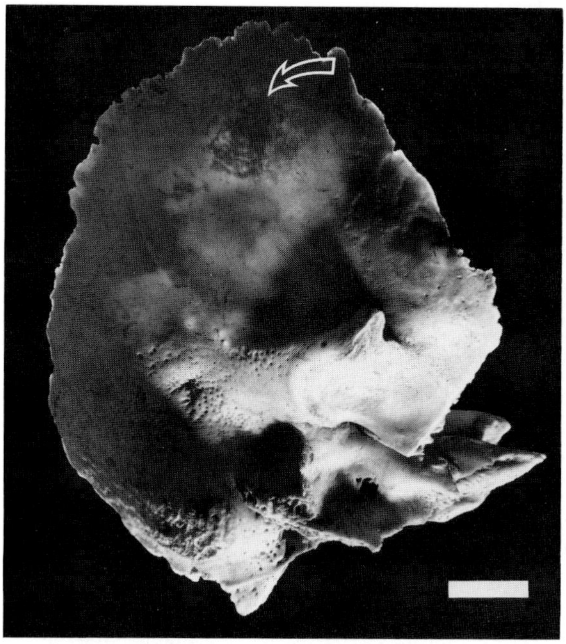

Fig. 6.30 Opacity caused by burning damage. This right temporal bone from an immature individual (1846) is lit from behind, the light visible through the thin bone of the translucent temporal squama. The mottled darkened patch in the center of the squama (arrow) is interpreted to indicate exposure to heat. Bar = 1 cm.

cussion activities. There is much evidence of thermal alteration. On the other hand, there is minimal evidence of geological alteration of the assemblage and no evidence of alteration by nonhuman mammals. In short, in Lyman's (1987a) terms, the context of the occurrence and the damage on the bones indicate that the primary, if not exclusive, agent of modification of the Mancos assemblage was human. The identification of this agent allows an assessment of the patterning of damage seen in the assemblage. This assessment may provide clues about prehistoric human behavior.

Fig. 6.31 A conjoined femoral specimen showing residue of soil attached to anhydrous bone next to the exfoliating bone (conjoining Set 59). This pattern of modification is interpreted to represent exposure to high thermal load. Bar = 1 cm.

CHAPTER

7

The Head

The background to the Mancos assemblage provided in Chapters 1 to 6 makes it appropriate to now turn to an element-by-element consideration of these human skeletal remains. This consideration of the maximally conjoined assemblage is aimed at a functional elucidation of the bone modification observed. The patterns of survival and damage for each element in the skeleton are assessed in Chapters 7 through 12. These chapters group skeletal elements into five body segments: the head (this chapter), the trunk (Chapter 8), the upper limb (Chapter 9), the lower limb (Chapter 10), and the hands and feet (Chapter 11). Figure 7.1 illustrates the relationships of these body segments.

In this chapter, as in Chapters 8 through 11, the analytical results stem from consideration of the Mancos assemblage in its maximally conjoined state. In other words, the analysis involved all *pieces* when they were maximally conjoined as well as those *specimens* for which no joins were found. To avoid confusion, the term ''specimen'' is used to refer to all unconjoined fragments. The term ''conjoining set'' refers to pieces comprising two or more conjoined specimens. Since the conjoined sets were treated as separate analytical units, the term ''piece'' is used to describe conjoining sets as well as to refer to specimens that did not participate in joins. Survival, fracture, toolmark, and burning patterns are described and interpreted on an element-by-element basis within the head, trunk, arm, leg, and hand/foot body segments. The assessment follows the methodology and standards introduced in Chapters 4 and 6.

Each element *Survival* section describes the maximally conjoined MNI values by age groups. Age groups are segregated in the analysis for functional reasons—the marrow content and fracture characteristics of a bone will change during ontogeny and this change may have implications for processing techniques. The *Survival* section details the representation of the various parts of each element. These descriptions give an idea of the relative survival of the individual bony element and its various parts. In the *Fracture* section the fracture patterns for each element are described in a qualitative, functional manner. The *Toolmarks* section provides a qualitative, functional account of the tool-associated bone modification for each element, with special reference to the soft tissues involved in the processing. The *Burning* section describes any patterns of thermal alteration on each element, again concentrating on the associated soft tissues. By reviewing the patterns of damage to bony elements and body segments in the Mancos collec-

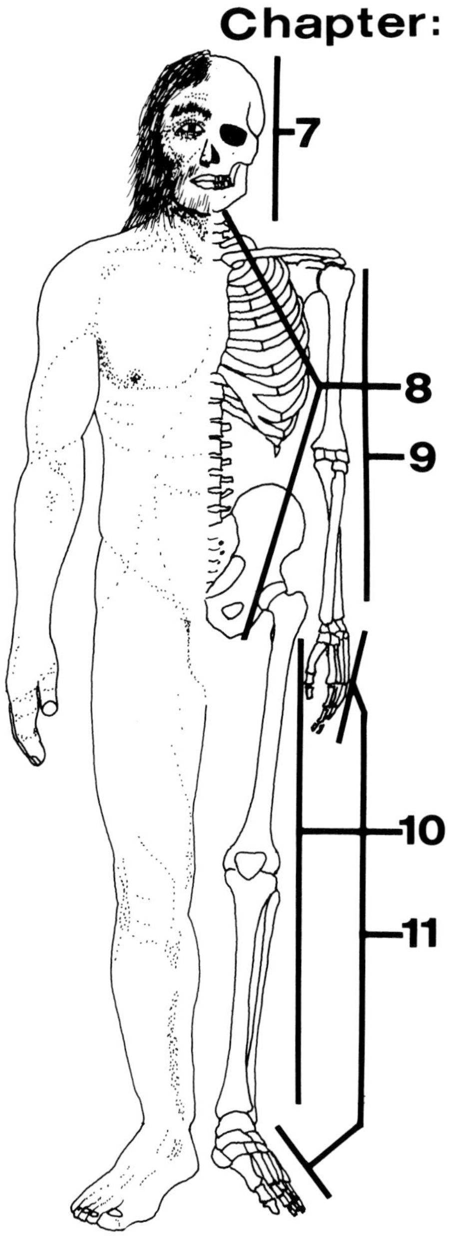

Fig. 7.1 Drawing of the skeleton, fleshed on one side. This chapter and the four to follow deal with the separate anatomical segments as indicated here. The reader may wish to consult this figure when conceptualizing the soft tissue coverage of the osteological elements described below.

tion in this detail, it is possible to elucidate the prehistoric activities that shaped this assemblage. The reader may, however, wish to proceed directly to the *Summary* section to gain an overall perspective on the processing techniques for each body segment.

The results presented in the element-by-element analyses of Chapters 7 through 11 are based on work performed on the collection after maximal conjoining. The minimum number of individuals represented by each skeletal element category is estimated (the most abundant elements give the MNI values reported in Table 5.1 for each room). The differential survival of various portions of each element is then described with reference to patterns of fracture, toolmarks, and burning. Each chapter is summarized with a consideration of the postmortem, prediscard treatment of the body segment. Chapters 7 through 11 thus represent an attempt to relate the observed patterns of archaeological bone modification to the overlying and underlying soft tissues of the human body. Quantitative results derived from a more traditional zooarchaeological assessment of the assemblage are presented in Appendix 2 and summarized in Chapter 12.

The most effective way to summarize survival and damage patterns in an osteological assemblage is to describe the entire assemblage on an element-by-element basis. Illustration plays a primary role in this endeavor. Dart's interpretations of the Makapansgat bone assemblage were questioned from the start, but photographic display of the patterns he observed proved invaluable to subsequent researchers. Dart's 1957 monograph, with its plates displaying dozens of specimens in different element categories, provides the reader with an effective overview of the material—an overview that conveys far more than simple statistics could.

A photographic record of the entire unconjoined Mancos assemblage is provided in the presentation to follow, with figures showing all unconjoined specimens in each skeletal element category. Patterns of element representation can be discerned simply by comparing these group photographs. Visual presentation of the unconjoined subassemblages allows the reader to assess readily the patterning in fragmentation and preservation on an element-by-element basis. Fracture, toolmark, and burning damage described in the text are illustrated by closeup views of individual specimens in each element category.

Shipman and Phillips-Conroy (1977) use the term "patterns" to describe what are actually breakage "kinds" or "types." In contrast, the current assessment of the Mancos assemblage seeks recurrences of survival or damage. It is these recurrences that I describe as patterns. These patterns are the clues to prehistoric activities. Several of the patterns can be observed within the photographs of each element category. Visual assessment of fracture patterning is greatly facilitated by this mode of presentation, a point recognized by Beyer *et al.* (1962), who presented fragmentation patterns of selected military ordnance (artillery and mortar shell fragments collected from experimentally controlled explosion) in an analogous manner. It is my conclusion that if more assemblages were presented in the comprehensive, nonselective, photographic manner employed in the chapters to follow, comparisons in zooarchaeology might be greatly facilitated (a point made by Lyman, 1976). Economic considerations weigh strongly against such complete visual presentation of most bone assemblages (as purchasers of this book appreciate), but computer-based imaging technology may provide an advantageous solution to this restriction.

THE SKULL: AN INTRODUCTION

In zooarchaeology, individual whole bones of the cranial vault ("elements," rather than "specimens") are rarely assessed independently. The mandible is the usual exception. The fact that bones such as the frontal, parietals, and occipital form much of a functional portion known as the cranial vault makes this procedure acceptable. For a more detailed, element-by-element analysis of the cranium, it is important to note that cranial vault specimens rarely consist of isolated elements. More commonly, cranial specimens consist of fragments that include parts of several different bony elements. For example, a fragment that is mostly frontal may include bits of parietal, sphenoid, ethmoid, lacrimal, and maxilla. Specimen identifications in Appendix 2 take note of this problem, listing the most intact element first, followed by a (+) to indicate that other elements are attached to the piece. Where more than one intact element is present, the specimen identification follows the order established in Table 6.2.

Cranial specimens with more than one element represented were assessed in each relevant round of the element-by-element analysis. For each element category, all specimens and pieces retaining portions of that element were assessed, resulting in some individual specimens figuring in discussions of different elements. Use of the data provided in Appendix 2 should take this into account. A consideration of the skull as a functional unit is provided at the end of this chapter.

Fig. 7.2 The Mancos 5MTUMR–2346 frontal bone subassemblage.

FRONTAL (FIGURE 7.2)

Survival

A total MNI of 17 in the maximally conjoined frontal bone assemblage includes 5 individuals younger than 12 years. No immature frontal is intact, and only 2 of the adults are nearly intact. The laterally projecting zygomatic process of the frontal is present only 3 times on the left and 6 times on the right. This structure, thin and exposed, is the frontal portion most susceptible to damage by fracture and burning. Detachment of the facial skeleton often involved breakage of the sphenoid/ethmoid/frontal plates, leaving some ethmoids in place, whereas others were removed with the facial/sphenoidal unit. Only one full face in the entire collection remains attached to the frontal.

Fracture

Of the 6 immature zygomatic processes of the frontal, 4 are broken back or chipped because of lateral blows. Many of the other pieces are burned, eliminating potential evidence of fracture trauma. One immature frontal (1631) shows small depressed areas that mimic carnivore tooth puncture, but in the absence of other dam-

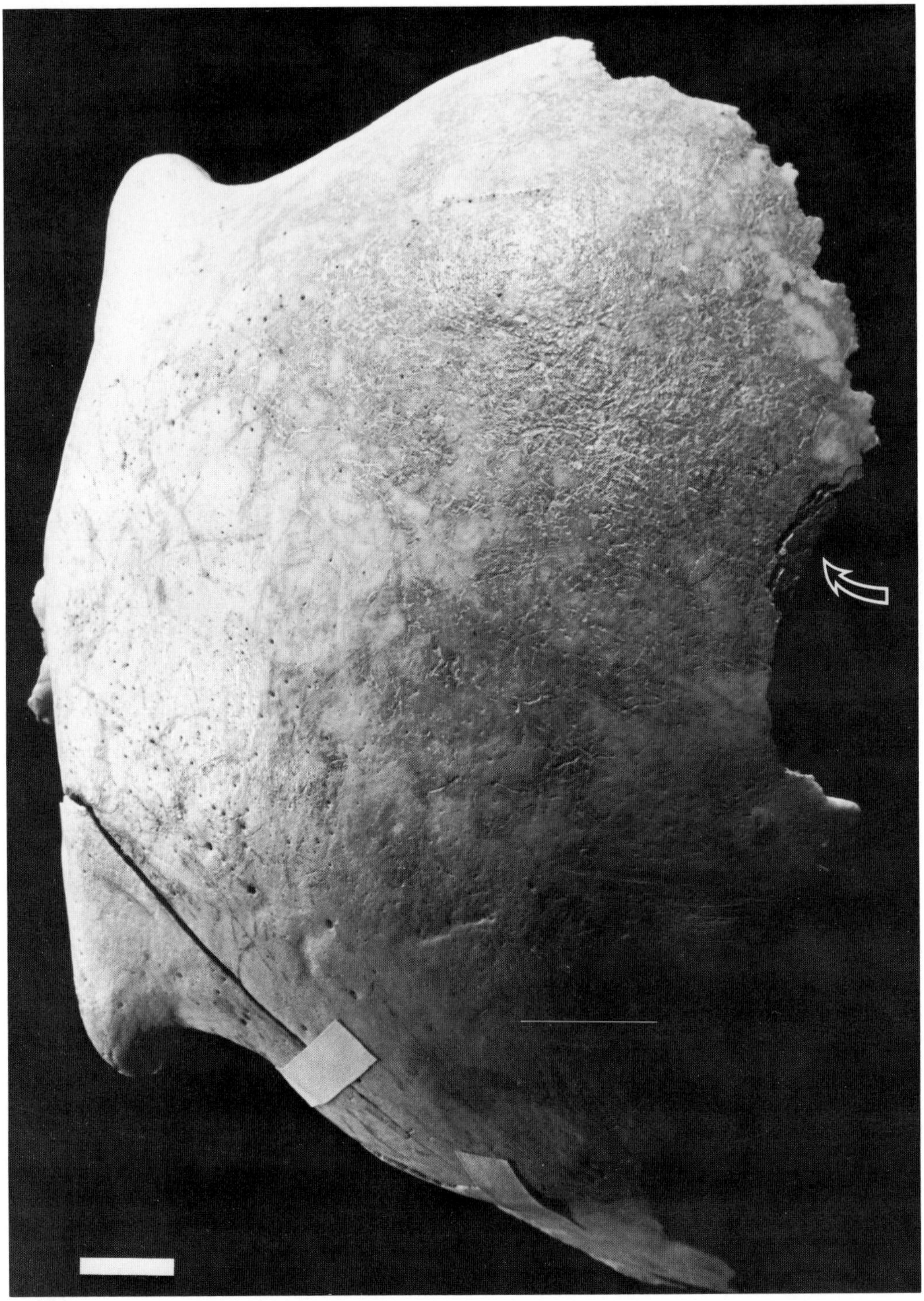

Fig. 7.3 Ectocranial percussion in the area of bregma (top of the cranial vault) and striae on the frontal bone (1671 conjoined with 1672; the reverse side is shown in Figure 4.4). Bar = 1 cm.

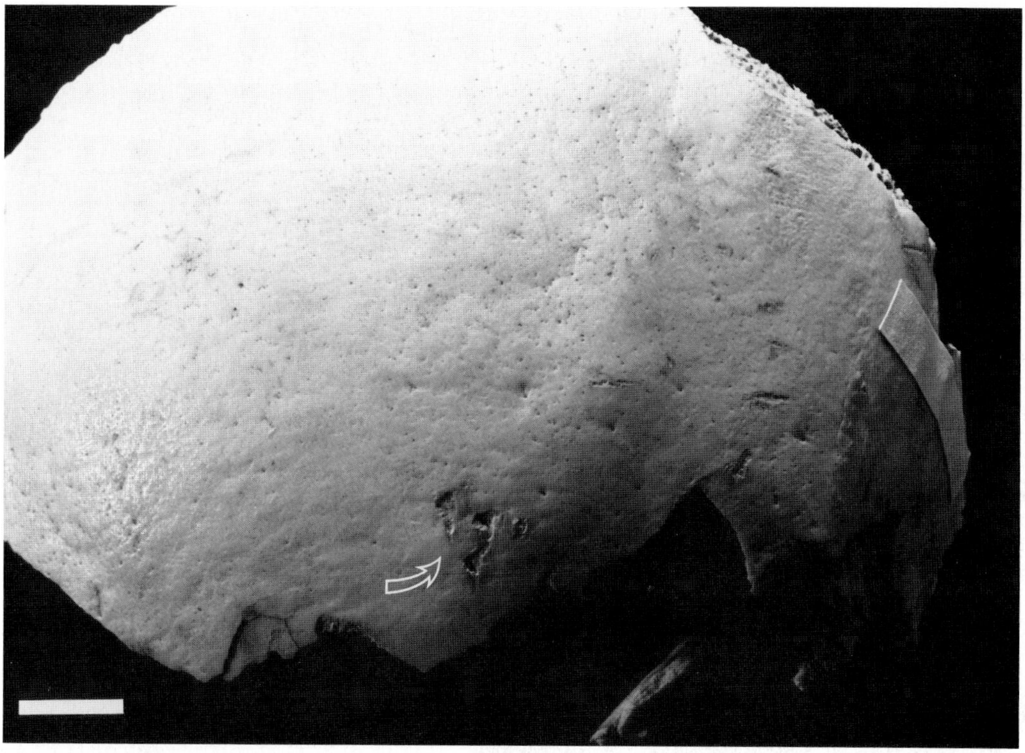

Fig. 7.4 Percussion damage to the frontal bone (1661 conjoined with 1662 and 1663). The view is toward the anterior (facial) surface of the frontal bone. Note the three successive impact points near the midline. See Figure 6.26 for Scanning Electron Micrograph images of this damage. Bar = 1 cm.

age, these are more likely to have been made by a blow from a pointed object.

Ectocranial percussion at bregma is evident on 3 of 6 adult pieces in the form of conchoidal scars, adhering flakes, or internal vault release (Figure 7.3). Ectocranial blows at a more anterior position, above glabella, are indicated for 5 other mature individuals. One piece (1661, Figure 7.4) illustrates how the vault breakage was accomplished by multiple hits with a sharp object on both sides of glabella above the supraorbitals. Of the 9 pieces where the region is preserved, 5 show hammer/anvil abrasion marks around glabella. One frontal (1629, from FA3, Room 8 of the more recent pueblo) exhibits a maze of randomly oriented striae across the ectocranial surface. The broken surfaces of this piece are rounded and polished. This unusual damage is also present on the only other cranial fragment from the same site feature, suggesting some abrasion unique to this feature. No adult frontals show percussion to the endocranial surface.

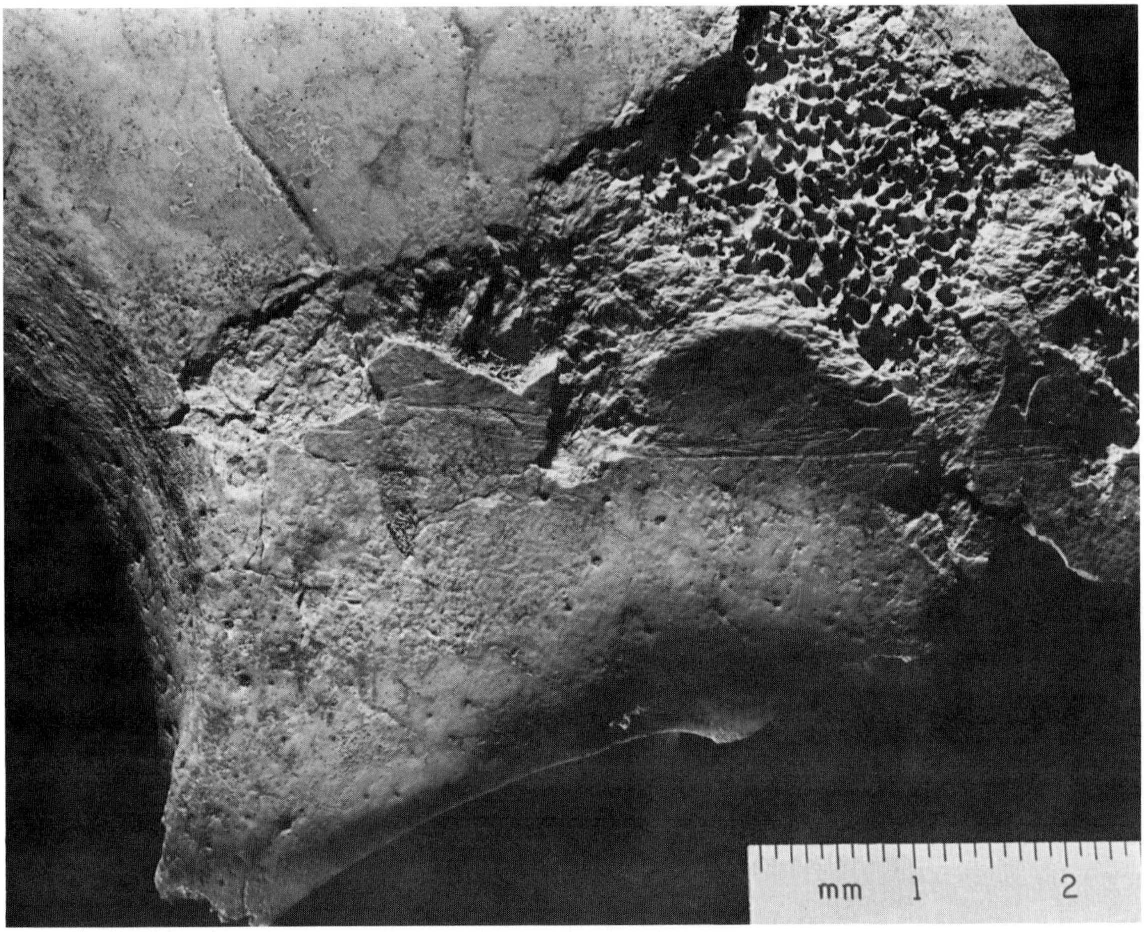

Fig. 7.5 Cutmarks on the frontal bone, transverse and in the temporal fossa (1656). View is from above, looking down onto the right supraorbital margin. Burning has resulted in exfoliation of the outer table of the cranial vault. The deep, sinuous grooves at upper frame left are vascular grooves, normal skeletal anatomy. The smaller scalar ticks are millimeters.

Toolmarks

Of the 10 available adult frontals, 3 show paracoronally directed slicing marks. One of these is set 2 cm anterior to the coronal suture, whereas the others are just above glabella, across the supratoral sulcus (Figure 7.5). Of the 7 observable adult frontals, only 1 (1641, Figure 7.6) shows parasagittal cutmarks. These marks are analogous to those described and illustrated by Villa *et al.* (1986b, Figures 13 and 14). Of the 14 available adult pieces, only 1 shows a vertical cutmark in the temporal fossa, possible evidence of the

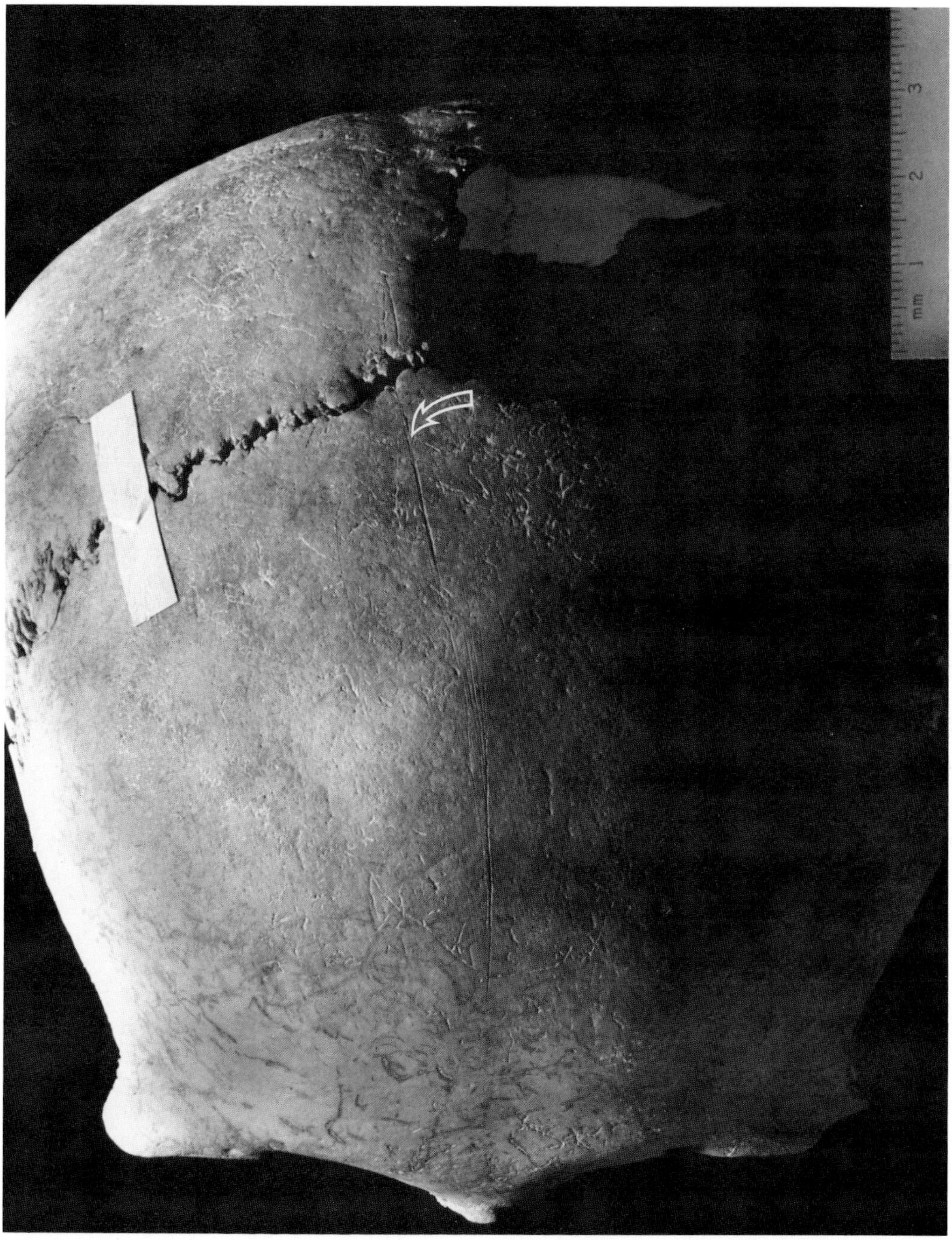

Fig. 7.6 Parasagittal cutmarks on the frontal bone and articulated parietal (1641 conjoined with 1642). View is from above, anterior is toward the bottom of the page.

removal of the temporalis muscle. No endocranial cutmarks were found on any frontal piece.

Many frontal pieces show abrasion on the ectocranial surface related to movement of a hammerstone or anvil across the bone during percussion. These marks, as described in Chapter 6, are superficial and occur in striae fields. They are not present endocranially in the Mancos assemblage.

Burning

All the immature MNI sets, and 7 of 9 other isolated immature pieces show evidence of burning as discoloration, cracking, charring, and exfoliation. The burning damage is focused on the frontal bosses and zygomatic processes, the two most projecting areas of this bone. Of the minimum 12 adult frontals, 8 show burning (Figure 7.7). This total includes slight effects at the frontal boss on 2 pieces and ''spillover'' damage from burning on the parietals near the coronal suture on another 4. Full burning involvement of the bone is seen on the remaining 2 pieces. The cutmarks on piece 1656 (Figure 7.5) were made prior to the time of burning. In contrast to the ectocranial burning damage, the endocranial surfaces of the Mancos frontals are unaffected by fire.

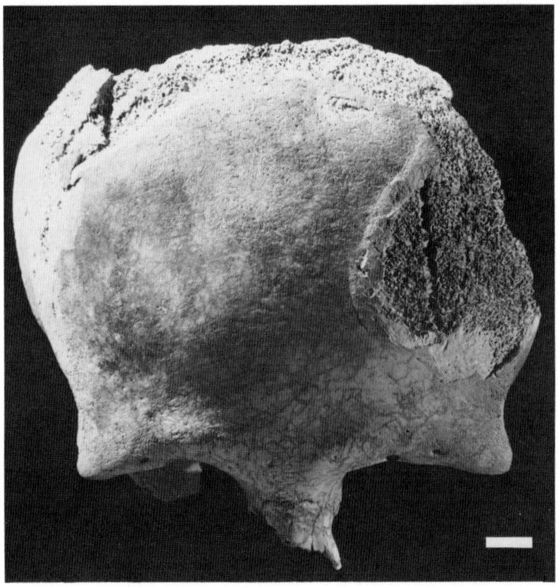

Fig. 7.7 Burning of the frontal bone at the frontal boss (1666). Bar = 1 cm.

PARIETALS (FIGURE 7.8)

Survival

A total MNI of 11 individuals was determined from the maximally conjoined assemblage of parietals. This includes 4 individuals younger than 12 years. Only 1 parietal (1736) remains intact. The more intact pieces are invariably attached to portions of the other parietal, temporal, and/or frontal bones.

Fracture

Ectocranial percussion damage is evident throughout the parietal sample. This damage is characterized by a roughly conchoidal impact fracture, the cone apex of which is located at the ectocranial impact point. This kind of fracture is most easily diagnosed on adult bone because of its thickness. Characteristics of ectocranial percussion include endocranial vault release and peeling, adhering flakes, percussion striae, and failed hammerstone pits in the outer bone table of the cranial vault. Most of the larger parietal pieces and conjoined sets show this kind of damage. Impact notches are often broad and poorly defined, with associated internal vault release (Figure 7.9). Broken edges and incipient fracture cracks on many pieces follow weaker paths through the bone, often along the meningeal impres-

Fig. 7.8 The Mancos 5MTUMR–2346 parietal bone subassemblage.

sions and sutures. This pattern of fracture is common in modern, medically documented cases of cranial trauma from blows by a blunt object either before or after death. There is no evidence of percussion to the endocranial surface in the Mancos parietal assemblage.

Toolmarks

Quantification of cutmarks on the parietal is extremely difficult, because fragmentation results in each piece preserving different parts of this bone. Immature pieces show no parietal cutmarks. Of the 7 adult parietals (5 individuals) where the region is observable, only 1 shows a paracoronal cut that scores the parietal in the region posterior to bregma (Figure 7.10). Of the 5 adult parietals where it is observable (3 individuals), there is a parasagittal cut down the midline in 1 (Figure 7.6). In addition, where the posterior half of the parietal is preserved in 8 pieces (7 individuals), cutmarks are seen on 5 (Figure 7.10). Of these, 3 show cutmarks oriented parallel to the lambdoidal suture. The remaining 2 individuals exhibit striae that pass anterosuperiorly from near asterion, within the attachment area of the temporalis muscle (Figure 7.11). Many isolated parietal fragments bear cutmarks, but it is difficult to assess more fully the patterning of the toolmark damage due to frag-

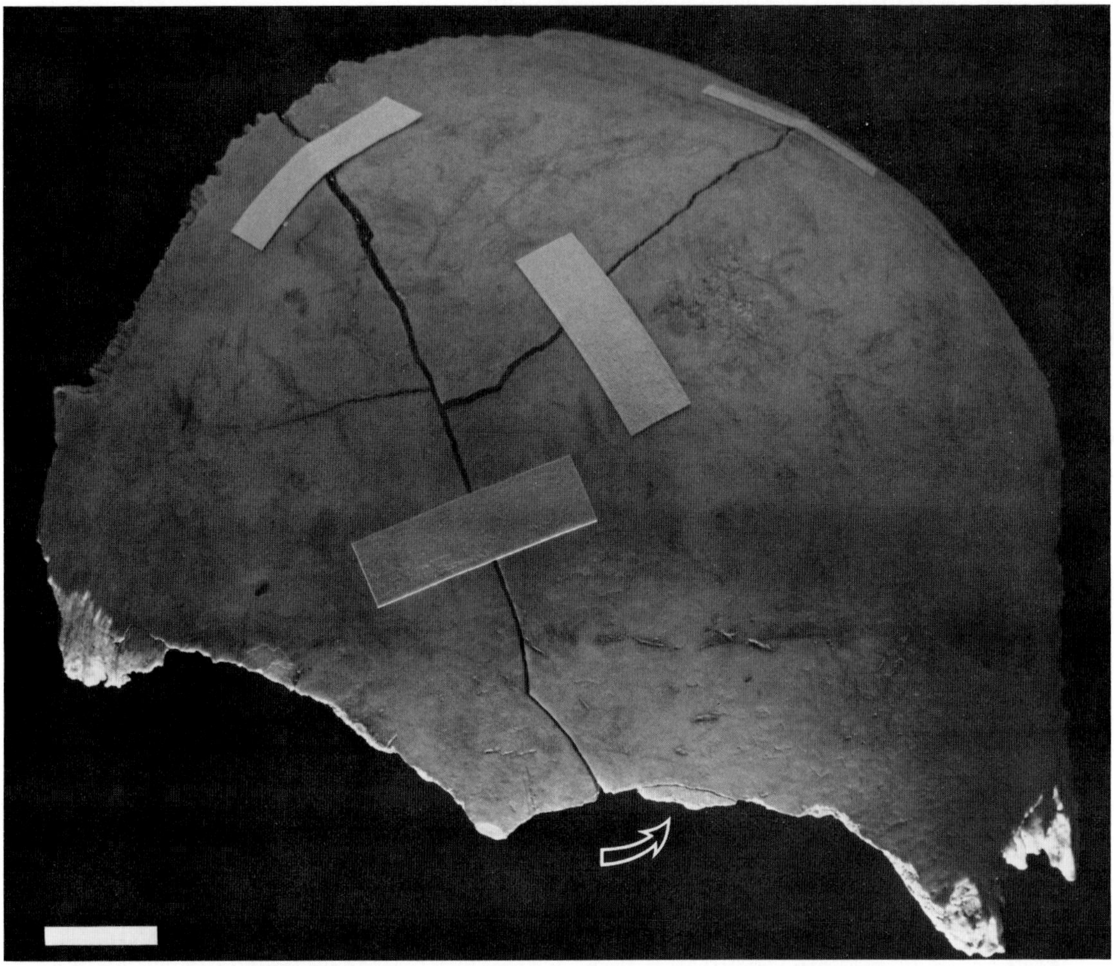

Fig. 7.9 Posterolateral view of a left parietal, with the squamous suture to the left. Impact notches and adhering flakes on the parietal indicate blows above the root of the mastoid process (1748–1750). Bar = 1 cm.

Opposite page top:

Fig. 7.10 Cutmarks and burning on a right parietal bone (1768). The view is from the side, with the anterior edge (coronal suture) of the bone at the right edge. Note that evidence of burning (exfoliation above, darkening below) extends across the subcutaneous area of the bone but stops at the temporal line, presumably because the temporalis muscle protected the underlying bone. Bar = 1 cm.

Opposite page bottom:

Fig. 7.11 Cutmarks and burning on a left parietal bone (1657). The view is similar to that of Figure 7.10. Note that the burning (darkened area along the upper edge) covers the subcutaneous area of the bone but is limited by the temporal line, below which the temporalis muscle seems to have protected the underlying bone. Note also the cutmarks on the submuscular surface. Bar = 1 cm.

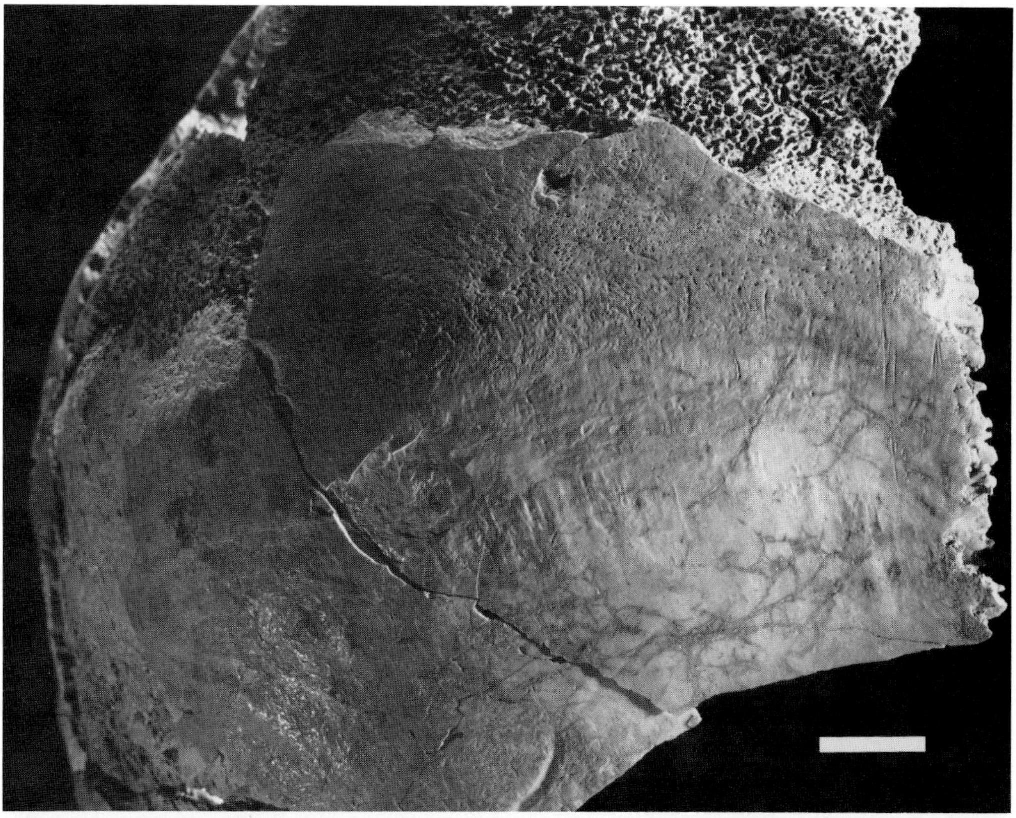

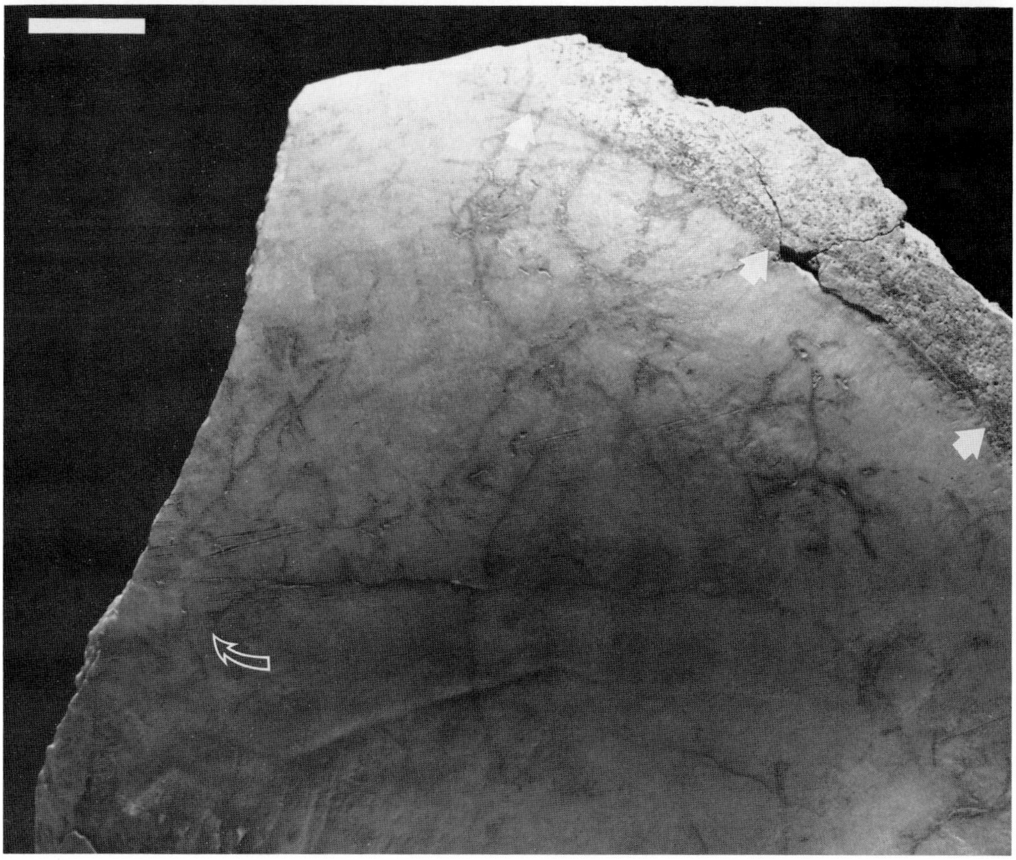

Fig. 7.12 Burning damage to the parietal bone (1684, 1761, 1829, 1837). Any cutmarks on the exfoliated surfaces would have been removed during the burning. Note that evidence of burning ranges from small patches of discoloration to nearly complete exfoliation. Bar = 1 cm.

mentation and heavy burning exfoliation. No cutmarks were found on the endocranial surface of the parietal.

Burning

Of the 23 isolated pieces of parietal from immature individuals, 18 are burned, whereas of the 48 adult isolated pieces, 27 are burned and 9 are indeterminate. All 4 large immature parietal segments show evidence of burning (Figure 7.12). Of the adults, only two of approximately 8 fairly complete pieces lack evidence of parietal burning. Only one of the two has burning on the accompanying frontal, whereas the other exhibits evidence of burning on the attached mastoid. Exfoliation of the outer table with consequent exposure of the diploe is especially common on the parietals. In many cases, however, the burning was not intense enough to cause exfoliation,

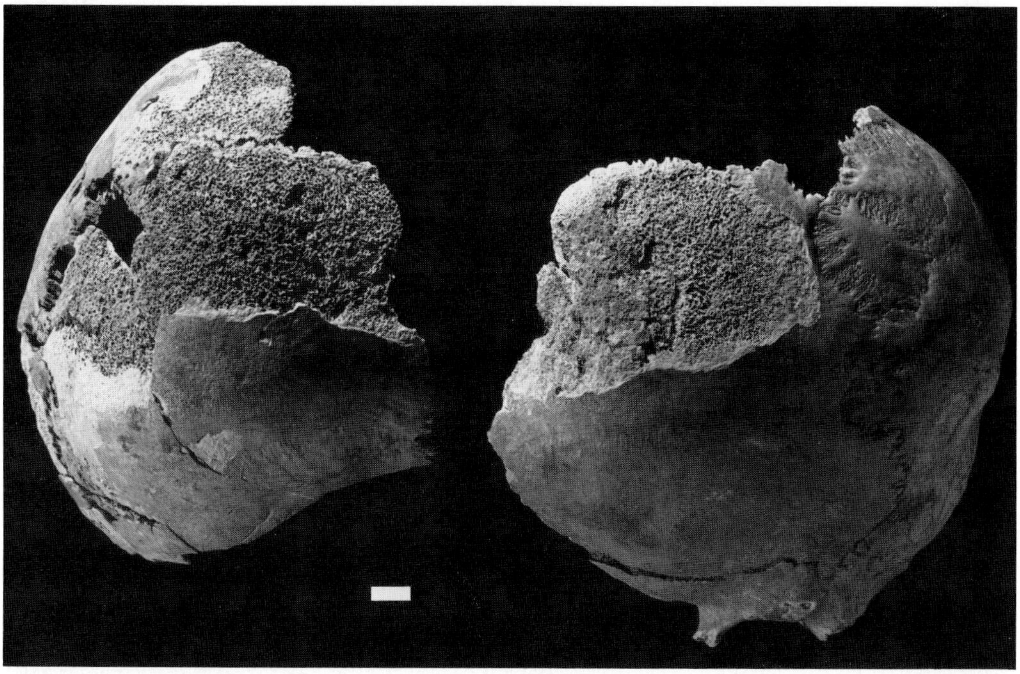

Fig. 7.13 Discoloration and exfoliation of the outer table of the cranial vault caused by burning to the parietal bone above the temporal line (1679, 1768). Perspective is from above and to the side of two cranial vaults, the sagittal sutures of the two specimens aligned horizontally in this view. Bar = 1 cm.

resulting instead in a discoloration and opacity to the bone (Figure 7.13).

A clear pattern of burning relative to the temporalis muscle cover on the parietal is seen in the assemblage. In specimens such as 1666, 1679, and 1657, the burning extends to the temporal line where it ceases. Of 14 adult parietal fragments with more than 20 cm of temporal line or adjacent bone preserved, half show the boundary of burning to be coincident with the temporal line. This is strong evidence that the adhering temporalis muscle protected the underlying vault during burning of the head, evidence that is consistent with the pattern of subcutaneous burning to be described for other vault bones in the sections to follow.

The predepositional condition of the burned parietal pieces probably differed substantially from their postexcavation and postcleaning condition today. This is because the burning weakened the bone to such an extent that the outer table, even if present over larger areas of the vault at deposition, has now been lost. The outer surface of these burned parietal bones is extremely fragile, in contrast to the unburned endocranial surface (Figures 7.14, 7.15). Among the many parietal pieces available, only one small fragment (1777) indicates burning after fracture of the vault (endocranial burning). The overwhelming majority of isolated parietal pieces with evidence of burning (n = 69) show only ectocranial involvement. The

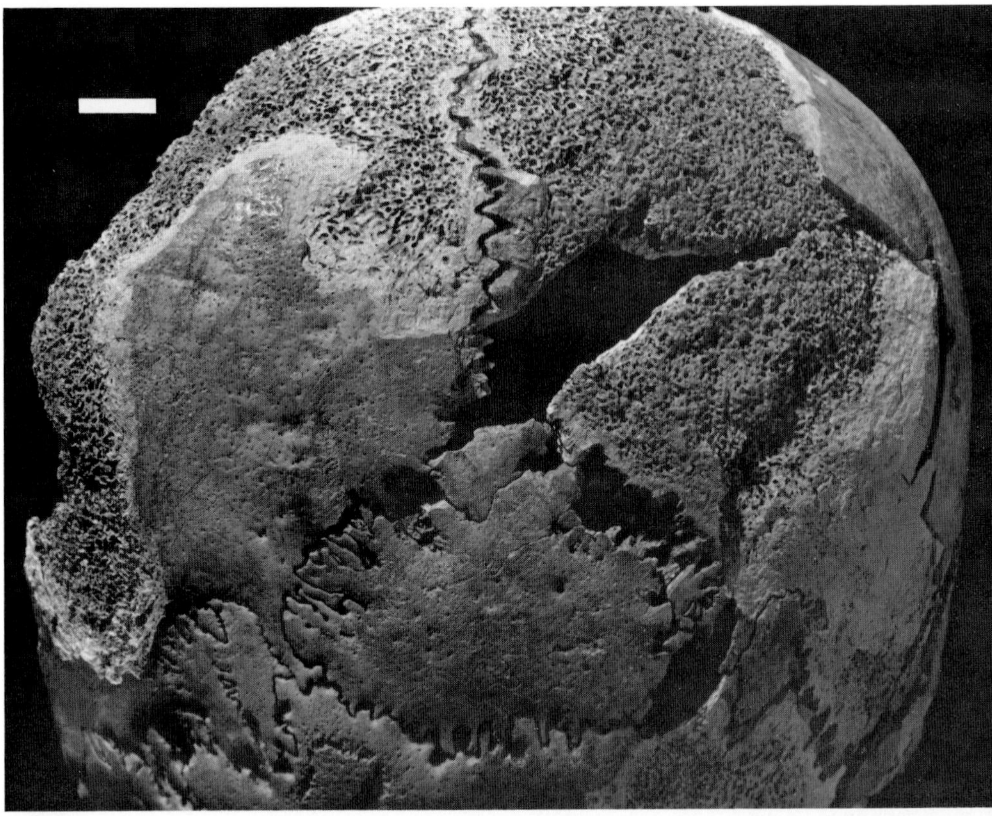

(a)

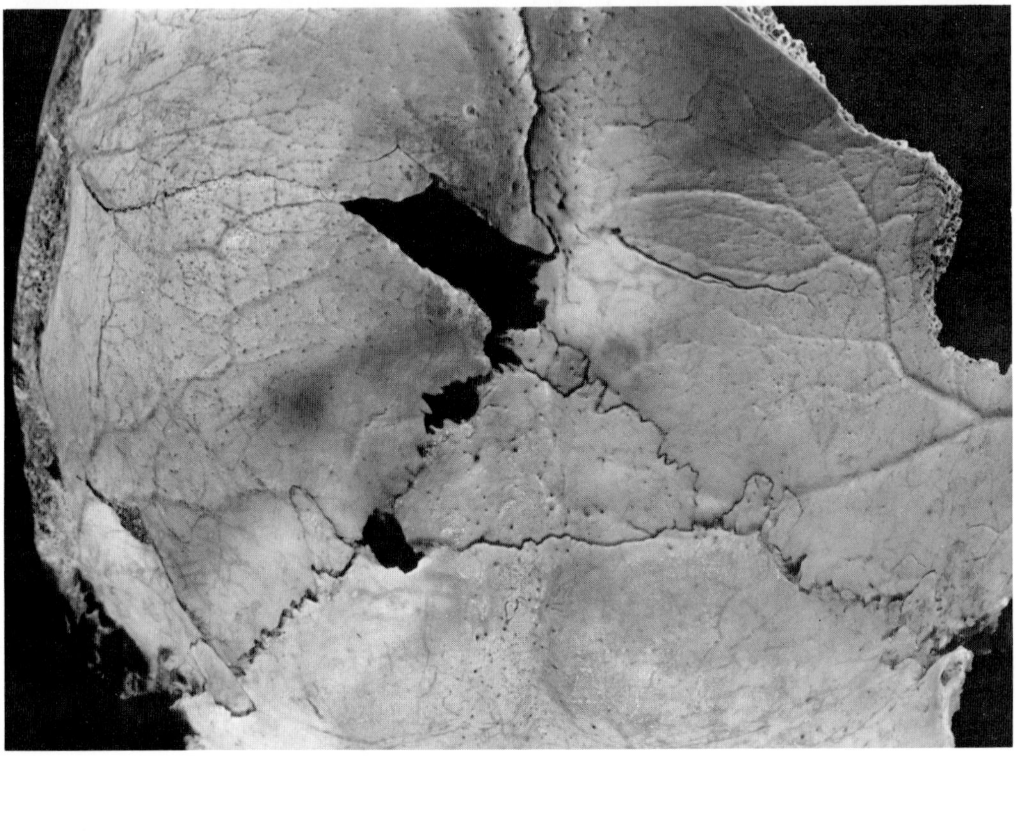

(b)

Opposite page:

Fig. 7.14 Ectocranial burning on the parietal bone (a) (1768). Endocranial burning on the same parietal bone (b) (1768). Note that the burning damage only extends to the endocranial surface as slight discoloration, even though the ectocranial surface is thoroughly exfoliated as a result of exposure to heat. Bar = 1 cm.

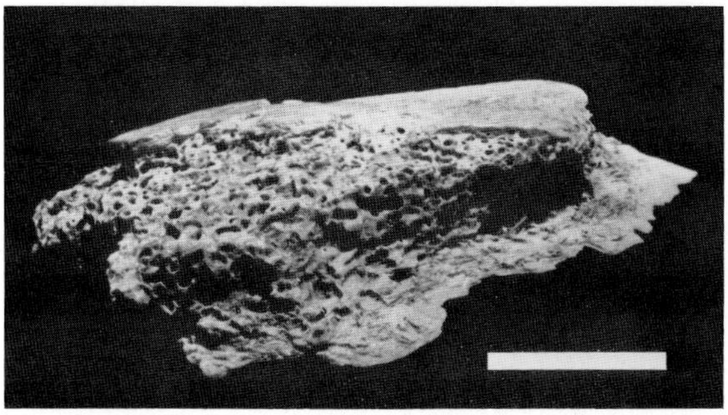

Fig. 7.15 Ectocranial burning and exfoliation are evident on this parietal bone fragment (1718), but the thin, unburned edge produced by internal vault release is not affected by burning. This is evidence for burning prior to fracture of the cranium. Bar = 1 cm.

differential between ectocranial and endocranial burning constitutes strong evidence for burning prior to fragmentation.

OCCIPITAL (FIGURE 7.16)

Survival

A MNI of 16 individuals was obtained from the maximally conjoined sample of occipital bones. This includes 4 individuals younger than age 12. Not a single occipital remains perfectly intact; one 18-year-old individual is nearly so, lacking only part of the asterionic corner and the left condyle. Only 9 intact condyles remain, and 6 of these are in 3 individuals each retaining both condyles. In 4 of the 5 adults where it can be examined, a paracoronal plane of fracture crosses the occipital at the level of the posterior half of the foramen magnum. This divides the occipital into larger squamal portions that often accompany the parietals to form larger vault fragments and smaller basioccipital/circumcondylar parts. This pattern of breakage characterizes 4 of 6 immature pieces and dominates the assemblage.

Fracture

Of the 7 condyles preserved well enough to indicate damage, 5 display crushing fracture (Figure 7.17). There is no clear evidence of percussion damage to the occipital besides this crushing. There is clear peeling damage on both endocranial and ectocranial surfaces adjacent to the transverse breakage at the rear of the foramen magnum (Figure 7.18).

Toolmarks

Of the 5 individuals with at least half the condylar region preserved, there is no evidence of cutmarks. Three individuals show cutmarks on the squama. These multiple, subparallel marks occur mostly in clusters, indicating a sawing motion with a flaked edge. Marks are present both above (Figure 7.19) and below (Figure 7.20) the superior nuchal line. Cutmarks below the nuchal line do not occur in any immature individual, but are present in 3 of 6 adults that retain more than half of the nuchal plane. There are no endocranial cutmarks in the sample.

Burning

None of the 5 adult or 4 immature pieces that preserve the basal and condylar portions show evidence of burning in this

7.16

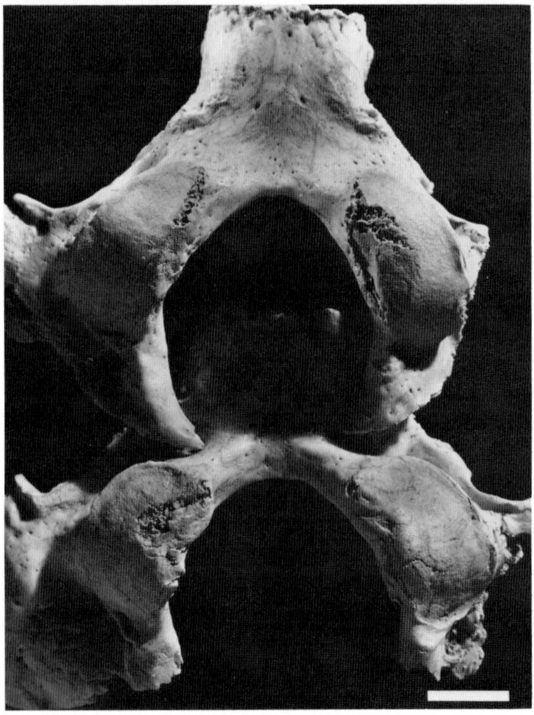
7.17

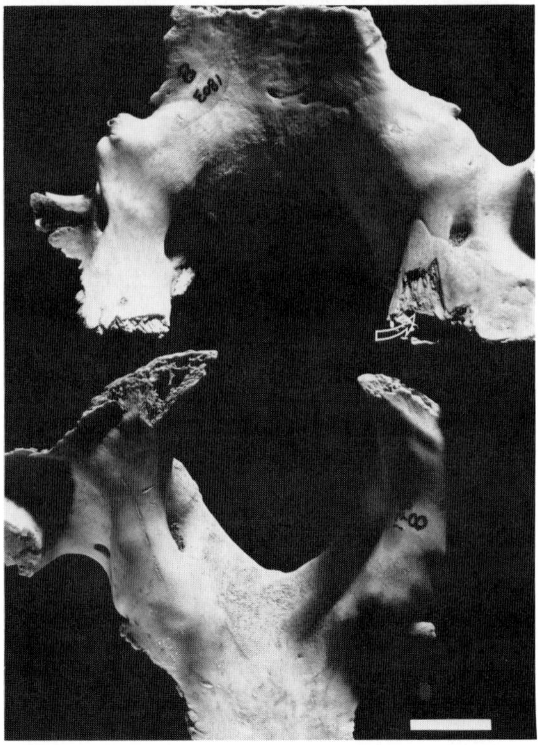
7.18

Opposite page:

Fig. 7.16 The Mancos 5MTUMR–2346 occipital bone subassemblage.

Fig. 7.17 Crushing damage to the occipital condyle (1679, 1785, 1803). Bar = 1 cm.

Fig. 7.18 Peeling damage around the broken edges of the foramen magnum produced when the occipital squama was levered away from the basilar portion of this bone (1803, 1785). Endocranial view. Bar = 1 cm.

Below:

Fig. 7.19 Cutmarks on an occipital bone fragment, both above and below the superior nuchal plane (1744). View is from behind, the lambdoidal suture up, and the nuchal plane in shadow. Bar = 1 cm.

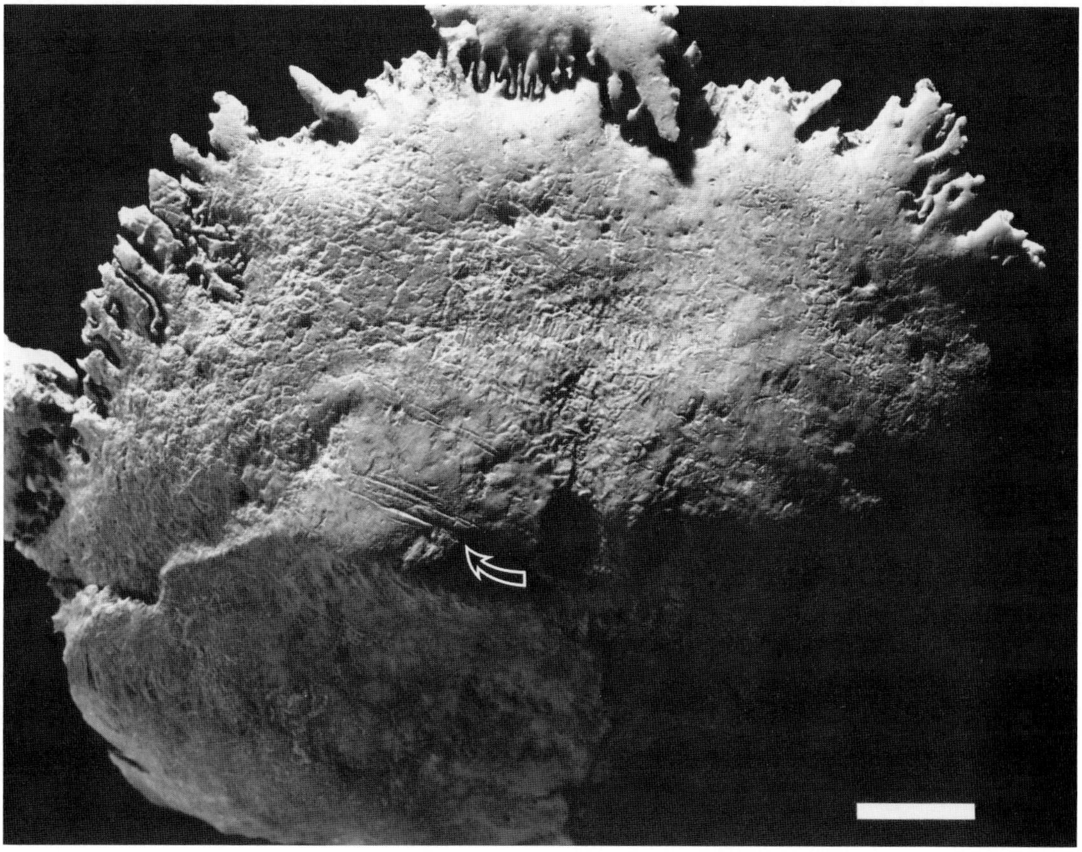

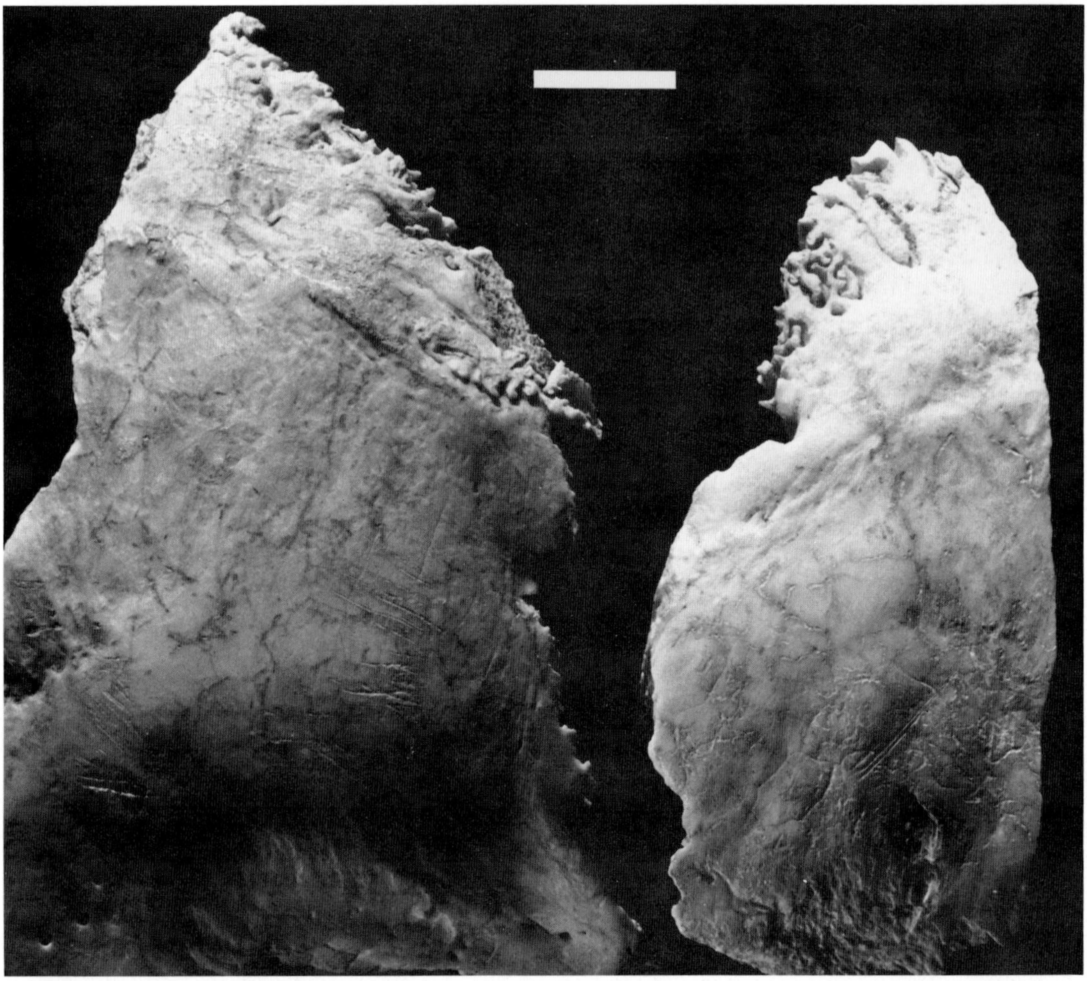

Fig. 7.20 Cutmarks below the superior nuchal line of the occipital bone (1797 and 1742). View is same as in Figure 7.19. Bar = 1 cm.

region. Conversely, almost all the occipitals with more than half the squama preserved show burning involvement. This burning centers on the upper scale. Three adult (1758, 1768, 1793) and one immature (1788) pieces show a clear demarcation between excellently preserved bone surface on the nuchal plane and poorly preserved, heavily burned, exfoliated bone surface just above the line (Figure 7.21). This is a good example of soft tissue protection of the underlying bone during thermal trauma. In this case, the thick mass of the nuchal musculature protected the bone surface inferior to the superior nuchal line. As was described for other vault bones above, evidence of endocranial burning is absent from the occipital.

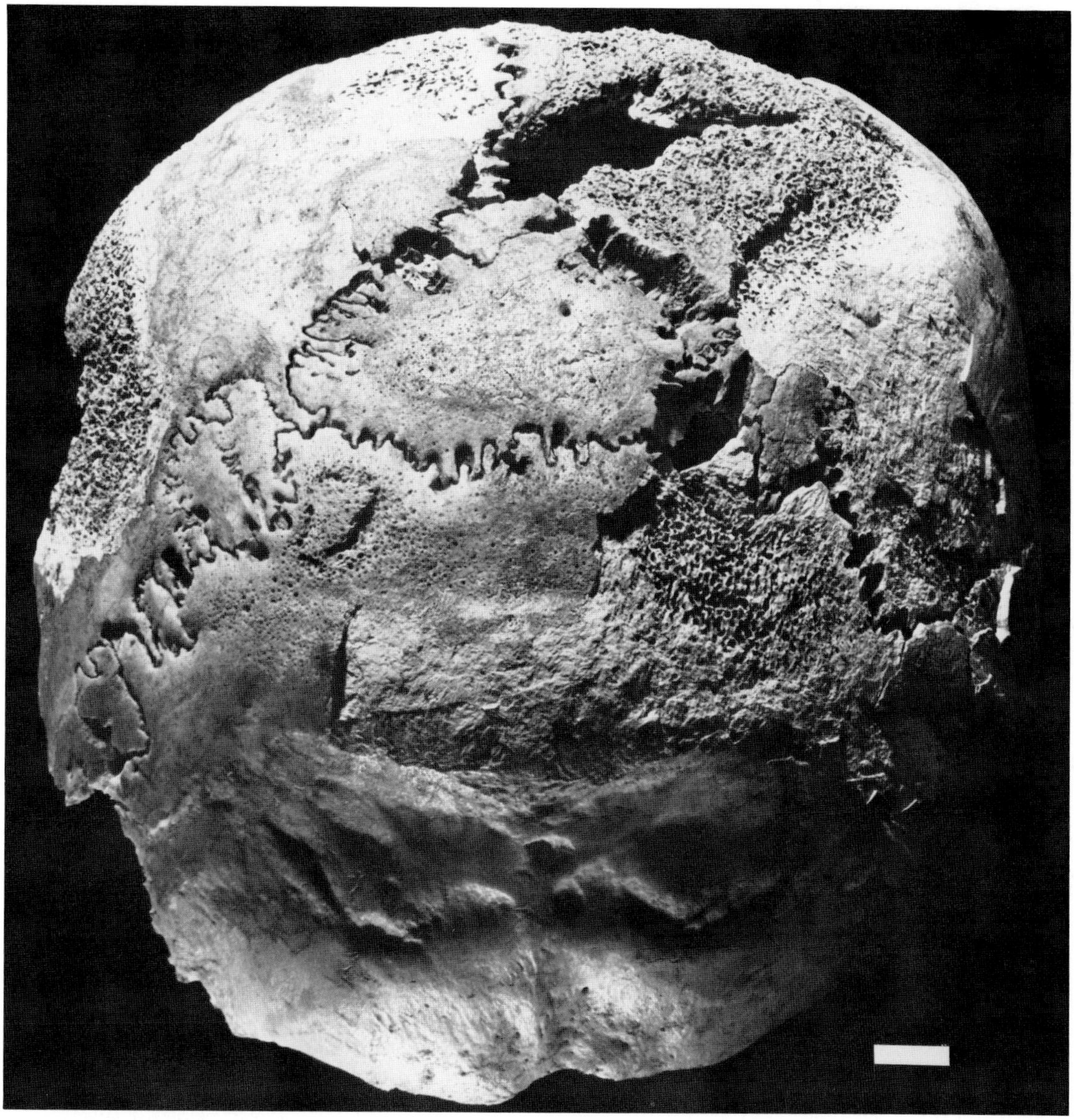

Fig. 7.21 Burning damage to the occipital bone (1768). View is from behind, along the sagittal plane, with the sagittal suture above the triangular inca bone. Exfoliation and discoloration extend across the subcutaneous portion of the bone, but the unaffected, perfectly preserved bone below the nuchal line indicates that this area was protected from thermal damage by the thick nuchal musculature. Bar = 1 cm.

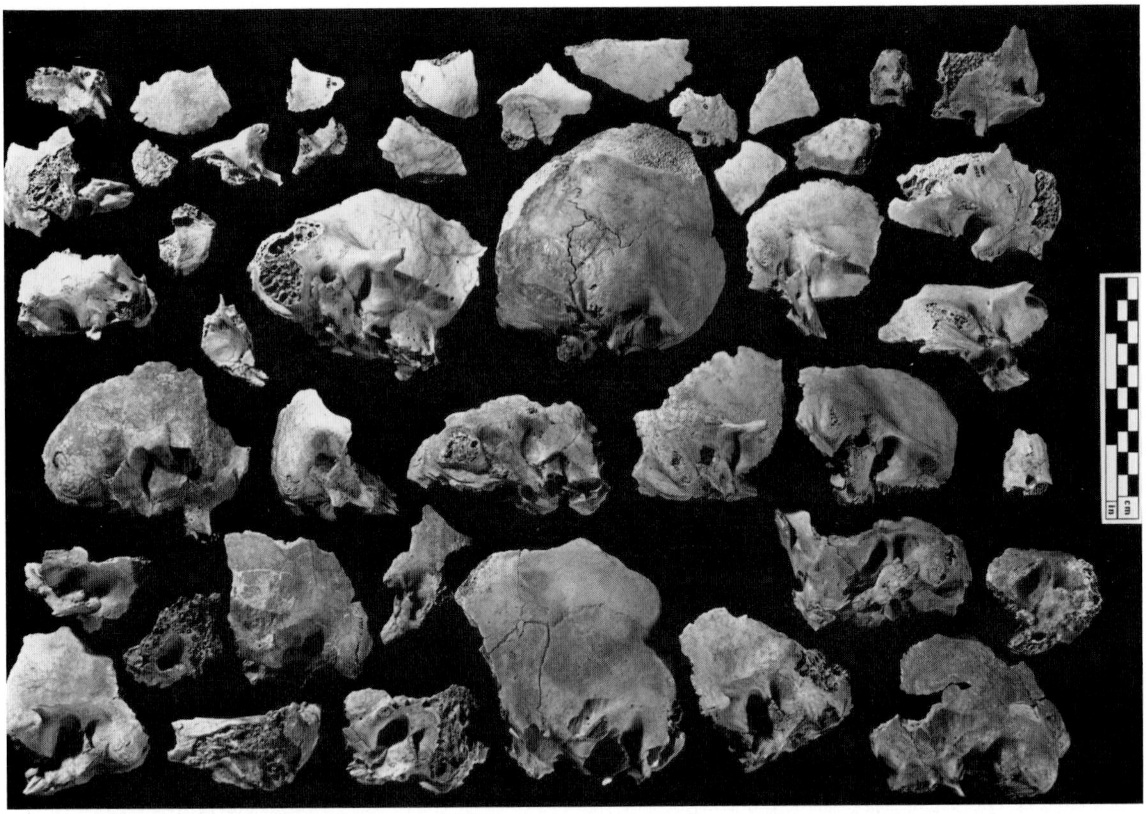

Fig. 7.22 The Mancos 5MTUMR–2346 temporal bone subassemblage.

TEMPORAL (FIGURE 7.22)

Survival

A total MNI of 17 individuals in the maximally conjoined assemblage of temporal bones includes 5 individuals younger than 12 years. All the temporals have the zygomatic process broken away; most of them show subsequent abrasion of the projecting stub. Of the 27 pieces (both sides included) with cranial temporomandibular joint surface (TMJ) preserved, 21 have an attached petrous. There are 5 additional isolated petrous portions. Of the 27 pieces with a TMJ, 16 retain more than half the squama, and 16 have pieces of sphenoid attached. Ten of the 27 pieces have attached segments of occipital. Only 2 of the 26 mastoid regions have intact mastoid processes; another 5 are slightly damaged, and the rest show some trauma.

Fracture

There is evidence of crushing in 6 of the 27 mastoids. One adult piece (1805, Figure 7.23) shows a chopmark and associated depressed fracture at the root of the zygomatic process, just behind the sphenotemporal suture. Many squamae show simple sutural release along the squamosal suture, but percussion to the ectocranial surface of the squama is indicated for some pieces (1805, 1809, 1810). Crushing and associated abrasion at the root of the zygomatic process are very common, this projecting stub having repeatedly contacted stone surfaces (Figure 7.24). There is no evidence of endocranial percussion.

Toolmarks

Of the 7 adult temporals, 1 piece (1836) shows deep vertical cuts, and another shows nicks in the root of the zygomatic process (1812, Figure 7.25). These marks may indicate ear removal because cutting strokes associated with such a practice

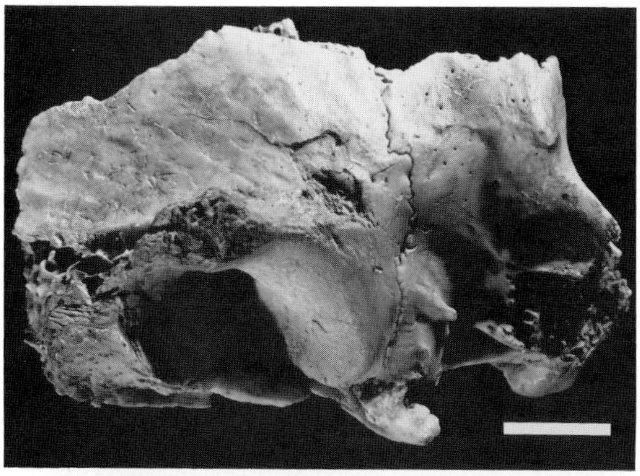

Fig. 7.23 A chopmark at the root of the zygomatic process of a right temporal bone (1805). View is from the lateral side, toward the ectocranial surface, and anatomical anterior is toward the right. The chopmark is centered in the bone, above the articular eminence. Bar = 1 cm.

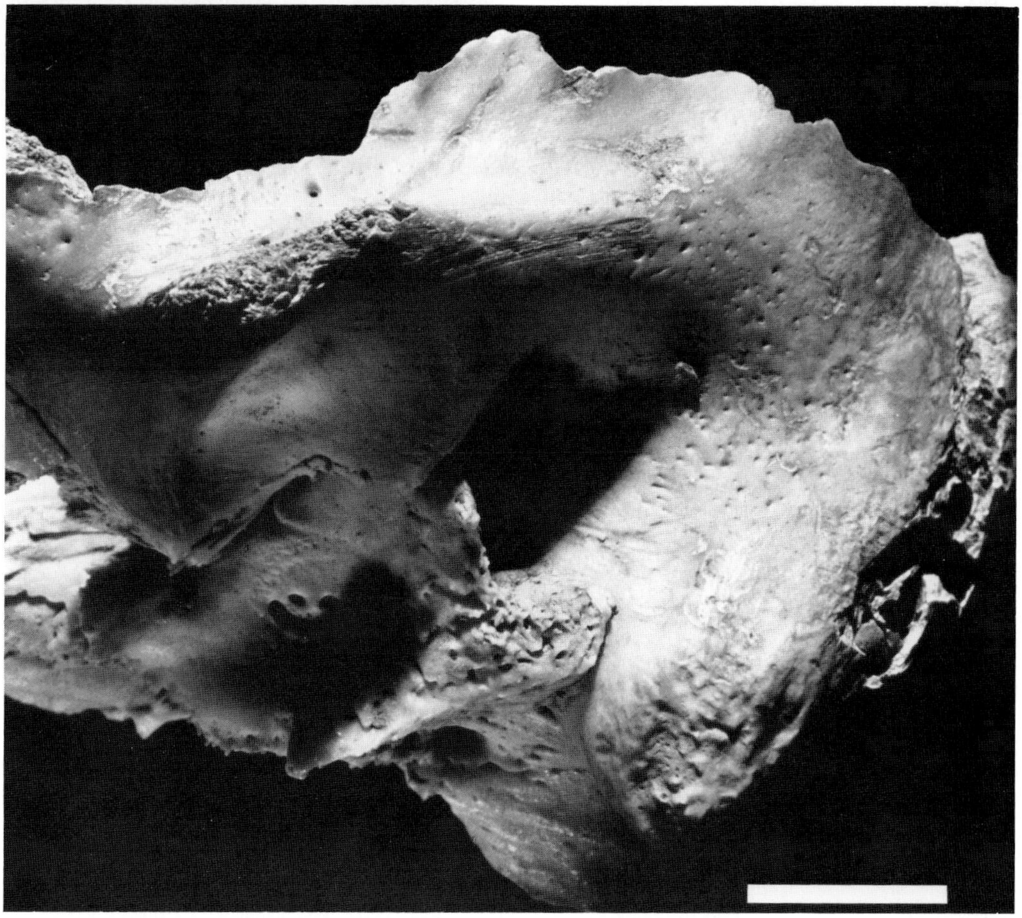

Fig. 7.24 Crushing and percussion striae at the root of the zygomatic process of a left temporal bone (1833). View is from the left side, toward the ectocranial surface, and anatomical anterior is to the left. Bar = 1 cm.

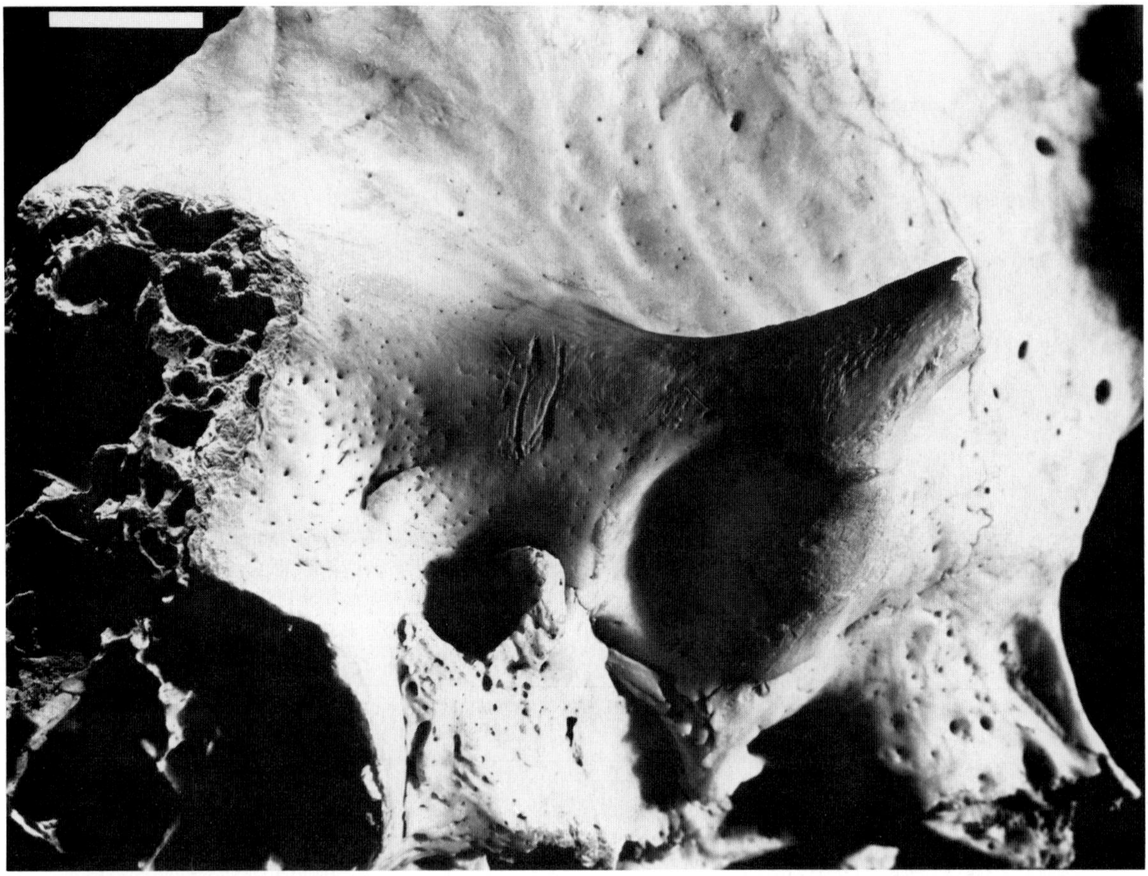

Fig. 7.25 Cutmarks on a right temporal bone, possibly associated with the removal of the ear from behind (1836). View is from the lateral side, toward the ectocranial surface, and anatomical anterior is toward the right. The cutmarks are vertical in orientation, set just above the external auditory meatus. Note that the burning damage to the mastoid process has exposed the mastoid air cells of the temporal. Bar = 1 cm.

would have been parallel to the side of the head, and the most laterally projecting bone surface likely to have contacted the blade in this region would have been the zygomatic process. The mastoid regions and TMJs show no cutmarks. No toolmarks were found on the immature pieces.

Burning

In the immature sample, 6 of 7 individuals preserving the mastoid region are burned here. In the adult sample, 16 of 18 individuals show such damage. The degree of burning ranges from discoloration to complete destruction with exposure of the mastoid air cells. In some pieces, the burning in this region was so intense that there is slight endocranial involvement (1836). The boss of the temporal just anterosuperior to the anterior edge of the zygomatic process is infrequently burned. This strong patterning (Figure 7.26) relates to the fact that the poorly protected, projecting, subcutaneous region mastoid portion of the cranium is highly vulnerable to burning.

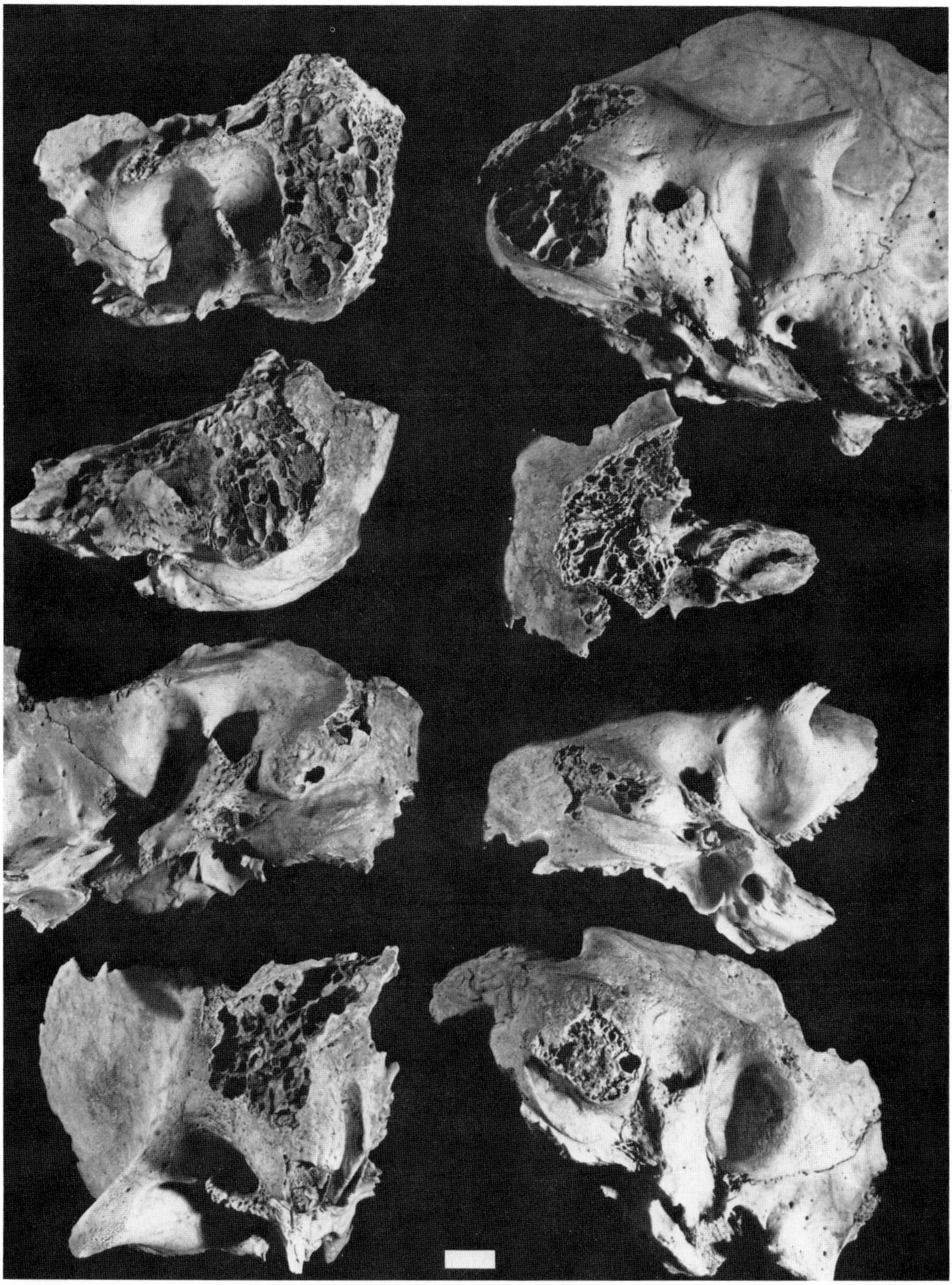

Fig. 7.26 Patterned burning damage to the subcutaneous mastoid area of a series of temporal bones from the left and right sides. This subcutaneous, projecting eminence is particularly susceptible to burning damage (left side, top to bottom: 1817, 1818, 1833, 1816; right side: 1836, 1651, 1848, 1809). Bar = 1 cm.

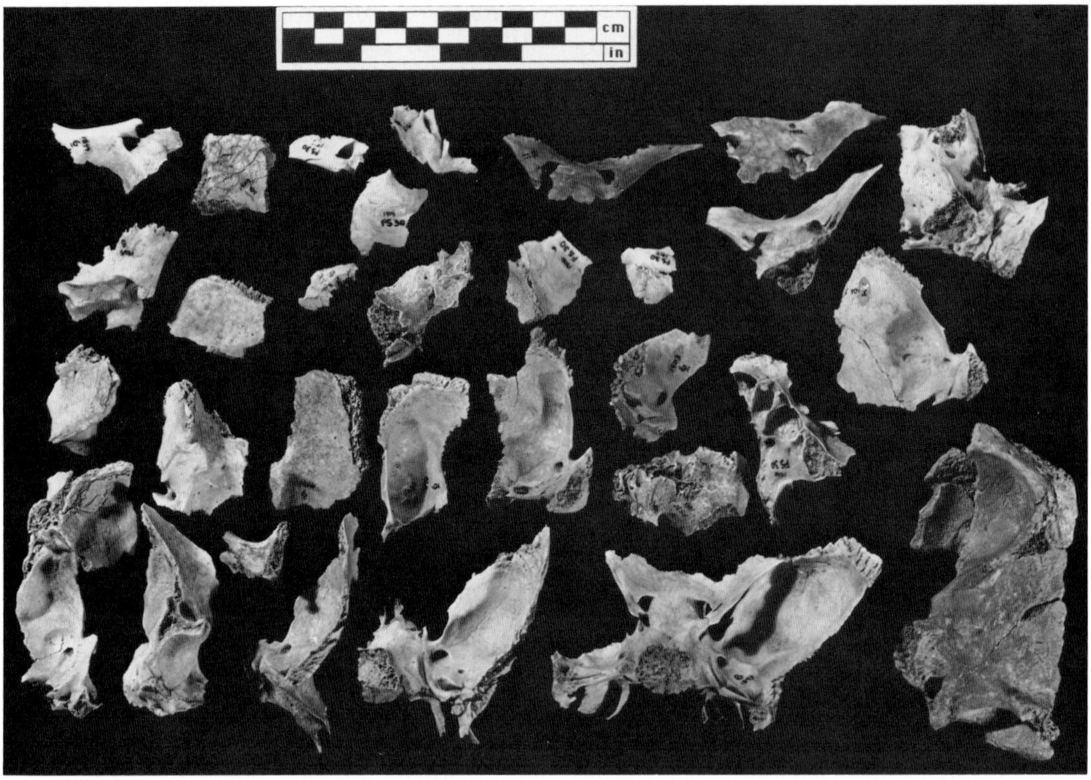

Fig. 7.27 The Mancos 5MTUMR–2346 sphenoid bone subassemblage.

SPHENOID (FIGURE 7.27)

Survival

A total MNI of 16 individuals was derived from the maximally conjoined assemblage of sphenoid bones, and includes both adult and immature individuals that were not further divided. There is not a single intact sphenoid in the assemblage; only three pieces retain both greater wings. Of the unconjoined sphenoid fragments, 17 are sphenoid alone (sometimes including portions of palatines, vomers, and ethmoids), and 22 adhere to other elements. Even highly fragmented sphenoids remain identifiable, so these numbers simply show that most sphenoid representation in the collection comes in pieces included in other element categories.

Fracture

The sphenoid, "buried" in the head between the face and vault, is commonly fractured in the assemblage, but was anatomically not susceptible to direct percussion. The most frequent fracture among the Mancos sphenoids was breakage through the sphenoidal sinuses of the body. When present in about half of the individuals, the pterygoid plates are not chipped along their posterior borders. The most patterned damage is in the region of the zygosphenoid suture on the anterolateral extent of the greater wing of the sphenoid. Where this suture is preserved, 4 of 11 rights and 1 of 10 lefts show crushing from the side, probably related to the smashing of the zygoma. An added temporal shows analogous fracture. These numbers are extremely conservative, including only cases where compressed flakes of bone are actually observed. There is often peeling in this region.

Toolmarks

No pieces of sphenoid show cutmarks on either the ectocranial or endocranial surfaces. One piece shows percussion striae in the area of the greater wing.

Burning

There is evidence of burning on 10 pieces. The area of burning corresponds to the point described above for most of the impact-fracture damage, the greater wing of the sphenoid between pterion and the temporal crest. The temporalis muscle and zygomatic arch both protect this area. Therefore, the burning indicates that these were removed prior to or by the burning process in the burned pieces. Burning, however, was not really intense or extensive on the sphenoid.

ZYGOMATIC (FIGURE 7.28)

Survival

A total MNI of 12 individuals was derived from the maximally conjoined zygomatic assemblage. This includes 5 individuals younger than 12 years. Only 1 adult and 3 immature zygomatics are perfectly intact. Most of the pieces are attached to the maxilla across the zygomaticomaxillary suture. Of the unconjoined fragments of this bone, only 2 of 13 had no other bone attached.

Fracture

In 6 of 9 pieces where observation is possible, there is fracture induced by a lateral blow at the maximum projection of the zygomatic arch. The result is a hairline fracture near jugale. Immature piece 1852 (Figure 7.29) is a fine example of this. The temporal process of the zygomatic is usually missing. Such fracture could result from the cranium having been dropped, hammered on, or anviled against a surface. Force came from a lateral direction and impact was not on the body of the zygomatic itself, as evidenced by collateral damage to adjacent bones. One piece shows evidence of peeling associated with the fracture.

Toolmarks

Most of the zygomatics, despite their very prominent, exposed position at the corner of the face, show no evidence of cutmarks. One 6-year-old and one adult show abrasion just inferolateral to the orbital rim. Only one piece shows slicing cutmarks. These cross from superolateral to inferomedial on both zygoma of individual 1875 + 1876 (Figure 7.30). The same area is present without cutmarks on 10 other pieces representing 8 individuals.

Burning

The zygomatic bone shows much evidence of burning. Heavily burned maxillae do not retain zygomatic fragments—the latter have presumably been completely incinerated on such pieces. Con-

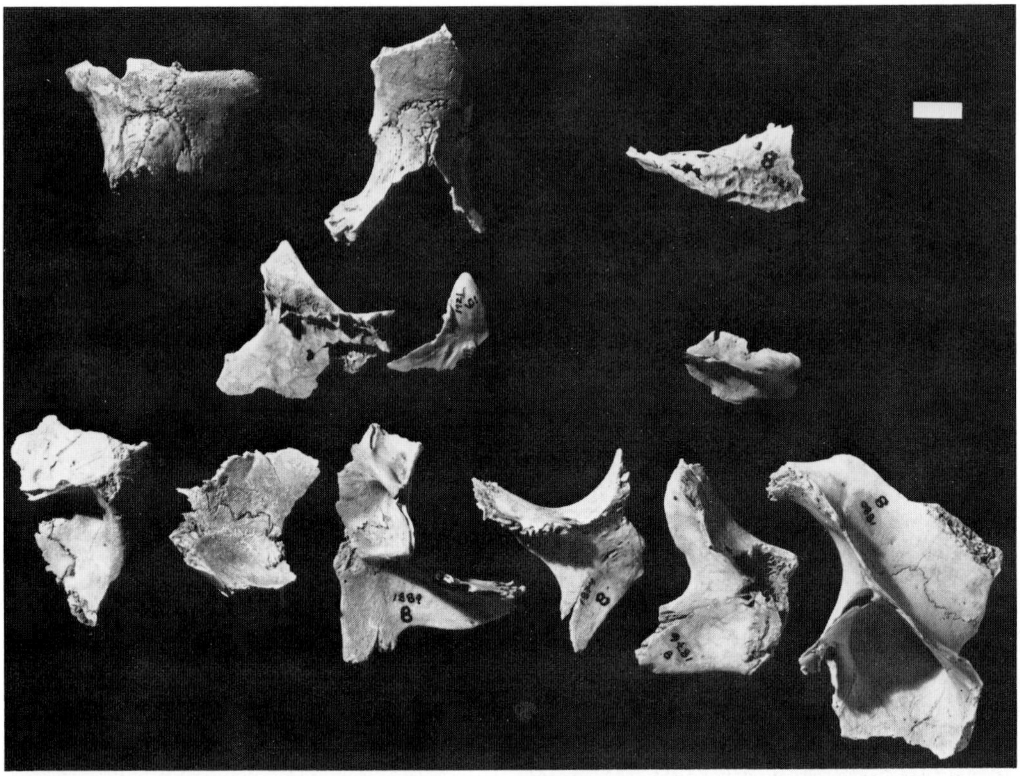

7.28

7.29

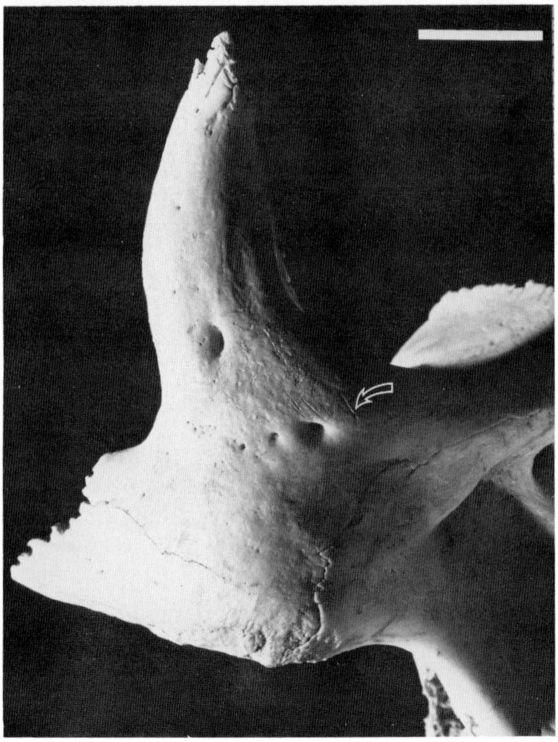

7.30

Opposite page:

Fig. 7.28 The Mancos 5MTUMR–2346 zygomatic and small facial bone subassemblage. Bar = 1 cm.

Fig. 7.29 A blow from the side fractured this zygomatic bone (1852). Note the concentrically arranged incipient fracture lines, and the evidence of spalled enamel on the canine and lateral incisor. Bar = 1 cm.

Fig. 7.30 Cutmarks on the zygomatic bone (1875). Bar = 1 cm.

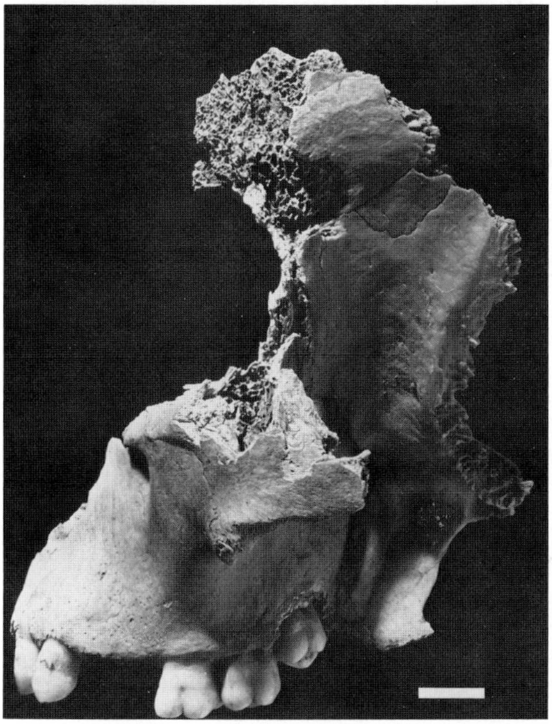

Fig. 7.31 Burning has affected the projecting portions of the frontal and zygomatic bones of this cranium (1863). Bar = 1 cm.

sistent with this pattern is the observation that heavily burned zygoma are attached to barely burned maxillae (1678, 1863; Figure 7.31). Six of the intact or fragmentary zygoma of 12 individuals show evidence of burning. Both adult and immature individuals display burning and there is no patterning with age. Of the 21 individuals represented facially by either right or left maxilla or zygomatic, or both, 15 show evidence of burning on one of these bones. All the other 6 crania could have been burned, the evidence subsequently broken or eroded away.

NASALS (FIGURE 7.28)

Survival

A total MNI of 14 individuals was obtained in the maximally conjoined assemblage. This total includes 3 individuals younger than age 12. The free inferior nasal edge is almost always broken away. The typical survival pattern is for the upper third of the right and left nasals to adhere to the frontal below glabella, held in place by adhering fragments of the frontal process of the maxilla. The inferior two-thirds of the nasals are usually missing due to fracture or burning.

Fracture

The survival pattern is related to breakage of the face from the vault. No direct percussion is indicated. Once the vault was removed, the projecting nasals would suffer further damage. A clean release of the vault and face across the frontomaxillary and frontonasal sutures rather than breakage across the nasals and maxillary frontal processes was only accomplished in 1 individual, an 11-year-old.

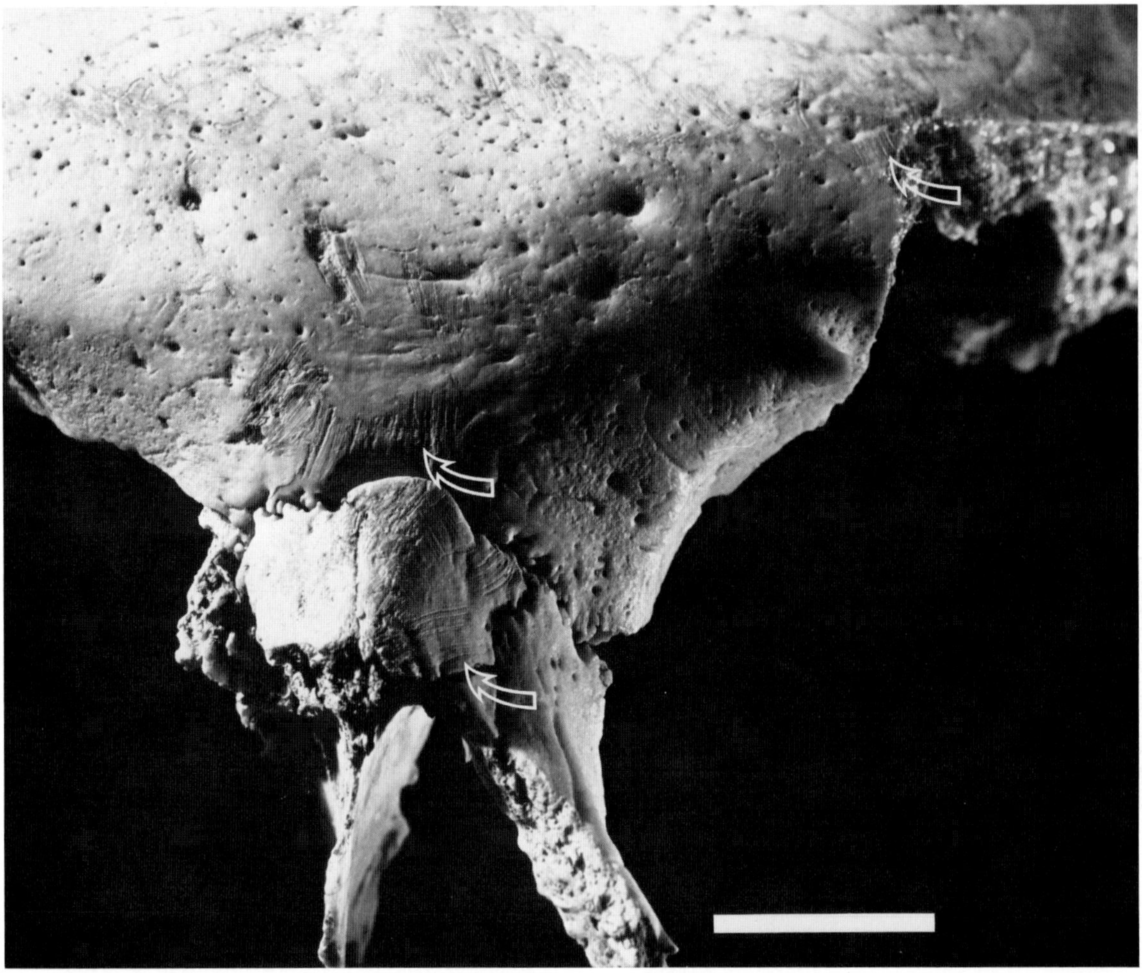

Fig. 7.32 Damage due to abrasion associated with percussion on the nasal bones (1670). View is from the front, along the sagittal plane. Bar = 1 cm.

Toolmarks

There is no evidence of slicing marks. The only marks are anvil or hammerstone abrasion on 6 individuals, and these show no pattern of orientation (Figure 7.32).

Burning

There is evidence of burning at the broken inferior edge of the nasals in 6 of 14 individuals, but this is an underestimate of burning damage because of postburning fracture and erosion.

MAXILLAE (FIGURE 7.33)

Survival

As noted in Chapter 4, a total count of 23 MNI was determined for the maximally

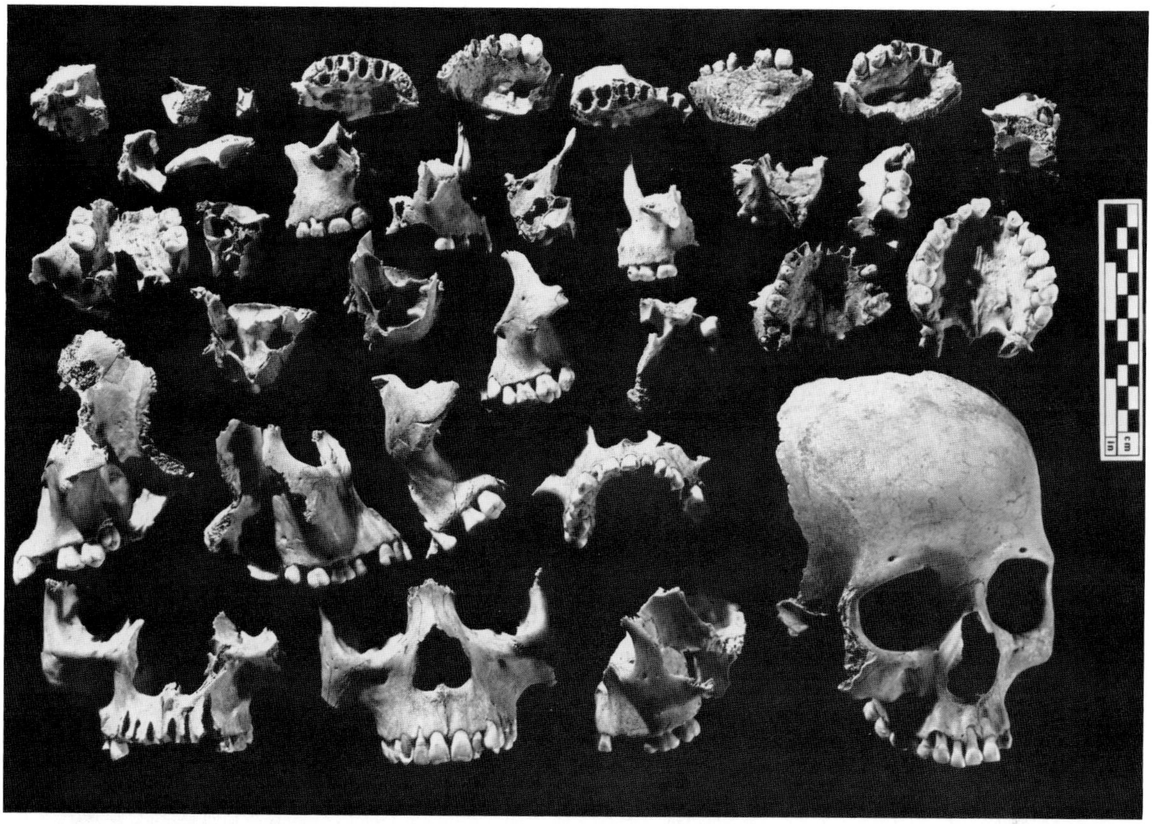

Fig. 7.33 The Mancos 5MTUMR–2346 maxilla subassemblage.

conjoined Mancos assemblage based on maxillae and maxillary dentition. Of these, 21 individuals are represented by maxillary bone, and 9 of these are 12 years or younger. Of the total 14 individuals represented by portions of both left and right maxillae, only 8 individuals retain articulation between the maxillary halves. Maxillae show the full range of preservation, from intact pieces within intact faces to very small, eroded alveolar sections. The full spectrum of damage is seen within the maxillary sample, and there is no typical survival class along this continuum.

Fracture

In the sample, the maxillary sinus is usually broken into, and loss of the zygomatic process is common. The palatine region is often missing, and the premaxillary region is often damaged. Alveolar bone buccal to the tooth roots is often missing and when teeth have been levered out (6 pieces) there is associated peeling of adjacent alveolar bone. The frontal process is usually broken. Of the total 42 frontal processes available for observation, only 6 are preserved intact. There is no obvious pattern of percussion damage,

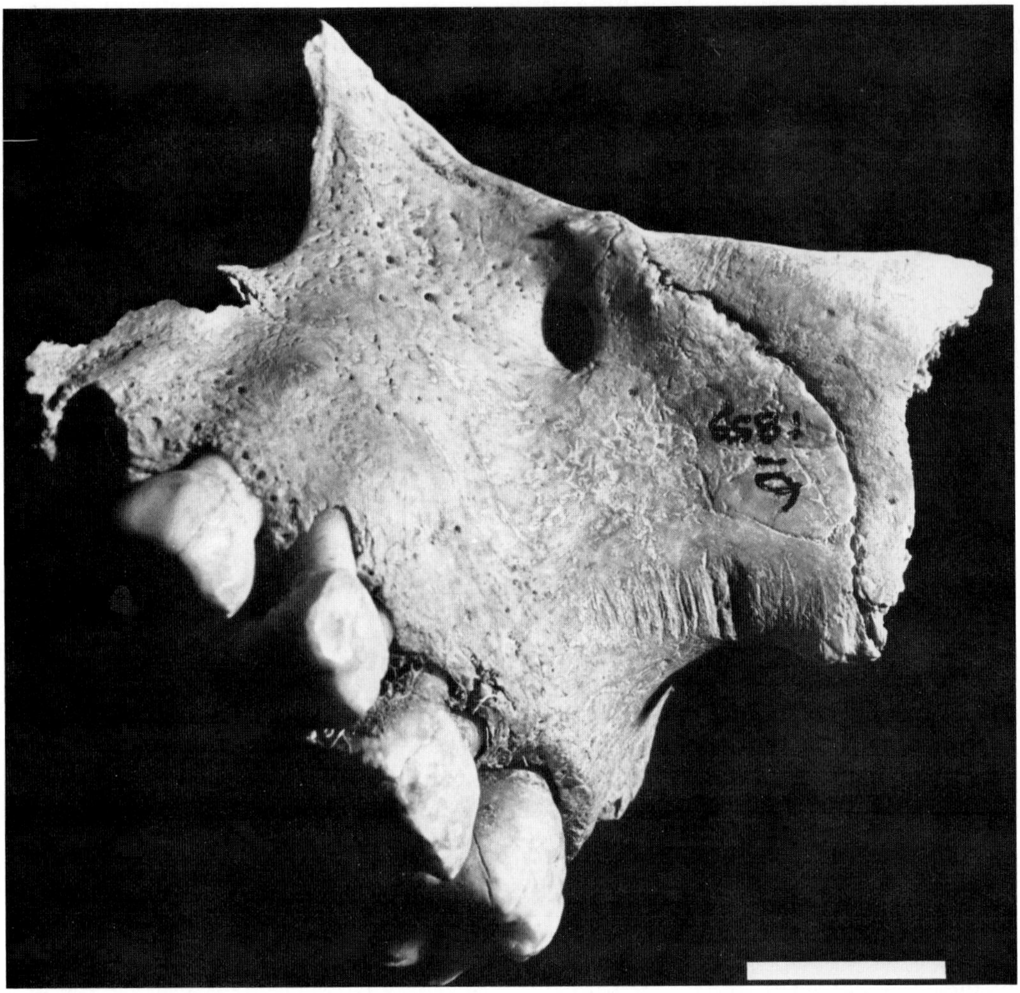

Fig. 7.34 Cutmarks consistent with a sawing motion of a stone tool, presumably used to remove the masseter muscle from this zygomaticomaxillary specimen (1859). Bar = 1 cm.

and most of the fracture seems incidental to the removal of the face from the cranial vault. Some pieces (1870, 1875) show evidence of heavy percussion to the alveolar process that resulted in forced dislocation of teeth.

Toolmarks

Cutmarks are rare on the maxillae, with only three major examples. A 6-year-old shows cutmarks made by a sawing motion on the anteroinferior root of the zygo-

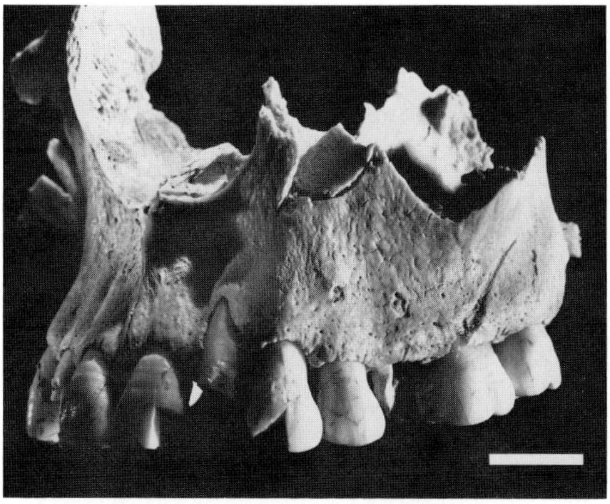

Fig. 7.35 Chopmarks to the maxilla (1877). The upper blow crushed a fragment of maxilla into the maxillary sinus, the lower blow left a long gouge in the alveolar region above the first and second molars. Bar = 1 cm.

matic, presumably associated with the removal of the masseter muscle (Figure 7.34; analogous to Binford's [1981] cutmark S-6). An adolescent shows a posterosuperior to anteroinferiorly oriented hackmark below the root of the zygomatic. A second blow is oriented in the same way at the root of the frontal process of the same piece (Figure 7.35). An adult shows a similar hackmark on the canine jugum near the base of the nasal aperture.

Burning

Burning damage to the maxillae ranges from extreme to slight. Of the 8 pieces from individuals 12 years and younger, 6 show evidence of burned maxillary bone. Of the 7 individuals between 12 and 18 years of age, only 2 lack burning, but both show evidence of burning on other articulated cranial bones. Of the 6 adults, only 2 lack evidence of burning. Thus, most maxillary pieces show evidence of burning. Burning is most intense on the frontal and zygomatic processes and on the alveolar bone over the incisors and canines. Alveolar bone over the third molars shows the least evidence of damage by fire.

MANDIBLE (FIGURE 7.36)

Survival

The mandibles and mandibular teeth yield a total MNI of 25 using the maximally conjoined assemblage. Of the 23 individuals with mandibular bone, 13 are represented by essentially complete mandibles, and 5 are represented by fragments that join to make nearly whole elements. Another 8 individuals are represented by mandibular halves. Of the 16 observable adults, 7 retain full mandibular dental arcades, and another 8 show fracture of the arcade near the symphysis. Besides joining near the midline, there is a notably small amount of joining in the mandible, corresponding to the relatively small number of mandibular fractures.

As noted by Nickens (1975), the mandible is the most abundant and intact skeletal element in the Mancos assemblage. Not only is the element itself represented abundantly with little breakage, but even the more fragile ramus has survived very well. Not a single individual in the MNI count has a corpus without its coronoid(s).

Fracture

Of the 12 adults represented in the anterior alveolar portion, 5 show crushing from anteriorly applied compression of the alveolar edges by a hammer or anvil (Figure 7.37). Some pieces show peeling of adjacent alveolar bone, but none of this

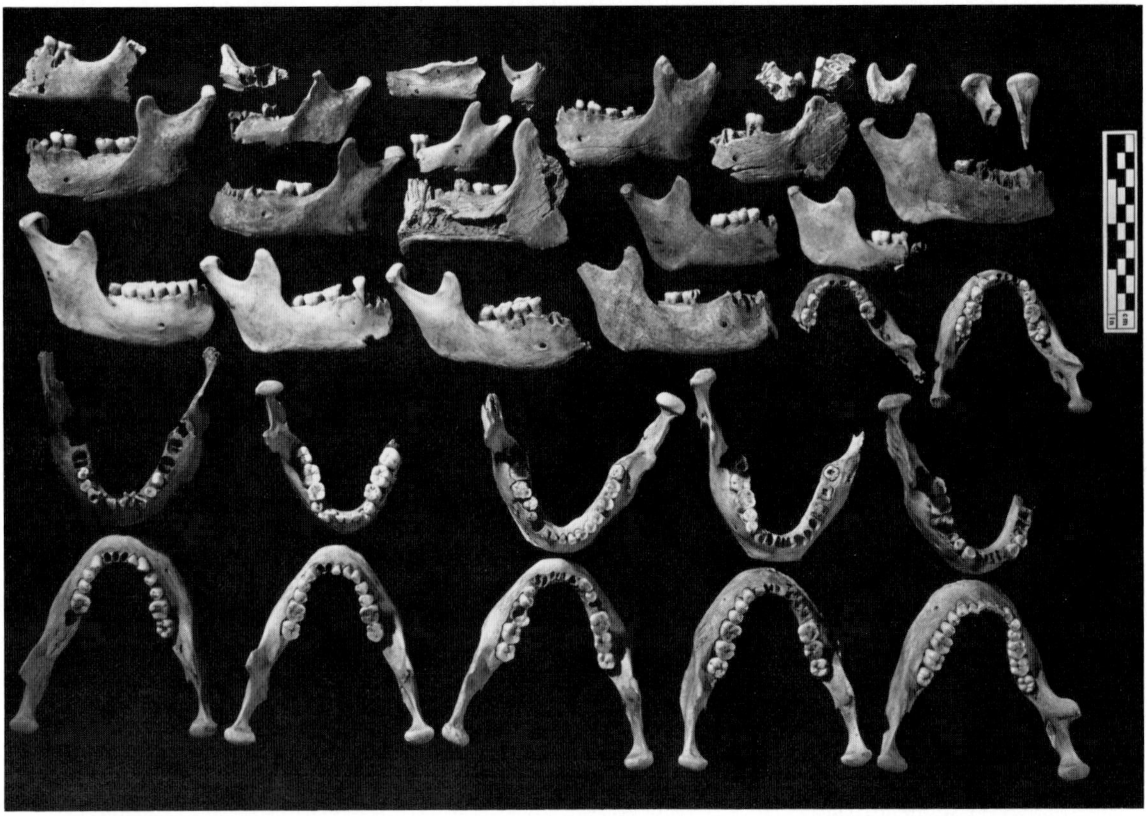

Fig. 7.36 The Mancos 5MTUMR–2346 mandible subassemblage. Note the relative completeness of this element relative to others in the overall assemblage.

damage indicates particularly heavy impact. The basal part of the corpus is often missing, mostly because of thermal damage. Only one (1937) of the 22 intact corpora, however, shows an adhering basal flake and associated fracture in the premolar region that corresponds to anvil fracture. Six adult individuals retain both condyles. Of the 22 intact adult condyles present, only 2 are ramus pieces detached from the adjacent corpus. Both show peeling on the anterior surface of the neck (Figure 7.38), and the nature of the broken ramus surface indicates that the mandible received laterally directed blows or leverage. The gonial angles and coronoids, when not burned, are not fractured.

Toolmarks

Few of the mandibular individuals display cutmarks; one of them is an adolescent, and the others are adults. There is very slight abrasion on the corpus prominence at the root of the ramus on 3 adult pieces (1926, 1932, 1936). Another piece (1951) shows true, but short, slicing marks in this area, oriented anterosuperiorly. There is minor basal abrasion on two other mandibles.

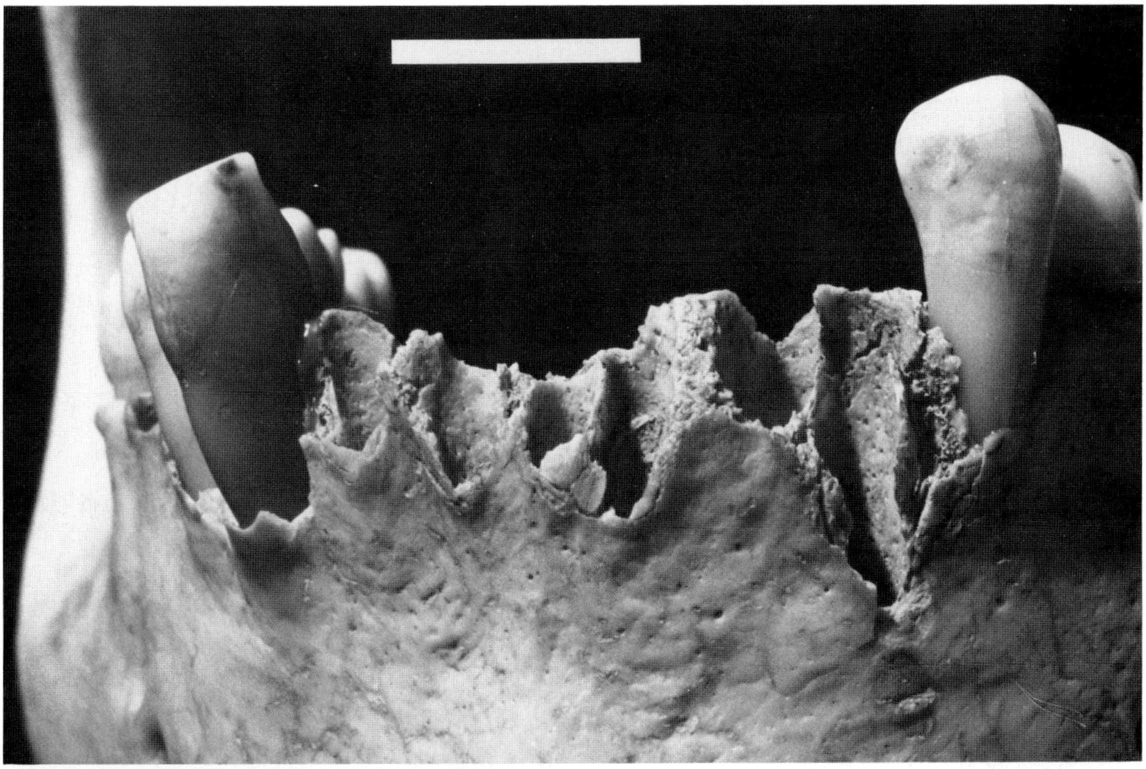

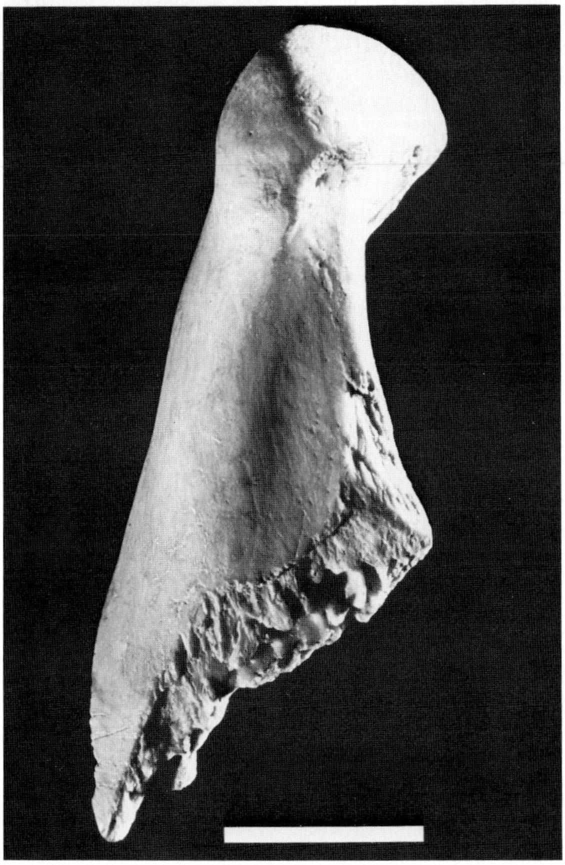

Fig. 7.37 Crushing in the anterior alveolar region of the mandible (1926). Bar = 1 cm.

Fig. 7.38 Peeling on the condylar neck of the mandible (1939). Bar = 1 cm.

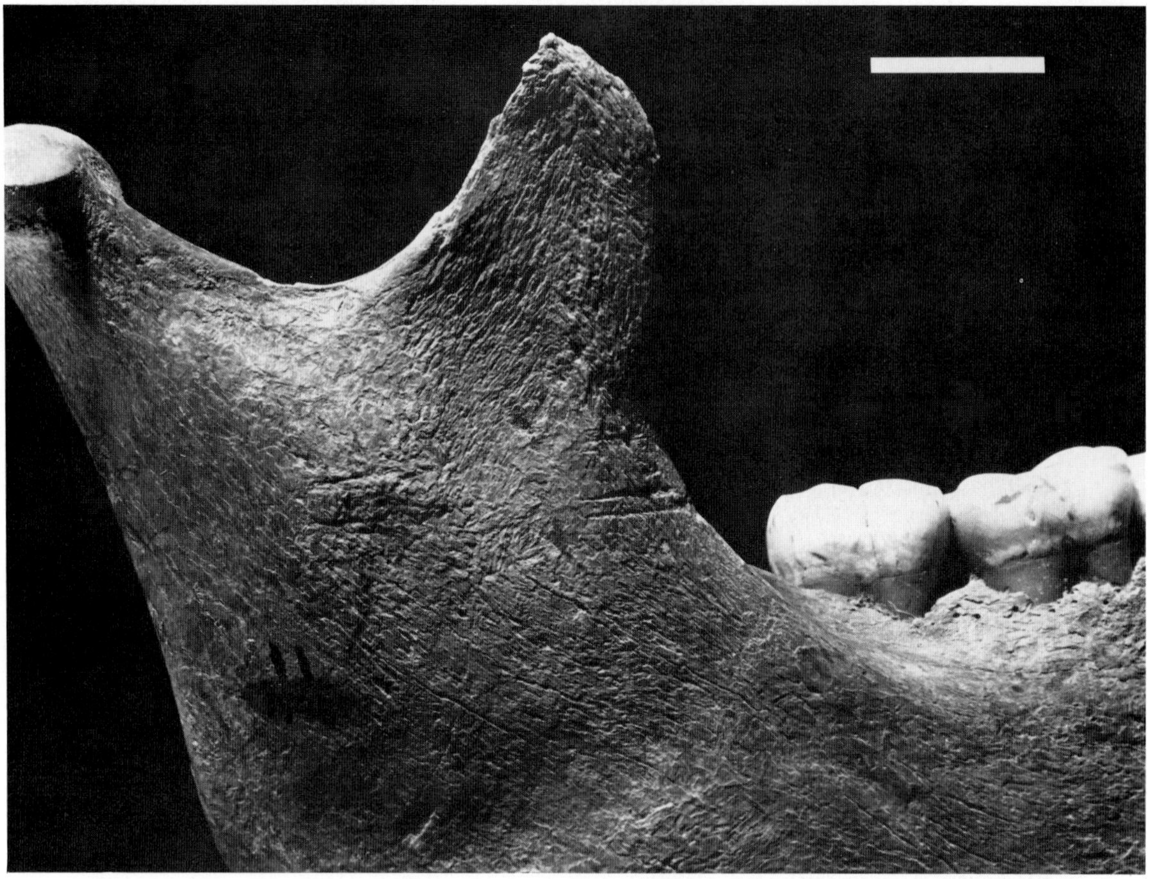

Fig. 7.39 Cutmarks on the mandibular ramus (1948), probably inflicted as a result of masseter muscle removal. Note the weathering damage to this specimen, one of the discolored, weathered specimens common to "Burial" 11. Bar = 1 cm.

Two mandibles, representing an adolescent and an adult, show slicing cutmarks on the lateral ramus caused by cuts through the fibers of the masseter muscle (analogous to cutmarks shown by Villa *et al.* [1986b, Figure 14.4]). The young individual shows this best (Figure 7.39), even though this piece is slightly eroded. One adult shows shallower marks that scar the lateral condylar neck and skip across to the anterior ramus edge (Figure 7.40; see Grayson [1988, Figure 14]). One of the isolated condylar pieces (1939) also shows similar cutmarks on the thin slip of ramus preserved below the condyle (cf. Binford's [1981] mark M-5; see Villa *et al.* [1986b, Figure 13.4]). Two adult pieces show subhorizontal marks at the base of the condyle (Figure 7.41).

Burning

Of the 33 intact or slightly damaged coronoids available for observation, only 1

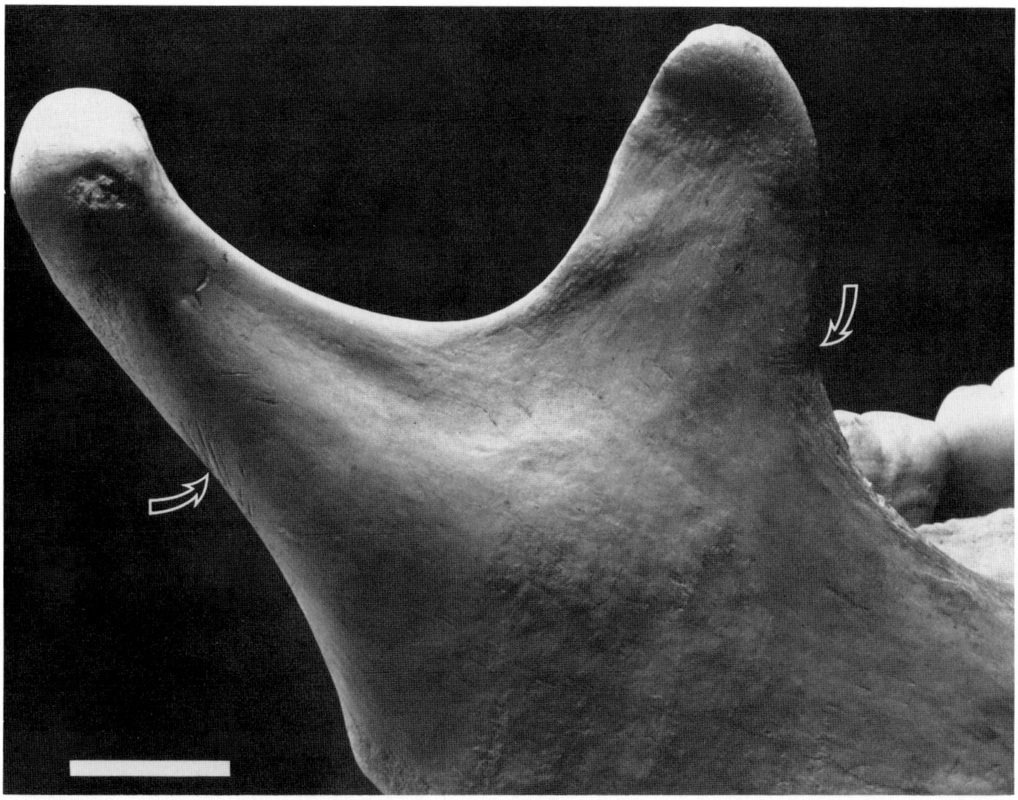

Fig. 7.40 Cutmarks on the mandibular ramus (1936), similar in placement and orientation to those illustrated in Figure 7.39. Bar = 1 cm.

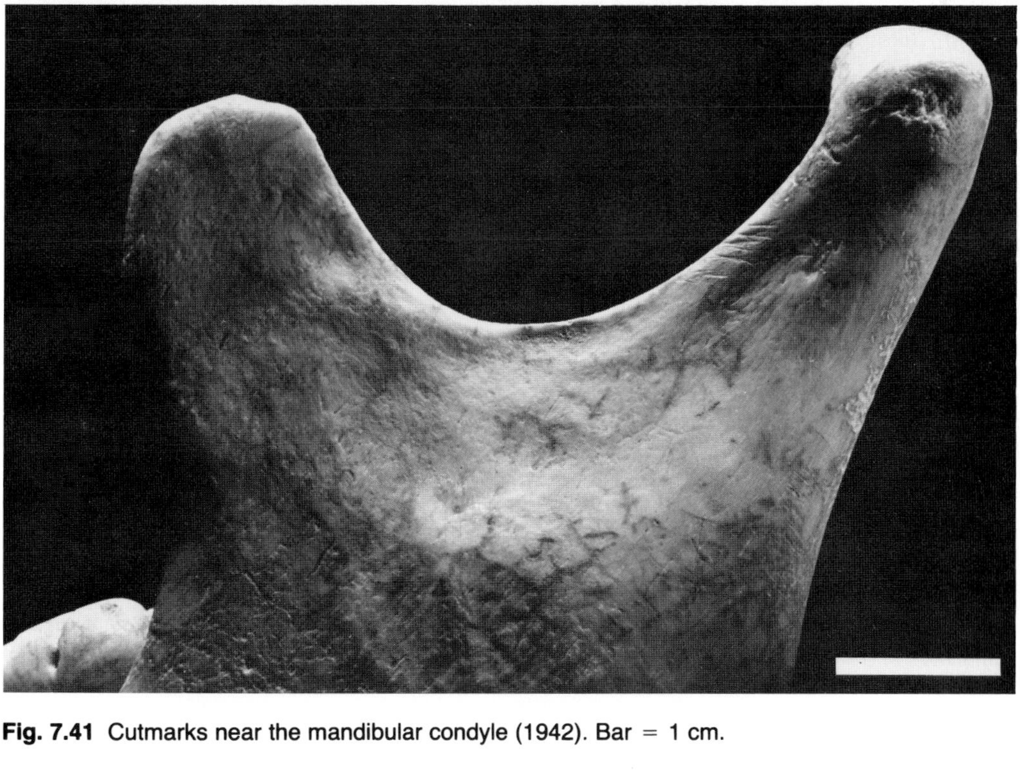

Fig. 7.41 Cutmarks near the mandibular condyle (1942). Bar = 1 cm.

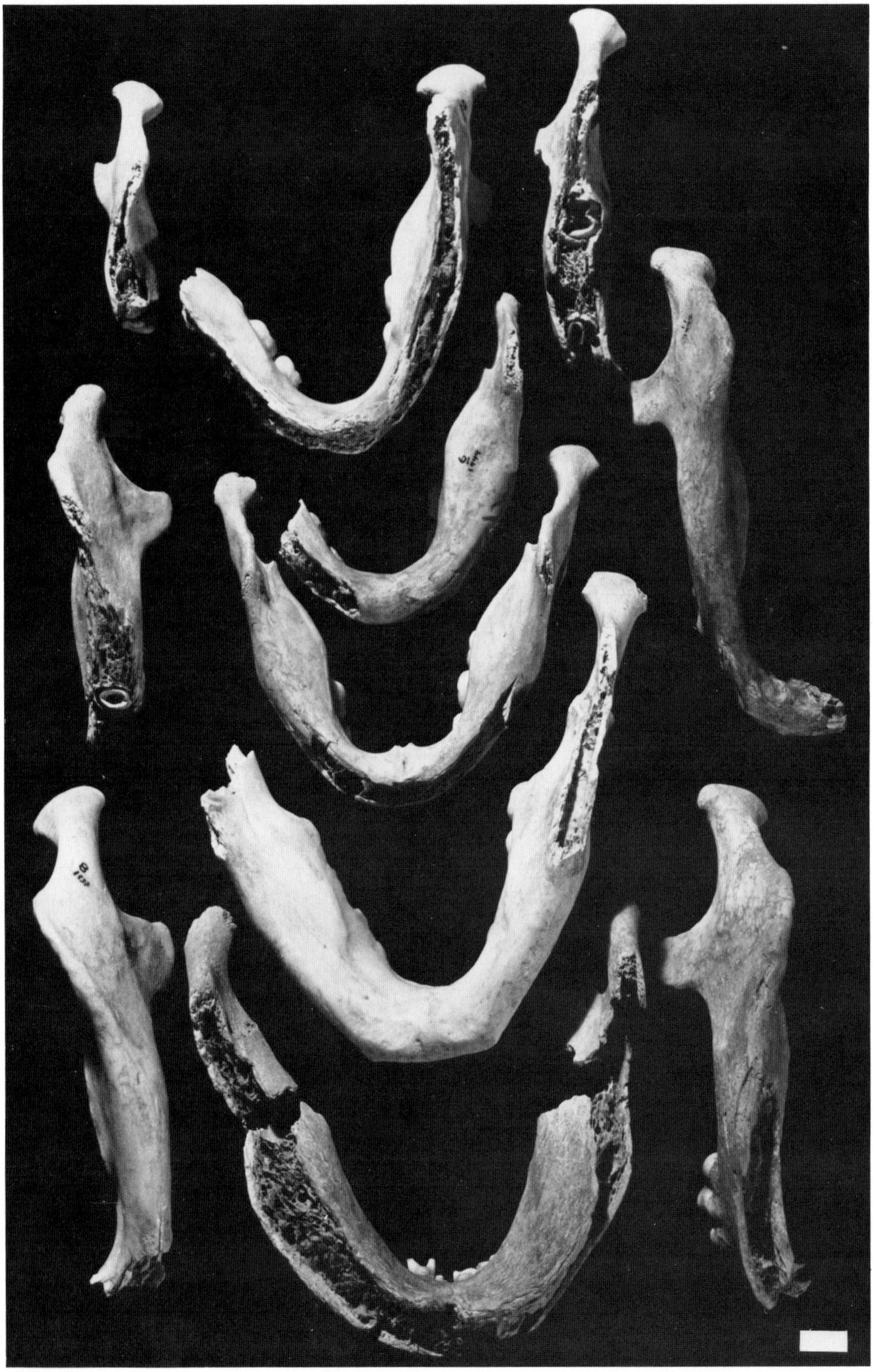

Opposite page:

Fig. 7.42 Patterned burning damage to the mandible. Note that the thermal damage is concentrated on the subcutaneous parts of the bone. Bar = 1 cm.

shows evidence of burning. Thus, the thinnest and most projecting portion of the mandible lacks significant burning damage. This contrasts with other areas of the bone; only 2 of the 23 mandibular individuals lack any evidence of burning on the mandible. The remaining 21 show burning on the gonial angle, base, or base and lateral corpus. Some pieces appear to be heavily weathered, but the distribution of this "weathering" matches the pattern of burning. With so many bases showing evidence of burning, only 6 pieces show molars with fire-caused exfoliation. Anterior teeth are so often missing that reliable counts on enamel exfoliation cannot be made from the mandibles. The patterning suggests, however, that the molar region and coronoid regions were protected from burning by overlying masseteric and temporal musculature. The subcutaneous portions of the mandible, the base and gonial angle, were the most susceptible to the effects of fire (Figures 7.42–7.45). This is strong evidence that the skull was burned as a unit.

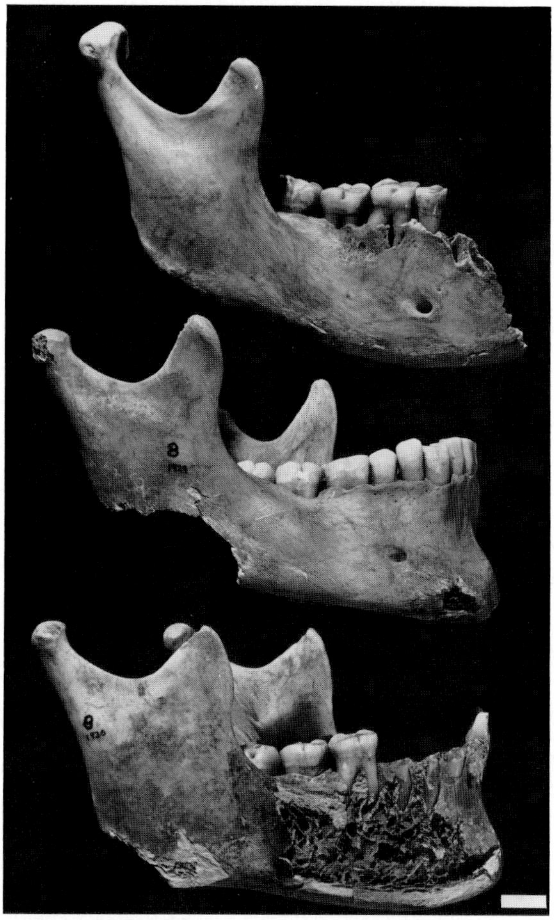

Fig. 7.43 Burning damage to the mandible (1936, 1929, 1930). This photograph is a cross-sectional sample that illustrates progressive destruction of the bone and teeth. Note that burning first affects the most prominent, subcutaneous portions of the bone. Although prominent and thin, the coronoids are not affected, presumably because they are invested with the temporalis muscle, deep within the zygomatic fossa of the cranium. Bar = 1 cm.

DENTITION (FIGURE 7.46)

Survival

Anterior and posterior teeth are absent in several maxillary and mandibular pieces. Evidence of peeling and percussion indicates that they were forced out while the bone was fresh. Table 7.1 provides a summary of dental survival, tabulating total

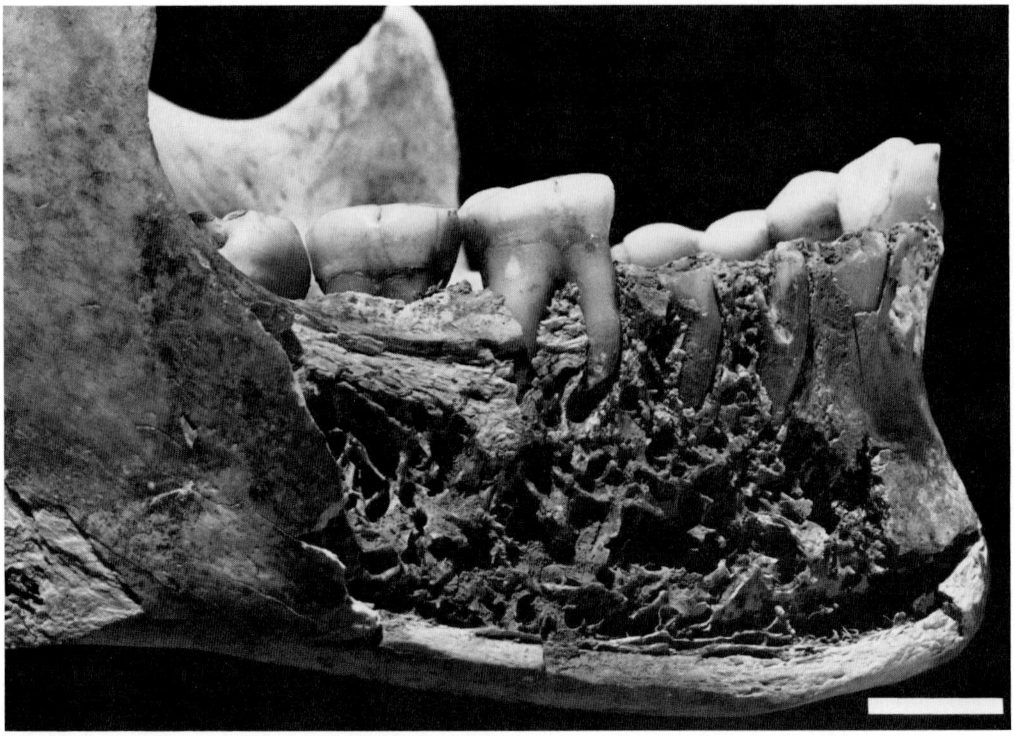

Fig. 7.44 Burning damage to the mandible (1930). This photograph shows the correspondence between burning and enamel exfoliation from the teeth. Note the char and discoloration below the anterior edge of the ramus and the exfoliation in the gonial area. Bar = 1 cm.

Fig. 7.45 Burning damage to the mandibular teeth. Note the spalling of enamel caused by differential expansion of dentine and enamel during burning (1950). Bar = 1 cm.

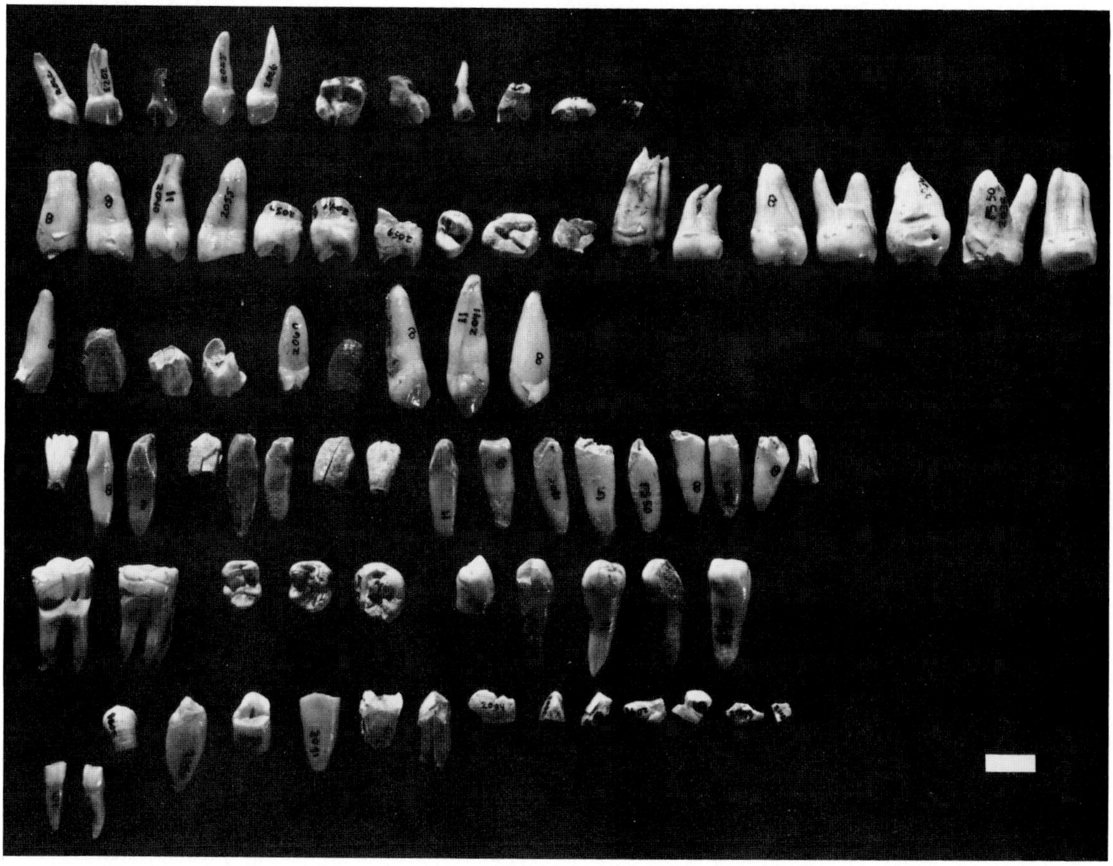

Fig. 7.46 The Mancos 5MTUMR–2346 subassemblage of isolated teeth. Bar = 1 cm.

identifiable isolated and implanted teeth from both sides of the body. Mandibular teeth are slightly more abundant than maxillary, following the representation of the bony elements. Single-rooted teeth (anteriors and premolars) are somewhat under-represented relative to their potential abundance in the normal dentition. This bias may reflect either recovery or perimortem factors.

Fracture

Most of the fragmentation seen in the dentition comes as a result of burning as described below. Some of it, however, is a result of hammerstone or anvil contact with the surfaces of the teeth. Table 7.1 shows the data for impact damage to the occlusal surfaces. This damage is illustrated in Figure 7.47, consisting of crushing and step fractures to the occlusal surfaces. This damage is concentrated in the permanent premolars and molars. It is most intense on the maxillary dentition, focused on the buccal cusps. It probably represents either anvil or hammerstone damage caused by blows directed normal to the tooth row. The damage is often bilateral. These blows probably were re-

Table 7.1

	TOTAL DECIDUOUS		TOTAL PERMANENT	
	LOWER	UPPER	LOWER	UPPER
CANINES AND INCISORS				
Total	10	12	52	40
Burned	4	3	24	21
Broken	0	0	1	0
PREMOLARS				
Total			38	33
Burned			4	11
Broken			0	9
MOLARS				
Total	14	16	65	58
Burned	4	7	24	15
Broken	0	0	4	14

Table 7.1 A summary of dental survival in the human assemblage from Mancos site 5MTUMR–2346. See the text for a discussion of the implications of these data.

sponsible for removing some teeth from their alveoli.

Burning

Table 7.1 tabulates data on burning damage to the Mancos dentition. Enamel and the underlying dentine respond differentially to heat, resulting in exfoliation of the enamel along the dentinoenamel junction of the crown (Furuhata and Yamamoto, 1967). This spalling of enamel is characteristic of burning damage, and is common in the Mancos sample. Upper and lower teeth suffer about equally from burning. Where the crown is only partially spalled, labial/buccal damage is more frequent than lingual damage, indicating burning of the outer crown half. In the deciduous dentition, the anterior and posterior teeth show about the same frequency of burning. In the permanent dentition, however, anterior teeth display more evidence of burning than posterior teeth. These facts correspond perfectly to the burning damage patterns seen on the bone of the maxilla and mandible. The most projecting, subcutaneous parts of the face are the most susceptible to burning damage. Because the permanent molars are shielded from heat by the overlying soft and hard tissues, thermal alteration of these teeth is far less frequent than for the anterior tooth crowns.

HEAD PROCESSING: AN INTERPRETIVE SUMMARY

Analysis of the individual bony elements that make up the skull has revealed patterns of survival, fracture, toolmarks, and burning. A breakdown of the skull into its element components reveals patterns of damage within each category. When the resulting information is synthesized by considering the skull as the bony foundation for the body's head segment, comprehensive, functionally explainable, and behaviorally significant patterns emerge. These allow a detailed reconstruction of the sequence of events that led to the characteristics displayed by the assemblage.

The minimum number of individuals represented by each of the skull's bony elements considered in this chapter ranges from lows of 11 and 12 individuals with the parietals and zygomatics, respectively, to highs of 23 and 25 with the maxillae and mandibles with their teeth. Most of the other bones cluster at around a minimum of 16 individuals represented. Many mandibles survive intact, as do many lower faces. Only a few faces and no vaults survive mostly intact. Only a tiny number of elements escape completely unscathed by fracture or burning. Percussion damage is widespread and particularly evident on subcutaneous bones

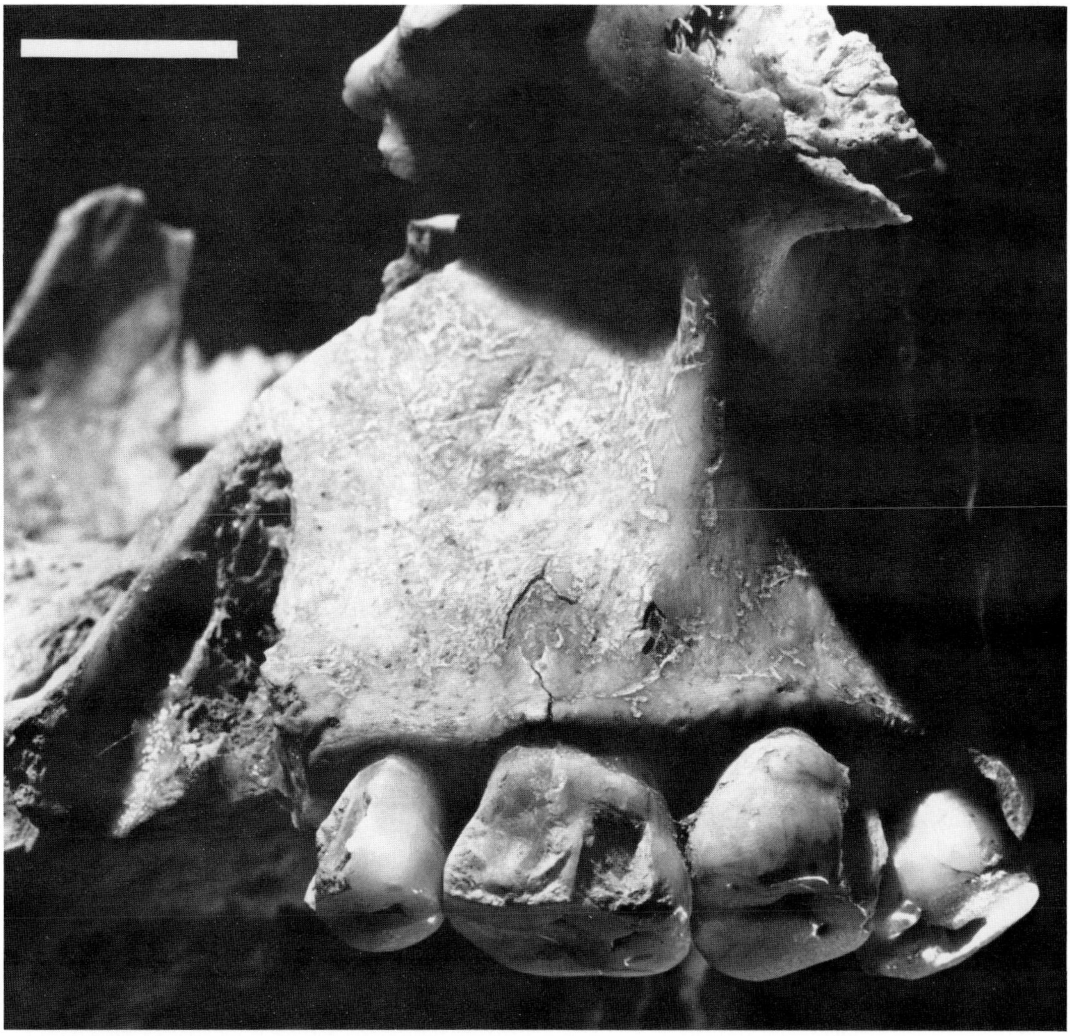

Fig. 7.47 Percussion damage (probably anvil-related) to the maxillary teeth (1875). Note that the more projecting, buccal cusps are flaked away. Bar = 1 cm.

of the vault. Evidence of crushing is minimal, probably because of the lack of spongy bone in the skull. Hammerstone pits are present on the vault, and abrasion, related to percussion, is ubiquitous. Adhering flakes and peeling are common. Cutmarks are relatively rare; chopmarks and scraping virtually absent. Evidence for burning is widespread, with the heaviest burning damage being found on projecting, subcutaneous, ectocranial surfaces.

Understanding the sequence of damage inflicted on the cranial segment of the anatomy is facilitated by considering the relationships between soft tissues and os-

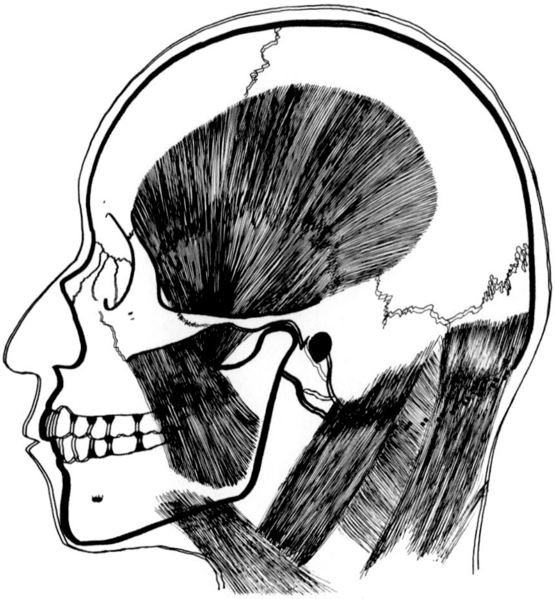

Fig. 7.48 Diagrammatic cutaway of hard and soft tissue anatomy of the human skull. Note the subcutaneous parts of the cranial skeleton along the base and angle of the mandible, at the mastoids, zygomatics, and vault bones that are not sheathed by muscle. These are the areas suffering from the most thermal damage as illustrated by the photographs above.

teological structures. Figure 7.48 illustrates these relationships, providing a guide to the subcutaneous bones of the skull. It is these subcutaneous elements that receive the greatest amount of tool and thermal damage. The sequence of head reduction as evidenced by the Mancos 5MTUMR–2346 assemblage is reconstructed below.

The lack of cutmarks near the occipital condyles and the low frequency of cutmarks in the nuchal region suggest that the skull and upper cervical vertebrae were removed from the body as a unit. As described in Chapter 8, the poorly preserved cervical vertebrae do not allow independent confirmation of this observation. The high incidence of cutmarks on the vault compared to a lower incidence of facial cutmarks suggests that the scalp was removed, at least from some of the heads. The superimposition of burning onto cutmarked surfaces suggests, for these pieces, that the scalp was removed prior to burning. Reasons for this removal might be functional (easier percussion after subjection to fire because the bone could be struck directly, without the blow being cushioned by adhering scalp and/or hair), aesthetic (to avoid the smell of burning hair; a practice of the Nunamiut [Binford, 1978]), or related to trophy acquisition. The overall low incidence of cutmarks, particularly on the mandibles, the temporals, and the nuchal region, suggests that muscle masses were infrequently removed or did not require cutting.

The pattern of burning damage to the subcutaneous parts of the head, particularly the gonial angle and mandible base, the zygomatic, and the zygomatic processes of the maxilla and frontal, indicates that masseter, temporalis, and nuchal muscles adhered to and protected the bone during heating of the intact head. This is confirmed by the lack of burning on the endocranial surface and the excellent, unburned preservation of the condyles, the thin pterygoid plates, and the delicate coronoid processes. Evidence for differential buccal versus lingual exfoliation of the teeth, and differential anterior versus posterior teeth burning corresponds to these observations. Evidence from the cranial parts cannot determine whether the head had been removed from the body prior to heating, but the cutmarks and lack of clavicular burning (see next chapter) suggest that removal preceded the thermal alteration of the skull.

There is great interindividual variation

in the degree to which various skull parts are burned. Interindividual variation in burning foci suggests that the head was placed directly on the coals, and perhaps shifted during heating. The heavy ectocranial burning and near lack of endocranial burning suggest that the aim of the burning was to heat the external musculature and/or cranial contents (mostly brain tissue). The overall patterning of thermal damage to the various parts of the skull within the Mancos assemblage overwhelmingly indicates that the head was heated while intact. Percussion therefore followed heating and was presumably directed toward removal of the brain tissues. The route of easiest entry, through the frontal and/or parietals, was followed. Percussion-related abrasion and damage to the dentition were coincident with fracture of the vault. The faces were uniformly removed from the vault at this time. Percussion was to the frontal and parietals. Heavy percussors such as the many manos and hammerstones found at the site, combined with anvils in the form of metates or other large stones would have been suited for the final breakage into the vault and the resultant trauma to the bones of the head.

Limited evidence from cutmarks in the temporal fossa and on the mandible ramus indicates that there was some postburning cutting of muscle tissue, but disarticulation of the mandible was usually not attempted or did not leave traces. The ubiquitous fracture of the zygomatic arches may be related either to general percussion of the vault or to a specific action to access the temporalis muscle.

The combined evidence from the cranial elements points to a focus on the heating of brain tissues, with limited incidental cutting aimed at scalp and muscle removal, and heavy percussion to open the cranial cavity. The presence of so many intact mandibles led Nickens (1975) to suggest that they had some special significance, perhaps similar to ethnographically documented cases from places such as New Guinea, where these elements were retained as trophies. The abundance of intact Mancos mandibles is perhaps better explained by the evidence that the head was heated with the mandible attached, the latter subsequently removed, and finally abandoned. The mandible's survival, like that of the maxillary alveolar portion, is attributable to the inherent robusticity of the bone and its teeth, and to the lack of nutritional value of this element.

The head, because it is so well represented osteologically in the Mancos assemblage, provides interpretable damage patterns that allow a reconstruction of prehistoric anatomical processing. In the chapters to follow, a similar reconstruction is attempted for other segments of the anatomy.

CHAPTER

8

The Thorax, Pelvis, and Shoulder Girdle

Osteologically, the elements of the thorax (vertebrae, ribs, and sternum), the pelvis (sacrum, os coxae, and coccyx), and the shoulder girdle (scapulae and clavicles) exist as isolated elements in the adult state and are therefore easier to treat systematically than cranial elements. For many postcranial elements, particularly the vertebrae, it is easy to sort young children from adults, but fragmentary vertebrae of 12-year-old children may be difficult to separate from those of small adults. Therefore, the age identifications on pieces representing postcranial elements are very rough approximations. The descriptions and interpretations that follow group the elements of the trunk by function. A summary of the body's trunk as a unit concludes the chapter.

HYOID

No hyoid specimens were recovered from the Mancos assemblage. This may be because this small, delicate element was fragmented during decapitation (see below) and/or was not identified or recovered during excavation.

ATLAS (FIGURE 8.1)

Survival

There was no conjoining among the atlas pieces. A total MNI of 10 includes 2 individuals younger than 12 years. The 2 children are represented by articular surfaces and posterior arches. Only 3 of the 10 adult pieces were intact, and two additional pieces lacked only the posterior ring. The other pieces are isolated articular or ring areas.

Fracture

All of the 13 preserved adult superior articular facets show damage to their rims. In 3 individuals, the damage is concentrated on the posterior edge, whereas 5 others show crushing of the sharp anterior edge. All the transverse processes show damage. Of these, 10 are judged to have been damaged when the bone was fresh. In the other 5, damage is of indeterminate antiquity. All 6 of the adult individuals where the posterior part of the arch is missing show a breakage pattern consistent with fresh bone. Two of the adult in-

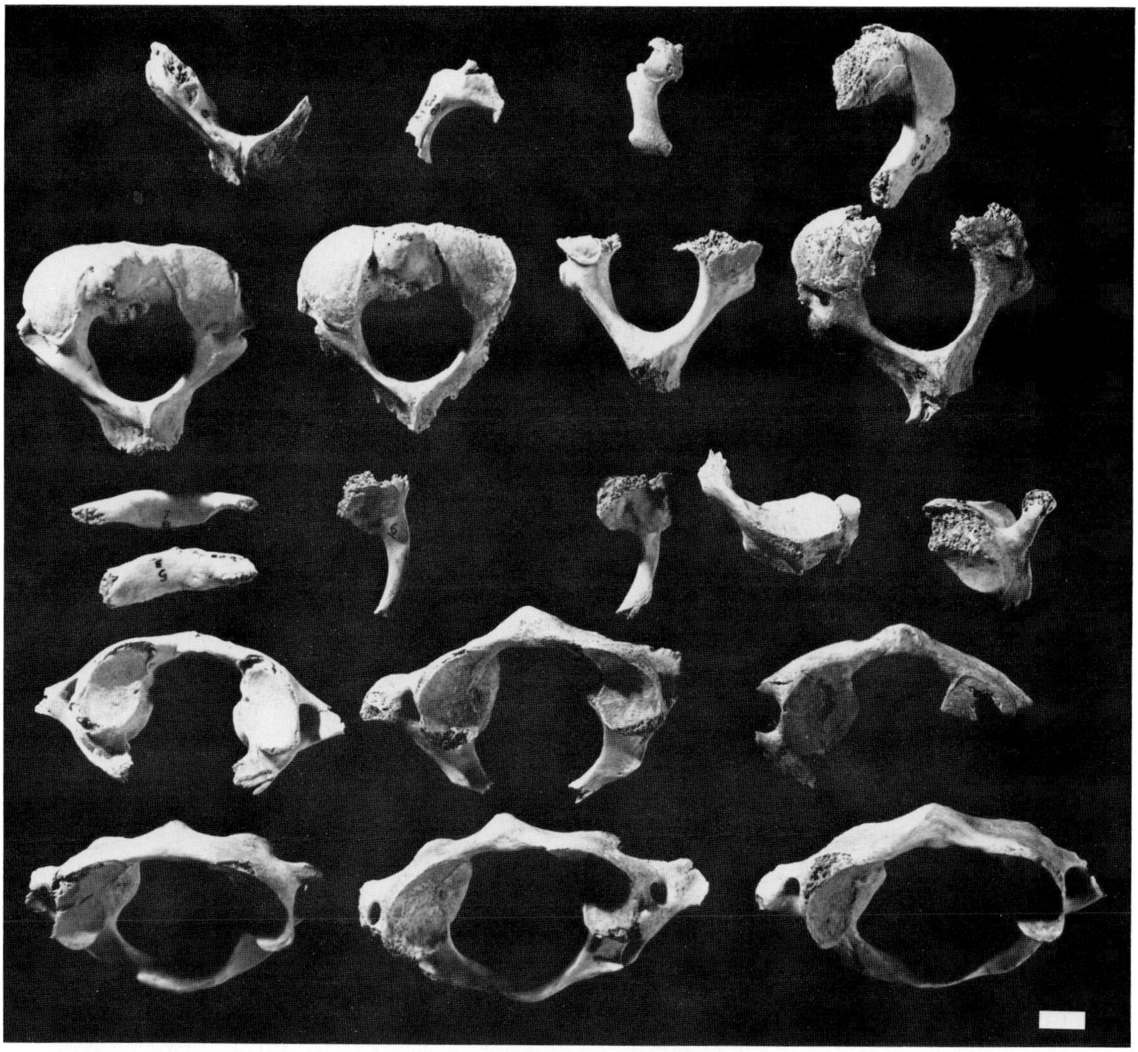

Fig. 8.1 The Mancos 5MTUMR–2346 atlas and axis subassemblage.

dividuals show anteroposterior crushing at the midline just in front of the axis articulation, and one of these also has a crushed area on the inferior edge of the anterior arch (Figure 8.2).

Of 13 adult inferior articular facets, 5 facets on 4 individuals show compression fracture, as if the bone were positioned, as it rests anatomically, on a flat surface, and then struck from above (Figure 8.2).

Toolmarks

No cutmarks are present, only abrasion associated with percussion fracture.

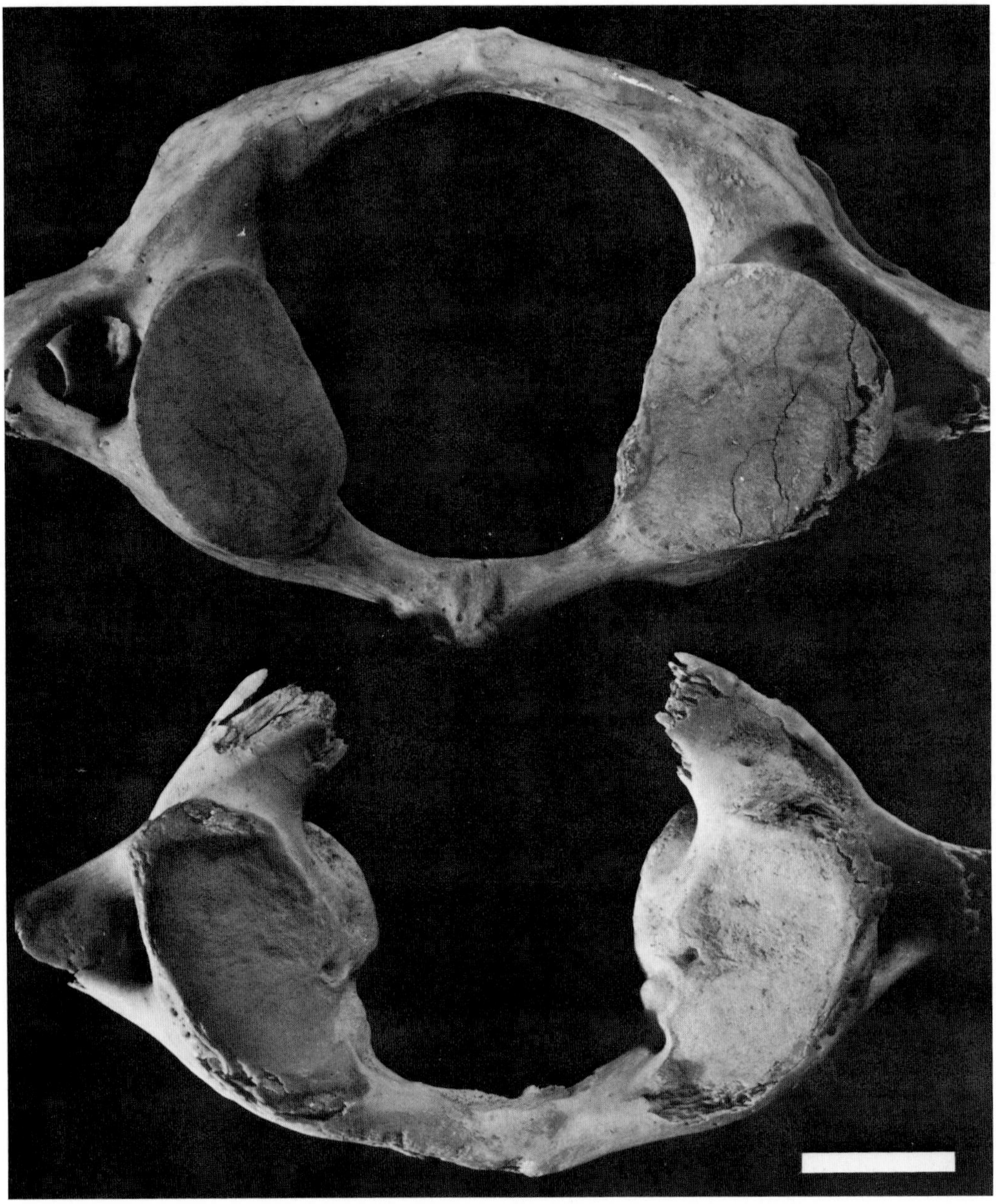

Fig. 8.2 Crushing and peeling of the atlas (0002 and 0004). Bar = 1 cm.

Burning

No unequivocal evidence of burning was found on the atlas.

AXIS (FIGURE 8.1)

Survival

A total postconjoining MNI of 6 individuals was derived from the maximally conjoined assemblage. This total includes 1 individual younger than 12 years. The pieces are variably intact, ranging along a gradient from complete (with minor damage at the tips of the transverse processes) to small segments of arch.

Fracture

One piece (0018) shows clear breakage of the arch from behind, with peeling fracture inside the neural arch. Another (0013) shows smashing of the body from above and crushing of the articular facets below. Not enough of a sample is available for a pattern to emerge.

Toolmarks

No toolmarks are present.

Burning

The best preserved piece (0014) shows obvious evidence of burning that has removed the posterior part of the spinous process. Damage to the 4 other individuals with this part preserved is consistent with such burning, but the coloration and disintegration are more equivocally fire-related in these cases. Enough of a pattern is present to conclude that the spines were charred; this makes anatomical sense because the spinous processes are the most subcutaneous parts of the element.

CERVICAL VERTEBRAE NUMBERS 3–7 (FIGURE 8.3)

Survival

A total MNI of 5 individuals was derived from the maximally conjoined assemblage. This number includes 2 individuals younger than age 12. This MNI is based on a total count of right superior articular facets. Further breakdown into numbered elements (vertebrae numbers 3–7) would certainly increase the total MNI. Fragmentation within the small sample, however, makes this kind of analysis unprofitable. The MNIs reported for the thoracic and lumbar vertebrae also follow this form of analysis and should be considered minimal MNIs.

Only 1 of 8 immature and 1 of 19 mature pieces had an intact body. Even these two bodies show peripheral damage. Vertebral bodies are entirely lacking for immature individuals for which 5 complete and 3 incomplete arches are preserved. In the adults, 9 arches are preserved, and 8 of these are whole. A major fragment of body (greater than half) is preserved on 3 of these, and the other 6 show only the posterior edge of the body. No adult spinous process is completely intact. Fracture is judged to be perimortem on 4 adults and indeterminate on the other 6. Only one immature piece shows an intact spinous process, and half of the 6 immature spinous processes were broken perimortem.

Fracture

The posterior half of the transverse foramen is usually present, but only 1 adult and 1 immature piece retain complete vertebral foramina. There is little damage to the posterior projecting edge of the inferior articular facet. This structure was ap-

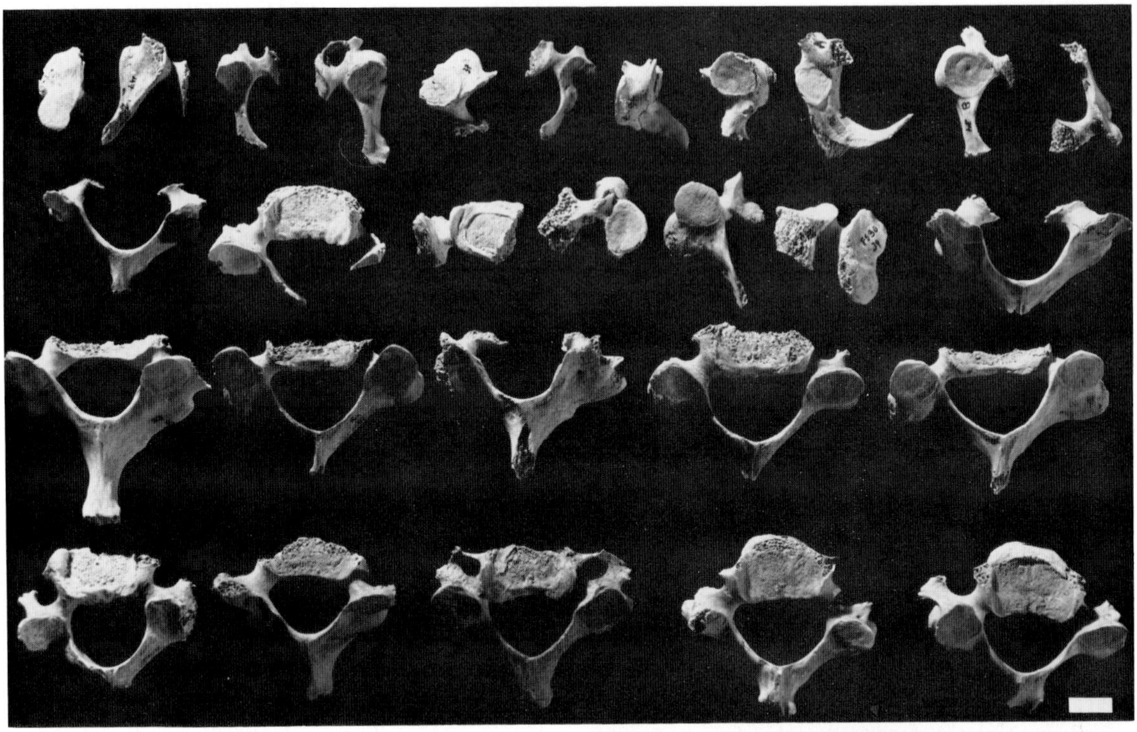

Fig. 8.3 The Mancos 5MTUMR–2346 cervical vertebrae subassemblage. Note the lack of intact vertebral bodies. Bar = 1 cm.

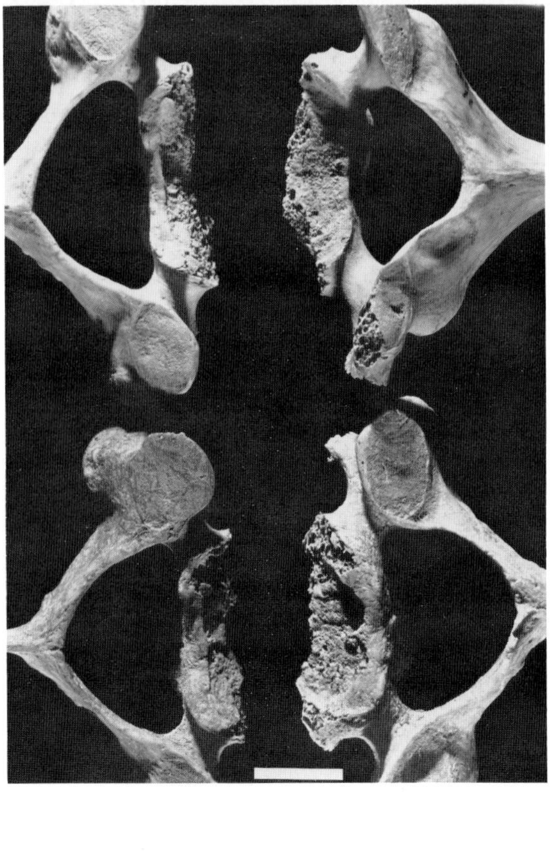

Fig. 8.4 Crushing damage to the bodies of cervical vertebrae (0028, 0029, 0030, 0031). Note that the anterior portions of the bodies are sheared away and the adhering edges demonstrate crushing damage. Bar = 1 cm.

parently protected from damage during crushing activity in which the tip of the spinous process and the anteroinferior edge of the body rested on an anvil, when percussion to the superior articular facets and upper surface of the body took place. The superior articular facets are crushed in several adult and immature pieces. Several adults show crushing damage to the superior surface of the body (Figure 8.4).

Fig. 8.5 The Mancos 5MTUMR–2346 thoracic vertebrae subassemblage. Note the lack of vertebral bodies and the dominance of spine and arch segments. Bar = 1 cm.

Toolmarks

No cutmarks are present on the preserved parts, but it should be noted that virtually no anterior surfaces of cervical bodies are preserved.

Burning

The tip of the spinous process is discolored and eroded in some pieces, suggestive of burning damage. The pattern is similar to that described for the axis.

THORACIC VERTEBRAE (FIGURE 8.5)

Survival

A total MNI of 5 individuals was calculated using the maximally conjoined assemblage. This total includes 2 subadults and 3 adults, and is based on superior articular facets. There is much fragmentation, and the resulting pieces range from small fragments to the most complete piece, an example lacking the entire body

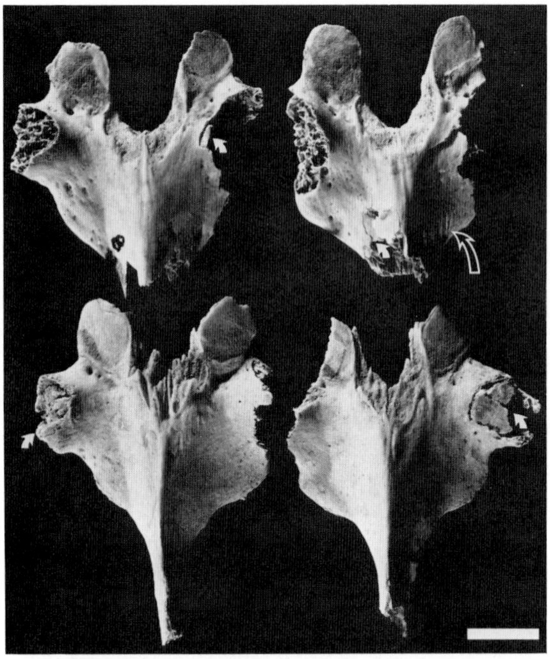

Fig. 8.6 Crushing (full arrows) and cutmarks (open arrow) at base of the spines of thoracic vertebrae (0064, 0066, 0073, 0075). Bar = 1 cm.

Fig. 8.7 Peeling on thoracic vertebrae (0063, 0064). Bar = 1 cm.

as well as the tips of the spinous and transverse processes. The general pattern is one dominated by loss of the transverse processes and body.

Fracture

Of the 53 adult and immature maximally conjoined pieces, the entire rear half of the arch (including one or both superior articular facets) is preserved in 36. Of the many superior articular facets preserved, most are undamaged, whereas 2 adults and 1 child show crushing damage. On the other hand, following the cervical pattern, there is not an intact spine tip among the 41 spinous processes where one might be expected. Transverse processes are also missing. Several pieces show crushing blows at the base of the spinous process, and evidence of percussion is present on the posterior surface of at least 10 vertebrae (Figure 8.6). The transverse processes were probably broken as part of rib slab removal (see below). Peeling is common, particularly on the pedicles and lamina (Figure 8.7).

razor + blades
backpack and work
jewelry
palm pilot
business cards
wallet + $$
Lauren's stuff

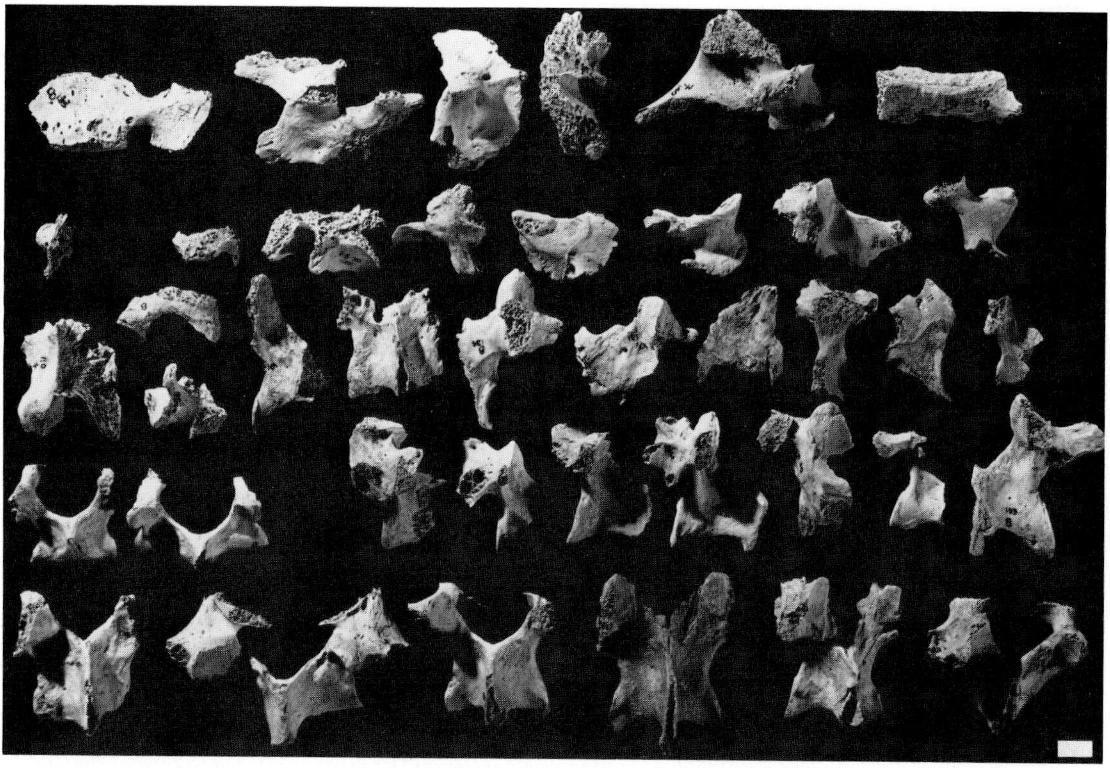

Fig. 8.8 The Mancos 5MTUMR–2346 lumbar and sacral vertebrae subassemblage. Note the absence of lumbar bodies and the dominance of spine and arch portions. Bar = 1 cm.

Toolmarks

Only 1 adult piece (0080) shows percussion-related abrasion, a scrape just above and anterior to the crushed spinous process. None of the 20 other pieces preserved in this region show such marks. Pieces 0073 and 0075, possibly adjacent thoracics from one individual, show vertically oriented, slicing striae on the right arch just lateral to the spinous process (Figure 8.6). These marks presumably relate to removal of the latissimus dorsi and other back muscles. In evaluating cutmark evidence, it must be remembered that transverse processes and bodies are absent from the sample.

Burning

There is only weak evidence, on a few spinous processes, for burning. Like the cervicals, however, the lack of most spinous processes is probably associated with either burning or battering or both.

LUMBAR VERTEBRAE (FIGURE 8.8)

Survival

A total postconjoining MNI of 4 individuals was derived from the maximally conjoined assemblage, and includes 1 subadult and 3 adults based on superior

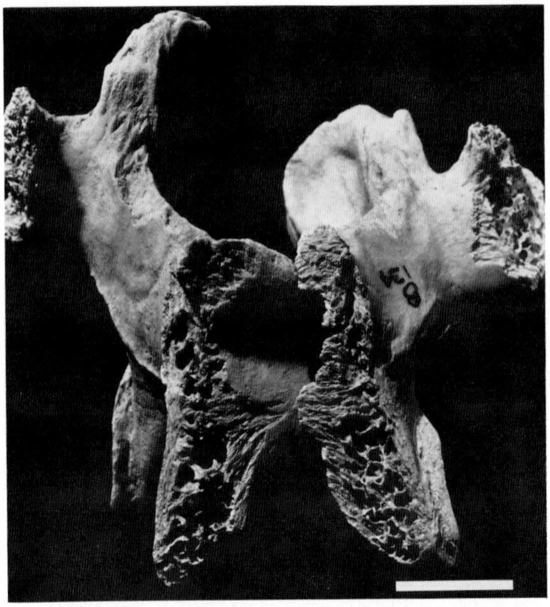

Fig. 8.9 Peeling on a lumbar vertebra (0133/134). Note that these pieces conjoin across the fracture surfaces that face the viewer. The piece on the right has been rotated around a vertical axis to demonstrate the motion that led to the peeling damage (see Figure 8.10). Bar = 1 cm.

articular facets. As with the thoracic vertebrae, there is much fragmentation and no lumbar piece is near to intact. The lumbar sample is smaller than the thoracic, but the same survival pattern is evident. Of the approximately 25 lumbar vertebrae represented in the Mancos assemblage, not one has a body. No transverse processes are intact. There are 2 immature and 10 adult lumbar arches preserved, but only 6 of these retain parts of all 4 articular facets. No spinous processes are preserved intact.

Fracture

There is peeling where the various processes have fractured (Figure 8.9). In 1 adult and 1 immature piece, the broken stump of the spinous process shows crushing from behind. Clearly the body was the element portion focused upon, and most of the other damage was incidental to removal of this segment.

Toolmarks

Conjoining Set 16 displays unilateral cutmarks between the superior and inferior articular facets—marks made by a very sharp edge (Figure 8.10). None of the 17 other anatomically analogous areas show similar marks.

Burning

One piece shows evidence of burning on its dorsal side, but this is only half of the arch. Several additional pieces are possibly burned, but as for the thoracic vertebrae, the evidence is weak.

SACRAL VERTEBRAE AND COCCYX (FIGURE 8.8)

Survival

The MNI of 3 includes 1 subadult and 2 adults. It is based on a total of only 6 sacral pieces. The remains of this element are very small fragments of the anterior face of the body, the dorsal spine, or articular facets. There is nothing in the assemblage that approaches even a good-sized fragment of sacrum. There were no coccygeal vertebrae recovered, perhaps owing to their small size and low relative density.

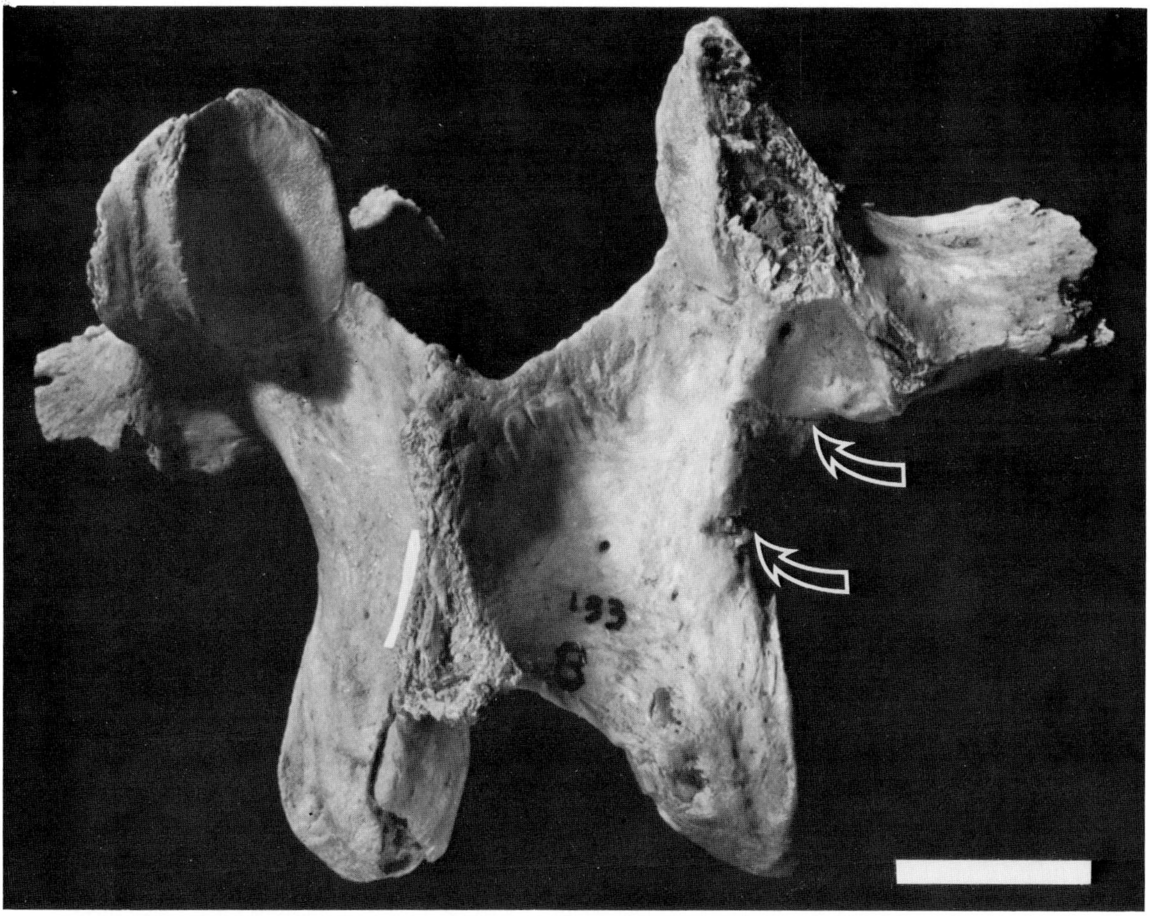

Fig. 8.10 Horizontally oriented chopmarks are seen just below the transverse process (arrow) on lumbar vertebrae (0133, 0134), shown here conjoined. Bar = 1 cm.

Fracture

There is peeling on the dorsal surface of both sacral spine pieces.

Toolmarks

No toolmarks are present.

Burning

There is no evidence of burning.

OS COXAE (FIGURE 8.11)

Survival

A total postconjoining MNI of 11 was derived from the maximally conjoined assemblage and was based on the acetabulum and the sacroiliac articulation. This total includes 5 subadult individuals. Not a single os coxae is preserved intact, and only 1 of the 8 adult pieces used for MNI

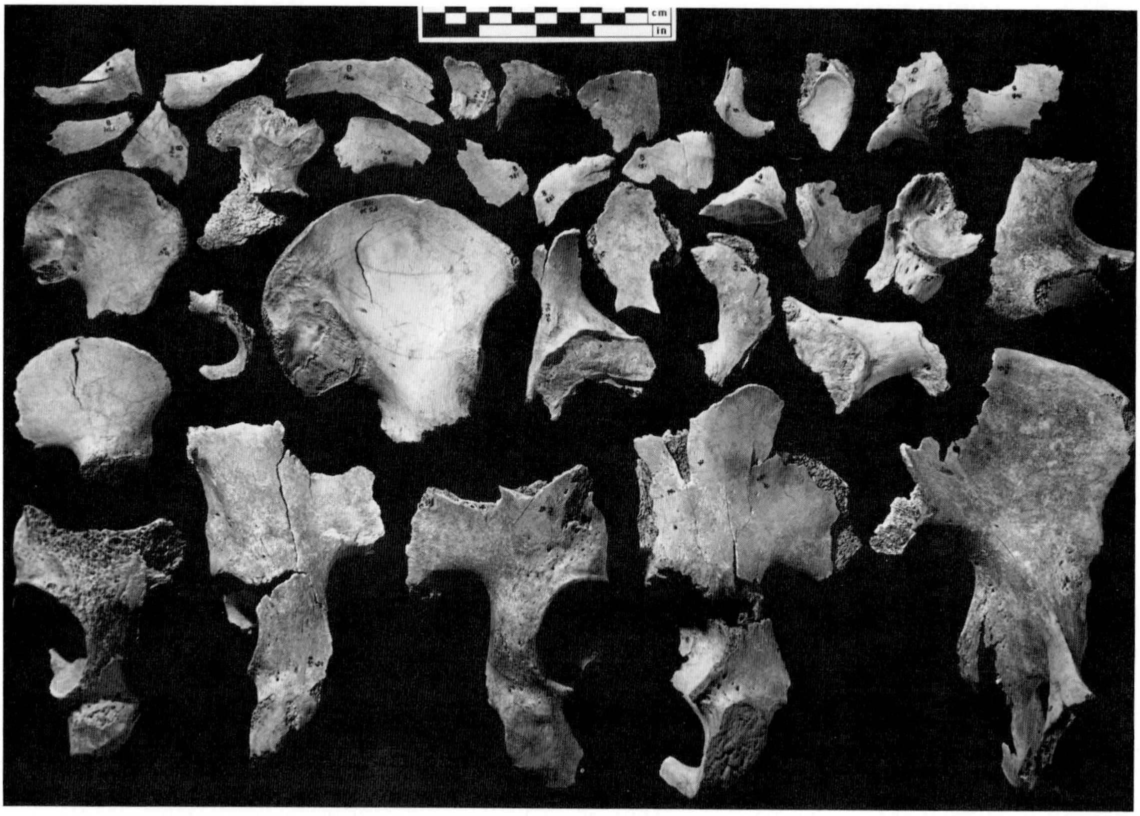

Fig. 8.11 The Mancos 5MTUMR–2346b os coxae subassemblage.

has half of the iliac crest intact. Pubic portions are invariably missing or damaged. This is also the case for the ischium.

Fracture

Much of the damage to the fragile broken edges of the os coxae is excavation- and transport-related. Some evidence of perimortem fracture remains, however. Of 5 available adults, 1 (0156) shows failed percussion points on the arcuate line just anterior to the apex of the auricular surface. Another adult (0161, Figure 8.12) shows adhering flakes with a concentric hairline fracture in the same region. This bone was probably placed on an anvil and struck medially to produce this damage. Immature piece 0168 shows similar damage.

On the lateral surface, opposite the auricular surface, one adult (0146, Figure 8.13) shows peeling, indicating removal of the posterior superior and inferior spine region. This piece also shows a depressed fracture centered in the lateral surface of its iliac blade. One superior pubic ramus (0147) shows peeling on its anterior surface.

As with the vertebrae, the general impression is one of percussion-induced fracture focused on the trabecular bone tissues of the os coxae.

Toolmarks

The medial surface of one adult piece (0157) shows four 2-cm long slicing marks traversing the iliac fossa vertically. None of 4 immature pieces and neither of the 2 other adults where this area can be observed show similar damage. On the lateral iliac surface, no marks are seen, but iliac blades are preserved on only 3 immature and 75 percent of 1 adult os coxae.

Four pieces show cutmarks around the acetabulum. All of them presumably involved slicing through hip musculature and ligaments in an effort to disarticulate the leg at the hip (see Binford, 1981, Table 4.04). A 12-year-old (0154, Figure 8.14) shows several cutmarks in the groove between the acetabulum and the ischium. Functionally, such cutmarks are consistent with slicing through the gluteal musculature. None of the 5 other pieces preserving this area show similar cutmarks. The second piece with circumacetabular cutmarks is an adult (0157) with horizontal marks at the superior, medial edge of the acetabulum, below the level of the anterior inferior iliac spine. None of 3 other pieces with this part preserved show similar marks. The third piece with circumacetabular cutmarks is another adult (0161, Figure 8.12) with cutmarks in the superior sciatic notch just below the preauricular sulcus. The fourth is a piece with slices at the inferior edge of the acetabular notch (0159, Figure 8.15). None of the three additional pieces preserving this part of the anatomy shows such cutmarks.

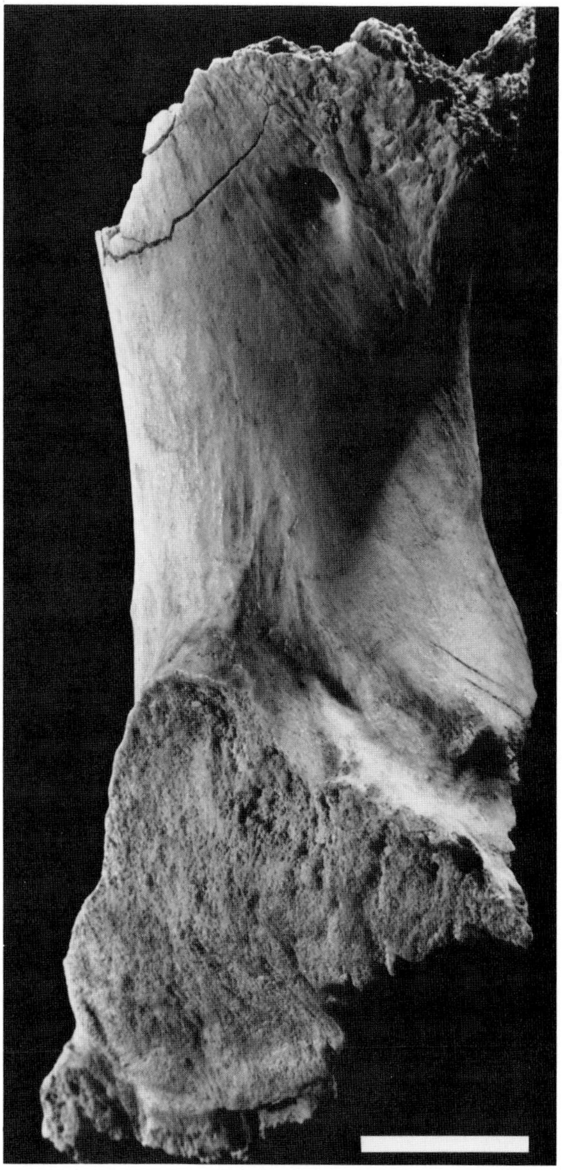

Fig. 8.12 Crushing and cutmarks on the os coxae (0161). Bar = 1 cm.

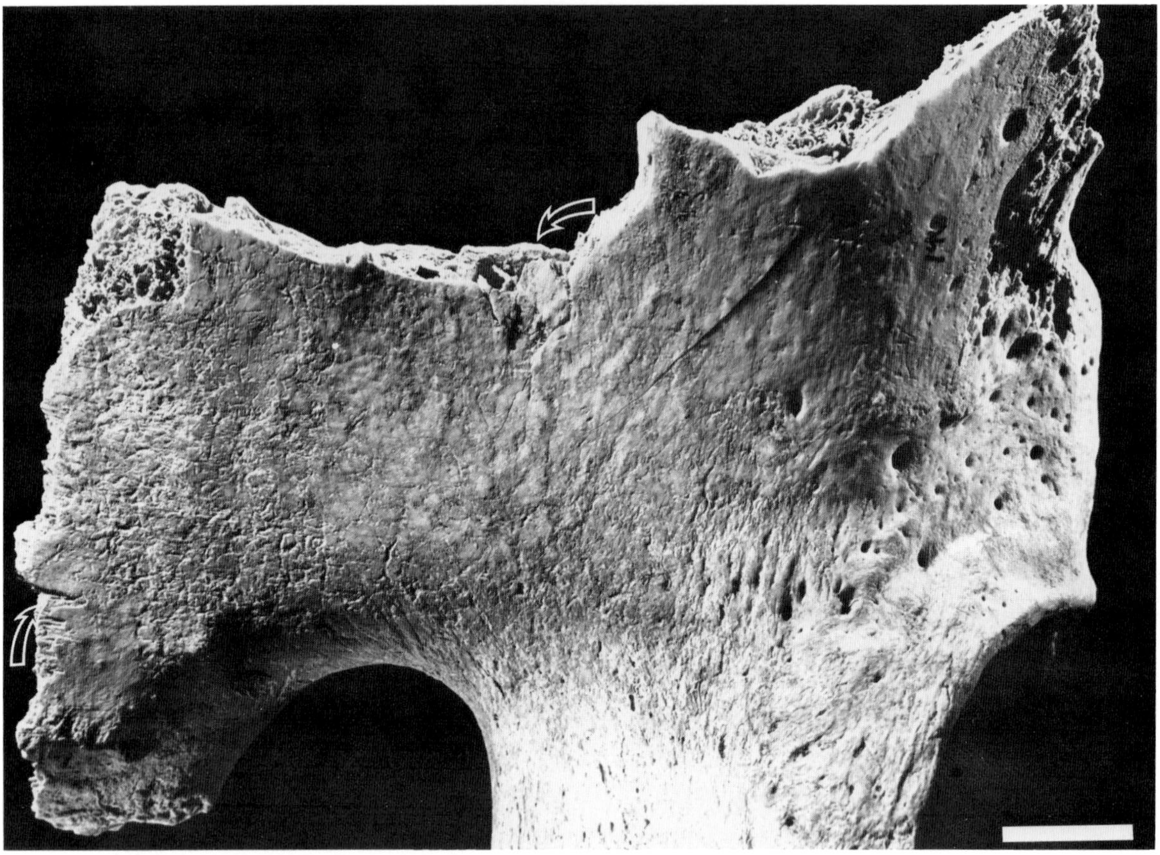

Fig. 8.13 Crushing and peeling on the lateral iliac blade (0146). Bar = 1 cm.

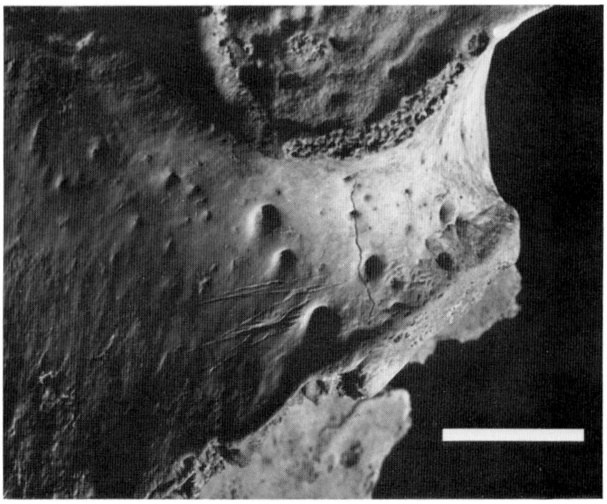

Fig. 8.14 Cutmarks on the os coxae (0154). Bar = 1 cm.

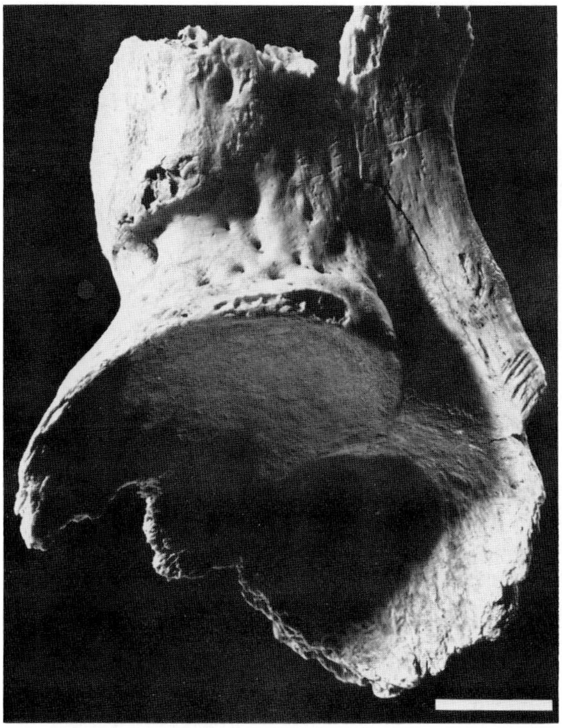

Fig. 8.15 Cutmarks around the acetabulum of the os coxae (0159). Bar = 1 cm.

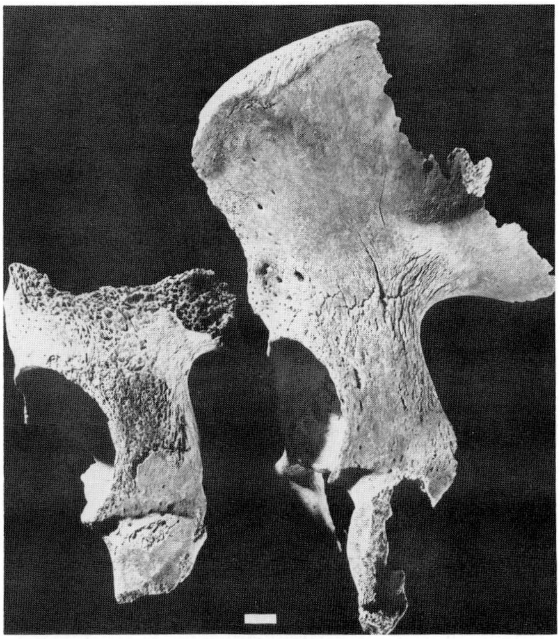

Fig. 8.16 Burning on the os coxae (0156, 0158). Note that the lateral portions of the bones show exfoliation and cracking concentrated just behind the acetabuli. Bar = 1 cm.

Burning

The iliac crest of the 12-year-old (154) and two other immature fragments are possibly burned. Of the adults, 5 pieces are definitely burned. Exfoliation of both inner and outer tables around the acetabulum is evident on these. The pattern, as described for the skull, is one where the projecting parts (crest, spines, pubes) are lost from crushing and/or burning. Statistical projections of burning for the os coxae are difficult because of the small sample and the variability in portions preserved. Of the 6 adult pieces with more than half of the acetabulum remaining, 4 show burning (Figure 8.16), and the evidence for the other 2 is ambiguous.

FIRST RIBS (FIGURE 8.17)

Survival

The overall rib MNI of 11 is based on the number of right first ribs. Out of a total of 21 maximally conjoined first rib pieces, the only one intact was from a 6-year-old.

Fracture

No pattern of first rib fracture is evident.

Toolmarks

Five first rib pieces show cutmarks. Of the 18 first rib pieces appropriately preserved, 2 show anteroposteriorly directed slicing

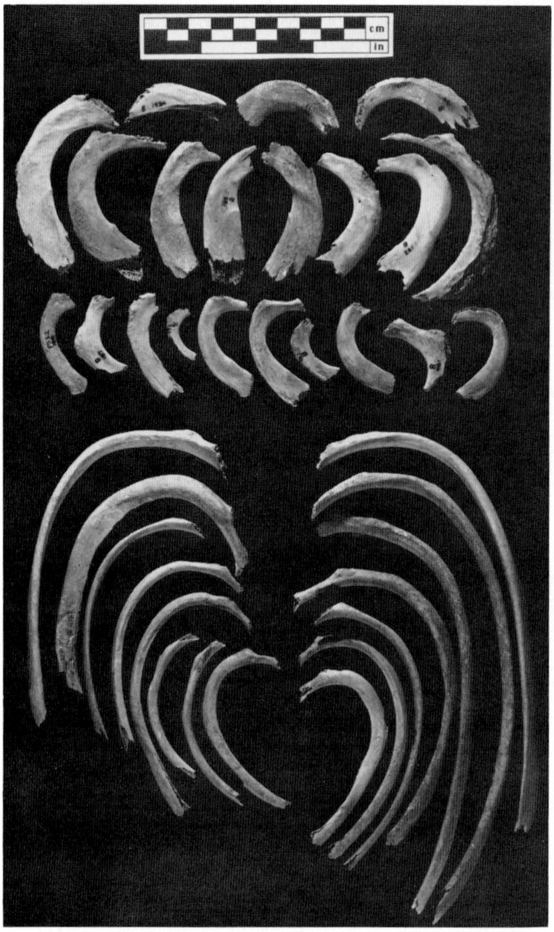

Fig. 8.17 The Mancos 5MTUMR–2346 Rib #1 (top half of frame) and Rib B (rib neck and tubercle, with more than half the shaft; bottom half) subassemblages.

marks across the subclavian surface (0193, 0196). A 4-year-old shows deep vertical cuts in the anterior rib edge at its deepest point of curvature (178). None of the 19 other pieces preserved in this area shows such cutmarks. Of the total of 16 first ribs on which the inferior surface is preserved, 2 show slicing marks (182, 185), and another 2 show abrasion.

Burning

No first rib piece showed obvious burning, but many pieces were equivocal.

RIBS 2–12 (FIGURES 8.17–8.20)

Survival

For ease of analysis, the degree of fragmentation was used to classify rib pieces (see Table 8.1). Of the total of 329 unconjoined rib pieces from ribs 2–12 in the Mancos assemblage, not a single one was preserved intact. Only 10 pieces closely approached the intact condition, preserving the head, neck, tubercle, and more than half of the shaft. The most abundant rib pieces were shaft fragments comprising less than half of a shaft (n = 174), and proximal rib ends (n = 75). It is evident that the more immature the rib, the greater the chance of its intact survival.

Table 8.1

Rib A: Head, Neck, Tubercle, and > 1/2 Shaft	0
Rib B: Neck, Tubercle, and > 1/2 Shaft	15
Rib C: > 1/2 Shaft only	65
Rib D: < 1/2 Shaft only	174
Rib E: Head, Neck, Tubercle, and < 1/2 Shaft	40
Rib F: Neck, Tubercle, and < 1/2 Shaft	35
Total Rib Specimens:	329

Table 8.1 Rib fragmentation. See the text for a discussion of the implications of these data.

Opposite page top:

Fig. 8.18 The Mancos 5MTUMR–2346 Rib C (more than half the shaft remaining, with no tubercle, neck, or head) subassemblage. Note the abundant rib shafts lacking heads.

Opposite page bottom:

Fig. 8.19 The Mancos 5MTUMR–2346 Rib D (less than half the shaft remaining, with no tubercle, neck, or head) subassemblage.

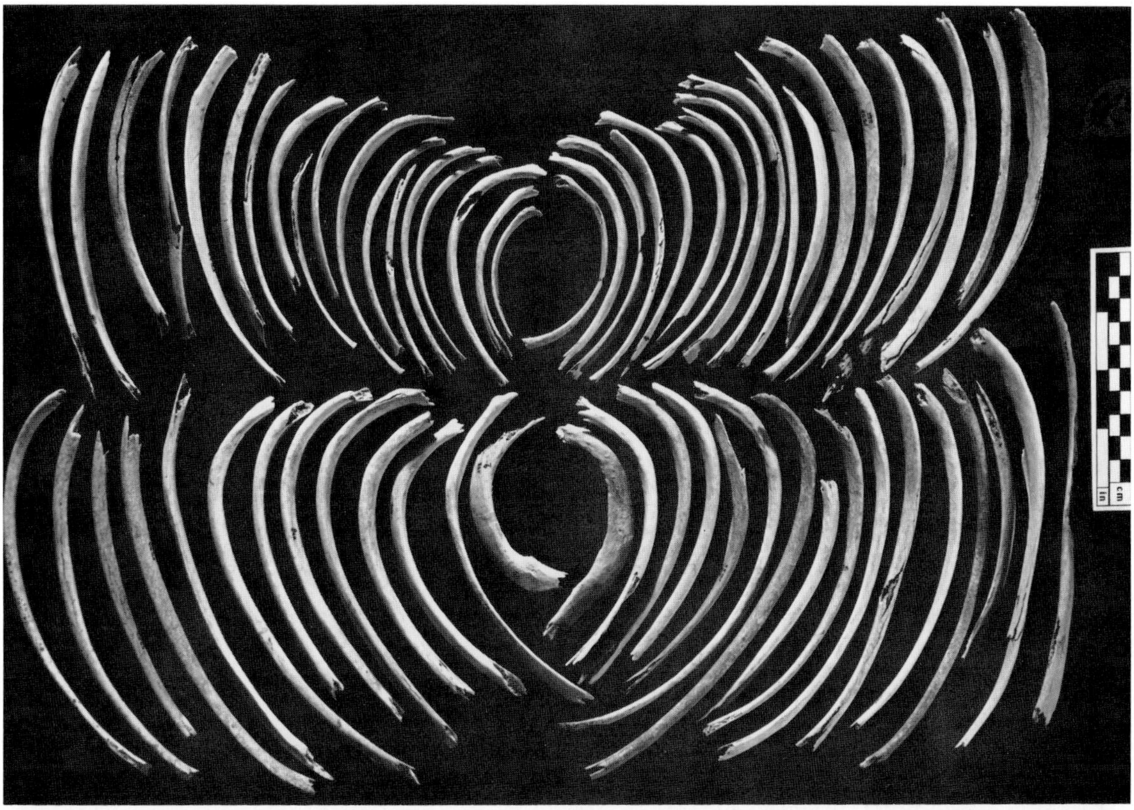
cm
in

cm
in

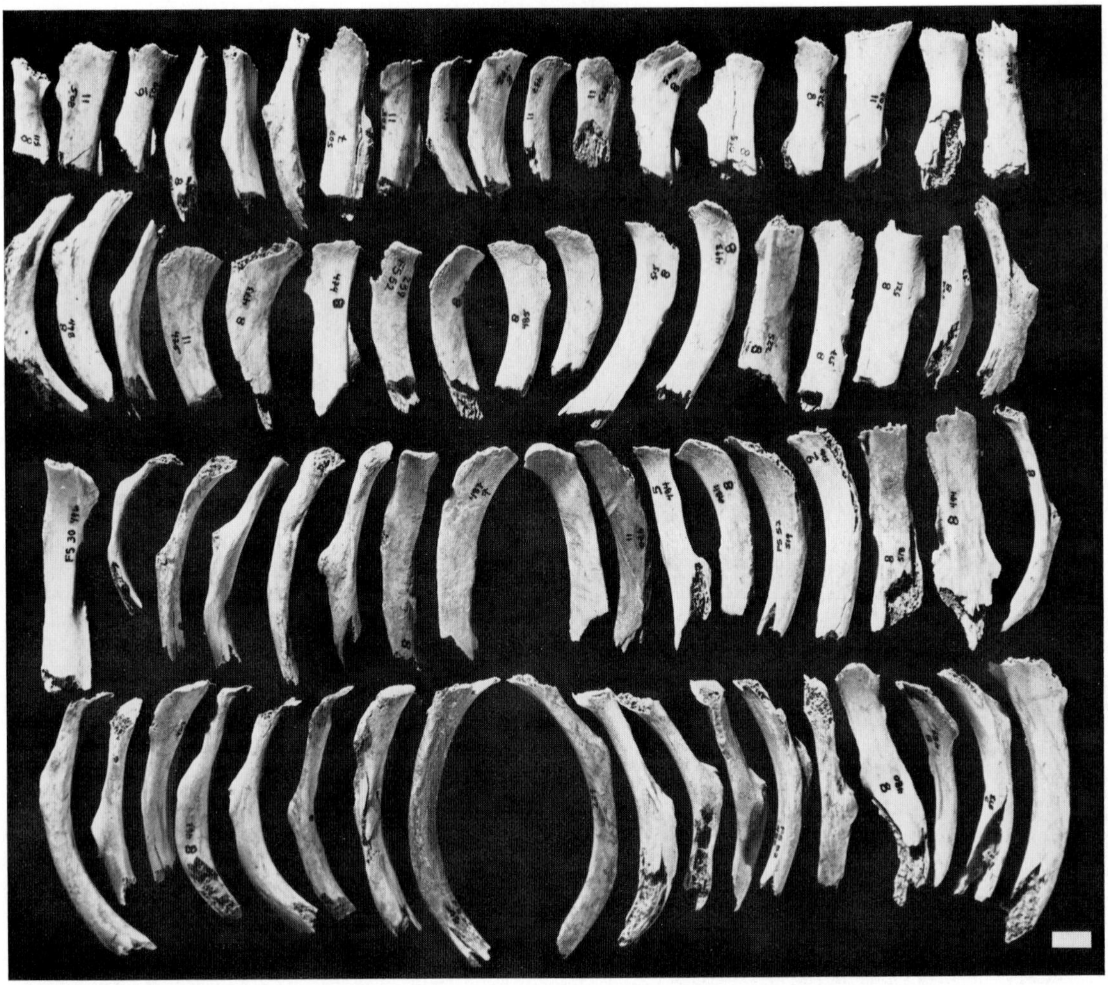

Fig. 8.20 The Mancos 5MTUMR–2346 Rib E (rib head, neck, and tubercle, with less than half the shaft) and F (rib neck and tubercle with less than half the shaft) subassemblages. Note how this subassemblage complements those illustrated in Figures 8.17–8.19 in demonstrating that ribs were removed in slabs, levered back against the transverse processes of thoracic vertebrae. Bar = 1 cm.

Fracture

Ubiquitous separation by fracture of the proximal end from the rest of the shaft shows clearly that the rib shafts, presumably as parts of rib slabs held together by fascia and intercostal musculature, were levered back against the transverse processes of the thoracic vertebrae (Figure 8.21). There is much peeling associated with this fracture; it is always on the superficial as opposed to the deep rib surface (Figure 8.22). The lack of rib heads may be due to destruction during this leverage,

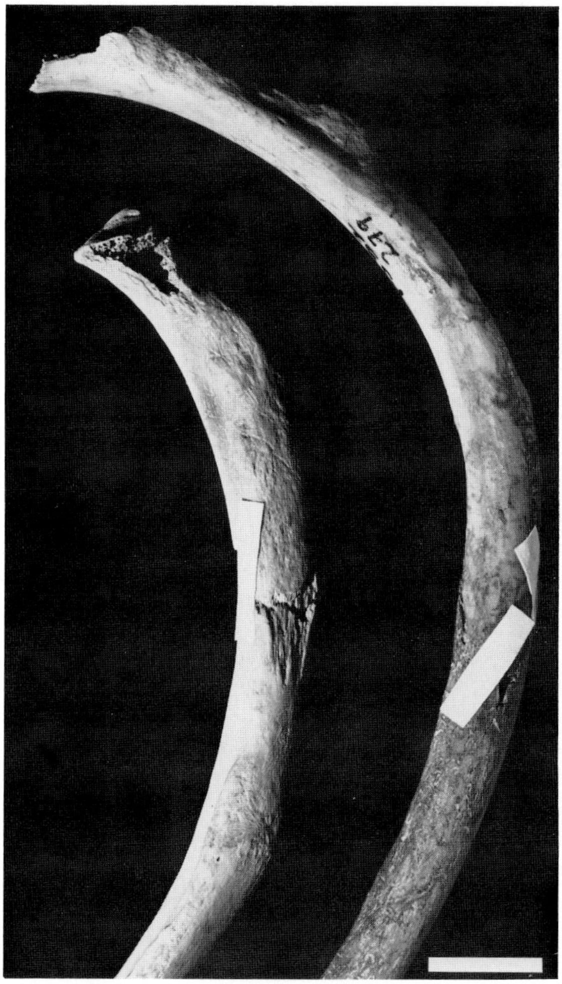

Fig. 8.21 Head and shaft breakage on ribs (0238 + 0239; 279 + 280). Bar = 1 cm.

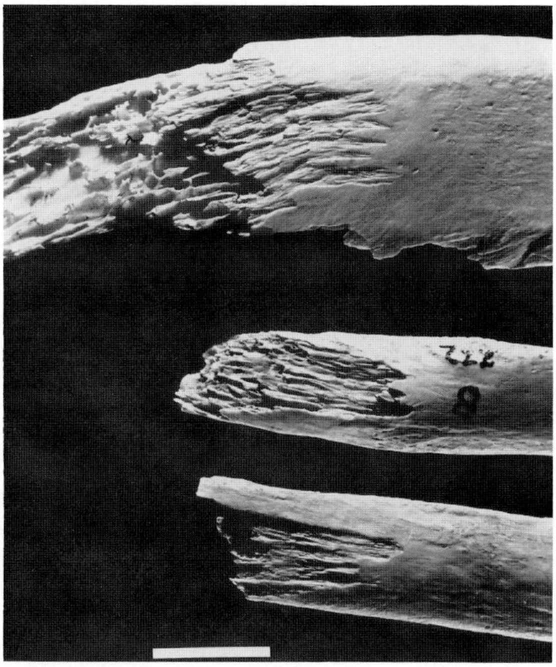

Fig. 8.22 Peeling on the ribs (268, 272, 281). Bar = 1 cm.

or may be due to crushing of this most trabecular part of the rib. Tubercles display crushing fracture in 6 of 75 proximal rib ends, whereas peeling is seen in 22 of these 75 pieces. Spiess (1979), Noe-Nygaard (1977), and Crader (1984) describe a similar pattern of many rib heads and attached proximal shafts in archaeological faunal remains. None describe peeling damage, but adjacent cutmarks have been interpreted as indicative of ribs being cut off. The damage pattern described is more consistent with the forced fracture described here and by Yellen (1977) and O'Connell *et al.* (1988). Binford (1984:119–120) provides an excellent ethnographic account of this process among the Nunamiut:

> Most commonly the ribs are removed during initial field butchering as a unit—a rib slab—and this is accomplished by breaking the rib unit back or up against the vertebrae (Figure 4.12) and then by cutting along the ventral surface of the broken ribs to free the slab from the vertebrae. This results in a characteristic break coupled with distinctive cut or slicing marks on the ventral surfaces of ribs.

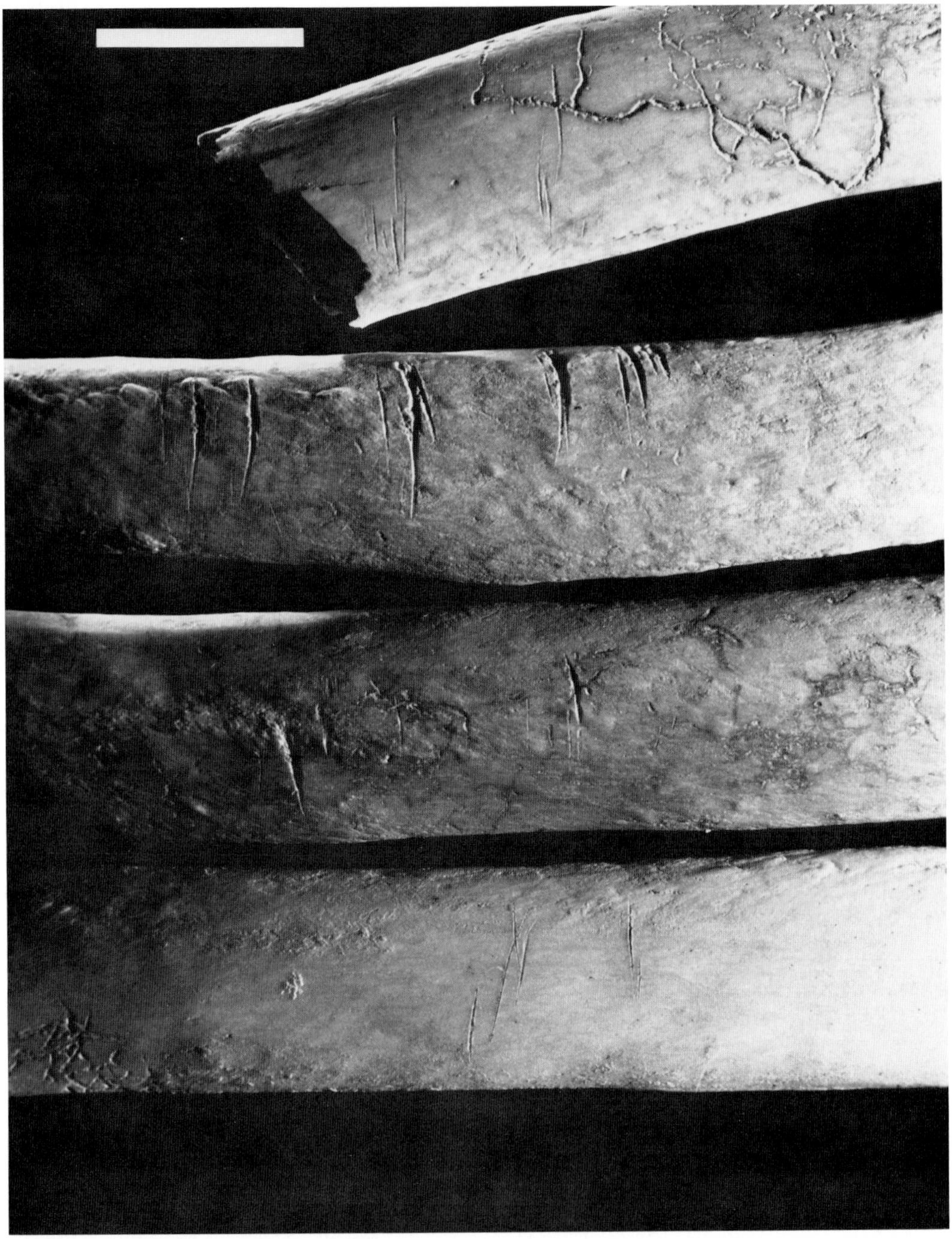

Fig. 8.23 Vertical cutmarks on the external surfaces of rib shafts (230, 232, 258, 332). These marks are probably related to the removal of pectoralis musculature and overlying soft tissues. Bar = 1 cm.

Toolmarks

In the immature ribs in the assemblage, 1 of 8 lefts and 2 of 9 rights show vertical slicing striae on the superficial surface about 2 cm from the sternal end. One other piece shows scrapes on the superior edge near the tubercle, and one shows several slicemarks oriented vertically at midshaft on the deep rib surface. The adult sample, a much larger collection of pieces, exhibits much tool-inflicted damage. Over half of the rib pieces that could be assigned to a body side showed either slicing marks or abrasion. These marks cluster in three areas on the rib.

The first area is on the superficial rib surface at midshaft. Here, the marks are typically slicing marks, vertical or oblique in orientation (Figure 8.23; see Grayson, 1988, Figure 15). They are often single but are sometimes multiple, and they sometimes mark the superior rib edge. Superficial (external) midshaft cutmarks were found on 25 of the 48 maximally conjoined rib shafts or shaft fragments that bore cutmarks. An additional 45 analogous rib pieces lack any marks. Because of uneven representation in the collection, a very rough estimate is that ⅓ to ½ of all ribs showed such cutmarks. The marks range in placement from near the sternum to near the proximal end. There are fewer cutmarks sternally, probably because the sternal rib end is not well represented. These slicing marks are presumably primarily associated with removal of skin, and removal of the pectoralis major and pectoralis minor muscles.

The second rib area with a distinctive tool-induced modification pattern is on the superficial rib surface just anterior to the tubercle (see Grayson, 1988, Figure 15). The marks here are usually more superficial than those at rib midshaft and appear to be more often percussion-related (for example, 0495, 0499). Of the 75 maximally conjoined ribs preserving this area, 27 show these marks. Some are clearly slicing marks (Figure 8.24), and their orientation and topography indicate that the tool came from behind, presumably to remove back musculature including the latissimus dorsi and trapezius muscles, as well as deeper soft tissue. Villa *et al.* (1986) refer to marks on the external surface of the Fontbrégoua ribs near the head that may be analogous. Binford (1981) refers to similar tenderloin filleting marks in ungulates (his code number RS-1).

The third area with strong evidence of tool-induced damage is opposite the second area, on the deep rib surface opposite the tubercle (see Grayson, 1988, Figure 15). This damage occurs in the deep curvature of the rib. The marks are best described as abrasion marks that verge, in some cases, on true scraping marks. These were clearly formed by blunt hammerstones or mauls being worked in multiple strokes in this area. There is occasionally crushing force associated with this action. Of the 172 observable maximally conjoined pieces from both sides that preserve the relevant area, 74 pieces show this damage (Figure 8.25). These marks could be related to scraping within the body cavity, but are more probably related to freeing the rib slab after the ribs have been levered against the thoracic transverse processes. Villa *et al.* (1986a) refer to similar marks on the Fontbrégoua ribs as defleshing marks.

Burning

Burning on the ribs is extremely difficult to establish. Two immature ribs are probably burned, and one is certainly burned. For the adults, burning is suggested on

Fig. 8.24 Proximal cutmarks on the external rib surface (513, 514), probably related to the removal of back musculature. Bar = 1 cm.

several fragments. There is a large enough sample to show that the ribs were definitely not burned with the same intensity as seen on either the mandibles or other cranial elements.

STERNUM (FIGURE 8.26)

Survival

Only two small sternal fragments remain, one fairly intact immature segment and one cortical flake of an adult.

Fracture

No patterns are evident.

Toolmarks

None are present.

Burning

None is visible.

CLAVICLE (FIGURE 8.27)

Survival

A total MNI of 18 individuals is derived from the maximally conjoined assemblage, and this includes 8 individuals younger than 12 years. A total of 6 of the 36 unconjoined pieces are fairly intact. Of the 12 sternal ends of adolescent or adult individuals, only 1 has a tiny fragment of articular surface remaining. Of the 16 acromial ends, only 1 (the same piece, conjoined) has a portion of the scapular articulation left. Only 5 of the 26 pieces greater than age 6 have intact midshafts.

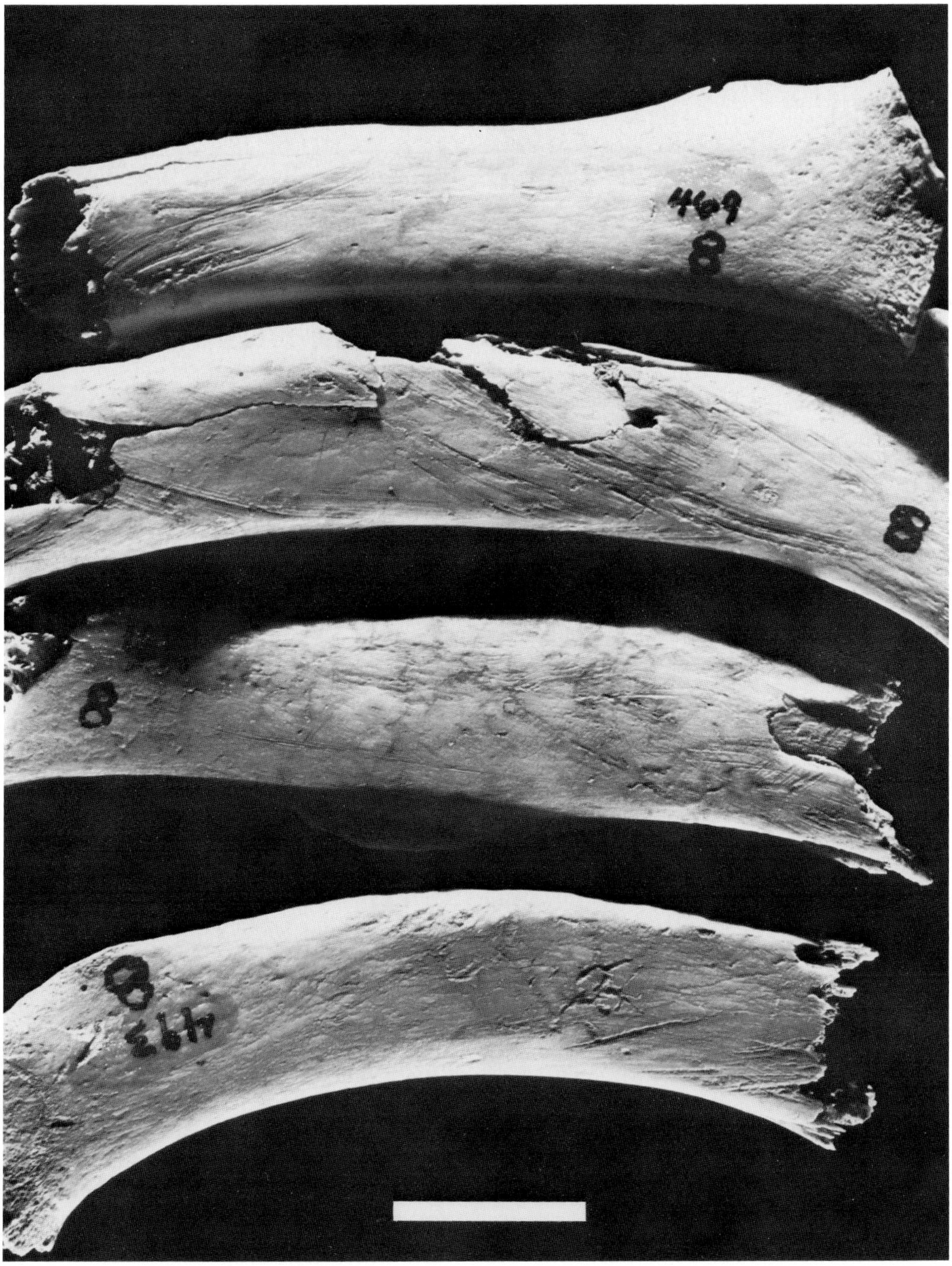

Fig. 8.25 Damage to the internal (body cavity) surface of the proximal rib ends in the form of percussion striae and crushing (460, 469, 491, 493). Bar = 1 cm.

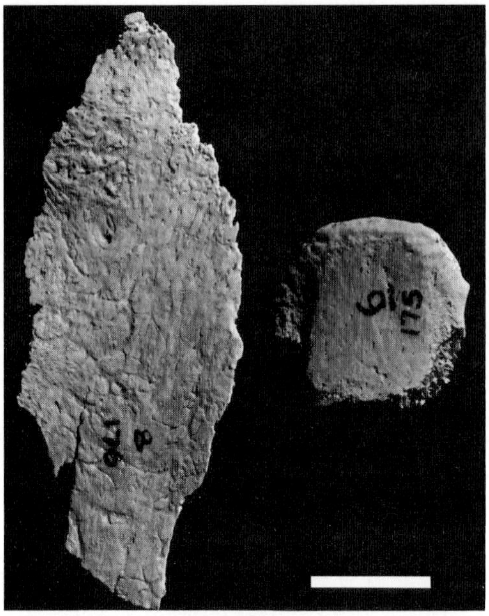

Fig. 8.26 The Mancos 5MTUMR–2346 sternum subassemblage. Bar = 1 cm.

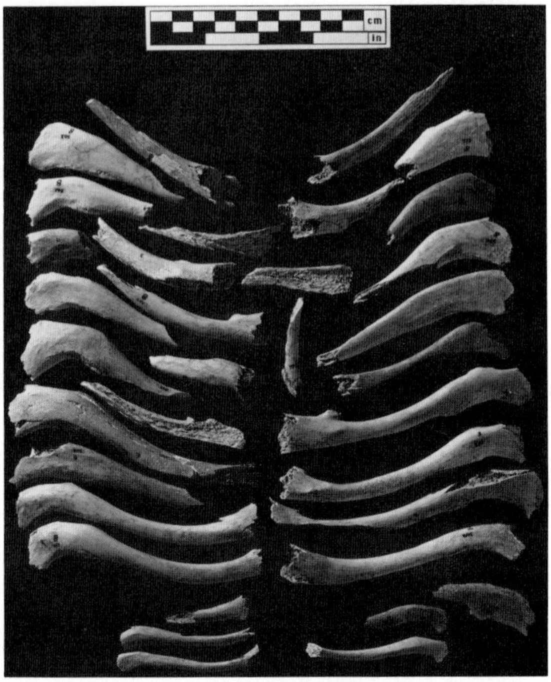

Fig. 8.27 The Mancos 5MTUMR–2346 clavicle subassemblage.

Fracture

Of the 16 acromial ends available for adolescent or adult individuals, 7 show bone flakes crushed in from above or below (Figure 8.28). Four of the 12 sternal ends show similar crushing, but the thinner cortex here makes detection of the direction of the blow(s) less clear. At midshaft, perimortem spiral fracture is ubiquitous, but no percussion points are evident. The single fully conjoined piece shows a breakage pattern that suggests fracture by simple forceful, 2-handed bending of the bone. Peeling is associated with the crushed acromial end of specimen 571.

Toolmarks

Of the 30 maximally conjoined pieces, only 11 lack cutmarks. Most of the unmarked pieces are very immature (n = 3), are acromial ends (n = 6), or are small shaft/sternal end fragments. All the large pieces representing individuals older than age 6, which preserve most of the shaft and proximal ends, show slicing marks. These marks vary in placement but are most concentrated on the cranial (superior in the biped) surface of the clavicle. There are 3 patterns of marks; these cutmark patterns differ slightly from those described by Villa *et al.* (1986b) and Poplin (1985, Fig. 112). The first Mancos pattern comprises marks with a posterolateral to anteromedial orientation. In some pieces, these cutmarks are superficial and look more like abrasion (0565), but in other, better expressed pieces, a sawing motion of the tool across the bone is demonstrated

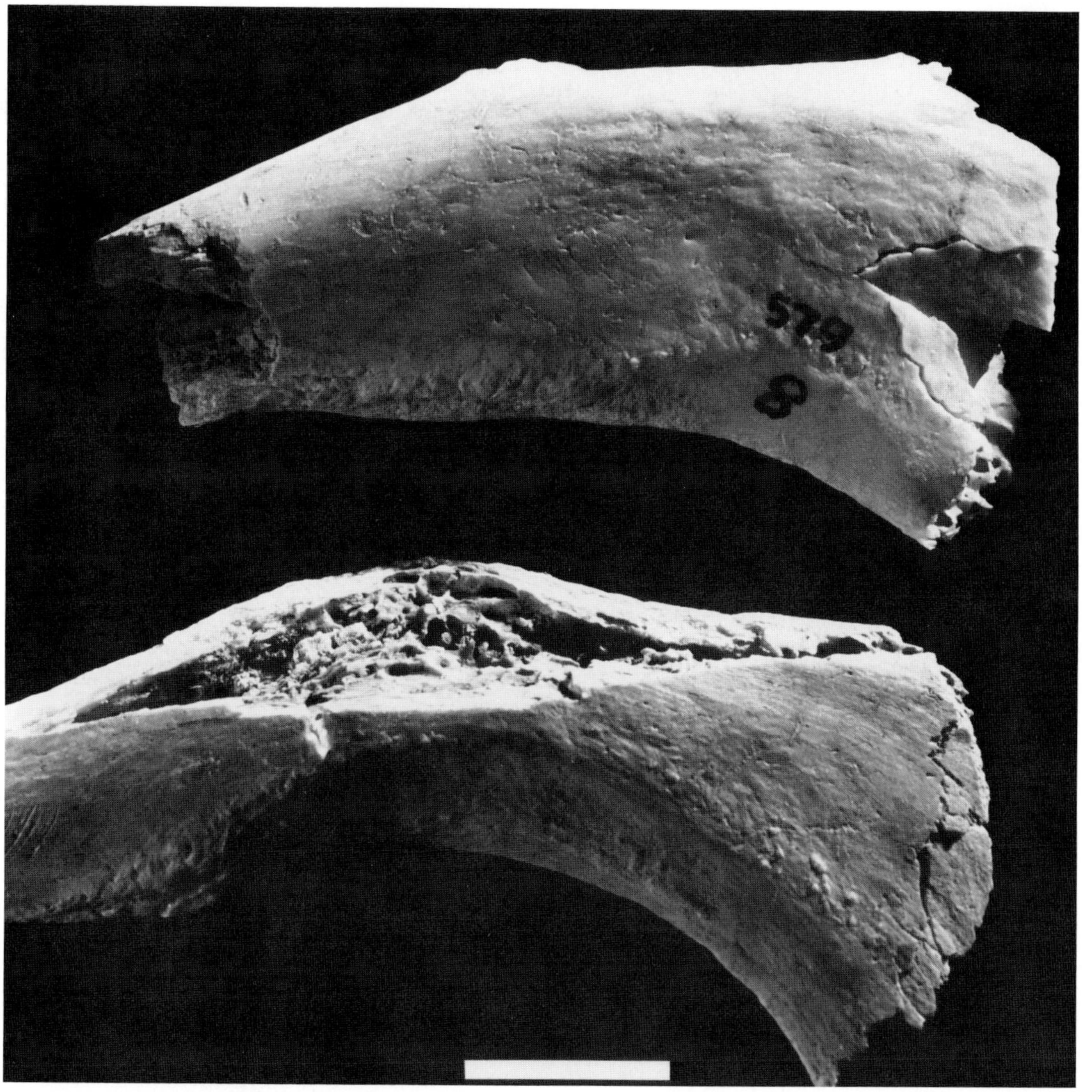

Fig. 8.28 Dorsoventral crushing of acromial ends of two left clavicles (569, 579). View is from above, lateral is toward the page bottom. Bar = 1 cm.

(Figure 8.29). Of the 11 adult pieces preserving the anterosuperior midshaft quadrant of the bone, 10 show such marks, along with two immature pieces. On 4 pieces, the cutmarks are more laterally placed, just above the acromial tubercle. These cutmarks on the superior and anterior clavicular surfaces are probably related to the removal of the platysma and sternocleidomastoid muscles, possibly during decapitation. In addition, vigorous cutting of the deltoideus muscle during

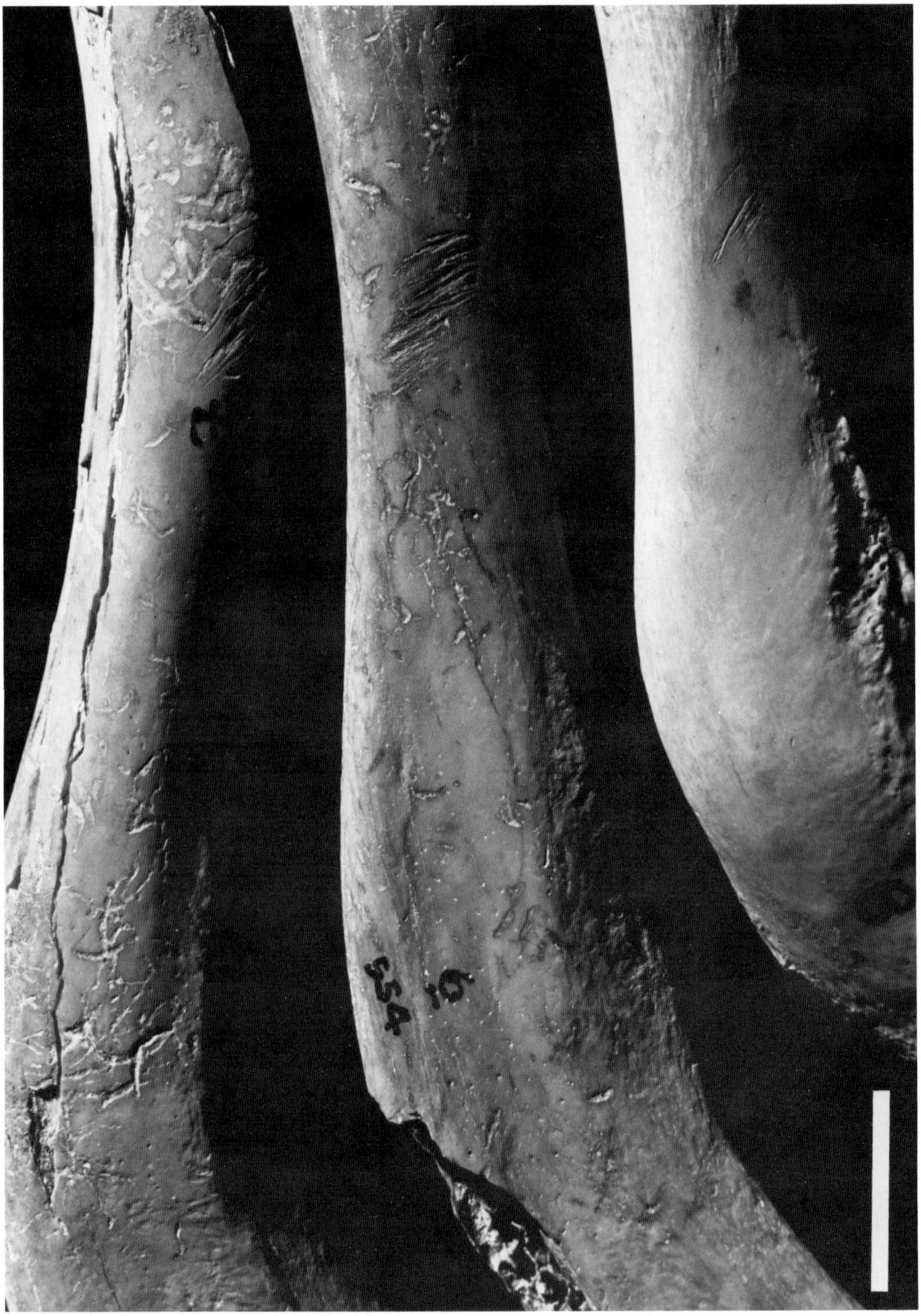

Fig. 8.29 Cranial (superior) surface cutmarks on three left clavicles (551, 553, 554). These marks may be related to decapitation. Acromial (lateral) end is toward the page bottom. Bar = 1 cm.

dismemberment could bring the stone tool edge into contact with the clavicle to form these marks.

The second cutmark pattern is seen on 2 of the 11 pieces, where additional hacking marks are set off 2 cm from the sternal end. On one of the pieces, the cutmarks described above hit the dorsal edge of the bone in addition to the cranial edge.

The third clavicular cutmark pattern is seen on 4 pieces where there are vertical slices on the anterior surface of the bone. These are not as frequent as the other marks mentioned above, appearing on only 4 of the 12 observable pieces. These marks may relate to the removal of the clavicular part of the pectoralis major muscle.

Burning

Only 2 maximally conjoined pieces show positive evidence of burning; both exhibit burning on the dorsal lateral shaft region. Of the remaining pieces, 9 show no burning, whereas the others show equivocal evidence.

SCAPULA (FIGURE 8.30)

Survival

A total MNI of 12 individuals was obtained from the maximally conjoined scapular assemblage, including 8 adults. Not a single scapula is intact. The acromion is missing or damaged on all pieces. The vertebral border is present on only 3 of the 5 children's scapulae; all adult vertebral borders are missing. Of the adults, 3 preserve fairly intact glenoids and spines. Only 2 coracoids (without tips) and one coracoid fragment are present in any scapular piece. The sample is small, and the destruction of adult scapulae ranges from a complete bone lacking the vertebral border, acromial tip, and coracoid, to pieces of axillary border or small glenoid parts.

Fracture

One adult piece shows that the spinous base of the acromion was broken away, crushed inferiorly, and peeled off anterosuperiorly (Figure 8.31). Massive crushing of the entire glenoid region is well illustrated in this piece. With slightly more crushing, the bone itself would have been obliterated. Three right adult pieces lack such damage, but the remaining 13 adult fragments consist of isolated scapular parts, such as axillary borders or acromions. Thus, there is a graded series showing the effects of crushing fracture to the glenoid region. One of the axillary borders shows that the inferior scapular angle also suffered crushing; none of these basal areas is preserved intact. On one of the fairly intact pieces (0530), a 1.5-mm, circular, depressed puncture occurs in the area just above the glenoid. In isolation, this puncture resembles a carnivore-induced feature, but there is no other evidence of gnawing on the piece.

Toolmarks

Only 1 of the 21 total scapular pieces shows cutmarks, but quantification of cutmarks in the assemblage is made difficult by differential representation. The cutmarked piece is the most complete scapula preserved. Two clear slicing strokes are indicated, slicing across the infraspinous fossa; one mark strikes the bony bar beneath the glenoid (Figure 8.32). Both marks run parallel to the scapular spine itself, bisecting the fossa. Similar marks are illustrated by Villa *et al.* (1986b, Fig-

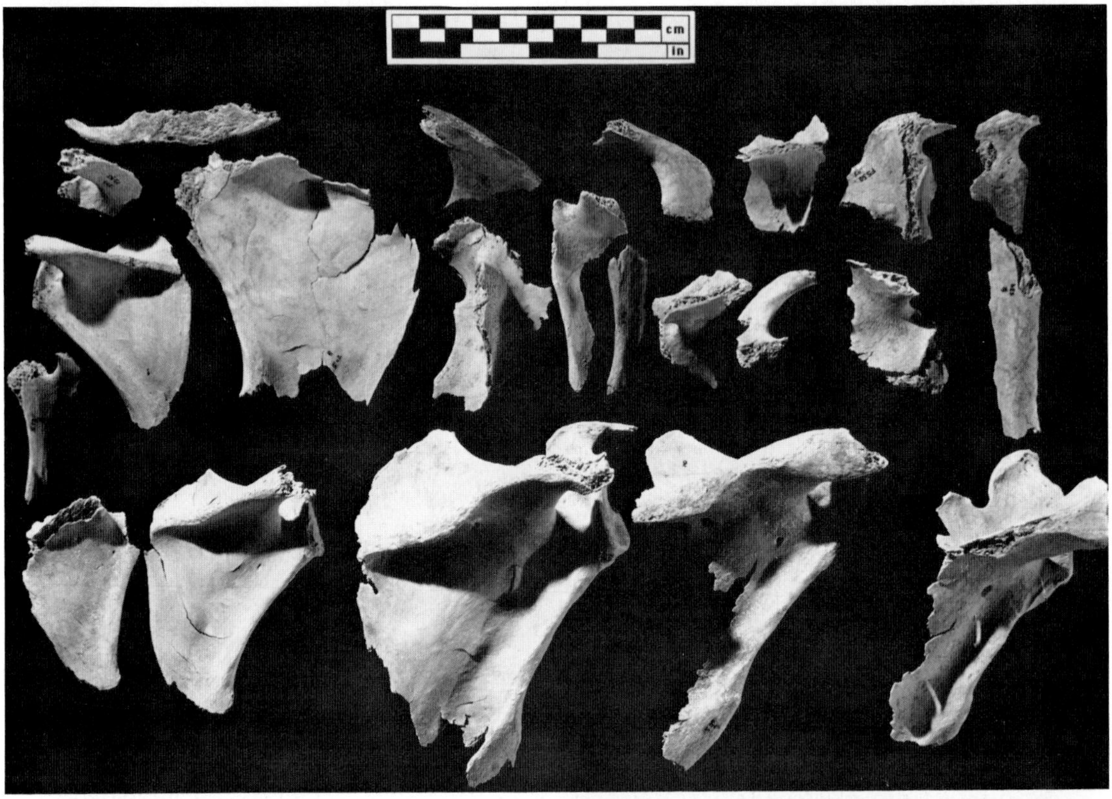

Fig. 8.30 The Mancos 5MTUMR–2346 scapula subassemblage.

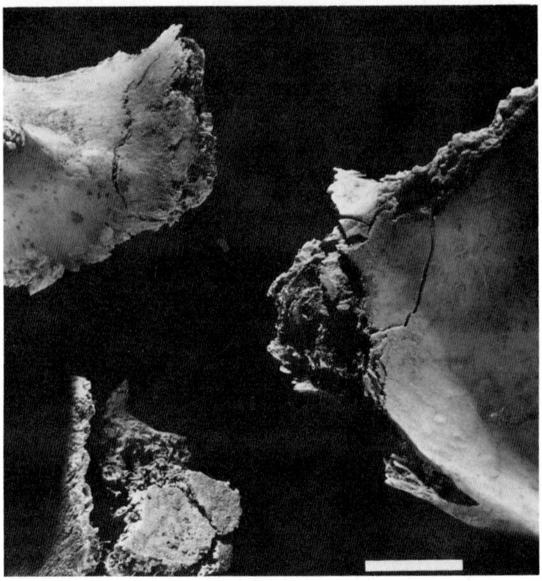

Fig. 8.31 Crushing and peeling on the scapula (532, 533, 542). Bar = 1 cm.

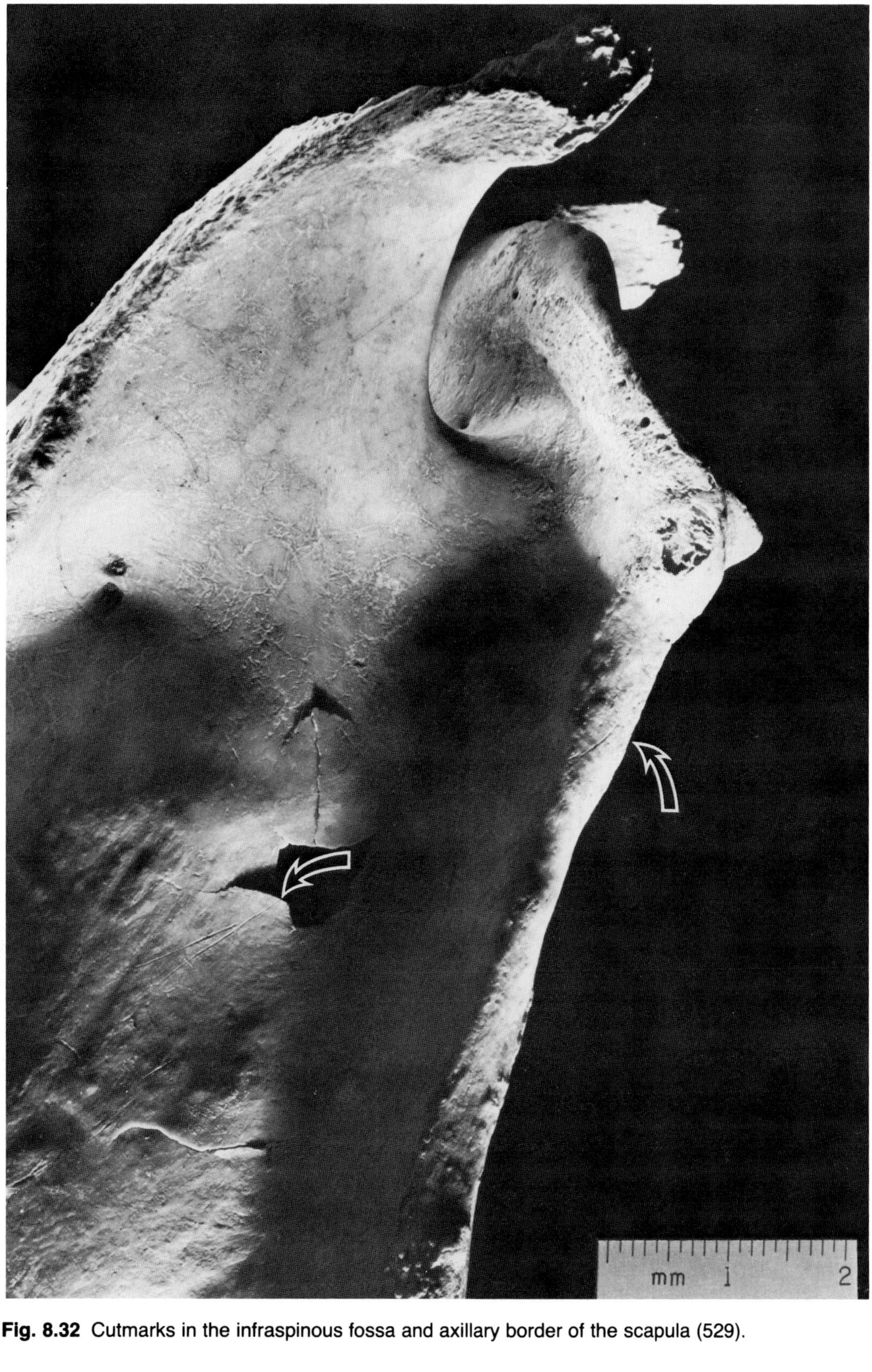

Fig. 8.32 Cutmarks in the infraspinous fossa and axillary border of the scapula (529).

ure 12.5.a) and Binford (1981, Figure 4.06). These marks obviously relate to defleshing in the form of removal of the infraspinatus muscle.

Burning

The nearly complete piece described above and illustrated in Figure 8.32 shows some of the best evidence of burning, on the tip of its acromion. Burning is evident on 2 additional pieces, both in the area of the acromion and spine. Of the other pieces, most show a kind of bone deterioration consistent with burning, but this cannot be established with confidence because multiple criteria and patterning of damage are not available.

TRUNK PROCESSING: AN INTERPRETIVE SUMMARY

The sequence of trunk processing is not as easy to interpret as that of the cranium. In the cranium, there is much fragmentation but not as much overall destruction, probably because trabecular bone is virtually absent above the neck. For this reason, the sequence of events is more easily reconstructed for the cranial anatomy. For the trunk, as for the cranium, there is evidence of disarticulation, burning, defleshing, and percussion. Yet it is the systematic absence of spongy bone tissue in trunk elements—inferred from adjacent fracture and peeling damage to be due to crushing—that provides insight into the processing. At the same time this patterned crushing renders details of the fracture, cutting, and burning sequence more difficult to establish.

Disarticulation of anatomical segments of the trunk is most clearly seen in the os coxae, where cutmarks around the acetabulum indicate femoral removal. There is no evidence of analogous removal of the humerus at the shoulder, but the sample of proximal humeri and scapular glenoids is small, and this joint is more easily disarticulated without intensive cutting immediately adjacent to the joint. The frequent cutmarks on the superior clavicular surface are probably associated with decapitation, and it is possible that the upper cervical vertebrae accompanied the head as a unit. The poor representation of all vertebral parts relative to cranial parts is probably because vertebral bodies were targets of processing for the spongy bone tissue that they contained.

The removal of skin and musculature is indicated by the frequency of cutmarks on external rib surfaces, by the parasagittal marks on the posterior surfaces of lumbar and thoracic vertebral arches, by the cutmarks on the inferior clavicular surfaces, and by cutmarks in the scapula's infraspinous fossa. Much cutmark evidence for disarticulation of bones at joints was probably lost when the adjacent spongy bone was crushed (see below), and, as a result, the disarticulation portion of processing is impossible to reconstruct accurately.

Removal of rib slabs is indicated by the fragmentation pattern within the ribs and associated damage to the vertebrae. Here, peeling on the superficial rib surfaces and crushing/abrasion damage to the deep rib surfaces near the neck/shaft junction suggest that the rib slabs were levered back against the thoracic transverse processes. Fracture patterns and peeling on some vertebral arches show that the spinal cord was exposed from behind, at least at some positions along the vertebral column. Clavicle shafts were broken open by both percussion and bending loads.

Crushing of spongy bone on both ends of the clavicle, in the scapular glenoid, the os coxae, the vertebral bodies, and presumably in the virtually missing sacra and sterna, is indicated by direct evidence in the form of adjacent crushed bone, peeling, and abrasion. Indirect evidence for such processing takes the form of highly skewed representations of different element portions. The ubiquitous absence of vertebral bodies is particularly telling in this regard.

Evidence of burning on the bones of the trunk correlates strongly with the depth of the soft tissue coverage (except for the ribs), but overall intensity and frequency of thermal damage are lower than that seen in the cranium. Therefore, vertebral spine tips and acromial processes show burning. Neither the trunk as a unit (with clavicle attached) nor rib slabs seem to have been exposed to intense heat in the way that the cranium was. On the other hand, the heavy burning around the acetabulum suggests that this anatomical unit was burned after removal of the protecting femur and associated gluteal musculature.

The general processing pattern discernible from an analysis of the trunk is one involving, in the following order, limited heating, disarticulation (segmentation), defleshing, and crushing of spongy bone portions. This pattern is repeated in the arm, hand, leg, and foot, as outlined in the following three chapters.

CHAPTER

9

The Arm

The elements of the arm—the humerus, radius, and ulna—are all long bones whose articular ends are easily identified, but whose shaft fragments are more difficult to attribute to element and side. Evidence for processing of the three arm bones is described from proximal to distal ends in the account that follows, and processing of the arm as a unit is described in the final section in this chapter.

HUMERUS (FIGURE 9.1)

Survival

The total postconjoining MNI of 17 individuals was derived from the maximally conjoined assemblage; 9 individuals are subadult. Conjoining has dramatic consequences for the humeral assemblage, allowing for the interpretation of the shaft fragmentation. Of the 9 postconjoining pieces from individuals younger than 6 years, 4 have intact shafts. Of these 4, the younger pieces retain unbroken shafts, whereas the 6-year-old pieces are broken like the adults. In adults, not one of the 24 available maximally conjoined pieces shows an intact shaft. Only 2 of the 7 isolated adult midshaft pieces preserve intact shaft circumferences.

Of the 8 pieces with shaft segments close to the head (individuals older than 6 years), not one retains any of the head's articular surface. On the other hand, of the 17 equivalent pieces with distal shaft, 12 preserve some segment of distal humeral articular surface. It is evident that shafts of individuals younger than age 5 were not broken, although their epiphyses and metaphyses are missing. For humeri of older individuals, shafts and heads were universally fractured, whereas the distal ends were less frequently broken.

Fracture

Shaft breakage was accomplished in two ways. The first involved hammerstone percussion, evidence of which is patent on 6 pieces in the form of conchoidal scars and adhering flakes both proximally and distally along the shaft (Figures 9.2, 9.3). The second shaft breakage technique was "over-anvil." This involved bending the bone atop or aside an anvil until it broke in a transverse, perpendicular, snap-break failure. This breakage pattern is seen on 7 of the pieces of individuals older than 6 years. Figure 9.4 shows that both fracture patterns are present on the conjoined humeri of conjoining Sets 20 and 30.

The pattern of relatively abundant distal humeral ends with attached distal shaft

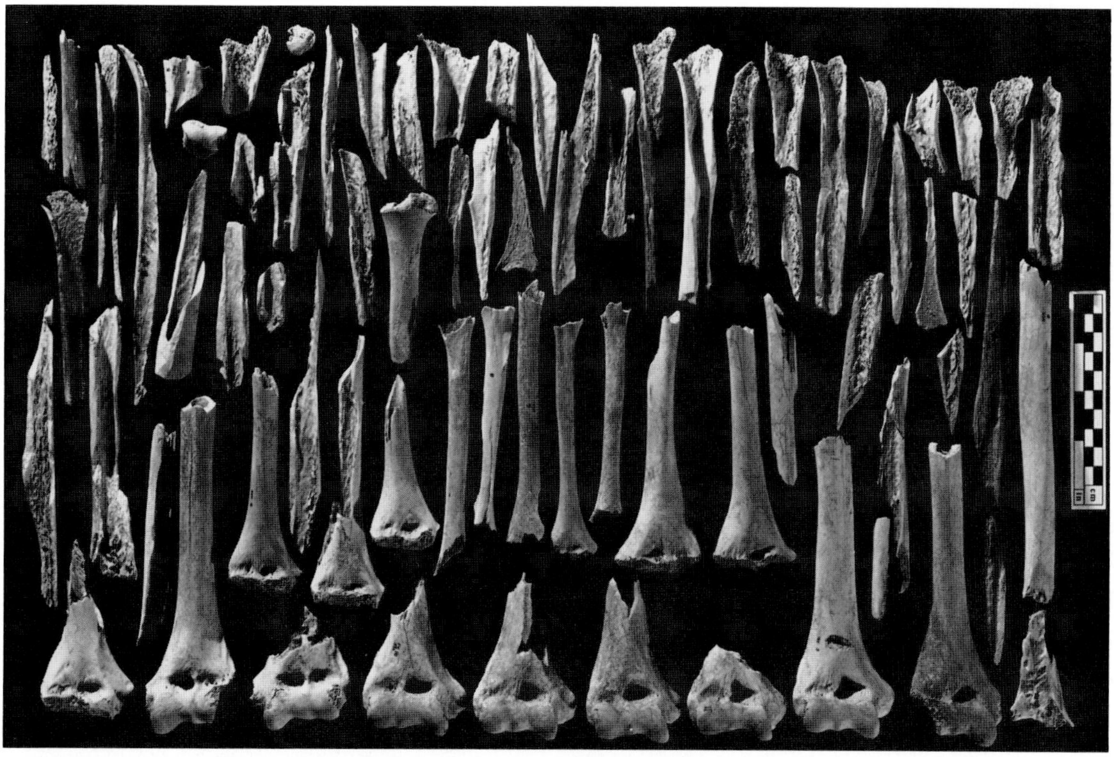

Fig. 9.1 The Mancos 5MTUMR–2346 humerus subassemblage. Note the patterning of fracture and representation, with the distal ends over-represented.

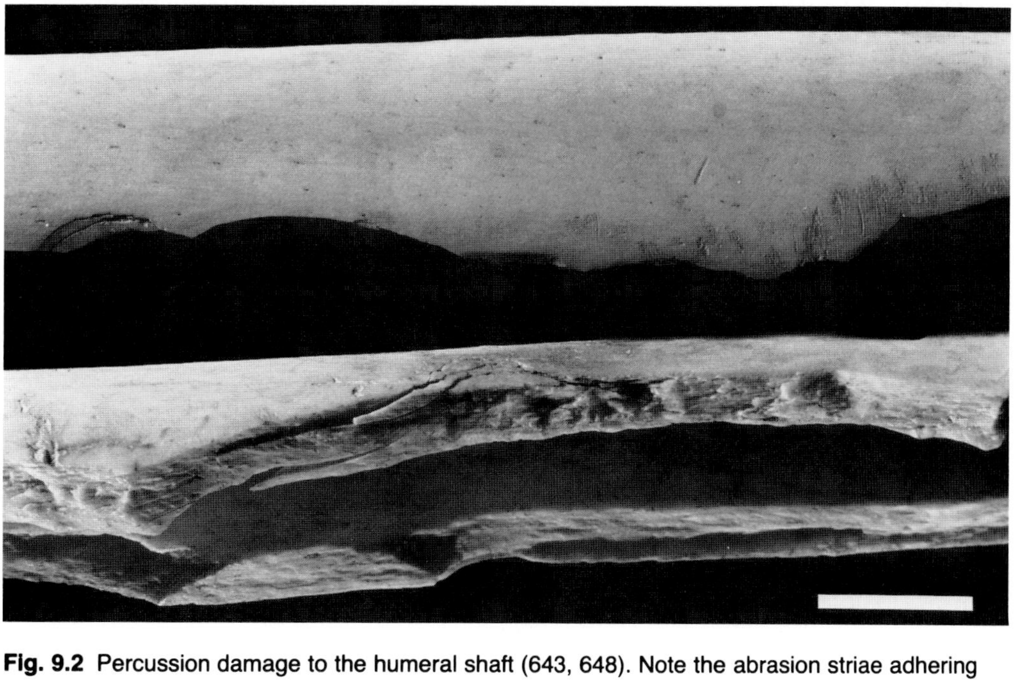

Fig. 9.2 Percussion damage to the humeral shaft (643, 648). Note the abrasion striae adhering flakes, and inner conchoidal flake scars. Bar = 1 cm.

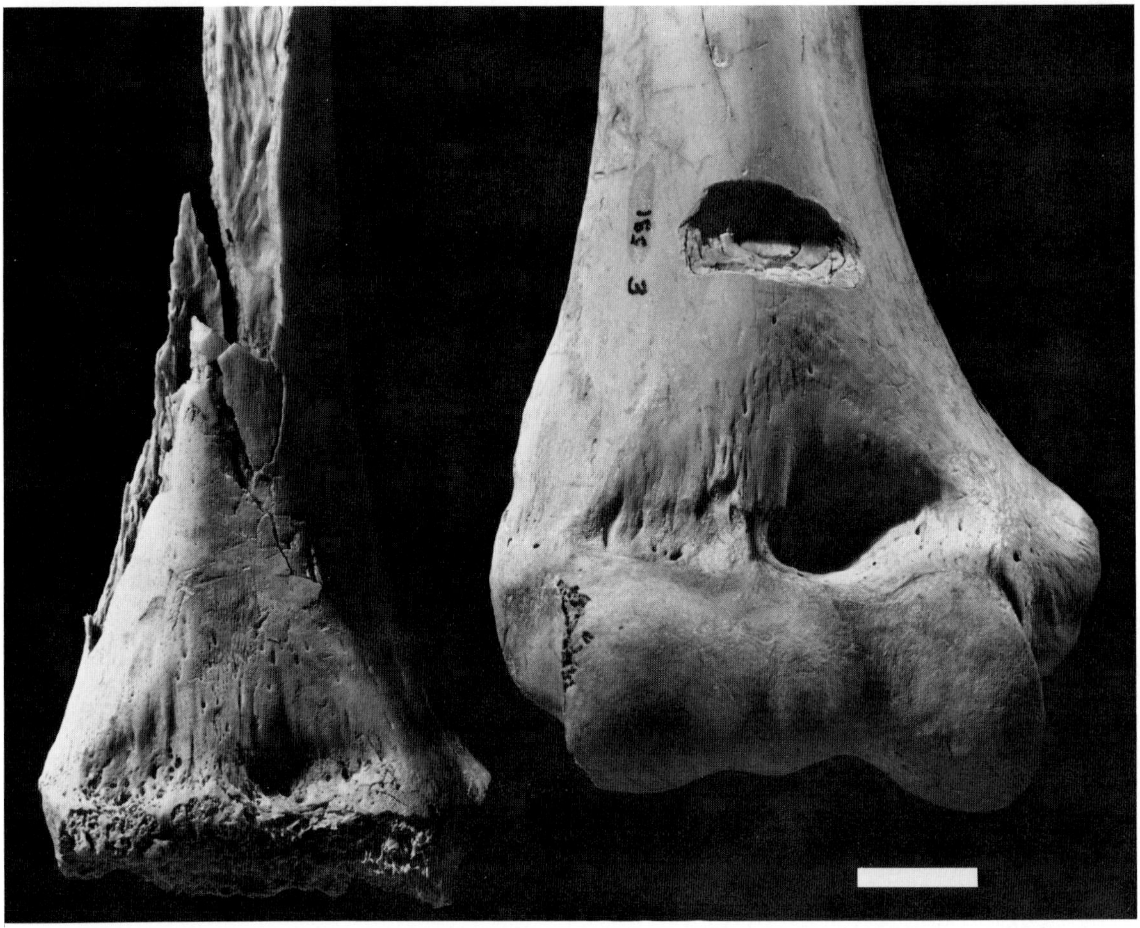

Fig. 9.3 Percussion damage to the distal humerus (590, 591). This part of the element is highly resistant to fragmentation by percussion. Bar = 1 cm.

cylinders (Figure 9.1) seems to relate to midshaft snap-fracture followed by percussion to the humeral head and proximal shaft. In 8 distal ends with spirally fractured shafts, however, blows to the anterior or posterior surfaces of the distal shaft are recorded (Figure 9.3). In the 7 pieces that preserve shaft near the humeral head in individuals older than 6 years, 4 show peeling at the broken surface, and 2 show evidence of crushing. Crushing is also seen in the denser, better represented distal humeral ends. The two most complete, probably antimeric, adult humeri show mirror-image damage in their transverse midshaft failure as well as their obliquely sheared distal lateral ends and spirally fractured proximal ends (Figure 9.4).

Toolmarks

Many maximally conjoined pieces have cutmarks, and where cutmarks are lacking, the pieces involved are very small or

Fig. 9.4 Humerus conjoining Sets 20 and 30. Note the midshaft perpendicular break and the spiral fracture proximal to this. Note also that the bone splinter toward the scale bears polish on its end, accumulated subsequent to fracture. Bar = 1 cm.

very immature. The most obvious and frequent mark is transverse, across the distal end (Figure 9.5). These marks are at various positions, but are invariably transverse, anterior, and proximal to the distal articular surface. They are related to tool edge contact with the high points of the distal shaft that lie below flexor tendons crossing the elbow joint. They are obviously disarticulation marks, and homologous marks are well documented in ursids by Guilday (1963), ungulates by Binford (1981, Figure 4.30, Hd-2), reindeer by Olsen (1987, Figure 2), mule deer by Lang and Harris (1984, Cut 14) and this study (see Chapter 13), and artiodactyls by Fisher (1984, Figures 42, 47). They are present in disarticulated hominid skeletal remains from both Neolithic (LeMort and Duday, 1987) and Pleistocene (Krapina and Vindija, personal observation) contexts. In the maximally conjoined Mancos assemblage, 10 of the 15 pieces that are moderately intact to intact in this anatomical area display these slicing marks. Similar marks are found on 1 adult piece on the posterior surface of the distal humerus.

Many of the humeral shaft fragments show abrasion striae, oriented mostly transversely. These are obviously percussion-related (caused by contact with hammer or anvil). One of the 2 fairly intact proximal ends shows slicing cutmarks circling the shaft below the neck. One piece (0642) displays polish on its broken distal end.

Burning

The sample is small, but there is evidence of burning. Four of the postconjoined fragments show definite burning, 25 are unburned, and 9 show equivocal evidence. The burned fragments are all shaft or shaft/distal end fragments; fractured

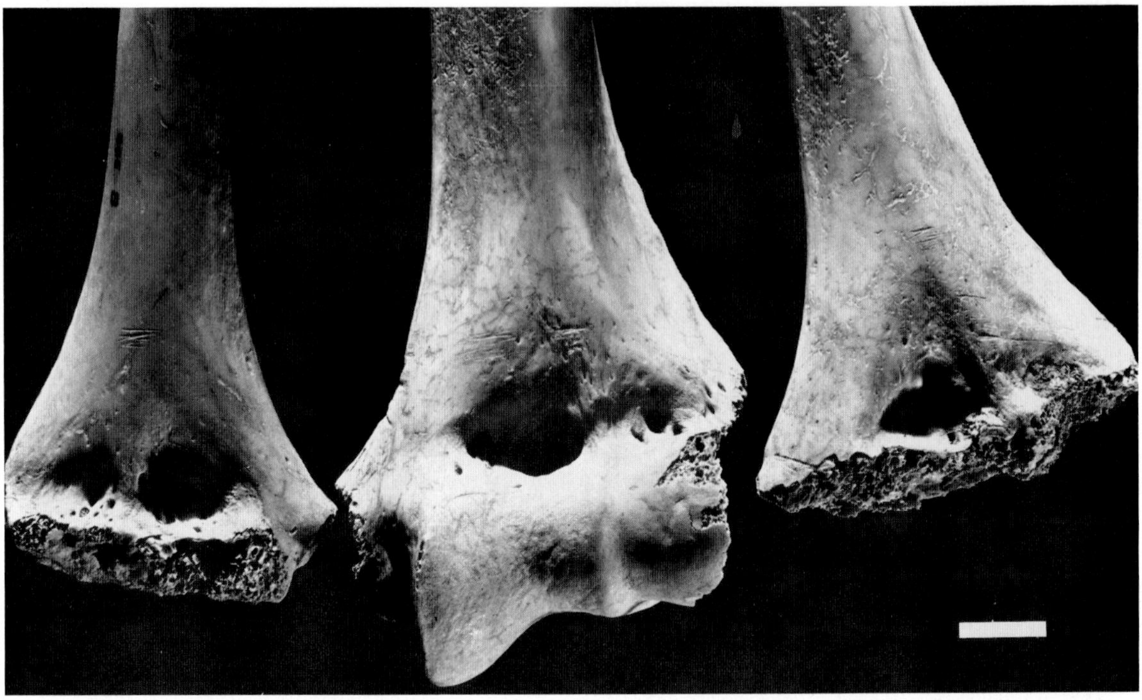

Fig. 9.5 Transverse cutmarks on the anterior surface of the distal humerus, presumably made when the flexor tendons crossing the elbow were severed with a stone tool. This damage, illustrated here by three specimens (588, 625, 641), is evident on many of the Mancos distal humeri. Bar = 1 cm.

ends and adjacent broken surfaces are unaltered by fire, indicating that the burning took place before the bones were broken. Differential burning along the shaft is probably related to the degree of soft tissue cover at the time of heating.

ULNA (FIGURE 9.6)

Survival

The total of 14 MNI includes 4 individuals younger than 6 years, 2 individuals between 6 and 9 years, and 9 people older than 12 years in the maximally conjoined assemblage. There are 8 unconjoined immature pieces that are relatively intact through the midshaft region, but only conjoined shafts of adults reach this level of completeness. There are 2 adult and 2 subadult pieces with fairly intact proximal ends. The remaining 5 adult and 8 immature head regions are heavily damaged or missing. Only 1 adult distal end is intact, whereas 5 of the immature pieces retain some epiphyseal surface in this region. As with the radius and humerus, adult ulnar midshafts are broken and both ends are usually missing.

Fracture

At the proximal ulnar end, all 4 rights and 3 of 6 lefts show mediolateral compres-

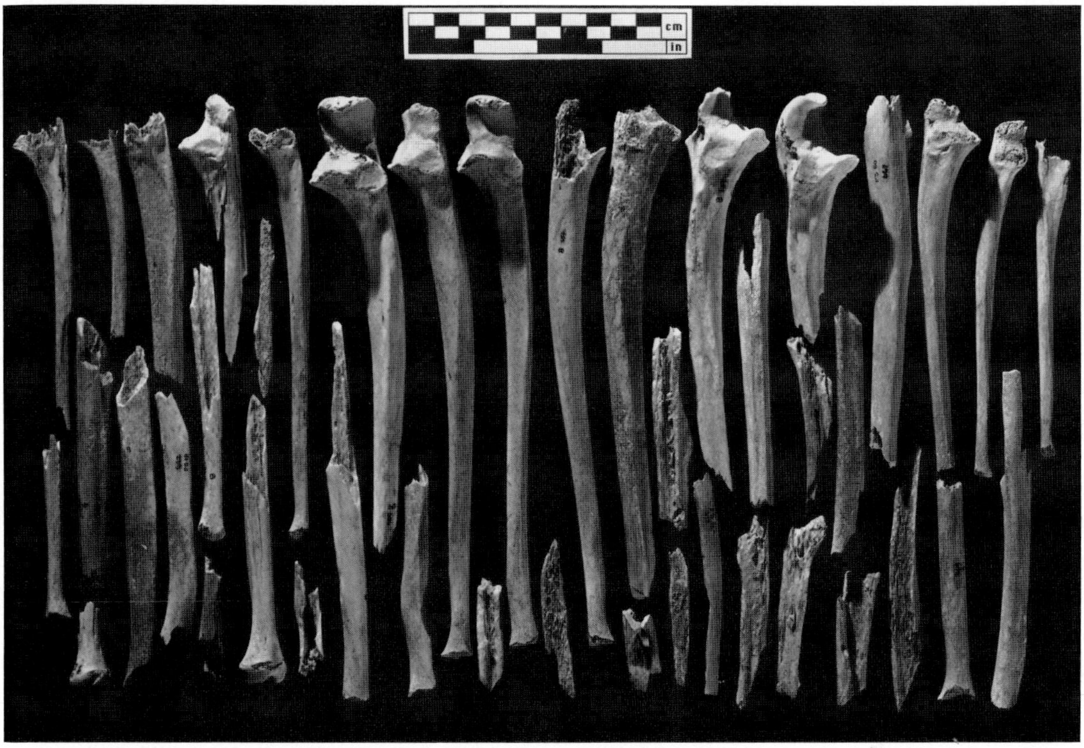

Fig. 9.6 The Mancos 5MTUMR–2346 ulna subassemblage.

sion of the heads. In the pieces representing younger individuals, the articular and epiphyseal surfaces are usually lost, but the crushing of the end results in a set of longitudinal splinters atop an intact shaft. These splinters remain in place after fracture, rebounding toward their original position. This is evidence of crushing (''mashing'') of the proximal ulna (see piece 652). Forcible removal of the crushed spongy bone is indicated by peeling down the coronoid process in piece 0671 (see Figure 9.8). In contrast, the adult proximal ulnae show broken shafts and lack evidence of head mashing in the form of rebounded splinters. In adults, the heads either are mostly intact (n = 4) or entirely missing.

For the ulnar shaft, pieces of individuals up to 12 years old are mostly intact. The shafts of older individuals are broken. Of the 11 pieces where it may be judged, 7 are spirally fractured, whereas 4 show perpendicular breaks. Both fracture types show clearly associated evidence of percussion, with adhering flakes and impact scars.

Of the 8 broken adult distal ends with some swelling toward the radial articulation, 1 retains the articular surface, and this is compressed by crushing fracture (0681). Another piece shows obvious crushing percussion of this region, with adhering flakes and hairline fractures (0674), whereas a third piece lacks such evidence but has peeling on the lateral surface of the shaft (0676). Figure 9.7 illustrates this damage.

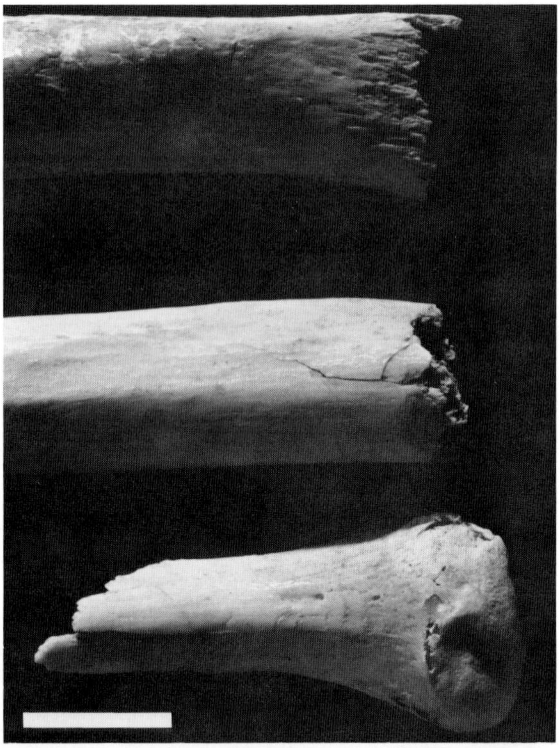

Fig. 9.7 Percussion damage and peeling of the distal ulna (674, 676, 681). Bar = 1 cm.

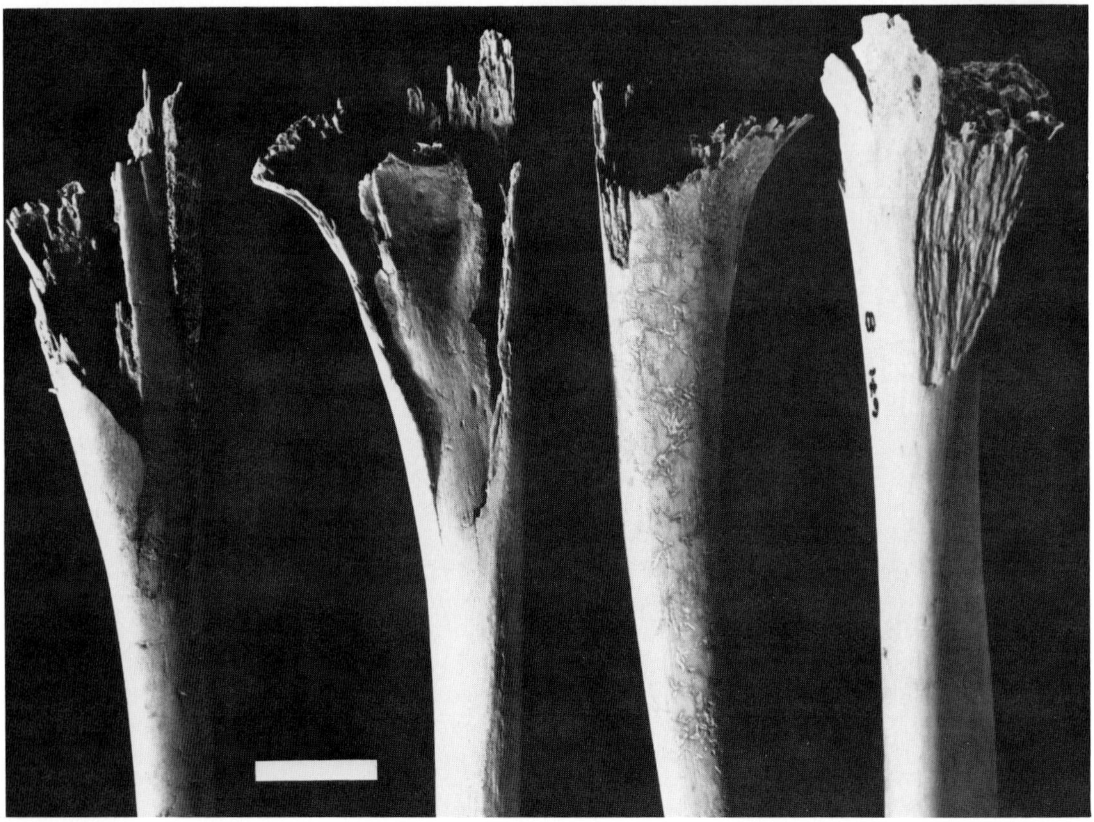

Fig. 9.8 Crushing (and resulting splintering damage) and peeling of the proximal juvenile ulnae (652, 669, 670, 671).

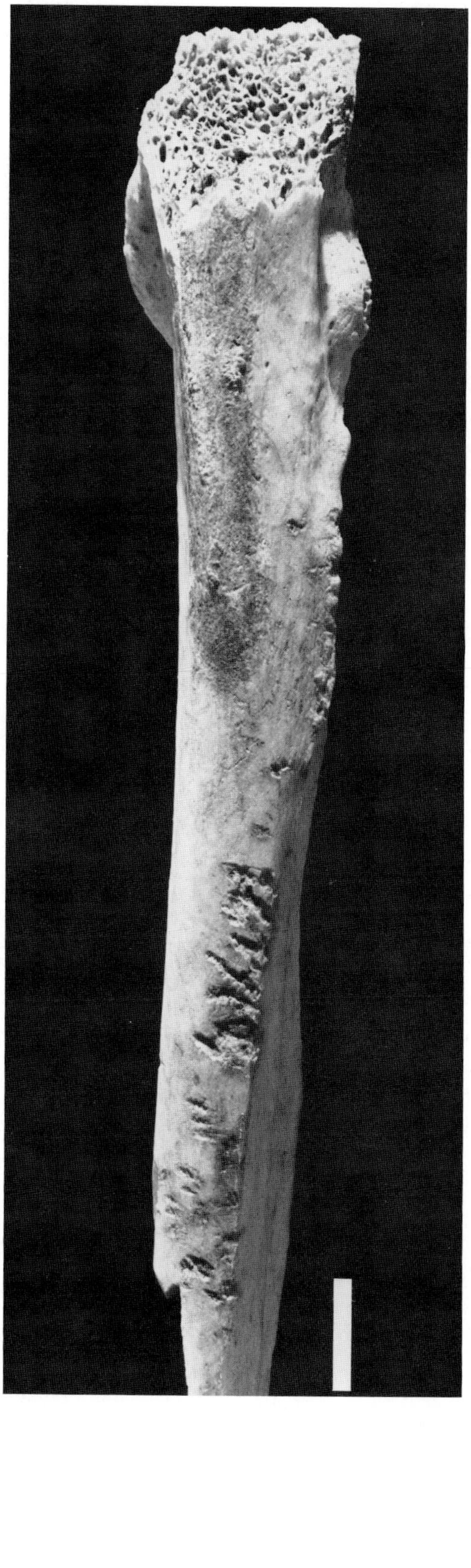

Fig. 9.9 Percussion and subcutaneous burning damage on the dorsal ulnar shaft (659).

Toolmarks

The strongest pattern, like that encountered with the humerus, is the nearly complete lack of cutmarks on immature pieces. One 10-year-old has percussion-related marks associated with proximal midshaft breakage. Of the 11 other maximally conjoined pieces with toolmarks, 5 are associated with shaft breakage (percussion striae from a hammerstone and/or an anvil), and only 3 are partially preserved slicing marks on small fragments. There is 1 hackmark on a distal interosseous crest (0662), 1 series of impact scars on the posterior ulnar ridge below the head (0659, Figure 9.9), and 1 case of obvious polish on the inner and outer cortical surfaces (0674).

Burning

Of the 37 maximally conjoined pieces, 15 show no evidence of burning, 8 show certain burning, and the others are more equivocal. In 4 of the 8 certainly burned pieces, burning was most intense along the posterior surface or on the posterior olecranon. Another piece, a 7-year-old, shows burning at both ends, but not in the shaft region. The sample is small, but when combined with observations on the radius (see next section), a patterned heating is indicated for the forearm.

RADIUS (FIGURE 9.10)

Survival

Of the total postconjoining MNI of 13 derived from the maximally conjoined as-

Fig. 9.10 The Mancos 5MTUMR–2346 radius subassemblage.

semblage, there are 3 individuals younger than 7 years, and 5 individuals between 7 and 12 years old. No piece is undamaged; there is only one intact adult piece. There are 3 adolescents and 4 juveniles with fairly intact, full shafts. The correlation of shaft destruction with individual age operates as it does for the humerus, but in the radius, a bone with a much smaller adult medullary cavity, pieces from individuals younger than 12 years are most often intact, whereas pieces of older individuals are broken in the midshaft region.

No adult radial head is intact, but 5 retain some articular surface. Four adult distal ends retain articular surface, and 7 show only a ragged broken edge at the distal end. The general indication is fair survival of the radius in individuals up to age 12, and poor survival of articular ends in adult individuals.

Fracture

Proximally, the radial sample is small; only 4 adult pieces are preserved in this area. The radial heads are partly intact and no crushing is indicated.

Midshaft fracture is dominantly of the leverage type, with perpendicular, jagged breaks in 10 of the 16 adult pieces. There is a small amount of spiral fracture, mostly distally; some pieces show percussion pitting; and conchoidal percussion scars are apparent on one shaft fragment. As with the humerus, it appears that both over-anvil bending and midshaft percussion breakage were employed to break the

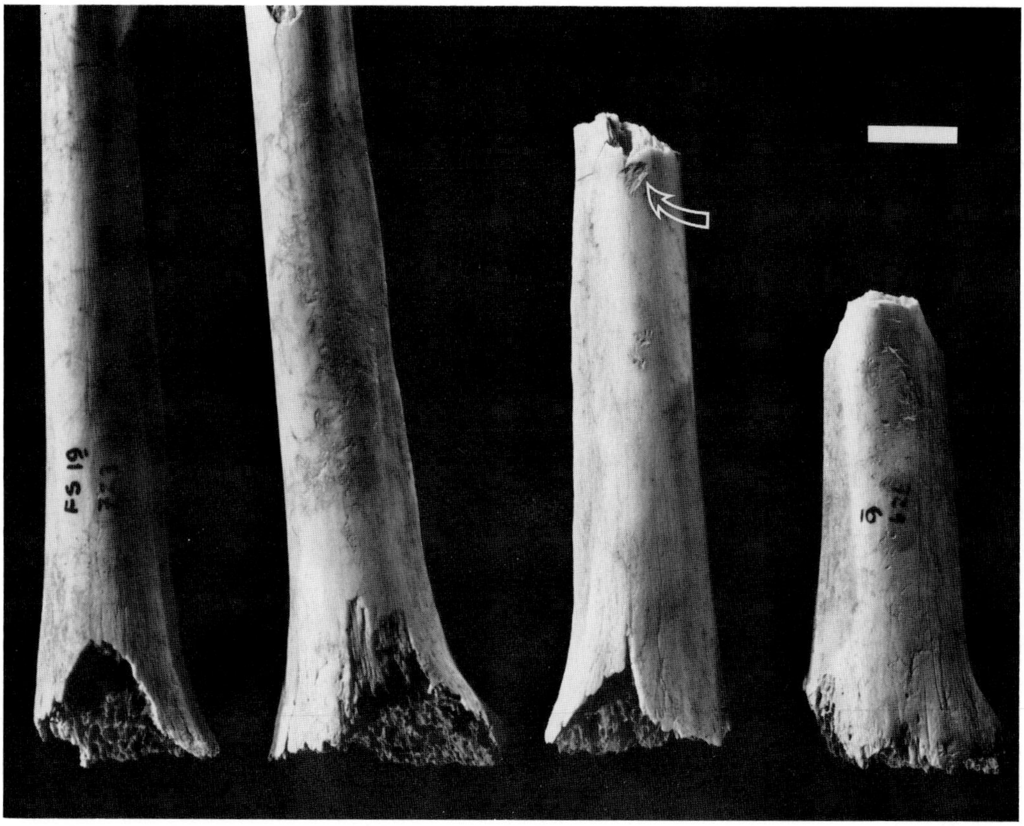

Fig. 9.11 Destruction and peeling of distal ends of the radius (708, 723, 724, 727). Note the percussion pit (arrow). Bar = 1 cm.

radii. The two pieces with percussion pits show the perpendicular breakage, indicating that percussion prior to or during bending may have provided the most effective means of fracturing the radial shaft.

Only 2 pieces show evidence of crushing to the distal radial end. Both show peeling up the shaft on the posterior surface, suggesting that the distal end was smashed, with percussion to the anterior surface and subsequent removal of the adhering mass of crushed bone and tissue (Figure 9.11).

Toolmarks

Two radius pieces show abrasion associated with hammerstone pits at midshaft (0707, 0708). Only 3 pieces show obvious slicing cutmarks. The first of these is a shaft and distal end with a series of oblique marks on the anterior surface that pass from superomedial to inferolateral (0723). The second piece is a shaft and partial head with transverse slices on the posteromedial corner of the radial tuberosity (0714). The third piece shows two sets of marks. One set goes transversely

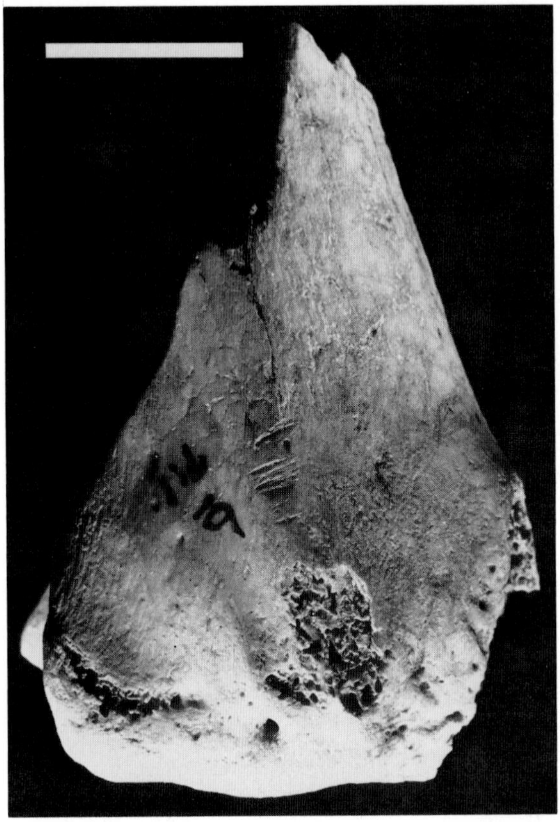

Fig. 9.12 Cutmarks on the distal dorsal radius (711), presumably related to the severing of the extensor tendons during detachment of the hand. Bar = 1 cm.

across the dorsal tubercles (distal end, dorsal surface), and is obviously related to cutting the tendons for the extrinsic extensor musculature of the hand, presumably directed at removal of the hand at the wrist. The second set is on the posterolateral corner oblique to the shaft axis (0711, Figure 9.12). None of the 5 other pieces with the same anatomical region preserved show these marks.

Burning

Of the maximally conjoined radial pieces, 9 show definite evidence of burning, 10 are equivocal, and 12 are unburned. The burning is highly patterned, being focused on the distal end (6 burned, 5 unburned) and shaft. The distal end suffered substantial fire-related destruction; the subcutaneous anterolateral shaft also suffered damage. Figure 9.13 illustrates this burning damage to the distal radius.

ARM PROCESSING: AN INTERPRETIVE SUMMARY

The foregoing analysis makes it possible to consider processing of the arm as an anatomical unit. The absence of proximal humeri renders any conclusions about disarticulation and burning at the shoulder impossible. Evidence in the form of abundant transverse slicing cutmarks on the distal humeri indicates segmentation of the arm at the elbow. Evidence for removal of the hand at the wrist is more limited due to the small sample size. Burning of the fleshed arm occurred, with the more subcutaneous parts of the forearm suffering most of the damage. Because of the degree of fragmentation, defleshing is impossible to document. Subsequent to burning, all bones of the arm were broken. Spongy bone parts with thin cortices (proximal humerus, proximal ulna, distal radius) were the targets of percussion damage as evidenced by crushing damage remaining at the broken bone ends of specimens; these element portions are poorly represented in the sample (for further quantification, see Chapter 12). The humeral shaft was the target of fracture on individuals older than 5 years, whereas the smaller diameter radial and ulnar shafts became susceptible to such fracture when individuals reached age 12. Fracture of the arm bones was accomplished by bending at midshaft and by percussion.

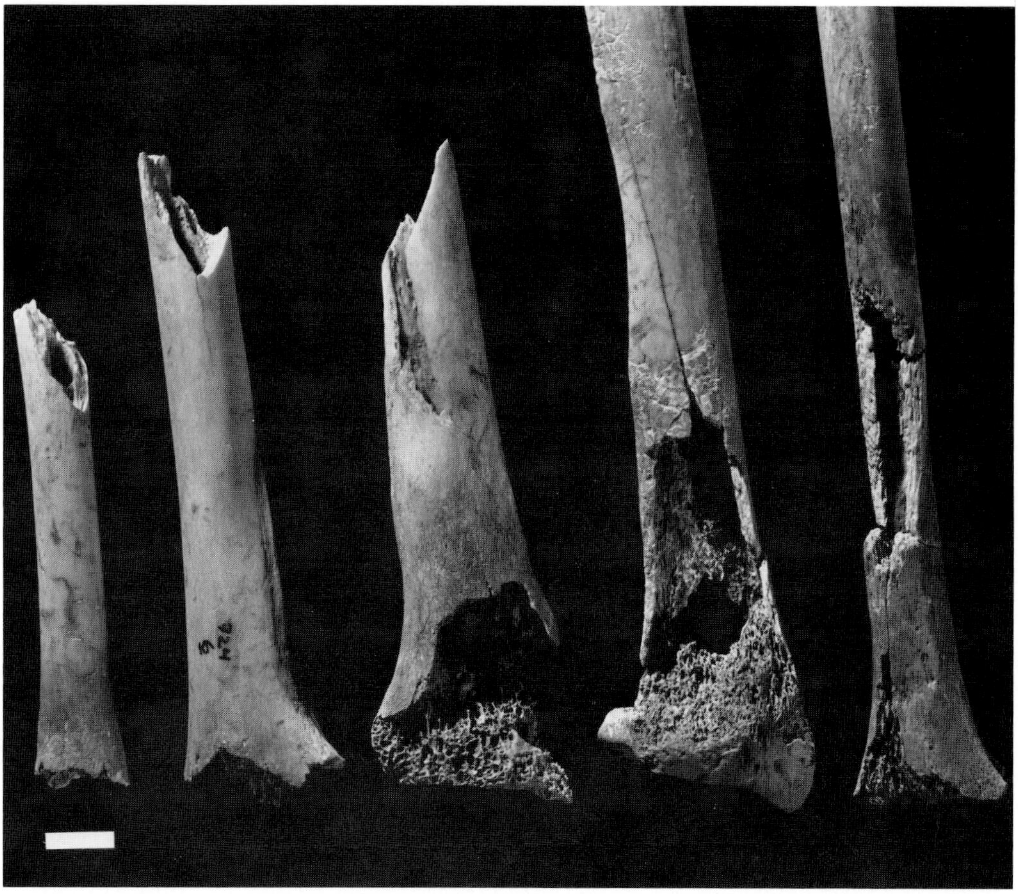

Fig. 9.13 Burning on the distal dorsal radius (698, 705, 712, 721, 729), concentrated on the subcutaneous surface of this bone. Bar = 1 cm.

CHAPTER

10

The Leg

The major leg elements—the femur, tibia, and fibula—are all long bones whose articular ends are easily identified. The patella is a large sesamoid bone. Evidence for processing of these four leg bones is described in the account that follows. Processing of the leg as a unit is described in the final section of the chapter.

FEMUR (FIGURES 10.1, 10.2)

Survival

Of the total MNI of 20 individuals derived from the maximally conjoined assemblage, 7 individuals were younger than 6 years at death, and 4 individuals were between 7 and 12 years. No femur is preserved intact, but survival of the immature specimens is far greater than survival of the adult femoral specimens. Only 1 adult partial femoral head is preserved. Two subadult femur head epiphyseal surfaces are preserved. Only 1 adult greater trochanter is preserved, this only partially.

Intact femur shafts are only present for very immature individuals. Adult shafts with intact cylindrical segments are extremely rare; almost all shaft specimens are bone splinters.

The distal femur end is intact in only one adult. Another adult piece lacks most of the distal articular surface. In summary, overall survival of the femur is poor. The femoral shaft is over-represented relative to the ends, but the shaft is universally fragmented. Identifiable maximally conjoined specimens and postconjoining pieces are well represented proximally, in the region just below the lesser trochanter. Distally, there are fewer pieces (the cortex is thinner here).

Fracture

It is useful to consider the pieces of the very young individuals (< 6 years) separately. On 6 of 8 observable maximally conjoined immature shafts, there is a basic, fairly perpendicular, jagged break at approximately midshaft. Associated with 2 of the 6 pieces are hammer or anvil pits close to the break. This looks like bending-induced breakage, probably initiated

Opposite page top:

Fig. 10.1 The Mancos 5MTUMR–2346 right femur subassemblage. Splinters attributable to femur, but not sided, are oriented horizontally.

Opposite page bottom:

Fig. 10.2 The Mancos 5MTUMR–2346 left femur subassemblage. Splinters attributable to femur, but not sided, are oriented horizontally.

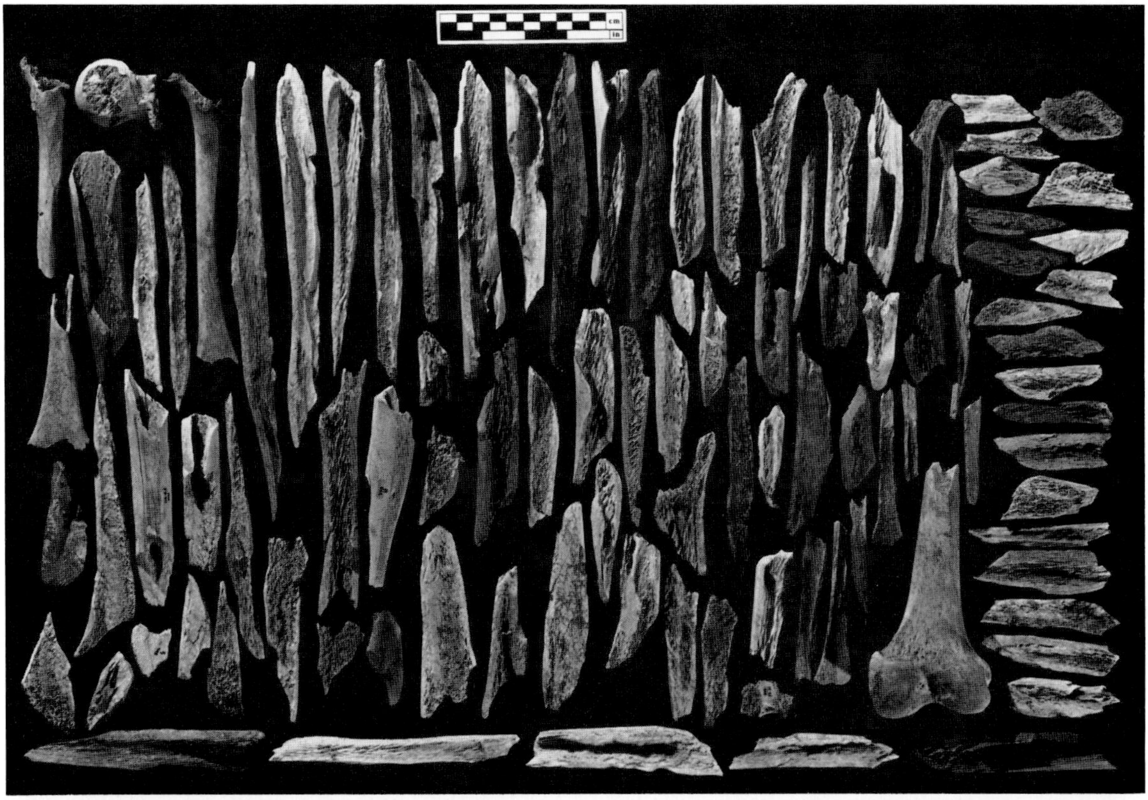
cm
in

cm
in

on an anvil or by initial weak percussion (Figure 10.3). There are no conchoidal scars or adhering flakes. Crushing of the metaphyses is indicated for several of these young femoral pieces.

The adult femoral shaft breakage pattern contrasts markedly with the situation in the very young pieces. In the adults, heavy percussion to the shaft was the rule, and spiral fractures are common. There are pieces with multiple successive impact scars (Figure 10.4, 10.5). Analysis of the percussion points throughout the sample shows them to occur on all four femoral shaft surfaces, with no apparent concentration on any side. When analysis of these impact points is made on a distal versus proximal basis, the samples become too small for statistically meaningful results.

Proximally, there is evidence for the "mashing" of the femoral end. Here, the head and trochanteric regions are underlain by spongy bone. One right femur head shows crushing and partial rebound, with both hammerstone and anvil contact points indented (Figure 10.6). Several immature individuals show evidence of the same action in the crushing of the lesser trochanter or distal neck edge; one left adult femur shows similar damage, with the head missing. Here, the trabecular bone exposed on the lesser and greater trochanters is surrounded by crushing damage (see Chapter 12 for illustration). The hammering actions recorded on these pieces seem responsible for eliminating most of the femoral ends in the Mancos assemblage.

The distal femoral ends are so thoroughly broken away that the thin-walled adjacent shaft is also usually lost. Several pieces show percussion flakes adhering in this distal shaft region. With the almost complete loss of distal femoral articular surface, however, there is no "rebound"

Fig. 10.3 Evidence of midshaft, over-anvil breakage of an immature individual's femur (744 + 745). Note the incipient fractures and percussion pit. Bar = 1 cm.

Fig. 10.4 Impact scars and conchoidal fracture of the femur shaft (conjoining Set 52). Bar = 1 cm.

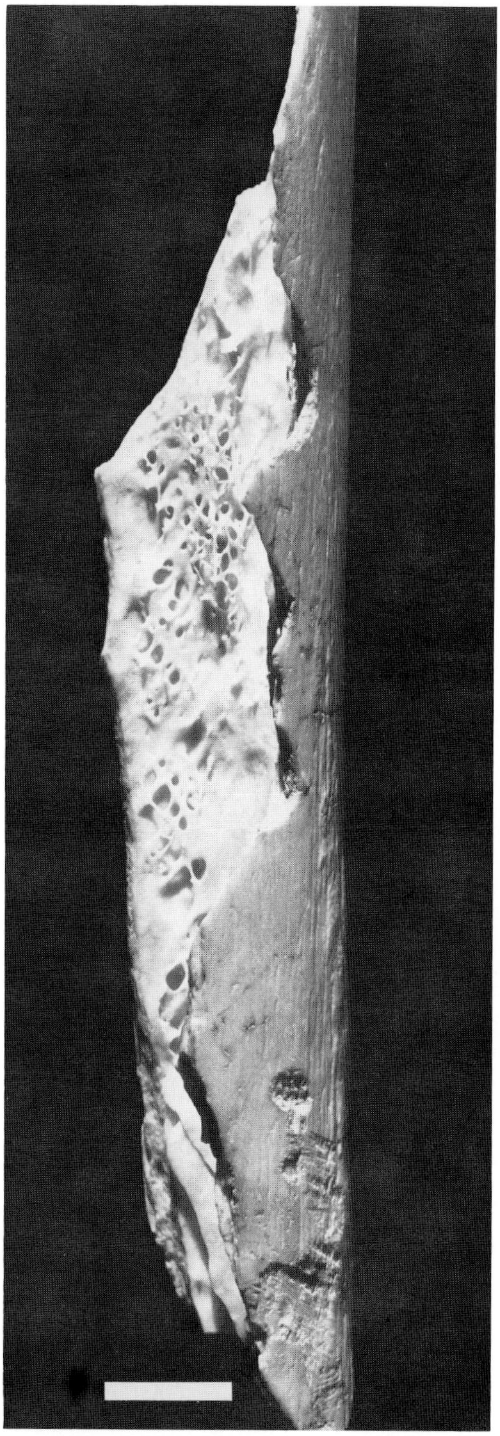

Fig. 10.5 Multiple percussor strikes recorded by damage to the femur shaft in the form of percussion pits and striae, and internally conchoidal scars (885).

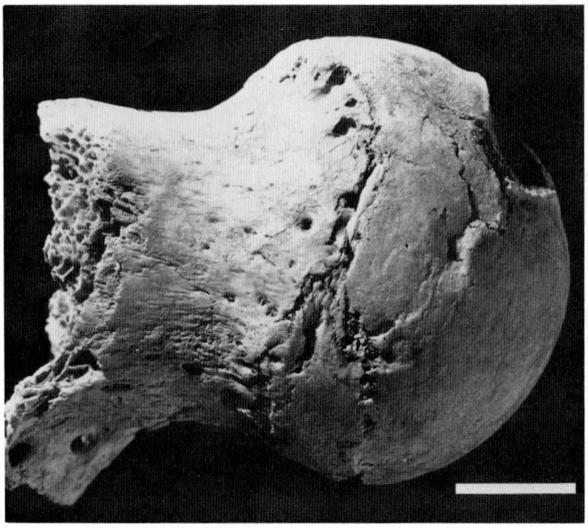

Fig. 10.6 Crushing of the femoral head (760). Bar = 1 cm.

crushing involved, and the entire distal end is usually simply missing. The only 2 adult pieces with any articular surface remaining include a virtually intact distal end with light percussion, and a segment centered on the patellar notch. Heavier crushing appears to have eliminated the other distal femora.

It is clear that the proximal and distal femoral ends from individuals older than 6 years were crushed, and the shafts broken open by percussion. This resulted in a collection of fragments that is heavily conjoined, but poorly identifiable in the preconjoined state.

Toolmarks

The paucity of proximal and distal femoral ends coupled with extreme shaft fragmentation makes interpretive, quantitative, and functional work on toolmarks very difficult.

Despite the good preservation and representation of the maximally conjoined pieces of individuals younger than 6 years, only about half of the shafts show toolmarks; most of them are abrasion related. There are a few slicing marks on the anterior and posterior shaft surfaces. Potential cutmarks associated with disarticulation are mostly unavailable due to the loss of the proximal and distal ends through crushing.

Of the more mature femoral pieces, 2 with unfused head epiphyses lack cutmarks around the neck. Only two fully adult pieces preserve any portion of the neck. One is the battered head illustrated in Figure 10.6. The second is a piece that displays three sets of slicing marks perpendicular to the neck axis on the anterior, posterior, and superior surfaces. These are clearly related to disarticulation at the hip. Similar marks are described and illustrated by Villa *et al.* (1986b) for humans and by Binford (1981, Figure 4.25, Fp-1) for ungulates. Of the 8 popliteal fossa fragments with one edge fairly intact, only 1 Mancos piece shows a transverse slicing mark.

The femur shaft, with its thick and resilient cortex, is a hammerstone target that accumulated a great deal of percussion signature in the form of hammerstone pitting and percussion-related abrasion (Figures 10.7, 10.8). Many striations on the femoral shafts are part of abrasion fields related to hammerstone and anvil contact. In some cases, the intense abrasion is so linear and deep that it mimics true slicing cutmarks (Figure 10.9). In other instances, the presence of deep, V-shaped pits on the bone surface indicates the use of a sharp-edged tool (Figure 10.10), but whether the objective was soft tissue removal via hacking, or fracture of the bone via hammering, is unresolvable. Several pieces show intense, heavy battering and hacking perpendicular to the linea aspera.

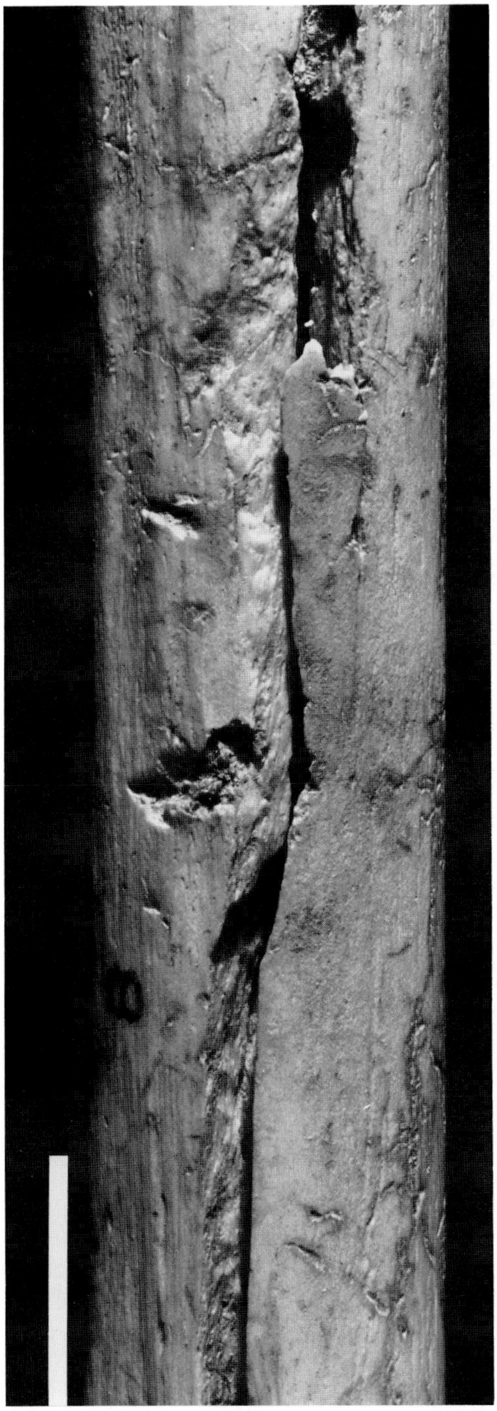

Fig. 10.7 Hammerstone impact points on a conjoined femur shaft (876, 877). Bar = 1 cm.

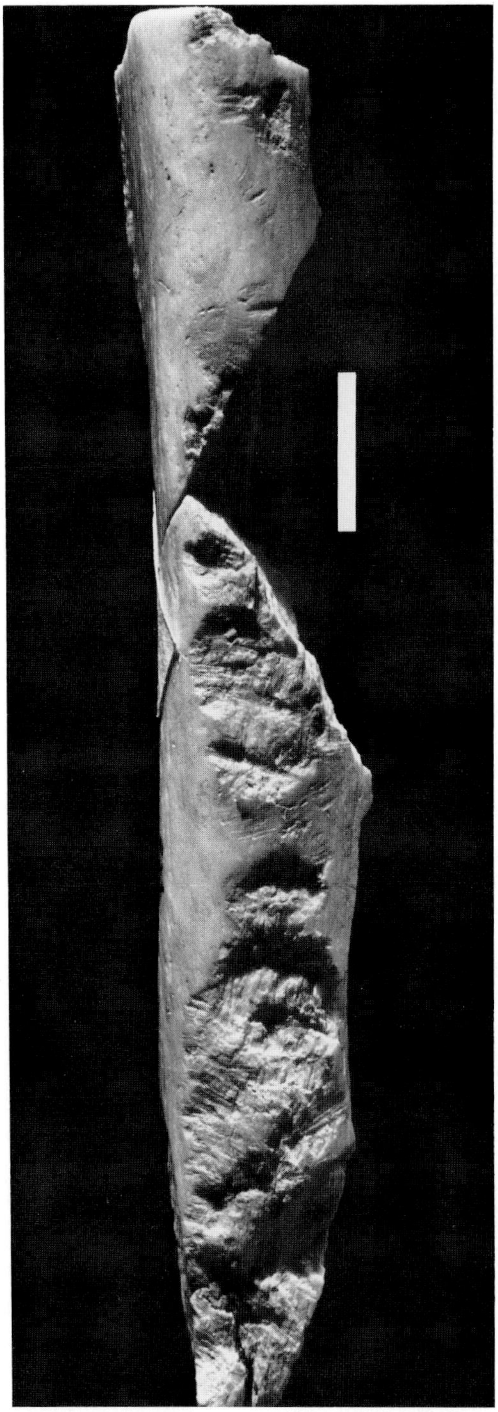

Fig. 10.8 Hammerstone impact points on the femur shaft (943, 944). Extremely heavy battering may have been required to fracture this specimen in the gluteal region, where the bone cortex was very thick. Bar = 1 cm.

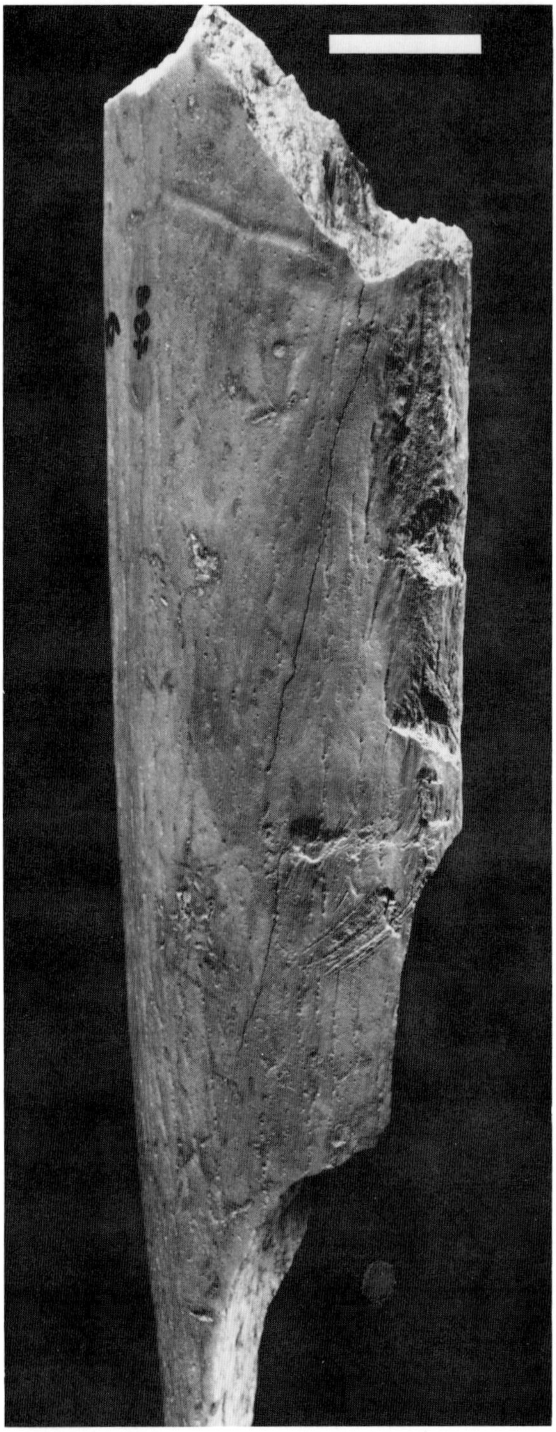

Fig. 10.9 Cutmark mimics in the form of abrasion striae associated with blows to the femur (887). Bar = 1 cm.

Fig. 10.10 Chopmarks on the femur shaft (792–794). Bar = 1 cm.

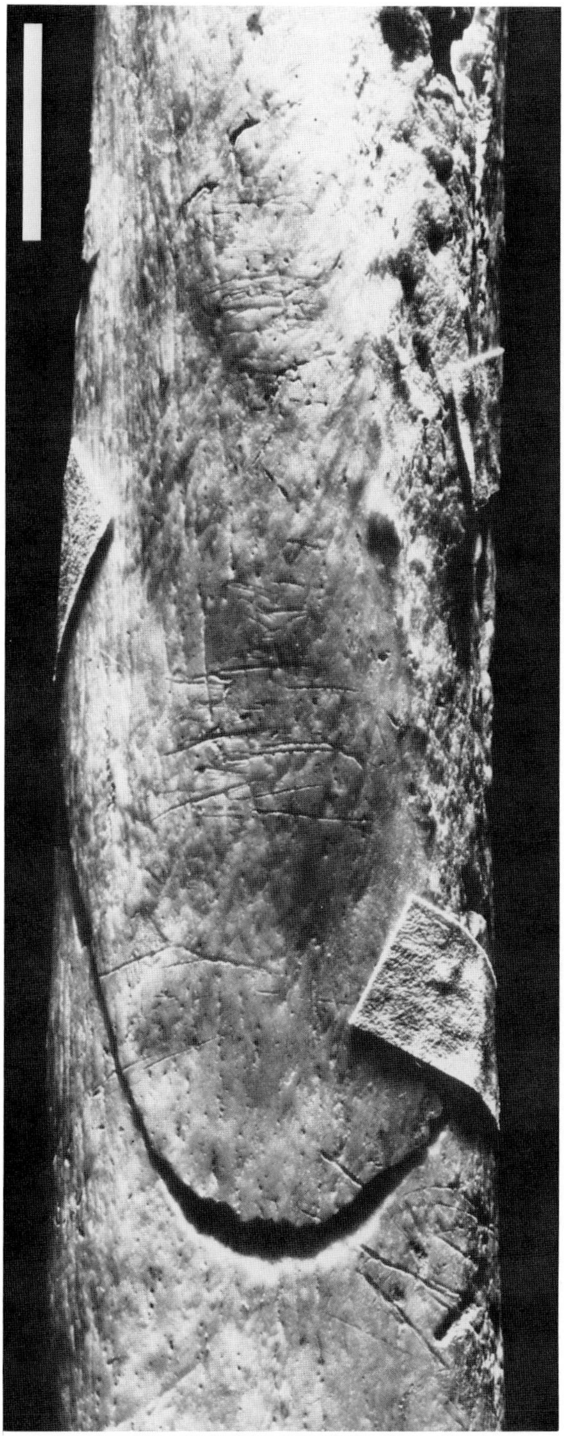

Fig. 10.11 Cutmarks on the femur (846–849). Note how one set crosses the spiral fracture. Bar = 1 cm.

Orientation of the true slicing marks on the femur shaft fragments varies from parallel to perpendicular to the shaft axis, but most marks are perpendicular to oblique (Figure 10.11). Several femur splinter pieces (0828, 0857, 0872) show edge polish and rounding (described in detail in Chapter 6).

Burning

Of the maximally conjoined assemblage, 1 of the 10 pieces from individuals younger than 6 years, and 14 of the pieces from older individuals show definitive evidence of burning. Roughly half of the femoral pieces, many from "Burial" 11, show evidence consistent with burning. The remainder, mostly from "Burial" 8, are unburned. From "Burial" 8 comes clear evidence of some burning after shaft fragmentation. Here, a burned and an unburned shaft fragment conjoining set provides this indication (Figure 10.12). Several other pieces suggest the same thing, but none are as well preserved as this set. There is no clear positional patterning to burning on the femur, but most burning is at midshaft, and most is anterior or lateral on the shaft. Some pieces, however, show burning to the posterior gluteal area or to the linea aspera itself. All of these shaft segments are deeply covered by soft tissue.

PATELLA (FIGURE 10.13)

Survival

The MNI of 7 is made up of 5 immature and 2 adult individuals, represented by fairly intact patellae.

Fig. 10.12 Burning damage to the femur. The conjoining pieces show that in this case, burning took place after fracture of this specimen (874 + 875). Note the percussion striae on the lighter piece, and the root etching of the burned fragment. Bar = 1 cm.

Fig. 10.13 The Mancos 5MTUMR–2346 patella subassemblage. Note the crushing damage to several of these specimens.

Fracture

The youngest individual shows a depressed puncture on the posterior patellar surface. Another immature piece and two adults show anteroposterior crushing damage, with compression and "rebound" on the articular surface. One adult is broken in half by such trauma. The other two damaged pieces, probably antimeres, show crushing on the medial and lateral sides instead of the anterior and posterior surfaces. The two remaining pieces show abrasion but no crushing.

Toolmarks

No tool-related marks except abrasion striae related to percussion are present.

Fig. 10.14 The Mancos 5MTUMR–2346 right tibia subassemblage. Splinters attributable to tibia, but not sided, are oriented horizontally.

Burning

One piece is very friable and possibly burned; the others are unburned.

TIBIA (FIGURES 10.14, 10.15)

Survival

Of the total MNI of 18 individuals in the maximally conjoined assemblage, 6 individuals were younger than 6 years at death, and 3 individuals were between ages 7 and 12. No tibia is preserved intact, but the survival of the immature specimens is better than the survival of the adult tibial specimens, following the pattern established above for the femur. Of the 11 maximally conjoined pieces from individuals younger than 6 years, 3 are intact shafts and one is a partial shaft. Of all the pieces representing individuals older than age 6, only one 9-year-old retains a complete, unconjoined shaft circumference at midshaft. The proximal epiphyseal surface is seen only on 4 immature pieces, and a tiny corner of articular surface remains on 1 adult. The distal epiphyseal surface is seen on only 1 individual, whereas that articular surface is preserved intact on 1 adult and partially preserved on 3 other adult tibiae. Thus, this overall pattern of nonsurvival of proximal and distal ends and splintering of the shafts is similar to that characterizing the femur.

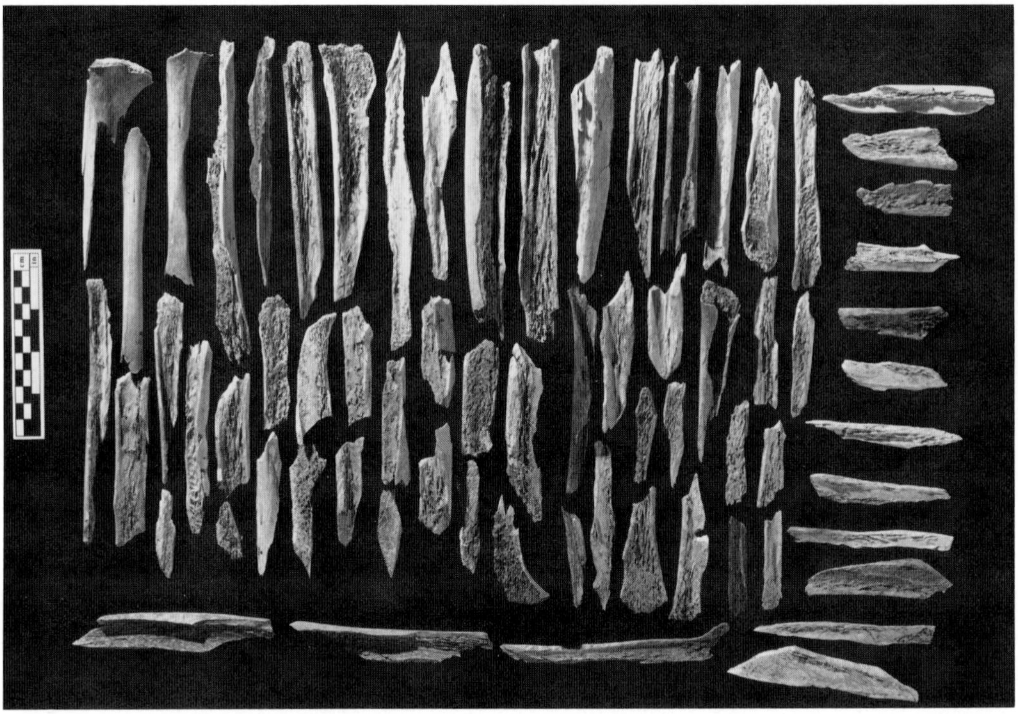

Fig. 10.15 The Mancos 5MTUMR–2346 left tibia subassemblage. Splinters attributable to tibia, but not sided, are oriented horizontally.

Fracture

Only 1 adult piece (1022 + 1023) retains evidence of crushing on the tibial plateau; it shows tiny crushed flakes adhering to the jagged broken proximal end and 3 concentric hairline fractures in the adjacent cortex. One subadult tibial tuberosity shows longitudinal peeling (1052); six tibial tuberosities remain among the adult pieces, but none show damage.

In immature pieces, the distal tibial end is almost always completely missing. One shaft shows peeling (1030), and none of the broken distal shaft ends show crushing damage. The 4 adults retaining distal ends all show slight or moderate abrasion, and 3 of these evidence crushing of the outer table down into the trabeculae (with some rebound), indicating that crushing on an anvil was the method of destruction.

Percussion was the favored mode of entry into the shaft, from the lateral, medial, or sometimes posterior surfaces. The lateral and posterior percussion scars indicate that soft tissue (muscular) cover that invests this area of the bone was already gone before percussion (this thick tissue would have cushioned the blow and made fracture impossible). There are numerous excellent examples of multiple blows, with conchoidal scars and adhering flakes demonstrating that percussion allowed access to the medullary cavity (Figures 10.16–10.18).

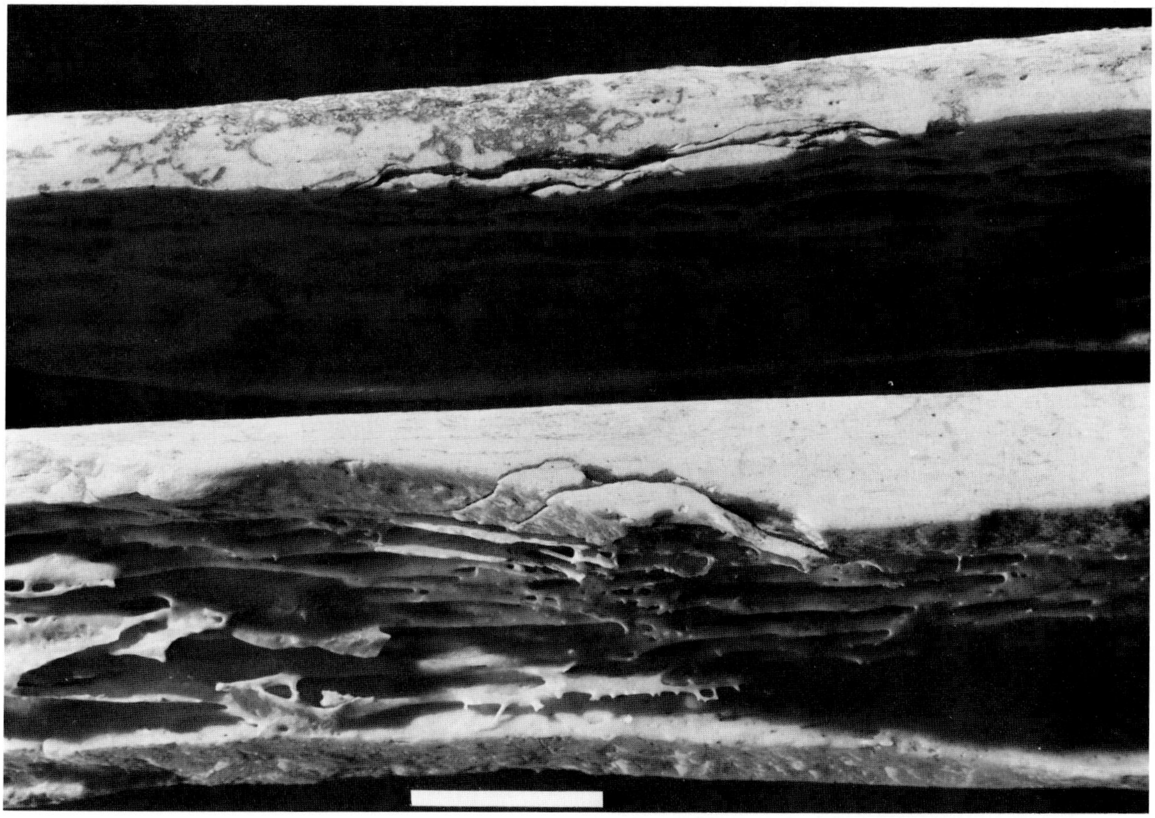

Fig. 10.16 Adhering flakes made by percussion to the tibial shaft (969, 1061). Bar = 1 cm.

Toolmarks

As is true for the femur, the paucity of proximal and distal tibial ends coupled with extreme shaft fragmentation makes interpretive, quantitative, and functional work on toolmarks very difficult. Tool-induced marks are frequent on both the maximally conjoined immature and adult pieces. These marks, particularly in the adults, are "hacking" marks on 3 pieces, a few slicing marks, and an abundance of anvil-hammer-related abrasion patches. In several cases these patches correspond to impact points.

Slicing cutmarks are rare, and no clear pattern is discernible. One immature piece (1037) shows hack/slicemarks across the superolateral popliteal compartment, probably for disarticulation of the proximal tibiofibular joint. Unfortunately, with the extremely poor representation of proximal and distal tibial ends, much disarticulation-related cutmark evidence is lost for the tibia.

Burning

There is excellent, patterned evidence of tibial burning throughout all age categories. Midshaft burning is most common,

Fig. 10.17 Percussion pitting on a conjoined tibial shaft piece (1020 + 1021). Bar = 1 cm.

seen on the medial (subcutaneous) surface of 5 immature and 15 adult maximally conjoined pieces. Only 1 immature and 1 adult midshaft showed a complete lack of burning, whereas 4 immature and 1 adult maximally conjoined tibial pieces show burning on the ends only, with no shaft involvement. Thus, for pieces from individuals older than age 7, virtually all the anterior tibial crests are present, and all pieces are burned on the medial surface (Figures 10.19, 10.20). This is strong evidence that the lower leg was burned whole, with the musculature attached. There is no case of burning after percussion fracture of the bone. This suggests that the subcutaneous medial tibial surface and anterior tibial crest were burned when the muscle-bound tibia was heated, followed by removal of the tissue, and percussion into the midshaft and crushing of the proximal and distal ends.

FIBULA (FIGURE 10.21)

Survival

Of the MNI count of 18 individuals in the maximally conjoined assemblage, 6 individuals were younger than 6 years at death, and 5 were between 7 and 12 years. The most complete fibula specimens are immature, as in the femur and tibia. Of the 7 individuals older than 12 years, only 2 have more than 2/3 of the shaft remaining intact. Shafts of individuals younger than 12 are usually intact, but only 5 of the immature pieces retain proximal or distal epiphyseal surfaces. No adult fibular piece retains the proximal articular surface, and only 1 adult maximally con-

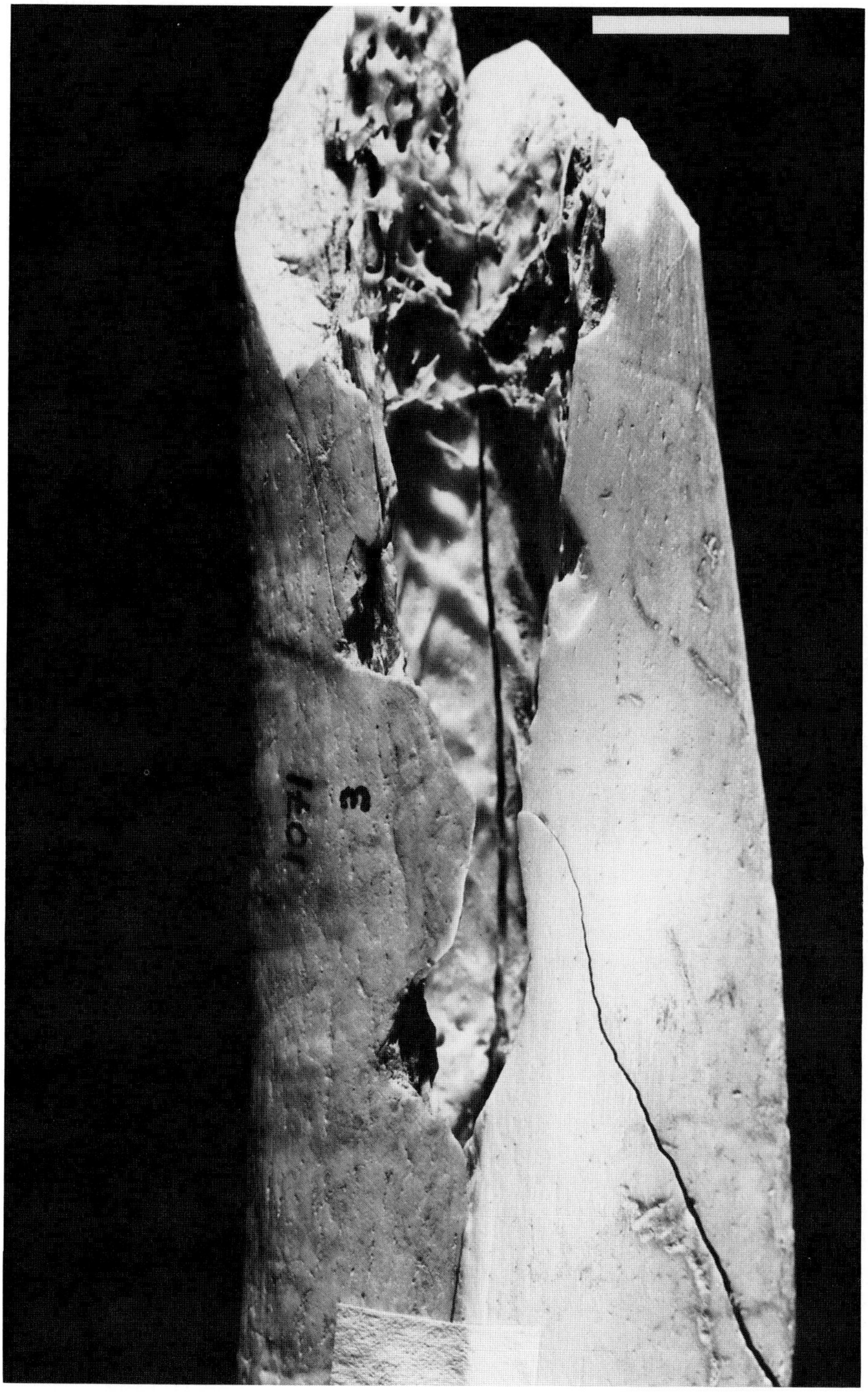

Fig. 10.18 Conchoidal scars on a conjoined tibial shaft piece (1070 + 1071). Bar = 1 cm.

Fig. 10.19 Some conjoining sets of right and left tibias, shown in the anterior view to illustrate patterned burning damage to the anteromedial surface (subcutaneous) of this bone (995, 987, 1009, 1003, 1014, 967, 1039, 1052, 1067, 1035, 1044, 1070). Note how the exfoliation and discoloration of burning is focused on the anterior tibial crest.

joined piece has a whole distal articular surface (4 adults retain slivers of this surface). Loss of the ends relates to fracture and burning (see below). The degree to which shaft circumferences are preserved stands in strong contrast to the situation documented above for the femur and tibia. In the fibula, the overwhelming majority of unconjoined specimens show midshaft segments that retain full shaft circumferences.

Fracture

Of the 10 adult pieces with fairly well-preserved proximal shaft regions, none retain heads. Two pieces show depressed flakes of cortical bone along the broken edge indicating crushing of the proximal end. The distal end is better represented; the same kind of evidence for crushing is also seen here (Figure 10.22). Several breaks along the fibula shafts of very

Fig. 10.20 Closeup of four anterior tibial surfaces to show the damage associated with burning (995, 1003, 1070, 1052). Upper numbers on scale are centimeters.

Fig. 10.21 The Mancos 5MTUMR–2346 fibula subassemblage. Note that in contrast to the tibia or femur subassemblages, the fibula shafts tend to be intact, the bones lacking only the proximal and distal ends.

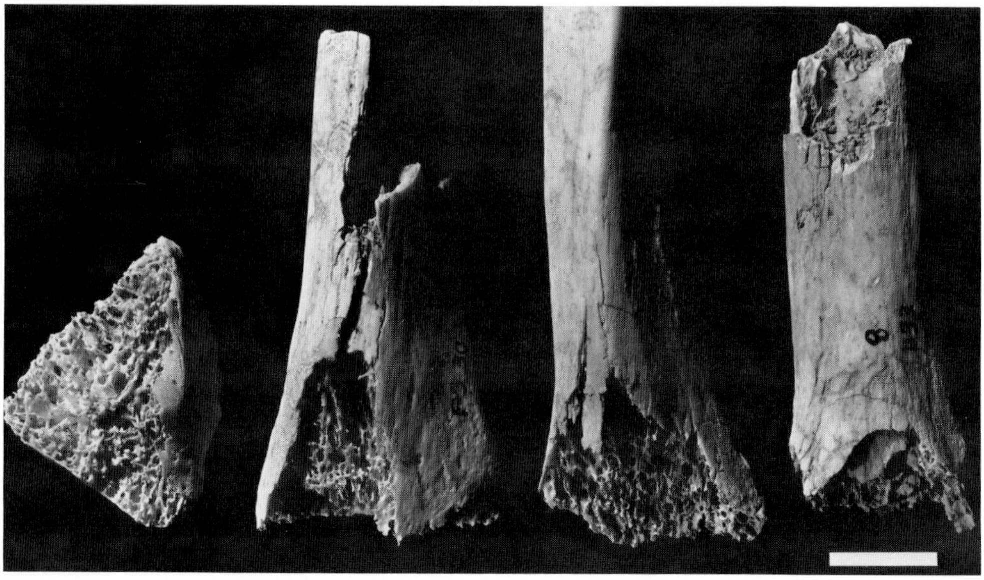

Fig. 10.22 Crushing damage of the distal fibula (1133, 1134, 1149, 1153). Note the trabecular bone exposed here. Bar = 1 cm.

young individuals (< 6 years) are associated with heavy burning damage. For the older immature material, there is one case of midshaft breakage. For the adults, there is considerable shaft fracture, but only 1 specimen shows obvious signs of conchoidal scarring associated with hammer strike. Some midshaft breaks are jagged and perpendicular to the shaft, but determining whether fracture was accomplished by leverage or by percussion breakage on an anvil is impossible.

Toolmarks

None of the 0- to 6-year-old individuals and only 1 of the 7- to 12-year-olds bear any cutmarks. On the adult fibulae, 8 pieces show toolmarks, but 7 of these are abrasion patches, usually associated with a fracture point on the bone. The fibula has remarkably few slicing cutmarks. If disarticulation of the bone from the tibia was accomplished by cutting, it should have shown up proximally and distally, but it did not, presumably because the disarticulation was done without cutting, perhaps by breaking the midshaft away from the fibular ends that remained articulated with the tibia.

Burning

Of the maximally conjoined pieces for which a side can be established, 18 are unburned, 12 bear ambiguous evidence, and 10 are definitely burned. All of the definitely burned specimens are heavily burned at an end (a broken midshaft end or the proximal or distal ends), whereas most of the remaining shaft is unburned. Most of the burned ends (7) are proximal and distal. If complete legs were being heated (whether disarticulated at the knee or not), both the subcutaneous proximal and distal fibular ends would have been exposed; hence the burning is to be expected.

LEG PROCESSING: AN INTERPRETIVE SUMMARY

Problems in interpreting the sequence of arm processing outlined in Chapter 9 are compounded in an analysis of the leg because the leg bones are so fragmented by fracture. Disarticulation of the leg at the hip is indicated by slicing marks around the acetabulum (see Chapter 8) and by anatomically related marks on the very limited femoral sample. Disarticulation of the leg at the knee or the foot at the ankle is impossible to evaluate because the spongy bone segments at these joints are missing in the Mancos assemblage.

Burning of the fleshed leg is best indicated in the tibial shafts, with a clear patterning of burning damage to the subcutaneous anteromedial surface adjacent to the unburned, protected posterior and lateral surfaces. Subsequent to burning of this bone, percussion fracture of the ends and the shaft was accomplished on an anvil. The same treatment is indicated for the femur, but the burning evidence is more limited for this element. There is a difference in the processing of young and old leg bone shafts. This is indicated by the fact that femoral and tibial shaft segments retain an intact circumference in only a handful of adult specimens, whereas very young specimens are consistently more intact. Furthermore, the fibula shaft circumferences for all age groups tend to be complete, indicating that fibula midshafts were ignored, whereas larger diameter limb-bone shafts were broken open.

CHAPTER

11

The Hand and Foot

Serial homology of the elements of the hand and foot makes it possible to present analytical results for the maximally conjoined assemblage of these anatomical units together in the same chapter. Separate summaries of hand and foot processing are included in this presentation.

CARPALS (FIGURE 11.1)

Survival

All the surviving carpals are from individuals older than 12 years. An MNI of 2 is indicated by mismatched right and left hamates. All the carpals are intact or slightly abraded.

Fracture

There is no indication of intentional fracture.

Toolmarks

There are no toolmarks.

Burning

None of the carpals are burned.

METACARPALS (FIGURE 11.1)

Survival

Minimum numbers estimates were made by sorting the specimens with best preservation into side and ray categories. Many shafts did not enter these calculations because shafts of the young could not always be sorted by ray. One individual younger than 6 years, 4 individuals between 7 and 12 years, and 5 adult individuals comprise the MNI. Heads and bases are poorly represented compared to the shafts. Only 9 specimens retain the shaft with more than half of the head and base, whereas 26 retain only the intact shaft.

Fracture

The patterning of fracture is obvious; the proximal and distal metacarpal ends are crushed, and the shafts remain fairly intact (Figure 11.1). Evidence that crushing resulted in this patterning takes the form of rebounded shaft splinters, outer bone table compaction, and downshaft peeling. On 14 adult and 5 immature specimens, the crushing blows were dorsoventral rather than mediolateral (Figure 11.2). No

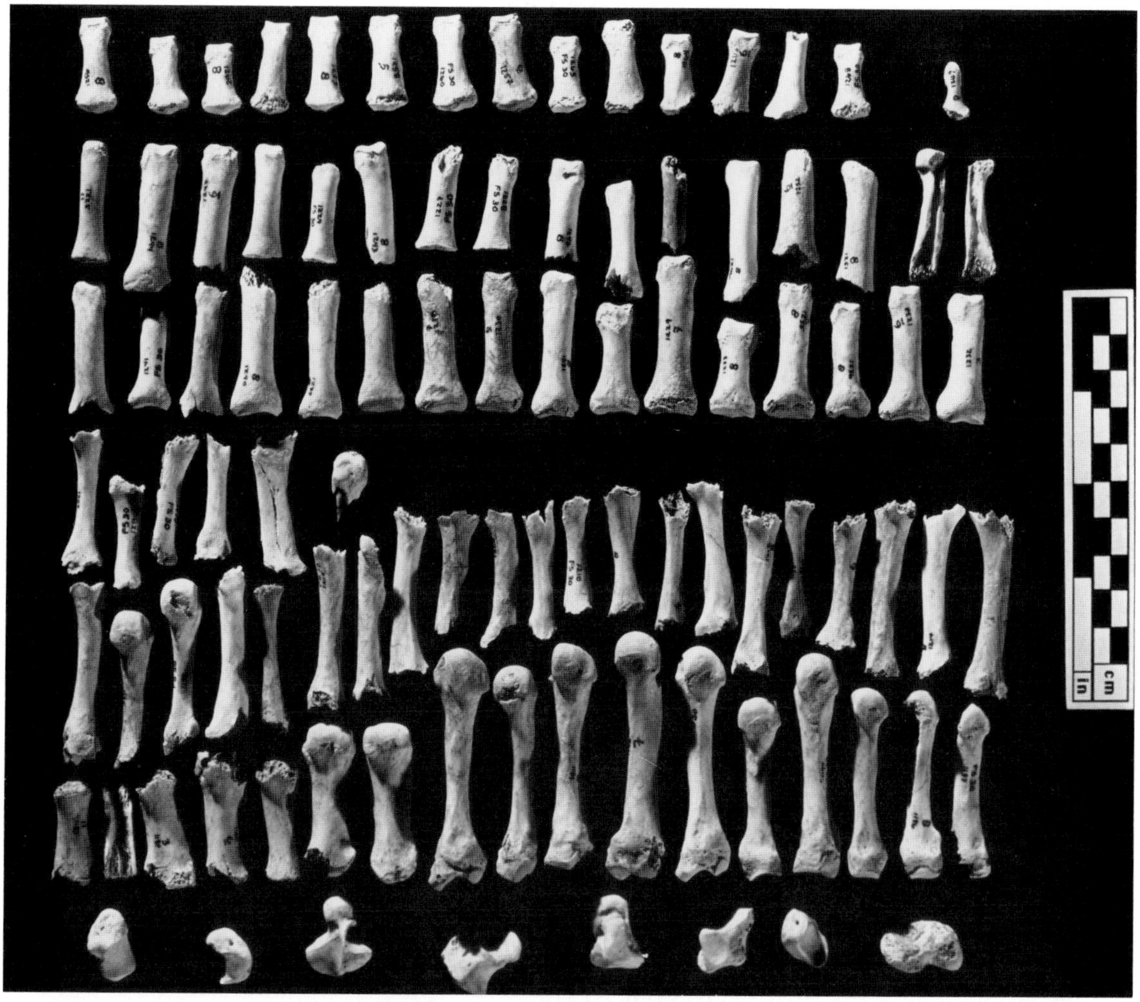

Fig. 11.1 The Mancos 5MTUMR–2346 hand subassemblage. Note the patterned damage to the metacarpal heads and phalangeal bases. Note also the relative paucity of carpal bones.

mediolateral crushing is indicated. The irregularity of damage (some pieces exhibit slight crushing, others lack the entire end) suggests a method using a hammer and anvil for crushing rather than intraoral processing, but the latter remains a possibility for some specimens, particularly in light of observations on Anasazi nonhuman faunal remains described and illustrated in the last chapter. A minor amount of the crushing could have resulted from forced disarticulation, but the bulk of the damage seems to be percussion-related. Only two metacarpals bear cutmarks, both short marks perpendicular to the shaft axis on the palmar surface.

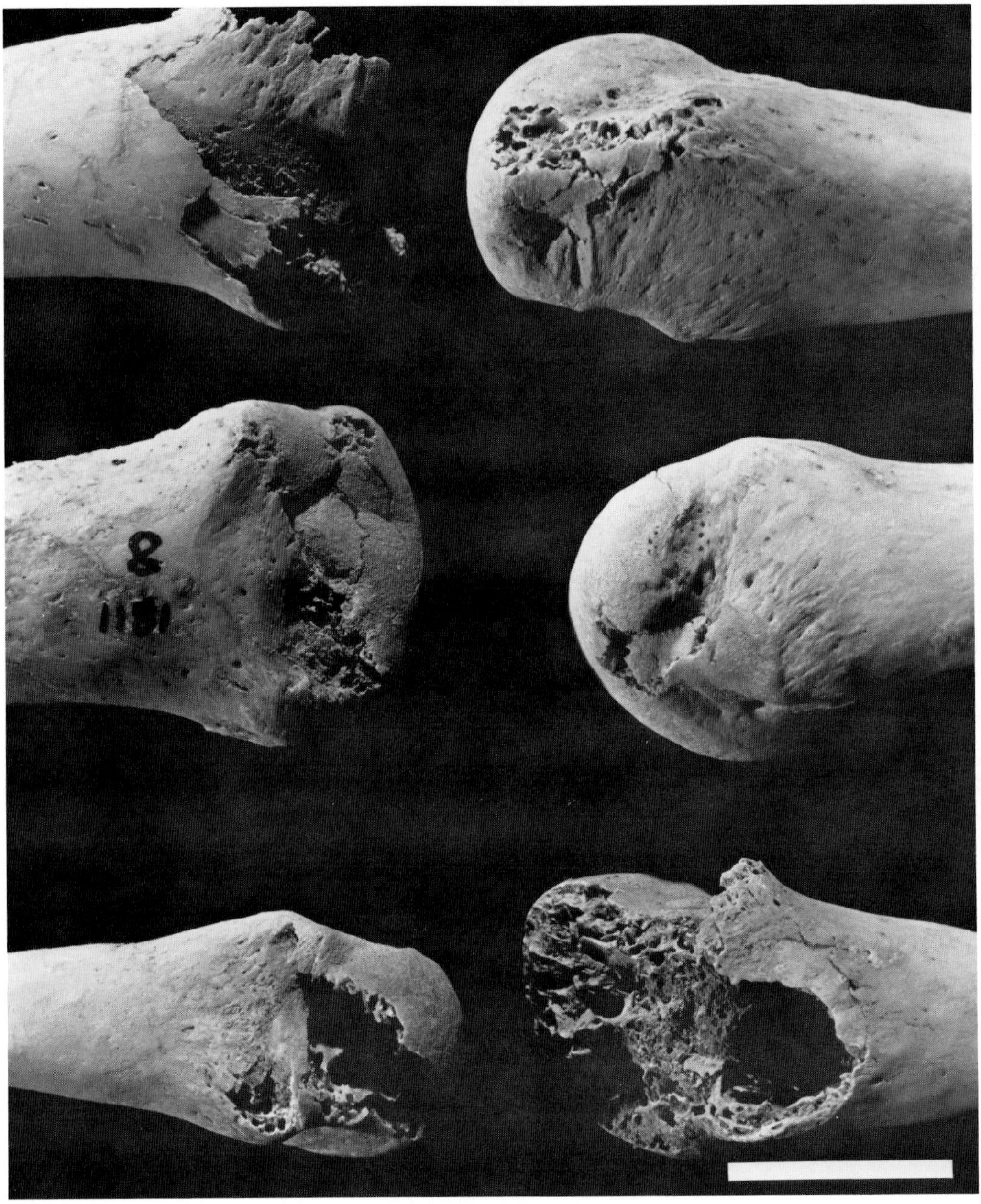

Fig. 11.2 Crushing of the metacarpal heads (1811, 1180, 1188, 1189, 1190, 1194). Bar = 1 cm.

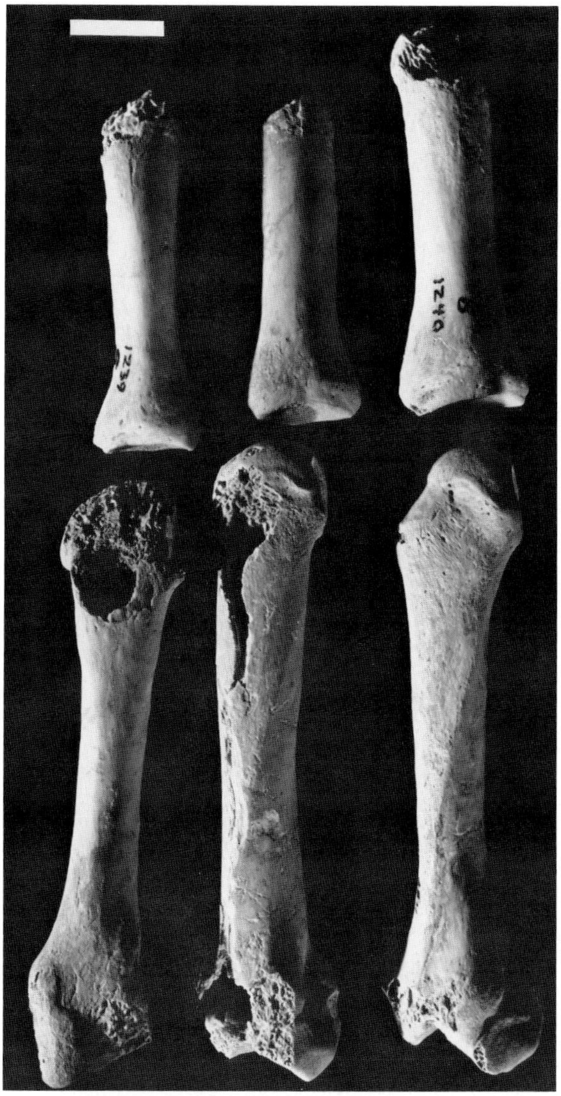

Fig. 11.3 Burning damage to the subcutaneous surfaces of metacarpals and hand phalanges (metacarpals 1186, 1187, 1189; phalanges 1229, 1250, 1239, 1240). Bar = 1 cm.

Burning

None of the 16 pieces representing individuals younger than age 10 show definite burning, but none are definitely unburned. Seven adult pieces are definitely burned, and 11 are definitely not burned. All of the 16 immature and the remaining 9 adult pieces show staining and/or weathering damage that may indicate fire. All of the adult metacarpals that are burned show dorsal burning, and all retain at least part of the base and head with the intact shaft (Figure 11.3). Burning on the dorsal surface is consistent with the thin cover of tissue here as opposed to the palmar surface.

HAND PHALANGES (FIGURE 11.1)

Survival

The MNI estimate for the assemblage of hand phalanges is 4—2 immature and 2 adult. This is a true minimum, estimated by a total count of proximal phalanges. There are 32 proximal phalanges, 13 intermediate phalanges, and only 1 distal phalanx. These numbers may reflect some bias against the smaller distal phalanges in recovery, but the large disparity between expected and observed proximal and intermediate phalanges is also explainable as indicating differential perimortem destruction of the intermediate phalanges, primarily by burning.

Twenty hand phalanges preserve more than half the base, more than half the head, and the entire shaft. Fourteen specimens lack only the base, whereas only 3 preserve only the base plus the shaft, and 6 are isolated shafts. Thus, a high proportion of the Mancos hand phalanges show basal damage but intact heads. The 3 pieces with base and shaft, but without the head, all show burning of the head region.

The overall survival pattern is similar to the metacarpals, with intact shafts preserved but bases and heads missing or damaged. Unlike the metacarpal situation, however, the phalangeal heads are not as heavily damaged as the bases. Loss of the phalangeal heads seems to be due primarily to burning rather than crushing (see below). To summarize, the loss of the phalangeal elements (proximal, intermediate, distal) increases distally. Within each phalangeal element category, the best survival is the distal segment (see Figure 11.1).

Fracture

Two shaft specimens without bases show circular, depressed fractures of 2 to 3 mm diameter on the dorsal surface just proximal to the phalangeal head. These may be related to intraoral or hammer-and-anvil preparation (Figure 11.4). Of the intact specimens, 3 show similarly directed percussion in the form of crushing on the dorsal surface of the base, and 3 of the shaft-plus-head pieces show similar evidence. Only two phalangeal shafts are split longitudinally.

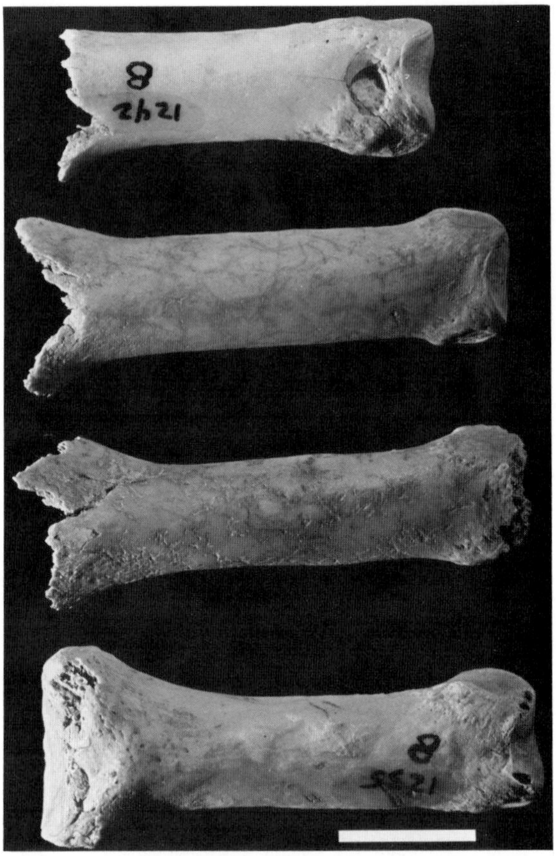

Fig. 11.4 Percussion damage to bases of the hand phalanges (1235, 1245, 1248, 1242). The puncture to specimen 1242 is discussed in Chapter 12 as possibly being due to human chewing. Bar = 1 cm.

Toolmarks

No hand phalanges show toolmarks.

Burning

The lone distal phalanx is unburned. There are 10 unburned, 16 ambiguous, and 19 definitely burned proximal and intermediate phalanges. Of the latter, only 5 are intermediates; 4 of these are burned distally, and one dorsally and distally (Figure 11.3). All of the remaining pieces have unburned bases and burned distal ends, with burning extending to the midshaft level on the dorsal shaft surface of 6 specimens. Where burning is unilateral, it is always on the dorsal surface. The burning is thus strongly patterned. The most intensively burned point is located, without exception, on the dorsal distal surface of each of the 19 definitely burned phalanges.

HAND PROCESSING: AN INTERPRETIVE SUMMARY

Slicing marks related to disarticulation and defleshing are notably absent in the hand elements. Burning is common, most marked on the subcutaneous dorsal distal surfaces of the metacarpals and phalanges. Evidence in the form of differential preservation or recovery (relative loss of carpals, metacarpal heads and bases, phalangeal bases) and direct observation indicates that the spongy bone covered with thin cortex was the target of hammer and anvil crushing.

CALCANEUS AND TALUS (FIGURE 11.5)

Survival

A minimum of 6 adults is represented by calcanei. Two specimens are fairly intact, but with major areas of damage. The other 4 left and 4 right specimens all retain edges or portions of their subtalar facets, but these lack the entire calcaneal tuberosity and all or part of the cuboid articular facet. The parts with highest survival are those centered on the groove between the talar facets.

The talus represents a minimum of 4 individuals, 3 adults and 1 immature. The adult specimens are all fairly intact, but the child lacks most of the head and the medial side.

Fracture

Six of the 10 calcaneal pieces show evidence of crushing fracture at the broken edges, and 2 show associated peeling damage. The best preserved, nearly intact specimen (1274) shows a massive compression fracture on the plantar surface on the edge of the anterior articular facet. The other intact specimen (1275) shows a similarly placed but smaller fracture that represents the same percussion action.

The medial side of the talar head is missing in all 4 specimens. In 2 adults (1282, 1283) it is simply sheared off, and in the third (1281) it is crushed in, with anvil marks perpendicular to the crushing. Edge crushing of the talus is seen in the other adults and in the immature specimen. The sample is small, but the pattern is clear.

Toolmarks

None are present on the calcaneus. The immature talar specimen (1280) has 2 hackmarks posteriorly, on the distal tibial and medial fibular articular surfaces.

Burning

Four calcaneal pieces are unburned, 5 show evidence consistent with burning, and 1 is definitely burned on the posterior, broken edge of the medial side of the tibial tuberosity. There is no burning on the talus.

OTHER TARSALS (FIGURE 11.5)

Survival

Only individuals older than 12 years are represented, a minimum number of 3. Only 3 cuneiforms and 1 navicular are more than half complete.

Fracture

Of the 9 available specimens, 3 cuneiforms and 2 naviculars show obvious evidence of compression. The presence of this crushing on the articular surfaces indicates that the bones were smashed individually after disarticulation. Breakage of the other pieces is also consistent with such fracture; 2 of the 3 intact cuneiforms are the specimens showing the compression fracture, indicating that even the more intact specimens were percussed.

Fig. 11.5 The Mancos 5MTUMR–2346 foot subassemblage. Note how the pattern of destruction of metacarpal heads and bases and phalangeal bases parallels that seen in the hand.

Toolmarks

No toolmarks are evident.

Burning

There is no evidence of burning.

METATARSALS (FIGURE 11.5)

Survival

A minimum numbers analysis performed as described for the hand indicates 2 individuals younger than 6 years, 3 individuals between 7 and 12 years, and 3 older individuals for a total MNI of 8. There are only 2 fairly intact metatarsals, and there were no isolated heads or bases. Only 7 specimens preserve more than half the head or the base along with the metatarsal shaft. In contrast, 43 specimens are shafts lacking either the head or the base (Figure 11.5).

Fracture

On the proximal end, 15 of the immature specimens show obvious crushing damage and this damage is mediolaterally oriented in every case. In the adults, 11 specimens show similar fracture and, in addition, 4 show peeling. The less obvious evidence of mashing the bone ends in adults stems from their greater rigidity—they are less prone to shatter into solid pieces. The immature metatarsals are softer, thinner-walled, more resilient, and therefore capable of better splinter "rebound" after crushing. Midshafts were much less susceptible to damage. The mediolaterally directed crushing damage to the proximal and distal metatarsals indicates disarticulation prior to breakage (Figure 11.6).

Toolmarks

Only one specimen (1300) displays an abrasion patch on its dorsal midshaft, and none of the metatarsals bear cutmarks.

Burning

There are 9 unburned, 5 definitely burned, and many ambiguous metatarsals. One 5th metatarsal has the distal and lateral shaft ends burned, one shows basal burning, and the others show burned midshafts on dorsal, medial, and lateral sides. This burning is much more poorly patterned than on the hand, and the overall impression is one of much less burning on the metatarsals than on the metacarpals.

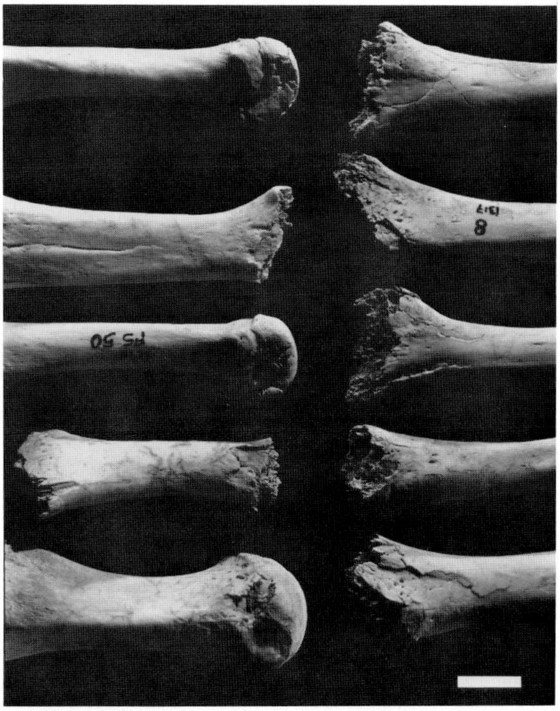

Fig. 11.6 Crushing of the metatarsal heads and bases shows postdisarticulation hammering of these elements (bases 1334, 1317, 1331, 1310, 1309; heads 1304, 1313, 1298, 1308, 1293). Bar = 1 cm.

FOOT PHALANGES (FIGURE 11.5)

Survival

Calculated as for the hand, the minimum number of individuals based on foot phalanges is 7, with 4 adults. Survival of these elements is very similar to the hands. There are 2 distal (both ray 1), no intermediate, and 42 proximal foot phalanges. The phalangeal bases are the foci of damage, and of the 2 specimens retaining the base but lacking the head, one shows basal crushing and the other shows distal burning. It is evident that hand and foot phalanges were treated, and are represented, in the same manner.

Fracture

Only 2 foot phalanges have shafts that are split longitudinally. Both proximal and distal ends in the assemblage show evidence of crushing fracture. Six of the adult phalangeal heads show evidence of dorsoventral crushing, whereas crushing

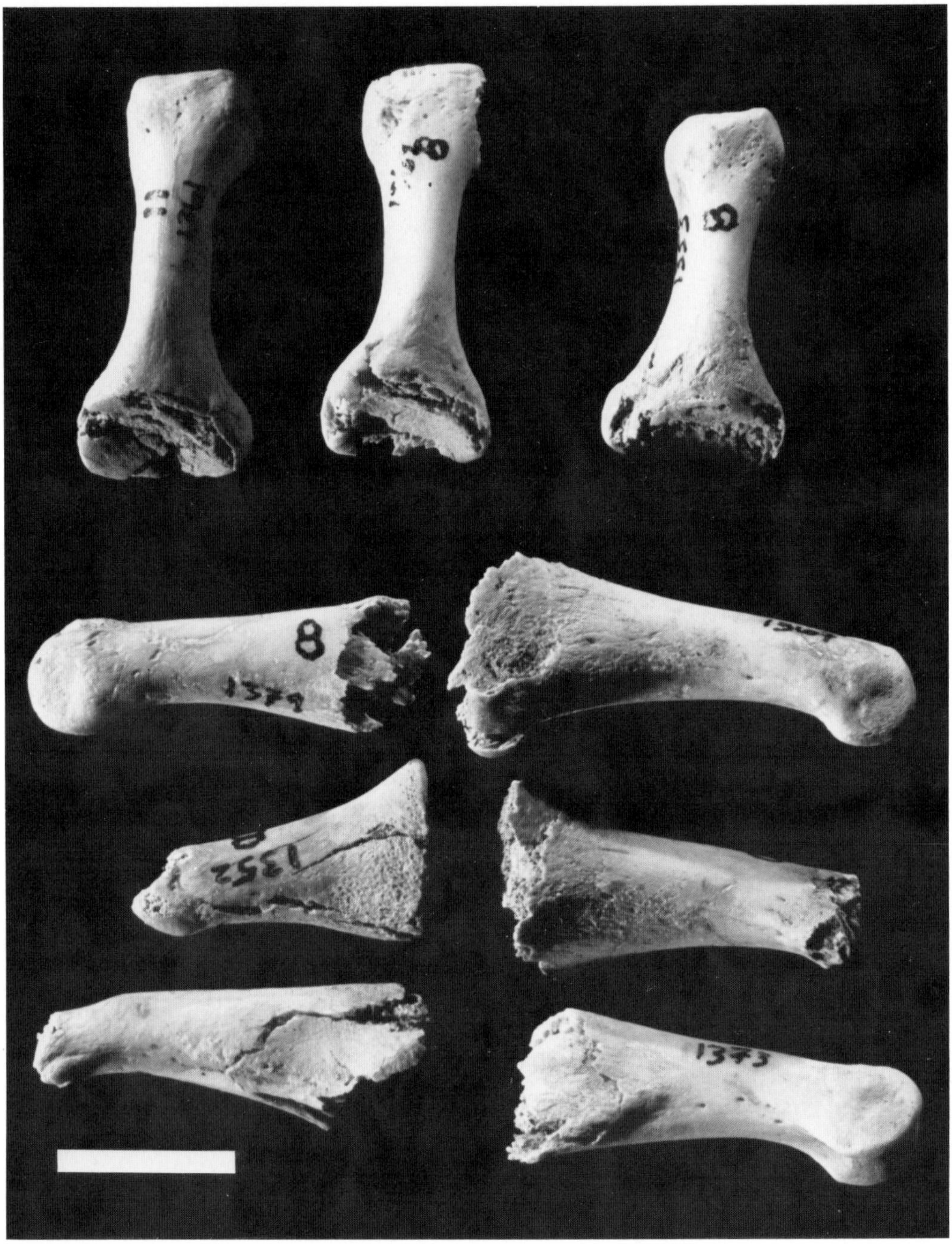

Fig. 11.7 Crushing of the foot phalanges (1361, 1369, 1353, 1352, 1379, 1359, 1374, 1373). Bar = 1 cm.

at the base was primarily mediolateral (Figure 11.7).

Toolmarks

There are no toolmarks on the foot phalanges.

Burning

Foot phalangeal burning follows the pattern established for the metatarsals versus metacarpals. Eighteen foot phalanges are unburned and only 1 is definitely burned, the head heavily damaged. The others are ambiguous. The foot was obviously subjected to less thermal damage than the hand.

FOOT PROCESSING: AN INTERPRETIVE SUMMARY

Like elements of the hand, the tarsals, metatarsals, and foot phalanges show virtually no evidence of toolmarks associated with disarticulation or defleshing. That disarticulation did occur, however, is certain. This is proven by the crushing damage to the foot's articular surfaces. Crushing in the foot, like that documented for the hand, focuses on the tarsals, the metatarsal heads and bases, and the phalangeal bases, all regions with a thin cortex and spongy bone below. Shafts of both the hand and foot bones, although considerably thinner-walled and easier to break than the humeral or femoral shafts, were left unbroken in almost all cases. Burning of the foot is less patterned than is the case for the hand.

To summarize, hand and foot elements were processed in a very similar manner. The processing documented for these elements is, in turn, very similar in several respects to that evidenced in other postcranial elements. Before turning to a summary of the processing evidence for the entire body and an interpretation of this evidence in light of the contextual data, it is necessary to provide a more explicitly quantitative analysis of the Mancos assemblage so that it might be compared to patterns of bone modification documented for other bone assemblages. This is done in Chapter 12.

CHAPTER

12

Comparative Analysis

The attributes recorded during the assessment of the Mancos 5MTUMR–2346 human bone assemblage were defined and described in Chapter 6. These attributes were employed in Chapters 7 to 11 in a segment-by-segment, functionally oriented analysis of the maximally conjoined Mancos skeletal assemblage. That study was made from the perspective of a human anatomist/physical anthropologist. It documented considerable evidence for human-induced modification of the Mancos assemblage, including burning of body segments, disarticulation, crushing of the spongy bone, and entry, via percussion, to the limb bones and endocranial cavity. Relationships between bone modification and the once-present soft tissues were demonstrated for many body segments, and the probable sequence of modification events was sometimes elucidated. The major types of bone modification characteristic of the Mancos assemblage are illustrated by the femoral specimen in Figure 12.1.

Because the analysis in Chapters 7 through 11 was done on an element-by-element basis, nonrefitted Mancos specimens that remained in the indeterminate cranial (ICR) and indeterminate postcranial (IP1–IP4) categories after maximal conjoining were not included or illustrated. These abundant, less identifiable specimens (illustrated in Figures 12.2–12.6) manifest the same kinds of modification.

Zooarchaeologists, who usually study taxonomically mixed assemblages, have not often pursued the level of functional, anatomical detail described in Chapters 7 through 11. Furthermore, they have not worked on maximally conjoined assemblages. Rather, data in standard archaeological faunal analyses have often been limited to specimen and individual counts and, sometimes, to percentages of modified specimens. The current chapter is an attempt to examine the unconjoined Mancos 5MTUMR–2346 assemblage from the perspective of an archaeological faunal analyst. The chapter is divided into five sections: "Identity and Survival," "Fracture," "Tool Modification," "Mammalian Chewing," and "Burning." Here, the data presented in Appendix 2 are used to explore the possibility that they can further elucidate the history of the Mancos assemblage. The chapter proceeds according to the attribute order used in Chapter 6 (Table 6.1) and Appendix 2. Its over-riding concern is with examining patterns of representation and modification of the human bones from Mancos 5MTUMR–2346 and comparing them to

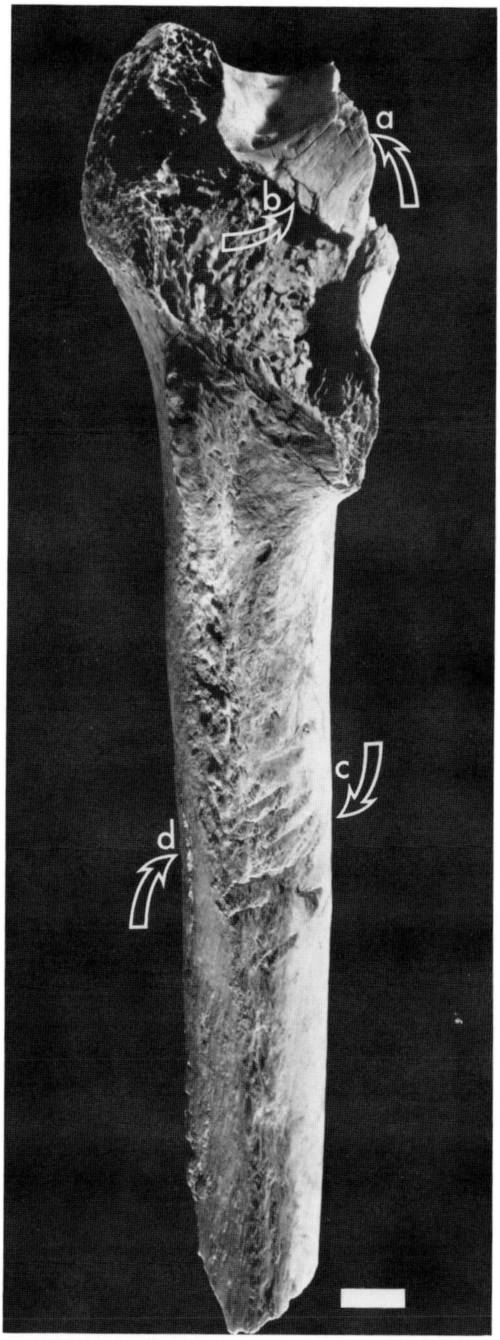

Fig. 12.1 This femoral specimen (870) illustrates the many kinds of damage observed on bones in the Mancos assemblage. Included are cutmarks on the femoral neck (a), crushing (b), chopmarks (c), and burning (d). Bar = 1 cm.

patterns documented for other human and zooarchaeological assemblages from the American Southwest.

THE COMPARATIVE BACKGROUND

Comparisons with published data from other archaeological bone assemblages are presented throughout this chapter. Table 12.1, supplemented by Appendix 1, describes attributes of the most significant assemblages used in the comparative analysis. These assemblages suffer from differential reporting of data. The sample is not meant to be inclusive, but, rather, representative of some of the best reported zooarchaeological and actualistic assemblages. These assemblages cross a wide range of types, including carnivore accumulations, forensic and cemetery collections, and archaeological assemblages spanning the globe from the Plio-Pleistocene to modern. Unfortunately, there are relatively few archaeological faunal assemblages as completely dominated by a single taxon as is the Mancos assemblage. Exceptions, of course, are butchering sites with the remains of large ungulates.

The last decade has seen rapid progress in the quantification and reporting of detailed zooarchaeological data, with many analysts embracing increasingly complete recovery and more sophisticated analytical techniques. Ironically, many of these practical and theoretical zooarchaeological advances have been made in Paleolithic contexts where the interpretation of faunal remains is basic to an understanding of human origins, but where the material culture of the hominids involved was comparatively undeveloped.

In contrast, Anasazi occurrences in the American Southwest represent an impres-

Fig. 12.2 The Mancos 5MTUMR–2346 indeterminate cranial fragment subassemblage.

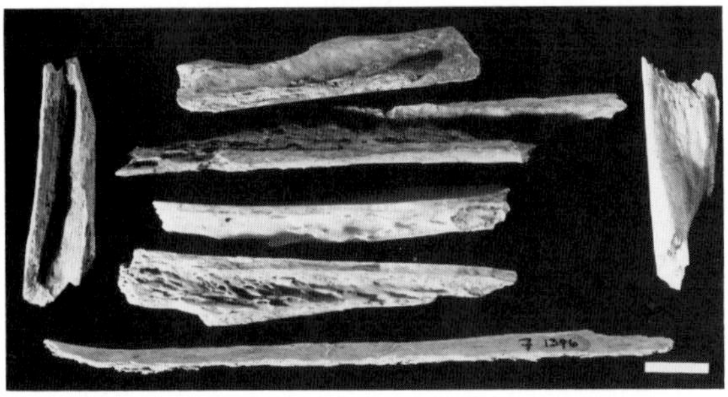

Fig. 12.3 The Mancos 5MTUMR–2346 IP1 (radius, or ulna, or fibula) subassemblage. Bar = 1 cm.

Opposite page top:

Fig. 12.4 The Mancos 5MTUMR–2346 IP2 (humerus, or tibia, or femur) subassemblage.

Opposite page bottom:

Fig. 12.5 The Mancos 5MTUMR–2346 IP3 (femur or tibia) subassemblage.

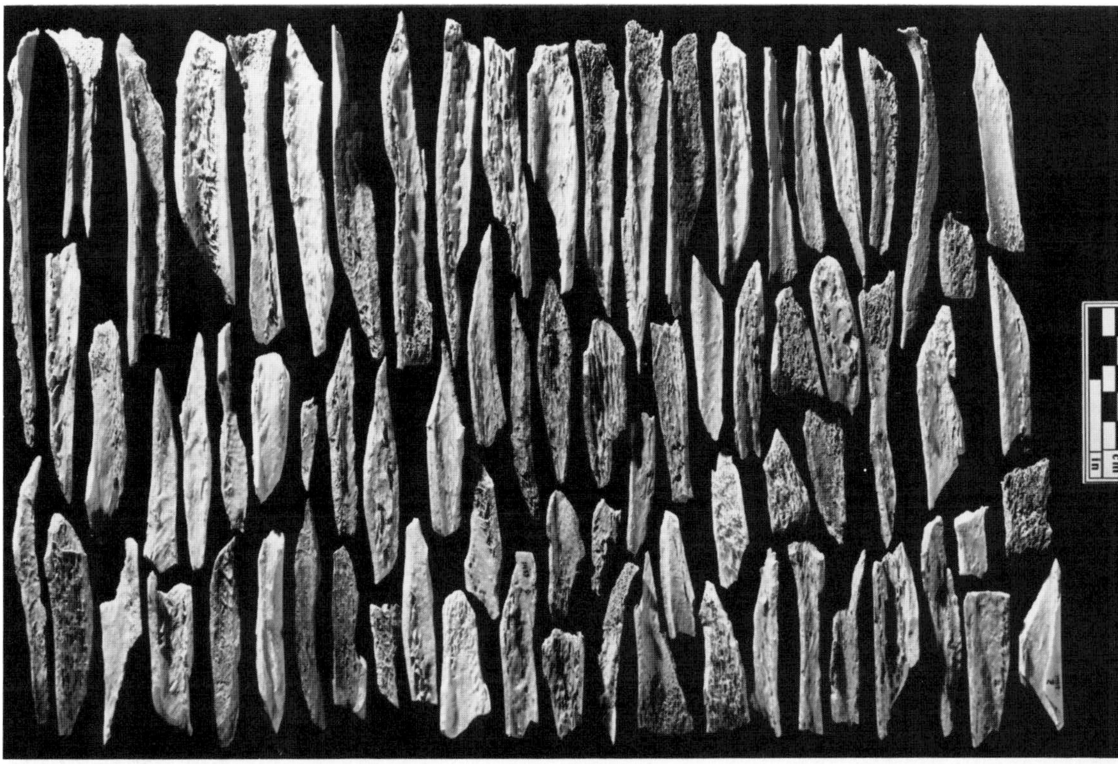

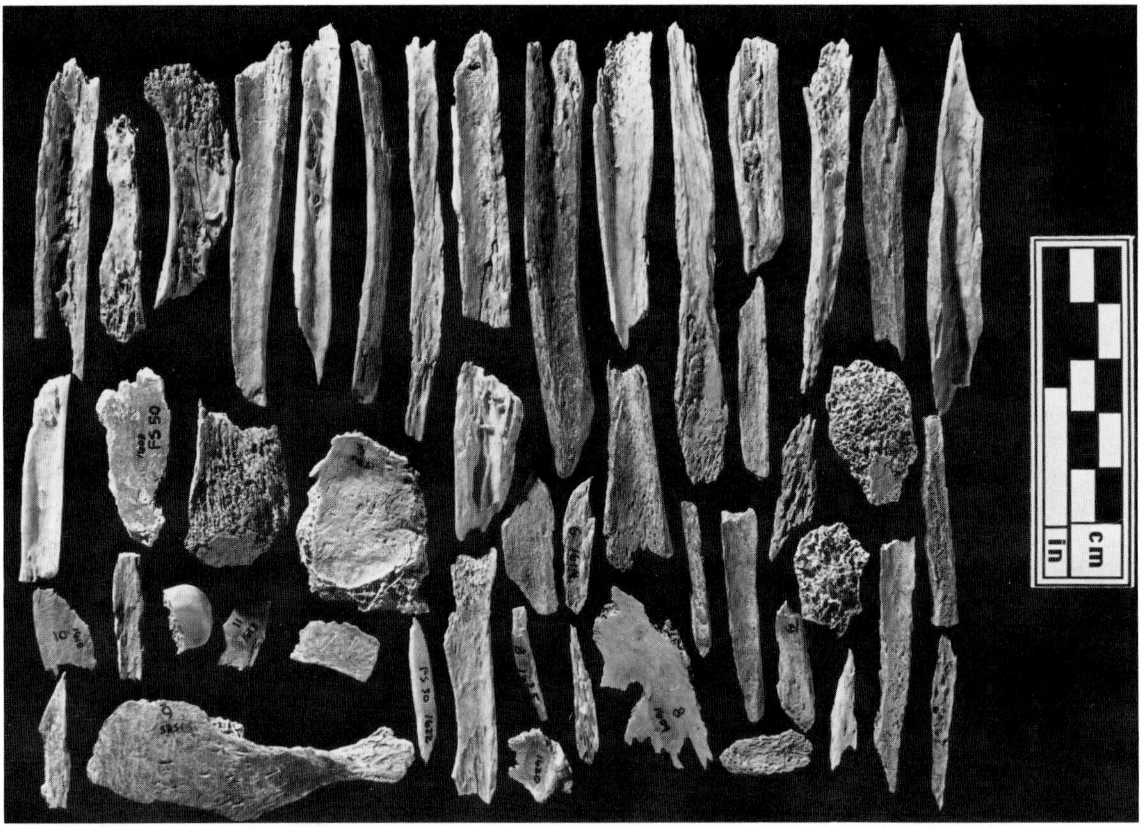

Fig. 12.6 The Mancos 5MTUMR–2346 IP4 (completely indeterminate) subassemblage.

sive material culture set in a physiographic, climatologic, and biotic context that remains relatively unchanged from what it was at the time of deposition. Collectively, these abundant sites have a comparatively limited time depth that is usually tightly controlled via ceramic seriation, C-14, and dendrochronology. The faunal component of some Southwestern sites has been biased during collection, with screening used intermittently, with bone tools garnering the most attention (Morris, 1939), and with many "unidentifiable" bones discarded in the field (Stein, 1963). Zooarchaeology in the Southwest has traditionally centered on taxonomic diagnosis, with few data compiled on MNI, NISP, element representation, or frequency of modification. The closest approximation to a detailed butchery analysis of a large nonhuman sample is Lang and Harris (1984), but Emslie's (1977) work on Mancos Canyon Anasazi faunal assemblages is also directly applicable to the current analysis.

Seen as a whole, the faunal analytical literature on the American Southwest is meagre in comparison to work on other archaeological dimensions of this region (see Lyman, 1979b for an example of how

Table 12.1 Faunal and Human Assemblages Used in the Comparative Analysis

I. Human Bones

A. "Cannibalized"

1. Southwest nonburial

Assemblage	*Geography*	*Age*	*Culture*	*Citation*
Yellow Jacket 5MT–3	Colorado	A.D. 1025–50	Anasazi	Malville (1989)
· Broken, scattered remains of 10 individuals (MNI) on a kiva floor, interpreted as representing food remains. NISP (zooarchaeologist): 389, TW NISP: 969.				
Burnt Mesa	New Mexico	A.D. 950	Anasazi	Flinn *et al.* (1976)
· Broken, scattered remains of 11 individuals (MNI) on a pithouse floor, interpreted as evidence of cannibalism. NISP: 1,114.				
Monument Valley	Arizona	Unknown	cf. Anasazi	Nass and Bellantoni (1982)
· Broken, mixed remains of 7 individuals (MNI) in a slab-lined pit interpreted as possible evidence of cannibalism. NISP: 436.				
Polacca Wash	Arizona	A.D. 1580	cf. Hopi	Turner and Morris (1970)
· Broken, mixed remains of 30 individuals (MNI), with no architectural association, interpreted as evidence of cannibalism. NISP: not recorded.				
Grinnell	Colorado	A.D. 1140	Anasazi	Luebben and Nickens (1982)
· Broken, mixed remains of 7 individuals (MNI) from a cist and recess in a kiva.				
Cottonwood Canyon	Utah	A.D. 900	Anasazi	Fettermann *et al.* (1988)
· Broken, mixed remains of 4 individuals (MNI) in shallow pit below floor surface of room. NISP: 61.				

2. European nonburial

Assemblage	*Geography*	*Age*	*Culture*	*Citation*
Fontbrégoua	France	4000–5000 B.C.	Early Neolithic	Villa *et al.* (1986a, 1986b)
· Clusters of human bone, deposited in pits in a temporary residential camp. The H1 sample of 7 individuals (MNI) is used in the comparative analysis here. Carnivore damage was observed on 1.5 percent of nontooth elements. Interpreted as evidence of cannibalism. Unfortunately, despite duplicate publication in French and American sources (Villa *et al.*, 1986a, 1986b), no preconjoining data were published on element representation. The author's request for these data was denied. NISP: In the H3 subassemblage, a single pit, the number of postconjoined specimens is 134.				

B. Archaeological cemetery

Assemblage	*Geography*	*Age*	*Culture*	*Citation*
CCO–138	N. California	A.D. 500–1500	Late Horizon	This study
· A typical archaeological cemetery skeletal population of 50 adults with disturbance by rodents. NISP: 3,044.				
Rom.-Br. Cemetery	London, England	A.D. 200–400	Roman	Waldron (1989)
· A typical archaeological cemetery population of 88 adults with poor to moderate preservation of elements. NISP: 6,209.				
Crow Creek	South Dakota	A.D. 1350	cf. Arikara	Gregg *et al.* (1981)
· A mass burial of nearly 500 individuals in a fortification ditch. Disarticulation was extensive, with evidence of carnivore modification. NISP: 13,024.				

Table 12.1 *(continued)*

C. Forensic

Assemblage	*Geography*	*Age*	*Culture*	*Citation*
Forensic/Carnivore	Seattle, Wash.	A.D. 1979–80	American	Haglund *et al.* (1988)

· Partially to fully skeletonized remains of 37 humans from outdoor locations. Carnivores (coyote and dog) had scavenged these individuals with 65 percent of the skeletons showing evidence of animal chewing. NISP: 1,527.

II. Nonhuman Bones

A. Nonarchaeological

1. Ancient carnivore/porcupine

Assemblage	*Geography*	*Age*	*Culture*	*Citation*
Makapansgat	South Africa	2.8 myr	None	Dart (1957b); Brain (1981a)

· The subassemblage analyzed comprises antelope remains from a deposit once linked to hominid behavior but now considered to be the result of carnivore and porcupine activity. NISP: 2,539.

Assemblage	*Geography*	*Age*	*Culture*	*Citation*
Swartkrans Mbr. I	South Africa	1.65 myr	None	Brain (1981a)

· The subassemblage analyzed comprises remains of 33 bovid individuals in size class III; without duplicate counting of the medium-size alcelaphines or indeterminate size III specimens. Archaeological evidence is present in the depository but it is thought that the assemblage results from carnivore activity. NISP: 356.

2. Modern carnivore/porcupine

Assemblage	*Geography*	*Age*	*Culture*	*Citation*
Syokimau Hyaena	Kenya	Recent	None	Bunn (1982)

· The subassemblage analyzed comprises the combined remains of *Giraffa, Taurotragus, Bos*, and bovid size classes III and IV. NISP: 184.

Assemblage	*Geography*	*Age*	*Culture*	*Citation*
Nossob Porcupine	South Africa	Recent	None	Brain (1981a)

· The subassemblage analyzed comprises the entire bovid sample, a minimum of 81 antelope individuals, from the lair. NISP: 815.

B. Ethnoarchaeological

Assemblage	*Geography*	*Age*	*Culture*	*Citation*
Navajo Summer	Arizona	1970	Navajo	Binford and Bertram (1977)

· The subassemblage analyzed comprises the remains of 11 sheep individuals who were butchered and whose remains were subjected to destruction by dogs over a six-month period. NISP: not reported.

Assemblage	*Geography*	*Age*	*Culture*	*Citation*
Kuiseb R. Hottentot	Namibia	1966	Hottentot	Brain (1981a)

· The assemblage analyzed comprises the remains of 64 goats (MNI) butchered, eaten, and discarded by the Hottentots. The bones were ravaged by dogs after discard. NISP: 1,155.

Assemblage	*Geography*	*Age*	*Culture*	*Citation*
Kwhee San	Botswana	1978	San	Bunn (1982)

· The subassemblage analyzed comprises the remains of *Giraffa, Taurotragus*, and bovid size class III individuals. The remains are from a temporary camp inhabited by 35 people. All were fresh when collected, and sample a five-day period of accumulation. Some specimens were refitted, and many were chopped into pieces by the San. No postdiscard taphonomic modification is noted. NISP: 413.

Table 12.1 *(continued)*

C. Archaeological mixed faunas[a]

1. Nonagriculturalists

Assemblage	*Geography*	*Age*	*Culture*	*Citation*
Dead Ind. Cr. Sheep	Wyoming	2000 B.C.	Mid. Plains Archaic	Fisher (1984)
· The vast majority of remains were from mule deer, but the sheep sample is also analyzed here. Remains were well preserved, with much evidence of processing on the minimum of 16 mountain sheep (MNI) analyzed. NISP: 304.				
Dead Indian Cr. Deer	See above			
· A minimum of c. 50 animals is represented in this subassemblage. NISP: 799.				
Chencherere	Malawi	400 B.C.–A.D. 1000	Late Stone Age	Crader (1984)
· The subassemblage analyzed comprised all of the bovid size class III remains (MNI = 22) from the combined strata of this rockshelter site. Evidence of hominid butchery is extensive. NISP: 567.				
Wilton	South Africa	2800 B.C.	Late Stone Age	Brain (1981a)
· The bovid remains from all LSA levels of this rock shelter were used in the analysis. Fragmentation is noted by Brain (1981a) as "extreme," attributed to cultural modification. NISP: 1,059.				
Last Supper Cave	Nevada	?B.C.	See below	Grayson (1988)
· The subassemblage analyzed comprised all of the bighorn sheep remains recovered from this cave site. The bulk of the remains derive from wood rat middens. A total of 2,194 specimens of *Ovis* were recovered, many bearing processing marks inflicted by people and marks made by rodents and carnivores. NISP: 1,311.				
Byeneskranskop	South Africa	3–10,500 B.C.	Late Stone Age	Klein (1980)
· The large-medium bovid subassemblage was used in the analysis. The assemblage is from a cave site whose strata sample about 10,000 years. NISP: unreported.				
Cueva del Juyo	Spain		Magdalenian	Klein and Cruz-Uribe (1987)
· The subassemblage analyzed comprises all of the remains of a minimum of 38 red deer individuals (MNI) from Level 6 of this cave. NISP: 1,268.				
Border Cave	South Africa	37–100,000 B.C.	Early LSA and MSA	Klein (1977)
· The subassemblage analyzed comprises all of the large-medium bovids from the combined Early LSA and MSA levels of this cave site. NISP: unreported.				
Klasies River Mouth	South Africa	35–135,000 B.C.	MSA	Klein (1976)
· The subassemblage analyzed comprises all the medium-large bovids (class III) from the MSA levels at this site. NISP: unreported.				
Ambrona	Spain	c. 0.5 myr	Acheulean	Klein (1987)
· The subassemblage analyzed comprises all of the red deer individuals (MNI = 9) from the Ambrona "Lower" "occupation." The assemblage shows nearly 20 percent rounding, indicating abrasion. Abrasion and corrosion have removed much superficial evidence, and how the assemblage relates to hominid activity is a matter of ongoing debate. NISP: unreported.				
Olorgesailie	Kenya	c. 0.7 myr	Acheulean	Koch (1986)
· The subassemblage analyzed is the giant baboon sample from DE/89. The assemblage has been attributed to hominid activity, but this seems doubtful after Koch's analysis. NISP: 1,826.				
Olduvai FLK 22	Tanzania	c. 1.8 myr	Oldowan	Bunn and Kroll (1986)
· The subassemblage analyzed is the large mammal sample (250+ lbs) from the FLK-22 "*Zinjanthropus*" floor. This assemblage is the subject of ongoing debate, and both hominid and carnivore activity are indicated for the bones. NISP: 1,288.				

Table 12.1 *(continued)*

2. Agriculturalists

Assemblage	*Geography*	*Age*	*Culture*	*Citation*
Antelope House	Arizona	A.D. 1200	Anasazi	Morris (1986)
· The subsample analyzed comprises mule deer from Late Pueblo III occupation. A minimum of 14 animals (MNI) was recovered. NISP: 503.				
Badger House	Colorado	A.D. 9–1100	Anasazi	Hayes and Lancaster (1975)
· The subsample analyzed comprises the pooled, primarily mule deer and bighorn sheep from the midden deposit of a pueblo inhabited primarily through Pueblo II times. NISP: 618.				
Emslie Mancos Canyon	Colorado	A.D. 800–1150	Anasazi	Emslie (1977)
· The subsample analyzed comprises the artiodactyl remains from four sites, 5MTUMR–2785–2346–2559, and–2347. NISP: 410.				
Converse 14:26	Arizona	A.D. 7–1100	Anasazi	Converse (pers. communication)
· The subsample analyzed comprises *Antilocapra americana* and other artiodactyls from a multicomponent Pueblo I and II site. NISP: 312.				
Guadalupe Ruin	New Mexico	A.D. 950–1350	Chaco/San Juan,M/V	Pippin (1987)
· The subsample analyzed comprises remains of deer, pronghorn, and bighorn pooled from both the Chacoan and San Juan/Mesa Verde components of the occupation. A minimum of 72 animals (MNI) is present. NISP: 1,312.				
Phillips	New Mexico	A.D. 1150	Corona Phase	Driver (1985)
· The subsample analyzed comprises medium antelope (deer and antelope) remains from one room of a 49-house unit settlement. Only 1.2 percent of the bones show carnivore modification. NISP: 1,676.				
Vista Shelter	Missouri	A.D. 1000	Mississippian	Wood (1968)
· The subsample analyzed comprises all of the deer bone from a shelter interpreted as a hunting station. Marrow processing is evident. NISP: unreported.				
Mapungubwe	South Africa	A.D. 970	Iron Age	Voigt (1983)
· The subassemblage analyzed comprises all of the bovid remains, a minimum of 199 animals, from K2/TS1/Level 2. The assemblage is from an Iron Age community and shows clear evidence of extensive butchery. NISP: 749.				
Ngamuriak	Kenya	B.C./A.D.	Elmenteitan	Marshall (1986a)
· The subassemblage analyzed comprises a minimum number of 68 caprine individuals (bovid size class II). The remains are from a 20–30-cm layer of sandy silts excavated in a village site interpreted as comprising homesteads made up of huts, middens, and stockholding areas. Preservation is sometimes poor, with bone broken up by plant action. NISP: 4,036.				
Prolonged Drift	Kenya	200 B.C.	Pastoral Neolithic	Gifford *et al.* (1980)
· The subassemblage analyzed comprises all of the large bovid remains (larger than Grant's gazelle and smaller than Cape buffalo) recovered from this open-air site. Bones had suffered much disintegration from clay soil cracking. NISP: 2,283.				
Alvastra	Sweden	3000 B.C.	Neolithic	During (1986)
· The subassemblage analyzed comprises all of the remains of elk/red deer and big ruminants (including *Bos tarus*) from the site, a pile dwelling situated in a spring mire. Carnivore gnawing, presumably dog, is evident on the bones. NISP: 917.				

Table 12.1 *(continued)*

D. Archaeological single-taxon faunas

Assemblage	*Geography*	*Age*	*Culture*	*Citation*
Eden-Farson	Wyoming	A.D. 1720	Shoshone	Frison (1971)
· The subsample analyzed comprises the remains of 84 antelope (MNI) from two lodges (6 and 9). The animals are interpreted as having been taken during a few weeks in the fall, as part of a communal trapping operation. It is a single-occurrence manifestation, the site only used one time. The processing is interpreted to have included fracture and crushing preparatory to boiling. NISP: 1,233.				
Lyman 17483	New Mexico	A.D. 1700–1775	Navajo	Lyman (1987a); Simmons (1983)
· This extensively used hunting camp yielded a collection of pronghorn remains, virtually all broken, with no geological fracture and less than 1 percent carnivore gnawing. NISP: 450.				
Garnsey	New Mexico	A.D. 1475	Late Prehistoric Plains	Speth (1983)
· The sample is from a site that was the locus of bison procurement activities in which at least 35 animals (MNI) were butchered and processed for transport to off-site villages. An unusually high proportion of males suggests preferential killing of bulls, but some male elements are under-represented at the site. Clear and consistent patterning related to processing decisions conditioned by utility. Destruction of elements by carnivores and rodents is not indicated. NISP: 2,075				
Gatecliff, Horizon 2	Nevada	A.D. 1300	cf. West. Shoshone	Thomas and Mayer (1983)
· A dense and patterned concentration, a "bone bed" of butchered bighorn sheep remains in a rockshelter. This assemblage is interpreted to represent a kill-butchering station, "a single behavioral and depositional event," in which a minimum of 24 sheep individuals were butchered. Butchery activity was restricted to primary dismemberment; the lack of secondary butchering marks and marrow-processing impact scars supports this. Roof collapse resulted in over half of the fragmentation in the assemblage. The assemblage was impacted heavily by nonhuman agents. NISP: 2,748.				
Lost Terrace	Montana	A.D. 900	NW Plains Bison Hunters	Davis and Fisher (1990)
· The pronghorn antelope subassemblage comprises remains of a MNI of 26 found in a thin "midden" generated from a site ". . . where bone breakage had been carried out relentlessly" (p. 276).				
Jurgens	Colorado	7100 B.C.	Paleoindian	Wheat (1979)
· The Area 1 subassemblage used in the analysis comprises the remains of 31 bison individuals (MNI) found in a bone bed. The assemblage was interpreted to represent evidence of a long-term camp. Cultural modification is evident, but evidence of carnivore action is unreported. NISP: 1,202.				
Horner	Wyoming	8000 B.C.	Paleoindian	Todd (1987a)
· The subassemblage analyzed comprises a minimum of 53 bison individuals from the Horner II bone bed, representing a single mass death of a relatively small group of bison. The bones show little evidence of cultural modification and little evidence of carnivore damage. NISP: 6,435.				

[a] Some or most of these assemblages are carnivore-ravaged; few are products of exclusively hominid activity.

Table 12.1 A listing of faunal and human assemblages used in the comparative quantitative analysis. These assemblages were selected because the data, particularly data on element representation, were reported in sufficient detail to allow comparison with the Mancos 5MTUMR–2346 assemblage.

few faunal reports were available for the Southwest a decade ago). Recent work has helped to rectify this (Breternitz *et al.*, 1986). The potential contributions that zooarchaeological work can make to solving important problems of Southwestern prehistory have recently brought calls for improved faunal analysis. For example, Bayham and Hatch (1985) recognized shortcomings of Southwestern zooarchaeology before 1985. They propose that site reports include, minimally, absolute bone frequencies by taxon, comparably determined MNI counts by taxon, modification frequencies by taxon (especially burning), and artiodactyl body part frequencies.

For the 5MTUMR–2346 analysis, medium-size artiodactyls (primarily deer) comprise the most appropriate comparative taxon because of the similarity in body size between these mammals and humans. Unfortunately, artiodactyl remains are far less abundant than the remains of smaller mammals and birds at most Anasazi sites (Emslie, 1983; Leonard, 1989). As one extreme example of this, Neusius (1986a) describes a mere 1.5 percent of the Aldea Sierritas mammal bone assemblage as artiodactyl. More typical of Anasazi zooarchaeological assemblages is the sample from Grass Mesa Village, where the most abundant mammals were rabbits, accounting for 34 percent of the total assemblage (20% were cottontail, 14% were jackrabbit), whereas artiodactyls constitute 14 percent of the assemblage (Neusius and Gould, 1988). Szuter (1989) reports a 14.5 percent artiodactyl composition for more southerly Hohokam faunal assemblages, and provides "lagomorph index" data (the ratio between identified artiodactyl and identified lagomorph specimens) for a variety of sites in south-central Arizona. She calls attention to ethnographic evidence from the Southwest that indicates that artiodactyl exploitation, from the hunt through the disposal of bones, is imbued with ritual that influences the final disposition of remains. She sees this as one difficulty in employing artiodactyl remains as subsistence indicators in the Southwest. Another difficulty, of course, is the fact that artiodactyl remains were often used for the production of bone tools and ornaments in this region.

A limited number of reports from Southwestern archaeological contexts provide relevant zooarchaeological data required for valid comparisons with the Mancos 5MTUMR–2346 human bone assemblage. These reports include Akins on Pueblo Alto (1982), Czaplewski (1982) on the Coronado Project, Lang and Harris (1984) on Arroyo Hondo Pueblo, Morris (1986) on Antelope House, Pippin (1987) on Guadalupe Ruin, and Neusius (1985a, 1986b, 1988), Sebastian (1986), and Neusius and Gould (1988) on Dolores Archaeological Program sites. A more comprehensive comparative background for human bone assemblages interpreted as evidence of cannibalism by Turner is available (Turner, 1983).

In an effort to overcome the obstacles to comparing the human 5MTUMR–2346 assemblage and nonhuman faunal remains from similar contexts, the author gathered data on the medium to large mammal components of Anasazi zooarchaeological remains from the Mesa Verde National Park. Key comparative attributes were recorded for the entire artiodactyl subassemblage from the Badger House midden (Site 1452; Hayes and Lancaster, 1975; n = 749 pieces). Furthermore, qualitative examination of similar remains from Long House (Site 1200) and Coyote Village (Site 820) was undertaken. The subassemblages assessed in this manner were overwhelmingly derived from mule deer

(*Odocoileus hemionus*) and bighorn (*Ovis canadensis*). The Badger House artiodactyl assemblage is particularly valuable for comparison with the Mancos 5MTUMR–2346 remains because of its large piece count, good bone preservation, recovery methodology (same as 5MTUMR–2346), complete midden excavation, age of the remains (A.D. 900–1100), and the fact that modification was scored by the same analyst (the author).

Throughout the following analysis, the most restrictive facet of zooarchaeology should be kept in mind—that assemblages are the products of complex past events that include, in addition to prehistoric human behavior, differentials in pre- and postdepositional bone modification, recovery, analysis, and reporting. Data published for other assemblages by other investigators must, therefore, be used judiciously in any comparative analysis. Characteristics that make the Mancos 5MTUMR–2346 assemblage unusual among archaeological faunas (and difficult to compare with them) include the unity of taxon (*Homo sapiens*), the dramatic skeletal differences between humans and medium to large ungulates, the lack of pre- and postdepositional modification by nonhuman agencies, and the good preservation of bone surfaces.

Comparisons among quantitative data reported for different vertebrate bone assemblages are often rendered ineffective or misleading because observational and recording standards differ so much among different investigators. Thus, comparisons of *identity* and *survival* of elements in assemblages depend upon the nature of recovery of the assemblages as well as on the skills, identification thresholds, and counting methods employed by the investigator. Quantitative comparisons among different *types of bone modification* in assemblages are affected by the same variables. The percentage of specimens in an assemblage reported to bear cutmarks is influenced, for example, by the recovery of the small bone component of the assemblage. The recovery and incorporation of thousands of tiny bone splinters into the denominator will depress any cutmark percentage figured on a total specimen basis because these small fragments are far less likely to bear cutmarks than the larger bone segments. Any reported cutmark percentage also depends upon what the conditions of observation were, what threshold of cutmark recognition was used by the investigator, and to what degree the original bone surfaces were preserved. All of these dimensions vary dramatically among different analyses. The present analyses of the Badger House ungulate remains and the Yellow Jacket 5MT–3 human remains were undertaken in an effort to control some of these variables. The study that follows reports data published for other assemblages, but the author is most confident in the comparability of data sets generated as part of the present research.

The analysis that follows does not include all possible manipulations of data. Some have undoubtedly been overlooked; others were judged not worth doing. The work attempts to fulfill the two most important conditions of any comparative assessment of archaeological faunal remains. First, the procedures through which the data were acquired are explicitly set forth in Chapters 4 and 6. Second, the data themselves are fully reported in Appendix 2.

IDENTITY AND SURVIVAL

Measures of abundance such as MNI and NISP are discussed in Chapters 5 and 6, and considered at length by Gilbert and

Singer (1982), Grayson (1984), Klein and Cruz-Uribe (1984), and Parmalee (1985). The survival of *specimens* in archaeological bone assemblages may be gauged against measures of *individuals* in the assemblage or against other *bones* or *portions of bones* in the assemblage.

Minimum Number of Individuals (MNI)

Chapter 5 provides a detailed analysis of the Mancos MNI, pointing out that this value is important in any further assessment of the assemblage. A minimum number of 29 individuals was determined for the 2,106-specimen Mancos human bone assemblage. This value is based on specimens from the upper and lower jaws that would all be considered "identifiable" by most zooarchaeologists. MNI values reported in zooarchaeology depend on analyst skill and methods. Considerable variation among analysts in these aspects undoubtedly has strong effects on reported MNI values. Because of the time and effort put into identifying the age, antimeric partners, and maxillary and mandibular nonmatches among the Mancos remains, the reported MNI value may be higher (by several individuals) than some practicing zooarchaeologists might calculate for this assemblage. As discussed in Chapter 4, the Mancos individuals comprising the minimum represent a wide spectrum of individual ages.

Total Number of Specimens

Table 12.2 provides data on MNI versus total specimen count for a series of single-taxon assemblages: Mancos, Gatecliff Shelter Horizon 2, and a variety of human bone assemblages for which published interpretations include cannibalism. The ratios between the total number of specimens in each assemblage and the minimum numbers of individuals represented show a wide range of values. It is impossible to ascertain whether this spread is real, or instead reflects the nonlinear relationship between MNI and total number of specimens. The spread also may be influenced by interassemblage differentials in recovery technique, refitting, and method of MNI calculation. Disentangling these influences is not possible without further information on each assemblage. The MNI:total specimen ratio is therefore not useful in comparing the degree of fragmentation among these sets. The data do, however, provide a good indication of how the Mancos assemblage compares to these other assemblages in overall size.

Number of Identified Specimens (NISP)

Problems inherent in identifying specimens and using these identifications to quantify abundance in the analysis of archaeological bone assemblages are discussed in Chapter 6. A series of pitfalls for any analyst is interposed between the human behaviors originally responsible for assemblage modification and the interpretation of quantitative results. These pitfalls include differentials in deposition and preservation, recovery method, and analyst skill.

Any comparative quantitative analysis of the Mancos assemblage must be sensitive to the fact that this is a single-taxon assemblage analyzed by an osteologist who specializes on that one taxon, *Homo sapiens*. Mechanisms to correct for these facts have been introduced in an effort to increase the validity of comparisons. As outlined in Chapter 6, Mancos specimens that many faunal analysts working on a mixed archaeological faunal collection would designate as identifiable (would set aside for a search of a comparative collec-

Table 12.2

ASSEMBLAGE	TOTAL # OF SPECIMENS	MNI	RATIO: TOTAL # OF SPECIMENS ÷ MNI
Leroux Wash	3,443	> 16	< 215.18
Burnt Mesa	3,389	11	308.09
Yellow Jacket 5MT–3	1,556	10	155.60
Mancos	**2,106**	**29**	**72.62**
Cottonwood Wash	693	4	173.25
Monument Valley	644	7	92.00
Marshview Hamlet	528	6	88.00
Sambrito Village	474	5	94.80
Polacca Wash	437	30	14.56
Grinnell	380	7	54.28
Ash Creek	212	5	42.40
Fontbrégoua H3[a]	> 134	6	> 22.43
Gatecliff Shelter (*Ovis*)	8,396	24	349.83

Sources: This study; Turner (1983); Thomas and Mayer (1983); and Villa *et al.* (1986a).
[a] These values are postrefitting and not directly comparable.

Table 12.2 A listing of MNI versus total specimen count for various assemblages.

tion) are recorded under Observations 4 through 8 in Appendix 2. Thus, the total count of these specimens (n = 721 in the Mancos assemblage) represents a NISP value in the sense of Grayson (1984) or Klein and Cruz-Uribe (1984).

The NISP values for a limited sample of mostly archaeological bone assemblages representing a wide range of time and contexts are displayed in Table 12.3. An attempt was made to select a sample of assemblages where recovery methods were fairly good and for which there were fairly reliable data on identification. Some of these assemblages are small, some very large. Among them there are wide differentials in antiquity and context, methods of recovery, the degree to which small mammals are included, and the confidence of identifications. Furthermore, the Mancos assemblage is difficult to compare with these other assemblages because of its single-taxon composition.

All other things being equal (a condition *certainly* not met in the select set of assemblages documented in Table 12.3), the higher the NISP:total specimen ratio, the more intact (less ravaged) the bones of an assemblage. Compared to most of the other human assemblages documented by Turner (1983) in the American Southwest (NISP:total specimen ratio mean [on gross count] = .57), the Mancos assemblage has a low ratio (.34). This comparison is very misleading, however, because Turner's (1983) "unidentifiable" category has few specimens. This is attributable to the taxonomic unity of the collections, Turner's expertise as a physical anthropologist, and the fact that he identified as "longbone" those specimens that fall into the Mancos "unidentified" category (remember that my NISP determinations were made from the viewpoint of a faunal analyst). Where identification was more comparable, in the cases of the Cottonwood and Yellow Jacket 5MT–3 assemblage data generated by the author, the Mancos NISP:total specimen ratio (0.34 for Mancos, .09 for Cottonwood, and .25 for Yellow Jacket 5MT–3) is relatively high. This is because this ratio is strongly influenced by the degree to which the small bone fragments are recovered during excavation. The large number of specimens belonging to the small element and fragment categories in the Cottonwood and Yellow Jacket assemblages inflate the denominator of the equation and lead to lower ratios. Unfortunately, reporting of only postconjoining data for the important Fontbrégoua assemblage makes it impossible to determine how specimen identifiability at Mancos compares with that for the European site. Comparison of the Mancos value with values from a range of Southwest archaeological faunal assemblages shows Mancos scoring on the high side. This may be because most of these archaeological faunas involved screening in the recovery phase, a procedure that rapidly inflates the unidentified specimen count, and therefore decreases the ratio, as noted above.

Table 12.3 provides a perspective on how the Mancos assemblage compares with a range of other assemblages in total specimen count and identifiability of elements. The wide range in values in the NISP:total specimen ratio results from prehistoric and historic human behaviors combining with a mixture of postdiscard value modifications derived from differentials in preservation, recovery, and analysis. The strong effects of the latter causes, often acting synergistically, are easily understood and certainly responsible for the wide disparity in ratios reported for the same assemblages (FLK Zinj at Olduvai, with ratios of 3.9, 8.8, and 31.0). Because of the fragmentation of the assemblage, Mancos specimens are far less identifiable than most human cemetery collections. Indeed, identifiability of the Mancos specimens falls squarely in the known range for archaeological faunal assemblages.

Element Representation

Elements of the skeleton usually occur in archaeological contexts in proportions that vary from those found in living animals. This observation has led students of prehistoric human behavior to focus considerable attention on the differential representation of elements in faunal assemblages. This approach has a long history, dating to at least the mid-19th century (Lubbock, 1865), with applications at many famous archaeological and paleontological sites. From *observations* of frequency data on elements and element portions, unwarranted *inferences* about prehistoric human behavior have been derived. These inferences, based on disproportions of elements and their parts, range from bone tool making by Pliocene hominids (Dart, 1957a) to the transport of animal parts by more recent humans (White, 1952; Perkins and Daly, 1968). For example, most workers have interpreted the lack of axial elements in archaeological assemblages as evidence of differential transport. A Southwest archaeological example comes with the work of Akins (1982), who noted the relative lack of thoracic, lumbar, and sacral vertebrae as well as ribs among the Pueblo Alto artiodactyl remains. She attributed this observation to the stripping and abandonment of these "low yield" portions at the kill site. It is now apparent that the disproportions themselves are often ambiguous in their meaning. The meaning and merits of ele-

Opposite page:

Table 12.3 A listing of NISP values for a variety of sites.

ASSEMBLAGE	ARCHAEOLOGY / TIME[1]	TOTAL SPECIMENS	TOTAL IDENTIFIED SPECIMENS (NISP)	NISP AS % OF TOTAL	SOURCE
THIS STUDY					
Mancos	**Pueblo III**	**2,106**	**721**	**34.2**	**This study**
SOUTHWEST HUMAN					
Yellow Jacket 5MT-3	Pueblo II	1,556	389	25.0	This study
Leroux Wash	Pueblo III	3,443	2,458	71.4	Turner (1983)[2]
Burnt Mesa	Pueblo II	3,389	1,114	32.9	Turner (1983)
Cottonwood Wash	Pueblo I	693	63	9.1	This study
Monument Valley	Anasazi indet.	644	436	67.7	Turner (1983)
Marshview Hamlet	Pueblo II/III	528	492	93.2	Turner (n.d.)
Sambrito Village	Pueblo II	474	309	65.2	Turner (1983)
Ash Creek	Pueblo IV	212	160	75.5	Turner (1983)
SOUTHWEST FAUNAL[3]					
Grass Mesa Village	Pueblo I	17,236	4,271	24.8	Neusius and Gould (1988)
McPhee Community Cluster	Pueblo I, II	28,484	7,579	26.6	Neusius (1988)
Navajo Reservoir Project	Pueblo IV	15,000	4,100	27.3	Harris (1963)
Pueblo Alto	Pueblo II	8,664	1,003	11.6	Akins (1982)
LeMoc Shelter (El. 1-5+)	Pueblo I	5,320	961	18.1	Neusius (1986b)
Arroyo Hondo (1-8)	Pueblo IV	3,794	1,095	28.9	Lang and Harris (1984)
Phillips	Pueblo III-IV	2,544	476	18.7	Driver (1985)
Bonnell	Pueblo II-IV	2,520	329	13.1	Driver (1985)
Antelope House	Pueblo II/III	2,030	359	17.7	Kelley (1975)
Ash Creek	Hohokam/Salado	410	40	9.8	Bayham and Hatch (1985)
Prince Hamlet	Pueblo I	384	37	9.6	Sebastian (1986)
OTHER NORTH AMERICAN FAUNAL					
Eshelman	Protohistoric	58,119	23,614	40.6	Guilday *et al.* (1962)
Fort Ligioner	British Army	40,537	3,537	8.7	Guilday (1970)
Tick Creek Cave	Archaic-Woodland	40,500	8,100	20.0	Parmalee (1965)
Quaker State Rockshelter	Woodland	29,159	4,227	14.5	Guilday and Tanner (1962)
Tehuacan Valley Sites	Pre A.D. 1500	11,000	4,713	42.8	Flannery (1967)
Eden-Farsen	Protohistoric	10,180	4,005	39.3	Frison (1971)
Gatecliff Shelter (*Ovis*)	Late Prehistoric	8,396	500	6.0	Thomas and Mayer (1983)
Garnsey	Late Prehistoric	6,937	2,549	36.7	Speth (1983)
Paxson Lake	Protohistoric	6,261	2,244	32.3	Yesner and Bonnichsen (1979)
EURASIAN HUMAN					
Fontbrégoua H3[4]	Neolithic	Unreported	134 postconjoining	--	Villa *et al.* (1986a)
EURASIAN FAUNAL					
Suberde	Neolithic	300,000	25,000	8.3	Perkins and Daly (1968)
Alvastra	Neolithic	87,000	4,414	5.1	During (1986)
Abri Pataud	Upper Paleolithic	45,362	455	1.0	Spiess (1979)
Birsmatten	Mesolithic	15,371	2,661	17.3	Schmid (1972)
Salzgitter-Lebenstedt	Middle Paleolithic	5,000	< 2,500	< 50.0	Staesche (1983)
Armeaux	Danubian	2,008	981	48.9	Poplin (1975)
AFRICAN FAUNAL					
Prolonged Drift	Neolithic	165,000	12,771	7.7	Gifford *et al.* (1980)
Mapungubwe	Iron Age	71,190	11,100	15.6	Voigt (1983)
Chencherere	Late Stone Age	68,174	2,727	4.0	Crader (1984)
Ngamuriak	Neolithic	62,508	14,302	22.9	Marshall (1986a)
Wilton	Late Stone Age	43,629	6,702	15.4	Brain (1981a)
Olduvai FLK Zinj	Oldowan	40,000	3,500	8.8	Bunn (1982)
Olduvai FLK Zinj	Oldowan	15,861	614	3.9	Potts (1988)
Olduvai FLK Zinj	Oldowan	3,510	1,088	31.0	Isaac and Crader (1981)
Olorgesailie DE/89	Acheulean	13,800	2,070	15.0	Isaac and Crader (1981)
Olorgesailie DE/89	Acheulean	9,231	2,190	23.7	Koch (1986)
Makapansgat Limeworks	Paleontological	7,159	2,599	36.3	Dart (1957a)
Mufulwe	Nachikufan	6,535	355	5.4	Gutin and Musonda (1985)
Swartkrans Member 2	Oldowan	5,894	1,039	17.6	Brain (1981a)
Kromdraai B	Indet.	4,985	613	12.3	Brain (1981a)
Bushman Rockshelter	MSA, LSA	4,819	1,775	36.8	Brain (1969a)
FxJj-20, Koobi Fora	Karari	4,570	416	9.1	Bunn (1982)
Olduvai BK	Developed Oldowan	2,957	1,597	54.0	Isaac and Crader (1981)
Swartkrans Member 1	Oldowan	2,381	1,188	49.9	Brain (1981a)
Amboseli	Modern hyaena	2,000	600	30.0	Hill (1984)
Syokiamu	Modern hyaena	1,124	640	57.0	Bunn (1982)

[1]The Pueblo I-IV designations indicate rough chronological placement rather than specific cultural attributes of the assemblages.

[2]The NISP values for Turner (1983) are inflated relative to others in this table. See text for details.

[3]Faunal counts for several Southwest sites exclude small mammals wherever these were tabulated separately in the original report.

[4]These values are post-refitting and not directly comparable.

ment representation data continue to be actively debated (Lyman, 1985; Metcalfe and Jones, 1988; Grayson, 1989; Klein, 1989; O'Connell *et al.*, 1990; Marshall and Pilgram, 1991).

Archaeological contexts spanning the Pliocene through recent have produced bone assemblages in which vertebrae and pelves are underrepresented relative to other elements. Archaeologists have most often attributed these disproportions to one of two processes—hominid selectivity in transport or postdiscard destruction by carnivores. Results of the Mancos analysis heighten the ambiguity in the meaning of archaeological bone element disproportions by suggesting that on-site, prediscard human processing may contribute to element disproportions in a similar fashion. Indeed, an overview of the literature from the perspective of the Mancos 5MTUMR–2346 analysis reveals that an unfortunate concentration on *proportional element representation* among Southwest human assemblages, as among zooarchaeological assemblages in general, has drawn attention away from the more subtle, but ultimately more significant, *bone modification attributes* that allow the investigator to assess the *cause* of the disproportions.

It is already evident that patterns of selective skeletal element representation in any assemblage can potentially derive from differentials in accumulation, predepositional sorting and destruction, and postdepositional destruction. Quantification of element survival as a guide to prehistoric behavior is therefore a difficult and treacherous endeavor. Osteological elements and their portions survive until archaeological analysis by escaping many agencies capable of altering the original proportions in the living animal's skeleton. Elements can be differentially introduced to a locality by selective hominid action. Alternatively, they can be differentially deleted by predators acting prior to hominid arrival. Once at the site of deposition (often different from the site of the animal's death), the skeletal elements can suffer differential destruction and disposal by the hands of hominids. Once disposed of, elements may be subjected to carnivore activity or wind and water action resulting in their destruction on the site, or their being carried off the site. Weathering, postdepositional leaching, and bioturbation are subsequent modifiers of element representation. Finally, differential recovery, identification (Lyman and O'Brien's [1987] "analytic absence of elements"), and reporting can alter the relative proportions of skeletal elements. Variation in these factors is usually independent. The zooarchaeologist, usually expected to unravel the history of bone assemblages formed through the interplay of these independent influences, is faced with a formidable challenge. When equipped with mere element frequencies, the task is daunting. For all of these reasons, the use of relative abundance data in isolation usually results in ambiguity or is downright misleading (Lyman, 1985). When conditioned by other evidence of bone modification and context, however, quantitative data on skeletal part representation may be informative.

One of the most effective means of presenting data on element and subelement representation is through the kind of element lot photographs used to illustrate Chapters 7 to 11. Because this technique of presentation is not yet widely employed, because of the subjectivity involved in interpreting the patterns in the images, and because a direct quantitative comparison of relative element and element portion abundance with other assemblages is desirable, element representation is quantified in more traditional fashion in this chapter.

Representation of each skeletal element in an archaeological bone assemblage may be measured by a simple specimen count (the NISP value by element), or the *percentage* of the total NISP that this value represents (%NISP). Alternatively, an estimate of how many individuals are represented by a particular element or element portion may be made (the actual, by-element MNI value, or the *percentage* of the total assemblage MNI that this by-element value represents [%MNI]). Table 12.4 provides a guide to element and element portion representation in the Mancos assemblage. Here, data are reported from both the physical anthropologist's perspective (the author's maximal identification in a conjoined, single-taxon assemblage; TW MNI, TW NISP, TW %MNI, TW %NISP), and a perspective perhaps more in line with some zooarchaeological analyses (zooarchaeological identification of specimens in a mixed-taxon assemblage).

A large set of values is used to describe element and element portion representation in zooarchaeological assemblages. Whatever the choice between MNI, MNE, MAU, and NISP, the variation among different analysts in what to identify as "identifiable" is of central importance. The difficulties in comparing physical anthropological identifications with faunal analytical identifications were previously discussed (see Chapter 6), but even among zooarchaeologists, decisions about the identifiability of specimens are highly subjective and the analytical results are therefore difficult to use in comparative work. The lack of standards in basic identification work probably renders many comparative quantitative analyses suspect.

Raw values for the number of identified specimens (NISPs) provide only indirect estimates of differential element survival because each individual's skeleton has dozens of representatives of some elements like hand phalanges, and only one or a few representatives of other elements such as the sacrum or atlas. Furthermore, different animals have different element complements in their skeletons (modern equids, for example, have single major metapodials on each appendage, whereas humans have five on each appendage). The minimum number of individuals per element, on the other hand, often provides samples of very small size. As a solution to this dilemma, some investigators have proposed other methods to estimate relative element abundance. For example, Binford (1978, 1984) created the "Minimal Animal Unit" (MAU) value by dividing the observed bone count for an element (or element portion) by the number of bones in the anatomy of a complete animal for that particular element (or element portion; NISP per element ÷ number of elements in the body). Grayson (1984) has noted problems with this approach.

In considering relative abundance, the "survival" of an element (or element portion) may be assessed by dividing the NISP value for a given element by the number of elements (or element portions) present in the animal times the minimum number of individual animals in the assemblage: element NISP ÷ [(# of elements) x (maximum MNI)]. This value is used by Brain (1981a) to assess survival, a value that he and Gifford-Gonzalez (1989a) call "percentage survival." Thus, a "survival" value for the talus in the Mancos assemblage equals the number of identifiable, surviving talus specimens (4) divided by the number of expected tali in 29 individuals (4 ÷ 58 = .068). Therefore, "survival" of the talus (at about 0.07) is poor relative to that of the maxilla (at 0.45). Were assemblages composed of only intact elements, "perfect" or "complete" survival would

ELEMENT	Total Specimens		Zooarchaeologically Identifiable specimens (NISP)		Minimum Number of Individuals (MNI)				ELEMENT
					TW		Zooarch.		
	total	adult	total	adult	total	adult	total	adult	
CRANIAL	474	336	229	168	29	20	29	20	CRANIAL
VAULT	331	229	92	64		-	-	-	*VAULT*
MAXILLA	31	19	26	16	21	12	21	12	*MAXILLA*
MANDIBLE	33	22	33	22	23	15	23	15	*MANDIBLE*
TOOTH	79	66	79	66	29	20	29	20	*TOOTH*
FREE VERTEBRAE	136	94	47	47	10	8	8	8	FREE VERTEBRAE
CERVICAL	48	35	25	25	10	8	8	8	*CERVICAL*
Atlas	12	9	8	8	10	8	8	8	*Atlas*
Axis	8	6	5	5	6	6	5	5	*Axis*
C3-7	28	20	12	12	5	3	4	2	*C3-7*
THORACIC	54	34	18	18	5	3	2	2	*THORACIC*
LUMBAR	34	25	4	4	4	3	1	1	*LUMBAR*
SACRUM	6	5	0	0	3	2	0	0	SACRUM
OS COXAE	34	28	10	6	11	7	8	5	OS COXAE
RIBS	350	277	101	76	8	5	8	5	RIBS
First rib	21	14	13	9	11	5	8	5	*First rib*
Rib A	0	0	0	0	-	-	-	-	*Rib A*
Rib B	15	6	15	6	-	-	-	-	*Rib B*
Rib C	66	43	17	6	-	-	-	-	*Rib C*
Rib D	174	142	2	2	-	-	-	-	*Rib D*
Rib E	40	38	36	35	-	-	-	-	*Rib E*
Rib F	34	34	18	18	-	-	-	-	*Rib F*
STERNUM	2	1	0	0	1	1	0	0	STERNUM
CLAVICLE	34	29	25	20	18	10	14	10	CLAVICLE
SCAPULA	22	16	7	4	12	8	8	5	SCAPULA
HUMERUS	71	58	19	13	17	8	17	8	HUMERUS
Proximal	-	-	0	0	-	-	0	0	*Proximal*
Distal	-	-	13	11	-	-	13	7	*Distal*
ULNA	44	36	12	9	14	6	9	6	ULNA
Proximal	-	-	7	6	-	-	7	6	*Proximal*
Distal	-	-	3	3	-	-	5	1	*Distal*
RADIUS	41	30	21	15	13	5	13	5	RADIUS
Proximal	-	-	9	8	-	-	10	5	*Proximal*
Distal	-	-	7	7	-	-	10	4	*Distal*
PATELLA	8	7	6	6	7	2	5	4	PATELLA
FEMUR	210	186	11	5	20	9	7	1	FEMUR
Proximal	-	-	5	2	-	-	7	1	*Proximal*
Distal	-	-	2	2	-	-	4	1	*Distal*
TIBIA	157	134	7	3	18	9	7	3	TIBIA
Proximal	-	-	1	0	-	-	4	0	*Proximal*
Distal	-	-	3	3	-	-	4	3	*Distal*
FIBULA	61	44	23	18	18	7	12	8	FIBULA
Proximal	-	-	2	1	-	-	5	4	*Proximal*
Distal	-	-	3	3	-	-	5	3	*Distal*
METACARPAL	44	44	43	43	10	5	8	6	METACARPAL
Proximal	14	14	14	14	-	-	-	-	*Proximal*
Distal	15	15	15	15	-	-	-	-	*Distal*
METATARSAL	54	43	45	38	8	3	8	6	METATARSAL
Proximal	16	15	15	14	-	-	-	-	*Proximal*
Distal	4	4	4	4	-	-	-	-	*Distal*
CARPAL	8	8	8	8	2	0	2	0	CARPAL
TARSAL	23	23	16	16	-	-	-	-	TARSAL
Astragalus	4	4	4	4	4	3	4	3	*Astragalus*
Calcaneus	10	10	7	7	6	6	5	5	*Calcaneus*
Other	9	9	5	5	3	0	3	0	*Other*
PROXIMAL PHALANX	75	69	74	68	4	2	4	2	PROXIMAL PHALANX
Hand	33	31	32	30	3	2	3	2	*Hand*
Foot	42	38	42	38	4	2	4	2	*Foot*
INTERMEDIATE PHALANX	13	13	13	13	2	1	2	1	INTERMEDIATE PHALANX
Hand	13	13	13	13	2	1	2	1	*Hand*
Foot	0	0	0	0	0	0	0	0	*Foot*
DISTAL PHALANX	4	4	3	3	2	1	2	1	DISTAL PHALANX
Hand	1	1	1	1	1	0	1	0	*Hand*
Foot	3	3	2	2	2	2	2	2	*Foot*
IP1	7	7	-	-	-	-	-	-	IP1
IP2	77	71	-	-	-	-	-	-	IP2
IP3	103	89	-	-	-	-	-	-	IP3
IP4	48	45	-	-	-	-	-	-	IP4
TOTAL	2106	1697	721	579	29	20	29	20	TOTAL

Note: permanent teeth scored as "adult".

Table 12.4 Element and element portion representation in the Mancos 5MTUMR–2346 assemblage.

equal 1.0, but the recovery of fragments of the same element from the same individual may inflate the result, often yielding survival values of greater than 1.0. A high survival value, when calculated in this manner, is inflated, particularly in a single-taxon assemblage, when a large diagnostic element such as the femur is highly fragmented. The "survival" approach used here only provides data on how elements survived relative to one another—differentials in this survival could have been introduced at the death locus, in differential transport, processing, discard, preservation, or recovery of the elements. Of course, a key factor in this method of element frequency determination is the equilibration involving the MNI of 29. Low survival values for different elements could imply that these elements never reached the site *or* that they were destroyed or lost on-site. Element representation data, by themselves, cannot resolve this. As Koch (1986) and Todd and Rapson (1988) point out, the mere documentation of patterns of differential destruction does not directly indicate the processes responsible for the observed disproportions. The relationships between %NISP, %MNI, and survival values for the Mancos 5MTUMR–2346 assemblage are shown in Figures 12.7 and 12.8.

Before comparing the Mancos 5MTUMR–2346 assemblage with others, it was necessary to attempt to investigate how assessment by a physical anthropologist might have altered the results on differential representation of different skeletal elements. Figure 12.9 shows the difference between final, postconjoining identification by a physical anthropologist and identification judged by the author to be typical in zooarchaeology (see Chapter

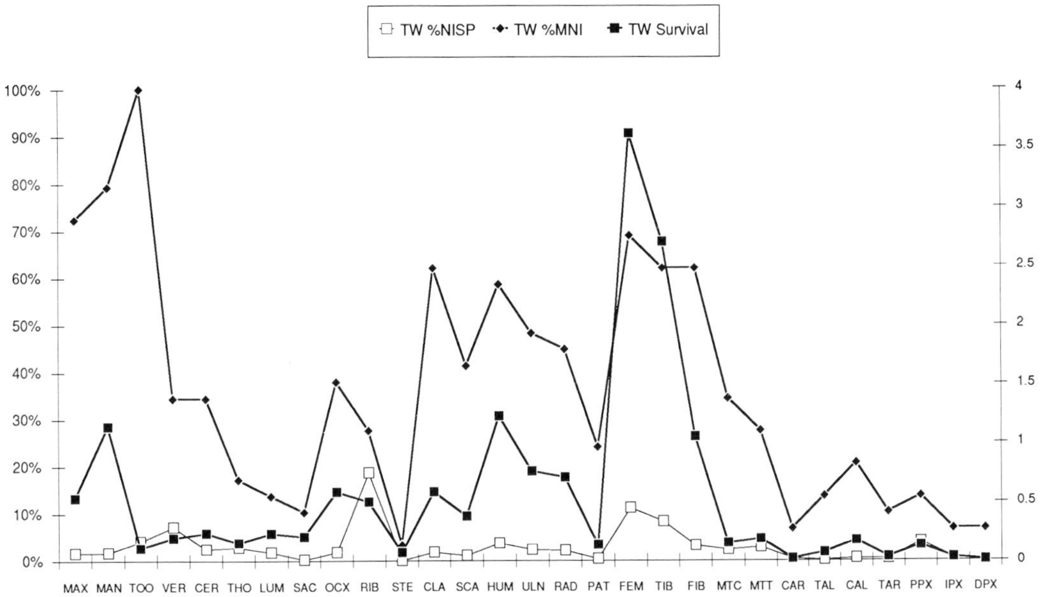

Fig. 12.7 Plot of relative element abundance as measured by TW %NISP, TW %MNI, and TW survival. For definitions of these values, see the text. Percentage values for NISP and MNI are on the left vertical axis, survival values are on the right vertical axis.

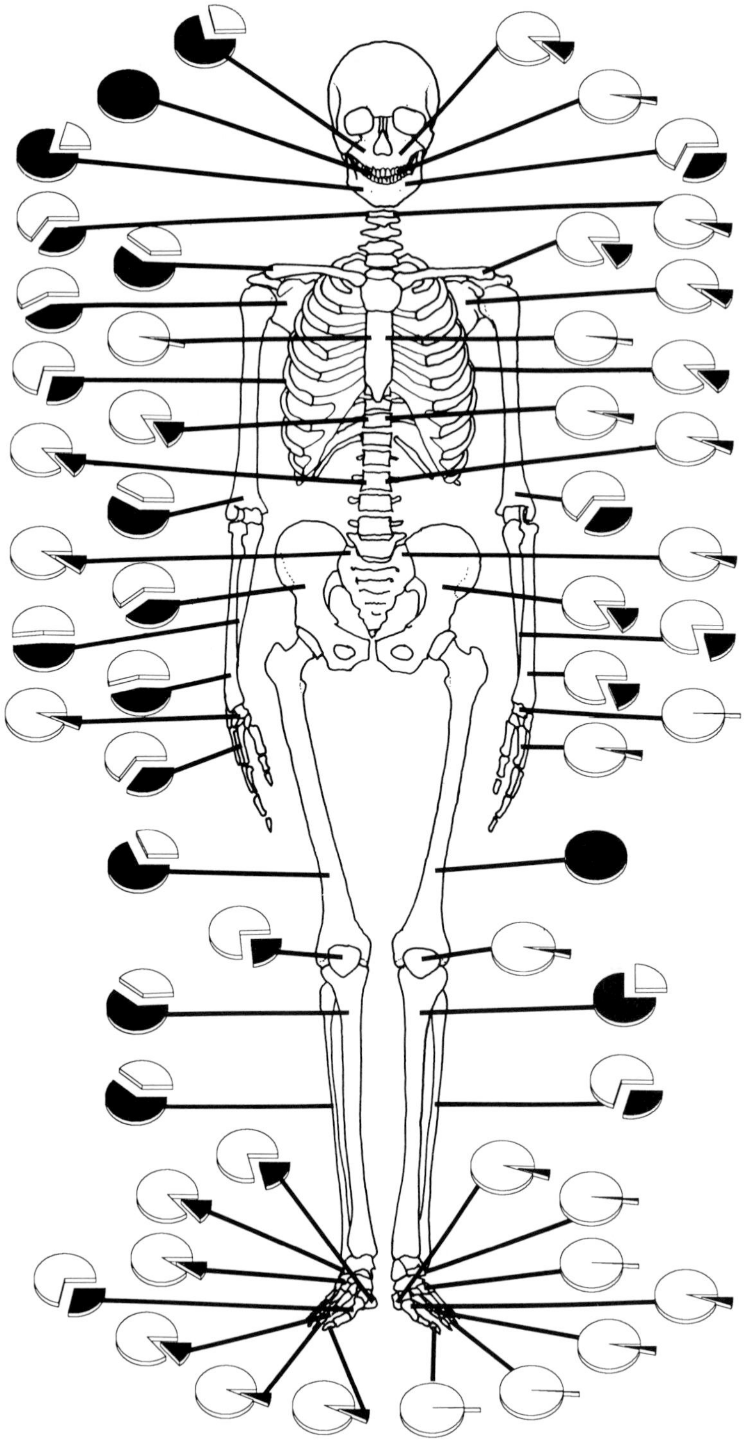

Fig. 12.8 Drawing summarizing relative skeletal element representation in the Mancos 5MTUMR–2346 assemblage. TW %MNI (viewer's left side) and TW survival values (viewer's right side) are indicated by the black pie slice for each element. Hand and foot phalanges are combined, shown under feet. Foot bones, from top to bottom on either side, are the calcaneus, talus, other tarsals, metatarsals, proximal phalanges, intermediate phalanges, and distal phalanges. %MNI values are relative to the 29 individuals represented by dental remains. Survival values are indicated as percentage value of the element with highest survival, the femur.

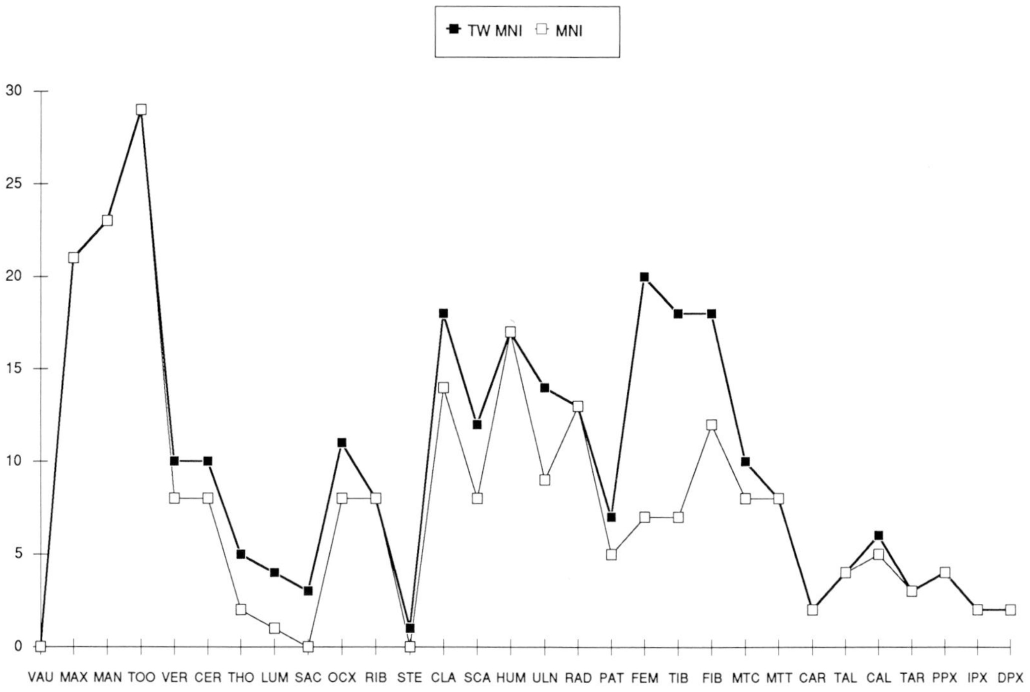

Fig. 12.9 Plot of physical anthropological versus zooarchaeological element representation by MNI. The left vertical axis shows minimum number of individuals as determined by each element. This plot shows that the greatest difference between final, postconjoining identification by a physical anthropologist and identification judged by me to be typical in zooarchaeology (see Chapter 6 for a full discussion), as measured by actual MNI values per element in the Mancos assemblage, is in the leg bones.

6 for a full discussion), as measured by actual MNI values per element in the Mancos assemblage. The resulting element representation curves are very similar, with the major differences at the femur, tibia, and fibula positions. Here, physical anthropological identification of broken shaft fragments doubles the relative representation of these limb elements. Figure 12.10 makes the same comparison with actual NISP values by element. A very similar but even more exaggerated effect is seen for lower limb elements, whereas the cranial vault, vertebral, and rib values also inflate dramatically with physical anthropological identification.

Finally, to gauge how differing levels of element identification affected results on relative element survival, the analysis compared "survival" values based on physical anthropological identifications with those based on the author's guess at "average zooarchaeological" identifications. The results are shown in Figure 12.11. Physical anthropological identification has very little effect on the survival values of cranial portions or hand and foot elements. It has limited effects on vertebral elements, and increasingly dramatic

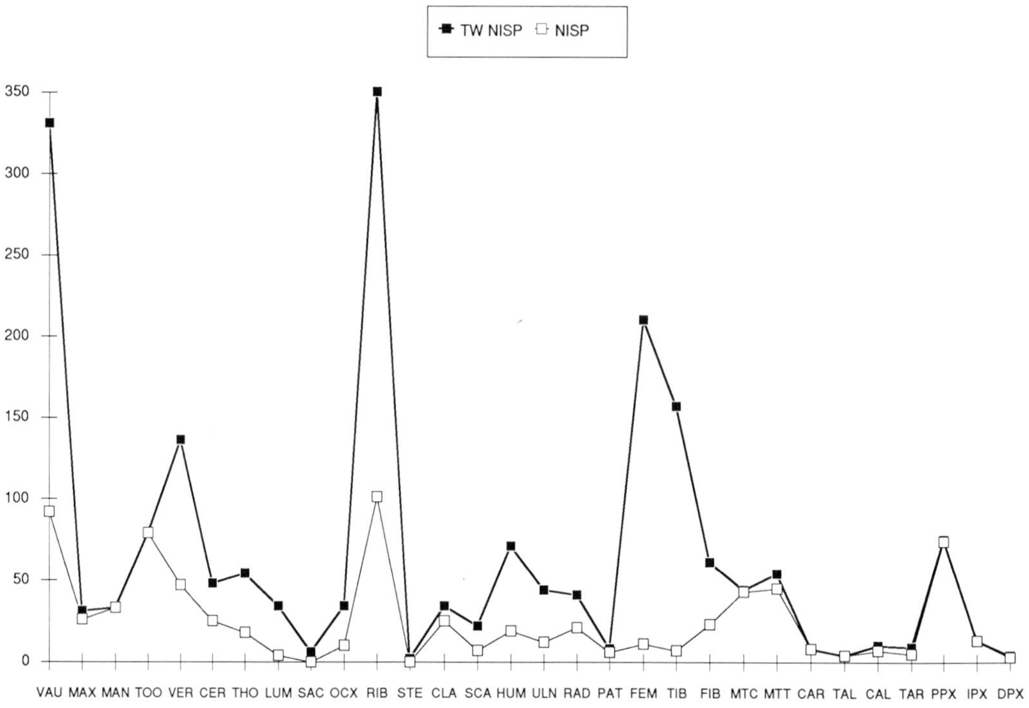

Fig. 12.10 Plot of physical anthropological versus zooarchaeological element representation by raw NISP values (specimen numbers shown on left vertical axis).

effects on scapular, costal, pelvic, forearm, upper arm, and leg elements. These effects result from the fact that the zooarchaeological faunal analyst is unlikely to element-identify limb shaft fragments in a mixed multitaxon assemblage, whereas the physical anthropologist often does identify them to element. Thus, it is evident that comparisons between the Mancos assemblage and other human assemblages from the American Southwest that were analyzed by physical anthropologists might be most effective when physical anthropological identifications are used. Comparisons with archaeological faunal assemblages, in contrast, might more appropriately use identifications that a faunal analyst would make for specimens in the Mancos assemblage.

The comparative analysis that follows employs data for the Mancos 5MTUMR–2346 assemblage derived from the total counts provided in Table 12.4. The limited effect of including subadult specimens was evaluated by plotting the adult specimens as a percentage of the total specimens in the assemblage (Figure 12.12).

To compare element survival among the assemblages summarized by Tables 12.1 and 12.2, a spreadsheet with all available data was constructed and used to generate histograms of element representation for each assemblage. For an assem-

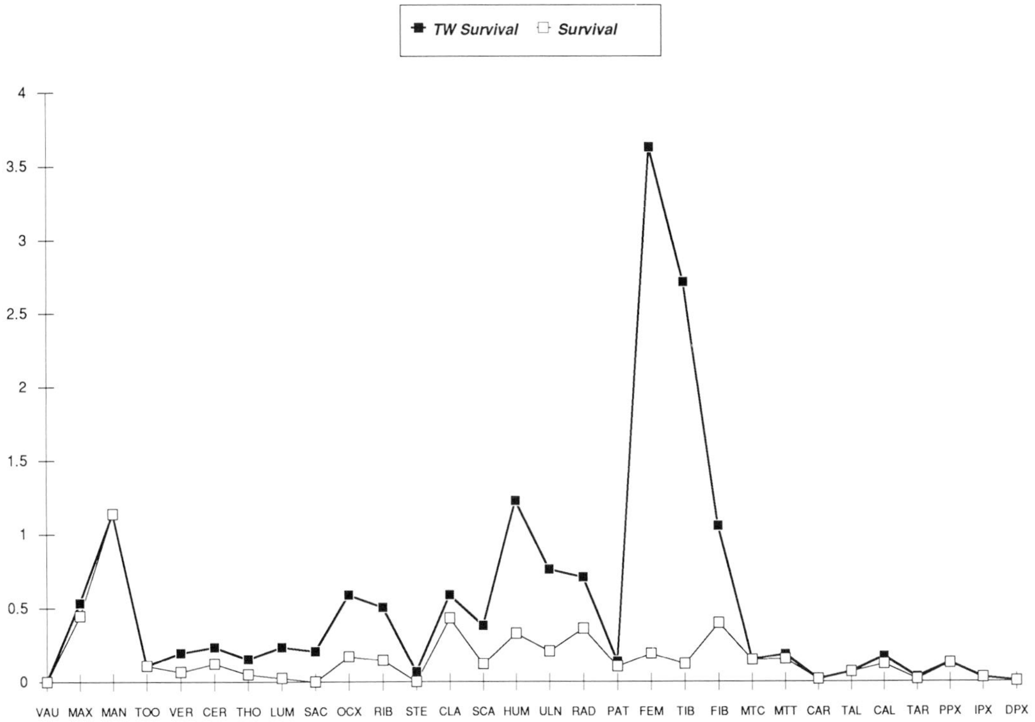

Fig. 12.11 Plot of physical anthropological versus zooarchaeological element representation by survival (element NISP ÷ [(# of elements) × (maximum MNI)]) values (survival values shown on left vertical axis). Note that like Figures 12.8 and 12.9, this plot shows that physical anthropological identification inflates the leg bone counts.

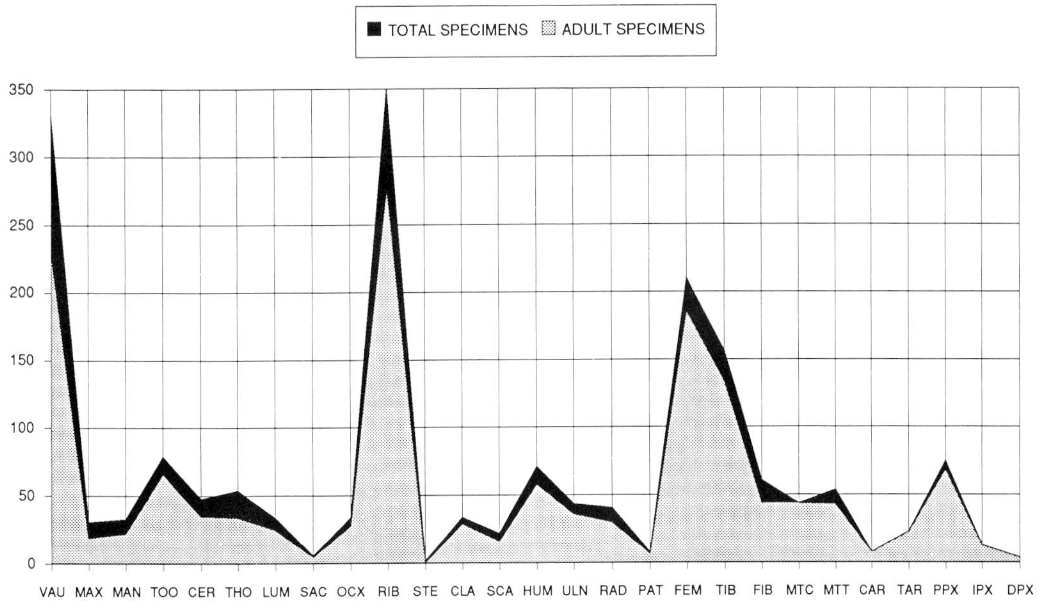

Fig. 12.12 Plot of adult specimens, by element as a proportion of total specimens. The age cutoff for this plot was c. 12 years. This plot shows that adult and immature skeletal elements are present at the expected proportions.

blage with a full data set, three separate histograms were plotted. The first plotted the percent NISP (NISP per element ÷ total assemblage NISP = %NISP), the second plotted the percent MNI (MNI per element ÷ total assemblage MNI = %MNI), and the third plotted ''survival'' (see above). Superimposition of histograms for different assemblages provides an excellent means of visually comparing element representation profiles. In the discussion that follows, the representation of different skeletal elements is addressed by comparing the Mancos 5MTUMR–2346 data with zooarchaeological data, and with data from the series of sites described as bearing possible evidence for cannibalism in the Southwest (as described in Chapter 3 and detailed in Appendix 1).

Before presenting the comparative archaeological data, it is necessary to gain a broader perspective on the susceptibility of bones to destructive agents. Such a perspective has been made available by the work of Brain (1981) and Lyman (1984b, 1985). A prime concern of zooarchaeology is to what degree the survival of different skeletal elements may be used to understand past hominid behaviors. Unfortunately, both human and nonhuman agents of destruction tend to produce similar patterns of element representation—a tendency conditioned by the fact that patterns of destruction *by any agent* are related to the structural properties of the bones themselves (Sutcliffe, 1970). In short, the elements and element portions most likely to survive best under the influence of *any* agency of destruction are the strongest, most dense, least trabecular ones.

Shipman (1981b) suggests that rather than bulk density, the ratio between spongy and compact bone in any element or element portion is the key variable affecting the bone's resistance to destruction. Unfortunately, comparative interelement and interelement portion density data are largely unavailable for the human skeleton, despite the availability of several techniques based on radiography and photon absorptiometry (Lyman, 1984b; Bowles *et al.*, 1985). The only source is Boaz and Behrensmeyer (1976), who report ''density'' values for archaeologically derived human skeletal remains. Only a few intact elements were measured by these authors, and no control for interindividual variation or organic content of the bones was attempted. This may explain why the Boaz and Behrensmeyer (1976) density values for the proximal ulna are greater than those for the distal humerus, and why the proximal and distal humerus are reported to be virtually identical in density (a most extraordinary conclusion given the anatomy of the human skeleton). Furthermore, there are no data available on marrow utility or grease utility (in the sense of Lyman, 1985) for the various elements in the human skeleton. These facts, coupled with the unreliability of the human density data, leave Lyman's results on ungulate element and element portion density the only available comparative base. This is unfortunate, because an artiodactyl skeleton differs substantially from a human one. Consider, for example, the difference in size, shape, and nutritive contents between a deer metapodial and a human metacarpal or metatarsal. Despite such differentials, as Figure 12.13 shows, there remains a strong relationship between Lyman's artiodactyl element bulk density values and the representation (measured by %MNI values) of different Mancos 5MTUMR–2346 human skeletal elements. A better measure of this relationship is shown by Figure 12.14, where the bones of the hand and foot are removed from consideration. Here, despite the very different anatomi-

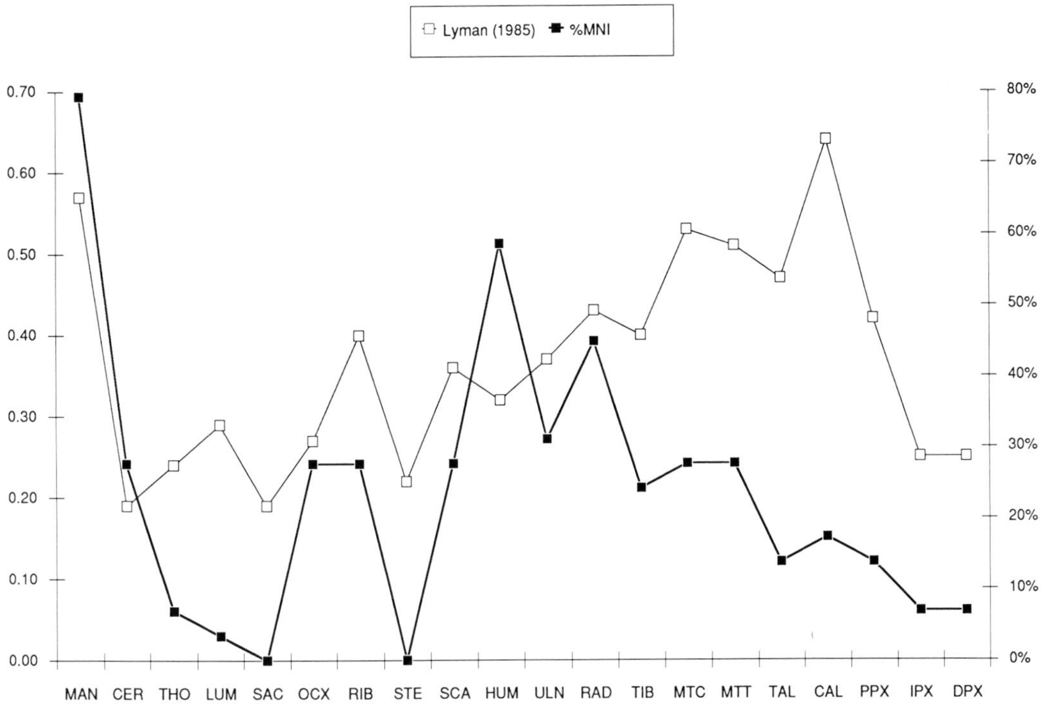

Fig. 12.13 Plot of the relationship between Lyman's (1985) ungulate skeletal element density values (indicated on the left vertical axis) and the %MNI values for the Mancos 5MTUMR–2346 assemblage (indicated on the right vertical axis). Note the correspondence between the highest (mandible) and lowest (cervical vertebra, sacrum, sternum) ungulate bone density values and the degree to which these elements are represented at 5MTUMR–2346. This is a reflection of the underlying plan of the vertebrate skeleton. Note that the high density values for the hand and foot bones do not predict the Mancos representation because human hand and foot bones are not as dense or as large, leading to increased deletion and decreased recovery.

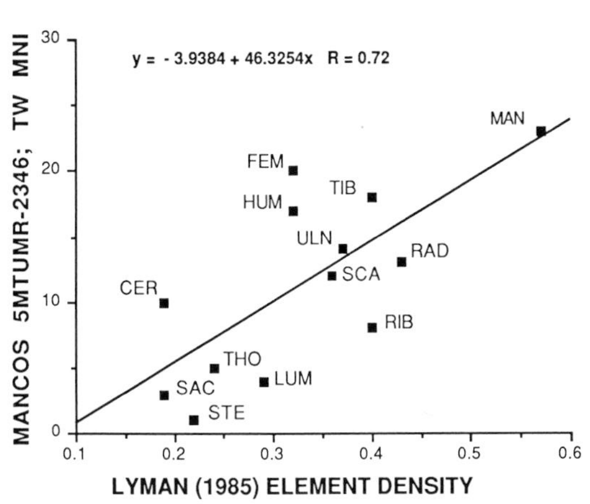

Fig. 12.14 Plot comparing Lyman's (1985) ungulate element bulk density values with the by-element TW MNI values for mandible, 4 vertebral types, ribs, sternum, scapula, humerus, ulna, radius, femur, and tibia in the Mancos 5MTUMR–2346 assemblage. These thirteen elements are considered to be the most anatomically similar between the two very different taxa. Note the relationship between the low MNI counts and low density. See the text for a fuller discussion of the application of ungulate density values to human remains.

cal construction of the 13 remaining elements, a reasonable relationship between ungulate element density and element representation in the Mancos assemblage is present. There is no doubt that this relationship will be greatly strengthened when comparable density data become available for the human skeleton.

An examination of the density values for element portions shows the same strong relationship with representation in the Mancos assemblage. When ratios between various element portions are considered for this assemblage (as measured by MNI and NISP), Lyman's (1985) distal versus proximal density values for the artiodactyl humerus, femur, and tibia are significant predictors of representation. Again, it is evident that the element part disproportions in the Mancos postcranial assemblage are strongly related to density. For example, the proximal humerus is much less dense (with thinner cortex and relatively more trabecular bone) than the distal humerus in most mammals. Humans are no exception to this rule. In the Mancos assemblage, no individuals are represented by proximal humeri, whereas 13 individuals are represented by distal humeri. The corresponding adult-only NISP values for Mancos are 0 and 11, respectively. Proximal:distal humerus NISP ratios approach a value of 1.0 (expected) in the Romano-British cemetery population (0.88; n = 100) and in the Horner (1.3; n = 92) bison assemblage, but many ethnographic, archaeological, carnivore-accumulated, and mixed assemblages have much lower ratios. For example, proximal humerus:distal humerus NISP ratio values range between 0.00 and 0.25 in such diverse assemblages as Makapansgat, Kuiseb, Emslie Mancos, Badger House, Converse, Eden-Farson, Dead Indian Creek, Mapungubwe, Last Supper, Cueva del Juyo, Prolonged Drift, and Olduvai FLK–22. Pippin (1987) attributes under-representation of the artiodactyl proximal humerus in the Guadalupe Ruin faunal remains to differential destruction by dogs or rodents, but in view of his suggestion that this assemblage could have been subjected to grease rendering, human involvement in the disproportion is possible. Because there is no evidence of carnivore destruction of the less dense element portions of the Mancos assemblage, because there is no evidence of postdepositional sorting or destruction of these less dense parts, because very fragile facial specimens are preserved fairly intact, and because there *is* substantial evidence of percussion-based crushing to the lighter, spongy bone portions of elements, it is inferred that humans were preferentially processing these lower-density parts of the Mancos human bones. This patterned elimination of spongy bone also reflects itself in disproportions in the overall element counts for the Mancos assemblage.

Most previous authors describing Southwestern human bone assemblages that have been interpreted as evidence of cannibalism did not focus their attention on the disproportions in *parts* of elements. Instead, they concentrated on the disproportions *among* various elements. Dittert *et al.* (1966) note that the Sambrito assemblage comprised predominantly skull and long-bone fragments. Turner and Morris (1970) plot element frequency for the Polacca Wash assemblage, noting the high incidence of cranial and scapular parts, and "suggesting some scavenger activity" (their Figure 1). They go on to explain the low frequency of vertebrae and pelves as follows: "They must have been carried away either by the assailants or by scavengers" (Turner and Morris, 1970:325). Nickens (1974, 1975) noted the disproportions in the 5MTUMR–2346 assemblage documented in Chapter 3, again suggesting that some body parts were left off-site.

Flinn *et al.* (1976) plot element frequency for the Burnt Mesa assemblage, noting the under-representation of pelvic portions and vertebrae. They attribute the lack of vertebrae, ribs, pelves, hand, and foot bones to their having been left outside, ". . . not, in general, brought in and subsequently deposited with the heads, arms, and legs. Clearly, this is suggestive of cannibalism" (Flinn *et al.*, 1976:313).

Luebben and Nickens (1982) note the low incidence or absence of postcranial material in the Grinnell assemblage. Nass and Bellantoni cite the latter two studies, and also note the relative scarcity of vertebrae, sacra, pectoral girdles, hands and feet, and sterni in the Monument Valley assemblage. They too suggest that these missing elements may have been left elsewhere, and imply that they are absent because of ". . . the difficulty of their dismemberment rather than initial carnivore activity or secondary burial" (Nass and Bellantoni, 1982:268). Turner (1983) compared identifiable skeletal elements in his sample of nine assemblages, finding differences among them in the degree to which various element groupings are preserved (his groupings are "skull, jaw"; "scapula, clavicle"; "vertebrae"; "rib, sternum"; "pelvis, sacrum"; "long bones"; "hand, foot, patella"; and "uncertain"). Turner (1983:232) reports Ash Creek to be low in skull and high in long-bone elements, Leroux Wash to be low in skull and vertebral elements, Monument Valley to be low in vertebral and long-bone elements, Mancos 5MTUMR–2346 to be low in skull, Burnt Mesa to be low in long-bone and high in skull, and Sambrito Village to be high in vertebrae. He goes on to note: "An unexplainable aspect of the mass burials is the marked deficiency of vertebral elements." Rice (1985) notes the under-representation of ribs, scapulae, clavicles, sacra, vertebrae, cranial bones, teeth, tarsals, metatarsals, carpals, metacarpals, and phalanges in the Ash Creek assemblage (Room 3, Tapia del Cerrito), attributing the abundance of limb elements to the taking of trophy limbs.

Malville (1989) cites the relative over-representation of atlas vertebrae and under-representation of thoracic and lumbar vertebrae and of the sternum, sacrum, and patellae in the Yellow Jacket 5MT–1 assemblage. For the nearby 5MT–3 assemblage, she notes that the most abundant element is the mandible, with under-representation of the sternum, sacrum, scapulae, ribs, patellae, and vertebrae. Grant (1989) notes under-representation of the bones of the spinal column, rib cage, pelves, hands, and feet in the Fence Lake assemblage. Finally, Villa *et al.* (1986a, 1986b) focus on bone modification rather than element representation in their analysis of the Fontbrégoua Cave human assemblage attributed to cannibalism. They do note a lack of most articular ends, however, suggesting that selected body parts were set aside for separate processing and consumption, thus being absent from the features excavated. Notable in their data is the under-representation of those elements that are also scarce in the Southwest assemblages described above.

Assessment of the relative proportions of element *portions* in the Southwestern human bone assemblages began with the work of Turner and Morris (1970), who observed a lack of articular ends in the Polacca assemblage. They concluded: "The second kind of damage to long bones (and irregular bones) is the cutting or breaking off distal and proximal ends, condyles, processes, and articular surfaces. This damage, while crude and perhaps due to inadequate tools or inaccurate knowledge of human anatomy, shows positively that the people had been dismembered . . .'' (Turner and Morris, 1970: 325). Nickens (1974, 1975) notes the lack of proximal and distal ends despite the large number of shaft splinters in the Mancos assemblage, and cites the Turner and Morris explanation. Malville (1989) describes the under-representation of vertebral bodies relative to arches and processes.

It is evident that the assemblages from the American Southwest that have been interpreted as evidence of cannibalism display dramatic element and element part disproportions, however measured. Similar disproportions are evident in a wide range of bone assemblages, and comparisons between the Mancos assemblage and a variety of other bone assemblages accumulated and modified by various agencies are appropriate.

Figure 12.7 summarizes the differential element representation in the Mancos assemblage. Elements with high TW representation values, however measured, include the femur, tibia, fibula, humerus, and mandible. With the exception of the mandible, these elements rank high because physical anthropological differentiation of even small shaft fragments of the limb bones was possible. Ranking below this are the radius, clavicle, and ulna. The lowest-ranking elements are, in contrast, the smallest (hand and foot intermediate and distal phalanges; tarsals, carpals), and least dense elements (sternum, vertebrae, patella).

Figure 12.15 compares relative element abundance for the Mancos and Yellow Jacket 5MT–3 assemblages using TW %NISP values. Data in this plot and the series of figures that follows in this chapter are derived from Table 12.4 or from

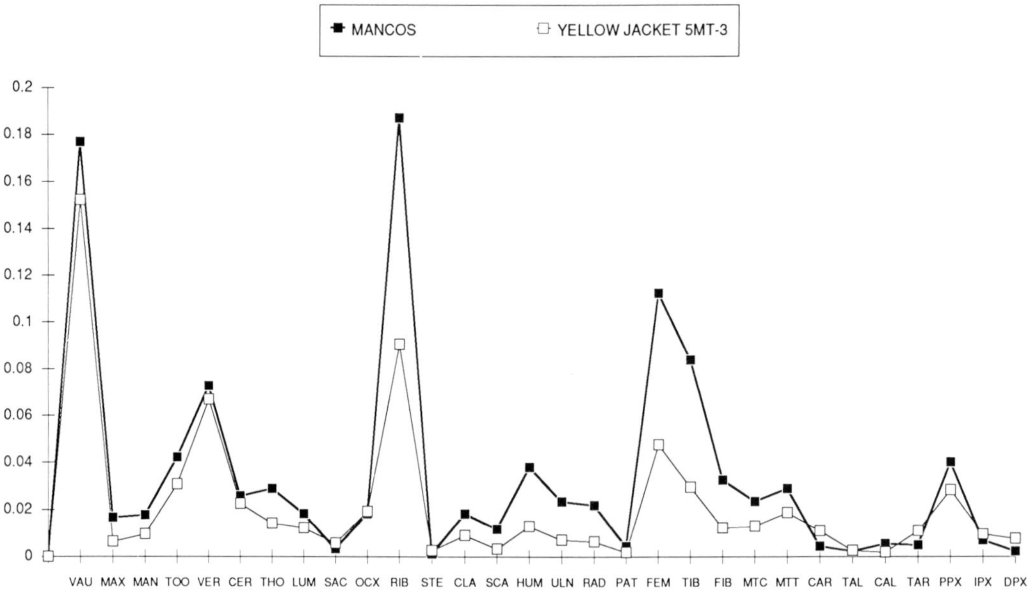

Fig. 12.15 Plot comparing relative skeletal element abundance for the Mancos 5MTUMR–2346 (TW NISP = 1871) and Yellow Jacket 5MT–3 (TW NISP = 1556) human bone assemblages using TW %NISP values. These values are indicated up the left vertical axis. Note the similar profiles of these two assemblages.

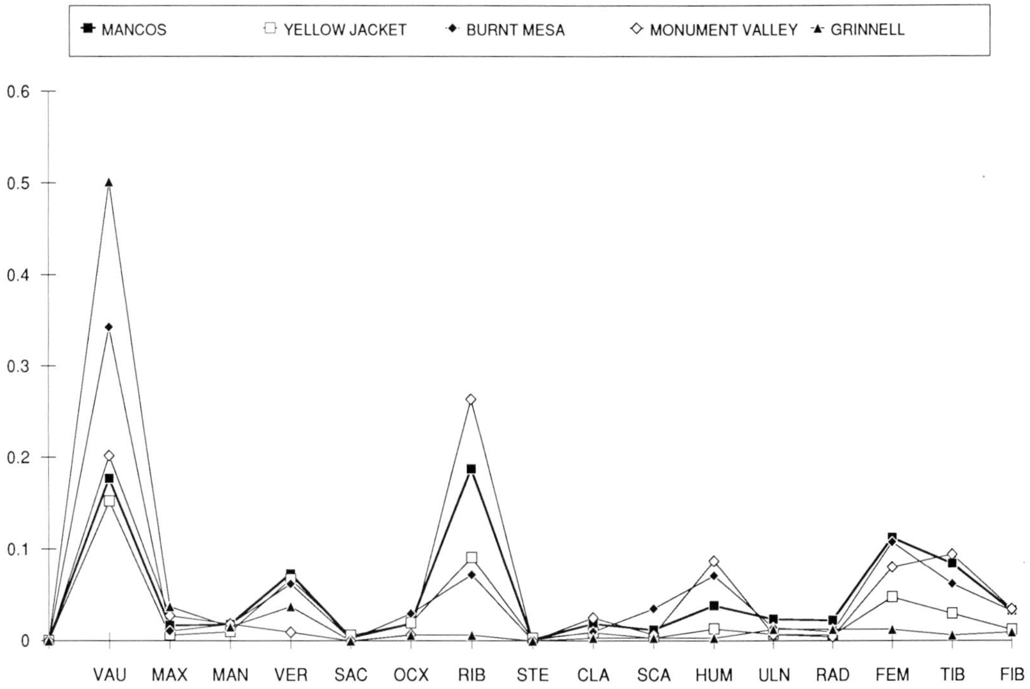

Fig. 12.16 Plot comparing relative skeletal element abundance for the Mancos 5MTUMR–2346 (TW NISP = 1871), Yellow Jacket 5MT–3 (TW NISP = 1556), Burnt Mesa (NISP = 1114), Monument Valley (NISP = 436), and Grinnell (NISP = 323) human bone assemblages using TW %NISP values. These values are indicated up the left vertical axis. Notable features of all these profiles include the large number of vault, rib, and femoral fragments. Also notable are the relative absence of specimens from the least dense elements, the sacra and sterna.

the assemblages described (with appropriate citations) in Table 12.1. Figure 12.16 uses the same values and incorporates data from the Burnt Mesa, Monument Valley, and Grinnell assemblages. Notable features of these %NISP profiles include the large number of vault, rib, and femoral fragments. Also notable is the relative absence of specimens from the least dense elements, the sacra and sterna. Figure 12.17 compares representation among various Southwest human bone assemblages based upon %MNI values. Here, the relative abundances noted above are also evident. The final graphic comparison between Southwest human bone assemblages that have been attributed to cannibalism is shown in Figure 12.18, which presents TW survival values by element. Again, as in the previous comparisons, mandibles, humeri, femora, and tibiae dominate, whereas vertebrae, sacra, and sternae are under-represented.

The comparisons presented above clearly demonstrate that the Mancos 5MTUMR–2346 assemblage closely matches other similar human bone assemblages from the American Southwest. In an effort to broaden the comparative base, the Mancos assemblage was compared with three other human bone assemblages. The first is a California archaeo-

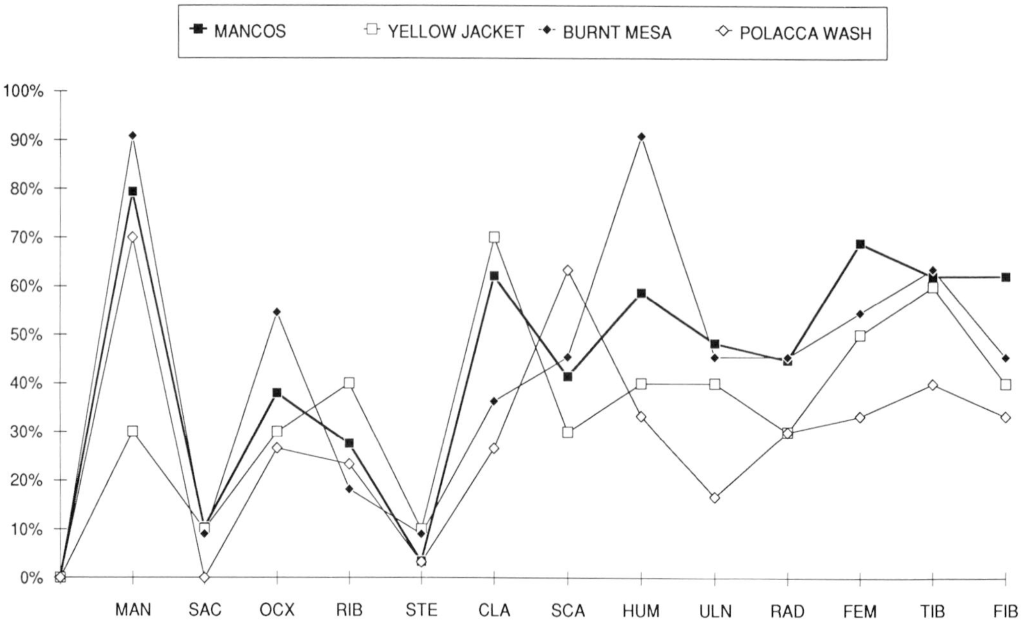

Fig. 12.17 Plot comparing %MNI values for skeletal elements in the 5MTUMR–2346 (TW MNI = 29), Yellow Jacket 5MT–3 (TW MNI = 10), Burnt Mesa (MNI = 10), and Polacca Wash (MNI = 30) human bone assemblages. The left vertical axis indicates the percentage of total assemblage MNI value that the by-element MNI values comprise.

logical cemetery population of 50 individuals (CCO–138). Burial of the 50 adults in a village midden was primary, and postdepositional disturbance by rodents was evident. Figure 12.19 shows some similarities between element representation profiles in a plot of TW %MNI, but the profiles are offset, with the cemetery population having a much greater average percentage representation. Broadening the perspective somewhat, Figure 12.20 compares the Mancos element representation with a modern forensic assemblage from the Pacific Northwest and two cemetery samples. These profiles are very disparate, another indication of the extreme disproportions seen in the Southwest assemblages. It is possible that the profile of the forensic assemblage might ultimately have come to more closely resemble the Mancos assemblage if the exposed skeletons had remained susceptible to continued scavenging by carnivores (particularly larger or more hungry carnivores).

This review indicates that the Southwest human assemblages described in Chapter 3 and detailed in Appendix 1 are similar in being characterized by element representations that depart strongly from what is ''expected'' based on representation in intact skeletons or skeletons derived from cemeteries. It is now appropriate to compare element representation in the Mancos assemblage with that expressed by a series of zooarchaeological faunal assemblages (Table 12.1).

Figure 12.21 compares the Mancos element representation profile with profiles

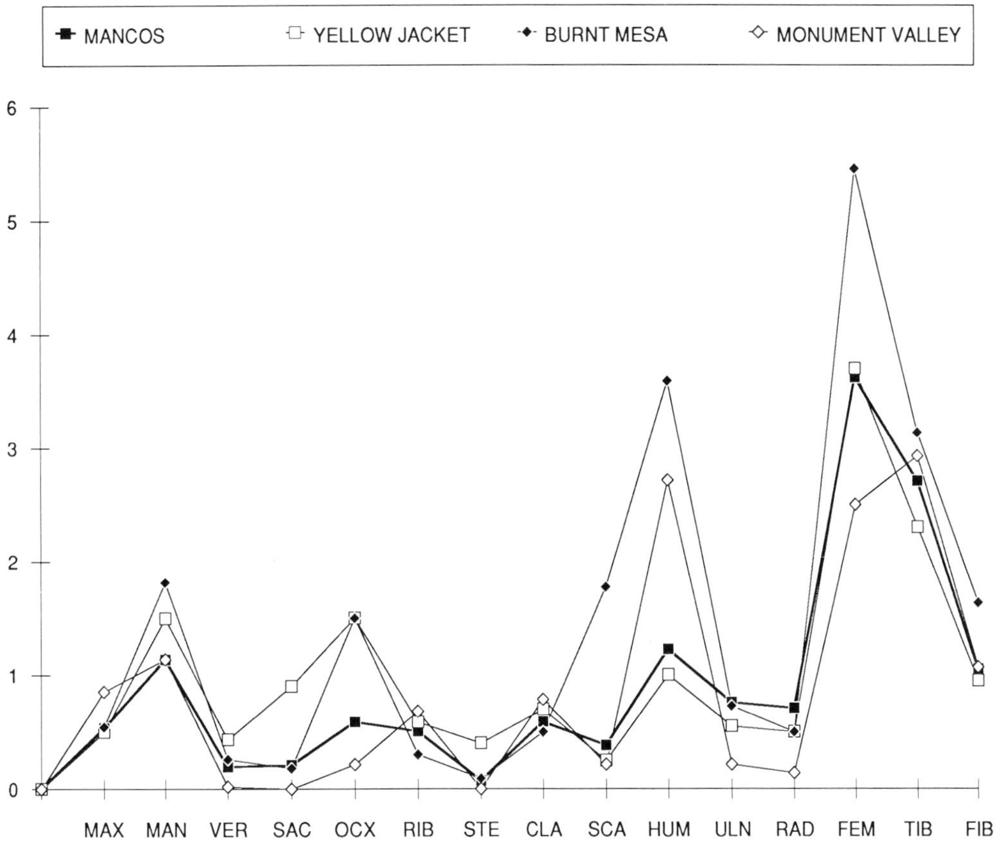

Fig. 12.18 Plot comparing TW survival values (on the left vertical axis) for various skeletal elements in the 5MTUMR–2346 assemblage with those from the Yellow Jacket 5MT–5, Burnt Mesa, and Monument Valley assemblages. Note the high representation of mandibles humeri, femora, and tibiae. Note the under-representation of vertebrae, sacra, and sternae.

of two roughly contemporary archaeological faunal samples from the Southwest, Guadalupe Ruin (NISP = 1,312, mostly deer, pronghorn, and bighorn sheep) and Antelope House (NISP = 503, mule deer). Survival profiles for these archaeological ungulate samples share a number of features with the Mancos assemblage profile. Vertebrae, ribs, patellae, carpals, and tarsals are notably under-represented in all three assemblages. Also notable is the great disparity between the Antelope House assemblage, where many limb elements have high survival values, and the Guadalupe Ruin assemblage, where the profile for postcranial elements more closely matches the Mancos assemblage. This comparison between Southwest nonhuman faunal assemblages and the Mancos 5MTUMR–2346 assemblage is continued in Figure 12.22. Here, the Mancos assemblage element representation profile is based on %NISP values in the Guadalupe Ruin, Antelope House, Emslie Man-

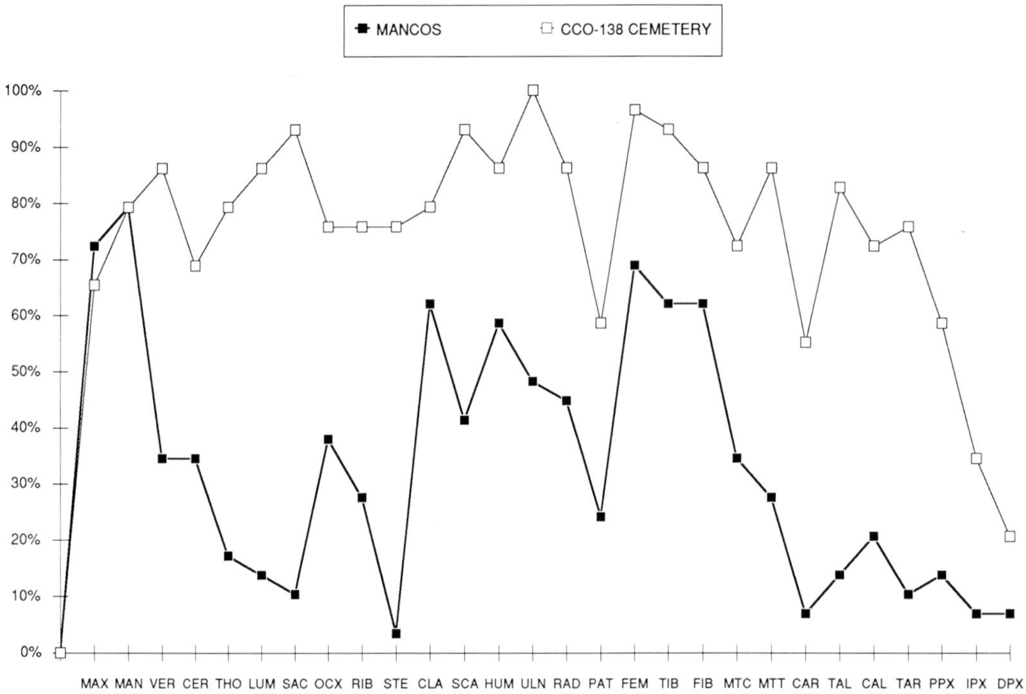

Fig. 12.19 Plot comparing TW %MNI values (on the left vertical axis) for various skeletal elements in the Mancos 5MTUMR–2346 and aboriginal Californian cemetery CCO–138 human bone assemblages. Note that the profiles are offset, indicating that much greater numbers of each element were present in the cemetery population, with over 80 percent of the expected elements appearing. Note also that most vertebrae, sacra, and sternae were recovered from the cemetery, unlike the situation for the Mancos assemblage.

cos, Badger House, and Converse assemblages. Relative to these assemblages, the Mancos assemblage has a high proportion of mandibular specimens and a low proportion of vertebral, scapular, and tibial specimens. The Mancos assemblage is not remarkable in the proportions of any of the other elements as measured by these %NISP values. Finally, Figure 12.23 compares element representation in the human bone assemblage with an extremely wide-ranging (spatially and temporally) set of zooarchaeological faunal assemblages (Table 12.1). The element representation profiles are broadly similar, characterized by highest survival of the mandibles and lowest survival of the vertebrae.

The descriptions of the Mancos 5MTUMR–2346 assemblage in Chapters 7 through 11 of this book go far toward explaining the human actions that resulted in the skeletal disproportions discussed here. Interpreting the disproportions to indicate off-site processing, trophy hunting, or other activities is probably unwarranted. Rather, the spongy bone portions are inferred to be "missing" from the Mancos assemblage because they were the focus of crushing activities by humans

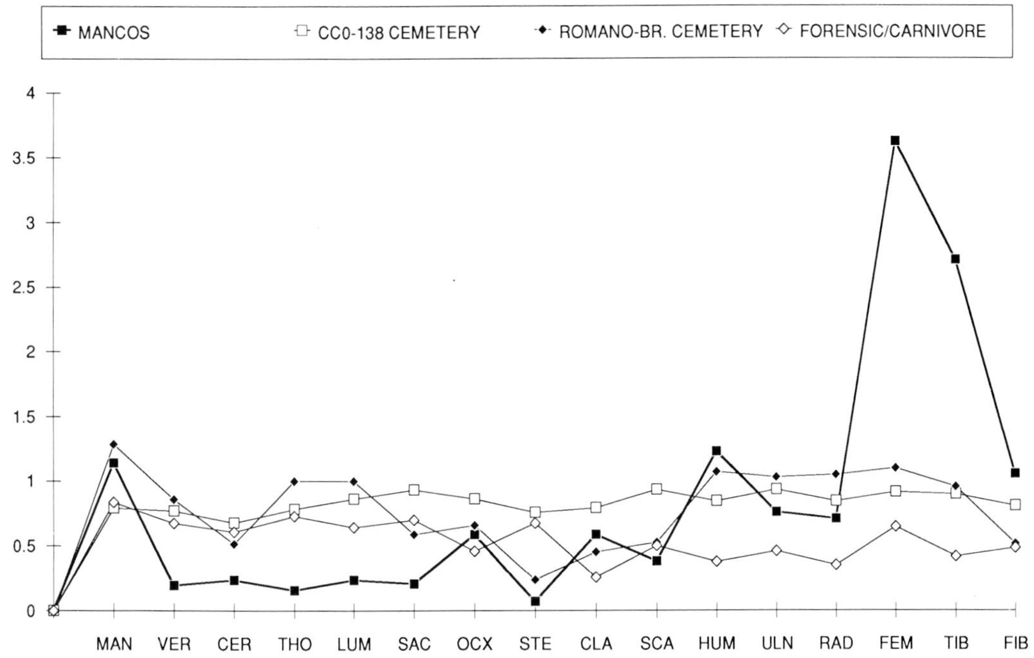

Fig. 12.20 Plot comparing TW survival values (on the left vertical axis) for various skeletal elements in the Mancos 5MTUMR–2346 assemblage and the CCO–138 and Romano-British cemetery populations. The forensic carnivore sample is from the remains of 37 carnivore-scavenged human individuals from the Pacific Northwest. For an assemblage comprising complete, intact skeletons, a single line crossing from left to right at the 1.0 value is expected. The cemetery populations follow this expectation fairly closely, the carnivore-scavenged assemblage departs from it to some degree, and the Mancos 5MTUMR–2346 assemblage shows an entirely different profile. Patterned element destruction is clearly indicated for the latter assemblage.

wielding hammerstones. This inference, however, does not explain why other element disproportions characterize this assemblage. For example, the 29 Mancos individuals were represented by 58 femoral shafts when alive. Estimates on how many shafts the available femoral fragments might make up are possible to make as follows. Assuming 15 fragments to each femoral shaft based on conjoining (see Chapter 4), 870 femoral splinters would be required to reconstruct the 58 indicated shafts. There are, maximally, only 438 available in the FEM and IP2, IP3, and IP4 categories. From these considerations, it is evident that at least half of the expected number of femoral shaft fragments of the 29 individuals represented in the assemblage are not accounted for. Another example of unexplained element disproportions may be found in the ribs, where 29 individuals would be expected to contribute 696 intact ribs. There are only 350 rib *fragments* in the Mancos assemblage. Explaining *these* disproportions is far more difficult than

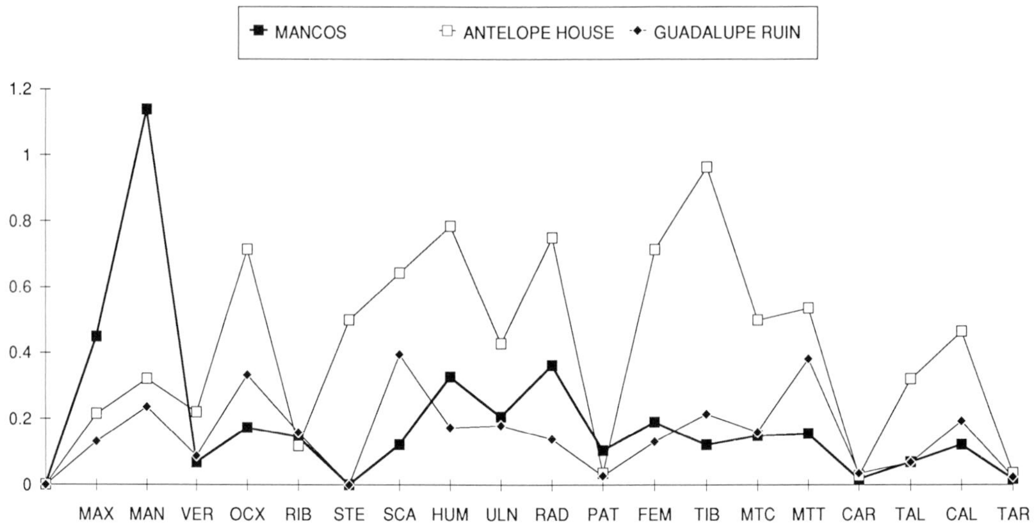

Fig. 12.21 Plot comparing the Mancos element representation profile with profiles of two roughly contemporary archaeological faunal samples from the Southwest, Guadalupe Ruin (NISP = 1,312, mostly deer, pronghorn, and bighorn sheep) and Antelope House (NISP = 503, mule deer). Survival values are indicated on the left vertical axis. Note that vertebrae, ribs, patellae, carpals, and tarsals are notably under-represented in all three assemblages. Note also the great disparity between the Antelope House assemblage and the Guadalupe Ruin assemblage, showing that there is not a single "pattern" of element representation in the Southwest, as judged from published data.

explaining the absence of spongy bone elements and element portions in the 5MTUMR–2346 assemblage.

Finally, following the spatially significant disproportions in the *ages* of individuals according to room (noted in Chapter 3), the evidence for spatially based disproportions among *elements* according to spatial provenance was examined. There appear to be no differentials in element representation by room in the Mancos pueblo.

Element disproportions in the Southwest human assemblages have been interpreted as a direct and exclusive result of human activity, but a wider perspective on the issue of element disproportions makes it clear that similar extreme disproportions are very common in ethnoarchaeological (Jones, 1984), carnivore-accumulated (Blumenschine, 1989), paleontological (Voorhies, 1969; Badgley, 1986b), and zooarchaeological assemblages (Bunn, 1982; Driver, 1984; Crader, 1984; Koch, 1986), where the agencies of bone modification differed dramatically. Identification of what agencies led to the disproportions may be investigated by examining the patterns of fracture, tool modification, chewing, and burning described in Chapters 7 to 11 and in the sections below. As Yellen (1977:328) recognized in an ethnoarchaeological context, "I am struck by the fact that interpretation based on the counting of anatomical parts provides the least

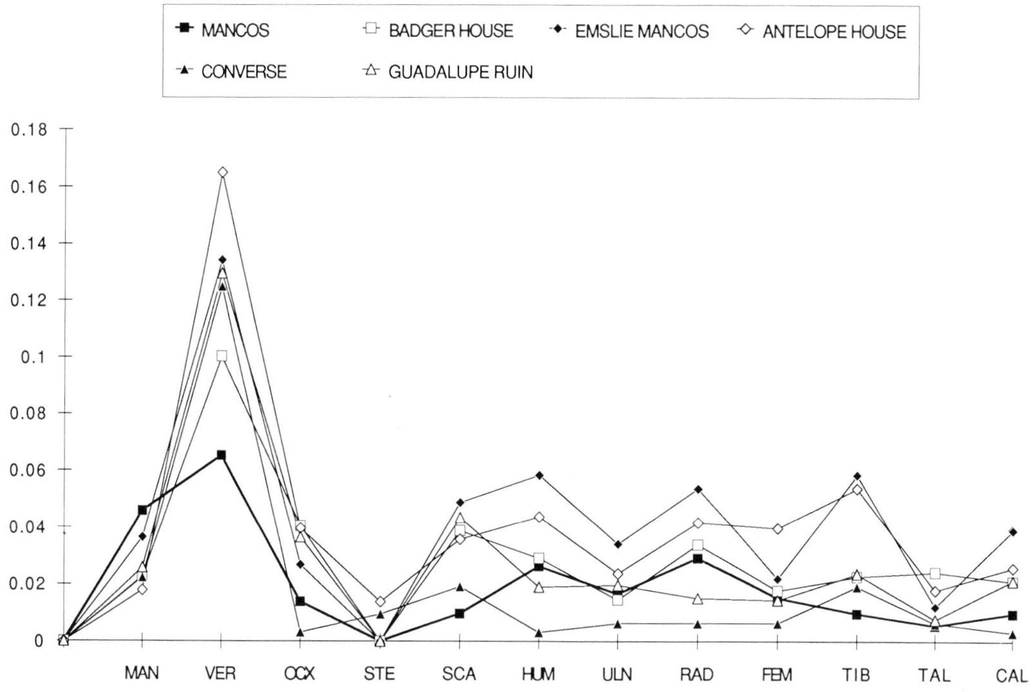

Fig. 12.22 Plot of element representation as measured by %NISP values for a series of Southwest zooarchaeological assemblages and the 5MTUMR–2346 human bone assemblage. The left vertical axis indicates %NISP values. Any interpretation of these profiles must consider that the values depend heavily upon the identification methodology used by the different faunal analysts involved in generating them. Nevertheless, the Mancos assemblage is characterized by disproportionately more mandibles and fewer scapulae and vertebrae than recorded in the faunal assemblages.

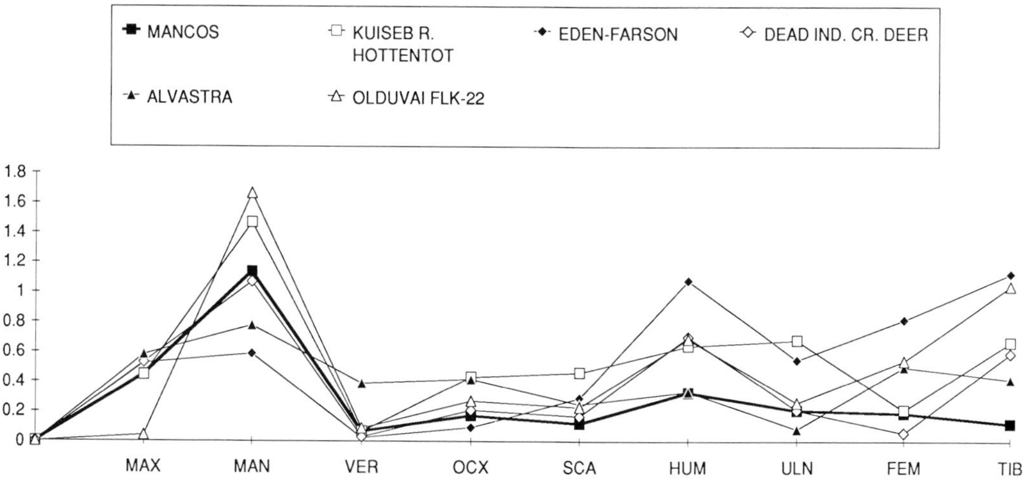

Fig. 12.23 Plot of element representation as measured by survival values for a series of ethnographic and archaeological faunal assemblages. Survival values are given on the left vertical axis. Note that all of these assemblages share with the Mancos assemblage the relatively high survival values for the mandible and relatively low survival values for the vertebrae, os coxae, and scapulae.

trustworthy information, while a more detailed analysis of the kind proposed here seems to yield not only more, but also more accurate, results.''

FRACTURE

Antiquity of Fracture

There is no evidence that bone fragmentation at Mancos 5MTUMR–2346 was the result of *in situ* fracture from sediment pressure or architectural collapse. In his initial report, Nickens (1974) noted the ''green'' fracture of bones in this assemblage. Fragmentation was judged to have been either predepositional or excavation-related. The latter fractures were readily distinguishable, and the Mancos assemblage, like most others, had its share of them. A total 494 of the 2,027 nontooth specimens showed evidence of modern fracture somewhere along the broken surfaces. This 24 percent figure is not an accurate reflection of overall fracture, however, because 353 of the 494 bones with evidence of modern fracture also show evidence of ancient fracture. Of the 2,027 Mancos specimens, 87 percent showed evidence of ancient fracture. Comparable figures for what Turner (1983) terms ''perimortem fracture'' lie between about 80 percent (Polacca Wash, Monument Valley) to near 100 percent (Leroux Wash, Burnt Mesa, etc.) among other human bone assemblages from the Southwest. The ''conservatism'' with which the investigator scores fracture as ancient or indeterminate, however, has total influence on these percentage values, making comparative results ambiguous. The most important conclusions about fracture antiquity relate to the fact that the overwhelming majority of bones comprising these assemblages were fractured before deposit and have been recovered from the encasing sediments largely intact.

Overall Completeness

Zooarchaeologists have recognized that the degree of fragmentation may provide clues to the means by which bone assemblages were generated. As an example of this line of examination, a recent ethnoarchaeological analysis demonstrated that only 10.4 percent of 2,800 mammal elements from one African campsite were complete (Gifford-Gonzalez, 1989a). Comparable data are rarely reported for archaeological assemblages, but in the Pueblo I, medium to large mammal subassemblage from Grass Mesa Village, 467 specimens were intact elements, 658 were one-third to two-thirds intact, and 5,986 were fragments representing less than a third of the original element (Neusius and Gould, 1988). Similar values are reported for the McPhee Community Cluster (Neusius, 1988). Among the Southwest human bone assemblages, it was the fragmentary nature of the bones found at various localities that originally led to the appreciation that these assemblages merited further examination. Sixty-seven years after the first of these assemblages was reported, Turner and Morris (1970) took steps to quantify this fragmentation, noting that the Polacca assemblage contained fewer than 10 percent unbroken specimens. Flinn, Turner and Brew (1976) noted that only 4 limb bones of the Burnt Mesa assemblage were intact. Nass and Bellantoni (1982), working with the Monument Valley assemblage, quantify ''whole'' versus ''fragment'' for various elements of the assemblage, and their data show that clavicles and hand and foot bones were most often preserved intact. These

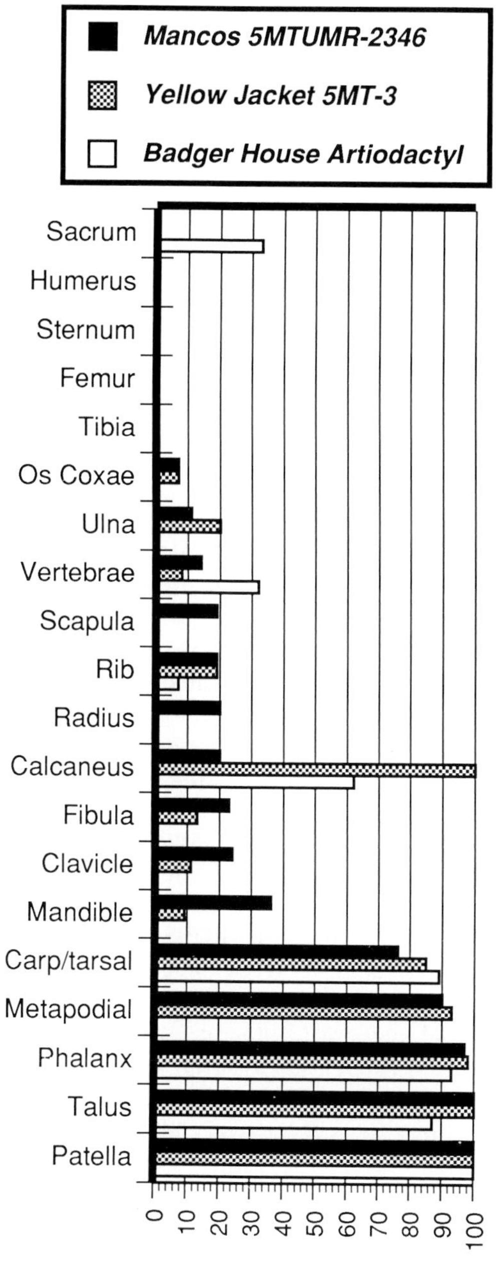

Fig. 12.24 Plot of "completeness" (percentage values) by element for two assemblages of human bones and the Badger House artiodactyl food remains. The relatively large number of complete vertebrae and calcanei and smaller numbers of complete metapodials in zooarchaeological remains of ungulates probably relate to the differences between artiodactyls and humans in the density of the former elements and to the fact that artiodactyl metapodials are anatomically (and nutritionally) very different from human ones.

authors note that the larger diameter limb bones (humerus, tibia, femur) were "severely fractured," whereas the radii, ulnae, and fibulae were "relatively undamaged."

To gain an approximation of how many and which elements were broken in the Mancos assemblage, elements were recorded as "W" when they were more than half complete (except for teeth). Crania in the Mancos assemblage were overwhelmingly fragmentary, as is the case for virtually all the other assemblages of human and zooarchaeological skeletal remains studied. Among the postcrania, elements that were relatively intact included only the patella and bones of the hand and foot. A very similar pattern of overall completeness is seen among both the Yellow Jacket 5MT–3 human bones and the ungulate remains from Badger House. Figure 12.24 illustrates this similarity. There are relatively larger numbers of complete vertebrae and calcanei and smaller numbers of complete metapodials in zooarchaeological remains of ungulates. These facts probably relate to the differences between artiodactyls and humans in the density of the former elements and to the fact that artiodactyl metapodials are anatomically (and nutritionally) very different from human ones.

Cranial Fracture

Bones of the human cranial vault are so different in size and shape from homologous bones of nonhuman mammals that qualitative and quantitative assessments are difficult. Jones (1983) notes that the modern Aché hunters of Paraguay opened all large vertebrate crania, juvenile cranial bones being disarticulated by prying the bones apart and adult crania being smashed from behind. The Badger House cranial bones were all fragmentary. The human bone assemblages from the American Southwest are noteworthy for the fact that the crania in them are universally fractured. In reporting on the faunal remains from Arroyo Hondo Pueblo, Lang and Harris (1984:132) state that "brain extraction was probably carried out on virtually all animals." Among the Mancos human vault bones, internal vault release was nearly six times more prevalent than external vault release, and disarticulation along the sutures was widespread. It may be inferred that the nutritious brain tissue was accessed by cranial vault fracture in all the taxa involved.

Vertebral Fracture

Mancos vertebral spines and arches usually lack attached bodies, which are generally missing except in some cervical specimens. The pattern of vertebral fracture is illustrated in Figure 12.25. Here, strong similarity between the Mancos vertebral assemblage fragmentation pattern (exclusive of atlas, axis, sacrum) and that of the Yellow Jacket 5MT–3 assemblage is seen. The Badger House vertebrae tend to be more complete, the bodies much more highly represented. This difference may be related to the relatively high density or low nutritive value of ungulate vertebrae, or to a difference in processing strategy. Despite the difference documented, the fact that bodies and arches are routinely separated from each other in these different assemblages is significant.

Rib Fracture

Turner and Morris (1970:327) described rib fragmentation in the Polacca Wash assemblage as one of the most unusual attributes of that assemblage, noting that the ribs were broken into "fragments of fairly uniform length, averaging about ten centimeters." They then compared this observation to others on ribs from Gran Quivira human skeletal remains (burials). They found that the Polacca fragments were shorter. They suggested that the Polacca Wash human ribs were intentionally fractured to fit in cooking vessels. This pattern of rib fragmentation is seen in a wide range of zooarchaeological remains.

Crader (1984) reports many rib heads and proximal shafts in the Chencherere Rockshelter ungulate remains, as does Losey (1973) in a historical archaeological context. Gilbert notes this pattern in River Basin Survey faunal remains (Gilbert, 1969). Binford (1984:120) describes rib fragmentation as follows:

> During my studies of hunting, butchering, and consumption of animal products by living peoples, I learned several things about breakage morphology and use of ribs. Most commonly the ribs are removed during initial field butchering as a unit—a rib slab—and this is accomplished by breaking the rib unit back or up against the vertebrae and then by cutting along the ventral surface of the broken ribs to free the slab from the vertebrae.

The functional account by Lang and Harris (1984:83), based on inferences from deer bone fragmentation at Arroyo Hondo, is also relevant in this regard:

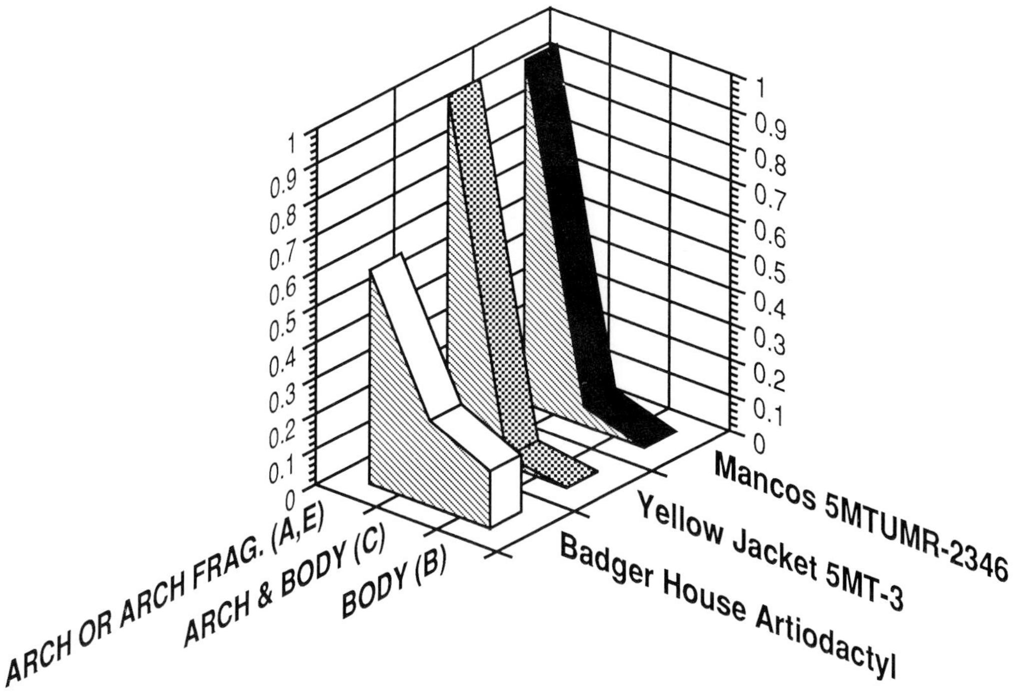

Fig. 12.25 Plot of vertebral portions preserved among the two human assemblages and the Badger House artiodactyl assemblage. Badger House ungulate vertebrae tend to be more complete, the bodies much more highly represented. This difference may be related to the relatively high density or low nutritive value of ungulate vertebrae, or to a difference in processing strategy. Note that bodies and arches were separated in all three assemblages.

> The remaining vertebral unit appears to have been detached from the rib cage by breaking through the ribs just below the articulation of the rib heads and thoracics. A similar procedure, possibly involving more cutting, apparently was applied to the breast zone, producing two large rib slabs, or racks, and a ventral thoracic cage, or breast unit. With this segmentation, primary butchering would have been completed.

Driver (1985), in another relevant archaeological context, provides quantification of the medium ungulates from the Phillips site, tabulating no complete ribs, 67 proximal rib ends, 38 distal rib ends, and 251 shaft fragments. This common pattern of rib fragmentation in archaeological assemblages is rarely quantified to this degree.

Patterns of rib fragmentation are illustrated in Figure 12.26. Here, the similarity between the Mancos and Yellow Jacket humans, and the Badger House artiodactyls is striking. All of the assemblages are dominated by specimens comprising less than half the shaft, and none of the assemblages have a significant number of intact ribs. Rather, fragments comprising either more than half of the shaft without the head, or a segment of the proximal end are the next most common

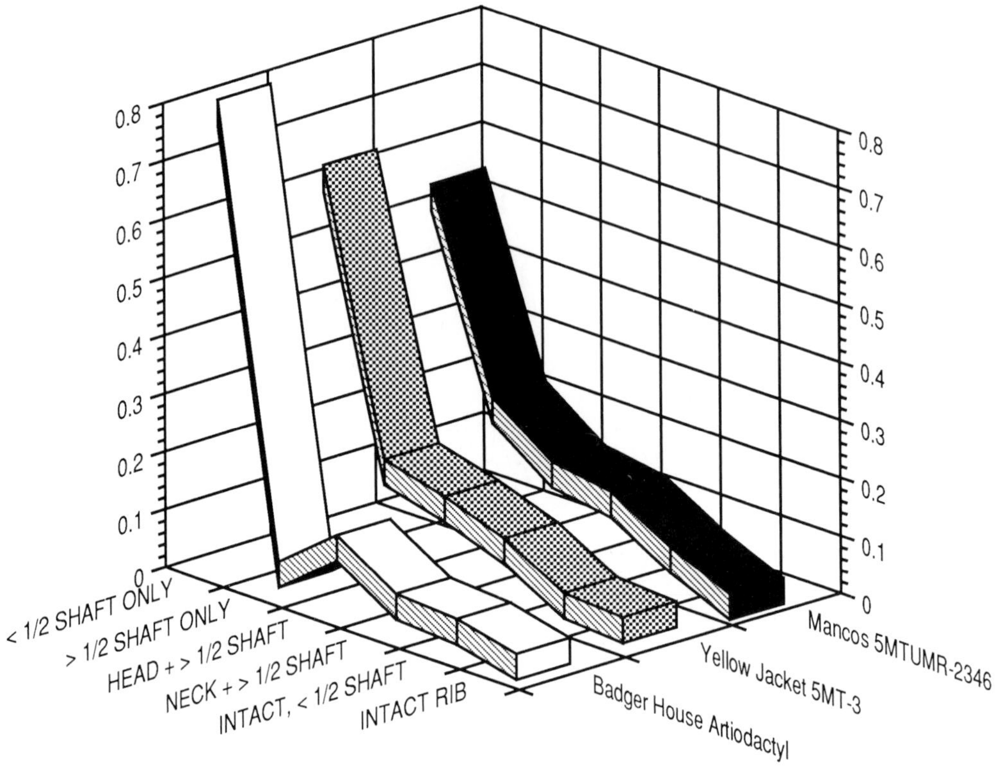

Fig. 12.26 Plot of rib fragmentation in the two human assemblages and the Badger House artiodactyl assemblage. All of the assemblages are dominated by specimens comprising less than half the shaft, and none of the assemblages have a significant number of intact ribs. See the text for an accounting for these parallels.

specimen types in all three assemblages. These data suggest that rib slabs were removed via leverage of the rib against the transverse process of the thoracic vertebrae, resulting in fracture of the rib near this point. Subsequent fracture of the rib shaft portions occurred in all three assemblages. It is not possible to determine the degree to which this reduction was intentionally aimed at producing fragments of uniform length.

Long-Bone Shaft Fracture

Quantification of the degree to which long-bone shafts are broken open has been attempted by Jones (1983). For the Aché hunters of Paraguay, Jones found that long-bone shafts containing less than 1 ml of marrow cavity were left unopened, whereas 65% of bones with 1 to 3 ml of space were opened and all bones with a greater marrow cavity volume were fractured. The Aché chewed the small bone ends off and sucked marrow out, leaving a cylindrical tube. Thus, for monkey bones, there were 94% tubular shafts. For the larger deer long bones, there were only 11% tubular shafts; the remaining shafts were broken open.

In archaeological contexts, it is often the case that larger limb-bone shaft fragments from medium- to large-sized ungulates are not found intact except at some kill and butchery sites. Bunn (1983, 1989) and Potts (1988) have attempted to quantify the fragmentation of limb-bone shafts. For example, for the FLK "Zinj" assemblage, Potts finds 12 cylinders among 894 long-bone specimens, concluding that a high frequency of cylinders, especially when coupled with low numbers of isolated articular ends, is "a clear indication of carnivore activity" (p. 124). Furthermore, Bunn (1989) notes higher degrees of limb-bone shaft fragmentation in African hunter-gatherer and archaeological assemblages compared to modern large carnivore accumulations.

For the Mancos assemblage, long-bone shafts were overwhelmingly represented by splinters. The best way to gain an appreciation of how shaft diameter correlates with fracture is to compare visually the Mancos femur subassemblage (Figures 10.1, 10.3, and 12.5) with the fibula subassemblage (Figure 10.21). Across the entire Mancos limb-bone assemblage, large diameter human limb-bone shafts are fragmented, whereas small diameter ones are not. For example, metatarsals, metacarpals, and phalanges account for 160 of the 223 recorded adult Mancos specimens with complete shaft circumferences. These long bones have short lengths and small midshaft diameters. Clavicles, ulnae, radii, and fibulae account for an additional 54 of the specimens, whereas the only 9 recorded specimens of humerus, femur, and tibiae retain intact shaft circumferences despite the greater bending strengths of these elements. Among 695 long-bone splinters representing sections of shaft in the Mancos assemblage, only 10.4 percent had complete circumferential enclosure of the medullary cavity anywhere along the shaft. This typical pattern of fragmentation, inferred to result from percussion-generated fracture directed at obtaining marrow from the larger limb bones, is also present in the Yellow Jacket 5MT–3 human and Badger House artiodactyl assemblages.

Fracture Surface Topography

Many investigators have called attention to the different kinds of topographies that characterize the broken ends of limb-bone shafts. Fracture patterns were scored for the Mancos long bones as described in Chapter 6. Of the 180 fracture surfaces so quantified among the limb bones (but not splinters), a dominance of "irregular" fractures was found. "Irregular" topographies comprised 81.1 percent of these fractures, followed by "irregular spiral" at 8.8 percent, "typical spiral" at 5.0 percent, "double-V" at 2.8 percent, and "typical perpendicular" at 1.7 percent. "Spiral" fractures, as least as defined here, are not dominant in this subassemblage.

Outer Conchoidal Scars

Only 9 specimens showed this damage in the Mancos assemblage. These were splinters, 5 from femora, three from tibiae, and one from an ulna.

Inner Conchoidal Scars

Evidence for percussion fracture of the Mancos limb bones is found in the presence of conchoidal scars located primarily on the medullary surface of long-bone cortices. Dittert *et al.* (1966) reported the presence of "impact percussion scars" for the Sambrito human bone assemblage, and Nickens (1974, 1975) recognized similar features for the Mancos assemblage. Villa *et al.* (1986a) report inner conchoidal scars on 20.7 percent of the postconjoined human long-bone fragments at Fontbrégoua.

Quantification of inner conchoidal scars is not widely reported in zooarchaeology, and among the best data are Binford's (1981) for the Nunamiut. Binford concludes that attention to a combination of the disposition and frequency of these scars, and to the gross breakage morphology of the bones, should elucidate the overall marrow-bone-breakage tactics evidenced by any assemblage. He reports percentages of these scars ranging from 14 to 17% on the bone splinters for six marrow-cracking experiments.

In the Mancos assemblage, 2.6 percent of 2,027 nontooth specimens exhibited internal conchoidal scars. These scars averaged 16.9 mm in diameter (range = 2–35 mm; a reminder that the mere dimensions of these features are unlikely to sort carnivore from hammerstone damage). Average thickness of bone associated with the scars was 3.4 mm. The total Yellow Jacket 5MT–3 human assemblage showed 2.4 percent of all specimens with inner conchoidal scars, and the Badger House artiodactyl assemblage showed 3.6 percent. Of the 51 adult Mancos specimens retaining this damage, 84.3 percent belonged to the tibia or femur, and 36 of these specimens showed only one scar (10 specimens showed 2 scars and 5 showed 3 scars). Similar distributions by element were observed in both the Yellow Jacket 5MT–3 and Badger House assemblages. Of the 561 adult bone "splinters" from the humerus, femur, tibia, IP2, and IP3 element categories of the Mancos 5MTUMR–2346 assemblage, 8.4 percent bore internal conchoidal scars.

Adhering Flakes

Adhering flakes were identified on 2.1 percent of the total Mancos nontooth assemblage. Analogous percentages for the Yellow Jacket 5MT–3 human and Badger House artiodactyl assemblages are 1.5 and 2.0 percent, respectively. When these flakes are examined among adult specimens on an element-by-element basis, it is evident that they are concentrated on the femur and tibia in all three assemblages. The percentage of specimens in the humerus + femur + tibia + IP2 + IP3 subassemblage at Mancos is 5.4 percent, whereas analogous values for Yellow Jacket 5MT–3 humans and Badger House artiodactyls are 6.5 and 4.4 percent, respectively.

Crushing

The incidence of crushing on a total nontooth assemblage basis is heavily dependent on the element and element portion composition of the assemblage. This is because this damage is most often observable in areas where the outer cortex of the bone is underlain by spongy bone that cushions the crushing blow and "suspends" the outer table that is crushed inward. Binford (1981) calculated the frequency of crushing ("depressed margins") among three populations of marrow-cracked bones collected among the Nunamiut, finding 23 percent in this sample of 206 specimens. In the total Mancos nontooth assemblage, crushing is observed on 16.4 percent of all specimens. Analogous values for Yellow Jacket 5MT–3 humans and Badger House artiodactyls are 13.3 and 4.7 percent, respectively. The low value for the artiodactyl remains may be related to a difference in processing strategy or to the higher density of articular ends of long bones and of vertebral bodies among these mammals compared to human bones. Another confounding factor may be the influence of carnivores at Badger House (expected to ravage already "crushed" ends and delete or modify the attribute). These possibilities are further discussed in the concluding chapter. In the Mancos assemblage, crushing is most common among axial elements and on bones of the hand and foot.

Peeling

The phenomenon of peeling has not been quantified elsewhere in the literature. In the Mancos assemblage, 6.8 percent of all specimens exhibit peeling. In the Yellow Jacket 5MT–3 human assemblage, this percentage is 5.6 percent, whereas in the Badger House artiodactyl assemblage, the value for peeling for the entire assemblage is 4.5 percent. In all three assemblages, peeling is focused on the axial parts of the postcranial skeleton, with 58.0 percent of all peeling in the Mancos assemblage confined to the ribs and vertebrae. This simply reflects the fact that fracture of these elements is more likely to be accompanied by peeling because of the bone structure.

Splinter Size

A variety of investigators have used data on long-bone splinter lengths to document or draw inferences about recent, paleontological, and archaeological bone assemblages (Brain, 1969b, 1975b, 1981; Fiorillo, 1988; Ghaleb, 1983). Whereas some investigators conclude that carnivore-accumulated assemblages are likely to have a larger proportion of longer bone fragments, Koch (1986) concludes that bone fragment length is of no value for determining the agents of fragmentation. When coupled with the fact that recovery technique has a strong bias on any distribution of fragment lengths in an archaeological bone assemblage, and with the observation that human long bones are of substantially different proportions than those of ungulates, it is evident that splinter length analysis is of little comparative value for this assemblage. It is important to note, however, that the high length to breadth values of complete human limb-bone shafts are predicted to make even midshaft *splinters* stand out as identifiable among midshaft splinters of artiodactyl bone.

Fracture Summary, with Comments on Marrow and Bone Grease Production

In *Homo sapiens*, as in other mammals, marrow functions as an organ in fat storage and hemopoetic potential. The distribution of this tissue, however, makes the study of marrow difficult. There are two kinds of marrow in humans: yellow (or fatty) marrow and red (or hemopoetic) marrow. Tavassoli and Yoffey (1983) suggest that red and fatty marrow each comprise approximately 2 percent body weight in adult humans.

The recognition by Lee (1979), Hayden (1981), and others that fatty tissue was a highly prized commodity among extant hunter-gatherers has been followed by the archaeological consideration of zooarchaeological remains from new perspectives (Speth, 1983, 1989, 1990; Speth and Spielmann, 1983). Limb bones of healthy, fat organisms represent reservoirs of fatty marrow tissue that are widely exploited for their contents. Bonnichsen and Will (1980) note that fatty marrow is the most concentrated energy source in the human diet, with the highest caloric value of any food.

The exploitation of bones for their marrow leaves osseous evidence in the form of element and element part disproportions and bone modifications. Ethnographic accounts show that marrow was regularly exploited among Australians (Spencer, 1896; Basedow, 1904; Sweeney, 1947; McArthur, 1960; Abbie, 1969), with bones being cracked open ''often enough by the teeth'' (Solomon, 1985:70). Tomita (1966) and O'Connell *et al.* (1988) note that the Hadza regularly crack ungulate long-bone shafts to gain access to marrow. Similar, older ethnohistorical accounts are known from all continents.

Accounts from Australia indicate that mammalian bones, particularly vertebrae, were regularly pulverized for direct consumption (Archer, 1977; Gould, 1980). Campbell (1939:13) reports such bone-eating behavior among native Australians as follows:

> During or after the cooking of a large animal, it is a common sight to see the natives breaking up with a stone pieces of bone—particularly the long bones—in order to extract the marrow, and in this process fragments of actual bone are also consumed. . . . This bone-eating habit, besides providing vigorous exercise for their teeth, no doubt has its value as a nutritional intake.

Binford (1987b) contends that this processing is the functional equivalent to the processing of bones for bone grease. Among the Southern Paiute, ''knee'' and ''ankle'' joints were pounded into a kind of food (Kelly, 1964). O'Connell *et al.* (1988) observed the Hadza gouging out and eating the cancellous bone in articular ends of ungulate limb bones. Brain (1969b, 1976) reports that the Hottentots regularly fracture goat limb bones for marrow and chew the spongy ends off. These behaviors contradict Blumenschine's (1986) and Speth's (1989) contention that many skeletal elements bear such small quantities of grease that they were not exploited before the late advent of grease-rendering technology in the form of fire and boiling containers. Furthermore, direct consumption of crushed spongy bone has important archaeological implications outlined in the concluding chapter.

In northern latitudes, the rendering of grease contained in bone tissue is documented for a variety of native people (Kehoe, 1967), including Laplanders (Lubbock, 1865), the Loucheux of Old Crow (Leechman, 1951), the Blackfeet (Leechman, 1951), the Kutenai and Omaha (Wheat, 1972), the Calling Lake Cree (Zierhut, 1967; Bonnichsen, 1973), the Tarahumara (Pastron, 1974), and other indigenous people (Peale, 1871; Vehik, 1977; Yesner and Bonnichsen, 1979). The rendered fat was often used in the production of pemmican (Reeves, 1990). Perhaps the best ethnographic description of grease rendering from the bones of large mammals is Binford's (1978:158) account of the associated activities among the Nunamiut. Here, for caribou bones, ''The procedure is to place an articulator end on the anvil and hold it with one hand while delivering a series of light blows aimed at crushing the outer surface of the articulator end. . . . Once the bone is seated heavy blows are delivered until the articulator end is pulverized into tiny chunks of bone tissue.'' The resulting pulverized bone mass and fragments are boiled in water to release the grease, which floats to the top of the container and may be skimmed off.''

Hurlburt's (1977) assessment of the faunal remains from the Hudson's Bay Company's Fort White Earth site in Canada notes the intensive fragmentation of bones, citing a variety of contemporary reports on aboriginal grease extraction and pemmican production. Walker's (1983) assessment of another fur trading post in northwestern Colorado draws similar conclusions from the historical archaeological bone assemblage recovered. The prehistoric archaeological manifestations of grease-rendering activity takes the form of stone boiling pits associated with scattered broken bones (Frison, 1978). Evidence of grease rendering is reported by Frison (1971) at the Eden-Farson site in the Upper Green River Basin of Wyoming. Frison attributes the lack of proximal humeri and proximal and distal femora in this antelope assemblage (representing more than 200 individuals from 12 lodges) to the destruction of these skeletal element portions during muscle removal. It is more likely that these spongy bone portions were deleted by the kind of processing activities described above. Davis and Fisher (1990:269) describe a similar occurrence at the Lost Terrace site of Montana, attributing the intensive processing-related damage they document on the antelope remains to "an unusual food shortage, probably in conjunction with severe winter weather." McKee (1988) reports evidence of the same activity on bison bones from the River Bend site, as does Wheat (1972, 1978, 1979) for the Paleoindian Olsen-Chubbuck and Jurgens sites. Yesner and Bonnichsen (1979) report similar findings for the caribou bones at Paxson Lake.

In the Southwest, there are fewer references to archaeological evidence of grease processing. Driver (1985) states that there is little evidence of this activity in the Sierra Blanca region because most long-bone ends exist as whole or large pieces. Lang and Harris (1984:84), however, note ". . . general battering of some highly cancellous epiphyses to expose the spongy bone containing red marrow . . ." on the artiodactyl remains from Arroyo Hondo. Young's (1980) work on the Tijeras Canyon artiodactyl remains postulates fragmentation and boiling of artiodactyl remains. Emslie (1977) illustrates deer remains from Mancos Canyon site 5MTUMR–2785 that have clear evidence of crushing of the humeral heads (his Figure 15).

Investigators of the assemblages of scattered and broken human bone from the Southwest have long noted the extensive fragmentation and disproportions among skeletal elements. Turner and Morris drew the analogy to cooking in ceramic vessels in 1970, but other investigators have been struck by the extreme fragmentation seen in the human remains. For example, Nass and Bellantoni (1982:268) ask ". . . why was it necessary to break the long bones into such small fragments to extract the marrow? . . . Less violence to those bones would have been sufficient for the same results." Malville (1989) suggested that the absence of cancellous elements among the Yellow Jacket human remains hinted at the possibility of bone grease rendering. In the Mancos assemblage, the patterns of element representation, the extensive evidence of percussion, and the signature of pot polish all warrant the inference that bone grease was rendered from the human remains in question.

Fragmentation of the Mancos assemblage of human bones closely follows what has been observed in many archaeological contexts. The fracture patterns are similar to those described for other human and nonhuman assemblages in the Southwest. Figure 12.27 summarizes data on "completeness," inner conchoidal scars, adhering flakes, and peeling in the human bone assemblages from Mancos 5MTUMR–2346 and Yellow Jacket 5MT–3, and in the artiodactyl assemblage from Badger House. The fracture-related attributes and their frequencies are very similar for these assemblages, suggesting that the bones of the skeletons were processed in similar manners.

TOOL MODIFICATION

Polish

As discussed and documented experimentally in Chapter 6, polish on the Mancos

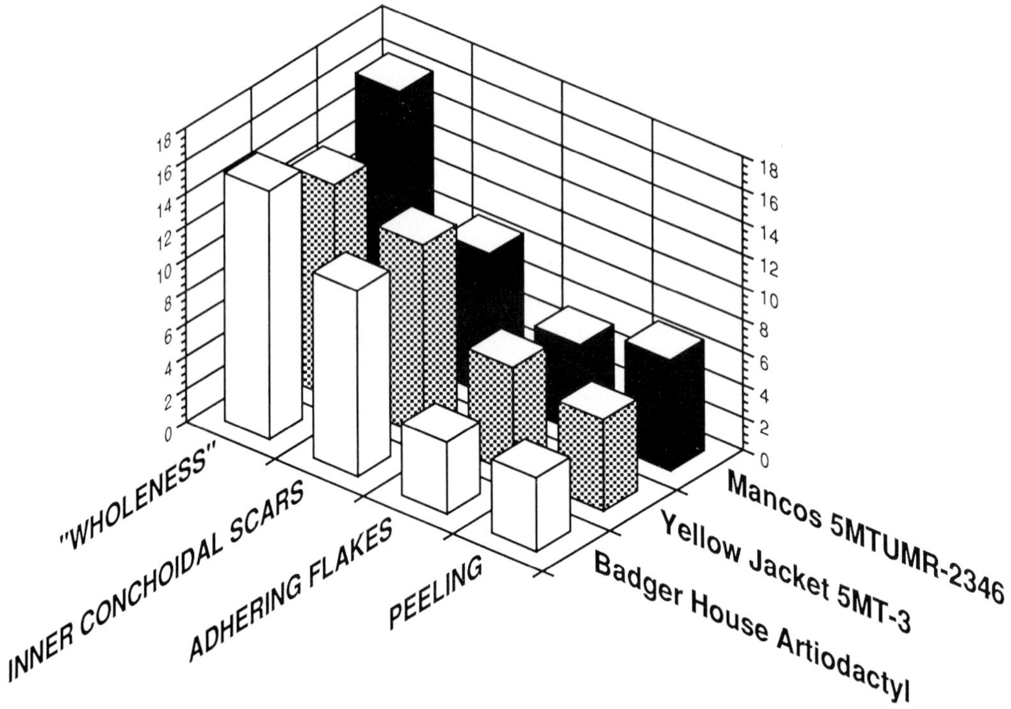

Fig. 12.27 Plot summarizing fragmentation patterns (percentage of specimens exhibiting each "modification") on the two human bone assemblages and the Badger House artiodactyl bone assemblage. This comparison is controlled for taxonomic differences by plotting only major limb elements (HUM + FEM + TIB + IP2 + IP3). Note the similar profiles.

assemblage is overwhelmingly confined to pot polish, damage manifested by the rounded and/or beveled ends of broken bones that are inferred to have been modified through contact with the inner walls of ceramic vessels. As noted in Chapter 6, it is possible that some analysts might have interpreted specimens here called pot-polished as intentionally or ''expediently'' made bone tools. A variety of polished bones have, at one time or another, been described as bone tools (Johnson, 1980; Brain, 1981a, 1989; Harrison and Medway, 1962; Sohn, 1988; Shipman *et al.* 1984), and some of these were undoubtedly intentionally modified by humans. Shipman and Rose (1988) note that carnivores, wind, water, and/or hominid use can all polish bone surfaces. Lyman (1984a) points out that context and modification are the two lines of evidence most important in identifying bone tools, and Binford and Stone (1987) provide a concise discussion on the recognition of bone tools. Turner's (n.d.:2) report on the Marshview Hamlet assemblage states that ''. . . very minor polishing of a few bone splinter tips may represent reaming activity, although post-excavational cleaning and handling might also have caused it.'' Malville (1989) reports a limb-bone shaft splinter modified as an awl from the 5MT–3 assemblage. She interprets the specimen as human.

Polished specimens from the Mancos assemblage are described and illustrated in some detail in Chapter 6. As noted there, the extent of this damage ranges across a continuum and any quantification of the attribute therefore depends entirely upon recognition threshold. For this reason, and until more work is done on this newly recognized bone modification, the *establishment* of this damage in an assemblage is probably far more significant than differences in the number of specimens so damaged. Even if more precise quantification of pot polish becomes possible, the degree of modification in any set of specimens will depend entirely upon the period of time during which bones are circulated in the vessel and how much they were agitated. The identification threshold for pot polish used in the analysis of the Mancos assemblage was fairly high (the author was conservative in making positive attributions). A total of 121 (6.0%) Mancos specimens with pot polish were identified out of the total 2,027 nontooth specimens in the assemblage. The Badger House totals were 100 of 749 (13.3%), but it is possible that the author's identification threshold was not so conservative for the artiodactyl remains. To better control the comparison between the artiodactyl and human assemblages, subassemblages of specimens from the major limb bones (humerus, femur, tibia, IP2, IP3) of the two assemblages were assessed. This comparison shows that 60.0 percent of the Badger House artiodactyl bone pot polish and 58.3 percent of the Mancos human bone pot polish were confined to these elements, mostly the splinter tips. Most of the other pot polish was concentrated on the broken rib ends in each assemblage. The Yellow Jacket 5MT–3 assemblage was not scored for pot polish.

Cutmarks

Cutmarks have long been recognized as human-induced bone modifications that can be quantified. Much of this quantification has recently been inspired by the ongoing debate over hominid behaviors in the late Pliocene (Binford, 1981; Bunn, 1982; Bunn and Kroll, 1986, 1988; Shipman, 1986; Lyman, 1987c; Gifford-Gonzalez, 1989b). Explanations of cutmark frequencies have often led investigators to novel conclusions. One investigator noted that low cutmark frequencies in Pliocene assemblages might result from *Homo habilis* butchers being particularly skilled in avoiding marking the bones with their stone tools (cited in LeMoine and MacEachern, 1983)! Another investigator, explaining the perceived low cutmark frequency in zooarchaeological deer remains from the Southwest, suggested that deer were hunted for raw material "rather than as items of consumption" (Olsen, 1980:275).

Cutmark quantification takes many forms, and there is a complex host of key postdiscard variables lurking behind reported cutmark "totals" for bone assemblages (to say nothing of prediscard variables such as experience of the butcher [Haynes, 1987], and the degree to which articular ends and their disarticulation cutmarks have been destroyed subsequent to cutmarking during the butchery process). The preservational characteristics of the bone surfaces, the fragmentation of the various elements, the presence or absence of shafts versus ends, the extent of rodent and/or carnivore chewing, the recognition criteria and thresholds used by the investigator, the recording procedures (whether the *total number* of marks or the number of specimens *with* marks is recorded), the lighting conditions and pace of analysis, the experience of the investigator, and the amount of percussion-related damage all carry the potential to influence reported cutmark frequencies.

Cutmark frequencies are reported for total assemblages, taxonomic subassemblages, and element subassemblages. Cutmark frequencies at Paleolithic sites include the values of 0.3 percent for 4,483 horse bones from Solutré, and 8.1 percent of reindeer bones from the same site (Olsen, 1989); 3.4 percent of 2,500 Olduvai Bed I bovid limb bones (Shipman, 1986); and 6.2 percent of 3,500 identifiable bones from Olduvai FLK ''Zinj'' (Bunn and Kroll, 1986). More recent zooarchaeological assemblages yield a comparable range of values, with 9.8 percent of the identifiable Ngamuriak specimens (Marshall, 1986a, 1986b); 4.0 percent of 355 identifiable Mufule Rock Shelter specimens (Gutin and Musonda, 1985); and 2.8 percent of Elmenteitan bones at Masai Gorge Rockshelter (Gifford-Gonzalez, 1985) showing these marks. The highest overall cutmark frequencies are reported from ethnoarchaeological studies, with 23 percent of 209 bones of deer butchered by the Aché (Jones, 1984); 31 percent of 83 bones of zebra butchered by the Dassanetch (Gifford-Gonzalez, 1989a); and 26.4 percent of 600 bones butchered by the San (Bunn, 1983). In Southwest zooarchaeology, cutmark frequencies reported for various large mammal subassemblages include 1 percent of 476 large mammal bones from Prairie Dog Hamlet (Emslie, 1986); 1.2 percent of the 17,236 bones at Grass Mesa Village (Neusius and Gould, 1988); 6 percent among deer bones from Grasshopper Pueblo (Olsen, 1980); and 7.0 percent of the 2,060 identifiable large mammal fragments from the McPhee Community Cluster (Neusius, 1988). Comparison between the large ungulates most often used in cutmark quantification studies and the human remains studied here is problematical for two reasons. First, the soft tissue anatomy differs substantially between humans and ungulates. Second, the lack of substantial hair across much of the human body is very different from the situation seen in other mammals, and it is possible that this difference may reflect itself in elevated or depressed cutmark frequencies.

Total assemblage cutmark frequencies have been summarized by Turner (1983) for many of the assemblages of broken, scattered human bones interpreted as evidence of cannibalism in the American Southwest. Overall cutmark frequencies in these assemblages as reported by Turner and others are provided in Table 12.5. The average overall assemblage value of 2.9 percent cutmarked specimens tabulated by Turner is well below the values observed for the Badger House artiodactyls (7.8%) and the Mancos 5MTUMR–2346 assemblages. Differentials in preservation, observational criteria, and recovery of tiny bone fragments probably combine to produce these differences. The very high value of 24 percent for the Emslie Mancos Canyon artiodactyl assemblage undoubtedly relates to the fact that this total was generated after only considering larger, identifiable specimens. This high percentage is thus inflated relative to the other values reported in Table 12.5. The reported cutmark values of 45.6 percent and 30.3 percent for two human bone lots from Fontbrégoua (Villa *et al.*, 1986a) are not approached among the other assemblages. Because the Fontbrégoua data represent postrefitting values, they are also likely to be inflated relative to other assemblages where cutmark values are recorded before refitting.

The variation seen in the values reported in Table 12.5 may be attributable to actual differences in defleshing and dis-

Table 12.5

ASSEMBLAGE	*TOTAL SPECIMENS*	*PERCENTAGE CUTMARKED*	*REFERENCE*
Sambrito Village (human)	474	4.6%	Turner (1983)
Burnt Mesa (human)	3,389	2.8%	Turner (1983)
Leroux Wash (human)	3,443	2.6%	Turner (1983)
Grinnell (human)	380	1.0%	Turner (1983)
Ash Creek (human)	212	3.3%	Turner (1983)
Marshview Hamlet (human)	528	2.6%	Turner (n.d.)
Yellow Jacket 5MT–1 (human)	500	8.6%	Malville (1990)
Yellow Jacket 5MT–3 (human)	1,516 (nontooth)	2.6%	This study
Fontebrégoua (human)	175	48.6%	Villa *et al.* (1986a)
Mancos 5MTUMR–2346 (human)	**2,027 (nontooth)**	**11.7%**	**This study**
Emslie Mancos Canyon (artiodactyl)	408	24%	Emslie (1977)
Badger House (artiodactyl)	749	7.8%	This study

Table 12.5 Cutmark frequencies reported for various human and artiodactyl bone assemblages. See the text for a discussion of these values.

articulation techniques of prehistoric people. Alternatively, they may reflect the influence of postprocessing factors outlined above. Differentials in preservational status and interobserver variation can be partially controlled for by restricting the comparisons among cutmark totals to the Yellow Jacket 5MT–3, Badger House, and Mancos 5MTUMR–2346 assemblages. Cutmarks in these assemblages were all recorded by the same analyst and the preservation is comparable. This comparison again reveals the Mancos humans (11.7%) and Badger House artiodactyls (7.8%) to have substantially higher assemblage cutmark frequencies than Yellow Jacket 5MT–3 human (2.6%) remains. Differential recovery is responsible for part of this difference. The 1,516-piece Yellow Jacket 5MT–3 assemblage has a total of only 40 cutmarked specimens. The total piece count is inflated by the fact that small bone fragments in the IP4 category comprise 30 percent of the total specimens in the Yellow Jacket assemblage, compared to only 2 percent of the Mancos 5MTUMR–2346 assemblage. These fragments, of course, are tiny splinters of bone that are less likely to bear cutmarks than fragments in other element categories. This difference in IP4 proportion between the assemblages is the result of differential recovery, but the effect on the cutmark frequencies is dramatic. This variable, differential recovery of small fragments can be controlled for by assessing cutmarks on particular elements.

An element-by-element cutmark distribution analysis of the adult specimens in two human (Mancos 5MTUMR–2346 and Yellow Jacket 5MT–3) and two artiodactyl (Emslie Mancos Canyon and Badger House) assemblages reveals both similarities and differences (Figure 12.28). The highest overall cutmark values are seen in the Emslie sample, for reasons described above. The difference between artiodactyl and human anatomy probably plays a large role in creating different cutmark

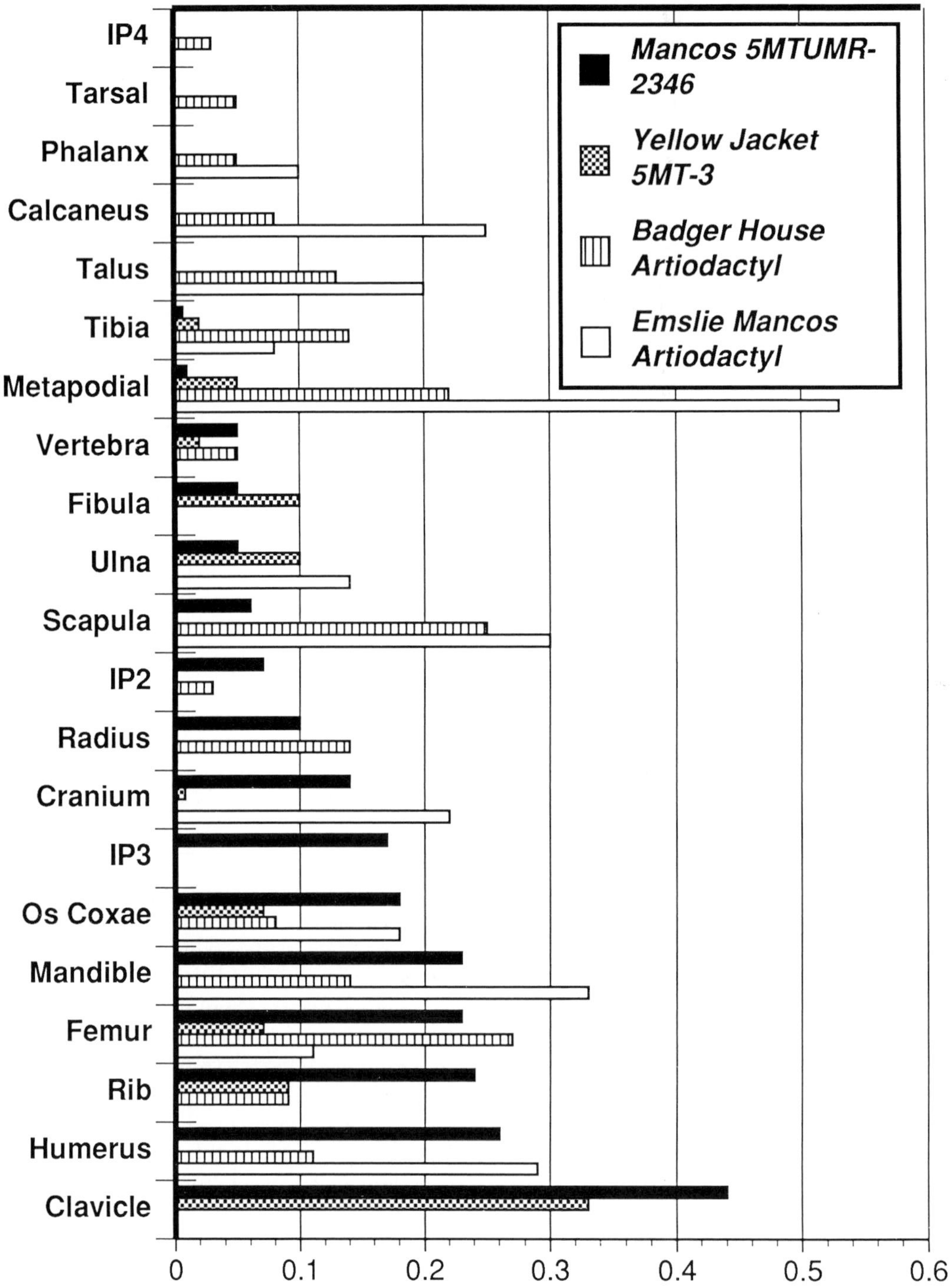

Fig. 12.28 Element-by-element plot of cutmark frequency on the adult specimens in two human (Mancos 5MTUMR–2346 and Yellow Jacket 5MT–3) and two artiodactyl (Emslie Mancos Canyon and Badger House) assemblages. See the text for a discussion of the differences.

frequency profiles for these assemblages. Obviously, the high cutmark frequency on the clavicles of the humans is not replicable among artiodactyls, which lack this skeletal element. The high frequency of metapodial cutmarks on the ungulate assemblages relate to the very different anatomy of this region. Beyond these anatomically conditioned differences in pattern, it is important to note the *similarities* in cutmark frequency patterns among the assemblages.

As a final controlled analysis, the frequencies of cutmarks in the combined adult humerus, femur, tibia, IP2, and IP3 element categories (major limb bones) were calculated for Mancos 5MTUMR–2346, Yellow Jacket 5MT–3, and Badger House. The lowest value was for Yellow Jacket humans at 2.4 percent. The Badger House artiodactyl value is intermediate, at 5.6 percent, and the Mancos 5MTUMR–2346 "major limb" assemblage has the highest cutmark frequency on these elements, at 14.5 percent. This is a real difference, because preservational and analytical conditions were held fairly constant. As outlined in Chapter 6, the average percentage intact surface value for Mancos was 94.9 percent, whereas for Yellow Jacket and Badger House the values were 98.7 and 90.8 percent, respectively. Therefore, the Badger House artiodactyl cutmark frequencies are probably depressed slightly relative to Mancos 5MTUMR–2346. The low cutmark frequency in the Yellow Jacket 5MT–3 assemblage cannot, however, be an artifact of preservation. The behavioral significance of these differences is not clear.

Chopmarks

Compared to the focus on cutmarks, considerably less attention has been given to the frequency of chopmarks on zooarchaeological and human bone assemblages. As outlined in Chapter 6, differentiating chopmarks from other kinds of surface modification is very difficult because recognition thresholds are often poorly defined. Gifford-Gonzalez (1989a) gives a further discussion of the differences and similarities between cutmarks and chopmarks, noting that cutmarks were more numerous than chopmarks on the ungulate bones in the Dassanetch ethnoarchaeological samples she studied. Here, however, the chopping tool was probably a metal blade responsible for the scarring of 17.9, 5.5, and 5.9 percent of zebra, cow, and caprine/small bovid long bones, respectively. Olsen's (1980:254) analysis of the Grasshopper Pueblo artiodactyl remains led to the recognition of damage to some elements, suggesting that they had been ". . . hacked through with a heavy, relatively blunt instrument such as a ground stone axe." In such cases, as with the Mancos assemblage, it may be difficult to differentiate chopping marks aimed at soft tissue from marks made by sharp-edged percussors aimed at fragmenting the bone itself.

Chopmarks were rare among the Mancos specimens, with only 15 being identified (0.7% of the total nontooth assemblage). In the Yellow Jacket 5MT–3 assemblage, the total of 12 chopmarks account for a total of only 0.7 percent of the entire assemblage. At Badger House, the 16 chopmarks account for 2 percent of the artiodactyl assemblage. When chopmarks are assessed on the subassemblage comprising the humerus, femur, tibia, IP2, and IP3, they are found to have frequencies of 1.3, 1.6, and 1.7 percent in the Mancos, Yellow Jacket, and Badger House assemblages, respectively.

Scrapemarks

Although scrapemarks are widely held to be a fairly common bone modification and have been documented to result from periosteum removal in ethnoarchaeological observations (Binford, 1978, 1981), they are very rare among the assemblages that the author has examined. Only 2 of the Mancos 5MTUMR–2346 specimens and 4 of the Yellow Jacket 5MT–3 specimens had scrapemarks; none of the Badger House specimens bore scrapemarks. Scraping of periosteum was apparently not part of the processing strategy involved with the generation of these assemblages.

Percussion Pits

Experimental work by Blumenschine and Selvaggio (1988) led to the recognition of "percussion marks" on 123 of 337 (37.6%) bone fragments modified by stone hammer-induced fracture to obtain marrow. Unfortunately, these authors do not provide separate data for the pits and striae (except on a small sample), but they do note that striae are more plentiful than pits. Turner (n.d.) mentions "percussion dents" on the Marshview Hamlet human bone assemblage, but does not quantify these features.

A total 4.0 percent of all specimens in the combined Mancos nontooth human bone assemblage bore at least one percussion pit. Values for the Yellow Jacket 5MT–3 and Badger House total assemblages are 9.2 and 3.3 percent, respectively. Nearly half of the specimens bearing percussion pits have at least two pits in all three of the assemblages. Percussion pits in the Mancos assemblage are found most frequently on the major limb bones, with 58 percent of the total 74 pitted specimens belonging to the femur or tibia. This pattern of percussion-pitting distribution by element is repeated in the Yellow Jacket and Badger House assemblages. When the percentages of specimens belonging to the humerus, femur, tibia, IP2, or IP3 categories and bearing percussion pits are calculated for these three assemblages, the Yellow Jacket 5MT–3 assemblage shows a frequency of 33 percent, followed by the Mancos assemblage with 9.3 percent and the Badger House artiodactyls with 6.6 percent. The explanation for these differences may lie in the somewhat less fragmented nature of the Yellow Jacket bones. An alternate explanation may lie in the fact that the sharper the tip of the percussor, the more likely the formation of a percussion pit rather than only abrasion striae. It is possible that the Yellow Jacket hammerstones used to fracture these limb elements had sharper tips. The latter explanation is consistent with the finding of more percussion striae on the Mancos 5MTUMR–2346 assemblage.

Percussion Striae

Percussion striae, although recognized as a bone modification attribute by Turner (1983), are not quantified in any work except that of Blumenschine and Selvaggio (1988). In the Mancos human bone assemblage, there is a high incidence of percussion striae, with a total specimen count of 376 specimens (18.5% of the total nontooth assemblage) exhibiting these marks. Values for the Yellow Jacket 5MT–3 and Badger House artiodactyl assemblages are 8.6 and 7.6 percent, respectively. As for cutmarks, the artiodactyl values may be depressed relative to the Mancos count, and an element-by-element assessment is warranted.

Figure 12.29 displays percussion striae by element for the Mancos and Yellow Jacket 5MT–3 human bones, and for the Badger House artiodactyl bones. Elements with consistently high frequencies are the major long bones. Percussion

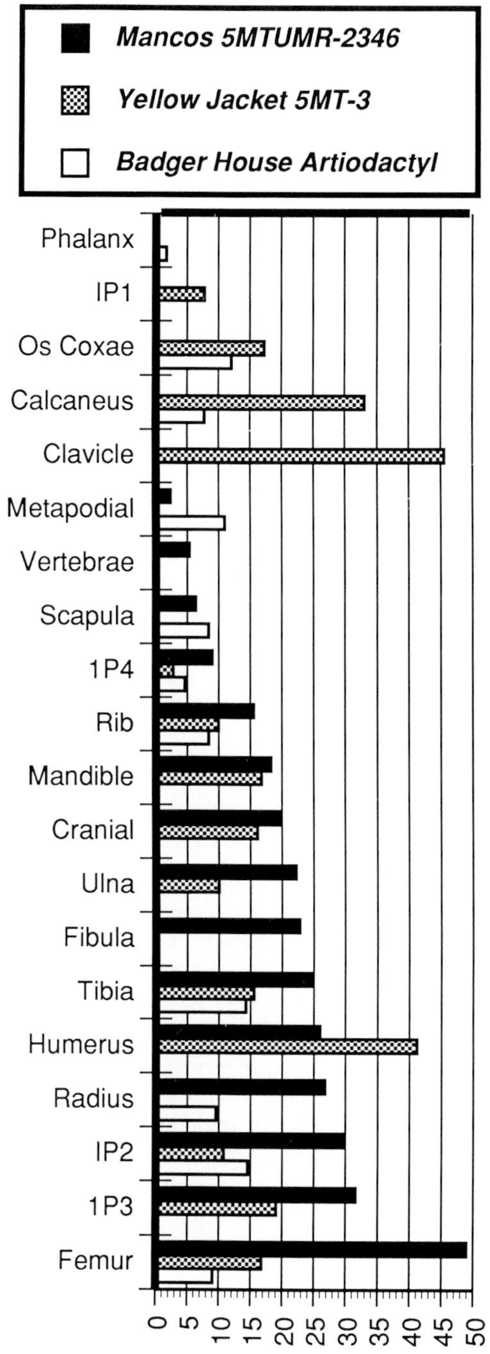

Fig. 12.29 Element-by-element plot of the percentages of adult specimens exhibiting percussion striae on the two human bone assemblages and the Badger House artiodactyl assemblage. See the text for a discussion of these data.

striae, theoretically, should occur most often on those elements requiring heavy, multiple impacts. The Mancos data conform to this prediction, with the most striae being documented on the femur. Smaller sample sizes for the other two assemblages make some comparisons problematical, but it is evident that the percussion striae distribution across the three assemblages is similar to what is seen with cutmarks, the Mancos assemblage showing higher incidence of the modification.

The combined humerus, femur, tibia, IP2, and IP3 subassemblages were used to assess the frequency of percussion striae to the major limb elements in the two human and one artiodactyl assemblages. These results show the Mancos assemblage with 34.9 percent of these elements carrying percussion striae, whereas 15.7 percent of the Yellow Jacket and 13.1 percent of the Badger House subassemblages show such damage. Because slight weathering can easily remove percussion striae, the Badger House frequency is probably depressed relative to the two other values because of differential preservation. Despite this difference, however, the percussion striae frequencies, like the cutmark data, suggest that the Mancos assemblage was more intensively processed than the two comparison assemblages.

Tool Modification Summary

Tool modification to the specimens constituting the Mancos 5MTUMR–2346 human bone assemblage closely follows what has been observed in many archaeological contexts. The patterns of tool modification are similar to those described for other human and nonhuman assemblages in the Southwest. Figure 12.30 summarizes data (controlled by major limb elements) on pot polish, cut-

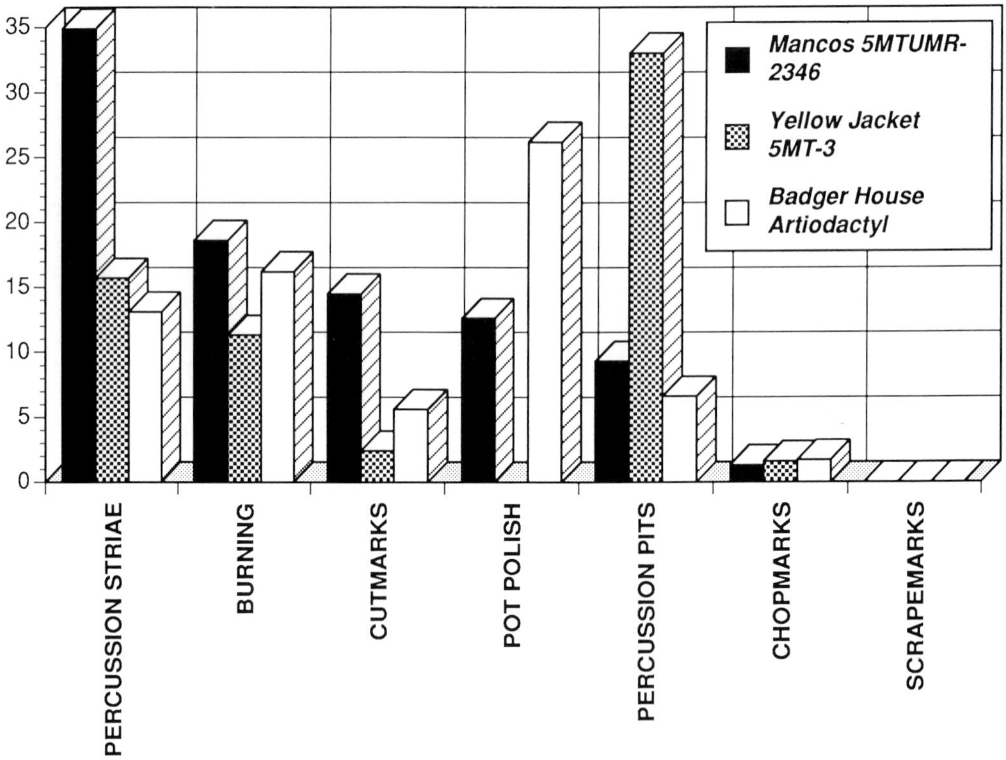

Fig. 12.30 Plot of the human-induced modifications to major limb elements (HUM + FEM + TIB + IP2 + IP3) in the Mancos 5MTUMR–2346 and Yellow Jacket 5MT–3 human bone assemblages compared to similar data for the Badger House artiodactyl bone assemblage. Scale indicates the percentage of specimens exhibiting the modification. Note that the Yellow Jacket assemblage was not scored for pot polish. See the text for a discussion of the significance of the similarities and differences summarized by this graphic.

marks, chopmarks, percussion striae, and burning in the human bone assemblages from Mancos and Yellow Jacket 5MT–3, and in the artiodactyl assemblage from Badger House. The modification-related attributes are shared among the assemblages where observed, and their frequencies are often very similar, suggesting that much bone processing was performed in the same manner. The Mancos assemblage shows elevated cutmark and percussion striae incidence, however, whereas the Yellow Jacket assemblage has elevated percussion pit incidence. The behavioral significance of these differences is unclear.

MAMMALIAN CHEWING

The nineteen human bone assemblages from Southwest archaeological contexts described in Chapter 3 and detailed in Appendix 1 show much fracture and many disproportions among skeletal elements. Wild and domestic canids (coyotes, wolves, dogs) are known to have coexisted with the Anasazi inhabitants of the Southwest during prehistoric times, and it is important to assess the degree to which these carnivores might have influenced the human bone assemblages. Carnivore influence over a bone assemblage can come in the portions of elements these animals delete by chewing, and in the marks and polish that they leave on bone surfaces. The presence or absence of the latter are critical in assessing carnivore damage, because the disproportions created by carnivore chewing may be similar to those created by hominid butchery practices—the results of both being conditioned in parallel by the structure of the bones themselves.

A considerable amount of forensic (Haglund *et al.*, 1988), ethnoarchaeological (Binford, 1978, 1981), and experimental work has been done on canid bone chewing. As summarized by Grayson (1988), canids prefer to attack the ends of major limb elements, whereas humans tend to "attack" the midshaft portions by percussion. This generalization (Potts, 1984) holds fairly well across a range of carnivore body sizes and bone-destruction capabilities, but the smashing of articular ends of some limb bones among humans as documented by the current study may render the generalization less universal.

In an effort to assess the signature of carnivore destruction of human skeletal remains, a sample of 25 human bone specimens from Wallace Ruin, Colorado, was examined (Bradley, 1988). Here, in a multistory, multicomponent pueblo site near Cortez, approximately 30–40 burials were disturbed by carnivore activity (presumably dogs, wolves, or coyotes). The remains were secondarily interred by the inhabitants after they had been disturbed and modified by carnivores. The subassemblage assessed was selected by Bradley and comprised femora, tibiae, fibulae, ulnae, humeri, and os coxae. The major limb elements followed the pattern of end-concentrated damage described by other workers. Punctures, tooth scoring, crushing, dimpled spongy bone, and denticulated edges were scored as present or absent on a total of 45 portions for the 25 specimens. Punctures, crushing, and dimpled spongy bone were present on more than half of all observations, and only 9 of the 45 observed areas lacked punctures, scoring, or notched edges, and 3 of the 9 showed crushing or dimpling. This damage patterning is unmistakable. No damage of this nature was observed on the Mancos or the Yellow Jacket 5MT–3 assemblages.

Akins (1986) notes that 19 percent of the 164 Chaco Canyon isolated human skeletal elements were carnivore-gnawed. Neusius (1988) reports that 0.7 percent of the nonhuman vertebrate bone fragments in the McPhee Community Cluster large mammal fauna show evidence of carnivore gnawing. Driver (1985) notes little evidence of carnivore activity on the Sierra Blanca zooarchaeological assemblages he studied, reporting less than 2 percent of specimens with traces of carnivore damage. Assessment of the Badger House artiodactyl fauna showed a frequency of 11.3 percent carnivore damage. This damage could have been imposed prior to acquisition by the Anasazi (by wild carnivores prior to Anasazi scavenging), or after the disposal of the bony pieces (presumably, by domestic dogs living at the site). The absence of carnivore damage from the Mancos human bone assemblage represents a significant difference from the Badger House artiodactyl assemblage.

As early as 1970, Turner and Morris

asked whether carnivores might have altered the Polacca Wash human bone assemblage. They concluded that despite the bone fragmentation, bone modifications diagnostic of carnivores, such as punctures, were absent from this sample. In his account, Turner (1983:221–225) suggests for the Polacca assemblage that ". . . some gnawing and bone removal by dogs, coyotes, and rodents probably occurred soon after the burial episode ended. . . ." Luebben and Nickens (1982) reported that two of the Grinnell specimens displayed evidence of rodent gnawing. Turner (1983) represents the only available published source of compiled comparative data on "possible gnawing" for Southwest human bone assemblages. He illustrates a puncture mark on an Ash Creek rib, noting that "Such damage is common in carcasses of animals dead of natural causes in the field but very rare in these Southwest mass burials" (Turner, 1983:224). He tabulates "possible gnawing" frequencies for many assemblages, giving the highest assemblage values to Ash Creek (5.2%) and Leroux Wash (3.0%). For all the assemblages that he considers, Turner (1983:234) concludes: "Possible animal gnawing and chewing occurs on only a small percentage of all elements, usually less than five percent. Some gnawing may have been done by humans and/or their dogs."

As noted in Chapter 6, criteria to diagnose between human and animal chewing have not been identified. A few of the Mancos 5MTUMR–2346 specimens, however, display damage on the ends that may have been produced by human chewing. One line of evidence that may support this suggestion comes from the lagomorph femora in the Badger House faunal assemblage. A random sample of 23 cottontail femora in this assemblage was examined. Two had their ends completely chewed off, one was burned only, and one lacked part of the condylar region but showed no other damage. The remaining distal femora were either completely intact and undamaged (n = 8) or displayed shallow punctures, often with loss of some of the condylar area (n = 11). The punctures were reminiscent of some displayed by metapodials and phalanges in the human assemblage from Mancos 5MTUMR–2346 (Figure 13.3). The finding that 47.8 percent of the lagomorph femora showed such punctures establishes a provocative pattern. It is possible to infer, on the basis of observed canid bone-chewing behavior, that canid chewing is unlikely to have been responsible for the observed pattern on the rabbit femora. This is because any canid chewing on the small, fragile lagomorph femur would have been likely to destroy the entire distal end of this bone, often with the carnivore subsequently ingesting the fragments.

Maguire *et al.* (1980:88) describe Hottentot chewing of goat bones described by Brain (1981a) as exhibiting

> Ragged-edged chewing, practically indistinguishable from that produced by hyaenas on the more frail skeletal elements. . . . Two types of damage not encountered on the bones from the hyaena dens were found on bones from the Hottentot sample: crushing by human teeth and knife-produced cut marks. The former category of damage can be reproduced by repeated crunching with the molars and premolars on a fairly soft bone, such as a chicken limb bone or immature goat or sheep bone, after the articular epiphyses have been removed so as to leave a splintery, inwardly depressed margin to the shaft.

Experiments by the author with cooked avian bones shows that the kind of puncture-crushing modification observed on the Mancos and Badger House bones is possible to replicate by means of human teeth. Ethnographic observations of people removing the articular ends of bones with their teeth are on record (Brain, 1981a; Jones, 1983). As Binford (1981) recognized in another context, more research is required.

BURNING

The variety of difficulties involved with the recognition and quantification of thermal damage to bones is discussed at length in Chapter 6 and by Gifford-Gonzalez (1989a). Many zooarchaeological analyses report frequencies of burned bone, but the recognition criteria are often left unspecified. Any comparative analysis using data from other sources must be cognizant of these limitations. As for other types of bone modification, assemblages analyzed by the same individual using the same recognition criteria will yield the most meaningful comparisons. The kind of element-by-element analysis of burning damage offered in previous chapters (and Gifford-Gonzalez, 1989a) is much more likely to yield insights into burning as related to food preparation than the by-assemblage or by-element quantitative analyses usually offered in zooarchaeological reports. Nevertheless, a brief review for the purposes of orientation is appropriate. Whole-assemblage burning frequencies range from 1 percent of the maximally identifiable specimens at Prolonged Drift (Gifford *et al.*, 1980), to 13 percent of the identifiable specimens at Jubilee Shelter (G. Turner, 1986), to 30.8 and 48.4 percent at the Turpin site (Theler and Harris, 1988), to 65 percent of the bone at Chencherere II (Crader, 1984). Gifford-Gonzalez reports burning frequencies in her Dassanetch samples of 20.5 percent (zebra), 44.0 percent (*Bos* and large bovid), and 52.9 percent (caprine and small bovid).

In the Southwest, zooarchaeological assemblages vary widely in the degree to which burning damage is present, from 47.3 percent of 3,887 Hohokam artiodactyl specimens (Szuter, 1989), to 32 percent of the total assemblage at the San Javier Bridge Site (Gillespie, 1987). A wide range of percentage burning values is reported for Coronado site artiodactyl assemblages (2.6%, 39.3%, 79.4%; Czaplewski, 1982), and 14 to 22 percent of deer bone at Pueblo Alto is reported to be burned (Akins, 1982). Neusius and Gould (1988) report that 16 percent of the large mammal bones from Grass Mesa Village were burned. For the McPhee Community Cluster fauna, 17.4 percent of the large mammal bones were burned. For the latter two assemblages, the overwhelming majority of the burned bones were listed as "completely burned," presumably calcined after fracture. In the artiodactyl assemblage recorded by Emslie (1977) from Mancos Canyon, 6.1 percent of the specimens showed evidence of burning.

Turner and Morris (1970) noted that some burning had occurred after dismemberment of the Polacca Wash human remains, and suggested that soft tissue cover of the mandibles may have mediated the burning damage pattern. Nickens (1974, 1975) notes similar patterning on the Mancos 5MTUMR–2346 remains. Flinn *et al.* (1976) noted that the Burnt Mesa remains included frontal and parietal specimens with exposed diploe, but they attribute this to heavy blows to the side and front of the head rather than to burning. These investigators count 36 percent of the fragmented bone as having been charred or calcined. They go on to note that bones at the top of the skull show the most evidence of burning, concluding that ''Perhaps the skull itself was used as a cooking utensil, being turned upside down so that it rested in the fire pit on the frontal and parietal sections, while the brain roasted within it'' (Flinn *et al.*, 1976:315). Nass and Bellantoni (1982) report that 12.6 percent of the Monument Valley specimens show evidence of burning. Turner's 1983 summary provides the most data relevant to an assessment of thermal alteration of the bone in the Southwest human assemblages. He reports percentages of specimens with evidence of burning that range from 1.7 percent at Leroux Wash to 35.4 percent at Burnt Mesa. In his summary, he implies that all of this burning damage took place after other processing had been completed: ''Burning after butchering and breaking is evident in two to 35 percent of all elements'' (Turner, 1983:234). This implication is considered to be very unlikely. It is true that in some assemblages (at least 5MT–3, Cottonwood Canyon) some postfragmentation incineration may be inferred from the presence of fully calcined shaft fragments. In the Mancos assemblage, however, the pattern of most fracture *prior* to burning is demonstrated by the observation that very few of the burned specimens in the assemblage show any evidence of burning on the endocranial surface or on the internal or fractured surfaces of postcranial specimens. Furthermore, documentation of soft tissue cover during thermal trauma (Chapters 7–11) constitutes evidence against a fracture-followed-by-burning sequence.

The overall burning percentage for the Mancos human assemblage is 21.5 percent. For the Yellow Jacket 5MT–3 human assemblage, the comparable value is 13.9 percent, and for the Badger House artiodactyl subassemblage, the percentage of burned specimens is 21.4 percent. It should be noted that a higher proportion of fragments that appeared to have been burned *after* the element they were part of was fractured were present in the latter two assemblages. It appears that small bone splinters were sometimes disposed of in hearths in both the human and nonhuman assemblages from various sites, resulting in many small calcined fragments entering into the burning totals. In contrast, this kind of burning was encountered only rarely in the Mancos assemblage, where most of the burning damage appears to have been done prior to fragmentation of the bones.

CHAPTER

13

Evaluation

During the first half of the twelfth century, the skeletal remains of seventeen adults and twelve children came to rest upon the floors and in the room fill of a small pueblo (now designated 5MTUMR–2346) in the Mancos Canyon of southwestern Colorado. Little is known about the canyon-bottom community of maize agriculturalists to whom this pueblo belonged. It is possible that the bony remains represent several individuals who did not reside at this particular pueblo, but there is no osteological evidence to indicate that the remains are not Anasazi.

Contextual data suggest that the remains were deposited simultaneously. Most of the bones show little or no weathering, indicating that surface exposure time was minimal. The remains themselves bear substantial evidence of human-induced modification in the form of thermal trauma, cutmarks, chopmarks, pot polish, and fracture and crushing by hammerstone percussion. There are very few nonhuman bones associated with the human remains. There is no evidence that carnivores manipulated the bones. The significance of these observations is assessed here from the local, regional, and global perspectives.

EVIDENCE FOR CANNIBALISM

History of Interpretation in the Prehistoric Southwest

In 1902, when Hough discovered a mass of broken skeletal remains of three individuals at the Canyon Butte Ruin 3 site in Arizona, he suggested (1903:313) that "Undoubtedly here was evidence of cannibalism, but as the find is unique so far in this region it probably only indicates anthropophagy from necessity." The possible motivations that might account for this and other similar assemblages recovered since are considered below. First, however, it is necessary to review the criteria that have been used to infer human cannibalism in the Southwest.

Hough (1903) was not explicit in linking the bone fragmentation patterns at Canyon Butte Ruin to those he observed on nonhuman faunal remains. Pepper reported in 1920 on results from the 1896–99 Hyde Excavations in Chaco Canyon. His descriptions of human skeletal remains from Rooms 61 and 80 of Pueblo Bonito, and from excavated fill at Penasco Blanco, are lacking in detail (and hence these occurrences are not included in my sample of 19 comparative assemblages). Pepper (1920:378) noted, however, that the Penasco Blanco remains "including portions of the skull, were charred, and the majority of the long bones had been cracked open and presented the same appearance as do the animal bones that have been treated in a similar way for the extraction of marrow."

The next investigator to report in detail about similar human bone assemblages in the Southwest was Morris (1939). He also inferred cannibalism for the La Plata Site 23 and Site 41 human remains, but the linkage of damage patterns with those observed on nonhuman bones remained inexplicit. Smith's (1949) description of the Big Hawk Valley assemblage was very tentative, suggesting that an interpretation of cannibalism was "tempting," but suggesting that other inferences also might be warranted. Although other similar assemblages were found through the 1960s, the 1970 Turner and Morris analysis of the Polacca Wash series set new standards that these and other occurrences would be measured against.

Turner and Morris (1970) were the first to compare in any detail damage patterns on the Southwestern human remains with those documented for analogous zooarchaeological bones—they assessed rib fragmentation from this perspective. These authors described the splinters of human long-bone shafts recovered from Polacca Wash as follows (1970:323): "These splinters are about the size and shape of prehistoric game remains found in Anasazi ruins." They noted the absence of carnivore damage, and used element representation, fracture patterns, cutmarks, and burning to argue that the inference of cannibalism was warranted. In 1976 Flinn, Turner, and Brew more formally proposed that seven criteria be used to recognize cannibalism in Southwestern human osteological assemblages: brain exposure, facial mutilation, burned bone, dismemberment, a pattern of missing elements, "greenstick" splintering of long-bone shafts, and cutmarks. Other investigators have inferred cannibalism when a match between this list and the damage attributes in other assemblages was found (Nass and Bellantoni, 1982).

In 1983 Turner proposed an expanded list of 14 "taphonomic characteristics of human butchering." The 14 characteristics were held by Turner (1983:233) to allow the inference, among human bone remains from the American Southwest, of "cannibalism (or flesh removal and disposal of osseous remains)." It should be noted that there may be a great difference between cannibalism and other mortuary practices involving flesh removal and bone disposal. Turner's summary made no comparative assessment of nonhuman faunal remains from ethnographic or archaeological contexts, hypothesizing that the damage and representation values "also apply to large non-human vertebrate food refuse." He noted that the types of damage found on the human remains in the Southwest could only have come as a result of human actions. He suggested (1983:219) that some of these characteristics ". . . be made the minimal requirement for identifying human modification of prehistoric animal bone lots." Turner closed his contribution by advocating a study of food refuse from archaeological sites.

Turner's 1983 list of features, reviewed in Chapter 3, has been adopted by other workers in the assessment of other assemblages of human bone inferred to represent evidence of cannibalism (Malville, 1989). Turner and Turner (1990:199) suggest that "violence and possible cannibalism" be inferred from "the minimal criteria of breaking, butchering, anvil abrasions, and burning.'' It is important to note that the Turner criteria represent descriptive commonalities among the human bone assemblages in the Southwest. The inference of cannibalism, however, should not be supported by these or any other criteria standing in isolation.

Recognizing Prehistoric Cannibalism

In reviewing the literature of the Southwest and beyond the author has noted a distinct tendency for archaeologists and physical anthropologists to initially interpret the presence of scattered, broken human remains as ''anything but'' cannibalism, often inferring from them secondary burial or carnivore disturbance. There are many archaeological examples of human remains in which the latter interpretations are clearly warranted by the contextual and osseous evidence. There are other cases in which the evidence is more ambiguous (Ravesloot, 1988).

The most explicit comparisons between human osteological remains inferred to represent cannibalism and zooarchaeological bones inferred to represent dietary practices are those of Villa and coworkers (1985, 1986a, 1986b, 1987, 1988). These authors write of having ''proven'' cannibalism ''beyond doubt'' (1988) by matching patterns of damage and representation of human and faunal remains found at the same French site. It could be questioned whether ''proof'' is the appropriate term to describe this linkage, but the Fontbrégoua inference of cannibalism is a very strong one. It meets the conditions for cannibalism recognition presented in Chapter 2. It was argued there that when archaeologists find *faunal* remains whose context, element representation, and damage patterns are in accordance with exploitation for nutritional benefit, the faunal remains may be interpreted to represent evidence of human consumption. When *human* remains are found in similar contexts, with similar patterns of exploitation, they are best interpreted as evidence of conspecific consumption, or cannibalism. Consumption, and its recognition, are the main issues.

Emphasis on the comparative analysis of human and faunal remains is the most appropriate approach to the recognition of cannibalism in the archaeological record. When damage patterns brought about by human efforts to prepare and remove tissues indicate a functional exploitation of the body and its elements consistent with the extraction of nutrition, the inference of cannibalism is warranted. Judgments on *what* patterns are consistent with nutritionally motivated processing may be assessed with reference to the zooarchaeological record or to ethnohistorical accounts.

Inferring cannibalism in archaeological contexts depends upon the comparative assessment of patterns of *processing* (cutmarks, percussion damage, fracture, burning) and *representation* of human bony remains. Given these principles, the enumeration of increasingly detailed descriptive criteria on which cannibalism is to be recognized (and that may not apply in different circumstances) is counterproductive. In practical terms, cutmarks and burning on a human bone assemblage are often held to be the primary signatures of cannibalism. As noted by Lyman (1987a), however, these alone are insufficient evidence on which to infer the consumption. It is the patterned bone destruction and associated signatures of percussion and postpercussion processing that constitute the best evidence warranting the inference that bone tissue was being manipulated to obtain nutrition.

The comparative approach advocated here emphasizes the analysis of multiple types of osteological damage, but it is very restrictive in the sense that it sets the threshold for cannibalism recognition at an artificially elevated level. The only higher level of inference would be that in which cannibalism was only to be inferred upon the recovery of human bones such as terminal phalanges from within demonstrably human coprolites. This is an unlikely scenario for most of the archaeological record, but one well within the bounds of possibility in the American Southwest—particularly when abandonment sometimes seems to have been coincident with the behavioral event involving the skeletal remains.

The stringent recognition criteria adopted here will render many, if not most, instances of prehistoric cannibalism invisible to the archaeologist. This is an unfortunate circumstance, for it means that we will seriously underestimate the practice in the past. Our gain is the removal of ambiguity, the increase in our confidence of recognition.

Comparison with Zooarchaeological Remains

The Mancos 5MTUMR–2346 human bone assemblage may be compared to zooarchaeological assemblages both qualitatively and quantitatively at both the global and regional levels. Chapter 12 presents a wide range of data to suggest that the Mancos human bones bear the same kinds of modifications seen on other zooarchaeological remains. Furthermore, the proportions of the specimens bearing these modifications are similar, in many cases, to those described for faunal remains across the entire archaeological record. Cutmarks and percussion damage are present in even the earliest bone assemblages inferred to have been exploited by hominids. These modifications indicate flesh removal, disarticulation, and marrow removal. Such activities are evidenced throughout the archaeological record by patterns of modification and representation. They are also evidenced on the human bones from Mancos 5MTUMR–2346.

Close parallels in the processing of human and nonhuman mammal remains are revealed by comparisons between the human bones from Mancos Canyon and artiodactyl remains from the greater Southwest, from the Mancos Canyon itself (Emslie, 1977), and from specifically chosen sites such as Badger House on nearby Mesa Verde.

A review of the relevant ethnohistorical documentation of mammalian carcass processing in the Southwest (Neusius, 1985b) has identified several cases of nonutilitarian treatment of animal bone remains among native peoples, including the nonfragmentation and ochre covering of antelope and mountain sheep limb bones (Beaglehole, 1936), ceremonial treatment of the head (Tyler, 1975), and off-site disposal of the bones of certain taxa such as ursids (Lange, 1959). Despite these ethnohistorical caveats, the archaeological record left by prehistoric people indicates that the processing of artiodactyls involved defleshing, segmentation, fracturing, and cooking practices that all left signatures on bone assemblages.

Lang and Harris (1984:84) provided a summary of the damage that they observed on artiodactyl bones from Arroyo Hondo Pueblo. The damage to postcranial skeletal elements included the following eight points:

> **(1)** spiral fracturing of the diaphyses of major long bones associated with yellow marrow extraction and preparation for rendering;

(2) depressed surface fractures marking the point of percussion impact of a relatively blunt object;

(3) short, broad cut marks or conchoidal fractures on ridged areas, caused by the impact of a sharp-edged object such as a chipped-stone chopper;

(4) splintered edges marking an impact point;

(5) short, sharply curved indentations along the margin of a bone splinter, suggesting fracturing by a supporting rock anvil;

(6) spalling of the relatively soft epiphyseal bone on the ends of femurs and humeri, probably incurred through contact with stone anvils that support each end of the long bone as it was broken by a powerful blow to the shaft;

(7) rib segmentation;

(8) general battering of some highly cancellous epiphyses to expose the spongy bone containing red marrow.

The Lang and Harris (1984) account also notes charring on the Arroyo Hondo artiodactyl skeletal remains. All of these kinds of damage are also seen on the human remains from Mancos 5MTUMR–2346, as well as the Badger House artiodactyls chosen for comparison with the Mancos human assemblage. Quantitatively, the Badger House assemblage differs from the Mancos human bone assemblage primarily in features related to postprocessing factors (Chapter 12). For example, Badger House artiodactyls have a higher frequency of carnivore gnawing, a higher frequency of heavy, whole-fragment calcining (probably related to disposal in hearths), and more widespread and relatively more advanced weathering damage. Processing-related differences between the Mancos human and Badger House artiodactyl bones are overwhelmingly related to the anatomical differences between human and artiodactyl skeletal elements. These differences include robusticity, size, shape, and marrow content of the phalanges, metatarsals, and hand and foot bones. Despite large anatomical differences between such phylogenetically disparate taxa as humans and artiodactyls, anatomical *similarities* condition the damage patterns in features such as proximal to distal humeral representation, and even in the placement and orientation of cutmarks (Figure 13.1).

In both the Mancos human and Badger House artiodactyl assemblages there is evidence that the body was partially or entirely skinned, segmented, roasted, and defleshed. In both assemblages the crania and postcranial skeletal elements were fractured, with a focus on the larger limb-bone shafts. This fracture is inferred to result from efforts to recover brain and yellow marrow tissue. There is no evidence of carnivores or sediment-weight contributing to this fracture.

Figure 13.2 summarizes data on the bone modifications that resulted from the processing described above for the Mancos 5MTUMR–2346 and Yellow Jacket 5MT–3 humans, and for the Badger House artiodactyls. The modification profiles are similar, with *both* of the human assemblages matching the Badger House artiodactyls in many modification percentages, and at least one of them matching in all categories except pot polish (where only the Mancos assemblage was conservatively scored; see Chapter 12). This *quantitative* correspondence was realized in a limited sample of three compared assemblages. Given the *qualitative* parallels with other artiodactyl assemblages from Anasazi contexts, it seems probable that many of the assemblages of human bones described here will fall well within the envelope of nonhuman bone modification and representation characteristic of food remains left by this culture.

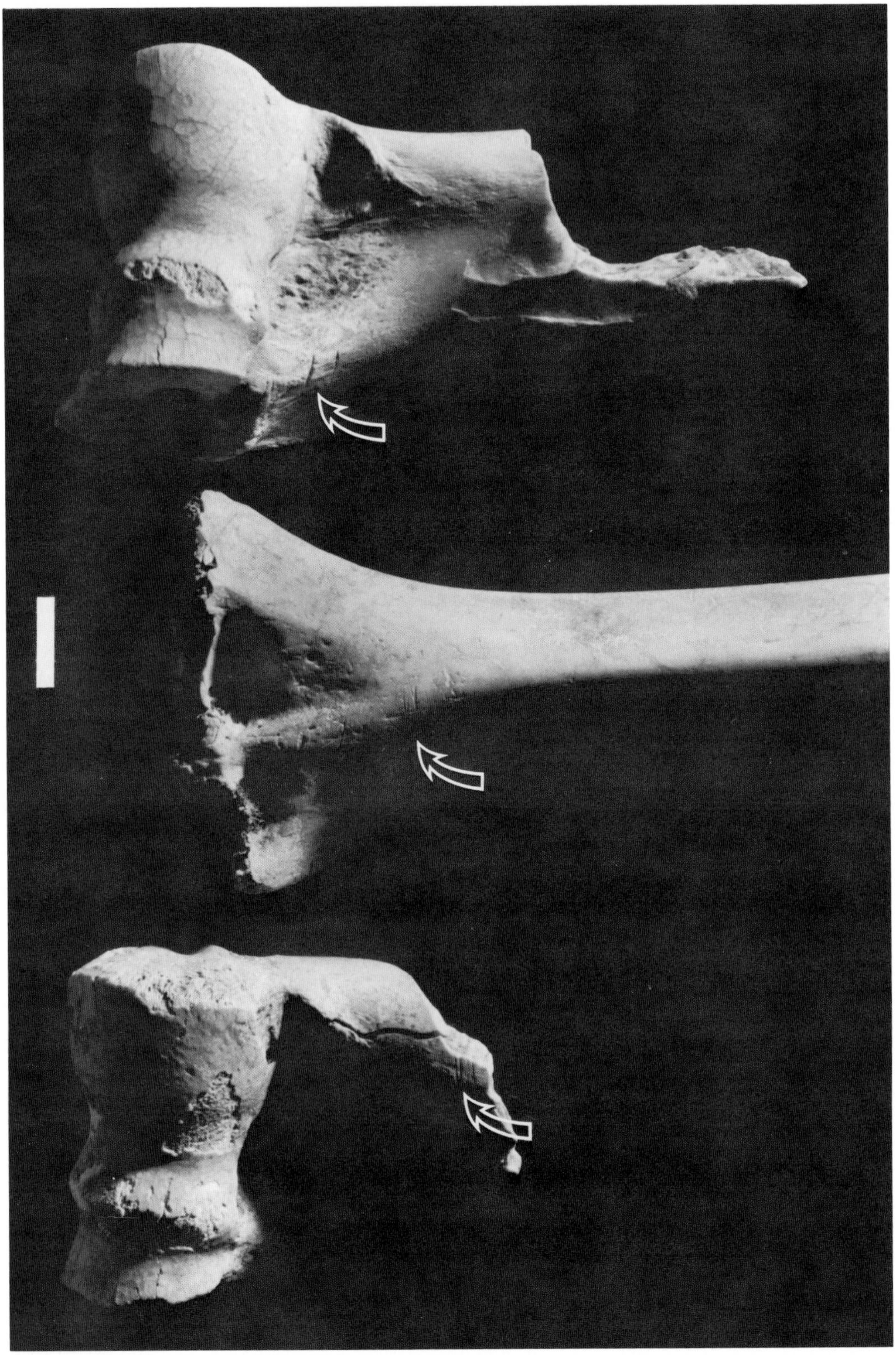

Opposite page:

Fig. 13.1 Similar anatomical placement of cutmarks on a human (center; Mancos 5MTUMR–2346 #625) and two artiodactyl (Badger House cervids: left, 7790/411; right, 27767b/706) distal humeri. These cutmarks were presumably made during slicing of the flexor tendons across the anterior part of the elbow joint during disarticulation of the forelimb. Bar = 1 cm.

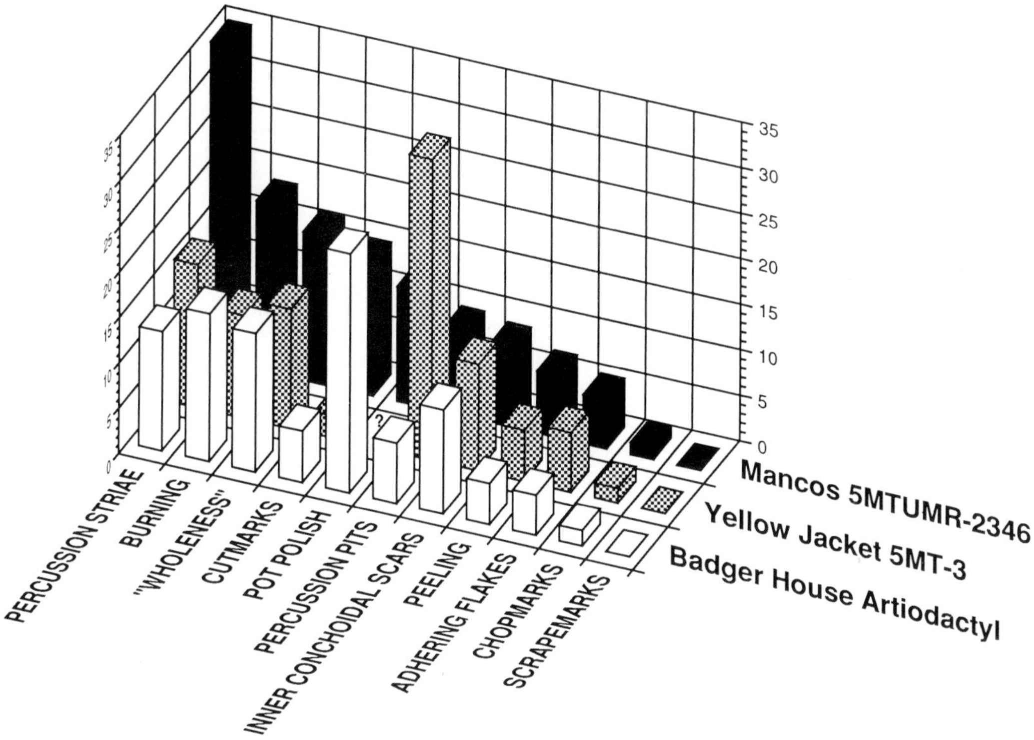

Fig. 13.2 A summary of data on the bone modifications from Chapter 12 for the Mancos 5MTUMR–2346 and Yellow Jacket 5MT–3 humans, and for the Badger House artiodactyls. The modification profiles are similar, with *both* of the human assemblages matching the Badger House artiodactyls in many modification percentages, and at least one of them matching in all categories except pot polish (where only the Mancos assemblage was conservatively scored; see Chapter 12).

Cannibalism or Mortuary Ritual?

Despite the parallels between the human and artiodactyl bone assemblages documented here, it is necessary to examine the possibility that the patterns observed among the human assemblages represent a kind of mortuary practice unrelated to consumption. For example, it might be argued that the heavy percussion to the Mancos bones documented by this analysis resulted from activities designed to *eliminate* identifiable bones, rather than to derive nutrition from them. This explanation is undermined by the fact that the mandible, one of the most diagnostic and recognizable human body parts, is the most intact bone in the assemblages. Large facial fragments are also often preserved fairly intact, in easily recognizable form, despite the fragility of the bones they comprise. In contrast, other elements such as vertebral centra (but not arches), sterna, and calcanei were eliminated or crushed almost beyond recognition. If the objective of fracture was to eliminate the bones, why were the most identifiable bones spared this treatment?

As Yellen (1991:19) documents in a different zooarchaeological context, "the perceived amount and quality of marrow can significantly affect how a bone is treated." In the human assemblages of the American Southwest, those long-bone shafts of small diameter (such as the adult fibula, radius, and ulna; and immature femur, tibia, and humerus) were discarded mostly unbroken, whereas every adult shaft of large diameter (and large marrow content) was fractured. This pattern implies that destruction of the bones was keyed to the acquisition of their nutritional contents. The patterning observed is most consistent with the inference that processing of the bones was not aimed at bone destruction, but rather at the "destruction" of exactly those parts whose large medullary cavities, or thin cortices with underlying spongy bone, held the most nutritional value.

Finally, the inference of mortuary ritual is considered to be substantially weakened by the demonstration that many Mancos 5MTUMR–2346 human bone specimens bear evidence of pot polish on their broken ends. This bone modification pattern is shared with the Badger House artiodactyls. It is attributed in Chapter 6 to circulation within a ceramic vessel. The inference that the human bones, once fragmented, were cooked in pots, like animal bones, represents a strong argument against attributing characteristics of the Mancos assemblage to noncannibalistic mortuary ritual.

ZOOARCHAEOLOGICAL IMPLICATIONS

This investigation was conducted with the goal of better understanding the archaeological signatures of cannibalism. During the investigation it also became evident that the results described here have implications for zooarchaeological research in the Southwest and beyond.

Differential Representation of Spongy Bone Parts

Among vertebrate bones, spongy elements or element portions (parts with thin cortices and substantial underlying spongy, or trabecular bone) are usually less resistant to damage and decay than segments of long-bone shaft, cranium, or mandible. As noted by the pioneer zooarchaeologist T. E. White in 1952, things that eliminate spongy bone parts include carnivore chewing (Binford, 1981; Haynes, 1981; D'Andrea and Gotthardt, 1984; Horwitz and Smith, 1988); butchery-related destruction (White, 1952; Lyman, 1978; Shipman *et al.*, 1981); natural *in situ* decay processes (faster in spongy bone; Leroi-Gourhan and Brezillon, 1972; Brown, 1974; Chase, 1986; Gordon and Buikstra, 1981); and behaviors resulting in the abandonment of axial portions at the death site (often tautologically inferred from the lack of such bones at *archaeology* sites—the now much-discredited Schlepp effect; A. Turner, 1989; O'Connell *et al.*, 1990). Choosing among these alternatives is known to be difficult, and one implication of the Mancos analysis is that it may be even more difficult than it already seems.

Although zooarchaeologists often attribute the deletion of softer, more friable spongy bone parts to abandonment, carnivore manipulation, or diagenetic processes, there is clear evidence that humans intentionally exploit these parts with and without grease-rendering technology. The problem of diagnosing between human and carnivore gnawing of spongy bone parts was discussed in the previous chapter. Conventional wisdom holds that carnivores chew off the ends of limb bones whereas humans without grease-rendering technology crack the shafts and leave the ends (Potts, 1988). Both organisms are attracted to the grease in the epiphyses of the long bones (Blumenschine, 1988). Unfortunately, the quantitative measures usually employed in isolation in zooarchaeology are often inadequate to distinguish between human and nonhuman factors leading to element and element part disproportions. Fortunately, however, hominid pulverization of spongy bone parts via percussion leaves characteristic but subtle traces in the form of abrasion and crushing—traces that are abundant on the 5MTUMR–2346 human remains. Assessment of other assemblages of zooarchaeological remains with attention to these details of modification may yield insights into the total butchery process practiced by prehistoric humans.

Hominid Exploitation of Spongy Bone

The use of spongy bone tissue is well documented ethnographically and archaeologically, with the former documentation mostly centered on modern people using container technology to render bone grease. Chapter 12 cited a variety of instances in which modern humans have been ethnographically observed to directly consume cancellous bone. From an archaeological perspective, in addition to the bone modification attributes noted above, the evidence from coprolites is important (Fry, 1985).

Preservational conditions in the Southwest have yielded an unparalleled record of human diet in the form of coprolites left by prehistoric people (Shafer *et al.*, 1989). Although none of the assemblages of broken and scattered human bone from the region are reported to have been associated with coprolites, data on bone matter in coprolites from other sites in the region is relevant to a consideration of how spongy bone tissue was used by the Anasazi. Stiger (1977) reports mammalian bone in 66.67 percent of the coprolites from Step House. In the analysis of coprolites from Chaco, Clary (1984) reports that 71 percent of samples contained bone fragments, and some still-articulated lagomorph joints were found in these coprolites. Morris (1986) reports bone fragments in more than 25 percent of coprolites from Glen Canyon. Fry and Hall (1975) and Morris (1986) both refer to the discovery of tiny, charred bone fragments in Antelope House coprolites. They interpret these remains as evidence for the consumption of bone cakes. It is possible that spongy bone was crushed by percussion and directly consumed or roasted in bone cakes before consumption. Spongy bone also could have been incorporated into the diet in the form of stews prepared with crushed bone. The coprolite evidence joins the ethnographic data to suggest that direct ingestion, by humans, of spongy bone tissue may have played a significant role in structuring the zooarchaeological record. Whether this bone tissue was directly consumed at Mancos 5MTUMR–

2346 is not possible to determine. Figure 13.3 illustrates the kind of bone modification described in Chapter 12 that is consistent with the idea that some bones were chewed by the Anasazi.

A deeper phylogenetic perspective on spongy bone exploitation is made possible by primatology. The hunting behavior of living common chimpanzees is increasingly well documented (Boesch and Boesch, 1989). These close relatives exploit both the brain tissue and the long-bone marrow of their mammalian prey. Marrow is described as being extracted with a stick tool after the bone's epiphysis has been removed with the teeth (Boesch and Boesch, 1989). Teleki's (1973:141) description of what the small-molared chimpanzees do to bones of their prey may cause the zooarchaeologist to take pause: "Small bones are thoroughly cleaned by sucking and scraping and are then chewed apart or discarded (and collected by others); large bones such as those of the arms and legs are cracked between the molars, and the marrow sucked out while the bones themselves are gradually consumed."

Implications

These observations on the exploitation of spongy bone tissue have implications for zooarchaeological analysis. First, the presence of tooth scoring and loss of spongy bone on zooarchaeological specimens is usually assumed to represent modification by members of the order Carnivora. The observations outlined above suggest that it would be wise to consider the role of habitually bipedal primates in the production of similar damage in some archaeological contexts. Furthermore, hominids wielding hammer and anvil technology could have accessed spongy bone tissue as well as the yellow marrow within limb-bone shafts, creating disproportions similar to those generated by other agencies, but leaving diagnostic modifications long before the advent of cooking container technology.

Analysts of the assemblages of broken and scattered human bones from the Southwest have long puzzled over the element disproportions that they observed, particularly the lack of vertebrae and the abundance of mandibles. The patterns of element representation and modification detailed in Chapter 12 imply that the spongy parts of human bones at Mancos 5MTUMR–2346 were processed in a manner consistent with exploitation for their nutritional content, and not with mortuary practice. Evidence in the form of preservation, pot polish, and spatial disposition suggests that the rendering of bone grease was one goal of processing (see Chapter 12 for a full discussion of this inference). The element disproportions so widely reported among the Southwestern human bone assemblages under review suggest that such rendering was a widespread practice.

THE REGIONAL PERSPECTIVE

The demonstration of similarity between the patterns of modification and representation of archaeological faunal remains and the assemblage of broken and scattered human bones from the Mancos 5MTUMR–2346 pueblo allows the inference of human cannibalism. Cannibalism is considered to be the behavior most likely responsible for the archaeological evidence. For the Mancos assemblage, like many other similar assemblages across the Southwest, this inference leads directly to a quest for explanation at both the local and regional levels. The difficulty of explaining *why* cannibalism oc-

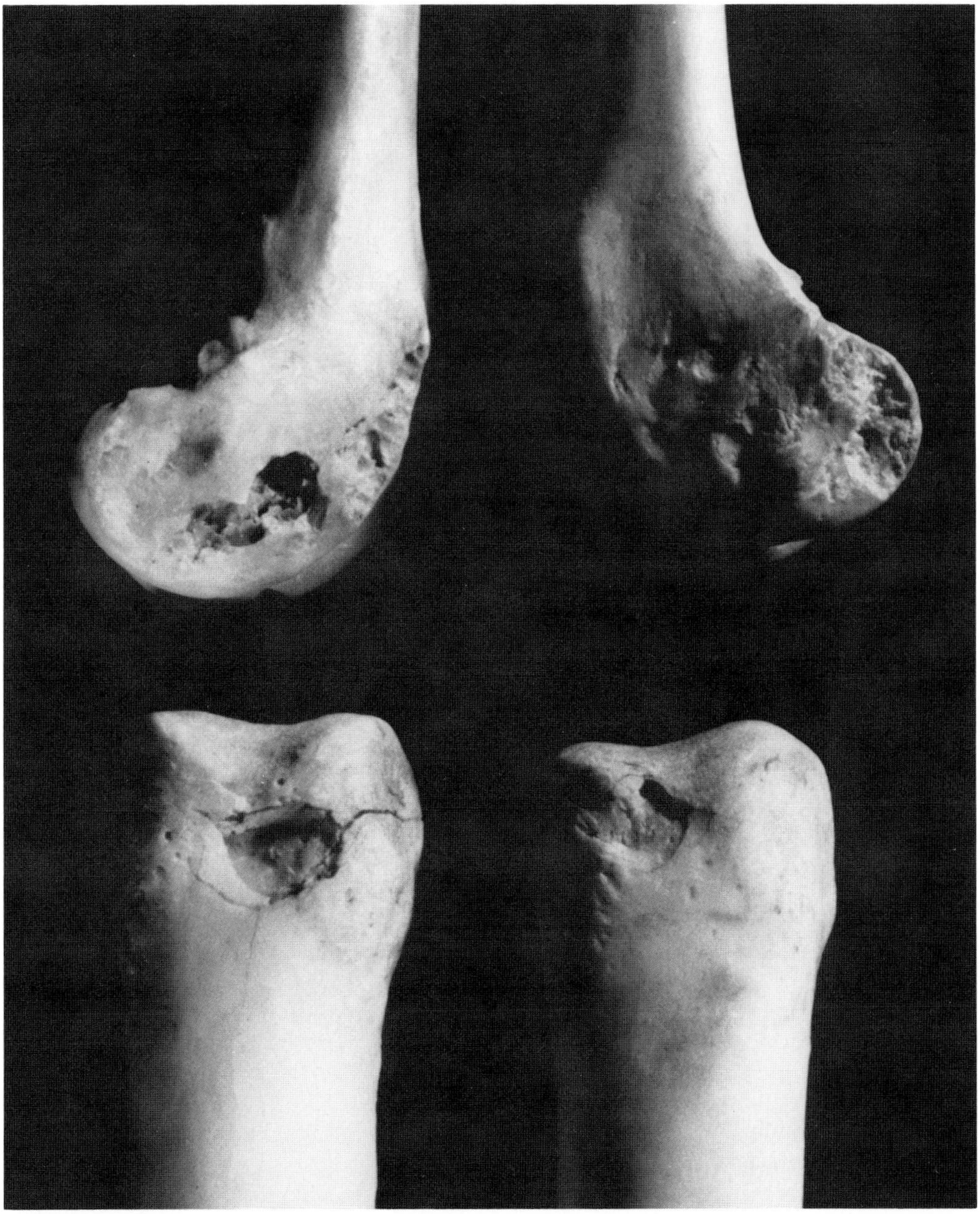

Fig. 13.3 The two distal femora at the top represent cottontail rabbits from the Badger House zooarchaeological assemblage (left, 29525p/706; right, 28459e/706). The two human phalanges below them are from the Mancos 5MTUMR–2346 assemblage of broken, scattered human bones. Note the punctures on the ends of all four specimens. This is possible evidence of human chewing. See the text for a discussion.

curred, however, is orders of magnitude greater than the difficulty of warranting the inference that it *did* occur.

The available osteological and contextual evidence from the Mancos 5MTUMR–2346 pueblo allows a wide range of possible explanations, ranging from the adoption of Hough's original (1903) inference of cannibalism in the region due to "necessity" to a host of other inferences constrained largely by the imagination.

The Anasazi who lived at 5MTUMR–2346 may have killed and eaten their enemies. They themselves may have been killed and eaten by such enemies. Alternatively, the people of a starving pueblo may have slowly consumed friends, relatives, acquaintances, or strangers who had died of starvation. The local circumstances under which any of these or other scenarios took place cannot be ascertained for the 5MTUMR–2346 assemblage except in the broadest terms. Any attempt to provide explanation and enhance understanding of the behaviors inferred to have taken place at 5MTUMR–2346 should address the greater record of such activities in the Southwest.

It is necessary to present a comparative summary of the various Southwestern human bone assemblages under review before outlining the possible explanations for the archaeological data. Chapter 3 and Appendix 1 describe 19 of the human assemblages used in the comparative work on Mancos 5MTUMR–2346, and several additional assemblages are now known (see below). There is a total MNI of 145 people in the comparative sample, represented by nearly 15,000 bone specimens that span 800 years of prehistory and tens of thousands of square kilometers of space.

Interassemblage Similarities in Composition and Context

More than one individual is present in 16 of the 19 assemblages of broken human bone introduced in Chapter 3 and detailed in Appendix 1 (Figure 3.1b). Each of these 16 assemblages comprises both immature (< 12 years) and adult individuals. Adult male and female individuals are present in all 7 assemblages in which more than two individuals are present and sex has been estimated. Beyond these basic biological parallels, there lies a great deal of variation in geographical, chronological, and contextual placement of the remains.

Interassemblage Differences in Composition and Context

Among the 19 human bone assemblages under review (Figure 3.1 and Appendix 1) there are 63 immature and 83 adult individuals. The minimum numbers of individuals in each sample range from 1 (Verdure Canyon) to 30 (Polacca Wash). Sex composition in the site samples is mixed, with 13 adults identified as probable females and 15 as probable males in the composite sample. The total piece count in these assemblages ranges from 202 at Bluff to 3,443 at Leroux Wash.

Of the 19 assemblages, 4 are unassociated with any architectural evidence (La Plata 23, Bluff, Polacca Wash, Verdure Canyon; ranging from MNIs of 1 to 30). The remaining 15 assemblages were found in or near structures that vary considerably in size and kind. Occurrences have been recovered from large, 20-room pueblos (Canyon Butte Ruin 3) and from smaller hamlets. There is one assemblage from a midden deposit (Canyon Butte Ruin 3) and one from an isolated stone-lined pit (Monument Valley). Three occurrences are from pits beneath rooms (La Plata 41, Yellow Jacket 5MT–1, Cottonwood Canyon). Five are from room floors or fills (Sambrito Village, Burnt Mesa, Mancos 5MTUMR–2346, Marshview Hamlet, Ash Creek). Two are from firepits or storage pits adjacent to pueblos (Big Hawk, Leroux Wash). In three instances some or all the remains are from kiva floors or fill (Mancos 5MTUMR–2346, Grinnell, Yellow Jacket 5MT–3; see Lekson, 1988 and Cater and Chenault, 1989 for critical discussions of the assumption that all kivas represent ceremonial centers). In two instances remains were recovered from fill in a ceramic jar (La Plata 23, Grinnell). This summary makes it clear that the disposal of the processed human remains took place in a variety of settings.

Interassemblage Similarities in Skeletal Representation and Bone Modification

Table 13.1 summarizes the kinds of bone modification shared between Southwestern human bone assemblages assessed in the present study and others reported in the literature. When combined with the quantitative data on element and element portion representation presented in Chapter 12, it is evident that the set of 19 assemblages introduced in Chapter 3 and detailed in Appendix 1 is characterized by many shared themes. Such comparisons, however, cannot fully express the degree of detailed similarity among these assemblages.

Many modification details seen in the 5MTUMR–2346 assemblage are shared with other human bone assemblages from the Southwest. Some examples of these shared details identified by the present study include parasagittal cutmarks on the Leroux Wash cranial vaults. The Mancos, Yellow Jacket 5MT–3, and Bluff assemblages share specimens with vertical cutmarks on the anterior clavicular surfaces, transverse cutmarks across the anterior distal humeral surfaces, and circumferential cutmarks around the femoral heads. Burning is concentrated on the zygomatic processes, gonial angles, and mandible bases in the Mancos and Yellow Jacket 5MT–3 assemblages. Completeness decreases inferiorly through the vertebral column from the atlas through the sacrum in most of the assemblages, and crushing at the bases of the proximal foot phalanges and the metapodials is present at Mancos as well as in the Leroux and Yellow Jacket 5MT–3 assemblages. There are scores of other detailed similarities between these and other assemblages examined by the author, and when the entire set of assemblages outlined in Appendix 1 has been studied in the manner of Chapters 7 through 11, it is predicted that the number of detailed similarities will increase dramatically.

The homogeneity in pattern of bone modification across the assemblages under consideration and the similarity of pattern between the artiodactyl and human assemblages studied may be inferred to represent culturally embedded rules of large mammal processing. On the other hand, the parallels may result from the anatomical constraints limiting the possible number of ways to effectively derive nutrition from a large body.

Interassemblage Differences in Skeletal Representation and Bone Modification

Many dimensions of element representation and bone modification are shared across the 19 Southwestern human bone assemblages under review. All 19 assemblages of broken and scattered human bones introduced in Chapter 3 contain specimens that have been burned. All 19

Table 13.1

MODIFICATION	*5MTUMR–2346*	*5MT–3*	*OTHER*
Preservation excellent	+	+	3, 5, 7, 9, 10, 11, 12, 13, 16
Perimortem Fracture:			All 19
Vault	+	+	2, 3, 5, 7, 8, 9, 10, 12, 13, 14, 18
Large diameter shaft focus	+	+	4, 5, 9, 10
Spongy bone crushing	+	+	7, 12, 17, 18
Peeling	+	+	7
Rib slab removal	+	+	7, 8, 9
Anvil damage to molars	+	+	
Over-anvil small diameter shafts	+	+	
Percussion:			
Striae	+	+	7, 14, 17
Inner conchoidal scars	+	+	6, 7, 8, 10, 13, 18, 19
Adhering flakes	+	+	7, 8, 13, 17, 18
Hammerstone pits	+	+	1, 7, 9, 14, 17
Cutmarks:			5-19
Scalping	+	+	5, 7, 9, 12, 18
Disarticulation	+	+	5, 7, 8, 9, 10, 18
Defleshing	+	+	7, 9, 10, 13
Pot Polish	+	?	?14, ?16
Burning:			All 19
Cranial subcutaneous	+	+	7, 8, 9, 12
Spalled anterior tooth enamel	+	+	
Postcranial subcutaneous	+	+	7

Table 13.1 A summary of the types of bone modification seen in the 19 assemblages of human bone from the Southwest. The "Other" category identifies the various assemblages by number, according to Figures 3.1 and 3.2. Modifications for each assemblage were observed by the author (Bluff, Mancos, Polacca Wash, Leroux Wash, Marshview Hamlet, Yellow Jacket 5MT–3, Cottonwood Canyon), or reported/illustrated in the appropriate publications. Note that observation for several attributes is unique to the present study, and that many publications do not report various kinds of modification. Key: 2 = La Plata 21, 3 = La Plata 41, 5 = Yellow Jacket 5MT–3, 6 = Sambrito Village, 7 = Bluff, 8 = Polacca Wash, 9 = Burnt Mesa, 10 = Monument Valley, 12 = Leroux Wash, 13 = Grinnell, 14 = Marshview Hamlet, 15 = Ash Creek, 17 = Cottonwood Canyon, 18 = Fence Lake Area, 19 = Verdure Canyon.

are characterized by considerable perimortem fracture of cranial and postcranial elements. Among the 19, all 15 reporting assemblages have specimens with cutmarks. Of the 15 cases where such damage is specified, 8 show no evidence of carnivore gnawing, one shows rodent gnawing only, and another 6 are said to show gnawing that may have been caused by humans and/or by carnivores (Turner, 1983). In the 11 cases where preservation of the bone is specified, it is excellent in 9.

Obviously, the kinds of human-induced alterations characterizing these assemblages are similar. Despite the common osteological threads that bind these occurrences together, the degree to which each assemblage is affected by the patterns of representation and modification differs significantly. A review of the literature and first-hand experience with the Bluff, Polacca Wash, Mancos 5MTUMR–2346, Leroux Wash, Marshview Hamlet, Yellow Jacket 5MT–3, and Cottonwood Canyon assemblages has revealed differences among the assemblages in the degree to which their components exhibit the kinds of alterations described here. This finding is reflected by the quantifiable variation among assemblages presented in the previous chapter.

The general bone fragmentation and the specific deletion of spongy bone portions of the Mancos assemblage are greater than seen in the Polacca Wash, Bluff, and Yellow Jacket 5MT–3 assemblages. For example, crushing damage to the spongy ends of the long bones is evident at Yellow Jacket 5MT–3, but relatively more of the articular ends are represented there than at Mancos. In the Bluff assemblage, large pieces of sacra and complete vertebrae are present, long-bone shafts are far less splintered than the Mancos remains, and long bones have been burned on their ends. From what can be garnered from published descriptions and firsthand assessment, there is a spectrum of bone destruction along which these assemblages lie, with the Mancos assemblage at the heavily impacted end of the spectrum.

Burning of the cranial bones is not as extensive in the Yellow Jacket 5MT–3 assemblage as it is among the Mancos specimens, with no burned mastoid processes and no clear correlation between soft tissue cover and burning at Yellow Jacket. The Yellow Jacket 5MT–3 assemblage lacks patterned burning on the tibia and metapodials. There were no bones found in articulation at Mancos, but articulated bones of the hand and foot were found *in situ* at Cottonwood and Bluff.

These largely qualitative dimensions of variation among the set of 19 assemblages were only partially revealed by the quantitative analysis of Chapter 12. This is because the relevant data are unavailable or have not been gathered in a manner adequate to discriminate among assemblages. Nevertheless, considerable variation is already apparent in the degree to which the bodies of men, women, and children in the 19 assemblages were processed.

Other axes of variation—cutmark intensity, for example—are also present among the assemblages, and in some cases this variation probably reflects real processing differences. When more control has been established over preservational and observational factors that might artificially bias results, a deeper analysis of interassemblage variation will be possible. Before moving to a consideration of explanations offered for the patterns documented here, it is useful to consider additional assemblages of broken human bones from the American Southwest that were not included in the 19 comparative sets.

OTHER POSSIBLE CASES

During the Mancos study other similar but unreported occurrences were found in the Southwest, making it certain that the 19 comparative assemblages of human bone used in the present study are not the only such assemblages known. Furthermore, some already discovered occurrences with skeletal evidence of interpersonal violence (Snider's Well, Mesa Verde, Charnel House Tower, West Pueblo at Aztec Ruin, Acowitz, Animas Valley, La Plata Site 33, Old Fort, Cottonwood Creek Cave 7, the Coombs Site, Bancos Village, Smokey Bear Ruin, Canyon de Chelly, Pueblo Bonito, Largo-Gallina) include articulated or partially articulated skeletons and evidence of violent perimortem trauma, including embedded projectile points. These occurrences were briefly considered in Chapter 3, where it was argued that their further assessment was beyond the scope of the present work. The limited descriptions available for many of these occurrences, however, leave open the possibility that some of them conform to the pattern described in this book. Further comparative analyses of the skeletal remains from these and other sites is urgently needed.

Human skeletal remains from Anasazi archaeological contexts are usually primary burials, and sometimes secondary burials and cremations. Standard archaeological research procedure in the region is to identify human skeletal material as "burial" remains, segregate such remains from the nonhuman fauna, and retain a physical anthropologist for their analysis. Departure from this standard field and analytical procedure has been made reluctantly, even in cases of large assemblages of broken human bones found scattered across dwelling spaces, as with many of the 19 assemblages described here. In Southwestern archaeology, the larger the broken and scattered human bone assemblage (the larger number of pieces and people represented), and the closer the assemblage is associated with an abandonment event, the greater the likelihood that it will be recognized by the excavators as extraordinary. Given the number of recognized occurrences, it is appropriate to ask whether only biased segments of a wide range of occurrences are being recognized archaeologically in the set of 19 comparative assemblages employed here.

Whenever people bury their dead beneath or near their dwelling places, the skeletal parts of these burials may become mixed with other occupational debris by biological or physical agents. The transport of human phalanges through the tunnels of burrowing rodents, for example, usually means that scattered and isolated human remains will be found at a site. These expectations are based on long experience of archaeologists, and most isolated human remains from the Southwest are interpreted as evidence of the artificial or natural disturbance of formal burials (Palkovich, 1980) or as cremations (Kelley, 1984). As one example of the magnitude of this, 37.4 percent of the Salado burial population reported by Rice (1985) was disturbed, and 53.6 percent of the disturbance was cultural.

If the bone-processing and discard behaviors that generated the 19 human bone assemblages under review here were regularly or intermittently being practiced during normal occupation of a habitation site, the assignment of scattered, isolated human bones at many sites to secondary burial, cremation, or artiodactyl remains could conceivably render a portion of such behaviors archaeologically invisible. At the same time, such assignments could be seriously biasing the overall record toward occurrences that are large and coincident with abandonment.

The high degree of fragmentation typical of the human bone assemblages described in this book might be expected to result in the archaeologist assigning the majority of the fragments to the indeterminate large mammal category. Identifiable human remains might be attributed to disturbance of formal burials and accordingly segregated. A good deal of research on the modification attributes of scattered and isolated human remains from Anasazi contexts needs to be done to assess the possibility that these predictions have merit. There is some evidence already available that suggests that they do (see below). Future research aimed at examining these possibilities must go beyond literature review, directly to the skeletal evidence itself.

During the literature search conducted in association with the present study, several sites were identified that may best fit, and possibly extend, the patterns of assemblage content, modification, and discard framed by the 19 occurrences named and assessed above. A brief introduction to the kinds of occurrences that need to be looked at from the perspective of nonburial disposal of human skeletal remains is appropriate.

In 1939 Kluckhohn and Reiter described an adult human skull found on a kiva floor at Chaco Canyon. The specimen was said to show signs of perimortem fracture and cutmarks at the skull base. A modified human femoral shaft fragment was also found. In 1956 Olson and Wasley reported the following about a kiva firepit found at Site LA–2699: "Within the fire pit were found a human parietal fragment and a burned section of mandible. An explanation for the presence of these bones is lacking" (Olson and Wasley, 1956:365).

Excavations at Periman Hamlet Area 1, a Pueblo I habitation of the Dolores Archaeological Project area (Site 5MT–4671; Wilshusen, 1986a), revealed small quantities of human bone from five different provenance units. For example, a cranial fragment was found in a hearth, and a humerus was found atop an ash pile near a central hearth of a pitstructure. Wilshusen (1986a:154) concludes that: "The presence of these bones is presumably better explained as resulting from ritual rather than culinary practices. . . . The meaning of isolated finds such as these can not be adequately dealt with at the site level: a pattern of such finds over a number of sites would allow a more complete explanation."

Excavations in Area 5 of the Grass Mesa Village site in the Dolores project area (Site 5MT–23; Lightfoot *et al.*, 1988) revealed the very fragmentary and burned remains of a juvenile and an adult in a roof and wall fall stratum of Room 13. These are interpreted as possibly representing bodies or bones that were placed on the roof and burned along with the structure. No further details are available. Scattered human remains have also been reported in structure fill at Black Mesa (Martin *et al.*, 1985).

These are just a few of what must be hundreds, if not thousands, of occurrences of isolated, fragmentary human skeletal remains in the Southwest. The majority of these may have nothing to do with, and include no evidence of, the kinds of processing documented for the Mancos human skeletal material. It is hoped that the documentation presented here, however, may prompt other researchers to examine from a new perspective the human remains that they recover.

Two examples of research conducted on previously recovered human skeletal remains witness to the utility of such a perspective. Both examples came to light during the time in which the Mancos 5MTUMR–2346 analysis was underway. The first was a study conducted by Turner on the skeletal remains from two individuals from a Pueblo I masonry site at Teec Nos Pos in northeastern Arizona. The partial skeletal remains of an adult human had been found lying face-down on a floor surface in 1969. They had been attributed to death by roof collapse. Turner's detailed analysis of these remains and an associated child's scapula demonstrated cutmarks and fracture patterns consistent with those seen among the 19 assemblages noted here. He interprets the remains as further evidence of social pathology and cannibalism (Turner, 1989). It is notable that the adult skeleton was largely articulated, but missing skeletal elements.

The second research example involves collections housed at the Mesa Verde National Park Research Center. In 1965 Lister reported on a skeletal occurrence at Mesa Verde Site 875. The scattered, partially disarticulated remains of several humans were found in Room 1 and interpreted to represent secondary burials (Stodder, 1987 notes similar occurrences at the Kin Tl'iish site of the Dolores project area). Maps and photographs of the Mesa Verde 875 occurrence suggested the possibility that this might be similar to what was described in the 19 assemblages, but a 1990 analysis of the bones showed only evidence of carnivore modification. These primary burials were disturbed by carnivores, and none of the element scattering and damage is attributable to human activity.

To test the possibility outlined above (that human remains displaying the patterns of representation and modification characterizing the Mancos and 19 other assemblages might be present at other already excavated sites), some of the human skeletal remains from other Mesa Verde sites (Bennett, 1975) were examined by the author in 1990. From Site 820 (J. Smith, in preparation), "Burial" 14 had been interpreted as the interment of an immature human, including bones of the cranial vault, right and left femora, os coxae, humeri, and other body parts. The fragmentary remains of this individual drew my attention because of the excellent bone preservation compared to the rest of the burials from the site (recovered from the same midden). Examination revealed evidence of perimortem fracture as well as hammerstone pits, abrasion, and possible burning on both cranial and postcranial elements from this individual. Peeling, crushing, and possible pot polish are present on the postcranial remains. Search of the faunal remains from this and nearby excavation units (FS186 and 11, 185, 213) revealed additional human bone fragments that probably belong to the same human child, including ribs and a left mandibular ramus with possible cutmarks. This combination of characteristics strongly suggests that this child was processed in a manner similar to that described in other assemblages.

These examples reveal the kind of additional research needed on collections of human skeletal remains already present in museums. As Turner (1989:152) notes, "Since there are far fewer physical anthropologists working on skeletal biology of the Southwest than archaeologists recovering human remains, it should not be surprising that skeletal studies lag far behind burial excavation." The current politically motivated concern with eliminating skeletal remains through "reburial" threatens to halt the acquisition of knowledge here as in many other areas.

Other research conducted during this study has resulted in still more occurrences of broken and scattered human remains that share many of the features characterizing the 19 human comparative assemblages described here. In southeastern Utah at Rattlesnake Ruin near Mustang Mesa, looters found a pit containing the fragmentary remains of 20 individuals. These were found adjacent to a small dwelling dated to A.D. 1050–1100. They bore cutmarks and impact signatures like those described for the 19 comparative assemblages used here (Shane Baker, Winston Hurst, personal communication). Multiple occurrences that also share characteristics with the 19 assemblages described in this book have recently been discovered as a result of work by the Office of Archaeological Studies of the Museum of New Mexico's La Plata Highway project (E. Blinman, personal communication). In June 1990, work near Towaoc at site 5MT–10207 revealed a concentration of human remains on a kiva floor. Some of the leg and foot bones were fairly intact and still in articulation with each other and with the os coxae (L. Hammack, C. Turner, personal communication). These discoveries bring the total number of known occurrences close to 25 as of the time this book was finished (September 1990).

EXPLAINING THE PATTERNS

The reader anticipating a neat, simple, comprehensive explanation for the assemblages of broken human bone from Southwestern archaeological contexts will be disappointed in what follows. As the next section points out, several such explanations have been offered, only to have been rendered implausible by the discovery of more, and often different occurrences.

History of Explanation

The first published inference of cannibalism and explanation of this behavior for the assemblages of intentionally broken human bones from the Southwest came from Hough (1902). As the first worker describing the first assemblage, his interpretation that the Canyon Butte Ruin 3 remains represented cannibalism called attention to the then unique nature of the discovery, noting that "... it probably only indicates anthropophagy from necessity." Pepper (1920:378) describes two other, possibly similar assemblages as due to cannibalism motivated by "stress of hunger or ... religious reasons." Morris (1939) and Smith (1952) subsequently described other assemblages as possibly representing cannibalism, but neither provided explanations, and Smith left a back door open by suggesting that a "vituperative grave digger" rather than cannibals might be responsible for the assemblage. Turner and Morris (1970) contended that the Polacca Wash remains represented the osseous evidence of a legendary massacre. They suggested that the Polacca Wash remains be "reasonably" interpreted as evidencing cannibalism. They did not speculate on whether this was "obligatory" or "ceremonial," but Nass and Bellantoni (1982) pointed out that if the series conformed to the legend, tribal warfare was involved. Nickens (1974, 1975) suggested that the cannibalism he inferred from the Mancos 5MTUMR–2346 assemblage was obligatory or emergency, but recommended that the question be left open. Hartman (1975:306) concluded that indications of cannibalism were not apparent until Pueblo III, and that "Archeological evidence of great stress during Pueblo III times is certainly supported by the presence of cannibalized human remains from this time period."

Flinn, Turner, and Brew (1976), in describing the Burnt Mesa assemblage, also invoked climatic change and social unrest, and attempted to draw a series of parallels with the then recently publicized case of cannibalism subsequent to an Andes airliner crash (Read, 1974). Turner (n.d.) goes on to suggest that "emergency" was the cause of the Burnt Mesa occurrence. Nass and Bellantoni (1982) contended that Late Pueblo II/Early Pueblo III represented "troubled times." They considered witchcraft as a possible explanation for the assemblages, but concluded that the demographic composition of many assemblages (interpreted to be family groups) was at odds with such an interpretation.

Turner's 1983 summary of the evidence from the Southwest does not attempt explanation of the cannibalism he infers. Rice (1985) suggested that the remains from Ash Creek represented "war trophies." Turner (n.d.:4) noted the lack of signs of warfare such as embedded projectile points in the Marshview Hamlet remains, concluding that ". . . emergency cannibalism most readily comes to mind as an explanation." Kane (1986:290) adopted this view, stating that "Most possible instances of Anasazi cannibalism appear to date to the 12th century, which may reflect increasing subsistence hardships during this period." Fetterman *et al.* (1988) presented a model based on climatic degradation and social unrest during the period A.D. 880–920. They cite evidence of contemporary "violence" at the Duckfoot and several Dolores sites. They suggest that food resources were scarce and individuals were eaten "in a time of desperation." Fink (1989) suggested that the Verdure occurrence might be associated with raiding, but noted that because of the long period spanned by the known assemblages, ". . . food stress is an unlikely cause." Turner and Turner (1990) suggest that these assemblages be interpreted as evidence of "violence," "chaos," and "social pathology."

These published explanations for the assemblages of broken human bones from Anasazi contexts are offered at two levels: the ultimate (climatically driven ecological and social instability) and the proximate (starvation, warfare/revenge). The two recurrent themes in the interpretations are a desire to attribute the behaviors that generated these assemblages to stress, and an inclination to seek ultimate causes through temporal correlation with other occurrences. The former theme remains strong, its tenacity possibly linked to the deeply ingrained historical tendency of Southwestern archaeology to explain cultural change with reference to climatic considerations. For the assemblages under review, the latter approach has been made more difficult to pursue as more spatially and temporally disparate occurrences have come to light. It is premature to offer comprehensive regional explanations for the assemblages under investigation, and there is no reason to conclude that the reasons behind them will not be multiple and independent. It is appropriate, however, to review some of the facts that an eventual comprehensive understanding of the assemblages will encompass.

Temporal Considerations

A popular anthropological pastime is to seek correlations among phenomena and infer causality from the correlations. For example, if all or most of the human bone assemblages under review came from a single period, anthropologists might seek regional climatic, environmental, demographic, architectural, or other changes to "explain" the assemblages. While such an approach is still possible on an assemblage-by-assemblage basis at the local level, the temporal distribution of assemblages under review shows the difficulty of searching for regional correlations as a means of circumscribing cause. As Plog *et al.* (1988:276) point out:

> In the traditional approach an event is identified, and environmental correlates are sought. There are two problems with such an ap-

> proach. First, all events have correlates, usually many. Identifying the specific correlate that caused the event becomes quite difficult. Secondly, the correlates of a specific event at a specific time and place may be different from the correlates of similar events at other times and places. Only by building independent records of environmental and behavioral patterns can one overcome this difficulty.

This, of course, is what now must be done for the assemblages under review. Figure 13.4 indicates the possible spans of the 19 assemblages used here for comparative purposes. The histograms below the bar chart represent an attempt to put an "envelope" around the possible "real" time distributions, using minimum, maximum, and midpoint estimations for each assemblage. Whatever the regional explanation offered for the assemblages, it must account for behaviors that may have been distributed fairly evenly throughout Pueblo II and III times in the region. As with most archaeological issues, better chronological control over the assemblages would facilitate analysis.

Demographic and Spatial Considerations

As outlined above, there is great variation in the number of individuals represented in each assemblage under study. Single individuals, possible family groups, and groups of up to 30 individuals are involved, and there is substantial variation along this range. Men, women, and children are, however, usually represented in the assemblages. There is little evidence that adult and immature individuals were treated differently except in ways consistent with variation in the nutritional value of their skeletons.

Contextual Considerations

The architectural contexts of the assemblages vary from none to rather large pueblos. The great variation surrounding the circumstances of disposal of the human remains indicates the lack of a uniform "routine" for disposal. There is no obvious pattern to indicate that the processing and discard of remains were tightly influenced by ceremonial considerations. On the other hand, the fact that so many of the occurrences of broken human bones comprise hundreds of specimens scattered across the floors and fills of rooms may be significant.

In Anasazi processing of large artiodactyl remains, the bone fragments were usually discarded in trash areas. The frequency of such midden discard for processed *human* bone cannot be determined now for reasons outlined above. Bony remains of large artiodactyls, however, are not generally found in the concentrations or spatial positions that many of the human assemblages occupy. These differences could reflect several factors. When humans were processed, several individuals were often involved and the processing period seems to have been brief. Artiodactyl procurement may not have commonly yielded multiple carcasses for butchery, and this would have reduced the probability of large numbers of bone fragments being simultaneously discarded. The archaeological visibility of artiodactyl processing would be correspondingly reduced.

The lack of much carnivore gnawing on the human remains as compared to the artiodactyl remains suggests that domestic carnivores did not greatly influence the human assemblages. Several investigators have noted the impact of domestic canids on bone assemblages in the Southwest and beyond (Lyon, 1970; Kent, 1981; Kelley, 1975). Domestic dogs were certainly present in the Mancos Canyon area, as evidenced by nearby dog burials (Emslie, 1978).

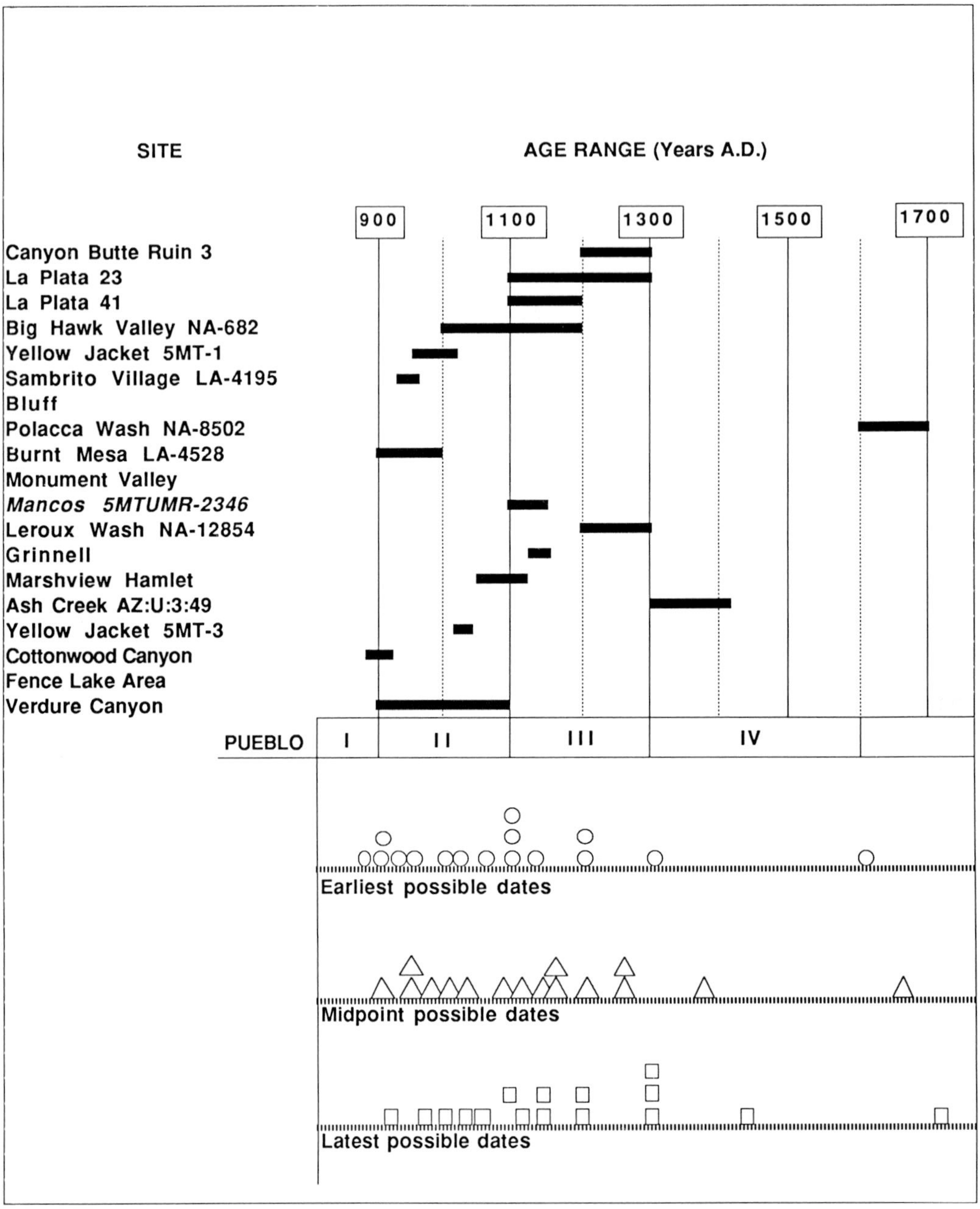

Fig. 13.4 The possible spans of the 19 assemblages of broken human bone from the Southwest are shown by horizontal black bars. The histograms below the bar chart attempt to put an "envelope" around the possible "real" time distributions, using minimum, maximum, and midpoint estimations for each assemblage.

The general lack of carnivore gnawing on the human remains under consideration could stem from several factors. First, if starvation was motivating the processing of human bones, it might be that the dogs would have already been consumed. Alternatively, if discard was rapidly followed by abandonment, domestic dogs might have departed with the occupants. Wild carnivores, however, might be expected to have been attracted to the bony remains. The intensive processing documented for some assemblages, however, would have left little to attract carnivores, particularly when the articular ends had been crushed, the bones had been rendered for grease, and most of the remains were rib and long-bone shaft fragments. For assemblages so thoroughly processed as the Mancos remains, the lack of carnivore damage might not be so behaviorally significant as the lack of such damage on assemblages containing more intact elements.

A final contextual observation concerns the lack of evidence that any of the human bone splinters were fashioned into artifacts. Fairly intensive bone tool production among the Anasazi is a well established fact, and the long, straight cortical bone sections of ungulate metapodials were consistently used to make awls. The long, thin cortical splinters so abundant in the human bone assemblages under review represent a potential source of bone material for the production of awls, needles, and scrapers—a source that was apparently untapped because of abandonment or behavioral restrictions, or both.

Variation in Bone Processing

A large component of variation in bone processing among the assemblages of human bone reviewed here relates to the fracture of long-bone shafts for marrow and to the crushing or deletion of the spongy parts of these and other bones. Olsen (1980) saw, in fragmentation variation among the deer bones at the Grasshopper Pueblo, evidence for intensification of marrow extraction and bone grease production through time. The variation of bone fragmentation among the Southwestern human bone assemblages reveals no such *temporal* pattern, but functional considerations related to bone marrow and grease rendering seem to have a great deal to do with the variation observed among assemblages.

As noted above, the major axis of interassemblage variation among the broken and scattered human remains from the Southwest was the amount of fragmentation and crushing. Some assemblages, such as that from Mancos, bear evidence of more processing than is seen in other assemblages. It is possible to infer that this spectrum of destruction may be related to different processing intensity conditioned by prehistoric choices about whether (or to what degree) bone grease was to be rendered. This would be the human analog of what Haynes (1982b) refers to as "motivational" factors affecting the degree of bone use by carnivores. Among the Kalam of the New Guinea highlands, Bulmer (1976) notes that the smaller and softer bones of larger animals were eaten to the extent that meat was available at the time and the extent to which the people were hungry. Whether these people bothered to smash long bones in order to extract the marrow depended on how much meat was available. It is likely that similar considerations hold across many human groups, although the fatty content of bones often makes them high-priority targets of exploitation.

From the variation seen in processing intensity among the Southwestern human bone assemblages, it is possible to infer that the results of a highly structured ceremonial mode of mortuary processing and discard are not being observed. Such treatment would be expected, in contrast, to lead to uniformity of assemblage composition and modification. The fact that processing and discard varied so greatly suggests that motivation was primarily nutritional and did not involve deeply embedded ritual.

Relating the Assemblages to "Warfare and Violence"

The terms "violence" and "mutilation" recur in the literature on the human bone assemblages under review here. This nomenclature has its roots in the Turner and Morris (1970) description of the Polacca Wash assemblage. The forensic osteologist is virtually never able to ascertain the cause of death from skeletal remains alone. The reason for this is made obvious by the imaginary case in which a murder is committed by poisoning and the deceased is subsequently shot through the skull. Embedded stone tool tips in skeletal remains have sometimes been used to infer that interpersonal violence led to death, as in the case of an Ash Creek rib with embedded point (Turner, 1983, his Figure 2). No embedded projectile points were observed in the human bone specimens that I have examined from the Mancos, Yellow Jacket, Bluff, and Cottonwood Canyon assemblages.

The Southwest ethnohistorical (Ellis, 1951) and archaeological records both provide evidence of interpersonal violence. Archaeologically, the "defensive" postures of some habitation sites, the discovery of intentionally burned structures, and the presence of skeletal remains of multiple individuals with evidence of trauma (but without formal burial) all indicate that amiable relations were not universal among the native peoples of this region (Eddy, 1974; Mackey and Green, 1979; Wilshusen, 1986b).

Turner and Morris (1970) argued that the presence of many small pieces of tooth and unweathered bone fragments suggested that death of the Polacca victims occurred at the burial site. They did state that this was not proven. Of the Polacca remains, they conclude (1970:327): "These individuals met a traumatic death, probably at their burial site, when each was mutilated, dismembered and smashed into small pieces." Noting the damage to the cranial pieces, particularly the "ablation" (knocking out) of the front teeth, they infer "violence" and "mutilation." Flinn *et al.* (1976:313) also note "mutilation" of the facial region of the Burnt Mesa remains, and Nass and Bellantoni (1982:268) suggest for the Monument Valley remains that ". . . less violence to the bones would have been sufficient for the same results."

The terms "violence" and "mutilation" have been based, in the assessment of Southwestern human bone assemblages, on evidence of percussion-driven fracture and scarring of the bones. Unfortunately, these terms carry with them implications that the processor(s) of these remains carried out their activities with an intent beyond mere economic processing. These terms, for example, are never applied to artiodactyl remains showing similar fragmentation patterns. The human bony remains, particularly from assemblages such as Mancos 5MTUMR–2346, show clear evidence of very heavy percussion. There is little evidence, however, that this percussion was intended for anything other than fragmentation of the bones, probably aimed at obtaining enclosed tissues. The opening of crania by percussion atop anvils could be responsible for most of the forced dislocation of anterior teeth (susceptible to this because of their prominence and single roots). The only possible evidence that percussion went beyond what was necessary to fracture the bone for direct or indirect acquisition of nutrition was observed in the form of repeated hammering to the anterior surface of one of the Bluff assemblage mandibles. To summarize and reiterate the discussion of Chapter 12, evidence is lacking that the human remains from the assemblages were manipulated for purposes other than the acquisition of nutrition.

The degree to which the cannibalism inferred for the Mancos and other related assemblages relates to warfare between indigenous groups is not possible to ascertain. It is, for example, plausible that climatically induced famine (see below) led to raiding bands of individuals preying upon and consuming other people. In this instance, the distal explanation for the bone assemblages would be climatic, a more proximal explanation would be famine, and the most local could be revenge and/or ritual associated with internecine warfare (Weisman and Milanich, 1976).

Possible Mesoamerican Influences

There is a large ethnohistorical record of cannibalism in Mesoamerica that is poorly verified archaeologically (see Chapter 2). The possibility that this behavior in the American Southwest represents an import from what is now Mexico, however, deserves consideration. Whereas previous discussions of Mesoamerican influence on the American Southwest tended to be polarized into whether there was *any* influence, more recent considerations have focused on the *degree* to which such influence was felt. The volume edited by Mathien and McGuire (1986) reflects this change, but there is no consensus on whether *pochteca* models for the north-south interaction are appropriate. Casas Grandes, the large, complex site in northwestern Chihuahua, Mexico, did not reveal clear evidence of cannibalism in its many skeletal remains (DiPeso, 1974). There is no evidence to indicate that cannibalism in the Southwest had a Mesoamerican connection, nor is there evidence to rule this possibility out.

Relating the Assemblages to Regional and Local Climatic Change

From the initial recognition that much of the Four Corners region had been abandoned by the Anasazi, archaeologists and others have advanced reasons to account for abandonment on both large and small scales. These reasons include disease, warfare, drought, invasion, and ritual (Nickens, 1981; Ambler and Sutton, 1989; Cameron, 1990).

The Southwest was a marginal environment for people such as the Anasazi whose subsistence depended on agriculture. For example, Decker and Tieszen (1989) indicate that an isotopic assessment of Mesa Verde diet from Basketmaker III to Pueblo III shows that diet was 70 to 80 percent corn for the entire occupational span. In the Colorado Plateau region, the most significant climatic variables for agriculturalists were precipitation and temperature, and the unpredictability of drought and frost made long-term farming in the region difficult (Wills, 1988). As Minnis (1985:193) puts it, the Southwest is:

> . . . generally marginal for maize-based horticulture and even minor changes in precipitation could substantially affect food production systems. Furthermore, the Southwest does not have particularly high biomass edible by humans, and with the lack of a widespread river

network and lack of beasts of burden, transportation was inefficient. Therefore, native populations with relatively low population densities may have been more vulnerable to fluctuations in food supply, and the range of responses available may have been more limited than in many other regions.

Dean *et al.* (1985) note that agricultural groups on the Colorado Plateau would have become more sensitive to environmental variation as their numbers approached carrying capacity for a given adaptive strategy. The relationship among climate, diet, and population in the prehistoric Southwest has been studied in detail for some sites such as Arroyo Hondo, where evidence of dietary stress from skeletal remains is evident (Palkovich, 1984; Wetterstrom, 1986). In other regions, the occupation of certain areas corresponds to episodes of high effective moisture (Matson *et al.*, 1988; Kohler and Matthews, 1988). Schlanger (1988) maintains that there was a smooth overall regional population increase in southwestern Colorado from A.D. 1 to 1100, but notes that local sequences register short-lived occupations and abandonments.

There is an increasingly detailed record of environmental change for the prehistoric Southwest in the form of dendrochronology, hydrological considerations, and pollen and faunal studies (Holbrook, 1975; Gumerman, 1988; Petersen, 1988). It is increasingly evident, as noted above, that the relationship between climate and human behavior is most appropriately first addressed on the local level.

For the Mancos 5MTUMR–2346 site, the best paleoenvironmental data are those of Nickens (1981). Nickens notes that dendrochronological, palynological, and contextual evidence combine to indicate a close correlation between periods of environmental stress and cultural activity in the nearby Johnson Canyon. He notes that a very important drought in the region came in the period A.D. 1140–1189. It is not possible to establish the relationship, if any, between this drought and the human bone assemblage (see Chapter 3 for a review of site chronology).

Starvation as Motivation

The effects of high-frequency processes, such as seasonal cycles and year-to-year variations (Dean, 1988), would have been regularly felt by the prehistoric inhabitants of the American Southwest. In this marginal environment, nutritional stress associated with crop or storage failure may be predicted to have been a fairly regular phenomenon. To reduce this stress, inhabitants would have turned to cultural buffering mechanisms involving demographic, productive, and organizational strategies (Cordell and Plog, 1979). Here in the Southwest, perhaps more than in most regions in the world, Colson's (1979:25) observation would have often been appropriate: "Despite all precautions, the bad years come." She notes that five devices can lessen vulnerability to the risks of these bad years: diversification of the resource base, storage, use of famine foods, conversion of surpluses to tradable goods, and cultivation of social relationships with other areas.

Hough's first attribution of an assemblage of broken human bones to nutritional stresses established a tradition of interpretation in the Southwest that remains strong today. Minnis (1985:41) contends that "The most highly publicized and overestimated response to food shortage is cannibalism." To what degree could the assemblages under study represent starvation-induced cannibalism—what Colson (1979) has termed "that last cruel resource of starving people"? There is no inconsistency between the temporal pattern so far established for the assemblages (Figure 13.4) and the idea that they represent manifestations of localized famine.

When lean years came to the Southwest in ethnographic times, the resulting famines made lasting impressions on indigenous people. Beaglehole (1936) cites Hopi eyewitness accounts of famine, and Cushing (1974:76) relates a Zuni legend about one bad winter as follows: "At last the corn was all gone. The people were pitiably poor. They were so weak that they could not hunt through the snow, therefore a great famine spread through the village. At last the people were compelled to gather old bones and grind them for meal." Historical accounts of starving explorers in other regions of the world eating shoes, leather, and old bones in the face of famine are not unusual (Franklin, 1823), and the thought of consuming conspecifics is never far away under these conditions. Starvation is the leading cause of modern-day instances of cannibalism. Although Garn and Block (1970) have doubted that regular cannibalism ever had much nutritional meaning, Vayda (1970) has called for research on this issue and Dornstreich and Morren (1974), Randall (1971), and Walens and Wagner (1971) have all noted the nutritional value of a human body—value that may mean the difference between life and death in certain circumstances.

For many of the Southwestern assemblages of human bone considered here, there is strong evidence that marrow was extracted and bone grease rendered. Marrow fat, unlike its extramedullary counterpart, is difficult to mobilize in humans (M. Tavassoli, personal communication). Fatty marrow is primarily a source of calories, as it is made mostly of fat, whereas red marrow is primarily a source of protein (although it has some fat in the normal state). Unfortunately, there are few studies on the nutritional content of normal human skeletons and even fewer studies on starved ones (Keys *et al.*, 1950). In conditions of starvation, some human fatty marrow can turn to red marrow (or gelatinous mucopolysaccharides, Tavassoli *et al.*, 1976), but how much is unknown (Tavassoli and Yoffey, 1983). Compounding the difficulty is the fact that there are no osteological markers reliably associated with starvation. This means that the osteologist is unable to assess whether the remains in the assemblages under study represent individuals who were starving when they died (contra Morris and Parkington, 1982).

The extremely intensive processing of human remains from Mancos 5MTUMR–2346 evidenced by patterns of representation and modification was noted in Chapter 12. If it could be shown that the processing of these bones was more intensive than that characteristically practiced on artiodactyl bones of the same size, density, and nutritional utility in all of the human assemblages under consideration, an argument for starvation-induced cannibalism might be more strongly supported. This is not, however, the case. As noted above, the Mancos assemblage lies at one end of a range of processing intensity, a range that overlaps extensively with that characterizing artiodactyl bone processing. Starvation may have been a motivating force in causing the prehistoric inhabitants of the region to cannibalize their fellows as Hough surmised 87 years ago, but the evidence acquired since then has not strengthened that explanation—

nor has it made it possible to choose among other alternatives.

FURTHER RESEARCH

At the Mancos 5MTUMR–2346 site, a 12th-century episode led to the deposition of fragmentary human bones that display evidence that humans were intentionally defleshed and disarticulated; that their crania and long-bone shafts were broken open by hammerstone and anvil percussion; that the trabecular portions of their skeletons were smashed by percussion; that body segments were roasted; and that bone fragments occupied ceramic vessels prior to disposal. The modification and representation of the human remains are consistent with that seen in faunal assemblages from a variety of related archaeological contexts. These observations support the inference that human cannibalism occurred in the prehistoric Mancos Canyon.

As for so many other prehistoric human behaviors in the American Southwest, there is not yet a satisfactory explanation for cannibalism inferred from the bony remains and their contexts. It is evident that a great deal of additional research must be done to elucidate this phenomenon here and in other places in the world. The present analysis has shown that the complexity of the record requires more than simplistic explanations, making the task of research at the regional, local, and global levels much more interesting.

The approach of forensic, crime-scene style investigation advocated by Turner (1983) will be a key component of future research in this area. A series of suggestions regarding methods of how relevant data may be acquired is the subject of Appendix 3. Attention to details such as bone chip distributions and coprolites may reveal important contextual data not yet available for the assemblages so far recovered. There is a great need for the recovery of a complete midden fauna from the same site yielding the fragmented human remains. Analysis of the human assemblages and similarly recovered faunal assemblages promises to better define the ranges of behaviors generating the human assemblages and to allow an understanding of the features, if any, that separate them from assemblages of similarly sized artiodactyls.

Research should not be driven by only the large, new, visible assemblages encountered in ongoing excavations. As noted above, a wealth of available data rests in museum collections. A concerted effort to see whether additional instances might have gone unrecognized is urgently needed to fathom the extent of the phenomena described here. Given the finding that so many fragments in the known assemblages might have been identified as "indeterminate mammal," both human and nonhuman bone assemblages will have to be assessed from this perspective. The fact that human limb bones tend to splinter into longer and straighter fragments than bones of similarly sized mammals may help in a search of the nonhuman assemblages.

There is a need for work with human cadavers to establish body part utility indices comparable to what is known for artiodactyls (Metcalfe and Jones, 1988). Biochemical techniques said to allow the taxonomic identification of blood residues on artifacts (Gurfinkel and Franklin, 1988; Loy and Wood, 1989; Hyland *et al.*, 1990) may prove useful in establishing more about the bone processing involved in the assemblages. Work on dental enamel composition holds out the promise of evaluating residence patterns among prehistoric populations (Schneider and Blakeslee, 1990), and might be applied in the Southwest to assess the affinity of individuals in the assemblages of broken human bones. It is possible that DNA could be extracted from both human hard and soft tissues, and that this DNA might be sequenced to allow local and regional genealogical assessment. Comparing skeletal remains comprising these assemblages with those from graves at the same and from nearby sites, and assessing all skeletal remains local to each assemblage from the biocultural perspective (Nickens, 1981; Martin *et al.*, 1985) will be important lines of research.

Context and dating will be key variables in the assessment of both old and new assemblages of broken human bone in the Southwest, but it is the recently acquired and yet-to-be discovered assemblages that hold the most potential to yield the necessary data. For example, research is underway on the very small bone flake component from the Yellow Jacket 5MT–3 excavation (Darling, personal communication). Combined with conjoining data, a fine-grained reconstruction of the activities that generated the assemblage (as in Lyman, 1980b; Dunnell and Stein, 1989) should be possible. Assessment of chemical residues on the associated lithic and ceramic components of this occurrence promises to shed new light on ancient activities.

Looking beyond the Southwest, there is a pressing need for archaeologists and physical anthropologists to work together to examine the evidence for ethnohistorical accounts of cannibalism. As outlined in the second chapter, this kind of research represents the only remaining pathway for anthropological assessment of the extent of human cannibalism, even in fairly recent times.

Finally, returning to the corner of anthropology from which this study grew, the analytical tools used in the study of cannibalism in the recent archaeological record need to be employed in an investigation of cannibalism in the more remote past.

Appendix 1

Catalog of Southwest Archaeological Sites with Evidence Interpreted as Indicating Cannibalism

SITE NAME: **Canyon Butte Ruin 3**.
SITE NUMBER: Unspecified.
SITE LOCATION: In northeastern Arizona, on a tributary that feeds the Little Colorado River at Woodruff, about 10 km SSE of the town of Carrizo.
EXCAVATOR(S): Walter Hough.
DATE(S) OF EXCAVATION: 1901.
COMPLETENESS OF EXCAVATION: The occurrence was in a cemetery associated with a pueblo. The amount excavated is not recorded.
PRIMARY ARCHAEOLOGICAL REPORT: Hough (1903).
PRIMARY SKELETAL REPORT: Hough (1903).
SITE TYPE: A sketch map accompanying the description indicates an oval pueblo with more than twenty rooms. The cemetery was placed to the northeast, in a thick refuse deposit.
AGE—LOCAL CHRONOLOGY: Undetermined.
AGE—REGIONAL CHRONOLOGY: Pottery from Canyon Butte figured in Hough (1903) suggests a safe placement between A.D. 1200 and 1300 (Pueblo III). Thanks are extended to Roberta Jewett for making the ceramic identifications and placing this site into the Pecos temporal framework.
CHRONOMETRIC AGE(S): None.
CONTEXT OF HUMAN REMAINS: "In the midst of the burials the workmen came upon a mass of broken human bones, which proved to be the remains of three individuals" (Hough, 1903:312–313).
NUMBER OF HUMAN SKELETAL PIECES: Unspecified.
NUMBER OF INDIVIDUALS: 3.
AGE AND SEX OF INDIVIDUALS: Unspecified.
DAMAGE PATTERN:
Burning: Traces on some.
Cutting: Unspecified.
Fracture: Percussion marks noted.
Gnawing: Unspecified.
Preservation: Unspecified.
EXCAVATOR'S INTERPRETATION: "Undoubtedly here was evidence of cannibalism, but as the find is unique so far in this region it probably only indicates anthropophagy from necessity" (Hough, 1903:313).
OTHER REPORTS AND INTERPRETATIONS: Smith (1952) merely cites Hough. Flinn, Turner, and Brew (1976) also cite Hough, indicating that some of the bones had cutmarks, but in Hough's account only percussion marks are noted. No mention of the Canyon Butte occurrence is made in Turner's 1983 summary.
DISCUSSION: This occurrence is incompletely documented, but the pattern described is consistent in many ways with other cases described below. In its day, it was unique in the Southwest beside the then unpublished Chaco discoveries (see Pepper, 1920; Chapter 13). Now Canyon Butte stands as an early discovery in a series.

SITE NAME: **La Plata 23 Rockshelter**.
SITE NUMBER: La Plata 23.

SITE LOCATION: Southwestern Colorado, on the west side of the La Plata River Valley, N of Pond's Arroyo.
EXCAVATOR(S): H. L. Shapiro.
DATE(S) OF EXCAVATION: 1927.
COMPLETENESS OF EXCAVATION: Unspecified.
PRIMARY ARCHAEOLOGICAL REPORT: Morris (1939).
PRIMARY SKELETAL REPORT: Morris (1939).
SITE TYPE: Open air, in front of a rock shelter dripline, between this line and the talus slope. A surface scatter of ceramics and bone led to excavation of a shallow firepit with slab walls. No other architecture was present.
AGE—LOCAL CHRONOLOGY: Undetermined.
AGE—REGIONAL CHRONOLOGY: The "highly evolved Pueblo wares" cited by Morris (1939) imply a Pueblo III placement for the occurrence. Reed (1948) identifies the jar with the bone material as PIII ware.
CHRONOMETRIC AGE(S): None.
CONTEXT OF HUMAN REMAINS: The fragments were found embedded in a burned layer in and adjacent to the firepit, and inside a large corrugated jar.
NUMBER OF HUMAN SKELETAL PIECES: Unspecified.
NUMBER OF INDIVIDUALS: 2.
AGE AND SEX OF INDIVIDUALS: One adolescent, one adult male.
DAMAGE PATTERN:
Burning: Many charred.
Cutting: Unspecified.
Fracture: Skulls broken open, long bones splintered.
Gnawing: Unspecified.
Preservation: Unspecified.
EXCAVATOR'S INTERPRETATION: "There can be little doubt that the two persons were cooked and eaten beneath the shelter of the ledge. Both skulls had been broken open, and most of the long bones splintered, just as would have been done to secure the brains and marrow" (Morris, 1939:75).
OTHER REPORTS AND INTERPRETATIONS: Reed (1948) and Flinn *et al.* (1976) acknowledge Morris, but Turner's 1983 summary makes no reference to this occurrence.
DISCUSSION: An analysis of this assemblage has never been published.

SITE NAME: **La Plata 41, Building XIV**.
SITE NUMBER: La Plata 41.
SITE LOCATION: Northwestern New Mexico, on the west side of the La Plata River, 3.5 km S of the Colorado border.
EXCAVATOR(S): Earl Morris.
DATE(S) OF EXCAVATION: 1930.
COMPLETENESS OF EXCAVATION: Complete, 100%.
PRIMARY ARCHAEOLOGICAL REPORT: Morris (1939).
PRIMARY SKELETAL REPORT: Morris (1939).
SITE TYPE: A unit pueblo with more than 13 rooms and two associated kivas.
AGE—LOCAL CHRONOLOGY: Unspecified.
AGE—REGIONAL CHRONOLOGY: Early Pueblo III by a large bowl, most of the pieces of which were found in direct association with the skeletal remains.
CHRONOMETRIC AGE(S): None.
CONTEXT OF HUMAN REMAINS: The remains were in a pit beneath two rooms. The pit was 2.45 m in diameter and 90 cm deep, and extended beyond the area beneath the rooms. The fill contained refuse, and the human remains were concentrated in a stratum 15 to 30 cm above the pit floor.
NUMBER OF HUMAN SKELETAL PIECES: Unspecified.
NUMBER OF INDIVIDUALS: 6.
AGE AND SEX OF INDIVIDUALS: Four adults, one adolescent, and one small child.
DAMAGE PATTERN:
Burning: "Browning" and charring present on "a minor portion" (Morris, 1939:105).
Cutting: Unspecified.
Fracture: "With few exceptions, the large bones and many small ones as well, had been split and cracked to pieces" (Morris, 1939:105). A photograph of assemblage elements (Morris, 1939, Plate 81) shows humeral and femoral shaft breakage, but, at least in some cases, both ends of these bones remained intact.
Gnawing: Unspecified.
Preservation: "They had the dead white appearance characteristic of bones that have been cooked, or freed from the soft parts before being covered with earth. This was not the bleach resulting from sunlight" (Morris, 1939:105).

EXCAVATOR'S INTERPRETATION: "All facts considered, it would be difficult to regard this mass of human remains as other than the residuum of a cannibalistic rite or orgy" (Morris, 1939:105).

OTHER REPORTS AND INTERPRETATIONS: None.

DISCUSSION: Morris (1939) illustrates this material (his Plate 81) and it is evident that his descriptions are accurate. The manner in which the bones were piled for the photograph, however, makes any further interpretation difficult.

SITE NAME: **Big Hawk Valley**.

SITE NUMBER: NA–682; "House of Tragedy."

SITE LOCATION: Northern Arizona, just S of the southern boundary of Wupatki National Monument, 1 mile E of U.S. Highway 89.

EXCAVATOR(S): Watson Smith.

DATE(S) OF EXCAVATION: 1948.

COMPLETENESS OF EXCAVATION: Complete, 100%.

PRIMARY ARCHAEOLOGICAL REPORT: Smith (1949, 1952).

PRIMARY SKELETAL REPORT: Smith (1952).

SITE TYPE: A one-story unit pueblo of 5 rooms, with a kiva and 4 associated storage pits.

AGE—LOCAL CHRONOLOGY: Tusayan, with strong Cohonina influence (Smith) or Klethla focus of Kayenta Anasazi (Turner and Turner, 1990).

AGE—REGIONAL CHRONOLOGY: Late Pueblo II or Early Pueblo III.

CHRONOMETRIC AGE(S): Unspecified.

CONTEXT OF HUMAN REMAINS: The remains found in the kiva include one skeleton with a "detached" left leg and an associated individual represented by scattered human bones. Bones from these individuals are not described as intentionally fractured and no trauma besides disarticulation is noted. Four storage pits were found nearby. One of these, Pit D, contained human remains buried under a sandstone slab.

NUMBER OF HUMAN SKELETAL PIECES: Unspecified.

NUMBER OF INDIVIDUALS: Unspecified.

AGE AND SEX OF INDIVIDUALS: Unspecified.

DAMAGE PATTERN:

Burning: Present.

Cutting: Present.

Fracture: Most long bones broken transversely, split longitudinally, and "hollowed out."

Gnawing: Absent.

Preservation: Unspecified.

EXCAVATOR'S INTERPRETATION: Smith (1949:48) suggests "An inference of cannibalism is tempting although perhaps unwarranted." His 1952 report reiterates this position, noting that an interpretation of cannibalism is "tempting," but going on to suggest that the bones might have even been reburied by a "particularly vituperative grave digger" (Smith, 1952:69).

OTHER REPORTS AND INTERPRETATIONS: Cited by Flinn *et al.* (1976) as a "similar example" in their analysis of Burnt Mesa (see below). Turner and Turner (1990:207) analyzed the available sample (Pit D remains could not be located) and found what they considered to be "the taphonomic signature of cannibalism."

DISCUSSION: Smith (1952) cites Morris' (1939) reports from La Plata, pointing out strong parallels in the patterning. As noted above, however, Smith is very tentative about attributing the Big Hawk evidence to cannibalism.

SITE NAME: **Yellow Jacket Porter Pueblo**.

SITE NUMBER: Site 5MT–1.

SITE LOCATION: In southwestern Colorado, between Cortez and Monticello, Utah, adjacent to U.S. Highway 666, at the head of Yellow Jacket Canyon. This site, the "Stevenson Site," is located c. 600 m SW of the southern end of the Yellow Jacket Ruin (5MT–5).

EXCAVATOR(S): University of Colorado Field School, under the direction of Joe Ben Wheat.

DATE(S) OF EXCAVATION: 1959.

COMPLETENESS OF EXCAVATION: Unspecified.

PRIMARY ARCHAEOLOGICAL REPORT: Swedlund (1969).

PRIMARY SKELETAL REPORT: Swedlund (1969).

SITE TYPE: Porter Pueblo is a residential site associated with a large ceremonial center.

AGE—LOCAL CHRONOLOGY: Early Mancos period.

AGE—REGIONAL CHRONOLOGY: Pueblo II.
CHRONOMETRIC AGE(S): C. A.D. 950–1025.
CONTEXT OF HUMAN REMAINS: Bones were found randomly distributed in a storage pit, in a 20-cm thick lens of ash and charcoal near the bottom of a 1.3-m diameter, 1-m deep storage pit cut into native clay and covered by a house floor. Some of the pieces were articulated, and the human remains were mixed with animal bone fragments, potsherds, a stone knife, hammerstones, bone awls, and other debris.
NUMBER OF HUMAN SKELETAL PIECES: Malville (1989) reports 500.
NUMBER OF INDIVIDUALS: 4.
AGE AND SEX OF INDIVIDUALS: The four individuals ranged in age from a four to five-year-old child to a 17-year-old.
DAMAGE PATTERN:
Burning: One cranial vault shows exfoliation of the outer table and evidence of thermal alteration, but Malville (1989) describes little evidence of burning.
Cutting: "Some striations occur on the long bones which might possibly be considered 'cutting' marks, but again the evidence is not clear" (Swedlund, 1969:108). Malville (1989) describes cranial cutmarks in detail, and it is clear that the crania were scalped. She also notes that slicing marks were more abundant than percussion marks on the Porter assemblage, while the reverse was true of the 5MT–3 assemblage (see below).
Fracture: Most long bones were split and fragmentary, many with spiral fractures. The crania, although broken into, were not as fragmented as reported in similar assemblages. Fracture was selective, focused on the larger diameter long bones.
Gnawing: Unspecified.
Preservation: Very good, with all the bones "bleached" to a light color, with minor plant root etching.
EXCAVATOR'S INTERPRETATION: Wheat (unpublished) interpreted the human bones to represent food remains. Swedlund (1969:107–108) cautiously considers that "The possibility that cannibalism was practiced is implied by the context of four individuals. . . ."
OTHER REPORTS AND INTERPRETATIONS: Malville (1989).
DISCUSSION: Although this represents a limited sample that has not been fully described, the data available make it clear that this assemblage shares many characteristics with the others described here.

SITE NAME: **Sambrito Village**.
SITE NUMBER: LA–4195.
SITE LOCATION: Northwestern New Mexico, on the west bank of the San Juan River, Rosa section, Navajo Reservoir District.
EXCAVATOR(S): F. W. Eddy and A. E. Dittert.
DATE(S) OF EXCAVATION: 1960, 1961.
COMPLETENESS OF EXCAVATION: Assisted by heavy equipment, excavation of the village was fairly complete, but the key occurrence in Pithouse 25 (see below) was recovered in a trench; the pithouse was not fully excavated.
PRIMARY ARCHAEOLOGICAL REPORT: Dittert *et al.* (1966).
PRIMARY SKELETAL REPORT: Bennett (1966).
SITE TYPE: A pithouse village of 38 houses, 25 surface structures, and 28 exterior pits, but no extensive refuse deposits.
AGE—LOCAL CHRONOLOGY: Piedra Phase.
AGE—REGIONAL CHRONOLOGY: Turner (1983) cites A.D. 950, which would place this site as Early Pueblo II.
CHRONOMETRIC AGE(S): Dendrochronology was employed, and one radiocarbon date was obtained. Ceramics indicated a 600-year occupation of the site. The radiocarbon date of 214 B.C. ± 264 was considered faulty by the investigators.
CONTEXT OF HUMAN REMAINS: A total of 17 collections of disarticulated bones representing 44 individuals was found scattered in the fill of features. Most individuals (n = 31) were in pithouses. Only 2 of these bone lots, from the "slump" of Pit houses 6 and 25, are described as cannibalized. These assemblages represent 3 and 12 individuals, respectively; the larger sample was found under a collapsed roof.
NUMBER OF HUMAN SKELETAL PIECES: 474 (Turner, 1983).
NUMBER OF INDIVIDUALS: From Pithouses 6 and 25, Dittert *et al.* (1966) report 15 individ-

uals, Bennett (1966) reports 14, and Turner (1983) tabulates 5 (possibly a misprint).

AGE AND SEX OF INDIVIDUALS: Bennett (1966) reports two adults and a child in Pithouse 6, five adolescents/young adults, four adults, and two age-indeterminate individuals from Pithouse 25.

DAMAGE PATTERN:

Burning: Turner (1983) reports 16.7 percent (79 of 474) burning.

Cutting: Turner (1983) reports that 4.6 percent (22 of 474) of the specimens show cutmarks.

Fracture: Turner (1983) reports 99.8 percent perimortem fracture and Dittert *et al.* (1966:248) describe the assemblages as showing ". . . long bones which were split lengthwise. Impact percussion scars suggest the use of a stone hammer to open the shafts. . . . This evidence indicates that the human bones were fleshed and broken open while the bone was still green."

Gnawing: Turner (1983) reports none.

Preservation: Unspecified.

EXCAVATOR'S INTERPRETATION: "Apparently these people were killed, cannibalized, and tossed onto the house floor, after which the structure was burned down upon them" (Dittert *et al.*, 1966:248).

OTHER REPORTS AND INTERPRETATIONS: Eddy (1974) suggests that the remains represent slaughtered members of a raiding party, but provides no evidence to support this claim. Flinn *et al.* (1976) note the proximity of the Sambrito and Burnt Mesa occurrences of perimortem trauma. Turner's independent analysis of the Sambrito Village remains (1983; presumably the pooled samples from Pithouses 6 and 25) resulted in an interpretation of cannibalism.

DISCUSSION: Despite multiple analyses, this material is not well illustrated or otherwise documented.

SITE NAME: **St. Christopher's Mission, Bluff, Utah.**

SITE NUMBER: Unspecified.

SITE LOCATION: In southeastern Utah, on the grounds of St. Christopher's Mission to the Navajo, near Bluff, Utah.

EXCAVATOR(S): Uncovered by bulldozer. Archaeologists Rudy, Lancaster, and Hewitt from Mesa Verde National Park went to observe the occurrence, and they salvaged the assemblage.

DATE(S) OF EXCAVATION: February 19, 1961.

COMPLETENESS OF EXCAVATION: Unspecified.

PRIMARY ARCHAEOLOGICAL REPORT: J. R. Rudy's "Investigation of a Site at Bluff, Utah" is a three-page, three-figure typescript report to the Mesa Verde National Park superintendent, dated February 28, 1961.

PRIMARY SKELETAL REPORT: Same.

SITE TYPE: Described in the report as "use area," with the suggestion of "some type of brush arbor-like structure," but without postholes and no definite house or room outline.

AGE—LOCAL CHRONOLOGY: Unspecified.

AGE—REGIONAL CHRONOLOGY: Indeterminate.

CHRONOMETRIC AGE(S): Unspecified.

CONTEXT OF HUMAN REMAINS: The remains were found jumbled together some 15 m south of the structure area, with no association except for three fortuitous Pueblo III sherds. Nothing suggested a direct link between the structure and the remains. The latter were encountered c. 1.3 m below the modern ground level. One adult tibia and fibula were found in articulation.

NUMBER OF HUMAN SKELETAL PIECES: There has been some postrefitting gluing of pieces together, particularly cranial parts. The current piece count is 202.

NUMBER OF INDIVIDUALS: At least five and possibly six or seven individuals were noted in the preliminary report, but my own preliminary reassessment in 1990 showed a MNI of 4 individuals.

NUMBER OF INDIVIDUALS: At least five and possibly six or seven individuals were noted in the preliminary report, but my own preliminary reassessment in 1990 showed a MNI of 4 individuals.

AGE AND SEX OF INDIVIDUALS: One adult (probable female) individual, one child of 6 years, one individual of 9–10 years, and one individual 6–10 years.

DAMAGE PATTERN:

Burning: Present on both cranial and postcranial elements; patterning corresponds to soft tissue cover; burning is focused on long-bone ends.

Cutting: Cutmarks noted on both cranial and postcranial elements.

Fracture: Fragmentation of cranial vaults is complete, but many long-bone shafts are complete.

Gnawing: Absent.

Preservation: Excellent.

EXCAVATOR'S INTERPRETATION: The primary report concludes that "The state of the bones recovered suggests cannibalism."

OTHER REPORTS AND INTERPRETATIONS: None; the author examined these remains in 1990 and found the patterning to be consistent in many details with that observed on other assemblages described here.

DISCUSSION: This occurrence was brought to the attention of current park archaeologist Jack Smith by Shane Baker of the Museum of Peoples and Cultures, B.Y.U., Provo, Utah. It is a relatively small collection in need of further analysis after deconjoining.

SITE NAME: **Polacca Wash.**

SITE NUMBER: NA–8502.

SITE LOCATION: In northeastern Arizona, on the left bank of Polacca Wash, about 10 miles S of the modern Hopi villages.

EXCAVATOR(S): Alan Olson and Edward Danson.

DATE(S) OF EXCAVATION: 1964.

COMPLETENESS OF EXCAVATION: Erosion had removed an indeterminate number of bones (see below), but those that remained were recovered.

PRIMARY ARCHAEOLOGICAL REPORT: Danson (1965) and Olson (1966).

PRIMARY SKELETAL REPORT: Olson (1966), reporting on the work of S. I. Rosen.

AGE—LOCAL CHRONOLOGY: The ceramic fragments include Tusayan corrugated utility ware, suggested by Danson to span A.D. 950 to 1275, and Tusayan black-on-red, dating between A.D. 1000 and 1300. These, of course, may not be contemporary with the bones. Olson (1966) suggests that the remains were deposited between A.D. 1000 and 1200.

AGE—REGIONAL CHRONOLOGY: See below.

CHRONOMETRIC AGE(S): A radiocarbon date on bone of 350 ± 95 B.P. places the site at c. A.D. 1580 (Turner and Morris, 1970), and their ethnohistorical conclusion (see below) places the site at A.D. 1700. They cite bone preservation as additional evidence for a more recent age than Pueblo III, but this should be discounted on the basis of uniformly good preservation among similar assemblages.

CONTEXT OF HUMAN REMAINS: The discovery was made when the bone bed was exposed around the periphery of a "hummock" in the center of a channel. Danson (1965) suggests and Olson (1966) interprets the spatial patterning as indicative of a purposeful oval arrangement of the bones, but preexcavation photographs show clearly that the bone bed was more extensive before erosion and that bones had obviously been carried away by moving water prior to the discovery. Only four potsherds and a *Neotoma* tibia were associated with the bone bed, lying at its base.

NUMBER OF HUMAN SKELETAL PIECES: Unspecified.

NUMBER OF INDIVIDUALS: 30.

AGE AND SEX OF INDIVIDUALS: 8 children from 1 year up, 4 adolescents, and eighteen adults. Of the adults, one male and three females could be identified (Turner, 1983).

DAMAGE PATTERN:

Burning: Turner (1983) reports 36% (156 of 437) burning. Olson (1966) notes charring on the internal surfaces of some bones.

Cutting: Present, not quantified.

Fracture: Turner and Morris (1970) describe two kinds of damage. The first is percussion of shafts to obtain marrow, and the second is breaking of long-bone ends and other processes, condyles, and articular surfaces. Percussion scars and adhering flakes are noted and illustrated. Crushing damage to the facial regions is also described. Turner (1983) reports 80.3 percent (351 of 437) perimortem fracture.

Gnawing: Turner and Morris (1970) rule out rodent or carnivore damage, and Turner (1983) notes the possible presence of gnawing.

Preservation: Some pieces that had been recently exposed showed a chalky, cracked, exfoliating surface. Others that had remained buried until excavation had more integrity.

EXCAVATOR'S INTERPRETATION: Olson (1966), interpreting the spatial patterning as a "formal arrangement," cautiously interprets the occurrence as evidence of a "magico-religious rite," describing it as a mass secondary burial ("secondary" clearly means, in this context, a lack of articulation of the bones). About cannibalism, Olson (1966:826) asks only: ". . . do the breakage and charring of the bone suggest cannibalism?"

OTHER REPORTS AND INTERPRETATIONS: Olson discounts a connection between the occurrence and the legend of the destruction of the Hopi pueblo of Awatobi. Turner and Morris (1970), however, conclude that the bones found at Polacca Wash represent 30 Hopi Indians of both sexes and all ages who were killed, dismembered, violently mutilated, and probably cannibalized. Furthermore, they make the case that the location, dismemberment, and age of the "burial" suggest that the bodies represent the captives taken in the legendary destruction of Awatobi Pueblo in A.D. 1700. These authors (1970:323) describe the assemblage as ". . . at present the most convincing evidence of cannibalism in all Southwestern archeology." They use this assemblage to generate a list of criteria for identification of cannibalism, including brain exposure, facial mutilation, burning, dismemberment, missing elements, shaft percussion, and cutmarks.

DISCUSSION: Fewkes' (1893) excavation of the abandoned village of Awatobi provided strong archaeological confirmation of the legend in the form of widespread evidence of a conflagration, including charred corn, as well as unburied skeletal remains on the kiva floor. Olson (1966) uses dating, skeletal makeup, and geographic location to discount the interpretation of the Polacca Wash occurrence as directly linked to Awatobi. Olson (1966) says that there is no evidence of violence, a point that Turner and Morris (1970) violently contend. The latter authors (1970:327) suggest that the individuals involved ". . . met a traumatic death, probably at their burial site, when each was mutilated, dismembered and smashed into small pieces."

It is impossible to determine the cause or nature of death from bony remains, but the Turner and Morris description of perimortem trauma is the more complete of the two available. Their interpretation of the Polacca evidence as the remains of the legendary Awatobi raid, however, must remain an unconfirmed possibility. Uncertainties over the dating, the incomplete recovery of the skeletal material, and the increased sample of other similar assemblages, all warrant caution in linking the occurrence with the legend. In this vein, Olson's (1966:826) closing paragraph has proven prophetic: "If this is a prehistoric occurrence, other examples may have been missed by those of us who comb pueblos and trash dumps without ranging too far afield from the specific site. If this is an ethnological practice, it may be imbedded in a matrix of practices that have thus far been incompletely explored."

SITE NAME: **Burnt Mesa.**

SITE NUMBER: LA–4528.

SITE LOCATION: In northwestern New Mexico, on Burnt Mesa, a plateau between the Pine and San Juan Rivers.

EXCAVATOR(S): Alan Brew.

DATE(S) OF EXCAVATION: 1969.

COMPLETENESS OF EXCAVATION: Complete, 100 percent.

PRIMARY ARCHAEOLOGICAL REPORT: Flinn *et al.* (1976).

PRIMARY SKELETAL REPORT: Flinn *et al.* (1976).

SITE TYPE: Three pithouses and associated surface structures.

AGE—LOCAL CHRONOLOGY: Late Piedra.

AGE—REGIONAL CHRONOLOGY: Early Pueblo II, based on ceramics and architecture.

CHRONOMETRIC AGE(S): Unspecified.

CONTEXT OF HUMAN REMAINS: One pithouse (Pit House 1) contained the occurrence; this pithouse was the only occupied structure at the time of the depositional event involving the skeletal remains. The occurrence represents a single depositional event, with bones found directly on the floor surface. The remains were subsequently buried by the collapse of the roof structure. Bone was found against and beneath metates on the floor, and most bone was found in a mound-shaped residential refuse deposit of ash and trash near the interior firepit. The primary investigators concluded that it was "quite possible" that the five metates on the floor of the pithouse were used as anvils for breaking and crushing the long bones.

NUMBER OF HUMAN SKELETAL PIECES: 3,389 (Turner, 1983).

NUMBER OF INDIVIDUALS: 11.

AGE AND SEX OF INDIVIDUALS: 1 infant, 2 children, 1 subadult, 7 adults, including 4 males and two females.

DAMAGE PATTERN:

Burning: Turner (1983) reports 35.4 percent (1,200 of 3,389) burning.

Cutting: Turner (1983) reports 2.8 percent (96 of 3,389) of the sample to have cutmarks. There are scalping marks on the cranial bones and disarticulation cutmarks on the postcrania.

Fracture: Turner (1983) reports 98 percent (3,321 of 3,389) perimortem fracture. The limb bones are splintered into long, angular fragments, and the proximal and distal pieces are broken or sheared off. Only four long bones are complete. The crania are broken, with radiating stress fractures.

Gnawing: 52 of the bones (1.5%) show evidence of gnawing.

Preservation: Described as good, with the unburned fragments being dense, nonfriable, and white to pale yellow.

EXCAVATOR'S INTERPRETATION: "Cannibalism is the most reasonable explanation for the patterned destruction" (Flinn *et al.* 1976:308).

OTHER REPORTS AND INTERPRETATIONS: Turner (1983) provides the same interpretation and lists the occurrence as evidence of "emergency" cannibalism.

DISCUSSION: The primary report on this large sample shows considerable sophistication in the methodology that Turner had developed to assess these assemblages. This methodology was first set out comprehensively in the Turner and Morris (1970) work on the Polacca Wash assemblage, and truly comparative work was possible in the early 1970s as a result of this development.

SITE NAME: **Monument Valley.**

SITE NUMBER: Unspecified.

SITE LOCATION: Northeastern Arizona or southeastern Utah, between the San Juan River and the Oljeto and Gypsum washes. The location of the occurrence in the valley was not established before the excavator's death.

EXCAVATOR(S): J. Lee Correll.

DATE(S) OF EXCAVATION: 1970.

COMPLETENESS OF EXCAVATION: The feature containing the bones was completely excavated.

PRIMARY ARCHAEOLOGICAL REPORT: Nass and Bellantoni (1982).

PRIMARY SKELETAL REPORT: Nass and Bellantoni (1982).

SITE TYPE: A 30-cm deep, slab-lined pit, approximately 0.61 m in diameter. An upright slab was placed on one side, and three other slabs covered most of the pit.

AGE—LOCAL CHRONOLOGY: Indeterminate.

AGE—REGIONAL CHRONOLOGY: Indeterminate.

CHRONOMETRIC AGE(S): Undetermined.

CONTEXT OF HUMAN REMAINS: Some of the sandstone slabs showed burning, and charcoal flakes were located throughout the pit. There were no nearby structures, and no cultural materials were present.

NUMBER OF HUMAN SKELETAL PIECES: 644.

NUMBER OF INDIVIDUALS: 7.

AGE AND SEX OF INDIVIDUALS: One infant, three adolescents, one adult male, and two elderly persons (one male and one female).

DAMAGE PATTERN:

Burning: Nass and Bellantoni (1982) report 12.6 percent burning, with 75 of the 644 charred and 6 calcined.

Cutting: 6 of the 644 (0.9%) had cutmarks.

Fracture: Almost all limb bones were fractured and splintered, the crania broken into.

Gnawing: Absent.

Preservation: The remains are reported as exhibiting neither weathering cracks nor sun-bleaching. The bones are reported as uncracked, unsplintered, and not brittle, retaining most of their organic matter and structure.

EXCAVATOR'S INTERPRETATION: The excavator died prior to publication.

OTHER REPORTS AND INTERPRETATIONS: Nass and Bellantoni (1982:269) conclude that "Without further evidence we suggest this was a family group that, for unknown reasons, fell victim to either ritual or survival cannibalism. . . ." Turner (1983) includes the assemblage in his survey.

DISCUSSION: The twelve-year period between discovery and publication, and the lack of chronological control served to diminish the impact of the discovery on other researchers.

SITE NAME: **Mancos Canyon 5MTUMR–2346.** NOTE: *This occurrence is the focus of the book. The data sketched in here are exclusively from Nickens (1975) and are provided at this juncture only to show how Mancos fits into the history of discovery and interpretation.*

SITE NUMBER: 5MTUMR–2346.

SITE LOCATION: Southwestern Colorado, just less than 1 km W of the Navajo Canyon and Mancos Canyon junction.

EXCAVATOR(S): J. A. Lancaster and L. V. Nordby, under the direction of David Breternitz.

DATE(S) OF EXCAVATION: 1973

COMPLETENESS OF EXCAVATION: Salvage, most of a unit pueblo.

PRIMARY ARCHAEOLOGICAL REPORT: Nordby (1974).

PRIMARY SKELETAL REPORT: Nickens (1974, 1975).

SITE TYPE: A unit pueblo with several rooms, a kiva, and an associated midden.

AGE—LOCAL CHRONOLOGY: McElmo Phase.

AGE—REGIONAL CHRONOLOGY: Early Pueblo III.

CHRONOMETRIC AGE(S): A.D. 1100–1150.

CONTEXT OF HUMAN REMAINS: The remains were scattered in the fill of several rooms.

NUMBER OF HUMAN SKELETAL PIECES: 1899 (Nickens, 1975).

NUMBER OF INDIVIDUALS: 33 (Nickens, 1975).

AGE AND SEX OF INDIVIDUALS: Identified as mostly adolescents and young adults.

DAMAGE PATTERN:

Burning: Present.

Cutting: Present.

Fracture: Perimortem.

Gnawing: Unspecified.

Preservation: Excellent.

EXCAVATOR'S INTERPRETATION: Cannibalism.

OTHER REPORTS AND INTERPRETATIONS: Cannibalism (Turner, 1983).

DISCUSSION: Chapter 3 is dedicated to a detailed consideration of the Mancos Canyon site, and the remainder of the book assesses the evidence.

SITE NAME: **Leroux Wash.**

SITE NUMBER: NA–12854.

SITE LOCATION: In northern Arizona, near Holbrook.

EXCAVATOR(S): Peter Pilles and Dana Hartman.

DATE(S) OF EXCAVATION: 1974.

COMPLETENESS OF EXCAVATION: Incomplete: pothunters had disturbed the occurrence and removed some of the skeletal remains.

PRIMARY ARCHAEOLOGICAL REPORT: Hartman's paper delivered at the annual American Association of Physical Anthropologists meeting constitutes the original report, but the published abstract (1975) does not specifically refer to the occurrence. Allen *et al.* (1985) cite Pilles (personal communication) in referring to bones cut into small pieces, with scorched ends and some cutmarked crania. Turner's 1983 summary provides data on the bone assemblage as outlined above but gives no other contextual information.

PRIMARY SKELETAL REPORT: Turner (1983).

SITE TYPE: A pit near a small pueblo contained the remains.

AGE—LOCAL CHRONOLOGY: Unspecified.

AGE—REGIONAL CHRONOLOGY: Late Pueblo III.

CHRONOMETRIC AGE(S): Turner (personal communication, 1983 letter) reports a collagen fraction date of A.D. 1065 ± 55.

CONTEXT OF HUMAN REMAINS: Commingled with charcoal and earth in a large pit.

NUMBER OF HUMAN SKELETAL PIECES: 3,443 (Turner, 1983).

NUMBER OF INDIVIDUALS: Allen *et al.* (1985) cite Pilles at 25–30. Turner (1983) reports more than 16.

AGE AND SEX OF INDIVIDUALS: Unspecified.

DAMAGE PATTERN:

Burning: Turner (1983) reports 1.7 percent (59 of 3,443) burning.

Cutting: Turner (1983) reports 2.6 percent (89 of 3,443) of the sample to have cutmarks.

Fracture: Turner (1983) reports 99.7 percent (3,434 of 3,443) perimortem fracture.

Gnawing: Turner (1983) reports 3.0 percent (102 of 3,443) gnawing.

Preservation: Good (Turner, 1983).

EXCAVATOR'S INTERPRETATION: Cannibalism.

OTHER REPORTS AND INTERPRETATIONS: See above.

DISCUSSION: This is a very important assemblage that deserves a fuller accounting despite the fact that it was disturbed and partly lost to pothunters.

SITE NAME: **Grinnell.**

SITE NUMBER: Unspecified.

SITE LOCATION: In extreme southwestern Colorado, about 15 km SW of Cortez, just SW of Yucca House National Monument on the Ray Ismay Ranch.

EXCAVATOR(S): Ralph Luebben.

DATE(S) OF EXCAVATION: 1974.

COMPLETENESS OF EXCAVATION: Complete, 100 percent.

PRIMARY ARCHAEOLOGICAL REPORT: Luebben and Nickens (1982).

PRIMARY SKELETAL REPORT: Luebben and Nickens (1982).

SITE TYPE: Termed "an unusual small ceremonial complex" by Luebben and Nickens, this site consisted of two kivas, a tunnel, a subterranean room, a circular tower, and two other surface structures.

AGE—LOCAL CHRONOLOGY: Early Mesa Verde Phase.

AGE—REGIONAL CHRONOLOGY: Early Pueblo III.

CHRONOMETRIC AGE(S): Dendrochronology and ceramic analysis place the site between A.D. 1135 and 1150.

CONTEXT OF HUMAN REMAINS: Cist 2, an oval cist of about 0.5 m cut into natural shale near the southeast recessed corner of Kiva 2, contained most of the human bones, two ceramic vessels, two hammerstones, and several other stones. Some bone was in the fill of a corrugated jar. Other human bone fragments were found on the adjacent kiva floor. A small amount of nonhuman bone (71 pieces, mostly bird and rodent) was also recovered.

NUMBER OF HUMAN SKELETAL PIECES: 380.

NUMBER OF INDIVIDUALS: 7

AGE AND SEX OF INDIVIDUALS: 2 children (8–10 years), 1 subadult (19 years), and 4 adults. At least one adult was female.

DAMAGE PATTERN:

Burning: Uncertain. Luebben and Nickens (1982) report burning on two shaft segments and 39 fragments of a parietal. Turner (1983) counts this as 41 burned pieces, 10.8 percent of the assemblage.

Cutting: 4 specimens show cutmarks (1 percent of the assemblage).

Fracture: Percussion fracture of long-bone shafts. Turner (1983) reports 97.9 percent (372 of 380) perimortem fracture.

Gnawing: Two bones show rodent gnawing.

Preservation: Excellent. The bone was dense and nonfriable, with sharp, angular, uneroded edges. On two-thirds of the fragments, cortex was intact and colored white and pale yellow.

EXCAVATOR'S INTERPRETATION: The authors describe the occurrence as similar to other mass interments but very cautiously avoid the conclusion that cannibalism was involved.

OTHER REPORTS AND INTERPRETATIONS: Turner includes this assemblage in his 1983 survey.

DISCUSSION: By the time that the Luebben and Nickens paper on Grinnell was published in 1982, the authors were able to refer to nearly a dozen "mass interments" that had been found in the Four Corners area. They note that this assemblage differed from the others only in its setting in a kiva, but refrain from interpreting the find as evidence of cannibalism, preferring instead the term "mass interment."

SITE NAME: **Marshview Hamlet.**
SITE NUMBER: 5MT–2235.
SITE LOCATION: Southwestern Colorado, in the Dolores Archaeological Project area, McPhee Reservoir.
EXCAVATOR(S): David Breternitz.
DATE(S) OF EXCAVATION: Between 1978 and 1980.
COMPLETENESS OF EXCAVATION: Unspecified.
PRIMARY ARCHAEOLOGICAL REPORT: Wiener (1984).
PRIMARY SKELETAL REPORT: Wiener (1984).
SITE TYPE: A large pitstructure.
AGE—LOCAL CHRONOLOGY: Sundial Phase and Marshview Subphase.
AGE—REGIONAL CHRONOLOGY: Mesa Verde Branch, Anasazi, Late Pueblo II Shill, Early Pueblo III.
CHRONOMETRIC AGE(S): A.D. 1050–1125 is given by Turner (1983), but the basis of the date is unspecified.
CONTEXT OF HUMAN REMAINS: On and near the floor of Pithouse 1, in the floor fill, upper fill, and outside of this large pitstructure. Some fragments from a firepit and some from a ventilator shaft.
NUMBER OF HUMAN SKELETAL PIECES: 528 (Turner, n.d.).
NUMBER OF INDIVIDUALS: 6.
AGE AND SEX OF INDIVIDUALS: Two children 2–12 years, one adolescent, and three older adults, one possible male and one female.
DAMAGE PATTERN:

Burning: Turner (n.d.) records 162 bones showing burning (30.7%), noting that most of the charred and calcined material was from a firepit.

Cutting: Turner (n.d.) records 14 specimens with cutmarks (2.6%).

Fracture: Percussion blows from hammer and anvil. Turner (n.d.) reports 99.9 percent perimortem fracture.

Gnawing: Turner (n.d.) reports 7 percent incidence of rodent and carnivore chewing, a figure higher than that seen in the other assemblages.

Preservation: Turner (n.d.) reports excellent, but Wiener (1984) and personal observation by the author agree that the preservation in this assemblage is not as good as that seen in other assemblages.

EXCAVATOR'S INTERPRETATION: Wiener (1984) initially displayed reluctance to label the Marshview Hamlet remains as evidence of cannibalism, interpreting them as a secondary burial, citing the presence of ceramic vessels and animal effigies as well as the relatively poor preservation of the bone.
OTHER REPORTS AND INTERPRETATIONS: Turner (n.d.) considers cannibalism to be the most "parsimonious" explanation for the assemblage that shares most features with the other occurrences described in this appendix.

SITE NAME: **Ash Creek (Tapia del Cerrito).**
SITE NUMBER: AZ:U:3:49 (ASU)
SITE LOCATION: Central Arizona, in the Tonto Basin, about 3 km N of the north end of Theodore Roosevelt Lake. This site is the farthest south of my sample and is referred to as "Salado" rather than "Anasazi."
EXCAVATOR(S): Glen Rice and John Hohmann.
DATE(S) OF EXCAVATION: 1982, 1983.
COMPLETENESS OF EXCAVATION: Total excavation of room spaces, sampling of extramural area, with full feature exposure.
PRIMARY ARCHAEOLOGICAL REPORT: Hohmann *et al.* (1985) and Rice (1985).
PRIMARY SKELETAL REPORT: Turner (1983).
SITE TYPE: A small unit pueblo of six masonry rooms, one long hallway, two small granaries, several free-standing walls, a roasting pit, and assorted extramural pits and hearths.
AGE—LOCAL CHRONOLOGY: Gila Phase, Salado.
AGE—REGIONAL CHRONOLOGY: Pueblo IV equivalent.
CHRONOMETRIC AGE(S): A.D. 1360 ± 60 by radiocarbon.
CONTEXT OF HUMAN REMAINS: Room 3, roughly 5 m × 5 m, burned, with roof collapse. Human long-bone fragments were found on the floor surface, both clustered and isolated, primarily along one edge of the

room. Some sorting by individual is suggested by the spatial patterning. Minor articulation is reported (one arm only). Two clusters of long-bone fragments suggest stacking with long axes of the bones parallel.

Bayham and Hatch (1985) report that non-human faunal remains were mixed with the human assemblage and that similar treatment (fracture, burning) of artiodactyl and human bone sometimes made identification difficult.

NUMBER OF HUMAN SKELETAL PIECES: 212.

NUMBER OF INDIVIDUALS: Conflicting accounts. Turner (1983) reports 5, Hohmann *et al.* (1985) report 10.

AGE AND SEX OF INDIVIDUALS: 1 adolescent, 4 adults (Turner, 1983).

DAMAGE PATTERN:

Burning: Turner (1983) reports 25.9 percent (55 of 212) burning.

Cutting: Turner (1983) reports 3.3 percent (7 of 212) of the sample to have cutmarks.

Fracture: Turner reports 97.6 percent (207 of 212) perimortem fracture.

Gnawing: Turner reports 5.2 percent (11 of 212) gnawing, with one illustrated rib perforation being carnivore-induced.

Preservation: Turner reports that the bones are not in good condition, but Hohmann *et al.* (1985) describe the bones as well preserved.

EXCAVATOR'S INTERPRETATION: Death of 10 individuals over an extended time period. Dismemberment after death with bone breakage caused by forced dismemberment. "Curation" in fleshed state, bundling of "trophy limbs," and bundles tied to structural beams in Room 3.

OTHER REPORTS AND INTERPRETATIONS: Turner (1983) interprets the assemblage as indicating cannibalism.

DISCUSSION: Turner's interpretation is based more on the data available. The Hohmann interpretation of "trophy limbs" is backed more by assertion than evidence.

SITE NAME: **Yellow Jacket 5MT–3.**

SITE NUMBER: Site 5MT–3.

SITE LOCATION: In southwestern Colorado, between Cortez and Monticello, Utah, adjacent to U.S. Highway 666, at the head of Yellow Jacket Canyon. This site is a residential site forming part of the Yellow Jacket complex, located ENE of 5MT–1, several hundred m SW of the large main Yellow Jacket ruin, site 5MT–5.

EXCAVATOR(S): A small amount was recovered by R. Coburn in 1985–86 but the bulk came from excavations by A. Darling, under overall direction of F. Lange.

DATE(S) OF EXCAVATION: 1985–86 and 1987.

COMPLETENESS OF EXCAVATION: The kiva was completely excavated.

PRIMARY ARCHAEOLOGICAL REPORT: Not available.

PRIMARY SKELETAL REPORT: Malville (1989).

SITE TYPE: A kiva.

AGE—LOCAL CHRONOLOGY: Early to Middle Mancos Phase.

AGE—REGIONAL CHRONOLOGY: Pueblo II.

CHRONOMETRIC AGE(S): c. A.D. 1025–1050.

CONTEXT OF HUMAN REMAINS: Bone fragments found over most of the kiva floor, with concentrations of larger pieces in the north and south areas, separated by a centrally placed fire hearth of c. 1 m diameter and adjacent corrugated vessel. A partial black-on-white bowl contained bone fragments. Associated faunal remains were very limited, comprising a few large ungulate shaft fragments (mostly modified) and turkey and rodent bones.

NUMBER OF HUMAN SKELETAL PIECES: 1,556. Malville (1989) reports 1,543.

NUMBER OF INDIVIDUALS: 10

AGE AND SEX OF INDIVIDUALS: The individual immature age range is c. 1.5, 2.0, 4.0, and 9.0 years old. The adults range from c. 25 years to c. 45 years. Included among the adults are at least two large, robust male individuals and at least one small, gracile female.

DAMAGE PATTERN:

Burning: Burning damage on some of the cranial pieces involves vault exfoliation and mandibular burning very similar to that seen in the Mancos 5MTUMR–2346 assemblage. In contrast to Mancos, there is a considerable amount of postfracture burning of isolated bone fragments; several of these pieces are included in conjoining sets.

Cutting: Cutmarks are evident on both cranial and postcranial elements.

Fracture: Fracture patterns are very similar to those documented for Mancos 5MTUMR–2346, but fracture is not as intensive.

Gnawing: No carnivore gnawing is present, and rodent gnawing is limited to the faunal remains.

Preservation: Preservation is excellent. There is no weathering on the bones, and root damage is minimal. Malville (1989) notes the dramatic difference between the condition of bones in this assemblage compared to the poorly preserved bone found in formal burials at the site.

EXCAVATOR'S INTERPRETATION: It was realized during excavation that this represented a possible case of cannibalism.

OTHER REPORTS AND INTERPRETATIONS: Malville (1989) interprets the material as representing "food remains" after her comparison with Turner's descriptions of other similar assemblages.

DISCUSSION: The excavators and University of Colorado Museum made this assemblage available for my use during 1988 and 1989. I performed basic curation on the collection, and used this opportunity to refine the discussion of techniques in the concluding chapter of this book. My analysis indicates that there is extremely high integrity to this assemblage. The great majority of femur specimens, for example, participated in conjoining, which resulted in the complete restoration of intact femur shafts for several individuals.

This sample is smaller than the Mancos one, but the parallels in bone modification are widespread and dramatic. The basic differences between the assemblages relate to the degree rather than the kind of treatment (burning, fracture, representation). Processing of the Yellow Jacket assemblage followed the same procedures but did not proceed to the same stages as seen with the Mancos assemblage. Because of the excellent preservation and reasonable sample from the Yellow Jacket assemblage, and because I was able to study this collection in some detail, I employ it comparatively in the text.

SITE NAME: **Cottonwood Canyon.**

SITE NUMBER: 42SA–12209.

SITE LOCATION: In southeastern Utah, 21 km NW of Blanding, in Cottonwood Canyon, watershed of the San Juan River.

EXCAVATOR(S): Jerry Fetterman.

DATE(S) OF EXCAVATION: 1987.

COMPLETENESS OF EXCAVATION: Mitigation work, partial excavation.

PRIMARY ARCHAEOLOGICAL REPORT: Fetterman *et al.* (1988).

PRIMARY SKELETAL REPORT: White (1988, in Fetterman *et al.*).

SITE TYPE: Seven surface rooms and a plaza were excavated. The human remains derive from Structure 3.

AGE—LOCAL CHRONOLOGY: Unspecified.

AGE—REGIONAL CHRONOLOGY: Pueblo I.

CHRONOMETRIC AGE(S): A.D. 890–920 based on ceramic analysis. Two radiocarbon dates predate known occupation and are therefore discarded by Fetterman *et al.* (1988).

CONTEXT OF HUMAN REMAINS: Structure 3 is a rectangular masonry room about 2 m long and 1.5 m wide. Only half of the room was excavated. The bones were found in Feature 3, partly contained within a shallow pit that extended below the floor surface in the west corner of the room. Bones were primarily in charcoal-stained, ashy fill, with refuse. Two stemmed projectile points were recovered among the remains, and one articulated hand/forearm unit was included. Root disturbance was evident. The excavator interprets the occurrence as an interment in the corner of the structure subsequent to occupation of the room.

NUMBER OF HUMAN SKELETAL PIECES: 693 specimens were recovered from the "feature."

NUMBER OF INDIVIDUALS: 4.

AGE AND SEX OF INDIVIDUALS: 2 immature individuals of c. 12 years and 2 elderly adults, one female and one male.

DAMAGE PATTERN:

Burning: White (1988) reports that burning ranges from intensive calcining to slight scorching. Totals are misleading because of root damage to the bones.

Cutting: The evidence is poor because of poor preservation, but a small number of cutmarks is reported by White (1988).

Fracture: Perimortem fracture is extensive,

with clear evidence of percussion of vault and limbs.

Gnawing: None is evident.

Preservation: Preservation is highly variable, with many specimen surfaces being extremely decalcified because of root activity.

EXCAVATOR'S INTERPRETATION: Cannibalism proposed as a result of environmental degradation and social unrest.

OTHER REPORTS AND INTERPRETATIONS: White (1990).

DISCUSSION: This assemblage is illustrative of how postdepositional conditions can dramatically influence the degree to which modification can be interpreted.

SITE NAME: **Fence Lake Area.**

SITE NUMBER: Unspecified.

SITE LOCATION: In the Fence Lake area of New Mexico, on private land 1 hour W of Grants, New Mexico, off Highway 117. c. 20 minutes from Fence Lake, ½ mile from lava flows.

EXCAVATOR(S): Pothunters.

DATE(S) OF EXCAVATION: 1986.

COMPLETENESS OF EXCAVATION: Unknown.

PRIMARY ARCHAEOLOGICAL REPORT: None.

PRIMARY SKELETAL REPORT: Grant (1989).

SITE TYPE: Unknown.

AGE—LOCAL CHRONOLOGY: Unknown.

AGE—REGIONAL CHRONOLOGY: Recovered ceramics of mostly black-on-white Tularosa type, with some black-on-red. Guesstimate of PIII.

CHRONOMETRIC AGE(S): None.

CONTEXT OF HUMAN REMAINS: From what may have been a firepit, no faunal remains associated.

NUMBER OF HUMAN SKELETAL PIECES: 1,088.

NUMBER OF INDIVIDUALS: 5.

AGE AND SEX OF INDIVIDUALS: Four adults represented by mandibles include two males and two probable females. The fifth individual is subadult.

DAMAGE PATTERN:

Burning: Only "smoke-blackening" noted on 5 specimens.

Cutting: Cutmarks noted on the cranial vault and on a mandibular ramus.

Fracture: Judged to be perimortem, with evidence of percussion pits and percussion abrasion.

Gnawing: None.

Preservation: Unspecified.

EXCAVATOR'S INTERPETATION: Unknown.

OTHER REPORTS AND INTERPRETATIONS: Grant interprets the remains as having been prepared for consumption, relying heavily on Turner's attributes.

DISCUSSION: This is a large assemblage, but the poor recovery considerably diminishes its value.

SITE NAME: **Verdure Canyon.**

SITE NUMBER: Site 42SA–3724.

SITE LOCATION: In Verdure Canyon, southeastern Utah.

EXCAVATOR(S): Woods Canyon Archaeological Consultants, Inc.

DATE(S) OF EXCAVATION: 1988.

COMPLETENESS OF EXCAVATION: Unspecified.

PRIMARY ARCHAEOLOGICAL REPORT: Fink (1989).

PRIMARY SKELETAL REPORT: Fink (1989).

SITE TYPE: The disarticulated remains of a single individual were found in a small cave/crevice.

AGE—LOCAL CHRONOLOGY: Unspecified.

AGE—REGIONAL CHRONOLOGY: Pueblo II.

CHRONOMETRIC AGE(S): c. A.D. 900–1100.

CONTEXT OF HUMAN REMAINS: Unspecified, except as noted above.

NUMBER OF HUMAN SKELETAL PIECES: 19.

NUMBER OF INDIVIDUALS: 1.

AGE AND SEX OF INDIVIDUALS: The individual was a young adult male.

DAMAGE PATTERN:

Burning: Differential burning on femur.

Cutting: Cutmarks noted on the femur.

Fracture: Percussion marks noted, and spiral fracture present.

Gnawing: The suggestion of carnivore gnawing is made, but evidence is not clearly set forth. Rodent gnawing is also evident.

Preservation: Slight "weathering" is noted.

EXCAVATOR'S INTERPRETATION: Unspecified.

OTHER REPORTS AND INTERPRETATIONS:

Fink (1989) interprets the damage as evidence of "social pathology," strongly suggesting that the individual died from a blow to the head (the cause of death, of course, is impossible to verify on the basis of bony trauma). Animal scavenging and possible mutilation and cannibalism are also posited.

DISCUSSION: Lacking are contextual details of the discovery.

Appendix 2

Mancos 5MTUMR–2346 Human Bone Specimen Databases

The five database files for the entire human bone assemblage from Mancos 5MTUMR–2346 are presented here. Each horizontal row represents a single, unconjoined specimen. Each vertical column represents a single observation. Specimens are numbered sequentially from 1 through 2100 in column 3. The 94 other attributes recorded comprise the other columns. Chapter 6 provides a full guide to these data, and Table 6.1 provides a working key to the observations recorded by the 5 databases presented in this appendix.

A: Axial

01	02	03	04	05	06	07	08	09	10	11	12	13	14	15	16	17	18	19	23	24	25	40	41	42	43	44	49	54	59	64	93	94	95
M	8	1	.	.	.	.	.	B	E	ATL	10	H	.	100	.	0	.	.	.	+	.	0	.	0	0	.	0	0	.	.	.	.	.
M	5	2	B	C	ATL	12	H	.	.	.	.	.	.	100	.	0	.	.	.	+	.	0	+	0	0	.	0	0	.	+	.	.	.
M	5	3	.	.	.	.	.	B	E	ATL	12	H	.	100	.	0	.	.	+	+	.	0	+	0	0	+	0	0	.	.	.	.	.
M	82	4	B	C	ATL	AD	H	.	.	.	.	.	.	100	.	0	.	.	.	+	.	0	+	0	0	.	0	0	.	+	.	.	.
M	8	5	B	C	ATL	AD	H	.	.	.	.	.	.	100	.	0	.	.	.	+	.	0	.	0	0	.	0	0	.	.	.	.	.
M	8	6	B	C	ATL	AD	H	.	.	.	.	.	.	100	.	0	.	.	.	+	.	0	+	0	0	.	0	0	.	.	.	.	.
M	6	7	B	A	ATL	AD	H	.	.	.	.	.	.	100	.	0	.	.	+	+	.	0	.	0	0	.	0	0	.	.	.	.	.
M	6	8	B	E	ATL	AD	H	.	.	.	.	.	.	100	.	0	.	.	.	.	+	0	.	0	0	.	0	0	.	.	.	.	.
M	6	9	.	.	.	.	.	R	E	ATL	04	.	.	100	.	0	.	.	.	+	.	0	.	0	0	.	0	0	.	.	.	.	.
M	8	10	.	.	.	.	.	R	E	ATL	04	H	.	100	.	0	.	.	.	+	.	0	.	0	0	.	0	0	.	.	.	.	.
M	8	11	R	E	ATL	AD	H	.	.	.	.	.	.	100	.	0	.	.	.	+	.	0	+	0	0	.	0	0	.	.	.	.	.
M	8	12	L	E	ATL	AD	H	.	.	.	.	.	.	100	.	0	.	.	.	+	.	0	.	0	0	.	0	0	.	.	.	.	.
M	8	13	B	A	AXI	12	H	.	.	.	.	.	.	100	.	0	.	.	+	+	.	0	+	0	0	.	0	0	.	.	.	.	.
M	8	14	B	C	AXI	AD	H	.	.	.	.	.	.	100	.	0	.	.	+	+	.	0	.	0	0	.	0	0	.	.	+	.	.
M	6	15	B	C	AXI	AD	H	.	.	.	.	.	.	100	.	0	.	.	+	.	+	0	.	0	0	.	0	0	.	.	.	.	.
M	6	16	B	A	AXI	AD	H	.	.	.	.	.	.	60	.	0	.	.	+	+	.	0	.	0	0	.	0	0	.	.	.	.	.
M	8	17	.	.	.	.	.	B	E	AXI	AD	H	.	100	.	0	.	.	.	+	.	0	.	0	0	+	0	0	.	.	.	.	.
M	30	18	R	E	AXI	AD	H	.	.	.	.	.	.	100	.	0	.	.	.	+	.	0	+	0	0	+	0	0	.	.	.	.	.
M	6	19	.	.	.	.	.	L	E	AXI	02	H	.	100	.	0	.	.	.	.	.	0	.	0	0	.	0	0	.	.	.	.	.
M	19	20	.	.	.	.	.	L	E	AXI	04	H	.	100	.	0	.	.	+	+	.	0	.	0	0	.	0	0	.	.	.	.	.
M	6	21	.	.	.	.	.	B	A	CER	04	H	.	100	.	0	.	.	.	.	+	0	.	0	0	.	0	0	.	.	.	.	.
M	6	22	.	.	.	.	.	B	A	CER	10	H	.	100	.	0	.	.	+	+	.	0	+	0	0	.	0	0	.	.	.	.	.
M	8	23	B	A	CER	12	H	.	.	.	.	.	.	100	.	0	.	.	.	+	.	0	.	0	0	.	0	0	.	.	.	.	.
M	8	24	B	C	CER	AD	H	.	.	.	.	.	.	100	.	0	.	.	.	.	+	0	.	0	0	.	0	0	.	.	.	.	.
M	8	24.1	B	C	CER	AD	H	.	.	.	.	.	.	100	.	0	.	.	+	.	.	0	.	0	0	.	0	0	.	.	.	.	.
M	8	25	B	F	CER	AD	H	.	.	.	.	.	.	100	.	0	+	.	+	+	.	0	.	0	0	.	0	0	.	.	.	.	.
M	6	26	B	C	CER	AD	H	.	.	.	.	.	.	100	.	0	.	.	+	+	.	0	.	0	0	.	0	0	.	.	.	.	.
M	6	27	B	C	CER	AD	H	.	.	.	.	.	.	80	.	0	.	.	.	+	.	0	.	0	0	.	0	0	.	.	.	.	.
M	11	28	B	C	CER	AD	H	.	.	.	.	.	.	100	.	0	.	.	.	+	.	0	+	0	0	.	0	0	.	.	.	.	.
M	6	29	B	C	CER	AD	H	.	.	.	.	.	.	90	.	0	.	.	.	+	.	0	.	0	0	.	0	0	.	.	.	.	.
M	6	30	B	A	CER	AD	H	.	.	.	.	.	.	100	.	0	.	.	.	+	.	0	.	0	0	.	0	0	.	.	.	.	.
M	6	31	B	A	CER	AD	H	.	.	.	.	.	.	90	.	0	.	.	.	+	.	0	.	0	0	.	0	0	.	.	.	.	.
M	19	32	.	.	.	.	.	B	A	CER	AD	H	.	100	.	0	.	.	.	+	.	0	.	0	0	.	0	0	.	+	.	.	.
M	8	33	.	.	.	.	.	R	E	CER	04	H	.	100	.	0	.	.	+	+	.	0	.	0	0	+	0	0	.	.	.	.	.
M	8	34	.	.	.	.	.	L	E	CER	08	H	13	100	.	0	.	.	.	+	.	0	.	0	0	.	0	0	.	.	.	.	.
M	8	35	.	.	.	.	.	R	E	CER	08	H	13	100	.	0	.	.	.	+	.	0	.	0	0	.	0	0	.	.	.	.	.
M	6	36	.	.	.	.	.	R	E	CER	10	H	.	100	.	0	.	.	.	.	+	0	.	0	0	.	0	0	.	.	.	.	.
M	8	37	.	.	.	.	.	R	E	CER	AD	H	.	100	.	0	.	.	+	+	.	0	.	0	0	.	0	0	.	.	.	.	.
M	3	38	.	.	.	.	.	R	E	CER	AD	H	.	100	.	0	.	.	+	+	.	0	.	0	0	.	0	0	.	.	.	.	.
M	30	39	R	E	CER	AD	H	.	.	.	.	.	.	100	.	0	.	.	.	+	.	0	+	0	0	.	0	0	.	.	.	.	.
M	50	40	.	.	.	.	.	R	E	CER	AD	H	.	100	.	0	.	.	+	+	.	0	.	0	0	+	0	0	.	.	.	.	.
M	8	41	.	.	.	.	.	L	E	CER	04	H	.	100	.	0	.	.	.	+	.	0	+	0	0	.	0	0	.	.	.	.	.
M	6	42	.	.	.	.	.	L	E	CER	04	H	.	100	.	0	.	.	+	.	.	0	.	0	0	.	0	0	.	.	.	.	.
M	8	43	L	E	CER	AD	H	.	.	.	.	.	.	100	.	0	.	.	.	+	.	0	+	0	0	+	0	0	.	.	.	.	.
M	50	44	.	.	.	.	.	L	E	CER	AD	H	.	100	.	0	.	.	.	+	.	0	+	0	0	.	0	0	.	.	.	.	.
M	30	45	.	.	.	.	.	L	F	CER	AD	H	.	100	.	0	.	.	.	.	+	0	.	0	0	.	0	0	.	.	.	.	.
M	7	46	.	.	.	.	.	L	E	CER	AD	H	.	100	.	0	.	.	+	.	.	0	.	0	0	.	0	0	.	.	.	.	.
M	8	47	.	.	.	.	.	L	E	CER	AD	H	.	100	.	0	.	.	+	+	.	0	.	0	0	+	0	0	.	.	.	.	.
M	6	48	.	.	.	.	.	B	A	THO	04	H	.	100	.	0	.	.	+	+	.	0	.	0	0	.	0	0	.	.	.	.	.
M	6	49	.	.	.	.	.	B	A	THO	04	H	.	100	.	0	.	.	+	.	+	0	+	0	0	.	0	0	.	.	.	.	.
M	6	50	.	.	.	.	.	B	A	THO	04	H	.	100	.	0	.	.	+	+	+	0	.	0	0	.	0	0	.	.	.	.	.
M	6	51	.	.	.	.	.	B	A	THO	04	H	.	100	.	0	.	.	.	+	.	0	.	0	0	.	0	0	.	.	.	.	.
M	6	52	.	.	.	.	.	B	A	THO	06	H	.	100	.	0	.	.	+	.	.	0	.	0	0	.	0	0	.	.	.	.	.
M	11	53	.	.	.	.	.	B	A	THO	06	H	.	100	.	0	.	.	.	.	+	0	.	0	0	.	0	0	.	.	.	.	.
M	6	54	.	.	.	.	.	B	A	THO	06	H	.	100	.	0	.	.	+	+	.	0	.	0	0	.	0	0	.	.	.	.	.
M	6	55	.	.	.	.	.	B	A	THO	06	H	.	100	.	0	.	.	+	+	.	0	.	0	0	.	0	0	.	.	.	.	.
M	6	56	.	.	.	.	.	B	A	THO	06	H	.	100	.	0	.	.	.	+	.	0	.	0	0	.	0	0	.	.	.	.	.
M	11	57	.	.	.	.	.	B	A	THO	08	H	.	100	.	0	.	.	.	.	+	0	.	0	0	.	0	0	.	.	.	.	.
M	8	58	.	.	.	.	.	B	A	THO	10	H	.	100	.	0	.	.	.	+	.	0	+	0	0	.	0	0	.	.	.	.	.

0.1	0.2	0.3	0.4	0.5	0.6	0.7	0.8	0.9	1.0	1.1	1.2	1.3	1.4	1.5	1.6	1.7	1.8	1.9	2.3	2.4	2.5	4.0	4.1	4.2	4.3	4.4	4.9	5.4	5.9	6.4	9.3	9.4	9.5
M	8	59	.	.	.	.	.	B	A	THO	10	H	.	100	.	0	.	.	.	+	.	0	.	0	0	.	0	0	.	.	.	.	.
M	8	60	.	.	.	.	.	B	A	THO	10	H	.	100	.	0	.	.	.	+	.	0	+	0	0	.	0	0	.	.	.	.	.
M	8	61	.	.	.	.	.	B	A	THO	10	H	.	100	.	0	+	.	.	+	.	0	.	0	0	.	0	0	.	.	.	.	.
M	8	62	B	A	THO	AD	H	.	.	.	.	.	.	100	.	0	.	.	.	+	.	0	+	0	0	.	0	0	.	.	.	.	.
M	8	63	B	A	THO	AD	H	.	.	.	.	.	.	100	.	0	.	.	.	+	.	0	.	0	0	+	0	0	.	.	.	.	.
M	6	64	B	A	THO	AD	H	.	.	.	.	.	.	100	.	0	.	.	.	+	.	0	+	0	0	+	0	0	.	.	.	.	.
M	6	65	B	A	THO	AD	H	.	.	.	.	.	.	100	.	0	.	.	.	+	.	0	+	0	0	.	0	0	.	.	.	.	.
M	6	66	B	A	THO	AD	H	.	.	.	.	.	.	100	.	0	.	.	+	+	.	0	+	0	0	.	0	0	.	.	.	.	.
M	8	67	B	A	THO	AD	H	.	.	.	.	.	.	100	.	0	.	.	.	+	.	0	.	0	0	.	0	0	.	.	.	.	.
M	6	68	B	A	THO	AD	H	.	.	.	.	.	.	100	.	0	.	.	.	+	.	0	.	0	0	.	0	0	.	.	.	.	.
M	6	69	B	A	THO	AD	H	.	.	.	.	.	.	100	.	0	.	.	.	+	.	0	.	0	0	.	0	0	.	.	.	.	.
M	8	70	B	A	THO	AD	H	.	.	.	.	.	.	100	.	0	.	.	.	+	.	0	+	0	0	.	0	0	.	.	.	.	.
M	6	71	B	A	THO	AD	H	.	.	.	.	.	.	100	.	0	.	.	+	.	+	0	.	0	0	.	0	0	.	.	.	.	.
M	8	72	B	A	THO	AD	H	.	.	.	.	.	.	100	.	0	.	.	.	+	.	0	+	0	0	.	0	0	.	.	.	.	.
M	8	73	B	A	THO	AD	H	.	.	.	.	.	.	100	.	0	.	.	.	+	.	0	+	0	0	.	1	0	.	.	.	.	.
M	8	74	B	A	THO	AD	H	.	.	.	.	.	.	100	.	0	.	.	.	+	.	0	+	0	0	.	0	0	.	.	.	.	.
M	8	75	B	A	THO	AD	H	.	.	.	.	.	.	100	.	0	+	.	.	+	.	0	+	0	0	.	3	0	.	.	.	.	.
M	6	76	.	.	.	.	.	B	A	THO	AD	H	.	100	.	0	.	.	.	+	.	0	+	0	0	.	0	0	.	.	.	.	.
M	8	77	B	A	THO	AD	H	.	.	.	.	.	.	100	.	0	.	.	.	+	.	0	+	0	0	.	0	0	.	.	.	.	.
M	8	78	B	A	THO	AD	H	.	.	.	.	.	.	100	.	0	.	.	.	+	+	0	+	0	0	+	0	0	.	.	.	.	.
M	6	79	.	.	.	.	.	B	A	THO	AD	H	.	100	.	0	.	.	.	+	.	0	.	0	0	+	0	0	.	.	.	.	.
M	8	80	.	.	.	.	.	B	A	THO	AD	H	.	100	.	0	.	.	.	+	.	0	+	0	0	.	0	0	.	+	.	.	.
M	8	81	.	.	.	.	.	B	A	THO	AD	H	.	100	.	0	.	.	+	+	+	0	.	0	0	.	0	0	.	.	.	.	.
M	8	82	.	.	.	.	.	B	A	THO	AD	H	.	100	.	0	.	.	.	+	.	0	.	0	0	.	0	0	.	.	.	.	.
M	6	83	.	.	.	.	.	B	A	THO	AD	H	.	100	.	0	.	.	.	+	.	0	.	0	0	.	0	0	.	.	.	.	.
M	8	84	.	.	.	.	.	B	A	THO	AD	H	.	100	.	0	.	.	.	+	.	0	.	0	0	.	0	0	.	.	.	.	.
M	8	85	.	.	.	.	.	B	A	THO	AD	H	.	100	.	0	.	.	+	+	.	0	.	0	0	.	0	0	.	.	.	.	.
M	8	86	.	.	.	.	.	B	A	THO	AD	H	.	100	.	0	.	.	.	+	.	0	.	0	0	.	0	0	.	.	.	.	.
M	52	87	.	.	.	.	.	R	A	THO	04	H	.	100	.	0	.	.	+	.	.	0	.	0	0	.	0	0	.	.	.	.	.
M	8	88	.	.	.	.	.	R	A	THO	08	H	.	100	.	0	.	.	.	+	.	0	.	0	0	.	0	0	.	.	.	.	.
M	8	89	.	.	.	.	.	R	A	THO	10	H	14	100	.	0	.	.	+	+	.	0	.	0	0	.	0	0	.	.	.	.	.
M	8	90	.	.	.	.	.	L	A	THO	10	H	14	100	.	0	.	.	.	+	.	0	.	0	0	.	0	0	.	.	.	.	.
M	8	91	.	.	.	.	.	R	A	THO	AD	H	.	100	.	0	.	.	+	+	.	0	.	0	0	.	0	0	.	.	.	.	.
M	8	92	.	.	.	.	.	R	A	THO	AD	H	.	100	.	0	.	.	.	+	.	0	+	0	0	.	0	0	.	.	.	.	.
M	8	93	.	.	.	.	.	R	A	THO	AD	H	.	100	.	0	.	.	.	+	.	0	+	0	0	.	0	0	.	.	.	.	.
M	8	94	R	A	THO	AD	H	.	.	.	.	.	.	100	.	0	.	.	+	+	.	0	+	0	0	+	0	0	.	.	.	.	.
M	8	95	.	.	.	.	.	R	A	THO	AD	H	.	100	.	0	.	.	+	.	.	0	.	0	0	.	0	0	.	.	.	.	.
M	8	96	.	.	.	.	.	L	A	THO	08	H	.	100	.	0	.	.	.	+	.	0	.	0	0	.	0	0	.	.	.	.	.
M	8	97	.	.	.	.	.	L	A	THO	10	H	.	100	.	0	.	.	.	+	.	0	.	0	0	.	0	0	.	.	.	.	.
M	8	98	.	.	.	.	.	L	A	THO	AD	H	.	100	.	0	.	.	.	+	.	0	.	0	0	+	0	0	.	.	.	.	.
M	8	99	.	.	.	.	.	L	A	THO	AD	H	.	90	.	0	.	.	.	+	.	0	.	0	0	.	0	0	.	.	.	.	.
M	6	100	L	A	THO	AD	H	.	.	.	.	.	.	100	.	0	.	.	.	+	.	0	.	0	0	.	0	0	.	.	.	.	.
M	8	101	.	.	.	.	.	L	A	THO	AD	H	.	100	.	0	.	.	.	+	.	0	+	0	0	.	0	0	.	.	.	.	.
M	8	102	.	.	.	.	.	B	A	LUM	04	H	.	100	.	0	.	.	.	+	.	0	.	0	0	.	0	0	.	.	.	.	.
M	8	103	.	.	.	.	.	B	A	LUM	06	H	.	100	.	0	.	.	.	+	.	0	.	0	0	.	0	0	.	.	.	.	.
M	8	104	B	A	LUM	AD	H	.	.	.	.	.	.	100	.	0	.	.	.	+	.	0	+	0	0	.	0	0	.	.	.	.	.
M	6	105	B	A	LUM	AD	H	.	.	.	.	.	.	80	.	0	.	.	.	+	.	0	.	0	0	.	0	0	.	.	.	.	.
M	6	106	B	A	LUM	AD	H	.	.	.	.	.	.	100	.	0	.	.	.	+	.	0	.	0	0	.	0	0	.	.	.	.	.
M	8	107	B	A	LUM	AD	H	.	.	.	.	.	.	100	.	0	.	.	.	+	.	0	.	0	0	.	0	0	.	.	.	.	.
M	6	108	.	.	.	.	.	B	A	LUM	AD	H	.	100	.	0	.	.	.	+	.	0	+	0	0	+	0	0	.	.	.	.	.
M	6	109	.	.	.	.	.	B	A	LUM	AD	H	.	100	.	0	.	.	+	+	.	0	.	0	0	.	0	0	.	.	.	.	.
M	7	110	.	.	.	.	.	B	A	LUM	AD	H	.	100	.	0	.	.	+	+	.	0	.	0	0	.	0	0	.	.	.	.	.
M	6	111	.	.	.	.	.	B	A	LUM	AD	H	.	100	.	0	.	.	+	+	.	0	.	0	0	.	0	0	.	.	.	.	.
M	8	112	.	.	.	.	.	R	A	LUM	10	H	.	100	.	0	.	.	.	+	.	0	.	0	0	.	0	0	.	.	.	.	.
M	30	113	.	.	.	.	.	R	A	LUM	10	H	.	100	.	0	.	.	.	+	.	0	.	0	0	+	0	0	.	.	.	.	.
M	30	114	.	.	.	.	.	R	A	LUM	AD	H	.	100	.	0	.	.	.	+	.	0	.	0	0	.	0	0	.	.	.	.	.
M	7	115	.	.	.	.	.	R	A	LUM	AD	H	.	100	.	0	.	.	.	+	.	0	.	0	0	.	0	0	.	.	.	.	.
M	6	116	.	.	.	.	.	R	A	LUM	AD	H	.	100	.	0	.	.	.	+	.	0	.	0	0	.	0	0	.	.	.	.	.

01	02	03	04	05	06	07	08	09	10	11	12	13	14	15	16	17	18	19	23	24	25	40	41	42	43	44	49	54	59	64	93	94	95
M	8	116.1	-	-	-	-	-	R	A	LUM	AD	H	-	100	-	0	-	-	-	+	-	0	-	0	0	-	0	0	-	-	-	-	-
M	8	117	-	-	-	-	-	L	F	LUM	04	H	-	100	-	0	-	-	-	+	-	0	-	0	0	-	0	0	-	-	-	-	-
M	30	118	-	-	-	-	-	L	F	LUM	08	H	-	100	-	0	-	-	+	+	-	0	-	0	0	-	0	0	-	-	-	-	-
M	5	119	-	-	-	-	-	L	A	LUM	10	H	-	100	-	0	-	-	-	+	-	0	-	0	0	-	0	0	-	-	-	-	-
M	6	120	-	-	-	-	-	L	A	LUM	10	H	-	100	-	0	-	-	-	+	-	0	-	0	0	-	0	0	-	-	-	-	-
M	8	121	-	-	-	-	-	L	A	LUM	10	H	-	100	-	0	-	-	-	+	-	0	-	0	0	-	0	0	-	-	-	-	-
M	8	122	-	-	-	-	-	L	A	LUM	AD	H	-	100	-	0	-	-	-	+	-	0	-	0	0	+	0	0	-	-	-	-	-
M	6	123	-	-	-	-	-	L	A	LUM	AD	H	-	100	-	0	-	-	-	+	-	0	-	0	0	-	0	0	-	-	-	-	-
M	8	124	-	-	-	-	-	L	A	LUM	AD	H	-	100	-	0	-	-	-	+	-	0	-	0	0	-	0	0	-	-	-	-	-
M	8	125	-	-	-	-	-	L	A	LUM	AD	H	-	100	-	0	-	-	-	+	-	0	+	0	0	-	0	0	-	-	-	-	-
M	8	126	-	-	-	-	-	L	A	LUM	AD	H	-	100	-	0	-	-	-	+	-	0	-	0	0	-	0	0	-	-	-	-	-
M	30	127	-	-	-	-	-	L	A	LUM	AD	H	-	100	-	0	-	-	+	+	-	0	-	0	0	-	0	0	-	-	-	-	-
M	19	128	-	-	-	-	-	L	A	LUM	AD	H	-	100	-	0	-	-	+	+	-	0	-	0	0	-	0	0	-	-	-	-	-
M	11	129	-	-	-	-	-	L	A	LUM	AD	H	-	100	-	0	-	-	-	+	-	0	-	0	0	-	0	0	-	-	+	+	-
M	8	130	-	-	-	-	-	L	A	LUM	AD	H	-	100	-	0	-	-	-	+	-	0	-	0	0	+	0	0	-	-	-	-	-
M	6	131	-	-	-	-	-	R	A	LUM	AD	H	15	100	-	0	-	-	+	+	-	0	-	0	0	+	0	0	-	-	-	-	-
M	6	132	-	-	-	-	-	L	A	LUM	AD	H	15	100	-	0	-	-	-	+	-	0	-	0	0	-	0	0	-	-	-	-	-
M	8	133	-	-	-	-	-	R	A	LUM	AD	H	16	100	-	0	-	-	-	+	-	0	-	0	0	+	2	0	-	-	-	-	-
M	8	134	-	-	-	-	-	L	A	LUM	AD	H	16	100	-	0	-	-	-	+	-	0	-	0	0	+	0	0	-	-	-	-	-
M	8	135	-	-	-	-	-	B	F	SAC	10	H	-	100	-	0	-	-	-	+	-	0	+	0	0	-	0	0	-	-	-	-	-
M	8	136	-	-	-	-	-	B	F	SAC	AD	H	-	100	-	0	-	-	+	+	-	0	-	0	0	+	0	0	-	-	-	-	-
M	8	137	-	-	-	-	-	B	F	SAC	AD	H	-	100	-	0	-	-	+	-	+	0	-	0	0	+	0	0	-	+	-	-	-
M	8	138	-	-	-	-	-	B	F	SAC	AD	H	-	100	-	0	-	-	-	+	-	0	-	0	0	-	0	0	-	-	-	-	-
M	19	139	-	-	-	-	-	B	F	SAC	AD	H	-	100	-	0	-	-	-	+	-	0	-	0	0	-	0	0	-	-	-	-	-
M	7	140	-	-	-	-	-	R	F	SAC	AD	H	-	100	-	0	-	-	+	+	-	0	-	0	0	-	0	0	-	-	-	-	-
M	8	141	R	F	OCX	04	H	-	-	-	-	-	-	100	-	0	-	-	+	+	-	0	-	0	0	-	0	0	-	-	-	-	-
M	6	142	-	-	-	-	-	R	F	OCX	06	H	-	100	-	0	-	-	-	+	-	0	-	0	0	-	0	0	-	-	-	-	-
M	8	143	R	F	OCX	06	H	-	-	-	-	-	-	100	-	0	-	-	-	+	-	0	+	0	0	-	0	0	-	-	-	-	-
M	6	144	R	F	OCX	06	H	-	-	-	-	-	-	100	-	0	-	-	+	+	-	0	-	0	0	-	0	0	-	-	-	-	-
M	6	145	-	-	-	-	-	R	F	OCX	AD	H	-	90	-	0	-	-	-	+	-	0	-	0	0	-	0	0	-	-	-	+	-
M	6	146	R	F	OCX	AD	H	-	-	-	-	-	-	80	-	0	-	-	-	+	-	1	+	0	0	+	0	0	-	-	-	-	-
M	6	147	-	-	-	-	-	R	F	OCX	AD	H	-	90	-	0	-	-	-	+	-	0	+	0	0	+	0	0	-	-	-	-	-
M	6	148	-	-	-	-	-	R	F	OCX	AD	H	-	100	-	0	-	-	-	+	-	0	-	0	0	-	0	0	-	-	-	-	-
M	50	149	-	-	-	-	-	R	F	OCX	AD	H	-	100	-	0	-	-	-	+	-	0	-	0	0	+	0	0	-	-	-	-	-
M	6	150	-	-	-	-	-	R	F	OCX	AD	H	-	100	-	0	-	-	+	+	-	0	-	0	0	-	0	0	-	-	-	-	-
M	6	151	-	-	-	-	-	R	F	OCX	AD	H	-	100	-	0	-	-	+	+	-	0	-	0	0	-	0	0	-	-	-	-	-
M	6	152	L	F	OCX	06	H	-	-	-	-	-	-	100	-	0	-	-	-	+	-	0	-	0	0	-	0	0	-	-	-	-	-
M	6	153	-	-	-	-	-	L	F	OCX	06	H	-	100	-	0	-	-	-	+	-	0	-	0	0	+	0	0	-	-	-	-	-
M	7	154	L	W	OCX	12	H	-	-	-	-	-	-	90	-	0	-	-	+	+	-	1	-	0	0	-	3	0	-	-	-	-	-
M	30	155	L	F	OCX	12	H	-	-	-	-	-	-	100	-	0	-	-	-	-	-	0	-	0	0	-	0	0	-	-	-	-	-
M	6	156	L	W	OCX	AD	H	-	-	-	-	-	-	70	-	3	-	-	+	-	-	0	-	3	0	-	0	0	-	-	-	-	-
M	6	157	L	F	OCX	AD	H	-	-	-	-	-	-	80	-	0	+	-	+	+	-	0	-	0	0	-	5	0	-	-	+	+	-
M	6	158	L	F	OCX	AD	H	-	-	-	-	-	-	10	-	0	-	-	+	+	-	0	+	0	0	-	0	0	-	-	+	+	+
M	6	159	-	-	-	-	-	L	F	OCX	AD	H	-	100	-	0	+	-	+	+	-	0	-	0	0	-	3	0	-	-	+	+	-
M	50	160	-	-	-	-	-	L	F	OCX	AD	H	-	100	-	0	-	-	-	+	-	0	-	0	0	-	0	0	-	-	+	-	-
M	8	161	-	-	-	-	-	L	F	OCX	AD	H	-	100	-	0	-	-	-	+	-	0	+	0	0	-	2	0	-	-	-	-	-
M	6	162	-	-	-	-	-	L	F	OCX	AD	H	-	100	-	0	-	-	-	+	-	0	-	0	0	+	0	0	-	-	-	-	-
M	6	163	-	-	-	-	-	L	F	OCX	AD	H	-	90	-	0	-	-	-	+	-	0	+	0	0	-	0	0	-	-	-	-	-
M	7	164	-	-	-	-	-	L	F	OCX	AD	H	-	100	-	0	-	-	-	+	-	0	-	0	0	-	0	0	-	-	-	-	-
M	8	165	-	-	-	-	-	L	F	OCX	AD	H	-	100	-	0	-	-	-	+	-	0	-	0	0	-	0	0	+	-	-	-	-
M	8	166	-	-	-	-	-	I	F	OCX	AD	H	-	100	-	0	-	-	+	+	-	0	-	0	0	-	0	0	-	-	-	-	-
M	8	167	-	-	-	-	-	I	F	OCX	AD	H	-	100	-	0	-	-	-	+	-	1	+	0	0	-	0	0	-	-	-	-	-
M	8	168	-	-	-	-	-	I	F	OCX	AD	H	-	100	-	0	-	-	+	+	-	0	-	0	0	-	0	0	-	-	-	-	-
M	6	169	-	-	-	-	-	I	F	OCX	AD	H	-	100	-	0	-	-	+	+	-	0	-	0	0	-	0	0	-	-	-	-	-
M	8	170	-	-	-	-	-	I	F	OCX	AD	H	-	100	-	0	-	-	-	+	-	0	-	0	0	+	3	0	+	-	-	-	-
M	50	171	-	-	-	-	-	I	F	OCX	AD	H	-	100	-	0	-	-	-	+	-	0	-	0	0	-	0	0	-	-	-	-	-
M	8	172	-	-	-	-	-	I	F	OCX	AD	H	-	100	-	0	-	-	+	+	-	0	-	0	0	-	0	0	-	-	-	-	-
M	8	173	-	-	-	-	-	I	F	OCX	AD	H	-	100	-	0	-	-	-	+	-	1	-	0	0	-	0	0	+	-	-	-	-

0.1	0.2	0.3	0.4	0.5	0.6	0.7	0.8	0.9	1.0	1.1	1.2	1.3	1.4	1.5	1.6	1.7	1.8	1.9	2.3	2.4	2.5	4.0	4.1	4.2	4.3	4.4	4.9	5.4	5.9	6.4	9.3	9.4	9.5
M	8	174	.	.	.	.	.	I	F	OCX	AD	H	.	100	.	0	.	.	.	+	.	0	.	0	0	.	0	0	.	.	.	.	.
M	6	175	.	.	.	.	.	B	F	STE	08	H	.	100	.	0	.	.	+	.	.	0	.	0	0	.	0	0	.	.	.	.	.
M	8	176	.	.	.	.	.	B	F	STE	AD	H	.	100	.	0	.	.	+	.	+	0	.	0	0	.	0	0	.	.	.	.	.
M	6	177	.	.	.	.	.	R	F	R#1	02	H	.	100	.	0	.	.	+	.	+	0	.	0	0	.	0	0	.	.	.	.	.
M	8	178	.	.	.	.	.	R	F	R#1	04	H	.	80	.	0	.	.	.	+	.	0	.	0	0	.	4	0	.	.	.	.	.
M	8	179	R	W	R#1	06	H	.	.	.	.	.	.	100	.	0	.	.	.	.	+	0	.	0	0	.	0	0	.	.	.	.	.
M	52	180	R	W	R#1	06	H	.	.	.	.	.	.	100	.	0	.	.	+	.	.	0	.	0	0	.	0	0	.	.	.	.	.
M	52	181	R	W	R#1	06	H	.	.	.	.	.	.	100	.	0	.	.	.	+	.	0	.	0	0	.	0	0	.	.	.	.	.
M	8	182	R	W	R#1	AD	H	.	.	.	.	.	.	100	.	0	.	.	+	+	.	0	.	0	0	.	4	0	.	.	.	.	.
M	9	183	R	W	R#1	AD	H	.	.	.	.	.	.	100	.	0	.	.	+	+	.	0	.	0	0	.	0	0	.	.	.	.	.
M	52	184	R	W	R#1	AD	H	.	.	.	.	.	.	60	.	0	.	.	+	+	.	0	.	0	0	.	0	0	.	.	.	.	.
M	52	185	.	.	.	.	.	R	F	R#1	AD	H	.	100	.	0	.	.	+	+	.	0	+	0	0	.	5	0	.	.	.	.	.
M	52	186	.	.	.	.	.	R	F	R#1	AD	H	.	100	.	0	.	.	.	+	.	0	.	0	0	.	0	0	.	.	.	.	.
M	8	187	R	F	R#1	AD	H	.	.	.	.	.	.	100	P	0	.	.	.	+	.	0	.	0	0	.	0	0	.	.	.	.	.
M	52	188	.	.	.	.	.	L	W	R#1	04	H	.	100	.	0	.	.	.	.	+	0	.	0	0	.	0	0	.	.	.	.	.
M	52	189	L	W	R#1	04	H	.	.	.	.	.	.	100	.	0	.	.	+	.	.	0	.	0	0	.	0	0	.	.	.	.	.
M	8	190	L	F	R#1	AD	H	.	.	.	.	.	.	100	.	0	.	.	.	+	.	0	.	0	0	.	0	0	.	.	.	.	.
M	8	191	L	W	R#1	AD	H	.	.	.	.	.	.	100	.	0	.	.	.	+	+	1	.	0	0	.	0	0	.	+	.	.	.
M	8	192	L	W	R#1	AD	H	.	.	.	.	.	.	100	.	0	.	.	.	.	+	0	.	0	0	.	0	0	.	.	.	.	.
M	8	193	L	F	R#1	AD	H	.	.	.	.	.	.	100	.	0	.	.	.	+	.	0	.	0	0	+	2	0	.	.	.	.	.
M	8	194	.	.	.	.	.	L	F	R#1	AD	H	.	100	.	0	.	.	.	.	+	0	.	0	0	.	0	0	.	.	.	.	.
M	52	195	L	F	R#1	AD	H	.	.	.	.	.	.	100	.	0	.	.	.	+	.	0	.	0	0	.	0	0	.	.	.	.	.
M	11	196	.	.	.	.	.	L	F	R#1	AD	H	.	80	.	2	+	.	+	+	.	0	.	0	0	.	2	0	.	.	.	.	.
M	8	196.1	.	.	.	.	.	I	F	R#1	AD	H	.	100	.	0	.	.	.	+	.	0	.	0	0	.	0	0	.	.	.	.	.
M	52	197	RB	B	RIB	04	H	.	.	.	.	.	.	100	.	0	.	.	+	+	.	0	.	0	0	.	2	0	.	.	.	.	.
M	52	198	R	B	RIB	04	H	.	.	.	.	.	.	100	.	0	.	.	.	+	.	0	.	0	0	.	0	0	.	.	.	.	.
M	52	199	R	B	RIB	04	H	.	.	.	.	.	.	100	.	0	.	.	+	.	+	0	.	0	0	.	0	0	.	.	.	.	.
M	52	200	R	B	RIB	04	H	.	.	.	.	.	.	90	.	0	.	.	.	+	+	0	.	0	0	.	0	0	.	.	.	.	.
M	52	201	R	B	RIB	04	H	.	.	.	.	.	.	100	.	0	.	.	.	+	+	1	.	0	0	.	0	0	.	.	.	.	.
M	52	202	R	B	RIB	04	H	.	.	.	.	.	.	100	.	0	.	.	+	.	+	0	.	0	0	.	0	0	.	.	.	.	.
M	8	203	R	B	RIB	AD	H	.	.	.	.	.	.	100	.	0	.	.	.	+	+	0	.	0	0	.	4	0	.	.	.	.	.
M	52	204	R	B	RIB	AD	H	.	.	.	.	.	.	100	.	0	.	.	+	+	.	1	.	0	0	.	9	0	+	.	.	.	.
M	52	205	L	B	RIB	04	H	.	.	.	.	.	.	50	.	0	.	.	+	.	+	0	+	0	0	.	0	0	.	.	.	.	.
M	52	206	L	B	RIB	04	H	.	.	.	.	.	.	100	.	0	.	.	.	.	+	0	+	0	0	.	0	0	.	.	.	.	.
M	52	207	L	B	RIB	04	H	.	.	.	.	.	.	90	.	0	.	.	+	.	+	1	.	0	0	.	0	0	.	.	.	.	.
M	52	208	L	B	RIB	12	H	.	.	.	.	.	.	80	.	0	.	.	+	.	+	0	.	0	0	+	0	0	.	.	.	.	.
M	52	209	L	B	RIB	AD	H	.	.	.	.	.	.	80	.	0	.	.	.	+	+	1	.	0	0	.	1	0	.	.	.	.	.
M	52	210	L	B	RIB	AD	H	.	.	.	.	.	.	100	.	0	.	.	+	+	+	1	.	0	0	.	1	0	.	.	.	.	.
M	52	211	L	B	RIB	AD	H	.	.	.	.	.	.	70	.	0	.	.	+	+	.	0	.	0	0	+	0	0	.	+	.	.	.
M	52	212	R	C	RIB	02	H	.	.	.	.	.	.	100	.	0	.	.	.	.	+	0	.	0	0	.	0	0	.	.	.	.	.
M	52	213	R	C	RIB	02	H	.	.	.	.	.	.	100	.	0	.	.	+	.	+	0	.	0	0	.	0	0	.	.	.	.	.
M	52	214	R	C	RIB	04	H	.	.	.	.	.	.	100	.	0	.	.	+	.	+	0	+	0	0	.	1	0	.	.	.	.	.
M	52	215	.	.	.	.	.	R	C	RIB	04	H	.	100	.	0	+	.	+	.	+	0	+	0	0	.	0	0	.	.	.	.	.
M	52	216	R	C	RIB	04	H	.	.	.	.	.	.	100	.	0	.	.	+	.	+	0	.	0	0	.	1	0	.	.	.	.	.
M	52	217	.	.	.	.	.	R	C	RIB	04	H	.	100	.	0	.	.	+	+	.	0	.	0	0	.	0	0	.	.	.	.	.
M	52	218	.	.	.	.	.	R	C	RIB	04	H	.	100	.	0	.	.	+	.	+	2	.	0	0	.	0	0	.	.	.	.	.
M	52	219	.	.	.	.	.	R	C	RIB	04	H	.	100	.	0	.	.	+	.	+	0	.	0	0	.	0	0	.	.	.	.	.
M	52	220	R	C	RIB	04	H	.	.	.	.	.	.	100	.	0	.	.	+	.	+	0	.	0	0	.	0	0	.	.	.	.	.
M	52	221	R	C	RIB	04	H	.	.	.	.	.	.	70	.	0	.	.	+	.	+	0	.	0	0	.	0	0	.	.	.	.	.
M	8	222	.	.	.	.	.	R	C	RIB	04	H	.	100	.	0	+	.	+	+	.	0	.	0	0	+	7	0	.	.	.	.	.
M	8	223	.	.	.	.	.	R	C	RIB	06	H	.	100	.	0	.	.	+	.	+	0	.	0	0	.	0	0	.	+	.	.	.
M	8	224	.	.	.	.	.	R	C	RIB	06	H	.	100	.	0	.	.	.	+	.	0	.	0	0	.	1	0	.	+	.	.	.
M	8	225	.	.	.	.	.	R	C	RIB	10	H	.	100	.	0	.	.	.	+	+	0	.	0	0	.	0	0	.	.	.	.	.
M	9	226	R	C	RIB	AD	H	.	.	.	.	.	.	100	.	0	.	.	.	+	.	0	.	0	0	+	1	0	.	.	.	.	.
M	52	227	R	C	RIB	AD	H	.	.	.	.	.	.	100	.	0	.	.	.	+	.	0	.	0	0	.	2	2	.	+	+	.	.
M	52	228	.	.	.	.	.	R	C	RIB	AD	H	.	90	.	0	.	.	.	+	.	0	.	0	0	.	0	0	.	+	.	.	.
M	52	229	.	.	.	.	.	R	C	RIB	AD	H	.	100	.	0	.	.	.	+	.	0	.	0	0	.	0	0	.	+	.	.	.
M	52	230	.	.	.	.	.	R	C	RIB	AD	H	.	100	.	0	.	.	+	+	.	1	.	0	0	.	8	0	.	.	.	.	.

01	02	03	04	05	06	07	08	09	10	11	12	13	14	15	16	17	18	19	23	24	25	40	41	42	43	44	49	54	59	64	93	94	95
M	8	231	-	-	-	-	-	R	C	RIB	AD	H	-	100	-	0	-	-	-	+	-	0	-	0	0	-	7	0	-	+	+	-	-
M	52	232	-	-	-	-	-	R	C	RIB	AD	H	-	100	-	0	-	-	+	-	-	0	-	0	0	-	9	0	-	+	-	-	-
M	9	233	-	-	-	-	-	R	C	RIB	AD	H	-	100	-	0	-	-	-	+	-	0	-	0	0	-	0	0	-	-	-	-	-
M	8	234	-	-	-	-	-	R	C	RIB	AD	H	-	100	-	0	-	-	-	+	-	0	-	0	0	-	1	0	-	-	-	-	-
M	8	235	-	-	-	-	-	R	C	RIB	AD	H	-	100	-	0	-	-	+	+	-	1	-	0	0	-	2	0	-	-	-	-	-
M	52	236	-	-	-	-	-	R	C	RIB	AD	H	-	60	P	0	-	-	+	+	-	0	-	0	0	-	0	0	-	+	-	-	-
M	8	237	-	-	-	-	-	R	C	RIB	AD	H	-	100	-	0	-	-	+	-	-	1	-	0	0	-	0	0	-	+	-	-	-
M	52	238	-	-	-	-	-	R	C	RIB	AD	H	2	100	P	0	-	-	-	+	-	0	-	0	0	+	1	0	-	+	-	-	-
M	52	239	-	-	-	-	-	R	E	RIB	AD	H	2	100	-	0	-	-	-	+	-	0	-	0	0	+	0	0	-	+	-	-	-
M	9	240	R	C	RIB	AD	H	-	-	-	-	-	3	100	-	0	-	-	-	+	-	0	-	0	0	-	1	0	-	+	-	-	-
M	9	241	-	-	-	-	-	R	D	RIB	AD	H	3	100	-	0	-	-	-	+	+	1	-	0	0	+	1	0	-	-	-	-	-
M	8	242	R	C	RIB	AD	H	-	-	-	-	-	4	100	-	0	+	-	-	+	-	0	-	0	0	-	0	0	-	-	-	-	-
M	8	243	-	-	-	-	-	R	D	RIB	AD	H	4	100	P	0	-	-	-	+	-	0	-	0	0	-	0	0	-	-	-	-	-
M	52	244	-	-	-	-	-	R	C	RIB	AD	H	5	90	P	0	+	-	+	-	+	0	+	0	0	-	0	0	-	+	+	+	+
M	52	245	-	-	-	-	-	R	F	RIB	AD	H	5	60	-	0	-	-	-	+	-	0	-	0	0	+	0	0	-	+	-	-	-
M	8	246	-	-	-	-	-	L	C	RIB	02	H	-	100	-	0	-	-	-	+	-	0	+	0	0	-	0	0	-	-	-	-	-
M	52	247	L	C	RIB	04	H	-	-	-	-	-	-	100	-	0	-	-	+	+	-	0	-	0	0	-	0	0	-	-	-	-	-
M	52	248	-	-	-	-	-	L	C	RIB	04	H	-	100	-	0	-	-	+	+	-	0	-	0	0	-	1	0	-	-	-	-	-
M	52	249	L	C	RIB	04	H	-	-	-	-	-	-	100	-	0	-	-	+	-	+	0	-	0	0	-	0	0	-	-	-	-	-
M	52	250	L	C	RIB	04	H	-	-	-	-	-	-	100	-	0	-	-	+	+	-	0	-	0	0	-	0	0	-	-	-	-	-
M	52	251	-	-	-	-	-	L	C	RIB	04	H	-	100	-	0	-	-	+	+	-	0	-	0	0	-	1	0	-	-	-	-	-
M	52	252	L	C	RIB	04	H	-	-	-	-	-	-	100	-	0	-	-	-	+	-	0	-	0	0	-	0	0	-	-	-	-	-
M	52	253	L	C	RIB	04	H	-	-	-	-	-	-	100	-	0	-	-	-	+	-	0	+	0	0	-	0	0	-	-	-	-	-
M	52	254	-	-	-	-	-	L	C	RIB	04	H	-	100	-	0	-	-	+	+	-	0	-	0	0	-	0	0	-	+	-	-	-
M	8	255	-	-	-	-	-	L	C	RIB	12	H	-	90	-	0	-	-	-	+	-	0	+	0	0	-	1	0	-	+	-	-	-
M	52	256	L	C	RIB	AD	H	-	-	-	-	-	-	20	-	1	-	-	+	+	-	0	-	0	0	-	1	0	-	-	-	-	-
M	52	257	L	C	RIB	AD	H	-	-	-	-	-	-	90	-	0	+	-	+	+	-	0	-	0	0	-	0	0	-	-	-	-	-
M	8	258	-	-	-	-	-	L	C	RIB	AD	H	-	100	P	0	+	-	+	+	-	0	-	0	0	-	3	0	-	-	-	-	-
M	8	259	-	-	-	-	-	L	C	RIB	AD	H	-	100	P	0	-	-	-	+	-	1	-	0	0	+	0	0	-	-	-	-	-
M	8	260	-	-	-	-	-	L	C	RIB	AD	H	-	100	-	0	-	-	+	+	-	0	-	0	0	-	0	0	-	-	-	-	-
M	52	261	-	-	-	-	-	L	C	RIB	AD	H	-	85	-	0	-	-	+	+	-	0	-	0	0	+	5	0	-	-	-	-	-
M	52	262	-	-	-	-	-	L	C	RIB	AD	H	-	100	-	0	-	-	+	+	-	0	-	0	0	-	6	0	-	+	-	-	-
M	7	263	-	-	-	-	-	L	C	RIB	AD	H	-	75	-	0	-	-	+	+	-	0	-	0	0	-	0	0	-	-	-	-	-
M	3	264	-	-	-	-	-	L	C	RIB	AD	H	-	90	P	0	-	-	+	+	-	0	-	0	0	+	1	0	-	+	-	-	-
M	9	265	-	-	-	-	-	L	C	RIB	AD	H	-	100	-	0	-	-	+	+	-	0	-	0	0	-	2	0	-	-	-	-	-
M	7	266	-	-	-	-	-	L	C	RIB	AD	H	-	100	-	0	-	-	-	+	-	0	-	0	0	+	6	0	-	+	-	-	-
M	52	267	-	-	-	-	-	L	C	RIB	AD	H	-	100	-	0	-	-	+	-	+	0	+	0	0	-	0	0	-	-	-	-	-
M	52	268	-	-	-	-	-	L	C	RIB	AD	H	-	100	-	0	-	-	-	+	-	0	-	0	0	+	2	0	-	+	-	-	-
M	9	269	-	-	-	-	-	L	C	RIB	AD	H	-	100	-	0	-	-	-	+	-	0	-	0	0	+	0	0	-	-	-	-	-
M	9	270	-	-	-	-	-	L	C	RIB	AD	H	-	100	P	0	-	-	-	+	-	0	-	0	0	+	0	0	-	-	-	-	-
M	8	271	-	-	-	-	-	L	C	RIB	AD	H	-	100	-	0	+	-	-	+	-	0	-	0	0	-	0	0	-	-	-	-	-
M	8	272	-	-	-	-	-	L	C	RIB	AD	H	-	100	-	0	-	-	-	+	-	0	+	0	0	-	0	0	-	+	-	-	-
M	52	273	-	-	-	-	-	L	C	RIB	AD	H	-	100	-	0	-	-	-	-	+	0	-	0	0	-	0	0	-	-	-	-	+
M	5	274	-	-	-	-	-	L	C	RIB	AD	H	-	100	-	0	-	-	+	+	-	0	-	0	0	-	0	0	-	-	-	-	-
M	8	275	-	-	-	-	-	L	C	RIB	AD	H	-	100	-	0	-	-	-	+	-	0	-	0	0	-	0	0	-	-	-	-	-
M	7	276	-	-	-	-	-	L	C	RIB	AD	H	-	75	-	0	-	-	+	+	-	0	-	0	0	-	4	0	-	-	-	-	-
M	52	277	-	-	-	-	-	L	C	RIB	AD	H	-	100	-	0	-	-	+	+	-	0	-	0	0	-	3	0	-	-	-	-	-
M	9	278	-	-	-	-	-	L	C	RIB	AD	H	-	100	-	0	-	-	+	+	-	0	+	0	0	-	0	0	-	-	-	-	-
M	52	279	-	-	-	-	-	L	C	RIB	AD	H	6	30	-	0	-	-	-	+	-	0	-	0	0	-	0	0	-	-	-	-	-
M	52	280	-	-	-	-	-	L	C	RIB	AD	H	6	100	-	0	-	-	-	+	-	0	-	0	0	-	0	0	-	-	-	-	-
M	8	281	-	-	-	-	-	L	C	RIB	AD	H	7	100	-	0	-	-	+	+	-	0	-	0	0	+	0	0	-	-	-	-	-
M	8	282	-	-	-	-	-	L	D	RIB	AD	H	7	100	-	0	-	-	-	+	+	0	-	0	0	-	0	0	-	-	-	-	-
M	52	283	-	-	-	-	-	R	D	RIB	04	H	-	100	-	0	-	-	+	-	-	0	-	0	0	-	0	0	-	-	-	-	-
M	52	284	-	-	-	-	-	R	D	RIB	04	H	-	100	-	0	-	-	-	+	-	0	-	0	0	-	0	0	-	-	-	-	-
M	52	285	-	-	-	-	-	R	D	RIB	04	H	-	100	-	0	-	-	+	-	+	0	-	0	0	-	0	0	-	-	-	-	-
M	8	286	-	-	-	-	-	R	D	RIB	06	H	-	100	-	0	-	-	-	+	-	1	-	0	0	+	0	0	-	+	-	-	-
M	52	287	-	-	-	-	-	R	D	RIB	06	H	-	100	-	0	-	-	-	+	-	0	+	0	0	-	0	0	-	+	-	-	-
M	52	288	-	-	-	-	-	R	D	RIB	06	H	-	100	P	1	-	-	+	+	-	0	-	0	0	+	0	0	-	-	-	-	-

01	02	03	04	05	06	07	08	09	10	11	12	13	14	15	16	17	18	19	23	24	25	40	41	42	43	44	49	54	59	64	93	94	95
M	8	289	-	-	-	-	-	R	D	RIB	12	H	-	100	-	0	-	-	-	+	+	0	-	0	0	+	0	0	-	+	-	-	-
M	30	290	-	-	-	-	-	R	D	RIB	12	H	-	100	-	0	-	-	+	+	-	2	+	0	0	-	0	0	-	+	-	-	-
M	8	291	-	-	-	-	-	R	D	RIB	12	H	-	100	-	0	-	-	-	+	+	2	+	0	0	-	0	0	-	-	-	-	-
M	8	292	-	-	-	-	-	R	D	RIB	12	H	-	100	-	0	-	-	+	+	-	0	+	0	0	-	1	0	-	-	-	-	-
M	52	293	-	-	-	-	-	R	D	RIB	AD	H	-	100	P	0	-	-	+	+	-	0	-	0	0	-	2	0	-	-	-	-	-
M	8	294	-	-	-	-	-	R	D	RIB	AD	H	-	100	-	0	-	-	-	+	-	0	-	0	0	-	1	0	-	+	-	-	-
M	8	295	-	-	-	-	-	R	D	RIB	AD	H	-	100	-	0	-	-	+	-	+	0	-	0	0	-	1	0	-	-	-	-	-
M	8	296	-	-	-	-	-	R	D	RIB	AD	H	-	100	-	0	-	-	-	+	-	0	+	0	0	-	0	0	-	-	-	-	-
M	8	297	-	-	-	-	-	R	D	RIB	AD	H	-	100	-	0	-	-	-	+	-	0	-	0	0	+	3	0	-	-	-	-	-
M	8	298	-	-	-	-	-	R	D	RIB	AD	H	-	100	-	0	-	-	-	+	-	1	+	0	0	-	0	0	-	+	-	-	-
M	8	299	-	-	-	-	-	R	D	RIB	AD	H	-	100	-	0	-	-	+	+	-	0	-	0	0	+	3	0	-	-	-	-	-
M	52	300	-	-	-	-	-	R	D	RIB	AD	H	-	100	-	0	-	-	+	+	-	0	-	0	0	-	0	0	-	-	-	-	-
M	52	301	-	-	-	-	-	R	D	RIB	AD	H	-	100	-	0	-	-	-	+	-	0	-	0	0	+	0	0	-	+	-	-	-
M	9	302	-	-	-	-	-	R	D	RIB	AD	H	-	100	-	0	-	-	-	+	-	1	-	0	0	-	0	0	-	-	-	-	-
M	8	303	-	-	-	-	-	R	D	RIB	AD	H	-	100	-	0	-	-	-	+	-	0	-	0	0	-	0	0	-	-	+	-	-
M	52	304	-	-	-	-	-	R	D	RIB	AD	H	-	100	-	0	-	-	-	+	-	0	-	0	0	+	1	0	-	+	-	-	-
M	52	305	-	-	-	-	-	R	D	RIB	AD	H	-	100	-	0	-	-	-	+	-	0	-	0	0	-	0	0	-	-	-	-	-
M	52	306	-	-	-	-	-	R	D	RIB	AD	H	-	100	-	0	-	-	+	+	-	0	-	0	0	-	0	0	-	+	-	-	-
M	52	307	-	-	-	-	-	R	D	RIB	AD	H	-	100	-	0	-	-	-	+	-	0	-	0	0	-	0	0	-	+	-	-	-
M	9	308	-	-	-	-	-	R	D	RIB	AD	H	8	100	-	0	-	-	+	+	+	2	-	0	0	-	0	0	-	-	-	-	-
M	9	309	-	-	-	-	-	R	D	RIB	AD	H	8	100	-	0	-	-	+	-	+	0	-	0	0	-	0	0	-	-	-	-	-
M	8	310	-	-	-	-	-	R	D	RIB	AD	H	9	100	-	0	-	-	+	+	-	1	-	0	0	-	0	0	-	-	-	-	-
M	8	311	-	-	-	-	-	R	D	RIB	AD	H	9	100	P	0	-	-	-	+	-	0	-	0	0	-	5	0	-	-	-	-	-
M	8	312	-	-	-	-	-	R	D	RIB	AD	H	10	100	-	0	-	-	+	+	-	1	-	0	0	+	1	0	-	-	-	-	-
M	8	313	-	-	-	-	-	R	D	RIB	AD	H	10	100	-	0	-	-	-	+	-	1	-	0	0	+	0	0	-	-	-	-	-
M	8	314	-	-	-	-	-	R	D	RIB	AD	H	11	100	-	0	-	-	-	+	-	0	-	0	0	-	0	0	-	-	-	-	-
M	8	315	-	-	-	-	-	R	F	RIB	AD	H	11	100	-	0	-	-	-	+	-	0	-	0	0	-	0	1	-	-	-	-	-
M	52	316	-	-	-	-	-	L	D	RIB	04	H	-	60	-	0	-	-	+	-	-	0	-	0	0	-	0	0	-	-	+	-	-
M	52	317	-	-	-	-	-	L	D	RIB	04	H	-	100	-	0	-	-	+	-	-	0	-	0	0	-	0	0	-	-	+	-	-
M	52	318	-	-	-	-	-	L	D	RIB	04	H	-	100	-	0	-	-	+	+	-	0	-	0	0	-	0	0	-	-	-	-	-
M	52	319	-	-	-	-	-	L	D	RIB	04	H	-	100	-	0	-	-	+	-	-	2	+	0	0	-	0	0	-	-	-	-	-
M	52	320	-	-	-	-	-	L	D	RIB	06	H	-	100	-	0	-	-	+	-	-	0	-	0	0	-	0	0	-	-	-	-	-
M	52	321	-	-	-	-	-	L	D	RIB	06	H	-	100	-	0	-	-	+	+	-	0	-	0	0	-	0	0	-	-	-	-	-
M	52	322	-	-	-	-	-	L	D	RIB	06	H	-	100	-	0	-	-	+	+	-	0	-	0	0	-	0	0	-	-	-	-	-
M	8	323	-	-	-	-	-	L	D	RIB	12	H	-	100	-	0	-	-	+	+	-	0	-	0	0	-	0	0	-	-	-	-	-
M	11	324	-	-	-	-	-	L	D	RIB	AD	H	-	100	-	0	-	-	-	+	-	0	-	0	0	-	0	0	-	-	+	-	+
M	8	325	-	-	-	-	-	L	D	RIB	AD	H	-	100	-	0	-	-	-	+	-	1	+	0	0	-	0	0	-	-	-	-	-
M	52	326	-	-	-	-	-	L	D	RIB	AD	H	-	100	-	0	-	-	-	+	-	4	+	0	0	-	0	0	-	-	-	-	-
M	8	327	-	-	-	-	-	L	D	RIB	AD	H	-	100	-	0	-	-	+	+	-	0	+	0	0	-	0	0	-	+	-	-	-
M	8	328	-	-	-	-	-	L	D	RIB	AD	H	-	100	-	0	-	-	-	+	-	0	+	0	0	-	0	0	-	-	-	-	-
M	8	329	-	-	-	-	-	L	D	RIB	AD	H	-	100	-	0	-	-	+	+	-	1	+	0	0	+	0	0	-	-	-	-	-
M	30	330	-	-	-	-	-	L	D	RIB	AD	H	-	100	-	0	-	-	-	+	-	0	-	0	0	-	1	0	-	+	-	-	-
M	9	331	-	-	-	-	-	L	D	RIB	AD	H	-	100	-	0	-	-	-	+	-	0	-	0	0	+	1	0	-	-	-	-	-
M	8	332	-	-	-	-	-	L	D	RIB	AD	H	-	100	-	0	-	-	-	-	+	1	+	0	0	-	4	0	-	-	-	-	-
M	52	333	-	-	-	-	-	L	D	RIB	AD	H	-	100	-	0	-	-	+	-	+	0	+	0	0	-	0	0	-	-	-	-	-
M	52	334	L	D	RIB	AD	H	-	-	-	-	-	-	100	-	0	-	-	-	+	-	0	-	0	0	+	0	0	-	-	-	-	-
M	9	335	-	-	-	-	-	L	D	RIB	AD	H	-	90	-	0	-	-	-	+	-	1	-	0	0	-	4	0	-	-	-	-	-
M	52	336	-	-	-	-	-	L	D	RIB	AD	H	-	100	-	0	-	-	-	+	-	2	-	0	0	+	0	0	-	+	-	-	-
M	9	337	-	-	-	-	-	L	D	RIB	AD	H	-	100	-	0	-	-	+	+	-	2	-	0	0	+	0	0	-	+	-	-	-
M	8	338	-	-	-	-	-	L	D	RIB	AD	H	-	100	-	0	-	-	+	+	-	0	-	0	0	+	0	0	-	+	-	-	-
M	8	339	-	-	-	-	-	L	D	RIB	AD	H	-	100	-	0	-	-	-	+	-	0	-	0	0	+	0	0	-	-	-	-	-
M	8	340	-	-	-	-	-	L	D	RIB	AD	H	-	100	-	0	-	-	-	+	-	0	-	0	0	-	3	0	-	-	-	-	-
M	8	341	-	-	-	-	-	L	D	RIB	AD	H	-	100	-	0	-	-	-	+	-	1	-	0	0	-	2	0	-	-	-	-	-
M	52	342	-	-	-	-	-	L	D	RIB	AD	H	-	90	-	0	-	-	+	+	-	1	-	0	0	-	0	0	-	-	-	-	-
M	9	343	L	D	RIB	AD	H	-	-	-	-	-	-	100	-	0	-	-	-	+	-	0	-	0	0	+	0	0	-	-	-	-	-
M	9	344	-	-	-	-	-	L	D	RIB	AD	H	-	90	-	0	-	-	+	+	-	1	-	0	0	-	0	0	-	-	-	-	-
M	11	345	-	-	-	-	-	L	D	RIB	AD	H	-	100	-	0	-	-	-	+	-	0	-	0	0	-	0	1	-	-	-	-	-
M	8	346	-	-	-	-	-	L	D	RIB	AD	H	-	100	-	0	-	-	-	+	-	1	-	0	0	-	0	0	-	-	-	-	-

01	02	03	04	05	06	07	08	09	10	11	12	13	14	15	16	17	18	19	23	24	25	40	41	42	43	44	49	54	59	64	93	94	95
M	8	347	.	.	.	.	.	L	D	RIB	AD	H	.	100	P	0	.	.	+	+	.	0	.	0	0	.	0	0	.	+	.	.	.
M	52	348	.	.	.	.	.	I	D	RIB	04	H	.	100	.	0	.	.	+	+	.	0	.	0	0	.	0	0	.	.	.	.	.
M	52	349	.	.	.	.	.	I	D	RIB	04	H	.	100	.	0	.	.	+	+	.	0	.	0	0	.	0	0	.	.	.	.	.
M	6	350	.	.	.	.	.	I	D	RIB	04	H	.	100	.	0	.	.	+	.	.	0	.	0	0	.	0	0	.	.	.	.	.
M	11	351	.	.	.	.	.	I	D	RIB	04	H	.	100	.	0	.	.	+	.	.	0	.	0	0	.	0	0	.	.	.	.	.
M	52	352	.	.	.	.	.	I	D	RIB	04	H	.	90	.	0	.	.	+	.	.	0	.	0	0	.	0	0	.	.	.	.	.
M	8	353	.	.	.	.	.	I	D	RIB	04	H	.	100	.	0	.	.	+	.	.	0	.	0	0	.	0	0	.	.	.	.	.
M	52	354	.	.	.	.	.	I	D	RIB	04	H	.	60	.	0	.	.	+	+	.	0	.	0	0	.	0	0	.	.	.	.	.
M	52	355	.	.	.	.	.	I	D	RIB	04	H	.	100	.	0	.	.	+	.	.	0	.	0	0	.	0	0	.	.	.	.	.
M	8	356	.	.	.	.	.	I	D	RIB	04	H	.	100	.	0	.	.	.	+	.	0	.	0	0	.	6	0	.	+	.	.	.
M	52	357	.	.	.	.	.	I	D	RIB	04	H	.	100	.	0	.	.	+	.	.	0	.	0	0	.	5	0	.	.	.	.	.
M	52	358	.	.	.	.	.	I	D	RIB	04	H	.	100	.	0	.	.	+	.	.	0	.	0	0	.	0	0	.	.	.	.	.
M	50	359	.	.	.	.	.	I	D	RIB	04	H	.	100	.	0	.	.	+	.	.	0	.	0	0	.	0	0	.	.	.	.	.
M	19	360	.	.	.	.	.	I	D	RIB	04	H	.	100	.	0	.	.	+	.	.	0	.	0	0	.	0	0	.	.	.	.	.
M	52	361	.	.	.	.	.	I	D	RIB	06	H	.	100	.	0	.	.	.	+	.	1	.	0	0	.	0	0	.	.	+	.	.
M	50	362	.	.	.	.	.	I	D	RIB	06	H	.	100	.	0	.	.	+	.	.	0	.	0	0	.	0	0	.	+	.	.	.
M	7	363	.	.	.	.	.	I	D	RIB	06	H	.	100	.	0	.	.	+	.	.	0	.	0	0	.	0	0	.	.	.	.	.
M	8	364	.	.	.	.	.	I	D	RIB	06	H	.	100	.	0	.	.	+	+	.	0	.	0	0	.	0	0	.	.	.	.	.
M	50	365	.	.	.	.	.	I	D	RIB	06	H	.	100	.	0	.	.	+	.	.	0	.	0	0	.	0	0	.	.	.	.	.
M	50	366	.	.	.	.	.	I	D	RIB	06	H	.	100	.	0	.	.	+	.	.	0	.	0	0	.	0	0	.	.	.	.	.
M	8	367	.	.	.	.	.	I	D	RIB	AD	H	.	100	.	0	.	.	+	+	.	0	.	0	0	.	0	0	.	.	.	.	.
M	9	368	.	.	.	.	.	I	D	RIB	AD	H	.	85	.	0	.	.	+	+	.	0	.	0	0	.	0	0	.	.	.	.	.
M	8	369	.	.	.	.	.	I	D	RIB	AD	H	.	100	.	0	.	.	+	+	.	0	.	0	0	.	0	0	.	.	.	.	.
M	8	370	.	.	.	.	.	I	D	RIB	AD	H	.	100	.	0	.	.	+	+	.	0	.	0	0	+	0	0	.	.	.	.	.
M	8	371	.	.	.	.	.	I	D	RIB	AD	H	.	100	.	0	.	.	+	+	.	0	.	0	0	+	0	0	.	+	.	.	.
M	8	372	.	.	.	.	.	I	D	RIB	AD	H	.	100	.	0	.	.	.	+	.	1	.	0	0	.	1	0	.	.	.	.	.
M	8	373	.	.	.	.	.	I	D	RIB	AD	H	.	100	.	0	.	.	.	+	.	0	.	0	0	+	0	0	.	.	.	.	.
M	52	374	.	.	.	.	.	I	D	RIB	AD	H	.	50	.	0	.	.	+	+	.	1	.	0	0	.	0	0	.	.	.	.	.
M	19	375	.	.	.	.	.	I	D	RIB	AD	H	.	80	.	0	.	.	.	+	.	1	.	0	0	.	0	0	.	.	.	.	.
M	3	376	.	.	.	.	.	I	D	RIB	AD	H	.	90	.	0	.	.	+	+	.	0	.	0	0	.	0	0	.	.	.	.	.
M	8	377	.	.	.	.	.	I	D	RIB	AD	H	.	100	.	0	.	.	.	+	.	0	.	0	0	.	0	0	.	.	.	.	.
M	8	378	.	.	.	.	.	I	D	RIB	AD	H	.	80	.	0	.	.	.	+	.	0	.	0	0	.	0	0	.	.	.	.	.
M	9	379	.	.	.	.	.	I	D	RIB	AD	H	.	100	.	0	.	.	.	+	.	0	.	0	0	.	0	0	.	.	.	.	.
M	8	380	.	.	.	.	.	I	D	RIB	AD	H	.	100	.	0	.	.	.	+	.	0	.	0	0	+	0	0	.	.	.	.	.
M	52	381	.	.	.	.	.	I	D	RIB	AD	H	.	100	.	0	.	.	.	+	.	1	.	0	0	.	0	0	.	.	.	.	.
M	8	382	.	.	.	.	.	I	D	RIB	AD	H	.	100	.	0	.	.	.	+	.	0	.	0	0	+	1	0	.	.	.	.	.
M	8	383	.	.	.	.	.	I	D	RIB	AD	H	.	100	.	0	.	.	+	+	.	0	.	0	0	.	0	0	.	.	.	.	.
M	52	384	.	.	.	.	.	I	D	RIB	AD	H	.	100	.	0	.	.	+	.	+	0	.	0	0	.	0	0	.	.	.	.	.
M	8	385	.	.	.	.	.	I	D	RIB	AD	H	.	70	.	0	.	.	.	+	.	0	.	0	0	.	0	0	.	.	.	.	.
M	9	386	.	.	.	.	.	I	D	RIB	AD	H	.	90	P	0	.	.	.	+	.	0	+	0	0	+	0	0	.	.	.	.	.
M	8	387	.	.	.	.	.	I	D	RIB	AD	H	.	100	.	0	.	.	.	+	+	0	.	0	0	.	0	0	.	.	.	.	.
M	8	388	.	.	.	.	.	I	D	RIB	AD	H	.	100	.	0	.	.	+	.	+	0	.	0	0	.	0	0	.	.	.	.	.
M	19	389	.	.	.	.	.	I	D	RIB	AD	H	.	80	.	0	.	.	.	+	.	0	.	0	0	.	0	0	.	.	.	.	.
M	52	390	.	.	.	.	.	I	D	RIB	AD	H	.	80	.	0	.	.	.	.	+	0	.	0	0	.	0	1	.	.	.	.	.
M	11	391	.	.	.	.	.	I	D	RIB	AD	H	.	100	.	0	.	.	.	+	.	1	.	0	0	.	4	0	.	.	.	.	.
M	19	392	.	.	.	.	.	I	D	RIB	AD	H	.	75	.	0	.	.	.	+	.	0	.	0	0	.	0	0	.	.	.	.	.
M	9	393	.	.	.	.	.	I	F	SCA	AD	H	.	10	.	0	.	.	.	.	.	0	.	0	0	.	0	0	.	.	.	.	.
M	8	394	.	.	.	.	.	I	D	RIB	AD	H	.	100	.	0	.	.	.	+	.	2	+	0	0	.	0	0	.	+	.	.	.
M	6	395	.	.	.	.	.	I	D	RIB	AD	H	.	40	.	0	.	.	.	.	+	0	.	0	0	.	0	0	.	.	.	.	.
M	8	396	.	.	.	.	.	I	D	RIB	AD	H	.	100	.	0	.	.	.	+	.	0	.	0	0	.	0	0	.	.	.	.	.
M	52	397	.	.	.	.	.	I	D	RIB	AD	H	.	100	.	0	.	.	.	+	.	0	.	0	0	.	0	0	.	.	.	.	.
M	6	398	.	.	.	.	.	I	D	RIB	AD	H	.	30	.	0	.	.	.	.	+	0	.	0	0	.	0	0	.	.	.	.	.
M	19	399	.	.	.	.	.	I	D	RIB	AD	H	.	100	.	0	.	.	.	+	.	1	.	0	0	.	0	0	.	.	.	.	.
M	19	400	.	.	.	.	.	I	D	RIB	AD	H	.	100	.	0	.	.	.	.	+	0	.	0	0	.	0	0	.	.	.	.	.
M	52	401	.	.	.	.	.	I	D	RIB	AD	H	.	100	.	0	.	.	+	.	+	0	.	0	0	.	0	0	.	+	+	.	.
M	8	402	.	.	.	.	.	I	D	RIB	AD	H	.	100	.	0	.	.	+	.	+	0	.	0	0	.	0	0	.	.	.	.	.
M	8	403	.	.	.	.	.	I	D	RIB	AD	H	.	100	.	0	.	.	.	.	+	0	.	0	0	.	0	0	.	.	.	.	.
M	9	404	.	.	.	.	.	I	D	RIB	AD	H	.	15	.	0	.	.	+	.	+	0	.	0	0	.	0	0	.	.	.	.	.

0.1	0.2	0.3	0.4	0.5	0.6	0.7	0.8	0.9	1.0	1.1	1.2	1.3	1.4	1.5	1.6	1.7	1.8	1.9	2.3	2.4	2.5	4.0	4.1	4.2	4.3	4.4	4.9	5.4	5.9	6.4	9.3	9.4	9.5
M	11	405	-	-	-	-	-	I	D	RIB	AD	H	-	90	-	0	-	-	-	-	+	0	-	0	0	-	0	0	-	-	-	-	-
M	8	406	-	-	-	-	-	I	D	RIB	AD	H	-	100	-	0	-	-	+	+	-	0	-	0	0	-	0	0	-	-	-	-	-
M	8	407	-	-	-	-	-	I	D	RIB	AD	H	-	100	-	0	-	-	+	-	+	0	-	0	0	-	0	0	-	-	-	-	-
M	19	408	-	-	-	-	-	I	D	RIB	AD	H	-	100	-	0	-	-	-	+	+	0	-	0	0	+	0	0	-	-	-	-	-
M	8	409	-	-	-	-	-	I	D	RIB	AD	H	-	100	P	0	-	-	-	+	-	0	-	0	0	-	1	0	-	-	-	-	-
M	8	410	-	-	-	-	-	I	D	RIB	AD	H	-	100	-	0	-	-	+	-	+	0	-	0	0	-	0	0	-	-	-	-	-
M	8	411	-	-	-	-	-	I	D	RIB	AD	H	-	100	-	0	-	-	-	+	-	0	-	0	0	-	0	0	-	-	-	-	-
M	8	412	-	-	-	-	-	I	D	RIB	AD	H	-	100	-	0	-	-	-	+	-	0	-	0	0	-	0	0	-	-	-	-	-
M	9	413	-	-	-	-	-	I	D	RIB	AD	H	-	100	-	0	-	-	-	+	-	0	+	0	0	+	2	0	-	-	-	-	-
M	9	414	-	-	-	-	-	I	D	RIB	AD	H	-	100	-	0	-	-	-	+	-	0	-	0	0	+	0	0	-	-	-	-	-
M	11	415	-	-	-	-	-	I	D	RIB	AD	H	-	100	-	0	-	-	-	+	-	0	-	0	0	-	0	0	-	-	-	-	-
M	8	416	-	-	-	-	-	I	D	RIB	AD	H	-	100	-	0	-	-	-	+	-	0	+	0	0	-	0	0	-	-	-	-	-
M	19	417	-	-	-	-	-	I	D	RIB	AD	H	-	100	-	0	-	-	+	-	+	0	-	0	0	-	0	0	-	-	-	-	-
M	8	418	-	-	-	-	-	I	D	RIB	AD	H	-	100	-	0	-	-	+	-	+	0	-	0	0	-	0	0	-	-	-	-	-
M	19	419	-	-	-	-	-	I	D	RIB	AD	H	-	100	-	0	-	-	+	+	-	0	-	0	0	+	0	0	-	-	-	-	-
M	19	420	-	-	-	-	-	I	D	RIB	AD	H	-	80	-	0	-	-	-	-	+	0	-	0	0	-	0	0	-	-	-	-	-
M	8	421	-	-	-	-	-	I	D	RIB	AD	H	-	100	-	0	-	-	-	+	-	0	+	0	0	-	0	0	-	-	-	-	-
M	11	422	-	-	-	-	-	I	D	RIB	AD	H	-	60	-	2	-	-	-	+	-	1	-	0	0	-	0	0	-	-	-	-	-
M	8	423	-	-	-	-	-	I	D	RIB	AD	H	-	100	-	0	-	-	-	+	-	0	-	0	0	-	0	0	-	-	-	-	-
M	6	424	-	-	-	-	-	I	D	RIB	AD	H	-	100	-	0	-	-	-	-	+	0	-	0	0	-	0	0	-	-	-	-	-
M	8	425	-	-	-	-	-	I	D	RIB	AD	H	-	100	-	0	-	-	-	+	-	0	-	0	0	+	0	0	-	-	-	-	-
M	7	426	-	-	-	-	-	I	D	RIB	AD	H	-	100	-	0	-	-	-	-	+	0	-	0	0	-	4	0	-	-	-	-	-
M	19	427	-	-	-	-	-	I	D	RIB	AD	H	-	100	-	0	-	-	-	+	-	0	-	0	0	+	0	0	-	-	-	-	-
M	8	428	-	-	-	-	-	I	D	RIB	AD	H	-	100	-	0	-	-	-	+	-	0	-	0	0	+	0	0	-	-	-	-	-
M	3	429	-	-	-	-	-	I	D	RIB	AD	H	-	100	-	0	-	-	+	+	-	0	-	0	0	+	0	0	-	-	-	-	-
M	30	430	-	-	-	-	-	I	D	RIB	AD	H	-	100	-	0	-	-	-	-	+	0	-	0	0	-	0	0	-	-	-	-	-
M	52	431	-	-	-	-	-	I	D	RIB	AD	H	-	100	-	0	-	-	+	+	-	0	-	0	0	-	0	0	-	-	-	-	-
M	7	432	-	-	-	-	-	I	D	RIB	AD	H	-	100	-	0	-	-	+	-	+	0	-	0	0	-	0	0	-	-	-	-	-
M	8	433	-	-	-	-	-	I	D	RIB	AD	H	-	100	P	0	-	-	+	-	+	0	-	0	0	-	0	0	-	-	-	-	-
M	6	434	-	-	-	-	-	I	D	RIB	AD	H	-	100	-	0	-	-	+	-	+	0	-	0	0	+	0	0	-	-	-	-	-
M	30	435	-	-	-	-	-	I	D	RIB	AD	H	-	100	-	0	-	-	-	+	+	0	-	0	0	+	0	0	-	-	-	-	-
M	8	436	-	-	-	-	-	I	D	RIB	AD	H	-	100	-	0	-	-	+	-	+	0	-	0	0	-	1	0	-	-	-	-	-
M	3	437	-	-	-	-	-	I	D	RIB	AD	H	-	100	-	0	-	-	-	+	-	0	-	0	0	-	0	0	-	-	-	-	-
M	8	438	-	-	-	-	-	I	D	RIB	AD	H	-	100	-	0	-	-	-	+	-	0	-	0	0	-	0	0	-	-	-	-	-
M	7	439	-	-	-	-	-	I	D	RIB	AD	H	-	100	-	0	-	-	-	-	+	0	-	0	0	-	2	0	-	-	-	-	-
M	11	440	-	-	-	-	-	I	D	RIB	AD	H	-	100	-	0	-	-	-	+	-	0	-	0	0	-	0	0	-	-	-	-	-
M	0	441	-	-	-	-	-	I	D	RIB	AD	H	-	0	-	0	-	-	-	-	+	0	-	0	0	-	0	0	-	-	-	-	-
M	52	442	-	-	-	-	-	I	D	RIB	AD	H	-	100	-	0	-	-	-	+	-	0	-	0	0	-	0	0	-	-	-	-	-
M	11	443	-	-	-	-	-	I	D	RIB	AD	H	-	100	-	0	-	-	+	+	-	0	-	0	0	-	0	0	-	-	+	-	-
M	8	444	-	-	-	-	-	I	D	RIB	AD	H	-	100	-	0	-	-	-	+	-	0	-	0	0	-	0	0	-	-	-	-	-
M	19	445	-	-	-	-	-	I	D	RIB	AD	H	-	100	-	0	-	-	-	+	-	0	-	0	0	-	0	0	-	-	-	-	-
M	11	446	-	-	-	-	-	I	D	RIB	AD	H	-	100	-	0	-	-	-	-	+	0	-	0	0	-	0	0	-	-	-	-	-
M	6	447	-	-	-	-	-	I	D	RIB	AD	H	-	100	-	0	-	-	-	+	-	0	-	0	0	-	0	0	-	-	-	-	-
M	6	448	-	-	-	-	-	I	D	RIB	AD	H	-	100	-	0	-	-	+	-	-	0	-	0	0	-	0	0	-	-	-	-	-
M	9	449	-	-	-	-	-	I	D	RIB	AD	H	-	100	-	0	-	-	-	-	+	0	-	0	0	-	0	0	-	-	-	-	-
M	9	450	-	-	-	-	-	I	D	RIB	AD	H	-	100	-	0	-	-	+	+	-	0	-	0	0	-	0	0	-	-	-	-	-
M	52	451	-	-	-	-	-	I	D	RIB	AD	H	-	10	-	0	-	-	+	+	-	0	-	0	0	-	0	0	-	-	-	-	-
M	0	452	-	-	-	-	-	I	D	RIB	AD	H	-	100	-	0	-	-	+	+	-	0	-	0	0	-	0	0	-	-	-	-	-
M	19	453	-	-	-	-	-	I	D	RIB	AD	H	-	100	-	0	-	-	+	+	-	0	-	0	0	-	0	0	-	-	-	-	-
M	8	454	-	-	-	-	-	I	D	RIB	AD	H	12	90	-	0	-	-	+	+	-	1	+	0	0	-	5	0	-	-	-	-	-
M	8	455	-	-	-	-	-	I	D	RIB	AD	H	12	100	-	0	-	-	+	+	-	0	-	0	0	-	0	0	-	-	-	-	-
M	52	456	R	E	RIB	04	H	-	-	-	-	-	-	100	-	0	-	-	+	+	-	0	-	0	0	-	0	0	-	-	-	-	-
M	11	457	-	-	-	-	-	R	E	RIB	06	H	-	100	-	0	-	-	-	+	-	0	-	0	0	-	1	0	+	-	-	-	-
M	8	458	R	E	RIB	12	H	-	-	-	-	-	-	100	-	0	-	-	-	+	-	0	-	0	0	-	2	0	+	-	-	-	-
M	8	459	R	E	RIB	12	H	-	-	-	-	-	-	100	-	0	-	-	-	+	-	0	-	0	0	+	0	0	-	-	-	-	-
M	8	460	R	E	RIB	AD	H	-	-	-	-	-	-	100	P	0	-	-	-	+	-	2	+	0	0	+	0	0	+	-	-	-	-
M	52	461	R	E	RIB	AD	H	-	-	-	-	-	-	100	-	0	-	-	-	+	-	0	-	0	0	+	0	0	-	-	-	-	-
M	8	462	R	E	RIB	AD	H	-	-	-	-	-	-	100	-	0	-	-	-	+	-	0	-	0	0	-	6	0	-	-	-	-	-

01	02	03	04	05	06	07	08	09	10	11	12	13	14	15	16	17	18	19	23	24	25	40	41	42	43	44	49	54	59	64	93	94	95
M	8	463	R	E	RIB	AD	H	.	.	.	.	.	.	100	.	0	.	.	.	+	.	0	.	0	0	.	0	0	.	.	.	.	.
M	8	464	R	E	RIB	AD	H	.	.	.	.	.	.	80	.	0	.	.	+	+	.	1	.	0	0	.	0	0	.	.	.	.	.
M	8	465	R	E	RIB	AD	H	.	.	.	.	.	.	100	.	0	.	.	.	+	.	0	.	0	0	.	1	0	.	.	.	.	.
M	8	466	R	E	RIB	AD	H	.	.	.	.	.	.	100	.	0	.	.	+	+	.	0	.	0	0	.	0	0	.	.	.	.	.
M	8	467	R	E	RIB	AD	H	.	.	.	.	.	.	100	.	0	.	.	.	+	.	0	.	0	0	.	2	0	.	+	.	.	.
M	8	468	R	E	RIB	AD	H	.	.	.	.	.	.	100	.	0	.	.	.	+	.	0	.	0	0	.	0	0	+	.	.	.	.
M	8	469	R	E	RIB	AD	H	.	.	.	.	.	.	100	.	0	.	.	.	+	.	0	.	0	0	.	0	0	+	.	.	.	.
M	11	470	R	E	RIB	AD	H	.	.	.	.	.	.	100	.	0	.	.	.	+	.	0	.	0	0	.	2	0	+	.	.	.	.
M	8	471	R	E	RIB	AD	H	.	.	.	.	.	.	100	.	0	.	.	.	+	.	0	.	0	0	.	0	0	+	.	.	.	.
M	8	472	R	E	RIB	AD	H	.	.	.	.	.	.	100	.	0	.	.	+	.	+	0	.	0	0	.	0	0	+	.	.	.	.
M	8	473	R	E	RIB	AD	H	.	.	.	.	.	.	100	.	0	.	.	.	+	.	0	.	0	0	.	0	0	+	.	.	.	.
M	8	474	R	E	RIB	AD	H	.	.	.	.	.	.	100	.	0	.	.	.	+	.	0	.	0	0	.	0	0	.	.	.	.	.
M	11	475	R	E	RIB	AD	H	.	.	.	.	.	.	100	P	0	+	.	.	+	.	0	.	0	0	.	0	0	.	.	.	.	.
M	8	476	R	E	RIB	AD	H	.	.	.	.	.	.	100	.	0	.	.	.	+	.	0	.	0	0	.	0	0	+	.	.	.	.
M	8	477	.	.	.	.	.	R	E	RIB	AD	H	.	100	P	0	.	.	.	+	.	0	.	0	0	.	0	0	+	.	.	.	.
M	8	478	L	E	RIB	AD	H	.	.	.	.	.	.	100	.	0	.	.	.	+	.	0	.	0	0	.	4	0	.	.	.	.	.
M	52	479	L	E	RIB	AD	H	.	.	.	.	.	.	100	.	0	.	.	.	+	.	0	.	0	0	.	0	0	.	.	.	.	.
M	8	480	L	E	RIB	AD	H	.	.	.	.	.	.	100	.	0	.	.	.	+	.	0	.	0	0	.	0	0	+	.	.	.	.
M	8	481	L	E	RIB	AD	H	.	.	.	.	.	.	100	.	0	.	.	+	+	.	0	.	0	0	.	0	0	.	.	.	.	.
M	52	482	L	E	RIB	AD	H	.	.	.	.	.	.	100	P	0	+	.	.	+	.	0	.	0	0	.	1	0	.	.	.	.	.
M	8	483	L	E	RIB	AD	H	.	.	.	.	.	.	100	P	0	.	.	.	+	.	0	.	0	0	.	0	0	+	.	.	.	.
M	5	484	L	E	RIB	AD	H	.	.	.	.	.	.	100	.	0	.	.	.	.	+	0	.	0	0	.	0	0	.	.	.	.	.
M	8	485	L	E	RIB	AD	H	.	.	.	.	.	.	100	P	0	.	.	.	+	.	0	.	0	0	.	0	0	.	.	.	.	.
M	8	486	L	E	RIB	AD	H	.	.	.	.	.	.	100	.	0	.	.	.	+	.	0	.	0	0	.	0	0	.	+	.	.	.
M	7	487	L	E	RIB	AD	H	.	.	.	.	.	.	100	.	0	.	.	+	+	.	0	.	0	0	.	0	0	.	.	.	.	.
M	8	488	L	E	RIB	AD	H	.	.	.	.	.	.	100	P	0	.	.	.	+	.	0	+	0	0	.	3	0	.	.	.	.	.
M	30	489	L	E	RIB	AD	H	.	.	.	.	.	.	100	.	0	.	.	.	+	.	0	.	0	0	.	0	0	.	.	.	.	.
M	8	490	.	.	.	.	.	L	E	RIB	AD	H	.	100	.	0	.	.	.	+	.	0	.	0	0	.	0	0	+	.	.	.	.
M	8	491	L	E	RIB	AD	H	.	.	.	.	.	.	100	.	0	.	.	.	+	.	0	+	0	0	.	0	0	+	.	.	.	.
M	8	492	L	E	RIB	AD	H	.	.	.	.	.	.	100	.	0	.	.	.	+	.	0	.	0	0	.	3	0	+	.	.	.	.
M	8	493	L	E	RIB	AD	H	.	.	.	.	.	.	100	.	0	.	.	.	+	.	0	.	0	0	.	0	0	+	.	.	.	.
M	8	494	L	E	RIB	AD	H	.	.	.	.	.	.	100	.	0	.	.	.	+	.	0	.	0	0	.	0	0	+	.	.	.	.
M	52	495	R	F	RIB	AD	H	.	.	.	.	.	.	100	.	0	.	.	.	+	.	0	+	0	0	+	0	0	+	.	.	.	.
M	30	496	R	F	RIB	AD	H	.	.	.	.	.	.	100	.	0	.	.	.	+	.	0	.	0	0	+	0	0	.	+	.	.	.
M	52	497	.	.	.	.	.	R	F	RIB	AD	H	.	100	.	0	.	.	.	+	.	0	.	0	0	+	0	0	.	.	.	.	.
M	8	498	R	F	RIB	AD	H	.	.	.	.	.	.	100	.	0	.	.	+	+	.	0	.	0	0	.	1	0	.	.	.	.	.
M	8	499	R	F	RIB	AD	H	.	.	.	.	.	.	100	.	0	.	.	.	+	.	0	.	0	0	+	0	0	.	.	.	.	.
M	8	500	R	F	RIB	AD	H	.	.	.	.	.	.	100	.	0	.	.	.	+	.	0	+	0	0	.	0	0	+	.	.	.	.
M	8	501	R	F	RIB	AD	H	.	.	.	.	.	.	100	.	0	.	.	.	+	.	0	.	0	0	+	0	0	+	.	.	.	.
M	9	502	R	F	RIB	AD	H	.	.	.	.	.	.	100	.	0	.	.	.	+	.	0	.	0	0	.	0	0	.	+	.	.	.
M	11	503	R	F	RIB	AD	H	.	.	.	.	.	.	100	P	0	.	.	.	+	.	0	.	0	0	.	0	0	.	.	.	.	.
M	52	504	.	.	.	.	.	R	F	RIB	AD	H	.	100	.	0	.	.	+	+	.	0	.	0	0	.	1	0	.	.	.	.	.
M	11	505	.	.	.	.	.	R	F	RIB	AD	H	.	100	P	0	.	.	.	+	+	0	.	0	0	.	0	0	.	.	.	.	.
M	8	506	R	F	RIB	AD	H	.	.	.	.	.	.	100	P	0	.	.	.	+	.	0	+	0	0	.	0	0	.	.	.	.	.
M	7	507	R	F	RIB	AD	H	.	.	.	.	.	.	100	.	0	.	.	.	+	+	0	.	0	0	+	0	0	.	+	.	.	.
M	11	508	.	.	.	.	.	R	F	RIB	AD	H	.	100	.	0	.	.	.	+	+	0	.	0	0	.	0	0	.	.	.	.	.
M	6	509	R	F	RIB	AD	H	.	.	.	.	.	.	100	.	0	.	.	.	+	.	0	.	0	0	+	0	0	.	.	.	.	.
M	8	510	.	.	.	.	.	R	F	RIB	AD	H	.	100	P	0	.	.	.	+	+	0	+	0	0	.	0	0	.	.	.	.	.
M	8	511	.	.	.	.	.	R	F	RIB	AD	H	.	100	.	0	.	.	.	+	.	0	.	0	0	.	0	0	.	.	.	.	.
M	8	512	L	F	RIB	AD	H	.	.	.	.	.	.	100	.	0	.	.	.	+	+	0	+	0	0	.	0	0	+	.	.	.	.
M	3	513	L	F	RIB	AD	H	.	.	.	.	.	.	100	.	0	.	.	.	+	.	0	.	0	0	+	3	0	.	.	.	.	.
M	8	514	L	F	RIB	AD	H	.	.	.	.	.	.	100	.	0	.	.	.	+	.	0	.	0	0	.	5	0	.	.	.	.	.
M	8	515	L	F	RIB	AD	H	.	.	.	.	.	.	100	P	0	.	.	.	+	.	0	.	0	0	.	0	0	.	.	.	.	.
M	9	516	L	F	RIB	AD	H	.	.	.	.	.	.	100	P	0	.	.	+	+	.	0	.	0	0	+	0	0	.	.	.	.	.
M	8	517	.	.	.	.	.	L	F	RIB	AD	H	.	100	.	0	.	.	+	+	+	0	+	0	0	.	0	0	+	.	.	.	.
M	8	518	.	.	.	.	.	L	F	RIB	AD	H	.	95	P	0	.	.	.	+	.	0	.	0	0	+	0	0	.	.	.	.	.
M	52	519	L	F	RIB	AD	H	.	.	.	.	.	.	100	P	0	.	.	+	+	+	0	.	0	0	.	0	0	+	.	.	.	.
M	52	520	L	F	RIB	AD	H	.	.	.	.	.	.	80	.	0	.	.	+	+	+	0	+	0	0	.	0	0	.	.	.	.	.

01	02	03	04	05	06	07	08	09	10	11	12	13	14	15	16	17	18	19	23	24	25	40	41	42	43	44	49	54	59	64	93	94	95
M	8	521	-	-	-	-	-	L	F	RIB	AD	H	-	100	P	0	-	-	-	+	-	0	+	0	0	-	0	0	-	-	-	-	-
M	8	522	-	-	-	-	-	L	F	RIB	AD	H	-	100	-	0	-	-	-	+	+	0	-	0	0	-	0	0	-	+	-	-	-
M	8	523	-	-	-	-	-	L	F	RIB	AD	H	-	100	-	0	-	-	-	+	-	0	+	0	0	-	0	0	-	+	-	-	-
M	8	524	-	-	-	-	-	L	F	RIB	AD	H	-	100	P	0	-	-	-	+	-	0	-	0	0	-	0	0	+	-	-	-	-
M	8	525	-	-	-	-	-	L	F	RIB	AD	H	-	100	P	0	-	-	-	+	-	0	-	0	0	-	0	0	-	-	-	-	-
M	11	526						L	F	RIB	AD	H	-	100	-	0	-	-	-	+	-	0	-	0	0	-	0	0	-	-	-	-	-
M	6	527	R	W	SCA	O6	H	-	-	-	-	-	-	95	-	0	-	-	+	+	-	0	-	0	0	-	0	0	-	-	+	-	-
M	8	528	R	W	SCA	10	H	-	-	-	-	-	-	100	-	0	-	-	+	-	-	0	-	0	0	-	0	0	-	-	-	-	-
M	6	529	R	W	SCA	AD	H	-	-	-	-	-	-	100	-	0	-	-	+	+	-	0	-	0	0	-	2	0	-	-	+	-	-
M	9	530	R	W	SCA	AD	H	-	-	-	-	-	-	80	-	0	-	-	+	+	-	0	+	0	0	-	0	0	-	-	-	-	-
M	8	531	R	W	SCA	AD	H	-	-	-	-	-	-	100	-	0	-	-	+	+	-	0	+	0	0	-	0	0	-	-	-	-	-
M	8	532	-	-	-	-	-	R	F	SCA	AD	H	-	100	-	0	-	-	+	+	-	0	+	0	0	+	0	0	-	-	-	-	-
M	6	533	-	-	-	-	-	R	F	SCA	AD	H	-	50	-	1	-	-	-	+	+	0	+	0	0	-	0	0	-	-	-	-	-
M	6	534	-	-	-	-	-	R	F	SCA	AD	H	-	100	-	0	-	-	-	+	-	0	+	0	0	-	0	0	-	-	-	-	-
M	50	535	R	F	SCA	AD	H	-	-	-	-	-	-	100	-	0	+	-	+	+	+	0	-	0	0	-	0	0	-	-	-	-	-
M	8	536	-	-	-	-	-	R	F	SCA	AD	H	-	100	-	0	-	-	+	+	-	0	-	0	0	-	0	0	-	-	-	-	-
M	6	537	-	-	-	-	-	R	F	SCA	AD	H	-	100	-	0	-	-	-	+	-	0	+	0	0	-	0	0	-	-	-	-	-
M	8	538	-	-	-	-	-	R	F	SCA	AD	H	-	100	-	0	-	-	-	+	-	0	-	0	0	-	0	0	-	-	+	+	+
M	6	539	-	-	-	-	-	L	F	SCA	04	H	-	100	-	0	-	-	-	+	-	0	-	0	0	-	0	0	-	-	-	-	-
M	5	540	L	W	SCA	06	H	-	-	-	-	-	-	100	-	0	-	-	-	-	-	0	-	0	0	-	0	0	-	-	-	-	-
M	3	541	-	-	-	-	-	L	F	SCA	10	H	-	100	-	1	-	-	+	+	-	0	-	0	0	-	0	0	-	-	-	-	-
M	8	542	-	-	-	-	-	L	F	SCA	AD	H	-	100	-	0	-	-	-	+	-	1	+	0	0	+	0	0	-	-	-	-	-
M	11	543	-	-	-	-	-	L	F	SCA	AD	H	-	100	-	0	-	-	-	+	-	0	-	0	0	-	0	0	-	-	-	-	-
M	11	544	-	-	-	-	-	L	F	SCA	AD	H	-	100	-	2	-	-	+	+	-	0	-	0	0	-	0	0	-	-	-	-	-
M	6	545	-	-	-	-	-	L	F	SCA	AD	H	-	100	-	0	-	-	-	+	-	0	+	0	0	-	0	0	-	-	+	-	-
M	11	546	-	-	-	-	-	L	F	SCA	AD	H	-	100	-	2	-	-	-	+	-	0	-	0	0	-	0	0	-	+	-	-	-
M	65	547	-	-	-	-	-	L	F	SCA	AD	H	-	100	-	1	-	-	-	-	+	0	-	0	0	-	0	0	-	-	-	-	-
M	30	945	R	W	PAT	12	H	-	-	-	-	-	-	100	-	0	-	-	-	+	-	0	+	0	0	-	0	0	-	-	-	-	-
M	8	946	R	W	PAT	AD	H	-	-	-	-	-	-	100	-	0	-	-	-	-	+	0	+	0	0	-	0	0	-	-	-	-	-
M	6	947	-	-	-	-	-	L	W	PAT	08	H	-	100	-	0	-	-	-	+	-	0	+	0	0	-	0	0	-	-	-	-	-
M	8	948	L	W	PAT	AD	H	-	-	-	-	-	-	100	-	0	-	-	-	-	+	0	+	0	0	-	0	0	-	-	-	-	-
M	8	949	L	W	PAT	AD	H	-	-	-	-	-	-	100	-	0	-	-	-	+	-	0	+	0	0	-	0	0	-	-	-	-	-
M	8	950	L	W	PAT	AD	H	-	-	-	-	-	-	100	-	0	-	-	-	-	-	0	-	0	0	-	0	0	-	-	-	-	-
M	11	951	L	W	PAT	AD	H	-	-	-	-	-	-	100	-	2	-	-	-	-	-	0	-	0	0	-	0	0	-	-	-	-	-
M	8	952	-	-	-	-	-	L	F	PAT	AD	H	-	100	-	0	-	-	-	+	-	0	+	0	0	-	0	0	-	-	-	-	-
M	8	1171	R	W	CAR	AD	H	-	-	-	-	-	-	80	-	0	-	-	-	-	+	0	-	0	0	-	0	0	-	-	-	-	-
M	30	1172	R	W	CAR	AD	H	-	-	-	-	-	-	100	-	0	-	-	-	-	-	0	-	0	0	-	0	0	-	-	-	-	-
M	6	1173	R	W	CAR	AD	H	-	-	-	-	-	-	20	-	0	-	-	-	-	-	0	-	0	0	-	0	0	-	-	+	-	+
M	30	1174	R	W	CAR	AD	H	-	-	-	-	-	-	100	-	0	-	-	-	-	-	0	-	0	0	-	0	0	-	-	-	-	-
M	30	1175	R	W	CAR	AD	H	-	-	-	-	-	-	100	-	0	-	-	-	-	-	0	-	0	0	-	0	0	-	-	-	-	-
M	30	1176	L	W	CAR	AD	H	-	-	-	-	-	-	100	-	0	-	-	-	-	-	0	-	0	0	-	0	0	-	-	-	-	-
M	30	1177	L	W	CAR	AD	H	-	-	-	-	-	-	100	-	0	-	-	-	-	-	0	-	0	0	-	0	0	-	-	-	-	-
M	30	1178	L	W	CAR	AD	H	-	-	-	-	-	-	100	-	0	-	-	-	-	-	0	-	0	0	-	0	0	-	-	-	-	-
M	30	1270	R	F	CAL	AD	H	-	-	-	-	-	-	100	-	0	-	-	-	+	-	0	+	0	0	+	0	0	-	-	-	-	-
M	8	1271	R	F	CAL	AD	H	-	-	-	-	-	-	100	-	0	-	-	-	+	+	0	+	0	0	-	0	0	-	-	+	+	+
M	6	1272	R	F	CAL	AD	H	-	-	-	-	-	-	80	-	0	-	-	-	+	-	0	-	0	0	+	0	0	-	-	-	-	-
M	6	1273	-	-	-	-	-	R	F	CAL	AD	H	-	100	-	0	+	-	+	+	-	0	-	0	0	-	0	0	-	-	+	+	-
M	6	1274	L	W	CAL	AD	H	-	-	-	-	-	-	100	-	0	-	-	-	-	-	0	-	0	0	-	0	0	-	-	-	-	-
M	6	1275	L	W	CAL	AD	H	-	-	-	-	-	-	100	-	0	-	-	-	-	+	0	+	0	0	-	0	0	-	-	-	-	-
M	6	1276	L	F	CAL	AD	H	-	-	-	-	-	-	100	-	0	-	-	-	+	-	0	-	0	0	-	0	0	-	-	-	-	-
M	8	1277	-	-	-	-	-	L	F	CAL	AD	H	-	100	-	0	-	-	-	+	-	0	-	0	0	-	0	0	-	-	-	-	-
M	8	1278	L	F	CAL	AD	H	-	-	-	-	-	-	100	-	0	-	-	-	+	-	0	+	0	0	-	0	0	-	-	-	-	-
M	30	1279	-	-	-	-	-	L	F	CAL	AD	H	-	100	-	0	-	-	-	+	-	0	+	0	0	+	0	0	+	-	-	-	-
M	5	1280	R	F	TAL	12	H	-	-	-	-	-	-	100	-	0	-	-	-	+	+	0	+	0	0	-	0	0	-	-	-	-	-
M	8	1281	R	W	TAL	AD	GH	-	-	-	-	-	-	100	-	0	-	-	-	+	-	0	+	0	0	-	0	0	-	-	-	-	-
M	6	1282	R	W	TAL	AD	H	-	-	-	-	-	-	90	-	0	-	-	-	+	-	0	+	0	0	-	0	0	-	-	-	-	-
M	6	1283	L	W	TAL	AD	H	-	-	-	-	-	-	100	-	0	-	-	-	+	-	0	+	0	0	-	0	0	-	-	-	-	-
M	8	1284	R	W	TAR	AD	H	-	-	-	-	-	-	100	-	0	-	-	-	+	+	0	+	0	0	-	0	0	-	-	-	-	-

01	02	03	04	05	06	07	08	09	10	11	12	13	14	15	16	17	18	19	23	24	25	40	41	42	43	44	49	54	59	64	93	94	95
M	8	1285	R	W	TAR	AD	H	-	-	-	-	-	-	100	-	0	-	-	-	+	-	0	+	0	0	-	0	0	-	-	-	-	-
M	8	1286	R	F	TAR	AD	H	-	-	-	-	-	-	100	-	0	-	-	-	+	-	0	+	0	0	-	0	0	-	-	-	-	-
M	8	1287	-	-	-	-	-	R	F	TAR	AD	H	-	100	-	0	-	-	-	+	-	0	+	0	0	-	0	0	-	-	-	-	-
M	11	1288	L	W	TAR	AD	H	-	-	-	-	-	-	100	-	0	-	-	-	-	+	0	-	0	0	-	0	0	-	-	-	-	-
M	6	1289	-	-	-	-	-	L	W	TAR	AD	H	-	100	-	0	+	-	+	+	-	0	-	0	0	-	0	0	-	-	-	-	-
M	8	1290	L	W	TAR	AD	H	-	-	-	-	-	-	100	-	0	-	-	-	+	-	0	+	0	0	-	0	0	-	-	-	-	-
M	8	1291	-	-	-	-	-	I	F	TAR	AD	H	-	100	-	0	-	-	-	+	-	0	-	0	0	-	0	0	-	-	-	-	-
M	8	1292	-	-	-	-	-	I	F	TAR	AD	H	-	100	-	0	-	-	-	+	-	0	+	0	0	-	0	0	-	-	-	-	-

01	02	03	04	05	06	07	08	14	15	16	17	18	19	20	21	22	23	24	25	29	30	31
M	6	548	R	W	CLA	04	H	.	100	.	0	.	.	CO	3	3	+	.	+	+	.	+
M	6	549	R	W	CLA	06	H	.	100	.	0	.	.	SO	3	3	.	+	.	.	+	.
M	11	550	R	F	CLA	06	H	.	100	.	0	.	.	PS	3	1	+	+	.	.	.	.
M	8	551	R	W	CLA	AD	H	.	100	.	0	.	.	SO	3	3	.	.	+	.	.	+
M	8	552	R	W	CLA	AD	H	.	100	.	0	.	.	SO	3	3	.	+	.	.	+	.
M	7	553	R	W	CLA	AD	H	.	100	.	0	.	.	SO	3	3	+	+	.	+	.	.
M	6	554	R	F	CLA	AD	H	.	100	.	0	.	.	SO	3	2	.	+	.	.	+	.
M	6	555	R	F	CLA	AD	H	.	100	.	0	.	.	SO	2	2	.	+	.	.	+	.
M	9	556	R	F	CLA	AD	H	.	100	.	0	.	.	DS	2	2	.	+	.	.	+	.
M	8	557	R	F	CLA	AD	H	.	100	P	0	.	.	PS	3	3	.	+	.	.	+	.
M	8	561	R	F	CLA	AD	H	17	100	.	0	.	.	SO	3	1	.	+	.	.	+	.
M	3	562	R	F	CLA	AD	H	17	80	.	0	.	.	SO	3	1	+	+	.	+	.	.
M	8	563	R	F	CLA	AD	H	18	100	.	0	.	.	DS	3	1	.	+	.	.	+	.
M	8	565	R	F	CLA	AD	H	18	100	.	0	.	.	PS	3	1	.	+	.	.	.	.
M	6	566	L	W	CLA	04	H	.	100	.	0	.	.	SO	3	3	+	.	.	+	.	.
M	11	567	L	F	CLA	06	H	.	100	.	0	.	.	SO	3	1	.	.	+	.	.	+
M	9	568	L	W	CLA	AD	H	.	100	.	0	.	.	SO	3	3	+	+	.	+	+	.
M	7	569	L	W	CLA	AD	H	.	100	.	0	.	.	SO	3	2	+	+	.	.	+	.
M	8	570	L	W	CLA	AD	H	.	100	.	0	.	.	SO	3	3	.	+	.	.	+	.
M	3	571	L	W	CLA	AD	H	.	80	.	0	.	.	SO	3	3	.	+	.	.	+	.
M	11	572	L	F	CLA	AD	H	.	100	.	0	+	.	SO	3	2	.	+	.	.	+	.
M	6	573	L	F	CLA	AD	H	.	100	.	0	.	.	SO	3	2	.	+	.	.	+	.
M	8	574	L	F	CLA	AD	H	.	100	.	0	.	.	SO	1	2	.	+	.	.	+	.
M	11	577	L	F	CLA	AD	H	.	100	.	0	.	.	SO	3	1	.	+	.	.	+	.
M	8	579	L	F	CLA	AD	H	.	100	.	0	.	.	SO	3	1	.	+	.	.	+	.
M	6	582	R	W	HUM	04	H	.	100	.	0	.	.	SO	3	3	.	+	+	.	.	+
M	6	583	R	W	HUM	04	H	.	40	.	0	.	.	SO	3	3	+	+	+	+	+	.
M	8	588	R	F	HUM	10	H	.	100	.	0	.	.	DS	3	1	.	+	.	.	+	.
M	8	589	R	F	HUM	10	H	.	100	.	0	.	.	DS	3	1	.	+	.	.	+	.
M	30	590	R	F	HUM	12	H	.	100	.	0	.	.	DS	1	2	.	+	.	.	+	.
M	3	591	R	F	HUM	AD	H	.	100	P	0	.	.	DS	3	2	+	+	.	+	+	.
M	50	592	R	F	HUM	AD	H	.	100	.	0	.	.	DO	1	1	.	+	.	.	+	.
M	19	593	R	F	HUM	AD	H	.	100	.	0	.	.	DO	1	1	.	+	.	.	+	.
M	6	595	R	F	HUM	AD	H	20	100	P	0	.	.	DS	3	2	.	+	.	.	+	.
M	6	607	R	F	HUM	AD	H	22	100	.	0	.	.	DS	1	1	.	+	.	.	+	.
M	30	610	R	F	HUM	AD	H	.	100	.	0	.	.	DS	1	1	.	+	.	.	+	.
M	8	613	R	F	HUM	AD	H	24	100	.	0	.	.	SO	3	2	.	+	.	.	+	.
M	19	615	R	F	HUM	AD	H	25	70	.	0	.	.	DS	1	1	.	+	.	.	+	.
M	6	619	L	W	HUM	04	H	.	100	.	0	.	.	SO	3	3	+	.	.	+	.	.
M	6	620	L	W	HUM	06	H	.	100	.	0	.	.	SO	3	3	+	+	.	+	.	.
M	8	624	L	F	HUM	AD	H	.	100	.	0	.	.	SO	3	3	.	+	.	.	+	.
M	8	625	L	F	HUM	AD	H	.	100	P	0	.	.	DS	3	1	.	+	.	.	+	.
M	50	626	L	F	HUM	AD	H	.	100	.	0	.	.	DO	1	1	+	+	.	.	+	.
M	6	641	L	F	HUM	AD	H	30	60	.	0	.	.	DS	3	2	.	+	.	.	+	.
M	8	654	R	W	ULN	06	H	.	100	.	0	.	.	SO	3	3	.	+	.	.	+	.
M	8	655	R	W	ULN	08	H	.	100	.	0	.	.	PS	3	3	.	+	.	.	+	.
M	8	657	R	W	ULN	AD	H	.	100	.	0	.	.	SO	3	3	+	+	.	+	+	.
M	7	658	R	W	ULN	AD	H	.	30	.	0	.	.	SO	3	3	.	+	.	.	+	.
M	8	659	R	F	ULN	AD	H	.	100	.	0	.	.	PS	3	1	.	+	.	.	+	.
M	8	660	R	F	ULN	AD	H	.	100	P	0	.	.	PS	3	1	.	+	.	.	.	.
M	8	671	L	W	ULN	10	H	.	100	.	0	.	.	SO	3	3	.	+	.	.	+	.
M	8	672	L	W	ULN	AD	H	.	100	.	0	.	.	CO	3	3	.	.	.	.	.	.
M	8	673	L	W	ULN	AD	H	.	100	.	0	+	.	CO	3	3	.	.	.	.	.	.
M	9	686	L	F	ULN	AD	H	37	100	.	0	.	.	PS	3	2	.	+	.	.	.	.
M	9	687	L	F	ULN	AD	H	37	100	.	0	.	.	DS	3	1	.	+	.	.	+	.
M	30	689	L	F	ULN	AD	H	38	100	.	0	.	.	PS	1	1	.	+	.	.	.	.
M	6	695	R	W	RAD	04	H	.	75	.	0	.	.	SO	3	3	.	+	.	.	+	.
M	6	696	R	W	RAD	04	H	.	100	.	0	.	.	SO	3	3	.	+	.	.	+	.
M	8	697	R	W	RAD	06	H	.	90	.	0	.	.	SO	3	3	.	+	.	.	+	.

03	32	33	34	35	36	37	38	39	40	41	42	43	44	45	46	47	48	50	51	52	53	55	56	57	58	60	61	62	63	81	82	83	84	85	86	87	88	89	90	91	92
548	.	.	.	.	.	0	0	.	0	.	0	0	.	2	0	0	0	0	0	0	0	.	.	.	.	.	.	.	.	.	.	.	.	.	.	.	.	.	.	.	.
549	IR	.	+	.	IR	0	0	.	0	.	0	0	.	2	2	0	1	0	0	0	0	.	.	.	.	.	.	.	.	.	.	.	.	.	.	.	.	.	.	.	.
550	.	.	+	.	ST	0	0	.	1	.	0	0	.	0	0	0	0	0	0	0	0	.	.	.	.	.	.	.	.	.	.	.	.	.	.	.	.	.	.	.	.
551	IR	.	.	+	IR	0	0	.	0	.	0	0	.	3	0	0	3	0	0	0	0	.	.	.	.	.	.	.	.	.	.	.	.	.	.	.	.	.	.	.	.
552	IR	.	+	.	IR	0	0	.	0	+	0	0	.	1	0	0	0	0	0	0	0	.	.	.	.	.	.	.	.	.	.	.	.	.	.	.	.	.	.	.	.
553	.	.	+	.	IR	0	0	.	3	.	0	0	.	0	0	0	1	0	0	0	0	.	.	.	.	.	.	.	.	.	.	.	.	.	.	.	.	.	.	.	.
554	IS	.	+	.	IR	0	0	.	0	.	0	0	.	0	0	0	1	0	0	0	0	.	.	.	.	.	.	.	.	.	.	.	.	.	.	.	.	.	.	.	.
555	TS	.	+	.	IR	0	0	.	0	+	0	0	.	0	0	0	0	0	0	0	0	.	.	.	.	.	.	.	.	.	.	.	.	.	.	.	.	.	.	.	.
556	IS	.	+	.	IR	0	0	.	0	+	0	0	.	0	0	0	0	0	0	0	0	.	.	.	.	.	.	.	.	.	.	.	.	.	.	.	.	.	.	.	.
557	IR	.	+	.	TS	0	0	.	0	.	0	0	.	3	0	0	1	0	0	0	0	.	.	.	.	.	.	.	.	.	.	.	.	.	.	.	.	.	.	.	.
561	IR	.	+	.	IR	0	0	.	0	.	0	0	.	0	0	0	0	0	0	0	0	.	.	.	.	.	.	.	.	.	.	.	.	.	.	.	.	.	.	.	.
562	.	.	+	.	IR	0	0	.	0	.	0	0	.	0	0	0	0	0	0	0	0	.	.	.	.	.	.	.	.	.	.	.	.	.	.	.	.	.	.	+	.
563	TS	.	+	.	IR	0	0	.	0	+	0	0	.	0	0	0	1	0	0	0	0	.	.	.	.	.	.	.	.	.	.	.	.	.	.	.	.	.	.	.	.
565	.	.	+	.	DV	0	0	.	0	+	0	0	.	2	0	0	0	0	0	0	0	.	.	.	.	.	.	.	.	.	.	.	.	.	.	.	.	.	.	.	.
566	.	+	.	.	.	0	0	.	0	.	0	0	.	0	0	0	0	0	0	0	0	.	.	.	.	.	.	.	.	.	.	.	.	.	.	.	.	.	.	.	.
567	IR	.	.	+	IR	0	0	.	0	.	0	0	.	0	0	0	0	0	0	0	0	.	.	.	.	.	.	.	.	.	.	.	.	.	.	.	.	.	.	.	.
568	IR	+	+	.	IR	0	0	.	0	+	0	0	.	1	1	0	0	0	0	0	0	.	.	.	.	.	.	.	.	.	.	.	.	.	.	.	.	.	.	.	.
569	IS	.	+	.	IR	0	0	.	0	+	0	0	.	0	2	0	0	0	0	0	0	.	.	.	.	.	.	.	.	.	.	.	.	.	.	.	.	.	.	.	.
570	IR	.	+	.	IR	0	0	.	0	+	0	0	.	0	1	0	1	0	0	0	0	.	.	.	.	.	.	.	.	.	.	.	.	.	.	.	.	.	.	.	.
571	IR	.	+	.	IR	0	0	.	0	.	0	0	+	1	0	0	0	1	0	0	0	.	.	.	.	.	.	.	.	.	.	.	.	.	.	.	.	.	.	.	.
572	IR	.	+	.	IR	0	0	.	0	.	0	0	.	0	0	0	0	0	0	0	0	.	.	.	.	.	.	.	.	.	.	.	.	.	.	.	.	.	.	.	.
573	IS	.	+	.	IR	0	0	.	0	+	0	0	.	0	0	0	0	0	0	0	0	.	.	.	.	.	.	.	.	.	.	.	.	.	.	.	.	.	.	.	.
574	TS	.	+	.	IR	0	0	.	0	.	0	0	.	0	0	0	0	0	0	0	0	.	.	.	.	.	.	.	.	.	.	.	.	.	.	.	.	.	.	.	.
577	TS	.	+	.	IR	0	0	.	0	.	0	0	.	0	0	0	1	0	0	0	0	.	.	.	.	.	.	.	.	.	.	.	.	.	.	.	.	.	.	.	.
579	IR	.	+	.	IR	0	0	.	0	+	0	0	.	0	0	0	0	0	0	0	0	.	.	.	.	.	.	.	.	.	.	.	.	.	.	.	.	.	+	+	+
582	IR	.	.	+	IR	0	0	.	0	.	0	0	.	0	2	0	0	0	0	0	0	.	.	.	.	.	.	.	.	.	.	.	.	.	.	.	.	.	.	.	.
583	IR	+	+	+	IR	0	0	.	0	.	0	0	.	0	0	0	0	0	0	0	0	.	.	.	.	.	.	.	.	.	.	.	+	+	+	.	.	.	.	.	.
588	IR	.	.	.	.	0	0	.	0	.	0	0	.	0	2	0	0	0	0	0	0	.	.	.	.	.	.	.	.	.	.	.	.	.	.	.	.	.	.	.	.
589	IS	.	.	.	.	0	0	.	3	.	0	0	.	0	0	0	0	0	0	0	0	.	.	.	.	.	.	.	.	.	.	.	.	.	.	.	.	.	.	.	.
590	TS	.	+	.	IR	0	0	.	2	+	0	0	.	0	1	0	0	0	1	0	0	.	.	.	.	.	+	.	.	.	.	.	.	.	.	.	.	.	.	.	.
591	IR	.	.	.	.	0	0	.	1	+	1	0	.	0	4	0	0	0	0	0	2	.	.	.	.	.	.	.	.	.	.	.	.	.	.	.	.	.	.	.	.
592	TS	.	.	.	.	0	0	.	4	.	0	0	.	0	1	0	0	0	0	0	0	.	.	.	.	.	.	.	.	.	.	.	.	.	.	.	.	.	.	.	.
593	IR	.	.	.	.	0	0	.	0	+	0	0	.	0	0	0	0	0	0	0	0	.	.	.	.	.	.	.	.	.	.	.	.	.	.	.	.	.	.	.	.
595	DV	.	.	.	.	0	0	.	0	+	0	0	.	0	1	0	0	0	0	0	0	.	.	.	.	.	.	.	.	.	.	.	.	.	.	.	.	.	.	.	.
607	IR	.	.	.	.	0	1	.	1	.	0	0	.	0	2	0	0	0	0	0	0	.	.	.	.	.	.	.	.	.	.	.	.	.	.	.	.	.	.	.	.
610	IR	.	.	.	.	0	0	.	1	.	0	0	.	0	1	1	0	0	0	0	0	.	.	.	.	.	.	.	.	.	.	.	.	.	.	.	.	.	.	.	.
613	DV	.	+	.	IR	0	0	.	2	+	0	0	.	0	0	0	0	0	0	0	0	.	.	.	.	.	.	.	.	.	.	.	.	.	.	.	.	.	.	.	.
615	DV	.	.	.	.	0	0	.	0	.	0	0	.	0	0	0	0	0	0	0	0	.	.	.	.	.	.	.	.	.	.	.	.	.	.	.	.	.	.	.	.
619	IR	+	.	.	IR	0	0	.	0	.	0	0	.	0	0	0	0	0	0	0	0	.	.	.	.	.	.	.	.	.	.	.	.	.	.	.	.	.	.	.	.
620	IR	+	+	.	IR	0	0	.	0	.	0	0	.	0	0	0	0	0	0	0	0	.	.	.	.	.	.	.	.	.	.	.	.	.	.	.	.	.	.	.	.
624	IR	.	+	.	IR	0	0	.	0	.	0	0	.	0	0	0	0	0	0	0	0	.	.	.	.	.	.	.	.	+	.	.	+	+	+	.	.	.	+	+	.
625	IR	.	+	.	IR	0	0	.	0	+	0	0	.	0	5	0	0	0	0	0	0	.	.	.	.	.	.	.	.	.	.	.	.	.	.	.	.	.	.	.	.
626	IR	+	+	.	IR	0	0	.	3	.	0	0	.	0	1	0	0	0	0	0	0	.	.	.	.	.	.	.	.	.	.	.	.	.	.	.	.	.	.	.	.
641	TP	.	+	.	IR	0	0	.	1	+	1	0	.	0	4	0	0	0	0	0	0	.	.	.	.	.	.	.	.	.	.	.	.	.	.	.	.	.	.	.	.
654	IR	.	+	.	IR	0	0	.	0	.	0	0	+	0	0	1	0	0	0	0	0	.	.	.	.	.	.	.	.	.	.	.	.	.	.	.	.	.	.	.	.
655	IR	.	+	.	IR	0	0	.	0	+	0	0	.	0	0	0	0	0	0	0	0	.	.	.	.	.	.	.	.	.	.	.	+	+	+	+	+	+	.	.	.
657	IR	+	+	.	IR	0	0	.	0	.	0	0	.	0	0	2	0	0	0	0	0	.	.	.	.	.	.	.	.	.	.	.	.	.	.	.	.	.	.	.	.
658	IR	.	+	.	TS	0	0	.	1	.	0	0	.	0	0	0	0	0	0	0	0	.	.	.	.	.	.	.	.	.	.	.	.	.	.	.	.	.	.	.	.
659	IR	.	+	.	IR	0	0	.	0	.	0	0	.	0	0	0	0	3	0	0	9	.	.	.	.	.	.	.	.	+	.	.	.	.	.	.	.	.	.	.	.
660	.	.	+	.	IS	0	0	.	2	.	0	0	.	0	0	0	0	0	0	0	0	.	.	.	.	.	.	.	.	.	.	.	.	.	.	.	.	.	.	.	.
671	IR	.	+	.	IR	0	0	.	0	.	0	0	+	0	0	0	0	0	0	0	0	.	.	.	.	.	.	.	.	.	.	.	.	.	.	.	.	.	.	.	.
672	.	.	.	.	.	0	0	.	0	.	0	0	.	0	0	0	0	0	0	0	0	.	.	.	.	.	.	.	.	.	.	.	.	.	.	.	.	.	.	.	.
673	.	.	.	.	.	0	0	.	0	.	0	0	.	0	0	0	0	0	0	0	0	.	.	.	.	.	.	.	.	.	.	.	.	.	.	.	.	.	.	.	.
686	.	.	+	.	IS	0	0	.	0	.	0	0	.	0	0	0	0	0	0	0	0	.	.	.	.	.	.	.	.	.	.	.	.	.	.	.	.	.	.	.	.
687	IS	.	.	.	.	0	0	.	3	.	0	0	+	0	0	0	0	0	0	0	0	.	.	.	.	.	.	.	+	.	.	.	.	.	.	.	.	.	.	.	.
689	.	.	+	.	IR	0	0	.	6	+	0	0	.	0	0	0	0	3	0	0	0	.	.	.	.	+	.	.	.	.	.	.	.	.	.	.	.	.	.	.	.
695	IR	.	+	.	IR	0	0	.	0	+	0	0	.	0	0	0	0	0	0	0	0	.	.	.	.	.	.	.	.	.	.	.	.	.	.	.	.	.	.	.	.
696	IR	.	+	.	IR	0	0	.	2	+	0	0	.	0	0	0	1	0	0	0	0	.	.	.	.	.	.	.	.	.	.	.	.	.	.	.	.	.	.	.	.
697	IR	.	+	.	IR	0	0	.	0	.	0	0	.	0	0	0	0	0	0	0	0	.	.	.	.	.	.	.	.	.	.	.	.	.	.	.	.	.	.	.	.

01	02	03	04	05	06	07	08	14	15	16	17	18	19	20	21	22	23	24	25	29	30	31	32	33	34	35	36	37	38	39
M	8	700	R	W	RAD	12	H	40	100	.	0	.	.	CO	3	3	.	.	.	.	.	.	.	.	.	.	.	0	0	.
M	8	701	R	F	RAD	12	H	40	100	.	0	.	.	DO	.	.	.	+	.	.	.	.	.	.	.	.	.	0	0	.
M	8	702	R	F	RAD	12	H	40	100	.	0	.	.	PO	.	.	.	+	.	.	.	.	.	.	.	.	.	0	0	.
M	8	703	R	F	RAD	AD	H	.	100	.	0	.	.	PS	3	1	.	+	.	.	.	.	.	.	+	.	TS	0	0	.
M	3	704	R	F	RAD	AD	H	.	90	.	0	.	.	DS	3	1	.	+	.	.	+	.	IS	.	.	.	.	0	0	.
M	8	705	R	F	RAD	AD	H	.	100	.	0	.	.	DS	3	1	.	+	.	.	+	.	IR	.	+	.	IR	0	0	.
M	6	711	R	F	RAD	AD	H	.	100	P	0	.	.	DO	1	1	.	+	.	.	+	.	IR	.	.	.	.	0	0	.
M	7	712	R	W	RAD	AD	H	41	50	.	0	.	.	DS	3	3	+	+	.	+	+	.	IR	+	+	.	IR	0	0	.
M	7	713	R	F	RAD	AD	H	41	15	.	0	.	.	PS	3	1	+	.	+	.	.	.	.	+	.	+	IR	0	0	.
M	8	714	R	W	RAD	AD	H	42	100	P	0	.	.	PS	3	2	.	+	.	.	.	.	.	.	+	.	IR	0	0	.
M	6	716	R	W	RAD	AD	H	43	100	P	0	.	.	PS	3	2	.	+	.	.	.	.	.	.	+	.	TP	0	0	.
M	6	718	L	W	RAD	08	H	.	100	.	0	.	.	SO	3	3	+	.	.	+	.	.	IR	+	.	.	IR	0	0	.
M	3	719	L	W	RAD	08	H	.	100	.	0	.	.	PS	3	2	+	.	+	.	.	.	.	+	.	+	IR	0	0	.
M	8	720	L	W	RAD	10	H	.	100	.	0	.	.	SO	3	3	.	+	.	.	+	.	IR	.	.	.	.	0	0	.
M	8	721	L	W	RAD	12	H	.	100	.	0	.	.	CO	3	3	+	.	.	.	.	.	.	+	.	.	IR	0	0	.
M	8	722	L	W	RAD	12	H	.	100	.	0	.	.	CO	3	3	.	.	.	.	.	.	.	.	.	.	.	0	0	.
M	50	725	L	F	RAD	AD	H	.	90	.	0	.	.	PS	2	1	.	+	.	.	+	.	IR	.	+	.	IR	0	0	.
M	6	726	L	F	RAD	AD	H	44	100	.	0	.	.	SO	3	2	.	+	.	.	+	.	IR	.	+	.	TP	0	0	.
M	6	736	R	W	FEM	04	H	.	90	.	0	.	.	SO	3	3	+	+	.	+	+	.	IR	+	+	.	IR	0	0	.
M	6	744	R	F	FEM	06	H	49	100	P	0	.	.	PS	3	1	.	+	.	.	+	.	IR	.	+	.	IS	0	0	.
M	6	745	R	F	FEM	06	H	49	100	.	0	.	.	SO	3	1	.	+	.	.	+	.	IS	.	+	.	IR	0	0	.
M	50	760	R	F	FEM	AD	H	.	100	.	0	.	.	PO	.	.	.	+	.	.	.	.	.	.	+	.	IR	0	0	.
M	6	792	R	F	FEM	AD	H	57	100	.	0	.	.	DS	3	1	.	+	.	.	+	.	IR	.	.	.	.	0	0	.
M	6	811	L	W	FEM	04	H	.	100	.	0	.	.	SO	3	3	.	+	.	.	+	.	IR	.	+	.	IR	0	0	.
M	6	819	L	F	FEM	08	H	.	90	.	0	.	.	PS	3	1	.	+	.	.	+	.	IR	.	+	.	IS	0	0	.
M	5	820	L	F	FEM	10	H	.	100	.	0	.	.	PS	3	1	.	+	.	.	.	.	.	.	+	.	IS	0	0	.
M	65	821	L	F	FEM	12	H	.	100	.	0	+	.	PS	2	1	+	+	.	.	.	.	.	.	.	.	.	0	0	.
M	6	830	L	F	FEM	AD	H	.	100	.	0	.	.	DO	.	.	+	+	.	+	+	.	IR	.	.	.	.	0	0	.
M	50	870	L	F	FEM	AD	H	74	90	.	0	.	.	SO	3	2	.	+	.	.	+	.	IR	.	+	.	VS	0	0	.
M	6	953	R	W	TIB	06	H	.	100	.	0	.	.	SO	3	3	.	+	.	.	+	.	IR	.	+	.	IR	0	0	.
M	3	961	R	F	TIB	10	H	.	80	.	0	.	.	SO	3	3	.	+	.	.	+	.	IR	.	+	.	IR	0	0	.
M	8	972	R	F	TIB	AD	H	.	100	.	0	.	.	DO	.	.	.	+	.	.	+	.	IR	.	+	.	IR	0	0	.
M	6	973	R	F	TIB	AD	H	.	75	P	0	.	.	DO	.	.	.	+	.	.	+	.	IR	.	+	.	IR	0	0	.
M	6	987	R	F	TIB	AD	H	97	100	.	0	.	.	DS	3	2	.	+	.	.	+	.	IS	.	.	.	.	0	0	.
M	6	1024	L	W	TIB	04	H	.	100	.	0	.	.	SO	3	3	.	+	.	.	+	.	IR	.	+	.	IR	0	0	.
M	8	1031	L	F	TIB	10	H	109	100	.	0	.	.	PS	1	1	+	+	.	+	+	.	IR	.	+	.	IS	0	0	.
M	6	1110	R	W	FIB	04	H	.	100	.	0	.	.	SO	3	3	+	+	.	.	+	.	IR	+	+	.	IR	0	0	.
M	6	1112	R	W	FIB	06	H	.	95	.	0	.	.	SO	3	3	+	+	.	+	+	.	IR	+	+	.	IR	0	0	.
M	6	1113	R	W	FIB	06	H	.	100	.	0	.	.	SO	3	3	+	+	.	+	+	.	IR	+	+	.	IR	0	0	.
M	8	1116	R	W	FIB	12	H	.	100	.	0	.	.	SO	3	3	.	+	.	.	+	.	IR	.	+	.	IR	0	0	.
M	8	1117	R	W	FIB	AD	H	.	100	.	0	.	.	DS	3	3	.	+	.	.	+	.	IR	.	.	.	.	0	0	.
M	8	1118	R	W	FIB	AD	H	.	100	.	0	.	.	DS	3	3	.	+	.	.	+	.	IR	.	.	.	.	0	0	.
M	7	1119	R	W	FIB	AD	H	.	90	.	0	.	.	SO	3	3	+	+	.	+	+	.	IR	.	+	.	IR	0	0	.
M	8	1120	R	W	FIB	AD	H	.	100	.	0	.	.	SO	3	3	.	+	.	.	+	.	IS	.	+	.	IR	0	0	.
M	8	1121	R	W	FIB	AD	H	.	100	.	0	.	.	SO	3	2	.	+	.	.	+	.	IR	.	+	.	IR	0	0	.
M	6	1122	R	F	FIB	AD	H	.	80	.	0	.	.	SO	3	2	.	+	.	.	+	.	IR	.	+	.	IR	0	0	.
M	6	1123	R	F	FIB	AD	H	.	100	P	0	.	.	SO	3	2	.	+	.	.	+	.	IS	.	+	.	IR	0	0	.
M	7	1129	R	F	FIB	AD	H	125	100	.	0	.	.	SO	3	1	.	+	.	.	+	.	IR	.	+	.	IR	0	0	.
M	6	1135	L	W	FIB	04	H	.	100	.	0	.	.	SO	3	3	+	.	.	+	.	.	IR	+	.	.	IR	0	0	.
M	6	1141	L	W	FIB	08	H	.	90	.	0	.	.	PS	3	2	+	+	.	.	.	.	.	+	+	.	IR	0	0	.
M	8	1144	L	W	FIB	12	H	.	80	.	1	.	.	SO	3	3	.	+	.	.	+	.	IR	.	+	.	IR	0	0	.
M	8	1145	L	F	FIB	12	H	.	100	.	0	.	.	PS	3	1	+	+	.	.	.	.	.	+	+	.	IR	0	0	.
M	8	1146	L	W	FIB	AD	H	.	100	.	0	+	.	SO	3	3	.	+	.	.	+	.	IR	.	+	.	IR	0	0	.
M	8	1147	L	W	FIB	AD	H	.	100	.	0	.	.	DS	3	3	.	+	.	.	+	.	IR	.	.	.	.	0	0	.
M	8	1148	L	W	FIB	AD	H	.	100	.	0	.	.	SO	3	2	+	+	.	.	+	.	IR	+	+	.	IR	0	0	.
M	19	1149	L	F	FIB	AD	H	.	100	P	0	.	.	SO	3	1	.	+	.	.	+	.	IR	.	+	.	IR	0	0	.
M	8	1150	L	F	FIB	AD	H	.	100	.	0	.	.	SO	3	2	+	+	.	+	+	.	IR	+	+	.	IR	0	0	.
M	8	1151	L	F	FIB	AD	H	.	100	.	0	.	.	SO	3	1	.	+	.	.	+	.	IR	.	+	.	IR	0	0	.
M	7	1159	L	F	FIB	AD	H	131	90	.	0	.	.	SO	3	1	+	+	.	+	+	.	IR	+	+	.	DV	0	0	.

03	40	41	42	43	44	45	46	47	48	50	51	52	53	55	56	57	58	60	61	62	63	81	82	83	84	85	86	87	88	89	90	91	92
700	0	.	0	0	.	0	0	0	0	0	0	0	0	.	.	.	.	.	.	.	+	.	.	.	.	.	.	.	.	.	+	.	.
701	0	.	0	0	.	0	0	0	0	0	0	0	0	.	.	.	.	.	.	.	.	.	.	.	.	.	.	.	.	.	.	.	.
702	0	.	0	0	.	0	0	0	0	0	0	0	0	.	.	.	.	.	.	.	.	.	.	.	.	.	.	.	.	.	.	.	.
703	0	.	0	0	.	0	0	0	0	0	0	0	0	.	.	.	.	.	.	.	+	.	.	.	.	.	.	.	.	.	.	.	.
704	0	+	0	0	.	0	0	0	0	0	0	0	0	.	.	.	.	.	.	.	.	.	.	.	.	.	.	.	.	.	+	+	+
705	1	+	0	0	.	0	0	0	0	0	0	0	0	.	.	.	.	.	.	.	.	.	.	.	+	.	.	.	.	.	.	.	.
711	2	.	0	0	.	0	0	1	0	0	0	0	0	.	.	.	.	.	.	.	.	.	.	.	.	.	.	.	.	.	.	.	.
712	0	.	0	0	.	0	0	0	0	0	0	0	0	.	.	.	.	.	.	.	+	.	.	.	.	.	.	.	.	.	.	.	.
713	0	.	0	0	.	0	0	0	0	0	0	0	0	.	.	.	.	.	.	.	.	.	.	.	.	.	.	.	.	.	.	.	.
714	0	+	0	0	.	1	0	0	0	0	0	0	0	.	.	.	.	.	.	.	.	.	.	.	.	.	.	.	.	.	.	.	.
716	0	.	0	0	.	0	0	0	0	0	0	0	0	.	.	.	.	.	.	.	.	.	.	.	.	.	.	.	.	.	.	.	.
718	0	.	0	0	.	0	0	0	0	0	0	0	0	.	.	.	.	.	.	.	.	.	.	.	.	.	.	.	.	.	.	.	.
719	2	.	0	0	.	0	0	0	0	0	0	0	4	.	.	.	.	.	.	.	.	.	.	.	.	.	.	.	.	.	.	.	.
720	0	.	0	0	.	0	0	0	0	0	0	0	0	.	.	.	.	.	.	.	.	.	.	.	.	.	.	.	.	.	.	.	.
721	0	+	0	0	.	0	0	0	0	0	0	0	0	.	.	.	.	.	.	.	.	.	.	.	+	+	+	.	.	.	.	.	.
722	0	.	0	0	.	0	0	0	0	0	0	0	0	.	.	.	.	.	.	.	.	.	.	.	.	.	.	.	.	.	.	.	.
725	0	.	0	0	.	0	0	0	0	0	0	0	0	.	.	.	.	.	.	.	.	.	+	.	.	.	.	.	.	.	.	.	.
726	0	.	0	0	.	0	0	0	0	0	0	0	0	.	.	.	.	.	.	.	+	.	.	.	.	.	.	.	.	.	.	.	.
736	0	.	0	0	.	0	0	0	0	0	0	0	0	.	.	.	.	.	.	.	.	.	.	.	.	.	.	.	.	.	.	.	.
744	2	.	3	0	.	0	0	0	0	0	0	0	0	.	.	.	.	.	.	.	+	.	.	.	.	.	.	.	.	.	.	.	.
745	3	+	1	0	.	0	1	0	0	0	0	0	0	.	.	.	.	.	.	.	+	.	.	.	.	.	.	.	.	.	.	.	.
760	0	+	0	0	.	0	0	0	0	0	0	0	0	.	.	.	.	+	.	.	.	.	.	.	.	.	.	.	.	.	.	.	.
792	0	+	2	0	.	0	3	0	0	0	3	0	0	.	.	.	.	.	.	.	.	.	.	.	.	.	.	.	.	.	.	.	.
811	0	+	0	0	.	0	0	0	0	0	0	0	0	.	.	.	.	.	.	.	.	.	.	.	.	.	.	.	.	.	.	.	.
819	0	+	0	0	.	5	0	0	0	0	0	0	0	.	.	.	.	.	.	.	.	.	.	.	.	.	.	.	.	.	.	.	.
820	3	.	0	0	.	0	0	0	0	0	0	0	0	.	.	.	.	.	.	.	.	.	.	.	.	.	.	.	.	.	.	.	.
821	0	.	0	0	.	1	0	0	0	0	0	0	0	.	.	.	.	.	.	.	.	.	.	.	.	.	.	.	.	.	.	.	.
830	1	.	0	0	.	0	0	0	0	0	0	0	0	.	.	.	.	.	.	.	.	.	.	.	.	.	.	.	.	.	.	.	.
870	1	+	6	0	.	3	0	3	0	9	0	0	0	.	.	.	.	+	.	.	.	.	.	.	.	.	.	.	.	.	+	+	+
953	0	.	0	0	.	0	0	0	0	0	0	0	0	.	.	.	.	.	.	.	.	.	.	.	+	.	.	.	.	.	.	.	.
961	3	.	0	0	+	0	0	0	0	0	0	0	0	.	.	.	.	.	+	.	.	.	.	.	.	.	.	.	.	.	.	+	.
972	0	.	0	0	.	0	0	0	0	0	0	0	0	.	.	.	.	.	.	.	.	.	.	.	.	.	.	.	.	.	.	.	.
973	1	+	0	0	.	0	0	0	0	0	0	0	0	.	.	.	.	.	.	.	.	.	.	.	.	.	.	.	.	.	.	.	.
987	0	.	0	0	.	0	0	0	0	0	0	0	0	.	.	.	.	.	.	.	.	.	.	.	.	.	.	.	.	.	+	.	.
1024	0	.	0	0	.	0	0	0	0	0	0	0	0	.	.	.	.	.	.	.	.	.	.	.	.	.	.	.	.	.	.	.	.
1031	2	.	0	0	.	0	0	0	0	0	0	0	0	.	.	.	.	+	.	.	.	.	.	.	.	.	.	.	.	.	.	.	.
1110	0	.	0	0	.	0	0	0	0	0	0	0	0	.	.	.	.	.	.	.	.	.	.	.	.	.	.	.	.	.	.	.	.
1112	0	.	0	0	.	0	0	0	0	0	0	0	0	.	.	.	.	.	.	.	.	.	.	.	.	.	.	.	.	.	.	.	.
1113	0	.	0	0	.	0	0	0	0	0	0	0	0	.	.	.	.	.	.	.	.	.	.	.	.	.	.	.	.	.	.	.	.
1116	0	+	0	0	.	0	0	0	0	0	0	0	0	.	.	.	.	.	.	.	.	.	.	.	.	.	.	.	.	.	.	.	.
1117	0	.	0	0	+	0	0	0	0	0	0	0	0	.	.	.	.	.	.	.	.	.	.	.	.	.	.	.	.	.	.	.	.
1118	0	.	0	0	.	0	0	0	0	0	0	0	0	.	.	.	.	.	.	.	.	.	.	.	.	.	.	+	+	+	.	.	.
1119	1	.	0	0	.	0	0	0	0	0	0	0	0	.	.	.	.	.	.	.	.	.	.	.	+	+	+	.	.	.	.	.	.
1120	0	.	0	0	.	0	0	0	0	0	0	0	0	.	.	.	.	.	.	.	.	.	.	.	+	+	+	.	.	.	.	.	.
1121	2	.	0	1	.	0	0	0	0	0	0	0	0	.	.	.	.	.	.	.	+	.	.	.	.	.	.	.	.	.	.	.	.
1122	0	.	0	0	.	0	0	0	0	0	0	0	0	.	.	.	.	.	.	.	.	.	.	.	.	.	.	.	.	.	.	.	.
1123	3	.	2	0	.	0	0	0	0	0	0	0	0	.	.	.	.	.	.	.	.	.	.	.	.	.	.	.	.	.	.	.	.
1129	1	.	0	0	.	0	0	0	0	0	0	0	0	.	.	.	.	.	.	.	.	.	.	.	.	.	.	.	.	.	.	.	.
1135	0	.	0	0	.	0	0	0	0	0	0	0	0	.	.	.	.	.	.	.	.	.	.	.	.	.	.	.	.	.	.	.	.
1141	2	.	0	0	.	0	0	0	0	0	0	0	0	.	.	.	.	.	.	.	.	.	.	.	+	+	+	.	.	.	.	.	.
1144	0	.	0	0	.	0	0	0	0	0	0	0	0	.	.	.	.	.	.	.	.	.	.	.	.	.	.	.	.	.	.	.	.
1145	0	.	0	0	.	0	0	0	0	0	0	0	0	.	.	.	.	.	.	.	.	.	.	.	.	.	.	.	.	.	.	.	.
1146	0	.	0	0	.	0	0	0	0	0	0	0	0	.	.	.	.	.	.	.	.	.	.	.	.	.	.	.	.	.	.	.	.
1147	0	.	0	0	.	0	0	0	0	0	0	0	0	.	.	.	.	.	.	.	.	.	.	.	.	.	.	.	.	.	.	.	.
1148	0	.	0	0	.	0	0	0	0	0	0	0	0	.	.	.	.	.	.	.	+	.	.	.	+	.	.	.	.	.	.	.	.
1149	0	+	0	0	.	0	0	0	0	0	0	0	0	.	.	.	.	.	.	.	.	.	.	.	.	.	.	.	.	.	.	.	.
1150	0	.	0	0	.	0	0	0	0	0	0	0	0	.	.	.	.	.	.	.	.	+	.	.	+	.	.	.	.	.	.	.	.
1151	1	+	0	0	.	0	0	0	1	0	0	0	0	.	.	.	.	.	+	.	.	.	.	.	.	.	.	.	.	.	.	.	.
1159	0	.	0	0	.	0	0	0	0	0	0	0	0	.	.	.	.	.	.	.	.	.	.	.	.	.	.	.	.	.	.	.	.

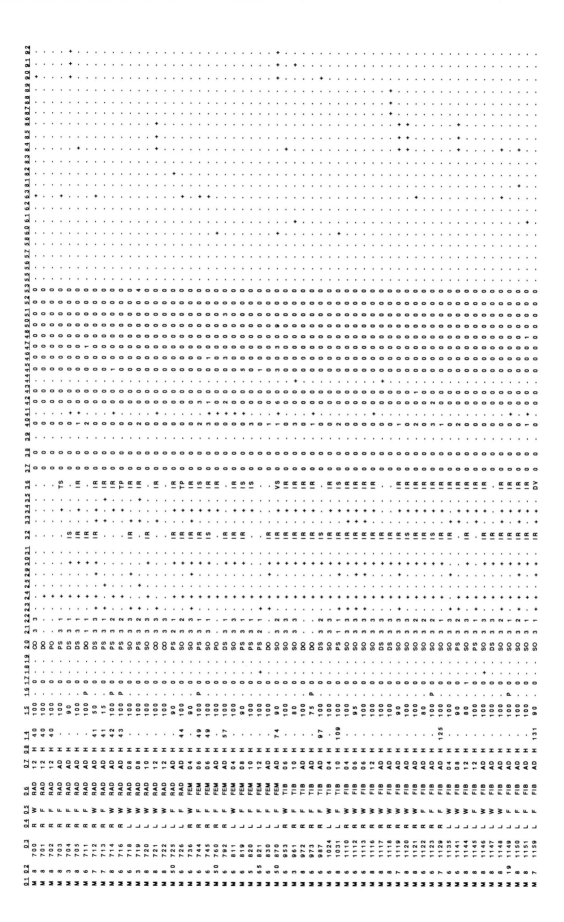

C: Splinters

01	02	03	09	10	11	12	13	14	15	16	17	18	19	20	23	24	25	37	38	40	41	42	43	44	49	54	59	64	93	94	95	96	97	98
M	11	558	R	F	CLA	AD	H	.	90	.	0	.	.	T	.	+	.	0	0	0	.	0	0	.	0	0	.	.	.	+	.			
M	6	559	R	F	CLA	AD	H	.	80	.	0	.	.	S	.	+	.	0	0	0	.	0	0	.	0	0	.	.	+	+	+	81	11	2
M	11	560	R	F	CLA	AD	H	.	100	.	1	.	.	T	.	+	.	0	0	0	.	0	0	.	0	0	.	.	.	.	.			
M	6	564	R	F	CLA	AD	H	18	100	.	0	.	.	S	.	+	.	0	0	0	.	0	0	.	0	0	.	.	.	.	.	46	8	2
M	11	575	L	F	CLA	AD	H	.	60	.	0	.	.	T	.	+	.	0	0	0	.	0	0	.	0	0	.	.	.	.	.			
M	6	576	L	F	CLA	AD	H	.	100	.	0	.	.	S	.	+	.	0	0	0	.	0	1	.	0	0	.	.	.	.	.	67	15	2
M	6	578	L	F	CLA	AD	H	.	90	.	0	.	.	T	.	+	.	0	0	0	.	0	0	.	0	0	.	.	+	+	+			
M	6	580	L	F	CLA	AD	H	.	100	.	0	.	.	S	.	+	.	0	0	0	.	0	0	.	4	0	.	.	.	.	.	53	13	2
M	6	581	L	F	CLA	AD	H	.	100	.	0	.	.	O	.	+	.	0	0	0	.	0	0	.	0	0	.	.	.	.	.			
M	6	584	R	F	HUM	04	H	19	100	.	0	.	.	S	.	+	.	0	1	2	.	0	0	.	0	0	.	+	.	.	.	130	11	2
M	6	585	R	F	HUM	04	H	19	100	.	0	.	.	S	.	+	.	0	0	0	.	0	0	.	0	0	.	+	.	.	.	80	16	2
M	6	586	R	F	HUM	04	H	19	100	.	0	.	.	S	.	+	.	0	0	0	.	0	0	.	0	0	.	+	+	+	.	86	10	2
M	11	587	R	F	HUM	06	H	.	100	.	1	.	.	T	.	+	.	0	0	1	.	0	0	.	0	0	.	.	.	.	.			
M	8	594	R	F	HUM	AD	H	.	100	.	0	.	.	O	.	+	.	0	0	0	+	0	0	.	0	0	.	.	.	.	.			
M	6	596	R	F	HUM	AD	H	20	80	.	0	.	.	S	.	+	.	0	0	0	.	0	0	+	0	0	.	+	.	.	.	148	21	4
M	8	597	R	F	HUM	AD	H	20	100	P	0	.	.	T	.	+	.	0	0	1	.	0	0	.	0	0	.	.	.	.	.			
M	6	598	R	F	HUM	AD	H	20	100	P	0	.	.	S	.	+	.	0	0	0	.	0	0	.	0	0	.	+	.	.	.	80	17	4
M	6	599	R	F	HUM	AD	H	20	20	.	0	.	.	S	.	+	.	0	0	0	.	0	0	.	0	0	.	.	.	.	.	107	12	4
M	6	600	R	F	HUM	AD	H	20	100	.	0	.	.	S	.	+	.	0	0	1	.	1	0	+	3	0	.	.	.	.	.	48	25	3
M	8	601	R	F	HUM	AD	H	21	100	P	0	.	.	S	.	+	.	0	0	0	.	0	0	.	4	0	.	.	.	.	.	184	13	2
M	8	602	R	F	HUM	AD	H	21	100	.	0	.	.	S	.	+	.	0	0	0	.	0	0	.	0	0	.	.	.	.	.	157	16	3
M	8	603	R	F	HUM	AD	H	21	100	.	0	.	.	S	.	+	.	0	0	0	.	0	0	.	0	0	.	.	.	.	.	138	20	3
M	8	604	R	F	HUM	AD	H	21	100	.	0	.	.	S	.	+	.	0	0	0	.	0	0	.	0	0	.	+	.	.	.	115	9	3
M	8	605	R	F	HUM	AD	H	21	100	.	0	.	.	S	.	+	.	0	0	0	.	0	0	.	0	0	.	.	.	.	.	95	15	3
M	8	606	R	F	HUM	AD	H	21	100	.	0	.	.	S	.	+	.	0	0	1	.	0	0	.	3	0	.	.	.	.	.	73	14	3
M	6	608	R	F	HUM	AD	H	22	100	.	0	.	.	S	.	+	.	0	0	0	.	0	0	.	0	0	.	+	.	.	.	101	18	3
M	6	609	R	F	HUM	AD	H	22	100	.	0	.	.	S	.	+	.	0	0	1	.	0	0	.	2	0	.	.	.	.	.	44	16	4
M	30	611	R	F	HUM	AD	H	23	100	.	0	.	.	O	.	+	.	0	0	0	+	0	0	.	0	0	.	.	.	.	.			
M	30	612	R	F	HUM	AD	H	23	100	.	0	.	.	O	.	+	.	0	0	0	.	0	0	.	0	0	.	.	.	.	.			
M	8	614	R	F	HUM	AD	H	24	100	.	0	.	.	S	.	+	.	0	1	0	.	0	0	.	0	0	.	.	.	.	.	119	13	3
M	19	616	R	F	HUM	AD	H	25	100	.	0	.	.	S	.	+	.	0	0	0	.	0	0	.	0	0	.	.	.	.	.	48	18	3
M	30	617	R	F	HUM	AD	H	26	100	.	0	.	.	S	.	+	.	0	0	0	.	0	0	.	5	1	.	.	.	.	.	90	14	3
M	30	618	R	F	HUM	AD	H	26	100	.	0	.	.	S	.	+	.	0	0	0	.	0	0	.	0	0	.	.	.	.	.	68	12	3
M	19	621	L	F	HUM	06	H	.	80	.	0	.	.	S	.	+	.	0	0	0	.	0	0	.	0	0	.	.	.	.	.	76	23	1
M	3	622	L	F	HUM	08	H	.	80	.	0	.	.	T	+	+	.	0	0	2	.	0	0	.	0	0	.	+	.	.	.			
M	6	623	L	F	HUM	08	H	.	100	.	0	.	.	S	.	+	.	0	0	0	.	0	0	.	0	0	.	+	.	.	.	87	11	2
M	8	627	L	F	HUM	AD	H	.	100	.	0	.	.	T	.	+	.	0	0	1	.	0	1	.	0	0	.	.	.	.	.			
M	6	628	L	F	HUM	AD	H	.	100	.	0	.	.	S	.	+	.	0	0	0	.	0	0	.	0	0	.	.	.	.	.	62	26	3
M	6	629	L	F	HUM	AD	H	27	100	.	0	.	.	S	.	+	.	0	0	0	.	0	0	.	0	0	.	+	.	.	.	87	18	4
M	6	630	L	F	HUM	AD	H	27	100	P	0	.	.	S	.	+	.	0	0	0	.	0	0	.	0	0	.	.	.	.	.	83	17	4
M	6	631	L	F	HUM	AD	H	27	100	.	0	.	.	S	.	+	.	0	0	0	.	0	0	.	0	0	.	.	.	.	.	65	22	3
M	6	632	L	F	HUM	AD	H	27	100	.	0	.	.	S	.	+	.	0	0	0	.	0	0	.	0	0	.	+	.	.	.	78	13	4
M	6	633	L	F	HUM	AD	H	27	100	.	0	.	.	S	.	+	.	0	0	0	.	0	0	.	0	4	.	+	.	.	.	76	12	3
M	11	634	L	F	HUM	AD	H	28	100	.	0	.	.	S	.	+	.	0	0	0	.	0	0	.	0	0	.	.	.	.	.	160	18	3
M	11	635	L	F	HUM	AD	H	28	100	.	0	.	.	S	.	+	.	0	0	0	.	0	0	.	0	0	.	.	+	.	.	111	23	2
M	11	636	L	F	HUM	AD	H	28	50	.	1	.	.	S	.	+	.	0	0	0	.	0	0	.	0	0	.	.	.	.	.	107	16	2
M	11	637	L	F	HUM	AD	H	28	100	.	0	.	.	S	.	+	.	0	0	0	.	0	1	.	0	0	.	.	.	.	.	56	14	3
M	6	638	L	F	HUM	AD	H	29	100	.	0	.	.	S	+	+	.	0	0	1	.	2	0	.	0	0	.	+	+	.	.	141	24	3
M	6	639	L	F	HUM	AD	H	29	90	.	0	.	.	S	.	+	.	0	0	1	.	0	0	.	0	0	.	+	+	+	+	99	15	3
M	6	640	L	F	HUM	AD	H	29	80	.	0	.	.	S	.	+	.	0	0	0	.	0	0	.	0	0	.	.	+	+	.	37	14	3
M	6	642	L	F	HUM	AD	H	30	100	P	0	.	.	S	.	+	.	0	2	0	.	1	1	.	0	0	.	+	.	.	.	136	20	4
M	8	643	L	F	HUM	AD	H	30	100	P	0	.	.	S	.	+	.	0	0	0	.	0	1	.	0	0	.	.	.	.	.	134	26	3
M	8	644	L	F	HUM	AD	H	31	100	.	0	.	.	S	.	+	.	0	0	0	.	0	0	.	1	0	.	.	.	.	.	57	27	3
M	8	645	L	F	HUM	AD	H	31	100	.	0	.	.	S	.	+	.	0	0	0	.	0	0	.	0	0	.	.	.	.	.	64	19	3
M	8	646	L	F	HUM	AD	H	32	100	.	0	.	.	O	.	+	.	0	0	0	+	0	0	.	0	0	.	.	.	.	.			
M	8	647	L	F	HUM	AD	H	32	100	.	0	.	.	O	.	+	.	0	0	0	.	0	0	.	0	0	.	+	.	.	.			
M	30	648	L	F	HUM	AD	H	33	100	P	0	.	.	S	.	+	.	0	3	0	.	0	2	.	0	0	.	+	.	.	.	160	17	3
M	30	649	L	F	HUM	AD	H	33	100	.	0	.	.	S	.	+	.	0	0	0	.	0	0	.	0	0	.	+	.	.	.	58	6	3
M	7	650	I	F	HUM	AD	H	.	100	.	0	.	.	S	.	+	.	0	0	0	.	0	0	.	0	0	.	+	.	.	.	94	14	3

01	02	03	09	10	11	12	13	14	15	16	17	18	19	20	23	24	25	37	38	40	41	42	43	44	49	54	59	64	93	94	95	96	97	98
M	7	651	I	F	HUM	AD	H	.	80	.	0	.	.	S	.	+	.	0	0	0	.	0	0	.	0	0	.	.	.	.	.	85	17	3
M	6	652	R	W	ULN	04	H	.	100	.	0	.	.	T	.	+	.	0	0	3	+	0	0	.	0	0	.	.	.	.	.			
M	52	653	R	F	ULN	04	H	.	80	.	0	.	.	T	.	+	.	0	0	0	.	0	0	.	0	0	.	.	+	+	+			
M	8	656	R	F	ULN	10	H	.	100	.	0	.	.	T	.	+	.	0	0	0	.	1	0	.	0	0	.	.	.	.	.			
M	6	661	R	F	ULN	AD	H	.	70	.	0	.	.	T	.	+	.	0	0	0	.	0	0	.	0	0	.	+	.	.	.			
M	19	662	R	F	ULN	AD	H	.	100	P	0	.	.	T	.	+	.	0	0	0	.	0	0	.	0	1	.	.	.	.	.			
M	6	663	R	F	ULN	AD	H	.	100	.	0	.	.	T	.	+	.	0	0	0	.	0	0	.	0	0	.	.	.	.	.			
M	6	664	R	F	ULN	AD	H	.	100	.	0	.	.	S	.	+	.	0	0	0	.	0	0	.	0	0	.	.	.	.	.	72	13	2
M	3	665	R	F	ULN	AD	H	34	90	.	0	.	.	T	+	+	.	0	0	2	.	0	0	.	0	0	.	.	+	+	+			
M	3	666	R	F	ULN	AD	H	34	10	.	0	.	.	S	+	+	.	0	0	0	.	0	0	.	0	0	.	.	+	+	.			
M	50	667	R	F	ULN	AD	H	35	100	.	0	.	.	T	.	+	.	0	0	0	.	0	0	.	0	0	.	.	.	.	.			
M	50	668	R	F	ULN	AD	H	35	100	.	0	.	.	S	.	+	.	0	0	0	.	0	0	.	0	0	.	.	.	.	.	69	14	3
M	6	669	L	F	ULN	04	H	.	100	.	0	.	.	T	.	+	.	0	0	0	.	0	0	.	0	0	.	.	+	.	.			
M	6	670	L	W	ULN	06	H	.	100	.	0	.	.	T	.	+	.	0	0	2	+	0	0	.	0	0	.	.	+	.	.			
M	8	674	L	F	ULN	AD	H	.	100	P	0	.	.	T	.	+	.	0	0	0	.	0	0	.	0	0	.	.	+	.	.			
M	FA1	675	L	F	ULN	AD	H	.	10	.	2	.	.	T	+	+	.	0	0	0	.	0	0	.	0	0	.	.	.	.	.			
M	6	675.1	L	F	ULN	AD	H	.	100	.	0	.	.	S	.	+	.	0	0	0	.	0	0	.	0	0	.	.	+	+	+	79	15	3
M	7	676	L	F	ULN	AD	H	.	100	P	0	.	.	T	+	+	.	0	0	0	+	0	0	+	0	0	.	.	+	.	.			
M	19	677	L	F	ULN	AD	H	.	100	P	0	.	.	T	.	+	.	0	0	0	.	0	0	.	0	0	.	.	.	.	.			
M	6	678	L	F	ULN	AD	H	.	100	.	0	.	.	T	.	+	.	0	0	0	.	0	0	.	0	0	.	.	.	.	.			
M	6	679	L	F	ULN	AD	H	.	100	.	0	.	.	S	.	+	.	0	0	0	.	1	0	.	2	0	.	.	.	.	.	76	13	2
M	6	680	L	F	ULN	AD	H	.	100	.	0	.	.	S	.	+	.	0	0	1	.	0	0	.	0	0	.	+	.	.	.	46	9	2
M	30	681	L	F	ULN	AD	H	.	100	.	0	.	.	O	.	+	.	0	0	0	+	0	0	.	0	0	.	.	.	.	.			
M	6	682	L	F	ULN	AD	H	.	100	.	0	.	.	T	+	+	.	0	0	0	.	0	0	.	0	0	.	.	.	.	.			
M	6	683	L	F	ULN	AD	H	36	80	.	0	.	.	T	.	+	.	0	0	0	.	0	1	.	0	0	.	+	.	.	.			
M	6	684	L	F	ULN	AD	H	36	100	.	0	.	.	S	.	+	.	0	0	0	.	0	0	.	0	0	.	.	.	.	.	53	14	3
M	6	685	L	F	ULN	AD	H	36	100	.	0	.	.	T	.	+	.	0	0	0	.	0	0	.	0	0	.	.	.	.	.			
M	8	688	L	F	ULN	AD	H	38	100	.	0	.	.	T	.	+	.	0	0	1	.	0	0	.	0	0	.	.	.	.	.			
M	FA1	690	I	F	ULN	AD	H	.	100	.	0	.	.	S	.	+	.	1	0	0	.	0	0	.	0	0	.	.	.	.	.	105	13	2
M	6	691	I	F	ULN	AD	H	.	100	.	0	.	.	S	.	+	.	0	0	0	.	0	0	.	0	0	.	.	.	.	.	44	10	2
M	6	692	I	F	ULN	AD	H	.	100	.	0	.	.	S	.	+	.	0	0	0	.	0	0	.	0	0	.	+	.	.	.	62	9	1
M	FA1	693	I	F	ULN	AD	H	39	100	.	0	.	.	S	.	+	.	0	0	0	.	0	0	.	0	0	.	+	.	.	.	69	7	2
M	FA1	694	I	F	ULN	AD	H	39	100	.	0	.	.	S	.	+	.	0	0	0	.	0	0	.	0	0	.	+	.	.	.	54	9	2
M	8	698	R	F	RAD	10	H	.	100	.	0	.	.	T	+	+	.	0	0	0	.	0	0	.	0	0	.	.	+	.	.			
M	8	699	R	F	RAD	12	H	.	100	.	0	.	.	T	.	+	.	0	0	0	.	0	0	.	0	0	.	.	.	.	.			
M	6	706	R	F	RAD	AD	H	.	80	.	0	.	.	T	.	+	.	0	0	0	.	0	0	.	0	0	.	.	+	+	+			
M	8	707	R	F	RAD	AD	H	.	100	.	0	.	.	T	.	+	.	0	0	1	.	2	0	.	0	0	.	.	.	.	.			
M	8	708	R	F	RAD	AD	H	.	100	.	0	.	.	T	.	+	.	0	0	1	.	3	0	.	0	0	.	+	.	.	.			
M	8	709	R	F	RAD	AD	H	.	80	.	0	.	.	T	.	+	.	0	0	0	.	0	0	.	0	0	.	.	+	+	+			
M	8	710	R	F	RAD	AD	H	.	100	P	0	.	.	T	.	+	.	0	0	0	.	0	0	.	0	0	.	+	.	.	.			
M	8	715	R	F	RAD	AD	H	42	100	P	0	.	.	S	.	+	.	0	0	0	.	3	0	.	0	0	.	+	.	.	.	41	14	2
M	6	717	R	F	RAD	AD	H	43	100	P	0	.	.	T	.	+	.	0	0	1	.	0	0	.	0	0	.	.	+	+	+			
M	19	723	L	F	RAD	AD	H	.	100	.	0	.	.	T	.	+	.	0	0	0	.	1	0	.	4	0	.	.	.	.	.			
M	6	724	L	F	RAD	AD	H	.	100	.	0	.	.	T	.	+	.	0	0	1	.	0	0	.	0	0	.	+	+	.	.			
M	6	727	L	F	RAD	AD	H	44	100	P	0	.	.	T	.	+	.	0	0	0	+	0	0	+	0	0	.	.	.	.	.			
M	6	728	L	F	RAD	AD	H	45	100	.	0	.	.	T	+	+	.	0	0	0	.	0	0	.	0	0	.	.	.	.	.			
M	6	729	L	F	RAD	AD	H	45	100	.	0	.	.	T	.	+	.	0	0	0	.	0	0	+	0	0	.	.	+	+	+			
M	6	730	L	F	RAD	AD	H	46	100	.	0	.	.	T	.	+	.	0	0	0	.	0	0	.	0	0	.	.	+	.	.			
M	6	731	L	F	RAD	AD	H	46	100	.	0	.	.	T	.	+	.	0	0	0	.	0	0	.	0	0	.	.	+	.	.			
M	50	732	I	F	RAD	AD	H	.	100	.	0	.	.	S	+	.	.	0	0	0	.	0	0	.	0	0	.	.	.	.	.			
M	8	733	I	F	RAD	IM	H	47	100	.	0	.	.	S	.	+	.	0	0	0	.	0	0	.	0	0	.	.	.	.	.	81	9	1
M	8	734	I	F	RAD	IM	H	47	100	.	0	.	.	S	.	+	.	0	0	0	.	0	0	.	0	0	.	.	.	.	.	80	8	1
M	30	735	I	F	RAD	IM	H	47	100	.	0	.	.	S	.	+	.	0	0	0	.	0	0	.	0	0	.	.	.	.	.	48	5	1
M	6	737	R	F	FEM	04	H	48	100	.	0	.	.	S	.	+	.	0	0	0	.	0	0	.	0	0	.	+	.	.	.	97	23	3
M	6	738	R	F	FEM	04	H	48	100	.	0	.	.	S	.	+	.	0	0	0	.	0	0	.	0	0	.	.	.	.	.	94	19	2
M	6	739	R	F	FEM	04	H	48	100	.	0	.	.	S	.	+	.	0	0	0	.	0	0	+	0	0	.	+	.	.	.	86	16	2
M	6	740	R	F	FEM	04	H	48	100	.	0	.	.	S	.	+	.	0	0	0	.	0	0	.	0	0	.	.	.	.	.	87	11	3
M	6	741	R	F	FEM	04	H	48	90	.	0	.	.	S	.	+	.	0	0	0	.	0	0	.	0	0	.	.	.	.	.	76	11	3

01	02	03	09	10	11	12	13	14	15	16	17	18	19	20	23	24	25	37	38	40	41	42	43	44	49	54	59	64	93	94	95	96	97	98
M	6	742	R	F	FEM	04	H	48	100	-	0	-	-	S	-	+	-	0	0	0	-	0	0	-	0	0	-	-	-	-	-	64	10	2
M	6	743	R	F	FEM	04	H	48	100	-	0	-	-	S	-	+	-	0	0	0	-	0	0	-	0	0	-	-	-	-	-	59	9	2
M	6	746	R	F	FEM	06	H	50	100	P	0	-	-	S	-	+	-	0	0	0	-	0	0	-	0	0	-	+	-	-	-	99	17	2
M	6	747	R	F	FEM	06	H	50	100	-	0	-	-	S	-	+	-	0	0	0	+	0	0	-	0	0	-	-	-	-	-	90	15	3
M	8	749	R	F	FEM	12	H	-	100	-	0	-	-	S	-	+	-	0	0	0	-	0	0	-	0	0	-	+	-	-	-	142	23	5
M	8	750	R	F	FEM	12	H	51	100	-	0	-	-	S	-	+	-	0	0	0	+	0	0	+	0	0	-	+	-	-	-	116	24	4
M	8	751	R	F	FEM	12	H	51	100	-	0	-	-	S	-	+	-	0	0	1	+	0	0	-	0	0	-	-	-	-	-	107	21	6
M	3	752	R	F	FEM	AD	H	-	100	-	0	-	-	S	+	+	-	0	1	0	-	1	0	-	7	0	-	+	+	+	+	187	24	6
M	8	753	R	F	FEM	AD	H	-	100	-	0	-	-	S	-	+	-	0	2	0	-	0	0	-	0	0	-	+	-	-	-	146	23	5
M	11	754	R	F	FEM	AD	H	-	100	-	0	-	-	S	-	+	-	0	0	0	-	0	0	-	0	0	-	-	+	+	+	150	20	6
M	8	755	R	F	FEM	AD	H	-	100	-	0	-	-	S	-	+	-	0	0	0	-	0	0	-	0	0	-	+	-	-	-	119	20	5
M	9	756	R	F	FEM	AD	H	-	100	-	0	-	-	S	-	+	-	0	1	0	-	0	1	-	0	0	-	+	-	-	-	107	23	4
M	8	757	R	F	FEM	AD	H	-	100	-	0	-	-	S	-	+	-	0	0	0	-	0	0	-	6	0	-	-	-	-	-	114	21	4
M	8	758	R	F	FEM	AD	H	-	100	-	0	-	-	T	-	+	-	0	0	2	-	0	0	-	5	0	-	+	-	-	-			
M	8	759	R	F	FEM	AD	H	-	100	-	0	-	-	S	-	+	-	0	1	0	-	0	0	-	0	0	-	+	-	-	-	112	33	5
M	8	761	R	F	FEM	AD	H	-	100	-	0	-	-	S	-	+	-	0	0	0	-	0	0	-	0	0	-	-	-	-	-	82	25	3
M	11	762	R	F	FEM	AD	H	-	100	-	0	-	-	S	-	+	-	0	0	0	-	0	0	-	0	0	-	+	-	-	-	64	22	6
M	8	763	R	F	FEM	AD	H	-	100	-	0	-	-	S	-	+	-	0	0	0	-	0	0	+	0	0	-	-	-	-	-	72	29	2
M	11	764	R	F	FEM	AD	H	-	100	-	0	-	-	S	-	+	-	0	0	0	-	0	0	-	2	0	-	+	-	-	-	67	22	5
M	8	765	R	F	FEM	AD	H	-	100	-	0	-	-	S	-	+	-	0	0	0	-	0	0	-	0	0	-	-	-	-	-	104	13	5
M	11	766	R	F	FEM	AD	H	-	100	-	0	-	-	S	-	+	-	0	0	1	-	1	0	-	2	0	-	+	-	-	-	51	23	4
M	8	767	R	F	FEM	AD	H	-	100	-	0	-	-	S	-	+	-	0	0	0	-	0	0	-	7	0	-	+	-	-	-	44	22	4
M	8	768	R	F	FEM	AD	H	-	100	-	0	-	-	S	-	+	-	0	0	0	-	0	1	-	0	0	-	+	-	-	-	48	18	5
M	6	769	R	F	FEM	AD	H	52	100	-	0	-	-	S	-	+	-	0	1	0	-	2	0	-	0	0	-	+	-	-	-	269	24	8
M	6	770	R	F	FEM	AD	H	52	100	-	0	-	-	S	-	+	-	0	0	0	-	0	0	-	0	0	-	+	-	-	-	159	25	4
M	8	771	R	F	FEM	AD	H	52	50	-	0	-	-	S	-	+	-	0	0	0	-	0	0	-	0	0	-	-	-	-	-	154	22	6
M	6	772	R	F	FEM	AD	H	52	80	-	0	-	-	S	-	+	-	0	0	0	-	0	0	-	0	0	-	+	-	-	-	152	12	6
M	6	773	R	F	FEM	AD	H	52	100	-	0	-	-	S	-	+	-	0	0	0	-	0	0	-	0	0	-	-	-	-	-	126	22	7
M	6	774	R	F	FEM	AD	H	52	100	-	0	-	-	S	-	+	-	0	0	0	+	0	0	-	0	0	-	+	-	-	-	108	25	3
M	6	775	R	F	FEM	AD	H	52	100	-	0	-	-	S	-	+	-	0	0	0	-	0	1	-	0	0	-	+	-	-	-	83	25	8
M	6	776	R	F	FEM	AD	H	52	100	-	0	-	-	O	-	+	-	0	0	0	-	0	0	-	0	0	-	-	-	-	-			
M	8	777	R	F	FEM	AD	H	53	100	P	0	-	-	S	-	+	-	0	0	0	-	0	0	-	0	0	-	+	-	-	-	189	20	6
M	8	778	R	F	FEM	AD	H	53	100	-	0	-	-	S	-	+	-	0	0	1	-	0	0	-	0	0	-	+	-	-	-	151	24	5
M	8	779	R	F	FEM	AD	H	53	100	P	0	-	-	S	-	+	-	0	0	0	-	0	0	-	0	0	-	+	-	-	-	153	17	6
M	8	780	R	F	FEM	AD	H	53	100	-	0	-	-	S	-	+	-	0	0	0	-	0	0	-	0	0	-	+	-	-	-	119	17	6
M	8	781	R	F	FEM	AD	H	54	100	P	0	-	-	S	-	+	-	0	0	0	-	0	0	-	1	0	-	-	-	-	-	98	20	4
M	8	782	R	F	FEM	AD	H	54	100	-	0	-	-	S	-	+	-	0	0	0	-	0	0	-	0	0	-	+	-	-	-	96	19	4
M	8	783	R	F	FEM	AD	H	54	100	-	0	-	-	S	-	+	-	0	0	0	-	0	0	-	1	0	-	-	-	-	-	80	18	4
M	8	784	R	F	FEM	AD	H	54	100	-	0	-	-	S	-	+	-	0	0	0	-	0	0	-	0	0	-	-	-	-	-	62	15	5
M	6	785	R	F	FEM	AD	H	55	100	-	0	-	-	S	-	+	-	0	0	0	-	0	0	-	1	0	-	-	+	+	+	84	30	4
M	3	786	R	F	FEM	AD	H	55	90	-	0	-	-	S	-	+	-	0	0	0	-	0	0	-	4	0	-	-	+	+	-	87	16	5
M	3	787	R	F	FEM	AD	H	55	100	-	0	-	-	S	-	+	-	0	0	0	-	0	0	-	1	0	-	-	-	-	-	71	22	5
M	3	788	R	F	FEM	AD	H	55	100	-	0	-	-	S	-	+	-	0	0	0	-	0	0	-	0	0	-	-	-	-	-	63	18	3
M	8	789	R	F	FEM	AD	H	56	100	P	0	-	-	S	-	+	-	0	1	0	-	2	0	-	0	0	-	+	-	-	-	225	23	5
M	6	790	R	F	FEM	AD	H	56	100	-	0	-	-	S	-	+	-	0	0	1	-	0	0	-	6	0	-	-	-	-	-	182	26	7
M	8	791	R	F	FEM	AD	H	56	100	-	0	-	-	S	-	+	-	0	0	0	-	0	1	-	0	0	-	+	-	-	-	128	15	4
M	3	793	R	F	FEM	AD	H	57	100	-	0	-	-	S	-	+	-	0	0	0	-	0	0	-	0	0	-	+	-	-	-	93	22	6
M	3	794	R	F	FEM	AD	H	57	100	-	0	-	-	S	-	+	-	0	0	0	-	0	0	-	0	2	-	+	-	-	-	59	20	6
M	11	795	R	F	FEM	AD	H	58	80	-	0	-	-	S	-	+	-	0	2	1	-	0	0	-	0	0	-	+	-	-	-	134	30	5
M	11	796	R	F	FEM	AD	H	58	100	-	0	-	-	S	-	+	-	2	1	0	-	0	0	-	0	0	-	+	-	-	-	123	23	5
M	11	797	R	F	FEM	AD	H	58	100	-	0	-	-	S	-	+	-	0	0	0	-	0	0	-	0	0	-	+	-	-	-	74	21	5
M	50	798	R	F	FEM	AD	H	59	80	-	0	-	-	T	-	+	-	0	0	2	-	0	0	-	0	0	-	-	+	+	+			
M	50	799	R	F	FEM	AD	H	59	80	-	0	-	-	S	-	+	-	0	0	0	-	0	0	-	0	0	-	-	+	+	+	91	24	4
M	50	800	R	F	FEM	AD	H	59	40	-	0	-	-	S	-	+	-	0	0	0	-	0	0	-	0	0	-	-	+	+	+	41	13	5
M	11	801	R	F	FEM	AD	H	60	70	-	0	-	-	S	-	+	-	1	0	0	-	0	0	-	0	0	-	-	-	-	-	189	22	5
M	11	802	R	F	FEM	AD	H	60	100	-	0	-	-	S	-	+	-	0	0	0	-	0	0	-	0	0	-	+	-	-	-	59	22	8
M	11	803	R	F	FEM	AD	H	61	100	-	0	+	-	S	-	+	-	0	0	1	-	0	0	-	0	0	-	-	-	-	-	121	24	4
M	11	804	R	F	FEM	AD	H	61	100	-	0	+	-	S	-	+	-	0	0	0	-	0	0	-	0	0	-	+	-	-	-	130	17	3

01	02	03	09	10	11	12	13	14	15	16	17	18	19	20	23	24	25	37	38	40	41	42	43	44	49	54	59	64	93	94	95	96	97	98
M	8	805	R	F	FEM	AD	H	62	100	-	0	-	-	S	-	+	-	0	1	1	-	0	1	-	3	0	-	-	-	-	-	125	28	5
M	6	806	R	F	FEM	AD	H	62	100	-	0	-	-	O	-	+	-	0	0	1	+	0	0	-	0	0	-	+	-	-	-			
M	8	807	R	F	FEM	AD	H	63	100	-	0	-	-	S	-	+	-	0	1	0	-	0	0	-	9	0	-	-	-	-	-	93	20	3
M	8	808	R	F	FEM	AD	H	63	100	-	0	-	-	S	-	+	-	0	0	0	-	0	0	-	1	0	-	+	-	-	-	79	20	2
M	7	809	R	F	FEM	AD	H	64	90	P	0	-	-	S	-	+	-	0	0	0	-	0	0	-	0	0	-	+	+	+	-	82	19	7
M	7	810	R	F	FEM	AD	H	64	100	P	0	-	-	S	-	+	-	0	0	1	-	0	0	-	0	0	-	+	-	-	-	66	23	6
M	6	812	L	F	FEM	04	H	-	100	-	0	-	-	T	-	+	-	0	0	1	-	0	0	-	0	0	-	+	-	-	-			
M	6	813	L	F	FEM	04	H	65	100	-	0	-	-	T	-	+	-	0	0	1	+	0	0	-	0	0	-	+	+	+	+			
M	6	814	L	F	FEM	04	H	65	100	-	0	-	-	S	-	+	-	0	0	0	-	0	0	-	0	0	-	+	-	-	-	88	10	1
M	6	815	L	F	FEM	04	H	65	100	-	0	-	-	S	-	+	-	0	0	0	-	0	0	-	3	0	-	+	-	-	-	78	14	2
M	6	816	L	F	FEM	04	H	65	100	-	0	-	-	S	-	+	-	0	0	0	-	0	0	-	0	0	-	+	-	-	-	76	10	2
M	6	817	L	F	FEM	04	H	65	100	-	0	-	-	S	-	+	-	0	0	0	-	0	0	-	3	0	-	-	+	-	-	58	10	2
M	8	818	L	F	FEM	06	H	-	100	-	0	-	-	T	+	+	-	0	0	2	-	0	0	-	0	3	-	-	+	+	+			
M	8	818.1	L	F	FEM	08	H	66	100	-	0	-	-	S	-	+	-	0	0	0	+	0	0	-	0	0	-	-	-	-	-	79	15	3
M	8	819.1	L	F	FEM	08	H	66	100	-	0	-	-	S	-	+	-	0	0	1	-	0	0	-	0	0	-	+	-	-	-	125	18	3
M	8	822	L	F	FEM	12	H	-	100	-	0	-	-	S	-	+	-	0	0	1	+	0	0	-	4	0	-	-	-	-	-	100	24	2
M	8	823	L	F	FEM	12	H	-	100	-	0	-	-	S	-	+	-	0	0	1	+	0	0	-	0	0	-	-	-	-	-	68	19	4
M	50	824	L	F	FEM	AD	H	-	100	-	0	-	-	S	-	+	-	0	2	1	-	0	0	-	9	0	-	-	-	-	-	221	21	5
M	50	825	L	F	FEM	AD	H	-	100	-	0	-	-	S	-	+	-	0	1	0	-	0	0	-	0	0	-	+	-	-	-	158	20	6
M	8	826	L	F	FEM	AD	H	-	100	-	0	-	-	S	-	+	-	0	0	0	-	0	0	-	0	0	-	+	-	-	-	137	16	6
M	8	827	L	F	FEM	AD	H	-	100	-	0	-	-	S	-	+	-	1	1	0	-	0	0	-	0	0	-	-	-	-	-	126	21	5
M	8	828	L	F	FEM	AD	H	-	100	P	0	-	-	S	-	+	-	0	0	0	-	0	0	-	0	0	-	-	-	-	-	141	23	6
M	8	829	L	F	FEM	AD	H	-	100	-	0	-	-	S	-	+	-	0	0	0	-	0	0	-	6	0	-	+	-	-	-	108	21	6
M	8	831	L	F	FEM	AD	H	-	100	P	0	-	-	S	-	+	-	0	0	0	-	0	0	-	0	0	-	-	-	-	-	81	14	4
M	8	832	L	F	FEM	AD	H	-	60	-	0	-	-	S	-	+	-	0	0	1	-	0	0	-	0	0	-	-	+	+	+	98	21	6
M	8	833	L	F	FEM	AD	H	-	100	-	0	-	-	S	-	+	-	0	0	0	-	0	0	-	0	0	-	+	-	-	-	67	19	6
M	8	834	L	F	FEM	AD	H	-	100	-	0	-	-	S	-	+	-	0	0	0	-	0	1	-	0	0	-	+	-	-	-	50	23	4
M	6	835	L	F	FEM	AD	H	67	80	-	0	-	-	S	-	+	-	0	0	0	-	0	0	-	0	0	-	+	-	-	-	233	22	7
M	6	836	L	F	FEM	AD	H	67	100	-	0	-	-	S	-	+	-	0	0	0	-	0	0	-	0	0	-	-	-	-	-	157	20	6
M	6	837	L	F	FEM	AD	H	67	100	-	0	-	-	S	-	+	-	0	0	0	-	0	0	-	0	0	-	+	-	-	-	112	20	5
M	6	838	L	F	FEM	AD	H	67	100	-	0	-	-	S	-	+	-	0	0	0	-	0	0	-	0	0	-	-	-	-	-	103	15	4
M	6	839	L	F	FEM	AD	H	67	100	-	0	-	-	S	-	+	-	0	0	0	-	0	0	-	0	0	-	-	-	-	-	77	19	6
M	6	840	L	F	FEM	AD	H	67	100	-	0	-	-	S	-	+	-	0	0	1	-	0	0	-	0	0	-	+	-	-	-	78	19	5
M	6	841	L	F	FEM	AD	H	67	70	-	0	-	-	S	-	+	-	0	0	0	-	0	0	-	0	0	-	-	-	-	-	48	27	3
M	6	842	L	F	FEM	AD	H	67	100	-	0	-	-	O	-	+	-	0	0	0	-	0	0	-	0	0	-	-	-	-	-			
M	6	843	L	F	FEM	AD	H	67	100	-	0	-	-	S	-	+	-	0	0	0	-	0	0	-	0	0	-	+	-	-	-	64	10	6
M	6	844	L	F	FEM	AD	H	67	100	-	0	-	-	S	-	+	-	0	0	0	-	0	0	-	0	0	-	-	-	-	-	44	18	3
M	6	845	L	F	FEM	AD	H	67	100	-	0	-	-	S	-	+	-	0	0	0	-	0	0	-	0	0	-	-	-	-	-	57	10	5
M	8	846	L	F	FEM	AD	H	68	100	-	0	-	-	T	-	+	-	0	0	0	-	0	0	-	6	0	-	+	-	-	-			
M	8	847	L	F	FEM	AD	H	68	100	-	0	-	-	S	-	+	-	0	1	0	-	1	0	-	9	0	-	+	-	-	-	124	27	5
M	8	848	L	F	FEM	AD	H	68	100	P	0	-	-	S	-	+	-	0	2	0	+	0	0	-	0	0	-	-	-	-	-	111	29	4
M	8	849	L	F	FEM	AD	H	68	100	-	0	-	-	S	-	+	-	0	0	0	-	0	0	-	0	0	-	-	-	-	-	97	17	4
M	8	850	L	F	FEM	AD	H	68	100	-	0	-	-	S	-	+	-	0	0	0	-	0	0	-	0	0	-	-	-	-	-	60	15	4
M	8	851	L	F	FEM	AD	H	69	100	-	0	-	-	S	-	+	-	0	0	1	-	0	0	-	2	0	-	-	-	-	-	148	17	5
M	8	852	L	F	FEM	AD	H	69	100	-	0	-	-	S	-	+	-	0	0	0	-	0	0	-	0	0	-	+	-	-	-	117	14	4
M	8	853	L	F	FEM	AD	H	69	100	-	0	-	-	S	-	+	-	0	0	0	-	0	0	-	0	0	-	-	-	-	-	117	16	5
M	8	854	L	F	FEM	AD	H	69	100	-	0	-	-	S	-	+	-	0	0	0	-	0	0	-	4	0	-	-	-	-	-	115	20	3
M	8	855	L	F	FEM	AD	H	69	100	-	0	-	-	S	-	+	-	0	0	1	-	0	0	-	2	0	-	+	-	-	-	95	25	3
M	7	856	L	F	FEM	AD	H	70	100	-	0	-	-	S	-	+	-	0	0	0	-	0	2	-	0	0	-	-	-	-	-	143	25	4
M	7	857	L	F	FEM	AD	H	70	100	-	0	-	-	S	-	+	-	0	0	0	-	0	0	-	3	0	-	+	-	-	-	108	17	4
M	7	858	L	F	FEM	AD	H	70	100	-	0	-	-	S	-	+	-	0	0	0	-	0	0	-	0	0	-	+	-	-	-	99	14	5
M	7	859	L	F	FEM	AD	H	70	100	-	0	-	-	S	-	+	-	0	0	0	-	0	0	-	0	0	-	+	-	-	-	92	14	5
M	8	860	L	F	FEM	AD	H	71	100	-	0	-	-	S	-	+	-	0	0	0	-	0	0	-	0	0	-	-	-	-	-	117	20	2
M	8	861	L	F	FEM	AD	H	71	100	P	0	-	-	S	-	+	-	0	0	0	-	0	0	-	0	0	-	+	-	-	-	98	17	2
M	8	862	L	F	FEM	AD	H	71	100	-	0	-	-	S	-	+	-	0	0	0	-	0	0	-	0	0	-	+	-	-	-	113	25	3
M	8	863	L	F	FEM	AD	H	71	100	-	0	-	-	S	-	+	-	0	0	0	-	0	0	-	0	0	-	+	-	-	-	79	18	2
M	8	864	L	F	FEM	AD	H	72	100	-	0	-	-	S	-	+	-	0	0	0	-	0	0	-	0	0	-	+	-	-	-	123	24	6
M	7	865	L	F	FEM	AD	H	72	100	-	0	-	-	S	-	+	-	0	0	0	-	0	0	-	0	0	-	-	-	-	-	81	28	6

01	02	03	09	10	11	12	13	14	15	16	17	18	19	20	23	24	25	37	38	40	41	42	43	44	49	54	59	64	93	94	95	96	97	98
M	7	866	L	F	FEM	AD	H	72	100	-	0	-	-	S	-	+	-	0	0	0	-	0	0	-	0	0	-	+	-	-	-	49	18	6
M	7	867	L	F	FEM	AD	H	73	30	-	0	-	-	S	+	+	-	0	0	0	-	0	0	-	0	0	-	-	+	+	+	-	26	5
M	7	868	L	F	FEM	AD	H	73	100	P	0	-	-	S	-	+	-	0	0	0	-	0	0	-	0	0	-	-	+	+	+	61	20	4
M	7	869	L	F	FEM	AD	H	73	100	-	0	-	-	S	-	+	-	0	0	0	-	0	0	-	0	0	-	-	-	-	-	59	18	6
M	6	871	L	F	FEM	AD	H	74	100	-	0	-	-	S	-	+	-	0	0	0	-	0	0	-	0	0	-	+	+	+	+	53	21	6
M	8	872	L	F	FEM	AD	H	75	100	P	0	-	-	S	-	+	-	0	0	0	-	0	0	-	0	0	-	-	-	-	-	134	16	5
M	8	873	L	F	FEM	AD	H	75	100	-	0	-	-	S	-	+	-	0	0	0	-	0	0	-	0	0	-	+	-	-	-	88	22	6
M	30	874	L	F	FEM	AD	H	76	100	-	0	+	-	S	-	+	-	0	0	0	-	0	0	-	2	0	-	-	+	-	-	107	23	5
M	30	875	L	F	FEM	AD	H	76	100	-	0	-	-	S	-	+	-	0	0	0	-	0	0	-	0	0	-	+	-	-	-	78	16	4
M	8	876	L	F	FEM	AD	H	77	100	-	0	-	-	S	-	+	-	0	0	0	-	1	0	-	0	0	-	+	-	-	-	121	12	4
M	8	877	L	F	FEM	AD	H	77	100	-	0	-	-	S	-	+	-	0	0	1	-	1	0	-	0	0	-	+	-	-	-	97	14	4
M	8	878	L	F	FEM	AD	H	78	100	-	0	-	-	S	-	+	-	0	0	0	-	2	0	-	0	0	-	-	-	-	-	50	23	5
M	8	879	L	F	FEM	AD	H	78	100	-	0	-	-	S	-	+	-	0	0	0	-	0	0	-	0	0	-	-	-	-	-	50	21	6
M	8	880	L	F	FEM	AD	H	79	100	-	0	-	-	S	-	+	-	0	0	0	-	0	0	-	0	0	-	-	-	-	-	64	17	2
M	30	881	L	F	FEM	AD	H	79	100	-	0	-	-	O	-	+	-	0	0	0	-	0	0	-	0	0	-	+	-	-	-			
M	8	882	I	F	FEM	AD	H	-	100	-	0	-	-	S	-	+	-	0	0	0	-	0	0	-	0	0	-	-	-	-	-	150	16	5
M	11	883	I	F	FEM	AD	H	-	100	P	0	-	-	S	-	+	-	0	0	0	-	0	0	-	0	0	-	+	-	-	-	129	21	6
M	11	884	I	F	FEM	AD	H	-	100	P	0	-	-	S	-	+	-	0	0	1	-	0	0	-	0	0	-	-	-	-	-	141	24	7
M	6	885	I	F	FEM	AD	H	-	100	-	0	-	-	S	-	+	-	0	3	0	-	2	0	-	0	0	-	+	-	-	-	119	26	3
M	9	886	I	F	FEM	AD	H	-	100	-	0	-	-	S	-	+	-	0	1	0	-	1	0	-	4	0	-	+	-	-	-	106	20	4
M	6	887	I	F	FEM	AD	H	-	100	-	0	-	-	S	-	+	-	0	0	1	-	4	0	-	0	0	-	+	-	-	-	89	26	7
M	8	888	I	F	FEM	AD	H	-	100	P	0	-	-	S	-	+	-	0	0	0	-	0	0	-	0	0	-	-	-	-	-	88	18	3
M	8	889	I	F	FEM	AD	H	-	100	-	0	-	-	S	-	+	-	0	0	0	-	0	0	-	0	0	-	-	-	-	-	86	19	4
M	19	890	I	F	FEM	AD	H	-	100	P	0	-	-	S	-	+	-	0	0	0	-	0	0	-	0	0	-	+	-	-	-	90	13	3
M	11	891	I	F	FEM	AD	H	-	100	-	0	-	-	S	-	+	-	0	0	0	-	0	0	-	2	0	-	+	-	-	-	76	21	3
M	8	892	I	F	FEM	AD	H	-	100	-	0	-	-	S	-	+	-	0	1	1	-	1	0	-	1	0	-	+	+	+	-	71	23	6
M	11	893	I	F	FEM	AD	H	-	30	-	0	-	-	S	-	+	-	0	0	0	-	0	0	-	0	0	-	-	+	+	-	73	22	6
M	11	894	I	F	FEM	AD	H	-	70	-	1	-	-	S	-	+	-	0	0	0	-	0	0	-	0	0	-	-	-	-	-	76	17	6
M	3	895	I	F	FEM	AD	H	-	100	P	0	-	-	S	-	+	-	0	0	1	-	0	0	-	0	0	-	-	-	-	-	64	25	4
M	30	896	I	F	FEM	AD	H	-	100	P	0	-	-	S	-	+	-	0	0	0	-	0	0	-	0	0	-	-	-	-	-	68	19	3
M	7	897	I	F	FEM	AD	H	-	100	-	0	-	-	O	-	+	-	0	0	0	-	0	0	-	0	0	-	-	-	-	-			
M	11	898	I	F	FEM	AD	H	-	50	-	1	-	-	S	-	+	-	0	0	0	-	0	0	-	0	0	-	-	-	-	-	66	16	3
M	11	899	I	F	FEM	AD	H	-	100	-	0	-	-	S	-	+	-	0	0	0	-	0	0	-	0	0	-	+	-	-	-	63	15	4
M	8	900	I	F	FEM	AD	H	-	100	P	0	-	-	S	-	+	-	0	0	1	-	0	0	-	4	0	-	+	-	-	-	64	18	3
M	8	901	I	F	FEM	AD	H	-	100	-	0	-	-	S	-	+	-	0	0	0	-	0	0	-	0	0	-	-	-	-	-	67	15	3
M	8	902	I	F	FEM	AD	H	-	80	-	0	-	-	S	-	+	-	0	0	0	-	0	0	-	0	0	-	-	-	-	-	64	18	2
M	8	903	I	F	FEM	AD	H	-	100	-	0	-	-	S	-	+	-	0	0	0	-	0	0	-	0	0	-	+	-	-	-	64	21	2
M	8	904	I	F	FEM	AD	H	-	100	-	0	-	-	S	-	+	-	1	0	0	-	0	0	-	0	0	-	+	-	-	-	53	21	4
M	7	905	I	F	FEM	AD	H	-	100	-	0	-	-	S	-	+	-	0	0	0	-	0	0	-	1	0	-	-	-	-	-	64	27	4
M	8	906	I	F	FEM	AD	H	-	100	-	0	+	-	S	-	+	-	0	0	0	-	0	0	-	0	0	-	-	-	-	-	49	23	6
M	8	907	I	F	FEM	AD	H	-	100	-	0	-	-	S	-	+	-	0	0	0	-	0	0	-	0	0	-	+	-	-	-	55	17	5
M	11	908	I	F	FEM	AD	H	-	100	-	0	-	-	S	-	+	-	0	0	0	-	0	0	-	0	0	-	-	-	-	-	54	15	3
M	50	909	I	F	FEM	AD	H	-	100	-	0	-	-	S	-	+	-	0	0	0	-	0	0	-	2	0	-	+	-	-	-	40	15	5
M	11	910	I	F	FEM	AD	H	-	90	-	0	-	-	S	-	+	-	0	0	0	-	0	0	-	0	0	-	-	+	+	+	34	20	3
M	8	911	I	F	FEM	AD	H	-	100	-	0	-	-	S	-	+	-	0	0	0	-	0	0	-	0	0	-	-	-	-	-	44	19	3
M	11	912	I	F	FEM	AD	H	-	80	-	0	-	-	S	-	+	-	0	0	0	-	0	0	-	0	0	-	-	+	+	+	37	21	3
M	6	913	I	F	FEM	AD	H	-	100	-	0	-	-	S	-	+	-	0	0	0	-	0	0	-	0	0	-	+	-	-	-	52	14	6
M	11	914	I	F	FEM	AD	H	-	90	-	0	-	-	S	-	+	-	0	0	0	-	0	0	-	8	0	-	-	+	+	-	38	14	4
M	11	915	I	F	FEM	AD	H	80	80	-	0	-	-	S	-	+	-	0	0	1	-	0	0	-	0	0	-	+	-	-	-	92	17	4
M	11	916	I	F	FEM	AD	H	80	90	-	0	-	-	S	-	+	-	0	0	0	-	0	0	-	0	0	-	+	+	+	-	95	14	4
M	11	917	I	F	FEM	AD	H	80	100	-	0	-	-	S	-	+	-	0	0	0	-	3	0	-	0	0	-	+	+	+	+	83	17	5
M	11	918	I	F	FEM	AD	H	80	100	-	0	-	-	S	-	+	-	0	0	0	-	0	0	-	4	0	-	-	-	-	-	84	13	4
M	11	919	I	F	FEM	AD	H	81	100	-	0	-	-	S	-	+	-	0	0	0	-	0	0	-	4	0	-	-	+	+	-	131	18	5
M	11	920	I	F	FEM	AD	H	81	100	-	0	-	-	S	-	+	-	0	0	0	-	0	0	-	0	0	-	-	+	+	-	118	21	7
M	11	921	I	F	FEM	AD	H	81	100	-	0	-	-	S	-	+	-	0	0	0	-	0	1	-	0	0	-	+	+	+	-	72	14	5
M	6	922	I	F	FEM	AD	H	82	0	-	3	-	-	S	-	+	-	0	0	0	-	0	0	-	0	0	-	-	-	-	-	76	24	7
M	6	923	I	F	FEM	AD	H	82	100	-	0	-	-	S	-	+	-	0	0	0	-	0	0	-	0	0	-	-	-	-	-	69	23	6
M	6	924	I	F	FEM	AD	H	82	100	-	0	-	-	S	-	+	-	0	0	1	-	0	0	-	0	0	-	+	+	-	-	62	19	5

01	02	03	09	10	11	12	13	14	15	16	17	18	19	20	23	24	25	37	38	40	41	42	43	44	49	54	59	64	93	94	95	96	97	98
M	8	925	I	F	FEM	AD	H	83	100	-	0	-	-	S	-	+	-	0	0	0	-	0	0	-	1	0	-	+	-	-	-	152	24	5
M	8	926	I	F	FEM	AD	H	83	90	-	0	-	-	S	-	+	-	0	0	0	-	0	0	-	1	0	-	-	+	+	-	107	20	7
M	8	927	I	F	FEM	AD	H	84	100	-	0	-	-	S	-	+	-	0	1	0	-	0	0	-	0	0	-	-	-	-	-	127	17	3
M	8	928	I	F	FEM	AD	H	84	100	-	0	-	-	S	-	+	-	2	0	0	-	0	0	-	4	0	-	-	-	-	-	100	18	5
M	8	929	I	F	FEM	AD	H	85	100	-	0	-	-	S	-	+	-	0	0	0	-	0	0	-	0	0	+	+	-	-	-	130	15	4
M	8	930	I	F	FEM	AD	H	85	90	-	0	-	-	S	-	+	-	0	0	0	-	0	0	-	1	0	-	-	-	-	-	84	14	3
M	8	931	I	F	FEM	AD	H	86	100	P	0	-	-	S	-	+	-	0	0	0	-	0	0	-	0	0	-	-	-	-	-	95	15	4
M	6	932	I	F	FEM	AD	H	86	100	P	0	-	-	S	-	+	-	0	1	0	-	0	0	-	0	0	-	-	-	-	-	88	21	4
M	8	933	I	F	FEM	AD	H	87	100	-	0	-	-	S	-	+	-	0	1	0	+	0	0	-	0	0	-	-	-	-	-	73	18	5
M	8	934	I	F	FEM	AD	H	87	100	-	0	-	-	S	-	+	-	0	0	1	-	0	0	-	0	0	-	+	-	-	-	57	18	5
M	6	935	I	F	FEM	AD	H	88	100	-	0	-	-	S	-	+	-	0	0	1	-	0	0	-	2	0	-	-	-	-	-	79	24	3
M	6	936	I	F	FEM	AD	H	88	100	-	0	-	-	S	-	+	-	0	1	0	-	0	0	-	0	0	-	-	-	-	-	72	20	3
M	8	937	I	F	FEM	AD	H	89	100	-	0	-	-	S	-	+	-	0	0	0	-	0	0	-	0	0	-	-	-	-	-	81	17	2
M	8	938	I	F	FEM	AD	H	89	100	-	0	-	-	S	-	+	-	0	0	0	-	0	0	-	0	0	-	-	-	-	-	41	15	3
M	11	939	I	F	FEM	AD	H	90	100	-	0	-	-	S	-	+	-	0	0	0	-	0	0	-	0	0	-	-	+	+	+	64	17	5
M	11	940	I	F	FEM	AD	H	90	90	-	0	-	-	S	-	+	-	0	0	0	-	0	0	-	0	0	-	+	+	+	+	66	12	3
M	50	941	I	F	FEM	AD	H	91	100	-	0	-	-	S	-	+	-	0	0	0	-	0	0	-	0	0	-	-	-	-	-	71	17	5
M	50	942	I	F	FEM	AD	H	91	100	-	0	-	-	S	-	+	-	0	0	0	-	0	0	-	0	0	-	+	-	-	-	51	15	5
M	8	943	I	F	FEM	AD	H	92	100	-	0	-	-	S	-	+	-	0	0	0	-	9	0	-	0	0	-	+	-	-	-	66	18	7
M	8	944	I	F	FEM	AD	H	92	100	-	0	-	-	S	-	+	-	0	0	0	-	3	0	-	0	0	-	+	-	-	-	38	20	8
M	6	954	R	F	TIB	06	H	-	100	-	0	-	-	S	-	+	-	0	0	1	-	0	0	-	0	0	-	-	-	-	-	56	17	1
M	6	955	R	F	TIB	06	H	93	100	-	0	-	-	T	-	+	-	0	0	2	-	0	0	-	0	0	-	-	-	-	-			
M	6	956	R	F	TIB	06	H	93	100	-	0	-	-	S	-	+	-	0	0	0	-	0	0	-	0	0	-	-	-	-	-	38	11	2
M	8	957	R	F	TIB	06	H	94	100	-	0	-	-	S	-	+	-	0	0	0	-	0	0	-	0	0	-	-	-	-	-	79	12	2
M	FS19	958	R	F	TIB	06	H	94	80	-	0	-	-	S	-	+	-	0	0	0	-	0	0	-	0	0	0	-	-	-	-	82	19	3
M	6	959	R	F	TIB	08	H	-	100	-	0	-	-	S	-	+	-	0	0	0	-	1	0	-	0	0	-	+	-	-	-	90	18	3
M	8	960	R	F	TIB	08	H	-	80	-	0	-	-	S	-	+	-	0	0	1	-	0	0	-	0	0	-	-	+	+	+	83	20	3
M	8	962	R	F	TIB	10	H	-	100	-	0	-	-	O	-	+	-	0	0	1	+	0	0	-	0	0	-	-	-	-	-			
M	8	963	R	F	TIB	12	H	95	100	-	0	-	-	S	-	+	-	0	0	0	-	0	0	-	0	0	-	-	-	-	-	136	15	4
M	8	964	R	F	TIB	12	H	95	100	-	0	-	-	S	-	+	-	0	0	0	-	0	0	-	0	0	-	-	-	-	-	82	12	2
M	8	965	R	F	TIB	12	H	95	100	-	0	-	-	S	-	+	-	0	0	0	-	0	0	-	0	0	-	-	-	-	-	94	10	3
M	8	966	R	F	TIB	AD	H	-	100	-	0	-	-	S	-	+	-	0	0	0	-	0	0	-	0	0	-	-	+	-	+	267	24	3
M	8	967	R	F	TIB	AD	H	-	90	-	0	+	-	S	-	+	-	0	0	0	-	0	0	-	0	0	-	-	+	+	+	151	18	3
M	8	968	R	F	TIB	AD	H	-	100	-	0	-	-	S	-	+	-	0	0	0	-	0	0	-	0	0	-	-	-	-	-	158	15	4
M	6	969	R	F	TIB	AD	H	-	100	-	0	-	-	S	-	+	-	0	1	0	-	0	1	-	0	0	-	-	+	+	-	151	22	5
M	8	970	R	F	TIB	AD	H	-	100	P	0	-	-	S	-	+	-	0	0	0	-	0	0	-	0	0	-	+	-	-	-	133	19	5
M	19	971	R	F	TIB	AD	H	-	100	-	0	+	-	S	-	+	-	0	0	1	-	0	0	-	0	0	-	+	-	-	-	99	24	4
M	8	974	R	F	TIB	AD	H	-	100	-	0	-	-	S	-	+	-	0	3	0	-	1	0	-	0	0	-	+	-	-	-	92	14	2
M	8	975	R	F	TIB	AD	H	-	100	-	0	-	-	O	-	+	-	0	0	0	+	0	0	-	0	0	-	-	-	-	-			
M	6	976	R	F	TIB	AD	H	-	100	-	0	-	-	O	-	+	-	0	0	0	+	0	0	-	0	0	-	-	-	-	-			
M	7	977	R	F	TIB	AD	H	96	100	-	0	-	-	S	-	+	-	0	0	0	-	0	0	-	0	0	-	-	-	-	-	93	12	3
M	7	978	R	F	TIB	AD	H	96	100	-	0	-	-	S	-	+	-	0	1	0	-	0	0	-	0	0	-	+	-	-	-	93	22	4
M	7	979	R	F	TIB	AD	H	96	100	-	0	-	-	S	-	+	-	0	0	0	-	0	0	-	0	0	-	-	-	-	-	82	20	6
M	7	980	R	F	TIB	AD	H	96	100	-	0	-	-	S	-	+	-	0	0	0	-	0	0	+	0	0	-	-	-	-	-	83	14	3
M	7	981	R	F	TIB	AD	H	96	100	-	0	-	-	S	-	+	-	0	0	1	-	0	0	-	0	0	-	+	-	-	-	71	27	7
M	7	982	R	F	TIB	AD	H	96	50	-	0	-	-	S	+	+	-	0	0	0	-	0	0	-	0	0	-	-	-	-	-	-	-	-
M	7	983	R	F	TIB	AD	H	96	100	-	0	-	-	S	-	+	-	0	0	0	-	0	0	-	0	0	-	+	-	-	-	72	18	5
M	7	984	R	F	TIB	AD	H	96	100	-	0	-	-	S	-	+	-	0	0	1	-	0	0	-	0	0	-	+	-	-	-	55	22	6
M	7	985	R	F	TIB	AD	H	96	100	-	0	-	-	S	-	+	-	0	0	1	-	0	0	-	0	0	-	-	-	-	-	71	15	5
M	7	986	R	F	TIB	AD	H	96	100	-	0	-	-	S	-	+	-	0	0	0	-	0	0	-	0	0	-	-	-	-	-	53	21	6
M	8	988	R	F	TIB	AD	H	97	100	-	0	-	-	S	-	+	-	0	0	1	-	0	0	-	0	0	-	-	-	-	-	105	17	5
M	8	989	R	F	TIB	AD	H	97	100	-	0	-	-	S	-	+	-	0	0	1	-	0	0	-	0	0	-	-	-	-	-	95	20	5
M	8	990	R	F	TIB	AD	H	97	100	-	0	-	-	O	-	+	-	0	0	1	+	0	0	-	0	0	-	-	-	-	-			
M	8	991	R	F	TIB	AD	H	97	100	-	0	+	-	S	-	+	-	0	0	2	-	0	0	-	0	0	-	+	+	+	-	65	20	5
M	8	992	R	F	TIB	AD	H	97	100	-	0	-	-	S	-	+	-	0	0	2	-	0	0	-	0	0	-	-	+	+	+	51	20	5
M	8	993	R	F	TIB	AD	H	98	100	-	0	-	-	S	-	+	-	0	0	2	-	0	0	-	0	0	-	-	-	-	-	229	23	4
M	8	994	R	F	TIB	AD	H	98	80	-	0	-	-	S	-	+	-	0	0	1	-	0	0	-	0	0	-	-	+	+	+	141	25	3
M	8	995	R	F	TIB	AD	H	98	100	-	0	-	-	S	-	+	-	0	0	0	-	0	0	-	0	0	-	-	-	-	-	152	11	3

01	02	03	09	10	11	12	13	14	15	16	17	18	19	20	23	24	25	37	38	40	41	42	43	44	49	54	59	64	93	94	95	96	97	98
M	8	996	R	F	TIB	AD	H	98	100	-	0	-	-	S	-	+	-	0	0	0	-	0	0	-	0	0	-	-	-	-	-	106	30	3
M	8	997	R	F	TIB	AD	H	98	100	-	0	-	-	S	-	+	-	0	0	0	-	0	0	-	0	0	-	+	-	-	-	75	33	5
M	6	998	R	F	TIB	AD	H	99	100	-	0	-	-	S	-	+	-	0	0	0	-	0	0	-	0	0	-	+	-	-	-	165	15	4
M	6	999	R	F	TIB	AD	H	99	100	-	0	-	-	S	-	+	-	0	0	0	-	3	0	-	0	0	-	+	-	-	-	128	20	4
M	6	1000	R	F	TIB	AD	H	99	100	-	0	-	-	S	-	+	-	0	0	1	-	0	0	-	0	0	-	+	-	-	-	89	25	3
M	6	1001	R	F	TIB	AD	H	99	100	P	0	-	-	S	-	+	-	1	1	0	-	1	0	-	0	0	-	+	-	-	-	99	15	3
M	6	1002	R	F	TIB	AD	H	99	100	-	0	-	-	S	-	+	-	0	0	0	-	0	0	-	0	0	-	-	-	-	-	82	16	3
M	6	1003	R	F	TIB	AD	H	100	30	-	0	-	-	S	-	+	-	0	0	0	-	0	0	-	0	0	-	-	+	+	+	222	16	3
M	6	1004	R	F	TIB	AD	H	100	100	-	0	-	-	S	-	+	-	0	0	0	-	1	0	-	0	0	-	-	-	-	-	128	21	4
M	6	1005	R	F	TIB	AD	H	100	90	-	0	-	-	S	-	+	-	0	0	0	-	0	0	-	0	0	-	-	+	+	+	111	16	4
M	6	1006	R	F	TIB	AD	H	100	100	-	0	-	-	S	-	+	-	0	0	0	-	0	0	-	0	0	-	+	-	-	-	89	12	3
M	6	1007	R	F	TIB	AD	H	100	100	-	0	-	-	S	-	+	-	0	0	0	-	0	0	-	0	0	-	-	+	+	+	51	10	3
M	3	1008	R	F	TIB	AD	H	101	100	-	0	-	-	S	-	+	-	0	0	1	-	0	0	-	0	0	-	-	+	+	+	186	18	3
M	8	1009	R	F	TIB	AD	H	101	100	-	0	-	-	S	-	+	-	0	0	0	-	0	0	-	0	0	-	-	+	+	+	171	18	3
M	8	1010	R	F	TIB	AD	H	101	100	-	0	-	-	S	-	+	-	0	0	1	-	0	0	-	0	0	-	+	-	-	-	83	20	4
M	8	1011	R	F	TIB	AD	H	101	100	-	0	-	-	S	-	+	-	0	0	0	-	0	0	-	0	0	-	-	-	-	-	82	12	3
M	50	1012	R	F	TIB	AD	H	102	100	-	0	-	-	S	-	+	-	0	0	0	-	0	0	-	0	0	-	-	-	-	-	156	20	4
M	11	1013	R	F	TIB	AD	H	102	100	-	0	-	-	S	-	+	-	0	0	0	-	0	0	-	0	0	-	+	+	+	+	152	20	7
M	8	1014	R	F	TIB	AD	H	103	100	P	0	-	-	S	-	+	-	0	1	1	-	0	0	-	0	0	-	+	+	+	+	126	23	6
M	8	1015	R	F	TIB	AD	H	103	100	-	0	-	-	S	-	+	-	0	0	0	-	0	0	-	0	0	-	-	-	-	-	90	18	7
M	8	1016	R	F	TIB	AD	H	104	100	-	0	-	-	S	-	+	-	0	0	1	-	0	0	-	0	0	-	+	-	-	-	116	17	3
M	8	1017	R	F	TIB	AD	H	104	100	-	0	-	-	S	-	+	-	0	0	0	-	0	0	-	0	0	-	-	-	-	-	91	14	3
M	8	1018	R	F	TIB	AD	H	105	100	-	0	-	-	S	-	+	-	0	0	0	-	0	0	-	0	0	-	-	-	-	-	72	24	4
M	8	1019	R	F	TIB	AD	H	105	100	P	0	-	-	S	-	+	-	0	0	0	-	0	0	-	0	0	-	-	-	-	-	58	17	4
M	8	1020	R	F	TIB	AD	H	106	100	P	0	-	-	S	-	+	-	0	0	0	-	1	0	-	0	0	-	-	-	-	-	50	18	4
M	8	1021	R	F	TIB	AD	H	106	100	-	0	-	-	S	-	+	-	0	1	0	-	2	0	-	0	0	-	-	-	-	-	34	16	4
M	30	1022	R	F	TIB	AD	H	107	100	-	0	-	-	O	+	+	-	0	0	0	-	0	0	-	0	0	-	-	-	-	-			
M	30	1023	R	F	TIB	AD	H	107	100	-	0	-	-	O	-	+	-	0	0	1	-	0	0	-	0	0	-	+	-	-	-			
M	6	1025	L	W	TIB	06	H	-	100	-	0	-	-	T	+	+	-	0	0	0	-	0	0	-	0	0	-	-	+	+	+			
M	8	1026	L	F	TIB	06	H	-	100	-	0	-	-	S	-	+	-	0	0	0	-	0	0	-	0	0	-	-	-	-	-	59	10	2
M	11	1027	L	F	TIB	06	H	108	80	-	1	-	-	S	-	+	-	0	0	0	-	0	0	-	0	0	-	-	-	-	-	124	14	2
M	11	1028	L	F	TIB	06	H	108	100	-	0	-	-	S	-	+	-	0	0	0	-	0	0	-	0	0	-	-	+	+	+	60	12	2
M	11	1029	L	F	TIB	06	H	108	100	-	0	-	-	S	-	+	-	0	0	0	-	0	0	-	0	0	-	-	-	-	-	60	11	1
M	8	1030	L	F	TIB	08	H	-	100	-	0	-	-	S	-	+	-	0	0	0	-	0	0	+	0	0	-	+	-	-	-	126	13	2
M	8	1032	L	F	TIB	10	H	109	100	-	0	-	-	S	-	+	-	0	2	1	-	0	1	-	0	0	-	-	+	+	+	161	13	3
M	8	1033	L	F	TIB	10	H	109	100	-	0	-	-	S	-	+	-	0	0	0	-	0	0	-	0	0	-	-	+	-	-	108	23	3
M	8	1034	L	F	TIB	10	H	109	100	-	0	-	-	S	-	+	-	0	0	1	-	0	1	-	0	0	-	-	+	-	-	79	14	3
M	8	1035	L	F	TIB	10	H	109	100	-	0	-	-	S	-	+	-	0	0	0	-	0	0	-	0	0	-	-	-	-	-	76	12	4
M	8	1036	L	F	TIB	10	H	109	100	-	0	-	-	S	-	+	-	0	0	0	-	0	0	-	0	0	-	+	-	-	-	55	14	3
M	6	1037	L	F	TIB	12	H	-	100	-	0	-	-	S	-	+	-	0	0	0	-	0	0	-	0	4	-	+	-	-	-	114	18	4
M	30	1038	L	F	TIB	12	H	110	90	-	0	-	-	S	-	+	-	0	0	0	-	0	0	-	0	0	-	-	+	+	+	120	20	2
M	5	1039	L	F	TIB	12	H	110	100	-	0	-	-	S	-	+	-	0	0	1	-	0	0	-	0	0	-	-	-	-	-	126	16	3
M	8	1040	L	F	TIB	AD	H	-	100	-	0	-	-	S	-	+	-	0	2	1	-	0	1	-	0	0	-	-	-	-	-	178	23	4
M	19	1041	L	F	TIB	AD	H	-	100	-	0	+	-	S	-	+	-	1	0	0	-	1	0	-	0	2	-	-	-	-	-	97	21	5
M	8	1042	L	F	TIB	AD	H	-	100	-	0	-	-	S	-	+	-	0	0	0	-	0	0	-	0	0	-	+	-	-	-	76	21	5
M	8	1043	L	F	TIB	AD	H	-	100	-	0	-	-	S	-	+	-	0	0	0	-	0	0	-	0	0	-	-	-	-	-	81	22	3
M	7	1044	L	F	TIB	AD	H	111	80	-	0	-	-	S	-	+	-	0	0	1	-	0	0	-	0	0	-	-	+	+	+	106	21	6
M	7	1045	L	F	TIB	AD	H	111	100	-	0	-	-	S	-	+	-	0	0	0	-	0	0	-	0	0	-	-	-	+	-	107	21	5
M	7	1046	L	F	TIB	AD	H	111	100	-	0	-	-	S	-	+	-	0	0	0	-	0	0	-	0	0	-	+	-	-	-	72	21	5
M	7	1047	L	F	TIB	AD	H	111	100	-	0	-	-	S	-	+	-	0	0	0	-	0	0	-	0	0	-	-	-	-	-	69	21	7
M	7	1048	L	F	TIB	AD	H	111	70	-	0	-	-	S	-	+	-	0	0	0	-	0	0	-	0	0	-	-	+	+	+	66	15	6
M	7	1049	L	F	TIB	AD	H	111	0	-	3	-	-	S	+	+	-	0	0	0	-	0	0	-	0	0	-	-	-	-	-	-	-	-
M	7	1050	L	F	TIB	AD	H	111	70	-	0	-	-	S	+	+	-	0	0	0	-	0	0	-	0	0	-	-	-	+	-	-	-	-
M	7	1051	L	F	TIB	AD	H	111	100	-	0	-	-	S	-	+	-	0	0	0	-	1	0	-	0	0	-	+	-	-	-	34	15	5
M	8	1052	L	F	TIB	AD	H	112	80	-	0	-	-	S	-	+	-	0	0	0	-	0	0	-	0	0	-	-	+	+	+	74	27	3
M	11	1053	L	F	TIB	AD	H	112	100	-	0	-	-	S	-	+	-	0	0	0	-	0	0	-	0	0	-	-	-	-	-	137	18	5
M	8	1054	L	F	TIB	AD	H	112	100	-	0	-	-	S	-	+	-	0	1	0	-	0	0	-	0	0	-	-	-	-	-	102	15	3
M	8	1055	L	F	TIB	AD	H	112	100	-	0	-	-	S	-	+	-	0	0	0	-	0	0	-	0	0	-	-	-	-	-	87	16	6

01	02	03	09	10	11	12	13	14	15	16	17	18	19	20	23	24	25	37	38	40	41	42	43	44	49	54	59	64	93	94	95	96	97	98
M	8	1056	L	F	TIB	AD	H	112	100	-	0	-	-	O	-	+	-	0	0	0	+	0	0	-	0	0	-	-	-	-	-			
M	30	1057	L	F	TIB	AD	H	113	100	-	0	-	-	S	-	+	-	1	0	0	-	0	0	-	0	0	-	-	-	-	-	151	32	2
M	30	1058	L	F	TIB	AD	H	113	100	P	0	-	-	S	-	+	-	0	0	0	-	0	1	-	0	0	-	-	+	+	-	189	17	3
M	30	1059	L	F	TIB	AD	H	113	100	-	0	-	-	S	-	+	-	0	0	0	-	0	2	-	0	0	-	-	-	-	-	141	22	2
M	30	1060	L	F	TIB	AD	H	113	100	-	0	-	-	S	-	+	-	0	0	0	-	0	0	-	0	0	-	-	+	-	-	62	13	5
M	6	1061	L	F	TIB	AD	H	114	60	-	0	-	-	S	-	+	-	0	0	0	-	0	3	-	0	0	-	-	-	-	-	165	19	4
M	6	1062	L	F	TIB	AD	H	114	70	-	0	-	-	S	-	+	-	0	0	0	-	0	0	-	0	0	-	+	-	-	-	77	29	4
M	6	1063	L	F	TIB	AD	H	114	100	-	0	+	-	S	-	+	-	0	0	0	+	0	0	-	0	0	-	-	+	+	-	88	17	3
M	6	1064	L	F	TIB	AD	H	114	100	-	0	-	-	S	-	+	-	0	0	0	-	0	0	-	0	0	-	-	-	-	-	53	15	3
M	11	1065	L	F	TIB	AD	H	115	50	-	0	-	-	S	-	+	-	0	1	0	-	0	1	-	0	0	-	-	+	+	+	149	17	3
M	11	1066	L	F	TIB	AD	H	115	100	-	0	-	-	S	-	+	-	0	0	2	-	0	0	-	0	0	-	-	+	+	+	120	20	4
M	11	1067	L	F	TIB	AD	H	115	30	-	0	-	-	S	-	+	-	0	0	0	-	0	0	-	0	0	-	-	+	+	+	57	14	3
M	7	1068	L	F	TIB	AD	H	116	100	-	0	-	-	S	-	+	-	0	0	3	-	0	0	-	0	0	-	-	+	+	+	192	20	3
M	7	1069	L	F	TIB	AD	H	116	100	-	0	-	-	S	-	+	-	0	0	1	-	0	0	-	0	0	-	-	-	-	-	64	13	2
M	3	1070	L	F	TIB	AD	H	117	90	-	0	-	-	S	-	+	-	0	3	1	-	0	1	-	0	0	-	-	+	+	+	141	24	5
M	3	1071	L	F	TIB	AD	H	117	100	-	0	-	-	S	-	+	-	0	2	2	-	0	0	-	0	0	-	+	-	-	-	117	17	5
M	8	1072	L	F	TIB	AD	H	118	100	-	0	-	-	S	-	+	-	0	0	0	-	0	0	-	0	0	-	-	-	-	-	81	20	5
M	19	1073	L	F	TIB	AD	H	118	90	-	0	+	-	S	-	+	-	0	0	0	-	0	0	-	0	0	-	-	-	+	-	71	18	4
M	8	1074	L	F	TIB	AD	H	119	100	-	0	-	-	S	-	+	-	0	0	0	-	0	0	-	0	0	-	+	-	-	-	81	23	3
M	8	1075	L	F	TIB	AD	H	119	100	-	0	-	-	S	-	+	-	0	0	0	-	0	0	-	0	0	-	+	-	-	-	70	21	2
M	8	1076	L	F	TIB	AD	H	120	100	P	0	-	-	S	-	+	-	0	0	0	-	0	0	-	0	0	-	-	+	-	-	77	17	8
M	8	1077	L	F	TIB	AD	H	120	90	-	0	-	-	S	-	+	-	0	0	0	-	0	1	-	0	0	-	-	+	+	+	67	18	8
M	8	1078	I	F	TIB	12	H	-	100	-	0	-	-	S	-	+	-	0	0	0	-	0	0	-	0	0	-	-	-	-	-	141	14	3
M	8	1079	I	F	TIB	12	H	-	100	P	0	-	-	S	-	+	-	0	0	0	-	0	0	-	0	0	-	+	+	+	+	152	16	3
M	6	1080	I	F	TIB	AD	H	-	100	-	0	-	-	S	-	+	-	0	0	1	-	0	0	-	0	0	-	-	-	-	-	127	24	3
M	8	1081	I	F	TIB	AD	H	-	80	-	0	-	-	S	+	+	-	0	0	0	-	0	0	-	0	0	-	-	-	-	-	-	19	2
M	30	1082	I	F	TIB	AD	H	-	100	-	0	-	-	S	-	+	-	0	0	0	-	0	0	-	0	0	-	-	-	-	-	117	23	5
M	7	1083	I	F	TIB	AD	H	-	40	-	0	-	-	S	-	+	-	0	0	0	-	0	0	-	0	0	-	-	+	+	+	107	16	7
M	30	1084	I	F	TIB	AD	H	-	100	-	0	-	-	S	-	+	-	0	0	0	-	0	0	-	0	0	-	-	+	+	+	101	17	5
M	8	1085	I	F	TIB	AD	H	-	100	P	0	-	-	S	-	+	-	0	0	0	-	0	0	-	0	0	-	-	-	-	-	90	21	3
M	8	1086	I	F	TIB	AD	H	-	100	-	0	-	-	S	-	+	-	0	0	0	-	0	0	-	0	0	-	+	+	-	-	100	9	3
M	8	1087	I	F	TIB	AD	H	-	100	-	0	-	-	S	-	+	-	0	0	0	-	0	0	-	0	0	-	-	-	-	-	90	19	4
M	8	1088	I	F	TIB	AD	H	-	100	-	0	-	-	S	-	+	-	0	0	0	-	2	0	-	0	0	-	-	-	-	-	90	23	4
M	8	1089	I	F	TIB	AD	H	-	100	-	0	-	-	S	-	+	-	0	0	0	-	0	0	-	0	0	-	-	-	-	-	86	16	3
M	8	1090	I	F	TIB	AD	H	-	100	-	0	-	-	S	-	+	-	0	0	0	-	0	0	-	1	0	-	+	-	-	-	65	23	4
M	8	1091	I	F	TIB	AD	H	-	100	P	0	-	-	S	-	+	-	0	0	0	-	2	0	-	0	0	-	+	-	-	-	86	20	4
M	8	1092	I	F	TIB	AD	H	-	100	-	0	-	-	S	-	+	-	0	0	1	-	2	0	-	0	0	-	+	-	-	-	70	23	6
M	30	1093	I	F	TIB	AD	H	-	100	P	0	-	-	S	-	+	-	0	0	0	-	0	0	-	0	0	-	+	-	-	-	95	13	5
M	11	1094	I	F	TIB	AD	H	-	90	-	0	-	-	S	-	+	-	0	0	0	-	0	0	-	0	0	-	-	+	+	+	56	21	4
M	8	1095	I	F	TIB	AD	H	-	100	-	0	-	-	S	-	+	-	0	0	0	-	0	0	-	0	0	-	-	+	+	-	65	16	3
M	8	1096	I	F	TIB	AD	H	-	100	-	0	-	-	S	-	+	-	0	0	0	-	0	0	-	0	0	-	-	+	+	-	68	17	6
M	6	1097	I	F	TIB	AD	H	-	60	-	0	-	-	S	-	+	-	0	0	0	-	0	0	-	0	0	-	-	+	+	+	66	19	5
M	6	1098	I	F	TIB	AD	H	-	50	-	0	+	-	S	-	+	-	0	0	0	-	0	0	-	0	0	-	-	+	+	+	68	18	3
M	6	1099	I	F	TIB	AD	H	-	70	-	0	-	-	S	-	+	-	0	0	0	-	0	0	-	0	0	-	-	+	+	+	60	16	5
M	19	1100	I	F	TIB	AD	H	-	100	-	0	-	-	S	-	+	-	0	0	0	-	0	0	-	0	0	-	-	-	-	-	66	11	3
M	8	1101	I	F	TIB	AD	H	-	100	-	0	-	-	S	-	+	-	0	0	0	-	0	0	-	0	0	-	-	-	-	-	67	8	3
M	11	1102	I	F	TIB	AD	H	-	50	-	0	-	-	S	-	+	-	0	0	0	-	0	0	-	0	0	-	-	+	+	+	59	14	3
M	8	1103	I	F	TIB	AD	H	-	100	-	0	-	-	S	-	+	-	0	1	0	-	0	0	-	0	0	-	-	-	-	-	54	18	3
M	7	1104	I	F	TIB	AD	H	-	100	-	0	-	-	S	-	+	-	0	0	0	-	0	0	-	0	0	-	-	-	-	-	48	16	6
M	30	1105	I	F	TIB	AD	H	-	100	-	0	-	-	S	-	+	-	0	0	0	-	0	0	-	0	0	-	-	+	+	+	51	17	5
M	30	1106	I	F	TIB	AD	H	121	100	-	0	-	-	S	-	+	-	0	0	0	-	0	0	-	0	0	-	-	-	-	-	110	11	2
M	30	1107	I	F	TIB	AD	H	121	100	-	0	-	-	S	-	+	-	0	0	1	-	0	0	-	0	0	-	-	-	-	-	129	19	3
M	8	1108	I	F	TIB	AD	H	122	100	-	0	-	-	S	-	+	-	0	0	0	-	0	0	-	0	0	-	-	-	-	-	93	22	3
M	8	1109	I	F	TIB	AD	H	122	100	-	0	-	-	S	-	+	-	0	0	0	-	0	0	-	0	0	-	-	-	-	-	102	18	3
M	8	1111	R	F	FIB	04	H	-	100	-	0	-	-	T	+	+	-	0	0	2	-	0	0	-	0	0	-	-	-	-	-			
M	30	1114	R	F	FIB	06	H	123	100	-	0	-	-	T	-	+	-	0	0	2	-	0	0	-	0	0	-	-	-	-	-			
M	30	1115	R	F	FIB	06	H	123	100	-	0	-	-	S	-	+	-	0	0	0	-	0	0	-	0	0	-	-	-	-	-	86	6	2
M	19	1124	R	F	FIB	AD	H	-	100	-	0	-	-	T	-	+	-	0	0	0	-	0	0	-	0	0	-	+	-	-	-			

01	02	03	09	10	11	12	13	14	15	16	17	18	19	20	23	24	25	37	38	40	41	42	43	44	49	54	59	64	93	94	95	96	97	98
M	5	1125	R	F	FIB	AD	H	-	100	-	0	-	-	S	-	+	-	0	0	0	-	0	0	-	0	0	-	-	+	+	+	44	12	1
M	8	1126	R	F	FIB	AD	H	124	100	P	0	-	-	T	-	+	-	0	0	0	-	2	0	-	0	0	-	+	-	-	-			
M	8	1127	R	F	FIB	AD	H	124	100	-	0	-	-	T	-	+	-	0	0	0	-	0	0	-	0	0	-	-	-	-	-			
M	8	1128	R	F	FIB	AD	H	124	100	-	0	-	-	S	-	+	-	0	0	0	-	0	0	-	0	0	-	-	-	-	-	36	12	2
M	7	1130	R	F	FIB	AD	H	125	100	-	0	-	-	S	-	+	-	0	0	1	-	0	0	-	0	0	-	-	-	-	-	58	12	2
M	8	1131	R	F	FIB	AD	H	126	100	-	0	-	-	S	-	+	-	0	0	0	-	1	0	-	0	0	-	-	-	-	-	68	9	3
M	8	1132	R	F	FIB	AD	H	126	100	-	0	-	-	S	-	+	-	0	0	0	-	0	0	-	0	0	-	+	-	-	-	56	7	4
M	30	1133	R	F	FIB	AD	H	127	100	-	0	-	-	O	-	+	-	0	0	0	+	0	0	-	0	0	-	-	-	-	-			
M	8	1134	R	F	FIB	AD	H	127	100	-	0	-	-	O	-	+	-	0	0	0	+	0	0	-	0	0	-	-	-	-	-			
M	8	1136	L	F	FIB	04	H	-	100	-	0	-	-	T	-	+	-	0	0	0	+	0	0	-	0	0	-	-	-	-	-			
M	6	1137	L	F	FIB	04	H	-	100	-	0	-	-	T	-	+	-	0	0	1	-	0	0	-	0	0	-	-	+	+	+			
M	8	1138	L	F	FIB	04	H	-	100	-	0	+	-	T	+	+	-	0	0	0	-	0	0	-	0	0	-	-	-	-	-			
M	11	1139	L	F	FIB	06	H	128	100	-	0	-	-	T	-	+	-	0	0	0	-	0	0	-	0	0	-	-	-	-	-			
M	11	1140	L	F	FIB	06	H	128	100	-	0	-	-	T	-	+	-	0	0	0	-	0	0	-	0	0	-	-	-	-	-			
M	50	1142	L	F	FIB	08	H	129	100	-	0	-	-	T	+	+	-	0	0	2	-	0	0	-	0	0	-	-	+	-	-			
M	6	1143	L	F	FIB	08	H	129	100	-	0	-	-	T	-	+	-	0	0	0	-	0	0	-	0	0	-	-	-	-	-			
M	8	1152	L	F	FIB	AD	H	-	100	-	0	-	-	T	-	+	-	0	0	0	-	0	0	-	0	0	-	-	-	-	-			
M	8	1153	L	F	FIB	AD	H	-	100	-	0	-	-	T	-	+	-	0	0	0	+	0	0	-	0	0	-	-	+	+	+			
M	8	1154	L	F	FIB	AD	H	-	100	-	0	+	-	T	-	+	-	0	0	0	-	0	0	-	0	0	-	-	+	+	+			
M	6	1155	L	F	FIB	AD	H	-	80	-	0	-	-	T	-	+	-	0	0	0	-	0	0	-	0	0	-	-	+	+	+			
M	6	1156	L	F	FIB	AD	H	130	90	-	0	-	-	T	-	+	-	0	0	2	-	2	0	-	0	0	-	+	+	+	-			
M	6	1157	L	F	FIB	AD	H	130	100	-	0	-	-	S	-	+	-	0	0	0	-	0	0	-	0	0	-	+	-	-	-	65	70	2
M	6	1158	L	F	FIB	AD	H	130	100	-	0	-	-	S	-	+	-	0	0	0	-	0	0	-	0	0	-	-	-	-	-	65	6	2
M	7	1160	L	F	FIB	AD	H	131	100	-	0	-	-	S	-	+	-	0	0	0	-	0	0	-	0	0	-	+	-	-	-	62	8	2
M	7	1161	L	F	FIB	AD	H	132	100	-	0	+	-	T	-	+	-	0	1	1	-	0	0	-	0	0	-	-	+	-	-			
M	7	1162	L	F	FIB	AD	H	132	100	-	0	-	-	S	-	+	-	0	0	0	-	0	0	-	0	0	-	-	-	-	-	71	6	1
M	6	1163	I	F	FIB	04	H	-	100	-	0	-	-	T	+	-	-	0	0	0	-	0	0	-	0	0	-	-	+	+	-			
M	11	1164	I	F	FIB	06	H	-	100	-	0	-	-	T	-	+	-	0	0	2	+	0	0	-	0	0	-	-	-	-	-			
M	11	1165	I	F	FIB	AD	H	-	100	-	0	+	-	S	-	+	-	0	0	1	-	0	0	-	0	0	-	-	-	-	-	97	13	3
M	19	1166	I	F	FIB	AD	H	-	100	-	0	-	-	T	-	+	-	0	0	0	-	0	0	-	0	0	-	-	-	-	-			
M	8	1167	I	F	FIB	AD	H	-	100	P	0	-	-	S	-	+	-	0	0	0	-	1	0	-	0	0	-	+	+	+	+	87	8	2
M	11	1168	I	F	FIB	AD	H	-	100	-	0	-	-	S	-	+	-	0	0	0	-	0	0	-	0	2	-	-	-	-	-	77	12	2
M	8	1169	I	F	FIB	AD	H	-	100	-	0	-	-	T	-	+	-	0	0	1	-	0	0	-	2	0	-	-	-	-	-			
M	7	1170	I	F	FIB	AD	H	-	100	-	0	-	-	S	-	+	-	0	0	0	-	0	0	-	0	0	-	-	+	+	+	66	12	2
M	6	1392	I	F	IP1	AD	H	-	100	-	0	-	-	S	-	+	-	0	0	0	-	0	0	-	0	0	-	-	-	-	-	80	9	3
M	3	1393	I	F	IP1	AD	H	-	100	P	0	-	-	S	-	+	-	0	0	0	-	0	0	-	0	0	-	-	+	+	-	62	10	3
M	30	1394	I	F	IP1	AD	H	-	100	-	0	-	-	S	-	+	-	0	0	0	-	0	0	-	0	0	-	-	-	-	-	54	7	2
M	7	1395	I	F	IP1	AD	H	-	30	-	2	-	-	S	-	+	-	0	0	0	-	0	0	-	0	0	-	-	-	-	-	38	11	2
M	7	1396	I	F	IP1	AD	H	-	80	-	0	-	-	S	-	+	-	0	0	0	-	0	0	-	0	0	-	-	-	-	-	98	6	1
M	8	1397	I	F	IP1	AD	H	-	100	-	0	-	-	S	-	+	-	0	0	0	-	0	0	-	0	0	-	-	+	+	+	47	8	2
M	8	1398	I	F	IP1	AD	H	-	100	-	0	-	-	S	-	+	-	0	0	0	-	0	0	-	0	0	-	-	-	-	-	35	11	3
M	7	1399	I	F	IP2	IM	H	-	100	-	0	-	-	S	-	+	-	0	0	0	-	0	0	-	0	0	-	-	-	-	-	148	9	1
M	8	1400	I	F	IP2	IM	H	-	100	-	0	-	-	S	-	+	-	0	0	0	-	0	0	-	0	0	-	-	-	-	-	75	16	2
M	8	1401	I	F	IP2	IM	H	-	100	-	0	+	-	S	-	+	-	0	0	0	-	0	0	-	0	0	-	-	-	-	-	84	9	2
M	6	1402	I	F	IP2	IM	H	-	100	-	0	-	-	S	-	+	-	0	0	0	-	0	0	-	0	0	-	+	-	-	-	74	9	2
M	8	1403	I	F	IP2	IM	H	133	100	P	0	-	-	S	-	+	-	0	0	0	-	0	0	-	0	2	-	-	-	-	-	111	18	3
M	8	1404	I	F	IP2	IM	H	133	100	-	0	+	-	S	-	+	-	0	0	0	-	1	0	-	0	0	-	-	-	-	-	90	9	2
M	8	1405	L	F	HUM	AD	H	-	100	-	0	-	-	S	-	+	-	0	0	0	-	0	0	-	0	0	-	+	+	+	+	136	20	3
M	30	1406	I	F	IP2	AD	H	-	100	-	0	-	-	S	-	+	-	0	0	0	-	0	0	-	0	0	-	+	-	-	-	98	18	4
M	9	1407	I	F	IP2	AD	H	-	100	-	0	-	-	S	-	+	-	0	0	1	-	0	1	-	0	0	-	-	-	-	-	118	15	2
M	30	1408	I	F	IP2	AD	H	-	100	-	0	-	-	S	-	+	-	0	0	0	-	0	0	-	0	0	-	-	-	-	-	88	18	2
M	8	1409	I	F	IP2	AD	H	-	100	-	0	-	-	S	-	+	-	0	0	1	-	0	0	-	0	0	-	-	-	-	-	125	13	3
M	8	1410	I	F	IP2	AD	H	-	100	-	0	-	-	S	-	+	-	0	0	0	-	0	0	-	0	0	-	-	-	-	-	118	13	3
M	8	1411	I	F	IP2	AD	H	-	100	P	0	-	-	S	-	+	-	0	2	1	-	0	0	-	0	0	-	+	-	-	-	119	14	3
M	8	1412	I	F	IP2	AD	H	-	100	P	0	-	-	S	-	+	-	0	0	0	-	0	0	-	0	0	-	+	-	-	-	123	14	3
M	8	1413	I	F	IP2	AD	H	-	100	-	0	-	-	S	-	+	-	0	0	0	-	0	0	-	0	0	-	-	-	-	-	114	18	2
M	8	1414	I	F	IP2	AD	H	-	100	-	0	-	-	S	-	+	-	0	0	0	-	0	0	-	0	0	-	-	-	-	-	126	14	3
M	8	1415	I	F	IP2	AD	H	-	100	-	0	-	-	S	-	+	-	0	0	0	-	0	0	-	0	0	-	+	-	-	-	90	13	2

01	02	03	09	10	11	12	13	14	15	16	17	18	19	20	23	24	25	37	38	40	41	42	43	44	49	54	59	64	93	94	95	96	97	98
M	8	1416	I	F	IP2	AD	H	-	100	-	0	-	-	S	-	+	-	0	0	0	-	0	2	-	0	0	-	-	-	-	-	93	14	3
M	8	1417	I	F	IP2	AD	H	-	100	-	0	-	-	S	-	+	-	0	0	0	-	0	0	-	0	2	-	+	-	-	-	98	13	2
M	9	1418	I	F	IP2	AD	H	-	100	-	0	-	-	S	-	+	-	0	0	0	-	0	0	-	0	0	-	-	-	-	-	95	7	2
M	8	1419	I	F	IP2	AD	H	-	100	-	0	-	-	S	-	+	-	0	0	1	-	0	0	-	0	0	-	-	+	-	-	101	15	3
M	8	1420	I	F	IP2	AD	H	-	100	P	0	-	-	S	-	+	-	0	0	0	-	0	0	-	3	0	-	-	-	-	-	93	12	3
M	30	1421	I	F	IP2	AD	H	-	100	-	0	-	-	S	-	+	-	0	0	0	-	0	0	-	0	0	-	-	-	-	-	80	13	3
M	8	1422	I	F	IP2	AD	H	-	100	-	0	-	-	S	-	+	-	0	0	0	-	0	0	-	0	0	-	+	-	-	-	78	15	4
M	6	1423	I	F	IP2	AD	H	-	100	-	0	-	-	S	-	+	-	0	0	0	-	0	0	-	0	0	-	+	-	-	-	72	12	3
M	30	1424	I	F	IP2	AD	H	-	100	-	0	-	-	S	-	+	-	0	0	0	-	0	0	-	0	0	-	-	-	-	-	72	15	2
M	6	1425	I	F	IP2	AD	H	-	100	-	0	+	-	S	-	+	-	0	0	0	-	0	0	-	0	0	-	-	-	-	-	56	17	3
M	8	1426	I	F	IP2	AD	H	-	100	-	0	-	-	S	-	+	-	0	0	0	-	0	0	-	0	0	-	+	-	-	-	77	12	2
M	8	1427	I	F	IP2	AD	H	-	80	-	0	-	-	S	-	+	-	0	0	0	-	0	0	-	0	0	-	-	-	-	-	70	16	3
M	8	1428	I	F	IP2	AD	H	-	90	-	0	-	-	S	-	+	-	0	0	0	-	0	0	-	0	0	-	-	-	-	-	57	15	2
M	9	1429	I	F	IP2	AD	H	-	100	-	0	-	-	S	-	+	-	0	0	0	-	0	0	-	0	0	-	-	-	-	-	61	14	3
M	7	1430	I	F	IP2	AD	H	-	100	-	0	-	-	S	-	+	-	0	0	0	-	0	0	-	0	0	-	+	-	-	-	97	13	2
M	30	1431	I	F	IP2	AD	H	-	100	-	0	-	-	S	-	+	-	0	0	0	-	0	0	-	0	0	-	-	-	-	-	78	12	2
M	8	1432	I	F	IP2	AD	H	-	100	P	0	-	-	S	-	+	-	0	0	0	-	0	0	-	0	0	-	-	-	-	-	71	13	3
M	9	1433	I	F	IP2	AD	H	-	100	-	0	-	-	S	-	+	-	0	0	0	-	0	0	-	4	0	-	-	-	-	-	65	12	2
M	8	1434	I	F	IP2	AD	H	-	100	-	0	-	-	S	-	+	-	0	0	0	-	0	0	-	0	0	-	-	-	-	-	74	10	3
M	11	1435	I	F	IP2	AD	H	-	100	-	0	-	-	S	-	+	-	0	0	0	-	0	0	-	2	0	-	-	-	-	-	81	10	3
M	8	1436	I	F	IP2	AD	H	-	100	P	0	-	-	S	-	+	-	0	0	0	-	0	0	-	0	0	-	+	-	-	-	73	8	3
M	50	1437	I	F	IP2	AD	H	-	100	-	0	-	-	S	-	+	-	0	0	0	-	0	0	-	0	0	-	-	-	-	-	79	11	3
M	11	1438	I	F	IP2	AD	H	-	40	-	1	-	-	S	-	+	-	0	0	0	-	0	0	-	0	0	-	-	-	-	-	76	13	2
M	11	1439	I	F	IP2	AD	H	-	100	-	0	-	-	S	-	+	-	0	0	0	-	0	0	-	0	0	-	-	+	+	+	60	15	4
M	8	1440	I	F	IP2	AD	H	-	100	P	0	-	-	S	-	+	-	0	0	1	-	0	0	-	0	0	-	+	-	-	-	71	14	3
M	19	1441	I	F	IP2	AD	H	-	100	-	0	-	-	S	-	+	-	0	0	0	-	0	0	-	0	0	-	-	-	-	-	80	12	3
M	11	1442	I	F	IP2	AD	H	-	100	-	0	+	-	S	-	+	-	0	0	0	-	0	0	-	0	0	-	-	-	-	-	83	8	3
M	8	1443	I	F	IP2	AD	H	-	100	-	0	-	-	S	-	+	-	0	0	0	-	0	0	-	0	0	-	-	-	-	-	66	12	3
M	8	1444	I	F	IP2	AD	H	-	100	P	0	-	-	S	-	+	-	0	0	0	-	0	0	-	0	0	-	-	-	-	-	52	18	4
M	8	1445	I	F	IP2	AD	H	-	100	-	0	-	-	S	-	+	-	0	0	0	-	0	0	-	0	0	-	-	-	-	-	59	13	2
M	11	1446	I	F	IP2	AD	H	-	100	-	0	-	-	S	-	+	-	0	0	0	-	1	0	-	0	0	-	+	+	-	-	60	14	3
M	3	1447	I	F	IP2	AD	H	-	100	-	0	-	-	S	-	+	-	0	0	0	-	0	0	-	0	0	-	-	-	-	-	52	15	3
M	8	1448	I	F	IP2	AD	H	-	100	-	0	-	-	S	-	+	-	0	0	1	+	0	0	+	0	0	-	+	-	-	-	65	19	2
M	8	1449	I	F	IP2	AD	H	-	100	-	0	-	-	S	-	+	-	0	0	0	-	0	0	-	0	0	-	+	-	-	-	65	9	2
M	50	1450	I	F	IP2	AD	H	-	100	-	0	-	-	S	+	+	-	0	0	0	-	0	0	-	0	0	-	+	-	-	-	-	-	-
M	50	1451	I	F	IP2	AD	H	-	100	-	0	-	-	S	-	+	-	0	0	0	-	0	0	-	0	0	-	-	+	-	-	69	12	3
M	8	1452	I	F	IP2	AD	H	-	100	P	0	-	-	S	-	+	-	0	0	0	-	0	0	-	0	0	-	+	-	-	-	70	10	2
M	8	1453	I	F	IP2	AD	H	-	100	-	0	-	-	S	-	+	-	0	0	0	-	0	0	-	1	0	-	-	-	-	-	66	12	4
M	30	1454	I	F	IP2	AD	H	-	100	-	0	-	-	S	-	+	-	0	0	0	-	0	2	-	0	0	-	-	-	-	-	66	10	2
M	9	1455	I	F	IP2	AD	H	-	100	-	0	-	-	S	-	+	-	0	0	0	-	0	0	-	2	0	-	+	-	-	-	45	11	3
M	6	1456	I	F	IP2	AD	H	-	80	-	0	-	-	S	-	+	-	0	0	0	-	0	0	-	0	0	-	-	+	+	+	46	13	1
M	6	1457	I	F	IP2	AD	H	-	90	-	0	-	-	S	+	+	-	0	0	1	-	0	0	-	0	0	-	-	-	-	-	-	-	-
M	8	1458	I	F	IP2	AD	H	-	100	-	0	-	-	S	-	+	-	0	0	3	-	0	0	-	0	0	-	-	+	+	+	38	15	2
M	6	1459	I	F	IP2	AD	H	-	70	-	0	-	-	S	-	+	-	0	0	0	-	0	0	-	0	0	-	-	-	-	-	52	14	2
M	7	1460	I	F	IP2	AD	H	-	100	-	0	-	-	S	-	+	-	0	0	1	-	0	0	-	0	0	-	-	-	-	-	40	17	2
M	8	1461	I	F	IP2	AD	H	-	100	-	0	-	-	S	-	+	-	0	0	0	-	0	0	-	0	0	-	-	-	-	-	50	12	2
M	8	1462	I	F	IP2	AD	H	-	100	-	0	-	-	S	-	+	-	0	0	0	-	0	0	-	0	0	-	-	-	-	-	51	10	2
M	8	1463	I	F	IP2	AD	H	-	100	-	0	-	-	S	-	+	-	0	0	0	-	0	0	-	0	0	-	+	-	-	-	38	14	1
M	50	1464	I	F	IP2	AD	H	-	100	-	0	-	-	O	-	+	-	0	0	0	+	0	0	-	0	0	-	+	-	-	-			
M	8	1465	I	F	IP2	AD	H	-	80	P	0	-	-	S	-	+	-	0	0	0	-	0	0	-	0	0	-	-	+	+	+	32	13	3
M	7	1466	I	F	IP2	AD	H	-	100	-	0	-	-	S	+	+	-	0	0	0	-	0	0	-	0	0	-	-	-	-	-	-	-	-
M	65	1467	I	F	IP2	AD	H	-	100	-	0	-	-	S	+	+	-	0	0	0	-	0	0	-	0	0	-	-	-	-	-	-	-	-
M	7	1468	I	F	IP2	AD	H	-	30	-	0	-	-	S	+	+	-	0	0	0	-	0	0	-	0	0	-	-	-	-	-	-	-	-
M	7	1469	I	F	IP2	AD	H	-	100	-	0	-	-	S	-	+	-	0	0	0	-	0	0	-	0	0	-	-	-	-	-	32	7	2
M	8	1470	I	F	IP2	AD	H	134	100	-	0	-	-	S	-	+	-	0	0	0	-	0	0	-	0	0	-	-	-	-	-	85	11	3
M	8	1471	I	F	IP2	AD	H	134	100	-	0	-	-	S	-	+	-	0	0	0	-	0	0	-	0	0	-	-	-	-	-	75	16	3
M	8	1472	I	F	IP2	AD	H	134	100	P	0	-	-	S	-	+	-	0	0	0	-	0	0	-	0	0	-	-	-	-	-	53	14	3
M	30	1473	I	F	IP2	AD	H	135	100	-	0	-	-	S	-	+	-	0	0	0	-	1	0	-	0	0	-	+	-	-	-	75	10	3

01	02	03	09	10	11	12	13	14	15	16	17	18	19	20	23	24	25	37	38	40	41	42	43	44	49	54	59	64	93	94	95	96	97	98
M	30	1474	I	F	IP2	AD	H	135	100	P	0	.	.	S	.	+	.	0	0	1	.	0	0	.	0	0	.	.	.	.	.	62	17	3
M	6	1475	I	F	IP2	AD	H	136	100	.	0	.	.	S	.	+	.	0	0	0	.	0	0	.	0	0	.	+	.	.	.	75	12	3
M	6	1476	I	F	IP2	AD	H	136	100	.	0	.	.	S	.	+	.	0	0	0	.	0	0	.	0	0	.	.	.	.	.	73	12	4
M	8	1477	I	F	IP3	IM	H	.	100	.	0	.	.	S	.	+	.	0	0	0	.	0	0	.	0	0	.	+	.	.	.	116	16	3
M	6	1478	I	F	IP3	IM	H	.	100	.	0	.	.	O	.	+	.	0	0	1	.	0	0	.	0	0	.	.	.	.	.			
M	8	1479	I	F	IP3	IM	H	.	100	.	0	.	.	S	.	+	.	0	0	2	.	0	0	.	0	0	.	.	.	.	.	58	22	2
M	6	1480	I	F	IP3	IM	H	.	100	P	0	.	.	S	.	+	.	0	0	0	.	0	0	.	0	0	.	+	.	.	.	83	17	3
M	6	1481	I	F	IP3	IM	H	.	100	.	0	.	.	S	.	+	.	0	0	0	.	0	0	.	0	0	.	+	.	.	.	81	18	3
M	11	1482	I	F	IP3	IM	H	.	100	.	0	.	.	S	.	+	.	0	0	1	.	0	0	.	0	0	.	+	.	.	.	78	15	3
M	11	1483	I	F	IP3	IM	H	.	100	.	0	.	.	S	.	+	.	0	0	0	.	0	0	.	0	0	.	+	.	.	.	65	16	2
M	30	1484	I	F	IP3	IM	H	.	100	.	0	.	.	S	.	+	.	0	0	0	.	0	0	.	0	0	.	+	.	.	.	66	15	3
M	30	1485	I	F	IP3	IM	H	.	100	.	0	.	.	S	.	+	.	0	0	0	.	0	0	.	0	0	.	.	+	+	.	50	17	2
M	8	1486	I	F	IP3	IM	H	.	100	.	0	.	.	S	.	+	.	0	0	0	.	0	0	.	0	0	.	+	+	.	.	64	10	2
M	8	1487	I	F	IP3	IM	H	.	100	.	0	.	.	S	.	+	.	0	0	0	.	0	0	.	0	0	.	.	.	.	.	55	16	2
M	8	1488	I	F	IP3	IM	H	.	100	.	0	.	.	S	.	+	.	0	0	0	.	0	0	.	4	0	.	.	.	.	.	38	17	3
M	7	1489	I	F	IP3	IM	H	.	100	P	0	.	.	S	.	+	.	0	0	1	.	0	0	.	0	0	.	+	+	.	.	63	15	2
M	19	1490	I	F	IP3	IM	H	.	100	.	0	.	.	S	.	+	.	0	0	0	.	0	0	.	0	0	.	+	.	.	.	64	12	2
M	30	1491	I	F	IP3	AD	H	.	100	.	0	.	.	S	.	+	.	0	0	0	.	0	0	.	0	0	.	.	.	.	.	123	18	3
M	11	1492	I	F	IP3	AD	H	.	40	.	1	+	.	S	.	+	.	0	0	1	.	0	0	.	3	0	.	.	.	.	.	99	26	7
M	30	1493	I	F	IP3	AD	H	.	100	.	0	.	.	S	.	+	.	0	0	0	.	0	0	.	0	0	.	.	+	+	.	112	18	4
M	8	1494	I	F	IP3	AD	H	.	100	P	0	.	.	S	.	+	.	0	0	0	.	0	0	.	0	0	.	+	.	.	.	117	17	6
M	8	1495	I	F	IP3	AD	H	.	100	.	0	.	.	S	.	+	.	0	0	0	.	0	0	.	0	0	.	.	.	.	.	106	19	4
M	11	1496	I	F	IP3	AD	H	.	100	P	0	.	.	S	.	+	.	0	0	1	.	0	0	.	3	0	.	+	.	.	.	88	23	6
M	11	1497	I	F	IP3	AD	H	.	100	.	0	.	.	S	+	+	.	0	2	0	.	0	0	.	0	0	.	.	.	.	.	.	18	6
M	8	1498	I	F	IP3	AD	H	.	100	.	0	.	.	S	.	+	.	0	0	0	.	0	0	.	1	0	.	+	.	.	.	110	16	6
M	8	1499	I	F	IP3	AD	H	.	100	P	0	.	.	S	.	+	.	0	0	0	.	0	0	.	1	0	.	.	.	.	.	93	21	3
M	30	1500	I	F	IP3	AD	H	.	100	.	0	.	.	S	.	+	.	0	0	0	.	0	0	.	0	0	.	.	.	.	.	99	20	3
M	11	1501	I	F	IP3	AD	H	.	100	P	0	.	.	S	.	+	.	0	0	0	.	0	0	.	5	0	.	+	.	.	.	114	17	6
M	11	1502	I	F	IP3	AD	H	.	20	.	0	+	.	S	.	+	.	0	0	1	.	0	0	.	0	0	.	.	.	.	.	78	22	5
M	8	1503	I	F	IP3	AD	H	.	100	.	0	.	.	S	.	+	.	0	0	1	.	0	0	.	0	0	.	.	+	+	.	91	16	3
M	30	1504	I	F	IP3	AD	H	.	100	P	0	.	.	S	.	+	.	0	0	0	.	5	0	.	0	0	.	+	.	.	.	81	18	2
M	11	1505	I	F	IP3	AD	H	.	100	.	0	.	.	S	.	+	.	0	0	0	.	0	0	.	0	0	.	.	+	.	.	64	28	2
M	3	1506	I	F	IP3	AD	H	.	100	.	0	.	.	S	.	+	.	0	1	0	.	0	0	.	3	0	.	.	.	.	.	69	21	3
M	8	1507	I	F	IP3	AD	H	.	100	.	0	.	.	S	.	+	.	0	3	1	.	0	0	.	0	0	.	.	.	.	.	73	22	4
M	8	1508	I	F	IP3	AD	H	.	100	P	0	.	.	S	.	+	.	0	1	0	.	0	1	.	0	0	.	.	.	.	.	101	14	4
M	50	1509	I	F	IP3	AD	H	.	100	.	0	.	.	S	.	+	.	0	0	1	.	0	0	.	3	0	.	+	.	.	.	103	14	3
M	8	1510	I	F	IP3	AD	H	.	100	P	0	.	.	S	.	+	.	0	0	0	.	0	0	.	4	0	.	+	.	.	.	89	16	4
M	6	1511	I	F	IP3	AD	H	.	100	.	0	.	.	S	.	+	.	0	0	0	.	0	0	.	0	0	.	.	+	+	+	82	16	4
M	6	1512	I	F	IP3	AD	H	.	100	.	0	.	.	S	.	+	.	0	0	0	.	0	0	.	0	0	.	+	.	.	.	74	21	4
M	8	1513	I	F	IP3	AD	H	.	100	.	0	.	.	S	.	+	.	0	0	0	.	0	0	.	0	0	.	.	.	.	.	76	16	3
M	30	1514	I	F	IP3	AD	H	.	100	.	0	.	.	S	.	+	.	0	0	1	.	0	0	.	0	0	.	.	.	.	.	86	15	3
M	8	1515	I	F	IP3	AD	H	.	100	.	0	.	.	S	.	+	.	0	0	0	.	3	0	.	0	0	.	+	.	.	.	79	15	6
M	8	1516	I	F	IP3	AD	H	.	100	.	0	.	.	S	.	+	.	0	0	0	.	3	0	.	0	0	.	.	.	.	.	72	17	5
M	11	1517	I	F	IP3	AD	H	.	60	.	0	.	.	S	.	+	.	0	0	0	.	0	0	.	2	0	.	.	+	+	.	77	15	3
M	8	1518	I	F	IP3	AD	H	.	100	P	0	.	.	S	.	+	.	0	0	0	.	0	0	.	0	0	.	.	.	.	.	85	13	2
M	30	1519	I	F	IP3	AD	H	.	100	.	0	.	.	S	.	+	.	0	0	0	.	0	0	.	0	0	.	.	.	.	.	83	11	3
M	8	1520	I	F	IP3	AD	H	.	100	.	0	.	.	S	.	+	.	0	0	0	.	0	0	.	0	0	.	.	.	.	.	86	13	4
M	11	1521	I	F	IP3	AD	H	.	90	.	0	.	.	S	.	+	.	0	0	0	.	0	0	.	0	0	.	.	+	+	.	64	16	5
M	8	1522	I	F	IP3	AD	H	.	100	.	0	.	.	S	.	+	.	0	0	0	.	0	0	.	0	0	.	.	.	.	.	74	15	3
M	7	1523	I	F	IP3	AD	H	.	100	.	0	.	.	S	.	+	.	0	0	0	.	0	0	.	0	0	.	+	+	.	+	76	17	4
M	50	1524	I	F	IP3	AD	H	.	50	.	0	.	.	S	.	+	.	0	0	0	.	0	0	.	3	0	.	.	+	+	.	67	18	5
M	8	1525	I	F	IP3	AD	H	.	100	.	0	.	.	S	.	+	.	0	0	0	.	1	0	.	1	4	.	.	.	.	.	72	16	5
M	8	1526	I	F	IP3	AD	H	.	100	.	0	.	.	S	.	+	.	0	0	0	.	0	0	.	0	0	.	+	.	.	.	75	16	5
M	7	1527	I	F	IP3	AD	H	.	100	.	0	.	.	S	.	+	.	0	0	0	.	0	0	.	0	0	.	+	.	.	.	67	18	6
M	11	1528	I	F	IP3	AD	H	.	60	.	0	.	.	S	.	+	.	0	1	0	.	0	0	.	0	0	.	.	+	+	+	54	19	2
M	8	1529	I	F	IP3	AD	H	.	100	.	0	.	.	S	.	+	.	0	0	0	.	0	0	.	0	0	.	+	.	.	.	61	18	2
M	8	1530	I	F	IP3	AD	H	.	100	P	0	.	.	S	.	+	.	0	1	0	.	1	0	.	0	0	.	.	.	.	.	52	18	4
M	8	1531	I	F	IP3	AD	H	.	100	.	0	.	.	S	.	+	.	0	1	0	.	4	0	.	0	0	.	.	.	.	.	53	18	5

0.1	0.2	0.3	0.9	1.0	1.1	1.2	1.3	1.4	1.5	1.6	1.7	1.8	1.9	2.0	2.3	2.4	2.5	3.7	3.8	4.0	4.1	4.2	4.3	4.4	4.9	5.4	5.9	6.4	9.3	9.4	9.5	9.6	9.7	9.8
M	7	1532	I	F	IP3	AD	H	-	20	-	0	+	-	S	-	+	-	0	0	0	-	0	0	-	0	0	-	-	+	+	+	52	18	5
M	11	1533	I	F	IP3	AD	H	-	100	-	0	-	-	S	-	+	-	0	0	0	-	0	0	-	0	0	-	-	-	-	-	51	22	5
M	7	1534	I	F	IP3	AD	H	-	100	-	0	-	-	O	-	+	-	0	0	0	-	0	0	-	0	0	-	-	-	-	-			
M	8	1535	I	F	IP3	AD	H	-	100	P	0	-	-	O	-	+	-	0	0	0	-	0	0	-	0	0	-	-	-	-	-			
M	6	1536	I	F	IP3	AD	H	-	100	-	0	-	-	S	-	+	-	0	0	1	-	0	0	-	0	0	-	+	-	-	-	62	16	3
M	11	1537	I	F	IP3	AD	H	-	100	P	0	-	-	S	-	+	-	0	0	0	-	0	0	-	0	0	-	+	-	-	-	80	11	3
M	11	1538	I	F	IP3	AD	H	-	70	-	0	-	-	S	-	+	-	0	0	0	-	0	0	-	0	0	-	-	+	+	-	-	16	4
M	8	1539	I	F	IP3	AD	H	-	100	-	0	-	-	S	-	+	-	0	0	0	-	0	0	-	0	0	-	-	-	-	-	54	17	4
M	8	1540	I	F	IP3	AD	H	-	100	-	0	-	-	S	-	+	-	0	1	0	-	1	0	-	0	0	-	-	-	-	-	54	18	4
M	8	1541	I	F	IP3	AD	H	-	90	-	0	-	-	S	-	+	-	0	0	0	-	0	0	-	0	0	-	+	-	-	-	53	17	3
M	11	1542	I	F	IP3	AD	H	-	100	-	0	-	-	S	-	+	-	0	0	0	-	0	0	-	0	0	-	+	-	-	-	61	14	2
M	8	1543	I	F	IP3	AD	H	-	100	-	0	-	-	S	-	+	-	0	0	0	-	0	0	-	0	0	-	-	-	-	-	87	10	5
M	30	1544	I	F	IP3	AD	H	-	100	-	0	-	-	S	-	+	-	0	0	0	-	0	0	-	0	0	-	-	-	-	-	76	12	2
M	8	1545	I	F	IP3	AD	H	-	100	-	0	-	-	S	-	+	-	0	0	0	-	1	0	-	0	0	-	+	+	-	-	35	17	3
M	8	1546	I	F	IP3	AD	H	-	100	-	0	-	-	S	-	+	-	0	0	0	-	0	0	-	4	0	-	-	-	-	-	39	21	4
M	8	1547	I	F	IP3	AD	H	-	100	-	0	-	-	S	-	+	-	0	0	0	-	0	0	-	0	0	-	-	-	-	-	56	13	2
M	7	1548	I	F	IP3	AD	H	-	20	-	0	-	-	S	-	+	-	0	0	0	-	0	0	-	0	0	-	-	-	+	-	43	19	3
M	8	1549	I	F	IP3	AD	H	-	100	-	0	-	-	S	-	+	-	0	0	0	-	0	0	-	0	0	-	-	-	-	-	63	15	2
M	7	1550	I	F	IP3	AD	H	-	100	-	0	-	-	S	-	+	-	0	0	0	-	0	0	-	0	0	-	+	-	-	-	62	12	2
M	19	1551	I	F	IP3	AD	H	-	100	-	0	-	-	S	-	+	-	0	0	0	-	0	0	-	0	0	-	+	-	-	-	45	20	3
M	8	1552	I	F	IP3	AD	H	-	100	-	0	-	-	S	-	+	-	0	0	0	-	3	0	-	0	0	-	-	-	-	-	33	17	5
M	8	1553	I	F	IP3	AD	H	-	100	-	0	-	-	S	-	+	-	0	0	0	-	0	0	-	0	0	-	+	-	-	-	51	14	4
M	8	1554	I	F	IP3	AD	H	-	100	-	0	-	-	S	-	+	-	0	0	0	-	0	0	-	0	0	-	-	-	-	-	53	17	4
M	11	1555	I	F	IP3	AD	H	-	100	-	0	-	-	S	-	+	-	0	1	0	-	0	0	-	2	0	-	-	-	-	-	50	21	4
M	8	1556	I	F	IP3	AD	H	-	100	-	0	-	-	S	-	+	-	0	0	0	-	1	0	-	0	0	-	-	-	-	-	58	14	2
M	8	1557	I	F	IP3	AD	H	-	100	-	0	-	-	S	-	+	-	0	0	0	-	0	0	-	0	0	-	-	-	-	-	49	14	4
M	9	1558	I	F	IP3	AD	H	-	100	-	0	-	-	S	-	+	-	0	0	0	-	0	0	-	0	0	-	+	+	-	+	39	17	5
M	8	1559	I	F	IP3	AD	H	-	100	-	0	-	-	S	-	+	-	0	0	0	-	1	0	-	0	0	-	-	-	-	-	43	16	4
M	8	1560	I	F	IP3	AD	H	-	100	-	0	-	-	S	-	+	-	0	0	0	-	0	0	-	0	0	-	-	-	-	-	44	19	4
M	7	1561	I	F	IP3	AD	H	-	100	-	0	-	-	S	-	+	-	0	0	0	-	0	0	-	0	0	-	-	-	-	-	39	14	5
M	8	1562	I	F	IP3	AD	H	-	100	-	0	-	-	S	-	+	-	0	0	0	-	0	0	-	0	0	-	-	-	-	-	38	18	3
M	7	1563	I	F	IP3	AD	H	-	100	-	0	-	-	S	-	+	-	0	0	3	+	0	0	-	0	0	-	+	-	-	-	48	13	4
M	8	1564	I	F	IP3	AD	H	-	100	-	0	-	-	S	-	+	-	0	0	0	-	2	0	-	0	0	-	+	-	-	-	44	9	4
M	30	1565	I	F	IP3	AD	H	-	100	-	0	-	-	O	-	+	-	0	0	1	-	0	0	-	0	0	-	-	-	-	-			
M	8	1566	I	F	IP3	AD	H	-	100	-	0	-	-	S	-	+	-	0	0	0	-	0	0	-	0	0	-	+	-	-	-	29	16	5
M	30	1567	I	F	IP3	AD	H	-	100	-	0	-	-	S	-	+	-	0	0	0	-	0	0	-	0	0	-	-	-	-	-	50	12	3
M	8	1568	I	F	IP3	AD	H	-	80	-	0	-	-	S	+	+	-	0	0	0	-	0	0	-	0	0	-	-	+	+	+	-	-	-
M	3	1569	I	F	IP3	AD	H	-	100	-	0	-	-	S	-	+	-	0	0	0	-	0	0	-	0	0	-	+	-	-	-	38	11	2
M	8	1570	I	F	IP3	AD	H	-	100	-	0	-	-	S	-	+	-	0	0	0	-	0	0	-	0	0	-	-	-	-	-	41	12	3
M	8	1571	I	F	IP3	AD	H	-	100	-	0	-	-	S	-	+	-	0	0	0	-	0	1	-	0	0	-	-	-	-	-	33	11	5
M	50	1572	I	F	IP3	AD	H	137	90	-	0	+	-	S	-	+	-	0	0	0	-	4	0	-	0	0	-	+	-	-	-	68	19	2
M	11	1573	I	F	IP3	AD	H	137	100	-	0	-	-	S	-	+	-	0	0	1	-	0	0	-	0	0	-	-	+	+	-	44	19	4
M	6	1574	I	F	IP3	AD	H	138	100	-	0	-	-	S	-	+	-	0	0	0	-	2	0	-	0	0	-	-	-	-	-	58	12	4
M	6	1575	I	F	IP3	AD	H	138	100	-	0	-	-	S	-	+	-	0	0	0	-	2	0	-	0	0	-	-	-	-	-	63	12	3
M	30	1576	I	F	IP3	AD	H	139	100	-	0	-	-	S	-	+	-	0	0	0	-	0	0	-	4	0	-	+	-	-	-	52	15	3
M	30	1577	I	F	IP3	AD	H	139	100	-	0	-	-	S	-	+	-	0	0	0	-	0	0	-	1	0	-	-	-	-	-	54	10	3
M	8	1578	I	F	IP3	AD	H	140	100	-	0	-	-	S	-	+	-	0	0	0	-	0	0	-	0	0	-	-	-	-	-	65	19	4
M	8	1579	I	F	IP3	AD	H	140	100	-	0	-	-	S	-	+	-	0	0	0	-	0	0	-	0	0	-	-	-	-	-	55	10	4
M	11	1580	I	F	IP4	IM	H	-	100	-	0	-	-	O	+	+	-	0	0	0	-	0	0	-	0	0	-	-	-	-	-			
M	8	1581	I	F	IP4	IM	H	-	100	-	0	-	-	S	-	+	-	0	0	0	-	0	0	-	0	0	-	-	-	-	-	58	12	1
M	8	1582	I	F	IP4	IM	H	-	100	-	0	-	-	S	-	+	-	0	0	1	-	0	0	-	0	0	-	-	-	-	-	47	9	1
M	8	1583	I	F	IP4	AD	H	-	100	-	0	-	-	S	-	+	-	0	0	0	-	0	0	-	0	0	-	-	-	-	-	85	9	2
M	11	1584	I	F	IP4	AD	H	-	100	-	0	-	-	S	-	+	-	0	0	0	-	0	0	-	0	0	-	-	+	-	-	81	11	3
M	6	1585	I	F	IP4	AD	H	-	80	-	0	-	-	O	-	+	-	0	0	0	-	0	0	-	0	0	-	-	-	-	-			
M	6	1586	I	F	IP4	AD	H	-	100	-	0	-	-	O	-	+	-	0	0	0	-	0	0	-	0	0	-	-	-	-	-			
M	50	1587	I	F	IP4	AD	H	-	100	-	0	-	-	S	-	+	-	0	0	0	-	1	0	-	0	4	-	-	-	-	-	70	10	2
M	6	1588	I	F	IP4	AD	H	-	90	-	0	-	-	S	-	+	-	0	0	1	-	0	0	-	0	0	-	+	-	-	-	67	10	2
M	7	1589	I	F	IP4	AD	H	-	100	-	0	-	-	S	-	+	-	0	1	0	-	0	0	-	0	0	-	-	+	+	+	60	10	2

01	02	03	09	10	11	12	13	14	15	16	17	18	19	20	23	24	25	37	38	40	41	42	43	44	49	54	59	64	93	94	95	96	97	98
M	8	1590	I	F	IP4	AD	H	-	100	-	0	-	-	S	-	+	-	0	0	1	-	0	0	-	0	0	-	-	-	-	-	45	12	2
M	30	1591	I	F	IP4	AD	H	-	100	-	0	-	-	S	-	+	-	0	0	0	-	0	0	-	0	0	-	+	-	-	-	66	7	3
M	7	1592	I	F	IP4	AD	H	-	100	-	0	-	-	S	-	+	-	0	0	1	-	0	0	-	0	0	-	-	-	-	-	74	5	2
M	6	1593	I	F	IP4	AD	H	-	100	-	0	-	-	S	-	+	-	0	0	0	-	0	0	-	0	0	-	-	-	-	-	66	6	2
M	30	1594	I	F	IP4	AD	H	-	100	-	0	-	-	S	-	+	-	0	0	0	-	0	0	-	0	0	-	+	-	-	-	65	8	2
M	7	1595	I	F	IP4	AD	H	-	20	-	0	-	-	S	+	+	-	0	0	0	-	0	0	-	0	0	-	-	+	+	+	-	-	-
M	11	1596	I	F	IP4	AD	H	-	100	-	0	-	-	S	-	+	-	0	0	0	-	0	0	-	0	0	-	-	-	-	-	57	8	2
M	7	1597	I	F	IP4	AD	H	-	100	-	0	-	-	S	-	+	-	0	0	0	-	0	0	-	0	0	-	-	-	-	-	43	8	3
M	6	1598	I	F	IP4	AD	H	-	100	-	0	-	-	S	-	+	-	0	0	0	-	0	0	+	0	0	-	-	-	-	-	38	12	3
M	8	1599	I	F	IP4	AD	H	-	100	-	0	-	-	S	-	+	-	0	0	0	-	0	0	-	0	0	-	-	-	-	-	43	8	2
M	8	1600	I	F	IP4	AD	H	-	100	-	0	-	-	S	-	+	-	0	0	0	-	0	0	-	0	0	-	-	-	-	-	38	7	2
M	50	1601	I	F	IP4	AD	H	-	100	-	0	-	-	S	-	+	-	0	0	0	-	0	0	-	0	0	-	-	-	-	-	33	11	2
M	6	1602	I	F	IP4	AD	H	-	100	-	0	-	-	O	-	+	-	0	0	0	-	0	0	-	0	0	-	-	-	-	-			
M	50	1603	I	F	IP4	AD	H	-	100	-	0	-	-	O	+	+	-	0	0	0	-	0	0	-	0	0	-	-	-	-	-			
M	8	1604	I	F	IP4	AD	H	-	100	-	0	-	-	O	-	+	-	0	0	1	-	0	0	-	0	0	-	-	-	-	-			
M	7	1605	I	F	IP4	AD	H	-	10	-	0	-	-	S	+	+	-	0	0	0	-	0	0	-	0	0	-	-	-	-	-	-	-	-
M	11	1606	I	F	IP4	AD	H	-	10	-	0	-	-	S	+	+	-	0	0	0	-	0	0	-	0	0	-	-	-	+	+	-	-	-
M	6	1607	I	F	IP4	AD	H	-	100	-	0	-	-	O	+	+	-	0	0	0	-	0	0	-	0	0	-	-	-	-	-			
M	11	1608	I	F	IP4	AD	H	-	0	-	0	-	-	S	+	+	-	0	0	0	-	0	0	-	0	0	-	-	-	-	-	-	-	-
M	19	1609	I	F	IP4	AD	H	-	100	-	0	-	-	S	-	+	-	0	0	0	-	0	0	-	0	0	-	-	-	-	-	27	7	1
M	6	1610	I	F	IP4	AD	H	-	100	-	0	-	-	O	-	+	-	0	0	0	-	0	0	-	0	0	-	-	-	-	-			
M	11	1611	I	F	IP4	AD	H	-	20	-	0	-	-	S	+	+	-	0	0	0	-	0	0	-	0	0	-	-	-	+	+	-	-	-
M	11	1612	I	F	IP4	AD	H	-	100	-	0	-	-	O	+	+	-	0	0	0	-	0	0	-	0	0	-	-	-	-	-			
M	11	1613	I	F	IP4	AD	H	-	100	-	0	-	-	O	+	+	-	0	0	0	-	0	0	-	0	0	-	-	-	-	-			
M	6	1614	I	F	IP4	AD	H	-	100	-	0	-	-	S	+	+	-	0	0	0	-	0	0	-	0	0	-	-	-	-	-	-	-	-
M	3	1615	I	F	IP4	AD	H	-	100	-	0	-	-	S	+	+	-	0	0	0	-	0	0	-	0	0	-	-	+	-	+	-	-	-
M	8	1616	I	F	IP4	AD	H	-	100	-	0	-	-	O	-	+	-	0	0	0	+	0	0	-	0	0	-	-	-	-	-			
M	6	1617	I	F	IP4	AD	H	-	50	-	0	-	-	S	+	+	-	0	0	0	-	0	0	-	0	0	-	-	-	-	-	-	-	-
M	6	1618	I	F	IP4	AD	H	-	50	-	0	-	-	S	+	+	-	0	0	0	-	0	0	-	0	0	-	-	+	+	-	-	-	-
M	6	1619	I	F	IP4	AD	H	-	60	-	0	-	-	O	-	+	-	0	0	0	-	0	0	-	0	0	-	-	-	-	-			
M	6	1620	I	F	IP4	AD	H	-	100	-	0	-	-	O	+	+	-	0	0	0	-	0	0	-	0	0	-	-	-	-	-			
M	6	1621	I	F	IP4	AD	H	-	100	-	0	-	-	S	+	+	-	0	0	0	-	0	0	-	0	0	-	-	-	-	-	-	-	-
M	30	1622	I	F	IP4	AD	H	-	100	-	0	-	-	S	-	+	-	0	0	0	-	0	0	-	0	0	-	-	-	-	-	27	4	1
M	11	1623	I	F	IP4	AD	H	-	100	-	0	-	-	S	+	+	-	0	0	0	-	0	0	-	0	0	-	-	-	-	-	-	-	-
M	5	1624	I	F	IP4	AD	H	-	100	-	0	-	-	S	-	+	-	0	0	0	-	0	0	-	0	0	-	-	-	-	-	22	4	1
M	8	1625	I	F	IP4	AD	H	-	80	-	0	-	-	S	+	+	-	0	0	0	-	0	0	-	0	0	-	-	-	-	-	-	-	-
M	6	1626	I	F	IP4	AD	H	141	100	-	0	-	-	S	-	+	-	0	0	0	-	0	0	-	0	0	-	+	-	-	-	45	6	2
M	6	1627	I	F	IP4	AD	H	141	100	-	0	-	-	S	-	+	-	0	0	0	-	0	0	-	0	0	-	-	-	-	-	38	6	5

D: Handfoot

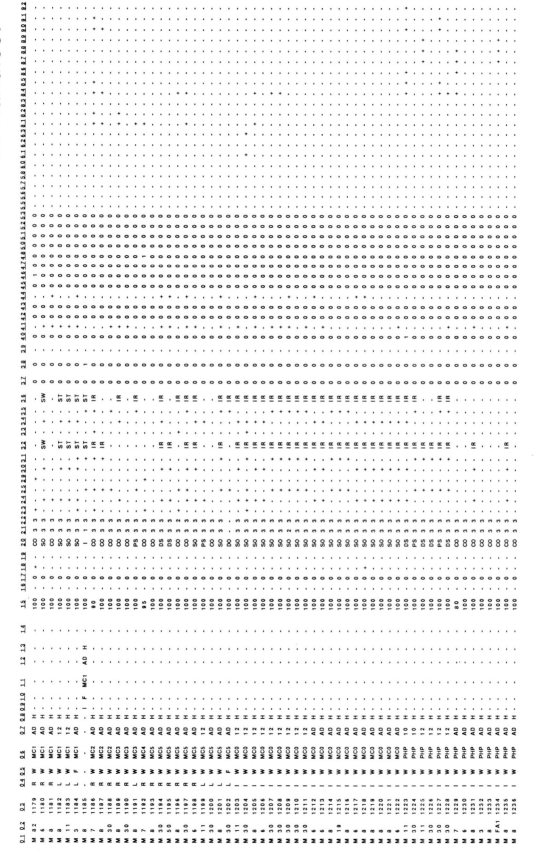

01	02	03	04	05	06	07	08	09	10	11	12	13	14	15	16	17	18	19	20	21	22	23	24	25	29	30	31	32	33	34	35	36	37	38	39	40	41	42	43	44	45	46	47	48	50	51	52	53	55	56	57	58	60	61	62	63	81	82	83	84	85	86	87	88	89	90	91	92
M	82	1179	R	W	MC1	AD	H	-	-	-	-	-	-	100	-	0	+	-	CO	3	3	+	-	-	+	-	-	-	-	-	-	-	0	0	-	0	-	0	0	-	0	1	0	0	0	0	0	0	-	-	-	-	-	-	-	-	-	-	-	-	-	-	-	-	-	-	-	-
M	6	1180	R	W	MC1	AD	H	-	-	-	-	-	-	100	-	0	-	-	SO	3	3	-	+	-	-	+	-	SW	-	+	-	SW	0	0	-	0	+	0	0	-	0	0	0	0	0	0	0	0	-	-	-	-	-	-	-	-	-	-	-	-	-	-	-	-	-	-	-	-
M	8	1181	R	W	MC1	AD	H	-	-	-	-	-	-	100	-	0	-	-	CO	3	3	-	+	-	-	-	-	-	-	-	-	-	0	0	-	0	+	0	0	+	0	0	0	0	0	0	0	0	-	-	-	-	-	-	-	-	-	-	-	-	-	-	-	-	-	-	-	-
M	8	1182	L	W	MC1	12	H	-	-	-	-	-	-	100	-	0	-	-	SO	3	3	-	+	-	-	+	-	ST	-	+	-	ST	0	0	-	0	+	0	0	-	0	0	0	0	0	0	0	0	-	-	-	-	-	-	-	-	-	-	-	-	-	-	-	-	-	-	-	-
M	11	1183	L	W	MC1	12	H	-	-	-	-	-	-	100	-	0	-	-	SO	3	3	-	+	-	-	+	-	ST	-	+	-	ST	0	0	-	0	+	0	0	-	0	0	0	0	0	0	0	0	-	-	-	-	-	-	-	-	-	-	-	-	-	-	-	-	-	-	-	-
M	3	1184	L	F	MC1	AD	H	-	-	-	-	-	-	100	-	0	-	-	SO	3	3	+	+	-	-	+	+	ST	-	+	-	ST	0	0	-	0	+	0	0	+	0	0	0	0	0	0	0	0	-	-	-	-	-	-	-	-	-	-	-	-	-	-	-	-	-	-	-	-
M	8	1185	-	-	-	-	-	I	F	MC1	AD	H	-	100	-	0	-	-	I	1	3	-	-	+	-	-	+	ST	-	-	+	ST	0	1	-	0	-	0	0	-	0	0	0	0	0	0	0	0	-	-	-	-	-	-	-	-	-	-	-	-	-	-	-	-	-	-	-	-
M	7	1186	R	W	MC2	AD	H	-	-	-	-	-	-	90	-	0	-	-	CO	3	3	+	-	+	-	-	+	IR	+	-	+	IR	0	0	-	0	-	0	0	-	0	0	0	0	0	0	0	0	-	-	-	-	-	-	-	-	+	+	-	+	+	-	-	-	-	+	+	-
M	8	1187	R	W	MC2	AD	H	-	-	-	-	-	-	100	-	0	-	-	CO	3	3	-	-	+	-	-	+	IR	-	-	-	-	0	0	-	0	-	0	0	-	0	0	0	0	0	0	0	0	-	-	-	-	-	-	-	-	+	-	-	+	-	-	-	-	-	+	-	-
M	30	1188	R	W	MC2	AD	H	-	-	-	-	-	-	100	-	0	-	-	CO	3	3	-	-	+	-	-	-	-	-	-	+	-	0	0	-	0	+	0	0	-	0	0	0	0	0	0	0	0	-	-	-	-	-	-	-	-	-	-	-	-	-	-	-	-	-	-	-	-
M	8	1189	R	W	MC3	AD	H	-	-	-	-	-	-	100	-	0	-	-	CO	3	3	-	+	-	-	-	-	-	-	+	-	IR	0	0	-	0	+	0	0	-	0	0	0	0	0	0	0	0	-	-	-	-	-	-	-	-	+	+	-	-	-	-	-	-	-	-	-	-
M	30	1190	R	W	MC3	AD	H	-	-	-	-	-	-	100	-	0	-	-	CO	3	3	-	-	-	-	-	-	-	-	-	-	-	0	0	-	0	+	0	0	-	0	0	0	0	0	0	0	0	-	-	-	-	-	-	-	-	-	-	-	-	-	-	-	-	-	-	-	-
M	8	1191	L	W	MC3	AD	H	-	-	-	-	-	-	100	-	0	-	-	PS	3	3	-	-	+	-	-	-	-	-	-	+	IR	0	0	-	0	-	0	0	-	0	0	0	0	0	0	0	0	-	-	-	-	-	-	-	-	+	-	-	-	-	-	-	-	-	-	-	-
M	7	1192	R	W	MC4	AD	H	-	-	-	-	-	-	95	-	0	-	-	CO	3	3	+	-	-	+	-	-	-	-	-	-	-	0	0	-	0	-	0	0	-	0	0	0	1	0	0	0	0	-	-	-	-	-	-	-	-	+	-	-	-	-	-	-	-	-	-	-	-
M	8	1193	R	W	MC5	AD	H	-	-	-	-	-	-	100	-	0	-	-	CO	3	3	-	-	-	-	-	-	-	-	-	-	-	0	0	-	0	-	0	0	-	0	0	0	0	0	0	0	0	-	-	-	-	-	-	-	-	-	-	-	-	-	-	-	-	-	-	-	-
M	30	1194	R	W	MC5	AD	H	-	-	-	-	-	-	100	-	0	-	-	DS	3	3	-	+	-	-	+	-	IR	-	+	-	IR	0	0	-	0	+	0	0	+	0	0	0	0	0	0	0	0	-	-	-	-	-	-	-	-	-	-	-	-	-	-	-	-	-	-	-	-
M	50	1195	R	W	MC5	AD	H	-	-	-	-	-	-	100	-	0	-	-	DS	3	3	-	+	-	-	+	-	IR	-	-	-	-	0	0	-	0	+	0	0	+	0	0	0	0	0	0	0	0	-	-	-	-	-	-	-	-	-	-	-	-	-	-	-	-	-	-	-	-
M	8	1196	R	W	MC5	AD	H	-	-	-	-	-	-	100	-	0	-	-	CO	3	2	+	-	+	-	-	-	-	+	-	-	IR	0	0	-	0	-	0	0	-	0	0	0	0	0	0	0	0	-	-	-	-	-	-	-	-	-	-	-	+	-	-	-	-	-	-	-	-
M	30	1197	R	W	MC5	AD	H	-	-	-	-	-	-	100	-	0	-	-	CO	3	3	-	+	+	-	+	-	IR	-	-	+	IR	0	0	-	0	+	0	0	+	0	0	0	0	0	0	0	0	-	-	-	-	-	-	-	-	+	-	-	+	-	-	-	-	-	-	-	-
M	6	1198	R	W	MC5	AD	H	-	-	-	-	-	-	100	-	0	-	-	SO	3	3	-	+	-	-	+	-	IR	-	+	-	IR	0	0	-	0	+	0	0	-	0	0	0	0	0	0	0	0	-	-	-	-	-	-	-	-	-	-	-	-	-	-	-	-	-	-	-	-
M	11	1199	L	W	MC5	12	H	-	-	-	-	-	-	100	-	0	-	-	PS	3	3	-	+	-	-	-	-	-	-	+	-	-	0	0	-	0	-	0	0	-	0	0	0	0	0	0	0	0	-	-	-	-	-	-	-	-	-	-	-	-	-	-	-	-	-	-	-	-
M	30	1200	L	W	MC5	AD	H	-	-	-	-	-	-	100	-	0	-	-	CO	3	3	-	-	-	-	-	-	-	-	-	-	-	0	0	-	0	-	0	0	-	0	0	0	0	0	0	0	0	-	-	-	-	-	-	-	-	-	-	-	-	-	-	-	-	-	-	-	-
M	8	1201	L	W	MC5	AD	H	-	-	-	-	-	-	100	-	0	-	-	SO	3	3	-	-	+	-	-	+	IR	-	-	+	IR	0	0	-	0	+	0	0	+	0	0	0	0	0	0	0	0	-	-	-	-	-	-	-	-	-	-	-	-	-	-	-	-	-	-	-	-
M	30	1202	L	F	MC5	AD	H	-	-	-	-	-	-	100	-	0	-	-	DO	-	-	-	-	+	-	-	-	-	-	-	+	IR	0	0	-	0	-	0	0	-	0	0	0	0	0	0	0	0	-	-	-	-	-	-	-	-	-	-	-	-	-	-	-	-	-	-	-	-
M	11	1203	I	W	MC0	12	H	-	-	-	-	-	-	100	-	0	-	-	SO	3	3	-	+	-	-	+	-	IR	-	+	-	IR	0	0	-	0	+	0	0	-	0	0	0	0	0	0	0	0	-	-	-	-	-	-	-	-	-	-	-	-	-	-	-	-	-	-	-	-
M	30	1204	I	W	MC0	12	H	-	-	-	-	-	-	100	-	0	-	-	SO	3	3	+	+	+	-	-	+	IR	+	+	-	IR	0	0	-	0	-	0	0	-	0	0	0	0	0	0	0	0	-	-	-	-	-	+	-	+	-	-	-	-	-	-	-	-	-	-	-	-
M	8	1205	I	W	MC0	12	H	-	-	-	-	-	-	100	-	0	-	-	SO	3	3	-	+	-	-	+	-	IR	-	+	-	IR	0	0	-	0	+	0	0	+	0	0	0	0	0	0	0	0	-	-	-	-	-	-	-	-	+	-	-	+	-	-	-	-	-	-	-	-
M	6	1206	I	W	MC0	12	H	-	-	-	-	-	-	100	-	0	-	-	SO	3	3	-	+	-	-	+	-	IR	-	+	-	IR	0	0	-	0	-	0	0	-	0	0	0	0	0	0	0	0	-	-	-	-	-	-	-	-	-	-	-	-	-	-	-	-	-	-	-	-
M	30	1207	I	W	MC0	12	H	-	-	-	-	-	-	100	-	0	-	-	SO	3	3	-	-	+	-	-	+	IR	-	-	+	IR	0	0	-	0	+	0	0	-	0	0	0	0	0	0	0	0	-	-	-	-	-	-	-	-	-	-	-	+	-	-	-	-	-	-	-	-
M	30	1208	I	W	MC0	12	H	-	-	-	-	-	-	100	-	0	-	-	SO	3	3	-	-	+	-	-	+	IR	-	-	+	IR	0	0	-	0	+	0	0	-	0	0	0	0	0	0	0	0	-	-	-	-	-	-	-	-	-	-	-	+	-	-	-	-	-	-	-	-
M	30	1209	I	W	MC0	12	H	-	-	-	-	-	-	100	-	0	-	-	SO	2	3	-	-	+	-	-	+	IR	-	-	+	IR	0	0	-	0	+	0	0	+	0	0	0	0	0	0	0	0	-	-	-	-	-	-	-	-	-	-	-	-	-	-	-	-	-	-	-	-
M	30	1210	I	W	MC0	12	H	-	-	-	-	-	-	100	-	0	-	-	SO	3	3	-	-	+	-	-	+	IR	-	-	+	IR	0	0	-	0	-	0	0	-	0	0	0	0	0	0	0	0	-	-	-	-	-	-	-	-	-	-	-	-	-	-	-	-	-	-	-	-
M	30	1211	I	W	MC0	12	H	-	-	-	-	-	-	100	-	0	-	-	SO	3	3	-	-	+	-	-	+	IR	-	-	+	IR	0	0	-	0	+	0	0	-	0	0	0	0	0	0	0	0	-	-	-	-	-	-	-	-	-	-	-	-	-	-	-	-	-	-	-	-
M	6	1212	I	W	MC0	AD	H	-	-	-	-	-	-	100	-	0	-	-	SO	3	3	-	+	-	-	+	-	IR	-	+	-	IR	0	0	-	0	-	0	0	+	0	0	0	0	0	0	0	0	-	-	-	-	-	-	-	-	-	-	-	-	-	-	-	-	-	-	-	-
M	6	1213	I	W	MC0	AD	H	-	-	-	-	-	-	100	-	0	-	-	SO	3	3	-	+	-	-	+	-	IR	-	+	-	IR	0	0	-	0	+	0	0	-	0	0	0	0	0	0	0	0	-	-	-	-	-	-	-	-	-	-	-	-	-	-	-	-	-	-	-	-
M	8	1214	I	W	MC0	AD	H	-	-	-	-	-	-	100	-	0	-	-	SO	3	3	-	-	+	-	-	+	IR	-	-	+	IR	0	0	-	0	-	0	0	-	0	0	0	0	0	0	0	0	-	-	-	-	-	-	-	-	-	-	-	-	-	-	-	-	-	-	-	-
M	19	1215	I	W	MC0	AD	H	-	-	-	-	-	-	100	-	0	-	-	SO	3	3	-	-	+	-	-	+	IR	-	-	+	IR	0	0	-	0	-	0	0	-	0	0	0	0	0	0	0	0	-	-	-	-	-	-	-	-	-	-	-	-	-	-	-	-	-	-	-	-
M	8	1216	I	W	MC0	AD	H	-	-	-	-	-	-	100	-	0	-	-	SO	3	3	-	-	+	-	-	+	IR	-	-	+	IR	0	0	-	0	-	0	0	-	0	0	0	0	0	0	0	0	-	-	-	-	-	-	-	-	-	-	-	-	-	-	-	-	-	-	-	-
M	6	1217	I	W	MC0	AD	H	-	-	-	-	-	-	100	-	0	-	-	SO	3	3	-	+	-	-	+	-	IR	-	+	-	IR	0	0	-	0	-	0	0	+	0	0	0	0	0	0	0	0	-	-	-	-	-	-	-	-	-	-	-	-	-	-	-	-	-	-	-	-
M	8	1218	I	W	MC0	AD	H	-	-	-	-	-	-	100	-	0	+	-	SO	3	3	-	+	-	-	+	-	IR	-	+	-	IR	0	0	-	0	-	0	0	+	0	0	0	0	0	0	0	0	-	-	-	-	-	-	-	-	-	-	-	-	-	-	-	-	-	-	-	-
M	8	1219	I	W	MC0	AD	H	-	-	-	-	-	-	100	-	0	-	-	SO	3	3	-	+	-	-	+	-	IR	-	+	-	IR	0	0	-	0	-	0	0	-	0	0	0	0	0	0	0	0	-	-	-	-	-	-	-	-	-	-	-	-	-	-	-	-	-	-	-	-
M	8	1220	I	W	MC0	AD	H	-	-	-	-	-	-	100	-	0	-	-	SO	3	3	-	+	-	-	+	-	IR	-	+	-	IR	0	0	-	0	-	0	0	-	0	0	0	0	0	0	0	0	-	-	-	-	-	-	-	-	-	-	-	-	-	-	-	-	-	-	-	-
M	8	1221	I	W	MC0	AD	H	-	-	-	-	-	-	100	-	0	-	-	SO	3	3	-	+	-	-	+	-	IR	-	+	-	IR	0	0	-	0	-	0	0	-	0	0	0	0	0	0	0	0	-	-	-	-	-	-	-	-	-	-	-	-	-	-	-	-	-	-	-	-
M	6	1222	I	W	MC0	AD	H	-	-	-	-	-	-	100	-	0	-	-	SO	3	3	-	+	-	-	+	-	IR	-	+	-	IR	0	0	-	0	+	0	0	-	0	0	0	0	0	0	0	0	-	-	-	-	-	-	-	-	-	-	-	-	-	-	-	-	-	-	-	-
M	11	1223	I	W	PHP	10	H	-	-	-	-	-	-	100	-	0	-	-	DS	3	3	-	+	-	-	+	-	IR	-	+	-	IR	0	0	-	1	-	0	0	-	0	0	0	0	0	0	0	0	-	-	-	-	-	-	-	-	-	-	-	+	+	+	-	-	-	+	-	+
M	30	1224	I	W	PHP	10	H	-	-	-	-	-	-	100	-	0	-	-	PS	3	3	-	-	+	-	-	+	IR	-	-	+	IR	0	0	-	0	-	0	0	-	0	0	0	0	0	0	0	0	-	-	-	-	-	-	-	-	-	-	-	-	-	-	-	-	-	-	-	-
M	11	1225	I	W	PHP	12	H	-	-	-	-	-	-	100	-	0	-	-	DS	3	3	-	-	+	-	-	+	IR	-	-	-	-	0	0	-	0	-	0	0	-	0	0	0	0	0	0	0	0	-	-	-	-	-	-	-	-	-	-	-	-	-	-	+	+	+	-	-	-
M	30	1226	I	W	PHP	12	H	-	-	-	-	-	-	100	-	0	-	-	DS	3	3	-	-	+	-	-	+	IR	-	-	-	-	0	0	-	0	-	0	0	-	0	0	0	0	0	0	0	0	-	-	-	-	-	-	-	-	-	-	-	-	-	-	-	-	-	-	-	-
M	30	1227	I	W	PHP	12	H	-	-	-	-	-	-	100	-	0	-	-	PS	3	3	-	-	+	-	-	+	IR	-	-	+	IR	0	0	-	0	-	0	0	-	0	0	0	0	0	0	0	0	-	-	-	-	-	-	-	-	-	-	-	+	+	-	-	-	-	+	+	-
M	30	1228	I	W	PHP	12	H	-	-	-	-	-	-	100	-	0	-	-	DS	3	3	-	-	+	-	-	+	IR	-	-	+	IR	0	0	-	0	+	0	0	-	0	0	0	0	0	0	0	0	-	-	-	-	-	-	-	-	-	-	-	+	-	-	-	-	-	-	-	-
M	7	1229	I	W	PHP	AD	H	-	-	-	-	-	-	80	-	0	-	-	CO	3	3	-	-	-	-	-	-	-	-	-	-	-	0	0	-	0	-	0	0	-	0	0	0	0	0	0	0	0	-	-	-	-	-	-	-	-	-	-	-	+	-	+	+	+	-	-	-	-
M	6	1230	I	W	PHP	AD	H	-	-	-	-	-	-	100	-	0	-	-	CO	3	3	-	-	-	-	-	-	-	-	-	-	-	0	0	-	0	-	0	0	-	0	0	0	0	0	0	0	0	-	-	-	-	-	-	-	-	-	-	-	-	-	-	-	-	-	-	-	-
M	8	1231	I	W	PHP	AD	H	-	-	-	-	-	-	100	-	0	-	-	CO	3	3	-	+	-	-	+	-	IR	-	-	-	-	0	0	-	0	+	0	0	-	0	0	0	0	0	0	0	0	-	-	-	-	-	-	-	-	-	-	-	-	-	-	-	-	-	-	-	-
M	3	1232	I	W	PHP	AD	H	-	-	-	-	-	-	100	-	0	-	-	CO	3	3	-	-	-	-	-	-	-	-	-	-	-	0	0	-	0	-	0	0	-	0	0	0	0	0	0	0	0	-	-	-	-	-	-	-	-	-	-	-	-	-	-	-	-	-	-	-	-
M	8	1233	I	W	PHP	AD	H	-	-	-	-	-	-	100	-	0	-	-	CO	3	3	-	-	-	-	-	-	-	-	-	-	-	0	0	-	0	-	0	0	-	0	0	0	0	0	0	0	0	-	-	-	-	-	-	-	-	-	-	-	-	-	-	-	-	-	-	-	-
M	FA1	1234	I	W	PHP	AD	H	-	-	-	-	-	-	100	-	0	-	-	CO	3	3	-	-	-	-	-	-	-	-	-	-	-	0	0	-	0	-	0	0	-	0	0	0	0	0	0	0	0	-	-	-	-	-	-	-	-	-	-	-	-	-	-	+	+	+	-	-	-
M	8	1235	I	W	PHP	AD	H	-	-	-	-	-	-	100	-	0	-	-	CO	3	3	-	+	-	-	+	-	IR	-	-	-	-	0	0	-	0	+	0	0	-	0	0	0	0	0	0	0	0	-	-	-	-	-	-	-	-	-	-	-	-	-	-	-	-	-	-	-	-
M	8	1236	I	W	PHP	AD	H	-	-	-	-	-	-	100	-	0	-	-	CO	3	3	-	-	-	-	-	-	-	-	-	-	-	0	0	-	0	-	0	0	-	0	0	0	0	0	0	0	0	-	-	-	-	-	-	-	-	-	-	-	-	-	-	-	-	-	-	-	-

01	02	03	04	05	06	07	08	09	10	11	12	13	14	15	16	17	18	19	20	21	22	23	24	25	28	30	31	32	33	34	35	36	37	38	39	40	41	42	43	44
M	6	1237	I	W	PHP	AD	H	-	-	-	-	-	-	100	-	0	-	-	CO	3	3	+	-	-	+	-	-	IR	-	-	-	-	0	0	-	0	-	0	0	-
M	6	1238	I	W	PHP	AD	H	-	-	-	-	-	-	90	-	0	-	-	CO	3	3	-	+	-	-	-	-	-	-	+	-	IR	0	0	-	0	-	0	0	-
M	8	1239	I	W	PHP	AD	H	-	-	-	-	-	-	100	-	0	-	-	CO	3	3	-	-	+	-	-	-	-	-	-	+	IR	0	0	-	0	-	0	0	-
M	8	1240	I	W	PHP	AD	H	-	-	-	-	-	-	100	-	0	-	-	PS	3	3	-	-	+	-	-	-	-	-	-	+	IR	0	0	-	0	-	0	0	-
M	30	1241	I	W	PHP	AD	H	-	-	-	-	-	-	100	-	0	-	-	PS	3	3	-	+	-	-	-	-	-	-	+	-	IR	0	0	-	0	-	0	0	-
M	8	1242	I	W	PHP	AD	H	-	-	-	-	-	-	100	-	0	-	-	DS	3	3	-	+	-	-	+	-	IR	-	-	-	-	0	0	-	0	+	0	0	-
M	8	1243	I	W	PHP	AD	H	-	-	-	-	-	-	100	-	0	-	-	DS	3	3	-	+	-	-	+	-	IR	-	-	-	-	0	0	-	0	+	0	0	-
M	8	1244	I	W	PHP	AD	H	-	-	-	-	-	-	100	-	0	-	-	DS	3	3	-	+	-	-	+	-	IR	-	-	-	-	0	0	-	0	-	0	0	-
M	6	1245	I	W	PHP	AD	H	-	-	-	-	-	-	100	-	0	-	-	DS	3	3	-	+	-	-	+	-	IR	-	-	-	-	0	0	-	0	+	0	0	-
M	8	1246	I	W	PHP	AD	H	-	-	-	-	-	-	100	-	0	-	-	DS	3	3	-	-	+	-	-	+	IR	-	-	-	-	0	0	-	0	-	0	0	-
M	6	1247	I	W	PHP	AD	H	-	-	-	-	-	-	100	-	0	-	-	DS	3	3	-	+	-	-	+	-	IR	-	-	-	-	0	0	-	0	-	0	0	-
M	6	1248	I	W	PHP	AD	H	-	-	-	-	-	-	100	-	0	-	-	DS	3	3	-	+	-	-	+	-	IR	-	+	-	IR	0	0	-	1	+	0	0	-
M	8	1249	I	W	PHP	AD	H	-	-	-	-	-	-	100	-	0	-	-	DS	3	3	-	+	-	-	+	-	IR	-	-	-	-	0	0	-	0	+	0	0	-
M	FA1	1250	I	W	PHP	AD	H	-	-	-	-	-	-	100	-	0	-	-	PS	3	3	-	+	-	-	-	-	-	-	+	-	IR	0	0	-	0	-	0	0	-
M	8	1251	I	W	PHP	AD	H	-	-	-	-	-	-	50	-	2	-	-	SO	3	3	-	-	+	-	-	+	IR	-	-	+	IR	0	0	-	0	-	0	0	-
M	6	1252	I	W	PHP	AD	H	-	-	-	-	-	-	60	-	0	-	-	SO	3	3	-	-	+	-	-	+	IR	-	-	+	IR	0	0	-	0	-	0	0	-
M	3	1253	I	W	PHP	AD	H	-	-	-	-	-	-	100	-	0	-	-	SO	3	3	-	+	-	-	+	-	IR	-	+	-	IR	0	0	-	0	-	0	0	-
M	6	1254	-	-	-	-	-	I	F	PHP	AD	H	-	100	-	0	-	-	I	2	3	-	+	-	-	+	-	IR	-	+	-	IR	0	0	-	0	-	0	0	+
M	8	1255	I	F	PHP	AD	H	-	-	-	-	-	-	100	-	0	-	-	DS	2	3	-	+	-	-	+	-	IR	-	+	-	IR	0	0	-	0	+	0	0	-
M	8	1256	I	W	IHP	AD	H	-	-	-	-	-	-	100	-	0	-	-	CO	3	3	-	-	-	-	-	-	-	-	-	-	-	0	0	-	0	+	0	0	-
M	6	1257	I	W	IHP	AD	H	-	-	-	-	-	-	100	-	0	-	-	CO	3	3	-	-	-	-	-	-	-	-	-	-	-	0	0	-	0	-	0	0	-
M	5	1258	I	W	IHP	AD	H	-	-	-	-	-	-	100	-	0	-	-	CO	3	3	-	-	-	-	-	-	-	-	-	-	-	0	0	-	0	-	0	0	-
M	8	1259	I	W	IHP	AD	H	-	-	-	-	-	-	100	-	0	-	-	CO	3	3	-	-	-	-	-	-	-	-	-	-	-	0	0	-	0	-	0	0	-
M	30	1260	I	W	IHP	AD	H	-	-	-	-	-	-	100	-	0	-	-	CO	3	3	-	-	-	-	-	-	-	-	-	-	-	0	0	-	0	-	0	0	-
-	8	1261	I	W	IHP	AD	H	-	-	-	-	-	-	100	-	0	-	-	CO	3	3	-	-	-	-	-	-	-	-	-	-	-	0	0	-	0	-	0	0	-
M	8	1262	I	W	IHP	AD	H	-	-	-	-	-	-	100	-	0	-	-	CO	3	3	-	-	-	-	-	-	-	-	-	-	-	0	0	-	0	-	0	0	-
M	30	1263	I	W	IHP	AD	H	-	-	-	-	-	-	100	-	0	-	-	CO	3	3	-	-	-	-	-	-	-	-	-	-	-	0	0	-	0	-	0	0	-
M	8	1264	I	W	IHP	AD	H	-	-	-	-	-	-	100	-	0	-	-	DS	3	3	-	+	-	-	+	-	IR	-	-	-	-	0	0	-	0	-	0	0	-
M	7	1265	I	W	IHP	AD	H	-	-	-	-	-	-	100	-	0	-	-	CO	3	3	-	-	+	-	-	+	IR	-	-	-	-	0	0	-	0	-	0	0	-
M	6	1266	I	W	IHP	AD	H	-	-	-	-	-	-	100	-	0	-	-	DS	3	3	-	+	-	-	+	-	IR	-	-	-	-	0	0	-	0	-	0	0	-
M	6	1267	I	W	IHP	AD	H	-	-	-	-	-	-	100	-	0	-	-	DS	3	3	-	-	+	-	-	+	IR	-	-	-	-	0	0	-	0	-	0	0	-
M	30	1268	I	W	IHP	AD	H	-	-	-	-	-	-	100	-	0	-	-	CO	3	3	-	-	-	-	-	-	-	-	-	-	-	0	0	-	0	-	0	0	-
M	8	1269	I	W	THP	AD	H	-	-	-	-	-	-	100	-	0	-	-	DS	3	3	-	-	+	-	-	+	IR	-	-	-	-	0	0	-	0	+	0	0	-
M	8	1293	R	W	MT1	AD	H	-	-	-	-	-	-	100	-	0	-	-	CO	3	3	-	-	-	-	-	-	-	-	-	-	-	0	0	-	0	+	0	0	-
M	8	1294	L	F	MT1	10	H	-	-	-	-	-	-	100	-	0	+	-	PS	3	3	-	+	-	-	-	-	-	-	+	-	IR	0	0	-	0	-	0	0	-
M	8	1295	L	W	MT1	AD	H	-	-	-	-	-	-	100	-	0	-	-	PS	3	3	-	+	-	-	-	-	-	-	+	-	IR	0	0	-	0	+	0	0	-
M	6	1296	L	W	MT1	AD	H	-	-	-	-	-	-	100	-	1	+	-	DS	3	3	+	-	+	+	-	+	IR	-	-	-	-	0	0	-	1	-	0	0	-
M	8	1297	-	-	-	-	-	I	F	MT1	AD	H	-	100	-	0	-	-	I	1	3	-	+	-	-	+	-	IR	-	+	-	IR	0	0	-	0	-	0	0	-
M	50	1298	R	W	MT2	AD	H	-	-	-	-	-	-	100	-	0	-	-	CO	3	3	+	+	+	-	+	-	IR	+	+	+	IR	0	0	-	0	+	0	0	-
M	8	1299	L	W	MT2	AD	H	-	-	-	-	-	-	100	-	0	-	-	PS	3	3	-	+	-	-	-	-	-	-	+	-	IR	0	0	-	0	+	0	0	-
M	8	1300	L	W	MT2	AD	H	-	-	-	-	-	-	100	-	0	-	-	PS	3	3	-	+	-	-	+	-	IR	-	+	-	IR	0	0	-	0	+	0	0	-
M	8	1301	R	W	MT3	AD	H	-	-	-	-	-	-	100	-	0	-	-	PS	3	3	-	+	-	-	+	-	IR	-	-	-	-	0	0	-	0	+	0	0	-
M	8	1302	R	W	MT3	AD	H	-	-	-	-	-	-	100	-	0	-	-	PS	3	3	-	-	-	-	-	-	-	-	-	-	-	0	0	-	0	+	0	0	-
M	50	1303	R	W	MT3	AD	H	-	-	-	-	-	-	100	-	0	-	-	PS	3	3	-	+	-	-	-	-	-	-	+	-	IR	0	0	-	0	+	0	0	-
M	5	1304	L	W	MT3	AD	H	-	-	-	-	-	-	100	-	0	-	-	CO	3	3	-	-	-	-	-	-	-	-	-	-	-	0	0	-	0	+	0	0	-
M	11	1305	L	F	MT3	AD	H	-	-	-	-	-	-	100	-	1	-	-	PS	3	3	-	+	+	-	-	+	IR	-	+	-	IR	0	0	-	1	-	0	0	-
M	8	1306	R	W	MT4	AD	H	-	-	-	-	-	-	100	-	0	-	-	PS	3	3	-	+	-	-	+	-	IR	-	+	-	IR	0	0	-	1	+	0	0	-
M	8	1307	R	W	MT4	AD	H	-	-	-	-	-	-	100	-	0	-	-	PS	3	3	-	+	-	-	+	-	IR	-	-	-	-	0	0	-	0	+	0	0	-
M	6	1308	R	W	MT5	AD	H	-	-	-	-	-	-	100	-	0	-	-	SO	3	3	-	+	-	-	+	-	IR	-	+	-	IR	0	0	-	0	+	0	0	+
M	30	1309	R	W	MT5	AD	H	-	-	-	-	-	-	100	-	0	-	-	SO	3	3	+	+	-	+	+	-	IR	-	+	-	IR	0	0	-	2	+	0	0	-
M	8	1310	I	W	MT0	AD	H	-	-	-	-	-	-	100	-	0	-	-	SO	3	3	-	+	-	-	+	-	IR	-	+	-	IR	0	0	-	0	+	0	0	-
M	8	1311	R	W	MT5	AD	H	-	-	-	-	-	-	100	-	0	-	-	SO	3	3	-	+	-	-	+	-	IR	-	+	-	IR	0	0	-	0	+	0	0	-
M	8	1312	R	W	MT5	AD	H	-	-	-	-	-	-	100	-	0	-	-	SO	3	3	-	+	-	-	+	-	IR	-	+	-	IR	0	0	-	0	+	0	0	-
M	8	1313	R	W	MT5	AD	H	-	-	-	-	-	-	100	-	0	-	-	SO	3	3	-	+	-	-	+	-	IR	-	+	-	IR	0	0	-	4	+	0	0	-
M	8	1314	R	W	MT5	AD	H	-	-	-	-	-	-	100	-	0	-	-	PS	3	3	-	-	-	-	-	-	-	-	-	-	-	0	0	-	0	+	0	0	-
M	8	1315	L	W	MT5	AD	H	-	-	-	-	-	-	100	-	0	-	-	SO	3	3	-	+	-	-	+	-	IR	-	-	-	-	0	0	-	0	+	0	0	-
M	8	1316	L	W	MT5	AD	H	-	-	-	-	-	-	100	-	0	-	-	SO	3	3	-	+	-	-	+	-	IR	-	+	-	IR	0	0	-	0	+	0	0	+
M	8	1317	L	W	MT5	AD	H	-	-	-	-	-	-	100	-	0	-	-	SO	3	3	-	+	-	-	+	-	IR	-	-	-	-	0	0	-	0	+	0	0	-
M	11	1318	L	W	MT5	AD	H	-	-	-	-	-	-	80	-	0	-	-	PS	3	3	-	+	-	-	+	-	IR	-	+	-	IR	0	0	-	0	+	0	0	-

03	45	46	47	48	50	51	52	53	55	56	57	58	60	61	62	63	81	82	83	84	85	86	87	88	89	90	91	92
1237	0	0	0	0	0	0	0	0	-	-	-	-	-	-	-	-	-	-	-	-	-	-	-	-	-	-	-	-
1238	0	0	0	0	0	0	0	0	-	-	-	-	-	-	-	-	-	-	-	+	-	+	+	+	+	-	-	-
1239	0	0	0	0	0	0	0	0	-	-	-	-	-	-	-	-	-	-	-	+	+	+	+	-	+	-	-	-
1240	0	0	0	0	0	0	0	0	-	-	-	-	-	-	-	-	-	-	-	+	+	+	+	-	-	+	+	+
1241	0	0	0	0	0	0	0	0	-	-	-	-	-	-	-	-	-	-	-	+	-	+	+	-	+	-	-	-
1242	0	0	0	0	0	0	0	0	-	-	-	-	-	-	-	-	-	-	-	-	-	-	-	-	-	-	-	-
1243	0	0	0	0	0	0	0	0	-	-	-	-	-	-	-	-	-	-	-	-	-	-	-	-	-	-	-	-
1244	0	0	0	0	0	0	0	0	-	-	-	-	-	-	-	-	-	-	-	-	-	-	-	-	-	-	-	-
1245	0	0	0	0	0	0	0	0	-	-	-	-	-	-	-	-	-	-	-	-	-	-	-	-	-	-	-	-
1246	0	0	0	0	0	0	0	0	-	-	-	-	-	-	-	-	-	-	-	-	-	-	-	-	-	-	-	-
1247	0	0	0	0	0	0	0	0	-	-	-	-	-	-	-	-	-	-	-	-	-	-	-	-	-	-	-	-
1248	0	0	0	0	0	0	0	0	-	-	-	-	-	-	-	-	-	-	-	-	-	-	+	-	+	-	-	-
1249	0	0	0	0	0	0	0	0	-	-	-	-	-	-	-	-	-	-	-	-	-	-	-	-	-	-	-	-
1250	0	0	0	0	0	0	0	0	-	-	-	-	-	-	-	-	-	-	-	+	+	+	-	-	-	-	-	-
1251	0	0	0	0	0	0	0	0	-	-	-	-	-	-	-	-	-	-	-	+	-	+	-	-	-	-	-	-
1252	0	0	0	0	0	0	0	0	-	-	-	-	-	-	-	-	-	-	-	+	+	-	-	-	-	-	-	-
1253	0	0	0	0	0	0	0	0	-	-	-	-	-	-	-	-	-	-	-	-	-	-	-	-	-	-	-	-
1254	0	0	0	0	0	0	0	0	-	-	-	-	-	-	-	-	-	-	-	-	-	-	-	-	-	-	-	-
1255	0	0	0	0	0	0	0	0	-	-	-	-	-	-	-	-	-	-	-	-	-	-	-	-	-	-	-	-
1256	0	0	0	0	0	0	0	0	-	-	-	-	-	-	-	-	-	-	-	-	-	-	-	-	-	-	-	-
1257	0	0	0	0	0	0	0	0	-	-	-	-	-	-	-	-	-	-	-	-	-	-	+	-	+	-	-	-
1258	0	0	0	0	0	0	0	0	-	-	-	-	-	-	-	-	-	-	-	-	-	-	+	+	-	-	-	-
1259	0	0	0	0	0	0	0	0	-	-	-	-	-	-	-	-	-	-	-	-	-	-	-	-	-	-	-	-
1260	0	0	0	0	0	0	0	0	-	-	-	-	-	-	-	-	-	-	-	-	-	-	+	-	-	-	-	-
1261	0	0	0	0	0	0	0	0	-	-	-	-	-	-	-	-	-	-	-	-	-	-	-	-	-	-	-	-
1262	0	0	0	0	0	0	0	0	-	-	-	-	-	-	-	-	-	-	-	-	-	-	-	-	-	-	-	-
1263	0	0	0	0	0	0	0	0	-	-	-	-	-	-	-	-	-	-	-	-	-	-	+	-	-	-	-	-
1264	0	0	0	0	0	0	0	0	-	-	-	-	-	-	-	-	-	-	-	-	-	-	-	-	-	-	-	-
1265	0	0	0	0	0	0	0	0	-	-	-	-	-	-	-	-	-	-	-	-	-	-	-	-	-	-	-	-
1266	0	0	0	0	0	0	0	0	-	-	-	-	-	-	-	-	-	-	-	-	-	-	-	-	-	-	-	-
1267	0	0	0	0	0	0	0	0	-	-	-	-	-	-	-	-	-	-	-	-	-	-	+	-	-	+	+	-
1268	0	0	0	0	0	0	0	0	-	-	-	-	-	-	-	-	-	-	-	-	-	-	-	-	-	-	-	-
1269	0	0	0	0	0	0	0	0	-	-	-	-	-	-	-	-	-	-	-	-	-	-	-	-	-	-	-	-
1293	0	0	0	0	0	0	0	0	-	-	-	-	-	-	-	-	-	-	-	-	-	-	-	-	-	-	-	-
1294	0	0	0	0	0	0	0	0	-	-	-	-	-	-	-	-	-	-	-	-	-	-	-	-	-	-	-	-
1295	0	0	0	0	0	0	0	0	-	-	-	-	-	-	-	-	-	-	-	-	-	-	-	-	-	-	-	-
1296	0	0	0	0	0	0	0	0	-	-	-	-	-	-	-	-	-	-	-	-	-	-	-	-	-	-	-	-
1297	0	0	0	0	0	0	0	0	-	-	-	-	-	-	-	-	-	-	-	-	-	-	-	-	-	-	-	-
1298	0	0	0	0	0	0	0	0	-	-	-	-	-	-	-	-	-	-	-	-	-	-	-	-	-	-	-	-
1299	0	0	0	0	0	0	0	0	-	-	-	-	-	-	-	-	-	-	-	-	-	-	-	-	-	-	-	-
1300	0	0	0	0	0	0	0	0	-	-	-	-	-	-	-	+	-	-	-	-	-	-	-	-	-	-	-	-
1301	0	0	0	0	0	0	0	0	-	-	-	-	-	-	-	-	-	-	-	-	-	-	-	-	-	-	-	-
1302	0	0	0	0	0	0	0	0	-	-	-	-	-	-	-	-	-	-	-	-	-	-	-	-	-	-	-	-
1303	0	0	0	0	0	0	0	0	-	-	-	-	-	-	-	-	-	-	-	-	-	-	-	-	-	-	-	-
1304	0	0	0	0	0	0	0	0	-	-	-	-	-	-	-	-	-	-	-	-	-	-	-	-	-	-	-	-
1305	0	0	0	0	0	0	0	0	-	-	-	-	-	-	-	-	-	-	-	-	-	-	-	-	-	-	-	-
1306	0	0	0	0	0	0	0	0	-	-	-	-	-	-	-	-	-	-	-	-	-	-	-	-	-	-	-	-
1307	0	0	0	0	0	0	0	0	-	-	-	-	-	-	-	-	-	-	-	-	-	-	-	-	-	-	-	-
1308	0	0	0	0	0	0	0	0	-	-	-	-	-	-	-	-	-	-	-	-	-	-	-	-	-	-	-	-
1309	0	0	0	0	0	0	0	0	-	-	-	-	-	-	-	-	-	-	-	-	-	-	-	-	-	-	-	-
1310	0	0	0	0	0	0	0	0	-	-	-	-	-	-	-	-	-	-	-	-	-	-	-	-	-	-	-	-
1311	0	0	0	0	0	0	0	0	-	-	-	-	-	-	-	-	-	-	-	-	-	-	-	-	-	-	-	-
1312	0	0	0	0	0	0	0	0	-	-	-	-	-	-	-	-	-	-	-	-	-	-	-	-	-	-	-	-
1313	0	0	0	0	0	0	0	0	-	-	-	-	-	-	-	-	-	-	-	-	-	-	-	-	-	-	-	-
1314	0	0	0	0	0	0	0	0	-	-	-	-	-	-	-	-	-	-	-	-	-	-	-	-	-	-	-	-
1315	0	0	0	0	0	0	0	0	-	-	-	-	-	-	-	-	-	-	-	-	-	-	-	-	-	-	-	-
1316	0	0	0	0	0	0	0	0	-	-	-	-	-	-	-	-	-	-	-	-	-	-	-	-	-	-	-	-
1317	0	0	0	0	0	0	0	0	-	-	-	-	-	-	-	-	-	-	-	-	-	-	-	-	-	-	-	-
1318	0	0	0	0	0	0	0	0	-	-	-	-	-	-	-	-	-	-	-	+	+	+	-	-	-	+	+	+

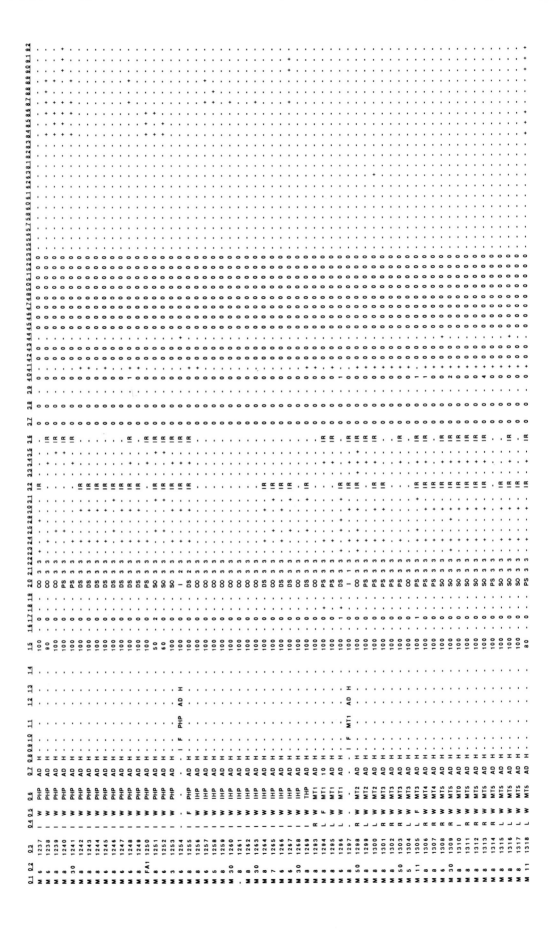

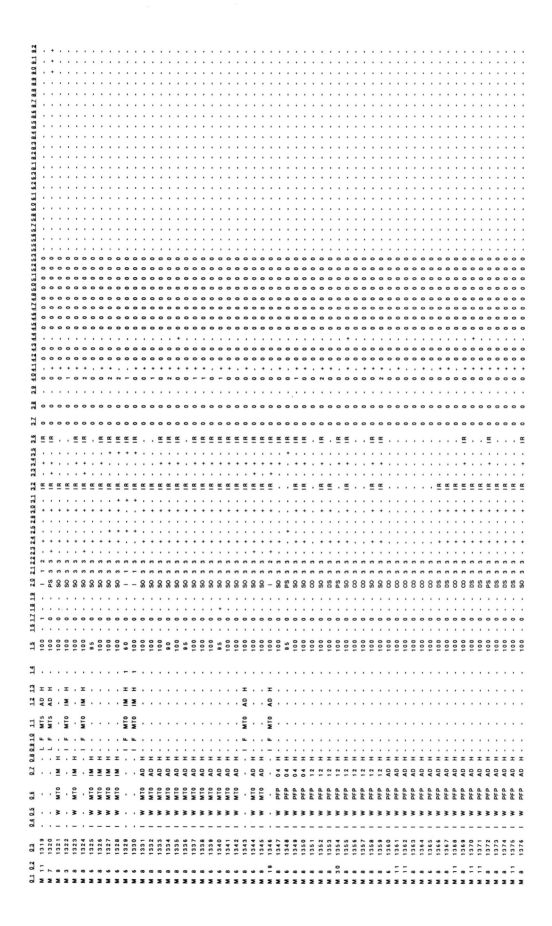

01	02	03	04	05	06	07	08	09	10	11	12	13	14	15	16	17	18	19	20	21	22	23	24	25	29	30	31	32	33	34	35	36	37	38	39	40	41	42	43	44	45	46	47	48	50	51	52	53	55	56	57	58	60	61	62	63	81	82	83	84	85	86	87	88	89	90	91	92
M	11	1319	-	-	-	-	-	L	F	MT5	AD	H	-	100	-	1	-	-	I	1	2	-	+	-	-	+	-	IR	-	+	-	IR	0	0	-	0	-	0	0	-	0	0	0	0	0	0	0	0	-	-	-	-	-	-	-	-	-	-	-	-	-	-	-	-	-	-	-	-
M	7	1320	-	-	-	-	-	L	F	MT5	AD	H	-	100	-	0	-	-	PS	3	3	+	+	-	-	+	-	IR	+	+	-	IR	0	0	-	0	+	0	0	-	0	0	0	0	0	0	0	0	-	-	-	-	-	-	-	-	-	-	-	-	-	-	-	-	-	+	+	+
M	9	1321	I	W	MTO	IM	H	-	-	-	-	-	-	100	-	0	-	-	SO	3	3	-	+	-	-	+	-	IR	-	-	-	-	0	0	-	0	+	0	0	-	0	0	0	0	0	0	0	0	-	-	-	-	-	-	-	-	-	-	-	-	-	-	-	-	-	-	-	-
M	3	1322	-	-	-	-	-	I	F	MTO	IM	H	-	100	-	0	-	-	SO	3	3	-	+	-	-	+	-	IR	-	-	-	-	0	0	-	1	+	0	0	-	0	0	0	0	0	0	0	0	-	-	-	-	-	-	-	-	-	-	-	-	-	-	-	-	-	-	-	-
M	8	1323	I	W	MTO	IM	H	-	-	-	-	-	-	100	-	0	-	-	SO	3	3	-	+	-	-	+	-	IR	-	+	-	IR	0	0	-	0	+	0	0	-	0	0	0	0	0	0	0	0	-	-	-	-	-	-	-	-	-	-	-	-	-	-	-	-	-	-	-	-
M	8	1324	-	-	-	-	-	I	F	MTO	IM	H	-	100	-	0	-	-	SO	3	3	+	+	-	-	+	-	IR	+	+	-	IR	0	0	-	2	+	0	0	-	0	0	0	0	0	0	0	0	-	-	-	-	-	-	-	-	-	-	-	-	-	-	-	-	-	-	-	-
M	6	1325	I	W	MTO	IM	H	-	-	-	-	-	-	95	-	0	-	-	SO	3	3	-	+	-	-	+	-	IR	-	-	-	-	0	0	-	0	-	0	0	-	0	0	0	0	0	0	0	0	-	-	-	-	-	-	-	-	-	-	-	-	-	-	-	-	-	-	-	-
M	8	1326	I	W	MTO	IM	H	-	-	-	-	-	-	100	-	0	-	-	SO	3	3	-	+	-	-	+	-	IR	-	+	-	IR	0	0	-	0	+	0	0	-	0	0	0	0	0	0	0	0	-	-	-	-	-	-	-	-	-	-	-	-	-	-	-	-	-	-	-	-
M	6	1327	I	W	MTO	IM	H	-	-	-	-	-	-	100	-	0	-	-	SO	3	3	-	+	+	-	+	-	IR	-	-	+	IR	0	0	-	2	+	0	0	-	0	0	0	0	0	0	0	0	-	-	-	-	-	-	-	-	-	-	-	-	-	-	-	-	-	-	-	-
M	6	1328	I	W	MTO	IM	H	-	-	-	-	-	-	100	-	0	-	-	SO	3	3	-	+	+	-	+	+	IR	-	-	+	IR	0	0	-	2	-	0	0	-	0	0	0	0	0	0	0	0	-	-	-	-	-	-	-	-	-	-	-	-	-	-	-	-	-	-	-	-
M	6	1329	-	-	-	-	-	I	F	MTO	IM	H	1	60	-	0	-	-	I	1	3	-	-	+	-	-	+	IR	-	-	+	IR	0	0	-	1	-	0	0	-	0	0	0	0	0	0	0	0	-	-	-	-	-	-	-	-	-	-	-	-	-	-	-	-	-	-	-	-
M	6	1330	-	-	-	-	-	I	F	MTO	IM	H	1	100	-	0	-	-	I	1	3	-	-	+	-	-	+	IR	-	-	+	IR	0	0	-	0	+	0	0	-	0	0	0	0	0	0	0	0	-	-	-	-	-	-	-	-	-	-	-	-	-	-	-	-	-	-	-	-
M	8	1331	I	W	MTO	AD	H	-	-	-	-	-	-	100	-	0	-	-	SO	3	3	-	+	-	-	+	-	IR	-	-	-	-	0	0	-	0	+	0	0	-	0	0	0	0	0	0	0	0	-	-	-	-	-	-	-	-	-	-	-	-	-	-	-	-	-	-	-	-
M	8	1332	I	W	MTO	AD	H	-	-	-	-	-	-	100	-	0	-	-	SO	3	3	-	+	-	-	+	-	IR	-	-	-	-	0	0	-	1	+	0	0	-	0	0	0	0	0	0	0	0	-	-	-	-	-	-	-	-	-	-	-	-	-	-	-	-	-	-	-	-
M	8	1333	I	W	MTO	AD	H	-	-	-	-	-	-	100	-	0	-	-	SO	3	3	-	+	-	-	+	-	IR	-	+	-	IR	0	0	-	0	+	0	0	-	0	0	0	0	0	0	0	0	-	-	-	-	-	-	-	-	-	-	-	-	-	-	-	-	-	-	-	-
M	8	1334	I	W	MTO	AD	H	-	-	-	-	-	-	90	-	0	-	-	SO	3	3	-	+	-	-	+	-	IR	-	+	-	IR	0	0	-	2	+	0	0	-	0	0	0	0	0	0	0	0	-	-	-	-	-	-	-	-	-	-	-	-	-	-	-	-	-	-	-	-
M	8	1335	I	W	MTO	AD	H	-	-	-	-	-	-	100	-	0	-	-	SO	3	3	-	+	-	-	+	-	IR	-	+	-	IR	0	0	-	0	+	0	0	+	0	0	0	0	0	0	0	0	-	-	-	-	-	-	-	-	-	-	-	-	-	-	-	-	-	-	-	-
M	8	1336	I	W	MTO	AD	H	-	-	-	-	-	-	95	-	0	-	-	SO	3	3	-	+	-	-	+	-	IR	-	-	-	-	0	0	-	0	+	0	0	-	0	0	0	0	0	0	0	0	-	-	-	-	-	-	-	-	-	-	-	-	-	-	-	-	-	-	-	-
M	8	1337	I	W	MTO	AD	H	-	-	-	-	-	-	100	-	0	-	-	SO	3	3	-	+	-	-	+	-	IR	-	+	-	IR	0	0	-	1	+	0	0	-	0	0	0	0	0	0	0	0	-	-	-	-	-	-	-	-	-	-	-	-	-	-	-	-	-	-	-	-
M	8	1338	I	W	MTO	AD	H	-	-	-	-	-	-	100	-	0	-	-	SO	3	3	-	+	-	-	+	-	IR	-	+	-	IR	0	0	-	1	+	0	0	-	0	0	0	0	0	0	0	0	-	-	-	-	-	-	-	-	-	-	-	-	-	-	-	-	-	-	-	-
M	6	1339	I	W	MTO	AD	H	-	-	-	-	-	-	100	-	0	-	-	SO	3	3	-	+	-	-	+	-	IR	-	+	-	IR	0	0	-	0	-	0	0	-	0	0	0	0	0	0	0	0	-	-	-	-	-	-	-	-	-	-	-	-	-	-	-	-	-	-	-	-
M	6	1340	I	W	MTO	AD	H	-	-	-	-	-	-	95	-	0	+	-	SO	3	3	-	+	-	-	+	-	IR	-	+	-	IR	0	0	-	1	+	0	0	-	0	0	0	0	0	0	0	0	-	-	-	-	-	-	-	-	-	-	-	-	-	-	-	-	-	-	-	-
M	8	1341	I	W	MTO	AD	H	-	-	-	-	-	-	100	-	0	-	-	SO	3	3	-	+	-	-	+	-	IR	-	+	-	IR	0	0	-	0	+	0	0	-	0	0	0	0	0	0	0	0	-	-	-	-	-	-	-	-	-	-	-	-	-	-	-	-	-	-	-	-
M	6	1342	I	W	MTO	AD	H	-	-	-	-	-	-	100	-	0	-	-	SO	3	3	-	+	-	-	+	-	IR	-	+	-	IR	0	0	-	0	-	0	0	-	0	0	0	0	0	0	0	0	-	-	-	-	-	-	-	-	-	-	-	-	-	-	-	-	-	-	-	-
M	8	1343	-	-	-	-	-	I	F	MTO	AD	H	-	100	-	0	-	-	SO	3	3	-	+	-	-	+	-	IR	-	+	-	IR	0	0	-	0	+	0	0	-	0	0	0	0	0	0	0	0	-	-	-	-	-	-	-	-	-	-	-	-	-	-	-	-	-	-	-	-
M	6	1344	I	W	MTO	AD	H	-	-	-	-	-	-	100	-	0	-	-	SO	3	3	+	+	-	-	+	-	IR	+	+	-	IR	0	0	-	0	-	0	0	-	0	0	0	0	0	0	0	0	-	-	-	-	-	-	-	-	-	-	-	-	-	-	-	-	-	-	-	-
M	9	1345	I	W	MTO	AD	H	-	-	-	-	-	-	100	-	0	-	-	SO	3	3	-	+	-	-	+	-	IR	-	+	-	IR	0	0	-	0	+	0	0	-	0	0	0	0	0	0	0	0	-	-	-	-	-	-	-	-	-	-	-	-	-	-	-	-	-	-	-	-
M	19	1346	-	-	-	-	-	I	F	MTO	AD	H	-	100	-	0	-	-	I	3	2	+	+	-	-	+	-	IR	+	+	-	IR	0	0	-	0	-	0	0	-	0	0	0	0	0	0	0	0	-	-	-	-	-	-	-	-	-	-	-	-	-	-	-	-	-	-	-	-
M	8	1347	I	W	PFP	04	H	-	-	-	-	-	-	100	-	0	-	-	SO	3	3	-	+	-	-	-	-	-	-	+	-	IR	0	0	-	0	+	0	0	-	0	0	0	0	0	0	0	0	-	-	-	-	-	-	-	-	-	-	-	-	-	-	-	-	-	-	-	-
M	6	1348	I	W	PFP	04	H	-	-	-	-	-	-	95	-	0	-	-	PS	3	3	-	-	+	-	-	-	-	-	-	+	IR	0	0	-	0	-	0	0	-	0	0	0	0	0	0	0	0	-	-	-	-	-	-	-	-	-	-	-	-	-	-	-	-	-	-	-	-
M	8	1349	I	W	PFP	04	H	-	-	-	-	-	-	100	-	0	-	-	SO	3	3	-	+	-	-	+	-	IR	-	+	-	IR	0	0	-	1	+	0	0	-	0	0	0	0	0	0	0	0	-	-	-	-	-	-	-	-	-	-	-	-	-	-	-	-	-	-	-	-
M	8	1350	I	W	PFP	04	H	-	-	-	-	-	-	100	-	0	-	-	SO	3	3	-	+	-	-	+	-	IR	-	+	-	IR	0	0	-	0	+	0	0	-	0	0	0	0	0	0	0	0	-	-	-	-	-	-	-	-	-	-	-	-	-	-	-	-	-	-	-	-
M	8	1351	I	W	PFP	12	H	-	-	-	-	-	-	100	-	0	-	-	CO	3	3	-	-	-	-	-	-	-	-	-	-	-	0	0	-	0	-	0	0	-	0	0	0	0	0	0	0	0	-	-	-	-	-	-	-	-	-	-	-	-	-	-	-	-	-	-	-	-
M	8	1352	I	W	PFP	12	H	-	-	-	-	-	-	100	-	0	-	-	SO	3	3	-	+	-	-	+	-	IR	-	+	-	IR	0	0	-	2	+	0	0	-	0	0	0	0	0	0	0	0	-	-	-	-	-	-	-	-	-	-	-	-	-	-	-	-	-	-	-	-
M	8	1353	I	W	PFP	12	H	-	-	-	-	-	-	100	-	0	-	-	DS	3	3	-	+	-	-	+	-	IR	-	-	-	-	0	0	-	0	+	0	0	-	0	0	0	0	0	0	0	0	-	-	-	-	-	-	-	-	-	-	-	-	-	-	-	-	-	-	-	-
M	30	1354	I	W	PFP	12	H	-	-	-	-	-	-	100	-	0	-	-	PS	3	3	-	+	-	-	-	-	-	-	+	-	IR	0	0	-	0	-	0	0	-	0	0	0	0	0	0	0	0	-	-	-	-	-	-	-	-	-	-	-	-	-	-	-	-	-	-	-	-
M	8	1355	I	W	PFP	12	H	-	-	-	-	-	-	100	-	0	-	-	SO	3	3	-	+	-	-	+	-	IR	-	+	-	IR	0	0	-	0	+	0	0	+	0	0	0	0	0	0	0	0	-	-	-	-	-	-	-	-	-	-	-	-	-	-	-	-	-	-	-	-
M	8	1356	I	W	PFP	12	H	-	-	-	-	-	-	100	-	0	-	-	CO	3	3	-	-	-	-	-	-	-	-	-	-	-	0	0	-	0	-	0	0	-	0	0	0	0	0	0	0	0	-	-	-	-	-	-	-	-	-	-	-	-	-	-	-	-	-	-	-	-
M	8	1357	I	W	PFP	12	H	-	-	-	-	-	-	100	-	0	-	-	CO	3	3	-	-	-	-	-	-	-	-	-	-	-	0	0	-	0	+	0	0	-	0	0	0	0	0	0	0	0	-	-	-	-	-	-	-	-	-	-	-	-	-	-	-	-	-	-	-	-
M	8	1358	I	W	PFP	12	H	-	-	-	-	-	-	100	-	0	-	-	SO	3	3	-	+	-	-	+	-	IR	-	+	-	IR	0	0	-	0	+	0	0	-	0	0	0	0	0	0	0	0	-	-	-	-	-	-	-	-	-	-	-	-	-	-	-	-	-	-	-	-
M	8	1359	I	W	PFP	12	H	-	-	-	-	-	-	100	-	0	-	-	SO	3	3	-	+	-	-	+	-	IR	-	+	-	IR	0	0	-	2	+	0	0	-	0	0	0	0	0	0	0	0	-	-	-	-	-	-	-	-	-	-	-	-	-	-	-	-	-	-	-	-
M	6	1360	I	W	PFP	AD	H	-	-	-	-	-	-	100	-	0	-	-	CO	3	3	-	-	-	-	-	-	-	-	-	-	-	0	0	-	0	-	0	0	-	0	0	0	0	0	0	0	0	-	-	-	-	-	-	-	-	-	-	-	-	-	-	-	-	-	-	-	-
M	11	1361	I	W	PFP	AD	H	-	-	-	-	-	-	100	-	0	-	-	CO	3	3	-	-	-	-	-	-	-	-	-	-	-	0	0	-	0	+	0	0	-	0	0	0	0	0	0	0	0	-	-	-	-	-	-	-	-	-	-	-	-	-	-	-	-	-	-	-	-
M	11	1362	I	W	PFP	AD	H	-	-	-	-	-	-	100	-	0	-	-	CO	3	3	-	-	-	-	-	-	-	-	-	-	-	0	0	-	0	-	0	0	-	0	0	0	0	0	0	0	0	-	-	-	-	-	-	-	-	-	-	-	-	-	-	-	-	-	-	-	-
M	8	1363	I	W	PFP	AD	H	-	-	-	-	-	-	100	-	0	-	-	CO	3	3	-	-	-	-	-	-	-	-	-	-	-	0	0	-	0	-	0	0	-	0	0	0	0	0	0	0	0	-	-	-	-	-	-	-	-	-	-	-	-	-	-	-	-	-	-	-	-
M	8	1364	I	W	PFP	AD	H	-	-	-	-	-	-	100	-	0	-	-	CO	3	3	-	-	-	-	-	-	-	-	-	-	-	0	0	-	0	+	0	0	-	0	0	0	0	0	0	0	0	-	-	-	-	-	-	-	-	-	-	-	-	-	-	-	-	-	-	-	-
M	6	1365	I	W	PFP	AD	H	-	-	-	-	-	-	100	-	0	-	-	CO	3	3	-	-	-	-	-	-	-	-	-	-	-	0	0	-	0	-	0	0	-	0	0	0	0	0	0	0	0	-	-	-	-	-	-	-	-	-	-	-	-	-	-	-	-	-	-	-	-
M	8	1366	I	W	PFP	AD	H	-	-	-	-	-	-	100	-	0	-	-	DS	3	3	-	+	-	-	+	-	IR	-	-	-	-	0	0	-	0	+	0	0	-	0	0	0	0	0	0	0	0	-	-	-	-	-	-	-	-	-	-	-	-	-	-	-	-	-	-	-	-
M	8	1367	I	W	PFP	AD	H	-	-	-	-	-	-	100	-	0	-	-	DS	3	3	-	+	-	-	+	-	IR	-	-	-	-	0	0	-	0	+	0	0	-	0	0	0	0	0	0	0	0	-	-	-	-	-	-	-	-	-	-	-	-	-	-	-	-	-	-	-	-
M	11	1368	I	W	PFP	AD	H	-	-	-	-	-	-	100	-	0	-	-	CO	3	3	-	+	-	-	+	-	IR	-	-	-	-	0	0	-	0	-	0	0	-	0	0	0	0	0	0	0	0	-	-	-	-	-	-	-	-	-	-	-	-	-	-	-	-	-	-	-	-
M	8	1369	I	W	PFP	AD	H	-	-	-	-	-	-	100	-	0	-	-	CO	3	3	-	+	-	-	+	-	IR	-	+	-	IR	0	0	-	0	+	0	0	-	0	0	0	0	0	0	0	0	-	-	-	-	-	-	-	-	-	-	-	-	-	-	-	-	-	-	-	-
M	11	1370	I	W	PFP	AD	H	-	-	-	-	-	-	100	-	0	-	-	DS	3	3	-	+	-	-	+	-	IR	-	-	-	-	0	0	-	0	+	0	0	+	0	0	0	0	0	0	0	0	-	-	-	-	-	-	-	-	-	-	-	-	-	-	-	-	-	-	-	-
M	11	1371	I	W	PFP	AD	H	-	-	-	-	-	-	100	-	0	-	-	DS	3	3	-	+	-	-	+	-	IR	-	-	-	-	0	0	-	0	+	0	0	-	0	0	0	0	0	0	0	0	-	-	-	-	-	-	-	-	-	-	-	-	-	-	-	-	-	-	-	-
M	8	1372	I	W	PFP	AD	H	-	-	-	-	-	-	100	-	0	-	-	PS	3	3	-	+	-	-	+	-	IR	-	+	-	IR	0	0	-	0	+	0	0	-	0	0	0	0	0	0	0	0	-	-	-	-	-	-	-	-	-	-	-	-	-	-	-	-	-	-	-	-
M	8	1373	I	W	PFP	AD	H	-	-	-	-	-	-	100	-	0	-	-	DS	3	3	-	+	-	-	+	-	IR	-	-	-	-	0	0	-	0	+	0	0	-	0	0	0	0	0	0	0	0	-	-	-	-	-	-	-	-	-	-	-	-	-	-	-	-	-	-	-	-
M	8	1374	I	W	PFP	AD	H	-	-	-	-	-	-	100	-	0	-	-	DS	3	3	-	+	-	-	+	-	IR	-	-	-	-	0	0	-	0	+	0	0	-	0	0	0	0	0	0	0	0	-	-	-	-	-	-	-	-	-	-	-	-	-	-	-	-	-	-	-	-
M	11	1375	I	W	PFP	AD	H	-	-	-	-	-	-	100	-	0	-	-	DS	3	3	-	+	-	-	+	-	IR	-	-	-	-	0	0	-	0	+	0	0	-	0	0	0	0	0	0	0	0	-	-	-	-	-	-	-	-	-	-	-	-	-	-	-	-	-	-	-	-
M	8	1376	I	W	PFP	AD	H	-	-	-	-	-	-	100	-	0	-	-	SO	3	3	-	+	-	-	+	-	IR	-	+	-	IR	0	0	-	0	+	0	0	-	0	0	0	0	0	0	0	0	-	-	-	-	-	-	-	-	-	-	-	-	-	-	-	-	-	-	-	-

01	02	03	04	05	06	07	08	09	10	11	12	13	14	15	16	17	18	19	20	21	22	23	24	25	29	30	31	32	33	34	35	36	37	38	39	40	41	42	43	44	45	46	47	48	50	51	52	53	55	56	57	58	60	61	62	63	81	82	83	84	85	86	87	88	89	90	91	92
M	8	1377	I	W	PFP	AD	H	-	-	-	-	-	-	100	-	0	-	-	DS	3	3	-	+	-	-	+	-	IR	-	-	-	-	0	0	-	0	+	0	0	+	0	0	0	0	0	0	0	0	-	-	-	-	-	-	-	-	-	-	-	-	-	-	-	-	-	-	-	-
M	8	1378	I	W	PFP	AD	H	-	-	-	-	-	-	100	-	0	-	-	SO	3	3	-	+	-	-	+	-	IR	-	+	-	IR	0	0	-	0	+	0	0	-	0	0	0	0	0	0	0	0	-	-	-	-	-	-	-	-	-	-	-	-	-	-	-	-	-	-	-	-
M	8	1379	I	W	PFP	AD	H	-	-	-	-	-	-	100	-	0	-	-	DS	3	3	-	+	-	-	+	-	IR	-	-	-	-	0	0	-	0	+	0	0	-	0	0	0	0	0	0	0	0	-	-	-	-	-	-	-	-	-	-	-	-	-	-	-	-	-	-	-	-
M	11	1380	I	W	PFP	AD	H	-	-	-	-	-	-	50	-	2	-	-	CO	3	3	-	-	-	-	-	-	-	-	-	-	-	0	0	-	0	-	0	0	-	0	0	0	0	0	0	0	0	-	-	-	-	-	-	-	-	-	-	-	-	-	-	-	-	-	-	-	-
M	19	1381	I	W	PFP	AD	H	-	-	-	-	-	-	100	-	0	-	-	CO	3	3	-	-	-	-	-	-	-	-	-	-	-	0	0	-	0	+	0	0	-	0	0	0	0	0	0	0	0	-	-	-	-	-	-	-	-	-	-	-	-	-	-	-	-	-	-	-	-
M	8	1382	I	W	PFP	AD	H	-	-	-	-	-	-	100	-	0	+	-	CO	3	3	-	-	-	-	-	-	-	-	-	-	-	0	0	-	0	-	0	0	-	0	0	0	0	0	0	0	0	-	-	-	-	-	-	-	-	-	-	-	-	-	-	-	-	-	-	-	-
M	8	1383	I	W	PFP	AD	H	-	-	-	-	-	-	100	-	0	-	-	CO	3	3	-	-	-	-	-	-	-	-	-	-	-	0	0	-	0	-	0	0	-	0	0	0	0	0	0	0	0	-	-	-	-	-	-	-	-	-	-	-	-	-	-	-	-	-	-	-	-
M	8	1384	I	W	PFP	AD	H	-	-	-	-	-	-	100	-	0	-	-	SO	3	3	-	+	-	-	+	-	IR	-	+	-	IR	0	0	-	0	+	0	0	-	0	0	0	0	0	0	0	0	-	-	-	-	-	-	-	-	-	-	-	-	-	-	-	-	-	-	-	-
M	8	1385	I	W	PFP	12	H	-	-	-	-	-	-	100	-	0	-	-	SO	3	3	-	+	-	-	+	-	IR	-	+	-	IR	0	0	-	0	+	0	0	-	0	0	0	0	0	0	0	0	-	-	-	-	-	-	-	-	-	-	-	-	-	-	-	-	-	-	-	-
M	8	1386	I	W	PFP	12	H	-	-	-	-	-	-	100	-	0	-	-	CO	3	3	-	-	-	-	-	-	-	-	-	-	-	0	0	-	0	-	0	0	-	0	0	0	0	0	0	0	0	-	-	-	-	-	-	-	-	-	-	-	-	-	-	-	-	-	-	-	-
M	8	1387	I	F	PFP	AD	H	-	-	-	-	-	-	100	-	0	-	-	I	1	3	-	+	-	-	+	-	IR	-	+	-	IR	0	0	-	0	+	0	0	-	0	0	0	0	0	0	0	0	-	-	-	-	-	-	-	-	-	-	-	-	-	-	-	-	-	-	-	-
M	8	1388	I	F	PFP	AD	H	-	-	-	-	-	-	100	-	0	-	-	PO	1	1	-	-	-	-	-	-	-	-	-	-	-	0	0	-	0	-	0	0	-	0	0	0	0	0	0	0	0	-	-	-	-	-	-	-	-	-	-	-	-	-	-	-	-	-	-	-	-
M	8	1389	I	W	TFP	AD	H	-	-	-	-	-	-	100	-	0	-	-	CO	3	3	-	-	-	-	-	-	-	-	-	-	-	0	0	-	0	+	0	0	-	0	0	0	0	0	0	0	0	-	-	-	-	-	-	-	-	-	-	-	-	-	-	-	-	-	-	-	-
M	8	1390	I	W	TFP	AD	H	-	-	-	-	-	-	100	-	0	-	-	CO	3	3	-	-	-	-	-	-	-	-	-	-	-	0	0	-	0	-	0	0	-	0	0	0	0	0	0	0	0	-	-	-	-	-	-	-	-	-	-	-	-	-	-	-	-	-	-	-	-
M	8	1391	-	-	-	-	-	I	F	TFP	AD	H	-	100	-	0	-	-	I	1	3	-	+	-	-	+	-	IR	-	+	-	IR	0	0	-	0	+	0	0	-	0	0	0	0	0	0	0	0	-	-	-	-	-	-	-	-	-	-	-	-	-	-	-	-	-	-	-	-

E: Cranial

0.1	0.2	0.3	0.4	0.5	0.6	0.7	0.8	0.9	1.0	1.1	1.2	1.3	1.4	1.5	1.6	1.7	1.8	1.9	2.3	2.4	2.5	2.6	2.7	2.8	4.0	4.1	4.2	4.3	4.4	4.9	5.4	5.9	6.4	9.3	9.4	9.5
M	6	1628	B	W	FRO	04	H	.	.	.	.	.	.	60	.	0	.	.	+	+	.	.	.	+	0	.	0	0	.	0	0	.	.	+	+	+
M	FA3	1629	B	W	FRO+	12	H	.	.	.	.	.	.	100	+	0	.	.	.	+	.	.	+	+	0	.	0	0	.	0	0	.	.	.	.	.
M	11	1630	.	.	.	.	.	B	F	FRO	IM	H	.	100	.	1	+	.	.	+	.	.	+	.	1	.	0	0	.	0	0	.	.	.	.	.
M	50	1631	R	F	FRO	06	H	.	.	.	.	.	.	100	.	0	.	.	+	+	.	.	.	.	0	+	0	0	.	0	0	.	.	.	.	.
M	8	1632	.	.	.	.	.	R	F	FRO	06	H	.	100	.	0	.	.	.	+	.	+	+	+	1	+	0	0	.	0	0	.	+	.	.	.
M	11	1633	R	F	FRO+	10	H	.	.	.	.	.	.	80	.	0	.	.	.	+	.	.	+	.	0	.	0	0	.	0	0	.	.	+	+	.
M	11	1634	.	.	.	.	.	R	F	FRO	AD	H	.	100	.	0	.	.	+	+	.	.	.	.	0	.	0	0	.	0	0	.	.	.	.	.
M	50	1635	L	F	FRO+	06	H	.	.	.	.	.	.	90	.	0	+	.	+	+	.	.	.	.	0	.	0	0	.	0	0	.	+	.	.	.
M	6	1636	.	.	.	.	.	L	F	FRO	08	H	.	100	.	0	.	.	+	+	.	.	.	+	0	.	0	0	.	0	0	.	.	.	.	.
M	6	1637	.	.	.	.	.	L	F	FRO	AD	H	.	100	.	0	.	.	+	+	.	.	.	.	0	.	0	0	.	0	0	.	.	.	.	.
M	FA1	1638	.	.	.	.	.	I	F	FRO	IM	H	.	100	.	0	.	.	.	+	.	.	.	.	0	.	0	0	.	0	0	.	.	.	.	.
M	6	1639	.	.	.	.	.	I	F	FRO	AD	H	.	100	.	0	.	.	+	+	.	.	.	+	0	.	0	0	.	0	0	.	.	.	+	.
M	8	1640	.	.	.	.	.	I	F	FRO	AD	H	.	100	.	0	.	.	.	+	.	.	+	.	0	.	2	0	.	0	0	.	+	.	.	.
M	6	1641	B	W	FRO+	AD	H	.	.	.	.	.	142	100	.	0	.	.	.	+	.	.	.	+	1	.	0	0	.	2	0	.	+	.	.	.
M	6	1642	R	W	PAR+	AD	H	.	.	.	.	.	142	100	.	0	.	.	+	+	.	.	+	+	1	.	0	0	.	7	0	.	+	.	.	.
M	6	1643	L	F	PAR	AD	H	.	.	.	.	.	142	100	.	0	.	.	+	+	.	.	.	+	0	.	0	0	.	9	0	.	+	+	+	.
M	6	1644	B	W	OCC+	AD	H	.	.	.	.	.	142	100	.	0	.	.	+	+	.	.	+	+	0	.	0	0	.	9	0	.	.	+	+	+
M	6	1645	L	W	TEM+	AD	H	.	.	.	.	.	142	90	.	0	.	.	+	+	.	.	.	+	0	+	0	0	.	0	0	.	.	+	+	+
M	6	1646	L	F	PAR	AD	H	.	.	.	.	.	142	100	.	0	.	.	+	+	.	.	+	+	0	.	0	0	.	7	0	.	+	.	.	.
M	8	1647	.	.	.	.	.	R	F	PAR	AD	H	142	100	.	0	.	.	.	+	.	.	.	+	1	.	0	0	.	1	0	.	+	.	.	.
M	6	1648	B	W	FRO+	06	H	.	.	.	.	.	143	100	.	0	.	.	+	+	.	.	.	+	2	.	0	0	.	0	0	.	.	+	+	+
M	6	1649	R	F	PAR	06	H	.	.	.	.	.	143	100	.	0	.	.	+	+	.	+	.	+	0	.	0	0	.	0	0	.	.	+	+	+
M	6	1650	B	F	OCC	06	H	.	.	.	.	.	143	100	.	0	.	.	+	+	.	.	.	+	0	.	0	0	.	0	0	.	.	+	.	.
M	6	1651	.	.	.	.	.	R	F	TEM	06	H	143	100	.	0	.	.	.	+	.	.	.	+	0	.	0	0	.	0	0	.	.	+	+	+
M	6	1652	.	.	.	.	.	L	F	TEM	06	H	143	100	.	0	.	.	+	+	.	.	.	+	0	.	0	0	.	0	0	.	.	+	+	+
M	6	1653	.	.	.	.	.	L	F	TEM	06	H	143	100	.	0	.	.	.	+	.	.	+	+	0	.	0	0	.	0	0	.	.	.	.	.
M	6	1654	.	.	.	.	.	L	F	OCC	06	H	143	100	.	0	.	.	.	+	.	.	.	+	0	.	0	0	.	0	0	.	.	.	.	.
M	6	1655	.	.	.	.	.	R	F	FRO	06	H	143	100	.	0	.	.	.	+	.	.	.	.	0	.	0	0	.	0	0	.	.	+	+	+
M	3	1656	B	F	FRO	AD	H	.	.	.	.	.	144	100	.	0	.	.	.	+	.	.	+	+	0	.	0	0	.	6	0	.	+	+	+	+
M	8	1657	R	F	PAR+	AD	H	.	.	.	.	.	144	100	.	0	.	.	.	+	.	.	+	+	0	.	0	0	.	9	0	.	.	+	+	+
M	3	1658	.	.	.	.	.	R	F	SPH+	AD	H	144	100	.	0	.	.	.	+	.	.	.	+	0	.	0	0	.	0	2	.	.	.	.	.
M	8	1659	.	.	.	.	.	R	F	PAR	AD	H	144	100	.	0	.	.	.	+	.	.	+	+	0	.	0	0	.	9	0	.	.	.	.	.
M	11	1660	.	.	.	.	.	B	F	FRO+	AD	H	144	100	.	0	.	.	+	+	.	.	.	+	0	.	0	0	.	0	0	.	.	+	+	.
M	8	1661	B	F	FRO	AD	H	.	.	.	.	.	145	100	.	0	.	.	.	+	.	.	+	+	0	+	9	1	.	0	0	.	+	+	+	.
M	8	1662	.	.	.	.	.	L	F	FRO	AD	H	145	100	.	0	.	.	.	+	.	.	.	+	0	+	2	0	.	0	0	.	+	.	.	.
M	8	1663	.	.	.	.	.	R	F	FRO	AD	H	145	100	.	0	.	.	.	+	.	.	+	.	0	+	2	0	.	0	0	.	+	+	+	.
M	8	1664	.	.	.	.	.	L	F	FRO	AD	H	145	100	.	0	.	.	.	+	.	.	.	+	0	+	0	0	.	0	0	.	+	.	.	.
M	3	1665	.	.	.	.	.	L	F	FRO	AD	H	145	100	.	0	.	.	.	+	.	.	.	.	0	.	0	1	.	0	0	.	+	.	.	.
M	6	1666	B	W	FRO+	AD	H	.	.	.	.	.	146	100	.	0	.	.	.	+	.	.	+	+	1	+	0	0	.	0	0	.	+	+	+	+
M	6	1667	.	.	.	.	.	R	F	PAR	AD	H	146	60	.	0	.	.	+	+	.	.	+	.	0	.	0	0	.	0	0	.	+	+	+	+
M	6	1668	.	.	.	.	.	L	F	PAR	AD	H	146	100	.	0	.	.	.	+	.	+	+	+	1	+	1	0	.	0	0	.	.	+	+	.
M	6	1669	.	.	.	.	.	R	F	PAR	AD	H	146	100	.	0	.	.	+	+	.	+	+	+	1	.	0	0	.	0	0	.	.	+	+	.
M	8	1670	B	W	FRO+	AD	H	.	.	.	.	.	147	100	.	0	.	.	.	+	.	.	+	+	1	+	0	0	.	6	0	.	+	.	.	.
M	8	1671	L	F	FRO	AD	H	.	.	.	.	.	147	100	.	0	.	.	.	+	.	.	.	+	0	+	0	0	.	0	0	.	+	.	.	.
M	8	1672	.	.	.	.	.	L	F	PAR	AD	H	147	100	.	0	.	.	.	+	.	.	.	+	1	+	0	1	.	0	0	.	.	.	.	.
M	8	1673	B	W	FRO	AD	H	.	.	.	.	.	148	100	.	0	.	.	.	+	.	.	.	+	0	.	0	0	.	0	0	.	+	.	.	.
M	8	1674	L	W	MAX+	AD	H	.	.	.	.	.	148	100	.	0	.	.	.	+	.	.	.	+	0	.	0	0	.	0	0	.	.	.	.	.
M	8	1675	L	W	TEM	AD	H	.	.	.	.	.	148	100	.	0	.	.	+	+	.	.	.	+	0	.	0	0	.	0	0	.	.	+	+	+
M	11	1676	R	F	FRO	08	H	.	.	.	.	.	149	100	.	0	.	.	+	+	.	.	.	+	1	.	0	0	.	0	0	.	+	+	+	+
M	11	1677	B	F	FRO+	08	H	.	.	.	.	.	149	100	.	0	.	.	+	+	.	.	.	.	0	.	4	0	.	0	0	.	+	+	+	+
M	8	1678	B	W	FRO+	AD	H	.	.	.	.	.	150	90	.	0	.	.	+	+	.	.	.	+	0	.	0	0	.	0	0	.	.	+	+	+
M	6	1679	B	W	OCC+	AD	H	.	.	.	.	.	150	100	.	0	.	.	+	+	.	.	.	+	0	.	0	0	.	0	0	.	.	+	+	+
M	8	1680	.	.	.	.	.	L	F	FRO	10	H	151	100	.	0	.	.	+	+	.	.	.	+	0	.	0	0	.	0	0	.	.	+	+	+
M	8	1681	.	.	.	.	.	L	F	SPH+	10	H	151	100	.	0	.	.	.	+	.	.	.	+	0	.	0	0	.	0	0	.	.	.	.	.
M	6	1682	.	.	.	.	.	R	F	PAR	IM	H	.	30	.	0	.	.	+	+	.	.	.	+	0	.	0	0	.	0	0	.	.	+	+	+
M	8	1683	.	.	.	.	.	R	F	PAR	AD	H	.	100	.	0	.	.	.	+	.	.	+	+	0	.	0	0	.	0	0	.	+	+	+	.
M	5	1684	R	F	PAR	AD	H	.	.	.	.	.	.	100	.	0	.	.	+	+	.	.	.	+	1	.	0	0	.	1	0	.	+	+	+	+
M	18	1685	R	F	PAR+	AD	H	.	.	.	.	.	.	10	.	2	.	.	.	+	.	.	+	+	0	.	0	0	.	0	0	.	.	.	.	.
M	11	1686	R	F	PAR	AD	H	.	.	.	.	.	.	80	.	0	.	.	.	+	.	.	.	+	0	.	0	0	.	0	0	.	.	+	+	+

01	02	03	04	05	06	07	08	09	10	11	12	13	14	15	16	17	18	19	23	24	25	26	27	28	40	41	42	43	44	49	54	59	64	93	94	95
M	8	1687	R	F	PAR	AD	H	-	-	-	-	-	-	100	-	0	-	-	-	+	-	-	-	+	0	-	0	0	-	0	0	-	-	+	-	-
M	8	1688	-	-	-	-	-	R	F	PAR	AD	H	-	100	-	0	-	-	-	+	-	+	-	+	0	-	1	0	-	0	0	-	+	-	-	-
M	6	1689	L	F	PAR	IM	H	-	-	-	-	-	-	40	-	0	-	-	+	+	-	-	-	+	0	-	0	0	-	0	0	-	-	+	+	+
M	8	1690	-	-	-	-	-	L	F	PAR	IM	H	-	80	-	0	-	-	+	+	-	-	+	+	0	-	0	0	-	0	0	-	-	+	+	+
M	11	1691	-	-	-	-	-	L	F	PAR	IM	H	-	100	-	0	-	-	-	+	-	-	+	+	0	-	0	0	-	0	0	-	-	-	-	-
M	6	1692	-	-	-	-	-	L	F	PAR	IM	H	-	70	-	0	-	-	+	-	+	-	-	+	0	-	0	0	-	0	0	-	-	+	+	+
M	11	1693	-	-	-	-	-	L	F	PAR	IM	H	-	100	-	0	-	-	-	+	-	-	+	+	0	-	0	0	-	0	0	-	-	+	-	-
M	6	1694	L	F	PAR	AD	H	-	-	-	-	-	-	100	-	0	-	-	-	+	-	-	+	+	0	-	2	0	-	0	0	-	+	-	-	-
M	8	1695	-	-	-	-	-	L	F	PAR	AD	H	-	100	-	0	-	-	-	+	-	-	+	+	1	-	0	0	-	0	0	-	-	+	+	-
M	8	1696	-	-	-	-	-	L	F	PAR	AD	H	-	100	-	0	-	-	+	+	-	-	-	+	0	-	0	0	-	1	0	-	-	+	+	+
M	6	1697	-	-	-	-	-	L	F	PAR	AD	H	-	100	-	0	-	-	+	+	-	-	-	+	0	-	0	0	-	0	0	-	-	+	+	-
M	8	1698	-	-	-	-	-	L	F	PAR+	AD	H	-	100	-	0	-	-	-	+	-	-	+	-	0	-	0	0	-	1	0	-	+	-	-	-
M	11	1699	-	-	-	-	-	L	F	PAR	AD	H	-	100	-	0	-	-	-	+	-	-	+	+	0	-	0	0	-	0	0	-	-	+	-	-
M	8	1700	-	-	-	-	-	L	F	PAR+	AD	H	-	100	-	0	-	-	-	+	-	-	-	-	0	-	0	1	-	4	0	-	-	-	-	-
M	8	1701	-	-	-	-	-	L	F	PAR	AD	H	-	100	-	0	-	-	-	+	-	-	+	+	0	-	0	0	-	0	0	-	-	+	+	+
M	6	1702	-	-	-	-	-	L	F	PAR	AD	H	-	100	-	0	-	-	+	+	-	-	-	+	0	-	0	0	-	0	0	-	-	+	+	+
M	65	1703	-	-	-	-	-	I	F	PAR	00	H	-	100	-	0	-	-	+	+	+	-	-	-	0	-	0	0	-	0	0	-	-	-	-	-
M	6	1704	-	-	-	-	-	I	F	PAR	IM	H	-	100	-	0	-	-	-	+	-	-	+	-	0	-	0	0	-	0	0	-	-	-	+	-
M	8	1705	-	-	-	-	-	I	F	PAR	IM	H	-	100	-	0	-	-	-	+	-	+	-	-	0	-	0	0	-	0	0	-	-	+	+	+
M	6	1706	-	-	-	-	-	I	F	PAR	IM	H	-	100	-	0	-	-	+	+	-	-	-	-	0	-	0	0	-	0	0	-	-	+	+	+
M	6	1707	-	-	-	-	-	I	F	PAR	IM	H	-	80	-	0	-	-	+	+	-	-	-	-	0	-	0	0	-	0	0	-	-	+	+	+
M	11	1708	-	-	-	-	-	I	F	PAR	IM	H	-	100	-	0	-	-	-	+	-	-	-	-	0	-	0	0	-	0	0	-	-	-	+	-
M	8	1709	-	-	-	-	-	I	F	PAR	IM	H	-	100	-	0	-	-	-	+	-	-	+	-	0	-	0	0	-	0	0	-	-	-	-	-
M	6	1710	-	-	-	-	-	I	F	PAR	IM	H	-	20	-	0	-	-	+	+	-	-	-	+	0	-	0	0	-	0	0	-	-	-	+	-
M	6	1711	-	-	-	-	-	I	F	PAR	IM	H	-	50	-	0	-	-	+	+	-	-	-	+	0	-	0	0	-	0	0	-	-	+	+	+
M	8	1712	-	-	-	-	-	I	F	PAR	IM	H	-	100	-	0	-	-	-	+	-	+	-	-	0	-	0	0	-	0	0	-	-	+	+	+
M	6	1713	-	-	-	-	-	I	F	PAR	IM	H	-	100	-	0	-	-	-	+	-	-	-	+	0	-	0	0	-	0	0	-	-	+	+	+
M	6	1714	-	-	-	-	-	I	F	PAR	IM	H	-	100	-	0	-	-	+	+	-	-	-	-	0	-	0	0	-	0	0	-	-	+	+	-
M	6	1715	-	-	-	-	-	I	F	PAR	IM	H	-	100	-	0	-	-	+	+	-	-	-	+	0	-	0	0	-	0	0	-	-	-	+	-
M	8	1716	-	-	-	-	-	I	F	PAR	AD	H	-	100	-	0	-	-	-	+	-	+	+	-	0	-	0	1	-	0	0	-	-	+	-	-
M	8	1717	-	-	-	-	-	I	F	PAR	AD	H	-	100	-	0	-	-	-	+	-	-	+	-	0	+	0	0	-	5	0	-	-	+	-	-
M	6	1718	-	-	-	-	-	I	F	PAR	AD	H	-	100	-	0	-	-	+	+	-	-	+	-	0	-	0	0	-	2	0	-	+	+	+	+
M	6	1719	-	-	-	-	-	I	F	PAR	AD	H	-	100	-	0	-	-	+	+	-	-	+	-	0	-	0	0	-	1	0	-	-	+	+	+
M	6	1720	-	-	-	-	-	I	F	PAR	AD	H	-	100	-	0	-	-	-	+	-	-	+	-	0	-	0	0	-	0	0	-	-	+	+	-
M	8	1721	-	-	-	-	-	I	F	PAR	AD	H	-	80	-	0	-	-	-	+	-	-	+	-	0	-	0	1	-	0	0	-	-	-	-	-
M	6	1722	-	-	-	-	-	I	F	PAR	AD	H	-	100	-	0	-	-	+	+	-	-	-	+	0	-	0	0	-	0	0	-	-	+	+	-
M	8	1723	-	-	-	-	-	I	F	PAR	AD	H	-	100	-	0	-	-	-	+	-	-	+	-	0	-	0	0	-	0	0	-	-	+	+	-
M	30	1724	-	-	-	-	-	I	F	PAR	AD	H	-	100	-	0	-	-	-	+	-	-	-	-	0	-	0	0	-	0	0	-	-	+	-	-
M	8	1725	-	-	-	-	-	I	F	PAR	AD	H	-	100	-	0	-	-	-	+	-	-	-	-	0	+	1	0	-	0	0	-	+	-	-	-
M	6	1726	-	-	-	-	-	I	F	PAR	AD	H	-	100	-	0	-	-	-	+	-	-	+	-	0	-	0	0	-	0	0	-	-	+	+	-
M	8	1727	-	-	-	-	-	I	F	PAR	AD	H	-	100	-	0	-	-	-	+	-	-	+	-	0	-	0	0	-	0	0	-	-	-	+	-
M	6	1728	-	-	-	-	-	I	F	PAR	AD	H	-	100	-	0	-	-	-	+	-	-	+	-	0	-	0	0	-	0	0	-	-	-	+	-
M	6	1729	-	-	-	-	-	I	F	PAR	AD	H	-	80	-	0	-	-	-	+	-	-	+	-	0	+	0	0	-	0	0	-	-	+	+	+
M	6	1730	-	-	-	-	-	I	F	PAR	AD	H	-	100	-	0	-	-	-	+	-	-	-	-	0	-	0	0	-	0	0	-	-	+	+	-
M	6	1731	-	-	-	-	-	I	F	PAR	AD	H	-	100	-	0	-	-	+	+	-	-	-	-	0	-	0	0	-	0	0	-	-	+	+	+
M	8	1732	-	-	-	-	-	I	F	PAR	AD	H	-	100	-	0	-	-	-	+	-	-	-	-	0	-	0	0	-	0	0	-	-	-	+	-
M	6	1733	-	-	-	-	-	I	F	PAR	AD	H	-	100	-	0	-	-	-	+	-	-	-	-	0	-	0	0	-	0	0	-	-	-	+	-
M	8	1734	-	-	-	-	-	I	F	PAR	AD	H	-	100	-	0	-	-	-	+	-	-	-	-	0	-	0	0	-	0	0	-	-	+	+	-
M	11	1735	-	-	-	-	-	I	F	PAR	AD	H	-	10	-	0	-	-	-	+	-	-	-	-	0	-	0	0	-	0	0	-	-	-	-	-
M	6	1736	R	W	PAR+	AD	H	-	-	-	-	-	152	100	-	0	-	-	-	+	-	-	-	+	2	-	0	0	-	9	0	-	+	+	+	+
M	6	1737	B	W	OCC+	AD	H	-	-	-	-	-	152	100	-	0	-	-	-	+	-	-	-	+	1	-	0	0	-	8	0	-	+	-	-	-
M	6	1738	R	W	TEM+	AD	H	-	-	-	-	-	152	100	-	0	-	-	-	+	-	-	-	-	0	+	0	0	-	0	0	-	-	-	-	-
M	6	1739	L	F	PAR	AD	H	-	-	-	-	-	152	100	-	0	-	-	-	+	-	-	-	+	0	-	0	0	-	0	0	-	-	-	-	-
M	6	1740	B	F	FRO	AD	H	-	-	-	-	-	152	100	-	0	-	-	-	+	-	-	+	+	0	-	0	1	-	0	0	-	+	+	-	-
M	6	1741	L	F	FRO+	AD	H	-	-	-	-	-	152	100	-	0	-	-	-	+	-	-	-	+	0	-	0	0	-	0	0	-	+	-	-	-
M	6	1742	R	F	OCC	AD	H	-	-	-	-	-	152	100	-	0	-	-	-	+	-	-	-	+	1	-	0	0	-	9	0	-	+	-	-	-
M	6	1743	L	F	PAR	AD	H	-	-	-	-	-	152	100	-	0	-	-	-	+	-	-	-	-	0	-	1	0	-	4	0	-	-	+	+	-
M	6	1744	L	F	PAR	AD	H	-	-	-	-	-	152	100	-	0	-	-	-	+	-	-	+	+	0	-	0	0	-	0	0	-	+	-	-	-

01	02	03	04	05	06	07	08	09	10	11	12	13	14	15	16	17	18	19	23	24	25	26	27	28	40	41	42	43	44	49	54	59	64	93	94	95
M	6	1745	L	F	PAR	AD	H	-	-	-	-	-	152	100	-	0	-	-	+	+	-	-	-	-	0	-	0	0	-	4	0	-	+	+	+	+
M	FA1	1746	R	W	PAR+	10	H	-	-	-	-	-	153	100	-	0	-	-	-	+	-	-	-	+	1	-	0	0	-	0	0	-	+	+	+	+
M	FA1	1747	B	W	OCC	10	H	-	-	-	-	-	153	100	-	0	-	-	+	+	-	-	-	+	0	-	0	0	-	0	0	-	+	+	+	+
M	FA1	1748	L	F	PAR	10	H	-	-	-	-	-	153	100	-	0	-	-	-	+	-	-	-	-	0	-	0	0	-	0	0	-	+	-	-	-
M	FA1	1749	L	F	PAR	10	H	-	-	-	-	-	153	100	-	0	-	-	+	+	-	-	-	+	0	-	0	0	-	0	0	-	+	-	-	-
M	FA1	1750	L	F	PAR	10	H	-	-	-	-	-	153	100	-	0	-	-	-	+	-	-	-	+	1	+	0	0	-	3	0	-	-	+	-	-
M	FA1	1751	R	F	PAR	10	H	-	-	-	-	-	153	90	-	0	+	-	+	+	-	-	-	+	1	-	0	0	-	0	0	-	-	-	-	-
M	FA1	1752	B	F	FRO	10	H	-	-	-	-	-	153	100	-	0	+	-	+	+	-	-	-	+	0	-	0	0	-	0	0	+	-	+	-	-
M	FA1	1753	-	-	-	-	-	L	F	FRO	10	H	153	50	-	0	-	-	+	+	-	-	-	+	0	-	0	0	-	0	0	-	+	+	-	+
M	11	1754	R	F	PAR+	AD	H	-	-	-	-	-	154	90	-	0	-	-	+	+	-	-	-	+	0	-	0	0	-	7	0	-	-	+	+	+
M	11	1755	R	F	PAR+	AD	H	-	-	-	-	-	154	90	-	0	-	-	+	+	-	-	-	+	1	-	0	0	-	0	0	-	+	+	+	+
M	11	1756	-	-	-	-	-	R	F	OCC	AD	H	154	100	-	0	-	-	-	+	-	-	-	+	0	-	0	0	-	0	0	-	-	+	+	+
M	11	1757	-	-	-	-	-	B	F	OCC	AD	H	154	60	-	0	-	-	-	+	-	-	-	+	0	-	0	0	-	0	0	-	-	+	+	+
M	11	1758	-	-	-	-	-	L	F	OCC	AD	H	154	100	-	0	-	-	-	+	-	-	-	+	0	-	0	0	-	0	0	-	-	+	+	+
M	11	1759	-	-	-	-	-	L	F	OCC	AD	H	154	100	-	0	-	-	-	+	-	-	+	-	0	-	0	0	-	0	0	-	-	+	+	+
M	11	1760	-	-	-	-	-	R	F	OCC	AD	H	154	100	-	0	-	-	-	+	-	-	-	+	0	-	0	0	-	0	0	-	-	-	-	-
M	8	1761	R	W	PAR	AD	H	-	-	-	-	-	155	100	-	0	-	-	-	+	-	+	-	+	0	-	0	0	-	0	0	-	-	+	+	+
M	8	1762	B	F	OCC+	AD	H	-	-	-	-	-	155	100	-	0	-	-	-	+	-	-	-	-	0	-	0	0	-	0	0	-	-	+	+	+
M	8	1763	R	F	PAR	AD	H	-	-	-	-	-	155	100	-	0	-	-	-	+	-	-	+	+	0	-	0	0	-	0	0	-	-	+	-	-
M	8	1764	-	-	-	-	-	L	F	PAR	AD	H	155	100	P	0	-	-	+	+	-	-	+	+	0	-	0	0	-	0	0	-	-	+	+	+
M	8	1765	-	-	-	-	-	R	F	TEM	AD	H	155	100	-	0	-	-	-	+	-	-	-	+	0	-	0	0	-	0	0	-	-	-	-	-
M	8	1766	-	-	-	-	-	R	F	PAR	AD	H	155	80	-	0	-	-	-	+	-	-	-	+	0	-	0	0	-	0	0	-	-	-	-	-
M	8	1767	-	-	-	-	-	R	F	PAR	AD	H	155	100	-	0	-	-	-	+	-	+	-	-	0	-	0	0	-	0	0	-	-	-	-	-
M	8	1768	R	W	PAR+	AD	H	-	-	-	-	-	156	100	-	0	-	-	+	+	-	-	+	+	1	-	0	0	-	9	0	-	+	+	+	+
M	8	1769	R	F	OCC	AD	H	-	-	-	-	-	156	100	-	0	-	-	+	+	-	-	-	+	0	-	0	0	-	0	0	-	-	+	-	-
M	8	1770	-	-	-	-	-	L	F	PAR	AD	H	156	100	-	0	-	-	-	+	-	-	-	+	0	-	0	0	-	0	0	-	-	-	+	-
M	8	1771	-	-	-	-	-	L	F	PAR	AD	H	156	100	-	0	-	-	-	+	-	-	-	+	0	-	0	0	-	0	0	-	-	-	+	-
M	30	1772	-	-	-	-	-	I	F	PAR	AD	H	157	100	-	0	-	-	-	+	-	-	+	-	0	-	0	1	-	0	0	-	+	+	+	+
M	8	1773	-	-	-	-	-	I	F	PAR	AD	H	157	100	-	0	-	-	-	+	-	-	-	-	0	-	0	0	-	0	0	-	-	+	+	+
M	8	1774	-	-	-	-	-	I	F	PAR	AD	H	157	100	-	0	-	-	-	+	-	-	+	-	0	-	0	1	-	0	0	-	-	+	-	-
M	11	1775	-	-	-	-	-	I	F	PAR	AD	H	158	100	-	0	-	-	+	+	-	-	-	-	0	-	0	0	-	0	0	-	-	+	-	+
M	11	1776	-	-	-	-	-	I	F	PAR	AD	H	158	100	-	0	-	-	+	+	-	-	-	-	0	-	0	0	-	0	0	-	-	+	+	+
M	6	1777	-	-	-	-	-	I	F	PAR	IM	H	159	100	-	0	-	-	+	+	-	-	-	+	0	-	0	0	-	0	0	-	-	+	-	-
M	6	1778	-	-	-	-	-	I	F	PAR	IM	H	159	100	-	0	-	-	+	+	-	-	-	-	0	-	0	0	-	0	0	-	-	+	-	-
M	11	1779	-	-	-	-	-	I	F	PAR	AD	H	160	20	-	0	-	-	-	+	-	-	-	+	0	-	0	0	-	0	0	-	-	-	+	-
M	11	1780	-	-	-	-	-	I	F	PAR	AD	H	160	100	-	0	-	-	-	+	-	-	-	+	0	-	0	0	-	0	0	-	-	-	+	-
M	8	1781	-	-	-	-	-	I	F	PAR	IM	H	161	100	-	0	-	-	-	+	-	-	-	-	0	-	0	0	-	0	0	-	-	+	-	-
M	8	1782	-	-	-	-	-	I	F	PAR	IM	H	161	100	-	0	-	-	+	+	-	-	-	-	0	-	0	0	-	0	0	-	-	+	-	-
M	8	1783	B	F	OCC	06	H	-	-	-	-	-	-	100	-	0	-	-	-	+	-	-	-	+	0	-	0	0	+	0	0	-	-	-	-	-
M	8	1784	-	-	-	-	-	B	F	OCC	06	H	-	100	-	0	-	-	-	+	-	-	+	-	1	-	0	0	+	0	0	-	-	-	-	-
M	8	1785	B	F	OCC	12	H	-	-	-	-	-	-	100	-	0	-	-	-	+	-	-	-	+	0	+	0	0	-	0	0	-	-	-	-	-
M	11	1786	-	-	-	-	-	B	F	OCC	IM	H	-	80	-	0	-	-	-	+	-	-	-	-	0	-	0	0	-	0	0	-	-	-	+	-
M	50	1787	-	-	-	-	-	B	F	OCC	AD	H	-	100	-	0	-	-	+	+	-	-	-	-	0	-	0	0	-	0	0	-	-	-	-	-
M	8	1788	B	F	OCC	AD	H	-	-	-	-	-	-	100	-	0	-	-	+	+	-	-	-	-	0	-	0	0	-	0	0	-	-	+	+	+
M	6	1789	-	-	-	-	-	B	F	OCC	AD	H	-	80	-	0	-	-	-	+	-	-	-	-	0	-	0	0	-	0	0	-	-	-	-	-
M	6	1790	-	-	-	-	-	R	F	OCC	06	H	-	100	-	0	-	-	-	+	-	-	-	-	0	-	0	0	-	0	0	-	-	-	-	-
M	8	1791	-	-	-	-	-	R	F	OCC	IM	H	-	100	-	0	-	-	+	+	-	-	-	+	0	-	0	0	-	0	0	-	-	+	+	+
M	8	1792	-	-	-	-	-	R	F	OCC	AD	H	-	100	-	0	-	-	-	+	-	-	-	-	0	+	0	0	-	0	0	-	-	-	-	-
M	30	1793	-	-	-	-	-	R	F	OCC	AD	H	-	100	-	0	-	-	-	+	-	-	+	+	0	-	0	0	-	0	0	-	-	+	+	+
M	6	1794	-	-	-	-	-	L	F	OCC	04	H	-	100	-	0	-	-	+	+	-	-	-	-	0	-	0	0	-	0	0	-	-	-	-	-
M	6	1795	-	-	-	-	-	L	F	OCC	04	H	-	100	-	0	-	-	+	+	-	-	-	-	0	-	0	0	-	0	0	-	-	-	-	-
M	8	1796	-	-	-	-	-	L	F	OCC	06	H	-	100	-	0	-	-	-	+	-	-	-	+	0	-	0	0	-	0	0	-	-	-	-	-
M	8	1797	-	-	-	-	-	L	F	OCC	AD	H	-	100	-	0	-	-	-	+	-	+	-	+	0	-	0	0	-	2	0	-	-	-	-	-
M	65	1798	-	-	-	-	-	L	F	OCC	AD	H	-	0	-	3	-	-	+	-	+	-	-	+	0	-	0	0	-	0	0	-	-	-	-	-
M	6	1799	-	-	-	-	-	I	F	OCC	IM	H	-	50	-	0	-	-	+	+	-	-	-	-	0	-	0	0	-	0	0	-	-	-	-	-
M	8	1800	-	-	-	-	-	I	F	OCC	IM	H	-	100	-	0	-	-	-	+	-	-	-	+	0	-	0	0	-	0	0	-	-	-	-	-
M	11	1801	-	-	-	-	-	I	F	OCC	IM	H	-	100	-	0	-	-	-	+	-	-	-	+	0	-	0	0	-	0	0	-	-	-	-	-
M	11	1802	-	-	-	-	-	I	F	OCC	AD	H	-	50	-	1	-	-	-	+	-	-	-	+	0	-	0	0	-	0	0	-	-	-	-	-

01	02	03	04	05	06	07	08	09	10	11	12	13	14	15	16	17	18	19	23	24	25	26	27	28	40	41	42	43	44	49	54	59	64	93	94	95
M	8	1803	B	F	OCC	12	H	-	-	-	-	-	162	100	-	0	-	-	-	+	-	-	+	+	0	+	0	0	+	0	0	-	+	-	-	-
M	8	1804	-	-	-	-	-	R	F	OCC	12	H	162	100	-	0	-	-	-	+	-	-	-	-	0	+	0	0	-	0	0	-	-	-	-	-
M	8	1805	R	F	TEM+	08	H	-	-	-	-	-	-	100	-	0	-	-	-	+	-	-	+	-	1	-	1	0	-	1	0	-	-	+	+	+
M	50	1806	R	F	TEM+	10	H	-	-	-	-	-	-	100	-	0	-	-	+	+	-	-	-	-	0	-	0	0	-	0	0	-	-	+	+	+
M	8	1807	R	W	TEM	12	H	-	-	-	-	-	-	100	-	0	-	-	-	+	-	-	-	+	0	-	0	0	-	0	0	-	-	+	+	+
M	8	1808	R	W	TEM	12	H	-	-	-	-	-	-	100	-	0	-	-	-	+	-	-	-	+	0	-	0	0	-	0	0	-	-	-	-	-
M	6	1809	R	W	TEM+	AD	H	-	-	-	-	-	-	100	-	0	-	-	-	+	-	-	-	+	0	-	0	0	-	0	0	-	+	+	+	+
M	8	1810	R	W	TEM	AD	H	-	-	-	-	-	-	100	-	0	-	-	-	+	-	-	-	+	0	+	0	0	-	0	0	-	-	+	+	+
M	8	1811	-	-	-	-	-	R	F	TEM	AD	H	-	100	-	0	-	-	-	+	-	-	-	+	0	-	0	0	-	0	0	-	-	-	-	-
M	8	1812	-	-	-	-	-	R	F	TEM	AD	H	-	100	-	0	-	-	-	+	-	-	+	-	0	-	0	0	-	2	0	-	+	-	-	-
M	6	1813	-	-	-	-	-	L	F	TEM	08	H	-	100	-	0	-	-	+	+	-	-	-	+	0	-	0	0	-	0	0	-	+	+	+	+
M	6	1814	-	-	-	-	-	L	F	TEM	10	H	-	100	-	0	-	-	+	+	-	-	-	+	0	-	0	0	-	0	0	-	-	+	+	+
M	FA3	1815	L	W	TEM+	AD	H	-	-	-	-	-	-	100	+	0	-	-	-	+	-	-	-	-	0	-	0	0	-	0	0	-	-	+	+	+
M	8	1816	L	W	TEM	AD	H	-	-	-	-	-	-	100	-	0	-	-	-	+	-	-	-	-	0	-	0	0	-	0	0	-	-	+	+	+
M	8	1817	L	W	TEM	AD	H	-	-	-	-	-	-	100	-	0	-	-	+	+	-	-	-	+	0	-	0	0	-	0	0	-	-	+	+	+
M	8	1818	-	-	-	-	-	L	F	TEM	AD	H	-	100	-	0	-	-	-	+	-	-	-	+	0	-	0	0	-	0	0	-	-	+	+	+
M	50	1819	-	-	-	-	-	L	F	TEM	AD	H	-	100	-	0	-	-	-	+	-	-	-	-	0	-	0	0	-	0	0	-	-	+	+	+
M	3	1820	-	-	-	-	-	L	F	TEM	AD	H	-	100	-	0	-	-	-	+	-	-	-	-	0	-	0	0	-	0	0	-	-	-	-	-
M	8	1821	-	-	-	-	-	I	F	TEM	IM	H	-	100	-	0	-	-	-	+	-	-	-	+	0	-	0	0	-	0	0	-	-	+	-	-
M	8	1822	-	-	-	-	-	I	F	TEM	AD	H	-	100	-	0	-	-	-	+	-	-	+	+	1	-	0	0	-	0	0	-	-	-	-	-
M	8	1823	-	-	-	-	-	I	F	TEM	AD	H	-	100	-	0	-	-	-	+	-	-	-	+	0	-	0	0	-	1	0	-	-	+	-	-
M	8	1824	-	-	-	-	-	I	F	TEM	AD	H	-	100	-	0	-	-	-	+	-	-	-	+	0	-	0	1	-	0	0	-	-	-	-	-
M	8	1825	-	-	-	-	-	I	F	TEM	AD	H	-	100	-	0	-	-	-	+	-	-	-	+	0	-	0	0	-	3	0	-	+	-	-	-
M	6	1826	-	-	-	-	-	I	F	TEM	AD	H	-	100	-	0	-	-	+	+	-	-	-	+	0	-	0	0	-	0	0	-	-	-	-	-
M	8	1827	-	-	-	-	-	I	F	TEM	AD	H	-	100	-	0	-	-	+	+	-	-	-	-	0	-	0	0	-	0	0	-	-	+	-	-
M	11	1827.1	-	-	-	-	-	I	F	TEM	AD	H	-	100	-	0	-	-	+	+	-	-	-	-	0	-	0	0	-	0	0	-	-	-	-	-
M	6	1828	R	W	TEM+	08	H	-	-	-	-	-	163	100	-	0	-	-	+	+	-	-	-	+	0	-	0	0	-	0	0	-	-	+	+	+
M	6	1829	R	F	PAR	08	H	-	-	-	-	-	163	100	-	0	-	-	+	+	-	-	-	+	0	-	0	0	-	0	0	-	-	+	+	+
M	6	1830	R	F	FRO	08	H	-	-	-	-	-	163	100	-	0	-	-	+	+	-	-	-	+	0	-	0	0	-	0	0	-	-	+	+	+
M	6	1831	-	-	-	-	-	R	F	SPH	08	H	163	100	-	0	-	-	+	+	-	-	-	+	0	-	0	0	-	0	0	-	-	-	-	-
M	6	1832	-	-	-	-	-	R	F	PAR	08	H	163	100	-	0	-	-	+	+	-	-	-	-	0	-	0	0	-	0	0	-	-	-	+	-
M	8	1833	L	W	TEM+	08	H	-	-	-	-	-	164	100	-	0	-	-	-	+	-	-	+	+	0	+	0	0	-	0	0	-	+	+	+	+
M	8	1834	-	-	-	-	-	R	F	SPH	08	H	164	100	-	0	-	-	-	+	-	-	-	+	0	+	0	0	-	0	0	-	-	-	-	-
M	8	1835	-	-	-	-	-	L	F	TEM	08	H	164	100	-	0	-	-	-	+	-	-	-	+	1	-	0	0	-	0	0	-	+	-	-	-
M	8	1836	R	W	TEM+	AD	H	-	-	-	-	-	165	100	-	0	-	-	-	+	-	-	-	+	0	-	0	0	-	3	0	-	-	+	+	+
M	8	1837	R	F	PAR	AD	H	-	-	-	-	-	165	100	-	0	-	-	-	+	-	-	-	+	0	-	0	0	-	3	0	-	-	+	+	+
M	8	1838	-	-	-	-	-	R	F	PAR	AD	H	165	100	-	0	-	-	-	+	-	-	-	-	0	-	0	0	-	0	0	-	-	-	-	-
M	8	1839	-	-	-	-	-	B	F	OCC	AD	H	165	100	-	0	-	-	-	+	-	-	+	+	0	-	0	0	-	0	0	-	-	+	-	-
M	FA1	1840	L	W	TEM	AD	H	-	-	-	-	-	166	80	-	0	-	-	+	+	-	-	-	+	0	-	0	0	-	0	0	-	+	-	-	-
M	FA1	1841	L	F	PAR	AD	H	-	-	-	-	-	166	80	-	0	-	-	-	+	-	-	-	+	0	-	0	0	-	0	0	-	-	-	+	-
M	FA1	1842	-	-	-	-	-	L	F	TEM	AD	H	166	100	-	0	-	-	+	+	-	-	-	+	0	-	0	0	-	0	0	-	-	-	+	-
M	FA1	1843	-	-	-	-	-	L	F	TEM	AD	H	166	0	-	3	-	-	+	+	-	-	-	-	0	-	0	0	-	0	0	-	-	-	-	-
M	65	1844	-	-	-	-	-	L	F	TEM+	08	H	167	100	-	0	-	-	-	+	-	+	-	+	0	-	0	0	-	0	0	-	-	-	-	-
M	5	1845	-	-	-	-	-	L	F	TEM	08	H	167	100	-	0	-	-	-	+	-	-	-	-	0	-	0	0	-	0	0	-	-	-	-	-
M	8	1846	R	W	TEM	10	H	-	-	-	-	-	168	100	-	0	-	-	-	+	-	-	-	+	0	-	0	0	-	0	0	-	-	+	-	-
M	8	1847	B	W	SPH	10	H	-	-	-	-	-	168	100	-	0	-	-	-	+	-	-	-	+	0	-	0	0	-	0	0	-	-	-	-	-
M	8	1848	R	W	TEM	12	H	-	-	-	-	-	169	100	-	0	-	-	-	+	-	-	-	+	0	+	0	0	-	0	0	-	-	+	+	-
M	8	1849	-	-	-	-	-	R	F	TEM	12	H	169	100	-	0	-	-	-	+	-	-	+	+	0	-	0	0	-	0	0	-	-	-	-	-
M	6	1850	-	-	-	-	-	R	F	MAX	04	H	-	100	-	0	-	-	-	+	-	-	-	+	0	-	0	0	-	0	0	-	-	-	-	-
M	6	1851	R	F	MAX+	06	H	-	-	-	-	-	-	100	-	0	-	-	+	+	-	-	-	+	0	-	0	0	-	0	0	-	-	+	+	+
M	8	1852	R	W	MAX	11	H	-	-	-	-	-	-	100	-	0	-	-	-	+	-	-	-	+	1	-	0	1	-	0	0	-	+	+	+	+
M	50	1853	R	F	MAX+	13	H	-	-	-	-	-	-	100	-	0	-	-	+	+	-	-	-	-	0	+	0	0	-	0	0	-	-	+	+	-
M	0	1854	R	F	MAX	AD	H	-	-	-	-	-	-	100	-	0	-	-	-	+	-	-	-	+	0	-	0	0	-	0	0	-	-	-	-	-
M	8	1855	R	F	MAX+	AD	H	-	-	-	-	-	-	100	-	0	-	-	-	+	-	-	-	+	0	-	0	0	-	0	0	-	-	-	-	-
M	8	1856	-	-	-	-	-	R	F	MAX	AD	H	-	100	-	0	-	-	-	+	-	-	-	+	0	-	0	0	-	0	0	-	+	-	-	-
M	8	1857	-	-	-	-	-	R	F	MAX	AD	H	-	100	-	0	-	-	-	+	-	-	-	+	0	-	0	0	-	0	0	-	-	+	+	-
M	6	1858	L	W	MAX+	04	H	-	-	-	-	-	-	100	-	0	-	-	+	+	-	-	-	+	0	-	0	0	-	0	0	-	-	-	-	-
M	6	1859	L	W	MAX+	07	H	-	-	-	-	-	-	100	-	0	-	-	+	+	-	-	-	+	0	-	0	0	-	9	0	-	+	-	-	-

01	02	03	04	05	06	07	08	09	10	11	12	13	14	15	16	17	18	19	23	24	25	26	27	28	40	41	42	43	44	49	54	59	64	93	94	95
M	6	1860	L	F	MAX	AD	H	-	-	-	-	-	-	90	-	0	-	-	+	+	-	-	-	+	0	-	0	0	-	0	0	-	-	+	+	-
M	50	1861	-	-	-	-	-	I	F	MAX	IM	H	-	100	-	0	-	-	+	+	+	-	-	-	0	-	0	0	-	0	0	-	-	-	-	-
M	6	1862	-	-	-	-	-	I	F	MAX	IM	H	-	100	-	0	-	-	+	+	-	-	-	-	0	-	0	0	-	0	0	-	-	-	-	-
M	8	1863	L	W	MAX+	AD	H	-	-	-	-	-	170	100	-	0	-	-	+	+	-	-	-	+	1	-	0	0	-	0	0	-	-	+	+	+
M	8	1864	R	W	MAX+	AD	H	-	-	-	-	-	170	100	-	0	-	-	-	+	-	-	-	+	0	-	0	0	-	0	0	-	-	+	+	+
M	8	1865	R	F	FRO+	AD	H	-	-	-	-	-	170	100	-	0	-	-	-	+	-	-	+	+	0	-	0	0	-	0	0	-	-	+	+	+
M	8	1866	L	F	FRO+	AD	H	-	-	-	-	-	170	100	-	0	-	-	-	+	-	-	-	+	0	-	0	0	-	0	0	-	+	+	+	+
M	8	1867	R	F	PAR	AD	H	-	-	-	-	-	170	100	-	0	-	-	+	+	-	-	-	+	0	-	0	0	-	0	0	-	-	+	+	+
M	8	1868	-	-	-	-	-	R	F	SPH	AD	H	170	100	-	0	-	-	-	+	-	-	-	+	0	-	0	0	-	0	0	-	-	-	-	-
M	8	1869	R	W	MAX+	15	H	-	-	-	-	-	171	100	-	0	-	-	+	+	-	-	-	+	0	-	0	0	-	0	0	-	-	+	+	+
M	8	1870	L	W	MAX+	15	H	-	-	-	-	-	171	100	-	0	-	-	-	+	-	-	-	+	0	-	0	0	-	0	0	-	-	+	+	+
M	8	1871	-	-	-	-	-	R	F	ZYG+	AD	H	171	100	-	0	-	-	-	+	-	-	-	+	0	-	0	0	-	0	0	-	-	+	+	+
M	8	1872	R	W	MAX+	05	H	-	-	-	-	-	172	100	-	0	-	-	-	+	-	-	-	+	0	-	0	0	-	0	0	-	-	-	-	-
M	8	1873	L	W	MAX	06	H	-	-	-	-	-	172	100	-	0	-	-	-	+	-	-	-	+	0	-	0	0	-	0	0	-	-	-	-	-
M	8	1874	L	W	ZYG	06	H	-	-	-	-	-	172	100	-	0	-	-	-	+	-	-	-	+	0	-	0	0	-	0	0	-	-	-	-	-
M	8	1875	R	W	MAX+	AD	H	-	-	-	-	-	173	100	-	0	-	-	-	+	-	-	-	+	1	-	0	0	+	4	0	-	-	-	-	-
M	8	1876	L	W	ZYG	AD	H	-	-	-	-	-	173	100	-	0	-	-	-	+	-	-	-	+	0	-	0	0	-	4	0	-	-	-	-	-
M	82	1877	R	W	MAX+	13	H	-	-	-	-	-	174	100	-	0	-	-	-	+	-	-	-	+	1	+	0	0	-	0	2	-	+	-	-	-
M	FA1	1878	B	F	FRO+	12	H	-	-	-	-	-	174	100	-	0	-	-	+	+	-	-	-	+	0	-	0	0	-	0	0	-	+	-	-	-
M	8	1879	L	W	MAX+	AD	H	-	-	-	-	-	175	100	-	0	-	-	-	+	-	-	-	+	1	-	0	1	-	0	0	-	-	-	-	-
M	8	1880	R	W	ZYG+	AD	H	-	-	-	-	-	175	100	-	0	-	-	-	+	-	-	-	+	0	-	0	0	-	0	0	-	+	-	-	-
M	8	1881	L	W	MAX+	10	H	-	-	-	-	-	176	100	-	0	-	-	-	+	-	-	-	+	0	+	0	0	-	0	0	-	-	-	-	-
M	8	1882	R	F	MAX+	10	H	-	-	-	-	-	176	100	-	0	-	-	-	+	-	-	-	+	0	-	0	0	-	0	0	-	-	-	-	-
M	6	1883	R	W	MAX+	04	H	-	-	-	-	-	177	100	-	0	-	-	+	+	-	-	-	+	0	-	0	0	-	0	0	-	-	+	+	+
M	6	1884	L	W	MAX+	04	H	-	-	-	-	-	177	100	-	0	-	-	-	+	-	-	-	+	0	-	0	0	-	0	0	-	-	-	-	-
M	6	1885	R	F	MAX	AD	H	-	-	-	-	-	178	100	-	0	-	-	-	+	-	-	-	+	0	+	1	0	-	0	0	-	+	+	+	+
M	6	1886	L	F	MAX	AD	H	-	-	-	-	-	178	100	-	0	-	-	-	+	-	-	-	+	0	-	2	0	-	0	0	-	+	+	+	+
M	8	1887	R	F	MAX+	AD	H	-	-	-	-	-	179	100	-	0	-	-	-	+	-	-	-	+	0	-	0	0	-	0	0	-	+	+	+	+
M	8	1888	L	F	MAX+	AD	H	-	-	-	-	-	179	100	-	0	-	-	+	+	-	-	-	+	0	-	0	0	-	0	0	-	-	+	+	+
M	8	1889	R	W	ZYG+	12	H	-	-	-	-	-	-	100	-	0	-	-	+	+	-	-	-	+	0	-	0	0	-	0	0	-	-	+	+	+
M	65	1890	L	W	ZYG+	AD	H	-	-	-	-	-	-	100	-	0	-	-	+	+	-	-	-	+	0	-	0	0	-	0	0	-	-	-	-	-
M	6	1891	R	F	ZYG+	AD	H	-	-	-	-	-	-	100	-	0	-	-	+	+	-	-	-	+	0	-	0	0	-	0	0	-	-	+	+	+
M	11	1892	-	-	-	-	-	B	F	SPH	10	H	-	100	-	0	-	-	-	+	-	-	-	+	0	-	0	0	-	0	0	-	-	-	-	-
M	8	1893	-	-	-	-	-	B	F	SPH	AD	H	-	100	-	0	-	-	-	+	-	-	-	+	0	-	0	0	-	0	0	-	-	-	-	-
M	6	1894	-	-	-	-	-	B	F	SPH+	AD	H	-	100	-	0	-	-	-	+	-	-	-	+	0	+	0	0	-	0	0	-	-	-	-	-
M	30	1895	-	-	-	-	-	R	F	SPH	08	H	-	100	-	0	-	-	-	+	-	-	-	+	0	+	0	0	-	0	0	-	-	-	-	-
M	6	1896	-	-	-	-	-	R	F	SPH	08	H	-	100	-	0	-	-	-	+	-	-	-	+	0	+	0	0	-	0	0	-	-	+	+	+
M	50	1897	-	-	-	-	-	R	F	SPH	08	H	-	90	-	0	-	-	-	+	-	-	-	+	0	-	0	0	-	0	0	-	-	-	-	-
M	50	1898	-	-	-	-	-	R	F	SPH+	AD	H	-	70	-	0	-	-	+	+	-	-	-	-	0	-	0	0	-	0	0	-	-	-	-	-
M	6	1899	-	-	-	-	-	R	F	SPH	AD	H	-	100	-	0	-	-	-	+	-	-	-	+	0	-	0	0	-	0	0	-	-	-	-	-
M	30	1900	-	-	-	-	-	R	F	SPH	AD	H	-	100	-	0	-	-	-	+	-	-	-	+	0	+	0	0	-	0	0	-	-	-	-	-
M	6	1901	-	-	-	-	-	L	F	SPH	04	H	-	100	-	0	-	-	+	+	-	-	-	+	0	-	0	0	-	0	0	-	-	-	-	-
M	8	1902	-	-	-	-	-	L	F	SPH+	06	H	-	100	-	0	+	-	+	+	-	-	-	-	0	-	0	0	-	0	0	-	-	+	+	+
M	6	1903	-	-	-	-	-	L	F	SPH	06	H	-	100	-	0	-	-	+	+	-	-	-	-	0	-	0	0	-	0	0	-	-	-	-	-
M	6	1904	-	-	-	-	-	L	F	SPH+	06	H	-	100	-	0	-	-	-	+	-	-	-	+	0	+	0	0	-	0	0	-	-	-	-	-
M	11	1905	L	F	SPH+	AD	H	-	-	-	-	-	-	100	-	0	-	-	+	+	-	-	-	-	0	-	0	0	-	0	0	-	-	+	+	+
M	6	1906	-	-	-	-	-	L	F	SPH	AD	H	-	100	-	0	-	-	-	+	-	-	-	+	0	-	0	0	-	0	0	-	-	-	-	-
M	8	1907	-	-	-	-	-	L	F	SPH	AD	H	-	100	-	0	-	-	+	+	-	-	-	+	0	-	0	0	-	0	0	-	-	+	+	+
M	8	1908	-	-	-	-	-	L	F	SPH	AD	H	-	100	-	0	-	-	-	+	-	-	-	-	0	+	0	0	-	0	0	-	-	-	-	-
M	6	1909	-	-	-	-	-	L	F	SPH+	AD	H	-	100	-	0	-	-	-	+	-	-	-	+	0	-	0	0	-	3	0	-	-	-	-	-
M	8	1910	-	-	-	-	-	I	F	SPH	AD	H	-	100	-	0	-	-	-	+	-	-	-	+	0	-	0	0	-	0	0	-	-	-	-	-
M	6	1911	-	-	-	-	-	I	F	SPH	AD	H	-	100	-	0	-	-	-	+	-	-	-	-	0	-	0	0	-	0	0	-	-	-	-	-
M	6	1912	-	-	-	-	-	I	F	SPH	AD	H	-	100	-	0	-	-	+	+	-	-	-	+	0	-	0	0	-	0	0	-	-	-	-	-
M	6	1913	-	-	-	-	-	I	F	SPH	AD	H	-	100	-	0	-	-	+	+	-	-	-	-	0	+	0	0	-	0	0	-	-	-	-	-
M	30	1914	-	-	-	-	-	I	F	SPH	AD	H	-	100	-	0	-	-	-	+	-	-	-	-	0	-	0	0	-	0	0	-	-	-	-	-
M	30	1915	-	-	-	-	-	I	F	SPH	AD	H	-	100	-	0	-	-	-	+	-	-	-	+	0	-	0	0	-	0	0	-	-	-	-	-
M	30	1916	-	-	-	-	-	L	F	SPH	08	H	180	100	-	0	-	-	-	+	-	-	-	+	0	-	0	0	-	0	0	-	-	-	-	-
M	30	1917	-	-	-	-	-	L	F	SPH	08	H	180	100	-	0	-	-	-	+	-	-	-	+	0	-	0	0	-	0	0	-	-	-	-	-

01	02	03	04	05	06	07	08	09	10	11	12	13	14	15	16	17	18	19	23	24	25	26	27	28	40	41	42	43	44	49	54	59	64	93	94	95
M	6	1918	-	-	-	-	-	R	F	NAS+	AD	H	-	100	-	0	-	-	-	+	-	-	-	-	0	-	0	0	-	0	0	-	-	+	+	+
M	8	1919	-	-	-	-	-	R	F	NAS+	AD	H	-	100	-	0	+	-	-	+	-	-	-	+	0	-	0	0	-	0	0	-	-	+	+	+
M	8	1920	-	-	-	-	-	B	F	ETH	AD	H	-	100	-	0	-	-	-	+	-	-	-	+	0	-	0	0	-	0	0	-	-	-	-	-
M	6	1921	-	-	-	-	-	B	F	ETH	AD	H	-	100	-	0	-	-	-	+	-	-	-	+	0	-	0	0	-	0	0	-	-	-	-	-
M	0	1922	-	-	-	-	-	B	F	VOM	AD	H	-	100	-	0	-	-	+	+	-	-	-	+	0	-	0	0	-	0	0	-	-	-	-	-
M	8	1923	-	-	-	-	-	I	F	INC	AD	H	-	100	-	0	-	-	-	+	-	-	-	+	0	-	0	0	-	0	0	-	-	-	-	-
M	8	1924	B	W	MAN	06	H	-	-	-	-	-	-	100	-	0	+	-	+	-	-	-	-	-	0	-	0	0	-	0	0	-	-	+	+	+
M	8	1925	B	W	MAN	10	H	-	-	-	-	-	-	100	-	0	-	-	+	-	+	-	-	-	0	-	0	0	-	0	0	-	-	+	+	+
M	8	1926	B	W	MAN	AD	H	-	-	-	-	-	-	100	-	0	-	-	-	+	-	-	-	-	0	+	0	0	-	0	0	-	-	-	-	-
M	5	1927	B	W	MAN	AD	H	-	-	-	-	-	-	100	-	0	-	-	-	-	-	-	-	-	0	-	0	0	-	0	0	-	-	-	-	-
M	8	1928	B	W	MAN	11	H	-	-	-	-	-	-	100	-	0	-	-	-	-	-	-	-	-	0	-	0	0	-	0	0	-	-	-	-	-
M	8	1929	B	W	MAN	AD	H	-	-	-	-	-	-	100	-	0	-	-	+	-	+	-	-	-	0	-	0	0	-	0	0	-	-	+	+	+
M	8	1930	B	W	MAN	AD	H	-	-	-	-	-	-	100	-	0	-	-	+	-	+	-	-	-	0	-	0	0	-	0	0	-	+	+	+	+
M	50	1931	B	W	MAN	AD	H	-	-	-	-	-	-	100	-	0	-	-	+	-	+	-	-	-	0	-	0	0	-	0	0	-	-	-	-	-
M	8	1932	B	W	MAN	AD	H	-	-	-	-	-	-	100	-	0	-	-	+	-	+	-	-	-	0	-	0	0	-	0	0	-	+	+	+	+
M	11	1933	B	W	MAN	AD	H	-	-	-	-	-	-	100	-	0	-	-	+	-	+	-	-	-	0	-	0	0	-	0	0	-	-	+	+	+
M	8	1934	B	W	MAN	AD	H	-	-	-	-	-	-	100	-	0	-	-	-	+	-	-	-	-	0	+	0	0	-	0	0	-	-	+	+	+
M	6	1935	R	F	MAN	09	H	-	-	-	-	-	-	0	-	0	-	-	+	-	+	-	-	-	0	-	0	0	-	0	0	-	-	-	-	-
M	6	1936	R	F	MAN	AD	H	-	-	-	-	-	-	100	-	0	-	-	+	-	+	-	-	-	0	-	0	0	-	6	0	-	-	+	+	+
M	8	1937	R	F	MAN	AD	H	-	-	-	-	-	-	100	-	0	+	-	-	+	-	-	-	-	0	-	0	0	-	0	0	-	-	+	+	+
M	6	1938	R	F	MAN	AD	H	-	-	-	-	-	183	40	-	2	+	-	+	-	+	-	-	-	0	-	0	0	-	0	0	-	-	-	-	-
M	6	1939	R	F	MAN	AD	H	-	-	-	-	-	-	100	-	0	-	-	-	+	-	-	-	-	0	-	0	0	+	0	0	-	-	-	-	-
M	6	1940	L	F	MAN	05	H	-	-	-	-	-	-	90	-	0	-	-	+	-	+	-	-	-	0	-	0	0	-	0	0	-	-	+	+	+
M	50	1941	L	F	MAN	07	H	-	-	-	-	-	-	100	-	0	-	-	+	-	+	-	-	-	0	-	0	0	-	0	0	-	-	+	-	-
M	6	1942	L	F	MAN	AD	H	-	-	-	-	-	-	40	-	0	-	-	+	+	+	-	-	-	0	-	0	0	-	5	0	-	-	+	+	+
M	6	1943	L	F	MAN	AD	H	-	-	-	-	-	-	100	-	0	-	-	-	+	-	-	-	-	0	-	0	0	-	0	0	-	-	-	-	-
M	6	1944	B	W	MAN	04	H	-	-	-	-	-	181	100	-	0	-	-	+	-	+	-	-	-	0	-	0	0	-	0	0	-	-	+	+	+
M	6	1945	L	F	MAN	04	H	-	-	-	-	-	181	100	-	0	-	-	+	+	+	-	-	-	0	-	0	0	-	0	0	-	-	+	+	+
M	6	1946	L	F	MAN	04	H	-	-	-	-	-	181	100	-	0	-	-	-	+	-	-	-	-	0	-	0	0	-	0	0	-	-	+	+	+
M	11	1947	L	F	MAN	14	H	-	-	-	-	-	182	100	-	0	+	-	-	+	-	-	-	-	0	+	0	0	-	0	0	-	+	+	+	+
M	11	1948	R	F	MAN	14	H	-	-	-	-	-	182	60	-	1	+	-	-	+	-	-	-	-	0	-	0	0	-	4	0	-	-	-	-	-
M	8	1949	R	F	MAN	AD	H	-	-	-	-	-	-	100	-	0	-	-	-	+	-	-	-	-	0	-	0	0	-	0	0	-	-	+	-	-
M	6	1950	L	F	MAN	AD	H	-	-	-	-	-	183	60	-	0	-	-	+	+	-	-	-	-	0	-	0	0	-	0	0	-	-	+	+	+
M	6	1951	R	F	MAN	AD	H	-	-	-	-	-	-	70	-	0	-	-	-	+	-	-	-	-	1	-	0	0	+	3	0	-	+	+	+	+
M	6	1952	L	F	MAN	AD	H	-	-	-	-	-	-	20	-	0	-	-	-	+	-	-	-	-	0	-	0	0	-	4	0	-	-	+	+	+
M	6	1953	B	F	MAN	AD	H	-	-	-	-	-	184	70	-	0	-	-	+	+	-	-	-	-	0	-	0	0	-	0	0	-	-	+	+	+
M	6	1954	L	F	MAN	AD	H	-	-	-	-	-	184	30	-	3	+	-	+	+	-	-	-	-	0	-	0	0	-	0	0	-	-	-	-	-
M	3	1955	R	F	MAN	09	H	-	-	-	-	-	185	100	-	0	-	-	+	-	+	-	-	-	0	-	0	0	-	0	0	-	-	+	+	+
M	6	1956	L	F	MAN	09	H	-	-	-	-	-	185	100	-	0	-	-	+	+	-	-	-	-	0	-	0	0	-	0	0	-	-	+	+	+
M	9	1957	-	-	-	-	-	I	F	ICR	IM	H	-	100	-	0	-	-	+	-	+	-	-	+	0	-	0	0	-	0	0	-	-	+	+	+
M	6	1958	-	-	-	-	-	I	F	ICR	IM	H	-	100	-	0	-	-	+	-	+	-	-	-	0	-	0	0	-	0	0	-	-	+	+	+
M	FA1	1959	-	-	-	-	-	I	F	ICR	IM	H	-	80	-	0	-	-	+	+	-	-	-	+	0	-	0	0	-	0	0	-	-	-	-	-
M	6	1960	-	-	-	-	-	I	F	ICR	IM	H	-	100	-	0	-	-	+	+	-	-	-	+	0	-	0	0	-	0	0	-	-	+	+	+
M	6	1961	-	-	-	-	-	I	F	ICR	IM	H	-	100	-	0	-	-	+	+	-	-	-	+	0	-	0	0	-	0	0	-	-	+	+	+
M	6	1962	-	-	-	-	-	I	F	ICR	IM	H	-	50	-	0	-	-	+	+	+	-	-	+	0	-	0	0	-	0	0	-	-	+	+	-
M	6	1963	-	-	-	-	-	I	F	ICR	IM	H	-	100	-	0	-	-	+	+	-	-	-	+	0	-	0	0	-	0	0	-	-	+	+	+
M	6	1964	-	-	-	-	-	I	F	ICR	IM	H	-	100	-	0	-	-	+	-	+	-	-	-	0	-	0	0	-	0	0	-	-	-	-	-
M	6	1965	-	-	-	-	-	I	F	ICR	IM	H	-	100	-	0	-	-	+	-	-	-	-	+	0	-	0	0	-	0	0	-	-	-	-	-
M	6	1966	-	-	-	-	-	I	F	ICR	IM	H	-	100	-	0	-	-	+	-	-	-	-	-	0	-	0	0	-	0	0	-	-	-	-	-
M	6	1967	-	-	-	-	-	I	F	ICR	IM	H	-	100	-	0	-	-	+	+	-	-	-	+	0	-	0	0	-	0	0	-	-	-	-	-
M	11	1968	-	-	-	-	-	I	F	ICR	AD	H	-	70	-	1	-	-	+	+	-	-	-	+	0	-	0	0	-	0	0	-	-	-	-	-
M	6	1969	-	-	-	-	-	I	F	ICR	AD	H	-	70	-	0	-	-	+	+	-	-	-	+	0	-	0	0	-	0	0	-	-	+	+	+
M	6	1970	-	-	-	-	-	I	F	ICR	AD	H	-	70	-	0	-	-	+	-	+	-	-	-	0	-	0	0	-	0	0	-	-	-	-	-
M	11	1971	-	-	-	-	-	I	F	ICR	AD	H	-	80	-	0	-	-	-	+	-	-	-	+	0	-	0	0	-	0	0	-	-	-	-	-
M	8	1972	-	-	-	-	-	I	F	ICR	AD	H	-	100	-	0	-	-	-	+	-	+	-	+	0	-	0	0	-	0	0	-	-	+	+	+
M	7	1973	-	-	-	-	-	I	F	ICR	AD	H	-	100	-	0	-	-	+	+	-	-	-	-	0	-	0	0	-	0	0	-	-	-	-	-
M	8	1974	-	-	-	-	-	I	F	ICR	AD	H	-	100	-	0	-	-	-	-	+	-	-	+	0	+	0	0	-	2	0	-	+	-	-	-
M	6	1975	-	-	-	-	-	I	F	ICR	AD	H	-	100	-	0	-	-	+	+	-	-	-	+	0	-	0	0	-	0	0	-	-	-	-	-

0.1	0.2	0.3	0.4	0.5	0.6	0.7	0.8	0.9	1.0	1.1	1.2	1.3	1.4	1.5	1.6	1.7	1.8	1.9	2.3	2.4	2.5	2.6	2.7	2.8	4.0	4.1	4.2	4.3	4.4	4.9	5.4	5.9	6.4	9.3	9.4	9.5
M	6	1976	-	-	-	-	-	I	F	ICR	AD	H	-	100	-	0	-	-	+	+	-	-	-	-	0	-	0	0	-	0	0	-	-	-	-	-
M	11	1977	-	-	-	-	-	I	F	ICR	AD	H	-	80	-	1	-	-	-	+	-	-	-	+	0	-	0	0	-	0	0	-	-	+	+	+
M	6	1978	-	-	-	-	-	I	F	ICR	AD	H	-	100	-	0	-	-	+	-	-	-	-	-	0	-	0	0	-	0	0	-	-	-	-	-
M	6	1979	-	-	-	-	-	I	F	ICR	AD	H	-	100	-	0	-	-	+	+	-	-	-	+	0	-	0	0	-	0	0	-	-	+	+	+
M	6	1980	-	-	-	-	-	I	F	ICR	AD	H	-	100	-	0	-	-	+	-	+	-	-	-	0	-	0	0	-	0	0	-	-	-	-	-
M	11	1981	-	-	-	-	-	I	F	ICR	AD	H	-	100	-	1	-	-	+	-	+	-	-	-	0	-	0	0	-	0	0	-	-	-	-	-
M	11	1982	-	-	-	-	-	I	F	ICR	AD	H	-	100	-	0	-	-	+	-	-	-	-	-	0	-	0	0	-	0	0	-	-	-	-	-
M	8	1983	-	-	-	-	-	I	F	ICR	AD	H	-	100	-	0	-	-	-	+	-	-	-	+	0	-	0	0	-	0	0	-	-	+	-	-
M	6	1984	-	-	-	-	-	I	F	ICR	AD	H	-	100	-	0	-	-	+	-	-	-	-	-	0	-	0	0	-	0	0	-	-	-	-	-
M	8	1985	-	-	-	-	-	I	F	ICR	AD	H	-	100	-	0	-	-	+	-	-	-	-	-	0	-	0	0	-	0	0	-	-	-	-	-
M	6	1986	-	-	-	-	-	I	F	ICR	AD	H	-	100	-	0	-	-	+	-	-	-	-	-	0	-	0	0	-	0	0	-	-	-	-	-
M	8	1987	-	-	-	-	-	I	F	ICR	AD	H	-	100	-	0	-	-	+	+	-	-	-	-	0	-	0	0	-	0	0	-	-	-	-	-
M	8	1988	-	-	-	-	-	I	F	ICR	AD	H	-	100	-	0	-	-	+	+	-	-	-	+	0	-	0	0	-	0	0	-	-	-	-	-
M	6	1989	-	-	-	-	-	I	F	ICR	AD	H	-	40	-	0	-	-	+	-	+	-	-	+	0	-	0	0	-	0	0	-	-	+	+	+
M	8	1990	-	-	-	-	-	I	F	ICR	AD	H	-	100	-	0	-	-	+	-	+	-	-	-	0	-	0	0	-	0	0	-	-	-	-	-
M	6	1991	-	-	-	-	-	I	F	ICR	AD	H	-	100	-	0	-	-	+	-	+	-	-	+	0	-	0	0	-	0	0	-	-	-	-	-
M	6	1992	-	-	-	-	-	I	F	ICR	AD	H	-	60	-	0	-	-	+	-	+	-	-	-	0	-	0	0	-	0	0	-	-	-	-	-
M	6	1993	-	-	-	-	-	I	F	ICR	AD	H	-	70	-	0	+	-	+	-	+	-	-	-	0	-	0	0	-	0	0	-	-	-	-	-
M	6	1994	-	-	-	-	-	I	F	ICR	AD	H	-	100	-	0	-	-	+	-	+	-	-	-	0	-	0	0	-	0	0	-	-	-	-	-
M	6	1995	-	-	-	-	-	I	F	ICR	AD	H	-	100	-	0	-	-	+	-	-	-	-	-	0	-	0	0	-	1	0	-	-	-	-	-
M	6	1996	-	-	-	-	-	I	F	ICR	AD	H	-	100	-	0	-	-	+	+	-	-	-	-	0	+	0	0	-	0	0	-	-	-	-	-
M	8	1997	-	-	-	-	-	I	F	ICR	AD	H	-	100	-	0	-	-	-	+	-	-	-	-	0	+	0	0	-	0	0	-	-	-	-	-
M	6	1998	-	-	-	-	-	I	F	ICR	AD	H	-	100	-	0	-	-	+	-	+	-	-	-	0	-	0	0	-	0	0	-	-	-	-	-
M	6	1999	-	-	-	-	-	I	F	ICR	AD	H	-	100	-	0	-	-	+	-	+	-	-	-	0	-	0	0	-	0	0	-	-	-	-	-
M	8	2000	-	-	-	-	-	I	F	ICR	AD	H	-	100	-	0	-	-	+	-	-	-	-	-	0	-	0	0	-	0	0	-	-	-	-	-
M	6	2001	-	-	-	-	-	I	F	ICR	AD	H	-	100	-	0	-	-	+	-	-	-	-	-	0	-	0	0	-	0	0	-	-	-	-	-
M	6	2002	-	-	-	-	-	I	F	ICR	AD	H	-	100	-	0	-	-	+	-	-	-	-	-	0	-	0	0	-	0	0	-	-	-	-	-
M	6	2003	-	-	-	-	-	I	F	ICR	AD	H	-	100	-	0	+	-	+	-	+	-	-	-	0	-	0	0	-	0	0	-	-	-	-	-
M	6	2004	-	-	-	-	-	I	F	ICR	AD	H	-	100	-	0	-	-	+	-	-	-	-	-	0	-	0	0	-	0	0	-	-	-	-	-
M	6	2005	-	-	-	-	-	I	F	ICR	AD	H	-	100	-	0	-	-	-	+	-	-	-	-	0	-	0	0	-	0	0	-	-	-	-	-
M	6	2006	-	-	-	-	-	I	F	ICR	AD	H	-	100	-	0	-	-	+	-	-	-	-	-	0	-	0	0	-	0	0	-	-	-	-	-
M	8	2007	-	-	-	-	-	I	F	ICR	AD	H	-	100	-	0	-	-	+	+	-	-	-	-	0	-	0	0	-	0	0	-	-	+	-	-
M	6	2008	-	-	-	-	-	I	F	ICR	AD	H	-	100	-	0	-	-	+	-	-	-	-	-	0	-	0	0	-	0	0	-	-	-	-	-
M	6	2009	-	-	-	-	-	I	F	ICR	AD	H	-	100	-	0	-	-	+	-	-	-	-	-	0	-	0	0	-	0	0	-	-	-	-	-
M	6	2010	-	-	-	-	-	I	F	ICR	AD	H	-	100	-	0	-	-	+	+	-	-	-	+	0	-	0	0	-	0	0	-	-	-	-	-
M	6	2011	-	-	-	-	-	I	F	ICR	AD	H	-	100	-	0	-	-	+	+	-	-	-	-	0	-	0	0	-	0	0	-	-	-	-	-
M	6	2012	-	-	-	-	-	I	F	ICR	AD	H	-	100	-	0	-	-	+	+	-	-	-	+	0	-	0	0	-	0	0	-	-	-	-	-
M	6	2013	-	-	-	-	-	I	F	ICR	AD	H	-	80	-	0	-	-	+	-	-	-	-	-	0	-	0	0	-	0	0	-	-	-	-	-
M	6	2014	-	-	-	-	-	I	F	ICR	AD	H	-	100	-	0	-	-	+	-	-	-	-	-	0	-	0	0	-	0	0	-	-	-	-	-
M	8	2015	-	-	-	-	-	I	F	ICR	AD	H	-	90	-	0	-	-	+	-	-	-	-	-	0	-	0	0	-	0	0	-	-	-	-	-
M	6	2016	-	-	-	-	-	I	F	ICR	AD	H	-	100	-	0	-	-	+	+	-	-	-	-	0	-	0	0	-	0	0	-	-	-	-	-
M	8	2017	-	-	-	-	-	I	F	ICR	AD	H	-	100	-	0	-	-	+	+	-	-	-	-	0	-	0	0	-	0	0	-	-	+	-	-
M	8	2018	-	-	-	-	-	I	F	ICR	AD	H	-	100	-	0	-	-	+	-	-	-	-	-	0	-	0	0	-	0	0	-	-	-	-	-
M	6	2019	-	-	-	-	-	I	F	ICR	AD	H	-	100	-	0	-	-	+	-	-	-	-	-	0	-	0	0	-	0	0	-	-	-	-	-
M	8	2020	-	-	-	-	-	I	F	ICR	AD	H	186	100	-	0	-	-	-	+	-	-	+	-	0	-	2	1	-	0	0	-	-	-	-	-
M	8	2021	-	-	-	-	-	I	F	ICR	AD	H	186	100	-	0	-	-	-	+	-	-	-	-	0	-	0	0	-	0	0	-	+	+	+	+
M	6	2022	R	W	DUT	IM	H																												-	-	-
M	6	2023	R	W	DUT	IM	H																												+	+	+
M	6	2024	L	W	DUT	IM	H																												-	-	-
M	6	2025	L	W	DUT	IM	H																												-	-	-
M	6	2026	L	W	DUT	IM	H																												+	+	-
M	6	2027	R	F	DUT	IM	H																												+	+	+
M	0	2028	R	F	DUT	IM	H																												-	-	-
M	0	2029	R	F	DUT	IM	H																												+	+	+
M	6	2030	I	F	DUT	IM	H																												+	+	+
M	6	2031	I	F	DUT	IM	H																												+	+	+
M	6	2032	I	F	DUT	IM	H																												-	-	-
M	6	2033	R	W	DLT	IM	H																												-	-	-

0.1	0.2	0.3	0.4	0.5	0.6	0.7	0.8	0.9	1.0	1.1	1.2	1.3	1.4	1.5	1.6	1.7	1.8	1.9	2.3	2.4	2.5	2.6	2.7	2.8	4.0	4.1	4.2	4.3	4.4	4.9	5.4	5.9	6.4	9.3	9.4	9.5
M	0	2034	R	W	DLT	IM	H																											.	.	.
M	8	2035	R	W	PUT	AD	H																											.	.	.
M	8	2036	R	W	PUT	AD	H																											+	.	.
M	6	2037	R	W	PUT	AD	H																											.	.	.
M	50	2038	R	W	PUT	AD	H																											.	.	.
M	5	2039	R	W	PUT	AD	H																											.	.	.
M	11	2040	R	W	PUT	IM	H																											.	.	.
M	11	2041	R	W	PUT	IM	H																											.	.	.
M	8	2042	R	W	PUT	AD	H																											+	+	.
M	8	2043	R	W	PUT	AD	H																											.	+	.
M	11	2044	R	W	PUT	AD	H																											+	+	+
M	6	2045	R	F	PUT	IM	H																											.	.	.
M	6	2046	R	F	PUT	IM	H																											.	.	.
M	6	2047	R	F	PUT	IM	H																											.	.	.
M	6	2048	R	F	PUT	IM	H																											+	+	+
M	6	2049	R	F	PUT	IM	H																											.	.	.
M	6	2050	R	F	PUT	AD	H																											.	.	.
M	6	2051	R	F	PUT	AD	H																											+	+	+
M	8	2052	L	W	PUT	AD	H																											.	.	.
M	8	2053	L	W	PUT	AD	H																											.	.	.
M	50	2054	L	W	PUT	AD	H																											+	+	+
M	8	2055	L	W	PUT	AD	H																											.	.	.
M	6	2056	L	F	PUT	IM	H																											.	.	.
M	8	2057	I	F	PUT	IM	H																											+	+	.
M	6	2058	I	F	PUT	IM	H																											.	.	.
M	6	2059	I	F	PUT	AD	H																											+	+	+
M	8	2060	L	W	PUT	AD	H																											.	.	.
M	11	2061	R	W	PLT	AD	H																											.	.	.
M	6	2062	R	W	PLT	AD	H																											+	+	+
M	0	2063	R	W	PLT	AD	H																											.	.	.
M	11	2064	R	W	PLT	AD	H																											.	.	.
M	50	2065	R	W	PLT	AD	H																											.	.	.
M	0	2066	R	F	PLT	IM	H																											.	.	.
M	0	2067	R	F	PLT	IM	H																											.	.	.
M	0	2068	R	F	PLT	IM	H																											.	.	.
M	8	2069	L	W	PLT	AD	H																											.	.	.
M	3	2070	L	W	PLT	AD	H																											.	.	.
M	11	2071	L	W	PLT	AD	H																											.	.	.
M	11	2072	L	W	PLT	AD	H																											.	.	.
M	6	2073	L	W	PLT	AD	H																											.	+	.
M	11	2074	L	W	PLT	AD	H																											.	.	.
M	0	2075	L	F	PLT	IM	H																											.	.	.
M	50	2076	L	F	PLT	IM	H																											.	.	.
M	0	2077	L	F	PLT	IM	H																											.	.	.
M	0	2078	L	F	PLT	IM	H																											.	.	.
M	50	2079	L	F	PLT	IM	H																											.	+	.
M	8	2080	I	F	PLT	AD	H																											.	.	.
M	6	2081	I	F	PLT	AD	H																											+	+	.
M	5	2082	I	F	PLT	AD	H																											+	+	+
M	50	2083	I	F	PLT	AD	H																											+	+	.
M	8	2084	I	F	PLT	AD	H																											+	+	.
M	6	2085	I	F	PLT	AD	H																											.	.	.
M	8	2086	I	F	PLT	AD	H																											+	+	.
M	6	2087	I	F	PLT	AD	H																											.	.	.
M	6	2088	I	F	ITO	IM	H																											.	.	.
M	8	2089	I	F	ITO	AD	H																											.	+	.
M	50	2090	I	F	ITO	AD	H																											.	.	.
M	8	2091	I	F	ITO	AD	H																											.	.	.

01	02	03	04	05	06	07	08	09	10	11	12	13	14	15	16	17	18	19	23	24	25	26	27	28	40	41	42	43	44	49	54	59	64	93	94	95
M	6	2092	I	F	ITO	AD	H																											+	+	+
M	6	2093	I	F	ITO	AD	H																											+	+	+
M	6	2094	I	F	ITO	AD	H																											+	+	-
M	0	2095	I	F	ITO	AD	H																											-	-	-
M	6	2096	I	F	ITO	AD	H																											-	-	-
M	6	2097	I	F	ITO	AD	H																											-	-	-
M	6	2098	I	F	ITO	AD	H																											-	-	-
M	6	2099	I	F	ITO	AD	H																											+	+	+
M	6	2100	I	F	ITO	AD	H																											-	-	-

Appendix 3

Procedures for the Recovery and Analysis of Broken and Scattered Human Bone from Archaeological and Forensic Contexts

Assemblages of human bone modified by humans are temporally and spatially widespread in the American Southwest, where further research is urgently needed to fully understand them. Opportunities to investigate the prehistoric behaviors that led to the accumulation of these assemblages will continue to grow as more field and laboratory work is accomplished. Now that these assemblages are becoming more widely known and investigated, their numbers are growing. During the years of this study, for example, the sample of recognized assemblages of this nature grew dramatically with the addition of several new sites (Bluff, Cottonwood Canyon, Yellow Jacket, Verdure Canyon, Teec Nos Pos; see also Chapter 13).

The Mancos analysis was begun before the logistical difficulties it entailed and the patterns of prehistoric behavior that it would reveal were fully appreciated. Now that the analysis has been done and documented, it is appropriate to record one of its most important lessons—recommendations for the recovery and analysis of similar collections that have already been recovered and those that remain undiscovered.

Some of the most important data on these assemblages are contextual. During excavation and recovery it is critical that close attention be paid to contextual details that will place the time of the assemblage deposition relative to the occupation/abandonment of the site and assist in conjoining studies. For older collections, contextual data are often inadequate. Finer recovery techniques in future excavations will be needed to elucidate the relationships among occupation, deposition of the assemblage, and abandonment of the site or structure.

Field workers encountering broken and scattered human bone whose preservation characteristics are similar to those described in this book are encouraged to proceed according to the steps outlined below. The major steps, in order, are: discovery, exposure, recording, labeling, lifting, transport, washing, sorting by element, attribute recording, refitting, anatomical analysis, photography, and curation.

Assemblages of the kind described here have come to light most frequently as the result of archaeological excavation, but vandalism and development have also revealed them. Subsequent to discovery, the first step to be taken is a careful exposure of as much of the *in situ* assemblage as possible. Because this exposure may take days or weeks of work with fine tools, great care should be taken to protect the bones from the effects of excavation trauma. For example, avoid scraping the bones with metal tools. Take care not to continually broom across broken bone edges. This may obscure important edge characteristics such as pot polish. Direct sunlight may rapidly weather newly exposed bones between exposure and lifting, so covers for the excavation should be sought. These assemblages usually contain large numbers of specimens whose good preservation and strength surpass bones in most formal burials. In the same assemblages, however, are burned specimens whose structural integrity, particularly the integrity of the surfaces, has been greatly weakened by thermal trauma. Great care must be taken to expose, remove, transport, and clean these fragile remains without further damage.

Each bone fragment should be piece-plotted before lifting, not lot-plotted unless the bone density warrants this. My recommendation is that each piece be bagged individually in the field. It is absolutely essential for analytical work (especially conjoining) that each separate specimen be given a unique identification number. These specimen numbers should be affixed permanently to each specimen. Designate with single numbers those specimens that are intact *in situ* but that may fracture upon removal. Glue the recently broken fragments back together immediately or bag them together and enclose a note to the effect that they are to be reglued to their *in situ* condition. Under no circumstances should bones be glued back together except in such cases —cases where it is certain that a single specimen was broken during or after recovery. All gluing should be done with water-soluble glue.

Great care should be taken to see that small bone flakes (true bone flakes, see Chapter 6) are recovered with provenance. A reasonable arbitrary cutoff point for giving unique numbers to individual specimens is 1 cm; specimens without any dimension larger than this can be counted and given lot numbers if necessary.

All earth associated with an assemblage of this kind should be wet-screened in window screen mesh before final disposal. If this is not possible, adequate samples with controlled spatial provenance should be wet-screened to recover the small fraction (''microartifacts''; see Dunnell and Stein [1989]). Because of the possibility that the assemblage represents an abandonment event, all stone artifacts in the proximity of the bones should be very carefully exposed and examined microscopically for bone residues. This is because the bone percussion and pulverization so widespread among these assemblages are predicted to result in bone residue being trapped in surface irregularities in any stones that could have functioned as hammers and anvils for processing of the bones. Several assemblages already on record (especially the Yellow Jacket 5MT–3 assemblage) have a degree of integrity so high as to indicate that such fine-grain behavioral information will be possible to extract from these sites, given sufficient care, patience, and attention to detail. The excavators should be especially vigilant of possible coprolite evidence.

Specimens recovered in the field should not be put in common bags for transport because adhering flakes can be dislodged and mixed, burned specimens are prone to disintegrate, and adjacent bones with grit-laden sediments interposed can rub against each other and introduce postexcavation abrasion and other trauma.

Upon arrival in the laboratory, all specimens should be washed in clean water before observation. Washing carries with it the danger that the bones might further disintegrate and/or that adhering tissue or other organic or inorganic materials could be lost. Each situation must, of course, be evaluated individually. Many attributes described in Chapter 6 of this book, however, are not visible until the specimen is washed—even a thin coating of grit can obscure percussion striae, cutmarks, and the like. If washing is judged not to endanger any data, the bones can be carefully rinsed clean. Care should be taken to see that small parts of specimens do not flake away and get lost during this operation. Burned specimens (specimens that are chalky, exfoliating, friable, and appear to be weathered) are particularly prone to damage during washing, and extreme caution should be used so that additional external bone table is not lost. With most unburned specimens, however, usually a simple rinsing of specimens between the fingers is all that is needed to adequately clean the fragments. Soft brushes may be employed where the bone can stand up to this treatment. Take great care to fix all loose tooth roots in their sockets with a drop of glue. Do not return isolated teeth to their sockets unless it is certain that they were in place in the jaw when it was *in situ* in the deposit. If bones disintegrate during washing, just keep the fragments together and glue them back together when they are dry.

After washing, the assemblage can be assessed as a unit, or in subassemblages. The first analytical step is identification, and this should be done by a physical anthropologist skilled at identifying very fragmentary specimens. Ratios between specimens allocated to the indeterminate categories employed here and specimens allocated to skeletal element should give rough ideas as to whether the identification of specimens within other assemblages has been performed to the greatest degree possible. On less fragmented assemblages, of course, these ICR and IP ratios should be even lower than those reported here. The group photographs of element categories in Chapters 7 to 12 should also assist in approximating the required level of specimen identification, although it should be borne in mind that some of the specimens in each photograph were identified only as a consequence of refitting.

All nonhuman specimens should be segregated from the human remains during sorting by element. In the assemblages the author has worked on (Mancos, Polacca, Leroux, Cottonwood Canyon, Yellow Jacket) the nonhuman component of the assemblage was extremely limited and easily diagnosed. In fact, errors of identifying human specimens as nonhuman are far more commonly encountered in sorting these assemblages.

If the entire assemblage is not yet available at this stage of the analysis, it is advisable to wait until it is. Much of the work described below is most effectively and efficiently done only when the entire assemblage is available. If part of it has been left in the ground pending further excavation, it is more efficient to wait until it is all available before proceeding any further with the analysis.

Once the assemblage has been sorted by element and side, examine all broken surfaces. Where fracture is clearly related to excavation or transport (such fracture is usually recognized as recent by lack of matrix and a much lighter color than the other anciently broken edges), check within the element category for the original *in situ* specimen that it belongs to. If

SPECIMEN NUMBER	____
CONJOINING SET NUMBER	____
PROVENANCE	____
FAUNAL ANALYST IDENTIFIABLE?	(+ or -)____
SIDE	(R, L, B, or I)____
FRAGMENTATION	(W or F)____
ELEMENT	(use 3-letter code)____
INDIVIDUAL AGE	(AD, IM, ??,L or #)____
INTACT EXTERNAL SURFACE	(give %)____
PERIMORTEM FRACTURE	(+, -, or ?)____
INTERNAL VAULT RELEASE	(+ or -)____
INNER CONCHOIDAL SCARS	(No.)____
CRUSHING	(+ or -)____
PERCUSSION PITS	(No.)____
ADHERING FLAKES	(No.)____
PEELING	(+ or -)____
CUTMARKS	(No.)____
CHOPMARKS	(No.)____
POLISH OR POT POLISH	(P or PP)____
INTENTIONAL SCRAPING	(+ or -)____
PERCUSSION STRIAE	(+ or -)____
RODENT GNAWING	(+ or -)____
CARNIVORE DAMAGE	(+ or -)____
BURNING	(+ or -)____

Table A3.1 A minimal list of observations recommended for each specimen from bone assemblages thought to be the product of hominid activities.

it is not there, it must be in one of the indeterminate categories (or, more tragically, it has been discarded at the site or lost in transport). Find all the recent fractures and glue them back together before proceeding with the analysis. As discussed above, never glue specimens together unless you are positive that they became detached from one another during excavation or later. If these recently broken specimens were mistakenly given separate numbers, delete one entry from the catalog and remove the appropriate number from the glued specimen. None of these joins may count as "joins" in the refitting analysis described below. When specimens with "recent" fractures remain after this analysis, if they are reckoned to represent more than half of the original *in situ* specimen, they should be treated as a separate specimen. When they clearly represent merely a small piece broken away from a larger specimen that cannot be found (usually these pieces are in the ICR, IP4, and IND categories), such recently broken, small fragments may be removed from further analysis. Do not glue isolated teeth back into jaws at this stage.

After all "recent" fractures have been eliminated in the manner described above, a preconjoining analysis designed to quantify bone modification is recommended. Table A3.1 lists a minimum of attributes recommended for recording during this stage of the analysis. This list includes those attributes found to be of most significance in the Mancos analysis. It will set a baseline for comparative studies among different assemblages. Attributes should be clearly defined by the analyst recording them. This stage of the analysis is best accomplished by two people working together, one working with the specimen and a hand lens under a harsh, unidirectional light, and the other entering data into the computer.

The full "zooarchaeological" quantification analysis recommended above has the important benefit of generating a full catalog of the assemblage. Once this has been done, a conjoining analysis is recommended. Chapter 4 of this book describes conjoining in detail, and procedures outlined there may be helpful in this work. I recommend, for reasons outlined in that chapter, that maximal conjoining be done within the femur, tibia, humerus, and all cranial element categories (except ICR), and between these and the relevant IP2 and IP3 categories. True bone flakes in the IP4 category might be profitably checked against shaft fragments during the conjoining. Refitting in all of the element categories is, of course, preferable to this minimal amount of conjoining, but the time costs in such a full refitting effort may prove to be prohibitive in larger collections. The larger the collection, the smaller the potential returns of such intensive conjoining.

When joins across ancient breaks are found, they should never be permanently fixed. Rather than gluing pieces together, it is recommended that temporary joins be forged with white masking tape. Make sure that the bone surface to which the tape will be affixed does not exfoliate—the bone may need strengthening with preservative prior to taping, particularly in the case of thermally damaged bone that has not yet exfoliated. Specimens may remain segregated by element during the conjoining exercise. After the conjoining exercise, a search for patterning of modification during disarticulation, percussion, and burning should be made within the maximally conjoined assemblage. Particular care should be paid to the anatomical relationships between bone modification and original soft tissue cover. Descriptions of all patterning and special trauma should be made, and photographs of the more important pieces in the maximally conjoined assemblage should be taken. During this stage of the analysis, determine the minimum number of individuals at each element position for the entire assemblage and for subassemblages as necessary. Note and assess all biological attributes of the specimens and of the assemblage in this maximally conjoined state.

After completing the analysis and necessary photography of the maximally conjoined assemblage, the individual specimens should be separated from one another, and the tape holding all joins together should be carefully removed. Do not leave specimens taped together for longer than three weeks. The final analytical step before curation of the assemblage should be photography. Each element set should be photographed in its deconjoined condition, in a format similar to that used in this book. This provides a graphic record of the entire assemblage. Storage of this kind of assemblage is best done on an element-by-element basis, with all specimens belonging to the same kind of element being kept together. For future investigators, it is helpful to have conjoining sets stored together, but do not attempt to store the remains in their conjoined state because the tape holding the joins together will deteriorate over time, leaving a residue on the bones.

Bibliography

Aaris-Sorensen, K. (1982) A classification code and computerized data analysis for faunal materials from archaeological sites. *Ossa* 8:3–19.

Abbie, A. (1969) *The Original Australians*. New York: American Elsevier.

Abler, T.S. (1980) Iroquois cannibalism: Fact not fiction. *Ethnohistory* 27:309–316.

Agrinier, P. (1978) A sacrificial mass burial at Miramar, Chiapas, Mexico. *New World Archaeological Foundation Papers* 42:1–52.

Aird, P.M. (1985) On distinguishing butchery from other post-mortem destruction: A methodological experiment applied to a faunal sample from Roman Lincoln. In: N.R. Fieller, D.D. Gilbertson and N.G. Ralph (eds.), *Palaeobiological Investigations: Research Design, Methods and Data Analysis*. British Archaeological Reports, International Series 266:5–18.

Akins, N.J. (1982) Analysis of faunal remains from Pueblo Alto, Chaco Canyon. Manuscript on file, Division of Cultural Research, National Park Service, Albuquerque.

Akins, N.J. (1986) A biocultural approach to human burials from Chaco Canyon, New Mexico. *Reports of the Chaco Center* 9. Santa Fe, Branch of Cultural Research, National Park Service.

Allen, J. and Guy, J.B.M. (1984) Estimations of individuals in archaeological faunal assemblages: How minimal is the MNI? *Archaeology in Oceania* 19:41–47.

Allen, W.H., Merbs, C.F. and Birkby, W.H. (1985) Evidence for prehistoric scalping at Nuvakewtaqa (Chavez Pass) and Grasshopper Ruin, Arizona. In: C.F. Merbs and R.J. Miller (eds.), *Health and Disease in the Prehistoric Southwest*. Tempe, Ariz.: Arizona State University Anthropological Research Papers, No. 34. pp. 23–42.

Allo, J. (1972) The Whangamata Wharf site (N49/2): Excavations on a Coromandel coastal midden. *Records of the Auckland Institute and Museum* 9:61–79.

Ambler, J.R. (1989) *The Anasazi: Prehistoric People of the Four Corners Region*. Flagstaff, Ariz.: Museum of Northern Arizona Press.

Ambler, J.R. and Sutton, M.Q. (1989) The Anasazi abandonment of the San Juan drainage and the Numic expansion. *North American Archaeologist* 10:39–55.

Andrews, P. and Cook, J. (1985) Natural modifications to bones in a temperate setting. *Man* (n.s.) 20:675–691.

Anglo, M. (1979) *Man Eats Man: The Story of Cannibalism*. London: Jupiter.

Anon. (1986) Cannibals shrink space alien's head. *Weekly World News* 8:4.

Archer, M. (1977) Faunal remains from the excavation at Puntutjarpa rockshelter. In: R.A. Gould (ed.), *The Archaeology of Puntutjarpa Rockshelter*. New York: American Museum of Natural History: Anthropological Papers 54:1:158–165.

Archer, M., Crawford, M. and Merrilees, D. (1980) Incisions, breakages, and charring, some probably man-made, in fossil bones from Mammoth Cave, western Australia. *Alcheringa* 4:115–131.

Arens, W. (1979) *The Man-eating Myth: Anthropology and Anthropophagy*. Oxford: Oxford University Press.

Armitage, P.L. (1978) A system for the recording and processing of data relating to animal remains from archaeological sites. In: D.R. Brothwell, K.D. Thomas and J. Clutton-

Brock (eds.), *Research Problems in Zooarchaeology*. University of London, Institute of Archaeology, Occasional Publication 3. pp. 39–45.

Avery, D.M. (1984) Sampling procedures and cautionary tales. In: M. Hall, G. Avery, D.M. Avery, M.L. Wilson and A.J.B. Humphreys (eds.), *Frontiers: Southern African Archaeology Today*. British Archaeological Reports, International Series 207:375–379.

Axtell, J. and Sturtevant, W.C. (1980) The unkindest cut, or who invented scalping. *William and Mary Quarterly* 37:451–472.

Baby, R. (1954) Hopewell cremation practices. *Ohio Historical Society Papers in Archaeology* 1:1–7.

Badgley, C. (1986a) Counting individuals in mammalian fossil assemblages from fluvial environments. *Palaios* 1:328–338.

Badgley, C. (1986b) Taphonomy of mammalian fossil remains from Siwalik rocks of Pakistan. *Paleobiology* 12:119–142.

Balme, J. (1980) An analysis of charred bone from Devil's Lair, western Australia. *Archaeology and Physical Anthropology in Oceania* 15:81–85.

Barker, G. (1975) To sieve or not to sieve. *Antiquity* 49:61–63.

Barrett, S. (1933) Ancient Aztalan. *Bulletin of the Milwaukee Public Museum* 13:1–402.

Bartel, B. (1982) A historical review of ethnological and archaeological analyses of mortuary practice. *Journal of Anthropological Archaeology* 1:32–58.

Basedow, H. (1904) *The Australian Aboriginal*. Adelaide: F.W. Preece and Sons.

Baud, C.A. (1982) La taphonomie. *Histoire et Archaeologie* 66:33–35.

Bayham, F.E. (1987) Review of J.C. Driver, 1985. *Kiva* 53:57–58.

Bayham, F.E. and Hatch, P. (1985) Hohokam and Salado animal utilization in the Tonto Basin. In: G. Rice (ed.), *Studies in the Hohokam and Salado of the Tonto Basin*. Tempe, Ariz.: Arizona State University, Office of CRM, OCRM Report No. 63:191–210.

Baynes, A., Merrilees, D. and Porter, J.K. (1975) Mammal remains from the upper levels of a Late Pleistocene deposit in Devil's Lair, western Australia. *Journal of the Royal Society of Western Australia* 61:33–65.

Beaglehole, E. (1936) Hopi hunting and hunting ritual. *Yale University Publications in Anthropology* 4:1–26.

Beck, C. and Jones, G.T. (1989) Bias and archaeological classification. *American Antiquity* 54:244–262.

Beebe, N.G. (1983) Evidence of carnivore activity in a Late Pleistocene/Early Holocene archaeological site (Bluefish Cave I), Yukon Territory, Canada. In: G.M. Lemoine and A.S. MacEachern (eds.), *A Question of Bone Technology*. Calgary: Archaeological Association, University of Calgary. pp. 1–14.

Behrensmeyer, A.K. (1978) Taphonomic and ecologic information from bone weathering. *Paleobiology* 2:150–162.

Behrensmeyer, A.K. (1987) Taphonomy and hunting. In: M.H. Nitecki and D.V. Nitecki (eds.), *The Evolution of Human Hunting*. New York: Plenum. pp. 423–450.

Behrensmeyer, A.K., Gordon, K.D. and Yanagi, G.T. (1986) Trampling as a cause of bone surface damage and pseudo-cutmarks. *Nature* 319:768–771.

Behrensmeyer, A.K., Gordon, K.D. and Yanagi, G.T. (1989) Nonhuman modification in Miocene fossils from Pakistan. In: R. Bonnichsen and M. Sorg (eds.), *Bone Modification*. Orono, Maine: Center for the Study of the First Americans, University of Maine. pp. 99–120.

Bell, L.S. (1990) Paleopathology and diagenesis: An SEM evaluation of structural changes using backscattered electron imaging. *Journal of Archaeological Science* 17:85–108.

Bennett, J.W. (1952) The prehistory of the northern Mississippi Valley. In: J.B. Griffin (ed.), *Archaeology of the Eastern United States*. Chicago: University of Chicago Press. pp. 108–123.

Bennett, K.A. (1966) Appendix B. Analysis of prehistoric human skeletal remains from the Navajo Reservoir District. In: F. Eddy (ed.), Prehistory in the Navajo Reservoir District, Northwestern New Mexico. *Museum of New Mexico, Papers in Anthropology* 15:523–546. Santa Fe: Museum of New Mexico Press.

Bennett, K.A. (1975) *Skeletal Remains from Mesa Verde National Park, Colorado*. U.S. Department of the Interior, National Park Service, Publications in Archeology 7F, Wetherill Mesa Studies.

Berrelleza, J.A.R. (1986) *El Sacrificio de Niños en Honor a Tlaloc*. M.A. Escuela Nacional de Antropologia e Historia (publ. I.N.A.H.; S.E.P.), Mexico City.

Berrizbeitia, E.L. (1989) Sex determination with the head of the radius. *Journal of Forensic Science* 34:1206–1213.

Berry, M.S (1982) *Time, Space and Transition in Anasazi Prehistory*. Salt Lake City: University of Utah Press.

Best, S.B. (1984) *Lakeba: The Prehistory of a Fijian Island*. Ph.D. diss., University of Auckland.

Beyer, J.C., Arima, J.K. and Johnson, D.W. (1962) Enemy ordnance materiel. In: J.C. Beyer (ed.), *Wound Ballistics*. Washington, D.C.: Office of the Surgeon General, Department of the Army. pp. 1–90.

Biddick, K.A. and Tomenchuck, J. (1975) Quantifying continuous lesions and fractures on long bones. *Journal of Field Archaeology* 2:239–249.

Binford, L.R. (1963) An analysis of cremations from three Michigan sites. *Wisconsin Archaeologist* 44:98–110.

Binford, L.R. (1978) *Nunamiut Ethnoarchaeology*. New York: Academic Press.

Binford, L.R. (1981) *Bones: Ancient Men and Modern Myths*. New York: Academic Press.

Binford, L.R. (1984) *Faunal Remains from Klasies River Mouth*. New York: Academic Press.

Binford, L.R. (1985) Human ancestors: Changing views of their behavior. *Journal of Anthropological Archaeology* 4:292–327.

Binford, L.R. (1987a) Were there elephant hunters at Torralba? In: M.H. Nitecki and D.V. Nitecki (eds.), *The Evolution of Human Hunting*. New York: Plenum. pp. 47–105.

Binford, L.R. (1987b) Researching ambiguity: Frames of reference and site structure. In: S. Kent (ed.), *Method and Theory for Activity Area Research*. New York: Columbia University Press. pp. 449–512.

Binford, L.R. (1988) Fact and fiction about the *Zinjanthropus* floor: Data, arguments, and interpretations. *Current Anthropology* 29:123–135.

Binford, L.R. (1990) Etude taphonomique des restes fauniques de la Grotte Vaufrey, Couche VIII. In: J.-Ph. Rigaud (ed.), *La Grotte Vaufrey: Paléoenvironnements, Chronologie, Activités Humaines. Mémoires S.P.F.* 19:535–563.

Binford, L.R. and Bertram, J.B. (1977) Bone frequencies—And attritional processes. In: L.R. Binford (ed.), *For Theory Building in Archaeology*. New York: Academic Press. pp. 77–153.

Binford, L.R. and Ho, C.K. (1985) Taphonomy at a distance: Zhoukoudian, "The Cave Home of Beijing Man?" *Current Anthropology* 26:413–442.

Binford, L.R. and Stone, N.M. (1986) Zhoukoudian: A closer look. *Current Anthropology* 27:453–474.

Binford, L.R. and Stone, N.M. (1987) On Zhoukoudian. Reply to Comments. *Current Anthropology* 28:102–105.

Black, D. (1931) Evidence of the use of fire by *Sinanthropus*. *Bulletin of the Geological Society of China* 11:107–108.

Black, G.A. (1967) *Angel Site: An Archaeological, Historical and Ethnological Study*. 2 vols. Indianapolis: Indiana Historical Society.

Blumenschine, R.J. (1986) Carcass consumption sequences and the archaeological distinction of scavenging and hunting. *Journal of Human Evolution* 15:639–659.

Blumenschine, R.J. (1988) An experimental model of the timing of hominid and carnivore influence on archaeological bone assemblages. *Journal of Archaeological Science* 15:483–502.

Blumenschine, R.J. (1989) A landscape taphonomic model of the scale of prehistoric scavenging opportunities. *Journal of Human Evolution* 18:345–371.

Blumenschine, R.J. and Selvaggio, M.M. (1988) Percussion marks on bone surfaces as a new diagnostic of hominid behavior. *Nature* 333:763–765.

Boaz, N.T. and Behrensmeyer, A.K. (1976) Hominid taphonomy: Transport of human skeletal parts in an artificial fluviatile environment. *American Journal of Physical Anthropology* 45:53–60.

Bobrowsky, P.T. (1982) An examination of Casteel's MNI behavior analysis: A reductionist approach. *Midcontinental Journal of Archaeology* 7:171–184.

Boesch, C. and Boesch, H. (1989) Hunting behavior of wild chimpanzees in the Tai National Park. *American Journal of Physical Anthropology* 78:547–573.

Bonnichsen, R. (1973) Some operational aspects of human and animal bone alterations. In: B.M. Gilbert (ed.), *Mammalian Osteoarchaeology: North America*. Columbia, Mo.: Missouri Archaeological Society. pp. 9–24.

Bonnichsen, R. (1979) *Pleistocene Technology in the Beringian Refugium*. Archaeological Survey of Canada, Paper No. 89.

Bonnichsen, R. (1983) The broken bone controversy: Some issues important for the study of early archaeological sites. In: G.M. Lemoine and A.S. MacEachern (eds.), *A Question of Bone Technology*. Calgary: Archaeological Association, University of Calgary. pp. 271–284.

Bonnichsen, R. and Sanger, D. (1977) Integrating faunal analysis. *Canadian Journal of Archaeology* 1:109–133.

Bonnichsen, R. and Will, R.T. (1980) Cultural modification of bone: The experimental approach to faunal analysis. In: B.M. Gilbert (ed.), *Mammalian Osteology*. 2d ed. Columbia, Mo.: Special Publication, Missouri Archaeological Society. pp. 7–30.

Bonucci, E. and Graziani, G. (1975) Comparative thermogravimetric, X-ray diffraction and electron microscope investigations of burnt bones from recent, ancient and prehistoric age. *Atti Della Academia Nazionale dei Lincei. Sci. Fis. Matem. Natur.* Ser. 8, 59:517–534.

Bouyssonie, A., Bouysonnie, J. and Bardon, L. (1913) La Station moustérienne de la "Bouffia" Bonneval à la Chapelle-aus-Saints. *L'Anthropologie* 24:609–634.

Bowden, R. (1984) Maori cannibalism: An interpretation. *Oceania* 55:2:81–99.

Bowler, J.M., Jones, R., Allen, H. and Thorne, A.G. (1970) Pleistocene human remains from Australia: A living site and human cremation from Lake Mungo, western New South Wales. *World Archaeology* 2:39–59.

Bowles, E.A., Weaver, D.S., Telewski, F.W., Wakefield, A.H., Jaffe, M.J. and Miller, L.C. (1985) Bone measurement by enhanced contrast image analysis: Ovariectomized and intact *Macaca fascicularis* as a model for human postmenopausal osteoporosis. *American Journal of Physical Anthropology* 67:99–103.

Bradley, B.A. (1988) Wallace Ruin interim report. *Southwestern Lore* 54:2:8–33.

Brady, I. (1982) Review of Arens, W. (1979) *American Anthropologist* 84:595–611.

Brain, C.K. (1969a) Faunal remains from the Bushman Rock Shelter, eastern Transvaal. *South African Archaeological Bulletin* 24:52–55.

Brain, C.K. (1969b) The contribution of Namib Desert Hottentots to an understanding of Australopithecine bone accumulations. *Scientific Papers of the Namib Desert Research Station* 39:13–22.

Brain, C.K. (1970) New finds at the Swartkrans Australopithecine site. *Nature* 225:1112–1119.

Brain, C.K. (1974) Some suggested procedures in the analysis of bone accumulations from southern African Quaternary sites. *Annals of the Transvaal Museum* 29:1–8.

Brain, C.K. (1975a) An introduction to the South African Australopithecine bone accumulations. In: A.T. Clason (ed.), *Archaeozoological Studies*. New York: American Elsevier. pp. 109–119.

Brain, C.K. (1975b) An interpretation of the bone assemblage from the Kromdraai australopithecine site, South Africa. In: R. Tuttle (ed.), *Paleoanthropology, Morphology and Paleoecology*. The Hague: Mouton. pp. 225–243.

Brain, C.K. (1976) Some principles in the interpretation of bone accumulations associated with man. In: G.L. Isaac and E.R. McCown (eds.), *Human Origins: Louis Leakey and the East African Evidence*. Menlo Park: W.A. Benjamin. pp. 96–116. (Cf. 1969b.)

Brain, C.K. (1980) Some criteria for the recognition of bone-collecting agencies in African caves. In: A.K. Behrensmeyer and A. Hill (eds.), *Fossils in the Making*. Chicago: University of Chicago Press. pp. 107–130.

Brain, C.K. (1981a) *The Hunters or the Hunted?* Chicago: University of Chicago Press.

Brain, C.K. (1981b) Presidential address: Taphonomy as an aid to African paleontology. *Palaeontologia Africana* 24:1–4.

Brain, C.K. (1985) Interpreting early hominid death assemblages: The rise of taphonomy since 1925. In: P.V. Tobias (ed.), *Hominid Evolution: Past, Present and Future*. New York: Alan R. Liss. pp. 41–46.

Brain, C.K. (1989) The evidence for bone modification by early hominids in Southern Africa. In: R. Bonnichsen and M. Sorg (eds.), *Bone Modification*. Orono, Maine: Center for the Study of Early Man, University of Maine. pp. 291–296.

Brain, C.K., Churcher, C.S., Clark, J.D., Grine, F.E., Shipman, P., Susman, R.L., Turner, A. and Watson, V. (1988) New evidence of early hominids, their culture and environment from the Swartkrans cave, South Africa. *South African Journal of Science* 84:828–835.

Brain, C.K. and Sillen, A. (1988) Evidence from the Swartkrans cave for the earliest use of fire. *Nature* 336:464–465.

Breternitz, D.A., Robinson, C.K. and Gross, G.T. (eds.) (1986) *Dolores Archaeological Program: Final Synthetic Report*. Denver: U.S. Department of the Interior, Bureau of Reclamation.

Breuil, H. (1938) The use of bone implements in the Old Paleolithic period. *Antiquity* 12:56–67.

Breuil, H. (1939) Bone and antler industry of the Choukoutien *Sinanthropus* site. *Paleontologia Sinica*, n.s. D., No. 6, Peking. Whole series #117.

Bromage, T.G. (1984) Interpretation of scanning electron microscopic images of abraded forming bone surfaces. *American Journal of Physical Anthropology* 64:161–178.

Bromage, T.G. and Boyde, A. (1984) Microscopic criteria for the determination of directionality of cutmarks on bone. *American Journal of Physical Anthropology* 65:359–366.

Brooks, A.S. and Yellen, J.E. (1987) The preservation of activity areas in the archaeological record: Ethnoarchaeological and archaeological work in northwest Ngamiland, Botswana. In: S. Kent (ed.), *Method and Theory for Activity Area Research*. New York: Columbia University Press. pp. 63–106.

Brose, D., Wentzel, G., Bluestone, H. and Essenpreis, P. (1976) Conneaut Fort, a prehistoric Whittlesey focus village in Ashtabula County, Ohio. *Pennsylvania Archaeologist* 46:4:29–77.

Brothwell, D.R. (1961) Cannibalism in early Britain. *Antiquity* 35:304–307.

Brothwell, D.R. (1969) The study of archaeological materials by means of the scanning electron microscope: An important new field. In: D. Brothwell and E. Higgs (eds.), *Science in Archaeology*. 2d ed. London: Thames and Hudson. pp. 564–566.

Brown, J.A. (1979) Charnel houses and mortuary crypts: Disposal of the dead in the Middle Woodland period. In: D. Brose and N. Greber (eds.), *Hopewell Archaeology: The Chillicothe Conference*. Kent, Ohio: Kent State University Press. pp. 211–219.

Brown, M.K. (1974) A preservative compound for archaeological materials. *American Antiquity* 39:469–473.

Brown, P. and Tuzin, D. (eds.) (1983) *The Ethnography of Cannibalism*. Washington, D.C.: Society for Psychological Anthropology.

Buckland, W. (1822) Account of an assemblage of fossil teeth and bones . . . etc. *Philosophical Transactions of the Royal Society of London* 122:171–237.

Buikstra, J.E. and Goldstein, L. (1973) The Perrins Ledge Crematory. *Reports of Investigation*. No. 28. Springfield, Ill.: Illinois State Museum.

Buikstra, J.E. and Mielke, J.H. (1985) Demography, diet, and health. In: R.I. Gilbert and J.H. Mielke (eds.), *The Analysis of Prehistoric Diets*. Orlando, Fla.: Academic Press. pp. 359–422.

Buikstra, J.E. and Swegle, M. (1989) Bone modification due to burning: Experimental evidence. In: R. Bonnichsen and M. Sorg (eds.), *Bone Modification*. Orono, Maine: Center for the Study of the First Americans, University of Maine. pp. 247–258.

Bulmer, R. (1976) Selectivity in hunting and disposal of animal bones by the Kalam of the New Guinea Highlands. In: G. de G. Sieveking, I.H. Longworth and K.E. Wilson (eds.), *Problems in Economic and Social Archaeology*. London: Duckworth. pp. 169–186.

Bunn, H.T. (1981) Archaeological evidence for meat-eating by Plio-Pleistocene hominids from Koobi Fora and Olduvai Gorge. *Nature* 291:574–577.

Bunn, H.T. (1982) *Meat-Eating and Human Evolution: Studies on the Diet and Subsistence Patterns of Plio-Pleistocene Hominids in East Africa*. Ph.D. diss., University of California at Berkeley.

Bunn, H.T. (1983) Comparative analysis of modern bone assemblages from a San hunter-gatherer camp in the Kalahari Desert, Botswana, and from a spotted hyaena den near Nairobi, Kenya. In: J. Clutton-Brock and C. Grigson (eds.), *Animals and Archaeology: 1. Hunters and Their Prey*. Oxford: British Archaeological Reports, International Series 163:143–148.

Bunn, H.T. (1989) Diagnosing Plio-Pleistocene hominid activity with bone fracture evidence. In: R. Bonnichsen and M. Sorg (eds.), *Bone Modification*. Orono, Maine: Center for the Study of the First Americans, University of Maine. pp. 299–315.

Bunn, H.T., Harris, J., Isaac, G.L., Kaufulu, Z., Kroll, E., Schick, K., Toth, N. and Behrensmeyer, A.K. (1980) FxJj 50: An early Pleistocene site in northern Kenya. *World Archaeology* 12:109–136.

Bunn, H.T. and Kroll, E.M. (1986) Systematic butchery by Plio/Pleistocene hominids at Olduvai Gorge, Tanzania. *Current Anthropology* 27:431–452.

Bunn, H.T. and Kroll, E.M. (1988) Fact and fiction about the *Zinjanthropus* floor: Data, arguments, and interpretations (reply to L.R. Binford). *Current Anthropology* 29:135–149.

Callow, P., Walton, D. and Shell, C.A. (1986) The use of fire at La Cotte de St. Brelade. In: P. Callow and J.M. Cornford (eds.), *La Cotte de St. Brelade 1961–1978: Excavations by C.B.M. McBurney*. Norwich: Geo Books. pp. 193–195.

Cameron, C.M. (1990) Pit structure abandonment in the Four Corners region of the American Southwest: Late Basketmaker III and Pueblo I periods. *Journal of Field Archaeology* 17:27–37.

Campana, D.V. and Crabtree, P.J. (1987) Animals—A C language computer program for the analysis of faunal remains and its use in the study of Early Iron Age fauna from Dun Ailinne. *Archaeozoologia* 1:57–68.

Campbell, T.D. (1939) Food, food values and food habits of the Australian aborigines in relation to their dental conditions. *Australian Journal of Dentistry* 43:1:1–15.

Casteel, R.W. (1971) Differential bone destruction: Some comments. *American Antiquity* 36:466–469.

Casteel, R.W. (1972) Some biases in the recovery of archaeological faunal remains. *Proceedings of the Prehistoric Society* 38:382–388.

Casteel, R.W. (1976–77) A consideration of the behaviour of the minimum number of individuals index: A problem in faunal characterization. *Ossa* 3–4:141–151.

Casteel, R.W. (1977) Characterization of faunal assemblages and the minimum number of individuals determined from paired elements: Continuing problems in archaeology. *Journal of Archaeological Science* 4:125–134.

Casteel, R.W. and Grayson, D.K. (1977) Terminological problems in quantitative faunal analysis. *World Archaeology* 9:235–242.

Cater, J.D. and Chenault, M.L. (1989) Kiva use reinterpreted. *Southwestern Lore* 54:3:19–32.

Chaplin, R.E. (1971) *The Study of Animal Bones from Archaeological Sites*. New York: Seminar Press.

Chase, P.G. (1986) *The hunters of Combe Grenal: Approaches to Middle Paleolithic Subsistence in Europe*. British Archaeological Reports, International Series 286:1–224.

Chmielewsky, W. (1958) Etat de conservation des ossements d'animaux receuillis dans la Grotte de Nietopersowa de Jerzmahovice. *Biuletyn Peryglacjalny* 6:279–283.

Clark, J. and Kietzke, K.K. (1967) Paleoecology of the Lower Nodular Zone, Brule Formation, in the Big Badlands of South Dakota. *Fieldiana: Geology Memoirs* 5:111–129.

Clark, J.D., Asfaw, B., Assefa, G., Harris, J.W.K., Kurashina, H., Walter, R.C., White,

T.D. and Williams, M.A.J. (1984) Palaeoanthropological discoveries in the Middle Awash Valley, Ethiopia. *Nature* 307:423–428.

Clarke, S.K. (1974) A method for the estimation of prehistoric pueblo populations. *Kiva* 39:283–287.

Clary, K.H. (1984) Anasazi diet and subsistence as revealed by coprolites from Chaco Canyon. In: J.W. Judge and J.D. Schelberg (eds.), *Recent Research on Chaco Prehistory*. Albuquerque, N. Mex.: U.S. Government Printing Office. pp. 265–279.

Clason, A.T. (1972) Some remarks on the use and presentation of archaeozoological data. *Helinium* 12:139–153.

Clason, A.T. and Prummel, W. (1977) Collecting, sieving and archaeozoological research. *Journal of Archaeological Science* 4:171–175.

Clutton-Brock, J. (1975) A system for the retrieval of data relating to animal remains from archaeological sites. In: A.T. Clason (ed.), *Archaeozoological Studies*. Amsterdam: North Holland. pp. 21–34.

Coe, M.D. and Diehl, R. (1980) *In the Land of the Olmec*. Vol. 1. Austin, Tex.: University of Texas Press.

Collins, S.M. (1983) The Anasazi and the district: Geography, management, or sociologie? In: J.E. Smith (ed.), *Proceedings of the Anasazi Symposium, 1981*. Cortez, Colo.: Cortez Printing and Mesa Verde Museum Association. pp. 37–41.

Colson, E. (1979) In good years and in bad: Food strategies of self-reliant societies. *Journal of Anthropological Research* 35:18–29.

Conroy, G.C., Jolly, C.J., Cramer, D. and Kalb, J.E. (1978) Newly discovered fossil hominid skull from the Afar Depression, Ethiopia. *Nature* 275:67–70.

Constandse-Westermann, T.S. and Meiklejohn, C. (1979) The human remains from Swifterbant. *Helinium* 19:237–266.

Cook, J. (1986) *The Application of Scanning Electron Microscopy to Taphonomic and Archaeological Problems*. British Archaeological Reports, International Series 296:143–163.

Cordell, L.S. (1984) *Prehistory of the Southwest*. Orlando, Fla.: Academic Press.

Cordell, L.S. and Plog, F. (1979) Escaping the confines of normative thought: A reevaluation of Puebloan prehistory. *American Antiquity* 44:405–429.

Cornwall, I.W. (1956) *Bones for the Archaeologist*. New York: Macmillan.

Coy, J.P. (1975) Iron Age cookery. In: A.T. Clason (ed.), *Archaeozoological Studies*. Amsterdam: North Holland. pp. 426–430.

Crader, D. (1984) Faunal remains from Chencherere II Rockshelter, Malawi. *South African Archaeological Bulletin* 39:37–52.

Cram, C.L. (1975) Osteoarchaeology in Oceania. In: A.T. Clason (ed.), *Archaeozoological Studies*. New York: American Elsevier. pp. 139–150.

Crapanzano, V. (1979) "We're what we eat": Review of Arens, W. (1979). *New York Times Book Review*, July 29, 1979.

Cruz-Uribe, K. and Klein, R.G. (1986) Pascal programs for computing taxonomic abundance in samples of fossil mammals. *Journal of Archaeological Science* 13:171–187.

Cushing, F.H. (1974) (reprint edition of 1920) Zuni breadstuff. *Indian Notes and Monographs*. Vol. 8. New York: Museum of the American Indian, Heye Foundation.

Czaplewski, N.J. (1982) Faunal analysis. In: R.E. Gasser (ed.), *The Coronado Project Archaeological Investigations*. Flagstaff, Ariz.: Museum of Northern Arizona. pp. 244–277.

Czaplicka, M. (1914) *Aboriginal Siberia, A Study in Social Anthropology*. Oxford: Clarendon Press.

Damuth, J. (1982) Analysis of the preservation of community structure in assemblages of fossil mammals. *Paleobiology* 8:434–446.

D'Andrea, A.C. and Gotthardt, R.M. (1984) Predator and scavenger modification of recent equid skeletal assemblages. *Arctic* 37:276–283.

Danson, E.B. (1965) *37th Annual Report of the Museum of Northern Arizona and Research Center, Flagstaff* 37:4:1–34.

Dart, R.A. (1957a) The osteodontokeratic culture of *Australopithecus prometheus*. *Transvaal Museum Memoirs*, Pretoria. No. 10.

Dart, R.A. (1957b) The Makapansgat Australopithecine osteodontokeratic culture. In: *Third Pan African Congress on Prehistory, Livingstone*. pp. 161–171.

Darwin, C. (1871) *The Descent of Man and Selection in Relation to Sex*. London: John Murray.

Davidson, J.M. (1979a) New Zealand. In: J. Jennings (ed.), *The Prehistory of Polynesia*. Cambridge: Harvard University Press. pp. 222–248.

Davidson, J.M. (1979b) Samoa and Tonga. In: J. Jennings (ed.), *The Prehistory of Polynesia*. Cambridge: Harvard University Press. pp. 82–109.

Davidson, J.M. (1984) *The Prehistory of New Zealand*. Auckland: Longeman Paul.

Davies, L.B. and Wilson, M. (eds.) (1978) Bison procurement and utilization: A symposium. *Plains Anthropologist* 23(82):2.

Davies, N. (1981) *Human Sacrifice: In History and Today*. New York: William Morrow.

Davis, L.B. and Fisher, J.W. (1990) A late prehistoric model for communal utilization of pronghorn antelope in the northwestern Plains region, North America. In: L.B. Davis and B.O.K. Reeves (eds.), *Hunters of the Recent Past*. London: Unwin Hyman. pp. 241–276.

Dean, J.S. (1988) A model of Anasazi behavioral adaptation. In: G.J. Gumerman (ed.), *The Anasazi in a Changing Environment*. Cambridge: Cambridge University Press. pp. 25–44.

Dean, J.S., Euler, R.C., Gumerman, G.J., Plog, F., Hevly, R.H. and Karlstrom, T.N.V. (1985) Human behavior, demography, and paleoenvironment on the Colorado Plateaus. *American Antiquity* 50:537–554.

Decker, K.W. and Tieszen, L. L. (1989) Isotopic reconstruction of Mesa Verde diet from Basketmaker III to Pueblo III. *Kiva* 55:33–47.

DeLaguna, F. (1934) *The Archaeology of Cook Inlet, Alaska*. Philadelphia: University Museum.

Dibble, H.J. and McPherron, S.P. (1988) On the computerization of archaeological projects. *Journal of Field Archaeology* 15:431–440.

Diehl, R. (1983) *Tula: The Toltec Capital of Ancient Mexico*. London: Thames and Hudson.

DiPeso, C.C. (1974) *Casas Grandes: A Fallen Trading Center of the Gran Chichimeca*. 8 vols. Flagstaff, Ariz.: Northland Press.

Dittert, A.E., Eddy, F.W. and Dickey, B.L. (1966) LA 4195, Sambrito Village. In: F.W. Eddy (ed.), *Prehistory in the Navajo Reservoir District, Northwestern New Mexico* (Museum of New Mexico Papers in Anthropology) 15:230–254. Santa Fe: Museum of New Mexico Press.

Dixon, E.J. (1984) Context and environment in taphonomic analysis: Examples from Alaska's Porcupine River caves. *Quaternary Research* 22:201–215.

Dokládal, M. (1970) Ergebnisse Experimenteller Verbremmungen zur Festellung von Form- und Grössenveränderungen von Menschenknochen unter dem Einfluss von Hohen Temperaturen. *Anthropologie* 8:3–17.

Dokládal, M. (1971) A further contribution to the morphology of burned human bones. A comparison of burned and non-burned bones of the same individuals. *Proceedings of the Tenth Congress of Czechoslovak Anthropologists in Humpolec 1969*. Edit. Academia, Praha.

Dornstreich, M.D. and Morren, S.E.B. (1974) Does New Guinea cannibalism have nutritional value? *Human Ecology* 2:1:1–12.

Driver, J.C. (1982) Minimum standards for reporting animal bones in salvage archaeology: Southern Alberta as a case study. In: P.D. Francis and E.C. Poplin (eds.), *Directions in Archaeology: A Question of Goals*. Calgary: University of Calgary Archaeological Association. pp. 199–209.

Driver, J.C. (1984) Zooarchaeology in the Sierra Blanca. In: S. Upham, F. Plog, D.G. Batcho and B.E. Kauffman (eds.), *Recent Research in Mogollon Archaeology*. Occasional Paper 10. Las Cruces: University Museum, New Mexico State University. pp. 140–155.

Driver, J.C. (1985) Zooarchaeology of six prehistoric sites in the Sierra Blanca region, New Mexico. *Research Reports in Archaeology* 12:1–103.

Duckworth, W.L.H. (1904) Note on the dispersive power of running water on skeletons: with particular reference to the skeletal remains of *Pithecanthropus erectus*. *Studies from the Anthropological Laboratory. The Anatomy School, Cambridge*. Cambridge: Cambridge University Press.

Ducos, P. (1968) L'origine des amimaux domestiques en Palestine. *Publications de l'Institute de Préhistoire de l'Université de Bordeaux*. Memoir 6.

Dunnell, R.C. and Stein, J.K. (1989) Theoretical issues in the interpretation of microartifacts. *Geoarchaeology* 4:31–42.

Durham, W.H. (1991) *Coevolution: Genes, Culture, and Human Diversity*. Stanford, Calif.: Stanford University Press.

During, E. (1986) The fauna of Alvastra. *Ossa* 12:1–210.

Eckholm, E. (1986) What is the meaning of cannibalism? *New York Times*, Dec. 9, 1986, p. 19.

Eddy, F.W. (1974) Population dislocation in the Navajo Reservoir District, New Mexico and Colorado. *American Antiquity* 39:75–84.

Eickhoff, S. and Herrmann, B. (1985) Surface marks on bones from a Neolithic collective grave (Odagsen, Lower Saxony): A study on differential diagnosis. *Journal of Human Evolution* 14:263–274.

Elkin, A.P. (1937) Beliefs and practices connected with death in north-eastern and western south Australia. *Oceania* 7:275–299.

Ellis, F.H. (1951) Patterns of aggression and the war cult of the southwestern pueblos. *Southwestern Journal of Anthropology* 7:177–201.

Ellis, F.H. (1968) An interpretation of prehistoric death customs in terms of modern Southwestern parallels. In: A.H. Schroeder (ed.), *Collected Papers in Honor of Lyndon Lane Hargraver*. Santa Fe: Museum of New Mexico Press (Archaeological Society of New Mexico Papers, No. 1).

Emslie, S.D. (1977) *Interpretation of Faunal Remains from Archaeological Sites in Mancos Canyon, Southwestern Colorado*. M.A. thesis, University of Colorado, Boulder.

Emslie, S.D. (1978) Dog burials from Mancos Canyon, Colorado. *Kiva* 43:167–182.

Emslie, S.D. (1983) Cultural and climatic implications in Anasazi faunal exploitation: A review and perspectives. In: J.E. Smith (ed.), *Proceedings of the Anasazi Symposium, 1981*. Cortez, Colo.: Cortez Printing and Mesa Verde Museum Association. pp. 119–123.

Emslie, S.D. (1984) Faunal analysis and archaeological research designs: A need for consistency. *American Archaeology* 2:132–139.

Emslie, S.D. (1986) Faunal report for Prairie Dog Hamlet. In: A.E. Kane and G.T. Gross (eds.), *Dolores Archaeological Program: Early Anasazi Sites in the Sagehen Flats Area*. Denver: U.S. Department of the Interior, Bureau of Reclamation. pp. 481–493.

Enloe, J.G. and David, F. (1989) Le remontage des os par individus: Le partage du renne chez les Magdaléniens de Pincevent (Le Grande Paroisse, Seine-et-Marne). *Bulletin de la Société Préhistorique Francaise* 86:275–281.

Euler, R.C. (1988) Demography and cultural dynamics on the Colorado Plateaus. In: G.J. Gumerman (ed.), *The Anasazi in a Changing Environment*. Cambridge: Cambridge University Press. pp. 192–229.

Fetterman, J., Honeycutt, L. and Kuckelman, K. (1988) Draft report on salvage excavations of 42SA12209, a Pueblo 1 habitation site in Cottonwood Canyon, Mati-Lasal National Forest, southeastern Utah.

Fewkes, J.W. (1938) A-wà-to-bi: An archaeological verification of a Tusayan legend. *American Anthropologist* 6:363–375.

Fieller, N.R. and Turner, A. (1982) Number estimation in vertebrate samples. *Journal of Archaeological Science* 9:49–62.

Fink, T.M. (1989) Analysis of human remains from Site 42SA3724, southeastern Utah. Soil Systems Technical Reports 89–04 (Phoenix, Ariz., Soil Systems, Inc., 1029 N. 1st St., Cory Dale Breternitz, president).

Finnegan, M. (1978) Non-metric variation of the infracranial skeleton. *Journal of Anatomy* 125:23–37.

Fiorillo, A.R. (1984) An introduction to the identification of trample marks. *Taphonomy Current Research* 1:47–48.

Fiorillo, A.R. (1987a) An attritional vertebrate fossil accumulation from a floodplain deposit. Geological Society of America Meeting Poster, Phoenix, Ariz.

Fiorillo, A.R. (1987b) Trample marks: Caution from the Cretaceous. *Current Research in the Pleistocene* 4:73–75.

Fiorillo, A.R. (1988) Taphonomy of Hazard Homestead Quarry (Ogallala Group), Hitchcock County, Nebraska. *Contributions to Geology, the University of Wyoming* 26:2:57–97.

Fiorillo, A.R. (1989) An experimental study of trampling: Implications for the fossil record.

In: R. Bonnichsen and M. Sorg (eds.), *Bone Modification*. Orono, Maine: Center for the Study of the First Americans, University of Maine. pp. 61–71.

Fisher, J.W. (1984) Medium-sized artiodactyl butchering and processing. *Wyoming Archaeologist* 27:1:63–82.

Flannery, K.V. (1967) The vertebrate fauna and hunting patterns. In: D.S. Byers (ed.), *The Prehistory of the Tehaucan Valley*. Vol. 1. Austin: University of Texas Press. pp. 132–178.

Flinn, L., Turner, C.G. and Brew, A. (1976) Additional evidence for cannibalism in the Southwest: The case of LA 4528. *American Antiquity* 41:308–318.

Forsyth, D.W. (1985) Three cheers for Hans Staden: The case for Brazilian cannibalism. *Ethnohistory* 32:1:17–36.

Fowler, W.R. (1984) Late Preclassic mortuary patterns and evidence for human sacrifice at Chalchuapa, El Salvador. *American Antiquity* 49:603–618.

Franchet, L. (1933) La coloration des os dans le sol: Le bouillage des cadavres au Moyen-Age, l'incineration et ses phenomens. *Revue Scientifique*. pp. 483–495, 520–532.

Franklin, J. (1823) *Narrative of a Journey to the Shores of the Polar Sea, in the Years 1819–1822*. London: John Murray.

Frayer, D.W. and Wolpoff, M.H. (1985) Sexual dimorphism. *Annual Reviews in Anthropology* 14:429–473.

Freeman, J.E. (1986) Aztalan: A Middle Mississippian village. *Wisconsin Archaeologist* 67:339–364.

Freeman, L.G. (1973) The significance of mammalian faunas from Paleolithic occupations in Catabrian Spain. *American Antiquity* 38:3–44.

Frison, G.C. (1971) Shoshonean antelope procurement in the Upper Green River Basin, Wyoming. *Plains Anthropologist* 16:258–284.

Frison, G.C. (1978) *Prehistoric Hunters of the High Plains*. New York: Academic Press.

Frison, G.C. and Todd, L.C., (eds.) (1987) *The Horner Site*. Orlando, Fla.: Academic Press.

Frison, G. C. and Walker, D.N. (eds.), (1984) The Dead Indian Creek site: An archaic occupation in the Absarokia Mountains in northeastern Wyoming. *Wyoming Archaeologist* 27(1–2).

Fry, G.F. (1985) Analysis of fecal material. In: R.I. Gilbert and J.H. Mielke (eds.), *The Analysis of Prehistoric Diets*. New York: Academic Press. pp. 127–154.

Fry, G. and Hall, H.J. (1975) Human coprolites from Antelope House: Preliminary analysis. *Kiva* 41:1:87–96.

Furuhata, T. and Yamamoto, K. (1967) *Forensic Odontology*. Tokyo: Ishiyaku.

Gamble, C. (1978) Optimising information from studies of faunal remains. In: J.F. Cherry, C. Gamble and S. Shennan (eds.), *Sampling in Contemporary British Archaeology*. British Archaeological Reports, International Series 50:321–353.

Garanger, J. (1972) Archéologie des Nouvelles Hébrides: Contribution à la connaissance des îles du Centre. *Publication de la Societé des Océanistes* 30.

Garn, S.M. and Block, W.D. (1970) The limited nutritional value of cannibalism. *American Anthropologist* 72:106.

Garn, S.M., Lewis, A.B., Swindler, D.R. and Kerewsky, R.S. (1967) Genetic control of sexual dimorphism in tooth size. *Journal of Dental Research* 46:963–972.

Gejvall, N.-G. (1969) Cremation. In: D.R. Brothwell and E. Higgs (eds.), *Science in Archaeology*. 2d ed. London: Thames and Hudson. pp. 468–479.

Ghaleb, B. (1983) *The Spotted Hyaena: Alterer of Bone: A Zoological Analysis of Two East African Bone Assemblages*. Ms.C. thesis, University of London, Institute of Archaeology.

Gifford, D. (1981) Taphonomy and paleoecology: A critical review of archaeology's sister disciplines. In: M.B. Schiffer (ed.), *Advances in Archaeological Method and Theory* 4:365–438.

Gifford, D.P. and Crader, D.C. (1977) A computer system for archaeological faunal remains. *American Antiquity* 42:225–238.

Gifford, D.P., Isaac, G.L. and Nelson, C.M. (1980) Evidence for predation and pastoralism at Prolonged Drift, a pastoral Neolithic site in Kenya. *Azania* 15:57–108.

Gifford, D. and Wright, B. (1986) A data management and table formatting system for vertebrate remains. D M Z III.3:137–164.

Gifford, E.W. (1951) Archaeological excavations in Fiji. *University of California Anthropological Records* 13:3.

Gifford, E.W. and Shutler, D. (1956) Archaeological excavations in New Caledonia. *University of California Anthropological Records* 18:1.

Gifford-Gonzalez, D. (1985) Faunal assemblages from Masai Gorge Rockshelter and Marula Rockshelter. *Azania* 20:69–88.

Gifford-Gonzalez, D. (1989a) Ethnographic analogues for interpreting modified bones: Some cases from East Africa. In: R. Bonnichsen and M. Sorg (eds.), *Bone Modification*. Orono, Maine: Center for the Study of Early Man, University of Maine. pp. 179–246.

Gifford-Gonzalez, D. (1989b) Shipman's shaky foundations. *American Anthropologist* 91:180–186.

Gilbert, A.S., Singer, G.H. and Perkins, D. (1981) Quantification experiments on computer-simulated faunal collections. *Ossa* 8:79–94.

Gilbert, A.S. and Singer, B.H. (1982) Reassessing zooarchaeological quantification. *World Archaeology* 14:21–40.

Gilbert, B.M. (1969) Some aspects of diet and butchering techniques among prehistoric Indians in South Dakota. *Plains Anthropologist* 14 (46):277–294.

Gillespie, W. (1987) Archaeology of the San Javier Bridge Site (AZ BB:13:14). Cultural Resource Management Division, Arizona State Museum. Archaeological Series 171, Pt. 3. Tucson: University of Arizona. pp. 271–301.

Goodman, A.H., Martin, D.L., Armelagos, G.J. and Clark, G. (1984) Indications of stress from bone and teeth. In: M.N. Cohen and G.J. Armelagos (eds.), *Paleopathology at the Origins of Agriculture*. Orlando, Fla.: Academic Press. pp.13–49.

Gordon, C.C. and Buikstra, J.E. (1981) Soil pH, bone preservation, and sampling bias at mortuary sites. *American Antiquity* 46:566–571.

Gordon-Grube, K. (1988) Anthropology in Post-Renaissance Europe: The tradition of medicinal cannibalism. *American Anthropologist* 90:405–409.

Gorecki, P.P. (1979) Disposal of human remains in the New Guinea Highlands. *Archaeology and Physical Anthropology in Oceania* 14:2:107–117.

Gould, R.A. (1980) *Living Archaeology*. Cambridge: Cambridge University Press.

Gould, S.J. and Lewontin, R.C. (1978) The spandrels of San Marco and the Panglossian paradigm: A critique of the adaptionist programme. *Proceedings of the Royal Zoological Society of London* 205:581–598.

Grant, S.S. (1989) Secondary burial or cannibalism: A New Mexico example (abstract of meetings paper). *American Journal of Physical Anthropology* 78:230–231.

Graves, James R. (1984) *The Indian Hills Site (33-WO-4): Archaeological Reflections of a Proto-historic Assistaeronon Town*. Unpublished M.A. and Ed. thesis in Anthropology, University of Toledo.

Grayson, D.K. (1973) On the methodology of faunal analysis. *American Antiquity* 38:432–439.

Grayson, D.K. (1978) Minimum numbers and sample size in vertebrate faunal analysis. *American Antiquity* 43:53–65.

Grayson, D.K. (1979) On the quantification of vertebrate archaeofaunas. In: M.B. Schiffer (ed.), *Advances in Archaeological Method and Theory* 2:199–237.

Grayson, D.K. (1981) A critical view of the use of archaeological vertebrates in paleoenvironmental reconstruction. *Journal of Ethnobiology* 1:28–38.

Grayson, D.K. (1984) *Quantitative Zooarchaeology*. Orlando, Fla.: Academic Press.

Grayson, D.K. (1988) Danger Cave, Last Supper Cave, and Hanging Rock Shelter: The faunas. *Anthropological Papers of the American Museum of Natural History* 66:1–130.

Grayson, D.K. (1989) Bone transport, bone destruction, and reverse utility curves. *Journal of Archaeological Science* 16:643–652.

Grayson, D.K. (1990) Donner party deaths: A demographic assessment. *Journal of Anthropological Research* 46:223–242.

Gregg, J.B., Zimmerman, L.J., Steele, J.P., Ferwerda, H. and Gregg, P.S. (1981) Antemortem osteopathology at Crow Creek. *Plains Anthropologist* 26 (94):287–300.

Grigson, C. (1978) Towards a blueprint for animal bone reports in archaeology. In: D.R. Brothwell, K.D. Thomas and J. Clutton-

Brock (eds.), *Research Problems in Zooarchaeology*. University of London, Institute of Archaeology, Occasional Publication 3. pp. 121–132.

Groff, A.C. (1960) California Indian cannibal tales. *Masterkey* 34:152–165.

Guilday, J.E. (1963) Bone refuse from the Oakfield site, Genessee County, New York. *Pennsylvania Archaeologist* 33:12–15.

Guilday, J.E. (1970) Animal remains from archaeological excavations at Fort Ligioner. *Annals of the Carnegie Museum* 42:177–186.

Guilday, J.E., Parmalee, P.W. and Tanner, D.P. (1962) Aboriginal butchering techniques at the Eschelman site (36 La 12), Lancaster County, Pa. *Pennsylvania Archaeologist* 32:59–83.

Guilday, J.E. and Tanner, D.P. (1962) Animal remains from the Quaker State Rockshelter (36VE27) Venango County, Pennsylvania. *Pennsylvania Archaeologist* 32:131–137.

Gumerman, G.J. (ed.) (1988) *The Anasazi in a Changing Environment*. Cambridge: Cambridge University Press.

Gurfinkel, D.M. and Franklin, U.M. (1988) A study of the feasibility of detecting blood residue on artifacts. *Journal of Archaeological Science* 15:83–97.

Guthrie, R. (1982) Cutmarks on Plio-Pleistocene bone: New evidence of hominid butchery? *Quarterly Review of Archaeology* 3:1:11–12.

Gutin, J.A. and Musonda, F. (1985) Faunal remains from Mufulwe Rock Shelter, Zambia, and their implications. *South African Archaeological Bulletin* 40:11–16.

Gzowski, P. (1980) *The Sacrament: A True Story of Survival*. New York: Atheneum.

Haas, J. (1990) Warfare and the evolution of tribal polities in the prehistoric Southwest. In: J. Haas (ed.), *The Anthropology of War*. Cambridge: Cambridge University Press. pp. 171–189.

Haglund, W.D., Reay, D.T. and Swindler, D.R. (1988) Tooth mark artifacts and survival of bones in animal scavenged human skeletons. *Journal of Forensic Sciences* 33:985–997.

Hakiel, N., Hakiel, B., Sydenstricker, K. and Huppe, K. (1983) Final report on the archery site (48SW52222): A Uinta Fremont site in southwest Wyoming. *Journal of Intermountain Archaeology* 3:77–94.

Hanihara, K. (1976) Statistical and comparative studies of the Australian aboriginal dentition. *Bulletin of the University of Tokyo Museum* 11:1–57.

Hare, P.E. (1980) Organic geochemistry of bone and its relation to the survival of bone in the natural environment. In: A.K. Behrensmeyer and A.P. Hill (eds.), *Fossils in the Making*. Chicago: University of Chicago Press. pp. 208–219.

Harner, M. (1977) The ecological basis for Aztec sacrifice. *American Ethnologist* 4:117–135.

Harris, A.H. (1963) Vertebrate remains and past environmental reconstruction in the Navajo Reservoir District. *Museum of New Mexico Papers in Anthropology* 11:1–71.

Harris, M. (1977) *Cannibals and Kings*. New York: Random House.

Harrison, T. and Medway, L. (1962) A first classification of prehistoric bone and tooth artefacts (based on material from Niah Great Cave). *Sarawak Museum Journal* 10:335–362.

Hartman, D. (1975) Preliminary assessment of mass burials in the Southwest. *American Journal of Physical Anthropology* 42:305–306.

Hassan, F.A. (1978) Demographic archaeology. *Advances in Archaeological Method and Theory* 1:49–103.

Hayden, B. (1981) Subsistence and ecological adaptations of modern hunter/gatherers. In: R.S. Harding and G. Teleki (eds.), *Omnivorous Primates: Gathering and Hunting in Human Evolution*. New York: Columbia University Press. pp. 344–421.

Hayes, A.C. and Lancaster, J.A. (1975) *Badger House Community, Mesa Verde National Park*. Washington, D.C.: U.S. Department of the Interior, National Park Service.

Haynes, G.A. (1980) Evidence of carnivore gnawing on Pleistocene and recent mammalian bones. *Paleobiology* 6:341–351.

Haynes, G.A. (1981) *Bone Modifications and Skeletal Disturbances by Natural Agencies: Studies in North America*. Ph.D. diss., Catholic University of America.

Haynes, G. (1982a) Utilization and skeletal disturbances of North American prey carcasses. *Arctic* 35:266–281.

Haynes, G. (1982b) Prey bones and predators: Potential ecologic information from analysis of bone sites. *Ossa* 7:75–97.

Haynes, G. (1983) Frequencies of spiral and green-bone fractures on ungulate limb bones in modern surface assemblages. *American Antiquity* 48:102–114.

Haynes, G. (1987) Elephant-butchering at modern mass-kill sites in Africa. *Current Research in the Pleistocene* 4:75–77.

Haynes, G. (1988) Longitudinal studies of African elephant death and bone deposits. *Journal of Archaeological Science* 15:131–157.

Haynes, G. and Stanford, D. (1984) On the possible utilization of *Camelops* by early man in North America. *Quaternary Research* 22:216–230.

Hegler, R. (1984) Burned remains. In: T.A. Rathburn and J.E. Buikstra (eds.), *Human Identification: Case Studies in Forensic Anthropology*. Springfield, Ill.: Charles C. Thomas. pp. 148–158.

Heidenreich, C.E. (1978) Huron. In: B.G. Trigger (ed.), *Handbook of North American Indians*, vol. 15, *Northeast*. Washington, D.C.: U.S. Government Printing Office. pp. 368–388.

Heizer, R. (1956) Archaeology of the Uyak site, Kodiak Island, Alaska. *Anthropological Records*. Berkeley and Los Angeles: University of California Press.

Helmuth, H. (1973) Cannibalism in paleoanthropology and ethnology. In: A. Montagu (ed.), *Man and Aggression*. New York: Oxford University Press. pp. 229–253.

Hendey, Q.B. and Singer, R. (1965) Part 3: The faunal assemblages from the Gamtoos Valley Shelters. *South African Archaeological Bulletin* 20:206–213.

Hesse, B. (1982) Bias in the zooarchaeological record: Suggestions for interpretation of bone counts in faunal samples from the Plains. In: D.H. Ubelaker and H.J. Viola (eds.), *Plains Indian Studies: A Collection of Essays in Honor of John C. Ewers and Waldo R. Wedel*. Smithsonian Contributions in Anthropology 30:157–172.

Heyerdahl, T. and Ferdon, E.N. (eds.) (1961) *Archaeology of Eastern Island: Report of the Norwegian Archaeological Expedition to Easter Island and the East Pacific*. School of American Research and Museum of New Mexico Monographs, No. 29. Vols. 1 and 2.

Hiatt, B. (1969) Cremation in aboriginal Australia. *Mankind* 7:104–119.

Hibbert, C. (1983) *Africa Explored: Europeans in the Dark Continent*. New York: W.W. Norton.

Higham, C.F.W. (1968) Faunal sampling and economic prehistory. *Zeitschrift für Säugetierkunde* 33:297–305.

Hill, A.P. (1976) On carnivore and weathering damage to bone. *Current Anthropology* 17:335–336.

Hill, A.P. (1980) Early postmortem damage to the remains of some contemporary East African mammals. In: A.K. Behrensmeyer and A.P. Hill (eds.), *Fossils in the Making*. Chicago: University of Chicago Press. pp. 131–152.

Hill, A.P. (1983) Hyaenas and early hominids. In: J. Clutton-Brock and C. Grigson (eds.), *Animals and Archaeology: 1. Hunters and Their Prey*. British Archaeological Reports, International Series 163:87–92.

Hill, A.P. (1984) Hyaenas and hominids: Taphonomy and hypothesis testing. In: R. Foley (ed.), *Hominid Evolution and Community Ecology*. London: Academic Press. pp. 111–128.

Hill, J.N. (1970) Broken K Pueblo. *University of Arizona Anthropological Papers* 18.

Hofman, J.L. (1986) Vertical movement of artifacts in alluvial and stratified deposits. *Current Anthropology* 27:163–171.

Hogg, G. (1966) *Cannibalism and Human Sacrifice*. New York: Citadel Press.

Hohmann, J., Fortin, P.I., Howard, J. and O'Brien, H. (1985) Site AZ:U:3:49 (ASU). In: J. Hohmann (ed.), Hohokam and Salado hamlets in the Tonto Basin: Site descriptions. Arizona State University, Office of Cultural Resource Management, OCRM Report No. 64.

Holbrook, S.J. (1975) *Prehistoric Paleoecology of Northwestern New Mexico*. Ph.D. diss., University of California at Berkeley.

Holtzman, R.C. (1979) Maximum likelihood estimation of fossil assemblage composition. *Paleobiology* 5:77–89.

Hooton, E.A. (1930) *The Indians of Pecos Pueblo*. New Haven: Yale University Press.

Horton, D.R. (1984) Minimum numbers: A consideration. *Journal of Archaeological Science* 11:255–271.

Horwitz, L.K. and Smith, P. (1988) The effects of striped hyaena activity on human remains. *Journal of Archaeological Science* 15:471–481.

Hough, W. (1902) Ancient peoples of the Petrified Forest of Arizona. *Harpers Monthly Magazine* 105:897–901.

Hough, W. (1903) Archaeological fieldwork in northeastern Arizona: Museum-Gates Expedition of 1901. U.S. National Museum Annual Report of 1901. pp. 279–358.

Hoyme, L.E. and Bass, W.M. (1962) Appendix: Human skeletal remains from the Tolifero (Ha6) and Clarksville (Mc14) sites, John H. Kerr Reservoir Basin, Virginia. *Bureau of American Ethnology Bulletin* 182:329–400.

Hrdlicka, A. (1944) *The Anthropology of Kodiak Island*. Philadelphia: Wistar Institute of Anatomy.

Huelsbeck, D.R. and Wesson, G. (1982) Thoughts on the collection, conservation and curation of faunal remains. *Northwest Anthropology Research Notes* 16:221–230.

Hummel, S., Schutkowski, H. and Herrmann, B. (1988) Advances in cremation research. Actes des 3èmes Journées Anthropologiques. *Notes et Monographies Techniques no. 24*. Paris: Éditions du CNRS. pp. 177–194.

Hurlburt, I. (1977) Faunal remains from Fort White Earth N.W. Co. (1810–1813). *Provincial Museum of Alberta, Human History Occasional Paper* 1:1–107.

Hyland, D.C., Tersak, J.M., Adovasio, J.M. and Siegel, M.I. (1990) Identification of the species of origin of residual blood on lithic material. *American Antiquity* 55:104–112.

Inskeep, R.R. and Hendey, Q.B. (1966) An interesting association of bones from the Elandsfontein fossil site. In: *Acts of the Fifth Panafrican Congress of Prehistory and Quaternary Studies*. Tenerife: Museo Arqueologico. pp. 109–124.

Isaac, G. and Crader, D. (1981) To what extent were early hominids carnivorous? An archaeological perspective. In: R. Harding and T. Teleki (eds.), *Omnivorous Primates*. New York: Columbia University Press. pp. 37–103.

Jacob, T. (1972) The problem of head-hunting and brain-eating among Pleistocene men in Indonesia. *Archaeology and Physical Anthropology in Oceania* 7:2:81–91.

James, S.R. (1989) Hominid use of fire in the Lower and Middle Pleistocene: A review of the evidence. *Current Anthropology* 30:1–26.

Jelinek, J. (1957) Anthropofagie a pohrebni ritus doby bronzove na podklade nálezu z moravy a z okolnich üzemi. *Acta Musei Moraviae* 42:1–133.

Johanson, D.C., Taieb, M. and Coppens, Y. (1982) Pliocene hominids from the Hadar Formation, Ethiopia (1973–1977): Stratigraphic, chronologic and paleoenvironmental contexts, with notes on hominid morphology and systematics. *American Journal of Physical Anthropology* 57:373–402.

Johnson, E. (1978) Paleo-Indian bison procurement and butchering patterns on the Llano Estacado. *Plains Anthropologist* 23(82):98–105.

Johnson, E. (1980) Updating comments on "Paleo-Indian procurement and butchering patterns on the Llano Estacado." *Plains Anthropologist* 25:83–85.

Johnson, E. (1983) A framework for interpretation in bone technology. In: G.M. LeMoine and A.S. MacEachern (eds.), *A Question of Bone Technology*. Calgary: University of Calgary Archaeological Association. pp. 55–93.

Jones, K.T. (1983) Forager archaeology: The Aché of eastern Paraguay. In: G.M. LeMoine and A.S. MacEachern (eds.), *A Question of Bone Technology*. Calgary: Calgary Archaeological Association. pp. 171–191.

Jones, K.T. (1984) *Hunting and Scavenging by Early Hominids: A Study in Archaeological Method and Theory*. Ph.D. diss., the University of Utah, Salt Lake City.

Jordan, R.H. (1988) Kodiak Island's Kachemak tradition: Violence and village life in a land of plenty. Annual Meetings of the Alaska Anthropological Association, Fairbanks, March 1988.

Kane, A.E. (1986) Prehistory of the Dolores River Valley. In: D.A. Breternitz, C.K. Robinson and C.T. Gross (eds.), *Dolores Archaeological Program: Final Synthetic Report*.

Denver: U.S. Department of the Interior, Bureau of Reclamation. pp. 353–435.

Kehoe, T.F. (1967) The Boarding School bison drive site. *Plains Anthropologist* 12 (35) Memoir No. 4: 1–165.

Kelley, J.C. and Kelley, E.A. (1975) An alternative hypothesis for the explanation of Anasazi culture history. *Papers of the Archaeological Society of New Mexico* 2:178–223.

Kelley, J.E. (1975) Zooarchaeological analysis at Antelope House: Behavioral inferences from distribution data. *Kiva* 41:81–85.

Kelley, J.H. (1984) The archaeology of the Sierra Blanca region of southeastern New Mexico. *University of Michigan, Museum of Anthropology, Anthropological Papers*. 74:1–527.

Kelly, L.T. (1964) Southern Paiute ethnography. *University of Utah Anthropological Papers* 69:1–194.

Kent, S. (1981) The dog: An archaeologist's best friend or worst enemy—The spatial distribution of faunal remains. *Journal of Field Archaeology* 8:367–372.

Keys, A., Brozer, J., Henschel, A., Michelson, O. and Taylor, H.L. (1950) *The Biology of Human Starvation*. Minneapolis: University of Minnesota Press.

Kidder, Alfred V. (1927) Southwestern Archaeological Conference. *Science* 68:489–491.

Kilman, E. (1959) *Cannibal Coast*. San Antonio: Naylor.

Kirch, P.V. (1973) Prehistoric subsistence patterns in the northern Marquesas Islands, French Polynesia. *Archaeology and Physical Anthropology in Oceania* 8:1:24–40.

Klapwijk, M. (1989) Pot- and pit-burials from the north-eastern Transvaal, South Africa. *South African Archaeological Bulletin* 44:65–69.

Klein, R.G. (1976) The mammalian fauna of the Klasies River Mouth sites, Southern Cape Province, South Africa. *South African Archaeological Bulletin* 31:75–98.

Klein, R.G. (1977) The mammalian fauna from the Middle and Later Stone Age (Late Pleistocene) levels of Border Cave, Natal Province, South Africa. *South African Archaeological Bulletin* 32:14–27.

Klein, R.G. (1980) The interpretations of mammalian faunas from stone age archaeological sites, with special reference to sites in the Southern Cape Province, South Africa. In: A.K. Behrensmeyer and A. Hill (eds.), *Fossils in the Making*. Chicago: University of Chicago Press. pp. 223–246.

Klein, R.G. (1981) Later Stone Age subsistence at Byeneskranskop Cave, South Africa. In: R.S.O. Harding and G. Teleki (eds.), *Omnivorous Primates: Gathering and Hunting in Human Evolution*. New York: Columbia University Press. pp. 166–190.

Klein, R.G. (1987) Reconstructing how early people exploited animals: Problems and prospects. In: M.H. Nitecki and D.V. Nitecki (eds.), *The Evolution of Human Hunting*. New York: Plenum. pp. 11–45.

Klein, R.G. (1989) Why does skeletal part representation differ between smaller and larger bovids at Klasies River Mouth and other archeological sites? *Journal of Archaeological Science* 6:363–381.

Klein, R.G. and Cruz-Uribe, K. (1984) *The Analysis of Animal Bones from Archaeological Sites*. Chicago: University of Chicago Press.

Klein, R. and Cruz-Uribe, K. (1987) La fauna mamifera del yacimiento de la Cueva de "El Juyo". Campañas de 1978 Y 1979. In: L. Barandiarán, L.G. Freeman, J. González Echegaray and R.G. Klein (eds.), *Centro de Investigacion y Museo de Altamira*. Monografias 14:99–120.

Kluckhohn, C. and Reiter, P. (1939) Preliminary report on the 1937 excavations Bc 50–51, Chaco Canyon, New Mexico. *University of New Mexico Bulletin* 345:3:2:38–39 (Anthropological Series, Albuquerque).

Knowles, F.H.S. (1937) Physical anthropology of the Roebuck Iroquois. *National Museum of Canada, Anthropological Series* 22:1–75.

Knowles, F.H.S. (1940) The torture of captives by Indians of eastern North America. *Proceedings of the American Philosophical Society* 82:151–225.

Koch, C.P. (1986) *The Vertebrate Taphonomy and Palaeoecology of the Olorgesailie Formation (Middle Pleistocene, Kenya)*. Ph.D. diss., University of Toronto.

Koch, K.F. (1970) Warfare and anthropophagy in Jalé society. *Anthropologica* (The Hague)

12:37–58.

Kohler, T.A. and Matthews, M.H. (1988) Long-term Anasazi land use and forest reduction: A case study from southwest Colorado. *American Antiquity* 53:537–564.

Kolata, G. (1986) Anthropologists suggest cannibalism is a myth. *Science* 232:1497–1500.

Krantz, G.S. (1968) A new method of counting mammal bones. *American Journal of Archaeology* 72:286–288.

Krantz, G.S. (1979) Oldest human remains from the Marmes site. *Northwest Anthropological Research Notes* 13:159–174.

Kroeber, A.L. (1927) Disposal of the dead. *American Anthropologist* 29:308–315.

Krogman, W.M. and Iscan, D.Y. (1986) *The Human Skeleton in Forensic Medicine*. 2d ed. Springfield, Ill.: Charles C. Thomas.

Kroll, E.M. and Isaac, G.L. (1984) Configurations of artifacts and bones at early Pleistocene sites in East Africa. In: H.J. Hietala (ed.), *Intrasite Spatial Analysis in Archaeology*. Cambridge: Cambridge University Press. pp. 4–31.

Lang, R.W. and Harris, A.H. (1984) *Faunal remains from Arroyo Hondo Pueblo*. Arroyo Hondo Archaeological Series, Vol. 5. Albuquerque: School of American Research Press.

Lange, C.H. (1959) *Cochiti: A New Mexico Pueblo, Past and Present*. Austin, Tex.: University of Texas Press.

Larsson, L., Meiklejohn, C. and Newell, R.R. (1981) Human skeletal material from the Mesolithic site of Ageröd 1: HC, Scania, southern Sweden. *Fornvannen* 76:161–168.

Lartet, E. (1860) On the coexistence of man with certain extinct quadrupeds, proved by fossil bones, from various Pleistocene deposits, bearing incisions made by sharp instruments. *Quarterly Journal of the Geological Society of London* 16(1):471–479. Reprinted in: R.F. Heizer (ed.) (1969) *Man's Discovery of His Past*. Palo Alto: Peek. pp. 122–131.

Lawrence, B. (1973) Problems in the inter-site comparison of faunal remains. In: J. Matolcsi (ed.), *Domestikations-forschkung und Geschichte der Haustiere*. Budapest: Akadémiai Kiadó. pp. 397–402.

Lawrence, D.R. (1968) Taphonomy and information loss in fossil communities. *Bulletin of the Geological Society of America* 79:1315–1330.

Leakey, M.D. (1945) Report on excavations at Hyrax Hill, Nakuru. *Transactions of the Royal Society of South Africa* 30:4:271–409.

Leakey, M.D. and Leakey, L.S.B. (1950) *Excavations at the Njoro River Cave*. Oxford: Clarendon Press.

Lee, R.B. (1979) *The !Kung San*. Cambridge: Cambridge University Press.

Leechman, D. (1951) Bone grease. *American Antiquity* 16:355–356.

Legge, A.J. (1978) Archaeozoology—Or zooarchaeology. In: D.R. Brothwell, K.D. Thomas and J. Clutton-Brock, J. (eds.), *Research Problems in Zooarchaeology*. University of London, Institute of Archaeology, Occasional Publications 3. pp. 129–132.

Lekson, S.H. (1988) The idea of the kiva in Anasazi archaeology. *Kiva* 53:213–234.

LeMoine, G.M. and MacEachern, A.S. (eds.) (1983) *A Question of Bone Technology*. Calgary: Archaeological Association of the University of Calgary.

LeMort, F. (1988) Cannibalisme ou rite funeraire? *Dossiers Histoire et Archaeologie* 124:46–49.

LeMort, F. and Duday, H. (1987) Traces de Décharnement sur un humérus dysmorphoque Néolithique. *Bulletin et Mémoire de la Societé d'Anthropologie de Paris* 4: Série 14:1:17–24.

Leonard, R.D. (1989) Anasazi faunal exploitation: Prehistoric subsistence on northern Black Mesa, Arizona. *Occasional Paper, Center for Archaeological Investigations, Southern Illinois University at Carbondale* 13:1–218.

Leroi-Gourhan, A. (1952) Étude des vestiges zoologiques. In: A. Laming-Emperaire (ed.), *La Découverte du Passe*. Paris: Picard. pp. 123–150.

Leroi-Gourhan, A. and Brezillon, M. (1972) Fouilles de Pincevent: Essai d'Analyse Ethnographique d'un Habitat Magdalenien (La Section 36). *Gallia Prehistoire Supplement* 7.

Lewin, R. (1981) Protohuman activity etched in fossil bones. *Science* 213:123–124.

Lie, R.W. (1980) Minimum number of individuals from osteological samples. *Norwegian Archaeological Review* 13:24–30.

Lightfoot, R.R., Emerson, A.M. and Blinman,

E. (1988) Excavations in Area 5, Grass Mesa Village (Site 5MT23). In: W.D. Lipe, J.N. Morris and T.A. Kohler (eds.), *Dolores Archaeological Program: Anasazi Communities at Dolores: Grass Mesa Village*. Denver: U.S. Department of the Interior, Bureau of Reclamation. pp. 1049–1135.

Lister, R.H. (1965) Contributions to Mesa Verde archaeology: II. Site 875, Mesa Verde National Park, Colorado. *University of Colorado Studies, Series in Anthropology* 11:1–112.

Lister, R.H. and Lister, F.C. (eds.) (1961) The Coombs site, Part 3, summary and conclusions. *University of Utah, Anthropological Papers* 41: 117–136.

Lobdell, J.E. (1975) Cottonwood Creek: Report on 1974 archaeological fieldwork. *University of Alaska Museum Newsletter* April 12–18. Paper presented at October 5, 1974 general meeting of the Kenai Penninsula Historical Association, Ninilchik, Alaska.

Loeb, E.M. (1923) The blood sacrifice complex. *American Anthropological Association Memoir* 30. Kraus Reprint, 1964.

Longacre, W.A. (1976) Population dynamics at the Grasshopper Pueblo, Arizona. In: E.B. Zubrow (ed.), *Demographic Anthropology*. Albuquerque: University of New Mexico Press. pp. 169–184.

Lopez, E.H. (1973) *The Highest Hell: The First Full Account of the Andes Air Crash*. London: Sidgwick and Jackson.

Losey, T.C. (1973) The relationship of faunal remains to social dynamics at Fort Enterprise, N.W.T. In: R.M. Getty and K.R. Fladmark (eds.), *Historical Archaeology in Northwestern North America*. Calgary, Alberta: University of Calgary Archaeological Association. pp. 133–143.

Lovejoy, C.O. (1985) Dental wear in the Libben population: Its functional pattern and role in the determination of adult skeletal age at death. *American Journal of Physical Anthropology* 68:47–56.

Lovejoy, C.O., Meindl, R.S., Pryzbeck, T.R., Barton, T.S., Heiple, K.G. and Kotting, D. (1977) Paleodemography of the Libben site, Ottawa County, Ohio. *Science* 198:291–293.

Loy, T.H. and Wood, A.R. (1989) Blood residue analysis at Cayönü Tepesi, Turkey. *Journal of Field Archaeology* 16:451–460.

Lubbock, J. (1865) *Prehistoric Times*. London: Williams and Norgate.

Luebben, R.A. and Nickens, P.R. (1982) A mass interment in an Early Pueblo III kiva in southwestern Colorado. *Journal of Intermountain Archaeology* 1:66–79.

Lumholtz, C. (1890) *Among Cannibals*. London: Murray.

Lyman, R.L. (1976) *A Cultural Analysis of Faunal Remains from the Alpowa Locality*. Unpublished MA thesis, Department of Anthropology, Washington State University, Pullman.

Lyman, R.L. (1978) Prehistoric butchering techniques in the lower Granite Reservoir, southeastern Washington. *Tebiwa* 13:1–25.

Lyman, R.L. (1979a) Faunal analysis: An outline of method and theory with some suggestions. *Northwest Anthropological Research Notes* 13:22–35.

Lyman, R.L. (1979b) Archaeological faunal analysis: A bibliography. *Occasional Papers of the Idaho Museum of Natural History* 31.

Lyman, R.L. (1980a) Archaeofauna. In: D.T. Kirkpatrick (ed.), *Prehistory and History of the Ojo Amarillo*. New Mexico State University Cultural Resources Management Division Report No. 276:1317–1388.

Lyman, R.L. (1980b) Inferences from bone distributions in prehistoric sites in the Lower Granite Reservoir area, southeastern Washington. *Northwest Anthropological Research Notes* 14:107–123.

Lyman, R.L. (1982) Archaeofaunas and subsistence studies. *Advances in Archaeological Method and Theory* 5:331–393.

Lyman, R.L. (1984a) Broken bones, bone expediency tools, and bone pseudotools: Lessons from the blast zone around Mount St. Helens, Washington. *American Antiquity* 49:315–333.

Lyman, R.L. (1984b) Bone density and differential survivorship of fossil classes. *Journal of Anthropological Archaeology* 3:259–299.

Lyman, R.L. (1985) Bone frequencies: Differential transport, *in situ* destruction, and the MGUI. *Journal of Archaeological Science* 12:221–236.

Lyman, R.L. (1987a) Archaeofaunas and butchery studies: A taphonomic perspective. *Ad-*

vances in Archaeological Method and Theory 10:249–337.

Lyman, R.L. (1987b) Zooarchaeology and taphonomy: A general consideration. *Journal of Ethnobiology* 7:93–117.

Lyman, R.L. (1987c) Hunting for evidence of Plio-Pleistocene hominid scavengers. *American Anthropologist* 89:710–715.

Lyman, R.L. (in press) Taphonomic problems with archaeological analyses of animal carcass utilization and transport.

Lyman, R.L. and Fox, G.L. (1989) A critical evaluation of bone weathering as an indication of bone assemblage formation. *Journal of Archaeological Science* 16:71–94.

Lyman, R.L. and O'Brien, M.J. (1987) Plowzone zooarchaeology: Fragmentation and identifiability. *Journal of Field Archaeology* 14:493–498.

Lyon, P.J. (1970) Differential bone destruction: An ethnographic example. *American Antiquity* 35:213–215.

McArthur, M. (1960) Nutritional report. In: C. Mountford (ed.), *Records of the American-Australian Scientific Expedition to Arnhem Land, Part 2, Anthropology and Nutrition.* Victoria: Melbourne University Press.

McArdle, J. (1975–77) A numerical (computerized) method for quantifying zooarchaeological comparison. *Paléorient* 3:181–190.

McCoy, P.C. (1979) Easter Island. In: J. Jennings (ed.), *The Prehistory of Polynesia.* Cambridge: Harvard University Press. pp. 135–166.

McDonald, J.A. (1976) *An Archaeological Assessment of Canyon de Chelly National Monument.* Tucson: National Park Services, Western Archaeological Center. Publications in Anthropology No. 5.

McKee, D.F. (1988) Bison hunting and processing at the River Bend Site (48NA202). *Wyoming Archaeologist* 31:13–32.

McKenzie, K. (1980) Waiting For Harry. A film of the Australian Institute of Aboriginal Studies. Distributed by the University of California Media Center, Berkeley (# 10727).

McKern, T.W. (1958) The use of short-wave ultra-violet rays for the segregation of commingled skeletal remains. Technical Report EP-98, Environmental Protection Research Division; Headquarters Quartermaster Research and Engineering Command, U.S. Army.

Mackey, J. and Green, R.C. (1979) Largo-Gallina towers: An explanation. *American Antiquity* 44:144–154.

McPherron, A. (1967) The Juntunen site and the Late Woodland prehistory of the Upper Great Lakes area. *Anthropological Papers of the Museum of Anthropology, the University of Michigan* No. 30.

Maguire, J., Pemberton, D. and Collett, M.H. (1980) The Makapansgat limeworks grey breccia: Hominids, hyaenas, hystricids or hillwash? *Palaeontologia Africana* 23:75–98.

Maltby, J.M. (1985) Assessing variations in Iron Age and Roman butchery practices: The need for quantification. In: N.R. Fieller, D.D. Gilbertson and N.G. Ralph (eds.), *Palaeobiological Investigations: Research Design, Methods of Data Analysis.* British Archaeological Reports, International Series 266:19–30.

Malville, N.J. (1989) Two fragmented human bone assemblages from Yellow Jacket, southwestern Colorado. *Kiva* 55:3–22.

Marshack, A. (1988) La pensée symbolique et l'art. *Dossiers Histoire et Archeologie* 124:80–90.

Marshall, F. and Pilgram, T. (1991) Meat versus within-bone nutrients: Another look at the meaning of body part representation in archaeological sites. *Journal of Archaeological Science* 18:149–163.

Marshall, F.B. (1986a) *Aspects of the Advent of Pastoral Economies in East Africa.* Ph.D. diss., University of California, Berkeley.

Marshall, F.B. (1986b) Implications of bone modification in a Neolithic faunal assemblage for the study of early hominid butchery and subsistence practices. *Journal of Human Evolution* 15:661–672.

Marshall, L.G. (1989) Bone modification and "The Laws of Burial." In: R. Bonnichsen and M. Sorg (eds.), *Bone Modification.* Orono, Maine: Center for the Study of the First Americans, University of Maine. pp. 7–24.

Martin, D.L., Goodman, A.H. and Armelagos, G.J. (1985) Skeletal pathologies as indicators of quality and quantity of diet. In: R. I. Gilbert and J. H. Mielke (eds.), *The Analysis of Prehistoric Diets.* Orlando, Fla.: Academic Press. pp. 227–279.

Martin, D.L., Piacentini, C. and Armelagos,

G.J. (1985) Paleopathology of the Black Mesa Anasazi: A biocultural approach. *Arizona State University, Anthropological Research Papers* 34:104–114.

Martin, H. (1907) *Recherches sur l'Evolution du Moustérien dans le Gisement de la Quina (Charente) I: Industrie Osseuse*. Paris 1907–1910. Schleicher Fréres, Éditeurs.

Martin, H. (1910) La percussion osseuse et les esquilles que en dérivent. Experimentation. *Bulletin Societe Prehistorique Francaise* 299–304.

Martin, P.S. (1929) The 1928 archaeological expedition of the State Historical Society of Colorado. *Colorado Magazine* 6:1–35.

Martin, P.S. and Plog, F. (1973) *The Archaeology of Arizona: A Study of the Southwest Region*. Garden City: Doubleday/Natural History Press.

Mathien, F.J. and McGuire, R.H. (eds.) (1986) *Ripples in the Chichimec Sea: New Considerations of Southwestern-Mesoamerican Interactions*. Carbondale: Southern Illinois University Press.

Matos Moctezuma, E. (1987) Symbolism of the Templo Mayor. In: E.H. Boone (ed.), *The Aztec Templo Mayor*. Washington, D.C.: Dumbarton Oaks. pp. 185–209.

Matson, R.G., Lipe, W.D. and Haase, W.R. (1988) Adaptational continuities and occupational discontinuities: The Cedar Mesa Anasazi. *Journal of Field Archaeology* 15:245–264.

Meadow, R.H. (1978) ''Bonecode''—A system of numerical coding for faunal data from Middle Eastern sites. *Peabody Museum Bulletin* 2:169–186.

Medlock, R.C. (1975) Faunal analysis. In: M.B. Schiffer and J.H. House (eds.), *Arkansas Archaeological Survey Research Series* 3:223–242.

Mensforth, R.P. and Lovejoy, C.O. (1985) Anatomical, physiological, and epidemiological correlates of the aging process: A confirmation of multifactorial age determination in the Libben skeletal population. *American Journal of Physical Anthropology* 68:87–106.

Mensforth, R.P., Lovejoy, C.O., Lallo, J.W. and Armelagos, G.J. (1978) The role of constitutional factors, diet and infectious disease in the etiology of porotic hyperostosis and periosteal reactions in prehistoric infants and children. *Medical Anthropology* 2:1–59.

Merbs, C.F. (1967) Cremated human remains from Point of Pines, Arizona: A new approach. *American Antiquity* 32:498–506.

Merbs, C.F. and Steadman, L.B. (1982) Kuru and cannibalism? *American Anthropologist* 84:611–627.

Metcalfe, D. and Jones, K.T. (1988) A reconsideration of animal body-part utility indices. *American Antiquity* 53:486–504.

Métraux, A. (1946) Tribes of the Middle and Upper Amazon River. In: J.H. Steward (ed.), *Handbook of South American Indians*. Washington, D.C.: Bureau of American Ethnology Bulletin 143:687–712.

Miles, J.S. (1975) *Orthopedic Problems of the Wetherill Mesa Populations*. Washington, D.C.: National Park Service, Wetherill Mesa Studies, Publications in Archaeology 7G.

Milner, G.R. and Smith, V.G. (1989) Carnivore alteration of human bone from a late prehistoric site in Illinois. *American Journal of Physical Anthropology* 79:43–49.

Minnis, P.E. (1985) *Social Adaptation to Food Stress: A Prehistoric Southwestern Example*. Chicago: University of Chicago Press.

Molto, J.E. (1983) Biological relationships of southern Ontario Woodland peoples: The evidence of discontinuous cranial morphology. *Archaeological Survey of Canada Paper* 119:1–396.

Molto, J.E., Spence, M.W. and Fox, W.A. (1986) The Van Oordt site: A case study in salvage osteology. *Canadian Review of Physical Anthropology* 5:49–61.

Montagu, A. (1937) Cannibalism and primitive man. *Science* 86:56–57.

Montagu, A. (1961) A brief excursion into cannibalism. In: A. Montague (ed.), *Man in Process*. Cleveland: World.

Morlan, R.E. (1984) Toward the definition of criteria for the recognition of artificial bone alterations. *Quaternary Research* 22:160–171.

Morris, A.G. and Parkington, J. (1982) Prehistoric homicide: A case of violent death on the Cape South Coast, South Africa. *South African Journal of Science* 78:167–169.

Morris, D.P. (1986) *Archaeological Investigations at Antelope House*. Washington, D.C.: National Park Service.

Morris, E.H. (1939) Archaeological studies in the La Plata District, southwestern Colorado and northwestern New Mexico. *Carnegie Institution of Washington*, Pub. 519.

Munthe, K. and McLeod, S.A. (1975) Collection of taphonomic information from fossil and recent vertebrate specimens, with a selected bibliography. *Paleobios* 19:1–12.

Myers, R.A. (1984) Island Carib cannibalism. *Nieuwe West-Indische Gids (New West Indian Guide)*. Utrecht, 58:(3/4):147–184.

Myers, T., Voorhies, M.R. and Corner, R.G. (1980) Spiral fractures and bone pseudotools at paleontological sites. *American Antiquity* 45:483–490.

Nass, G.G. and Bellantoni, N.F. (1982) A prehistoric multiple burial from Monument Valley evidencing trauma and possible cannibalism. *Kiva* 47:257–271.

Needham, R. (1980) Review of Arens, W. (1979). *The Times Literary Supplement*, Jan. 25, 1980.

Nelson, C.T. (1938) The teeth of the Indians of Pecos Pueblo. *American Journal of Physical Anthropology* 23:261–298.

Nelson, N.C. (1928) Pseudo-artifacts from the Pliocene of Nebraska. *Science* 67:316–317.

Neuman, G.G. (1987) How we became (in)human. In: G.G. Neuman (ed.), *Origins of Human Aggression*. New York: Human Sciences Press. pp. 78–104.

Neusius, S.W. (1985a) The Dolores Archaeological Program faunal data base. In: K.L. Petersen, V.L. Clay, M. H. Matthews and S.W. Neusius (eds.), *Dolores Archaeological Program: Studies in Environmental Archaeology*. Denver: U.S. Department of the Interior, Bureau of Reclamation. pp. 117–126.

Neusius, S.W. (1985b) Faunal resource use: Prespectives (sic) from the ethnographic record. In: K.L. Petersen, V.L. Clay, M. H. Matthews and S.W. Neusius (eds.), *Dolores Archaeological Program: Studies in Environmental Archaeology*. Denver: U.S. Department of the Interior, Bureau of Reclamation. pp. 101–115.

Neusius, S.W. (1986a) Faunal remains from Aldea Sierritas. In: A.E. Kane and G.T. Gross (eds.), *Dolores Archaeological Program: Early Anasazi Sites in the Sagehen Flats Area*. Denver: U.S. Department of the Interior, Bureau of Reclamation. pp. 381–397.

Neusius, S.W. (1986b) Faunal remains from LeMoc Shelter. In: T.A. Kohler, W.D. Lipe and A.E. Kane (eds.), *Dolores Archaeological Program: Anasazi Communities at Dolores: Early Small Settlements in the Dolores River Canyon and Western Sagehen Flats Area*. Denver: U.S. Department of the Interior, Bureau of Reclamation. pp. 279–296.

Neusius, S.W. (1988) Faunal exploitation during the McPhee Phase: Evidence from the McPhee Community Cluster. In: A.E. Kane and C.K. Robinson (eds.), *Dolores Archaeological Program: Anasazi Communities at Dolores: McPhee Village*. Denver: U.S. Department of the Interior, Bureau of Reclamation. pp. 1209–1291.

Neusius, S.W. and Gould, M. (1988) Faunal remains: Implications for Dolores Anasazi adaptations. In: W.D. Lipe, J.N. Morris and T.A. Kohler (eds.), *Dolores Archaeological Program: Anasazi Communities at Dolores: Grass Mesa Village*. Denver: U.S. Department of the Interior, Bureau of Reclamation. pp. 1049–1135.

Nichol, R.K. and Creak, G.A. (1979) Matching paired elements among archaeological bone remains. *Newsletter of Computer Archaeology* 14:6–16.

Nickens, P.R. (1974) Analysis of prehistoric human skeletal remains from the Mancos Canyon, southwestern Colorado. Ms. Report, Dept. of Anthropology, Univ. of Colorado, Boulder. 84 pp.

Nickens, P.R. (1975) Prehistoric cannibalism in the Mancos Canyon, southwestern Colorado. *Kiva* 40:283–293.

Nickens, P.R. (1981) Pueblo III communities in transition: Environment and adaptation in Johnson Canyon. *Colorado Archaeological Society Memoir* 2:1–62.

Noe-Nygaard, N. (1977) Butchering and marrow fracturing as a taphonomic factor in archaeological deposits. *Paleobiology* 3:218–237.

Noe-Nygaard, N. (1987) Taphonomy in archaeology with special emphasis on man as a biasing factor. *Journal of Danish Archaeology* 6:7–62.

Noe-Nygaard, N. (1989) Man-made trace fossils

on bones. *Human Evolution* 4:461–491.

Nordby, L.V. (1974) The excavation of sites 5MTUMR–2343, –2345 and –2346, Mancos Canyon, Ute Mountain, Ute Homelands, Colorado. Bureau Indian Affairs, Contract MOOC14201337 Report.

O'Connell, J.F., Hawkes, K. and Blurton Jones, N. (1988) Hadza hunting, butchering, and bone transport and their archaeological implications. *Journal of Anthropological Research* 44:113–161.

O'Connell, J.F., Hawkes, K., and Blurton Jones, N. (1990) Reanalysis of large mammal body part transport among the Hadza. *Journal of Archaeological Science* 17:301–316.

Olivier, J.S. (1989) Analogues and site context: Bone damages from Shield Trap Cave (24CB91), Carbon County, Montana, U.S.A. In: R. Bonnichsen and M. Sorg (eds.), *Bone Modification*. Orono, Maine: Center for the Study of the First Americans, University of Maine. pp. 73–98.

Olsen, J.W. (1980) *A Zooarchaeological Analysis of Vertebrate Faunal Remains from the Grasshopper Pueblo, Arizona*. Ph.D. diss., University of California, Berkeley.

Olsen, S.J. (1961) The relative value of fragmentary mammalian remains. *American Antiquity* 26:538–540.

Olsen, S.J. (1971) *Zooarchaeology: Animal Bones in Archaeology and Their Interpretation*. New York: Addison-Wesley.

Olsen, S.J. and Olsen, J.W. (1981) A comment on nomenclature in faunal studies. *American Antiquity* 46:192–194.

Olsen, S.L. (1987) Magdalenian reindeer exploitation at the Grotte des Eyzies, Southwest France. *Archaeozoologia* 1:171–182.

Olsen, S.L. (ed.) (1988) *Scanning Electron Microscopy in Archaeology*. British Archaeological Reports, International Series 452.

Olsen, S.L. (1989) Solutré: A theoretical approach to the reconstruction of Upper Paleolithic hunting strategies. *Journal of Human Evolution* 18:295–327.

Olsen, S.L. and Shipman, P. (1988) Surface modifications on bone: Trampling versus butchery. *Journal of Archaeological Science* 15:535–553.

Olson, A.P. (1966) A mass secondary burial from northern Arizona. *American Antiquity* 31:822–826.

Olson, A.P. and Wasley, W.W. (1956) An archaeological traverse survey in west-central New Mexico. In: F. Wendorf, N. Fox, and O.L. Lewis (eds.), *Pipeline Archaeology*. Santa Fe and Flagstaff: Laboratory of Anthropology and Museum of Northern Arizona. pp. 256–390.

Ortiz de Montellano, B.R. (1978) Aztec cannibalism: An ecological necessity? *Science* 200:611–617.

O'Shea, J. (1984) *Mortuary Variability*. Orlando, Fla.: Academic Press.

O'Shea, J.M. and Bridges, P.S. (1989) The Sargent Site Ossuary (25CU28), Custer County, Nebraska. *Plains Anthropologist* 34:123:7–21.

Owsley, D.W., Berryman, H.E. and Bass, W.M. (1977) Demographic and osteological evidence for warfare at the Larson site, South Dakota. *Plains Anthropologist* 22 (78:2):119–131.

Paine, R.R. (1989) Model life tables as a measure of bias in the Grasshopper Pueblo skeletal series. *American Antiquity* 54:820–824.

Palkovich, A.M. (1980) *Pueblo Population and Society: The Arroyo Hondo Skeletal and Mortuary Remains*. Santa Fe: School of American Research Press. Arroyo Hondo Archaeological Series, Vol. 3.

Palkovich, A.M. (1984) Agriculture, marginal environments, and nutritional stress in the prehistoric Southwest. In: M.N. Cohen and G.J. Armelagos (eds.), *Paleopathology at the Origins of Agriculture*. New York: Academic Press. pp. 425–438.

Parmalee, P.W. (1960) Animal remains from the Aztalan Site, Jefferson County, Wisconsin. *Wisconsin Archaeologist* 41:1–10.

Parmalee, P.W. (1965) The food economy of Archaic and Woodland peoples at Tick Creek Cave Site, Missouri. *Missouri Archaeologist* 27:1:1–34.

Parmalee, P.W. (1977) The avifauna from prehistoric Arikara sites in South Dakota. *Plains Anthropologist* 22:189–222.

Parmalee, P.W. (1985) Identification interpretation of archaeologically derived animal remains. In: R.I. Gilbert and J.H. Mielke (eds.),

The Analysis of Prehistoric Diets. New York: Academic Press. pp. 61–95.

Pastron, A.G. (1974) Preliminary ethnoarchaeological investigations among the Tarahumara. In: C.B. Donnan and C.W. Clewlow (eds.), *Ethnoarchaeology*. Los Angeles: UCLA Institute of Archaeology, Monograph 4. pp. 93–114.

Pastron, A.G. and Clewlow, C.W. (1974) Ethnoarchaeological observation on human burial decomposition in the Chihuahua Sierra. *UCLA Institute of Archaeology Monograph* 4:177–181.

Payne, S. (1972a) Partial recovery and sample bias—The results of some seiving experiments. In: E.S. Higgs (ed.), *Papers in Economic Prehistory*. Cambridge: Cambridge University Press. pp. 49–64.

Payne, S. (1972b) On the interpretation of bone samples from archaeological samples. In: E.S. Higgs (ed.), *Papers in Economic Prehistory*. Cambridge: Cambridge University Press. pp. 65–81.

Payne, S. (1975) Partial recovery and sample bias. In: A.T. Clason (ed.), *Archaeozoological Studies*. Amsterdam: North Holland. pp. 7–17.

Payne, S. (1983) Bones from cave sites: Who ate what? Problems and a case study. In: J. Clutton-Brock and C. Grigson (eds), *Animals and Archaeology: 1. Hunters and Their Prey*. British Archaeological Reports, International Series 163:149–162.

Peale, T.R. (1871) On the uses of the brain and marrow of animals among the Indians of North America. *Annual Report of the Smithsonian Institution for 1870*: 390–391. Washington, D.C.

Pearce, J.E. (1932) The archaeology of east Texas. *American Anthropologist* 34:670–687.

Pearce, J.E. (1935) Tales that dead men tell. *University of Texas Bulletin* 3537:1–2.

Pei, W.C. (1938) Le Role des animaux et des causes naturelles dans le cassure des os. *Palaeontologica Sinica*, n.s. D., No. 7. Peking.

Pepper, G.H. (1920) Pueblo Bonito. *Anthropological Papers of the American Museum of Natural History* 27:1–398.

Perkins, D. and Daly, P. (1968) A hunters' village in Neolithic Turkey. *Scientific American* 219:5:96–106.

Perzigian, A.J. (1976) The dentition of the Indian Knoll skeletal population: Odontometrics and cusp number. *American Journal of Physical Anthropology* 44:113–122.

Petersen, K.L. (1988) Climate and the Dolores River Anasazi. *University of Utah, Anthropological Papers* 113:1–152.

Pfeiffer, S. (1986) Morbidity and mortality in the Uxbridge Ossuary. *Canadian Review of Physical Anthropology* 5:23–31.

Phelps, D.S. and Burgess, R. (1964) A possible case of cannibalism in the Early Woodland period of eastern Georgia. *American Antiquity* 30:199–202.

Pietrusewsky, M. (1985) Human cranial collections from the Pacific and Asia preserved in Dresden, Berlin and Leipzig and information on collections outside the German Democratic Republic. *Abhandlungen und Berichte des Staatlichen Museums für Volkerkuknde Dresden* 42. Dresden, GDR.

Pijoan, C.M.-A. and Mansilla, J. (1990) Evidencias rituales en restos humanos del Norte de Mesoamerica. In: F.S. Miranda (ed.), *Mesoamerica Norte de Mexico: Siglo IX–XII*. Mexico City: Museo Nacional de Antropología, Instituto Nacional de Antropología e Historia. pp. 467–478.

Pijoan, C.M.-A., Mansilla, J. and Pastrana, A. (in press) Uno caso de desmembramiento. Tlatelolco, D.F. *Estudios de Antropología Biológica* (Mexico City: Instituto Nacional de Antropología e Historia-Universidad Nacional Autonoma de Mexico) 5.

Pijoan, C.M.-A. and Pastrana, A. (1985) Evidencias de antropofagia y sacrificio humano en restos óseos. In: *Avances en Antropología Física* (Mexico City: Instituto Nacional de Antropología e Historia; Cuadernos de Trabajo) 2:37–45.

Pijoan, C.M.-A. and Pastrana, A. (1987) Método para el registro de marcas de corte en huesos humanos: El caso de Tlatelcomila, Tetelpan, D.F. *Estudios de Antropología Biológica* (Mexico City: Instituto Nacional de Antropología e Historia-Universidad Nacional Autonoma de Mexico) 3:419–435.

Pijoan, C.M.-A. and Pastrana, A. (1989) Evidencias de acrividades rituales en restos oseos humanos en Tlatelcomila, D.F. In: M.C. Macias (ed.), *El Preclasico o Formativo: Avances y Perspectivas*. Mexico City: Museo Nacional de Antropología, Instituto Nacional de Antropologia e Historia. pp. 287–306.

Pijoan, C.M.-A., Pastrana, C. and Maquívar, M. (1989) El Tzompantli de Tlatelolco: Una Evidencia de Sacrificio Humano. *Estudios de Antropología Biológica* (Mexico City: Instituto Nacional de Antropología e Historia-Universidad Nacional Autonoma de Mexico) 3:561–583.

Pippin, L.C. (1987) Prehistory and paleoecology of Guadalupe Ruin, New Mexico. *University of Utah Anthropological Papers* 112:1–265.

Plog, F. (1975) Demographic studies in Southwestern prehistory. In: A.C. Swedlund (ed.), *Population Studies in Archaeology and Biological Anthropology*, Society for American Archaeology, Memoirs 30:94–103.

Plog, F. (1979) Prehistory: Western Anasazi. In: A. Ortiz (ed.), *Handbook of North American Indians*, vol. 9, *The Southwest*. Washington, D.C.: U.S. Government Printing Office. pp. 108–130.

Plog, F., Gumerman, G.J., Euler, R.C., Dean, J.S., Hevly, R.H. and Karlstrom, T.N.V. (1988) Anasazi adaptive strategies: The model, predictions, and results. In: G.J. Gumerman (ed.), *The Anasazi in a Changing Environment*. Cambridge: Cambridge University Press. pp. 230–276.

Plug, C. and Plug, I. (1990) MNI counts as estimates of species abundance. *South African Archaeological Bulletin* 45:53–57.

Polis, G.A., Myers, C.A. and Hess, W.R. (1984) A survey of intraspecific predation within the class Mammalia. *Mammal Review* 14:187–198.

Poplin, F. (1975) La faune néolithique d'Armeaux (Yonne, France): Ses donnés sur l'activité humaine. In: A.T. Clason (ed.), *Archaeozoological Studies*. New York: American Elsevier. pp. 179–192.

Poplin, F. (1981) Un problème d'ostéologie quantitative: Calcul d'effectif initial d'après appariements. Généralisation aux autres types de remontages et à d'autres materiéls archéologiques. *Revue d'Archéométrie* 5:159–165.

Poplin, F. (1983) Essai d'ostéologie quantitative sur l'estimation du nombre d'individus. *Kölner Jahrbuch für Ur- und Frügeschichte* 16:(1978–79):153–164.

Poplin, F. (1985) Les Galois dépecés de Gournay-sur-Aronde. *Review Archeologique de Picardie: Special No. "Gournay 1, Les Fouilles sur le Sanctuaire et l'Oppidium."* pp. 147–166.

Potts, R. (1982) *Lower Pleistocene Site Formation and Hominid Activities at Olduvai Gorge, Tanzania*. Ph.D. diss., Harvard University.

Potts, R. (1984) Hominid hunters? Problems of identifying the earliest hunter/gatherers. In: R. Foley (ed.), *Hominid Evolution and Community Ecology*. London: Academic Press. pp. 129–166.

Potts, R. (1986) Temporal span of bone accumulations at Olduvai Gorge and implications for early hominid foraging behavior. *Paleobiology* 12(1):25–31.

Potts, R. (1987) On butchery by Olduvai hominids. *Current Anthropology* 28:95–98 (with a reply from Bunn and Kroll).

Potts, R. (1988) *Early Hominid Activities at Olduvai*. New York: Aldine De Gruyter.

Potts, R. and Shipman, P. (1981) Cutmarks made by stone tools on bones from Olduvai Gorge, Tanzania. *Nature* 291:577–580.

Poulsen, J. (1968) Archaeological excavations on Tongatapu. In: I. Yawata and K.Y.H. Sinoto (eds.), *Prehistoric Culture in Oceania: A Symposium. 11th Pacific Congress, Tokyo, 1966*. Honolulu: Bishop Museum Press. pp. 85–92.

Rackham, J. (1983) Faunal sample to subsistence economy. In: M. Jones (ed.), *Integrating the Subsistence Economy*. British Archaeological Reports, International Series 181:251–277.

Randall, M.E. (1971) Comment on "The limited nutritional value of cannibalism." *American Anthropologist* 73:269.

Rathje, W.L. (1981) Emperor cannibal. *Early Man* 3:4:11.

Rathje, W.L. (1985) The cannibal debate. *Wilson Quarterly*. Spring 1985:134–135.

Ravesloot, J.C. (1988) Mortuary practices and social differentiation at Casas Grandes, Chihuahua, Mexico. *Anthropological Papers of the University of Arizona* 49:1–113.

Read, P.P. (1974) *Alive: The Story of the Andes Survivors*. Philadelphia: Lippincott.

Rechtman, R.B. (1991) *The Evolution of Sociopolitical Complexity in the Fiji Islands*. Ph.D. diss., University of California at Los Angeles.

Redding, R.W., Pires-Ferreira, J.W. and Zeder, M.A. (1977) A proposed system for computer analysis of identifiable faunal material from archaeological sites. *Paleorient* 3:191–205.

Redding, R.W., Zeder, M.A. and McArdle, J. (1978) Bonesort II: A system for the computer processing of identifiable faunal material. In: R.H. Meadow and M.A. Zeder (eds.), *Approaches to Faunal Analysis in the Middle East. Peabody Museum Bulletin* 2:135–147.

Redmond, B.G. (1982) Drilled skulls and eyes of clay: Late Woodland burial ceremonialism in the western Lake Erie basin. *Toledo Area Aboriginal Research Bulletin* 11:1–36.

Reed, C.A. (1963) Osteo-archaeology. In: D. Brothwell and E.S. Higgs (eds.), *Science in Archaeology*. London: Thames and Hudson. pp. 204–216.

Reed, E.K. (1948) Fractional burials, trophy skulls and cannibalism. *National Park Service Region 3, Anthropological Notes* 79.

Reeves, B.O. (1990) Communal bison hunters of the northern Plains. In: L.B. Davis and B.O. Reeves (eds.), *Hunters of the Recent Past*. London: Unwin Hyman. pp. 168–194.

Reitz, E.J., Scott, S.L. and Moore, K. (1987) Zooarchaeological theory and method. *Tennessee Anthropological Association, Miscellaneous Paper* 12:27–65.

Rice, G. (ed.) (1985) Studies in the Hohokam and Salado of the Tonto Basin. Arizona State University, Office of Cultural Resource Management, OCRM Report No. 63.

Richardson, P. (1980) Carnivore damage to antelope bones and its archaeological implications. *Palaeontologia Africana* 23:109–125.

Riley, C. L. and Hedrick, B. (eds.) (1978) *Across the Chichimec Sea*. Carbondale: Southern Illinois University Press.

Rivière, P.G. (1980) Review of Arens, W. (1979). *Man* 15:1:203–205.

Robbins, L. (1974) Prehistoric people of the Mammoth Cave area. In: P.J. Watson (ed.), *Archaeology of the Mammoth Cave Area*. New York: Academic Press. pp. 137–162.

Robinson, C.K. (1974) *Human Skeletal Remains from 1975 Archaeological Excavations in Mancos Canyon, Colorado*. M.A. thesis, University of Colorado at Boulder.

Roman-Berrelleza, J.A. (1986) *El sacrificio de niños en honor a Tlaloc (La oferenda no. 48 del Templo Mayor)*. Master's Thesis, Escuela Nacional de Antropologia e Historia, I.N.A.H., S.E.P., Mexico City.

Rose, J.C., Condon, K.W. and Goodman, A.H. (1985) Diet and dentition: Developmental disturbances. In: R.I. Gilbert and J.H. Mielke (eds.), *The Analysis of Prehistoric Diets*. Orlando, Fla.: Academic Press. pp. 281–305.

Ruff, C.B. (1981) A reassessment of demographic estimates for Pecos Pueblo. *American Journal of Physical Anthropology* 54:147–151.

Russell, M.D. (1987) Mortuary practices at the Krapina Neanderthal site. *American Journal of Physical Anthropology* 72:381–397.

Russell, M.D. and LeMort, F. (1986) Cutmarks on the Engis 2 calvaria? *American Journal of Physical Anthropology* 69:503–509.

Russell, M.D., Shipman, P. and Villa, P. (1985) Abstract only. *American Journal of Physical Anthropology* 66:223.

Sadek-Kooros, H. (1972) Primitive bone fracturing: A method of research. *American Antiquity* 37:369–382.

Sadek-Kooros, H. (1975) Intentional fracturing of bone: Description of criteria. In: A.T. Clason (ed.), *Archaeozoological Studies*. New York: American Elsevier. pp. 139–150.

Sagan, E. (1974) *Cannibalism—Human Aggression and Cultural Form*. New York: Harper and Row.

Sahlins, M. (1978) Culture as protein and profit. *New York Review of Books* 25:18:45–53.

Sahlins, M. (1979) Cannibalism: An exchange. *New York Review of Books* 26:4:4–47.

Sahlins, M. (1983) Raw women, cooked men, and other "great things" of the Fiji Islands. In: P. Brown and D. Tuzins (eds.), *The Ethnography of Cannibalism*. Washington, D.C.: Society for Psychological Anthropology. pp. 72–93.

Sanday, P.R. (1986) *Divine Hunger: Cannibal-*

ism as a Cultural System. Cambridge: Cambridge University Press.

Sanders, W.T. (1972) Life in a classic village. In: *Teotihuacan, Onceava Mesa Redonda, 1966*. Mexico City: Sociedad Mexicana de Antropologia.

Saul, F.P. (1968) The human skeletal remains of the Sheep Rock Shelter. In: J.W. Michels and J.S. Dutt (eds.), *Archaeological Investigations of Sheep Rock Shelter*. Occasional Papers in Anthropology, Department of Anthropology, Pennsylvania State University 5:199–220.

Saunders, S.R. (1989) Nonmetric skeletal variation. In: M.Y. Işçan and K.A.R. Kennedy (eds.), *Reconstruction of Life from the Skeleton*. New York: Alan R. Liss. pp. 95–108.

Schick, K.D., Toth, N. and Daeschler, E. (1989) An early paleontological assemblage as an archaeological test case. In: R. Bonnichsen and M. Sorg (eds.), *Bone Modification*. Orono, Maine: Center for the Study of the First Americans, University of Maine. pp. 121–136.

Schiffer, M.B. (1987) *Formation Processes of the Archaeological Record*. Albuquerque: University of New Mexico Press.

Schild, R. (1976) The final Paleolithic settlements of the European Plain. *Scientific American* 234:2:88–99.

Schlanger, S.H. (1987) Population measurement, size, and change, A.D. 600–1175. In: K.L. Petersen and J.D. Orcutt (eds.), *Dolores Archaeological Program: Supporting Studies: Settlement and Environment*. Denver: U.S. Department of the Interior, Bureau of Reclamation. pp. 569–605.

Schlanger, S.H. (1988) Patterns of population movement and long-term population growth in southwestern Colorado. *American Antiquity* 53:773–793.

Schmid, E. (1972) *Atlas of Animal Bones*. Amsterdam: Elsevier.

Schneider, K.N. and Blakeslee, D.J. (1990) Evaluating residence patterns among prehistoric populations: Clues from dental enamel comparison. *Human Biology* 62:71–83.

Schrire, C. (1982) The Alligator Rivers: Prehistory and ecology in western Arnhem Land. Terra Australis (Australian National University, Department of Prehistory, Research School of Pacific Studies, Canberra) No. 7.

Schryer, D.R. (1986) Existence of cannibalism, a response to Kolata (1986). *Science* 233:926.

Scott, G.R. (1973) *Dental Morphology: A Genetic Study of American White Families and Variation in Living Southwest Indians*. Ph.D. diss., Arizona State University, Tempe.

Scott, G.R. and Dahlberg, A.A. (1982) Microdifferentiation in tooth crown morphology among Indians of the American Southwest. In: B. Kurtén (ed.), *Teeth: Form, Function, and Evolution*. New York: Columbia University Press. pp. 259–291.

Scott, K. (1986) The bone assemblages of Layers 3 and 6. In: P. Callow and J.M. Cornford (eds.), *La Cotte de St. Brelade 1961–1978: Excavations by C.B.M. McBurney*. Norwich: Geo Books. pp. 159–183.

Scott, L. and Klein, R.G. (1981) A hyaena-accumulated bone assemblage from Late Holocene deposits at Deelpan, Orange Free State. *Annals of the South African Museum* 86:217–227.

Sebastian, L. (1986) Excavations at Prince Hamlet (Site 5MT2161). In: T.A. Kohler, W.D. Lipe and A.E. Kane (eds.), *Dolores Archaeological Program: Anasazi Communities at Dolores: Early Small Settlements in the Dolores River Canyon and Western Sagehen Flats Area*. Denver: U.S. Department of the Interior, Bureau of Reclamation. pp. 333–442.

Seeman, M.F. (1986) Adena "houses" and their implications for Early Woodland settlement models in the Ohio Valley. In: K.B. Farnsworth and T.E. Emerson (eds.), *Early Woodland Archaeology*. Kampsville, Ill.: Center for American Archaeology Press. pp. 564–580.

Shafer, H.J., Marek, M. and Reinhard, K.J. (1989) A Mimbres burial with associated colon remains from the NAN Ranch Ruin, New Mexico. *Journal of Field Archaeology* 16:17–30.

Shankman, P. (1969) Lévi Strauss's theory of cannibalism. *American Anthropologist* 71:54–69.

Shipman, P. (1981a) Applications of Scanning Electron Microscopy to taphonomic problems. *Annals of the New York Academy of Science* 276:357–385.

Shipman, P. (1981b) *Life History of a Fossil*. Cambridge: Harvard University Press.

Shipman, P. (1983) Early hominid lifestyle:

Hunting and gathering or foraging and scavenging. In: J. Clutton-Brock and C. Grigson (eds.), *Animals and Archaeology: 1. Hunters and Their Prey*. British Archaeological Reports, International Series 163:51–62.

Shipman, P. (1984) Scavenger hunt. *Natural History* 93(4):20–27.

Shipman, P. (1986) Scavenging or hunting in early hominids: Theoretical framework and tests. *American Anthropologist* 88:27–43.

Shipman, P. (1987) The myths and perturbing realities of cannibalism. *Discover*, March 1987:70–76.

Shipman, P. (1988) Actualistic studies of animal resources and hominid activities. In: S.L. Olsen (ed.), *Scanning Electron Microscopy in Archaeology*. Oxford: British Archaeological Reports, International Series 452:261–285.

Shipman, P., Bosler, W. and Davis, K.L. (1981) Butchering of giant geladas at an Acheulian site. *Current Anthropology* 22:257–268.

Shipman, P., Bosler, W. and Davis, K.L. (1982) Reply to Binford and Todd. *Current Anthropology* 23:110–111.

Shipman, P., Fisher, D.C. and Rose, J.J. (1984) Mastodon butchery: Microscopic evidence of carcass processing and bone tool use. *Paleobiology* 10:358–365.

Shipman, P., Foster, G. and Schoeninger, M. (1984) Burnt bones and teeth: An experimental study of color, morphology, crystal structure and shrinkage. *Journal of Archaeological Science* 11:307–325.

Shipman, P. and Phillips-Conroy, J. (1977) Hominid tool-making versus carnivore scavenging. *American Journal of Physical Anthropology* 46:77–87.

Shipman, P., Potts, R. and Pickford, M. (1983) Lainyamok, a new Middle Pleistocene hominid site. *Nature* 306:365–368.

Shipman, P. and Rose, J. (1983) Early hominid hunting, butchering, and carcass-processing behaviors: Approaches to the fossil record. *Journal of Anthropological Archaeology* 2:57–98.

Shipman, P. and Rose, J.J. (1984) Cutmark mimics on modern and fossil bovid bones. *Current Anthropology* 25:116–117.

Shipman, P. and Rose, J.J. (1988) Bone tools: An experimental approach. In: S.L. Olsen (ed.), *Scanning Electron Microscopy in Archaeology*. Oxford: British Archaeological Reports, International Series 452:303–335.

Shipman, P., Walker, A., van Couvering, J., Hooker, P. and Miller, J. (1981) The Fort Ternan hominoid site, Kenya: Geology, age, taphonomy and paleoecology. *Journal of Human Evolution* 10:49–72.

Shotwell, J.A. (1955) An approach to the paleoecology of mammals. *Ecology* 36:327–337.

Simmons, A.H. (1983) Excavations at prehistoric sites on the Navajo Indian Irrigation Project, northwestern New Mexico. *Journal of Field Archaeology* 10:155–176.

Singer, R. (1956) The "bone tools" from Hopefield. *American Anthropologist* 58:1127–1134.

Sinoto, Y.A. (1979) The Marquesas. In: J. Jennings (ed.), *The Prehistory of Polynesia*. Cambridge: Harvard University Press. pp. 110–134.

Skinner, A.B. (1919) An ancient Algonkian fishing village at Cayuga, New York. *Indian Notes and Monographs* 2:43–57. New York: Museum of the American Indian, Heye Foundation.

Smith, W. (1949) Excavations in Big Hawk Valley. *Plateau* 21:3:42–48.

Smith, W. (1952) Excavations in Big Hawk Valley, Wupatki National Monument, Arizona. *Museum of Northern Arizona Bulletin* 24:1–203.

Snow, C.E. (1948) Indian Knoll skeletons. *University of Kentucky Reports in Anthropology* 4:371–545.

Snow, C.E. (1974) *Early Hawaiians: An Initial Study of Skeletal Remains from Mokapu, Oahu*. Lexington: University of Kentucky Press.

Sohn, P. (1988) Bone tools of Yonggul Cave at Chommal, Korea. In: E.K. Chen (ed.), *The Paleoenvironment of East Asia from the Mid-Tertiary*, vol. 2, *Oceanography, Palaeozoology, and Palaeoanthropology*. Hong Kong: University of Hong Kong, Centre of Asian Studies. pp. 1124–1185.

Solomon, S. (1985) *People and Other Aggravations: Taphonomic Research in Australia*. B.A. thesis, Department of Prehistory and Archaeology, University of New England.

Somers, A.N. (1892) Prehistoric cannibalism in America. *Popular Science Monthly* 42:203–207. Reprinted in *Wisconsin Archaeologist* 19:1:20–24.

Spencer, B. (1896) *Report on the Work of the Horn Expedition to Central Australia,* pt. 4, *Anthropology*. London: Dulan.

Spennemann, D.H.R. (1987) Cannibalism in Fiji: The analysis of butchering marks on human bones and the historical record. *Domodomo*: Fiji Museum Quarterly. 1&2:29–46.

Spenneman, D.H. and Colley, S.M. (1989) Fire in a pit: The effects of burning on faunal remains. *Archaeozoologia* 3:51–64.

Speth, J.D. (1983) *Bison Kills and Bone Counts: Decision Making by Ancient Hunters*. Chicago: University of Chicago Press.

Speth, J.D. (1989) Early hominid hunting and scavenging: The role of meat as an energy source. *Journal of Human Evolution* 18:329–343.

Speth, J.D. (1990) Seasonality, resource stress, and food sharing in so-called egalitarian foraging societies. *Journal of Anthropological Archaeology* 9:148–188.

Speth, J.D. and Spielmann, K.A. (1983) Energy source, protein metabolism and hunter-gatherer subsistence strategies. *Journal of Anthropological Archaeology* 2:1–31.

Spiess, A.E. (1979) *Reindeer and Caribou Hunters*. New York: Academic Press.

Spitz, W.U. (1980) Thermal injuries. In: W.U. Spitz and R.S. Fischer (eds.), *Medicolegal Investigation of Death*. Springfield, Ill.: Charles C. Thomas. pp. 295–319.

Springer, J.W. (1980) Review of Arens, W. (1979) *Anthropological Quarterly* 53:148–150.

Staesche, U. (1983) Aspects of the life of Middle Paleolithic hunters in the N.W. German Lowlands, based on the site Salzgitter-Lebenstedt. In: J. Clutton-Brock and C. Grigson (eds.), *Animals and Archaeology: 1. Hunters and Their Prey*. British Archaeological Reports, International Series 163:173–181.

Stahl, P.W. and Zeidler, J.A. (1988) The spatial correspondence of selected bone properties and inferred activity areas in an early formative dwelling structure (S20) at Real Alto, Ecuador. In: N.J. Saunders and O. de Montollin (eds.), *Recent studies in Pre-Columbian Archaeology*. British Archaeological Reports, International Series 421:275–298.

Stein, W.T. (1963) Mammal remains from archaeological sites in the Point of Pines region, Arizona. *American Antiquity* 29:213–220.

Stewart, T.D. (1979) *Essentials of Forensic Anthropology*. Springfield, Ill.: Charles C. Thomas.

Stiger, M.A. (1977) *Anasazi Diet: The Coprolite Evidence*. M.A. thesis, Department of Anthropology, University of Colorado at Boulder.

Stodder, A.N.W. (1986) Complexity in Early Anasazi mortuary behavior: Evidence from the Dolores Archaeological Program. Paper presented at 51st Annual Meeting of the Society for American Archaeology, New Orleans, La., April 24, 1986.

Stodder, A.N.W. (1987) The physical anthropology and mortuary practice of the Dolores Anasazi: An early Pueblo population in local and regional context. In: K.L. Petersen and J.D. Orcutt (eds.), *Dolores Archaeological Program: Supporting Studies: Settlement and Environment*. Denver: U.S. Department of the Interior, Bureau of Reclamation. pp. 339–504.

Stothers, D.M., Graves, J.R. and Redmond, B.G. (1982) Cannibalism in the Great Lakes: Evidence from the Sandusky Tradition. *Toledo Area Aboriginal Research Bulletin* 11:37–60.

Straus, L.G. (1977) Of deerslayers and mountain men: Palaeolithic faunal exploitation in Cantabrian Spain. In: L.R. Binford (ed.), *For Theory Building in Archaeology*. New York: Academic Press. pp. 41–76.

Straus, W.L. (1957) Saldanha man and his culture. *Science* 125:973–974.

Susini, A., Baud, C.A. and Tochon-Danguy, H.J. (1988) Actes des 3èmes Journées Anthropologiques. *Notes et Monographies Techniques no. 24*. Paris: Éditions du CNRS. pp 43–67.

Sutcliffe, A.J. (1970) Spotted hyaena: Crusher, gnawer, digester and collector of bones. *Nature* 227:1110–1113.

Sutton, D. (1990) Organisation and ontology: The origins of the northern Maori chiefdom, New Zealand. *Man* 25:667–692.

Swedlund, A.C. (1969) *Human skeletal material from the Yellow Jacket Canyon Area, Southwestern Colorado*. Masters thesis, University of Colorado at Boulder.

Sweeney, G. (1947) Food supplies of a desert tribe. *Oceania* 17:289–299.

Szuter, C. (1989) *Hunting by Prehistoric Horticulturalists in the American Southwest*. Ph.D. diss., University of Arizona, Tucson.

Tannahill, R. (1975) *Flesh and Blood: A History of the Cannibal Complex*. New York: Stein and Day.

Tanner, J. (1830) *A Narrative of the Captivity and Adventures of John Tanner during Thirty Years Residence among the Indians in the Interior of North America*. New York: G. and C.H. Carvill.

Tavassoli, M., Eastlund, D.T., Yam, L.T., Neiman, R.S. and Finkel, H. (1976) Gelatinous transformation of bone marrow in prolonged self-induced starvation. *Haematology* 16:311–319.

Tavassoli, M. and Yoffey, J.M. (1983) *Bone Marrow. Structure and Function*. New York: A.R. Liss.

Teleki, G. (1973) *The Predatory Behavior of Wild Chimpanzees*. Lewisburge: Bucknell University Press.

Theler, J. and Harris, S. (1988) Faunal remains from the Turpin Site (33HA 19), Hamilton County, Ohio. *West Virginia Archeologist* 40:2:1–23.

Thomas, D.H. and Mayer, D. (1983) Behavioral faunal analysis of selected horizons. *Anthropological Papers of the American Museum of Natural History* 59: 353–391.

Thurman, M.D. and Willmore, L.J. (1981) A replicative cremation experiment. *North American Archaeologist* 2:275–283.

Tobias, P.V. (1987a) On the relative frequencies of hominid maxillary and mandibular teeth and jaws as taphonomic indicators. *Human Evolution* 2:297–309.

Tobias, P.V. (1987b) Preliminary report on new hominid tapho-data, a new taphonomic hypothesis and two new taphonomic rations. *Palaeoecology of Africa* 18:395–401.

Todd, L.C. (1987a) Taphonomy of the Horner II bone bed. In: G.C. Frison and L.C. Todd (eds.), *The Horner Site*. Orlando, Fla.: Academic Press. pp. 107–198.

Todd, L.C. (1987b) Analysis of kill-butchery bonebeds and interpretation of Paleoindian hunting. In: M.H. Nitecki and D.V. Nitecki (eds.), *The Evolution of Human Hunting*. New York: Plenum. pp. 225–266.

Todd, L.C. and Rapson, D.J. (1988) Long bone fragmentation and interpretation of faunal assemblages: Approaches to comparative analysis. *Journal of Archaeological Science* 15:307–325.

Tomasevic, N. (ed.) (1981) *Tibet*. Belgrade: Jugoslovenska Revija; New York: McGraw-Hill.

Tomenchuk, J. and Tomenchuck, S. (1976) Quantifying continuous lesions and fractures on long bones: The design and operation of an inking collar. *Journal of Field Archaeology* 3:353–355.

Tomita, K. (1966) The sources of food for the Hadzapi tribe: The life of a hunting tribe in East Africa. *Kyoto University African Studies* 1:157–171.

Toth, N. (1989) Molluscan shell knives and experimental cut-marks on bones. *Journal of Field Archaeology* 16:250–255.

Trinkaus, E. (1985) Cannibalism and burial at Krapina. *Journal of Human Evolution* 14:203–216.

Tucci, G. (1967) *Tibet Land of Snows*. New York: Stein and Day.

Tuck, J.A. *Onondage Iroquois Prehistory: A Study in Settlement Archaeology*. Syracuse: Syracuse University Press.

Turner, A.T. (1981) Minimum number estimation offers minimal insight in faunal analysis. *Ossa* 7:199–201.

Turner, A.T. (1983) The quantification of relative abundances in fossil and sub-fossil bone assemblages. *Annals of the Transvaal Museum* 33:311–321.

Turner, A.T. (1984) Behavioural inferences based on frequencies in bone assemblages from archaeological sites. In: M. Hall, G. Avery, D.M. Avery, M.L. Wilson and A.J.B. Humphreys (eds.), *Frontiers: Southern African Archaeology Today*. British Archaeological Reports, International Series 207:362–366.

Turner, A.T. (1989) Sample selection, Schlepp effects and scavenging: The implications of partial recovery for interpretations of the terrestrial mammal assemblage from Klasies River Mouth. *Journal of Archaeological Science* 16:1–11.

Turner, C.G. (1979) Dental anthropological indications of agriculture among the Jomon people of central Japan. X. Peopling of the Pacific. *American Journal of Physical Anthropology* 51:619–635.

Turner, C.G. (1983) Taphonomic reconstructions of human violence and cannibalism based on mass burials in the American Southwest. In: G.M. LeMoine and A.S. MacEachern (eds.), *A Question of Bone Technology*. Calgary: University of Calgary Archaeological Association. pp. 219–240.

Turner, C.G. (1986a) What is lost with skeletal reburial? I. Adaptation. *Quarterly Review of Archaeology* 7:1–3.

Turner, C.G. (1986b) The first Americans: The dental evidence. *National Geographic Research* 2:1:37–46.

Turner, C.G. (1989) Teec Nos Pos: More possible cannibalism in northeastern Arizona. *Kiva* 54:147–152.

Turner, C.G. (n.d.) Another prehistoric Southwest mass human burial suggesting violence and cannibalism: Marshview Hamlet, Colorado. In: G.T. Gross and A.E. Kane (eds.), *Aceramic and Late Occupation at Dolores*. Denver: Bureau of Reclamation.

Turner, C.G. and Morris, N.T. (1970) A massacre at Hopi. *American Antiquity* 35:320–331.

Turner, C.G. and Turner, J.A. (1990) Perimortem damage to human skeletal remains from Wupatki National Monument, Northern Arizona. *Kiva* 55:187–212.

Turner, G. (1986) Faunal remains from Jubilee Shelter, Transvaal. *South African Archaeological Bulletin* 41:63–68.

Twain, M. (1871) A brace of brief lectures on science. In: C. Neider (ed.), *Life as I Find It*. New York: Harper and Row.

Tyler, H.A. (1975) *Pueblo Animals and Myths*. Norman, Okla.: University of Oklahoma Press.

Ubelaker, D.H. (1989) *Human Skeletal Remains*. 2d ed. Washington, D.C.: Taraxacum.

Uerpmann, H.-P. (1978) The "Knocod" system for processing data on animal bones from archaeological sites. *Peabody Museum Bulletin* 2:149–168.

Ullrich, H. (1986) Manipulations on human corpses, mortuary practice and burial rites in Paleolithic times. *Fossil Man—New Facts, New Ideas: Anthropos* 23:227–236.

Upham, S. (1987) The tyranny of ethnographic analogy in southwestern archaeology. *Arizona State University Anthropological Research Papers* 38:265–279.

Vayda, A.P. (1970) On the limited nutritional value of cannibalism. *American Anthropologist* 72:1462–1463.

Vehik, S.C. (1977) Bone fragments and bone grease manufacturing: A review of their archaeological use and potential. *Plains Anthropologist* 22:169–182.

Vigne, J. and Marinval-Vigne, M. (1983) Methode pour la mise en evidence de la consommation du petit gibier. In: J. Clutton-Brock and C. Grigson (eds.), *Animals and Archaeology: 1. Hunters and Their Prey*. British Archaeological Reports, International Series 163:239–242.

Villa, P. (1982) Conjoinable pieces and site formation processes. *American Antiquity* 47:276–290.

Villa, P. (1990) Torralba and Aridos: Elephant exploitation in Middle Pleistocene Spain. *Journal of Human Evolution* 19:299–309.

Villa, P., Bouville, C., Courtin, J., Helmer, D., Mahieu, E., Shipman, P., Belluomini, G. and Branca, M. (1986a) Cannibalism in the Neolithic. *Science* 233:431–436.

Villa, P., Courtin, J., Helmer, D., Shipman, P., Bouville, C. and Mahieu, E. (1986b) Un cas de cannibalisme au Néolithique. *Gallia Préhistoire* 29:143–171.

Villa, P., Courtin, J., Helmer, D. and Shipman, P. (1987) Cannibalisme dans la grotte de Fontbrégoua. *Sommaire* 223:40–52.

Villa, P., Courtin, J. and Helmer, D. (1988) Cannibalism in Old World prehistory. *Rivista di Antropologia* (Rome). Supplemento del Vol. 66:47–64.

Villa, P., Helmer, D. and Courtin, J. (1985)

Restes osseux et structures d'habitat en grotte: L'apport des remontages dans la Baume Fontbrégoua. *Bulletin Societe Prehistorique Francaise* 82:389–421.

Vivian, R.G. (1990) *The Chacoan Prehistory of the San Juan Basin*. San Diego, Calif.: Academic Press.

Voigt, E.A. (1983) *Mapungubwe: An Archaeozoological Interpretation of an Iron Age Community*. Pretoria: Transvaal Museum Monograph 1.

Volhard, E. (1939) *Kannibalismus*. Stuttgart: Strecker and Schroder.

Von den Driesch, A. and Boessneck, J. (1975) Schnittspuren an neolithischen Tierknochen. *Germania* 53:1–23.

Von Endt, D.W. and Ortner, D.J. (1984) Experimental effects of bone size and temperature on bone diagenesis. *Journal of Archaeological Science* 11:247–253.

Voorhies, M.R. (1969) Taphonomy and population dynamics of an early Pliocene vertebrate fauna, Knox County, Nebraska. *Contributions to Geology, University of Wyoming Special Paper Number 1*.

Wagner, U. (1979) Review of Arens, W. (1979) and Lumholtz, C. (1979). *Ethnos* 3–4:267–270.

Waldron, T. (1989) The relative survival of the human skeleton: Implications for paleopathology. In: A. Boddington, A.N. Garland and R.C. Janaway (eds.), *Death, Decay and Reconstruction*. Manchester: Manchester University Press. pp. 54–78.

Walens, S. and Wagner, R. (1971) Pigs, proteins and people-eaters. *American Anthropologist* 73:269–270.

Walker, D.N. (1983) Faunal remains and subsistence practices at 5FM605; A fur trading post in northwestern Colorado. *Southwestern Lore* 49:1:6–29.

Walker, P.L. (1985) Anemia among prehistoric Indians of the American Southwest. In: C.F. Merbs and R.J. Miller (eds.), *Health and Disease in the Prehistoric Southwest*. Tempe, Ariz.: Arizona State University Anthropological Research Papers 34:139–164.

Walker, P.L. and Long, J.C. (1977) An experimental study of the morphological characteristics of tool marks. *American Antiquity* 42:605–616.

Wall, S.M., Musgrave, J.H. and Warren, P.M. (1986) Human bones from a late Minoan 1B house at Knossos. *Annual, British School of Archaeology at Athens* 81:333–388.

Watson, J.P. (1972) Fragmentation analysis of animal bone samples from archaeological sites. *Archaeometry* 14:221–227.

Watson, J.P. (1979) The estimation of relative frequencies of mammalian species: Khirokitia 1972. *Journal of Archaeological Science* 6:127–137.

Watson, P.J. (1974) Prehistoric horticulturalists. In: P.J. Watson (ed.), *Archaeology of the Mammoth Cave Area*. New York: Academic Press. pp. 233–238.

Weigand, P. C., Harbottle, C. and Sayre, E.V. (1977) Turquoise sources and source analysis: Mesoamerica and the Southwestern USA. In: T.K. Earl and J.E. Erickson (eds.), *Exchange Systems in Prehistory*. New York: Academic Press. pp. 15–34.

Weisman, B. and Milanich, J.T. (1976) Dietary scarcity: A stimulus for warfare among southeastern United States horticulturalists during the historic period. *Florida Journal of Anthropology* 1:1:31–37.

Wells, C. (1960) A study of cremation. *Antiquity* 34:29–37.

Welsh, W.B.M. (1988) A case for the practice of human sacrifice among the Classic lowland Maya. In: N.J. Saunders and O. de Montollin (eds.), *Recent Studies in Pre-Columbian Archaeology*. British Archaeological Reports, International Series 421:275–298.

Wetherill, R. (1894) Snider's Well (Letter to the Editor). *The Archaeologist* (Ohio State Archaeological and Historical Society) 2:288–289.

Wetterstrom, W. (1986) *Food, Diet, and Population at Prehistoric Arroyo Hondo Pueblo, New Mexico*. Santa Fe, N. Mex.: School of American Research.

Wheat, J.B. (1972) The Olsen–Chubbuck site, a Paleo-Indian bison kill. *Society of American Archaeology Memoir* 26:1–179.

Wheat, J.B. (1978) Olsen–Chubbuck and Jurgens sites: Four aspects of Paleo-Indian bison economy. *Plains Anthropologist* 23 (82):84–89.

Wheat, J.B. (1979) The Jurgens site. *Plains Anthropologist Memoir* 15:1–153.

White, T.D. (1985) Acheulian man in Ethiopia's Middle Awash Valley: The implications of cutmarks on the Bodo cranium. Kroon Memorial Lecture, 1985. Albert Egges van Giffen Instituut voor Prae-en Protohistorie van de Universiteit van Amsterdam. Harlem, Netherlands: Enschede en Zonen. pp. 1–33.

White, T.D. (1986) Cutmarks on the Bodo cranium: A case of prehistoric defleshing. *American Journal of Physical Anthropology* 69:503–509.

White, T.D. (1987) Cannibals at Klasies? *Sagittarius: Magazine of the South African Museum* 2:2:6–9.

White, T.D. (1988) Cottonwood Wash, southeastern Utah: Human osteology of Feature 3, FS#27, Site 42SA12209. In: J. Fetterman, L. Honeycutt and Kristin Kuckelman (eds.), *Report on Salvage Excavations of 42SA12209, a Pueblo I habitation site in Cottonwood Canyon, Mati-Lasal National Forest, Southeastern Utah*. U.S. National Forest Service, Contract 53-84627-7-10024.

White, T.D. (1991) *Human Osteology*. Orlando, Fla.: Academic Press.

White, T.D. and Toth, N. (1991) The question of ritual cannibalism at Grotta Guattari. *Current Anthropology* 32: 118–124.

White, T.E. (1952) Observations on the butchering technique of some aboriginal peoples. *American Antiquity* 17:337–338.

White, T.E. (1953) A method of calculating the dietary percentage of various food animals utilized by aboriginal peoples. *American Antiquity* 18:396–398.

White, T.E. (1956) The study of osteological materials in the plains. *American Antiquity* 21:401–404.

Whitlam, R.G. (1982) Archaeological taphonomy: Implications for defining data requirements and analytical procedures. In: P.D. Francis and E.C. Poplin (eds.), *Directions in Archaeology: A Question of Goals*. Calgary: University of Calgary Archaeological Association. pp. 145–154.

Wiener, A.L. (1984) Appendix E: Human skeletal remains. In: D. Breternitz (ed.), *Dolores Archaeological Program: Synthetic Report 1978–1981*. Technical Report No. 191. Denver: U.S. Department of the Interior, Bureau of Reclamation, Engineering and Research Center. pp. 239–248.

Wild, C.J. and Nichol, R.K. (1983a) A note on Rolf Lie's approach to estimating minimum numbers from osteological samples. *Norwegian Archaeological Review* 16:45–49.

Wild, C.J. and Nichol, R.K. (1983b) Estimation of the original number of individuals from paired bone counts using estimators of the Krantz type. *Journal of Field Archaeology* 10:337–344.

Willey, G.R. (1966) *An Introduction to American Archaeology,* vol. 1, *North and Middle America*. Englewood Cliffs, N.J.: Prentice-Hall.

Wills, W.H. (1988) Early agriculture and sedentism in the American Southwest: Evidence and interpretations. *Journal of World Prehistory* 2:445–488.

Wilshusen, R.H. (1986a) Excavations at Periman Hamlet (Site 5MT4671), Area 1, a Pueblo I habitation. In: A.E. Kane and C.K. Robinson (eds.), *Dolores Archaeological Program: Anasazi Communities at Dolores: Middle Canyon Area* (Book 1 of 2). Denver: U.S. Department of the Interior, Bureau of Reclamation. pp. 25–177.

Wilshusen, R.H. (1986b) The relationship between abandonment mode and ritual use in Pueblo I Anasazi protokivas. *Journal of Field Archaeology* 13:245–254.

Wilson, M.C. (1983) Candid scavengers and butchering patterns: Evidence from a 3600-year-old bison bone bed in Alberta. In: G.M. LeMoine and A.S. MacEachern (eds.), *A Question of Bone Technology*. Calgary: University of Calgary Archaeological Association. pp. 95–139.

Wintemberg, W.J. (1936) Roebuck Prehistoric Village Site, Greenville County, Ontario. *National Museum of Canada, Bulletin* 83.

Wintemberg, W.J. (1939) Lawson Prehistoric Village Site, Middlesex County, Ontario. *National Museum of Canada, Bulletin* 94. pp. 1–104.

Wiseman, R.N. (ed.) (1976) *Multidisciplinary Investigations at the Smokey Bear Ruin (LA2112), Lincoln County, New Mexico.* Las Cruces: COAS.

Wobst, H.M. (1978) The archaeo-ethnology of hunter-gatherers or the tyranny of the ethnographic record in archaeology. *American Antiquity* 43:303–309.

Wood, W.R. (1968) Mississippian hunting and butchering patterns: Bone from the Vista Shelter, 23SR–20, Missouri. *American Antiquity* 33:170–179.

Wright, J.V. (1966) The Ontario Iroquois Tradition. *National Museum of Canada Bulletin* 210.

Wyckoff, R.W. (1972) *The Biochemistry of Animal Fossils.* Briston, England: Scientechnica.

Wyman, J. (1874) Report of the Curator. *Seventh Annual Report of the Trustees of the Peabody Museum of American Archaeology and Ethnology.* Cambridge: Salem Press. pp. 7–37.

Yellen, J. (1977) Cultural patterning in faunal remains: Evidence from the !Kung bushmen. In: D. Ingersoll, J. Yellen and W. MacDonald (eds.), *Experimental Archaeology.* New York: Columbia University Press. pp. 271–331.

Yellen, J.E. (1991) Small mammals: !Kung San utilization and the production of faunal assemblages. *Journal of Anthropological Archaeology* 10:1–26.

Yesner, D.R. (1978) Animal bones and human behavior. *Reviews in Anthropology* 5:333–355.

Yesner, D.R. and Bonnichsen, R. (1979) Caribou metapodial shaft splinter technology. *Journal of Archaeological Science* 6:303–308.

Young, G. (1980) Analysis of faunal remains. In: L.S. Cordell (ed.), *Tijeras Canyon: Analysis of the Past.* Albuquerque: University of New Mexico Press. pp. 88–120.

Zegwaard, G. (1959) Headhunting practices of the Asmat of Netherlands New Guinea. *American Anthropologist* 61:1020–1041.

Ziegler, A.C. (1973) Inference from prehistoric faunal remains. *Addison Wesley Module in Anthropology* 43. Reading, Mass.: Addison Wesley.

Zierhut, N.W. (1967) Bone breaking activities of the Calling Lake Cree. *Alberta Anthropologist* 1:33–36.

Zimmerman, L., Emerson, T., Willey, P., Swegle, M., Gregg, J., Gregg, P., White, E., Smith, C., Haberman, T. and Bumsted, M.P. (1980) The Crow Creek site (39BF11) massacre: A preliminary report. Report to the U.S. Army Corps of Engineers, Omaha District.

Zimmerman, L.J. and Alex, R. (1981) The Crow Creek Experience. *Early Man* 3:3:3–10.

Index